The
DA CAPO
OPERA
MANUAL

The DA CAPO OPERA MANUAL

෨

by
Nicholas Ivor Martin

෨

DA CAPO PRESS • New York

CONTENTS

INTRODUCTION

This tome would have been called *The Opera Cookbook* had I not feared that the enduring cliché of the 400-pound diva would make readers think of pasta and cream sauce instead of a serious opera reference work for professionals and aficionados alike.

Nevertheless, my earliest memories of the performing arts involve food. One of my first jobs in opera as a little boy was to consume a loaf of French bread in a Wolf Trap Opera production of *Le Prophète,* where I soon discovered that completing my assignment depended on protecting my fresh nightly prop from my fellow performers. In a production of *The Duchess of Malfi,* I watched the leading man devour an entire chicken onstage every night. And in this same production one of the choristers prepared herself for the lunatic scene by sitting in the canteen chewing on her own hair.

The serious reason for using the word "cookbook" in the title was that it best represents the work itself: each entry includes a list of "ingredients" necessary to produce an opera. For opera professionals and academics, this book can help both in selecting works to produce and in the preparation for actual production. For the opera-goer, the book is a way to get information about operas, much of which is otherwise available only from crumbling scores that have to be hunted down in libraries and opera archives. The breadth of information about each opera and the number of operas covered is, I believe, unique among currently published opera reference works.

Even the most extensive reference book can only give the barest flavor of the works it covers, but it is my hope that *The Da Capo Opera Manual* will help its users find new things to suit their taste and tempt them to sample some that they might not otherwise have considered.

EXPLANATORY NOTES

Tens of thousands of operas have been written since the form was first invented about 400 years ago. Since my purpose was to provide background information on operas for production, I gave preference to works that seemed likely to be performed. At the risk of oversimplifying the decision-making process, this meant: (1) the "standard" works that are performed constantly; (2) all works, where practical, by major composers (no, not every Donizetti work is included); (3) works that were extremely popular at the time, even if they have since been neglected (e.g., *L'Oracolo* by Leoni); (4) works by composers who were famous, but not for their operas (e.g., Rachmaninov, Copland); and (5) small-scale works that are frequently performed in schools even if they do not make their way to major operatic stages.

Preference was also given to works for which the scores are available. (Research for this book was done in the Library of Congress, several of the major university libraries, the important Chicago-area libraries and Lyric Opera of Chicago's library.) If the only copy of the score is hidden in the attic of a cottage in the Pyrenees, it is not going to be produced very often.

❧

Each opera is listed by its original-language title and, where different, its English title. A few conventions: As a general rule, I have tried to avoid Anglicizing names. In the case of Russian and Czech operas, this was unavoidable, and those operas are alphabetized by their English-language titles. If a name is itself a word or phrase in the original language, it seemed best to translate it (e.g., "Poet's Wife"). In some cases, I bowed to tradition: It just looked wrong to list the *commendatore* as "commander" in *Don Giovanni*. English-language rules are used for capitalization: While *Il barbiere di Siviglia* may be correct, it seemed unnecessarily confusing to switch style every time I switched language.

Each introductory paragraph gives a brief summary of the opera's history and structure: the composer and his or her birth and death date, the librettist, the original language of the piece, the source for the story, the premiere date and location, the setting of the piece, the type (grand opera, operetta, etc.), the structure (set numbers or through composed—an often subjective distinction for works written in the past hundred years), and any additional notes. The premiere given is usually the stage premiere; if the broadcast premiere is earlier, it is listed separately.

Sets shows how many different locations are called for in the score, often a matter of interpretation and artistic judgment. For example, are the prologue and "opera within the opera" of *Ariadne* in different locations? How many different rooms are there in *Finta Semplice*? The numbers shown are a best guess from the descriptions given in the score.

Acts gives the number of acts and scenes in the opera, often with notations for major revisions of the work. Unless otherwise noted, prologues and epilogues are counted as separate scenes but not separate acts. Thus *Esclaramonde* is in 4 acts, 8 scenes, there being one scene each in acts I and IV; two scenes each in acts II and III; and one scene each for the prologue and epilogue. Act designations follow the composer's manuscript, including some odd examples, e.g., Prokofiev's four-hour *War and Peace* in a single act. Scene designations are more subjective. In many of the older works, where scenes were demarcated very freely in the score (and often added by the editor, not the composer), I have generally reduced the scene breaks to changes of location. It simply did not seem useful to have *Barbiere di Siviglia* in twenty or more scenes. For modern works, scenes generally follow the score even if there is no change of venue.

Length is an approximate timing in minutes as culled from recordings and performances. For all of the better-known pieces, multiple timings were available and those shown represent what I believe to be a sensible middle ground. When act timings were not available, the complete running time is shown with all acts listed together, so that "I, II, III: 130," means that acts I, II and III together contain 130 minutes of music (i.e., exclusive of intermission time).

Arias lists the major arias in each piece. My apologies to anyone whose favorite aria I have omitted.

Hazards indicates unusually difficult stage business, such as the destruction of the universe, singers transformed into frogs or buildings falling on peoples' heads.

Scenes lists the location of each scene as given in the most authoritative score available. Since scene numbers are shown elsewhere, every attempt has been made here to simplify the scene listing. Therefore, when all the acts of a scene occur in a single location, only the act number is listed, e.g., "I. A temple," rather than, "Ii – Ix. A temple." Multiple scenes in the same location are not listed individually, thus "Ii – Iiii. A temple," indicates that the first three scenes all occur in this location.

Categorization of roles as "major," "minor" and "bit" is necessarily subjective. Bit parts generally indicate roles of a few lines at most (e.g., the shepherd in *Pelleas*, the Prince of Persia in *Turandot* and the Slave in *Salome*). In most cases, speaking roles are merely indicated as such. However, in operas where there are many speaking roles, some of them quite small (several of the French operettas, for example), "speaking bits" are listed separately. "Treble" means a child singer. "Mute" denotes a non-speaking, non-singing role such as the Executioner in *Turandot*. Since these roles can usually be easily added or removed by the stage director, no listing of "supernumeraries" as such seemed feasible. Many—if not most—operas with large choruses have some supernumeraries, but this is not indicated unless there is no chorus. When does a singing part become a role rather than a small group in the chorus? The general rule used here is that the individual must sing at least one solo line, but the answers depend upon the opera and past practice.

Chorus parts shows the subdivisions within the chorus and is therefore an extremely rough indication of minimum numbers. In addition to S, A, T and B for soprano, alto, tenor and bass, Ba means baritone and M means mezzo (only used when the composer has specifically so designated the parts, generally in modern works).

Chorus roles lists the different persons choristers portray. Where child choristers are involved, the number of divisions is generally noted, e.g., "in two parts."

Dance/movement is an attempt to flag any dance or special movement in the piece. Full-scale ballet is easy enough to spot, but this is another area where the extent and difficulty of the dance can be drastically changed from one production to the next. Puppets, gymnasts, acrobats, etc. all fall under this heading. "Dance/movement: None" is not meant as a slur on the dramatic pacing of the opera so listed.

Orchestra gives the orchestration with appropriate notes in cases where multiple orchestrations exist, or where the orchestration was not done by the composer. Original instruments are generally listed, even though modern substitutions are the norm (e.g., tuba instead of cimbasso). The abbreviations are:

> fl - flute
> picc - piccolo
> ob - oboe

     Eng hrn - English horn
     cl - clarinet
     bsn - bassoon
     cont bsn - contrabassoon
     hrn - horn
     trp - trumpet
     trb - trombone
     perc - percussion
     timp - timpani
     vln - violin
     vla - viola
     vlc - cello
     bs - string bass

There are a few modifiers:

     bs - bass
     ten - tenor

Doublings are indicated with parentheses, thus "picc, 2 fl (picc)," means there are three musicians: one plays piccolo, one plays flute and one plays both. Similarly "fl (alto fl, picc)" shows one person playing three instruments. Where the number of strings is specified by the composer, this is shown by section, i.e., "8-6-8-6-4" indicates 8 first violins, 6 second violins, 8 violas, 6 cellos and 4 basses.

Stageband shows what backstage musicians are called for in each act. Organ is listed as stageband if the score explicitly indicates this, otherwise it is included in the pit listing.

Publisher is a very incomplete list of companies that publish each opera and is only meant as a guide of where to start looking for a score.

Rights gives the copyright information on each score. The rule of thumb for copyright is that works are protected to the later of (a) 75 years from the publication date or (b) 50 years from the composer's death. But since most of the relevant copyright law is governed by international treaty—and these treaties have changed repeatedly during the life of some of these operas—it is always best to check with the publisher to see what is protected and what is public domain.

Acknowledgments

I would like to thank David Hendin and my editor, Yuval Taylor, both of whom were instrumental in putting this book together. For their extensive effort and encouragement, Lisa Bury and Marina Vecci have my heartfelt gratitude. I would also like to thank David Kleinberg, Bruno Bartoletti, William Mason, Thomas Blandford, Donna Brunsma, Josie Campbell, John Coleman, Michael Dost, Crozet Duplantier, Ursula Eggers Carroll, Craig Ewington, Magda Krance, Julie Griffin-Meadors, James Johnson, Jacobina Martin, Caroline Moores, Philip Morehead, Donald Palumbo, Roger Pines, Francis Rizzo, Peter Russell, Timothy Shaindlin and Marc Verzatt. The music staff at the Library of Congress were both knowledgeable and helpful and have my thanks: William Harvey, Alicia Patterson, Sam Peryman, Charles Sens, Wayne D. Shirley, Stephen Soderberg, and Walter Zvonchenko.

Operas by Title

Operas by Composer

L'Abandon d'Ariane • The Abandonment of Ariane

Composed by Darius Milhaud (September 4, 1892 – June 22, 1974). Libretto by Henri Hoppenot. French. Based on Greek mythology. Premiered Wiesbaden, Wiesbaden Opera, April 20, 1928. Set in Naxos in legendary times. Satire. Through composed.

Sets: 1. **Acts:** 1 act, 5 scenes. **Length:** I: 10. **Hazards:** None. **Scenes:** I. A deserted spot on the island of Naxos.

Major roles: Dionysos (baritone), Ariane (soprano), Thésée (tenor). **Minor roles:** Three shipwrecked sailors (tenor, baritone, bass), Three Bacchanites (soprano, mezzo, contralto), Phèdre (soprano).

Chorus parts: N/A. **Chorus roles:** None. **Dance/movement:** None. **Orchestra:** 2 fl, ob, 2 cl, bsn, hrn, 2 trp, timp, perc, strings (1-1-1-1-1). **Stageband:** None. **Publisher:** Universal Edition. **Rights:** Copyright 1928 by Universal Edition. Renewed 1956.

Ii. Ariane is shipwrecked with her sister, Phèdre, and her fiancé, Thésée. She loathes Thésée, but Phèdre loves him. Iii. The god Dionysos appears, disguised as an old man and the sisters give him alms. Iiii. Dionysos drugs Thésée so that he sets sail without Ariane. Iiv. Dionysos tells Ariane of her rescue. Iv. He grants her request to join Diana as a constellation in the night sky.

Abu Hassan

Composed by Carl Maria von Weber (November 18, 1786 – June 5, 1826). Libretto by Franz Karl Hiemer. German. Based on a story in "A Thousand and One Nights." Premiered Munich, Residenztheater, June 4, 1811. Set in Bagdad in an unspecified time. Comedy. Set numbers with recitative and spoken dialogue. Overture.

Sets: 1. **Acts:** 1 act, 1 scene. **Length:** I: 55. **Arias:** "Was nun zu machen" (Abu Hassan), "Wird Philomele trauern" (Fatime). **Hazards:** None. **Scenes:** I. Abu Hassan's room in the palace of the caliph.

Major roles: Abu Hassan (tenor), Fatime (soprano), Omar (bass). **Speaking:** Caliph Harun al Raschid, Zobeïde, Mesrur, Zemrud.

Chorus parts: SATTB. Chorus roles: Believers, retinue of the caliph, followers of Zobeïde. Dance/movement: None. Orchestra: 2 fl (picc), 2 ob, 2 cl, 2 bsn, 2 hrn, 2 trp, trb, timp, perc, 2 guitar, strings. Stageband: I: 2 ob, 2 hrn. Publisher: C.F. Peters, Gregg International Publishers. Rights: Expired.

I. Abu Hassan and his wife, Fatime, are pressed by their creditors. Each privately decides to report the other's death to their respective masters and so collect the customary burial payment. Hassan gets money from the banker Omar—who is in love with Fatime. When Omar woos her, Fatime is upset, but plays along. Hassan returns and Fatime locks Omar in the closet. The calpih's agents come to find out who is dead—husband or wife. The caliph himself arrives and Hassan explains that Omar paid the debts. Omar is released from the closet and the Caliph pardons Hassan and Fatime.

The Abduction from the Seraglio

See "Die Entführung aus dem Serail" entry.

Acis and Galatea

Composed by George Frederic Handel (February 23, 1685 – April 14, 1759). Libretto by John Gay, Alexander Pope and John Hughes. English. Based on the John Dryden translation of Ovid's "Metamorphoses." Premiered Cannons, Court Theater, c. 1718. Set in a rural landscape in ancient times. Serenata, masque or pastoral opera. Set numbers with recitative. Overture. Revised and premiered on June 10, 1732, at the King's Theater in the Hay-Market, London: expanded to 3 acts. Revised by W. A. Mozart, 1788.

Sets: 1. Acts: 2 acts, 2 scenes. Length: I, II: 120. Arias: "As when the dove laments" (Galatea), "Love sounds th'alarm" (Acis). Hazards: II: Acis crushed under a rock and turned into a stream. Scenes: I – II. A rural landscape with rocks, groves and a river.

Major roles: Galatea (soprano), Acis (tenor or soprano), Damon (tenor, alto or countertenor), Polyphemus (bass). Minor roles (all missing from original version): Clori (soprano), Sylvio (tenor), Filli (alto), Dorinda (alto), Eurilla (soprano).

Chorus parts: SATTB (briefly SATTTB, although 1st tenor line often sung by altos); also done SATB. Chorus roles: Nymphs and shepherds. Dance/movement: None. Orchestra: 2 fl (picc), 2 ob, strings, organ, carillon, harpsichord, continuo (in original version; 2 trp, cembalo added in London version). **Stageband:** None. **Publisher:** Novello, Ewer and Co., German Handel Society. **Rights:** Expired.

I. The nymph Galatea longs to be reunited with her lover, the shepherd Acis. Acis's friend, Damon, tries to get his mind off Galatea. The lovers are reunited.

II. Polyphemus the giant falls in love with Galatea, but she rejects him. Damon counsels Polyphemus to woo gently. Acis challenges Polyphemus and is crushed under a rock. Galatea saves him by turning him into a stream.

Admeto

Composed by George Frederic Handel (February 23, 1685 – April 14, 1759). Libretto possibly by Nicola Francesco Haym. Italian. Possibly based on "L'Antigone Delusa da Alceste" by Aurelio Aureli. Premiered London, King's Theater, January 31, 1727. Set in Tessaglia in an unspecified time. Comedy. Set numbers with recitative. Overture (sinfonia) before I, II.

Sets: 6. **Acts:** 3 acts, 28 scenes. **Length:** I, II, III: 180. **Arias:** "Ah, sì, morrò" (Admeto). **Hazards:** I: Statue of Apollo speaks. II: Ercole throws Cerebus into a deep abyss. **Scenes:** Ii – Iiii. Royal apartments. Iiv. A wood. Iv. The inside walks of a garden. Ivi. The royal apartments and the garden. Ivii – Iix. The wood. IIi. Hell. IIii – IIiv. The garden. IIv – IIix. The wood. IIIi – IIIiii. A courtyard. IIIiv – IIIx. A square.

Major roles: King Admeto of Thessaly (contralto or countertenor), Alceste (soprano), Princess Antigona (soprano). **Minor roles:** Orindo (mezzo), Ercole (bass), Apollo (bass), Prince Trasimede (alto or countertenor). **Mute:** Cerebus, two furies, page, guards, huntsmen, soldiers.

Chorus parts: N/A. **Chorus roles:** None. **Dance/movement:** None. **Orchestra:** 2 ob, 2 hrn, traversa, strings, continuo. **Stageband:** None. **Publisher:** Gregg Press Ltd. **Rights:** Expired.

Ii. King Admeto is ill. Iii. Ercole tells the king he must leave soon. Iiii. Admeto prays for health, but the statue of Apollo speaks and says he will have no relief until a friend is willing to die for him. Iiv. Princess Antigona loves Admeto. He once loved her and she hopes to get into the palace by disguising herself as a shepherdess. Iv. Admeto's queen Alceste gives up her life for Admeto's. Ivi. Admeto recovers, but, finding Alceste dead, asks Ercole to bring her back. Ivii. Antigona's servant

Meraspe brings her the news. Iviii. Antigona plays on Prince
Trasimede's love for her to gain admittance to the palace. She convinces
him she is not Antigona, merely someone who looks like her. Iix.
Antigona begins to hope.

IIi. Ercole rescues Alceste from the underworld. IIii. Antigona rejects
Trasimede. IIiii. Admeto finds Trasimede's portrait of Antigona. IIiv.
Still disguised, Antigona is introduced to Admeto. IIv. Alceste decides to
test her husband's fidelity by returning disguised as a soldier. IIvi.
Admeto longs for death. IIvii. Trasimede abducts Antigona, but she convinces him to free her. IIviii. Trasimede's page mistakenly steals a portrait of the king (not the one of Antigona). IIix. The page drops the portrait, which Antigona finds, and Alceste overhears Antigona declaring
her love to the portrait.

IIIi. Not realizing that Trasimede freed Antigona, Meraspe appeals to
the king to save her. He reveals Antigona's true identity. IIIii. Admeto's
love for Antigona revives. IIIiii. When Ercole tells Admeto he was
unable to free Alceste, he is surprised the king is not upset. IIIiv. Alceste
angrily takes Admeto's picture from Antigona. IIIv. The king's soldiers
arrest Alceste, believing her to be Antigona's abductor. IIIvi. Ercole frees
Alceste. IIIvii. Realizing Admeto means to marry Antigona, Trasimede
decides to kill Admeto first. IIIviii. Admeto proposes to Antigona.
Alceste disarms Trasimede before he can kill the king, and the soldiers
mistakenly arrest her. IIIix. Alceste reveals her true identity. IIIx.
Admeto pardons Trasimede and Antigona resigns her claim on Admeto
to Alceste.

Adriana Lecouvreur

Composed by Francesco Cilèa (July 26, 1866 – November 20, 1950).
Libretto by Arturo Colautti. Italian. Based on a drama by Eugène Scribe
and Ernest Legouvé. Premiered Milan, Teatro Lirico, November 6, 1902.
Set in Paris in 1730. Tragedy. Set numbers with accompanied recitative.
Ballet. Brief prelude before each act.

Sets: 4. **Acts:** 4 acts, 4 scenes. **Length:** I: 36. II: 32. III: 28. IV: 34. **Arias:** "Io
son l'umile ancella" (Adriana), "Poveri fiori" (Adriana). **Hazards:** None.
Scenes: I. Backstage at the Comédie Française. II. A lodge on the
grounds of the Grange Batelière. III. A state reception room in the palace
of Bouillon. IV. An elegant salon in Adriana's house.

Major roles: Stage manager Michonnet (baritone), Adriana Lecouvreur
(soprano), Count Maurizio (tenor), Princess de Bouillon (mezzo). **Minor
roles:** Jouvenot (soprano), Poisson (tenor), Dangeville (mezzo), Quinault

(bass), Abbott of Chazeuil (tenor), Prince de Bouillon (bass). **Bit part:** Major domo (tenor or speaking). **Mute:** Maid. **Dancers:** Paride, Mercurio, Giunone, Pallade, Venere.

Chorus parts: SSATTBB. **Chorus roles:** Actors, ladies, gentlemen, off-stage voices, people of the theater, pastoral chorus, guests. **Dance/movement:** III: Pastoral ballet. **Orchestra:** picc, 2 fl, 2 ob, Eng hrn, 2 cl, 2 bsn, 4 hrn, 3 trp, 3 trb, tuba, timp, perc, harp, celeste, strings. **Stageband:** None. **Publisher:** Casa Musicale Sonzogno, E. Sonzogno. **Rights:** Copyright 1903 by Edoardo Sonzogno.

I. Michonnet, the stage manager of the Comédie Française, cajoles the actors before their performance. The prince comes to visit Duclos, his mistress, but she is busy writing a letter. Michonnet tries to tell Adriana he loves her, but is prevented by her confession that she loves Maurizio, a young soldier of the count's who is in the audience. The prince intercepts Duclos's love letter to Maurizio, but does not realize Duclos is actually arranging a meeting on behalf of the princess. Maurizio eventually gets the letter and postpones his date with Adriana.

II. The princess loves Maurizio and is mortified that his only interest in her is political. Hearing the prince coming, she hides. The prince thinks he has caught Maurizio with Duclos and is glad for the excuse to break with her. Adriana is shocked to learn Maurizio is no commoner but a count. She helps him smuggle out the princess.

III. The prince gives a reception at which the princess recognizes Adriana's voice and tries to humiliate her. The guests are entertained with a pastoral, and Adriana uses her dramatic recitation to retaliate against the princess.

IV. Adriana receives withered flowers, ostensibly from Maurizio. The count denies this and proposes. Only when Adriana's mind begins to wander does anyone realize the flowers were poisoned—by the princess. Adriana dies in Maurizio's arms.

Die Ägyptische Helena • The Egyptian Helen

Composed by Richard Strauss (June 11, 1864 – September 8, 1949). Libretto by Hugo von Hofmannsthal. German. Based on "Helen in Egypt" by Euripides and other classical legends. Premiered Dresden, Staatsoper, June 6, 1928. Set in Egypt shortly after the Trojan War. Romantic opera. Through composed. Prologue.

Sets: 2. **Acts:** 2 acts, 9 scenes (including prologue). **Length:** Prologue,

I: 60. II: 70. **Hazards:** II: Hermione appears on horseback. **Scenes:**
Prologue – I. A hall in Aithra's palace. II. A tented pavilion opening
wide onto a palm grove with the Atlas mountains rising in the background.

Major roles: Aithra (soprano), Helena (soprano), Menelas (tenor). **Minor
roles:** All-knowing Mussel (contralto), First servant (soprano), Second
servant (mezzo), Hermione (soprano), First elf (soprano), Second elf
(soprano), Third elf (contralto), Altair (baritone), Da-ud (tenor).

Chorus parts: SSAATTTT. **Chorus roles:** Altair's desert warriors, maidens, youths and slaves, Poseidon's warriors, eunechs, husbands, wives.
Dance/movement: None. **Orchestra:** 4 fl (2 picc), 2 ob, Eng hrn, 3 cl, bs
cl, 3 bsn (cont bsn), 6 hrn, 6 trp, 3 or 4 trb, tuba, 2 harp, timp, perc,
celeste, organ, strings (16-14-10-10-8). **Stageband:** I: perc, organ. II: 6 ob,
6 cl, 4 hrn, 4 trp, 2 trp, perc, timp, organ. **Publisher:** Adolph Fürstner.
Rights: Copyright 1928, 1933 by Adolph Fürstner. Renewed 1955, 1960.
Assigned to Boosey & Hawkes.

Prologue. The Trojan war is over and Menelas sails home with his wife,
Helena. He intends to kill her, but is prevented by the enchantress,
Aithra, who raises a storm and shipwrecks the Greeks. Ii. In Aithra's
palace, Helena tries to lessen Menelas's anger. Iii. He is about to kill her
when Aithra's elves distract him and lure him away. Iiii. Aithra restores
Helena's youthful beauty. Iiv. The elves fool Menelas into thinking he
has killed Helena. When he meets Aithra, she tells him that the woman
Paris ran off with was not Helena, but a replica of her created by the
gods. When she returns the "real" Helena to him, Menelas is convinced.
Since Helena does not want to return home, Aithra promises to send
them to an enchanted pavilion at the foot of Mount Atlas. She gives
Helena lotus juice that will suppress Menelas's memory of the past.

IIi. Menelas concludes Helena must be a phantom. IIii. Prince Altair and
his son, Da-ud, bring presents to Helena. Altair falls in love with Helena
and to get rid of Menelas, persuades him to go hunting with his warriors. IIiii. Aithra realizes that she inadvertently gave Helena a juice that
makes one remember the past. She comes to retrieve it, but Helena
decides that restoring Menelas's memory is her only hope. Menelas mistakes Da-ud for Paris and kills him. IIiv. Helena offers Menelas the
remembrance potion. He believes it is poison, but takes it anyway.
Menelas remembers everything—including his love of Helena. Altair
orders his men to seize Menelas so Altair can have Helena for himself.
Aithra's warriors defeat Altair and restore Helena and Menelas's daughter, Hermione, to her parents.

L'Africaine • The African Woman

Composed by Giacomo Meyerbeer (September 5, 1791 – May 2, 1864). Libretto by Eugène Scribe. French. Based on historical characters. Premiered Paris, Opéra, April 28, 1865. Set in Portugal and India in the late 15th century. Grand opera. Set numbers with recitative. Overture. Entr'acte before each act. Ballet.

Sets: 6. **Acts:** 5 acts, 6 scenes. **Length:** I: 40. II: 30. III: 20. IV: 35. V: 20. **Arias:** Adamastor (Nélusko), Ô Paradis (Vasco di Gama). **Hazards:** None. **Scenes:** I. The council chamber of the King of Portugal. II. The prison of the inquisition at Lisbon. III. The between decks of a large ship. IV. Before an Indian temple and palace. Vi. The queen's gardens. Vii. A promontory overlooking the sea.

Major roles: Inez (soprano), Vasco di Gama (tenor), Sélika (soprano or mezzo), Nélusko (baritone). **Minor roles:** Don Diego (bass), Don Pédro (bass), Grand Inquisitor (bass), Don Alvar (tenor), Four sailors (2 tenor, 2 bass), High Priest of Brama (bass baritone). **Bit part:** Anna (mezzo). **Mute:** Usher, Priest.

Chorus parts: SSAATTBB. **Chorus roles:** Bishops, members of the royal council, ushers, courtiers, sailors, soldiers, Indians, priests. **Dance/movement:** IV: Procession and ballet of the priests and soldiers. **Orchestra:** picc, 3 fl (picc), 2 ob, 2 Eng hrn, 2 cl, bs cl, 4 bsn, Eb sax, 4 hrn, 2 cornet, 2 trp, 3 trb, ophicléide, 3 timp, 3 harp, 3 perc, strings. **Stageband:** III: military drum, bells. IV: 2 little sax, 4 sop sax, 4 alto sax, 2 bar sax, 6 bs sax, 4 trp, military drums, 2 ob, 2 hrn, 2 bsn. V: 2 fl, 2 cl, 2 bsn, 2 hrn, 2 harp, harmonium. **Publisher:** G. Ricordi, Garland Publishing. **Rights:** Expired.

I. Inez anxiously awaits the return of her lover, the explorer Vasco di Gama. But Inez's father, Don Diego, tells Inez she must marry Don Pedro. His case is strengthened by news that Vasco has died on Bernard Diaz's expedition. Don Pedro convenes the royal council to consider Diaz's fate. As witness to Diaz's disaster, Don Alvar produces Vasco di Gama, who survived and promises to succeed where Diaz failed: If they give him a ship, he will round the cape. As proof that there are lands—and races—as yet undiscovered, Vasco produces two Indian slaves he procured in Africa, Nelusko and Selika. When the council rejects Vasco's petition, he calls them fools and is imprisoned.

II. In prison, Selika contemplates her love for Vasco—and the throne she left behind. Nelusko loves Selika and wants to kill Vasco, but Selika prevents him. Selika shows Vasco the correct route around the cape. Inez has procured Vasco's liberty, but Don Pedro, who has now married Inez, means to sail around the cape himself. Vasco gives his slaves to his beloved Inez to prove that Selika means nothing to him. Pedro decides to use the slaves as guides.

III. Nelusko guides Pedro's ships around the cape, singing to the sailors the legend of Adamastor, monarch of the deep. Vasco arrives in his own ship and warns Pedro that they are on a fatal course. Pedro orders Vasco shot, but is forced to relent when Selika takes Inez hostage. The ship is captured by Indians.

IV. Now back in her native land, Selika is crowned while Nelusko gives orders for Vasco's death. Vasco rejoices in the country's beauty even as he is readied for execution. To save Vasco, Selika swears she married him and Nelusko reluctantly confirms her story. Vasco falls in love with Selika and does marry her.

Vi. Selika is furious at finding Vasco with Inez. Inez swears that both she and Vasco honor his marriage to Selika, but it is clear that the two are still in love. Selika tells Nelusko to put Vasco and Inez on a ship, adding that she will go to the promontory at the cape. He warns her against the mancanilla tree whose fragrance induces delirium and death. Vii. Selika gathers the leaves of the tree while Vasco escapes home. She dies in Nelusko's arms and he falls, lifeless.

Agrippina

Composed by George Frederic Handel (February 23, 1685 – April 14, 1759). Libretto by Vincenzo Cardinal Grimani. Italian. Original work based on historical incidents. Premiered Venice, Teatro San Giovanni Crisostomo, December 26, 1709. Set in Rome in the 1st century AD Drama for music. Set numbers with recitative. Overture. Ballet.

Sets: 6. **Acts:** 3 acts, 7 scenes. **Length:** I, II, III: 180. **Hazards:** None. **Scenes:** Ii. Agrippina's apartments. Iii. The square of the capitol. Iiii. Popea's room. IIi. A street. IIii. A garden with fountains. IIIi. Popea's room. IIIii. The imperial salon.

Major roles: Agrippina (soprano), Nerone (soprano or countertenor), Ottone (contralto), Poppea (soprano), Emperor Claudio (bass). **Minor roles:** Pallante (bass), Narciso (contralto or countertenor), Lesbo (bass). **Bit part:** Giunone (alto).

Chorus parts: N/A. **Chorus roles:** None. **Dance/movement:** III: Ballet of gardeners, gardeners, cavaliers, ladies. **Orchestra:** 2 recorders, 2 ob, 2 trp, timp, strings, continuo. **Stageband:** None. **Publisher:** Gregg Press Ltd. **Rights:** Expired.

Ii. Agrippina decides to make use of Emperor Claudio's absence to put her son by her first marriage, Nerone, on the throne. She calls two prospective suitors, Pallante and Narciso, one after the other, and tells each of them that Claudio has drowned and she will marry him if he induces the people to proclaim Nerone emperor. Iii. No sooner is Nerone declared emperor—with the help of extensive bribery—than news comes that Ottone has saved Claudio. Ottone tells Agrippina he loves Poppea and that for saving his life, Claudio has named him the heir. Agrippina promises to help him win Poppea. Iiii. Claudio, Ottone and Nerone all love Poppea; she loves Ottone. Agrippina tells Poppea that Ottone has traded her to Claudio in return for being named heir. Furious at Ottone for his faithlessness, Poppea follows Agrippina's advice: She makes Claudio jealous of Ottone. Claudio determines to disinherit Ottone. His advances on Poppea are cut short by the timely return of Agrippina.

IIi. Claudio publicly brands Ottone a traitor. IIii. Poppea and Ottone talk and clear up their misunderstanding. She decides to revenge herself on Agrippina, who, meanwhile, has persuaded her lovers (Pallante and Narciso) to murder each other—and Ottone. Poppea makes an assignation with Claudio and Nerone to further her plans. Agrippina persuades Claudio to name Nerone his successor.

IIIi. Poppea hides Ottone in her room so he can overhear her meetings with Claudio and Nerone. When Nerone arrives, Poppea promises she loves him, but makes him hide, telling him that Agrippina is coming. Claudio now woos Poppea. She makes him jealous of Nerone and exposes Nerone's hiding place to prove her accusations. With Nerone disgraced, Poppea tells Claudio he must protect her from Agrippina if he is to have her love. IIIii. Nerone appeals to Agrippina to intercede for him with Claudio, which she agrees to do after he renounces Poppea. Agrippina's suitors admit their treachery to Claudio. Claudio summons everyone before him, hoping to learn who is telling the truth. He proclaims Ottone his successor and orders Poppea to marry Nerone. Ottone refuses the throne, which convinces Claudio to change his mind. Poppea marries Ottone; Nerone is named the heir.

Aïda

Composed by Giuseppe Verdi (October 9, 1813 – January 27, 1901). Libretto by Antonio Ghislanzoni. Italian. After Camille du Locle work based on summary by Egyptologist Auguste Mariette Bey. Premiered Cairo, Italien Theatre, December 24, 1871. Set in Memphis and Thebes in Pharaonic times. Tragedy. Set numbers with accompanied recitative. Ballet. Prelude.

Sets: 7. **Acts:** 4 acts, 7 scenes. **Length:** I: 40. II: 40. III: 30. IV: 40. **Arias:** "Celeste Aïda" (Radamès), "Ritorna vincitor!" (Aïda), "O cieli azzurri" / "O patria mia" / Nile aria (Aïda). **Hazards:** Large cast (triumphal scene). **Scenes:** Ii. Room in the king's palace at Memphis. Iii. Inside the temple of Vulcan at Memphis. IIi. Hall in the apartments of Amneris. IIii. Before a gate of the city of Thebes. III. On the bank of the Nile before the temple of Isis. IVi. Hall in the king's palace. IVii. Crypt under the temple of Vulcan.

Major roles: Amneris (mezzo), Aïda (soprano), Radamès (tenor), Amonasro (baritone). **Minor roles:** King (bass), Ramfis (bass), Priestess (soprano or mezzo), Messenger (tenor).

Chorus parts: SSAATTTTBBBB. **Chorus roles:** Priests, priestesses, ministers, captains, soldiers, officials, Ethiopian slaves and prisoners, Egyptian people, fan bearers, standard bearers. **Dance/movement:** Iii: Ballet of the priestesses. IIi: Ballet of the Moorish slaves. IIii: Ballet girls. **Orchestra:** 3 fl (picc), 2 ob, Eng hrn, 2 cl, bs cl, 2 bsn, 4 hrn, 2 trp, 3 trb, cimbasso, timp, perc, harp, strings. **Stageband:** I: harp. II: band, 6 Egyptian trp. IV: 4 trp, 4 trb, perc, harp. **Publisher:** Schirmer, Kalmus. **Rights:** Expired.

Ii. Egypt and Ethiopia are at war. Aïda, daughter of the Ethiopian King Amonasro, has been captured by the Egyptians and forced to serve the Egyptian princess Amneris. Amneris fears that the Egyptian general Radamès loves Aïda and not herself. Iii. The Egyptians pray for success in the war.

IIi. Amneris tricks Aïda into admitting she loves Radamès, then, furious, swears to ruin Aïda. IIii. Radamès and the Egyptian army return in triumph, leading their Ethiopian captives. What they do not realize is that one of the captives is actually the Ethiopian King Amonasro. Amonasro swears Aïda to silence. As a reward for his victory, the Egyptian King gives Amneris to Radamès. Still in love with Aïda, Radamès negotiates the return of most of the Ethiopian captives.

III. Amonasro convinces Aïda to find out from Radamès what route the Egyptian army will take. When he tells her, Amonasro and Aïda flee to Ethiopia to defeat the Egyptian army. Radamès realizes—too late—that he has betrayed his country. He surrenders himself.

IVi. Amneris offers to save Radamès from execution if he will renounce Aïda, but he refuses. Nor will he defend his actions. Radamès is condemned to be buried alive under the altar of Vulcan. IVii. Aïda joins Radamès in the crypts. They renew their vows of love before suffocating.

Akhnaten

Composed by Philip Glass (b. January 31, 1937). Libretto by Philip Glass, Shalom Goldman, Robert Israel, Richard Riddell. Egyptian, English, Hebrew, Accadian. Drawn from various Biblical and ancient Egyptian texts. Premiered Stuttgart, Württembergischer Staattstheater, March 24, 1984. Set in Egypt in the 1300s BC and the present day. Portrait opera. Through composed. Some spoken lines. Prelude. Epilogue. Orchestral preludes and interludes before acts and between scenes.

Sets: 6. **Acts:** 3 acts, 11 scenes. **Length:** I, II, III: 135. **Hazards:** II: Destruction of the temple of Amon. **Scenes:** Ii – Iii. Thebes. Iiii. A windowed balcony in the palace of the pharaohs. IIi – IIii. The temple of Amon. IIiii – IIiv. The city of Akhnaten. IIIi – IIIii. The palace and immediate environs. IIIiii – IIIiv. The city of Akhnaten in the present day.

Major roles: Akhnaten (counter tenor), Queen Tye (soprano), Nefertiti (contralto). **Minor roles:** Aye (bass), High Priest Amon (tenor), Horemhab (baritone). **Speaking:** Amenhotep the scribe.

Chorus parts: SATB. **Chorus roles:** People of Thebes, funeral attendants (8 men), priests of Amon and of Aten, soldiers, daughters of Akhnaten (3 soprano, 3 alto). **Dance/movement:** II: Dances in honor of the opening of the city of Akhnaten. **Orchestra:** 2 fl (picc), 2 cl, bs cl, 2 ob (ob d'amore), 2 bsn, 2 hrn, 2 trp, 2 trb, tuba, 3 perc, celeste, synthesizer, strings. **Stageband:** None. **Publisher:** Dunvagen Music Publishers. **Rights:** Copyright 1983 by Dunvagen Music Publishers.

Ii. The pharaoh, Amenhotep III, is buried according to Egyptian custom. Iii. His son, Akhnaten, is crowned. Iiii. Akhnaten, his queen, Nefertiti, and his mother, Queen Tye, pray.

IIi. Akhnaten and his fellow Aten worshippers attack and destroy the temple of Amon. IIii. Akhnaten and Nefertiti sing together. IIiii. Akhnaten's followers celebrate the opening of a new city named after the pharaoh. IIiv. The pharaoh expresses his devotion to his god Aten.

IIIi. The pharaoh is isolated from his people. His domains are overrun by his enemies. IIIii. The people burst into the palace and carry off the pharaoh and his family, ending Akhnaten's reign. IIIiii. In the present day, tourists swarm around the ruins of Akhnaten's city. IIIiv. The ghosts of Akhnaten and his family follow the funeral procession of Amenhotep III.

Albert Herring

Composed by Benjamin Britten (November 22, 1913 – December 4, 1976). Libretto by Eric Crozier. English. Based on a short story by Guy de Maupassant. Premiered Glyndebourne, Glyndebourne Opera House, June 20, 1947. Set in Loxford, a small market-town in East Suffolk in April and May of the year 1900. Comic opera. Set numbers with recitative. Musical interlude between scenes in I, II. Entr'acte before II, III.

Sets: 3. **Acts:** 3 acts, 5 scenes. **Length:** I: 53. II: 55. III: 30. **Hazards:** None. **Scenes:** Ii. The breakfast room in Lady Billows's house. Iii. Mrs. Herring's green grocery shop. IIi. Inside a marquee set up in the vicarage garden. IIii – III. Inside the shop.

Major roles: Lady Billows (soprano), Florence Pike (contralto), Miss Wordsworth (soprano), Mr. Gedge (baritone), Mayor Upfold (tenor), Superintendent Budd (bass), Sid (baritone), Albert Herring (tenor), Nancy (mezzo), Mrs. Herring (mezzo). **Minor roles:** Emmie (child soprano), Cis (child soprano), Harry (treble).

Chorus parts: N/A. **Chorus roles:** None. **Dance/movement:** None. **Orchestra:** fl (picc), ob, cl (bs cl), bsn, hrn, perc, harp, piano, string quintet, piano (can be played by conductor). **Stageband:** I: bouncing ball (handled by performers but notated rhythmically in score). **Publisher:** Boosey & Hawkes. **Rights:** Copyright 1947, 1948 by Hawkes & Son.

Ii. The village leaders cannot find a girl virtuous enough to be the May Queen. In desperation, they nominate the simple-minded Albert Herring. Iii. Albert's friend Sid chides a group of children for stealing from Mrs. Herring's green grocery. He teases Albert about his moral fastidiousness and flirts with the pretty Nancy. Albert himself wonders if his mother is a bit too strict. Lady Billows and the village leaders arrive to tell Albert he has been named May King. Albert thinks the whole thing is daft. He wants to turn it down but his mother insists.

IIi. While the villagers are preparing for the May celebration, Sid and Nancy spike Albert's lemonade with rum. Speeches and presentations are made all around. The feast begins and Albert greedily downs his lemonade. IIii. Albert returns to the shop, drunk. He overhears Nancy and Sid, who (between kisses) feel sorry for Albert. Taking his prize money, Albert rushes out into the night. His mother comes home and, assuming Albert is fast asleep, closes the shop.

III. The whole town is out searching for Albert. Nancy feels guilty about the rum. Albert's orange blossom from the celebration is discovered on the road, crushed, and Mrs. Herring is convinced Albert is dead. Just as the confusion reaches its height, Albert appears and admits he spent the night drinking and fighting. But it wasn't much fun, he adds. Things return to normal, and Albert returns to work. Nancy gives him a kiss and he gives peaches to the children.

Alceste

Composed by Christoph Willibald Gluck (July 2, 1714 – November 15, 1787). Libretto by Ranieri di Calzabigi and Le Blanc du Roullet. Italian and French (two versions). Based on a libretto by Philippe Quinault. Premiered Vienna, Burgtheater, December 26, 1767. Set in Thessaly in legendary times. Tragedy. Set numbers with recitative. Overture. Ballet. Revised French version premiered in Paris, April 23, 1776.

Sets: 5. **Acts:** 3 acts, 20 scenes. **Length:** I: 55. II: 55. III: 40. **Arias:** "Divinités du Styx" (Alceste). **Hazards:** None. **Scenes:** Ii – Iii. A public place before the palace of Admète. Iiii – Ivii. The temple of Apollon. II. A vast room in the palace. IIIi – IIIii. A court in the palace. IIIiii – IIIix. A desolate, wild place.

Major roles: Alceste (soprano), High priest of Apollon (bass baritone), Admète (tenor). **Minor roles:** Four voices (soprano, alto, tenor, bass), Évandre (tenor), Hercule (bass), Thanatos god of the underworld (bass), Apollon (baritone). **Bit parts:** Herald (bass), Oracle (bass). **Mute:** Two children of Admète and Alceste.

Chorus parts: SSAATTBB. **Chorus roles:** Officers of the palace, ladies in waiting, people of Phère, devils, priests and priestesses of Apollon. **Dance/movement:** I: Cultic dances of the priests. II: Ballet. III: Andante, march, minuet, gavotte and chaconne. **Orchestra:** 2 fl, 2 cl, 2 ob, 2 bsn, 4 hrn, 2 trp, 3 trb, timp, strings. **Stageband:** I: 2 ob, 2 cl, 2 bsn, 4 trb. II: 4 trb, 2 harp. III: 4 trb, 4 hrn. **Publisher:** Bärenreiter Kassel, Boieldieu. **Rights:** Expired.

Ii. The people await news of Admète, their dying king. Iii. Alceste, the queen, is grief stricken over her husband's condition. Iiii. The high priest of Apollon prays for the king's recovery. Iiv. The oracle announces that the king will die today unless someone agrees to die in his place. Iv. Alceste agrees to sacrifice herself. Ivi. The high priest announces the god's acceptance. Ivii. Alceste is elated by love.

IIi. The people celebrate Admète's return to health. IIii. Admète is perturbed to learn that his health was bought with the death of an unknown subject. IIiii. He is reunited with his wife. When Admète learns the truth, he determines to prevent his wife's sacrifice. IIiv. Alceste calls on the gods to honor the trade.

IIIi. The people weep for their ruler. IIIii. Hercule returns and vows to save the queen. IIIiii. Alceste descends to the gates of Hades. IIIiv. Admète begs her to reconsider. Both appeal to the gods, but the god Thanatos says the decision is up to Alceste. IIIv. Alceste is saved by Hercule. IIIvi. Apollon approves what Hercule has done. IIIvii. The gates of Hades vanish. IIIviii. All thank the god. IIIix. The people exalt Hercule and their king and queen.

Alcina

Composed by George Frederic Handel (February 23, 1685 – April 14, 1759). Libretto by Antonio Marchi. Italian. Based on Ariosto's "Orlando Furioso." Premiered London, Royal Opera House, Covent Garden, April 16, 1735. Set on a magic island in an unspecified time. Comedy. Set numbers with recitative. Overture. Symphony before III. Ballet.

Sets: 8. **Acts:** 3 acts, 38 scenes. **Length:** I, II, III: 210. **Arias:** "Verdi prati" (Ruggiero). **Hazards:** I: mountain disintegrates revealing Alcina's palace. II: palace transformed back into a desert. Melisso transforms himself into Ruggiero's nursemaid. Lion approaches and lies at Oberto's feet. Palace transformed into a seascape. **Scenes:** Ii. A desert place terminated by high craggy mountains at the foot of which opens a little cave. Iii – Ivii. The palace of Alcina. Iviii – Ixiv. A gallery leading to the apartments of Alcina. IIi. A rich and splendid hall of the enchanted palace of Alcina and the desert. IIii – IIiii. The desert. IIiv – IIxii. A place leading to the royal gardens with a statue of Circe. IIxiii. A subterranean apartment. IIIi – IIIv. A court of the palace. IIIvi – IIIxi. A prospect of the palace surrounded with trees, statues, obelisks, trophies and dens of wild beasts. A seascape.

Major roles: Bradamante (contralto), Morgana (soprano), Alcina (soprano), Ruggiero (soprano, mezzo or countertenor). **Minor roles:** Melisso (bass), Oberto (soprano), Oronte (tenor).

Chorus parts: SATB. **Chorus roles:** Pages, knights, ladies, wild beasts, Alcina's lovers. **Dance/movement:** I: Courtly dances. II: spirits dance. **Orchestra:** picc, 2 fl, 2 ob, 2 bsn, 2 hrn, cembalo or harpsichord, strings. **Stageband:** None. **Publisher:** Gregg International Publishers. **Rights:** Expired.

Ii. Disguised as a man, Bradamante comes to rescue her husband, Ruggiero, from the sorceress Alcina, whose sister, Morgana, falls in love with Bradamante. Iii. Bradamante is welcomed at the palace. Iiii. The knight Oberto is searching for his father. Iiv. Ruggiero has forgotten Bradamante for Alcina. Iv. Alcina's general, Oronte, loves Morgana. Ivi. Morgana favors Bradamante. Ivii. She scorns Oronte. Iviii. Oronte explains to Ruggiero that Alcina turns her old lovers into beasts—and makes him jealous of Bradamante. Iix. Ruggiero accuses Alcina of faithlessness. Ix. She denies his accusation. Ixi. Bradamante rebukes Ruggiero for forgetting her. Ixii. Bradamante's ally, Melisso, worries that Ruggiero will seek revenge. Ixiii. Morgana soon reports that Ruggiero has asked Alcina to turn Bradamante into a beast. Ixiv. Bradamante lets Morgana believe she loves her.

IIi. Melisso recalls Ruggiero to his duty and wife. IIii. But Ruggiero drives Bradamante away, believing she is a ghost. IIiii. He is wracked with doubt. IIiv. Alcina decides to harm Bradamante. IIv. But Morgana stops her. IIvi. Ruggiero tells Alcina he is going off to hunt. IIvii. Alcina promises to help Oberto find his father. IIviii. Oronte warns Alcina of Ruggiero's betrayal. IIix. He is again scorned by Morgana. IIx. Oronte resolves to get over Morgana. IIxi. Bradamante tells Oberto that his father was changed into a lion by Alcina and promises to undo the spell. IIxii. Ruggiero and Bradamante make up. IIxiii. Alcina raises her enchanted troops.

IIIi. Oronte wins Morgana by pretending to have forgotten her. IIIii. Alcina confronts Ruggiero, who rejects her. IIIiii. Melisso arms Ruggiero against Alcina's magic. IIIiv. Bradamante determines to free Alcina's captives. IIIv. Oronte tells Alcina that Ruggiero is winning. IIIvi. Alcina tries to get Oberto to kill a lion, but Oberto refuses, realizing it is his father. IIIvii. Alcina and Bradamante argue. IIIviii. Ruggiero defeats Alcina's forces. IIIix. Bradamante tries to shatter Alcina's magic by destroying her magic urn. IIIx. She is prevented by Morgana. IIIxi. But Ruggiero succeeds and Alcina's captives are freed.

Alfonso und Estrella • Alfonso and Estrella

Composed by Franz Schubert (January 31, 1797 – November 19, 1828). Libretto by Franz von Schober. German. Original work. Premiered Weimar, Hoftheater, June 24, 1854. Set in Northern Spain in legendary times. Romantic opera. Through composed. Overture. Introduction before III.

Sets: 4. **Acts:** 3 acts, 6 scenes. **Length:** I, II, III: 165. **Hazards:** None. **Scenes:** Ii. In a valley before Troila's house. Iii. A room in the palace of King Mauregato. IIi. A woods on a mountain. IIii. Near the city gate. IIiii. The room in the palace. III. The woods.

Major roles: Troila (baritone), Alfonso (tenor), Estrella (soprano), Adolfo (bass), King Mauregato of Leon (baritone). **Minor roles:** Girl (soprano), Youth (tenor), Bodyguard leader (tenor). **Bit parts:** Two peasants (contralto, tenor).

Chorus parts: SSAATTTBBB. **Chorus roles:** Peasants, women, youths, soldiers, conspirators, servants, hunters. **Dance/movement:** II: March. **Orchestra:** picc, 2 fl, 2 ob, 2 cl, 2 bsn, 4 hrn, 2 trp, 3 trb, timp, perc, strings. **Stageband:** I: 2 cl, 2 bsn 2 hrn, harp, perc. II: 2 hrn, 2 trp. III: 2 ob, 2 cl, 2 bsn, 2 hrn, 2 trp. **Publisher:** J. N. Fuchs, Breitkopf & Härtel. **Rights:** Expired.

Ii. The peasants of the valley express their gratitude to Troila who has spent his life ministering to the sick. They do not know that Troila was king of Leon until he was overthrown by his minister, Mauregato, and banished to this valley. Troila's son, Alfonso, chaffs at being confined to the valley, but Troila counsels patience and gives him a golden chain. Iii. In the palace of Mauregato, the king's victorious general, Adolfo, proposes to Princess Estrella who refuses. Adolfo appeals to Mauregato, who says that only the man who returns the chain of St. Eurich to his possession may marry the princess.

IIi. Lost while out hunting, Estrella meets Alfonso. They fall in love and Alfonso gives the princess the chain. IIii. Adolfo raises a band of conspirators to overthrow the king. IIiii. Mauregato is worried about Estrella, but she eventually returns. When Adolfo's revolt begins, the king advises his supporters to flee, but they insist on putting up a fight.

III. The king's men are put to flight. Adolfo, who finds Estrella in the woods, threatens to kill her if she will not marry him. She is rescued by Alfonso and his huntsmen. Alfonso rallies the king's forces and leads a counterattack against the conspirators. Mauregato, who has fled into the woods, is overcome with guilt for usurping Troila's throne, but Troila forgives him. Mauregato gives Estrella's hand to the victorious Alfonso, and Mauregato and Troila name him King of Leon.

Alzira

Composed by Giuseppe Verdi (October 9, 1813 – January 27, 1901). Libretto by Salvatore Cammarano. Italian. Based on the play "Alzire" by Voltaire. Premiered Naples, Teatro San Carlo, August 12, 1845. Set in Peru in the mid-16th century. Lyric tragedy. Set numbers with recitative. Overture. Prologue.

Sets: 6. **Acts:** 2 acts, 6 scenes (or 3 acts if prologue is considered a separate act). **Length:** Prologue: 15. I: 40. II: 35. **Arias:** Alzira's cavatina (Alzira). **Hazards:** None. **Scenes:** Prologue. A vast plain irrigated by the Rima River. Ii. The main square in Lima. Iii. Ataliba's apartment in the governor's palace. IIi. Inside the fortifications at Lima. IIii. A frightful cavern. IIiii. The great hall in the governor's residence.

Major roles: Zamoro (tenor), Gusmano (baritone), Alzira (soprano). **Minor roles:** Otumbo (tenor), Alvaro (bass), Ataliba (bass), Zuma (soprano), Ovando (tenor).

Chorus parts: SATTB. **Chorus roles:** Indian warriors and women, Spanish officials and soldiers, wedding guests. **Dance/movement:** None. **Orchestra:** picc, 2 fl, 2 ob, 2 cl, 2 bsn, 4 hrn, 2 trp, 3 trb, cimbasso, timp, perc, harp, strings. **Stageband:** I: band. II: band, perc. **Publisher:** G. Ricordi, University of Chicago Press. **Rights:** Expired.

Prologue. Alvaro, the Spanish Governor of Peru, is taken prisoner by the Incas in retaliation for the supposed murder of their chief, Zamoro, by Alvaro's son, Gusmano. But Zamoro is not dead. He returns and orders Alvaro's release. Zamoro intends to lead all the tribes against the Spaniards to free his fiancée, Alzira.

Ii. The Spanish soldiers promise to fight for their king. Alvaro abdicates in favor of Gusmano and Alzira's father, Ataliba, swears loyalty to him. Gusmano wants to marry Alzira. Iii. Alzira dreams of Zamoro, who she thinks is dead. Ataliba tells Alzira to marry Gusmano for the good of the tribe, but she refuses. Zamoro sneaks into the palace in disguise. He presents himself to Alzira and they swear their love. Gusmano has Zamoro arrested. Alvaro recognizes Zamoro and asks his son to spare the chieftain. An Indian army demands Zamoro's release, and Gusmano lets him go.

IIi. The Spanish soldiers celebrate their victory over the Indians. Zamoro has been captured and condemned. Gusmano tells Alzira she must marry him to save Zamoro's life. Alzira considers suicide. IIii. Zamoro escapes. He hears that Alzira is marrying Gusmano. IIiii. The wedding celebration commences. A soldiers stabs Gusmano at the altar. It is Zamoro. Gusmano forgives him and dies in Alvaro's arms.

Amahl and the Night Visitors

Composed by Gian Carlo Menotti (b. July 7, 1911). Libretto by Gian Carlo Menotti. English. Inspired by Hieronymous Bosch's painting "The Adoration of the Magi." Premiered New York City, NBC Television Opera Theater, December 24, 1951. Set near Bethlehem in the 1st century

AD. Miracle play. Through composed. First stage performance Indiana, February 21, 1952.

Sets: 1. **Acts:** 1 act, 1 scene. **Length:** I: 45. **Hazards:** None. **Scenes:** I. Amahl's and his mother's cottage and the surrounding countryside.

Major roles: Amahl (boy soprano), Amahl's mother (soprano), King Kaspar (tenor), King Melchior (baritone), King Balthazar (bass). **Bit part:** Page (bass or baritone).

Chorus parts: SATB. **Chorus roles:** Shepherds and villagers. **Dance/movement:** I: Shepherds folk dance for the kings. **Orchestra:** fl, 2 ob, cl, bsn, hrn, trp, harp, piano, perc, strings. **Stageband:** None. **Publisher:** G. Schirmer. **Rights:** Copyright 1951, 1952 by G. Schirmer, Inc.

I. Amahl's mother puts him to bed. She does not believe his tales of a huge star with a flaming tail and wonders how they will live now that there is nothing left to sell. A knock on the door awakens them: Three kings are asking for shelter. Mother gets wood for the fire and sends for the other shepherds to bring food and gifts. The kings explain they are following a star that will lead them to the Child. The shepherds dance. After everyone has gone to sleep, the mother tries to steal the kings' gold, but their page catches her. Amahl defends his mother and the kings let her keep the gold. When Amahl offers to send the Child his crutch as a gift, he finds that his lameness has disappeared. With his mother's blessing, Amahl joins the kings on their journey.

Amelia al Ballo • Amelia Goes to the Ball

Composed by Gian Carlo Menotti (b. July 7, 1911). Libretto by Gian Carlo Menotti. Italian and English. Original work Premiered Philadelphia, Academy of Music, April 1, 1937. Set in Milan around 1910. Comic opera. Set numbers with continuous recitative. Prelude.

Sets: 1. **Acts:** 1 act, 1 scene. **Length:** I: 60. **Hazards:** I: Husband fires a pistol at lover. Amelia breaks a vase over her husband's head. **Scenes:** I. The luxurious bedroom of Amelia.

Major roles: Amelia (soprano), Husband (baritone), Lover (tenor). **Minor roles:** Friend (contralto), Chief of police (bass). **Bit parts:** Two chambermaids (2 mezzo). **Mute:** Stretcher bearers.

Chorus parts: SATB (briefly SSAATB). **Chorus roles:** Neighbors and passersby. **Dance/movement:** None. **Orchestra:** picc, 2 fl, 2 ob, 2 cl, 2 bsn, 4 hrn, 3 trp, 3 trb, tuba, timp, perc, celeste, glockenspiel, harp, xylophone, strings. **Stageband:** None. **Publisher:** G. Schirmer, G. Ricordi & Co. **Rights:** Copyright 1938 by G. Ricordi & Co. New copyright 1952. Renewed 1965.

I. Amelia is about to leave for the ball when her husband accuses her of infidelity, showing a letter from her lover. When the husband agrees to let Amelia go to the ball, she confesses she is indeed having an affair with their upstairs neighbor. Furious, the husband locks Amelia in the apartment and goes upstairs to shoot the lover. But Amelia screams a warning out the window and her lover slides down a rope into the apartment—and proposes that they run away. Amelia agrees: they will bolt *after* the ball. The husband returns and tries to shoot the lover, but the pistol misfires. The two men get into a long discussion—to Amelia's intense annoyance. She breaks a vase over her husband's head, knocking him out. When the police arrive, Amelia tells them her lover is a robber. Both men now disposed of, Amelia goes to the ball with the chief of police.

L'Amico Fritz • Friend Fritz

Composed by Pietro Mascagni (December 7, 1863 – August 2, 1945). Libretto by Nicola Daspuro. Italian. Based on the novel by Émile Erckmann and Alexandre Chatrian. Premiered Rome, Teatro Costanzi, October 31, 1891. Set in Alsace in the late 19th century. Lyric comedy. Set numbers with recitative. Prelude. Intermezzo before III.

Sets: 2. **Acts:** 3 acts, 3 scenes. **Length:** I, II: 60. III: 30. **Hazards:** None. **Scenes:** I. Fritz Kobus's dining room. II. Courtyard of a farm. III. The dining room.

Major roles: Fritz Kobus (tenor), Rabbi David (baritone), Suzel (soprano). **Minor roles:** Hanezò (bass), Caterina (soprano), Beppe (mezzo). **Bit part:** Federico (tenor).

Chorus parts: SATB. **Chorus roles:** Offstage farmers and children. **Dance/movement:** None. **Orchestra:** 3 fl (picc), 2 ob, 2 cl, 2 bsn, 4 hrn, 2 trp, 3 trb, tuba, timp, perc, harp, strings. **Stageband:** I: ob, band, vln. **Publisher:** Casa Musicale Sonzogno. **Rights:** Expired.

I. Rabbi David persuades Fritz Kobus, a rich farmer, to lend him money for dowries for several matches he is arranging. Fritz and his friends, Hanezò and Federico, sit down to eat. Suzel, the steward's daughter, brings Fritz violets and Beppe plays and sings for them. The men laugh about how soon Suzel will find a husband, but Fritz is not amused.

David bets Fritz that Suzel will be married shortly. A group of children cheers Fritz.

II. Suzel picks cherries for Fritz. They talk about the birds' singing. Fritz's friends join them. Relying on the biblical story of Rebecca and Eleazar, David suggests to Suzel that she marry Fritz. When David tells Fritz that he means to find Suzel a husband, Fritz is furious, because he is determined not to fall in love. He leaves with his friends and Suzel bursts into tears.

III. Fritz cannot stop thinking of Suzel. Beppe's attempts to cheer him up fail: Fritz is in love. David worries Fritz by telling him that Suzel's marriage is all arranged—she has consented. Suzel, too, is sad. She is convinced Fritz does not care for her. They meet and admit their love. David has won his bet—Fritz's farm—but he gives it to Suzel.

L'Amore dei Tre Re • The Love of Three Kings

Composed by Italo Montemezzi (August 4, 1875 – May 15, 1952). Libretto by Sem Benelli. Italian. Based on the play by Benelli. Premiered Milan, Teatro alla Scala, April 10, 1913. Set in a remote castle in Italy in the Middle Ages, forty years after a barbarian invasion. Tragedy. Through composed. Orchestral introduction before II.

Sets: 3. **Acts:** 3 acts, 3 scenes. **Length:** I: 30. II: 40. III: 20. **Hazards:** None. **Scenes:** I. A spacious hall in the castle. II. A circular terrace high on the castle walls. III. The crypt in the castle chapel.

Major roles: Archibaldo (bass), Avito (tenor), Fiora (soprano), Manfredo (baritone). **Minor role:** Flaminio (tenor). **Bit parts:** Handmaiden Ancella (soprano), Offstage boy (treble), Young girl (soprano), Youth (tenor), Old woman (mezzo).

Chorus parts: SSSAAAATTTBBBB. **Chorus roles:** Inhabitants of Altura: men, women, youths and old women. **Dance/movement:** None. **Orchestra:** 3 fl (picc), 2 ob, Eng hrn, 2 cl, 3 bsn (cont bsn), 4 hrn, 3 trp, 3 trb, tuba, timp, perc, celeste, harp, strings. **Stageband:** I: fl. II: 3 trp. III: bells. **Publisher:** G. Ricordi Inc. **Rights:** Copyright 1913 by G. Ricordi.

I. Forty years ago, Archibaldo defeated the Italians to build himself a kingdom. His son Manfredo married Fiora, an Italian princess. Now old and blind, Archibaldo awaits Manfredo's return. Fiora was once engaged to Avito and has taken him as a lover. Archibaldo suspects Fiora but does not want to know the truth. Manfredo returns from the war: He could not wait to see Fiora.

II. Manfredo takes his leave, asking Fiora to wave goodbye to him from the tower. She is overcome by his love and renounces Avito, but Avito's love wins her over. Archibaldo discovers the lovers and though he cannot see, he hears Avito's escape. He demands to know the name of Fiora's lover. When she refuses to answer, Archibaldo strangles her. Manfredo returns and his father tells him the truth.

III. The people mourn Fiora. Avito kisses the corpse, but Archibaldo has coated Fiora's lips with poison. Manfredo kills himself by also kissing Fiora. He is discovered by Archibaldo.

L'Amore Medico • Doctor Cupid

Composed by Ermanno Wolf-Ferrari (January 12, 1876 – January 21, 1948). Libretto by Enrico Golisciani. Italian. Based on "L'Amour Médecin" by Molière. Premiered Dresden, Dresden Opera, December 4, 1913. Set near Paris in the 17th century. Comedy. Set numbers with accompanied recitative. Overture. Intermezzo before II.

Sets: 2. **Acts:** 2 acts, 15 scenes. **Length:** I, II: 90. **Hazards:** None. **Scenes:** I. The garden of Arnolfo's villa. II. A spacious, handsome salon in Arnolfo's house.

Major roles: Arnolfo (bass), Lucinda (soprano), Lisetta (soprano), Clitandro (tenor). **Minor roles:** Tomes (baritone), Desfonandres (baritone), Macroton (baritone), Bahis (tenor), Notary (baritone).

Chorus parts: SSATTTBB. **Chorus roles:** Arnolfo's friends and servants, gardeners, pages, apothecaries, children, peasants, musicians, dancing girls. **Dance/movement:** II: Wedding dance. **Orchestra:** picc, 2 fl, 2 ob, Eng hrn, 2 cl, bs cl, 2 bsn, 4 hrn, 3 trp, 3 trb, tuba, timp, perc, harp, celeste, strings. **Stageband:** fl, picc, 2 cl, 2 bsn, 2 hrn, trp, 4 vln, 2 vlc, 2 bs, spinet, perc. **Publisher:** G. Schirmer. **Rights:** Copyright 1913 by Josef Weinberger. Copyright 1914 by G. Schirmer.

Ii. Arnolfo's daughter, Lucinda, pines for love because her father has kept her secluded from any possible suitors. Iii. He tries to cheer her up with presents. Iiii. The maid, Lisetta, points out that Lucinda needs a husband. Iiv. The young cavalier Clitandro serenades Lucinda. She loves him, but does not know what to do. Lisetta forms a plan. Iv. Arnolfo contemplates moving to an even more secluded spot. Ivi. Lisetta reports that Lucinda has taken ill. Arnolfo sends for help.

IIi. Four doctors prescribe four different courses of treatment for Lucinda. IIii. Lisetta insults the doctors. IIiii. They leave. IIiv. Lisetta dis-

guises Clitandro as a doctor. IIv. She introduces him to Arnolfo. IIvi.
Clitandro brings Lucinda flowers. IIvii. Clitandro tells Arnolfo that
Lucinda's sickness can only be cured by marriage. He proposes to "pretend" to marry her, to which Arnolfo readily agrees. IIviii. A real marriage contract is drawn up and signed. IIix. Clitandro arranges a wedding celebration and while everyone is dancing, he and Lucinda run
away.

Andrea Chénier

Composed by Umberto Giordano (August 28, 1867 – November 12,
1948). Libretto by Luigi Illica. Italian. Based on events in the life of the
poet Andrea Chénier. Premiered Milan, Teatro alla Scala, March 28,
1896. Set in France in 1789 through 1794. Historical verismo opera. Set
numbers with accompanied recitative.

Sets: 4. **Acts:** 4 acts, 4 scenes. **Length:** I: 30. II: 25. III: 40. IV: 15. **Arias:** Un
dì all'azzurro spazio (Chénier), Vivere in fretta (Bersi), La mamma morta
(Maddalena), Nemico della patria (Gérard), Come un bel dì di Maggio
(Chénier). **Hazards:** None. **Scenes:** I. Winter garden in the Chateau di
Coigny. II. The Cafe Hottot on the Seine, Paris. III. Headquarters of the
revolutionary tribunal. IV. Courtyard in the prison of St. Lazare.

Major roles: Andrea Chénier (tenor), Carlo Gérard (baritone),
Maddalena di Coigny (soprano). **Minor roles:** Bersi (mezzo), Countess
di Coigny (mezzo), Pietro Fléville (bass or baritone), Abbe (tenor),
Incredibile (tenor), Roucher (bass or baritone), Schmidt (bass), Mathieu
(baritone), Madelon (mezzo), Fouquiertinville (bass or baritone). **Bit
parts:** Major Domo (bass), Dumas (bass). **Speaking bit:** Boy. **Mute:** Old
Gérard, Flando Fiorinelli (pianist), Orazio Coclite, Robespierre, Roger
Albert (boy).

Chorus parts: SSSSAATTBB. **Chorus roles:** Lackeys, ladies, gentlemen,
clerics, musicians, gendarmes, shepherds, shepherdesses, cavaliers, beggars, citizens, revolutionary soldiers, revolutionary judges and jurors,
prisoners, newsboys. **Dance/movement:** I: Gavotte. **Orchestra:** picc, 2 fl,
2 ob, Eng hrn, 2 cl (bs cl), 2 bsn, 4 hrn, 3 trp, 3 trb, tuba, timp, perc, harp,
strings. **Stageband:** I: piano (played by Fiorinelli character). I, III, IV:
drums. **Publisher:** Casa Musicale Sonzogno, Kalmus. **Rights:** Copyright
1896 by Edoardo Sonzogno. 1959 by Casa Musicale Sonzogno.

I. Carlo Gérard, a lackey, looks forward to the revolution, but this does
not prevent him from admiring the aristocrat Maddalena di Coigny.
Maddalena asks her mother, the countess, about the evening's guests
and complains that French fashions are suffocating. The guests arrive,

including the novelist Pietro Fléville, the pianist Fiorinelli and the poet Andrea Chénier. The Abate arrives with news of the political agitations in Paris, but is upstaged by a pastoral tableaux presented by Fléville. Chénier declines to recite one of his poems, so Fiorinelli plays the piano instead. Maddalena embarrasses Chénier: She has bet her friends that Chénier will speak to her of love—which is exactly what he does when she asks for a poem. He tells her that she knows nothing of love and recites a poem about the cruelty of the ancient regime. The guests are scandalized but Maddalena apologizes. The party is interrupted by a crowd of beggars whom Gérard has admitted to the house. The countess is furious and Gérard and his father leave with the beggars.

II. Recognizing Incredibile as one of Robespierre's spies, Bersi toasts the free life of the revolutionary. Incredibile is suspicious of Chénier who is clearly waiting for someone. Chénier's friend Roucher arrives with a passport that will get Chénier safely out of the country, but Chénier is here to meet a mysterious woman who has been writing him letters. He loves her, he says, and cannot leave. Roucher convinces Chénier that his lady is a Parisian of easy virtue and persuades him to take the passport. The crowd cheers the arrival of Gérard and Robespierre. Gérard is searching for Maddalena and Incredibile promises to locate her. Bersi tells Chénier to wait by the statue of Marat for his mysterious correspondent who turns out to be Maddalena. She begs Chénier to protect her. The two swear never to part but Incredibile has seen them and brings Gérard. Roucher chases off Incredibile while Chénier wounds Gérard in a sword fight. Chénier flees before Incredibile returns with an angry mob.

III. The people are unimpressed by Mathieu's call to support the revolution until Gérard adds his voice. Madelon, an old woman who has lost her son and oldest grandson to the revolution, volunteers her remaining grandson. Incredibile reports the capture of Chénier. He assures Gérard that Maddalena will be found soon and urges him to compose criminal charges against Chénier. Gérard reluctantly does so, sad that his dreams have come to this. Maddalena comes to plead for Chénier's life and realizing Gérard's desire for her, she offers herself to him. Her devotion convinces Gérard to try to save Chénier. The tribunal is convened. Fouquier Tinville, the public prosecutor, charges Chénier as a traitor. Chénier is condemned in spite of Gérard's confession that he accused Chénier falsely.

IV. Roucher bribes Schmidt, Chénier's jailer, so that he may speak to Chénier. Maddalena and Gérard bribe Schmidt to substitute Maddalena for one of the condemned women. The lovers console each other as they are led off to the guillotine.

Angélique

Composed by Jacques Ibert (August 15, 1890 – February 5, 1962). Libretto by Michel Weber (Nino). French. Original work. Premiered Paris, Théâtre Bériza, January 28, 1927. Set in a French port at an unspecified time. Farce. Set numbers with spoken dialogue. Introduction.

Sets: 1. **Acts:** 1 act, 1 scene. **Length:** I: 50. **Hazards:** I: devil magically appears. **Scenes:** I. A public place.

Major role: Angélique (soprano). **Minor roles:** Boniface (baritone), First godmother (soprano), Second godmother (mezzo), Italian (tenor), Charlot (baritone), Englishman (tenor), Moor (bass), Devil (tenor). **Speaking bits:** Neighbors.

Chorus parts: N/A. **Chorus roles:** None. **Dance/movement:** None. **Orchestra:** 2 fl (picc), ob, cl, bsn, hrn, trp, trb, timp, perc, piano, strings. **Stageband:** None. **Publisher:** Heugel & Co. **Rights:** Copyright 1926 by Heugel.

I. Infuriated by his shrewish young wife, Angélique, the China-shop owner, Boniface, decides to sell her. She is bought, in turn, by an Englishman, an Italian and a Moor, but all three quickly return her. When the men all wish Angélique to the devil, the devil appears and purchases her. No sooner have the men rejoiced in their good fortune, however, then the devil returns. He, too, cannot put up with Angélique's ways. Back with her husband, Angélique promises to behave.

Aniara

Composed by Karl-Birger Blomdahl (October 19, 1916 – June 14, 1968). Libretto by Erik Lindegren. Swedish. Based on an epic poem by Harry Martinson. Premiered Stockholm, Royal Opera, May 31, 1959. Set aboard the spaceship Aniara in the future. Space opera. Through composed. Musical interludes between scenes. Prelude before IIiii.

Sets: 5. **Acts:** 2 acts, 7 scenes. **Length:** I, II: 105. **Hazards:** I: Flashbacks to evacuation of Earth. Ship swerves to avoid an asteroid. The Mima displays three "Mima tapes," images and sound depicting the destruction of earth. **Scenes:** Ii. Galactic space and earth. Iii. Midsummer dance in the great assembly hall aboard the spaceship Aniara. Iiii. In front of curtain and the Mima hall. IIi. The Mima hall. IIii. The hall of mirrors. IIiii. The hall of the light year. IIiv. Galactic space.

Major roles: The Mimarobe (baritone). **Minor roles:** Daisi Doody (soprano), Comedian Sandon (comic tenor), Chief technician 1 (lyric tenor), Chief technician 2 (tenor), Chief technician 3 (baritone), Chefone the dictator (baritone), Blind poetess (high soprano). **Bit part:** Passenger (baritone). **Mute:** Deaf man. **Dancers:** Isagel the pilot, Yaal, Libidel, Chebeba, Gena, reflection of Yaal, reflection of Libidel, reflection of Chebeba, reflection Gena.

Chorus parts: SATB. **Chorus roles:** Emigrants from Doris/passengers, space cadets, mourning women. **Dance/movement:** I: Ballet. Pantomime of the deaf man. II: Yaal, Libidel, Chebeba and Gena perform a lascivious dance. Isagel dances her death. **Orchestra:** 3 fl (picc), 3 ob (Eng hrn), 3 cl (bs cl, 2 cl in A), alto sax (cl), 3 bsn (2 cont bsn), 4 hrn, 4 trp (bs trp), 3 trb, tuba, timp, harp, piano, vibraphone, 4 perc, strings. **Stageband:** None. **Publisher:** Schott & Co. Ltd. **Rights:** Copyright 1959 by Schott & Co. Ltd.

Ii. The Mimarobe recalls the evacuation of earth after a nuclear holocaust. Iii. The midsummer dance aboard the spaceship Aniara is interrupted when the ship swerves to avoid hitting an asteroid. The chief technician explains that the ship cannot reach its destination, but must continue on through interstellar space. Iiii. The passengers consult/worship the Mima, a technical marvel kept by the Mimarobe. The Mimarobe comments on the beauty of Isagel, the female pilot. The Mima shows the destruction of earth. A blind man and a deaf man communicate their experience of the destruction.

IIi. Mima dies of sorrow. Chefone, dictator of Aniara, accuses Mimarobe of causing Mima's death and has him imprisoned. IIii. The passengers repent their sins. IIiii. They celebrate the twentieth anniversary of Aniara's launch. The first engineer dies and the body is shot into space. IIiv. One by one, the passengers die of old age.

Anna Bolena

Composed by Gaetano Donizetti (November 29, 1797 – April 8, 1848). Libretto by Felice Romani. Italian. Based on the play by Alessandro Pepoli and Marie-Joseph de Chénier's "Enrico VIII" (translated by Ippolito Pindemonte). Premiered Milan, Teatro Carcano, December 26, 1830. Set in Windsor in 1536. Tragedy. Set numbers with recitative. Overture.

Sets: 6. **Acts:** 2 acts, 6 scenes. **Length:** I: 75. II: 75. **Arias:** "Al dolce guidami" (Anna), "Vivi tu" (Riccardo Percy). **Hazards:** None. **Scenes:** Ii. A brightly lit chamber in the queen's apartments in Windsor castle. Iii. The great park of Windsor. Iiii. An anteroom in Windsor castle leading to the queen's apartments. IIi. The tower of London. IIii. A vestibule giving onto the chamber in which the peers are closeted. IIiii. The prison.

Major roles: Giovanna Seymour (mezzo), Anna Bolena (soprano), King Enrico VIII (bass), Lord Riccardo Percy (tenor). **Minor roles:** Smeton (mezzo), Lord Rochefort (bass), Sir Hervey (tenor).

Chorus parts: SATTB. **Chorus roles:** Courtiers, lords and ladies, huntsmen, pages, grooms, maids of honor, soldiers. **Dance/movement:** None. **Orchestra:** 2 fl (picc), 2 ob, 2 cl, 2 bsn, 4 hrn, 2 trp, 3 trb, timp, perc, strings. **Stageband:** None. **Publisher:** Belwin Mills. **Rights:** Expired.

Ii. King Enrico has fallen in love with Giovanna di Seymour and everyone knows it is only a matter of time before he disposes of his wife, Anna Bolena. Anna, who left Lord Riccardo Percy for Enrico, warns Giovanna not to repeat her mistake. But Giovanna has decided: She convinces Enrico to marry her as soon as Anna is gone. Iii. Anna's brother, Lord Rochefort, welcomes Percy back from exile. Percy still loves Anna and Enrico duplicitously explains that he has recalled Percy for Anna's sake. Iiii. The musician Smeton overhears Rochefort convince Anna to see Percy. Percy forgives Anna, but she begs him to go away. They are surprised by the king who accuses her of infidelity. Smeton's attempt to defend the queen backfires. Enrico has them all arrested.

IIi. Giovanna counsels Anna to "confess" to her supposed crime: Her guilt would dissolve her marriage to Enrico—which is the only way Enrico might let her live. Anna is impressed by Giovanna's earnestness, although she suspects her motives. IIii. Enrico has tricked Smeton into confessing by promising to spare Anna. Anna and Percy defy the king. While Giovanna begs the king to forgive Anna, the royal council condemns Anna, Percy and Rochefort. The king commutes Percy and Rochefort's sentences, but they spurn his clemency. IIiii. Anna is delirious, remembering happier times. The condemned are led off to execution as the sounds of Enrico's wedding are heard in the background.

Antony and Cleopatra

Composed by Samuel Barber (March 9, 1910 – January 23, 1981). Libretto by Franco Zeffirelli. English. Based on the play by Shakespeare. Premiered New York City, Metropolitan Opera Association, September 16, 1966. Set in Rome in the 1st century BC. Tragedy. Through composed with prologue. Musical interludes between scenes.

Sets: 11. **Acts:** 3 acts, 15 scenes. **Length:** Prologue, I, II, III: 115. **Hazards:**

None. **Scenes:** Prologue. Unspecified. Ii. Cleopatra's palace in Alexandria. Iii. The Senate in Rome. Iiii. Cleopatra's palace. Iiv. A Roman banquet hall. IIi. The Senate. IIii. Cleopatra's garden. IIiii. Outside Antony's battlefield tent. IIiv. Inside Antony's tent. IIv. The battlefield at Actium. IIvi. Cleopatra's palace. IIvii. A battlefield. IIviii. Antony's ruined tent. IIIi. Cleopatra's monument. IIIii. Inside the monument.

Major roles: Cleopatra (soprano), Antony (baritone or high bass), Enobarbus (bass). **Minor roles:** Charmian (mezzo), Iras (contralto), Caesar Octavius (tenor), Agrippa (bass), Eros (tenor or high baritone), Soldier of Caesar (baritone), Rustic (baritone or bass), Messenger (tenor), Soothsayer (bass), Alexas (bass), First guard (baritone), Second guard (tenor), Third guard (bass), Dolabella (baritone). **Bit parts:** Fourth guard (bass), First watchman (bass), Second watchman (bass), Thidias (tenor or high baritone), Lepidus (tenor), Maecenas (bass). **Speaking:** Octavia.

Chorus parts: SSSAATTBB. **Chorus roles:** Egyptian courtiers, Roman senators and soldiers. Several small groups. **Dance/movement:** I: Dance of Egyptian girls and of slaves. **Orchestra:** 3 fl (2 picc, alto fl), 2 ob, Eng hrn, 2 cl, bs cl, 2 bsn, cont bsn, 4 hrn, 3 trp, 3 trb, tuba, timp, 6 perc, piano, celeste, 2 harp, guitar (optional), strings. **Stageband:** I, III: 4 trp, 4 trb. II: hrn (optional), 4 trp, 2 trb, tuba, organ (optional), perc. **Publisher:** Schirmer. **Rights:** Copyright 1966, 1976 by G. Schirmer.

Prologue. The chorus condemns Antony's life of luxury in Egypt. Ii. Antony realizes that life with Cleopatra is enervating him and he reluctantly takes his leave. Iii. The Roman Senate welcomes Antony, but Caesar Octavius is angry that Antony ignored his request for troops and suspects him of treason. The senator Agrippa suggests that peace be restored by having Antony marry Caesar's sister, Octavia. Iiii. Cleopatra pines for Antony. When news arrives of his marriage, Cleopatra is so angry she flogs the messenger. The messenger redeems himself by assuring Cleopatra she is fairer than Octavia. Iiv. Dolabella remarks that now that Antony is married, he will have to give up Cleopatra, but Antony's friend, Enobarbus, doubts that. Enobarbus recalls Antony's first encounter with Cleopatra. A vision of the Egyptian queen appears to Antony and he swears to return to her.

IIi. Caesar tells the Senate that Antony has given Cyprus, Lydia and lower Syria to Cleopatra. Rome prepares for war. IIii. Charmian and Iras tease Cleopatra's attendant Alexas. They have Alexas's friend the soothsayer tell their fortune. The soothsayer promises they will outlive their mistress. Antony's and Cleopatra's professions of love are interrupted by Enobarbus with news of Caesar's conquests. Cleopatra intends to accompany the army, but Enobarbus warns her that she distracts

Antony too much. IIiii. Antony's guards hear unearthly music in the camp, which they take to be an evil omen. IIiv. Antony reluctantly disengages himself from Cleopatra's embrace and prepares for the coming battle. IIv. In the midst of the battle, Cleopatra sails for home. The Egyptian army is demoralized and defeated. IIvi. Cleopatra is humble with Caesar's ambassador, Thidias, but Thidias's impertinence infuriates Antony. Antony feels that Cleopatra has abandoned him to the young Caesar. On a sudden inspiration, Cleopatra hurries off to her monument and orders Alexas to inform Antony she has committed suicide. IIvii. Enobarbus despairs. IIviii. Upon hearing of Cleopatra's death, Antony asks his shield bearer Eros to kill him. Eros slays himself instead. Antony falls on his sword, only to learn that Cleopatra lives.

IIIi. Antony is brought into Cleopatra's presence where he dies. Griefstricken, Cleopatra recounts a dream in which she saw Antony as Emperor of Rome. Caesar arrives and assures Cleopatra of his friendship. She promises obedience and Caesar laments Antony's passing. IIIii. Dolabella confesses to Cleopatra that Caesar means to lead her before his chariot in his triumphal entry into Rome. Using a poisonous asp, Cleopatra, Iras and Charmian all commit suicide. Cleopatra is borne off to be buried with Antony.

Arabella

Composed by Richard Strauss (June 11, 1864 – September 8, 1949). Libretto by Hugo von Hofmannsthal. German. Based on Hofmannsthal's novel "Lucidor." Premiered Dresden, Staatsoper, July 1, 1933. Set in Vienna in 1860. Lyric comedy. Through composed. Prelude before III. Brief spoken dialogue in III. Opus 79.

Sets: 3. **Acts:** 3 acts, 3 scenes. **Length:** I: 60. II: 45. III: 45. **Arias:** "Er ist der Richtige nicht für mich!" (Arabella), "Er mein—ich sein" (Arabella), "Das war sehr gut" (Arabella). **Hazards:** None. **Scenes:** I. A drawing room in a Vienna hotel. II. A public ballroom. III. An open hall with staircase in the hotel.

Major roles: Adelaide (mezzo), Zdenka (soprano), Matteo (tenor), Arabella (soprano), Mandryka (baritone). **Minor roles:** Fortune teller (soprano), Count Elemer (tenor), Count Waldner (bass), Count Dominik (baritone), Count Lamoral (bass), Fiakermilli (coloratura soprano). **Bit parts:** Waiter (tenor), Three gamblers (3 bass). **Speaking bits:** Welko, Jankel, Djura. **Mute:** Arabella's companion, Doctor, Groom.

Chorus parts: STB. **Chorus roles:** Coachmen, guests at the ball, hotel residents, waiters. **Dance/movement:** II: ballroom dancing. **Orchestra:** 3 fl (picc), 2 ob, Eng hrn, C-cl, 2 B- (A-) cl, bs cl, 3 bsn (cont bsn), 4 hrn, 3 trp, 3 trb, tuba, timp, harp, strings. **Stageband:** None. **Publisher:** Boosey & Hawkes, B. Schott Söhne. **Rights:** Copyright 1933 by R. Strauss. Assigned 1955 to Franz Strauss. Renewed 1970 by Dr. Franz Strauss.

I. Adelaide consults a fortune teller about how to repair the family fortunes. The only hope is for their daughter Arabella to marry well. There is another daughter, Zdenka, but she is forced to dress as a boy because the family cannot afford to bring up two ladies. The disguise has not stopped Zdenka from falling in love with Matteo, a young officer. But it does put her in an awkward position when Matteo confesses to her that he loves Arabella. Zdenka dutifully tries to plead Matteo's case with Arabella. Meanwhile, Arabella's father, Count Waldner, continues to gamble—and lose. To salvage his position, Waldner hits on the expedient of fixing Arabella up with a rich old army comrade. The comrade is unfortunately dead, but his nephew Mandryka, charmed by a picture of Arabella, comes in his place. Mandryka lends Waldner money and is promised Arabella's hand.

II. Arabella is introduced to Mandryka at a ball and the two fall in love. Matteo is heartbroken, but Zdenka cheers him up by giving him a key, which she tells him is to Arabella's room. Mandryka overhears and when Arabella leaves the ball, he follows her.

III. The key is really to Zdenka's room and it is she to whom Matteo has unwittingly made love. He runs into Arabella on the stairs and is maddened by her inexplicable aloofness. Arabella's parents and Mandryka demand explanations. Zdenka finally confesses. Matteo admits he suspected Zdenka's disguise all along and the two pairs of lovers forgive one another.

Ariadne auf Naxos • Ariadne of Naxos

Composed by Richard Strauss (June 11, 1864 – September 8, 1949). Libretto by Hugo von Hofmannsthal. German. Original work initially meant to be performed with the play "Le Bourgeois Gentilhomme" by Molière. Premiered Stuttgart, Hoftheater, October 25, 1912. Set in Vienna in the 18th century. Lyric comedy. Through composed. Set numbers with recitative in "opera." Prologue. Overture before I, II. Intermezzo in I. Opus 60. First act is the "prologue" before the "performance" (2nd act). Revised version (including prologue) first performed Vienna, October 4, 1916.

Sets: 1 or 2. **Acts:** 2 act, 2 scenes. **Length:** I: 35. II: 80. **Arias:** "Grossmächtige Prinzessin" (Zerbinetta), Composer's aria (Composer).

Hazards: None. **Scenes:** Prelude. A room in the house of a nobleman. I. A stage set of a small desert island.

Major roles: Composer (soprano), Tenor/Bacchus (tenor), Zerbinetta (high soprano), Prima donna/Ariadne (soprano). **Minor roles:** Music master (baritone), Lackey (bass), Dancing master (tenor), Naiad (high soprano), Dryad (contralto), Echo (soprano), Brighella (high tenor), Harlekin (baritone), Scaramuccio (tenor), Truffaldin (bass). **Bit part:** Officer (tenor), Wig maker (high bass). **Speaking:** Major domo.

Chorus parts: N/A. **Chorus roles:** None. **Dance/movement:** I: Zerbinetta and her troupe dance. **Orchestra:** 2 fl (picc), 2 ob, 2 cl, 2 bsn, 2 hrn, trp, trb, piano, 2 harps, harmonium, celeste, timp, perc, strings (6-4-4-2). **Stageband:** None. **Publisher:** Boosey & Hawkes. **Rights:** Copyright 1912, 1916, 1922, 1940 Fürstner. Assigned Boosey & Hawkes, 1943, 1944.

Prelude. A nobleman has planned a balanced evening's entertainment for his guests: a composer and singer have been retained to perform the new opera seria "Ariadne," after which a comedy troupe will provide lighter fare. The composer and his music master are not pleased to be double-billed with vulgar entertainers. But when the nobleman orders the two entertainments to be performed simultaneously, they are positively scandalized. They try to make it work, but compromise seems impossible: The commediene Zerbinetta tells the composer that his heroine, Ariadne, just needs a new boyfriend. Horrified by her levity, the composer runs out of the room.

I. The hybrid entertainment begins. Ariadne pines for Theseus and death. The others try to cheer her up. Zerbinetta recounts her past love affairs. The men woo Zerbinetta, who goes off with Arlecchino. The nymphs welcome Bacchus, who has just escaped the witch Circe. And Ariadne falls in love with Bacchus.

Ariane et Barbe-Bleue • Ariane and Bluebeard

Composed by Paul Dukas (October 1, 1865 – May 17, 1935). Libretto by Maurice Maeterlinck. French. Based on a story by Charles Perrault. Premiered Paris, Opéra Comique, May 10, 1907. Set inside Bluebeard's castle in Medieval times. Symbolist drama. Through composed. Prelude before I, II, III.

Sets: 2. **Acts:** 3 acts, 3 scenes. **Length:** I, II, III: 120. **Hazards:** I: Blinding light and rivers of gems behind the first six doors. **Scenes:** I. A semi-circular hall in Bluebeard's castle. II. A vast underground hall with vaults supported by numerous pillars. III. The semi-circular hall.

Major roles: Nurse (contralto), Ariane (mezzo). **Minor roles:** Barbe-Bleue/Bluebeard (bass or bass baritone), Sélysette (mezzo), Ygraine (soprano), Mélisande (soprano), Bellangère (soprano), Old peasant (bass). **Bit parts:** Second peasant (tenor), Third peasant (bass). **Mute:** Alladine.

Chorus parts: SATTTBBB. **Chorus roles:** Peasants, people. **Dance/movement:** None. **Orchestra:** 3 fl (2 picc), 2 ob, Eng hrn, 2 cl, bs cl, 3 bsn, cont bsn, 4 hrn, 3 trp, 3 trb, tuba, timp, perc, celeste, 2 harp, strings. **Stageband:** None. **Publisher:** A. Durand & Fils. **Rights:** Expired.

I. After marrying Bluebeard, Ariane comes to his castle. Sure he loves her, she ignores the gloomy warnings of the crowd. Together with her nurse, Ariane opens six mysterious doors in the castle and discovers rich troves of gems. Bluebeard is angry with her for trying to discover his secrets. When the crowd, enraged at Bluebeard, breaks into the castle, Ariane calms them down.

II. While Bluebeard is away, Ariane finds his five previous wives imprisoned, but alive. She frees them.

III. The wives are unable or unwilling to escape from the castle so they instead adorn themselves with Bluebeard's jewels. When Bluebeard returns, he is attacked by the crowd, which ties him up and turns him over to the wives for punishment. Ariane frees Bluebeard, but decides she must leave him. The other wives remain.

Ariodante

Composed by George Frederic Handel (February 23, 1685 – April 14, 1759). Libretto by Antonio Salvi. Italian. From "Orlando Furioso" by Ludovico Ariosto. Premiered London, King's Theater, January 8, 1735. Set in Scotland in medieval times. Comedy. Set numbers with recitative. Overture. Ballet. Symphony before II. Intermezzo before Iiv, IIIvi, IIIxii.

Sets: 9. **Acts:** 3 acts, 36 scenes. **Length:** I, II, III: 180. **Arias:** Con l'ali di costanza (Ariodante), Scherza infida (Ariodante), Cieca notte (Ariodante), Dopo notte (Ariodante). **Hazards:** None. **Scenes:** Ii – Iiv. Royal apartments. Iv – Ixi. A royal garden. Ixii – Ixiii. A beautiful valley. IIi – IIv. An old, ruined palace. IIvi – IIx. A gallery. IIIi – IIIiii. A wood. IIIiii – IIIvi. The royal garden. IIIvii – IIIx. A tournament field. IIIxi – IIIxii. An apartment allotted for the confinement of Ginevra. IIIxiii. A royal hall with a grand staircase.

Major roles: Ginevra (soprano), Dalinda (soprano), Polinesso (alto or countertenor or bass baritone), Ariodante (contralto or mezzo). **Minor roles:** Odoardo (tenor), Lurcanio (tenor), King of Scotland (bass). **Mute:** Two assassins.

Chorus parts: SATB. **Chorus roles:** Shepherds, nymphs, guards, knights, ladies, attendants. **Dance/movement:** I: ballet of shepherds and nymphs. II: ballet. III: Wedding ballet at court. **Orchestra:** 2 fl, 2 ob, 2 bsn, 2 hrn, 2 trp, traversa, strings, continuo. **Stageband:** III: 2 ob, 2 bsn. **Publisher:** Gregg Press. **Rights:** Expired.

Ii. Ginevra tells Dalinda that she loves Ariodante—and that her father, the king, approves. Iii. She rejects Polinesso, who loves her. Iiii. Dalinda loves Polinesso. Iiv. Polinesso swears to defeat his rival. Iv. Ariodante tells Ginevra he is unworthy of her, but Ginevra disagrees. Ivi. The king blesses the couple. Ivii. He makes Ariodante his heir. Iviii. Ariodante is happy. Iix. Polinesso agrees to marry Dalinda and tells her to disguise herself as Ginevra. Ix. Ariodante's brother, Lurcanio, declares his love for Dalinda. Ixi. Dalinda rejoices in her love. Ixii. Ariodante admires the landscape. Ixiii. Shepherds and nymphs celebrate the coming nuptials.

IIi. Alone, Polinesso admits he is deceiving Dalinda. IIii. He convinces Ariodante that Lurcanio has betrayed him by making love to Dalinda—who is dressed like Ginevra. IIiii. Ariodante considers suicide. IIiv. Polinesso promises to love Dalinda. IIv. He revels in his success. IIvi. Odoardo tells the king Ariodante is dead. IIvii. On hearing the news, Ginevra faints. IIviii. Lurcanio produces a letter from Ariodante accusing Ginevra and demands justice. IIix. The king denounces Ginevra. IIx. She loses her sanity.

IIIi. Fleeing Polinesso's assassins, Dalinda encounters Ariodante and tells him the truth. IIIii. Dalinda is angry with Polinesso. IIIiii. Polinesso volunteers to fight for Ginevra's honor. IIIiv. The king softens towards his daughter. IIIv. She kisses his hand. IIIvi. And prepares herself for death. IIIvii. Lurcanio fights and kills Polinesso. IIIviii. Ariodante returns. IIIix. He explains everything. IIIx. Lurcanio reiterates his love for Dalinda. IIIxi. Ginevra is released. IIIxii. She and Ariodante are reunited. IIIxiii. They marry.

Arlecchino • Harlequin

Composed by Ferruccio Busoni (April 1, 1866 – July 27, 1924). Libretto by Ferruccio Busoni. German. Original work based on Italian commedia dell'arte figures and situations. Premiered Zürich, Stadttheater, May 11, 1917. Set in Bergamo in the 18th century. Theatrical caprice. Set numbers with recitative and spoken dialogue. Prologue.

Sets: 1. **Acts:** 1 act, 5 scenes. **Length:** Prologue, I: 65. **Hazards:** I: Arlecchino jumps out a window. **Scenes:** Prologue. Before the curtain. I. A steep and tortuous street in the upper town of Bergamo.

Major roles: Ser Matteo del Sarto (baritone), Abbott Cospicuo (baritone), Dr. Bombasto (bass), Colombina (mezzo), Leandro (tenor). **Speaking:** Arlecchino. **Mute:** Annunziata, Two soldiers.

Chorus parts: N/A. **Chorus roles:** None. **Dance/movement:** I: Annunziata and Arlecchino dance a "short, lively dance." **Orchestra:** 2 fl (picc), 2 ob (Eng hrn), 2 cl (bs cl), 2 bsn, 3 hrn, 2 trp, 3 trb, timp, perc, celeste, strings. **Stageband:** None. **Publisher:** Breitkopf & Härtel. **Rights:** Copyright 1918 by Breitkopf & Härtel.

Prologue. Arlecchino introduces the play. Ii. Matteo the tailor works and reads Dante, unaware that Arlecchino is sleeping with Matteo's wife, Annunziata. Arlecchino makes his escape by brazenly jumping out the window right in front of Matteo. While making off with Matteo's keys, Arlecchino tells the distraught husband that the barbarians are attacking the town. The abbate thanks the doctor for sending so many of his flock on to heaven. They discuss women. Matteo tells them of the supposed invasion, but they go to the tavern. Iii. Arlecchino masquerades as a recruiting officer and drafts Matteo. He returns Matteo's keys, which he has copied. Iiii. Arlecchino's wife, Colombina, chides him for his unfaithfulness, but Arlecchino runs off. Leandro woos Colombina until Arlecchino challenges him to fight. Leandro is wounded. Iiv. The abbate, the doctor and Colombina discover Leandro. They put him on a donkey cart and take him off to the hospital. Arlecchino runs off with Annunziata before Matteo returns home. Arlecchino and Annunziata dance.

Armida

Composed by Franz Joseph Haydn (March 31, 1732 – May 31, 1809). Libretto by Jacopo Durandi. Italian. Based on the epic poem "Gerusalemme liberata" by Torquato Tasso. Premiered Esterháza, Court Theater, February 26, 1784. Set in Damascus during the crusades. Heroic drama. Set numbers with recitative. Overture.

Sets: 6. **Acts:** 3 acts, 7 scenes. **Length:** I: 50. II: 60. III: 30. **Hazards:** III: A myrtle tree opens and Armida steps out. She conjures up a magic bridge, whereupon the wood is replaced by the European encampment. An infernal charioteer appears and attacks Rinaldo. **Scenes:** Ii. Council chamber in the royal palace of Damascus. Iii. A steep mountain on the peak of which Armida's castle can be seen. Iiii. Armida's apartment. IIi.

A garden in Armida's palace. IIii. The Europeans' encampment. IIIi. A dark, forbidding grove in the middle of which is a very thick myrtle tree. IIIii. The encampment.

Major roles: Idreno (bass), Armida (soprano), Rinaldo (tenor), Ubaldo (tenor), Zelmira (soprano), Clotarco (tenor). **Mute:** Soldiers, nymphs and furies.

Chorus parts: N/A. **Chorus roles:** None. **Dance/movement:** None. **Orchestra:** 2 fl, 2 ob, 2 cl, 2 bsn, 2 hrn, timp, strings, continuo. **Stageband:** None. **Rights:** Expired.

Ii. The Christian knight Rinaldo has fallen in love with the heathen sorceress Armida. He agrees to fight for her uncle, King Idreno, against the Christians. Iii. Armida's magic does not stop the Christian soldiers, who are led by Ubaldo and Clotarco. Idreno sends Zelmira, the daughter of the Egyptian sultan, out to lead the Christians into a trap, but she falls in love with Clotarco. Iiii. Ubaldo reminds Rinaldo of his duty, but is unable to shake Armida's enchantment.

IIi. Zelmira is unable to dissuade Idreno from his plan of ambushing the Christians. The king pretends to agree to Clotarco's demand that the Christian knights enchanted by Armida be released. With great reluctance, Rinaldo leaves with Ubaldo. IIii. Armida asks for refuge in Ubaldo's camp but is refused.

IIIi. Prophesy says that only Rinaldo can overcome the enchanted woods. Armida emerges from the magic myrtle tree that Rinaldo has entered the woods to cut down. Rinaldo defeats Armida's furies and cuts down the tree. IIIii. Armida sends an infernal chariot against Rinaldo, but he escapes.

Armide

Composed by Christoph Willibald Gluck (July 2, 1714 – November 15, 1787). Libretto by Philippe Quinault. French. Based on "Gerusalemme Liberata" by Torquato Tasso. Premiered Paris, Académie Royale de Musique, September 23, 1777. Set in Damascus in 1099. Heroic drama. Set numbers with recitative. Overture. Ballet.

Sets: 7. **Acts:** 5 acts, 23 scenes. **Length:** I – V: 150. **Arias:** "Plus j'observe ces lieux" (Renaud). **Hazards:** III: Armide visits Hades. IV: Ubalde and Danish knight fight monsters and wild beasts. The beasts sink out of sight and the landscape is transformed. V: Demons destroy the palace. **Scenes:** I. A hall in the palace of Armide. IIi. A desert.

IIii – IIv. Enchanted woods. IIIi – IIIii. A rough and wild landscape. IIIiii – IIIiv. Hades. IIIv. The wild landscape. IVi. The wild landscape and an agreeable country scene. IVii – IViv. The enchanted wood. V. The palace garden.

Major roles: Armide (soprano), Renaud (tenor). **Minor roles:** Phénice (soprano), Sidonie (soprano), King Hidraot (baritone), Aronte (bass), Artemidore (tenor), Nyad (soprano), Fury of hate (mezzo or contralto), Ubalde (baritone), Danish knight (tenor), Demon as Lucinde (soprano), Demon as Melissa (soprano).

Chorus parts: SATB. **Chorus roles:** People of Damascus, demons disguised as shepherds and shepherdesses, furies, demons disguised as peasants, pleasures, happy lovers, demons. **Dance/movement:** I: Dance of the Damascans. II: Dance of the Nyads. III: Dance of the furies. IV: Dance. V: Chaconne, gavotte, minuet and Sicilian dance. **Orchestra:** 2 fl, 2 ob, 2 cl, 2 bsn, 2 hrn, 2 trp, 2 trb (optional), timp, strings. **Stageband:** None. **Publisher:** G. Ricordi, Bureau de Journal de Musique. **Rights:** Expired.

Ii. Armide's magic has triumphed over Godfrey's knights. But Armide worries that her conquest is incomplete because Renaud does not love her. Iii. King Hidraot hopes Armide, who is his niece, will marry. Iiii. The people of Damascus celebrate their victory. Iiv. Renaud frees Armide's prisoners.

IIi. Renaud has been banished from Godfrey's camp. A knight warns him to beware Armide's charms. IIii. Armide lures Renaud into a forest. IIiii. He falls asleep. IIiv. He dreams of nymphs and shepherds. IIv. Armide cannot bring herself to kill the helpless knight.

IIIi. Armide loves Renaud. IIIii. But she still wants revenge. IIIiii. She fetches Hate to aid her. IIIiv. Armide changes her mind, offending Hate. IIIv. She returns to the world.

IVi. Ubalde and a Danish knight defeat Armide's monster guardians with the help of a magic scepter. IVii. The Danish knight meets a demon disguised as his beloved Lucinde. IViii. Ubalde saves the knight. IViv. The two men resolve not to be distracted again.

Vi. Armide fears she will lose Renaud, but he assures her of his love. Vii. The lovers are entertained by Pleasure and her attendants. Viii. Ubalde and the Danish knight recall Renaud to his duty. Viv. Renaud takes his leave of the heartbroken—and angry—Armide. Vv. She destroys her palace and pursues Renaud with her demons.

Aroldo

Composed by Giuseppe Verdi (October 9, 1813 – January 27, 1901). Libretto by Francesco Maria Piave. Italian. Based on "Le Pasteur" by Souvestre and Bourgeois. Premiered Rimini, Teatro Nuovo, August 16, 1857. Set in England and Scotland in the 12th century. Melodrama. Set numbers with recitative. Overture. Reworking of Verdi's "Stiffelio" with alternate final scene in III and new "Loch Lomond" fourth act.

Sets: 5. **Acts:** 4 acts, 5 scenes. **Length:** I: 50. II: 25. III: 25. IV: 25. **Hazards:** IV: Mina and Egberto's boat comes ashore in a storm. **Scenes:** Ii. A parlor in Egberto's dwelling. Iii. A hall brightly lit for a party. II. The old cemetery of the castle of Kent. III. An antechamber in Egberto's home. IV. A deep valley in Scotland.

Major roles: Mina (soprano), Aroldo (tenor), Egberto (baritone). **Minor roles:** Godvino (tenor), Briano (bass). **Bit parts:** Enrico (tenor), Elena (mezzo). **Mute:** Jorg.

Chorus parts: SSATTBB. **Chorus roles:** Crusaders, ladies and noblemen, servants, pages, heralds, hunters, villagers, Saxons, offstage congregation. **Dance/movement:** None. **Orchestra:** 2 fl, 2 ob, 2 cl, 2 bsn, 4 hrn, 2 trp, 3 trb, tuba, timp, perc, organ, strings. **Stageband:** I: hrn. IV: hrns, bell. **Publisher:** G. Ricordi & Co. **Rights:** Expired.

Ii. Aroldo is welcomed home from Palestine. In his absence, his wife, Mina, has had an affair with Godvino. Aroldo introduces Briano, a holy man who saved his life. Mina wants to tell Aroldo the truth, but Mina's father, Egberto, insists it is her duty to remain silent and be faithful from now on. Iii. Godvino leaves a letter for Mina. It is intercepted by Aroldo, but Egberto takes it before Aroldo can read it. Egberto challenges Godvino.

II. Godvino finds Mina in the cemetery and says he still loves her. Egberto challenges Godvino, who reluctantly agrees to fight. Aroldo separates the combatants. The truth comes out. Briano prevents Aroldo from fighting Godvino.

III. Godvino flees, but is recaptured. Aroldo forces Mina to sign divorce papers, although she says she still loves him. Egberto kills Godvino.

IV. Aroldo and Briano become hermits in Scotland. Mina and Egberto arrive by boat in a storm. Aroldo forgives Mina.

Ascanio in Alba

Composed by Wolfgang Amadeus Mozart (January 27, 1756 – December 5, 1791). Libretto by Giuseppe Parini. Italian. Based on a play by Count Claudio Nicolò Stampa. The piece is meant to represent the wedding for which it was written. Premiered Milan, Teatro Regio Ducal, October 17, 1771. Set in Alba in classical times. Festa teatrale. Set numbers with recitative. Overture.

Sets: 1. **Acts:** 2 acts, 2 scenes. **Length:** I, II: 160. **Arias:** "Sì, ma d'un altro Amore" (Silvia). **Hazards:** I: Venere's chariot ascends into the clouds. II: Trees are transformed into columns. Altar is enveloped by clouds out of which appear Venere, graces and spirits. **Scenes:** I – II. An expanse of ground bordered by a ring of oak trees.

Major roles: Venere (soprano), Ascanio (soprano), Silvia (soprano). **Minor roles:** Fauno (soprano), Aceste (tenor).

Chorus parts: SSATB. **Chorus roles:** Spirits, graces, shepherds, shepherdesses, spirits, nymphs. **Dance/movement:** I: graces and spirits dance, nymphs dance. **Orchestra:** 2 fl, 2 ob, 2 bsn, 2 hrn, 2 trp, 2 serpents, timp, strings, continuo. **Stageband:** None. **Publisher:** Breitkopf & Härtel. **Rights:** Expired.

I. The Goddess Venere has promised the people of Alba that her son, Ascanio, will rule over them and marry Sylvia, the daughter of the priest Aceste. Venere tells Ascanio to enter Alba incognito. Ascanio does not see why his identity should be secret, but follows his mother's advice. He meets the shepherd Fauno and sees Sylvia. Sylvia confesses to her father that she has fallen in love with a man she has seen only in her dreams. Aceste suspects (correctly) that the vision is of Ascanio. Venere tells her son to keep his secret a little longer.

II. Sylvia awaits Ascanio. She sees the man in her vision, but does not know if he is her fiancé. Through Fauno, Aceste invites Ascanio to the wedding. Sylvia overhears and is crushed: she concludes that Ascanio is not her fiancé. Ascanio is impatient to tell Sylvia the truth. Sylvia decides to honor her commitment to Ascanio. Ascanio realizes how lucky he is. Venere reveals Ascanio's identity and blesses the lovers.

The Aspern Papers

Composed by Dominick Argento (b. October 27, 1927). Libretto by Dominick Argento. English. Based on the novella by Henry James. Premiered Dallas, The Dallas Opera, November 19, 1988. Set in a village

near the northern end of Lake Como in 1835 and 1895. Tragedy.
Through composed. Prologues before I and II. Barcarole text from
Longfellow's poem, "Cadenabbia."

Sets: 4. **Acts:** 2 acts, 10 scenes. **Length:** Prologue, I: 60. II: 55. **Hazards:**
Frequent changes of time. **Scenes:** Prologue – Ii. The terrace and garden
of the villa. Iii – Iiii. The exterior wall of the music room and terrace.
Iiv – Iv. Interior of the music room. Prologue. Creon's palace and
Medea's house. IIi – IIii. Exterior of the music room and terrace. IIiii –
IIiv. Interior of the music room. (Scenes alternate between 1895 and
1835.)

Major roles: Juliana Bordereau (soprano), Aspern (tenor), Tina (mezzo),
Lodger (baritone). **Minor roles:** Barelli (bass baritone), Sonia (mezzo),
Pasquale/Painter (bass), Olimpia/Voice of Juliana in the prologue
(soprano).

Chorus parts: SATB. **Chorus roles:** Offstage. **Dance/movement:** None.
Orchestra: 2 fl (picc), 2 ob (Eng hrn), 2 cl (bs cl), 2 bsn (cont bsn), 3 hrn, 2
trp, 2 trb, tuba, timp, 2 perc, piano (celeste), harp, strings. **Stageband:**
None. **Publisher:** Boosey & Hawkes. **Rights:** Copyright 1988 by Boosey
& Hawkes.

Prologue. Juliana remembers her singing career—and the love of her life,
the composer Aspern who drowned in Lake Como sixty years ago.
Ii. She rents rooms to a lodger. He is a writer and presses Juliana's niece,
Tina, for information about Aspern. Iii. In a flashback, Aspern's portrait
is being painted. The composer discusses his new opera, Medea, with
Barelli the impresario while Juliana practices. Iiii. After two months, the
lodger has learned nothing. He decides to woo the daughter—which
Juliana encourages. Juliana shows the lodger Aspern's portrait, which he
pretends not to recognize. Tina refuses to help him get ahold of Aspern's
papers. Iiv. In a flashback, Juliana coaches Sonia, Barelli's new protegée
(and mistress). When Juliana goes out, Aspern embraces Sonia. The two
feel guilty at betraying Juliana. She overhears them. Iv. Tina returns
from a romantic evening with the lodger. She promises to help him.
Juliana has fallen sick. The lodger attempts to go through her things, but
Juliana catches him. She faints.

Prelude. The lodger does not believe that Aspern's opera Medea was
destroyed by the composer hours before he drowned. He thinks Juliana
has it. IIi. In a flashback, Aspern has finished Medea. Realizing he means
to pay a nocturnal visit to Sonia, Juliana sets the boat adrift. Aspern
swims out to get it. IIii. Juliana has died. Tina gives the lodger Aspern's
picture. She hints that he can have the music if he marries her. IIiii.
Juliana tells Barelli that Aspern burned "Medea" before his death—and

that she is retiring from the stage. IIiv. The lodger has decided to marry
Tina when she tells him that she burnt the manuscript. The lodger flees.
Now Tina really burns the manuscript.

Assassinio nella Cattedrale • Assassination in the Cathedral

Composed by Ildebrando Pizzetti (September 20, 1880 – February 13,
1968). Libretto by Alberto Castelli. Italian. Based on the play "Murder in
the Cathedral" by T. S. Eliot. Premiered Milan, Teatro alla Scala, March
1, 1958. Set in Canterbury in December 2, 1170 and December 29, 1170.
Tragedy. Through composed. Intermezzo.

Sets: 3. **Acts:** 2 acts, 4 scenes (including intermezzo). **Length:** I, II: 100.
Hazards: None. **Scenes:** Ii. Before the cathedral. Iii. The archbishop's
study. Intermezzo. Inside the cathedral. II. Before the cathedral.

Major role: Archbishop Tommaso Becket (bass). **Minor roles:** Two
women (soprano, mezzo), Three priests (tenor, baritone, bass), Herald
(tenor), Four tempters (tenor, 3 baritone), Four cavaliers of the king
(tenor, 2 baritone, bass).

Chorus parts: SSAATTBB. **Chorus roles:** Women of Canterbury, priests,
mysterious voices of the air, children. **Dance/movement:** None.
Orchestra: 3 fl (picc), 2 ob, Eng hrn, 2 cl, bs cl, 2 bsn, cont bsn, 4 hrn, 3
trp, 3 trb, tuba, timp, harp, celeste, perc, strings. **Stageband:** I: bells.
Publisher: G. Ricordi. **Rights:** Copyright 1958 by G. Ricordi & Co.

Ii. The people of Canterbury mourn the absence of their archbishop,
Thomas à Becket, who has fled to France to avoid the wrath of King
Henry II after a disagreement over royal interference in church matters.
Word arrives of Becket's return. Iii. The archbishop resists temptors who
are sent to seduce him.

Intermezzo. Becket gives a Christmas sermon on martyrdom. II. Four
knights, sent by Henry II, murder Becket. They attempt to justify their
actions in historical terms.

At the Boar's Head

Composed by Gustav Holst (September 21, 1874 – May 25, 1934).
Libretto by Gustav Holst. English. After the play "Henry IV" by William
Shakespeare Premiered Manchester, British National Opera Company,
April 3, 1925. Set in Eastcheap in the 15th century. Musical interlude. Set

numbers with recitative. Music based on old English melodies.
Sets: 1. **Acts:** 1 act, 1 scene. **Length:** I: 60. **Arias:** "I know you all" (Hal).
Hazards: None. **Scenes:** I. Upper room of The Boar's Head Tavern.

Major roles: Falstaff (bass), Prince Hal (tenor). **Minor roles:** Bardolph (baritone), Peto (tenor), Gadshill (tenor), Poins (bass), Mistress Quickly (soprano), Doll Tearsheet (mezzo), Pistol (baritone). **Bit parts:** Pistol's two companions (2 baritone). **Mute:** A drawer.

Chorus parts: Ba. **Chorus roles:** Offstage soldiers. **Dance/movement:** None. **Orchestra:** picc, fl, ob, Eng hrn, 2 cl, 2 bsn, 2 hrn, 2 trp, tuba or euphonium, timp, strings. **Stageband:** None. **Publisher:** Novello & Co. **Rights:** Copyright 1925 by Novello & Co.

I. Falstaff and his men steal 1,000 pounds, only to be robbed of it themselves. They return to the Boar's Head Inn where they tell the story to Prince Hal, grossly exaggerating the strength and numbers of their assailants. Hal admits that it was he and Poins who robbed them. A messenger tells Hal to return to court: Percy has started a rebellion. To amuse themselves, Falstaff and Hal take turns play-acting the king—and praising or abusing Falstaff. Doll Tearsheet says farewell to Falstaff. Hal and Poins disguise themselves as servants and everyone joins in a song. When a group of soldiers passes by, Hal throws off his disguise and joins them. Pistol argues with Falstaff and Falstaff's men drive him out of the tavern. Falstaff himself flees into the night.

Atalanta

Composed by George Frederic Handel (February 23, 1685 – April 14, 1759). Libretto by an anonymous author. Italian. Based on the pastoral "La Caccia in Etolia" by Belisario Valeriani. Premiered London, King's Theater, May 12, 1736. Set in Arcadia in legendary times. Opera seria or pastoral. Set numbers with recitative. Overture. Orchestral interludes in I and III. Sinfonia before III.

Sets: 1. **Acts:** 3 acts, 3 scenes. **Length:** I: 45. II: 50. III: 45. **Arias:** "Care selve" (Meleagro). **Hazards:** I: Wild boar hunt. Atalanta kills the boar. III: Mercurio descends on a cloud surrounded by graces and cupids. Backdrop opens to reveal bonfires. **Scenes:** I – III. Open meadows with a few huts and woods on either side.

Major roles: Meleagro (soprano or countertenor), Aminta (tenor), Irene (contralto), Atalanta (soprano). **Minor roles:** Nicandro (bass), Mercurio (bass).

Chorus parts: SATB. **Chorus roles:** Nymphs, shepherd, loves, graces. **Dance/movement:** None. **Orchestra:** 2 ob, 2 hrn, 3 trp, timp, strings, continuo. **Stageband:** None. **Publisher:** Gregg Press Inc. **Rights:** Expired.

I. Meleagro, the King of Etolia, has disguised himself as the shepherd Tirsi to woo Amarillis. Aminta loves Irene. She returns his love, but tries to make him jealous of Meleagro. When her father, Nicandro, asks about her behavior, Irene explains that she wishes to test Aminta's love. Aminta tries to throw himself in front of a wild boar, but his fellow shepherds prevent him. Amarillis is really Atalanta, the princess of Arcadia, in disguise. She kills the boar.

II. Atalanta loves Meleagro, but cannot marry him because he is only a shepherd. When Meleagro overhears Atalanta confessing this truth, he tries to tell her he is really a king, but she will not listen. Irene agrees to plead Meleagro's case with Atalanta. He gives her a ribbon for Atalanta, which Irene uses to make Aminta jealous. Atalanta gives Aminta an arrow to give to Meleagro.

III. Irene gives Atalanta the ribbon. Aminta uses Atalanta's arrow to make Irene jealous. Meleagro overhears and fears that Atalanta loves Aminta. Meleagro rebukes Atalanta for her infidelity until she admits she loves him. Nicandro reveals Atalanta and Meleagro's true identities. Irene and Aminta declare their love. Mercurio descends from the heavens to bless the couples

Attila

Composed by Giuseppe Verdi (October 9, 1813 – January 27, 1901). Libretto by Temistocle Solera. Italian. Based on "Attila, König der Hunnen" by Zacharias Werner. Premiered Venice, Teatro la Fenice, March 17, 1846. Set in Aquileia, Adriatic lagoons, Rome in the mid-5th century. Lyric drama. Set numbers with recitative. Overture. Prologue.

Sets: 6. **Acts:** 3 acts, 8 scenes. **Length:** Prologue: 15. I: 15. II: 30. III: 40. **Arias:** "Dagl' immortali vertici" (Ezio). **Hazards:** None. **Scenes:** Prologue i. A square in Aquileia. Prologue ii. High water in the Adriatic lagoons. Ii. A forest near Attila's camp. Iii. Attila's tent. Iiii. Attila's camp. IIi. Ezio's camp. IIii. Attila's camp. III. The forest.

Major roles: Attila (bass), Ezio (baritone), Odabella (soprano), Foresto (tenor). **Minor roles:** Uldino (tenor), Leone (bass).

Chorus parts: SSAATTBB. **Chorus roles:** Soldiers, Huns, Herulians, Ostrogoths, Odabella's attendants, Druid priestesses, virgins and children, refugees, hermits, slaves, captains, nobles, people. **Dance/move-ment:** None. **Orchestra:** 2 fl (picc), 2 ob (Eng hrn), 2 cl, 2 bsn, 4 hrn, 2 trp, 3 trb, cimbasso, timp, perc, harp, strings. **Stageband:** I: trps. II: trps. **Publisher:** Belwin Mills. **Rights:** Expired.

Prologue i. Attila's soldiers prostrate themselves before their leader, Atilla, amidst the ruins of conquered Aquileia. Against Attila's orders, his slave Uldino has spared Odabella (daughter of the late lord of Aquileia). Smitten by her defiance, the great warrior grants her one request. When she demands a sword, Attila gives her his. Attila is pleased that Ezio is the Roman envoy, but refuses when Ezio offers to join forces in return for Italy, and they part. Prologue ii. The hermits of San Giacomo praise God. Foresto, arriving with a group of refugees from Aquileia, is tormented by the realization that Odabella is in Attila's harem.

Ii. Odabella misses Foresto. He returns disguised, but reproaches Odabella with unfaithfulness. She swears she means to murder Attila. Iii. Attila tells Uldino of his dream in which the gods warn him to retreat, which he refuses to do, instead ordering his troops forward. Iiii. As Leone and a group of virgins and children approach the army, Attila recognizes in Leone the vision from his dream.

IIi. Ezio is ordered home by the feeble child-ruler, Valentinian: Rome has made a truce with Attila. But first Attila asks him to visit his camp. As Ezio is preparing to do so, he is accosted by Foresto who plans to kill Attila. When you see a fire on the mountain, attack, Foresto tells him. Ezio agrees to do so. IIii. Attila's army celebrates. They welcome Ezio, but the Druids foresee disaster for Attila. Foresto has poisoned Attila's cup, but Odabella warns him before he can drink: She reserves revenge for herself. Attila gives Foresto to Odabella for punishment and announces his intention to marry her.

III. Uldino warns Foresto that Attila's marriage is imminent, and Foresto curses Odabella. The army is ready, Ezio reports. Odabella flees the wedding, protesting she still loves Foresto. Attila follows her and is slain by her, Foresto and Ezio. Roman troops destroy the Hun's army.

Atys

Composed by Jean-Baptiste Lully (November 28, 1632 – March 22, 1687). Libretto by Philippe Quinault. French. Based on Ovid's "Fasti." Premiered Saint Germain en Laye, Court Theater, January 10, 1676. Set in Phrygia in legendary times. Tragedy. Set numbers with recitative. Prologue. Overture.

Sets: 7. **Acts:** 5 acts, 8 scenes. **Length:** Prologue: 20. I: 35. II: 25. III: 35. IV: 25. V: 30. **Arias:** "Ciel! Quelle vapeur m'environne" (Atys), "Espoir si cher et si doux" (Cybèle). **Hazards:** III: Atys dreams. V: Atys is transformed into a pine tree. **Scenes:** Prologue. The palace of Time. I. A mountainside consecrated to Cybèle. II. The temple of Cybèle. IIIi. The palace of Cybèle's high priest. IIIii. A cavern surrounded by poppies and brooks. IIIiii. The palace of the high priest. IV. The palace of the river Sangar. V. Delightful gardens.

Major roles: Atys (tenor), Sangaride (soprano), Goddess Cybèle (soprano), King Célénus of Phrygia (baritone). **Minor roles:** God of time (baritone), Goddess Flore (soprano), Zephyr (tenor), Melpomène (soprano), Iris (soprano), Idas (bass), Nymph Doris (soprano), Priestess Mélisse (soprano), God of Sleep (tenor), Morphée (tenor), Phobétor (bass), Phantase (tenor), God of the river Sangar (bass), Fury Alecton (bass). **Dancers:** Heroes (Hercule, Antée, Etheocle, Polinice, Castor, Pollux).

Chorus parts: SATB. **Chorus roles:** Twelve hours of day, twelve hours of night, nymphs, Phrygians, nations, zephyrs, river, spring and stream gods, woodland divinities, corybantes. **Dance/movement:** Prologue: nymphs dance. III: pleasant dreams convey goddess's love for Atys. **Orchestra:** 2 fl/recorders, 3 ob, bsns, strings, continuo. **Stageband:** None. **Rights:** Expired.

Prologue. The gods remember the fates of the great heroes. I. Atys worships the Goddess Cybèle. His friend Idas realizes Atys is in love, although Atys denies this to the nymph Sangaride. Sangaride is engaged to the king of Phrygia, but she secretly loves Atys. The Phrygians arrive for the wedding and Atys admits to Sangaride that he is dying of love for her. She tells him she returns his love. Everyone waits for Cybèle to appear. The goddess accepts their homage.

II. King Célénus and Atys await Cybèle's choice of a high priest. Célénus fears he has a rival for Sangaride. Cybèle chooses Atys, admitting to her priestess Mélisse that she loves Atys. Cybèle's choice is announced.

IIIi. Atys pines. Doris and Idas persuade Atys to tell Cybèle his problem. Atys struggles with his conscience until he is overcome by sleep. IIIii. He learns of Cybèle's love in his dreams. IIIiii. Talking to Cybèle, Atys realizes the truth of his dream. Cybèle agrees to prevent Sangaride's marriage, beginning to suspect that Atys and the nymph are in love. Cybèle asks why love has betrayed her.

IV. Believing that Atys has fallen in love with Cybèle, Sangaride determines to marry Célénus, who loves her, but does not want to marry her unless she loves him. He interprets her remarks as assurances of her love. Sangaride and Atys fight, but are reconciled. Sangaride's father, the god of the river Sangar, invites everyone to his daughter's wedding. Atys uses his powers as high priest to prevent the wedding.

V. Célénus complains to Cybèle, who promises to avenge both of them. They confront the guilty lovers. The god Alecton confuses Atys so that he mistakes Sangaride for a monster and kills her. His reason restored, Atys is horrified by his crime and stabs himself. Cybèle, wracked by remorse, transforms the dying Atys into a pine tree. She calls on all nature to mourn and honor the tree.

Aufstieg und Fall der Stadt Mahagonny • The Rise and Fall of the City of Mahagonny

Composed by Kurt Weill (March 2, 1900 – April 3, 1950). Libretto by Bertolt Brecht. German. Original work. Premiered Leipzig, Neues Theater, March 9, 1930. Set in a fictitious town in Alabama in the 1920s. Satire. Set numbers with recitative and spoken dialogue. Prelude before I, II. Two versions: original "Singspiel" version smaller in scope.

Sets: 11. **Acts:** 3 acts, 21 scenes. **Length:** I: 65. II: 40. III: 40. **Hazards:** I: A truck drives onstage. Projections on the front scrim. Jimmy fires a gun in the air. II: Voice heard over loudspeaker. Projections. III: City in flames. Projections. **Scenes:** Ii – Iiv. A desolate place. Iv – Ivi. The wharf of Mahagonny. Ivii. Inside the Hotel for Rich Men. Iviii. The wharf. Iix – Ixi. In front of the hotel. IIi – IIiii. A road outside Mahagonny. IIiii. Mandalay brothel. IIiv. A boxing ring. IIv. A pool hall. IIIi. A street in Mahagonny. IIIii. A courtroom. IIIiii – IIIiv. A view of the city. IIIv. The city in flames.

Major roles: Trinity Moses (baritone), Leokadja Begbick (contralto or mezzo), Jenny Smith (soprano), Jim Mahoney (tenor). **Minor roles:** Fatty the bookkeeper (tenor), Jack (tenor), Bankbook Billy (baritone), Alaska Wolf Joe (bass). **Bit parts:** Man (tenor), Woman (soprano), Toby Higgins (tenor).

Chorus parts: SATTBB. **Chorus roles:** Men and women of Mahagonny (includes a small group of six men and six women). **Dance/movement:** None. **Orchestra:** 2 fl, ob, cl, alto sax, ten sax, 2 bsn (cont bsn), 2 hrn, 3 trp, 2 trb, tuba, timp, perc, banjo, bs guitar, bandoneon, piano, harmonium, strings. **Stageband:** I: piano. II: 2 picc, 2 cl, 3 sax, 2 bsn, 2 hrn, 2 trp, 2 trb, tuba, 3 vln, 3 sax, perc, banjo, piano, zither, bandoneon. **Publisher:** Universal Edition. **Rights:** Copyright 1929, 1930 by Universal. Renewed 1956 by Mrs. Karoline Weill.

I. Fatty, Moses and the widow Begbick flee the police. Their truck breaks down in the desert and they decide to found a city: Mahagonny. Although people move in, they do not stay for long. Jimmy arrives from Alaska, but quickly gets bored. A hurricane is reported heading for the city. Jimmy convinces Begbick that it is of no use to forbid people from doing anything they want.

II. The hurricane misses the city. With all things now permissible, Mahagonny grows into a thriving city. The inhabitants eat, fight and visit the brothels. Jimmy's friend Joe is killed in a fight with Trinity Moses. When Jimmy is arrested for debt, his girlfriend, Jenny, refuses to lend him money.

III. In court, an unrepentant murderer is freed, while Jimmy is condemned. He says goodbye to Jenny and his friend Bill and is hanged. The people of Mahagonny despair and set fire to the city. They carry Jimmy's coffin through the streets.

The Ballad of Baby Doe

Composed by Douglas Moore (August 10, 1893 – July 25, 1969). Libretto by John Latouche. English. Original work based on historical figures. Premiered Central City, Colorado, Central City Opera House, July 7, 1956. Set in Colorado and Washington, D.C. in 1880 through 1899. Folk opera. Set pieces with accompanied recitative and spoken dialogue. Orchestral interludes between scenes.

Sets: 10. **Acts:** 2 acts, 11 scenes. **Length:** I: 70. II: 65. **Arias:** Willow song (Baby Doe), Letter aria (Baby Doe), Silver aria (Baby Doe), Augusta's lament (Augusta), "Warm as the autumn night" (Horace Tabor).
Hazards: None. **Scenes:** Ii. Outside the Tabor Opera House, Leadville, 1880. Iii. Outside the Clarendon Hotel. Iiii. The Tabor apartment, several months later. Iiv. The lobby of the Clarendon Hotel. Iv. Augusta's parlor in Denver, a year later. Ivi. A suite in the Willard Hotel, Washington, D.C., 1883. IIi. The Windsor Hotel, Denver, 1893. IIii. A club room in Denver, 1895. IIiii. The Matchless Mine, 1896. IIiv. Augusta's parlor, November 1896. IIv. The stage of the Tabor Grand Theatre, April, 1899.

Major roles: Horace Tabor (bass baritone), Augusta (mezzo), Mrs. Elizabeth (Baby) Doe (lyric soprano), Mama McCourt (contralto). **Minor roles:** Four friends of Augusta (2 sopranos, 2 mezzos), Four cronies of Tabor (2 tenors, 2 baritones), McCourt family (soprano, contralto, tenor, bass), Four dandies (2 tenors, 2 baritones), Old silver miner (tenor), Stage doorman (tenor), Bouncer (baritone), Politician (baritone), Kate (soprano), Meg (mezzo), William Jennings Bryan (bass or bass baritone).
Bit parts: President Chester A. Arthur (tenor), Father Chapelle (tenor), Hotel clerk (tenor), Mayor (tenor), Bellboy (baritone), Footman (baritone), Child Elizabeth (child soprano), Adult Silver Dollar (mezzo), Augusta's maid Samantha (mezzo), Two offstage newsboys (2 tenor).
Mute: Child Silver Dollar.

Chorus parts: SATB. **Chorus roles:** Dance hall girls, foreign diplomats, miners and their wives. **Dance/movement:** I: Miners and dance hall girls, wedding dance. II: polka. **Orchestra:** 2 fl (picc), ob, 2 cl, bsn, 2 hrn, 2 trp, 2 trb, tuba, timp, perc, harp, piano, strings. **Stageband:** None.
Publisher: Chappell & Co. **Rights:** Copyright 1956 by Douglas Moore and John Latouche.

Ii. Horace Tabor has struck it rich mining silver in Colorado and now owns most of Central City. He has built an opera house to show off his newfound wealth and while he and his cronies attend the opening night concert, the miners drink and carouse outside. The bouncer at the bar tries to quiet the miners, but one of them brags that Tabor will let him do anything: the miner owns the Matchless Silver Mine, which Tabor is hot to buy. The concert ends and Tabor and his men emerge from the opera house. They scandalize their wives by dancing with the bar girls. While this is going on, the young Baby Doe arrives in Central City and asks Tabor for instructions to the Clarendon Hotel. Iii. Tabor's wife, Augusta, goes home, but Tabor lingers outside the Clarendon Hotel. He overhears some of the local girls criticizing Baby Doe's pretensions and listens to Baby Doe singing at her hotel room window. When Tabor applauds, Baby Doe comes to the window and they talk. Tabor's wife calls him in. Iiii. Augusta discovers a pair of lace gloves and a tender note to Baby Doe in Tabor's desk. She is heartsick, but when Tabor returns, she first argues with him about his purchase of the Matchless Mine. At last she admits that she knows Tabor is having an affair with Baby Doe. Tabor defends Baby Doe but Augusta swears to run her out of town. Iiv. The clerk of the Clarendon Hotel sends to warn Tabor that Baby Doe is leaving. In a long letter to her mother, Baby Doe recounts her divorce from Harvey Doe and her decision not to break up Tabor's marriage—even though she loves him. Not realizing Baby Doe has decided to leave Central City, Augusta threatens her. They discuss Tabor. Baby Doe is convinced he is a great man, but Augusta knows that his successes have been pure luck. As soon as Augusta is gone, Tabor rushes in and convinces Baby Doe to remain. Iv. Augusta insists she will do nothing about Tabor's liaison with Baby Doe—unless Tabor tries to divorce her. Ivi. But Tabor divorces her anyway. He has now become a U.S. Senator and is about to marry Baby Doe. At the wedding, Tabor's dandies warn him to sell his mines while he can: the silver standard is doomed. Tabor dismisses their advice. He has purchased Queen Isabella's jewels, which he presents to his bride. The wedding is almost spoiled when the priest storms out after learning that both Tabor and Baby Doe are divorced. But the appearance of President Arthur saves the festivities.

IIi. Ten years have passed, but Augusta's friends still refuse to be in the same room with Baby Doe: When Tabor and Baby Doe attend the governor's ball, Augusta's friends walk out. Augusta herself makes up with Baby Doe and tries to convince her that Tabor must sell his mine: the president is about to sign a bill that will ruin the price of silver. Unfortunately, Tabor overhears. He angrily sends Augusta away and makes Baby Doe promise never to sell the mine. IIii. Over a game of poker, Tabor's cronies discuss his sinking fortunes. They refuse to invest in Tabor's holding company and are appalled that he means to support William Jennings Bryan for president. IIiii. The workers of the Matchless Mine listen to a speech by Bryan against the evils of the gold standard. IIiv. Bryan is defeated. Baby Doe's mother begs Augusta to help the bankrupt Tabors, but Augusta refuses. IIv. The stage doorman of the Tabor Opera House tries to stop Tabor from entering until he realizes who it is. When Tabor hallucinates about his earlier days, the doorman runs to get help. A vision of Augusta appears to Tabor. It tells him he will die a failure and shows him his daughter Silver Dollar as a drunken flapper. Baby Doe arrives and comforts her husband.

Un Ballo in Maschera • A Masked Ball

Composed by Giuseppe Verdi (October 9, 1813 – January 27, 1901). Libretto by Antonio Somma. Italian. Based on Scribe libretto for Auber's opera "Gustave III." Premiered Rome, Teatro Apollo, February 17, 1859. Set in Boston in the 17th century. Melodrama. Set numbers with accompanied recitative. Prelude. Opera originally concerned the assassination of King Gustave of Sweden in 1792.

Sets: 5. **Acts:** 3 acts, 5 scenes. **Length:** I: 50. II: 35. III: 45. **Arias:** "Eri tu" (Renato), "Là rivedrà nell'estasi" (Riccardo), "Ma se m'è forza perderti" (Riccardo), "Morrò, ma prima in grazia" (Amelia), "Ecco l'orrido campo" (Amelia), "Rè dell'abisso" (Ulrica), "Volta la terrea" (Oscar). **Hazards:** None. **Scenes:** Ii. Reception room in the governor's house. Iii. Dwelling of the fortune teller. II. Lonely field in the suburbs of Boston. IIIi. Study in Renato's house. IIIii. Sumptuous room in the count's quarters.

Major roles: Riccardo/Gustavus (tenor), Renato/Ankerström (baritone), Amelia (soprano), Ulrica/Madam Arvidson (contralto). **Minor roles:** Oscar (soprano), Silvano/Christian (bass), Samuel/Count Ribbing (bass), Tom/Count Horn (bass), Judge (tenor). **Bit part:** Servant to Amelia (tenor). (Second name is that in Swedish setting.)

Chorus parts: SSATTBBB. **Chorus roles:** Deputies, officers, sailors, guards, people, noblemen, partisans of Samuel and Tom, servants, masked people and dancing couples. **Dance/movement:** III: Ballroom dancing. **Orchestra:** 2 fl (picc), 2 ob (Eng hrn), 2 cl, 2 bsn, 4 hrn, 2 trp, 3 trb, cimbasso, timp, perc, harp, strings. **Stageband:** III: military band, string orchestra. **Publisher:** Kalmus, G. Ricordi. **Rights:** Expired.

Ii. Riccardo accepts petitions from his constituents while Tom and Samuel plot to assassinate him. Looking at the guest list for the ball reminds Riccardo of his love for Amelia—the wife of Renato, his closest advisor. Renato has information on the conspirators, but Riccardo will not listen. A magistrate presents an order for the deportation of the fortune teller Ulrica. Oscar defends Ulrica, and Riccardo decides to visit her in disguise. Iii. Ulrica predicts that the sailor Silvano will get a promotion. Hearing this, Riccardo slips a promotion into Silvano's pocket. All are amazed at Ulrica's powers. Amelia's servant asks Ulrica to meet with his mistress privately. Riccardo hides. Amelia begs Ulrica to make her forget her fatal love for Riccardo. Beneath the gallows grows an herb that will make you forget him, Ulrica says. The crowd returns and Riccardo asks about his future. Ulrica tells him he will be murdered by the first friend he shakes hands with. When Renato arrives, Riccardo shakes his hand to disprove the prophecy. Ulrica suspects Tom and Samuel. Riccardo reveals his identity and the crowd hails him. Tom and Samuel realize they will have missed their chance.

II. As Amelia searches under the gallows for the magic herb, she is surprised by Riccardo. Swearing their guilty love, the lovers are interrupted by Renato, who has followed Riccardo to warn him the assassins are closing in. Renato does not recognize Amelia through her veil. He begs Riccardo to flee. Riccardo makes Renato swear to get Amelia to safety—without asking any questions—and leaves. The conspirators catch Renato and Amelia. Realizing their mistake, they try to unveil Amelia. Renato draws his sword to prevent this, but Amelia herself removes the veil. The conspirators have a good laugh, but Renato is heartbroken. He asks Tom and Samuel to visit him tomorrow morning.

IIIi. Renato threatens to kill Amelia. She begs for one last visit with her son, which he grants. Renato joins Tom and Samuel, pledging his son as a hostage for his good faith. Unable to agree on who will do the assassination, the conspirators put their names in a vase from which the unsuspecting Amelia pulls out Renato's name. Oscar invites Renato and Amelia to a masked ball given by Riccardo and Renato accepts, intending to assassinate Riccardo there. Amelia realizes what he intends. IIIii. Riccardo, having decided he must renounce his love for Amelia, writes orders for Renato and his wife to be sent overseas. He ignores a letter warning him of the assassination attempt. At the ball, Renato tricks Oscar into revealing Riccardo's disguise. Amelia begs Riccardo to leave, but he refuses. He tells her he is sending her and Renato to England. Renato stabs Riccardo. The crowd closes in on Renato, intending to kill him, but the dying Riccardo intervenes. He forgives Renato and swears to him that Amelia is innocent. All mourn Riccardo's death.

Der Barbier von Bagdad • The Barber of Bagdad

Composed by Peter Cornelius (December 24, 1824 – October 26, 1874). Libretto by Peter Cornelius. German. Based on "The Tale of the Tailor" in "The Thousand and One Nights." Premiered Weimar, Hoftheater, December 15, 1858. Set in Bagdad in legendary times. Comic opera.

Through composed. Overture. Entr'acte before II. Revised version by F. Mottl premiered at Karlsruhe on February 1, 1884.

Sets: 2. **Acts:** 2 acts, 16 scenes. **Length:** I: 55. II: 45. **Arias:** "Bin Akademiker" (Abul). **Hazards:** None. **Scenes:** I. A room in Nureddin's house. II. A room in the cadi's house.

Major roles: Nureddin (heldentenor), Abul Hassan Ali Ebn Bekar the barber (bass), Margiana (high soprano). **Minor roles:** Bostana (mezzo), Cadi Baba Mustapha (lyric tenor), Caliph (baritone). **Bit parts:** Three Muezzins (2 tenor, bass), Offstage slave (tenor).

Chorus parts: SSSAAATTTTTBBBBB. **Chorus roles:** Nureddin's servants, friends of the cadi, people of Bagdad, women, followers of the cadi. **Dance/movement:** None. **Orchestra:** picc, 2 fl, 2 cl, 2 ob, 2 bsn, 4 hrn, 2 trp, 3 trb, tuba, timp, 2 perc, harp, strings. **Stageband:** None. **Publisher:** C.F. Kahnt Nachfolger. **Rights:** Expired.

Ii. Nureddin is sick with love. Iii. He dreams of his beloved Margiana. Iiii. Margiana agrees to see Nureddin while her father is at prayer. In preparation for the rendezvous, Nureddin sends for a barber. Iiv. He is ecstatic at the thought of seeing Margiana. Iv. The barber, Abul Hassan Ali Ebn Bekar, wants to predict Nureddin's future, but Nureddin just wants a shave. Ivi. He tries to turn the barber out. Ivii. Abul disapproves of Margiana's father, Cadi Baba Mustapha, because he shaves himself. Iviii. It was love that killed Abul's brothers, he recalls. Iix. Over Nureddin's protests, Abul resolves to stay with Nureddin and protect him. Nureddin pretends Abul is sick and loads him down with doctors and medications.

IIi. The cadi has promised Margiana's hand to an old friend who has sent Margiana rich presents. She is unimpressed. IIii. Nureddin and Margiana swear eternal love. IIiii. The cadi returns and beats a slave for breaking a vase. Margiana and Bostana hide Nureddin in a chest. IIiv. Abul accuses the cadi of murdering his friend and claims that the chest contains the body. IIv. The cadi answers that the chest contains presents for Margiana. IIvi. The caliph himself investigates. IIvii. The chest is opened. Abul revives Nureddin and the caliph promises to see Nureddin and Margiana wed.

Il Barbiere di Siviglia • The Barber of Seville

Composed by Giovanni Paisiello (May 9, 1740 – June 5, 1816). Libretto by Giuseppe Petrosellini. Italian. Based on the play by Pierre Augustin

Caron de Beaumarchais. Premiered St. Petersburg, Hermitage Imperial
Theater, September 26, 1782. Set in Seville in the 18th century. Comic
opera. Set numbers with recitative. Overture.

Sets: 3. **Acts:** 4 acts, 4 scenes. **Length:** I, II, III, IV: 120. **Arias:** "Scorsi già
molti paesi" (Figaro), "La calunnia, mio signor" (Basilio), "Veramente ha
torto" (Bartolo), "Già riede primavera" (Rosina). **Hazards:** None. **Scenes:**
Ii. A street in Seville. II. Rosina's apartment in Bartolo's house. III.
Rosina's apartment. IV. Another room in Bartolo's house.

Major roles: Count Almaviva (tenor), Figaro (baritone), Rosina (soprano), Bartolo (bass). **Minor roles:** Svegliato (bass), Giovinetto (tenor), Don
Basilio (baritone). **Bit parts:** Notary (bass), Mayor (tenor). **Mute:** servants.

Chorus parts: N/A. **Chorus roles:** None. **Dance/movement:** None.
Orchestra: 2 fl, 2 ob, 2 cl, 2 bsn, 2 hrn, strings, timp, mandolin, continuo.
Stageband: None. **Publisher:** G. Ricordi. **Rights:** Expired.

I. Disguised as the poor Lindoro, Count Almaviva woos Rosina. He
meets his old servant, Figaro. Rosina drops a letter from her balcony for
Almaviva. Rosina is Bartolo's ward—and Bartolo hopes to marry her.
Figaro suggests Almaviva get into Bartolo's house by disguising himself
as a soldier. Bartolo goes out. Figaro and Almaviva plan to meet later.

II. Rosina writes a second letter for Almaviva, which she entrusts to
Figaro. Bartolo suspects Figaro. He abuses his servants. He asks if there
have been any visitors. The servants do not know. Rosina admits that
Figaro visited, but maintains her innocence. Almaviva arrives disguised
as a drunken soldier quartered upon Bartolo. Almaviva passes Rosina a
letter. Bartolo and Almaviva quarrel, and Bartolo throws Almaviva out.
Bartolo tries to find out about the letter from Almaviva, but Rosina convinces him there wasn't one. Rosina reads Almaviva's letter, which
instructs her to pick a fight with her guardian.

III. Bartolo is appalled by Rosina's temper. Almaviva pretends to be a
pupil of Don Basilio's come to give Rosina a music lesson since Basilio is
sick. He wins Bartolo over by showing him a love letter from Rosina—
which he says he means to use to convince Rosina that her lover,
Almaviva, is unfaithful. Almaviva is exultant. He and Rosina flirt.
Figaro comes to shave Bartolo. He tries to get Bartolo's keys so he can
copy them and Bartolo hands them over. Figaro breaks all the china and
when Bartolo goes out to investigate, Almaviva asks Rosina to elope.
Bartolo and Figaro return. Basilio's arrival threatens to upset the lovers'
plans, but they tell Basilio he looks ill and send him home. While Figaro
shaves Bartolo, Almaviva plans his elopement with Rosina, but Bartolo

catches Almaviva and throws him out. Bartolo sends Basilio for a notary.

IV. Rosina goes to the rendezvous, but finds Bartolo in the room. He tells her that her lover—who she still knows only as Lindoro—means to betray her to the count. Furious, Rosina agrees to marry Bartolo. She decides to confront Lindoro with his treachery. Figaro and the count sneak into the house and Almaviva explains everything to Rosina. They are reconciled. Basilio returns with the notary—who marries Almaviva and Rosina. Bartolo discovers that he is too late.

Il Barbiere di Siviglia • The Barber of Seville

Composed by Gioachino Rossini (February 29, 1792 – November 13, 1868). Libretto by Cesare Sterbini. Italian. Based on the play by Pierre-Augustin Caron de Beaumarchais. Premiered Rome, Teatro Argentina, February 20, 1816. Set in Seville in the 18th century. Comic melodrama. Set numbers with recitative. Overture. Orchestral interlude (storm sequence).

Sets: 3. **Acts:** 2 acts, 4 scenes. **Length:** I: 90. II: 60. **Arias:** "Largo al facto-tum" (Figaro), "Una voce poco fa" (Rosina), "La calunnia" (Basilio), "A un dottor" (Bartolo), "Cessa di più resistere" (Almaviva), "Ecco ridente" (Almaviva), "Il vecchioto cerca moglie" (Berta). **Hazards:** None. **Scenes:** Ii. A square in Seville. Iii – IIi. A room in Don Bartolo's house. IIii. A room with a balcony. (Often played in three acts, Iii and IIi becoming act II.)

Major roles: Count Almaviva (tenor), Figaro (baritone), Rosina (mezzo; originally soprano). **Minor roles:** Fiorello (baritone), Dr. Bartolo (bass baritone), Basilio (bass), Berta (mezzo or soprano), Sergeant (tenor or baritone). **Bit parts:** Ambroggio (bass or mute). **Mute:** Notary.

Chorus parts: TTB. **Chorus roles:** Musicians, soldiers. **Dance/movement:** None. **Orchestra:** 2 fl (picc), 2 ob, 2 cl, 2 bsn, 2 hrn, 2 trp, bs drum, triangle, strings, harpsichord. **Stageband:** I: guitar. **Publisher:** Ricordi, Francois Castil-Blaze. **Rights:** Expired.

Ii. Almaviva meets Fiorello and his musicians in front of Dr. Bartolo's house and they serenade Rosina. The count pays and dismisses the noisy musicians. Figaro arrives, bragging how popular he is, and Almaviva enlists his help. Rosina and Bartolo appear on the balcony and Rosina drops a letter to her lover. Bartolo intends to marry Rosina himself so as to get her money, Figaro tells Almaviva. Rosina now appears at the balcony alone and Almaviva tells her he is Lindoro, a poor student who loves her. Figaro advises Almaviva to pose as a drunken soldier who has been quartered on the doctor. Figaro gives Almaviva directions to his shop and they part. Fiorello grumbles that Almaviva has told him to wait and then gone off without him.

Iii. Rosina points out that no one pushes her around and gets away with it. Bartolo learns from Basilio that it is Count Almaviva who woos his ward. Basilio suggests slandering Almaviva, but Bartolo prefers to hurry on his own wedding. Figaro, who has overheard their conversation, reports it to Rosina. She asks about Lindoro and Figaro suggests she write him a letter. He is surprised to find the letter already written. Bartolo quizzes Rosina about her letter writing and locks her in her room. Almaviva arrives in his disguise, ignoring Bartolo's protest that he is exempt from quartering soldiers. Almaviva slips a letter to Rosina. Although Bartolo sees the letter, Rosina swaps it with the laundry list before he can read it. He and Almaviva fight, bringing the police down on them. The officer tries to arrest Almaviva, but draws back when he learns who the count really is.

IIii. Almaviva returns to Bartolo's house disguised as Don Alonso, a pupil of Basilio's. Since Basilio is sick, he says, he will give Rosina her singing lesson. To win Bartolo's trust, he gives him one of Rosina's letters and promises to tell Rosina that he got it from the count's mistress. During the lesson, Bartolo decides he dislikes Rosina's choice of arias and sings one of his own favorites. Figaro, arriving for Bartolo's shave, steals the key to the balcony from the doctor's key ring and breaks some dishes to lure Bartolo out of the room. Almaviva proposes to Rosina, who accepts him. Basilio arrives but Almaviva convinces Bartolo that Basilio's presence is dangerous since he does not know about Rosina's letter. They all tell Basilio he looks sick and send him home. The music lesson resumes while Figaro shaves the doctor. Almaviva arranges to elope with Rosina at midnight, but they are discovered before he can admit to giving her letter to the doctor. Bartolo throws the men out of the house. Berta wonders at all the commotion. Bartolo sends Basilio off for a notary to perform his marriage. Meanwhile, Bartolo uses Almaviva's letter to convince Rosina that the count intended to seduce and betray her. Furious, Rosina reveals the elopement plans and agrees to marry him. Bartolo rushes off to fetch the police.

IIiii. When Figaro and Almaviva arrive, Rosina confronts Almaviva who reveals that he is the count. Their rejoicing is cut short when Figaro realizes their ladder has been stolen. Basilio enters with the notary, who Figaro persuades to wed Rosina and Almaviva while the count bribes and threatens Basilio into acting as a witness. Bartolo arrives too late: The lovers are married. He is concerned about the dowry, but when Almaviva tells him to keep the money, Bartolo blesses the happy couple.

Prodaná Nevěsta • The Bartered Bride

Composed by Bedřich Smetana (March 2, 1824 – May 12, 1884). Libretto by Karel Sabina. Czech. Original work. Premiered Prague, Provisional Theater, May 30, 1866. Set in a Bohemian village in the 19th century. Comic opera. Set numbers with recitative. Overture. Furiant before IIii. Originally in 2 acts with dialogue but without dances; revised 3-act version premiered in Prague, September 25, 1870.

Sets: 2. **Acts:** 3 acts, 3 scenes. **Length:** I: 45. II: 45. III: 40. **Arias:** "Were I ever to learn that you had ceased to care" (Mařenka), "Ma-ma-ma-ma, so dear" (Vašek), "Ah, love's sweet dream" (Mařenka). **Hazards:** None. **Scenes:** I. The main square of a village on a feast day in spring. II. Inside a country inn. III. The main square of the village.

Major roles: Mařenka or Marie (soprano), Vašek (tenor), Jeník (tenor), Kecal (bass). **Minor roles:** Krušina (baritone), Ludmila (soprano), Mícha (bass), Háta (mezzo), Company manager (tenor), Esmeralda (soprano). **Bit part:** Indian (tenor). Speaking bits: Two boys ("The bear is loose" and "The bear's gone wild").

Chorus parts: SATTBB. **Chorus roles:** Villagers, children, actors. **Dance/movement:** I: Villagers' dance. Polka. III: Dance of the comedians/circus performers. **Orchestra:** picc, 2 fl, 2 ob, 2 cl, 2 bsn, 4 hrn, 2 trp, 3 trb, timp, perc, strings. **Stageband:** III: picc, trp, perc. **Publisher:** Schirmer, Smetana Museum. **Rights:** Expired.

I. The villagers sing about the dangers of love. Jeník assures Marie that her parents will not succeed in parting them. He tells her he was driven from home by his step-mother. They pledge their love. Kecal, the marriage broker, persuades Marie's doubting parents, Krušina and Ludmila, to put Marie's fate in his hands. Marie will marry Tobias Mícha's son, he says. Mícha's son by his first marriage has disappeared; his younger son is Vašek. Kecal praises Vašek and his wealth. Marie takes the news badly. Kecal assures Krušina that he will not need to break his promise to Mícha. The villagers dance.

II. At the inn, the village men drink and dance. The stuttering Vašek fears that people will make fun of him. He does not know who Marie is when she approaches him and tells him that his intended loves another. She would cheat on you, Marie says, leading him on. Vašek is attracted to the mysterious girl, but is unsure what to do as his mother insists that he marry Marie. Kecal tells Jeník that romance cannot withstand poverty. Give up Marie, he advises, and I will find you a rich and pretty woman free of charge. When he offers to pay Jenik 300 ducats outright, Jeník agrees—on condition that Marie marry only a son of Tobias Mícha.

Jeník thinks of his and Marie's future happiness. The chorus is scandalized that Jeník has bartered his bride for gold, but Jeník signs the contract.

III. Vašek fears the planned wedding will kill him. When the circus
director introduces his show, Vašek is enchanted by one member of the
troupe, the lovely Esmeralda, who returns his affection. The Indian
warns the circus director that the man who plays the bear is too drunk to
perform and Esmeralda and the director talk Vašek into taking his place.
Vašek shocks his parents by telling them he will not marry Marie. He is
more interested in the girl who warned him about Marie. Marie discovers Jeník's apparent treachery, but still says she will not marry Vašek.
Vašek, in turn, realizes the girl he likes is Marie. Marie laments Jeník's
betrayal. He tries to explain the situation to her, but she will not listen.
Jeník angers her further by promising Kecal—in Marie's presence—that
Marie will marry a son of Mícha. When the parents arrive, Háta and
Mícha immediately recognize Jeník as his son by his first marriage. Háta
is furious at Jeník's plan to cheat her son, but the contract is written and
Jeník prevails. Two boys announce that the bear has escaped from the
circus, but it is only Vašek in his costume. The parents and villagers
bless the happy couple.

Die Bassariden • The Bassarids

Composed by Hans Werner Henze (b. July 1, 1926). Libretto by W. H.
Auden and Chester Kallman. German. Based on the play "The Bacchae"
by Euripides. Premiered Salzburg, Grosses Festspielhaus, August 6,
1966. Set in Thebes shortly after the founding of the city. Opera seria.
Through composed. Classical intermezzo. Original libretto written in
English, but translated into German.

Sets: 3. **Acts:** 1 act, 5 scenes. **Length:** I: 120. **Hazards:** Iiii: Earthquake and
fire. Iiv: Pentheus' dismembered body shown although actual dismem-
berment is not seen. Palace consumed by flame and vines sprout on the
ruins. **Scenes:** Ii – Iii. The courtyard of the royal palace of Thebes.
Intermezzo. A garden. Iiii. Mount Cytheron. Iiv. The courtyard.

Major roles: King Pentheus of Thebes (baritone), Dionysus/Voice/
Stranger (tenor), Tiresias/Calliope (tenor), Cadmus (bass), Agave/
Venus (mezzo). **Minor roles:** Beroë (mezzo), Captain of the royal guard/
Adonis (baritone), Autonoë/Proserpine (spinto soprano). **Bit parts:**
Bacchanite (bass; hums his part). **Mute:** Young slave woman, Child.

Chorus parts: SSAATTBB. **Chorus roles:** Citizens of Thebes, Bassarids
(Maenads and Bacchanites), guards, servants, musicians. **Dance/move-**

ment: Stylized bacchanite dances throughout. **Orchestra:** 4 fl (3 picc), 2 ob, 2 Eng hrn, 4 cl (2 sax), bs cl (sax), 4 bsn (cont bsn), 6 hrn, 4 trp (bs trp), 3 trb, 2 tuba, timp, perc, 2 harp, celeste, 2 piano, strings. **Stageband:** I: 4 trp, 2 mandolin, guitar. **Publisher:** B. Schott's Söhne. **Rights:** Copyright 1993 by B. Schott's Söhne.

Ii. The citizens of Thebes pay tribute to their new king, Pentheus, grandson of their founder, Cadmus, and son of Agave. They run off to welcome the god Dionysus. Tiresias counsels Cadmus and Agave to follow Pentheus, but they doubt the new god. As his first royal act, Pentheus douses the flame on Semele's tomb to silence the voice of superstition. Agave and her sister, Autonoe, heed the call of Dionysus. Iii. Cadmus tells Pentheus to worship Dionysus, but Pentheus refuses. He orders the bassarids arrested and tortured for information about Dionysus. An earthquake frees the prisoners. Pentheus is bewitched by the stranger (Dionysus) and rescinds his orders to recapture and kill the bassarids.

Intermezzo. Agave and Autonoe argue over the favors of the captain of the guard. To settle their quarrel, Tiresias has them present "The Judgment of Calliope." Disguised as Calliope, Tiresias satisfies the claims of Venus (Agave) and Proserpine (Autonoe) for the mortal Adonis (the captain) by giving him to each for part of the year.

Iiii. Dionysus persuades Pentheus to seek out the bassarids disguised as a woman. Beroe begs Dionysus to spare Pentheus, but he refuses, pointing out that no one spared his mother, Semele. Dionysus takes Pentheus to Mount Cytheron where he is hunted and dismembered by the Maenads. Iiv. Agave returns with the head of Pentheus, whom she mistakes for a lion. Cadmus shows her the truth: that she has killed her own son. Dionysus banishes Cadmus and his daughters and sets fire to the palace. He calls Semele to dwell with him among the immortals.

Bastien und Bastienne • Bastien and Bastienne

Composed by Wolfgang Amadeus Mozart (January 27, 1756 – December 5, 1791). Libretto by Friedrich Wilhelm Weiskern. German. Parody of Rousseau by Marie-Justine-Benoîte Favart. Premiered Vienna, Private residence, September 1768. Set in a French village in the 18th century. Singspiel puppet opera. Set numbers with spoken dialogue. Overture.

Sets: 1. **Acts:** 1 act, 7 scenes. **Length:** I: 40. **Arias:** "O Bastien" (Bastienne). **Hazards:** None. **Scenes:** I. The edge of a village.

Major roles: Bastienne (soprano), Colas (bass), Bastien (tenor).

Chorus parts: N/A. **Chorus roles:** None. **Dance/movement:** None.
Orchestra: 2 fl, 2 ob, 2 hrn, strings. **Stageband:** None. **Publisher:**
Universal Edition, Breitkopf & Härtel. **Rights:** Expired.

Ii. Bastien leaves his girlfriend, Bastienne. Iii. She is distraught and asks
Colas to help her forget her sadness. He assures Bastienne that Bastien
really loves her; he is merely vain. Iiii. Feign indifference, Colas suggests. Iiv. When Bastien decides he wants Bastienne back, Colas tells him
she already has a rich lover. Iv. Bastien is upset. Ivi. He goes to
Bastienne but she orders him away. When Bastien threatens to kill himself, Bastienne relents and takes him back. Ivii. Bastien and Bastienne
praise Colas's sagacity.

Ba-ta-clan

Composed by Jacques Offenbach (June 20, 1819 – October 5, 1880).
Libretto by Ludovic Halévy. French. Original work. Premiered Paris,
Théâtre des Bouffes Parisiens, December 29, 1855. Set in China at an
unspecified time. Operetta. Set numbers with spoken dialogue.
Orchestral introduction.

Sets: 1. **Acts:** 1 act, 1 scene. **Length:** I: 40. **Hazards:** None. **Scenes:** I. The
gardens of the emperor's palace in China.

Major roles: Fé-an-nich-ton (soprano), Ké-ki-ka-ko (tenor), Ko-ko-ri-ko
(baritone), Fé-ni-han (tenor). **Minor roles:** Two conspirators (2 falsetto
tenors).

Chorus parts: SATB. **Chorus roles:** Conspirators, mandarins and man-
darines. **Dance/movement:** I: Conspirators' dance. **Orchestra:** 2 fl (picc),
ob, 2 cl, bsn, 2 hrn, 2 trp, trb, timp, perc, strings. **Stageband:** None.
Publisher: Belwin Mills. **Rights:** Expired.

I. The mandarin Ké-ki-ka-ko and the mandarine Fé-an-nich-ton each discover that the other is not Chinese at all, but French. Both were abducted
and given high positions in the Chinese court, but both miss Paris. They
agree to escape. The emperor, Fé-ni-han, worries about the presence of
conspirators in his court. He, too, is originally French and homesick. Ké-
ki-ka-ko and Fé-an-nich-ton are captured when they try to escape.
Discovering that they, too, are French, the emperor tells how the real
emperor threatened him with impalement if he did not assume the
throne. He tries to force Ké-ki-ka-ko to become emperor, but Ké-ki-ka-ko
refuses. The three hold off the conspirators by singing a chorus from
"Les Huguenots." Ko-ko-ri-ko admits that he, too, is French, but he does

want to be emperor. Fé-ni-han abdicates in Ko-ko-ri-ko's favor and the new emperor helps his fellow countrymen escape.

La Battaglia di Legnano • The Battle of Legnano

Composed by Giuseppe Verdi (October 9, 1813 – January 27, 1901). Libretto by Salvatore Cammarano. Italian. Based on "La Battaille de Toulouse" by Joseph Méry. Premiered Rome, Teatro Argentina, January 27, 1849. Set in Milan and Como in 1176. Lyric tragedy. Set numbers with recitative. Overture.

Sets: 7. **Acts:** 4 acts, 7 scenes. **Length:** I: 40. II: 15. III: 40. IV: 15. **Arias:** "Ah! m'abbraccia d'esultanza" (Rolando), "Se al nuovo dì pugnando" (Rolando). **Hazards:** None. **Scenes:** Ii. Near the city walls of Milan. Iii. A shady spot amid groups of trees near the moat that surrounds the ramparts. II. A magnificent room in the town hall of Como. IIIi. Subterranean vaults in the basilica of S. Ambrogio in Milan. IIIii. Apartments in Rolando's castle. IIIiii. A room high up in the tower. IV. A square in Milan with the porch of a church in view.

Major roles: Arrigo (tenor), Rolando (baritone), Lida (soprano). **Minor roles:** Second consul (bass), Imelda (mezzo), Marcovaldo (baritone), Federico Barbarossa (bass). **Bit parts:** First consul (bass), Mayor of Como (bass), Herald/Squire (tenor). **Mute:** Rolando's son.

Chorus parts: SSATTTTBBB. **Chorus roles:** Knights of death, magistrates, ladies in waiting, people of Milan, senators, League and German soldiers, soldiers, officers, old men. **Dance/movement:** None. **Orchestra:** 2 fl, 2 ob, 2 cl, 2 bsn, 4 hrn, 2 trp, 3 trb, tuba or cimbasso, timp, perc, harp, organ, strings. **Stageband:** I, II, III, IV: 6 trp, 4 trb, 2 drums. IV: bells. **Publisher:** G. Ricordi & Co. **Rights:** Expired.

Ii. The army of the Lombard League assembles. Rolando is surprised to see his friend Arrigo, whom everyone believed dead. Iii. Lida mourns Arrigo and her parents. She has married Rolando and has a son but is deeply unhappy. The prisoner Marcovaldo loves her, but she sends him away. Arrigo accuses Lida of being unfaithful to him.

II. Rolando and Arrigo try to persuade the Italians of Como to fight with the league. They are defeated by the arrival of Federico Barbarossa with his army.

IIIi. Arrigo joins the Lombard knights who have sworn to defeat Federico or die in the attempt. IIIii. Lida writes a letter to Arrigo.

Rolando asks Arrigo to take care of Lida and his son if he dies in battle. Marcovaldo intercepts Lida's letter and shows it to Rolando. IIIiii. Lida tells Arrigo she still loves him. They are discovered by Rolando. Rather than kill Arrigo, Rolando locks him in the tower: Arrigo will be dishonored when he misses the battle. Arrigo jumps from the balcony.
IV. The army returns victorious, but Arrigo has been mortally wounded. He swears Lida is innocent. Rolando forgives both of them. Arrigo dies.

The Bear

Composed by William Walton (March 29, 1902 – March 8, 1983). Libretto by Paul Dehn and William Walton. English. Based on a story by Anton Chekhov. Premiered Aldeburgh, English Opera Group, June 3, 1967. Set in Russia in 1888. Extravaganza. Through composed.

Sets: 1. **Acts:** 1 act, 1 scene. **Length:** I: 50. **Hazards:** None. **Scenes:** I. The drawing room of Madam Popova's country house.

Major roles: Yeliena Ivanovna Popova (mezzo), Grigory Stepanovitch Smirnov (baritone). **Minor role:** Luka (bass). **Mute:** Cook, Groom.

Chorus parts: N/A. **Chorus roles:** None. **Dance/movement:** None. **Orchestra:** fl, ob, cl, bsn, hrn, trp, trb, perc, harp, piano, strings. **Stageband:** None. **Publisher:** Oxford University Press. **Rights:** Copyright 1968, 1977 by Oxford University Press.

I. Luka tries to convince his mistress, Madam Popova, to stop mourning her husband, but she plans to mourn forever. Smirnov insists on being admitted. He lent money to Popova's husband and needs it back to pay his own creditors. Popova promises to pay him at the end of the week. Smirnov is furious. He starts drinking and threatens to stay until he gets his money. Popova asks him to be quiet. They end up discussing Popova's husband's infidelities. Smirnov is unimpressed by Popova's chastity, pointing out that she does not forget her makeup. Popova accuses him of being a bear and a brute. Smirnov challenges Popova to a duel, which she accepts. At her request, he shows her how to fire a pistol. Smirnov falls in love with Popova's ferocious strength. He proposes, but Popova still wants to fight. Popova's resistance overcome, the couple embraces.

Béatrice

Composed by André Charles Prosper Messager (December 30, 1853 – February 24, 1929). Libretto by Robert de Flers and Gaston-A. de

Caillavet. French. Based on a story by Charles Nodier. Premiered Monte Carlo, Théâtre de Monte Carlo, March 21, 1914. Set in Sicily in the 16th century. Lyric legend. Set numbers. Introduction. Prelude before II, IV.

Sets: 3. **Acts:** 4 acts, 4 scenes. **Length:** I, II, III, IV: 150. **Arias:** "Quand l'atteindrai je donc" (Lorenzo), "C'est ici" (Béatrice). **Hazards:** I, IV: Statue turns into a woman. **Scenes:** I. A convent courtyard. II. A terrace opening onto the sea. III. A fisherman's bar on the shore. IV. The convent courtyard.

Major roles: Béatrice (dramatic soprano), Virgin (soprano), Musidora (mezzo), Bohemian girl (mezzo or contralto), Mother Superior (mezzo), Lorenzo (tenor). **Minor roles:** Frosine (soprano), Lélia (soprano), Sister Odile (soprano), Sister Blandine (soprano), Sister Monique (soprano), Tibério (baritone), Bishop (bass), Fabrice (tenor), Beppo (baritone), Fabio (tenor). **Bit parts:** Voice of a fisherman (tenor), Gardener (tenor), Old fisherman (bass), Second fisherman (tenor), Third fisherman (bass).

Chorus parts: SATB. **Chorus roles:** Monks, nuns, fishermen, angels. **Dance/movement:** III: Béatrice dances for the fishermen. **Orchestra:** 3 fl, 2 ob, Eng hrn, 2 cl, bs cl, 3 bsn, 4 hrn, 3 trp, 3 trb, tuba, harp, organ, bells, timp, perc, strings. **Stageband:** None. **Publisher:** Adolph Fürstner. **Rights:** Expired.

I. Béatrice has entered a convent, honoring a vow she made to the Virgin, whom she credits with saving the life of Lorenzo, a dear friend, in the recent war. Lorenzo believes she loves him and abducts her from the convent. A statue of the Virgin comes to life and takes Béatrice's place in the convent.

II. Lorenzo grows bored with Béatrice and, after a party, runs off with Musidora. In despair, Béatrice gives herself to the revellers.

III. Years have passed, and Lorenzo, downtrodden and despairing, wanders into a fisherman's bar. There he discovers Béatrice, whose dances drive the fishermen to fight for her. Lorenzo begs her to come back to him, but she refuses. In their brawling, the fishermen kill one of their own, causing them to turn on Béatrice.

IV. Remorseful for the suffering she has caused, Béatrice hears a heavenly choir. She returns to the convent, where the statue of the Virgin forgives her and accepts her back.

Beatrice di Tenda • Beatrice of Tenda

Composed by Vincenzo Bellini (November 3, 1801 – September 23, 1835). Libretto by Felice Romani. Italian. Based on the play by Carlo Tebaldi-Fores. Premiered Venice, Teatro la Fenice, March 16, 1833. Set in Binasco castle near Milan in 1418. Lyric tragedy. Set numbers with recitative. Prelude.

Sets: 6. **Acts:** 2 acts, 6 scenes. **Length:** I, II: 165. **Arias:** "Rimorso in lei?" (Filippo). **Hazards:** None. **Scenes:** Ii. Great hall of the castle of Binasco. Iii. Agnese's apartments. Iiii. Grove in the ducal palace garden. Iiv. Remote courtyard in the palace of Binasco. IIi. Gallery in the castle of Binasco. IIii. Ground floor vestibule opening onto the castle prisons.

Major roles: Duke Filippo Maria Visconti (baritone), Agnese of Maino (mezzo), Orombello (tenor), Beatrice of Tenda (soprano). **Minor role:** Anichino (tenor). **Bit part:** Rizzardo del Maino (tenor).

Chorus parts: SATTBB. **Chorus roles:** Courtiers, ladies in waiting, guards, soldiers, judges. **Dance/movement:** None. **Orchestra:** 2 fl (picc), 2 ob, 2 cl, 2 bsn, 4 hrn, 2 trp, 3 trb, timp, perc, harp, strings. **Stageband:** None. **Publisher:** G. Ricordi, Inc., Pietro Pittarelli & Co. **Rights:** Expired.

Ii. Filippo Visconti is tired of his wife, Beatrice, and annoyed that he owes his position to her. He loves Beatrice's lady-in-waiting Agnese. Iii. Agnese thinks of the young nobleman she loves, Orombello. She lures him into her apartments. Misunderstanding Agnese's words, Orombello admits his love for Beatrice. Furious, Agnese sends him away. Iiii. Beatrice berates herself for bestowing her love and kingdom on Filippo. She prays. Filippo orders Agnese's brother, Rizzardo, to keep an eye on Beatrice. Producing incriminating documents, he taxes Beatrice with betrayal—which she hotly denies. Iiv. The soldiers, having noted Filippo's strange behavior, vow to watch him. Orombello has gathered troops to defend Beatrice and he begs her to flee with him, but she refuses. Orombello is discovered by Filippo kneeling at Beatrice's feet. Filippo orders the pair imprisoned.

IIi. The courtiers reveal how Orombello—after extensive torture—confessed and implicated Beatrice. Orombello's friend Anichino begs Filippo not to condemn Beatrice, pointing out that the people are on her side. Filippo entrusts the trial to a panel of judges. Beatrice declares that Filippo is not fit to judge her. Brought before the court, Orombello declares Beatrice's innocence. He and Beatrice are condemned to be tortured. Overcome with guilt at having planted the documents that incriminated Beatrice, Agnese asks Filippo to pardon his wife. He tells Agnese he means to marry her. Beatrice has admitted nothing under torture and Filippo hesitates to sign Beatrice's death warrant. Upon hearing that troops loyal to Beatrice are besieging the castle, Filippo signs the warrant. IIii. Beatrice's friends and ladies-in-waiting bewail her fate. Beatrice rejoices that she goes to death innocent. Agnese begs forgiveness, which Orombello and Beatrice grant. Beatrice conjures her friends to pray for their enemies.

Béatrice et Bénédict • Béatrice and Bénédict

Composed by Hector Berlioz (December 11, 1803 – March 8, 1869). Libretto by Hector Berlioz. French. Based on the play "Much Ado About Nothing" by Shakespeare. Premiered Baden Baden, Neues Theater, August 9, 1862. Set in Sicily in the 16th century. Comedy. Set numbers with recitative and spoken dialogue. Overture. Entr'acte before II.

Sets: 2. **Acts:** 2 acts, 2 scenes. **Length:** I: 80. II: 55. **Arias:** "Je vais le voir" (Héro), "Dieu! que viens-je d'entendre" / "Il m'en souvient" (Béatrice). **Hazards:** None. **Scenes:** I. The park of the governor of Messina. II. A large room in the governor's palace.

Major roles: Héro (soprano), Béatrice (mezzo), Bénédict (tenor). **Minor roles:** Don Pedro (bass), Claudio (baritone), Somarone (bass), Ursule (contralto). **Speaking:** Léonato. **Speaking bits:** Messenger, Two maids, Musician, Offstage voice, Scrivener.

Chorus parts: SATTBB. **Chorus roles:** People of Sicily, musicians, choristers, lords and ladies of the governor's court. **Dance/movement:** I: National dance "sicilienne." **Orchestra:** 2 fl (picc), 2 ob (Eng hrn), 2 cl, 2 bsn, 4 hrn, 2 trp, 2 cornet, 3 trb, timp, guitar, perc, 2 harp, strings. **Stageband:** I: 2 ob, 2 bsn, 2 trp, cornet, perc, 2 guitar. **Publisher:** Kalmus Music. **Rights:** Expired.

I. The people of Sicily cheer Don Pedro's victory over the moors. Héro waits for her fiancé, Claudio, while Béatrice makes derisive inquiries after Bénédict. Béatrice and Bénédict tease and insult one another. Bénédict assures Claudio and Pedro that he will never marry. Privately, Pedro and Claudio decide Bénédict should marry Béatrice. Somarone rehearses the choristers and musicians in a work he has composed in honor of Claudio's wedding. Knowing that Bénédict is listening, Léonato assures Pedro that Béatrice loves Bénédict. Bénédict determines to return her love. Héro has played a similar trick on Béatrice. Héro cries at her own happiness.

II. Somarone improvises verses praising Syracusian wine. Béatrice realizes she loves Bénédict, but refuses to confess when Héro baits her. With a show of reluctance, Béatrice and Bénédict agree to marry. Claudio marries Héro.

Beatrix Cenci

Composed by Alberto Ginastera (April 11, 1916 – June 25, 1983). Libretto by Alberto Ginastera and William Shand. Spanish. Based on historical persons, "Chroniques Italiennes" by Stendhal and "The Cenci" by Percy Bysshe Shelley. Premiered Washington, D.C., Opera Society of Washington, September 10, 1971. Set in Rome and Petrella at the end of the 16th century. Historical tragedy. Through composed with some spoken lines.

Sets: 13. **Acts:** 2 acts, 14 scenes. **Length:** I, II: 90. **Hazards:** I, II: Cenci's vicious dogs are heard (taped) and seen. II. Cenci sees the ghosts of his victims. **Scenes:** Ii. Before Rome. Iii. A chamber in the Cenci palace in Rome. Iiii. Another chamber. Iiv. A grove in the palace gardens. Iv. The banquet hall. Ivi. Beatrix's chamber. Ivii. Bernardo's room. IIi. A terrace in the castle of Petrella. IIii. A dark corridor in the castle. IIiii. The dining hall. IIiv. The count's antechamber and bedroom. IIv. A chamber in the Cenci palace in Rome. IIvi. The torture chamber in the Castel Sant' Angelo. IIvii. A prison cell.

Major roles: Count Francesco Cenci (bass), Beatrix Cenci (lyric soprano). **Minor roles:** Andrea (baritone), Lucrecia (contralto), Orsino (tenor), Bernardo (treble), Giacomo (bass baritone). **Bit parts:** Three guests, Prison guard (bass). **Speaking:** Olimpio, Marzio.

Chorus parts: SATB. **Chorus roles:** People of Rome, ladies in waiting, Cenci's guests, judges. **Dance/movement:** I: Ballroom dancing at Cenci's party. **Orchestra:** 3 fl (picc), 3 ob, 3 cl, 2 bsn, cont bsn, 4 hrn, 4 trp, 4 trb, tuba, harp, organ, celeste, mandolin, timp, 3 perc, strings, taped sound effects. **Stageband:** I: bells. **Publisher:** Boosey & Hawkes. **Rights:** Copyright 1971 by Boosey & Hawkes.

Ii. The chorus bemoans the cruelty of Count Cenci. Iii. Cenci receives good news from Salamanca and orders a celebration. Iiii. Cenci's daughter, Beatrix, and wife, Lucrecia, have evil forebodings. Iiv. Beatrix asks her former suitor, Orsino, to take a letter to the Pope. He agrees, but tears it up. Iv. At the party, Cenci announces his good news: Two of his sons are dead. He makes advances on Beatrix who runs away. Ivi. Orsino tells Beatrix the Pope refused her letter. Cenci rapes her. Ivii. Lucrecia keeps her son, Bernardo, company.

IIi. Beatrix and her brother Giacomo plot revenge. IIii. They hire two assassins. IIiii. Cenci suspects his danger. IIiv. The assassins stab him to death in his bed. IIv. Orsino warns Beatrix of her imminent arrest before escaping himself. IIvi. Beatrix is tortured by the authorities. IIvii. She is unnerved by a vision of hell, but recovers and goes peacefully to her execution.

Beauty and the Beast

Composed by Vittorio Giannini (October 19, 1903 – November 28, 1966). Libretto by Robert A. Simon. English. Based on the fairy tale. Premiered Hartford, Connecticut, Julius Hartt School of Music, February 14, 1946. Set in the father's home and outside beast's castle in legendary times. Fairy tale. Through composed. Musical interlude between scenes. Radio premiere by CBS Radio, November 24, 1938.

Sets: 3. **Acts:** 1 act, 6 scenes. **Length:** I: 60. **Hazards:** None. **Scenes:** Ii. The father's home. Iii – Iiii. Before the castle of the beast. Iiv. The father's home. Iv. Before the castle. Ivi. The beast's garden beside the river.

Major roles: Father (baritone), Beauty (soprano), Beast (tenor). **Minor roles:** Story teller (mezzo), First daughter (mezzo), Second daughter (contralto), Gardener (tenor), Offstage voices (2 tenor, 1 baritone).

Chorus parts: N/A. **Chorus roles:** None. (The "chorus" marked in the final five bars of the opera is sung by the soloists.) **Dance/movement:** None. **Orchestra:** 2 fl, ob, 2 cl, bsn, 2 hrn, 2 trp, 2 trb, timp, perc, strings. **Stageband:** None. **Publisher:** Franco Colombo, Inc. **Rights:** Copyright 1951 by G. Ricordi & Co.

Ii. The father of three girls sees his fortunes improve after a period of poverty. Two of the daughters demand expensive presents, but the youngest—Beauty—wants only a rose. Iii. On his way to the city, the father stops to talk to the gardener of a hideous man (the beast). The gardener lets him pluck a rose for Beauty. The beast is furious. He turns the gardener to stone and demands Beauty as his bride. Iiii. Beauty tells the beast she cannot marry him, but he believes she will change her mind. Iiv. Worried that her father is ill, Beauty comes home. She remembers the beast in a dream. Iv. As she promised she would, Beauty returns to the beast. Ivi. She finds him dying and admits she loves him. The beast has Beauty free the gardener. The beast is transformed into a handsome young man: Beauty's love has removed the curse on him.

The Beggar's Opera

Composed by Johann Pepusch (1667 – July 20, 1752). Libretto by John Gay. English. Original work created from existing ballads. Premiered London, Lincoln's Inn Fields, January 29, 1728. Set in London in the 18th century. Ballad opera. Set numbers with recitative and spoken dialogue. Overture. Musical interludes between scenes. Only overture and song tunes with figured bass extant of original. Many of the songs were pre-existing ballads that Pepusch incorporated into the work. The materials were "fleshed out" by several composers including Frederic Austin (for the Lyric Theatre, Hammersmith in 1920) and Benjamin Britten. Because of the age and nature of the piece, many realizations and arrangements exist.

Sets: 4. **Acts:** 3 acts, 4 scenes. **Length:** I, II, III: 150. **Arias:** "What shall I do to show how much I love?" (Polly), "Oh London is a fine town" (Mrs. Peachum), "Pretty Parrot, say" (Macheath), South sea ballad (Lucy), "Bonny Dundee" (Macheath) **Hazards:** None. **Scenes:** I. Peachum's house. Iii. A tavern near Newgate. Iiii. Newgate prison. III. A gaming house.

Major roles: Peachum (bass), Mrs. Peachum (mezzo), Polly Peachum (soprano), Macheath (tenor), Lucy Lockit (soprano). **Minor roles:** Filch (tenor), Jenny Diver (contralto), Lockit the jailer (baritone or bass). **Bit parts:** Matt of the Mint (tenor), Mrs. Vixen (mezzo), Molly Brazen (mezzo), Gambler (tenor), Diana Trapes (soprano). **Speaking:** Beggar, Player.

Chorus parts: SSATTB. **Chorus roles:** Macheath's gang (Jemmy Twitcher, Crook-fingered Jack, Wat Dreary, Robin of Bagshot, Nimming Ned, Harry Padington, Ben Budget), women of the town (Mrs. Coaxer, Dolly Trull, Betty Doxy, Mrs. Slammekin, Suky Tawdry), gamblers. (Bit solo parts come from chorus, although names are not repeated.) **Dance/movement:** II: women of the town dance. III: final dance. **Orchestra:** fl, 2 ob, bsns, strings, continuo. (Many orchestrations and arrangements exist.) **Stageband:** None. **Publisher:** Boosey & Hawkes. **Rights:** Expired.

I. Peachum claims that everyone is a rogue out to cheat his brother. He and his wife are upset with Polly's expensive tastes and superior ways. Polly confesses that she loves—and has married—Macheath, who is condemned to die for his crimes. Polly and Macheath declare their love.

Iii. Peachum has informed on Macheath. Polly warns Macheath, but he carouses with his gang and is arrested. Iiii. In prison, Macheath concludes that no action so inescapably dooms a man as getting involved with a woman. His two wives—Polly and Lucy—visit him. Lucy helps Macheath escape.

III. Macheath finds that none of his friends will help him and he is recaptured. Lucy decides to revenge herself on Polly. Both women appeal to Macheath. He is led to the gallows, but is reprieved at the last moment.

La Belle Hélène • The Beautiful Helen

Composed by Jacques Offenbach (June 20, 1819 – October 5, 1880). Libretto by Henri Meilhac and Ludovic Halévy. French. Original work inspired by Greek legend. Premiered Paris, Théâtre des Variétés, December 17, 1864. Set in Sparta and Nauplia before the Trojan War. Operetta. Set numbers with recitative and spoken dialogue. Introduction. Entr'acte before II, III.

Sets: 3. **Acts:** 3 acts, 3 scenes. **Length:** I: 45. II: 30. III: 25. **Arias:** "Amours divins" (Hélène). **Hazards:** I: A dove delivers a letter to Calchas. III: High priest of Venus (Paris) arrives in a ship. **Scenes:** I. A public square outside the temple of Jupiter in Sparta. II. A luxurious room in the queen's private suite in the palace. III. On the beach at Nauplia.

Major roles: Hélène (soprano), High Priest Calchas (bass), Pâris (tenor). **Minor roles:** Oreste (mezzo or tenor), Parthoenis (soprano), Leoena (mezzo), First Ajax (tenor), Second Ajax (tenor), Ménélas (tenor), Achille (tenor), Agamemnon (bass baritone), Bacchis (soprano). **Bit parts:** Two young girls (soprano). **Speaking:** Philocòme, Euthycles.

Chorus parts: SATTBB. **Chorus roles:** People, followers of Adonis, guards, slaves, princes, princesses, Hélène's waiting women. **Dance/movement:** III: dances, ballet. **Orchestra:** 2 fl (picc), 2 ob, 2 cl, 2 bsn, 4 hrn, 2 trp, 3 trb, tuba (optional), timp, perc, strings. **Stageband:** None. **Publisher:** Heugel & Co. **Rights:** Expired.

I. Calchas, the high priest of Jupiter, is disappointed by the people's offerings. He talks to Hélène about the young Pâris, who judged the three goddesses, Minerva, Juno and Venus. Pâris chose Venus and the goddess has promised him the most beautiful woman in the world as a reward. Hélène admires Pâris, but means to stay faithful to her husband, Ménélas. Venus enlists Calchas to help Pâris. The high priest tells Ménélas that Jupiter wants him to go to Crete.

II. Calchas gambles with the kings of Greece and wins by cheating. Pâris sneaks into Hélène's bedroom disguised as a slave. She resists his advances, but Ménélas interrupts and makes a scene. Pâris is banished.

III. Venus takes revenge against Ménélas by making Spartan husbands and wives unfaithful. Hélène tells Ménélas that nothing happened between her and Pâris. Agamemnon and Calchas tell Ménélas that he should give Hélène to Pâris for the good of his subjects, but Ménélas objects. Ménélas sends for the High Priest of Venus to get a second opinion. Pâris arrives disguised as the high priest. He takes Hélène away, ostensibly to appease Venus with sacrifices.

Benvenuto Cellini

Composed by Hector Berlioz (December 11, 1803 – March 8, 1869). Libretto by Léon de Wailly and Auguste Barbier. French. Based on the autobiography of Benvenuto Cellini. Premiered Paris, Opéra, September 10, 1838. Set in Rome in 1532. Comedy. Set numbers with recitative. Overture. Entr'acte before II, III. Originally in 2 acts. Condensed and changed to 3 acts for premiere in Weimar, March 20, 1852.

Sets: 4. **Acts:** 3 acts, 4 scenes. **Length:** I, II, III: 155. **Arias:** "Ah! qui pourrait me résister" (Fieramosca), "Seul pour lutter" (Cellini). **Hazards:** III: Casting of Cellini's statue. **Scenes:** I. A room in Balducci's splendid house. IIi. The courtyard of a tavern. IIii. The Piazza Colonna at the corner of the Via Corso. III. Cellini's sculpture studio in the Roman Coliseum.

Major roles: Balducci (bass), Teresa (soprano), Benvenuto Cellini (tenor), Fieramosca (baritone), Ascanio (mezzo). **Minor roles:** Francesco (tenor), Bernardino (bass), Innkeeper (tenor), Pompeo (baritone), Cardinal Salviati (bass). **Bit part:** Officer (baritone).

Chorus parts: SSAATTTTBBBB. **Chorus roles:** Maskers, neighbors and servants of Balducci, people of Rome, workmen and friends of Cellini, members of a theatrical troupe, monks, members of the cardinal's suite. **Dance/movement:** II: Dance of the theatrical performers. **Orchestra:** 2 fl (picc), 2 ob, 2 cl, 4 bsn, 4 hrn, 4 trp, 2 cornet, 3 trb, ophicléide, timp, perc, harp, strings. **Stageband:** II: choristers with drums and perc. III: 2 guitar, 2 trp (guitars and trps can be in orchestra), anvil. **Publisher:** Enoch & Co., Choudene & Son. **Rights:** Expired.

I. The pope's treasurer, Balducci, wonders why the pope employs such a ne'er-do-well as Benvenuto Cellini. Cellini loves Balducci's daughter Teresa and visits her when Balducci is out. Fieramosca, sculptor to the pope, who also loves Teresa, overhears Cellini persuading Teresa to elope. Cellini plans to disguise himself as a monk. Balducci returns and beats Fieramosca.

IIi. Cellini and his fellow goldsmiths toast their art, but are unable to pay their bar bill. When Cellini's apprentice, Ascanio, arrives with gold meant as payment for the casting of a statue, Cellini uses it to buy more wine. Cellini and his friends plan to embarrass Balducci in retribution for his sending such a meager payment. Fieramosca's friend Pompeo persuades him to preempt Cellini's plan and abduct Teresa himself. IIii. Balducci and his daughter attend a play in the piazza. At Cellini's urging, the players parody Balducci himself. While the infuriated Balducci creates a scene, Cellini and Fieramosca descend on Teresa, both disguised as monks. A fight ensues, in which Cellini kills Pompeo. A cannon sounds, signaling the end of carnival, and in the confusion Fieramosca is arrested for Pompeo's murder.

III. Ascanio brings Teresa to Cellini's studio. Cellini joins them there, having eluded his pursuers by slipping into a chorus of real monks. Balducci demands the return of his daughter, whom he has promised to Fieramosca. They are interrupted by the cardinal, who is furious that Cellini has not yet cast the statue. He orders Cellini arrested, but when Cellini threatens to destroy the model of the statue, the cardinal relents. He gives Cellini one hour to cast the statue—or be hanged. Lacking sufficient gold to finish the job, Cellini melts down all his other creations. The statue is completed and the cardinal forgives him—and grants him Teresa's hand.

Bertha

Composed by Ned Rorem (b. October 23, 1923). Libretto by Kenneth Koch. English. Original work parodying Shakespeare's histories. Premiered New York City, Alice Tully Hall, November 26, 1973. Set in Oslo at an unspecified time. Satire. Through composed.

Sets: 8. **Acts:** 1 act, 10 scenes. **Length:** I: 25. **Hazards:** I: Boy and girl are killed in an explosion. **Scenes:** Ii. The ramparts. Iii. A study in the castle. Iiii. Bertha's summer lodge. Iiv. A little Scotch frontier town on the battle lines. Iv. The council chamber. Ivi. A rose garden. Ivii – Iviii. The throne room. Iix. A public place. Ix. The throne room.

Major role: Bertha (mezzo). **Minor roles:** Noble/Teacher/First Scotchman/Man/Barbarian chieftain ("medium high," e.g., tenor), Counselor/Third Scotchman ("low," e.g., bass), Old man/Second Norwegian citizen ("medium low," e.g., baritone or bass), Messenger/Girl ("high," e.g., soprano), Officer/Second Scotchman/First Norwegian citizen/Common Norwegian soldier ("medium," e.g., tenor).

Chorus parts: SATB. **Chorus roles:** Barbarians and Norwegians.
Dance/movement: None. **Orchestra:** Piano. **Stageband:** None.
Publisher: Boosey & Hawkes. **Rights:** Copyright 1973 by Boosey &
Hawkes Inc.

Ii. Bertha commands her dispirited troops to attack the barbarians and
inspires them to victory. Iii. Bertha beheads her teacher for asking what
distinguishes her Norwegians from the barbarians. Iiii. Bertha orders an
attack on Scotland. Iiv. She is victorious. Iv. Bertha's counselors object to
her useless wars. Ivi. A man and girl meet in Bertha's rose garden. She
arranges for them to be blown up. Ivii. In old age, Bertha meditates on
her greatness. Iviii. She orders the country surrendered to the barbarians
so she can conquer it back. Iix. The barbarians take over. Ix. Bertha
reconquers Norway and drops dead.

Der Besuch der alten Dame • The Visit of the Old Lady

Composed by Gottfried von Einem (January 24, 1918 – July 12, 1996).
Libretto by Friedrich Dürrenmatt. German. Based on the play by
Dürrenmatt. Premiered Vienna, Staatsoper, May 23, 1971. Set in Güllen,
a small town, in the present. Tragedy. Through composed. Introductions
before each act. Interludes between scenes (8 interludes total). Opus 35.

Sets: 7. **Acts:** 3 acts, 10 scenes. **Length:** I, II, III: 135. **Hazards:** I: Train
arrives onstage. Claire has a false left leg, which she displays. II: Claire
has a false hand. **Scenes:** Ii. The railway station. Iii. Konrad's village
wood. Iiii. The inn "The Golden Apostle." IIi. The general store. IIii. The
sacristy. IIiii. The station. IIIi. Petersen's farm shed. IIIii. The general
store. IIIiii. Konrad's village wood. IIIiv. Auditorium in "The Golden
Apostle."

Major roles: Mayor (helden tenor), Schoolmaster (baritone), Alfred Ill
(high baritone), Claire Zachanassian nee Wäscher (mezzo). **Minor roles:**
Priest (bass baritone), Railway Guard (bass), Policeman (bass baritone),
Koby (tenor), Loby (tenor), Doctor Nüsslin (baritone), Butler (tenor), Ill's
wife Mathilde Blumhard (lyric soprano), Ill's son (tenor), Ill's daughter
(mezzo), Hofbauer (tenor), Two women customers (2 soprano),
Helmesberger (baritone), Cameraman (bass). **Bit parts:** Conductor
(tenor), Station master (bass baritone), Husband IX (tenor), Voice (tenor).
Mute: Husband VII, Mayor's wife Annette Dummermuth, Sexton.
Speaking: Reporter. **Speaking bits:** Two Manhattan gangsters (Toby
and Roby).

Chorus parts: SAATB. **Chorus roles:** Citizens of Güllen, voices of the woods. **Dance/movement:** III: citizens dance for joy over Ill's death. **Orchestra:** picc, 2 fl, 2 ob, 2 cl, 2 bsn, 4 hrn, 3 trp, 3 trb, tuba, timp, perc, strings. **Stageband:** I: bells, station bell, fire bell. II: bells. III: guitar (can be in pit). **Publisher:** Boosey & Hawkes. **Rights:** Copyright 1970, 1971 by Boosey & Hawkes.

Ii. The unemployed men of Güllen sit in the station, awaiting the return of an Armenian oil millionairess, Claire Zachanassian. The citizens—and Alfred Ill, who loved Claire forty years ago—hope she will help the town. Claire introduces her seventh husband. She has brought a coffin with her. Iii. In the woods, Claire and Ill reminisce. Ill married rich, as did Claire, but Ill is now bankrupt like the town. Claire agrees to help. Ill kisses her hand—and discovers that it, like her left leg, is fake. Iiii. The citizens give a dinner for Claire in "The Golden Apostle." The mayor speaks about Claire's childhood generosity, but she sets the record straight. Claire agrees to give the town a huge sum of money on one condition. Forty years ago, Ill betrayed her by claiming her child was not his own. She was forced into prostitution and now she demands that someone murder Ill. The mayor rejects Claire's offer, but Claire says she will wait.

IIi. Customers flood Ill's store, buying items on account. Ill realizes that the whole town is out on a spending spree. IIii. Ill confesses his fears to the priest, who asks if Ill fears that, as he betrayed Claire for money, the people will now betray him for the same reason. The priest has bought a new bell. He tells Ill to flee. IIiii. Ill goes to the station, but the people will not let him leave.

IIIi. The schoolmaster and the doctor tell Claire the town is now hopelessly in debt. They ask her to buy up the factories to rejuvenate the economy, but it seems she already owns everything. IIIii. Ill has bought new things for his store and his family has new clothes. The mayor brings Ill a gun and obliquely suggests he shoot himself. Ill agrees to abide by the decision of the town, but will not kill himself. IIIiii. Claire and Ill reminisce and she tells him about the tomb she has built for him. IIIiv. At a town meeting, the schoolmaster argues that Claire's money is irrelevant: justice must be done. Everyone votes to take the money. The mayor hurries the press out of the auditorium and has the doors locked. When the reporter returns, he is told Ill died of a heart attack. Claire retrieves the body and pays the mayor. The people dance for joy.

Betrothal in a Convent

Composed by Sergei Prokofiev (April 27, 1891 – March 5, 1953). Libretto by Mira Mendelssohn-Prokofieva and Sergei Prokofiev. Russian. Based on the play "The Duenna" by Richard Brinsley Sheridan. Premiered Prague, Narodni Divadlo Theater, May 5, 1946. Set in Seville in the 18th century. Lyric comedy. Set numbers with recitative. Overture.

Sets: 8. **Acts:** 4 acts, 9 scenes. **Length:** I, II, III, IV: 150. **Hazards:** None. **Scenes:** I. A plaza in front of Don Jerome's house. IIi. Louisa's apartment in her father's house. IIii. The waterfront. IIiii. A room in Don Jerome's house. IIIi. Mendoza's lodgings. IIIii. Don Jerome's house. IIIiii. A convent garden. IVi. A monastery. IVii. Ballroom in Don Jerome's house. **Major roles:** Don Jerome (tenor), Mendoza (bass), Antonio (tenor), Louisa (soprano). **Minor roles:** Ferdinand (baritone), Lopez (tenor), Three maskers (tenor, baritone, bass), Duenna Margaret (contralto), Three fishwives (soprano, mezzo, contralto), Clara (mezzo), Rosina (contralto or mezzo), Don Carlos (baritone), Lauretta (soprano), Brother Chartreuse (baritone), Brother Benedictine (bass), Brother Elixir (tenor), Father Augustine (baritone). **Bit parts:** Pedro (tenor), Pablo (tenor), Michael (bass), Two monks (bass), First servant (tenor), Second servant (tenor). **Mute:** Friend who plays the cornet, Servant who plays the bass drum, page boy.

Chorus parts: SSAATTBB. **Chorus roles:** Nuns, monks, guests, tradespeople. **Dance/movement:** I: dance of the maskers. **Orchestra:** picc, 2 fl, 2 ob, Eng hrn, 2 cl, bs cl, 2 bsn, cont bsn, 4 hrn, 3 trp, 3 trb, tuba, timp, perc, harp, strings. **Stageband:** I: guitar, 4 vln, 2 vla, 3 vlc, perc. III: fl, alto sax, 2 vln, 3 vla, 2 vlc, 2 bs. IV: 2 cl, trp, 2 hrn, trb, tuba, perc. **Publisher:** Leeds Music Corp., State Music Publishers. **Rights:** Copyright 1948, 1954 by Leeds Music Corp.

I. Don Jerome plots with Mendoza to corner the fish market in Seville. To seal the bargain, Mendoza will marry Jerome's daughter Louisa. But Louisa loves Antonio, while Jerome's son Ferdinand loves Clara. Jerome finds Antonio with Louisa and chases him away.

IIi. Louisa's duenna, Margaret, promises to help her by marrying the rich Mendoza herself. Ferdinand and Louisa argue with their father about Mendoza, but Jerome is adamant that Louisa marry him. Margaret lets Jerome find one of Antonio's love letters so he will fire her. Louisa then leaves the house, disguised as Margaret. IIii. Clara, too, has run away from home. She is angry with Ferdinand for being too free towards her and means to hide in the convent. Louisa introduces herself to Mendoza as Clara, saying she is looking for Antonio. Mendoza agrees to help. IIiii. He pays a call on Jerome where he meets Margaret—who claims to be Louisa. She insists they elope.

IIIi. Mendoza finds Antonio for Louisa. IIIii. Mendoza's friend Don Carlos brings Jerome a message from Mendoza telling him of the completed elopement and asking his blessing to marry. Amused at all the subterfuge, Jerome agrees. Receiving a separate—but similar—letter from Louisa, Jerome consents to this also and makes arrangements for a celebration. IIIiii. Ferdinand sees Louisa with Antonio, but mistakes her for Clara, impressing the real Clara with his jealousy.

IVi. In the monastery, the monks drink and carouse. Antonio, Louisa, Mendoza and Margaret come to be married. Ferdinand fights Antonio, but Clara separates them. All three couples wed. IVii. At Jerome's party, all true identities are revealed. Since Clara is rich, Jerome is reconciled to the poor Antonio. Everyone but Mendoza is happy.

Der Bettelstudent • The Beggar Student

Composed by Karl Millöcker (April 29, 1842 – December 31, 1899). Libretto by F. Zell (Camillo Walzel) and Richard Genée. German. Based on "Les Noces de Fernande" by Victorien Sardou and "The Lady of Lyons" by Edward Bulwer-Lytton. Premiered Vienna, Theater an der Wien, December 6, 1882. Set in Kracow, Poland in 1704. Operetta. Set numbers with recitative and spoken dialogue. Overture. Entr'acte before III.

Sets: 4. **Acts:** 3 acts, 4 scenes. **Length:** I, II, III: 90. **Arias:** "Ich hab' kein Geld" (Symon). **Hazards:** None. **Scenes:** Ii. Courtyard of a military prison at Kracow. Iii. An inn. II. The grand salon in the palace of Countess Palmatica. III. The palace garden.

Major roles: Ollendorf (comic bass), Symon Symonovicz (tenor), Jan (tenor), Laura (soprano). **Minor roles:** Enterich (baritone), Piffke (tenor), Puffke (tenor), Bronislava (soprano), Palmatica (mezzo), Onuphrie (bass), Eva (mezzo), Richthofen (tenor), Lieutenant Wangenheim (tenor), Lieutenant Schweinitz (bass), Captain Heinrici (bass), Bugomil (bass).

Chorus parts: SATTBB. **Chorus roles:** Prisoners and their wives, wedding guests. **Dance/movement:** None. **Orchestra:** 2 fl (picc), 2 ob, 2 cl, 2 bsn, 4 hrn, 2 trp, 3 trb, timp, perc, harp, strings. **Stageband:** I: military band, drums. **Publisher:** Edition Cranz. **Rights:** Expired.

Ii. The Saxons have captured Kracow and the prisons are filled with Polish political prisoners. Enterich the jailer is besieged by wives wanting to see their imprisoned husbands. He agrees to the visits, but helps himself to the wives' presents. Iii. General Ollendorf is mad at Laura for having rejected his kisses. He avenges himself by paying a poor, imprisoned student, Symon, to court her, disguised as a prince. Symon and Laura fall in love.

II. While the countess tells Laura how to rule a husband, Symon's friend Janitsky makes love to Laura's sister, Bronislava. Symon asks Laura if she would love him if he were poor and she swears she would. He sends her a letter explaining everything, but it is intercepted by Ollendorf. After the wedding, Symon's true identity is revealed before everyone.

III. The women scorn Symon. Janitsky takes money from Ollendorf to betray the Polish grand duke, but uses it to win over the citadel for the Poles. As a cover, he has Symon pretend to be the grand duke. For his part in the victory, Symon is knighted by the Polish king and reconciled to his mother-in-law.

Billy Budd

Composed by Benjamin Britten (November 22, 1913 – December 4, 1976). Libretto by E. M. Forster and Eric Crozier. English. Based on the story by Herman Melville. Premiered London, Royal Opera House, Covent Garden, December 1, 1951. Set onboard the "Indomitable," a seventy-four-gun ship, during the French and English wars of 1797. Tragedy. Through composed with prologue and epilogue. Orchestral interludes between scenes. First version in four acts.

Sets: 4. **Acts:** 2 acts, 7 scenes. **Length:** I: 82. II: 76. **Arias:** "Billy Budd, king of the birds!" (Budd), "I accept their verdict" (Vere), "I'm sleepy" (Budd). **Hazards:** I, II: Set on a ship at sea. II: Budd hanged. **Scenes:** Ii. The main deck and quarter-deck of H.M.S. Indomitable. Iii. The captain's cabin. Iiii. The berth-deck. IIi. The main deck and quarter-deck. IIii. The captain's cabin. IIiii. A bay of the upper gun-deck. IIiv. The main deck and quarter-deck.

Major roles: Captain Edward Fairfax Vere (tenor), Billy Budd (baritone), John Claggart (bass). **Minor roles:** Mr. Redburn (baritone), Mr. Flint the sailing master (bass baritone), Lieutenant Ratcliffe (bass), Red Whiskers (tenor), Donald (baritone), Dansker (bass), Novice (tenor), Squeak (tenor), Bosun (baritone), First mate (baritone), Second mate (baritone), Maintop (tenor), Novice's friend (baritone), Arthur Jones (baritone). **Bit parts:** Four midshipmen (boys). **Speaking part:** Cabin boy.

Chorus parts: TTTTBBBB. **Chorus roles:** Officers, sailors, powder monkeys, drummers, marines, gunners, seamen, after-guardsmen. Two solo lines in Iii (bass & baritone). **Dance/movement:** None. **Orchestra:** 4 fl (picc), 2 ob, Eng hrn, 2 cl (bs cl), bs cl, alto sax, 2 bsn, cont bsn, 4 hrn, 4 trp, 3 trb, tuba, timp, 5 perc, harp, strings. **Stageband:** II: 4 drums. **Publisher:** Boosey & Hawkes. **Rights:** Copyright 1951, 1952 by Hawkes & Son (London) Ltd.

Prologue. Vere thinks back to the French wars when he was captain of the Indomitable. Ii. On board the Indomitable, the Bosun has a novice flogged. Ratcliffe returns with three men he has impressed into service: Red Whiskers, Arthur Jones and Billy Budd. Claggart, the master at arms, and First Lieutenant Redburn question the recruits. Billy Budd is excellent sailor material, they realize—in spite of his stammer. Budd is thrilled to be assigned to the foretop, but his farewell to his old ship, "The Rights of Man," is misunderstood as a political statement. Claggart tells Squeak to harass and keep an eye on Budd. The novice's spirit has been broken by the flogging. Donald warns Budd about Claggart. All praise their captain. Iii. Vere invites Redburn and Flint into his cabin for a drink. They complain about the French and worry about mutiny. Iiii. It is night and the men sing sea shanties. When Budd discovers Squeak going through his things, they fight. Squeak pulls a knife but Budd decks Squeak. Claggart has Squeak thrown in irons. Claggart is bothered by Budd's goodness and vows to destroy him. He promises to protect the novice from further floggings if he entraps Budd into mutiny. Using Claggart's money, the novice tries to bribe Budd, but Budd sends him away. Dansker warns Budd of Claggart's hatred, but Budd is happy with his new life and thinks everyone loves him.

IIi. A heavy mist blankets the ship. Claggart tries to report Budd to the captain, but is interrupted by the sighting of an enemy frigate. The Indomitable gives chase but is forced to stand down when the mist reappears. Claggart tells the captain that Budd is a mutineer, but the captain is skeptical. Claggart shows him the gold that he claims Budd used to bribe Squeak. IIii. Alone in his cabin, the captain reflects that Claggart is evil. Budd is admitted. He is ecstatic, since he thinks he is being promoted. The captain gently sets him straight and calls in Claggart. When Claggart accuses Budd of mutiny, Budd is so shocked he stammers and cannot reply. He strikes the master at arms, killing him. Vere is overcome by the dilemma that now confronts him. He convenes a drum head court composed of Flint, Redburn and Ratcliffe. Budd is interviewed by the court. He begs the captain to save him. The court consults. None of them liked Claggart but the law is clear: failing in their plea to the captain to intervene, they condemn Budd to be hanged from the yard-arm. Vere wonders how he can live with himself. IIiii. Budd contemplates death. Dansker brings him a mug of grog and tells him about the disaffection in the ranks. Reconciled to his fate, Budd warns Dansker that the sailors must not try to save him. IIiv. The first lieutenant reads out the articles of war. Budd blesses Captain Vere and is hanged. Epilogue. Vere, now an old man, is finally reconciled to what happened.

Boccaccio

Composed by Franz von Suppé (April 18, 1819 – May 21, 1895). Libretto by F. Zell (Camillo Walzel) and Richard Genée. German. Based on the play by Jean-François-Antoine Bayard, Adolphe de Leuven, Léon Lévy Brunswick and Arthur de Beauplan. Premiered Vienna, Carltheater, February 1, 1879. Set in Florence in 1331. Operetta. Set numbers with spoken dialogue and recitative. Prelude. Introduction before III.

Sets: 3. **Acts:** 3 acts, 3 scenes. **Length:** I, II, III: 105. **Arias:** "Ich sehe einen jungen Mann dort stehn" (Boccaccio). **Hazards:** I: People burn Boccaccio's books. **Scenes:** I. A public square in Florence. II. The houses and gardens of Lotteringhi and Lambertuccio. III. The garden of the ducal palace in Florence.

Major roles: Leonetto (tenor), Giovanni Boccaccio (tenor or baritone), Fiametta (soprano), Pietro (tenor). **Minor roles:** Checco (bass), Fratelli the bookseller (baritone), Lotteringhi the cooper (tenor), Lambertuccio the grocer (tenor), Scalza the barber (bass), Beatrice (soprano), Isabella (mezzo), Peronella (soprano), Stranger (baritone). **Bit parts:** Chichibio, Tofano, Fresco, Guido, Cisti, Federico, Giotto, Rinieri, Major Domo Cascio, Donna Jancofiere, Eliza, Marietta, Donna Pulci.

Chorus parts: SATTBB (briefly SSAA). **Chorus roles:** Beggars, students, journeymen, Donna Pulci's daughters. **Dance/movement:** III: Pantomime. **Orchestra:** 2 fl (picc), 2 ob, 2 cl, 2 bsn, 4 hrn, 2 trp, 3 trb, timp, perc, strings. **Stageband:** II: 6 trp. **Publisher:** Oliver Ditson Co. **Rights:** Expired.

I. The Florentines are angry with Boccaccio for ridiculing them in his books. Boccaccio's friend Leonetto loves Beatrice, but her father, Scalza, does not approve. Leonetto visits Beatrice while Scalza is out of town, but is surprised when Scalza returns early. Boccaccio helps Leonetto escape. Meanwhile, Boccaccio himself loves Lambertuccio's adopted daughter, Fiametta. Boccaccio meets Pietro, the prince of Palermo, who is in town to marry the duke's daughter. While Boccaccio woos Fiametta, Pietro woos Lotteringhi's wife, Isabella. The crowd burns Boccaccio's books.

II. Boccaccio, Leonetto and Pietro woo their loves. Mistaking Pietro for Boccaccio, the Florentines beat him.

III. Fiametta is really the duke's daughter—and is thus engaged to Pietro. Boccaccio is asked to write a comedy to be performed for the duke's entourage. He uses the opportunity to satirize Pietro. Pietro forgives him and helps him with Fiametta.

La Bohème • The Bohemian

Composed by Ruggero Leoncavallo (April 23, 1857 – August 9, 1919). Libretto by Ruggero Leoncavallo. Italian. Based on the romance "Scènes de la Vie de Bohème" by Henri Murger. Premiered Venice, Teatro la Fenice, May 6, 1897. Set in Paris from December 1837 to 1838. Lyric comedy. Set numbers with recitative.

Sets: 3. **Acts:** 4 acts, 4 scenes. **Length:** I, II, III, IV: 135. **Arias:** "Musette svaria sulla bocca viva" (Mimì), "Da quel suon soavemente" (Musette). **Hazards:** II: Tenants throw potatoes and water on Musette's guests. **Scenes:** I. The first floor of the Café Momus. II. The courtyard of the Musette's house. III – IV. Marcello's garret.

Major roles: Schaunard (baritone), Marcello (tenor), Rodolfo (baritone), Mimì (lyric soprano), Musette (mezzo). **Minor roles:** Gaudenzio (tenor), Loafer (tenor), Gustavo Colline (baritone), Eufemia (mezzo), Barbemuche (comic bass), Durand (tenor), Gentleman on the first floor (tenor), Viscount Paolo (baritone). **Bit parts:** Old woman (mezzo), Clerk (bass), Wife (mezzo), Apothecary (tenor), Two women (mezzo). **Mute:** Waiters, Three scullions.

Chorus parts: SSAATTTTBBBB. **Chorus roles:** Students, grisettes, tenants, servants, cooks, porters. **Dance/movement:** II: Ballroom dancing. **Orchestra:** 2 fl (picc), 2 ob (Eng hrn), 2 cl, 2 bsn, 4 hrn, 3 trp, 3 trb, tuba, timp, perc, piano, harp, strings. **Stageband:** I: bells. **Publisher:** Edoardo Sonzogno. **Rights:** Expired.

I. Gaudenzio rebukes Schaunard and his artist friends, Marcello and Rodolfo, for their behavior in his café. Schaunard promises to reform and convinces Gaudenzio to prepare a Christmas Eve feast for the artists and their lady friends. The artists eat but cannot pay and Gaudenzio refuses to let them leave. Barbemuche introduces himself and offers to pay the bill. The artists are offended and refuse. They suggest a game of billiards with the loser paying. Barbemuche accepts and loses to Schaunard.

II. Musette is evicted from her apartment since her old lover refuses to pay the rent now that she is with Marcello. The party Musette has planned is almost ruined, but she decides to hold it in the courtyard where all of her furniture has been dumped. The party is a success until the angry tenants pelt the guests with potatoes. In the confusion, Mimì agrees to run off with Viscount Paul.

III. Schaunard and Rodolfo have been jilted and Musette is leaving Marcello. Mimì begs Rodolfo to forgive her, but he refuses.

IV. The men's Christmas Eve dinner is interrupted by Mimì, who has been sent away from the hospital. She is dying. Musette arrives and sends Schaunard off to pawn her jewels and buy medicine. Mimì dies in Rodolfo's arms.

La Bohème • The Bohemian

Composed by Giacomo Puccini (December 22, 1858 – November 29, 1924). Libretto by Giuseppe Giacosa and Luigi Illica. Italian. Based on novel "Scènes de la Vie de Bohème" by Henry Murger. Premiered Turin, Teatro Regio, February 1, 1896. Set in Paris about 1830. Tragedy. Through composed.

Sets: 3. **Acts:** 4 acts, 4 scenes. **Length:** I: 35. II: 18. III: 25. IV: 29. **Arias:** "Che gelida manina" (Rodolfo), "Mi chiamano Mimì" (Mimì), "Vecchia zimarra"/Coat song (Colline), Musetta's aria (Musetta). **Hazards:** None. **Scenes:** I. A garret, Christmas Eve. II. A square in the Latin quarter of Paris before the Café Momus. III. The barrier d'Enfer. IV. In the garret.

Major roles: Marcello (baritone), Rodolfo (tenor), Mimì (soprano), Musetta (soprano). **Minor roles:** Colline (bass), Schaunard (baritone), Benoit (bass), Parpignol (tenor), Alcindoro (bass). **Bit parts:** Boy (treble), Custom house sergeant (bass), Customs officer (bass).

Chorus parts: SSAATTTTBB. **Chorus roles:** Townspeople, soldiers, servants, students, street vendors, cafe customers, midinettes, waiters, working girls, gendarmes, street sweepers, customs officers, children (in 2 parts). **Dance/movement:** None. **Orchestra:** 3 fl (picc), 2 ob, Eng hrn, 2 cl, bs cl, 2 bsn, 4 hrn, 3 trp, 3 trb, bs trb, timp, perc, xylophone, harp, strings. **Stageband:** II: 4 picc, 6 trp, 6 drums. III: chimes. **Publisher:** Schirmer, Ricordi. **Rights:** Expired.

I. Marcello and Rodolfo complain about the cold in their garret and Rodolfo uses his old manuscripts to make a fire. Colline joins them. The men are surprised when Schaunard arrives with provisions and explains that an English peer hired him to play music until the peer's parrot died. "I played for three days and then poisoned the parrot," Schaunard explains. He insists they dine out. Benoit, the landlord, comes for the rent. The young artists pretend to be offended that he has a mistress and eject him. When the men head out to the Café Momus, Rodolfo stays behind briefly to finish some writing. Mimi appears. She needs her candle lit, but is faint from the exertion of climbing the stairs. She loses her key. The wind blows out all the candles. Rodolfo has secretly pocketed the key and he persuades Mimi to stay and talk with him. Mimi and Rodolfo kiss.

II. The streets are crowded with Christmas revelers. Parpignol is selling children's toys. Mimi shows off the bonnet Rodolfo has bought her. Marcello's ex-girlfriend, Musetta, appears, her elderly suitor, Alcindoro, in tow. She causes a scene to attract the attention of the young men. Her behavior scandalizes Alcindoro, but Musetta sends him off on an errand. She escapes with Marcello and his friends amidst the soldiers' procession—sticking Alcindoro with the bill.

III. Mimi asks Marcello for help. She plans to leave Rodolfo since his jealousy is making things impossible. Marcello has a talk with Rodolfo, who admits he loves Mimi passionately, but knows that his life of poverty is hastening on her consumption. When Mimi's cough reveals that she has been eavesdropping, Rodolfo tries to comfort her. The lovers postpone their parting until spring. Marcello and Musetta have a falling out.

IV. Marcello and Rodolfo pretend not to care that their loves have found wealthy suitors. Colline and Schaunard bring bread and herring for dinner. The men pretend to be nobles at a feast and ball. This becomes a mock duel until it is interrupted by Musetta. She has brought Mimi— who is dying. They put Mimi to bed. Musetta tells Marcello to pawn her earrings and fetch a doctor. She herself goes to get Mimi a muff to warm her hands. Colline sells his beloved overcoat. The lovers have a last caress. Marcello returns with medicine; Musetta with a new muff. Mimi dies, plunging her friends into despair.

The Bohemian Girl

Composed by Michael William Balfe (May 15, 1800 – October 20, 1870). Libretto by Alfred Bunn. English. Based on the French ballet pantomime "La Gipsy" by Joseph Marzilier and Jules-Henri Vernoy de Saint-Georges. Premiered London, Drury Lane, November 27, 1843. Set in Pressburg and environs in the 18th century. Romantic opera. Set numbers with recitative and dialogue. Overture. Introduction before III.

Sets: 6. **Acts:** 3 acts, 6 scenes. **Length:** I, II, III: 150. **Arias:** "I dreamt that I dwelt in marble halls" (Arline). **Hazards:** None. **Scenes:** I. The château and grounds of Count Arnheim on the Danube. IIi. A street in Presburg, 12 years later. IIii. Another street in Presburg. IIiii. The public square in Presburg. IIiv. The interior of Count Arnheim's apartments in the hall of justice. III. A splendid salon in the castle of Count Arnheim.

Major roles: Count Arnheim (baritone), Thaddeus (tenor), Arline (soprano). **Minor roles:** Devilshoof (bass), Florestein (tenor), Queen of the gypsies (mezzo). **Bit parts:** Buda (soprano), Captain of the guard (bass), Officer (tenor). **Speaking:** Gypsy, Servant.

Chorus parts: SSATTBB. **Chorus roles:** Count's retainers, huntsmen, pages, nobles, gypsies, peasants, soldiers, citizens. **Dance/movement:** I: Entertainment at the count's banquet (waltz and gallop). II: Gypsy dances. **Orchestra:** 2 fl, 2 ob, 2 cl, basset hrn, 2 bsn, 2 hrn, 2 trp, 3 trb, ophicléide, timp, perc, harp, strings. **Stageband:** II: trp. **Publisher:** Schirmer. **Rights:** Expired.

I. The count and his retainers hunt. Thaddeus—an enemy of Austria from her war with Poland—eludes a troop of Austrian soldiers by joining a gypsy band. The count's nephew, Florestein, reports that the count's six-year-old daughter, Arline, has been attacked by a wild animal. Thaddeus saves her. In gratitude, the count invites him to dinner. When the count toasts the emperor's health, Thaddeus causes a scene. Though outraged, the count protects Thaddeus from his still more outraged guests. The gypsy Devilshoof intervenes. He is arrested, but escapes and kidnaps Arline.

IIi. Twelve years have passed. The gypsies rob Florestein, but their queen insists on giving him back his property. Arline presses her lover, Thaddeus, for an explanation of her origins. The gypsy queen also loves Thaddeus. Devilshoof has retained Florestein's medallion, which the queen takes from him. IIii. Arline and the gypsies go off to the fair. IIiii. Florestein is attracted to Arline but she laughs at him. She is wearing his medallion—which the queen gave her—so he takes his revenge by accusing her of theft. The gypsies fight to protect Arline, but she is captured. IIiv. Arline is brought before the chief magistrate—who is the count. She explains how she got the medallion. The count is sympathetic, but is forced to condemn her nonetheless. Arline draws a dagger and tries to stab herself, but is prevented by the count. He sees the scar from the wild animal on her arm and realizes she is his long-lost daughter. He is ecstatic.

III. Florestein begs Arline's forgiveness. Thaddeus and Devilshoof ask Arline to return with them, but she refuses to desert her father. When the count and his guests arrive, Thaddeus hides. His hiding place is betrayed by the queen of the gypsies who enters in disguise. Arline begs the count to accept Thaddeus, but the count is repulsed by his gypsy heritage. Only when Thaddeus reveals his true identity as a Polish nobleman does the count relent. The queen orders a gypsy to shoot Thaddeus, but Devilshoof throws off his aim and the queen dies instead.

Bomarzo

Composed by Alberto Ginastera (April 11, 1916 – June 25, 1983). Libretto by Manuel Mujica Láinez. Spanish. Based on Láinez's novel. Premiered

Washington, D.C., Opera Society of Washington, May 19, 1967. Set in Bomarzo, Florence and Rome in the 16th century. Melodrama. Through composed but mostly recitative. Prelude. Interludes between scenes.

Sets: 12. **Acts:** 2 acts, 15 scenes. **Length:** I: 80. II: 50. **Hazards:** I: Images of Pier Francesco in the courtesan's mirrors mock him. Silvio's incantation. Girolamo falls off a precipice. Ghost of Pier Francesco's father appears to him. Vision of a devil in a mirror. II: Pier Francesco's nightmare. Statues of alchemists dance. Silvio's laboratory collapses. Pier Francesco's spirit ascends from his body. **Scenes:** Ii. The park of the castle of Bomarzo. Iii. A room in the castle of Bomarzo. Iiii. The private study of the young Pier Francesco Orsini. Iiv. The chamber of the courtesan Pantasilea in Florence. Iv. The bank of the river Tiber in the countryside around Bomarzo. Ivi. The great hall of the castle of Bomarzo. Ivii. The terrace outside the great hall. Iviii. Pier Francesco's study. IIi. Hall in the Farnese palace in Rome. IIii. A bed chamber in the castle of Bomarzo. IIiii. The bed chamber at a distance. IIiv. The gallery of the castle. IIv. The castle garden. IIvi. Silvio's laboratory in the cellars of the castle. IIvii. The castle park.

Major roles: Duke Pier Francesco Orsini of Bomarzo (tenor), Astrologer Silvio de Narni (baritone). **Minor roles:** Voice of shepherd boy (treble), Nicolas Orsini (contralto or tenor), Diana Orsini (contralto), Child Maerbale (treble), Child Girolamo (treble), Child Pier Francesco (treble), Gian Corrado Orsini (bass), Messenger (baritone), Pantasilea (mezzo), Girolamo (baritone), Maerbale (baritone), Julia Farnese (soprano). **Mute:** Abul. **Dancer:** Skeleton.

Chorus parts: SATB. **Chorus roles:** Prelates, courtiers, pages, servants, astrologers, monsters, demons. **Dance/movement:** I: Dancing animated skeleton. II: Court "passamezzo." Ritual dance of the alchemists. **Orchestra:** 2 fl (picc), 2 ob (Eng hrn), 2 cl (2 bs cl), 2 bsn (cont bsn), 3 hrn, 3 trp, 3 trb, 4 timp, mandolin, harp, clavicembalo, piano (celeste), harpsichord, xylophone, 3 perc, strings (vla d'amore). **Stageband:** I: Sound of peacocks. **Rights:** Copyright 1967 by Boosey & Hawkes Inc.

Ii. Pier Francesco, the hunchbacked duke of Bomarzo, drinks a magic potion intended to confer immortality. Iii. As a boy, Pier Francesco's brothers, Girolamo and Maerbale, tease him and get him in trouble with their father, Gian Conrado Orsini. Pier Francesco sees a dancing skeleton. Iiii. The astronomer Silvio de Narni tells the young Pier Francesco that he will be immortal. Pier Francesco knows that his father means to kill him and agrees to let Silvio perform an incantation. His father returns from battle mortally wounded. Iiv. Pier Francesco, still a virgin, is sent to the Florentine courtesan Pantasilea. Images of himself mock him from the mirrors and he flees. Iv. Diana Orsini comforts her grand-

son, Pier Francesco. Girolamo falls off a precipice and dies. Ivi. Pier
Francesco is crowned duke and Diana introduces him to Julia Farnese.
He sees a ghost of his father. Ivii. Pier Francesco rejoices in his new title.
Iviii. He wishes Julia loved him and sees a vision of the devil.
IIi. Maerbale loves Julia. Pier Francesco spills red wine on Julia's dress.
IIii. Julia and Pier Francesco are married. He is haunted by a mosaic of
the devil that no one else can see. IIiii. Pier Francesco sees monsters in
his nightmares. IIiv. Frustrated with love and his deformity, Pier
Francesco embraces the statue of the minatour in the castle gallery. IIv.
At his order, Silvio tempts Maerbale into visiting Julia in her room. She
resists, but Pier Francesco has Maerbale killed. IIvi. Pier Francesco has
commissioned monstrous statues for the park. Silvio brews an immortality potion for Pier Francesco, but his laboratory is destroyed by the
magic. IIvii. Nicolas Orsini has poisoned the potion. Pier Francesco takes
it and dies, his spirit joining the monsters in the garden.

The Boor

Composed by Dominick Argento (b. October 27, 1927). Libretto by John
Olon-Scrymgeour. English. Based on the comedy by Anton Chekhov.
Premiered Rochester, Eastman School of Music, May 6, 1957. Set in the
countryside in 1890. Comic opera. Through composed. Overture.

Sets: 1. **Acts:** 1 act, 11 scenes. **Length:** I: 55. **Hazards:** None. **Scenes:** I.
The drawing room of a widow's house in the country.

Major roles: Widow (soprano), Boor (bass baritone). **Minor role:** Old
servant (tenor).

Chorus parts: N/A. **Chorus roles:** None. **Dance/movement:** None.
Orchestra: fl (picc), ob (Eng hrn), 2 cl (bs cl), bsn, 2 hrn, trp, piano, perc,
strings. **Stageband:** None. **Publisher:** Boosey & Hawkes. **Rights:**
Copyright 1960 by Boosey & Hawkes Inc.

Ii. A young widow remains in mourning a year after her husband died.
Iii. She remembers how faithless he was when alive. Iiii. A boorish man
pushes his way past the servant. Iiv. He demands payment on a loan he
made to the widow's husband. Iv. His house is about to be foreclosed
on, but the widow explains she cannot get the money immediately. Ivi.
She ends the interview. Ivii. The boor decides to try again. Iviii. When
the servant refuses to let him pass, the boor threatens to remain in the
house until he is paid. Iix. He makes noise, which brings the widow out
to berate him. They argue about the fickleness of women and the faithlessness of men. The boor challenges the widow to a duel. Ix. She
impresses the boor by accepting. Ixi. The boor shows the widow how to

use a gun, but refuses to fire at her: He has fallen in love. He proposes. The widow returns his affection.

Boris Godunov

Composed by Modest Mussorgsky (March 21, 1839 – March 28, 1881). Libretto by Modest Mussorgsky. Russian. Based on the epic poem by Alexander Pushkin and "History of the Russian State" by Nicolai Mikhailovich Karamzin. Premiered St. Petersburg, Maryinsky Theater, February 8, 1874. Set in Russia and Poland from 1598 to 1605. Music drama. Set numbers with recitative. Prologue. Several versions exist with major differences. The so-called Polish scenes (IIIi and IIIii) were added later by Mussorgsky and can be omitted. Some versions omit only IIIi. Prologue ii and Ii can be swapped, as can IVi and IVii. Orchestrations exist by Moussorgsky (7-scene version premiered Leningrad, February 16, 1928), Rimsky-Korsakov (premiered St. Petersburg, December 10, 1896) and Shostakovich (premiered Leningrad, November 4, 1959). Incomplete Mussorgsky version given in charity performance February 17, 1873.

Sets: 9. **Acts:** 4 acts, 9 scenes. **Length:** Prologue: 20. I: 35. II: 30. III: 40. IV: 45. **Arias:** "I have attained the highest power" (Boris). **Hazards:** None. **Scenes:** Prologue i. Courtyard of the Novodievitchi monastery. Prologue ii. A square in the Moscow Kremlin. Ii. A cell in the Chudov monastery. Iii. An inn near the Lithuanian border. II. The tsar's apartments in the Kremlin. IIIi. Marina Mnishek's boudoir at Sanomir. IIIii. The garden of the Mnishek castle. IVi. An assembly hall in the Kremlin. IVii. A clearing in a forest near Kromy. (See notes.)

Major roles: Duke Vassili Ivanovich Shuisky (tenor), Boris Godunov (bass baritone), Pimen (bass), Grigori/Pretender Dimitri (tenor), Marina Mnishek (mezzo or soprano). **Minor roles:** Constable (baritone), Andrei Schelkhalov (baritone), Innkeeper/Hostess (mezzo), Varlaam (bass), Missail (tenor), Border guard (bass), Xenia (soprano), Nurse (mezzo), Fyodor (mezzo or treble), Jesuit Rangoni (baritone or bass), Idiot (tenor), Jesuit Lovitzky (bass), Jesuit Tscherniakovsky (bass). **Bit parts:** Mitiuk (bass), Two peasants (alto, soprano), Nikitich (bass), Boyar Khrushchov/Messenger (tenor). (In the original 7-scene version, Grigori is a minor role, while Rangoni and Marina do not exist.)

Chorus parts: SSAATTBBB. **Chorus roles:** Peasants, pilgrims, monks, police, boyars, Polish knights and ladies (in IIIii only), young girls (in IIIi), vagrants, urchin children (in 2 parts). **Dance/movement:** IIIi: Clapping game. IIIii: Polonaise. **Orchestra:** 3 fl (picc), 2 ob (Eng hrn), 2 cl (bs cl), 2 bsn, 4 hrn, 3 trp, 3 trb, tuba, timp, perc, harp, piano (4 hands), strings. **Stageband:** Prologue: 2 or 4 trp, bells. I: tam tam. IV: trps, chimes, tam tam. **Publisher:** Belwin Mills, Affiliated Music Corporation. **Rights:** Expired.

Prologue i. A police officer bullies the crowd into pleading with Boris to become tsar. Prologue ii. Boris is hailed tsar, but the death of the rightful tsarevitch disturbs his conscience.

Ii. The monk Pimen has almost completed his history. His young companion, Gregori, wakes from a dream in which he is jeered at by all Moscow. He envies Pimen's worldly experience, but Pimen praises the peacefulness of the monastery. Hearing that the young tsarevitch murdered by Boris was his own age, Gregori vows to punish the tsar. Iii. Two itinerant monks, Varlaam and Missail, stop at an inn on the Lithuanian border. They drink and Varlaam recounts the siege of Kazan. Grigori has fled the monastery. When he questions the innkeeper about the border crossing, she warns him that it is guarded by soldiers, but tells him about a secret path. The police come looking for Grigori, but as they cannot read the written description of him, Grigori fools them into arresting Varlaam. By the time Varlaam sets the police straight, Grigori has fled.

II. Boris's daughter, Xenia, mourns her dead fiancé while his son, the tsarevitch Fyodor, and the nurse play. The tsar laments that all of his good intentions are thwarted by an angry providence. He is warned of Grigori's pretensions to the throne by Prince Shuisky, whose loyalty the tsar doubts. Haunted by Grigori's assumption of the name of the dead tsarevitch Dimitri, Boris questions Shuisky about Dimitri's death. Shuisky assures Boris that he saw the real Dimitri dead.

IIIi. The Polish princess Marina is entertained by her ladies in waiting. She consults her confidant, the Jesuit Rangoni. IIIii. Grigori goes to Poland to raise troops. There he falls in love with Marina. Rangoni encourages Grigori, although the young pretender distrusts the priest. Marina promises Grigori her love—if he can defeat Boris and make himself tsar.

IVi. The boyars curse and condemn the false Dimitri. Shuisky undermines Boris by telling the boyars of the tsar's guilt-ridden visions. Pimen tells how his sight was restored by the spirit of the murdered tsarevitch. Overcome, Boris calls for his son and dies in his arms. IVii. A crowd taunts and beats a boyar while the children rob a simpleton. Missail and Varlaam incite them against Boris. They capture and murder two Jesuits. The simpleton weeps for the people of Russia.

Braniboři v Čechách • Brandenburgers in Bohemia

Composed by Bedřich Smetana (March 2, 1824 – May 12, 1884). Libretto by Karel Sabina. Czech. Based on scenes from Czech history. Premiered Prague, Provisional Theater, January 5, 1866. Set in Bohemia in 1279. Historical drama. Set numbers with recitative. Ballet. Prelude.

Sets: 4. **Acts:** 3 acts, 6 scenes. **Length:** I, II, III: 150. **Arias:** "It was a beautiful dream" (Ludiše), "Your picture" (Tausendmark). **Hazards:** None. **Scenes:** Ii. A garden in front of the house on Olbramovič's estate. Iii. A square in Prague. IIi. A village square. IIii. A courtroom in Prague. IIiii. The garden. III. The village square.

Major roles: Lord Mayor Volfram Olbramovič (bass), Junoš (tenor), Ludiše (soprano), Jan Tausendmark (baritone), Jíra (tenor). **Minor roles:** Oldřich Rokycanský (baritone), Vlčenka (soprano), Děčana (contralto), Captain Varneman (tenor), Villager (bass), Town crier (bass).

Chorus parts: SSAATTBB. **Chorus roles:** Knights, soldiers, villagers, vagabonds, beggars, judges. **Dance/movement:** I: ballet. **Orchestra:** picc, 2 fl, 2 ob, 2 cl (bs cl), 2 bsn, 4 hrn, 2 trp, 3 trb, tuba, timp, perc, strings. **Stageband:** II: trp, drum. **Rights:** Expired.

Ii. The regent of Bohemia has called in Prince Brandenburg and his men to protect Bohemia from its enemies. But the Brandenburgers have behaved like an invading army. The knight Oldřich is unable to persuade Volfram to lead a rising against the Brandenburgers. Junoš brings word that the Brandenburgers have sacked Prague, and Volfram goes to the rescue. Volfram's daughter Ludiše, sorry to have missed her sweetheart, Junoš, rejects the advances of Tausendmark. He takes revenge by persuading the Brandenburgers to loot her father's estate. Tausendmark plans to abduct Ludiše. Iii. Vagabonds join in the looting of Prague. They crown the run-away serf, Jíra, their king. Ludiše and her sisters have been taken captive by the Brandenburgers and appeal to the beggars to help her. Jíra negotiates with Tausendmark until Volfram arrives. Tausendmark says that Jíra abducted Volfram's daughters. Jíra is arrested.

IIi. In a nearby town, Czech peasants flee the onslaught of the Brandenburgers, who take control of the town. Prince Brandenburg orders his men to leave Bohemia within three days. IIii. Jíra is tried and found guilty. A messenger arrives from the Brandenburg soldiers demanding ransom for Volfram's daughters. Volfram sends Tausendmark. IIiii. Volfram's daughters hope to be rescued; Junoš assures them help is on the way. The captain of the Brandenburgers decides to take the girls with him if he is forced to leave before the ransom arrives.

III. The captain gladly takes Tausendmark's money in exchange for Volfram's daughters, but he refuses to protect Tausendmark from his enemies. Tausendmark means to leave with Ludiše. The daughters wonder if they should make a break for it. Tausendmark takes Ludiše, but leaves the other daughters behind. The captain prepares to depart when Junoš arrives with his men and Jíra, whom he has freed from prison. They find the captain, but not Ludiše. Jíra rescues Ludiše from Tausendmark, for which Volfram thanks Jíra.

Les Brigands • The Brigands

Composed by Jacques Offenbach (June 20, 1819 – October 5, 1880). Libretto by Henri Meilhac and Ludovic Halévy. French. Original work. Premiered Paris, Théâtre des Variétés, December 10, 1869. Set in Mantua and environs at an unspecified time. Operetta. Set numbers with recitative and spoken dialogue. Overture. Entr'acte before II, III.

Sets: 3. **Acts:** 3 acts, 3 scenes. **Length:** I: 45. II: 40. III: 25. **Arias:** "Après avoir pris à droite" (Fiorella), "Falsacappa voici ma prise" (Fragoletto). **Hazards:** None. **Scenes:** I. A rocky landscape in the province of Mantua. II. Outside a country inn on the border of Mantua and Granada. III. The great hall in the palace of the duke of Mantua.

Major roles: Falsacappa (tenor), Fiorella (soprano), Fragoletto (soprano). **Minor roles:** Domino (baritone), Barbavano (bass), Carmagnola (tenor), Fiametta (soprano), Zerlina (soprano), Bianca (mezzo), Cicinella (mezzo), Pietro (baritone), Prince (tenor), Pipo the innkeeper (tenor), Captain of the guard (bass), Baron of Campo Tasso (tenor or baritone), Tutor of the Princess of Granada (bass), Count of Gloria-Cassis (tenor), Adolphe of Valladolid (tenor), Princess of Granada (soprano), Treasurer (tenor). **Bit parts:** Brigand (tenor), Pipetta (soprano), Pipa (mezzo), Duchess (soprano), Marchioness (contralto). **Speaking bits:** Pipetto, Journalist, Antonio, Court usher. **Mute:** Royal courier, Notary.

Chorus parts: SATTTBBB. **Chorus roles:** Brigands, soldiers, peasants, cooks, Italian nobles, pages and servants, Spanish nobles and ladies of the court, Spanish pages and servants, nobles and ladies of the court of the Duke of Mantua, four girls. **Dance/movement:** III: Dances. **Orchestra:** 2 fl (picc), 2 ob, 2 cl, 2 bsn, 4 hrn, 2 trp, 3 trb, timp, perc, strings. **Stageband:** None. **Publisher:** Boosey & Co. **Rights:** Expired.

I. The brigands complain to their chief, Falsacappa, that their robberies do not pay very well. Falsacappa's daughter Fiorella has fallen in love with Fragoletto, a chocolate maker they recently robbed, but who is now willing to become a brigand for Fiorella. While Fragoletto is being tested, the prince comes in asking for directions. Since he is cute, Fiorella helps him escape before the brigands return. Fragoletto passes his test: He abducts a royal courier bearing news of the prince's upcoming marriage. Falsacappa decides to steal the bride-to-be's dowry. He substitutes a picture of his daughter for that of the prince's fiancée and sends the messenger on his way. Fragoletto is officially made a brigand.

II. The brigands take over an inn. They lock up the princess and her escort and head for court, intending to impersonate them, but the prisoners escape.

III. The prince's treasurer admits he has embezzled the dowry money. The prince recognizes the "princess" as Fiorella. The real princess arrives and the prince orders Falsacappa and his men hanged, but when Fiorella reminds the prince that she saved his life, he frees the brigands. The treasurer bribes the princess's escort to avoid paying the dowry.

The Burning Fiery Furnace

Composed by Benjamin Britten (November 22, 1913 – December 4, 1976). Libretto by William Plomer. English. Based on the Book of Daniel in the Old Testament. Premiered Suffolk, English Opera Group, Orford Church, June 9, 1966. Set in Babylon in the 6th century BC. Parable for church performance. Through composed with spoken lines. Opus 77.

Sets: 1. **Acts:** 1 act, 1 scene. **Length:** I: 64. **Hazards:** I: The Israelites are thrown into a burning, fiery furnace but remain unscathed. **Scenes:** I. Nebuchadnezzar's palace in Babylon.

Major roles: Abbot/Astrologer (baritone), Herald and leader of the courtiers (baritone), Ananias (baritone), Misael (tenor), Azarias (bass), Nebuchadnezzar (tenor). **Minor roles:** Two acolytes/Assistants (treble). **Bit part:** Angel/Assistant (treble). (Principals and choristers are drawn from a group of 1 abbot, 12 monks and 4 acolytes, including roles and chorus.)

Chorus parts: TBaB. **Chorus roles:** Courtiers (3 tenor, 2 baritone, 2 bass), Assistants (4 treble, which includes the two acolytes and the angel). **Dance/movement:** I: Two acolytes dance for the king. **Orchestra:** fl (picc), hrn, alto trb, vla, db bs (Babylonian drum), harp (little harp), perc, chamber organ (cymbals). (Performed by 8 lay brothers.)

Stageband: None. **Publisher:** Faber Music Ltd. **Rights:** Copyright 1966 by Faber Music Ltd.

I. The abbot and monks introduce the story of the burning fiery furnace and don their costumes for the pageant. Nebuchadnezzar has chosen three princes of Israel to rule over three provinces of Babylon. He renames them Shadrach, Meshach and Abednego and all but the three Israelites sit down to a feast. They are entertained by two acolytes. The astrologer draws attention to the fact that the three Israelites are not eating. The three politely decline, citing Hebrew law, but the king is insulted. The astrologer warns Nebuchadnezzar that he has endangered his kingdom by appointing these strangers. The king demands that the Israelites bow down before the god of Babylon. They refuse. The king has them cast into a burning fiery furnace, but an angel protects them. Nebuchadnezzar converts to the god of the Israelites and sends away his astrologer. The abbot and monks draw the moral.

La Calisto • Calisto

Composed by Pier Francesco Cavalli (February 14,
1602 – January 14, 1676). Libretto by Giovanni
Faustini. Italian. Based on Ovid's "Metamorphoses."
Premiered Venice, Teatro S. Apollinaire, November
28, 1651. Set in Pelasgia in the Peloponnese in mythical times. Drama for music. Set numbers with recitative. Prologue.
Realized by Raymond Leppard.

Sets: 7. **Acts:** 2 acts, 7 scenes. **Length:** I, II: 160. **Arias:** "Lucidissima face"
(Endimione), "Ardo, sospiro e piango" (Diana). **Hazards:** I: Jove brings
forth a stream and is transformed into Diana. II: Giunone turns Calisto
into a bear and Giove turns her back. **Scenes:** Prologue. The cave of eternity. I. A parched forest by the dried-up source of the Ladone. IIi. The
summit of Mount Latmos. IIii. The plain of Erymantho. IIiii. The source
of the Ladone. IIiv. Another part of the forest. IIv. The Empireo.

Major roles: Giove (bass), Mercurio (baritone), Calisto (soprano),
Endimione (counter tenor), Diana (mezzo), Linfea (tenor travesty role).
Minor roles: Goddess of nature (mezzo), Goddess of eternity (soprano),
Goddess of destiny (soprano), Satirino (soprano), Pane (bass), Sylvano
(bass baritone), Giunone (soprano), Echo (soprano).

Chorus parts: SSAATTB. **Chorus roles:** Furies, satyrs and heavenly spirits. **Dance/movement:** I, II: Optional dances. **Orchestra:** strings, continuo. **Stageband:** None. **Publisher:** Faber Music Ltd. **Rights:** Expired.

Prologue. The goddesses agree to give Calisto a place among the stars. I.
Giove descends to save earth from a fire and drought. He is captivated
by the nymph Calisto's beauty, but she is determined to remain a virgin.
Mercurio counsels Giove to disguise himself as the goddess Diana and
kiss Calisto, which he does. Endimione loves Diana. She cares for him
but is sworn to chastity. Calisto greets the real Diana, but the goddess
rebukes her for her talk of kisses. Satirino is rejected by Linfea while
Diana rejects Pane.

IIi. Satirino is amazed to find Diana encouraging Endimione's love. IIii.
Calisto confides in Giove's jealous wife, Giunone, who bitterly reproves
her husband. Pane attacks his rival, Endimione. IIiii. Giunone turns
Calisto into a bear. IIiv. Diana saves Endimione from Pane and admits
her love. IIv. Giove breaks Giunone's spell and makes Calisto immortal.

La Cambiale di Matrimonio • Marriage by Promissory Note

Composed by Gioachino Rossini (February 29, 1792 – November 13, 1868). Libretto by Gaetano Rossi. Italian. Based on a play by Camillo Federici. Premiered Venice, Teatro San Moisè, November 3, 1810. Set in England in the 18th century. Farce. Set numbers with recitative. Overture.

Sets: 1. **Acts:** 1 act, 1 scene. **Length:** I: 80. **Arias:** "Grazie, grazie" (Slook), "Vorrei spiegarvi il giubilo" (Fanny). **Hazards:** None. **Scenes:** I. A room in Tobia Mill's house.

Major roles: Tobia Mill (bass), Edoardo Milfort (tenor), Fanny (soprano), Slook (bass). **Minor roles:** Norton (bass), Clarina (mezzo). **Mute:** servants.

Chorus parts: N/A. **Chorus roles:** None. **Dance/movement:** None. **Orchestra:** fl, 2 ob, 2 cl, bsn, 2 hrn, strings, continuo. **Stageband:** None. **Publisher:** G. Ricordi, James E. Matthew. **Rights:** Expired.

I. Edoardo and Fanny, Tobia Mill's daughter, are in love, but since Edoardo is poor, they have not told Mill. Mill has engaged his daughter to an American, Mr. Slook, giving Slook a promissory note for Fanny. Fanny and Edoardo threaten Slook into renouncing his marriage. Not knowing why Slook has changed his mind, Mill is mortified and challenges Slook to a duel. Deciding to help Fanny and Edoardo, Slook signs the promissory note over to Edoardo and names him his heir. Mill and Slook are about to fight when Edoardo presents the promissory note and demands Fanny. Slook reconciles Mill and the lovers.

La Campana Sommersa • The Sunken Bell

Composed by Ottorino Respighi (July 9, 1879 – April 18, 1936). Libretto by Claudio Guastalla. Italian. Based on the drama by Gerhart Hauptmann. Premiered Hamburg, Municipal Theater, November 18, 1927. Set in Germany in legendary times. Symbolist drama. Through composed. Introduction before III.

Sets: 3. **Acts:** 4 acts, 4 scenes. **Length:** I, II, III, IV: 130. **Hazards:** None. **Scenes:** I. A mountain meadow surrounded by pine trees. II. The living room of Heinrich's house. III. A forsaken glass blower's hut not far from the snow caves. IV. The mountain meadow.

Major roles: Rautendelein (soprano), Enrico (tenor). **Minor roles:**

Nickelmann (baritone), Faun (tenor), Witch (mezzo), Barber (tenor), School master (baritone), Curate (bass), First elf (soprano), Second elf (soprano), Third elf (mezzo), Magda (soprano), Neighbor (mezzo). **Speaking bits:** Two children, Dwarf. **Mute:** Goblins, Neighbors, Villagers. **Dancers:** Elves.

Chorus parts: SSAA. **Chorus roles:** Elves, children (1 part). **Dance/movement:** I: Dance of the elves. **Orchestra:** 3 fl, pan pipes, 3 ob, 3 cl, 2 bsn, 4 hrn, 3 trp, 3 trb, tuba, timp, perc, xylophone, celeste, organ, harp, strings. **Stageband:** None. **Publisher:** Bote & Bock. **Rights:** Copyright 1927 by Bote & Bock.

I. A faun tells Nickelmann, the old man of the well, that a church is being constructed nearby. Since elves hate the sound of bells, the faun casts the bell and its maker, Heinrich, into the lake. The young elf Rautendelein finds the dying Heinrich and tries to help him. The barber, the schoolmaster and the pastor take Heinrich home. Rautendelein watches the elves dance and decides to follow Heinrich.

II. Heinrich is brought home to his wife, Magda. When she goes off to find a cure for him, Rautendelein appears and heals and rejuvenates Heinrich.

III. Rautendelein lures Heinrich up to the mountains where he enslaves the dwarves and sets to work on a church for a new religion. The pastor reminds him of his wife, but Heinrich refuses to give up his newfound vigor unless the bell that sunk into the lake rings. A band of men attacks Heinrich, but he defeats them. Heinrich's children tell him that Magda has drowned herself in the lake. Heinrich hears the sunken bell ringing and repents.

IV. Heinrich returns to Rautendelein and dies in her arms.

Il Campanello • The Night Bell

Composed by Gaetano Donizetti (November 29, 1797 – April 8, 1848). Libretto by Gaetano Donizetti. Italian. Based on "La Sonnette de Nuit" by Léon Lévy Brunswick, Mathieu-Barthélemy Troin and Victor Lhérie. Premiered Naples, Teatro Nuovo, June 1, 1836. Set in Foria, a suburb of Naples, in the early 19th century. Comic melodrama. Set numbers with recitative. Prelude.

Sets: 1. **Acts:** 1 act, 1 scene. **Length:** I: 55. **Arias:** "Bella cosa" (Annibale). **Hazards:** I: Annibale steps on small firecrackers, setting them off. **Scenes:** I. The room behind an apothecary's store.

Major roles: Don Annibale Pistacchio (bass), Serafina (soprano), Enrico (baritone). **Minor roles:** Spiridione (tenor), Madame Rosa (mezzo).

Chorus parts: SATTBB. **Chorus roles:** Don Annibale's relations, wedding guests and servants. **Dance/movement:** I: Guests dance the "gallop." **Orchestra:** 2 fl, 2 ob, 2 cl, 2 bsn, 2 hrn, 2 trp, 3 trb, timp, strings. **Stageband:** None. **Publisher:** International Music Company. **Rights:** Expired.

Ii. The apothecary, Don Annibale, celebrates his wedding to Serafina, who is young and beautiful. Annibale tells Serafina's mother, Madame Rosa, that he must leave tomorrow for Rome to hear the reading of his aunt's will. He does not care for Rosa's dashing young nephew, Enrico, who arrives with firecrackers. Enrico dances with Serafina and each accuses the other of faithlessness. Annibale interrupts. He is furious, but Enrico tells him they were rehearsing a play. Enrico sings a drinking song. The guests leave and Annibale prepares for bed. A new regulation requires apothecaries to respond to the night bell in person. Enrico, disguised as a French dandy, rings the bell, demanding wine. While Annibale is mixing a sedative, Enrico rearranges the furniture in the darkened room. He tells Annibale he is better and leaves. Annibale feels his way around. Enrico returns, disguised as a singer with throat problems. He infuriates Annibale by singing at the top of his lungs and Annibale throws him out. Annibale finds a letter warning that an enemy of the apothecary means to have revenge upon him. Spiridione suggests putting some of Enrico's firecrackers on the floor to alert them to intruders. Enrico brings an impossibly complicated prescription. While going to bed, Annibale accidentally sets off the firecrackers and the noise wakes the household. It is morning and Enrico and the guests return to see Annibale off to Rome. Annibale warns Serafina not to answer the night bell.

Il Campiello • The Square

Composed by Ermanno Wolf-Ferrari (January 12, 1876 – January 21, 1948). Libretto by Mario Ghisalberti. Italian. Based on the play by Carlo Goldoni. Premiered Milan, Teatro alla Scala, February 12, 1936. Set in Venice in the mid-18th century. Lyric comedy. Through composed. Introduction. Intermezzo before II. Ballet. Ritornello before III.

Sets: 1. **Acts:** 3 acts, 3 scenes. **Length:** I: 40. II: 35. III: 30. **Hazards:** Note that Cate and Pasqua are played by men. III: rocks thrown during fight. **Scenes:** I – III. A square with several houses.

Major roles: Gasparina (soprano), Cavalier Astolfi (baritone), Lucieta (soprano), Gnese (soprano). **Minor roles:** Anzoleto the haberdasher (bass), Donna Cate Panciana (comic tenor), Donna Pasqua Polegana (comic tenor), Orsola the street vendor (mezzo), Zorzeto (tenor), Fabrizio dei Ritorti (bass). **Mute:** Sansuga, Orbi, Giovanni, Facchini, porters.

Chorus parts: SATBB. **Chorus roles:** People. **Dance/movement:** I: Cavalier dances with the ladies. II: ballet of the inn maidens, wedding party dance. **Orchestra:** picc, 2 fl, 2 ob, 2 cl, 2 bsn, 4 hrn, 3 trp, 3 trb, tuba, timp, perc, harp, piano, organ, celeste, strings. **Stageband:** II: beggars play tambourines, etc. **Publisher:** G. Ricordi & Co. **Rights:** Copyright 1935, 1936 by G. Ricordi & Co.

I. Cavalier Astolfi flirts with Gasparina, but is equally attracted to Lucieta and Gnese. Lucieta loves the haberdasher Anzoleto and is jealous when she sees Anzoleto with Gnese. Lucieta's mother, Cate, and Gnese's mother, Pasqua, both plan to remarry as soon as they marry off their daughters. Gnese and Zorzeto are in love. When Zorzeto talks to Lucieta, Anzoleto gets jealous and starts a fight. The cavalier Astolfi breaks up the fight.

II. Gasparina's uncle Fabrizio chastises the women for making so much noise. Anzoleto and Lucieta get engaged. The cavalier treats them to a celebratory dinner. Fabrizio forbids Gasparina to attend. The beggars feast on polenta. The cavalier learns that Gasparina will have a substantial dowry, but Fabrizio knows that the cavalier is bankrupt.

III. Fabrizio decides to move to get away from the noise. The cavalier asks to marry Gasparina and Fabrizio agrees. Anzoleto, again jealous of Zorzeto, slaps Lucieta, but they make up. Anzoleto insults Zorzeto and a fight ensues. The cavalier reconciles everyone by inviting them to dinner. He announces his engagement to Gasparina.

Candide

Composed by Leonard Bernstein (August 25, 1918 – October 14, 1990). Libretto by Lillian Hellman and Hugh Wheeler. English. Based on the story by Voltaire. Premiered New York City, Martin Beck Theater, December 1, 1956. Set in various cities in the old and new worlds in the 18th century. Comedy. Set numbers with spoken dialogue. Overture. Several versions with significant differences, including long opera house version (premiered New York City Opera, October 13, 1982 and shown in this entry) and short Broadway version.

Sets: 22. **Acts:** 2 acts, 23 scenes. **Length:** I: 80. II: 65. **Arias:** "Glitter and be Gay" (Cunegonde). **Hazards:** I: Pangloss hanged. II: Candide's boat sinks. Quick scene changes. **Scenes:** Ii. Dr. Voltaire's traveling freak show. Iii. The schoolroom, castle and gardens. Iiii. A desolate hearth. Iiv. The baronial chapel. Iv. A meadow by moonlight and the battlefield. Ivi. Cunegonde's room. Ivii. Destroyed village. Iviii. Central square in Lisbon. Iix. A Lisbon street. Ix. Cunegonde's room. Ixi. A room in the inn at Cadiz. Ixii. Central plaza at Cadiz. IIi. Plaza Grande, Cartagena. IIii. A ship at sea. IIiii. Montevideo cathedral. IIiv. A jungle. IIv. Eldorado and a jungle. IIvi. A jungle and sheep meadow. IIvii. Ballroom in Cartagena and the dock. IIviii. A desert island. IIix. The private gaming room in the palace of the prefect of Constantinople. IIx. The cave of the wisest man. IIxi. Candide's farm. (Different versions order scenes differently. Can be Venice instead of Constantinople.)

Major roles: Voltaire/Dr. Pangloss/Businessman/Governor/Second Gambler/Police Chief/Sage (tenor or baritone), Candide (tenor), Maximilian (baritone), Cunegonde (soprano), Paquette (soprano), Old lady (mezzo). **Minor roles:** Three judges (tenor, baritone, bass), Six dons (3 tenors, 3 baritones), Two pink sheep (sopranos), Pasha-Prefect (baritone). **Bit part:** Lion (bass), First gambler (baritone). **Speaking:** Huntsman, Baron, Baroness, Servant of Maximilian, Two Bulgarian soldiers, Two Westphalian soldiers, Heresy agent, Grand Inquisitor, Don Issachar the Jew, Governor's aide, Slave driver, Father Bernard, Four sailors. **Mute:** Calliope player, Two inquisition agents, Two pirates. [Above is for opera house version. Other versions have additional bit parts, e.g., Bear keeper, Alchemist, Junkman, Cosmetic merchant, Prince Charles Edward, King Hermann Augustus, Sultan, Tsar, etc.]

Chorus parts: SSAATTBB. **Chorus roles:** Medieval church singers, Lisbonites, Jesuits, ball guests, slaves, gamblers, dancing girls, people. **Dance/movement:** Ixii: Old lady dances for the dons. IIvii: Governor's waltz. **Orchestra:** 2 fl (picc), ob (Eng hrn), 2 cl (bs cl, soprano sax), bsn, 2 hrn, 2 trp, 2 trb, tuba, timp, 3 perc, harp, strings. **Stageband:** None. **Publisher:** Amberson Enterprises, Boosey & Hawkes. **Rights:** Copyright 1955, 1957, 1958, 1976, 1982 by Leonard Bernstein.

Ii. Voltaire introduces Candide, a bastard cousin who lives with the baron's family; Paquette, the sexy young maid; and the baron's son and daughter, Cunegonde and Maximilian. Iii. Dr. Pangloss instructs the youngsters that everything is for the best in this best of all possible worlds. After class, Cunegonde watches as Pangloss teaches the cooperative Paquette "advanced physics." Cunegonde repeats this experiment with Candide, but Maximilian catches them and the baron banishes Candide. Iiii. Two Bulgarian soldiers conscript Candide. Iiv. Bulgarian soldiers sack the baronial castle, raping and killing its inhabitants. Iv. Cunegonde and Candide remember happier times. Ivi. Cunegonde becomes the mistress of both the rich Jew Don Issachar and the Grand

Inquisitor. Ivii. Candide finds Pangloss in an earthquake-ravaged city. Iviii. The doctor's philosophy gets Candide and himself condemned by the Inquisition. While Cunegonde looks on, Candide is flogged and Pangloss hanged. Iix. Candide is nursed by an old lady. Ix. He is reunited with Cunegonde and kills both Don Issachar (accidentally) and the inquisitor (intentionally). With the old lady's help, the lovers escape to Cadiz. Ixi. The trio is robbed. Ixii. Trying to repair their fortunes, the old lady offers herself—without success—to six rich old dons. Candide is hired as captain of an expedition to rescue the Jesuits of Montevideo. The three sail for the New World.

IIi. Paquette and Maximilian are offered at auction as female slaves. The Spanish governor buys Maximilian and propositions him. Upon discovering that Maximilian is a man, he orders him strung up. IIii. On board ship, the old lady tells Candide and Cunegonde that she was born a princess. Her story is interrupted by pirates, who abduct the women. IIiii. Candide proceeds to Montevideo alone where he is reunited with Paquette and Maximilian. Maximilian is furious at the thought of Cunegonde marrying Candide (a bastard). He attacks Candide but is himself accidentally killed. IIiv. Paquette and Candide escape into the jungle. IIv. They stumble upon Eldorado but are bored with its tranquility. IIvi. Loading two pink sheep with gold, they return to Cartagena. IIvii. Candide finds the old lady, who tells him that Cunegonde has been taken to Constantinople. The boat they leave on sinks. IIviii. Candide, Paquette, the old lady and the sheep are marooned on a desert island from which they are eventually rescued. IIix. In Constantinople the prefect complains that he has no sooner cheated someone than he is himself cheated. Candide and company attempt to buy Cunegonde. The prefect agrees to a gamble, which Candide wins because Maximilian is the croupier. IIx. Unsure what to do now, Candide and the rest visit the cave of the wisest man. From him they learn that the highest wisdom is to work. IIxi. Candide and Cunegonde start a farm.

Capriccio

Composed by Richard Strauss (June 11, 1864 – September 8, 1949). Libretto by Clemens Krauss and Richard Strauss. German. Original work. Premiered Munich, Königliches Hof- und Nationaltheater, October 28, 1942. Set in a château near Paris about 1775 ("at the time when Gluck began his reform of opera"), afternoon into evening. Conversation piece for music. Through composed using a variety of forms: ballet, bel canto duet, octet, sonnet, recitative, aria, etc. Difficult solo lines in orchestra. Opus 85.

Sets: 1. **Acts:** 1 act, 13 scenes. **Length:** I: 135. **Arias:** Countess's final scene

(Countess), La Roche's aria (La Roche). **Hazards:** None. **Scenes:** I. Salon of a rococo castle overlooking a park.

Major roles: Countess (soprano), Count (baritone), Flamand (tenor), Olivier (baritone), La Roche (bass), Clairon (contralto). **Minor roles:** Monsieur Taupe (tenor), Italian singer (soprano), Italian tenor (tenor), Major-Domo (bass). **Bit parts:** Eight servants (4 tenors, 4 basses). **Mute:** Young Dancer.

Chorus parts: N/A. **Chorus roles:** None. **Dance/movement:** I: Gavotte by a solo ballerina. **Orchestra:** 3 fl (picc), 2 ob, Eng hrn, 3 cl, basset hrn, bs cl, 3 bsn (cont bsn), 4 hrn, 2 trp, 3 trb, timp, perc, 2 harps, cembalo, strings (16-16-10-10-6). **Stageband:** String sextet (2 vln, 2 vla, 2 vcl) and trio (vla, vlc, cembalo). **Publisher:** B. Schott's Söhne, Boosey and Hawkes, Johannes Oertet, Berlin. **Rights:** Copyright 1942 by Richard Strauss.

I. The widowed countess sits rapt, listening to the new string sextet composed by Flamand. The composer and the poet Olivier discover that they are rivals for her affections—and attention. Together, they rail at the theater director La Roche who has slept through the composition. La Roche awakes and the three men discuss current fashions in opera. The great actress Clairon will be coming soon to read through Olivier's new play with the countess's brother, the count, La Roche reveals. Olivier insists that he still admires Clairon's talent although he is no longer in love with her. Olivier, Flamand and La Roche retire to prepare the stage for the afternoon's rehearsal. The Countess praises Flamand's music but evades the Count's questions about her romantic interest in the composer and poet. La Roche returns and praises the birthday celebration he has arranged for the Countess. Clairon arrives and reads through Olivier's play with the Count. She is impressed with the Count and the group retires offstage to rehearse. Olivier repeats the love sonnet from his play, addressing it to the Countess. Flamand sits down to set the sonnet to music while the Countess flirts with Olivier. The composer is soon done. He plays his work and the three wonder about the struggle between words and music. La Roche comes to fetch Olivier: he needs permission to make some cuts to the play. Olivier goes out with him and the Flamand pours out his love for the Countess. She promises him an interview in the library at eleven o'clock the next morning. The Countess remains alone onstage while the rehearsal can be heard in the background. The Count returns and he and the Countess discuss their various amours. "Words or Music?" the Countess asks. The players return, their rehearsal finished. While chocolate is served, the guests are entertained by a dancer and musicians provided by La Roche. Olivier approaches Clairon during the dance, but after a brief exchange they part in anger. Olivier and Flamand again spar over the importance of their respective arts. Is rhythm or verse more constraining? Is the abstraction of music or the clarity of language more expressive? It is pointed out that opera is a fusion of all forms. La Roche introduces two Italian singers who perform a duet for the company's amusement. The Count invites Clairon to accompany him to Paris; she accepts. After some urging, La Roche reveals something of the birthday celebration he is planning. There will be a living tableau, "The Birth of Pallas Athene," acting out the birth of Athene from the forehead of Zeus. In an octet, the guests amuse themselves at the expense of La Roche's grandiose idea. Attempting to appease the offended theater director, the Countess coaxes out of him the second part of the program: "The Fall of Carthage." In a long oration, La Roche challenges the artists to produce something worthy of the theater. "I preserve the art of your fathers," he explains, "and I discover—and support—the talent of tomorrow. It is easy for you to rail at the theater when you only produce dry, academic trifles." The guests are convinced; the Countess challenges the poet and composer to produce an opera. After some discussion it is agreed to make an opera of the events of the afternoon. Everyone but the Countess leaves for Paris. The servants clear the room while making fun of the afternoon's goings-on. Monsieur Taupe, the prompter, appears. He has fallen asleep and been left behind. The major domo takes him off to the kitchen for some refreshment and promises to get him a coach to Paris. The Countess appears and the major domo informs her that Olivier has asked to meet her in the library tomorrow at eleven. The Countess is amused that Olivier and Flamand are destined to be inseparable now. She sings the sonnet that the two men have written for her and wonders aloud which she will pick, words or music?

I Capuleti e i Montecchi • The Capulets and the Montagues

Composed by Vincenzo Bellini (November 3, 1801 – September 23, 1835). Libretto by Felice Romani. Italian. Based on the play "Romeo and Juliet" by Shakespeare. Premiered Venice, Teatro la Fenice, March 11, 1830. Set in Verona in the 13th century. Lyric tragedy. Set numbers with recitative. Overture.

Sets: 6. **Acts:** 2 acts, 18 scenes. **Length:** I, II: 130. **Arias:** "O quante volte" (Giulietta). **Hazards:** None. **Scenes:** Ii – Iiii. Gallery in Capellio's palace. Iiv – Ivi. Giulietta's apartments. Ivii – Iix. Internal atrium in Capellio's palace. IIi – IIiv. Apartments in Capellio's palace. IIv – IIvii. Remote place. IIviii – IIix. The tombs of the Capulets.

Major roles: Tebaldo (tenor), Capellio (bass), Lorenzo (bass), Romeo (mezzo), Giulietta (soprano).

Chorus parts: SATTB. **Chorus roles:** Capulets, Montagues, young ladies, soldiers, guards. **Dance/movement:** None. **Orchestra:** 2 fl (picc), 2 ob, 2 cl, 2 bsn, 4 hrn, 2 trp, 3 trb, timp, perc, harp, strings. **Stageband:** I: 2 trp II: 2 trp, harmonium (winds and brass can move to stage from pit). **Publisher:** Kalmus, G. Ricordi & Co. **Rights:** Expired.

Ii. The Capulets gather. Iii. The Montagues offer peace, but Capellio wants revenge on Romeo for killing his son. Tebaldo is to marry Capellio's daughter, Giulietta. Iiii. Romeo's peace embassy fails. Iiv. Giulietta calls for her Romeo. Iv. Lorenzo brings him. Ivi. Romeo asks Giulietta to flee but she cannot. Ivii. The celebrations for Giulietta's wedding begin. Iviii. Armed Montagues interrupt the festivities. Iix. Capellio and Tebaldo find Romeo with Giulietta, but Romeo is extricated by his allies.

IIi. Giulietta anxiously awaits news of the fighting. IIii. Romeo is safe. Lorenzo convinces Giulietta to take a potion that simulates death, promising to reunite her with Romeo. IIiii. Giulietta begs her father to forgive her but he is adamant. IIiv. Capellio doubts Lorenzo's loyalty. IIv. Romeo awaits Lorenzo. IIvi. He is discovered by Tebaldo. IIvii. The two men hear of Giulietta's death. IIviii. Romeo visits Giulietta's tomb and takes poison. IIix. Giulietta wakes to have Romeo die in her arms. She dies. Capulets and Montagues discover the bodies.

Cardillac

Composed by Paul Hindemith (November 16, 1895 – December 28, 1963). Libretto by Ferdinand Lion. German. Based on "Das Fräulein von Scuderi" by E.T.A. Hoffmann. Premiered Dresden, Staatsoper, November 9, 1926. Set in Paris in the 17th century. Tragedy. Set numbers with recitative. Overture. Ballet. Introduction before IV. Revised version premiered in Zürich, June 20, 1952. Reduced to 4 acts (original version included performance of Lully's "Phaeton").

Sets: 4. **Acts:** 4 acts, 4 scenes (5 acts in original version). **Length:** I, II, III, IV: 90. **Hazards:** III: Cardillac works gold into jewelry. **Scenes:** I. An open space in the city. II. The singer's bedroom. III. Cardillac's workshop. IV. In the street outside the opera.

Major roles: First singer of the opera (soprano), Cardillac the goldsmith (baritone), Cardillac's daughter (soprano). **Minor roles:** Gold merchant (bass), Provost marshall (bass), Officer (tenor), Young cavalier (tenor), Journeyman (tenor), Phaeton (tenor), Apollo (bass), Klymene (contralto) (last three omitted in later version). **Mute:** Rich marquis. **Bit part:** Chorister (baritone).

Chorus parts: SATB. **Chorus roles:** City mob, police, tavern goers, people, theater personnel. **Dance/movement:** II: pantomime of the courtier and lady making love. IV: ballet. **Orchestra:** 2 fl (picc), ob, Eng hrn, 2 cl, bs cl, tenor sax, 2 bsn, cont bsn, hrn, 2 trp, 2 trb, tuba, piano, 4 perc, strings (6-0-4-4-4). **Stageband:** IV: fl, ob, bsn, harp, cembalo, vln, vla, vlc, bs. **Publisher:** B. Schott's Söhne. **Rights:** Copyright 1926, 1952 by Schott & Co. Ltd.

I. The crowd honors the goldsmith Cardillac. But they also pity him: Everyone who buys his jewelry is mysteriously murdered. A lady promises herself to a courtier if he brings her one of Cardillac's creations.

II. The courtier brings her a golden girdle. While he is making love to the lady, a masked figure kills him and steals the girdle.

III. A gold merchant believes Cardillac is in league with the devil and spies on him to get proof. The goldsmith's daughter tells Cardillac she is in love with a young officer. Cardillac blesses their marriage. He begs the officer not to purchase one of his jewels, but the officer insists.

IV. Cardillac attacks the officer, but fails to kill him. The officer begs Cardillac to flee. When the gold merchant raises the alarm, the officer accuses the gold merchant himself of being his assailant. Cardillac confesses his guilt and the crowd kills him. The officer mourns Cardillac.

Carmen

Composed by Georges Bizet (October 25, 1838 – June 3, 1875). Libretto by Henri Meilhac and Ludovic Halévy. French. Based on a novel by Propser Mérimée. Premiered Paris, Opéra Comique, March 3, 1875. Set in Seville and environs in 1820. Tragedy. Set numbers with recitative or spoken dialogue (original version used spoken dialogue). Prelude. Entr'acte before II, III and IV. Optional ballet.

Sets: 3. **Acts:** 4 acts, 4 scenes. **Length:** I: 50. II: 40. III: 35. IV: 20. **Arias:** "L'amour est un oiseau rebelle" (Carmen), "La fleur que tu m'avais jetée" / Flower song (José), "Je dis que rien" (Micaëla), "Près des remparts de Séville" / Seguidilla (Carmen), "Votre toast" / Toreador's song (Escamillo), "Les tringles des sistres tintaient" (Carmen). **Hazards:** None. **Scenes:** I. Plaza in Seville. II. Tavern of Lillas Pastia. III. Wild mountain pass. IV. Plaza in Seville.

Major roles: Don José (tenor), Carmen (mezzo), Micaëla (soprano). **Minor roles:** Escamillo (baritone), Zuniga (bass), Moralès (baritone),

Frasquita (soprano), Mercédès (mezzo), Dancaïro (tenor or baritone), Remendado (tenor). **Bit part:** Girl (mezzo). **Mute:** Lillas Pastia.

Chorus parts: SSATTBB. **Chorus roles:** Soldiers, gypsies, cigarette girls, street boys (children), smugglers, young men, townspeople. **Dance/movement:** II: Dance of gypsy girls and Carmen. IV: Ballet (optional). **Orchestra:** 2 fl (2 picc), 2 ob (Eng hrn), 2 cl, 2 bsn, 4 hrn, 2 trp, 3 trb, timp, perc, harp, strings. **Stageband:** I: trp. II: 2 trp. IV: 2 trp, 3 trb. **Publisher:** Schirmer, C. F. Peters. **Rights:** Expired.

I. Micaëla approaches Morales and the dragoons, looking for José. His company will be here soon, the soldiers tell Micaëla and she decides to return later. The street boys follow the changing of the guard. Zuniga asks José about the girls who work in the cigarette factory, but he is more interested in his beloved Micaëla. The factory takes a break and the square is swarmed by young men courting the cigarette girls. The men's favorite is Carmen, who teases them and tosses a flower at José's feet. Micaëla arrives, bringing José a letter and a kiss from his mother. She goes before he can read the letter in which his mother charges him to marry Micaëla (which José is quite willing to do). Screaming offstage announces a fight between Manuela and Carmen. José breaks it up and—at Zuniga's order—jails Carmen. Carmen tantalizingly convinces José to free her, promising to meet him at Lillas Pastia's tavern later. Bewitched, he helps her stage her escape.

II. Carmen sings a gypsy song at Lillas Pastia's tavern. Zuniga—who is having an affair with Carmen—tells her that José was jailed for letting her escape and has just been released. The crowd cheers the entrance of the toreador Escamillo. He woos Carmen, who is unimpressed. Dancaïro and Remendado are planning another smuggling run, but they need the help of the women—all agree that women are indispensable for double-dealing. Carmen waits for José. She dances for him. When José hears the bugle calling him back to camp for the night, Carmen demands he stay—as proof of his love. Zuniga comes back for Carmen, but his discovery of the smugglers prompts them to kidnap him. José realizes he cannot go back to his post.

III. José is remorseful about disappointing his mother. The gypsy women tell their futures, but Carmen's always comes up death. When the smugglers move off, leaving José behind as a guard, Micaëla emerges. She is frightened when she hears gunfire: José has fired at Escamillo. The toreador is looking for Carmen and José challenges him to a knife fight. Escamillo accepts, but the fight is interrupted by the return of the smugglers. Escamillo invites everyone to the bullfight. Since Carmen is getting tired of José, she is only too pleased when Micaëla asks him to come away with her. José is reluctant and swears he will never let Carmen go. Only Micaëla's revelation that José's mother is dying convinces him to accompany her home.

IV. The bullfight is beginning. Carmen swears she loves Escamillo and ignores her friends' warning that José is close by—and dangerous. Carmen waits for José and tells him plainly that it is over. Finding his pleas unavailing, José kills Carmen with his knife.

Carry Nation

Composed by Douglas Moore (August 10, 1893 – July 25, 1969). Libretto by William North Jayme. English. Original work based on historical events. Premiered Lawrence, Kansas, University of Kansas Theatre, April 28, 1966. Set in Kansas and Missouri in the 1860s. Historical drama. Set numbers. Prologue. Orchestral interlude before Ii, Iii.

Sets: 7. **Acts:** 2 acts, 8 scenes. **Length:** Prologue, I: 60. II: 60. **Hazards:** None. **Scenes:** Prologue. A plush "joint" in Topeka, Kansas around the turn of the century. Ii. An afternoon in late spring 1865. The parlor of the parents' home in Belton, Missouri. Iii. A churchyard in Belton. Iiii. A barn in Belton decorated for a hoe-down. IIi. Charles' and Carry's home in Holden, Missouri, 1867. IIii. The mother's bedroom. IIiii. A saloon in Holden. IIiv. The churchyard in Belton.

Major roles: Carry Nation (mezzo), Father (bass baritone), Mother (soprano), Charles (baritone). **Minor roles:** First man (baritone), Second man (tenor), City Marshall (baritone), Belton Preacher (baritone), Young man (tenor), Girl (soprano), Boy (boy soprano), Edna Maud (alto), First lady auxiliary member (soprano), Saloon quartet (2 tenors, 2 basses), Caretaker (baritone). **Bit parts:** Second and third ladies' auxiliary members (sopranos). **Dancer:** Saloon boy.

Chorus parts: SSATTBB. **Chorus roles:** Saloon patrons, dancing hall girls, Carry's women, boys and girls (in 2 parts), members of the ladies' auxiliary. **Dance/movement:** I: Saloon dance, square dance. **Orchestra:** 2 fl (picc), 2 ob (Eng hrn), 2 cl, 2 bsn, 3 hrn, 2 trp, 3 trb, timp, perc, piano, harp, strings. **Stageband:** I: prayer bell. **Publisher:** Galaxy Music Corporation. **Rights:** Copyright 1968 by Galaxy Music Corporation.

Prologue. Carry Nation and her women go around Kansas destroying saloons in the cause of Prohibition. They are arrested in Topeka. Ii. Thirty years before, Carry grows up in Belton, Missouri. She remembers her first religious experience. Carry and her father worry that their mother will object to a boarder. They have rented a room to Dr. Charles Gloyd who has just left the army. Iii. Charles hates the town's religious fervor, but loves Carry. Carry's father discovers him talking to Carry. He calls him a drunkard and throws him out of the house. Iiii. Charles finds Carry at the square dance and tells her he has gotten a practice in a near-by town. When Carry's father rejects his request for Carry's hand, he proposes publicly. Carry's father calls Charles a drunk, but Carry forgives him and accepts.

IIi. Carry entertains the women of the ladies' auxiliary who pity her. Charles drinking has hurt his practice and they remain poor. Carry asks him to give up drinking. She is pregnant. IIii. Carry sends her mother a letter, begging for money. Her father sees it and goes to fetch Carry home. IIiii. Charles gets drunk in the saloon and remembers how he let a Confederate boy bleed to death during the war. Carry comes to get him. Her father enters and she agrees to leave Charles. IIiv. Carry learns that Charles has died. She is furious with herself for abandoning him and decides to devote her life to the cause of Prohibition.

Casanova's Homecoming

Composed by Dominick Argento (b. October 27, 1927). Libretto by Dominick Argento. English. Original work interweaving scenes from Casanova's memoirs. Premiered St. Paul, Minnesota, Minnesota Opera, April 12, 1985. Set in Venice in the first week of carnival, 1774. Comic opera. Set numbers with recitative.

Sets: 8. **Acts:** 3 acts, 9 scenes. **Length:** I: 50. II: 45. III: 40. **Hazards:** Fanciful scene changes. II: gale in the lagoon. III: fireworks. **Scenes:** Ii. In the piazza San Marco. Iii. At the opera. Iiii. A large gambling hall on the ridotto. IIi. In Madame d'Urfé's laboratory. IIii. In Giulietta Croce's kitchen. IIiii. On the lagoon. IIIi. In Casanova's bedroom. IIIii. In the inquisitors' chambers. IIIiii. In the piazza San Marco.

Major roles: Casanova (baritone), Lorenzo (baritone), Giulietta (soprano), Bellino/Teresa (mezzo), Madame d'Urfé (contralto). **Minor roles:** Montebank (bass), Vendor (contralto), Charlatan (tenor), Marcantonio (treble or soprano), Marquis of Lisle (tenor), Gianpaolo (contralto), Businello (bass baritone), Barbara (lyric soprano), Gabrielle/Gondolier (lyric tenor), Timante (contralto), Dircea (soprano), King Demofoonte (tenor), Cherinto (soprano), Girl in Casanova's bed (soprano), Chief of police (bass), First inquisitor/Pulcinello (tenor), Second Inquisitor/Tartaglia (bass), Third Inquisitor/Spanish captain (bass). **Bit parts:** Lady whose purse is stolen (soprano), Young woman in Casanova's bed (contralto), Police officer (tenor), Junior police officer (tenor), Two guards (2 bass), Madame d'Urfé's servant (soprano), Matusio (contralto), Matron in Casanova's bed (soprano). **Mute:** Girl of Marcantonio's age.

Chorus parts: SATB. **Chorus roles:** Carnival revelers, party guests, funeral attendants (Min. 24). **Dance/movement:** I: Venetian furlana. **Orchestra:** 2 fl (picc), 2 ob (Eng hrn), 2 cl (bs cl), 2 bsn, 2 hrn, 2 trp, trb, tuba, timp, perc, harp, harpsichord (celeste), strings. **Stageband:** None. **Publisher:** Boosey & Hawkes. **Rights:** Copyright 1985 by Boosey and Hawkes, Inc.

Ii. Casanova asks the Abbé Lorenzo about the crazy old alchemist, Madame d'Urfé, and her profligate nephew—and heir—the Marquis de Lisle. When the 13-year-old Marcantonio steals a purse from a passing lady, Casanova grabs him and returns the purse. Casanova takes the boy into his service. The marquis suspects Casanova of planning to swindle his aunt and plots with his friend Businello to discredit Casanova. Giulietta welcomes Casanova home and introduces her daughter Barbara. Giulietta was the wife of an old associate of Casanova's—and Barbara is Casanova's god-child. When Giulietta explains that she is without money for Barbara's dowry, Casanova promises to help. Iii. At the opera, the marquis persuades the castrato Bellino to dress as a woman and pass a love letter to Casanova. Iiii. Casanova comes to the ridotto to seduce Bellino, who leads him on before admitting he is a castrato. The guests and revelers laugh at Casanova. In fact, Bellino is a woman named Teresa, which she admits to Casanova in private. Passing herself off as a castrato is the only way Teresa could support herself. Casanova promises to keep her secret if she helps him.

IIi. Madame d'Urfé hopes to use her alchemical powers to remake herself as a male infant—with the help of Casanova's own magical powers. But her confidence in him has been broken. Casanova restores it by presenting Bellino, who he claims to have turned from a man into a woman. IIii. Casanova explains his plan to Lorenzo, Marcantonio, Giulietta and Teresa: He will tell Madame d'Urfé to gather seven pounds of each of the seven precious metals. Casanova will row her out into the lagoon where Casanova's four accomplices will appear as spirits. They will tell Madame d'Urfé to throw the metals into the lagoon. IIiii. Casanova brings Madame d'Urfé out into the lagoon, but a real storm terrifies the conspirators. In the confusion, Casanova and Madame d'Urfé fall into the water.

IIIi. Lorenzo is amazed they got Madame d'Urfé home. As he is talking to Casanova, a funeral procession passes by: Madame d'Urfé has died of pneumonia. The police arrest Casanova. IIIii. The marquis accuses Casanova of sorcery and murder. Casanova gets off by saying Madame d'Urfé paid him to sleep with her. IIIiii. In the piazza, a group of performers parody Casanova's adventures, but his good nature and generosity silence them. Barbara and Gabrielle return from their wedding. They thank Casanova and Barbara reveals that Casanova is really her father. Lorenzo embraces Teresa. Marcantonio seduces a passing girl. Fireworks mark the new year.

Castor et Pollux • Castor and Pollux

Composed by Jean-Philippe Rameau (September 25, 1683 – September 12, 1764). Libretto by Pierre Joseph Bernard. French. Greek mythology. Premiered Paris, Théâtre de l'Académie Royale de Musique, October 24, 1737. Set in Sparta, Hades and heaven in legendary times. Tragedy. Set numbers with recitative. Overture. Prologue. Symphony before Iiv. Entr'acte before V. Ballet. Revised version premiered January 11, 1754 in Paris.

Sets: 6. **Acts:** 5 acts, 28 scenes. **Length:** Prologue: 30. I: 30. II: 30. III: 15. IV: 30. V: 30. **Arias:** "Tristes apprêts" (Télaïre), "Séjour de l'éternelle paix" (Castor). **Hazards:** V: Jupiter descends on his eagle. Skies open to reveal the sun chariot and the palace of Olympus. **Scenes:** Prologue. A portico in ruins where the Arts and Pleasures are assembled. I. A monument erected for the funeral of Castor. II. The temple of Jupiter. III. The entrance to hell. IV. The Elysian fields. V. The surroundings of Sparta.

Major roles: Phébé (soprano), Télaïre (soprano), Pollux (bass or baritone), Castor (tenor). **Minor roles:** Minerve (soprano), Amour (tenor), Mars (bass), Vénus (soprano), First athlete (tenor), Second athlete (bass), High Priest of Jupiter (tenor), Jupiter (bass), Follower of Hébé (soprano), Happy spirit (soprano), Planet (soprano). **Mute:** Mercure.

Chorus parts: SSATTB. **Chorus roles:** Arts and celestial pleasures, Spartans, athletes, priests, Hébé and her attendants, demons, people, happy spirits, stars, planets, satellites, gods. **Dance/movement:** V: Celestial chaconne. **Orchestra:** 2 fl, 2 ob, 2 bsn, trp, timp, strings, continuo. **Stageband:** None. **Publisher:** A. Durand & Fils. **Rights:** Expired.

Prologue i. The arts and pleasures call on Vénus to subdue Mars, the god of war. Prologue ii. She does so.

Ii. A troop of Spartans mourns Castor. Iii. Phébé assures Castor's love, Télaire, that Castor's immortal brother Pollux will revenge him. Iiii. Télaire reflects that revenge is small consolation. Iiv. Pollux brings in the corpse of Lincée, Castor's murderer. Iv. Pollux admits he loves Télaire. She asks him to intervene with his father, Jupiter, to bring Castor back to life.

IIi. Pollux is torn between love and friendship. IIii. He considers Castor lucky to have Télaïre's love. IIiii. The high priest of Jupiter calls the god forth. IIiv. Jupiter tells Pollux that he can only save Castor by taking his place in the underworld. IIv. The celestial pleasures show Pollux what he would miss if he gave up his immortality.

IIIi. Phébé tries to prevent Pollux from going. IIIii. When he insists, Phébé says she will follow him. IIIiii. Télaire encourages Pollux. IIIiv. With the help of Mercure, Pollux defeats the demons guarding the entrance to hell. IIIv. Phébé is upset at not being able to follow him.

IVi. In the Elysian fields, the dead Castor remembers his love. IVii. A group of happy spirits try to cheer up Castor. IViii. Pollux enters. IViv. He takes Castor's place, but Castor promises to return in one day, after seeing Télaire.

Vi. Phébé plots revenge. Vii. Castor explains to Télaire that he cannot remain with her. Viii. He sends away the Spartans who come to congratulate him. Viv. Télaire argues with Castor. Vv. Jupiter decrees that Castor and Pollux shall share their immortality. Vvi. Pollux returns. Vvii. A heavenly divertissement is given for the heroes and they are admitted into the zodiac.

Caterina Cornaro

Composed by Gaetano Donizetti (November 29, 1797 – April 8, 1848). Libretto by Giacomo Sacchero. Italian. Based on the opera "La Reine de Chypre" by Halévy. Premiered Naples, Teatro San Carlo, January 12, 1844. Set in Venice and Cyprus in the 15th century. Lyric tragedy. Set numbers with recitative. Prologue. Prelude before prologue and each act. Revised version premiered February 2, 1845 in Parma. Originally named "La Regina di Cipro."

Sets: 5. Acts: 2 acts, 5 scenes. Length: Prologue, I, II: 115. Arias: "Io trar non voglio" (Gerardo). Hazards: None. Scenes: Prologue i. A room in the Cornaro palace. Prologue ii. Caterina's room. Ii. A square in Nicosia. Iii. The queen's apartments. II. An atrium in Lusignano's palace.

Major roles: Gerardo (tenor), Caterina Cornaro (soprano), Ambassador Mocenigo (bass), King Lusignano (baritone). Minor roles: Andrea Cornaro (bass), Matilde (soprano), Strozzi (tenor), Knight (tenor).

Chorus parts: SATTBB. Chorus roles: Knights, ladies, gondoliers, assassins, ladies-in-waiting, soldiers, guards. Dance/movement: None. Orchestra: 2 fl (picc), 2 ob, 2 cl, 2 bsn, 4 hrn, 2 trp, 3 trb, bs trb, timp, perc, harp, strings. Stageband: None. Publisher: Egret House. Rights: Expired.

Prologue i. Caterina Cornaro's marriage to a young Frenchman, Gerardo, is interrupted by Mocenigo, the Venetian Ambassador to Cyprus. He orders Caterina's father to call off the marriage: The government intends to cement its alliance with Cyprus by marrying Caterina to the Cyprian King Lusignano. The lovers are furious. Prologue ii. Mocenigo orders Caterina to renounce Gerardo—or Mocenigo's assassins will kill Gerardo on the spot. When she does so, Gerardo curses her.

Ii. Mocenigo learns that Gerardo has followed him to Cyprus. He orders Strozzi to kill him. Lusignano intends to preserve Cyprus from Venetian rule. He pities Caterina and saves Gerardo from Mocenigo's assassins. The two swear brotherhood. Iii. Gerardo warns Caterina that Mocenigo has poisoned Lusignano. The Venetian ambassador insists Caterina rule Cyprus under instructions from Venice. Lusignano orders Mocenigo arrested and declares war on Venice.

II. Gerardo leads the Cypriot soldiers into battle. Venice is defeated, but Lusignano is slain. The Cypriots swear allegiance to Caterina.

I Cavalieri di Ekebù • The Knights of Ekebù

Composed by Riccardo Zandonai (May 30, 1883 – June 5, 1944). Libretto by Arturo Rossato. Italian. Based on the novel "Gösta Berlings Saga" by Selma Lagerlöf. Premiered Milan, Teatro alla Scala, March 7, 1925. Set in Ekebù in Switzerland long ago. Lyric drama. Through composed.

Sets: 4. **Acts:** 4 acts, 4 scenes. **Length:** I: 35. II: 30. III: 25. IV: 25. **Hazards:** IV: Smith fires are lit. **Scenes:** I. The inside of an inn and the adjoining clearing. II. A large hall in the castle of Ekebù. III. The interior of a smithy. IV. A courtyard in the castle. (Note that a scene before the smithy and Sintram's house is sometimes added as IIIii.)

Major roles: Gösta Berling (tenor), Anna (soprano), Commandant (mezzo). **Minor roles:** Sintram (bass), Samzelius (bass), Christian (baritone), Girl (soprano), Lilliecrona or Liecrona (tenor). **Bit parts:** Hostess of the inn (mezzo). (Lilliecrona becomes a bit part if his aria is cut. Mother only appears in IIIii, which is often cut.)

Chorus parts: SSATTTTBBBB. **Chorus roles:** Girls, knights, people. **Dance/movement:** I: Knights dance. **Orchestra:** 3 fl, 3 ob, 3 cl, 2 bsn, 4 hrn, 3 trp, 3 trb, tuba, timp, perc, celeste, harp, strings. **Stageband:** II: cl, 2 hrn, 2 trb. **Publisher:** G. Ricordi & Co. **Rights:** Copyright 1925 by G. Ricordi & Co.

I. It is Christmas Eve and Gösta has lost his position as pastor because of drunkenness. The sinister Sintram finds him in the tavern and gives him money for drink: He is furious that Gösta loves his daughter, Anna, and only too happy to see Gösta ruining himself. Anna and her friends pass by on their way to a party at the castle. The commander of the castle and ironworks asks Gösta to be one of her "knights." Being forced to marry a man she did not love has permanently embittered the commander. She runs the ironworks and collects the weak and destitute in her castle, calling them her knights. When Gösta hears that Anna will be at the castle, he agrees to go.

II. Anna and the girls prepare a skit to entertain the guests. Gösta is to play Anna's lover. The girls tease Anna and she cries. Left alone with Gösta, Anna rebukes him for his drinking. Gösta uses the skit to tell Anna how much he loves her and she answers in kind. Sintram stops the performance and disowns Anna.

III. The knight Lilliecrona cries for the wife and son he deserted. Midnight strikes and Sintram appears to the knights as the devil. He tells them he gives the commander power in exchange for the soul of one knight a year. Her castle and money are presents of her dead lover, he adds. The infuriated knights go to the commander's husband who throws the commander out.

IV. The crowd blames Anna for the poverty and starvation that have fallen on the town since the commander left. Gösta tells them Anna is innocent and promises to bring back the commander. Anna is about to leave Gösta when the knights return with the dying commander. She blesses and forgives everyone, and at her wish they start up the ironworks again.

Cavalleria Rusticana • Rustic Chivalry

Composed by Pietro Mascagni (December 7, 1863 – August 2, 1945). Libretto by Giovanni Targioni-Tozzetti and Guido Menasci. Italian. Based on the play by Giovanni Verga. Premiered Rome, Teatro Costanzi, May 17, 1890. Set in Sicily in 1880. Verismo. Set numbers with accompanied recitative. Prelude and symphonic intermezzo.

Sets: 1. **Acts:** 1 act, 1 scene. **Length:** I: 70. **Arias:** "Viva il vino"/Drinking song (Turiddù), "Voi lo sapete o mamma" (Santuzza). **Hazards:** None. **Scenes:** I. Village square with church and home of Mamma Lucia.

Major roles: Santuzza (dramatic soprano), Mamma Lucia (contralto or mezzo), Alfio (baritone), Turiddù (tenor). **Minor role:** Lola (mezzo). **Bit parts:** Three women (soprano).

Chorus parts: SSATTB. **Chorus roles:** Villagers and peasants. Children. **Dance/movement:** None. **Orchestra:** 2 picc, 2 fl, 2 ob, 2 cl, 2 bsn, 4 hrn, 2 trp, 3 trb, tuba, timp, perc, 2 harp, strings. **Stageband:** I: church bells, organ, harp. **Publisher:** Schirmer, Bote and G. Bock. **Rights:** Expired.

I. Offstage, Turiddu sings that he would love his sweetheart even if it destroyed him. The peasants and villagers come out of church, singing of spring and love. Santuzza asks Mamma Lucia where she can find Turiddu, and is told he is away. When Mamma Lucia relents and asks Santuzza into her house, Santuzza says she cannot enter because she is a sinner and an outcast. Mamma Lucia asks if Turiddu is in trouble. Alfio joyously returns home, and Mamma Lucia learns from him that Turiddu is still in town. She voices surprise, but Santuzza hushes her. The villagers pray and return to church. Santuzza explains to Mamma Lucia that Turiddu loved Lola but returned from the army to find her married to Alfio. Trying to forget his pain, Turiddu turned to Santuzza. But when Lola became his mistress, he forgot about Santuzza. Turiddu arrives and Santuzza warns him that Alfio knows of his affair. She begs forgiveness for the things she has said and vents her fury on the scheming Lola. Turiddu refuses to forgive her but they are interrupted by the arrival of Lola, asking after Alfio. When Lola acts surprised that they are not in church, Santuzza tells her only those who have not sinned should go to Mass. Lola says she has not sinned and goes in. Santuzza again begs Turiddu's forgiveness, but he leaves in disgust. Santuzza curses him, intercepts Alfio on his way to church and tells him of Lola's infidelity. When he swears revenge, Santuzza is stricken with remorse. The service over, Turiddu and Lola lead the villagers in a toast to love. Alfio bites Turiddu's ear, challenging him to fight. Turiddu admits his guilt to Alfio and wonders what will happen to Santuzza if he dies. He asks his unsuspecting mother for her blessing and commends Santuzza to her care. He leaves and the villagers soon return with the news of his death. Santuzza faints.

La Cena delle Beffe • The Jesters' Supper

Composed by Umberto Giordano (August 28, 1867 – November 12, 1948). Libretto by Sem Benelli. Italian. Based on the play by Benelli. Premiered Milan, Teatro alla Scala, December 20, 1924. Set in Florence in the 15th century. Lyric drama. Through composed.

Sets: 3. **Acts:** 4 acts, 4 scenes. **Length:** I, II, III, IV: 90. **Arias:** "Sempre così sul margine del sogno" (Ginevra). **Hazards:** None. **Scenes:** I. The dining hall in the house of Tornaquinci. II. Ginevra's antechamber. III. A subterranean room in the Medici palace. IV. Ginevra's antechamber.

Major roles: Giannetto Malespini (tenor), Neri Chiaramantesi (baritone), Ginevra (soprano). **Minor roles:** Tornaquinci (bass), Gabriello Chiaramantesi (tenor), Cintia (mezzo), Fazio (baritone), Doctor (comic baritone), Trinca (comic tenor), Laldomine (mezzo), Fiammetta (soprano), Lisabetta (mezzo or soprano), Offstage singer (tenor). **Bit parts:** Calandra (baritone), Lapo (tenor), Offstage voice (tenor), Offstage voice (bass). **Speaking bit:** Offstage men (scream at end of II). **Mute:** Footmen of the Medici, servants of Tornaquinci.

Chorus parts: N/A. **Chorus roles:** None. **Dance/movement:** None. **Orchestra:** 3 fl (picc), 2 ob, Eng hrn, 2 cl, bs cl, 2 bsn, 4 hrn, 3 trp, 3 trb, tuba, timp, perc, harp, celeste, xylophone, piano, strings. **Stageband:** IV: 2 mandolin, vla, vlc, bs, harp. **Publisher:** Casa Musicale Sonzogno. **Rights:** Copyright 1924 by Casa Musicale Sonzogno.

I. At the command of Lorenzo de Medici, Tornaquinci gives a dinner and invites Giannetto Malespini and Giannetto's enemies Neri and Gabriello Chiaramantesi. Neri and Gabriello have beaten Giannetto, and Neri has stolen Ginevra, the woman Giannetto loves. The men make peace, but Giannetto lets slip his suspicion that Gabriello, too, loves Ginevra. Gabriello leaves for Pisa. When Neri boasts of his fearlessness, Giannetto challenges him to appear before Ceccherino in Vacchereccia. Neri accepts.

II. Giannetto has given it out that Neri is mad and Ginevra's maid tells Ginevra how Neri tried to kill everyone at Vacchereccia and has been imprisoned. Ginevra discovers the man she slept with last night was Giannetto, not Neri. Giannetto has almost convinced Ginevra to go back to bed with him when Neri returns, having escaped from prison. Giannetto collects a group of Medici retainers and recaptures Neri.

III. Everyone now believes Neri to be mad. Giannetto brings a doctor who advises that the patient be confronted with painful memories to shock him into sanity. The people whom Neri has tricked and betrayed berate him. Neri feigns madness. Giannetto allows Lisabetta to lead Neri away and tells Neri that he himself is going to visit Ginevra.

IV. Neri arrives at Ginevra's before Giannetto and forces Ginevra to help lay a trap. He kills Ginevra with the first man who enters her room. Giannetto appears and Neri, realizing he has killed his own brother Gabriello, staggers out into the night.

Cendrillon • Cinderella

Composed by Jules-Emile-Frédéric Massenet (May 12, 1842 – August 13,

1912). Libretto by Henri Cain. French. After story by Charles Perrault. Premiered Paris, Théâtre National de l'Opéra Comique, May 24, 1899. Set in a mythical kingdom in mythical times. Grand opera. Set numbers with recitative. Introduction. Ballet.

Sets: 5. **Acts:** 4 acts, 20 scenes. **Length:** I, II, III, IV: 145. **Hazards:** None. **Scenes:** I. The home of Countess de la Haltière. II. The hall of festivities at court. IIIi – IIIiv. The home of Countess de la Haltière. IIIv – IIIvi. The fairy's home in the woods. IVi – IViii. The terrace of Cinderella's home. IViv. The palace.

Major roles: Pandolfe (bass baritone), Countess de la Haltière (mezzo or contralto), Cinderella (mezzo), Prince Charming (soprano or tenor). **Minor roles:** Noémie (soprano), Dorothée (mezzo), Fairy (coloratura soprano), Master of ceremonies (baritone), King (baritone), Dean of the faculty (baritone), First minister (bass), Six spirits (4 soprani, 2 contralti). **Speaking bit:** Herald.

Chorus parts: SSSSAATTBB. **Chorus roles:** Servants, tailors, hair-dressers, courtiers, doctors, ministers, lords and ladies, spirits, young girls, people. Many small groups and solo lines. **Dance/movement:** IIiii: Presentation of the daughters of the nobility. III: Dance of the fairies. IViv: March of the princesses. **Orchestra:** 3 fl (picc), 2 ob (Eng hrn), 2 cl, 2 bsn, 4 hrn, 2 trp, 3 trb, tuba, 2 harp, timp, perc, strings. **Stageband:** II: glass fl, vla d'amore, harp, lute. III: glass fl, ob, celeste, harmonium, harp, timp. IV: ob, trps, perc. **Publisher:** Heugel & Co. **Rights:** Expired.

Ii. The servants rush to fulfill the Countess de la Haltière's orders. Iii. Pandolfe remembers his peaceful life as a widower and berates himself for remarrying. He pities his daughter and determines to be master in his own house—some day. Iiii. The countess coaches her two daughters, Noémie and Dorothée, on how they should act when presented to the king. Iiv. She supervises her daughters' dressing. Iv. Cinderella wishes she were going to the ball. She finishes her chores and falls asleep. Ivi. The fairy provides Cinderella with a dress and carriage, but warns her to leave the ball before midnight.

IIi. The courtiers, doctors and ministers try, unsuccessfully, to amuse the prince. IIii. The prince longs for love. IIiii. The daughters of the nobility are presented, but Cinderella outshines them all. IIiv. The prince declares his undying love for her. The clock strikes midnight and Cinderella flees.

IIIi. Cinderella runs home from the ball, having lost one of her glass slip-pers. IIIii. Pandolfe is berated by his new family for admiring the myste-rious woman at the ball. They say the court was scandalized. IIIiii.

Pandolfe comforts Cinderella and tells her to pack: They are returning to their beloved farm. IIIiv. Cinderella flees the house alone. IIIv. She and the prince separately find their way to the woods where the fairy keeps them from seeing each other. IIIvi. The fairy grants the lovers' wish and reunites them. She charms them to sleep.

IVi. Cinderella is recovering from a long illness, which began the night Pandolfe found her in the woods asleep. She is convinced her trip to the ball was only a dream. IVii. Spring returns. IViii. In hopes of finding his love, the prince calls on ladies from all over the world to try on the glass slipper left behind by Cinderella at the ball. IViv. Cinderella goes to the palace and is greeted by the prince and people as their future queen. The countess embraces her stepdaughter.

La Cenerentola • Cinderella

Composed by Gioachino Rossini (February 29, 1792 – November 13, 1868). Libretto by Jacopo Ferretti. Italian. Based on a libretto by Charles-Guillaume Étienne. Premiered Rome, Teatro Valle, January 25, 1817. Set in Salerno in the 18th century. Comedy. Set numbers with recitative. Overture.

Sets: 5. **Acts:** 2 acts, 6 scenes. **Length:** I, II: 150. **Arias:** "Una volta c'era un re" (Angelina), "Miei rampolli femminili" (Magnifico). **Hazards:** None. **Scenes:** Ii. Old fashioned room in the castle of Don Magnifico. Iii. A small room in the palace. Iiii. A drawing room in the palace. IIi. The small room in the palace. IIii. Hall in Magnifico's house. IIiii. A hall with a throne.

Major roles: Clorinda (soprano), Thisbe (mezzo), Angelina/Cenerentola (alto), Don Magnifico (bass), Don Ramiro (tenor), Dandini (bass). **Minor roles:** Alidoro (bass).

Chorus parts: TTBB. **Chorus roles:** Courtiers, guests of Don Ramiro. **Dance/movement:** None. **Orchestra:** 2 fl (picc), 2 ob, 2 cl, 2 bsn, 2 hrn, 2 trp, trb, timp, perc, strings, continuo. **Stageband:** None. **Publisher:** Colombo, Kalmus. **Rights:** Expired.

Ii. Alidoro disguises himself as a beggar. Cenerentola's two stepsisters, Clorinda and Thisbe, rebuff him, but Cenerentola gives him food. Courtiers invite the stepsisters to a ball at which the prince, Don Ramiro, will choose his bride. Clorinda and Thisbe run Cenerentola ragged making her help them prepare for the ball. The noise wakes their father, Don Magnifico. The prince arrives, disguised as a servant so as to find a girl who loves him for himself. His servant Dandini pretends to be the prince. Ramiro and Cenerentola fall in love. Dandini explains that by the terms of the late king's will he must marry or lose his inheritance. When Cenerentola begs to go to the ball, Don Magnifico cruelly refuses. Alidoro presents the register showing that Don Magnifico has three daughters, but Magnifico claims the third daughter died. Using his magic powers, Alidoro sends Cenerentola to the ball anyway, warning her to leave the ball by midnight. Iii. Dandini gets Don Magnifico drunk. Iiii. The courtiers toast Don Magnifico, who has been promoted to wine steward by Dandini. Dandini warns Ramiro that Don Magnifico's daughters are conceited and silly. The two women indignantly reject the suggestion that one of them marry the prince's servant (Ramiro). Everyone admires Cenerentola. Her relatives are surprised by her resemblance to Cenerentola but dismiss it.

IIi. Don Magnifico tells his daughters he is in debt and one of them must wed the prince to redeem the family name. He daydreams about the bribes he will collect as the prince's father-in-law. Dandini loves Cenerentola but she admits she loves his servant. Ramiro is overjoyed and proposes, but Cenerentola puts him off until they meet again. The clock strikes midnight and Cenerentola flees, leaving behind a glass slipper. Ramiro vows to find his beloved. Dandini reveals his true identity to Magnifico. Alidoro is pleased his plans for Cenerentola are working. IIii. Magnifico and his daughters return home in a funk. After a brief thunderstorm, Dandini and Ramiro arrive. The stepsisters are mortified to learn Ramiro is the prince. The slipper fits Cenerentola. Her stepsisters heap abuse on her and she leaves with the prince. Alidoro tells the step sisters to beg Cenerentola for mercy. IIiii. They do and are forgiven.

The Christmas Rose

Composed by Frank Bridge (February 26, 1879 – January 10, 1941). Libretto by Frank Bridge. English. Based on the play for children by Margaret Kemp-Welch and Constance Cotterell. Premiered London, Royal College of Music, December 8, 1931. Set in Bethlehem and environs in the 1st century AD. Miracle play. Through composed. Orchestral introduction.

Sets: 3. **Acts:** 1 act, 3 scenes. **Length:** I: 50. **Hazards:** I: Roses grow up through the snow. Stable doors open miraculously. **Scenes:** Ii. At night on the hills near Bethlehem. Iii. The way to Bethlehem. Iiii. Before the inn.

Major roles: Third shepherd (bass baritone), Miriam (soprano), Reuben (mezzo). **Minor roles:** First shepherd (tenor), Second shepherd (baritone).

Chorus parts: SSSSAATB. **Chorus roles:** Peasants, offstage women.
Dance/movement: None. **Orchestra:** 2 fl, 2 ob, 2 cl, 2 bsn, 2 hrn, 2 trp,
trb, timp, perc, harp, strings. **Stageband:** None. **Publisher:** Augener.
Rights: Copyright 1931 by Augener Ltd.

Ii. Three shepherds are visited by an angel who tells them the Savior has
been born in Bethlehem. They decide to seek him. Miriam, the daughter
of one of the shepherds, is left behind to look after her brother, Reuben.
Reuben and Miriam disobey their father and set out to see the Child. Iii.
They get lost, but a star appears to guide them. Iiii. The children arrive
at the stable. They are afraid to enter without a gift. Roses miraculously
appear in the snow and the children gather them up. The stable doors
open and the children enter.

Le Cid • The Cid

Composed by Jules-Emile-Frédéric Massenet (May 12, 1842 – August 13,
1912). Libretto by Adolphe D'Ennery, Louis Gallet and Édouard Blau.
French. Based on a play by Pierre Corneille and "Las Mochedades del
Cid" by Guillen de Castro y Bellvis. Premiered Paris, Opéra, November
30, 1885. Set in Spain in the 12th century. Grand opera. Set numbers with
recitative. Overture. Ballet.

Sets: 9. **Acts:** 4 acts, 10 scenes. **Length:** I, II, III, IV: 145. **Arias:** "Ô souverain" (Rodrigue), "Pleurez mes yeux" (Chimène). **Hazards:** III: vision
of St. Jacques. **Scenes:** Ii. A room in the house of the Count of Gormas.
Iii. A gallery in the royal palace. IIi. A street in Burgos. IIii. The main
square of Burgos. IIIi. Chimène's chamber. IIIii. Rodrigue's camp. IIIiii.
Rodrigue's tent. IIIiv. The camp. IVi. A room in the royal palace in
Grenada. IVii. The great hall of the palace.

Major roles: Chimène (dramatic soprano), Don Diègue (bass), Don
Rodrigue (tenor). **Minor roles:** Count of Gormas (bass baritone), Don
Arias (tenor), Don Alonzo (bass), Infante (soprano), King of Spain (bari-
tone). **Bit parts:** St. Jacques (baritone), Moorish envoy (bass or baritone).

Chorus parts: SSATTTTTTBBBBB. **Chorus roles:** Lords, pages, people,
monks, girls, soldiers, officers, celestial voices, ladies, priests.
Dance/movement: II: Ballet of native dances—castillane, andalouse,
aragonaise, aubade, catalane, madrilene, navarraise. III: ballet.
Orchestra: 2 fl, 2 ob (Eng hrn), 2 cl, 2 bsn, 4 hrn, 2 cornet, 2 trp, 3 trb,
tuba, timp, 4 perc, 2 harps, organ, strings. **Stageband:** I, II, III, IV: 4 trp, 4
cornet, 2 saxhrn, 2 timp, perc, 2 harp. **Publisher:** Heugel & Co. **Rights:**
Expired.

Ii. The dons discuss the anticipated promotions of Rodrigue and the Count de Gormas. The count's daughter, Chimene, loves Rodrigue. The Infante, too, loves Rodrigue, but he is beneath her station and she promises him to Chimene. Iii. The people celebrate Spain's triumph over the Moors. Rodrigue is knighted. Passing over the count, the king appoints Rodrigue's father, Don Diègue, guardian of the Infante. The count is furious. Diègue proposes that Chimene marry his son, Rodrigue, but the count publicly insults Diègue. Rodrigue reluctantly agrees to avenge his father.

IIi. Rodrigue fights and kills the count. Chimene vows revenge on her father's killer—only to learn he is Rodrigue. IIii. The Infante distributes alms. Chimene asks the king to punish Rodrigue, while his friends plead for his pardon. A Moorish envoy declares a renewal of the war. The king appoints Rodrigue commander of the army.

IIIi. Rodrigue says farewell to Chimene. Realizing she still loves him, he swears to return victorious. IIIii. On the eve of battle, Rodrigue speaks to his men. IIIiii. He prays and a vision of St. Jacques, patron saint of Spain, appears, assuring him of victory. IIIiv. The battle is joined.

IVi. Deserters falsely report Rodrigue's death to Diègue, but Rodrigue and his army return, victorious. IVii. Rodrigue is hailed as the Cid. Chimene forgives him.

La Clemenza di Tito • The Clemency of Titus

Composed by Wolfgang Amadeus Mozart (January 27, 1756 – December 5, 1791). Libretto by Caterino Mazzolà. Italian. Based on a libretto by Pietro Metastasio. Premiered Prague, Gräflich Nostitzsches Nationaltheater, September 6, 1791. Set in Rome in the 1st century AD. Opera seria. Set numbers with recitative. Overture.

Sets: 6. **Acts:** 2 acts, 7 scenes. **Length:** I, II: 135. **Arias:** "Non più di fiori" (Vitellia), "Parto, parto" (Sesto). **Hazards:** I: Arsonists set fire to the capitol. **Scenes:** Ii. Vitellia's apartments. Iii. A part of the Roman forum. Iiii. A retreat in the imperial residence on the Palatine Hill. Iiv. The capitol. IIi. The retreat in the imperial residence. IIii. A large hall designed for public hearings. IIiii. The entrance to the amphitheater.

Major roles: Vitellia (soprano), Sesto (mezzo), Annio (contralto or tenor), Tito Vespasiano (tenor). **Minor roles:** Publio (bass), Servillia (soprano).

Chorus parts: SATB. **Chorus roles:** Roman senators, legates, lictors,

patricians, plebeians and Praetorian guards. **Dance/movement:** None.
Orchestra: 2 fl, 2 ob, 2 cl, basset hrn, 2 bsn, 2 hrn, 2 trp, timp, strings,
continuo. **Stageband:** None. **Publisher:** Bärenreiter Kassel. **Rights:**
Expired.

Ii. Vitellia loves Emperor Tito, but is also angry that his father overthrew
hers. She is jealous of Tito's love for Queen Berenice, a barbarian. Vitellia
pressures Sesto—who loves her—to kill Tito, but Sesto is reluctant
because Tito is a good emperor and his friend. Annio announces the
departure of Berenice. He asks Sesto to petition the emperor to approve
Annio's marrying Sesto's sister Servillia. Iii. The provinces present their
tribute to the emperor. Titus accepts the gifts on behalf of victims of the
eruption of Vesuvius. Tito announces his intention to marry Servillia.
Sesto is too surprised to speak, but Annio selflessly blesses the match
and breaks the news to Servillia. Iiii. Servillia admits her love to Tito,
who immediately relinquishes his claim. Vitellia has heard of the
planned marriage and is insulted. She persuades Sesto to kill Tito—only
to learn that Tito now wishes to marry her. Iiv. Sesto's coconspirators set
fire to the capitol while Sesto stabs the emperor.

IIi. Sesto is relieved to learn that Tito lives. Annio counsels him to stay
and beg forgiveness, but Vitellia insists he fly. Sesto is arrested. IIii. Tito
can hardly believe Sesto's guilt though confirmed by the prisoner himself. Annio pleads for him. Tito talks with Sesto, but Sesto cannot bring
himself to implicate Vitellia. He orders Sesto brought with him to the
arena, thus convincing Vitellia that he means to throw Sesto to the lions.
IIiii. Vitellia confesses everything to the emperor who forgives her and
all the other conspirators.

Cléopâtre • Cleopatra

Composed by Jules-Emile-Frédéric Massenet (May 12, 1842 – August 13,
1912). Libretto by Louis Payen (penname of Albert Liénard). French.
Loosely based on Shakespeare's play and historical incident. Premiered
Monte Carlo, Théâtre de Monte Carlo, February 23, 1914. Set in Egypt
and Rome at the time of the civil wars. Lyric drama. Set numbers with
recitative. Prelude before I, IV. Ballet.

Sets: 5. **Acts:** 4 acts, 5 scenes. **Length:** I, II, III, IV: 120. **Hazards:** None.
Scenes: I. Marc-Antoine's camp at Tarsus in Asia Minor on the banks of
the Cydnus. Iii. At Rome in the atrium of Marc-Antoine's house. Iiii.
Tavern of Amnhès in Alexandria. III. Cléopâtre's gardens. IV. Terrace of
the royal crypt.

Major roles: Marc-Antoine (baritone), Spakos (tenor), Cléopâtre (mezzo), Octavie (soprano). **Minor roles:** Charmion (soprano), Ennius (baritone), Sévérus (baritone), Amnhès (baritone). **Bit parts:** Slave at the door (baritone), Second slave (baritone), Voice (baritone). **Mute:** Octave. **Dancer:** Adamos.

Chorus parts: SATB. **Chorus roles:** Roman soldiers and officers, Greek and Egyptian slaves, bridal procession, crowd in the tavern, servants of Cléopâtre. **Dance/movement:** II: Adamos's tavern dance. III: Ballet of Cléopâtre's slaves. **Orchestra:** 3 fl (picc), 3 ob (Eng hrn), 3 cl (bs cl), 3 bsn, 4 hrn, 3 trp, 3 trb, tuba, timp, perc, 2 harp, strings. **Stageband:** I, III, IV: 6 trp. II: picc, 2 ob, 10 darboukas, timp, perc. **Publisher:** Heugel & Co. **Rights:** Expired.

I. Marc-Antoine receives delegations from the people his armies have conquered. The queen of Egypt, Cléopâtre, comes in person, attended by slaves bearing gifts. Despite his protests of indifference, Marc-Antoine is overcome by Cléopâtre's beauty. The Roman Senate calls Marc-Antoine home, but he instead accompanies Cléopâtre to Egypt.

IIi. Marc-Antoine has returned to Rome to marry Octavie, Octave's sister. He asks Ennius about Cléopâtre and is upset she has found another lover. Marc-Antoine deserts the loving Octavie to return to Egypt. IIii. Amnhès the tavern owner tries to amuse the jaded Cléopâtre, who has come disguised as a young boy. The queen has grown tired of her slave lover, Spakos, and is attracted to the dancer Adamos. Spakos attacks the dancer, infuriating the taverngoers. Cléopâtre saves herself by revealing her true identity. Cléopâtre hears of Marc-Antoine's return and intends to go to him. When Spakos objects, Cléopâtre has him arrested.

III. Cléopâtre wonders that Marc-Antoine does not lead his armies against Octave. The lovers are surprised by Octavie, who begs Marc-Antoine to return to Rome and make peace with her brother. Cléopâtre seconds Octavie's arguments, but the jealous Marc-Antoine refuses. He determines to fight Octave and Cléopâtre supports his decision.

IV. The Romans have defeated the Egyptians. Rather than be led in disgrace to Rome, Cléopâtre decides to kill herself. Spakos pleads for her love, but Cléopâtre loves Marc-Antoine. Spakos admits he sent Marc-Antoine word that Cléopâtre was dead. The queen stabs Spakos, who dies. Rather than live without Cléopâtre, Marc-Antoine has given himself a mortal wound. He dies in Cléopâtre's arms. She poisons herself as Octave's army approaches.

Il Combattimento di Tancredi e Clorinda • The Combat of Tancredi and Clorinda

Composed by Claudio Monteverdi (May 15 [baptized], 1567 – November 29, 1643). Libretto by Torquato Tasso. Italian. Setting of Canto XII from "La Gerusalemme liberata" by Torquato Tasso. Premiered Venice,

Private home, 1624. Set in Palestine in the late 11th century. Dramatic scene. Dramatic recitative.

Sets: 1. **Acts:** 1 act, 1 scene. **Length:** I: 25. **Hazards:** None. **Scenes:** I. The crest of a hill.

Major roles: Narrator (tenor), Clorinda (soprano), Tancredi (tenor).

Chorus parts: N/A. **Chorus roles:** None. **Dance/movement:** None. **Orchestra:** strings, keyboard continuo (Luciano Berio version: 3 vla, vlc, cont bs, clavicembalo; Malipiero version: clavincembalo, strings; Ghedini version: harp, harpsichord, 3 vla, vlc, cb). **Stageband:** None. **Publisher:** Universal Edition, Oxford University Press. **Rights:** Expired.

I. Tancredi, believing Clorinda to be a man, challenges her to fight. After a long battle, he kills her. Too late, he realizes he has killed his beloved.

Veselohra no mostě • Comedy on the Bridge

Composed by Bohuslav Martinů (December 8, 1890 – August 28, 1959). Libretto by Bohuslav Martinů. Czech. Based on the comedy by Václav Kliment Klicpera. Premiered Prague, Czech Radio, March 18, 1937. Set on a bridge in the first half of the 19th century. Comedy. Set numbers with recitative and lines spoken over music. Prelude. Radio opera. Stage premiere Zürich, March 31, 1952.

Sets: 1. **Acts:** 1 act, 1 scene. **Length:** I: 35. **Hazards:** None. **Scenes:** I. A bridge across a river separating two opposing armies.

Major roles: Popelka sometimes known as Josephine (soprano), Bedroň the brewer (bass), John (baritone), Eva (contralto), Schoolmaster (tenor). **Speaking:** Enemy sentry, Friendly sentry, Friendly officer.

Chorus parts: N/A. **Chorus roles:** None. **Dance/movement:** None. **Orchestra:** fl (picc), ob, cl, bsn, 2 hrn, trp, trb, timp, perc, piano, strings. **Stageband:** None. **Publisher:** Boosey & Hawkes. **Rights:** Copyright 1951, 1952 by Boosey & Hawkes.

I. Popelka is allowed onto the bridge by the enemy sentry, but the friendly sentry won't let her off and the enemy sentry won't let her go back. She is trapped, as is Bedroň the hops-grower. Bedroň wonders why Popelka's fiancé, John, is not jealous of her going to the enemy camp. Bedroň kisses Popelka just as John approaches the bridge. John, Bedroň's wife, Eva, and the schoolmaster get trapped on the bridge. John rejects Popelka. The cease fire runs out and shots are heard. The schoolmaster is pondering a riddle told him by a friendly officer. Popelka explains she went to the enemy camp to find her dead brother. Bedroň went to talk to the officials about a secret plan for victory. Bedroň and Popelka are forgiven by their spouses—who confess that they are not perfect themselves. The friendly army is victorious, Popelka's brother is alive and the officer orders them all off the bridge.

Le Comte Ory • The Count Ory

Composed by Gioachino Rossini (February 29, 1792 – November 13, 1868). Libretto by Eugène Scribe and Charles Gaspard Delestre-Poirson. French. Based on a one-act play, itself derived from a medieval legend set down by Pierre Antoine de la Place. Premiered Paris, Opéra, August 20, 1828. Set in France circa 1200. Comic opera. Set numbers with recitative. Prelude.

Sets: 2. **Acts:** 2 acts, 2 scenes. **Length:** I: 55. II: 55. **Arias:** "Veiller sans cess" (Tutor), "En proie à la tristesse" (Countess). **Hazards:** None. **Scenes:** I. Countryside before the castle of Formoutiers. II. A large room in the castle.

Major roles: Raimbaud (bass), Ragonde (contralto), Tutor of the count (bass), Count Ory (tenor), Countess Adèle (soprano). **Minor roles:** Alice (soprano), Isolier (mezzo), Cavalier (tenor).

Chorus parts: SSAATTBB. **Chorus roles:** Cavaliers, ladies in waiting, men disguised as female pilgrims, villagers. **Dance/movement:** None. **Orchestra:** picc, 2 fl, 2 ob, 2 cl, 2 bsn, 4 hrn, 2 trp, 3 trb, timp, perc, strings. **Stageband:** None. **Publisher:** G. Ricordi, Troupenas. **Rights:** Expired.

I. Raimbaud announces that a wise hermit (actually Count Ory in disguise) will visit the village to offer counsel. The castle is filled with women waiting for their husbands to return from the crusades. Ory's page Isolier is in love with the countess, who has sworn herself to chastity while her brother is at war. The count's tutor complains that he spends all his time chasing after the energetic count. Isolier confides his love to the hermit —who is also in love with the countess—and explains his plan to sneak into the castle disguised as a female pilgrim. The countess consults the hermit about a cure for her melancholia. He proposes she fall in love, which she promptly does—with Isolier. The count warns her not to trust the page. When the tutor reveals Ory's identity, everyone is shocked. The countess receives a letter announcing her brother's return.

II. The countess and her attendants admit a group of female pilgrims who seek shelter from the storm. The pilgrims are really Ory and his men in disguise. Ory thanks the countess profusely. Missing something to drink with dinner, Raimbaud breaks into the castle wine cellar and returns with enough for everyone. They toast the countess's absent brother. Isolier tells the women that their husbands will be back by midnight—and gives away the count's disguise. After everyone is in bed, the count enters the countess's room. He woos her, not realizing in the dark that it is Isolier's hand he is holding. The husbands return. Isolier reveals himself and helps smuggle the count out of the castle.

The Consul

Composed by Gian Carlo Menotti (b. July 7, 1911). Libretto by Gian Carlo Menotti. English. Original work. Premiered Philadelphia, Schubert Theater, March 1, 1950. Set somewhere in Europe in the 1940s. Tragedy. Through composed with orchestral interludes between scenes. The voice on the record is often done with a recording provided by the publisher.

Sets: 2. **Acts:** 3 acts, 6 scenes. **Length:** I: 40. II: 50. III: 25. **Arias:** "To this we've come" (Magda). **Hazards:** II, III: Magda's visions. **Scenes:** Ii. The Sorel home, early morning. Iii. The consulate, later the same day. IIi. The Sorel home in the evening a month later. IIii. The consulate, a few days later. IIIi. The consulate, late afternoon, several days later. IIIii. The Sorel home, that night.

Major roles: John Sorel (baritone), Magda Sorel (soprano), Mother (contralto), Secretary (mezzo). **Minor roles:** Voice on the Record (soprano), Secret Police Agent (bass), Mr. Kofner (bass baritone), Foreign Woman (soprano), Magician Nika Magadoff (tenor), Vera Boronel (contralto), Anna Gomez (soprano), Assan (baritone). **Mute:** First plainclothesman, Second plainclothesman.

Chorus parts: N/A. **Chorus roles:** None. **Dance/movement:** II: Ball in the consulate waiting room. III: Waltz in Magda's vision. **Orchestra:** fl, ob, cl, bsn, 2 hrn, 2 trp, trb, timp, perc, harp, piano, strings. **Stageband:** III: telephone bell. **Publisher:** Schirmer. **Rights:** Copyright 1950 by G. Schirmer Inc.

Ii. John Sorel drags himself into his apartment, having been shot by the police while escaping from a secret political meeting. Hearing the police coming, John hides. The policeman interrogates Magda who says she has not seen her husband for two weeks. Their neighbor, Michael the shoemaker, is dragged off to prison. John emerges from hiding and begins to pack, intending to slip across the border that night. Go to the consulate, he advises Magda, and tell them our story. He warns her not to call on any of his friends and arranges to get messages to her via Assan the glass cutter. Iii. At the consulate, the secretary discovers that Mr. Kofner has again failed to bring the right documents. Since the foreign woman does not speak the language, Mr. Kofner translates. The foreign woman wants to go to her daughter who ran away three years ago, but is now ill. The secretary tells her to fill out an application and wait—it may take three or four months for a visa to be approved. Magda asks to speak to the consul but is rebuffed. She begs the secretary to tell the consul her story, but the secretary only gives her forms to fill out. Nicholas Magadoff the magician performs magic tricks to pass the time.

IIi. A month has passed with no news from John and no help from the consulate. Magda's mother sings to the baby, who is sick. Magda has a nightmare in which John returns with the secretary. Magda is afraid of the secretary and begs John to send her away. He will not, claiming she is his sister. Magda wakes. A rock sails through the window—the arranged signal—and the relieved women call Assan the glass cutter. The secret police agent returns, but Magda throws him out. Assan tells the women that John is still hiding in the mountains and will not cross the border until he knows that they can get out too. Magda tells him to go ahead—everything will be fine. The mother discovers that the baby has died. Assan sees this, but the mother swears him to silence. Only after Assan leaves does Magda discover the truth. The women mourn. IIii. Back in the consulate, Anna Gomez, a concentration camp survivor without a home, is put off by the secretary. Magda arrives, frantic, but is told to wait in line. The magician, finding that art and fame are no substitute for a visa, hypnotizes everyone in the waiting room and makes them dance. The secretary is terrorized and forces the magician to leave. Magda screams at the secretary who agrees to get her in to see the consul. When the secret police agent comes out of the consul's office, Magda faints.

IIIi. Magda is in the consulate again, but still has not seen the consul. The secretary goes through Vera Boronel's papers with her. Assan comes in to tell Magda that John has heard about the death of his son and mother and insists on coming home. Magda writes out a note for Assan to give to John that will persuade him not to recross the border. Magda leaves and the secretary is haunted by the names and faces of all the people waiting for visas. John appears. He has been followed by the secret police, who come into the consulate to get him. Outraged, the secretary promises to report this violation of international law to the consul. John asks to call Magda but is told he can do it from the police station. IIIii. Magda opens the gas vents in the stove to kill herself. She sees visions of John, her mother and the visitors to the consulate who tell her that the kingdom of death has no visas. Magda tries to follow them, but cannot. She dies. The phone rings.

Le Contes d'Hoffmann • The Tales of Hoffmann

Composed by Jacques Offenbach (June 20, 1819 – October 5, 1880). Libretto by Jules Barbier and Michel Carré. French. Based on the stories of E. T. A. Hoffmann. Premiered Paris, Opéra Comique, February 10, 1881. Set in Nuremburg, Paris, Munich and Venice in the early 19th century. Grand opera. Set numbers with recitative (originally intended to have spoken dialogue). Prelude, prologue and epilogue. Interlude between III and epilogue. Entr'actes. Completed after Offenbach's death with recitatives by Ernest Guiraud and barcarole from Offenbach's opera-ballet "Die Rheinnixen." Several alternate versions with transposition of second and third acts and/or omission of Muse, Lindorf, Stella and/or Andres.

Sets: 4. **Acts:** 3 acts, 5 scenes (sometimes done in 4 acts). **Length:** Prologue: 25. I: 35. II: 30. III: 45. Epilogue: 8. **Arias:** "Scintille diamant"/Diamond aria (Dappertutto), "Elle a fui" (Antonia), "Jour et nuit" (Franz), "Il était une fois à la cour d'Eisenbach"/La légende de Kleinzach (Hoffmann), "Les oiseaux dans la charmille" (Olympia). **Hazards:** II: Hoffmann's reflection "stolen" in a mirror. III: Vision of Antonia's mother. **Scenes:** Prologue. Luther's Tavern adjoining the opera house. I. Elegant parlor of a scientist. II. Exterior of a gallery in a palace overlooking the grand canal in Venice. III. Crespel's house in Munich. Epilogue. Luther's tavern.

Major roles: Lindorf/Dr. Miracle/Coppélius/Dappertutto (bass baritone), Hoffmann (tenor), Olympia (soprano), Giulietta (mezzo), Antonia (soprano). **Minor roles:** Nicklausse (mezzo), Spalanzani (tenor), Crespel (bass), Franz (tenor), Andrès (tenor), Luther (bass or baritone), Nathanael (tenor), Hermann (baritone), Cochenille (tenor), Schlemiel (baritone or bass), Voice of Antonia's mother (mezzo). **Bit parts:** Pittichinaccio (tenor). **Speaking:** Stella, Muse. (Nicklausse can double muse. Olympia, Giulietta, Antonia and Stella ocassionally played by same performer. Pitichinaccio, Franz, Cochenille and Adres can be sung by same performer.)

Chorus parts: SATTBB. **Chorus roles:** Spirits of beer and wine, students,

Spalanzani's guests, Giulietta's guests. **Dance/movement:** I (Olympia): waltz. **Orchestra:** 2 fl (picc), 2 ob, 2 cl, 2 bsn, 4 hrn, 2 trp, 3 trb, timp, perc, harp, strings. **Stageband:** I: harp, fl, cl (all 3 can be from orchestra). III: piano. **Publisher:** Schirmer. **Rights:** Expired.

Prologue. Stella, an opera singer, has sent a letter and key to the poet Hoffmann through Andres. Councillor Lindorf bribes Andres and gets both, intending to supplant Hoffman in Stella's affections. Students enter Luther's tavern demanding beer. Hoffmann sings a song about the dwarf Kleinzack and is carried away in mid-song by a vision of his love. When Hoffmann denies he is in love, Lindorf laughs. The two men trade insults, and Hoffmann accuses Lindorf of being his nemesis. He praises Stella and begins the tales of his past loves.

I. The scientist Spalanzani hopes to use his creation, Olympia (a mechanical doll), to win back the 500 ducats he lost when the bank of Elias went bankrupt. He greets Nicklausse and Hoffmann. The poet's real interest is in Olympia, whom he believes to be Spalanzani's daughter: He has apprenticed himself to the scientist to be near her. Coppélius sells Hoffmann glasses. He has come to claim payment from Spalanzani for providing Olympia's eyes. Spalanzani gets rid of him with a check for 500 ducats drawn on Elias's bank. Spalanzani's guests arrive for the presentation of Olympia, who charms everyone with a song. Hoffmann catches a moment alone with his love. Nicklausse tries to warn him but to no avail. Realizing he has been cheated, Coppélius returns and sabotages Olympia. She dances wildly and is smashed to bits, revealing that she is a puppet.

II. Dappertutto hopes Hoffmann will fall for the Venetian courtesan Giulietta just as Schlemiel did before him. He has charmed Giulietta with a diamond and orders her to steal Hoffmann's reflection. This she does. Hoffmann fights and kills Schlemiel for the key to Giulietta's bedroom only to find she has fled with Pittichinaccio. Nicklausse drags Hoffmann away as the police arrive.

III. Antonia sings of her absent lover. Her father, Crespel, begs her not to sing as it endangers her frail health. Crespel has come to Munich to get his daughter away from Hoffmann. He tells the servant Franz to admit no one while he is out, but Franz is deaf and misunderstands. In his master's absence, Franz indulges his fondness for singing and dancing. Hoffmann and Antonia sing together until Antonia faints. Crespel comes in and Hoffmann hides. Dr. Miracle is announced and Crespel tries unsuccessfully to keep the quack out. The doctor has Antonia sing and prescribes pills. All three men leave, but Miracle returns and, aided by the voice of Antonia's dead mother, persuades the girl to sing. Father and lover return to find Antonia dead. Epilogue. Hoffmann's audience now realize that his three loves are all aspects of Stella. Hoffmann drinks to drown his sorrows. Stella, finding him dead drunk, leaves with Lindorf. (Alternately, the muse of poetry comes to comfort Hoffmann.)

Le Convenienze ed Inconvenienze Teatrali

See "Viva la Mamma" entry.

Coq d'Or

See "The Golden Cockerel" entry.

Der Corregidor • The Magistrate

Composed by Hugo Wolf (March 13, 1860 – February 22, 1903). Libretto by Rosa Mayreder-Obermayer. German. Based on "El Sombrero de Tres Picos" by Pedro de Alarcón. Premiered Mannheim, Nationaltheater, June 7, 1896. Set in Andalusia in 1804. Comedy. Through composed. Overture. Brief prelude before II. Entr'acte before III, IV.

Sets: 5. **Acts:** 4 acts, 27 scenes. **Length:** I: 35. II: 45. III: 25. IV: 20. **Arias:** "Herz, verzage nicht geschwind" (Zuniga). **Hazards:** None. **Scenes:** I. A paved square at the mill. Ii – IIvi. The kitchen of the mill. IIvii – IIxi. Room in the alkalde's house. IIIi – IIIiii. A road in hilly country. IIIiiii – IIIvi. The kitchen of the mill. IV. Street at night in front of the magistrate's house.

Major roles: Tio Lukas (baritone), Frasquita (mezzo), Repela (bass), Magistrate Don Eugenio de Zuniga (tenor). **Minor roles:** Neighbor (tenor), Tonuelo (bass), Juan Lopez (bass), Manuela (mezzo), Pedro (tenor), Donna Mercedes (soprano), Duenna (alto). **Bit part:** Night watchman (baritone).

Chorus parts: SSAATTBB (briefly BBB). **Chorus roles:** Bishop and his retinue, corrigedors, alguacils, musicians, rabble. **Dance/movement:** None. **Orchestra:** 3 fl (picc), 2 ob, Eng hrn, 2 cl, bs cl, 2 bsn, 4 hrn, 3 trp, 3 trb, tuba, timp, perc, harp, strings. **Stageband:** I: 3 trp, 2 hrn. **Publisher:** C. F. Peters, Lauterbach and Kuhn. **Rights:** Expired.

Ii. A neighbor of Tio Lukas's compliments him on his beautiful wife, Frasquita. Iii. Lukas knows that the magistrate is in love with Frasquita, but wonders why the magistrate is coming to his mill. He and Frasquita agree that he will hide in the bushes to eavesdrop. Iiii. The magistrate's servant Repela checks that Frasquita is alone before fetching his master.

Iiv. Frasquita asks the magistrate to nominate her nephew as court secretary. When he bends to kiss her, she ducks and he falls over. Iv. The magistrate determines to get even.

IIi. Lukas and Frasquita are happy. IIii. The drunken Tonuelo tells Lukas he is needed by the alcalde. Frasquita reluctantly agrees to stay behind. IIiii. She is afraid but opens the door for the magistrate, thinking he is Lukas. IIiv. The magistrate has fallen into the brook and is freezing. Frasquita is suspicious and unimpressed by both the magistrate's offer to nominate her nephew and his threats. IIv. She summons Repela to look after the magistrate while she goes into town to find Lukas. IIvi. Fearing Frasquita means to alert his wife, the magistrate sends Repela after her. IIvii. Juan Lopez, the alcalde, plots to humiliate Lukas. IIviii. He tries to get him drunk, but Lukas out drinks him. IIix. Lukas then jumps out the window to escape. IIx. Manuela sounds the alarm. IIxi. Tonuelo and Pedro chase after Lukas.

IIIi. Frasquita hurries into town. IIIii. Repela overtakes and accompanies her. IIIiii. Lukas returns home and is surprised to find the door unlocked—and the magistrate in his bed. IIIiv. He puts on the magistrate's clothes and leaves his own. IIIv. The magistrate puts on Lukas's clothes. IIIvi. Lopez, his confederates and Frasquita find the magistrate alone at the mill. They run after Lukas.

IVi. The night watchman makes his rounds. IVii. The magistrate finds he is locked out of his own house. IViii. Frasquita worries what her husband might have done in his jealous fury. IViv. He has, it turns out, gotten into the magistrate's bed with the magistrate's wife, Mercedes. IVv. Everyone is furious, but Mercedes and Frasquita explain everything and all recriminations are buried.

Il Corsaro • The Corsair

Composed by Giuseppe Verdi (October 9, 1813 – January 27, 1901). Libretto by Francesco Maria Piave. Italian. Based on the poem by Lord Byron. Premiered Trieste, Teatro Grande, October 25, 1848. Set on an island in the Aegean and in the city of Corone in the 19th century. Tragedy. Set numbers with recitative. Prelude.

Sets: 6. Acts: 3 acts, 7 scenes. Length: I, II, III: 95. Hazards: II: Seid's navy and palace are set ablaze. III: Corrado throws himself into the sea. Scenes: Ii. The sea shore of the corsairs' island in the Aegean. Iii. Medora's room in the old turret facing the sea. IIi. A room in Seid's harem. IIii. A magnificent pavilion on the shore of the harbor of Coron. IIIi. Seid's apartments. IIIii. Inside a tower. IIIiii. The sea shore.

Major roles: Corrado (tenor), Medora (soprano), Gulnara (soprano), Pasha Seid of Coron (baritone). **Minor roles:** Giovanni (bass), Selimo (baritone or tenor). **Bit parts:** Black eunuch (tenor), Slave (tenor), Anselmo (bass).

Chorus parts: SSATTBB. **Chorus roles:** Corsairs, guards, Turks, slaves, odalisques, Medora's ladies in waiting. **Dance/movement:** None. **Orchestra:** picc, fl, 2 ob, 2 cl, 2 bsn, 4 hrn, 2 trp, 3 trb, cimbasso, timp, perc, harp, strings. **Stageband:** None. **Publisher:** Kalmus. **Rights:** Expired.

Ii. Corrado tells his pirate gang that he means to lead them in battle against Pasha Seid. Iii. He takes leave of his beloved Medora.

IIi. Seid's favorite slave, Gulnara, loathes him. IIii. Corrado presents himself to Seid as an escaped prisoner of the pirates. His men set fire to the pasha's navy and palace. When Corrado removes his disguise and attacks, he is captured. Seid threatens Corrado with a painful death.

IIIi. Gulnara makes Seid jealous by asking him to spare Corrado. IIIii. She kills Corrado's prison guard and frees Corrado. IIIiii. Believing Corrado dead, Medora poisons herself. Corrado returns and Medora dies in his arms. He throws himself into the sea.

Così fan tutte • Women Are Like That

Composed by Wolfgang Amadeus Mozart (January 27, 1756 – December 5, 1791). Libretto by Lorenzo Da Ponte. Italian. Original work. Premiered Vienna, Burgtheater, January 26, 1790. Set in Naples in the 18th century. Opera buffa. Set numbers with recitative. Overture.

Sets: 7. **Acts:** 2 acts, 34 scenes. **Length:** I: 80. II: 70. **Arias:** "Un'aura amorosa" (Ferrando), "Come scoglio" (Fiordiligi), "Una donna di quindici anni" (Despina), "In uomini" (Despina), "Per pietà" (Fiordiligi), "Tradito schernito" (Ferrando). **Hazards:** None. **Scenes:** Ii. A room in a café. Iii – Ivii. A garden at the seashore. Iviii – Ixiii. A pretty room. Ixiv – Ixvi. A flower garden. IIi – IIiii. A room in the sisters' home. IIiv – IIix. A garden at the seashore. IIx – IIxiv. A room. IIxv – IIxviii. A hall, richly decorated and illuminated.

Major roles: Fiordiligi (soprano), Dorabella (mezzo), Guglielmo (baritone), Ferrando (tenor), Despina (soprano), Don Alfonso (bass).

Chorus parts: SATB. **Chorus roles:** Soldiers, servants, sailors, wedding guests, people. **Dance/movement:** None. **Orchestra:** 2 fl, 2 ob, 2 cl, 2 bsn,

2 hrn, 2 trp, timp, strings, continuo. **Stageband:** None. **Publisher:** Schirmer, Ernst Eulenburg. **Rights:** Expired.

Ii. Don Alfonso bets Ferrando and Guglielmo that their girlfriends, Dorabella and Fiordiligi, are not as faithful as the men think. Iii. The women praise their sweethearts. Iiii. Don Alfonso tells the women that Ferrando and Guglielmo must go off to war. Iiv. The lovers say their goodbyes. Iv. Ferrando and Guglielmo board ship with the other soldiers. Ivi. Fiordiligi, Dorabella and Don Alfonso wave goodbye. Ivii. Don Alfonso impugns the fidelity of woman. Iviii. Tired of being the maid, Despina drinks some of the ladies' chocolate. Iix. She discounts the ladies' grief and their men's fidelity. Ix. Don Alfonso bribes Despina and brings her in on his scheme. Ixi. Ferrando and Guglielmo are presented to Dorabella and Fiordiligi, disguised as Albanians. The women are only prevented from throwing the men out by the arrival of Don Alfonso who claims them as his dearest friends. The women leave. Ixii. Don Alfonso reminds the men that the bet is not over. Ixiii. Despina assures Don Alfonso that the women will give in eventually. Ixiv. The women are in the garden, still lamenting their loss. Ixv. Ferrando and Guglielmo prove their love to the ladies by drinking poison. It is not real poison, but the women are frightened and call for help. Ixvi. Despina enters, disguised as a doctor, and cures the men. The ladies spurn their new lovers' kisses.

IIi. Despina softens Dorabella's and Fiordiligi's resolve. IIii. The sisters agree to allow a flirtation and unknowingly choose each other's lovers. IIiii. Don Alfonso invites the women into the garden. IIiv. The lovers walk arm in arm. IIv. Dorabella accepts a locket from Guglielmo and gives him her portrait of Ferrando in return. IIvi. Ferrando has less luck with Fiordiligi. IIvii. Fiordiligi admits to herself that the stranger attracts her. IIviii. Ferrando reports Fiordiligi's rejection to Guglielmo—who in turn relates Dorabella's capitulation. Guglielmo berates womankind. IIix. Ferrando is distraught. IIx. Despina is ready to be married to her new lover and chides Fiordiligi's pangs of conscience. IIxi. Fiordiligi decides to disguise herself as a soldier and search out Ferrando and Guglielmo. IIxii. Guglielmo, who has overheard her plans, is impressed. But Ferrando renews his suit and Fiordiligi's defenses crumble. IIxiii. It is now Guglielmo's turn to rage at his betrayal. Don Alfonso advises them to marry their sweethearts anyway. All women are weak, he says. IIxiv. Despina announces the women's willingness to marry. IIxv. Despina and Don Alfonso direct the wedding preparations. IIxvi. The couples have dinner. IIxvii. Despina, disguised as a notary, presents the wedding contracts, which the lovers sign. Everyone panics when Don Alfonso announces the return of Ferrando and Guglielmo. IIxviii. The men return and "discover" the wedding contracts. They berate their faithless lovers. Dorabella and Fiordiligi admit their guilt but say

Despina and Don Alfonso set them up to it. Don Alfonso reveals the plot. The women beg forgiveness, which their lovers readily grant.

Countess Maritza

See "Gräfin Maritza" entry.

The Crucible

Composed by Robert Ward (b. September 13, 1917). Libretto by Bernard Stambler. English. Based on the play by Arthur Miller. Premiered New York City, New York City Opera, October 26, 1961. Set in Salem, Massachusetts in 1692. Tragedy. Through composed. Orchestral interludes.

Sets: 5. **Acts:** 4 acts, 5 scenes. **Length:** I: 30 II: 25. III: 25. IV: 25. **Hazards:** None. **Scenes:** I. Reverend Parris's house. II. The kitchen of John Proctor's farmhouse. IIIi. A small woods before Parris's house. IIIii. The town meetinghouse transformed into a courtroom. IV. A great dank, inner hall, vaguely circular, within the town blockhouse and jail.

Major roles: Abigail Williams (soprano), John Proctor (baritone), The Reverend John Hale (bass), Elizabeth Proctor (mezzo). **Minor roles:** Tituba (contralto), The Reverend Samuel Parris (tenor), Thomas Putnam (baritone), Ann Putnam (soprano), Rebecca Nurse (contralto), Giles Corey (tenor), Ezekiel Cheever (tenor), Mary Warren (soprano), Judge Danforth (tenor), Sarah Good (soprano). **Bit parts:** Francis Nurse (bass).

Chorus parts: SSATB. **Chorus roles:** Girls (Betty Parris, mezzo; Ruth Putnam, coloratura soprano; Susanna Walcott, contralto; Mercy Lewis, contralto; Martha Sheldon, soprano; Bridget Booth, soprano), people of Salem. **Dance/movement:** None. **Orchestra:** 2 fl (picc), 2 ob (Eng hrn), 2 cl (bs cl), 2 bsn (cont bsn), 4 hrn, 2 trp, 2 trb, timp, perc, harp, strings. (Taped sound in III.) **Stageband:** None. **Publisher:** Galaxy Music Corporation. **Rights:** Copyright 1962 by Bernard Stambler and Robert Ward.

I. Abigail admits to her uncle, the Reverend Samuel Parris, that she and Betty Parris went dancing in the woods with Tituba. When Betty—and the Putnam girl—fall ill, people claim it is witchcraft and call Reverend Hale. Hale frightens Abigail into saying that Tituba was making a pact with the devil. Tituba, when questioned, admits to conversing with the devil and implicates Sarah Good.

II. John's wife, Elizabeth, tells him that people are being executed for witchcraft on the testimony of Abigail and her friends. She asks John to expose Abigail as a fraud, but he fears that his affair with Abigail will open him to revenge. Hale finds a voodoo doll in Elizabeth's house, which he takes as evidence that Elizabeth is a witch. John demands that the servant Mary explain that she framed Elizabeth, but Mary fears Abigail.

IIIi. John confronts Abigail, but she still loves him and refuses to free Elizabeth from jail. IIIii. In court, Giles Corey accuses Thomas Putnam of branding people as witches so he can grab their land. When Giles refuses to support his accusation by naming people who heard Putnam's plan—and cannot produce any evidence—he is arrested on contempt of court. John accuses Abigail and the girls of fraud, producing Mary as a witness, and Abigail denies the charge. John admits having an affair with Abigail, but Elizabeth is brought in and denies it. Hale believes John, but the girls throw fits and claim he is the devil.

IV. John has been imprisoned. Abigail asks him to flee with her, but he refuses. Hale begs Judge Danforth to delay the hangings, but he will not do so—even when Parris reports that Abigail has fled with his money. After a tearful reunion with Elizabeth, John agrees to confess. However, he refuses to implicate others in his confession or to sign a written confession, so Danforth condemns him.

Cumberland Fair

Composed by Alec Wilder (February 16, 1907 – December 24, 1980). Libretto by Arnold Sundgaard. English. Original work. Premiered Montclair, New Jersey, Montclair State Teachers College, May 22, 1953. Set on a street in Sycamore Hill and on the grounds of Cumberland Fair on an October day. Jamboree. Set numbers with spoken dialogue.

Sets: 2. **Acts:** 1 act, 2 scenes. **Length:** I: 25. **Hazards:** None. **Scenes:** Ii. A street in Sycamore hill. Iii. Cumberland fair.

Major roles: Ben Blake (baritone), Phoebe (mezzo), Billy Barlow (baritone), Reuben Ranzo (tenor), Polly Oliver (soprano). **Minor role:** Fourth barker (tenor). **Speaking:** Three barkers.

Chorus parts: SAATTBB. **Chorus roles:** Fair goers. **Dance/movement:** I: Jamboree. **Orchestra:** fl, 4 cl, 2 trp, bs, guitar, piano, perc. **Stageband:** None. **Publisher:** Hollis Music. **Rights:** Copyright 1953 by Hollis Music.

Ii. Polly Oliver has promised Ben Blake, Billy Barlow and Reuben Ranzo that she will go to Cumberland Fair with each of them. No one has asked her cousin, Phoebe. Reuben is disappointed and asks Phoebe instead. Iii. At the fair, Polly flirts with Reuben while Ben and Billy fuss over Phoebe. Reuben wins a shawl, which he gives to Phoebe. Polly leaves in a huff. The others dance the jamboree.

Příhody Lišky Bystroušky • The Cunning Little Vixen

Composed by Leoš Janáček (July 3, 1854 – August 12, 1928). Libretto by Leoš Janáček. Czech. Based on a story by Rudolf Těsnohlídek. Premiered Brno, National Theater, November 6, 1924. Set in a forest and surroundings in legendary times. Folk opera. Through composed. Entr'actes before each act. Preludes.

Sets: 7. **Acts:** 3 acts, 9 scenes. **Length:** I: 25. II: 35. III: 30. **Hazards:** Most principal characters are forest animals. **Scenes:** Ii. A dark, dry gully in the wood. Iii. Courtyard of the "Lakeside" forester's lodge. IIi. The forest by the badger's house. IIii. The Páseks' Inn. IIiii. A forest pathway leading uphill. IIiv. The Vixen's lair. IIIi. The edge of a clearing. IIIii. The Páseks' Inn. IIIiii. The dark, dry gully.

Major roles: Forester (baritone), Vixen Sharp Ears (soprano). **Minor roles:** Lapák the dog (mezzo), Cock (soprano), Hen (soprano), Priest (bass), Schoolmaster (tenor), Fox (soprano or tenor), Harašta (bass). **Bit parts:** Cricket (treble), Grasshopper (treble), Mosquito (treble), Frog (treble), Forester's wife (contralto), Frantík (soprano or treble), Pepík (soprano or treble), Badger (bass), Innkeeper Pásek (tenor), Owl (contralto), Jay (soprano), Woodpecker (contralto), Young vixen (treble), Innkeeper's wife (soprano). (Priest can double as badger.)

Chorus parts: SAATTBB. **Chorus roles:** Hens, animals of the forest, fox cubs. **Dance/movement:** Ii: Ballet of the animals. IIiv: Second animal ballet. IIIi: Fox cub ballet. **Orchestra:** 4 fl, 3 ob, 3 cl, 3 bsn, 4 hrn, 3 trp, 3 trb, tuba, timp, perc, harp, celeste, strings. **Stageband:** None. **Publisher:** Universal Edition. **Rights:** Copyright 1924 by Universal Edition.

Ii. The napping forester is awakened by the animals. Seeing the vixen, the forester grabs her and takes her home. Iii. The vixen is left in the backyard with Lapák the dog, who talks of love. When he makes a pass at the vixen, she hits him. The children Pepík and Frantík tease the vixen and hit her with a stick. She bites Pepík and tries to run away, but Frantík catches her and the forester ties her up. Night passes. The vixen tries to convince the hens that they can live without the greedy old cock, but they only brag about their productivity. She digs a hole—pretending to bury herself alive—and when the curious hens approach she kills every one. The forester beats the vixen, but she escapes into the woods.

IIi. The badger hits the vixen for intruding on his home, so she urinates on him, chases him away, and moves in. IIii. The forester, the priest and the school teacher drink and play cards. The forester teases his friend the school teacher about having a girlfriend. He curses the vixen. IIiii. The school teacher drunkenly stumbles towards home. He mistakes a sunflower for his lovely Theresa and passes out in the undergrowth. The priest comes along next, recalling how his only love ran away with the butcher's boy. He and the school master are roused by the shouting of the forester, who is once again in pursuit of the vixen. IIiv. The vixen is transfixed by a handsome fox. He walks her home and she tells him about her adventures in the forester's household. They fall in love. After making love, they are married by the woodpecker.

IIIi. The forester encounters Harašta, who is going to be married to Theresa. He lays a trap for the vixen, who has killed another hare. The vixen and her growing family of cubs smell the trap and avoid it. Harašta chases the vixen, who eludes him. He falls down and, in frustration, fires his gun at the foxes, mortally wounding the vixen. IIIii. The schoolmaster is dejected that his beloved Theresa is marrying someone else. His friend the forester contemplates old age. IIIiii. The forester takes a nap in the woods. He tries to catch one of the vixen's cubs, but she is just as tricky as her mother.

Dalibor

Composed by Bedřich Smetana (March 2, 1824 –
May 12, 1884). Libretto by Josef Wenzig. Czech.
Based on historical events. Premiered Prague, Czech
Theater, May 16, 1868. Set in Prague in the 15th cen-
tury. Rescue opera. Set numbers with recitative. Interludes between
scenes.

Sets: 6. **Acts:** 3 acts, 7 scenes. **Length:** I: 50. II: 50. III: 50. **Arias:** Goaler
aria (Beneš), Joy aria (Milada), "What magic is this?" (Dalibor). **Hazards:**
None. **Scenes:** I. A courtyard at the royal castle. IIi. A street in the lower
town with an inn. IIii. The interior of the castle with the living quarters
of the jailer. IIiii. A dark jail. IIIi. An illuminated royal chamber. IIIii. The
jail. IIIiii. In front of the tower.

Major roles: Milada (soprano), Dalibor (tenor). **Minor roles:** Jitka
(soprano), King Vladislav (baritone), Budivoj commander of the castle
guard (baritone), Beneš the jailer (bass), Vítek (tenor). **Bit part:** Judge
(bass). **Mute:** Zdeněk's ghost.

Chorus parts: SATTBB. **Chorus roles:** Judges, royal mercenaries, mercenaries and servants of Dalibor, people, monks, women. **Dance/move-
ment:** None. **Orchestra:** picc, 2 fl, 2 ob, 2 cl, 2 bsn, 4 hrn, 2 trp, 3 trb, tuba,
timp, perc, harp, strings. **Stageband:** I: 4 trp. **Publisher:** Hudební
Matice, Josef Weinberger. **Rights:** Expired.

I. Dalibor is accused of treason and his ward, Jitka, fears he will be condemned. King Vladislav opens the trial and Milada gives evidence that
Dalibor attacked her brother's castle and killed the brother. Dalibor
explains that Milada's brother murdered his friend. He is sentenced to
life imprisonment. The king refuses Milada's plea for leniency. Milada
loves Dalibor and she and Jitka determine to free him.

IIi. Jitka's beloved Vítek has gathered Dalibor's mercenaries, planning to
free Dalibor. IIii. Milada has disguised herself as a boy to insinuate herself into the service of Dalibor's jailer, Beneš. Beneš complains about the
mournfulness of a jailer's life. Out of pity he agrees to Dalibor's request
for a violin. Milada prays for success in freeing Dalibor. IIiii. The jailer
sends her into the cell with the violin. Dalibor dreams of his dead friend.
Milada reveals herself to Dalibor who falls in love with her.

IIIi. Milada flees the jail when Beneš realizes she is a spy. Dalibor's
judges convince the king to have Dalibor slain. IIIii. Dalibor cuts off his

shackles with the tools Milada has left him, but the guards come for Dalibor before he can escape. They inform him he will be executed immediately. IIIiii. Realizing Dalibor is still a prisoner, Milada and Dalibor's men attack the castle. Milada is mortally wounded in the attack, but Dalibor's men are victorious.

La Damnation de Faust • The Damnation of Faust

Composed by Hector Berlioz (December 11, 1803 – March 8, 1869). Libretto by Hector Berlioz and Almire Gandonnière. French. Based on Gérard de Nerval's adaptation of "Faust" by Johann von Goethe. Premiered Monte Carlo, Théâtre de Monte Carlo, February 18, 1893. Set in Hungary and Germany in the 16th century. Dramatic legend. Set numbers with recitative. Ballet. Concert premiere in Paris, December 6, 1846.

Sets: 10. **Acts:** 4 acts, 20 scenes. **Length:** I, II, III, IV: 125. **Arias:** Chanson de la Puce (Méphistophélès), "Merci doux crépuscule" (Faust). **Hazards:** IV: Horseback ride to hell, bloody rain & dancing skeletons. **Scenes:** I. The plains of Hungary. Iii – Iiii. Faust's study in northern Germany. IIiii. Auerbach's cellar in Leipzig. IIiv. Bushy meadows on the banks of the Elbe. IIv. Before Margarita's house. IIIi – IVi. Margarita's chamber. IVii – IViii. Cavern and forest. IViv. Descent into hell. IVv. In hell. IVvi. On earth and in heaven.

Major roles: Faust (tenor), Méphistophélès (bass baritone), Marguerite (mezzo). **Minor roles:** Brander (bass).

Chorus parts: SATTBB. **Chorus roles:** Peasants, villagers, tavern goers, gnomes and sylphs, soldiers, students, spirits of hell, seraphim and heavenly spirits, boys (in 2 parts). **Dance/movement:** I: Peasant dance. II: Sylph ballet. III: Will-o'-the-wisps ballet. **Orchestra:** 3 fl (2 picc), 2 ob (Eng hrn), 2 cl, bs cl, 4 bsn, 4 hrn, 2 trp, 2 cornets, 3 trb, tuba, ophicléide, timp, perc, 2 harp, strings. **Stageband:** IV: 2 hrn, 2 trp. **Publisher:** Schirmer, Richault. **Rights:** Expired.

Ii. Faust rejoices in the spring. Iii. He observes a peasant celebration. Iiii. The Hungarian army marches by.

IIi. Unsatisfied by life, Faust contemplates suicide but is stopped by the sounds of an Easter hymn. IIii. Méphistophélès appears and offers Faust riches and fame. IIiii. He transports Faust to Leipzig where they drink and carouse. Faust is unimpressed, so they hurry off to the banks of the Elbe. IIiv. Nymphs and Sylphs give Faust a vision of Marguerite. IIv. Soldiers and students promenade.

IIIi. With the aid of Méphistophélès, Faust enters Marguerite's chamber. IIIii. He hears her coming and hides. IIIiii. As she prepares for bed, Marguerite daydreams about her predestined love. IIIiv. Méphistophélès summons the willow-o'-the-wisps to his aid. IIIv. Marguerite recognizes Faust as the man in her dreams. IIIvi. They exchange vows of love. IIIvii. The villagers have learned of Faust's nocturnal visit and come to investigate. Méphistophélès warns the lovers and helps Faust escape.

IVi. Marguerite pines for Faust. IVii. Faust finds comfort in nature. IViii. He learns from Méphistophélès that Marguerite is imprisoned for poisoning her mother: The potion that Faust gave Marguerite to put her mother to sleep during their nightly meetings killed her. Faust agrees to sign a contract to serve Méphistophélès as the price of saving Marguerite. IViv. Horses appear and Méphistophélès and Faust ride to hell. IVv. The spirits of hell welcome Faust. Epilogue. Marguerite is forgiven and admitted into heaven.

The Dangerous Liaisons

Composed by Conrad Susa (b. April 26, 1935). Libretto by Philip Littell. English. Based on the novel "Les Liaisons Dangereuses" by Pierre Choderlos de Laclos. Premiered San Francisco, War Memorial Opera House, San Francisco Opera, September 10, 1994. Set in France in the 18th century. Tragedy. Set numbers with recitative. Overture. Orchestral interludes between scenes. Prelude before II.

Sets: 7. **Acts:** 2 acts, 8 scenes. **Length:** I, II: 170. **Hazards:** None. **Scenes:** Ii. Madame de Rosemonde's salon. Iii. Various bedrooms. Iiii. Wooded area at Rosemonde's estate. IIi. Merteuil's bedroom in Paris. IIii. Valmont's bedroom. IIiii. Merteuil's secret pleasure pavilion. IIiv. Convent and entrance to the park of Vincennes. IIv. Before the curtain.

Major roles: Madame de Merteuil (mezzo), Valmont (baritone), Madame de Tourvel (soprano), Cecile (soprano), Danceny (tenor). **Minor roles:** Madame de Volanges (mezzo), Madame de Rosemonde (sorpano), Bertrand, Azolan. **Bit parts:** Emilie, Victoire, Julie, First man, Second man. **Mute:** Father Anselme.

Chorus parts: SATB. **Chorus roles:** Offstage (group of 12 people who also sing smaller roles). **Dance/movement:** None. **Orchestra:** 3 fl (3 picc), 3 ob (Eng hrn), 3 cl (bs cl), 3 bsn (cont bsn), 4 hrn, 3 trp (flugelhrn), 3 trb, tuba, timp, 3 perc, harp, synthesizer, strings. **Stageband:** None. **Publisher:** G. Schirmer. **Rights:** Copyright 1994 by G. Schirmer, Inc.

Ii. Madame de Merteuil is furious that her former lover, Gercourt, is marrying Cecile. Cecile and the chevalier Danceny are in love, but their love is chaste. Merteuil exacts revenge by persuading Valmont to seduce Cecile. In return, she holds out the hope that she will sleep with him. Valmont himself loves the virtuous Madame de Tourvel. She is impressed with his arranged show of virtue. Merteuil gets Danceny out of the way by telling Cecile's mother, Volanges, that he loves Cecile. Iii. Merteuil writes to Valmont about her love affairs. She and Cecile correspond over Valmont's seduction of Cecile. Valmont writes a love letter to Tourvel. Iiii. Valmont woos Tourvel.

IIi. Merteuil insists Valmont break off his affair with Tourvel. IIii. He does so but Tourvel's grief drives her mad. IIiii. Valmont finds Danceny in bed with Merteuil. He declares war on her for reneging on their bargain. Danceny learns that Valmont seduced Cecile and challenges him to a duel. IIiv. Danceny mortally wounds Valmont. Valmont asks him to publish his letters—which incriminate Merteuil. He declares his love for Tourvel and dies. Tourvel dies. IIv. Merteuil is disgraced by the letters.

Daphne

Composed by Richard Strauss (June 11, 1864 – September 8, 1949). Libretto by Josef Gregor. German. Partly based on the "Metamorphoses" of Ovid. Premiered Dresden, Staatsoper, October 15, 1938. Set in Thessaly in legendary times. Bucolic tragedy. Through composed. Introduction.

Sets: 1. **Acts:** 1 act, 1 scene. **Length:** I: 105. **Hazards:** I: A strange radiance emanates from Apollo. Apollo kills Leukippos with his bow. **Scenes:** I. Near the hut of Peneios on the river bank.

Major roles: Daphne (soprano), Leukippos (tenor), Apollo (tenor). **Minor roles:** First shepherd (baritone), Second shepherd (tenor), Gaea (contralto), First maid (soprano), Second maid (soprano), Peneios (bass). **Bit parts:** Third shepherd (bass), Fourth shepherd (bass).

Chorus parts: SATBB. **Chorus roles:** Shepherds, masked figures, maids. **Dance/movement:** I: Dances in honor of Dionysus by shepherds, Thrysus bearers. **Orchestra:** 3 fl (picc), 2 ob, Eng hrn, 3 cl, basset horn, bs cl, 3 bsn, cont bsn, 4 hrn, 3 trp, 3 trb, tuba, timp, perc, 2 harp, strings (16-16-12-10-8). **Stageband:** I: organ, alpine horn. **Publisher:** Johannes Vertel, A. Fürstner. **Rights:** Copyright 1938 by Richard Strauss.

I. The shepherds prepare for the festival of Dionysus, but Daphne is communing with nature. She scorns Leukippos's love for her. Daphne's maids dress Leukippos as a maid so he can dance with Daphne. Apollo comes to the festival disguised as a cattleman and falls in love with Daphne. Jealous of Leukippos, he kills him. Daphne is heartbroken. The god repents and calls on the gods to take Leukippos to Olympus. He turns Daphne into her favorite tree.

The Daughter of the Regiment

See "La Fille du Régiment" entry.

Death in Venice

Composed by Benjamin Britten (November 22, 1913 – December 4, 1976). Libretto by Myfanwy Piper. English. Based on the novel by Thomas Mann. Premiered The Maltings, Snape, Aldeburgh Festival, June 16, 1973. Set in Munich and Venice in 1911. Tragedy. Set numbers with recitative. Overture between Iii and Iiii. Opus 88.

Sets: 9. **Acts:** 2 acts, 17 scenes. **Length:** I: 80. II: 65. **Hazards:** Onboard a moving ship and gondola. **Scenes:** Ii. Entrance to a cemetery in Munich. Iii. On the boat to Venice. Iiii. In a gondola on the way to the Lido. Iiv. The hotel hall. Iv. On the beach. Ivi. In a gondola on the way to Venice. Ivii. On the beach. IIi. The hotel barber shop. IIii. In a gondola. IIiii. The terrace outside the hotel. IIiv. A travel bureau. IIv. The hotel. IIvi. A dark stage. IIvii. The empty beach. IIviii. The barber shop. IIix. A street in Venice. IIx. The hotel hall.

Major roles: Gustav von Aschenbach (tenor), Traveler/Elderly fop/Old gondolier/Hotel manager/Hotel barber/Leader of the players/Voice of Dionysus (bass baritone). **Minor roles:** Hotel porter (tenor), Hotel waiter (bass), Strawberry seller (soprano), Lace seller (soprano), Glass maker (tenor), Voice of Apollo (countertenor), Strolling player (soprano), Strolling player (tenor), English clerk in the travel bureau (bass or baritone). **Bit parts:** Three youths on the boat (2 tenor, 1 baritone), Ship's steward (bass), Four girls (2 soprano, 2 alto), Lido boatman (bass), French girl (soprano), French mother (contralto), Two Americans (2 tenor), German mother (contralto), German father (baritone), Polish father (baritone), Russian nanny (contralto), Danish lady (soprano), English lady (soprano), Russian mother (soprano), Russian father (bass), Two offstage voices at the beach (soprano, alto), Beggar woman (contralto), Restaurant waiter (bass), Three gondoliers (2 tenor, 1 bass), Guide (bass), Newspaper seller (soprano), Priest in St. Mark's (bass). **Mute:** Beggar woman's child. **Dancers:** Polish mother, Tadzio, Two daughters, Governess, Jaschiu, boys, girls, strolling players, beach attendants.

Chorus parts: SATB. **Chorus roles:** Youths and girls, hotel guests and waiters, gondoliers and boatmen, street vendors, beggars, citizens of Venice, choir in St. Mark's, tourists, followers of Dionysus. **Dance/movement:** I: Sports competition of Tadzio and his friends. II: Acrobats perform a pantomime for hotel guests. **Orchestra:** 2 fl (2 picc), 2 ob, 2 cl (bs cl), 2 bsn, 2 hrn, 2 trp, 2 trb, tuba, harp, piano, timp, 5 perc, strings (min. 6-4-3-3-2). **Stageband:** II: Players' fl, guitar, trp are mimed onstage and played from pit. **Publisher:** Faber Music Ltd. **Rights:** Copyright 1973, 1974, 1975 by Faber Music Limited.

Ii. Aschenbach, a famous novelist, is world-weary. A traveler convinces him to go south. Iii. He takes a boat to Venice. Iiii. The gondolier insists on taking Aschenbach to the Lido and the novelist acquiesces. Iiv. He is greeted by the hotel manager, watches the hotel guests go into dinner and marvels at the beauty of the boy Tadzio. Iv. He sees Tadzio again on the beach. Ivi. Overpowered by the sights and smells of Venice, Aschenbach decides to return home. Seeing Tadzio changes his mind. Ivii. Tadzio competes with his friends at sports and wins every time. Aschenbach realizes he is in love with the boy.

IIi. Aschenbach is afraid to introduce himself to Tadzio. While Aschenbach is having his hair cut, the barber makes a fleeting reference to a sickness that is driving people away. IIii. Aschenbach hears rumors of plague. He follows Tadzio's family around. IIiii. The hotel guests watch a pantomime. Aschenbach asks the leader of the players if there is plague in Venice, but is laughed off. IIiv. The tourists flee Venice and the plague. Aschenbach consults with an English clerk who says the authorities do not want to admit the existence of the plague because it will ruin business. IIv. Aschenbach decides to warn Tadzio's mother, but cannot bring himself do it. IIvi. In his dream, Dionysus and Apollo argue. IIvii. Aschenbach decides to stay. IIviii. The barber spruces up Aschenbach's appearance. IIix. Aschenbach eats a tainted strawberry. IIx. Tadzio's family is leaving. He beckons to Aschenbach, but the writer is dying.

Dèbora e Jaéle • Dèbora and Jaéle

Composed by Ildebrando Pizzetti (September 20, 1880 – February 13, 1968). Libretto by Ildebrando Pizzetti. Italian. Based on the Biblical Book of Judges. Premiered Milan, Teatro alla Scala, December 16, 1922. Set in Israel in Biblical times. Tragedy. Through composed. Prelude before I, III.

Sets: 3. **Acts:** 3 acts, 3 scenes. **Length:** I, II, III: 165. **Hazards:** III: Jaéle drives a stake through Sìsera's head. **Scenes:** I. The great square in the city of Kèdesh. II. A terrace in the palace of King Sìsera in Haròscet. III. An open grassy space in the forest of Saananim.

Major roles: Jaéle (dramatic soprano), Dèbora (mezzo), King Sìsera (tenor). **Minor roles:** Blind man of Kinnèreth (bass), Scillèm (tenor), Mara (mezzo), Azriél (tenor), Nabì (baritone), Hèver (bass), Jèsser (baritone), Baràk (bass), Jafía (tenor), Piràm (baritone), Talmài (bass), Adonisèdek (baritone). **Bit parts:** Shepherd (baritone), Three crowd members (tenor, baritone, bass), Slave (tenor), Israelite (baritone).

Chorus parts: SSAATTBaBaBB (briefly TTT). **Chorus roles:** Old men, officers, guards, Israelites. **Dance/movement:** None. **Orchestra:** 3 fl (picc), 2 ob, Eng hrn, 3 cl (bs cl), 3 bsn, 4 hrn, 3 trp, 3 trb, tuba, timp, perc, celeste, 2 harp, strings. **Stageband:** I, II: 4 trp. **Publisher:** G. Ricordi. **Rights:** Copyright 1922 by G. Ricordi & Co.

I. King Sìsera has defeated the Jews, who now appeal to their prophetess, Dèbora, for advice. The people revile Jaéle, who is suspected of having been Sìsera's mistress. Dèbora protects Sìsera and tells the leader of the Jewish army, Baràk, to lead the army up Mount Tabor, promising victory to the army.

II. Jaéle's husband, Hèver, offers to spy for Sìsera, but the honorable king refuses. He receives Jaéle, who apologizes for scorning his previous advances and tells him the Jewish army is small and weak. Sìsera learns that this is not the case, but disdains to punish Jaéle. He releases her.

III. The Jewish army has been victorious and Sìsera flees to Jaéle's tent. Rather than let him be captured by his enemies, Jaéle slays Sìsera by driving a stake through his head while he is sleeping.

Le Dernier Sauvage • The Last Savage

Composed by Gian Carlo Menotti (b. July 7, 1911). Libretto by Gian Carlo Menotti. French (original libretto Italian). Original work. Premiered Paris, Opéra Comique, October 21, 1963. Set in India and Chicago in the mid-20th century. Comedy. Set numbers with recitative. Prelude. Interlude before Iii. Often performed in Italian or English.

Sets: 6. **Acts:** 3 acts, 6 scenes. **Hazards:** None. **Scenes:** Ii. A room in the palace of the Maharajah. Iii. The great court of the palace. IIi. Kitty's boudoir in Scattergood's penthouse in Chicago. IIii. The garden of the Maharajah's palace. IIiii. A large living room in Scattergood's penthouse. III. The remotest depths of the Indian jungle.

Major roles: Maharajah of Rajaputana (bass), Mr. Scattergood (bass baritone), Maharanee of Rajaputana (contralto), Prince Kodanda (tenor), Kitty (soprano), Sardula (soprano), Abdul (baritone). **Minor roles:** Two Indian scholars (tenor, baritone), Two American tailors (tenor, baritone), English tailor (tenor), Catholic priest (bass), Black Protestant minister (baritone), Rabbi (tenor), Orthodox priest (tenor), Philosopher (baritone), Physician (baritone), Painter (tenor), Poet (tenor), Composer (baritone), Concert singer (soprano), Scientist (tenor), Society woman (contralto), Business woman (soprano). **Mute:** Major Domo.

Chorus parts: SSAATTBB. **Chorus roles:** Hunters, Indian princes, ladies-in-waiting, palace attendants, journalists, military and civilian authorities, politicians, society women, debutantes, guests, soldiers, servants. **Dance/movement:** None. **Orchestra:** 3 fl (picc), 2 ob, 3 cl (bs cl), 3 bsn (cont bsn), 4 hrn, 3 trp, 3 trb, tuba, timp, perc, piano, 2 harp, strings. **Stageband:** I: hrn, trp. II: vln, vla, vlc. **Publisher:** Belwin Mills. **Rights:** Copyright 1963, 1973 by Belwin Mills Publishing Corp.

Ii. The maharaja and Mr. Scattergood compare assets and decide that a marriage between their children would be acceptable. Of the maharajah's 27 wives, only one has borne him a child, a blond, blue-eyed son, Kodanda. Kodanda is as reluctant to marry Scattergood's daughter Kitty as she is to marry him. Kitty is looking for the last primitive caveman as part of her Ph.D. work. Kodanda insists that Kitty give up her quests, while Kitty insists she be allowed to continue. The parents pay Abdul to pose as Kitty's caveman. The maharanee thinks she has met Scattergood before. Iii. Kodanda loves the serving girl Sardula, but she is engaged to Abdul. Kitty captures Abdul. She wins a delay of her marriage while she takes Abdul to the States for study. Abdul does not want to be away from Sardula, but she reminds him of the money.

IIi. Kitty arranges a party to introduce Abdul. Three tailors take his measurements. She teaches him "the art of love." IIii. Kodanda believes that Sardula is beginning to love him. IIiii. Scattergood secretly arranges with Abdul for his return to India. At Kitty's party, Abdul is introduced to politicians, professionals and clergy. Disgusted by society, he leaves.

III. Abdul has retreated to the jungle, but cannot stop thinking of Kitty. Kitty, the maharajah, Scattergood et al. come searching for Abdul. Kodanda proposes to Sardula—who accepts. The maharanee finally recognizes Scattergood: they had an affair years ago in Egypt. Kodanda is really Scattergood's son—and Kitty's brother. Abdul is located but refuses Scattergood's money. With the help of the maharanee and Scattergood, Kitty becomes engaged to Abdul and Kodanda to Sardula. Kitty agrees to stay in the jungle with Abdul. Privately, she assures her father that she will bring Abdul around to a less primitive existence.

The Desert Song

Composed by Sigmund Romberg (July 29, 1887 – November 9, 1951). Libretto by Otto Harbach, Oscar Hammerstein II and Frank Mandel. English. Original work. Premiered New York City, Casino Theater, November 30, 1926. Set in North Africa in 1925. Musical comedy. Set numbers with spoken dialogue. Prelude. Entr'acte before II.

Sets: 8. **Acts:** 2 acts, 8 scenes. **Length:** I, II: 90. **Arias:** Sabre song (Margot). **Hazards:** None. **Scenes:** Ii. Retreat of the Red Shadow in the Riff mountains. Iii. Outside General Birabeau's house. Iiii. A room in General Birabeau's house. IIi. The harem of Ali Ben Ali. IIii. A corridor outside Margot's suite. IIiii. The room of the silken couch in Ali's palace. IIiv. The edge of the desert. IIv. The courtyard of General Birabeau's house.

Major roles: Sid El Kar (tenor), Pierre Birabeau/The Red Shadow (baritone), Captain Paul Fontaine (baritone), Susan (soprano), Margot Bonvalet (soprano). **Minor roles:** Mindar (bass or speaking), Ali Ben Ali (bass), Clementina (mezzo). **Bit parts:** Lieutenant La Vergne (any voice), Sergeant De Boussac (baritone), Edith (soprano), First girl (soprano). **Speaking:** Hadji, Hassi, Neri, Benjamin Kidd, Sentinel, Azuri, General Birabeau, Soldier, Guard, Riff.

Chorus parts: SSAATTBB. **Chorus roles:** French girls, Spanish cabaret girls, soldiers wives, native dancers, servants of General Birabeau, soldiers of the French Legion, members of the Red Shadow's band, soldiers of Ali. **Dance/movement:** I: Dancing at General Birabeau's party. II: Spanish dance. **Orchestra:** fl, ob, cl, bsn, 2 hrn, 2 trp, trb, harp, perc (timp), strings. **Stageband:** I: bugle. **Publisher:** Harms, Inc. **Rights:** Copyright 1927 by Malem Corp. Renewed 1954, 1959 by Harbach, Hammerstein and Mandel.

Ii. Paul Fontaine, a captain in the French Foreign Legion in Morocco, is unable to capture the Red Shadow, a popular bandit. Only two of the Red Shadow's trusted henchmen know that he is really Pierre Birabeau, a Frenchman—and the son of Governor General Birabeau. Pierre became the Red Shadow in reaction to the cruelty of the previous governor, Paul's father, and is in love with Paul's fiancée, Margot. Pierre's men capture Bennie Kidd, a British society reporter turned war correspondent, and release him on condition that he join their band. Paul discovers the Shadow's hideout and sets an ambush. Azuri, a Moroccan girl, is angry that Paul has thrown her over for Margot. Iii. Bennie's secretary, Susan, who is in love with him, welcomes him back. Iiii. Margot throws a party at which she admits to Birabeau that she is disappointed in the unromantic Paul. Evading Paul, Pierre slips into the party. To maintain his disguise, Pierre has adopted a wimpy persona with whom Margot is unimpressed. Only when he returns as the Red Shadow—and kisses her—does Pierre get her attention. Margot reports his appearance to Paul who gives chase. The Red Shadow again appears to Margot, who pulls a gun on him, but cannot bring herself to shoot.

IIi. Kidnaping Margot and Susan, Pierre seeks refuge with his old friend Ali Ben Ali. Margot is furious. After a run-in with one of Ali's harem girls, Bennie dresses as a woman to get away. Pierre's men try to convince him that kidnapping Margot was foolish. IIii. Bennie is discovered before he can escape and he and Susan are put out in the desert to die. IIiii. Margot tells the Red Shadow she loves Pierre, but when Pierre visits her, she says she loves the Shadow. Azuri produces Birabeau, who challenges Pierre to a fight. Pierre refuses. IIiv. Pierre's dishonor dissolves his followers' oaths and they regretfully expose him in the desert. IIv. Birabeau returns home with Margot and orders Paul to kill the Red Shadow. Susan and Bennie return unharmed—and in love. Azuri claims her reward and admits that the Shadow is Birabeau's son Pierre. Birabeau is horrified. Paul returns with Pierre, who claims to have killed the Shadow. In private, father and son make up. Margot is heartbroken until Pierre changes back into his Shadow disguise. The lovers fall into each others' arms.

Osud • Destiny

Composed by Leoš Janáček (July 3, 1854 – August 12, 1928). Libretto by Leoš Janáček and Fedora Bartošová. Czech. Based on historical incident with autobiographical aspects. Premiered Brno, Brno Theater, October 25, 1958. Set in Moravia in the late 19th century. Tragedy. Through composed. Brief introduction. Radio premiere Brno Radio, September 18, 1934.

Sets: 3. **Acts:** 3 acts, 3 scenes. **Length:** I: 30. II: 15. III: 30. **Arias:** "From a clear sky" (Živný). **Hazards:** II: Míla and her mother falling off a balcony. **Scenes:** I. The spa of Luhačovice, Moravia. II. Živný's study, four years later. III. The great hall of the conservatory, fourteen years later.

Major roles: Míla Válková (soprano), Živný the composer (tenor), Míla's mother (contralto). **Minor roles:** Poet/Student/Conservatory student Hrazda (tenor), Dr. Suda (tenor), Lhotský (bass), Konečný (baritone), Child Doubek (treble), Adult Doubek (tenor), Conservatory student Verva (baritone), Conservatory student Součková (soprano), Miss Stuhlá (soprano), Conservatory student Kosinská (contralto). **Bit parts:** First lady (soprano), Second lady (soprano), Old Slovak woman (contralto), Major's wife (soprano), Councillor's wife (contralto), Miss Pacovská/

Fanča (soprano), First guest (tenor), Second guest (baritone), Waiter (tenor), Engineer (tenor), Young widow (contralto), First gentleman (baritone), Second gentleman (baritone). **Mute:** Žán, Nána.

Chorus parts: SATB. **Chorus roles:** School mistresses, students, school-girls, guests at the spa, conservatory students. **Dance/movement:** III: Dance of the female students. **Orchestra:** picc, 2 fl, 2 ob, Eng hrn, 2 cl, bs cl, 2 bsn, cont bsn, 4 hrn, 3 trp, 3 trb, tuba, perc, timp, harp, piano, organ, strings. **Stageband:** I: band. **Publisher:** Dilia. **Rights:** Copyright 1958 by Dilia, Praha.

I. The inhabitants of the spa bask in the sunshine. Lhotský´, Konečný and Dr. Suda flatter Míla. They are approached by the composer Živný who has just finished a revenge opera about unrequited love. When Živný and Míla trade veiled barbs, the others discreetly withdraw. Míla asks if Živný has come to claim his child. Yes, and his mother too, Živný answers. Miss Stuhlá collects her choir together for rehearsal. Miss Pacovská and the students persuade Dr. Suda to accompany them on their excursion. Suda, Lhotský and the students make fun of Miss Stuhlá's choir. Míla's mother is looking for her. Míla and Živný return after everyone else has gone, sit down in the restaurant and talk of their past love. Živný remembers how Míla's mother objected to him. "She forced us apart," Míla says, "but I still loved you." The lovers realize it is best to stay and face the others when they return.

II. Živný and Míla are now married. He wonders if he should premiere his revenge opera—to exorcise its power to hurt his wife Míla. He begins to play from the score, but Míla's mother can be heard in the background, mockingly repeating Živný's words. The composer remembers his pain at Míla's betrayal. Their four-year-old son, Doubek, tells his mother she does not know love because she does not behave "like John and the nanny." Realizing that her mother has been left unattended, Míla runs off in search of her. The mother appears, clutching her jewel box and ranting about disinheriting them. There is a struggle in which mother and daughter fall off the balcony and are killed.

III. Verva, Hrazda, Součková and the students play through Živný´'s latest opera only to discover it has no ending. They are talking about the premiere and the work's autobiographical flavor when Živný arrives. In talking about the opera, Živný is reminded of his misfortunes. A storm is brewing outside and Živný tells how he sees his dead wife's face in the storm. He faints. The concerned students send for a doctor. Verva wonders about the music for the final scene, but Živný says he intends to leave the opera unfinished.

The Devil and Daniel Webster

Composed by Douglas Moore (August 10, 1893 – July 25, 1969). Libretto by Douglas Moore. English. Based on a story by Stephen Vincent Benét. Premiered New York City, Martin Beck Theater, May 18, 1939. Set in New Hampshire in the 1840s. Folk opera. Set numbers with dialogue.

Sets: 1. **Acts:** 1 act, 1 scene. **Length:** I: 55. **Hazards:** I: White moth flies out of Scratch's box. Ghostly jury appears. **Scenes:** I. Home of Jabez Stone, Cross Corners, New Hampshire.

Major roles: Jabez Stone (bass), Mary Stone (mezzo or soprano), Daniel Webster (baritone), Mr. Scratch (tenor). **Minor roles:** Voice of Miser Stevens (tenor), Clerk (baritone). **Bit parts:** Two women (sopranos), Two men (baritones), Old man (tenor), Old woman (mezzo), Third woman (soprano), Third man (baritone), Simon Girty (tenor), King Philip (bass), Blackbeard Teach (baritone). **Speaking:** Fiddler. **Speaking bit:** Fourth man, Justice Hathorne, Walter Butler.

Chorus parts: SATTBB. **Chorus roles:** Jurors, men and women of Cross Corners. **Dance/movement:** I: Square dance at the wedding. **Orchestra:** Full: 2 fl (picc), 2 ob (Eng hrn), 2 cl (bs cl), 2 bsn (cont bsn), 2 hrn, 2 trp, trb, timp, perc, harp, strings. Reduced: fl, ob, cl, bsn, hrn, trp, trb, perc, piano, strings. **Stageband:** None. **Publisher:** Boosey & Hawkes. **Rights:** Copyright 1943 by Boosey & Hawkes.

I. Jabez and Mary Stone celebrate their wedding and are toasted by Daniel Webster. The devil appears in the form of Mr. Scratch, a Boston lawyer, who plays the violin and frightens the guests. He carries a box out of which escapes a white moth—the soul of Miser Stevens, one of Scratch's victims. Jabez now confesses that he owes his prosperity to the devil. Webster agrees to get Jabez out of his unusual "mortgage." He argues with Scratch and demands a trial. Scratch produces a jury of twelve dead scoundrels, but Webster's eloquence wins them over. Jabez's neighbors drive the devil out of New Hampshire.

Čert a Káča • The Devil and Kate

Composed by Antonín Dvořák (September 8, 1841 – May 1, 1904). Libretto by Adolf Wenig. Czech. Based on the fairy tales of Božena Němcová. Premiered Prague, National Theater, November 23, 1899. Set in a Czech village in legendary times. Comedy. Through composed. Overture. Entr'acte before II and III. Opus 112.

Sets: 3. **Acts:** 3 acts, 3 scenes. **Length:** I: 55. II: 30. III: 30. **Arias:** "I, an unhappy shepherd" (Jirka), "It is a little far" (Marbuel), "How sad it is in the castle" (Princess). **Hazards:** I: Marbuel and Káča disappear to hell. **Scenes:** I. Hall in a village inn. II. A gloomy hall in hell. III. A hall in the princess's castle.

Major roles: Jirka (tenor), Káča (mezzo), Devil Marbuel (bass). **Minor roles:** Káča's mother (mezzo), Lucifer (bass), Infernal porter (bass or baritone), Infernal Court Marshall (bass or baritone), Princess (soprano), Chamber maid (soprano). **Bit part:** Musician (tenor or baritone).

Chorus parts: SATTBB. **Chorus roles:** Villagers, devils, courtiers, musicians. **Dance/movement:** I: Villagers waltz. Káča dances with Marbuel. II: Devils' ballet and Káča dances with Jirka. **Orchestra:** picc, 2 fl, 2 ob, Eng hrn, 2 cl, bs cl, 2 bsn, cont bsn, 4 hrn, 3 trp, 3 trb, tuba, timp, perc, harp, strings. **Stageband:** None. **Publisher:** Národní Hudební Vydavatelství. **Rights:** Expired.

I. During a peasant holiday, the shepherd Jirka takes leave of his friends to return to work. The villagers curse their heartless princess and her bailiff. No one will dance with Káča because she talks too much; she swears she would dance with the devil. The Devil Marbuel appears and, after inquiring about the bailiff and his princess, dances with Káča and asks her to run away with him. She agrees and they disappear in a cloud of smoke. The villagers realize Marbuel was a devil and Jirka—who has been fired by the bailiff—agrees to rescue Káča.

II. In hell, a chorus of devils carouses. They wake up Lucifer who bawls them out and asks if Marbuel has returned after being sent for the bailiff and the princess. He returns instead with Káča, who is furious at having been tricked. She grabs Marbuel by the neck and does not let go until they bribe her with a gold necklace. Jirka comes to fetch her. Marbuel now reports on the princess and the bailiff. Lucifer condemns the princess, but decides to let the bailiff off with a warning. He tells Marbuel to carry the hefty Káča home. Exhausted, Marbuel cuts a deal with Jirka: If Jirka can get rid of Káča for him, Marbuel will tell the bailiff he must follow him to hell. Jirka can then intervene and "save" the bailiff, who will henceforth be in his debt. He warns Jirka not to try and save the princess. At Jirka's orders, the devils feed Káča and give her gold. Jirka then dances her back out of hell.

III. Marbuel's plan has worked and the princess sadly awaits her fate. She asks Jirka to save her, which he agrees to do when she frees the serfs. Jirka brings in Káča, who is burning for revenge since Marbuel's gold necklace has turned to leaves. When Marbuel comes for the princess, Jirka warns him that Káča is coming to get him. Marbuel flees. The princess rewards Jirka and Káča.

The Devil Take Her

Composed by Arthur Benjamin (September 18, 1893 – April 10, 1960). Libretto by Alan Collard and John B. Gordon. English. Original work. Premiered London, Royal College of Music, December 1, 1931. Set in London in the 15th century. Comedy. Through composed. Prologue spoken over overture.

Sets: 1. **Acts:** 1 act, 2 scenes. **Length:** I: 45. **Hazards:** None. **Scenes:** I. The living room of the poet in London, which opens onto the street.

Major roles: Poet (tenor), Wife (mezzo), Doctor/Devil (bass). **Minor roles:** Watchman (baritone), Neighbor (baritone), Maid (soprano), Doctor's first attendant (bass), Doctor's second attendant (soprano), First woman (soprano), Second woman (mezzo), Third woman (contralto). **Bit parts:** Orange seller (contralto), Sweep (baritone), Blind beggar (baritone). **Mute:** Bird seller.

Chorus parts: N/A. **Chorus roles:** None. **Dance/movement:** None. **Orchestra:** 2 fl, 2 ob, 2 cl, 2 bsn, 4 hrn, 2 trp, 3 trb, tuba, timp, perc, piano, strings. **Stageband:** None. **Publisher:** Boosey & Hawkes. **Rights:** Copyright 1932 by Boosey & Co. Ltd.

Ii. A poet draws inspiration from his mute wife, but longs to hear her speak. Iii. He completes a song commissioned by his neighbor. The neighbor tells the poet about a doctor who can cure muteness. The poet's wife is cured and, with her newfound voice, tells her husband how boring his poetry is, attacks the crowd that has gathered to hear her speak—and fires the maid. The poet calls on the devil to carry his wife away, but the devil refuses. The poet leaves with the devil. Alone, the wife tells the audience the moral: better for a wife to be silent than to scold.

Dialogues des Carmélites • Dialogues of the Carmelites

Composed by Francis Poulenc (January 7, 1899 – January 30, 1963). Libretto by Francis Poulenc. French. Based on the play by Georges Bernanos (itself based on the novel of Gertrude von le Fort) and scenario of Father Bruckberger and Philippe Agostini. Premiered Milan, Teatro alla Scala, January 26, 1957. Set in France from 1789 through 1794. Lyric tragedy. Through composed. Interludes before Iiii, Iiiii, IIIii, IIIiii, IIIiv.

Sets: 9. **Acts:** 3 acts, 12 scenes. **Length:** I: 55. II: 45. III: 45. **Hazards:** Chorus of nuns beheaded. **Scenes:** Ii. The library of the Marquis de la

Force. Iii. The parlor of the Carmelite convent. Iiii. The workroom of the convent. Iiv. The infirmary. IIi. The chapel. IIii. The chapter room. IIiii. The parlor. IIiv. The sacristy. IIIi. The chapel. IIIii. The library of the Marquis de la Force. IIIiii. The conciergerie. IIIiv. Place de la Révolution.

Major roles: Blanche de la Force (lyric soprano), Chevalier de la Force (tenor), Madame de Croissy the prioress (contralto), Madame Lidoine the new prioress (soprano), Mother Marie of the Incarnation (mezzo), Sister Constance of St. Denis (light soprano). **Minor roles:** Marquis de la Force (baritone), Mother Jeanne of the Child Jesus (contralto), Sister Mathilde (mezzo), Father Confessor (tenor), First officer (tenor), Second officer (baritone), Jailer (baritone). **Bit parts:** Thierry (baritone), Javelinot (baritone). **Speaking:** Two old women, old man.

Chorus parts: SSAATTBB + Carmelites (SMC). **Chorus roles:** Nuns (Mother Gerald, Sisters Claire, Antoine, Catherine, Felicity, Gertrude, Alice, Valentine, Anne of the Cross, Martha, St. Charles), officials of the municipality, officers, policemen, prisoners, guards, townsfolk. **Dance/movement:** None. **Orchestra:** picc, 2 fl, 2 ob, Eng hrn, 2 cl, bs cl, 2 bsn, cont bsn, 4 hrn, 3 trp, 3 trb, tuba, timp, 2 harp, perc, piano, celeste, xylophone, strings. (Many string subdivisions and string solos.) **Stageband:** I, II, III: bells. **Publisher:** G. Ricordi & Co. **Rights:** Copyright 1957 by G. Ricordi & Co.

Ii. The chevalier bursts in on his father (the marquis) to report that his sister, Blanche, is in danger, her carriage surrounded by screaming peasants. The Marquis assures him the carriage has weathered worse and discounts the possibility of a revolution. Blanche returns intact, but is terrified by the shadow of their valet, Thierry. Seeking escape from her fears, Blanche asks her father's permission to become a nun. Iii. Blanche is interviewed by Madame de Croissy, the prioress of the Carmelite convent. Iiii. Sister Constance chatters over her ironing until Blanche reminds her that the prioress lies dying. Constance has a premonition that she and Blanche will die young—and on the same day. Her buoyant good spirits grate on Blanche. Iiv. Mother Marie attends the prioress in the infirmary. The prioress worries about Blanche and commends her to Marie's protection. When Blanche arrives, the prioress blesses her and tells her to face her trials with courage. She becomes delirious, imagining the convent in ruins, the flagstones covered with blood. She dies.

IIi. Sister Constance and Blanche are in the chapel, praying and watching the body. When Constance goes to find their replacements, Blanche is afraid and leaves. Mother Marie forgives her. Interlude. Constance does not think the prioress's death was fitting. IIii. Madame Lidoine, the new prioress, warns her charges that the future will be difficult. Interlude. The chevalier visits his sister. IIiii. He tries, unsuccessfully, to persuade her to fly the country with him. Blanche wonders that everyone treats her like a child. IIiv. The father confessor comes to the convent to offer a prayer before he goes into hiding. The police enter the convent and read the declaration of expulsion. The first commissioner (who used to be a sacristan) agrees to dismiss the patrol for the rest of the day. The prioress leaves for Paris.

IIIi. In the prioress's absence, Mother Marie proposes the sisters take a vow of martyrdom. A secret ballot reveals only one sister in opposition. Constance admits she voted against the vow, but has now changed her mind. The father confessor administers the vow. Interlude. On being warned that the state will be watching the sisters closely, the prioress decides against having the father confessor say mass. IIIii. Blanche has returned to her father's house after his execution. When Blanche laments her own cowardice, Mother Marie tells her where to go to be safe. Interlude. Blanche hears of the arrest of the Carmelites on the streets of Paris. IIIiii. In jail, the prioress joins her convent in the vow of martyrdom. They all wonder where Blanche is, but Constance is convinced she will return. The jailer reads out the sisters' sentence of death. Interlude. The father confessor relays the news to Mother Marie who feels guilty at going free. IIIiv. Blanche joins the sisters at the guillotine.

Dido and Æneas

Composed by Henry Purcell (c. 1659 – November 21, 1695). Libretto by Nahum Tate. English. Based on the Aeneid of Virgil. Premiered London, Josias Priest's School for Young Gentlewomen, December 1689. Set in Carthage after the Trojan War. Tragedy. Set numbers with recitative. Overture. Only extant manuscripts post-date the premiere by a century. Music for the prologue and the last six lines of act II are missing.

Sets: 4. **Acts:** 3 acts, 4 scenes. **Length:** Prologue, I: 15. II: 20. III: 20. **Arias:** "When I am laid in earth" (Dido). **Hazards:** Prologue opens at sea. **Scenes:** Prologue. Over the sea. I. The palace. II. The cave. III. The ships.

Major roles: Belinda (soprano), Dido/Elissa (soprano), Æneas/Phœbus (tenor or high baritone), Sorceress/Spring (mezzo). **Minor roles:** Second woman/Venus (mezzo), First witch/First woman (soprano), Second witch (soprano). **Bit parts:** Sailor (tenor).

Chorus parts: SSAATTBB. **Chorus roles:** Courtiers, witches, spirits, sailors. **Dance/movement:** Prologue: Dance of the Tritons, nymphs and shepherds. I: Dance of Dido's attendants. II: Dance of sailors, enchantresses and fairies. Dance of Dido's attendants to entertain Æneas. III: Dance of sailors and enchantresses. Dance of Cupid.

Orchestra: guitars, strings, continuo (harpsichord, cembalo or piano with single cello). **Stageband:** None. **Publisher:** Oxford University Press, Novello. **Rights:** Expired.

Prologue. Shepherds, shepherdesses and nymphs hail love and celebrate spring.

I. Dido's confidante, Belinda, and her ladies-in-waiting assure her that her love for Æneas is reciprocated.

II. A sorceress, jealous of Dido, plans to trick Æneas into deserting his love. The sorceress conjures up a storm. Appearing to Æneas in the likeness of Mercury, she orders him to sail for Italy. III. Watching Æneas's ships preparing to depart, the sorceress and her minions dance in triumph. Æneas offers to stay, but Dido sends him away and gives herself up to death.

Le Docteur Miracle • Doctor Miracle

Composed by Georges Bizet (October 25, 1838 – June 3, 1875). Libretto by Léon Battu and Ludovic Halévy. French. Original work. Premiered Paris, Théâtre des Bouffes Parisiens, April 9, 1857. Set in Padua in the 19th century. Operetta. Set numbers with spoken dialogue. Overture.

Sets: 1. **Acts:** 1 act, 1 scene. **Length:** I: 60. **Hazards:** None. **Scenes:** I. The mayor's house.

Major roles: Lauretta (soprano), Mayor (baritone), Véronique (soprano), Captain Silvio/Pasquin/Dr. Miracle (tenor).

Chorus parts: N/A. **Chorus roles:** None. **Dance/movement:** None. **Orchestra:** 2 fl (picc), ob, 2 cl, bsn, 3 hrn, 2 trp, trb, timp, perc, strings. **Stageband:** I: cl, trb, perc. **Publisher:** Editions Françaises de Musique. N/A. **Rights:** Expired.

I. The mayor of Padua, his wife, Véronique, and his daughter, Lauretta, are awakened by a racket in the square. The mayor thinks it is Lauretta's objectionable suitor, Captain Silvio, but he is deceived by Silvio's disguise as Dr. Miracle. The mayor hires a new servant, Pasquin, who is really Silvio in another disguise. Pasquin serves up a horrible omelette for the mayor's breakfast. Alone with Lauretta, Silvio removes his disguise. The mayor catches them and expels Silvio. Silvio now reveals that the omelette was poisoned and the horrified mayor calls in Dr. Miracle. The doctor promises to save the mayor if he can marry Lauretta. After the mayor consents, Silvio reveals there was no poison.

Doktor Faust • Doctor Faust

Composed by Ferruccio Busoni (April 1, 1866 – July 27, 1924). Libretto by Ferruccio Busoni. German. Based on "Doctor Faustus" by Marlowe. Premiered Dresden, Sächsisches Staatstheater, May 21, 1925. Set in Wittenberg, Parma and Münster in the 16th century. Poem for music. Through composed. Overture. Six scenes: two prologues (first half), one intermezzo and three scenes (second half).

Sets: 5. **Acts:** 1 act, 6 scenes. **Length:** I: 155. **Arias:** "Traum der Jugend" (Faust). **Hazards:** Second prologue: pale green light and six tongues of flame that float about the room. A raven flies into Faust's room with a pen in its beak. i: Faust makes a swarm of fawnlike devils appear; day is changed to night. King Solomon, the Queen of Sheba, Samson and Dalila are conjured up. Mephistopheles' hand appears as a claw. ii: Duchess's dead baby turns into a straw doll. Helen of Troy appears. Three students disappear. iii: Duchess and soldier vanish. Crucifix is transformed into Helen. **Scenes:** Prologue i – ii. Faust's study in Wittenberg. Intermezzo. An ancient Romanesque chapel in Münster. i. The ducal park at Parma. ii. A tavern in Wittenberg. iii. A street in Wittenberg.

Major roles: Faust (baritone), Dark spirit / Herald / Chaplain / Courier / Night watchman / Mephistopheles (tenor), Duchess of Parma (soprano). **Minor roles:** Wagner (baritone), Three students from Kracow (1 tenor, 2 bass), Soldier (baritone), Lieutenant (tenor), Master of ceremonies (bass), Duke of Parma (tenor), Five Wittenberg students (4 tenor, 1 baritone), Student of the natural sciences (baritone). **Bit parts:** Voice of the spirit Gravis (bass), Voice of the spirit Levis (bass), Voice of the spirit Asmodus (baritone), Voice of the spirit Beelzebuth (tenor), Voice of the spirit Megäros (tenor), Three voices (soprano, mezzo, contralto), Theologian (bass), Jurist (bass), Shy person (bass). **Mute:** King Solomon, Queen of Sheba, Samson, Dalila, John the Baptist and his executioner, Salome, Helen of Troy.

Chorus parts: SSAATTTBBB. **Chorus roles:** Churchgoers, soldiers, courtiers, hunters, farmers, Catholic and Lutheran students, peasants. **Dance/movement:** I: Courtly dances. **Orchestra:** picc, 2 fl, 2 ob (Eng hrn), 2 cl, bs cl, 3 bsn (cont bsn), 5 hrn, 3 trp, 3 trb, tuba, timp, perc, 2 harp, celeste, organ, strings. **Stageband:** Prologue: hrn, bells. Intermezzo: drums and trps. i: harp, hrn, 3 trp. **Publisher:** Breitkopf & Härtel. **Rights:** Copyright 1926 by Breitkopf & Härtel.

First prologue. Faust is working on alchemical experiments when Wagner brings in three students from Krakow who give Faust an important book on magic. After they depart, Faust asks Wagner about the students, but he denies having seen them. Second prologue. Faust uses the book to call evil spirits to serve him. Mephistopheles agrees to do so in exchange for Faust's soul, but Faust refuses. The devil points out that Faust is plagued by creditors and after he kills a few for him, Faust signs the devil's contract. Intermezzo. Faust has dishonored a soldier's sister and the soldier seeks revenge. Mephistopheles offers to kill the soldier, but Faust insists he do it indirectly. Disguised as a friar, Mephistopheles warns the soldier to confess. A lieutenant and his patrol kill the soldier.

i. Faust is presented to the Duke and Duchess of Parma as a learned magician. He conjures up various historical personages and seduces the duchess. She runs off with him, and Mephistopheles, disguised as the court chaplain, persuades the duke to let her go. ii. Faust drinks and philosophizes with a group of students. Mephistopheles reports that the duchess is dead and brings Faust the body of their dead child. When they investigate further, the baby turns into straw. Mephistopheles conjures up Helen of Troy, but she vanishes when Faust tries to touch her. The three students tell Faust his time is up, but he makes them disappear. iii. Wagner has taken Faust's university position and his house. Faust despairs. He sees the duchess who gives him his dead child. He tries to pray, but Mephistopheles blocks his entrance into the church. Faust uses his magic to give his own life force to the child.

Dom Sébastien

Composed by Gaetano Donizetti (November 29, 1797 – April 8, 1848). Libretto by Eugène Scribe. French. Based on "Dom Sébastien de Portugal" by Paul-Henri Foucher. Premiered Paris, Opéra, November 13, 1843. Set in Portugal and Fez in 1578. Grand opera. Set numbers with recitative. Ballet. Prelude before each act. Revised several times by the composer.

Sets: 7. **Acts:** 5 acts, 7 scenes. **Length:** I, II, III, IV, V: 150. **Arias:** "Seul sur la terre" (Sébastien), "O Lisbonne" (Camoëns). **Hazards:** None. **Scenes:** I. The port of Lisbon near the royal palace. IIi. The house of Ben-Selim in Fez. IIii. The field of Alcazar Kebir after the battle. IIIi. A room in the royal palace in Lisbon. IIIii. The great square in Lisbon. IV. The hall of the high tribunal. V. Apartment in the tower of Lisbon.

Major roles: Camoëns (baritone), Dom Sébastien (tenor), Zaïda (mezzo). **Minor roles:** Dom Antonio (tenor), Dom Juan de Sylva the grand inquisitor (bass), Ben Selim (bass), Abayaldos (baritone), Dom Henrique (bass), Don Luigi (tenor). **Bit parts:** Three inquisitors (2 tenor, bass).

Chorus parts: SATTB. **Chorus roles:** Courtiers, soldiers and sailors of Portugal, Arab soldiers and women, judges of the supreme court, members of the inquisition, people. **Dance/movement:** II: Ballet of Ben Selim's servants dancing for Zaïda. **Orchestra:** 2 fl (picc), 2 ob, 2 cl, 2 bsn, 4 hrn, 4 trp, 3 trb, ophicléide, timp, perc, strings. **Stageband:** I: 3 trp, drums. III: 2 trp, drums, bells. V: 2 hrn, 2 bsn, harp. **Publisher:** Bureau Central de Musique, Garland Publishing. **Rights:** Expired.

I. King Sébastien of Portugal leaves his uncle, Dom Antonio, as regent while he leads an expedition to Africa. Antonio allies himself with Dom Juan, the grand inquisitor. The poet Camoëns asks to accompany Sébastien. At Camoëns's urging, Sébastien frees the condemned African princess Zaïda.

IIi. Zaïda returns to Africa. She has fallen in love with Sébastien. Her father, Ben Selim, tries to comfort her. The warrior chieftain Abayaldos hopes to win Zaïda's love by defeating Sébastien in battle. IIiii. Sébastien is wounded and Abayaldos victorious. Dom Henrique claims to be Sébastien so that he can die in his place. Zaïda discovers the wounded king and confesses her love. She buys Sébastien's freedom by agreeing to marry Abayaldos.

IIIi. Juan welcomes Abayaldos to Portugal. Abayaldos realizes Zaïda never loved him. IIIii. Camoëns returns to Lisbon. The king is believed dead. Camoëns swears to remain loyal. He and Sébastien are reunited. Sébastien reveals himself to the army.

IV. Sébastien is arrested. Zaïda bears witness that Sébastien is the king, but Juan orders her arrested and tortured.

V. Antonio and Juan agree to make Portugal subject to Spain. Juan tells Zaïda he will spare Sébastien if he abdicates. Zaïda hopes to save Sébastien. Sébastien refuses to abdicate. Camoëns brings news of a popular uprising. He, Zaïda and Sébastien try to escape out the window. Antonio observes them fall to their deaths.

Domino Noir • The Black Domino

Composed by Daniel François Esprit Auber (January 29, 1782 – May 12, 1871). Libretto by Eugène Scribe. French. Original work. Premiered Paris, Opéra Comique, December 2, 1837. Set in Madrid in the 19th century. Comic opera. Set numbers with recitative and spoken dialogue. Overture. Entr'acte before II, III.

Sets: 3. **Acts:** 3 acts, 3 scenes. **Length:** I: 35. II: 40. III: 30. **Hazards:** None. **Scenes:** I. The queen's apartments in the palace of Madrid. II. A dining room in the house of Juliane. III. The parlor of the convent of St. Rosa.

Major roles: Juliane (tenor), Count Horace of Massarena (tenor), Angèle (soprano or mezzo). **Minor roles:** Lord Elfort (bass), Brigitte/Sister Gertrude (mezzo or soprano), Jacinthe (mezzo), Gil Perez (bass), Sister Ursule (mezzo or soprano). **Speaking bits:** Melchior, Offstage voice.

Chorus parts: SATTBB. **Chorus roles:** Noblemen and ladies of the court of Nonnes, friends of Juliane, nuns. **Dance/movement:** None. **Orchestra:** 2 fl (picc), 2 ob, 2 cl, 2 bsn, 4 hrn, 2 trp, 3 trb, timp, perc, harp, strings. **Stageband:** I: 2 fl, 2 ob, 2 bsn, 2 hrn, harp, strings. III: 2 cl, 2 bsn, 2 hrn, harp, strings. **Publisher:** G. Brandus, Troupenas & Co. **Rights:** Expired.

I. Lord Elfort has come to a ball without his wife, who is sick. He loses at whist to Count Horace. Horace is betrothed to the ambassador's niece, but he admits to his friend, Juliane, that he loves a mysterious woman in a black domino. The woman is Angèle and Horace dances with her while Juliane distracts her companion, Brigitte. Elfort mistakes Angèle for his wife. Midnight strikes and Angèle flees.

II. Angèle loses her way and takes shelter with Juliane's porter, Jacintha. Jacintha passes Angèle off as her niece, but Horace is not fooled. He has a bracelet Angèle dropped at the ball, which one of Juliane's friends identifies as belonging to the queen. Angèle panics when Elfort is announced. She persuades Jacinthe's suitor, Gil Perez, to give her the keys to the convent of which he is porter. She flees, leaving Horace as mystified as ever.

III. Angèle is the queen's cousin and is about to be sworn in as abbess of the convent. Sister Ursule is jealous of her and tries, unsuccessfully, to find out what she has been doing. Horace pays Angèle a visit. She receives a letter that her uncle has left her his fortune. Now rich, Angèle agrees to marry Horace and Ursule becomes abbess.

Don Carlo

Composed by Giuseppe Verdi (October 9, 1813 – January 27, 1901). Libretto by Camille du Locle and François Joseph Méry. French and Italian. Play by Friedrich von Schiller. Premiered Paris, Opéra, March 11, 1867 (original version). Set in Spain in about 1560. Tragedy. Set numbers with accompanied recitative. Prelude before the second act. Verdi reworked score in 1883, condensing five acts into four by placing material from the original first act into act two. Libretto reworked by Ghislanzoni.

Sets: 6 (7 in 5-act version). **Acts:** 4 acts, 7 scenes (5 acts, 8 scenes in original version). **Length:** I: 65. II: 40. III: 55. IV: 20. (In 5-act version I: 30.) **Arias:** "Nel giardin del bello"/Veil song (Eboli), "Non pianger, mia compagna" (Elisabetta), "Tu che la vanità conoscesti del mondo" (Elisabetta), "Ella giammai m'amò" (Filippo), "Io la vidi" (Carlo), "Io morrò" (Rodrigo), "O don fatale" (Eboli). **Hazards:** None. **Scenes:** Ii. Cloister of the monastery of St. Just. Iii. The garden adjoining the monastery. IIi. The Queen's gardens in Madrid. IIii. Square before the cathedral. IIIi. The King's study in Madrid. IIIii. The prison of Don Carlo. IVi. Cloister of the monastery of St. Just. (In 5-act version, act I is set in forest of Fontainebleau.)

Major roles: Filippo II (bass), Don Carlo (tenor), Rodrigo (baritone), Elisabetta of Valois (soprano), Grand Inquisitor (bass), Princess of Eboli (mezzo). **Minor roles:** Count of Lerma (tenor), Friar (bass), Tebaldo (soprano). **Bit parts:** Royal herald (tenor), Celestial voice (soprano). **Mute:** Countess of Aremberg.

Chorus parts: SSATTBBB. **Chorus roles:** Six Flemish deputies (6 basses), Inquisitors, gentlemen and ladies of the court of Spain, pages, guards, friars, members of the Holy Office, soldiers, magistrates, monks, people. **Dance/movement:** Ballet in original version. **Orchestra:** 3 fl (picc), 2 ob (Eng hrn), 2 cl (bs cl), 4 bsn (cont bsn), 4 hrn, 4 trp, 3 trb, ophicléide, timp, perc, harp, strings. **Stageband:** I (5-act version): 4 hrn. Four-act version: I: chimes. II: organ or harmonium, band, perc, harp. **Publisher:** Schirmer, Kalmus. **Rights:** Expired.

Ii. Monks pray before the tomb of Charles V. Don Carlo is upset because his father, King Filippo II, has remarried—and to the Don's own intended. He thinks he recognizes King Charles V's voice among the friars. Carlo's friend Rodrigo tells him that the people of Flanders are calling for him. He is horrified by Don Carlo's revelation that he loves his stepmother, Queen Elisabetta. All the more reason to hurry off to Flanders, Rodrigo advises. Iii. The Princess of Eboli, accompanied by Tebaldo, sings the Song of the Veil for the amusement of the ladies of the court. Rodrigo enters with a letter for the Queen, which he says is from the Queen Mother. It is actually from Carlo, instructing the Queen to trust Rodrigo. She grants Rodrigo a favor for his efforts and Rodrigo begs an audience for Don Carlo. When Elisabetta agrees, Tebaldo brings in Don Carlo. Eboli wonders if the don is in love with her (Eboli). Carlo begs permission to depart for Flanders. He declares his love for the queen but she silences him. During the interview, the Countess of Aremberg and the other ladies-in-waiting have demurely faded into the background. The king, finding the queen alone, is furious at this dereliction of duty and orders the Countess back to France. The queen bids the countess a tearful farewell. The king taxes Rodrigo with his resignation from the army and warns him about his pride. Rodrigo recounts the destruction and hunger in Flanders, but the king says it was necessary to subdue the rebellion. The king confesses his suspicions of the queen and Carlo.

IIi. It is night and Don Carlo waits for the queen. Eboli arrives instead and Don Carlo declares his love before he realizes who it is. Eboli guesses whom Carlo really loves and swears revenge. Rodrigo considers killing Eboli but is restrained by Carlo. He swears his fidelity to Carlo and takes the don's letters and papers for safe keeping. IIii. The people sing Filippo's praises while those condemned by the Inquisition are led away. The procession is interrupted by six Flemish deputies who, led by Don Carlo, beg mercy for their country. The king denounces them as traitors. When Carlo again asks to be sent to Flanders, the king refuses. Carlo draws his sword. The king commands the guards to disarm Carlo, but when they do not move, Rodrigo does it himself. A heavenly voice calls the deputies to heaven. The autodafé begins.

IIIi. Elisabetta never loved me, the king realizes. The blind Grand Inquisitor is led in. He agrees that religion will sanction the sacrifice of Don Carlo and then demands the sacrifice of Rodrigo. The queen appears, looking for her jewel casket, which the king has. She refuses to open it, so the king breaks it open—and discovers a portrait of Carlo. The queen maintains her innocence. After the king's departure, Eboli confesses to the queen that she spied on her and stole the casket. She begs forgiveness and is offered the choice of exile or a convent. Alone, Eboli wonders if it is not too late to save Carlo's life. IIIii. Rodrigo visits Carlo in prison and predicts that he will die in the don's place. They discovered your papers on me, Rodrigo explains, and they now believe it was I who planned the Flemish rebellion. Meanwhile, an agent of the Inquisition has crept in unobserved. He shoots Rodrigo, who falls, entrusting the cause of Flanders to Carlo. The king comes to set Carlo free, but Carlo is furious over Rodrigo's death. Outside, a rebellion is in progress. The king orders the doors opened and the people rush onstage demanding Don Carlo. The situation is saved by the Grand Inquisitor, who awes the crowd into submission.

IV. Elisabetta kneels before the tomb of Charles V and implores God to ease her suffering. Don Carlo comes to say farewell. He is going to Flanders to raise the standard of rebellion. The would-be lovers are caught by the king and the Grand Inquisitor. Before the guards can seize Carlo, Charles V appears and takes Don Carlo with him into the cloister.

Don Giovanni

Composed by Wolfgang Amadeus Mozart (January 27, 1756 – December 5, 1791). Libretto by Lorenzo Da Ponte. Italian. Based on Giovanni Bertati libretto for Giuseppe Gazzaniga opera and the legends of Don Juan. Premiered Prague, National Theater, October 29, 1787. Set in

Seville in the mid-17th century. Drama. Set numbers with recitative. Overture.

Sets: 10. **Acts:** 2 acts, 10 scenes. **Length:** I: 85. II: 79. **Arias:** "Madamina! Il catalogo è questo"/Catalog aria (Leporello), "Ah fuggi il traditor!" (Elvira), "Or sai, chi l'onore" (Anna), "Dalla sua pace" (Ottavio), "Finch' han dal vino"/Champagne aria (Giovanni), "Batti, batti, o bel Masetto" (Zerlina), "Vedrai, carino" (Zerlina), "Il mio tesoro intanto" (Ottavio), "Mi tradì quell'alma ingrata" (Elvira), "Non mi dir" (Anna), "Deh vieni alla finestra" (Giovanni). **Hazards:** II: Statue of the Commendatore moves. Giovanni dragged off to hell by demons. **Scenes:** Ii. The garden of the commendatore's house. Iii. A street. Iiii. The open country. Iiv. A garden. Iv. Brilliantly lit ballroom in Giovanni's mansion. IIi. A street before Elvira's house. IIii. A cemetery. IIiii. An enclosed churchyard. IIiv. A darkened room in Anna's house. IIv. A lighted hall in Giovanni's mansion.

Major roles: Don Giovanni (bass baritone), Leporello (bass), Donna Anna (soprano), Donna Elvira (soprano), Don Ottavio (tenor), Zerlina (soprano). **Minor roles:** Commendatore (bass), Masetto (bass or baritone). **Mute:** Peasant.

Chorus parts: SATB. **Chorus roles:** Peasants (mute), musicians, servants, offstage demons. **Dance/movement:** I: Peasant wedding dance and ballroom dancing. **Orchestra:** 2 fl, 2 ob, 2 cl, 2 bsn, 2 hrn, 2 trp, 3 trb, timp, mandolin, strings, continuo (cembalo). **Stageband:** I: Orchestra I—2 ob, 2 hrn, vlns, vla, vlc, bs; Orchestra II—vlns, vlc, bs; Orchestra III—vlns, vlc, bs. II: 2 cl, 2 ob, 2 bsn, 2 hrn, 3 trb, vlc, bs. **Publisher:** Schirmer, Dover. **Rights:** Expired.

Ii. Leporello stands watch while Giovanni seduces Anna, whose screams wake her father, the commendatore. He challenges Giovanni who kills him. Without knowing who did it, Anna makes Ottavio swear to avenge her father's death. Iii. Elvira swears to expose her faithless lover if he does not come back to her. Giovanni seeks to comfort her until he realizes he is the faithless lover and flees. Leporello shows Elvira the ridiculously long list of Giovanni's romantic conquests. Iiii. Giovanni encounters the celebrations for Zerlina and Masetto's wedding. He invites the guests to his castle, being sure to separate Masetto from his fiancée. Giovanni overcomes Zerlina's scruples, but is thwarted by Elvira, who warns Zerlina not to believe his promises of love. Anna and Ottavio come to Giovanni for help, but Anna realizes it was Giovanni who killed her father. Leporello reports to Giovanni that he has gotten all the peasants drunk. Iiv. Masetto is angry with Zerlina but she brings him around. She wants to hide from Giovanni, but Masetto insists she meet him while he hides to observe. Giovanni attempts to seduce Zerlina until

Masetto interrupts. Ottavio, Anna and Elvira arrive masked. Iv. Giovanni dances with Zerlina and drags her into another room while Leporello distracts Masetto. Zerlina cries for help. Ottavio breaks down the door and Giovanni tries unsuccessfully to throw the blame on Leporello. The crowd turns on Giovanni but he makes his escape.

IIi. Giovanni and Leporello exchange clothes so Giovanni can woo Elvira's maid. When Elvira comes to the balcony, Giovanni swears his love for her, leaving Leporello to act out his part. Giovanni himself scares Elvira and Leporello off by pretending to be a bandit. He then serenades Elvira's maid. Masetto arrives with a band of armed peasants looking for Giovanni. Giovanni—pretending to be Leporello—offers to help, but instead disperses Masetto's followers and beats Masetto. Zerlina comforts her fiancé. IIii. Leporello tries to escape from Elvira but is confronted by Zerlina, Masetto, Ottavio and Anna. Elvira begs mercy for Giovanni, but Leporello reveals his true identity. Zerlina ties him up, but he escapes. IIiii. Giovanni and Leporello meet up in the graveyard where the commendatore is buried. Giovanni invites the commendatore's statue to dinner and it accepts. IIiv. Anna declares she will not marry Ottavio until she has her revenge. IIv. Giovanni boldly begins his dinner alone. When Elvira begs Giovanni to repent, he laughs. The statue of the commendatore arrives. When they shake hands, Giovanni cannot free himself from the statue's grip. The statue drags him down to hell. Anna, Elvira and Ottavio arrive too late to exact revenge. They reflect that all seducers end so.

Don Pasquale

Composed by Gaetano Donizetti (November 29, 1797 – April 8, 1848). Libretto by Giovanni Ruffini. Italian. Based on libretto by Angelo Anelli for Stefano Pavesi's "Ser Marcantonio." Premiered Paris, Théâtre Italien, January 3, 1843. Set in Rome in the early 19th century. Comedy. Set numbers with accompanied recitative. Overture.

Sets: 4. **Acts:** 3 acts, 5 scenes. **Length:** I: 40. II: 30. III: 40. **Arias:** "Bella siccome un angelo" (Malatesta), "Cercherò lontana terra" (Ernesto), Com'è gentil" (Ernesto), "So anch'io la virtù magica" (Norina). **Hazards:** None. **Scenes:** Ii. A room in Don Pasquale's house. Iii. A room in Norina's house. II. Don Pasquale's drawing room. IIIi. Don Pasquale's drawing room. IIIii. A small grove in Don Pasquale's garden.

Major roles: Don Pasquale (comic bass), Ernesto (tenor), Dr. Malatesta (baritone), Norina (soprano). **Minor role:** Notary (tenor, baritone or bass).

Chorus parts: SATTB. **Chorus roles:** Servants and maids. Solo lines in IIIi. **Dance/movement:** None. **Orchestra:** 2 fl (picc), 2 ob, 2 cl, 2 bsn, 4 hrn, 2 trp, 3 trb, timp, perc, harp (mandolin), strings. **Stageband:** None. **Publisher:** Ricordi. **Rights:** Expired.

Ii. Don Pasquale wonders what his nephew, Ernesto, will think of his plan to marry Malatesta's sister. Aquiver with anticipated love, he insists Malatesta bring his sister for a visit at once. Ernesto keeps resisting Pasquale's attempts to marry him off, since he is in love with Norina, and the exasperated old gentleman announces he is disowning his nephew and getting married himself. Astounded, Ernesto begs him to consult Malatesta. "I have," Pasquale reports, "and he approves." Since Norina is poor, Ernesto realizes that being disinherited means the end of his own plans. That his friend Malatesta is encouraging Pasquale makes it worse. Iii. Norina brags about her feminine wiles. Malatesta returns, pleased at the joke he is to play on Pasquale. Norina loses heart when she receives a letter from Ernesto bidding her farewell, but Malatesta lets her in on the joke: Because Pasquale cannot be dissuaded from marrying, Malatesta plans to pass Norina off as his sister. She will agree to marry Pasquale, but they will fake the marriage contract. Then it is up to Norina to drive her supposed husband crazy. The doctor promises to tell Ernesto what they are up to. "Be bashful and simple-minded with Pasquale," the doctor counsels her.

II. Distraught, Ernesto decides to flee to some distant country. Norina is presented to Pasquale under the name Sofronia. She charms him with her extreme modesty and accepts his proposal of marriage. Ernesto— who has not been warned of the plot— is astounded when he is called upon to witness the marriage of his Norina to Pasquale. Once the contract is signed, Norina starts bossing Pasquale around. Ernesto quickly figures out the joke. The new bride insists on more servants, a carriage and new furnishings—all of which the hapless Pasquale is to pay for.

IIIi. Servants and milliners rush about with Norina's purchases. When Pasquale objects to Norina's plans to attend the theater, she slaps him and goes anyway. Pasquale threatens to divorce her. Once she is gone, he discovers a love letter addressed to her and calls for Malatesta to help him expose his wife's infidelity. The servants wonder at the chaos of Pasquale's domestic life. While Malatesta attends Pasquale, Ernesto heads for the garden disguised as Norina's lover. The doctor, who pretends to disbelieve Pasquale until he produces the love letter, proposes that they conceal themselves in the garden. He agrees that if they overhear anything incriminating, they will send Norina away. IIIii. It is night and Ernesto and Norina are in the garden, exchanging vows of love. They are overheard by Malatesta and Pasquale, but Ernesto hides before they can catch him. Malatesta and Norina now convince Pasquale that his wife (Norina/Sophronia) hates Ernesto's beloved (Norina). If Ernesto plans to marry her, Norina (Sophronia) says she will leave. Overjoyed at the opportunity to rid himself of his pesky wife, Pasquale agrees to have Ernesto marry his beloved on the spot. His enthusiasm is not diminished when the others explain the trick they have played on him. The moral, they tell Pasquale, is: act your age.

Don Quichotte

Composed by Jules-Emile-Frédéric Massenet (May 12, 1842 – August 13, 1912). Libretto by Henri Cain. French. Based on the Jacques le Lorrain drama (itself based on Cervantes). Premiered Monte Carlo, Théâtre de Monte Carlo, February 19, 1910. Set in Spain in the 15th century. Lyric tragedy. Set numbers with accompanied recitative. Prelude. Entr'acte before each act.

Sets: 5. **Acts:** 5 acts, 5 scenes. **Length:** I, II, III, IV, V: 120. **Arias:** "Quand la femme a vingt ans" (Dulcinée), "C'est vers ton amour" (Quichotte). **Hazards:** II: Quichotte fights a windmill. **Scenes:** I. Public square in Spain. II. Countryside. III. In the sierra. IV. Courtyard of Dulcinée's house. V. Road through the gorge of an ancient forest.

Major roles: Dulcinée (mezzo), Don Quichotte (bass), Sanche (baritone). **Minor roles:** Pedro (soprano), Garcias (mezzo), Rodriguez (tenor), Juan (tenor), Bandit chief (baritone). **Bit parts:** Two servants (baritone, bass). **Speaking:** Four bandits.

Chorus parts: SAATTBB. **Chorus roles:** People, beggars, bandits, Dulcinée's guests. **Dance/movement:** I: Villagers dance. IV: Dance of Dulcinée's guests. **Orchestra:** 3 fl (picc), 3 ob (Eng hrn), 3 cl (bs cl), 3 bsn, 4 hrn, 3 trp, 3 trb, tuba, timp, perc, 2 harp, organ, strings. **Stageband:** I: 2 fl, perc, celeste, piano, harp. IV: fl, ob (Eng hrn), celeste, perc, harp, timp, cont bs, guitar (score says imperative guitar played by Dulcinée herself). V: vln, vla, harp. **Publisher:** Heugel & Co. **Rights:** Expired.

I. Dulcinée's suitors flatter her. As the crowd cheers the arrival of Don Quichotte and Sanche, Quichotte orders Sanche to give alms to the beggars. Night falls and Quichotte sends Sanche away so he can serenade Dulcinée. He is overheard by Juan, one of Dulcinée's suitors, who challenges him. The fight is broken up by Dulcinée, who flirts with Quichotte to annoy Juan. If you really love me, Dulcinée says, you will retrieve my necklace that was stolen by the brigand chief. Dulcinée goes off with Juan, laughing at Quichotte.

II. Quichotte composes verses for Dulcinée. He is unconvinced by

Sanche's revelation that the foes they vanquished yesterday were really pigs and sheep. Sanche complains they have no food and that Dulcinée sends them on hopeless errands to make fun of Quichotte. He abuses womankind. Quichotte, mistaking a group of windmills for giants, charges them and is thrown from his horse. III. He fights the brigands who stole Dulcinée's necklace. He is soundly defeated, but his piety charms the brigands, who return the necklace and ask for his blessing.

IV. Dulcinée is bored by her suitors. Sanche announces Quichotte and punishes two servants for making fun of his master. Quichotte promises Sanche great riches as reward for his loyalty. Dulcinée and her guests laugh at Quichotte since they cannot believe he escaped from the bandits. They are stunned when he produces the necklace. Quichotte proposes, but Dulcinée only laughs. Then she repents and tries to be kind. Her suitors ridicule Quichotte, but Sanche tells them they are nothing compared to Quichotte's noble soul. V. Quichotte dies in his faithful Sanche's arms.

Don Rodrigo

Composed by Alberto Ginastera (April 11, 1916 – June 25, 1983). Libretto by Alejandro Casona. Spanish. Original work. Premiered Buenos Aires, Teatro Cólon, July 24, 1964. Set in Toledo in the 8th century. Tragedy. Through composed. Twelve-tonal. Orchestral interludes between scenes.

Sets: 8. **Acts:** 3 acts, 9 scenes. **Length:** I: 30. II: 30. III: 40. **Hazards:** II: Rodrigo dreams of Ceuta and the Moorish ships. **Scenes:** Ii. The hall of honor of the palace of Toledo. Iii. The cathedral of Toledo. Iiii. A crypt in Toledo known as the cave of Hercules. IIi. A shady garden in the palace of Toledo. IIii – IIiii. Florinda's apartments at night. IIIi. Rodrigo's chamber and the battlements of Ceuta. IIIii. Rodrigo's battlefield tent in the encampment at Guadalete. IIIiii. A hillside before a hermit's dwelling.

Major roles: Florinda (dramatic soprano), Teudiselo (bass), Don Julian (baritone), Don Rodrigo (dramatic tenor). **Minor roles:** First maiden (soprano), Second maiden (mezzo), First page/First locksmith/First messenger (tenor), Second page/Second locksmith/Second messenger (baritone), Fortuna (mezzo), Bishop/Blind hermit (baritone). **Bit parts:** Voice in the dream (bass), Young messenger (contralto), Young boy Rapaz (tenor), Young girl Zagala (soprano).

Chorus parts: SSAATTBB. **Chorus roles:** Heralds, pages, maidens, ladies, nobles, captains, Spanish and Arab soldiers, watchmen, people, peasants, woodcutters, shepherds, workmen. **Dance/movement:** None. **Orchestra:** 3 fl (picc), 3 ob (Eng hrn), 3 cl (bs cl), 3 bsn (cont bsn), 6 hrn, 4 trp, 4 trb, tuba, 2 timp, 6 perc, glockenspiel (xylophone), celeste, vla d'amore, mandolin, harp, strings. **Stageband:** I: 8 trp, perc, bells. II: 12 hrn. III: 12 hrn, 8 trp, Moorish pipes, bells. **Publisher:** Boosey and Hawkes. **Rights:** Copyright 1967 by Boosey & Hawkes.

Ii. The people of Toledo await Don Rodrigo, who has defeated his father's murderers and returns to be crowned king of Spain. Don Julian introduces his daughter Florinda to Rodrigo. She is to return with her father to Africa after the coronation, but wants to remain in Spain. Rodrigo promises to keep her at court. Iii. During Rodrigo's coronation, Florinda drops the crown, which everyone takes as a bad omen. Iiii. All of the kings of Spain since ancient times have respected the secret locked inside a chest in the cave of Hercules, but Rodrigo insists on forcing the chest open. Inside he finds a Moorish flag and a scroll prophesying that the Moors will enslave Spain.

IIi. Rodrigo's tutor, Teudiselo, warns him of the Moorish preparations for war, but Rodrigo is confident that Don Julian can keep the Moors in check. Florinda and her maidens bathe naked in the fountain until Rodrigo discovers them. IIii. The king enters Florinda's chamber at night and seduces her. IIiii. Furious at the king both for seducing her and for leaving her, Florinda writes her father demanding revenge.

IIIi. In his dreams, Rodrigo sees Julian raising a rebellion. IIIii. After bitter fighting, Julian's army defeats Rodrigo's. IIIiii. Escaping, Rodrigo wanders through the mountains until he finds a hermit. He prays for forgiveness for his sins. Florinda returns and tries to comfort him before he dies.

La Donna del Lago • The Lady of the Lake

Composed by Gioachino Rossini (February 29, 1792 – November 13, 1868). Libretto by Andrea Leone Tottola. Italian. Based on the poem by Sir Walter Scott. Premiered Naples, Teatro San Carlo, September 24, 1819. Set in Scotland in the 16th century. Opera seria. Set numbers with recitative. Overture.

Sets: 7. **Acts:** 2 acts, 7 scenes. **Length:** I: 85. II: 55. **Arias:** "Taci, lo voglio e basti" (Douglas), "Ah si pera" (Malcolm), "Oh fiamma soave" (Uberto). **Hazards:** I: Elena appears in a boat on the lake. A brilliant meteor flashes across the sky. **Scenes:** Ii. The rock of Benledi covered at the summit by a thick wood and sloping down to a broad valley. Iii. Elena's home. Iiii. A plain surrounded by towering mountains. IIi. A thick wood with a cavern on one side. IIii. Inside the cavern. IIiii. A room in the palace at Stirling. IIiv. The throne room.

Major roles: Elena (soprano), King Giacomo V of Scotland/Uberto (tenor), Malcolm (contralto), Douglas d'Angus (bass). **Minor roles:** Albina (soprano), Serano (tenor), Rodrigo (tenor). **Bit part:** Bertram (tenor).

Chorus parts: SSAATTTTBB. **Chorus roles:** Shepherds and shepherdesses, hunters, Elena's friends, clansmen, bards, lords and ladies, officers and soldiers. **Dance/movement:** None. **Orchestra:** picc, 2 fl (picc), 2 ob, 2 cl, 2 bsn, 2 or 4 hrn, 2 trp, 3 trb, timp, perc, harp, strings. **Stageband:** I: band (hrn, trps). **Publisher:** Edizioni Musicale Otos, Laffillé. **Rights:** Expired.

Ii. Shepherds and hunters go about their work. Elena loves the highlander Malcolm. A hunter tells her he has lost his way. It is King Giacomo, disguised under the name Uberto. Uberto's men search for him. Iii. Elena tells Uberto how her father, Douglas of Angus, was driven from King Giacomo's court. Fearing he will be discovered, Uberto leaves. Malcolm contemplates his love for Elena. Douglas wants Elena to marry Rodrigo, leader of the highlanders. Elena and Malcolm pledge their mutual love. Iiii. Presented to Elena, Rodrigo is disappointed by her lack of enthusiasm. Malcolm pledges to fight with Rodrigo. A meteor flashes across the sky (a good omen) as they go into battle.

IIi. Douglas has hidden Elena in a cave for her protection. Uberto finds her and declares his love. He gives her a jewel-encrusted ring, which he tells her to present to the king if she ever needs to obtain a pardon for her father or lover. Rodrigo interrupts them and challenges Uberto. IIii. The highlanders are defeated and Rodrigo slain. IIiii. Elena goes to the king to save her father. She does not realize that Uberto is the king. IIiv. The king pardons both Douglas and Malcolm.

Le Donne Curiose • The Inquisitive Women

Composed by Ermanno Wolf-Ferrari (January 12, 1876 – January 21, 1948). Libretto by Luigi Sugana. Italian (premiered in German). Based on the play by Carlo Goldoni. Premiered Munich, November 27, 1903. Set in Venice in the mid-18th century. Comedy. Through composed. Overture. Intermezzo before IIii.

Sets: 4. **Acts:** 3 acts, 6 scenes. **Length:** I: 45. II: 30. III: 35. **Hazards:** III: Gondola crosses the stage. **Scenes:** Ii. A large meeting room in a clubhouse. Iii. A room in Ottavio's house. IIi. A room in Lelio's house. IIii. The room in Ottavio's house. IIIi. A street in Venice with a view of a canal. IIIii. A room within the clubhouse.

Major roles: Ottavio (bass), Florindo (tenor), Pantalone (comic baritone), Arlecchino (comic bass), Beatrice (mezzo), Rosaura (soprano), Eleonora (soprano), Colombina (soprano). **Minor roles:** Leandro (tenor), Lelio (baritone). **Bit parts:** Asdrubale (tenor), Almorò (tenor), Alvise (tenor), Lunardo (bass), Mòmolo (bass), Mènego (bass), Two gondoliers (2 bass or baritone). **Mute:** Servant.

Chorus parts: SATTB. **Chorus roles:** Servants, gondoliers, people. **Dance/movement:** III: Minuet, furlana. **Orchestra:** 2 fl (picc), 2 ob, 2 cl, 2 bsn, 2 hrn, 2 trp, timp, 1 or 2 perc, harp, piano, strings. **Stageband:** I: clock tower bell. III: 2 mandolin, 2 guitar, bs. IV: vln. **Publisher:** Josef Weinberger. **Rights:** Copyright 1903 by G. Schirmer Inc.

Ii. A group of friends meet at their club to talk and play games. Pantalone arranges a supper for the members, putting his servant, Arlecchino, in charge of preparations. Pantalone swears that the club will never admit women. Iii. Ottavio's wife, Beatrice, and his daughter, Rosaura, wonder what goes on at the club. Rosaura fears they keep mistresses there; Beatrice believes they gamble. Lelio's wife, Eleonora, tells them the men are practicing alchemy. Arlecchino's girlfriend, Colombina, says they are using sorcery to find buried treasure. When Arlecchino pays a call on Colombina, the women force him to tell them about the club. His remarks confirm each woman in her own suspicions. Ottavio refuses to tell Beatrice about the club. Rosaura threatens to break up with Florindo if he does not tell her what happens at the club, and pretends to faint. Florindo is so upset he tells Colombina the club password.

IIi. Eleonora gets the key to the club out of her husband's pocket and fights with him because he will not tell her about the club. IIii. Rosaura and Colombina tell Beatrice the password. Beatrice tries to get her husband's key. Colombina gets it by spilling coffee on Ottavio and switching his keys while she cleans his coat. Colombina disguises herself as a man and goes to the clubhouse with Beatrice. Rosaura pines for Florindo. He returns to her and she persuades him to give her his key.

IIIi. Pantalone buys candles for dinner, and Arlecchino assures him the meal will be a feast. Arlecchino surprises Eleonora by the clubhouse and confiscates her key. Beatrice and Colombina find the clubhouse and Colombina approaches Pantalone, but he realizes she is a woman and takes her key. Lelio realizes he does not have his key; Ottavio and Florindo are also without keys. Pantalone returns the lost keys. Wondering what Rosaura did with his key, Florindo sees her and takes it back. Rosaura faints in Arlecchino's arms. All of the women beat Arlecchino until he gives them a key. IIIii. Pantalone warns the men never again to part with their keys. The women sneak into the club.

They find the men having dinner. The women are discovered. The men forgive the women and everyone dances.

Double Trouble

Composed by Richard Mohaupt (September 14, 1904 – July 3, 1957). Libretto by Roger Maren. English. After "Menaechmi" by Plautus. Premiered Louisville, Kentucky, Louisville Orchestra, December 4, 1954. Set on a Mediterranean island at an unspecified time. Comedy. Set numbers with recitative and some spoken lines. Choral interludes between scenes. Prologue. Epilogue.

Sets: 1. **Acts:** 1 act, 16 scenes. **Length:** I: 65. **Hazards:** I: Hocus and Pocus are identical twins. **Scenes:** I. A street with two houses.

Major roles: Hocus (bass baritone), Erotia (coloratura soprano), Dr. Antibioticus (comic tenor), Pocus (bass baritone). **Minor roles:** Naggia (mezzo), Cynthia (soprano), Lucio (tenor). **Speaking bit:** Chorister. **Mute:** Slaves.

Chorus parts: SATB. **Chorus roles:** Greek chorus. **Dance/movement:** None. **Orchestra:** 2 fl (picc), ob (Eng hrn), cl (bs cl), bsn (db bsn), 2 hrn, 2 trp, 2 trb, 2 pianos, 3 perc, timp, strings. **Stageband:** None. **Publisher:** Associated Music Publishers. **Rights:** Copyright 1954 by Associated Music Publishers.

Ii. The chorus introduces Hocus, who was lost as a boy by his father on a business trip. Hocus's twin brother, Pocus, has spent his life searching for Hocus. Iii. Hocus is married to Naggia, but is having an affair with the courtesan Erotia. Naggia catches Hocus giving Erotia her own mink coat and diamond ring. Iiii. Hocus refuses to let his daughter Cynthia marry her beloved Lucio. Iiv. The chorus announces Pocus's arrival. Iv. While searching for his brother, Pocus has found time for a romance in every port. Ivi. Erotia mistakes Pocus for Hocus and takes him home with her. Ivii. The men of the chorus are amused, but the women are scandalized. Iviii. Naggia's friend (and Lucio's father) Dr. Antibioticus shares his medical theories. Iix. Cynthia and Lucio appeal to Dr. Antibioticus for help. He tells them everything will work out since Naggia has hired him to cure all of Hocus's faults. Ix. Lucio and Cynthia overhear Pocus taking leave of Erotia and try to blackmail him. The confused Pocus happily agrees to let them marry. Ixi. Naggia's slaves gag and bind Pocus in preparation for Dr. Antibioticus's treatment. Ixii. Erotia is confused when Hocus asks her to give back the coat and ring, since she gave them to Pocus. Hocus and Erotia fight. Ixiii. Hocus is furious to discover that Lucio and Cynthia are married. Ixiv. Pocus runs into

Hocus while escaping from Dr. Antibioticus's treatment. Naggia's slaves capture Hocus and Pocus, who explain that they are brothers. Ixv. Hocus decides to go home with Pocus and auctions off everything he and Naggia own, giving away Naggia herself. Ixvi. The chorus asks for applause and says good night.

Down in the Valley

Composed by Kurt Weill (March 2, 1900 – April 3, 1950). Libretto by Arnold Sundgaard. English. Original work. Premiered Bloomington, Indiana, Indiana University, July 15, 1948. Set in Birmingham city in the present. Tragedy. Set numbers with spoken dialogue.

Sets: 5. **Acts:** 1 act, 7 scenes. **Length:** I: 45. **Hazards:** None. **Scenes:** Ii. A jail cell. Iii. Jennie's front porch and a field. Iiii. Inside the church. Iiv. In front of the church and a street. Iv. Shadow Creek Café. Ivi. The porch and field. Ivii. The jail cell.

Major roles: Brack Weaver (tenor or high baritone), Jennie Parsons (lyric soprano). **Minor roles:** Leader (baritone), Preacher (baritone), Thomas Bouché (bass). **Speaking:** Jennie's father. **Speaking bits:** Guard, Peters, two men, two women.

Chorus parts: SSAATTBB. **Chorus roles:** People, congregation, dancers. **Dance/movement:** I: square dancing. **Orchestra:** 2 fl, ob, 2 cl, alto sax, ten sax, bsn, 2 hrn, 2 trp, 2 trb, guitar, piano, perc, strings (vlns in 3 parts; no vlas; not less than 2-2-2-2-1). **Stageband:** None. **Publisher:** G. Schirmer. **Rights:** Copyright 1948 by Kurt Weill and Arnold Sundgaard.

Ii. The chorus introduces the story of Brack Weaver. The night before he is to be executed, Brack waits for a letter from his love, Jennie Parsons, then escapes. Iii. Jennie ignores her father's advice to forget Brack. Brack tracks her down and they declare their love. Iiii. They remember how they met in church. Iiv. After church, Brack walks Jennie home. He asks her to a dance and she accepts. Bouché also asks Jennie. Jennie's father forbids her to go to the dance with Brack. He is grateful to Bouché for helping him get an extension on his loans. Iv. Brack and Jennie attend the dance. Bouché attacks Brack with a knife, but Brack kills him. Ivi. Brack turns himself in. Ivii. He returns to jail, satisfied to await his execution

Die Dreigroschenoper • The Three Penny Opera

Composed by Kurt Weill (March 2, 1900 – April 3, 1950). Libretto by

Bertolt Brecht. German. Based on "The Beggar's Opera" by John Gay. Premiered Berlin, Theater am Schiffbauerdamm, August 31, 1928. Set in London in 1837. Satire. Set numbers with recitative and spoken dialogue. Overture. Prologue. Interludes before IIii and IIIii.

Sets: 4. **Acts:** 3 acts, 8 scenes. **Length:** I: 25. II: 30. III: 20. **Arias:** "Mac the Knife" (Macheath). **Hazards:** None. **Scenes:** Ii. Peachum's beggars' shop. Iii. An empty stable. Iiii. Peachum's beggars' shop. IIi. The empty stable. IIii. Whorehouse in Turnbridge. IIiii. Jail cell in the old bailey. IIIi. Peachum's beggars' shop. IIIii. Jail cell in the old bailey.

Major roles: Macheath/Mac the Knife (tenor), Polly Peachum (soprano), Jenny (soprano). **Minor roles:** Street singer (baritone), Mr. Peachum (baritone), Mrs. Peachum (mezzo), Tiger Brown (baritone), Lucy (soprano).

Chorus parts: SATB. **Chorus roles:** Beggars, poor people, gang members, whores, police. (Various speaking bits.) **Dance/movement:** None. **Orchestra:** tenor sax (sop sax, bsn, cl), alto sax (fl, cl), 2 trp, trb (bs), banjo (vlc, guitar, bandoneon), perc, timp, harmonium (celeste), piano. **Stageband:** None. **Publisher:** Universal Edition. **Rights:** Copyright 1928 by Universal Edition. Renewed 1956 by Mrs. Karoline Weill-Davis.

Prologue. No one ever seems to catch Mac the Knife at his crimes, the street singer notes. Ii. Polly Peachum does not come home, having secretly married Mac the Knife. Iii. They are toasted by members of Mac's gang. Mac and his old friend, chief of police Brown, reminisce about the men they knew who went into the army. Iiii. Polly recounts all the nice men she turned down. She accepted Mac because he was not nice. Mr. and Mrs. Peachum point out the world is poor and man is bad—and therefore one should not marry for love.

IIi. Mac takes his leave of Polly, who realizes he is not coming back. Mrs. Peachum offers Jenny ten shillings to report Mac to the police. He will be out looking for sex, Mrs. Peachum is sure. IIii. Jenny cleans the glasses and makes the beds in the house of prostitution, but daydreams about the day when she can kill them all. Jenny and Mac fondly remember the six months when they kept house. She turns him in to the police. IIiii. In jail, Mac decides that only the rich live pleasantly. Polly and Mac's new girlfriend, Lucy, fight over Mac. IIiv. Lucy decides to poison Polly. IIv. Jenny and Mac agree that morals come after food.

IIIi. Peachum tells Brown that man is not smart enough to do anything right. IIIii. All the great men and women of history have come to bad ends, Jenny says. What will become of Mac and me? IIIiii. Preparing for the gallows, Mac calls on his friends to save him; then forgives them for not doing so. IIIiv. As Mac is being led to the gallows, a messenger appears with a pardon. In view of the Queen's coronation, Mac has been forgiven and elevated to the peerage. The street singer reflects that we generally forget the poor—who are not saved at the last minute by messengers from the king.

I Due Foscari • The Two Foscari

Composed by Giuseppe Verdi (October 9, 1813 – January 27, 1901). Libretto by Francesco Maria Piave. Italian. Based on the historical play by Lord Byron. Premiered Rome, Teatro Argentina, November 3, 1844. Set in Venice in 1457. Lyric tragedy. Set numbers with recitative. Prelude before I, II.

Sets: 6. **Acts:** 3 acts, 8 scenes. **Length:** I: 40. II: 37. III: 28. **Arias:** "O vecchio cor, che batti" (Doge), "Non maledirmi" (Jacopo), "Più non vive!" (Lucrezia), "Al infelice veglio conforta" (Jacopo). **Hazards:** None. **Scenes:** Ii. A room in the Doge's palace. Iii. A room in the Foscari palace. Iiii. The room in the Doge's palace. Iiv. Private apartments of the Doge. IIi. The state prison. IIii. The chambers of the council of ten. IIIi. The piazzetta. IIIii. The private apartments of the Doge.

Major roles: Jacopo Foscari (tenor), Lucrezia Contarini (soprano), Doge Francesco Foscari (baritone). **Minor roles:** Barbarigo (tenor), Jacopo Loredano (bass), Officer of the council of ten (tenor), Pisana (soprano). **Bit part:** Servant of the Doge (bass). **Mute:** Two sons of Jacopo Foscari, officers, gondoliers, sailors, pages.

Chorus parts: SSATTBB. **Chorus roles:** Members of the Council of Ten, senators, attendants of Lucrezia, Venetian ladies, people of Venice and maskers, guards, jailers, gondoliers, sailors, pages, servants. **Dance/movement:** III: Optional dance during barcarole. **Orchestra:** 2 fl, 2 ob, 2 cl, 2 bsn, 4 hrn, 2 trp, 3 trb, tuba, timp, perc, harp, strings. **Stageband:** II: band. III: trps, bells. **Publisher:** G. Ricordi. **Rights:** Expired.

Ii. Jacopo Foscari is called before the Council of Ten by his father, Doge Francesco Foscari. Iii. Jacopo's wife, Lucrezia, pleads on her husband's behalf. Iiii. But Jacopo is sent back into exile. Iiv. The doge feels for his son, but cannot allow himself to be moved by Lucrezia's pleas.

IIi. Lucrezia and the doge visit Jacopo in prison and tell him his sentence. Loredano comes to take Jacopo to Crete. He orders Lucrezia to stay behind. IIii. The council discusses Jacopo's supposed crime of killing a Donato and siding with Venice's enemies. Lucrezia makes one final plea, but is again rejected.

IIIi. The Venetians celebrate. Jacopo takes leave of his wife and children. IIIii. Barbarigo gives the doge proof of Jacopo's innocence, but Jacopo has died on his way into exile. The Council of Ten deposes the doge. Francesco Foscari's enemy, Malipiero, is proclaimed doge. Foscari drops dead.

Il Duello Comico • The Comic Duel

Composed by Giovanni Paisiello (May 9, 1740 – June 5, 1816). Libretto by Giovanni Battista Lorenzi. Italian (or French). Original work Premiered Naples, Teatro Nuovo, Spring 1774. Set in Naples in the 18th century. Comedy. Set numbers with recitative and spoken dialogue. Overture.

Sets: 1. **Acts:** 1 act, 1 scene. **Hazards:** None. **Scenes:** I. A street before Bettina's house and Fortunata's inn.

Major roles: Bettina (soprano), Leandro (tenor), Topo (bass), Dr. Policronio (bass), Dr. Simone (bass), Clarice (soprano). **Minor roles:** Violetta (soprano), Fortunata (soprano).

Chorus parts: N/A. **Chorus roles:** None. **Dance/movement:** None. **Orchestra:** 2 fl, 2 ob, 2 cl, 2 bsn, 2 hrn, 2 trp, strings. **Stageband:** None. **Publisher:** Le Duc. **Rights:** Expired.

I. Bettina's brother, Simone, and Leandro laugh at Bettina's preference for French over her native tongue. Leandro proposes to Bettina, but she prefers Don Policronio. She sends Simone for a marriage license. Desperate, Leandro bribes the servants, Violetta and Topo, into helping him. Topo suggests Leandro fight a duel with Policronio. The pistols will not be loaded, but Policronio will be made to believe he has killed Leandro. Topo will persuade Policronio to flee rather than face the consequences. Clarice has been abandoned by Leandro. She confides in Fortunata. Topo delivers Leandro's challenge. The duel occurs and Policronio flees as planned. Leandro pretends to have gone mad because he could not have Bettina. Topo convinces Bettina that Policronio is a drunk and a womanizer and she agrees to marry Leandro. Policronio returns and tries to speak to Bettina, but Topo hurries him away. Bettina warns Leandro that she will not tolerate jealousy in a husband. Clarice and Fortunata call the police on Policronio. But Simone points out that Leandro is not dead—and he is about to marry Bettina. The plot being revealed, Bettina goes back to Policronio and Leandro marries Clarice.

The Duenna

See "Betrothal in a Convent" entry.

A Kékszakállú Herceg Vará • Duke Bluebeard's Castle

Composed by Béla Bartók (March 25, 1881 – September 26, 1945). Libretto by Béla Balázs. Hungarian. Based on a fairy tale. Premiered Budapest, Budapest Opera, May 24, 1918. Set in Bluebeard's castle at an unspecified time. Fantasy opera. Through composed. Spoken prologue.

Sets: 1. **Acts:** 1 act, 1 scene. **Length:** I: 63. **Hazards:** None. **Scenes:** I. Vast circular Gothic hall.

Major roles: Count Bluebeard (bass baritone), Judith (soprano or mezzo). **Speaking:** Prologue. **Mute:** Bluebeard's three former wives.

Chorus parts: N/A. **Chorus roles:** None. **Dance/movement:** None. **Orchestra:** 4 fl (2 picc), 2 ob, Eng hrn, 3 cl (bs cl), 4 bsn (cont bsn), 4 hrn, 4 trp, 4 trb, tuba, 2 harp, celeste, organ, timp, perc, strings. **Stageband:** I: 4 trp, 4 trb. **Publisher:** Universal Edition. **Rights:** Copyright 1921, 1925 by Universal Edition. Renewed by Boosey and Hawkes.

I. Judith loves Bluebeard. She has left her family for him and is not discouraged by Bluebeard's dark and gloomy castle, where she insists that seven locked and bolted doors be thrown open. Behind the first is Bluebeard's torture chamber, the walls dripping with blood. Bluebeard wonders why Judith wishes to pry into every corner. "Because I love you," she answers. He warns her to be careful. Judith opens the armory, the treasury and the secret garden. All are stained with blood. Behind the fifth door, she finds Bluebeard's kingdom. Bluebeard asks her not to open the final two doors, but Judith insists. The sixth door conceals a flood of tears. Bluebeard tells Judith to kiss him and not ask any more questions. Having guessed what is behind the seventh door, Judith inquires about Bluebeard's former wives. The seventh door conceals Bluebeard's former wives, who have bled to feed his garden, armory and torture chamber. Judith is locked in with the former wives.

Dvakrát Alexandr • Alexandr Twice

Composed by Bohuslav Martinů (December 8, 1890 – August 28, 1959). Libretto by André Wurmser. Czech. Original work. Premiered Mannheim, Opera house, February 18, 1964. Set in Paris in 1900. Comic opera. Set numbers with spoken dialogue. Prelude. Libretto originally written in German, but translated into Czech.

Sets: 1. **Acts:** 1 act, 11 scenes. **Length:** I: 40 **Hazards:** I: Alexandr's portrait sings. Armanda's dream. **Scenes:** I. A middle-class drawing room in Paris.

Major roles: Filoména/female narrator/goddess of matrimony (contralto), Alexandr II (baritone), Armanda (soprano), Portrait/male narrator/Alexandr I (bass). Minor role: Oskar (tenor).

Chorus parts: Speaking. **Chorus roles:** Extremely brief offstage chorus. **Dance/movement:** I: Demons dance. **Orchestra:** fl, ob, cl, bsn, hrn, trp, trb, piano, strings. **Stageband:** None. **Publisher:** Bärenreiter Kassel. **Rights:** Copyright 1937 by Bärenreiter Kassel.

Ii. The chambermaid, Filoména, contemplates love. Iii. Alexandr returns for his suitcase. Iiii. His wife, Armanda, worries that Alexandr will not be back in time to greet his American cousin. Iiv. Alexandr tells Filoména to keep quiet about the suitcase. Iv. The maid and Alexandr's own portrait condemn him for abandoning Armanda. Ivi. Oskar calls on Armanda. Ivii. He tells her of Alexandr's betrayal, but she does not believe him. Oskar loves Armanda, but she is faithful to Alexandr. Iviii. The American cousin—Alexandr's exact double—arrives and seduces Armanda. Iix. Wracked with guilt Armanda dreams she and the cousin have murdered her husband. She sees demons. Ix. The cousin was Alexandr himself. Ixi. When Alexandr leaves for work, Armanda goes out with Oskar.

Edgar

Composed by Giacomo Puccini (December 22, 1858 – November 29, 1924). Libretto by Ferdinando Fontana. Italian. Based on the play "La Coupe et les Lèvres" by Alfred de Musset. Premiered Milan, Teatro alla Scala, April 21, 1889. Set in Flanders in 1302. Lyric drama. Set numbers with recitative. Brief introduction before I. Prelude before III. Revised version (reduced from 4 acts to 3) premiered in Ferrara, February 28, 1892.

Sets: 3. **Acts:** 3 acts, 3 scenes. **Length:** I: 35. II: 20. III: 40. **Arias:** "Questo amor" (Frank), "Tu il cuor mi strazi" (Tigrana), "O soave vision" (Edgar), "Nel villaggio d'Edgar" (Fidelia). **Hazards:** I: Edgar burns down his house. **Scenes:** I. Square of a Flemish village. II. A terrace near a garden and street. III. The battlements of a fortress with the city of Courtray in the distance.

Major roles: Fidelia (soprano), Edgar (tenor), Tigrana (mezzo). **Minor roles:** Frank (baritone), Gualtiero (bass).

Chorus parts: SSATTTBBB. **Chorus roles:** Farmers, courtiers, banquet guests, soldiers, monks (12 bass), people, children (1 part), ushers. **Dance/movement:** None. **Orchestra:** 3 fl (picc), 2 ob (Eng hrn), 2 cl (bs cl), 2 bsn, 4 hrn, 3 trp, 3 trb, tuba, timp, 2 perc, harp, organ, strings. **Stageband:** II: drums, trps. III: trps. **Publisher:** G. Ricordi & Co. **Rights:** Expired.

I. Fidelia greets Edgar and gives him a twig from an almond tree. Tigrana reminds Edgar of his dead passion for her. She scorns her adoptive brother Frank's love for her (she was abandoned and brought up by Frank's parents). Tigrana's singing offends the devout peasants, but Edgar defends her. He sets fire to his house and is about to run off with Tigrana when Frank challenges him. Frank's father, Gualtiero, is unable to prevent a fight. Edgar wounds Frank and leaves with Tigrana.

II. Edgar is weary of Tigrana's dissipated life. She points out that he is dependent on her, having burned his father's house. Frank's military company passes by and Edgar joins them. Tigrana swears revenge.

III. Edgar is believed dead and is buried with great ceremony. Only a friar (Edgar himself in disguise) says bad things about the deceased. He convinces all but Fidelia that he was a bad man. Tigrana comes to mourn. Edgar pays her to slander himself publicly. When she does so, he removes his disguise and curses Tigrana. Tigrana stabs Fidelia.

Une Education Manquée • A Defective Education

Composed by Emmanuel Chabrier (January 18, 1841 – September 13, 1894). Libretto by Eugene Leterrier and Albert Vanloo. French. Original work. Premiered Paris, Cercle de la Presse, May 1, 1879. Set in France during the reign of Louis XVI. Comedy. Set numbers with spoken dialogue. Overture.

Sets: 1. **Acts:** 1 act, 1 scene. **Length:** I: 45. **Hazards:** None. **Scenes:** I. Gontran's home.

Major roles: Pausanias (bass), Gontran de Boismassif (tenor), Hélène de la Cerisaie (soprano).

Chorus parts: N/A. **Chorus roles:** None. **Dance/movement:** None. **Orchestra:** fl, picc, ob, cl, bsn, hrn, cornet, timp, perc, strings. **Stageband:** None. **Publisher:** Enoch & Co., Éditions Musicales du Marais. **Rights:** Expired.

I. Gontran brings his new bride, Hélène, home from the convent. His drunken tutor, Pausanias, announces Hélène's aunt. Gontran is terrified to learn that his grandfather has sent a letter instead of coming in person to advise on the wedding night. Neither the letter nor Hélène's aunt has any pertinent advice but the newlyweds are convinced there must be something more than kissing to be done. Gontran sends for Pausanias. Hélène retires to bed. Pausanias and Gontran review Gontran's education, but the tutor is forced to admit he knows nothing about the topic that interests Gontran. He promises to find out. A storm breaks. Hélène emerges from her bedroom, frightened by the lightening. Gontran comforts her and they learn what they were supposed to know. When Pausanias returns, Gontran sends him away.

Einstein on the Beach

Composed by Philip Glass (b. January 31, 1937). Libretto by Christopher Knowles, Lucinda Childs and Samuel M. Johnson. English. Original work with spoken texts by Christopher Knowles, Samuel Johnson and Lucinda Childs. Premiered Avignon, France, Festival of Avignon, July 25, 1976. Set in a train, courtroom and spaceship at an unspecified time. Minimalist opera. Through composed with various spoken texts. Lacking in a conventional plot, the piece centers on visual themes. Acts separated by "knee plays." Piece is a general meditation on the dangers and possibilities of Einstein's theory of relativity. Three central themes are of a train (used by Einstein to describe relativity); a trial (the cost of nuclear weapons); and a spaceship (the possibilities of science). "On the beach" is a reference to a novel about nuclear holocaust by Nevil Shute.

Sets: 7. **Acts:** 4 acts, 9 scenes, 5 knee plays. **Length:** I, II, III, IV: 270. **Hazards:** None. **Scenes:** Knee play 1. Ii. A train. Iii. A trial. Knee play 2. IIi. Field with spaceship. IIii. Night train. Knee play 3. IIIi. Trial and prison. IIIii. Field with spaceship. Knee play 4. IVi. Building and train. IVii. Bed. IViii. Spaceship. Knee play 5.

Major roles: Tenor and soprano soloists. Four actors, dancers, solo violinist/Einstein.

Chorus parts: SATB + SATTBB. **Chorus roles:** Small chorus (SATTBB; 6 people total) and large chorus (14 people). **Dance/movement:** II, III: Dance in field with spaceship. **Orchestra:** Soprano saxophone (flute), electric organ, flute (soprano sax, bs cl), sound mix, alto sax (flute), electric organ (synthesizer bs, additional keyboards). **Stageband:** I, II, III, IV: Einstein is a violinist. **Rights:** Copyright 1976 by G. Schirmer.

No plot in the conventional sense.

Elegie für junge Liebende • Elegy for Young Lovers

Composed by Hans Werner Henze (b. July 1, 1926). Libretto by W. H. Auden and Chester Kallman. German. Original work. Premiered Schwetzingen, Schlosstheater, May 20, 1961. Set in the Austrian alps in 1910. Tragedy. Through composed. Some spoken lines. Orchestral interlude in IIIvi during blizzard.

Sets: 3. **Acts:** 3 acts, 34 scenes. **Length:** I, II, III: 150. **Hazards:** III: Blizzard on the mountain. **Scenes:** I – IIIv. Parlor and terrace of "Der Schwarze Adler," an inn in the Austrian alps. IIIvi – IIIviii. On the Hammerhorn. IIIix. Dressing room and stage of a theater in Vienna.

Major roles: Hilda Mack (coloratura soprano), Carolina Countess of Kirchstetten (contralto), Dr. Wilhelm Reischmann (bass), Toni Reischmann (lyric tenor), Gregor Mittenhofer (baritone), Elisabeth Zimmer (soprano). **Speaking:** Josef Mauer. **Mute:** servants.

Chorus parts: N/A. **Chorus roles:** None. **Dance/movement:** None. **Orchestra:** fl (picc, alto fl), Eng hrn (ob), cl (bs cl), alto sax, bsn, hrn, trp, trb, timp, perc, cow bell (taped), celeste, flexatone, marimbaphone, vibraphone, mandolin, guitar, harp, piano, 2 vln, vla, vlc, cont bs. **Stageband:** I: perc. **Publisher:** B. Schott's Söhne. **Rights:** Copyright 1961 by B. Schott's Söhne.

Ii. Hilda Mack waits for her husband, who left to climb the Hammerhorn forty years ago and never returned. Iii. Carolina and Dr. Reischmann read the latest, mostly favorable, reviews of Mittenhofer's poetry. Carolina hides money for Mittenhofer to find—one of many ways in which she and the doctor tend Mittenhofer and keep him going. Iiii. The doctor's son, Toni, joins them. Iiv. Toni is introduced to Mittenhofer's young lover, Elisabeth. Hilda has a vision. Iv. Hilda's visions inspire Mittenhofer's poetry. The poet reduces Carolina to tears because of typos in his proofs. Weakened by flu, she faints. Ivi. Mittenhofer finds Carolina's money. Ivii. The doctor examines Carolina. Iviii. Josef Mauer reports that the body of Hilda's husband has been discovered, preserved in the Alpine ice. Iix. Carolina and the doctor decide Elisabeth should tell Hilda. Ix. Elisabeth tells Hilda. Ixi. Toni remembers his mother's final days. Ixii. Hilda accepts her husband's death.

IIi. Elisabeth and Toni are in love. IIii. Carolina and the doctor disapprove and scold them. IIiii. The lovers are resentful. IIiv. Carolina discovers Mittenhofer already knows the truth. IIv. Using self deprecation and an appeal for his art, Mittenhofer convinces Elisabeth to stay. IIvi. Toni asks about the interview. IIvii. Elisabeth admits she cannot leave Mittenhofer. IIviii. Toni confronts Mittenhofer who leaves the decision up to Elisabeth. IIix. Hilda has been drinking. She comforts Elisabeth. Elisabeth proposes to Toni, who accepts. Mittenhofer overrides the doctor's objections. IIx. He quotes to them from his new poem. IIxi. "Stay one more day until I have completed it," Mittenhofer begs Elisabeth. She agrees. IIxii. All look forward to the coming day. IIxiii. In private, Mittenhofer vents his contempt for his companions.

IIIi. The young lovers go hiking on the mountain while Mittenhofer has writer's block. IIIii. Before going, Hilda makes her peace with Carolina. IIIiii. The doctor leaves to prepare the town house. IIIiv. Carolina thinks Mittenhofer is better off without Elisabeth. He wonders how long it will be before the young lovers get bored with each other. A storm is coming on and Mauer asks Mittenhofer if he knows of anyone up on the mountain. The poet lies and says "no." IIIv. Carolina determines to stay with Mittenhofer. IIIvi. Elizabeth and Toni try to find shelter from the blizzard. IIIvii. They pretend to look back on forty years of marriage. IIIviii. The lovers die in the blizzard. IIIix. Mittenhofer reads his elegy for Elisabeth and Toni.

Die Englische Katze • The English Cat

Composed by Hans Werner Henze (b. July 1, 1926). Libretto by Edward Bond. German. Based on "Peines de Coeur d'une Chatte Anglaise" by Honoré de Balzac. Premiered Schwetzingen, Württemberg State Theater, June 2, 1983. Set in London about 1900. Comedy. Through composed. Dances between scenes.

Sets: 5. **Acts:** 2 acts, 7 scenes. **Length:** I, II: 125. **Arias:** "The world is wide" (Minette), "Man makes his world" (Tom). **Hazards:** Main characters are all animals. **Scenes:** Ii. Mrs. Halifax's drawing room. Iii. The roof of Mrs. Halifax's house. Iiii. Mrs. Halifax's private chapel. IIi. The drawing room. IIii. Divorce court. IIiii. The drawing room. IIiv. Lawyer's chambers in Lincoln's Inn Fields.

Major roles: Lord Puff/Offstage serenader (light spinto tenor), Minette (light soprano), Tom/Offstage serenader (lyric baritone). **Minor roles:** Peter/Mr. Keen/Defense counsel/Lucian/Parson/Offstage serenader (lyric tenor), Jones the money lender/Mr. Fawn/Judge/Offstage serenader (baritone), Miss Crisp/Star/Jury member (soprano), Mr. Plunkett/Prosecution counsel/Offstage serenader (bass baritone), Arnold/Offstage serenader (bass), Mrs. Gomfit/Star/Jury member (soprano), Lady Toodle/Star/Jury member (mezzo), Babette/Moon/Jury member (mezzo), Louise/Star/Jury member (soprano). (All characters are cats except (a) Louise is a mouse; (b) Jury members are birds; (c) Lucian is a fox; (d) prosecution and defense counsels and judge are dogs; (d) the parson is a sheep.)

Chorus parts: N/A. **Chorus roles:** None. **Dance/movement:** I: Counter dance, collages. II: Tempesta, courante, anglaise. **Orchestra:** 2 fl (2 picc, 2 recorders), 2 ob (2 Eng hrn, heckelphone), 2 cl (bs cl, cont bs cl), 2 bsn (cont bsn), 2 hrn, trp, trb, 3 perc, harp, chamber organ, celeste, piano, strings (6-4-3-3-1). **Stageband:** None. **Publisher:** Schott. **Rights:** Copyright 1983 by B. Schott's Söhne.

Ii. Mrs. Halifax wants her cat, Lord Puff, to marry Minette. This upsets Puff's nephew, Arnold, who hopes to inherit Puff's fortune. Minette is introduced to Puff and the other feline members of the Royal Society for the Protection of Rats (RSPR). Iii. On the roof of the house, Minette meets Peter, a stray cat who declares his love for her. Iiii. Arnold tries to poison Puff. When this fails, he accuses Minette of having a lover (Tom). Puff is disturbed, but goes ahead with the wedding for fear that a scandal will ruin his chance at the presidency of the RSPR.

IIi. Minette gives money to her sister, Babette, who has been evicted. Tom joins the army to forget Minette, but deserts. She loves him. Puff's

friends discover them together and insist Puff divorce Minette. IIii. Tom
disguises himself as the defense counsel and argues that Puff and
Minette's marriage was never consummated. The judge is biased and
fines Tom. Privately, Tom explains to Minette how he escaped from his
regiment after being lashed 99 times. Tom's disguise is exposed and he
is taken into custody. The prosecuting counsel recognizes Tom as the
long lost son of Lord Fairport: he is rich. IIiii. Upset by the scandal, Mrs.
Halifax has ordered Minette to be put in a sack and tossed into the river.
Tom falls in love with Babette and obtains Minette's blessing for him to
marry Babette. IIiv. The RSPR murder Tom to get his money. Louise the
mouse runs off with the money she has collected for the RSPR.

Elektra

Composed by Richard Strauss (June 11, 1864 – September 8, 1949).
Libretto by Hugo von Hofmannsthal. German. Based on the play by
Sophocles. Premiered Dresden, Semper Opernhaus, January 25, 1909. Set
in Mykene after the Trojan war. Music drama. Through composed. Opus
58.

Sets: 1. **Acts:** 1 act, 1 scene. **Length:** I: 105. **Hazards:** None. **Scenes:** I. The
inner courtyard bounded by the back of the palace.

Major roles: Klytemnästra (mezzo), Elektra (dramatic soprano),
Chrysothemis (soprano), Orest (baritone). **Minor roles:** Overseer (soprano), Five maid servants (contralto, 2 mezzos, 2 sopranos), Young servant
(tenor), Aegisth (tenor). **Bit parts:** Confidante (soprano), Train bearer
(soprano), Old servant (bass), Guardian/Tutor of Orest (bass).

Chorus parts: SSAATTBB. **Chorus roles:** Offstage servants.
Dance/movement: I: Elektra's dance of triumph. **Orchestra:** picc, 3 fl (2
picc), 3 ob (Eng hrn), heckelphone, 5 cl, 2 basset hrn, bs cl, 3 bsn, cont
bsn, 8 hrn (4 Wagner tuba), 6 trp, bs trp, 3 trb, cont bs trb, cont bs tuba, 2
timp, 3 or 4 perc, glockenspiel, celesta, 2 harp, strings (8-8-8-6-6-6-6-8:
three divisions in vlns and vlas). **Stageband:** None. **Publisher:** Boosey &
Hawkes. **Rights:** Copyright 1916, 1943 Adolph Fürstner. Assigned 1943
to Boosey & Hawkes.

I. The maid servants discuss the abuse heaped on them by Elektra, the
mad daughter of Queen Klytemnästra. Elektra recalls the murder of her
father by Klytemnästra. Elektra's sister Chrysothemis warns her that the
queen and her new husband, Aegisth, mean to imprison Elektra.
Chrysothemis begs Elektra to forget her hatred so that both sisters may
lead normal lives, bearing and rearing children. Sounds are heard within. The queen has dreamed that her son, Orest, was pursuing her.

Disgusted with her own infirmities and the useless counsels of her advisers, Klytæmnestra talks with Elektra. She confesses she is plagued by nightmares and visions and asks what sacrifice will end the nightmares. Only one sacrifice will work, Elektra tells her: your own death. She guesses that Klytæmnestra is terrified at the thought of Orest's return. News arrives of Orest's death. Elektra tells Chrysothemis they must now kill Aegisth and Klytæmnestra themselves, but Chrysothemis refuses. Elektra digs up the axe with which her father was murdered, but is interrupted by Orest—whom she does not recognize. He says he has news for the queen of Orest's death. When Elektra gives her name, Orest confesses his own. Orest kills Klytæmnestra. Aegisth returns and is likewise murdered. Elektra dances and falls lifeless to the ground.

Elisabetta

Composed by Gioachino Rossini (February 29, 1792 – November 13, 1868). Libretto by Giovanni Federico Schmidt. Italian. Based on a play by Carlo Federici. Premiered Naples, Teatro San Carlo, October 4, 1815. Set in England in the late 16th century. Lyric drama. Set numbers with recitative. Overture.

Sets: 5. Acts: 2 acts, 5 scenes. Length: I: 75. II: 65. Arias: "Qui sosteniamo" / "Che intesi" (Norfolk). Hazards: None. Scenes: Ii. The royal hall. Iii. The royal apartments. IIi. A room in the palace. IIii. A hall adjacent to the prison. IIiii. The dungeon.

Major roles: Duke of Norfolk (tenor), Elisabetta (soprano), Leicester (tenor). Minor roles: Guglielmo (tenor), Matilde (soprano), Enrico (contralto).

Chorus parts: SATTB. Chorus roles: Knights, people, soldiers, guards. Dance/movement: None. Orchestra: 2 fl (picc), 2 ob, Eng hrn, 2 cl, 2 bsn, 2 hrn, 2 trp, 3 trb, timp, perc, strings, continuo. Stageband: None. Publisher: Belwin Mills. Rights: Expired.

Ii. Leicester is welcomed home from a victorious war in Scotland by Queen Elisabetta. Norfolk is jealous. Leicester is horrified to find his wife, Matilde, and her brother, Enrico, among his prisoners. She followed Leicester after hearing of Elisabetta's love for him. Leicester points out that Matilde's kinship with Maria Stuarda puts her at grave risk. Iii. Leicester tells Norfolk his secret. Norfolk immediately betrays him to the queen, and the queen has Leicester arrested.

IIi. The queen is unable to persuade Leicester to renounce Matilde. She banishes Norfolk. IIii. Norfolk incites Leicester's soldiers to free their beloved general. IIiii. Leicester is horrified that Norfolk wants him to start a rebellion and refuses. Elisabetta offers to let Leicester escape, but he begs for Matilde's and Enrico's lives. The queen tells Leicester that Norfolk betrayed him. Overhearing this, Norfolk attacks the queen but Enrico and Matilde disarm him; Norfolk is arrested and the queen pardons Leicester, Matilde and Enrico.

L'Elisir d'Amore • The Elixir of Love

Composed by Gaetano Donizetti (November 29, 1797 – April 8, 1848). Libretto by Felice Romani. Italian. Based on libretto "Le Philtre" by Eugène Scribe. Premiered Milan, Teatro della Canobbiana, May 12, 1832. Set in a small Italian village in the 19th century. Melodrama. Set numbers with recitative. Brief prelude.

Sets: 4. **Acts:** 2 acts, 4 scenes. **Length:** I: 66. II: 51. **Arias:** "Una furtiva lagrima" (Nemorino), "Come paride" (Belcore), "Quanto è bella" (Nemorino), "Udite, udite o rustici" (Dulcamara). **Hazards:** None. **Scenes:** Ii. Outside Adina's farm. Iii. The village square. IIi. Inside Adina's farmhouse. IIii. A courtyard.

Major roles: Adina (soprano), Nemorino (tenor), Belcore (baritone), Dr. Dulcamara (comic bass). **Minor roles:** Giannetta (soprano).

Chorus parts: SATTB. **Chorus roles:** Villagers, soldiers. **Dance/movement:** II: Peasant dance sometimes done in wedding scene. **Orchestra:** 2 fl (picc), 2 ob, 2 cl, 2 bsn, 2 hrn, 2 trp, 2 or 3 trb, timp, harp, piano, strings. **Stageband:** I: drum, cornet. II: band. **Publisher:** G. Ricordi. **Rights:** Expired.

Ii. The peasant Nemorino is in love with Adina who seems to be attracted to Sergeant Belcore. Iii. In hopes of winning over Adina, Nemorino buys what he thinks is a magic love potion from the quack Dr. Dulcamara (it's actually Bordeaux).

IIi. Nemorino's feigned indifference to Adina infuriates her and she agrees to marry Belcore. In desperation, Nemorino enlists in Belcore's regiment so that he can buy more love potion with the enlistment bonus. IIii. Meanwhile, Nemorino's uncle has died (offstage), leaving him a rich man. Nemorino hasn't heard the news, but the village girls have and they mob him—which only convinces him that the potion is finally working. Adina buys back Nemorino's enlistment papers and confesses her love for him.

Das Ende einer Welt • The End of a World

Composed by Hans Werner Henze (b. July 1, 1926). Libretto by Wolfgang Hildescheimer. German. Original work. Premiered Hamburg, Radio, December 4, 1953. Set on a man made island in the Venetian lagoon in the present. Radio opera. Set numbers with recitative. Spoken prologue. Originally written for radio. Revised for stage and premiered in Frankfurt, November 30, 1965.

Sets: 2. **Acts:** 1 act, 2 scenes. **Length:** I: 50. **Hazards:** I: palace sinks into the sea. Fallersleben escapes by gondola. **Scenes:** Ii. The hall of the Montetristo palace. Iii. Outside the palace.

Major role: Fallersleben (tenor). **Minor roles:** Major domo (baritone), Signora Sgambati (coloratura soprano), Marchioness Montetristo (contralto), Madam Dombrowska (tenor), Professor Kuntz-Sartori (baritone), Golch (bass).

Chorus parts: SSSATB. **Chorus roles:** Guests, servants. **Dance/movement:** None. **Orchestra:** recorder, fl, ob, cl, bsn, hrn, trp, trb, harmonium, grand piano, harp, guitar, 3 timp, perc, strings (mostly soloists). **Stageband:** I: trp, cembalo, fl. **Publisher:** B. Schott's Söhne. **Rights:** Copyright 1965 by B. Schott's Söhne.

Ii. Fallersleben attends a literary soiree given by the Marquise Montetristo on her manmade island near Venice. The guests are entertained with a flute concerto. The island begins to sink, but the performance goes on. Iii. Fallersleben and the servants leave, but the other guests stay to the end and are drowned.

L'Enfant et les Sortilèges • The Child and the Visions

Composed by Maurice Ravel (March 7, 1875 – December 28, 1937). Libretto by Sidonie-Gabrielle Colette. French. Original work. Premiered Monte Carlo, Théâtre de Monte Carlo, March 21, 1925. Set in Normandy in the present. Lyric fantasy. Through composed. Ballet.

Sets: 2. **Acts:** 1 act, 2 scenes. **Length:** I: 45. **Arias:** "Toi, le coeur de la rose" (Child). **Hazards:** I: Scenery is to scale for a small child; animated furniture and animals; princess swallowed by the earth; walls of the room fly away to reveal the garden; dragonflies and moths fly. Shepherds come to life from wallpaper. **Scenes:** Ii. A room in the country opening on a garden. Iii. The garden.

Major role: Child (mezzo). **Minor roles:** Mama/Chinese cup/Dragonfly (mezzo contralto), Black cat/Comtoise clock (baritone), Armchair/Tree (bass), Shepherdess/Screech owl (soprano), Black Wedgwood teapot (tenor), Fire/Princess/Nightingale (soprano), Little old man/ Arithmetic/Tree frog (tenor), White cat/squirrel (mezzo), Bat (soprano). **Bit parts:** Bench (treble), Couch (treble), Stool (treble), Wicker chair (treble), Shepherd (contralto), Shepherdess (soprano), Four animals (alto, tenor, soprano, bass). **Mute:** Cinder, lambs, blue dog, book pages.

Chorus parts: SSAATTBB. **Chorus roles:** Shepherds, shepherdesses, men, women, numbers (children in 3 parts), trees, animals. **Dance/movement:** I: Armchair and bergère do a "measured and grotesque" dance. Teapot and cup dance. Brief pastoral ballet. Numbers dance. Dragonflies and moths dance. Frogs dance and play. **Orchestra:** picc, 2 fl, 2 ob, Eng hrn, 3 cl, bs cl, 2 bsn, cont bsn, 4 hrn, 3 trp, 3 trb, tuba, timp, perc, xylophone, celeste, harp, piano, strings. **Stageband:** I: fl. **Publisher:** A. Durand & Fils. **Rights:** Copyright 1925, 1932 by Durand.

Ii. Ignoring his mother's admonitions, a child breaks things and pulls the cat's tail. The furniture comes to life and gets revenge by terrorizing the child. The fire chases him and the shepherds painted on the wall paper scold him. The princess from his favorite childhood book—which the child ripped to pieces—is swallowed by the earth. Arithmetic rises up out of one of the torn books and torments him. Iii. The child is transported into the garden, where the trees and animals attack him for his cruelty. So anxious are they to hurt the child that they fight amongst themselves for the privilege. The child tends a wounded squirrel though he is himself hurt. Impressed, the animals carry him home.

L'Enfant Prodigue • The Prodigal Son

Composed by Claude Debussy (August 22, 1862 – March 25, 1918). Libretto by E. Guinand. French. Based on the Bible. Premiered Paris, Conservatory (Prix de Rome), 1884. Set near Lake Génézareth in Biblical times. Lyric scene. Set numbers with accompanied recitative. Prelude

Sets: 1. **Acts:** 1 act, 1 scene. **Length:** I: 35. **Arias:** "L'année en vain" (Lia), "Ces airs joyeux" (Azaël), "Mon fils est revenu" (Siméon). **Hazards:** None. **Scenes:** I. A village near the sea of Génézareth.

Major roles: Lia (soprano), Azaël (tenor). **Minor role:** Siméon (baritone). **Mute:** Young people.

Chorus parts: N/A. **Chorus roles:** None. **Dance/movement:** I: dance of the young men and maidens. **Orchestra:** 3 fl (picc), 2 ob, Eng hrn, 2 cl, 2

bsn, 4 hrn, 2 trp, 3 trb, tuba, timp, perc, 2 harp, strings. **Stageband:** None. **Publisher:** A. Durand & Fils. **Rights:** Expired.

I. Lia still misses her son, Azaël, and wonders why he left. Exhausted and broken, Azaël returns to his ancestral home. His parents welcome and forgive him.

L'Enlèvement d'Europe • The Abduction of Europe

Composed by Darius Milhaud (September 4, 1892 – June 22, 1974). Libretto by Henri Hoppenot. French. Based on Greek mythology. Premiered Baden Baden, Town Hall, July 17, 1927. Set in Thebes in legendary times. Satire. Through composed.

Sets: 1. **Acts:** 1 act, 7 scenes. **Length:** I: 9. **Hazards:** I: Jupiter is disguised as a bull. **Scenes:** I. Before the house of Agénor in the country.

Major roles: Pergamon (baritone), King Agénor (bass), Jupiter (tenor), Europe (soprano). **Minor roles:** Three servant girls (soprano, mezzo, contralto), Three soldiers/workers (tenor, baritone, bass).

Chorus parts: N/A. **Chorus roles:** None. **Dance/movement:** None. **Orchestra:** fl, ob, cl, bsn, trp, perc, strings (1-0-1-1-1). **Stageband:** None. **Publisher:** Universal Edition. **Rights:** Copyright 1927 by Universal Edition. Renewed 1955.

Ii. Europe refuses to marry Pergamon. Iii. He complains to her father, King Agénor, that she prefers her cattle to him. Iiii. The men hide to watch her. Iiv. Disguised as a bull, Jupiter woos Europe, who promises to meet him in the field after dark. Iv. The chorus relates how Pergamon attacks Jupiter. Ivi. Pergamon is mortally wounded. Ivii. Europe leaves with Jupiter.

Die Entführung aus dem Serail • The Abduction from the Seraglio

Composed by Wolfgang Amadeus Mozart (January 27, 1756 – December 5, 1791). Libretto by Gottlieb Stephanie. German. Based on libretto by Christoph Friedrich Bretzner. Premiered Vienna, Burgtheater, July 16, 1782. Set in the country palace of the Pasha in the mid-16th century. Comic opera/singspiel. Set numbers with recitative. Overture. Spoken dialogue.

Sets: 3. **Acts:** 3 acts, 28 scenes. **Length:** I: 40. II: 50. III: 40. **Arias:** "Ach ich liebte" (Konstanze), "Ha wie will ich triumphieren" (Osmin), "Ich baue ganz" (Belmonte), "Martern aller Arten" (Konstanze), "Traurigkeit" (Konstanze), "Welche Wonne, welche Lust" (Blöndchen). **Hazards:** None. **Scenes:** I. A square in front of the Pasha's palace on the seashore. II. A garden in Pasha Selim's palace. IIIi – IIIv. The square in front of the Pasha's palace. IIIvi – IIIix. The Pasha's chamber.

Major roles: Konstanze (soprano), Belmonte (tenor), Blöndchen or Blonde (soprano), Pedrillo (tenor), Osmin (bass). **Speaking:** Pasha Selim, Klaas the boatman. **Mute:** a mute.

Chorus parts: SATB. **Chorus roles:** Guards, slaves, janissaries (chorus only appears in two scenes and can be offstage). **Dance/movement:** None. **Orchestra:** picc, 2 fl, 2 ob, 2 cl (basset horn), 2 bsn, 2 hrn, 2 trp, timp, perc, strings (solo fl, ob, vln and vlc quartet in IIiii). **Stageband:** None. **Publisher:** International, Broude Brothers. **Rights:** Expired.

Ii. Belmonte longs to free his beloved Konstanze from the harem of the Pasha Selim. Iii. He approaches Osmin, who reluctantly confirms that this is the pasha's house. When Belmonte asks after Pedrillo (his servant, who is now the pasha's slave), Osmin chases him away. Iiii. Osmin threatens Pedrillo and storms off. Iiv. Belmonte returns and Pedrillo admits he had almost given up hope of rescue. "After we were captured by the pirates," Pedrillo explains, "the pasha bought Konstanze, her maid Blöndchen and me as slaves." They plot their escape. Iv. Belmonte longs to be reunited with Konstanze. Ivi. Pasha Selim returns, accompanied by his Janissaries. Ivii. Konstanze tells Pasha Selim she does not return his love. She appeals to his good nature and begs for time. Iviii. Pedrillo introduces Belmonte to Pasha Selim as an architect looking for work. Iix. He promises Belmonte to arrange an interview with Konstanze. Ix. Osmin tries, unsuccessfully, to prevent Pedrillo and Belmonte from entering the garden.

IIi. Blöndchen gives Osmin a piece of her mind and chases him away. IIii. Konstanze bemoans her fate and is consoled by Blöndchen. IIiii. Pasha Selim confronts Konstanze, but she declares she will never love him. She assures him that torture and death will not change her mind, but asks him to show mercy. IIiv. Pasha Selim is impressed by her firmness. IIv. Blöndchen wonders if she would be so resolute in her mistress's place. IIvi. Pedrillo tells Blöndchen that Belmonte means to rescue them tonight. He gives her sleeping powder for Osmin, keeping some if he should see Osmin first. IIvii. Pedrillo works up his courage for the escape. IIviii. He persuades Osmin to have a glass of wine—into which he has poured the sleeping potion. The two men toast Bacchus and womankind. The potion begins to take effect. IIix. Pedrillo and

Blöndchen arrive and Konstanze and Belmonte are reunited. The women are offended when the men doubt they have been true. The men beg forgiveness.

IIIi. Klaas the boatman and Pedrillo set up ladders to help the ladies escape. IIIii. Pedrillo makes a last check of the area. IIIiii. Belmonte anticipates success. IIIiv. Pedrillo signals the women. IIIv. A mute alerts the drunken Osmin to the escape attempt and summons help. The four lovers are captured. Osmin gloats over his plans to torture and execute them. IIIvi. Konstanze and Belmonte are led before the pasha, who is vengefully pleased to learn that Belmonte is the son of his worst enemy, the commandant of Oran. IIIvii. Konstanze and Belmonte agree it is better to die together than to live apart. IIIviii. Pedrillo and Blöndchen are brought in. IIIix. Rather than repay the commandant's wrong with another, the pasha decides to release the four. They express their gratitude and everyone praises Pasha Selim.

Ernani

Composed by Giuseppe Verdi (October 9, 1813 – January 27, 1901). Libretto by Francesco Maria Piave. Italian. Based on the play by Victor Hugo. Premiered Venice, Teatro la Fenice, March 9, 1844. Set in Spain in the early 16th century. Lyric drama. Set numbers with recitative. Prelude.

Sets: 5. **Acts:** 4 acts, 5 scenes. **Length:** I: 45. II: 30. III: 20. IV: 15. **Arias:** "Ernani involami" (Elvira), "Infelice, e tu credevi" (Silva). **Hazards:** None. **Scenes:** Ii. Mountains of Aragon. Iii. Elvira's room in Silva's castle. II. A magnificent hall in Silva's palace. III. Underground vaults in Aix-la-Chapelle containing the tomb of Charlemagne. IV. A terrace in Don Juan of Aragon (Ernani)'s palace in Saragozza.

Major roles: Ernani (tenor), Don Carlo (baritone), Don Ruy Gomez de Silva (bass), Elvira (soprano). **Minor roles:** Giovanna (mezzo), Don Riccardo (tenor), Jago (bass).

Chorus parts: SSATTBB. **Chorus roles:** Rebel mountaineers, brigands, Elvira's attendants, knights and servants of Silva, conspirators, electors, nobles, ladies. **Dance/movement:** None. **Orchestra:** 2 fl, 2 ob, 2 cl, bs cl, 2 bsn, 4 hrn, 2 trp, 3 trb, tuba, timp, perc, harp, strings. **Stageband:** II: picc, Ab cl, Eb cl, 2 B cl, 2 hrn, 4 trp, 2 flügelhrn, bombarini, 3 trb, drums. IV: 3 trp. **Rights:** Expired.

Ii. Ernani's fellow brigands exhort him to drink and be merry. Ernani loves Elvira, the fiancée of Don Ruy Gomez de Silva. The brigands agree to abduct her. Iii. In Silva's castle, Elvira longs for Ernani to save her from the loathsome Silva. Don Carlo (the king) also loves Elvira, but she scorns him and draws a dagger to defend herself. Ernani confronts Carlo, his mortal enemy, with the murder of Ernani's father. Returning to find two would-be seducers in his home, Silva challenges them both. Silva's ardor diminishes when he realizes one of the men is his king. Ernani tells Elvira his plan to rescue her while Carlo enlists Silva in his quest to be Holy Roman Emperor.

II. It is Silva and Elvira's wedding day. Ernani offers his life to Silva. Elvira and Ernani embrace but are separated by Silva. Carlo arrives looking for Ernani, but Silva hides him, wishing to punish the brigand himself. The king demands—and gets—Elvira. Silva now challenges Ernani, but Ernani refuses to fight an old man. Ernani points out that they now have a common enemy—the king. He suggests they join forces and promises to kill himself when Silva chooses.

III. Carlo hides in Charlemagne's tomb to spy on those conspiring against him. The conspirators draw lots to determine who will assassinate Carlo and Ernani is chosen. Cannon sound, announcing Carlo's election as emperor. He orders the conspirators executed, but Elvira pleads for mercy. Carlo pardons everyone and orders Elvira and Ernani to wed. Silva is furious.

IV. Elvira and Ernani are celebrating their marriage when Silva appears and reminds Ernani of his oath to die when Silva chose. Ernani stabs himself.

Erwartung • Expectation

Composed by Arnold Schönberg (September 13, 1874 – July 13, 1951). Libretto by Marie Pappenheim. German. Original work. Premiered Prague, Neues Deutsches Theater, June 6, 1924. Set in a woods at night in the present. Monodrama. Through-composed, atonal. Opus 17.

Sets: 3. **Acts:** 1 act, 4 scenes. **Length:** I: 30. **Hazards:** None. **Scenes:** Ii. The edge of a wood. Roads and fields visible in the moonlight. Iii – Iiii. A broad path in the woods. Iiv. A road before a house.

Major role: Woman (soprano or mezzo).

Chorus parts: N/A. **Chorus roles:** None. **Dance/movement:** None. **Orchestra:** picc, 3 fl (picc), 4 ob (Eng hrn), 4 cl, bs cl, 3 bsn, cont bsn, 4 hrn, 3 trp, 4 trb, tuba, harp, celeste, glockenspiel, xylophone, timp, perc, strings (16-14-10 to 12-10 to 12-8 to 10). **Stageband:** None. **Publisher:** Universal Edition. **Rights:** Copyright 1924 by Universal Edition.

Ii. It is night and the woman runs into the woods. Iii. Every noise and movement terrifies her. Iiii. She calls out to her darling whom she is trying to find. Iiv. Emerging from the woods, she discovers the dead body of her beloved. She remembers her love for him—and the white-armed woman with whom he betrayed her. As the sun rises, she wonders what she should do.

Esclarmonde

Composed by Jules-Emile-Frédéric Massenet (May 12, 1842 – August 13, 1912). Libretto by Alfred Blau and Louise de Gramont. French. Based on the medieval romance "Parthenopoeus de Blois." Premiered Paris, Opéra Comique, May 14, 1889. Set in Byzantium and France in the Middle Ages. Romantic opera. Set numbers with recitative. Prologue. Epilogue. Entr'actes before each act. Musical interludes between scenes. Ballet.

Sets: 7. **Acts:** 4 acts, 8 scenes. **Length:** I, II, III, IV: 155. **Hazards:** I: Esclarmonde's incantation. Tripod transformed into chariot. II: Vision of virgins of St. George. IV: Magical summons of Esclarmonde. **Scenes:** Prologue. The basilica at Byzantium. I. A terrace of the palace at Byzantium. Iii. An enchanted island. Iiii. A room in an enchanted palace. IIIi. A public square in Blois. IIIii. Roland's chamber in Cléomer's palace. IV. The forest of Ardennes. Epilogue. The basilica.

Major roles: Emperor Phorcas (bass), Princess Esclarmonde (soprano), Parséïs (mezzo), Count Roland (tenor). **Minor roles:** Énée (tenor), King Cléomer (bass), Bishop of Blois (bass baritone), Byzantine herald (tenor). **Bit part:** Saracen envoy (bass).

Chorus parts: SSAATTBB. **Chorus roles:** Dignitaries, knights, guards, monks, priests, penitents, warriors, virgins, children, spirits, courtiers, people, nymphs. **Dance/movement:** II: spirits' dance. IV: ballet of the wood spirits. **Orchestra:** 3 fl (picc), 2 ob, Eng hrn, 2 cl, bs cl, 2 bsn, cont bsn (or sarrusophone), 4 hrn, 3 trp, 3 trb, tuba, timp, perc, harps, strings. **Stageband:** Prologue, epilogue: organ. III: 3 trb, 3 tuba, perc, organ. IV: 4 trp, 3 trb, 3 tuba, perc. **Publisher:** Kalmus, Hartmann. **Rights:** Expired.

Prologue. Emperor Phorcas abdicates in favor of his daughter, Esclarmonde, to pursue his studies of magic. Until she turns twenty, he decrees, Esclarmonde must not be seen by a man. At that time, a tournament will be held, the victor to claim both Esclarmonde and empire.

I. Esclarmonde confesses her love for the hero Roland to her sister Parséïs, who suggests Esclarmonde use her own magic powers to summon him. Parséïs's love, Énée, returns, having fought abroad and been beaten only by Roland. He thinks the French King Cléomer means to wed Roland to his daughter. Esclarmonde sends Roland a magic boat.

IIi. Esclarmonde brings Roland to a magic island and offers to become his wife, but he must decide without knowing her name or seeing her face. IIii. Roland weds Esclarmonde, but promises to keep the nuptials secret. She gives him the sword of St. George, which will protect him so long as he is faithful. He goes to save his king from the Saracens.

IIIi. Roland defeats the Saracens, but refuses the hand of King Cléomer's daughter. IIIii. The bishop persuades Roland to confess his secret. He concludes that Roland has been enslaved by the devil. When Esclarmonde appears to Roland, the bishop bursts in on them and Esclarmonde's face is revealed. She curses Roland and disappears. Roland's sword breaks.

IV. Parséïs and Énée go to the Ardennes in search of Phorcas: The tournament for Esclarmonde's hand is in preparation but Esclarmonde has disappeared. Furious, Phorcas summons Esclarmonde and orders her to renounce Roland—or he will die. Reluctantly, Esclarmonde obeys. Epilogue. Hoping to die in battle, Roland enters the tournament for Esclarmonde's hand—and wins. He refuses the prize until Esclarmonde removes her veil, revealing her true identity.

Des Esels Schatten • The Donkey's Shadow

Composed by Richard Strauss (June 11, 1864 – September 8, 1949). Libretto by Hans Adler. German. Based on the novel "The Abderites" by Christoph Martin Wieland. Premiered Ettal, Bavaria, Gymnasium of the Benedictine Abbey, June 7, 1964. Set in Abdera in Thrace in the 5th century BC. Singspiel. Set numbers with spoken dialogue. Prelude. Orchestrated and completed by Karl Haussner after Strauss's death.

Sets: 6. **Acts:** 1 act, 6 scenes. **Length:** I: 90. **Arias:** "Ich möchte" (Philippides), "Da bilden sich die guten Leute" (Kenteterion). **Hazards:** I: donkey appears onstage. **Scenes:** Ii. A road crossing a plain near Abdera. Iii. Office of the municipal judge. Iiii. Kenteterion's workshop. Iiv. Hall in the house of Agathyrsus. Iv. The frog pond of the temple of Latona. Ivi. The market square of Abdera.

Major roles: Antrax a donkey driver (tenor), Struthion the dentist (bass), Judge Philippides (baritone). **Minor roles:** Physignatus the lawyer (tenor), Polyphonus the lawyer (bass), Kenteterion (bass), Krobyle (contralto), Gorgo (soprano). **Speaking:** Court usher, Manservant to Agathyrsus, Agathyrsus, Strobylus, Two priests of Latona.

Chorus parts: SATB. **Chorus roles:** People of Abdera, municipal guards. **Dance/movement:** Iv: A frog pantomime. **Orchestra:** 2 fl, 2 ob, 2 cl, 2 bsn, 2 hrn, 2 trp, 2 trb, timp, perc, xylophone, glockenspiel, piano, strings. **Stageband:** None. **Publisher:** Boosey & Hawkes. **Rights:** Copyright 1967 by Boosey & Hawkes.

Ii. The dentist Struthion rents Antrax's donkey to make the long, hot journey to the county fair. The two men rest and Struthion sits in the shadow of the donkey. Antrax protests, as Struthion has rented the donkey, but not his shadow. They return to Abdera to seek judgment. Iii. The two men plead their case before Judge Philippides. The judge attempts to effect a compromise, but his efforts fail when two lawyers step in. Iiii. The case has dragged on for months, attracting public attention. Struthion comes to Kenteterion, head of the cobblers' guild, for help. (Dentists in Abdera belong to the cobbler's guild.) The cobbler agrees. Iiv. Antrax appeals to the aged Agathyrsus, leader of the temple of Jason, offering his young daughter, Gorgo, to Agathyrsus to persuade him to help. Iv. Struthion counters by winning over Strobylus, leader of the rival temple of Latona. Strobylus is furious with Agathyrsus for keeping storks that eat the frogs sacred to Latona. Ivi. The lawyers make their cases before the council of four hundred. Philippides orders the donkey brought in. It is discovered that the donkey has starved to death, no one having remembered to feed it. Philippides dismisses the case and pays the court costs out of the public treasury. Agathyrsus gives Antrax two new donkeys.

Esther

Composed by Hugo Weisgall (October 13, 1912 – March 11, 1997). Libretto by Charles Kondek. English. Based on the Biblical story. Premiered New York City, New York City Opera, October 3, 1993. Set in Persia in Biblical times. Drama. Through composed with recitative.

Sets: 16. **Acts:** 3 acts, 37 scenes. **Length:** I, II, III: 110. **Hazards:** I: Ten corpses hanging from gibbets. **Scenes:** Ii. The foot of a hill before eleven corpses hanging in gibbets. Iii. The home of Mordecai. Iiii –
Iiv. Unspecified. Iv. Haman's house. Ivi – Ivii. Xerxes' palace. Iviii – Iix. Xerxes' harem. Ix. The den of the astrologers. Ixi. Haman's house. Ixii. In the presence of the king. IIi. Unspecified. IIii. A prison cell. IIiii – IIiv. Unspecified. IIv – IIvi. Xerxes' bed chamber. IIvii. Haman's house. IIviii. Esther's apartment in the palace. IIix. Unspecified. IIx. Xerxes' bed

chamber. IIxi. A hall leading to the throne room. IIxii. The throne room. IIxiii – IIIi. Unspecified. IIIii – IIIvii. The great hall of the palace. IIIviii. On the way to the gallows. IIIix. A meeting place. IIIx. The terrace of the palace. IIIxi. Unspecified. IIIxii. The foot of the hill.

Major roles: Mordecai (bass baritone), Esther (soprano), King Xerxes of Persia (baritone). **Minor roles:** Grave digger (bass), Vashti (mezzo), Bigthan (tenor), Teresh (baritone), Zeresh (contralto), Prime Minister Haman (tenor), Hegai keeper of the harem (countertenor), Reader (tenor). **Bit parts:** Servant (tenor), Young girl (mezzo).

Chorus parts: SSAATTBB. **Chorus roles:** Mob, harem girls, astrologers (3 tenors, 3 basses), Jews, children (three parts), elders, people. **Dance/movement:** III: Wild celebratory dance. **Orchestra:** 3 fl (picc), 2 ob (Eng hrn), 2 cl (bs cl), 2 bsn, 4 hrn, 3 trp, 2 trb, tuba, timp, perc, harp, strings. **Stageband:** None. **Publisher:** Theodore Presser Co. **Rights:** Copyright 1993 Theodore Presser Co.

Ii. A hooded figure visits the site where a man and his ten sons have been hanged. Iii. In a flashback to Esther's youth, Esther's uncle Mordecai tells her she has been chosen for King Xerxes' harem. Iiii. Xerxes' chamberlains, Bigthan and Teresh, plot to restore Xerxes' banished queen, Vashti, by poisoning Xerxes. Iiv. A servant tells Mordecai. Iv. Mordecai warns the king. Prime Minister Haman, who is jealous, takes the advice of his wife, Zeresh, to move against all the Jews—not just Mordecai. Ivi. Haman tells Xerxes that the Jews are a subversive influence. Ivii. Xerxes longs for a new wife. Iviii. The harem girls tell Esther about the king. Iix. Hegai, the keeper of the harem, brings Esther to the king. Ix. Haman learns from the astrologers what day Mordecai will die. Ixi. Haman and Zeresh plot. Ixii. Xerxes follows Haman's advice and orders the extermination of the Jews.

IIi. Mordecai fears for his people. IIii. Imprisoned after the failed coup, Vashti remembers how Xerxes humiliated her. IIiii. Vashti and Zeresh wonder about the new queen, Esther. IIiv. Esther is frightened at her coronation. IIv. Xerxes listens to a recital of the plot against him. IIvi. Xerxes honors Mordecai for saving his life. IIvii. Haman swears revenge on Mordecai. IIviii. Esther refuses Mordecai's plea to intervene with Xerxes on behalf of her people. IIix. She comes to realize that the Jews are her responsibility. IIx. In a flashback, Esther is brought to Xerxes' bed chamber for the first time. He falls in love with her and promises to make her queen. IIxi. Esther decides to make her appeal to Xerxes. IIxii. The king promises to call the people together and grant the queen a wish even though he does not know what it will be. IIxiii. Esther realizes she has found her destiny.

IIIi. The Jews pray. IIIii. The king calls the people together. IIIiii. Xerxes grants Esther her wish. IIIiv. She asks mercy for the Jews—and reveals that she is a Jew. IIIv. Esther demands the execution of Haman and his ten sons. IIIvi. The king agrees and makes Mordecai prime minister. Xerxes cannot revoke his previous decree, but he allows the Jews to arm and defend themselves. IIIvii. Haman is arrested. IIIviii. A band of mocking children accompany him to the gallows. IIIix. Mordecai consults with the Jewish elders about defending themselves. IIIx. Esther and the king look back on the day of the massacre. Many died, but many survived. They reaffirm their love. IIIxi. The people acclaim Mordecai. IIIxii. Back in the present, the hooded figure admits to the grave digger that she is Esther.

Yevgeny Onyegin • Eugene Onegin

Composed by Peter Ilyitch Tchaikovsky (May 7, 1840 – November 6, 1893). Libretto by Konstantin Shilovsky and Peter Ilyitch Tchaikovsky. Russian. Based on the verse novel by Alexander Pushkin. Premiered Moscow, Moscow Conservatoire, March 29, 1879. Set in Russia in the 1820s. Lyric scenes. Set numbers with accompanied recitative. Introduction.

Sets: 7. **Acts:** 3 acts, 7 scenes. **Length:** I: 70. II: 40. III: 35. **Arias:** "Ah, Tanya, Tanya" (Olga), "Were I a man whom fate intended" (Onegin), Letter aria (Tatyana), Lenski's aria (Lenski). **Hazards:** None. **Scenes:** Ii. The garden of the Larin country estate. Iii. Tatyana's room. Iiii. Another part of the garden in the Larin estate. IIi. The principal reception room of the Larin house. IIii. A rustic water mill on the banks of a wooded stream. IIIi. A salon adjoining the ballroom of a nobleman's mansion in St. Petersburg. IIIii. The drawing room of Prince Gremin's house in St. Petersburg.

Major roles: Tatyana (soprano), Vladimir Lenski (tenor), Eugene Onegin (baritone). **Minor roles:** Olga (contralto), Madame Larina (mezzo), Nurse Filipyevna (mezzo), Captain (bass), Mr. Triquet (tenor), Zaretsky (bass), Prince Gremin (bass). **Mute:** Monsieur Guillot.

Chorus parts: SSAATTBB. **Chorus roles:** Peasants, guests of Madame Larina, guests at a ball in St. Petersburg, officers, servants, landowners. **Dance/movement:** I: peasant dance. II: ballroom dancing. III: polonaise. **Orchestra:** picc, 2 fl, 2 ob, 2 cl, 2 bsn, 4 hrn, 2 trp, 3 trb, timp, harp, strings. **Stageband:** None. **Publisher:** Richard Schauer, D. Rahter. **Rights:** Expired.

Ii. Tatyana and Olga sing duets while Madame Larina reminisces about her youth. The peasants have gathered in the harvest, and dance to amuse their mistress. Olga's suitor, Lenski, brings his friend Onegin. Iii. Tatyana asks Filipyevna about her marriage and writes a passionate love letter to Onegin, which Filipyevna agrees to deliver. Iiii. Onegin rejects Tatyana, telling her he was not meant to marry.

IIi. At Lenski's insistence, Onegin attends Tatyana's name day ball. When people gossip about him, he takes revenge on Lenski by flirting with Olga. Lenski is angry and picks a fight with Onegin. Reluctantly, Onegin agrees to fight a duel. IIii. Lenski wonders if Olga will shed a tear if he dies. Onegin kills Lenski in the duel.

IIIi. Onegin is bored with life. He attends a ball in St. Petersburg where he encounters Tatyana—now married to Prince Gremin. Tatyana's transformation from a country girl to a dazzling princess captivates him. IIIii. Tatyana accuses Onegin of loving her now only because she is rich and famous. She still loves him, but she decides to be faithful to Gremin: She sends Onegin away.

Euridice

Composed by Jacopo Peri (August 20, 1561 – August 12, 1633). Libretto by Ottavio Rinuccini. Italian. Based on Greek mythology. Premiered Florence, Palazzo Pitti, October 6, 1600. Set in ancient Greece in mythic times. Comic opera. Set numbers with recitative. Prologue. Musical contributions by Giulio Caccini.

Sets: 2. **Acts:** 3 acts, 3 scenes. **Length:** I, II, III: 90. **Arias:** "Antri ch'a miei lamenti" (Orfeo), "Nel pur ardor" (Tirsi), "Non piango e non sospiro" (Orfeo), "Funeste piagge, ombrosi orridi campi" (Orfeo), "Gioite al canto mio" (Orfeo). **Hazards:** None. **Scenes:** I. A pastoral setting. II. The underworld. III. The pastoral setting.

Major roles: Arcetro (contralto), Euridice (soprano), Orfeo (tenor), Dafne (soprano). **Minor roles:** Tragedy (soprano), Shepherd (tenor), First nymph (soprano), Aminta (tenor), Second nymph (soprano), Tirsi (tenor), Venere (soprano), Plutone (bass), Proserpina (soprano), Caronte (bass), Radamante (tenor).

Chorus parts: SSATB. **Chorus roles:** Nymphs, shepherds, ghosts and gods of the underworld. **Dance/movement:** I: Nymphs and shepherds dance to celebrate Euridice's return. **Orchestra:** 3 fl, 2 ob, 3 trp, 2 trb, 3 vla, vla da gamba, violone, 2 lutes, harpsichord (one possible realization: actual score shows only vocal lines and basso continuo). **Stageband:** None. **Publisher:** Otos Edition. **Rights:** Expired.

I. Orfeo and Euridice marry. Dafne reports that Euridice has died of a poisoned snake bite. Orfeo's friend Arcetro tells the wedding party how Orfeo was comforted by the goddess Venere. II. The goddess takes Orfeo to the underworld to reclaim Euridice. Orfeo pleads with Plutone—who relents when his wife, Proserpina, takes Orfeo's side. III. Orfeo and Euridice return to the world of the living.

Euryanthe

Composed by Carl Maria von Weber (November 18, 1786 – June 5, 1826). Libretto by Helmina von Chézy. German. Based on the 13th-century romance "L'Histoire du Très-noble et Chevalereux Prince Gérard, Comte de Nevers." Premiered Vienna, Kärntnerthor-theater, October 25, 1823. Set in France in the early 12th century. Romantic opera. Set numbers with recitative. Overture.

Sets: 4. **Acts:** 3 acts, 6 scenes. **Length:** I: 65. II: 35. III: 40. **Arias:** "Glöcklein im Thale" (Euryanthe), "O mein Leid" (Eglantine), "Bethörte!" (Eglantine), "Wo berg' ich mich?" (Lysiart), "Wehen mir Lüfte Ruh!" (Adolar), "Zu ihm! zu ihm!" (Euryanthe). **Hazards:** III: Serpent attacks Adolar (can be done offstage). **Scenes:** Ii. The hall of the royal castle. Iii – IIi. The garden of the castle of Nevers. IIii. The hall of the royal castle. IIIi. A barren ravine ringed with thick scrub. IIIii. An open space surrounded by trees in front of the castle of Nevers.

Major roles: Count Adolar of Nevers (tenor), Count Lysiart of Foret (baritone), Euryanthe of Savoyen (soprano), Eglantine of Puiset (mezzo). **Minor roles:** King Louis VI (bass), Bertha (soprano). **Bit part:** Rudolf (tenor).

Chorus parts: SATTBB. **Chorus roles:** Knights, ladies, peasants, Euryanthe's attendants, nobles, hunters. **Dance/movement:** I: Court dance. III: Peasant May dance. **Orchestra:** 2 fl, 2 ob, 2 cl, 2 bsn, 4 hrn, 2 trp, 3 trb, timp, strings. **Stageband:** I: 4 trp. III: 2 picc, 2 ob, 2 cl, 2 bsn, 4 hrn, 2 trp, 3 trb, timp. **Publisher:** C. F. Peters, Schlesinger. **Rights:** Expired.

Ii. Adolar sings to the court about his faithful love, Euryanthe. Lysiart bets Adolar that he can prove Euryanthe is faithless. Iii. Euryanthe takes in Eglantine, a young girl abandoned because of her father's treason. Euryanthe breaks her vow of silence and tells Eglantine the secret of Adolar's dead sister, Emma. Eglantine loves Adolar and plots to betray Euryanthe.

IIi. Lysiart, who also loves Euryanthe, has qualms about what he is doing. But he joins forces with Eglantine, who gives him the ring she has taken from Emma's tomb. IIii. Euryanthe is received by the king and reunited with Adolar. Lysiart produces Emma's ring as proof that Euryanthe betrayed Adolar's secret, and the court condemns Euryanthe.

IIIi. Adolar and Euryanthe wander in the desert. He means to kill her, but instead abandons her after she tries to save him from a serpent. The king finds Euryanthe, learns the truth and promises to help her. IIIii. Eglantine and Lysiart are engaged, but Eglantine is driven mad by her guilt. The king lets everyone believe that Euryanthe died. Eglantine triumphantly reveals her treachery and Lysiart stabs her. Euryanthe returns and is reunited with Adolar.

Výlet pana Broučka do XV století/Výlet pana Broučka do Měsíce • The Excursions of Mr. Brouček on the Moon and in the 15th century

Composed by Leoš Janáček (July 3, 1854 – August 12, 1928). Libretto by Viktor Dyk (Moon) and František Procházka (15th century). Czech. Based on novelettes by Svatopluk Čech. Premiered Prague, National Theater, April 23, 1920. Set in Prague and on the moon in the late 19th century and 1420. Comedy. Through composed. Overture. Introduction before each act. The two sections of the work can be done independently.

Sets: 9. **Acts:** 4 acts, 11 scenes. **Length:** I: 35. II: 35. III: 20. IV: 35. **Arias:** "Now I flee" (Etherea). **Hazards:** I, II: Brouček flies to and from the moon. Flying horse (Pegasus). Azurean weeps cheese. IV: Burning barrel transforms into a candle. **Scenes:** Ii. Vikárka St. in front of St. Vitus Cathedral. Iii. Old castle steps. Iiii. The moon. IIi. The throne room of Wonderglitter in the temple of arts. IIii. Vikárka street. IIIi. King Wenceslas IV's treasure chamber. IIIii. The old town square, early morning, 1420. IIIiii. Before Domšík's house. IVi. A room in Domšík's house. IVii. Old town square. IViii. Courtyard of the Vikárka Inn, 1888.

Major roles: Mr. Brouček (tenor), Mazal/Azurean (tenor), Málinka/Etherea/Kunka (soprano), Sexton of St. Vitus's/Lukristan/Domšík (bass baritone), Würfl/Wonderglitter/Kostka (bass). **Minor roles:** Boy in the inn/Minister of culture/Scholar (soprano), Minister/Fanny Nowak/Františka (alto), Svatopluk Čech (tenor), Train conductor/Works minister/Miroslav (tenor), Vacek (baritone). **Bit parts:** Two voices from above (tenor, baritone), Two Taborites (tenor, bass). **Mute:** John Žižka.

Chorus parts: SSAATTBB (briefly TTTBBB). **Chorus roles:** People at the inn, moon maidens, people, children (in 1 part), voices from the depth below, Etherea's maids, musicians, Taborites. **Dance/movement:** II: Dance of the artists. **Orchestra:** 4 fl (picc), 2 ob, Eng hrn, 2 cl, bs cl, 2 bsn, cont bsn, 4 hrn, 4 trp, 3 trb, tuba, timp, perc, celeste, glockenspiel, organ, harp, strings. **Stageband:** I: bagpiper (or in pit). **Publisher:** Universal Edition. **Rights:** Copyright 1919 by Universal Edition. Renewed 1947.

Ii. It is night and the sexton catches his daughter, Málinka, out with the painter, Mazal. Málinka complains to Brouček, the landlord, that no one will marry her. The artists are drinking and singing in the inn. Málinka goes home but Mazal calls her out and they walk to the old castle, talking of love. Brouček has forgotten to buy sausages for the inn and the apprentice chases after him. Iii. Brouček muses about how peaceful the moon is compared to earth. He finds himself floating up into the sky. Iiii. Waking on the moon, Brouček meets Azurean, who he thinks is Mazal. Azurean says Brouček has never known love and calls on Etherea. Brouček mistakes Etherea for Málinka. The moon people talk only of love and poetry. Etherea flies off with Brouček on Pegasus. Etherea's father, Lunigrove, reads from his book of aesthetics while Azurean laments the loss of Etherea.

IIi. Wonderglitter explains that he is a patron of the arts because he lacks the talent to be an artist. Etherea arrives with Brouček and asks for Wonderglitter's protection. Lunigrove arrives and catches Etherea in a net. The artists dance to welcome Brouček and invite him to supper. They put the disoriented Czech to sleep with their poetry and art. The moon people are offended when Brouček uses the word "nose." Rainbowglory shows Brouček his painting but Brouček again offends everyone by eating his sausages. (The moon people eat flowers.) Explaining what sausages are only makes things worse. Fed up with Etherea's advances, Brouček blows her up and flies off on Pegasus. The artists praise Wonderglitter. IIii. There is a musical interlude during which earth and Vikárka Street reappear. It is morning. The artists are praising Würfl the innkeeper; the lovers return. The apprentice waiter announces that they are carrying Brouček home.

IIIi. Brouček believes there is a secret tunnel under the castle. In searching through the cellar of the inn, he stumbles into King Wenceslas IV's treasure chamber and then exits into the old town square. An image of the poet Svatopluk Čech appears and asks when the Czech people will again be great. IIIii. Brouček gets into an altercation with a town councillor. A crowd gathers and concludes that Brouček must be a spy of King Sigismund's. Brouček realizes that King Žižka and his enemy Sigismund are alive—and that the year is not 1880, but 1420. IIIiii. Brouček is brought before Domšík, the judge, for questioning. He claims to have returned from Turkey. The judge tells Brouček that now, on the eve of battle with Sigismund, all brave men are welcome.

IVi. Brouček has stayed the night in Domšík's house. With the help of Kedruta the housewife, Domšík dresses Brouček in period attire. His daughter, Kunka, returns from church with Vacek, Vojta, Miroslav and a student. The guests toast one another's health and lament how the Czechs are always slandered and attacked. They swear to defend themselves against the heresies of the church and the usurpations of the king. Vacek and the student argue about the Taborites. Brouček admits he does not care about the political situation and refuses to fight, upsetting the others. Peter announces the arrival of the enemy crusading army and everyone else goes out to fight. Kedruta, Kunka and Brouček nervously await the outcome of the battle. IVii. The victorious Hussites and Taborites return to town to celebrate. Brouček meets two Taborites and lies to them about his part in the fight. He is caught and exposed by Peter. Domšík has died gloriously. Infuriated by Brouček's cowardice, the people stuff him in a barrel and set it on fire. IViii. The barrel gradually changes into a candle held by Würfl the innkeeper. He helps Brouček off to bed.

Sorochinskaya Yarmarka • The Fair of Sorochintzy

Composed by Modest Mussorgsky (March 21, 1839 – March 28, 1881). Libretto by Modest Mussorgsky. Russian. Based on the story by N. V. Gogol. Premiered Moscow, Free Theater, October 21, 1913. Set in Little Russia (Ukraine) in the mid-19th century. Comedy. Set numbers with accompanied recitative. Overture. Ballet. Completed by Cui and premiered St. Petersburg, October 13, 1917. Other attempts to complete the work by Anatoly Lyadov, Vyacheslav Karatygin, Sakhnovsky, Vissarion Shebalin and Nikoly Tcherepnin. Reconstructed from the composer's manuscript by P. Lamm.

Sets: 3. **Acts:** 3 acts, 3 scenes. **Length:** I, II, III: 130. **Arias:** The peasant lad's Dumka (Gritzko). **Hazards:** None. **Scenes:** I. The fair at Sorochintzy. II. Tcherevik's cottage. III. The village square.

Major roles: Parassia (soprano), Tcherevik (bass), Gritzko (tenor), Khivria (mezzo). **Minor roles:** Gypsy (bass), Old crony (bass), Pastor's son (tenor), Three guests (2 tenor, 1 baritone) [or Two guests (2 tenor), Two Jews (2 tenor), Two gypsies (2 bass)].

Chorus parts: SSAAATTBB. **Chorus roles:** Youths, maidens, gypsies, vendors, Cossacks, Jews. **Dance/movement:** III: Villagers dance a "hopak." **Orchestra:** picc, 2 fl, 2 ob (Eng hrn), 2 cl, 2 bsn, 4 hrn, 2 trp, 3 trb, timp, perc, harp, strings (Cui version). **Stageband:** None. **Publisher:** State Publishers Music. **Rights:** Expired.

I. The peasant Tcherevik brings his daughter, Parassia, to the fair, and the young Gritzko convinces Tcherevik to let him marry her. Tcherevik has a drink with an old crony of his. His wife, Khivria, finds him and objects to Parassia's marrying Gritzko. A gypsy promises Gritzko he will get Parassia if he sells his donkey to the gypsy cheap. Parassia appears and admits she loves Gritzko.

II. Khivria fights with Tcherevik and orders him out of the house. She invites in her lover, the pastor's son, and when Tcherevik returns with some friends, the pastor's son hides in the attic. Tcherevik's crony recounts the story of the scarlet jacket: A man was once kicked out of hell and took to drinking. He pawned his scarlet jacket with a Jew to pay his bar bill, but the Jew sold the jacket. For this, the Jew was tormented by demon pigs. Tcherevik's friends think they see a pig, but it is the pastor's son. He is exposed and Khivria embarrassed. III. Tcherevik overrules Khivria and lets Parassia marry Gritzko.

The Fairy Queen

Composed by Henry Purcell (c. 1659 – November 21, 1695). Libretto by an anonymous author. English. Based on "A Midsummer Night's Dream" by Shakespeare. Premiered London, Queen's Theatre, Dorset Gardens, May 2, 1692. Set in Athens in legendary times. Masque. Set numbers with spoken dialogue. Overture. Prelude before I, V. Overture. Symphony before IV. Music is confined to "masques" separated by spoken scenes.

Sets: 4. **Acts:** 5 acts, 6 scenes. **Length:** Overtures: 7. I: 10. II: 25. III: 20. IV: 25. V: 35. **Arias:** "Thus the gloomy world" (Chinese man), "One charming night" (Secrecy), "Thrice happy lovers" (Juno), The Plaint (Juno). **Hazards:** III: A bridge appears and vanishes. V: dancing monkeys. **Scenes:** I. Palace of the Duke of Athens. II – III. A forest. IV. A garden of fountains. Vi. A forest. Vii. A Chinese garden.

Major roles are the speaking parts of the Shakespeare play. **Minor roles:** Drunken poet (baritone), First fairy (soprano), Second fairy (soprano), Man (tenor), First woman (soprano), Night (soprano), Phoebus (tenor), Mystery (soprano), Secrecy (contralto or countertenor), Sleep (bass), Second woman (soprano), Coridon (bass), Mopsa (soprano or countertenor), Nymph (soprano), Third woman (contralto), Attendant (soprano), Spring (soprano), Summer (contralto or countertenor), Autumn (tenor), Winter (bass), Juno (soprano), Chinese man (countertenor), Chinese woman (soprano), Hymen (bass). (Unnamed male and female parts can be variously assigned.)

Chorus parts: SATB. **Chorus roles:** Fairies, nymphs, hay makers, Chinese men and women. **Dance/movement:** I: hornpipe, rondeau, jig. II: Fairy dances. III: Fairies, swans, green men and hay makers dance. V: Chinese and monkeys dance. **Orchestra:** 2 fl, 2 ob, 2 trp, timp, strings, continuo (harpsichord). **Stageband:** None. **Publisher:** Kalmus, Novello & Co. **Rights:** Expired.

I. Hermia's father, Egeus, demands his daughter marry Demetrius even though she loves—and is loved by—Lysander. The duke takes the side of the father and Hermia and Lysander decide to flee Athens. A group of tradesmen prepare a play for Hermia's wedding. The fairy king, Oberon, is angry with his queen, Titania, for keeping an Indian boy Oberon wants. A group of fairies torment a drunken poet. Titania hides the Indian boy.

II. Titania and Oberon fight. The fairy king decides to humiliate Titania and sends Puck in search of a magic love-inducing flower. As Oberon watches, Demetrius enters the woods in pursuit of Hermia—and pursued by Helena. The fairy king instructs Puck to use the flower to make Demetrius love Helena. The fairies dance and Titania sleeps. Puck unknowingly uses the philter on Lysander instead of Demetrius.

III. Lysander falls in love with Helena. The tradesmen rehearse their play. Puck fixes an ass's head on Bottom and uses the flower to make Titania fall in love with Bottom. Oberon orders Puck to fix his mistake with the Athenian lovers. Green men, fairies and swans dance. The hay maker Coridon tries to kiss Mopsa.

IV. Oberon makes Demetrius love Helena. The two mortal men fight over Helena until Puck releases Lysander from the spell. Oberon releases Titania. The seasons celebrate Oberon's birthday.

Vi. Egeus and the duke discover the lovers in the forest and agree to let them marry their respective loves. Bottom is released and the tradesmen hurry back to Athens to perform at the weddings. Juno blesses the lovers. Vii. Chinese and monkeys dance and call forth Hymen, the god of marriage.

Falstaff

Composed by Giuseppe Verdi (October 9, 1813 – January 27, 1901). Libretto by Arrigo Boito. Italian. Based on Shakespeare's "The Merry Wives of Windsor" and "Henry IV." Premiered Milan, Teatro alla Scala, February 9, 1893. Set in Windsor in the 15th century. Lyric comedy. Through composed.

Sets: 5. **Acts:** 3 acts, 6 scenes. **Length:** I: 35. II: 45. III: 45. **Arias:** "Dal labbro" (Fenton), "È sogno?" (Ford), "L'onore! Ladri!"/Honor monologue (Falstaff), "Sul fil d'un soffio" (Nannetta), "Mondo ladro" (Falstaff). **Hazards:** IIii: Basket thrown out the window with Falstaff in it. **Scenes:** Ii. Inside the Garter Inn. Iii. A garden outside Ford's house. IIi. At the Garter Inn. IIii. A room in Ford's house. IIIi. An open square. IIIii. Windsor Park.

Major roles: Sir John Falstaff (baritone), Fenton (tenor), Ford (baritone), Alice Ford (soprano), Nannetta (soprano), Dame Quickly (mezzo). **Minor roles:** Dr. Caius (tenor), Bardolfo (tenor), Pistola (bass), Meg Page (mezzo). **Mute:** Falstaff's page Robin, Innkeeper of the Garter, Ford's servants (Ned, Tom, Will and Jack).

Chorus parts: SSSAATTBB. **Chorus roles:** Burghers and commoners, Ford's servants, masqueraders as goblins, fairies and witches. **Dance/ movement:** III: Elves and fairies dance. **Orchestra:** 3 fl (picc), 2 ob, Eng hrn, 2 cl, bs cl, 2 bsn, 4 hrn, 3 trp, 3 trb, bs trb, timp, perc, harp, guitar, strings. **Stageband:** III: chime, hrn. **Publisher:** Schirmer, Dover, G. Ricordi. **Rights:** Expired.

Ii. Dr. Cajus accuses Bardolfo and Pistola of getting him drunk and robbing him. Falstaff and his men deny the charge and chase the doctor off. Wondering how to refill his purse, Falstaff muses that Alice Ford and Meg Page are both attractive (and married)—and both control the purse strings at home. Falstaff gives Bardolfo and Pistola love letters to deliver to the ladies, but they refuse the dishonorable task and the page goes instead. Falstaff lectures on the meaninglessness of honor. Iii. Meg and Alice share their identical protestations of love from Falstaff. Ford is assailed by Dr. Cajus, Fenton, Bardolfo and Pistola, all telling tales on Falstaff. "He's after your wife," they warn Ford. Nannetta and Fenton kiss. Alice sends Dame Quickly to Falstaff to arrange a rendezvous. Unaware of the women's plan to entrap Falstaff, Ford arranges to be presented to Falstaff under an assumed name.

IIi. Dame Quickly tells Falstaff that Alice and Meg are both madly in love with him. "You can visit Alice between two and three when her husband is out," she says. Falstaff receives Ford disguised as a Mr. Brook. "All my riches have failed to win me the virtuous Alice," Ford confesses. He pays Falstaff to seduce Alice—on the theory that one seduction will make a second easier. Falstaff admits he already has an appointment with Alice, making Ford furious. IIii. Dame Quickly reports to Alice and Meg, who prepare for Falstaff's arrival. Nannetta enters in tears because her father wants her to marry Dr. Cajus. The women promise to fix things. As Falstaff sweettalks Alice, he is interrupted by Dame Quickly announcing the arrival of Meg. He hides behind a screen. Following their plan, Meg warns Alice that her husband has learned about Falstaff, but the women are surprised when Ford returns in a fury. While Ford searches the house, the women stuff Falstaff into a laundry basket. Fenton and Nannetta are discovered kissing behind the screen. The servants dump the laundry basket—Falstaff and all—into the river amid general hilarity.

IIIi. Falstaff feels betrayed but Dame Quickly cajoles him into another assignation with Alice. He is to come to the park at midnight, she says, disguised as the Black Huntsman whose ghost haunts the park. Ford repents of his jealousy and the men and women join forces against Falstaff. Not knowing that he is being overheard by Dame Quickly, Ford tells Dr. Cajus to wear a hood and promises that after the joke is sprung on Falstaff, he will wed him to Nannetta. IIIii. In Windsor Park, Alice and Nannetta, who have been tipped off, dress Fenton in a hood. Falstaff arrives on the stroke of midnight. Disguised as fairies, the plotters torment him until he begs for mercy. Bardolfo's disguise comes off, giving away the joke. Ford performs the wedding of—he thinks—Dr. Cajus and Nannetta along with another couple. In fact, the Nannetta is Bardolfo in disguise. The second couple is Fenton and the real Nannetta. The subterfuge is revealed. Ford forgives the lovers and everyone has a good laugh.

La Fanciulla del West • The Girl of the Golden West

Composed by Giacomo Puccini (December 22, 1858 – November 29, 1924). Libretto by Guelfo Civinini and Carlo Zangarini. Italian. Based on the play by David Belasco. Premiered New York City, Metropolitan Opera Association, December 10, 1910. Set in a mining camp at the foot of the Cloudy Mountains in California from 1849 to 1850. Melodrama. Through composed. Brief prelude.

Sets: 3. **Acts:** 3 acts, 3 scenes. **Length:** I: 62. II: 41. III: 27. **Arias:** "Ch'ella mi creda" (Dick Johnson). **Hazards:** III: Men chase Ramerrez on horseback and Minnie arrives on horseback. **Scenes:** I. Inside the "Polka" bar. II. Inside Minnie's cabin. III. A mining camp in a forest clearing.

Major roles: Minnie (soprano), Sheriff Jack Rance (baritone), Dick Johnson/Ramerrez (tenor). **Minor roles:** Ashby (bass), Nick the bartender (tenor), Sonora (baritone), Trin (tenor), Sid (baritone), Handsome (baritone), Harry (tenor), Joe (tenor), Happy (baritone), Larkens (bass), Billy Jackrabbit (bass), Wowkle (mezzo), Jake Wallace (baritone), José Castro (bass). **Bit parts:** Post boy (tenor), Offstage miner (baritone).

Chorus parts: TTBB (briefly TTTT, extra parts taken by four miners). **Chorus roles:** Miners, Wells Fargo men, men of the camp. Small solo groups. **Dance/movement:** I: Minnie and Johnson. **Orchestra:** picc, 3 fl, 3 ob, Eng hrn, 3 cl, bs cl, 3 bsn, cont bsn, 4 hrn, 3 trp, 3 trb, bs trb, 2 harps, timp, perc, glockenspiel, celeste, strings. **Stageband:** I: harp. II: bells, wind machine. **Publisher:** G. Ricordi. **Rights:** Expired.

I. It is the end of the day and the miners file into the Polka bar. Jack Wallace sings a song. Larkens, who is homesick, decides to give up mining and the miners take up a collection to pay for his trip home. When Sid is caught cheating at cards, the miners want him strung up. But Rance instead affixes the two of hearts to Sid's chest and warns that if he ever removes the card, he will be hanged. The agent of the Wells Fargo company, Ashby, is after the "greaser" Ramerrez and his band of outlaws. A fight breaks out when Sonora tells Rance that Minnie—the owner of the Polka—is only toying with him, but Minnie breaks up the fight. Courted by the miners, she gives them their nightly schooling. The post boy arrives with a letter from Ramerrez's former girlfriend, Nina, informing Ashby that he can catch Ramerrez at the "Palmetto" tonight. Ashby is overjoyed, but Rance does not trust Nina. Rance is interested in Minnie, but she rebuffs him. A stranger, Dick Johnson, arrives. He and Minnie have met before and she intervenes with the miners when they demand to know his plans. When Minnie dances with Johnson, Rance is furious. Ashby returns, having captured Castro, a greaser in Ramerrez's gang. The men want to hang Castro but he offers to betray Ramerrez. Ramerrez is actually Johnson, but the miners don't know this and they accept Castro's offer. Castro alerts Johnson that his men are outside waiting to rob the bar, then leads the miners off on a wild goose chase. Minnie is concerned about the gold the miners leave with her for safe-keeping, but Johnson promises her it will be safe. They declare their love.

II. Billy Jackrabbit and his squaw, Wowkle, discuss getting married as they help Minnie prepare her cabin for Johnson's arrival. Minnie tells Johnson about her life and the lovers kiss. Overcome by the knowledge of his secret, Johnson tries to leave but is prevented by the snow. He swears his eternal love. Pistol shots and voices are heard in the background. Rance, Nick and Ashby arrive on the trail of Ramerrez. Minnie hides Johnson, and is shocked to learn from them that Johnson is Ramerrez. When they warn her that Ramerrez is nearby, Minnie sends them on their way before she confronts Johnson. "I would never have robbed you," Johnson swears, explaining that he has reformed. He leaves and is shot. Ignoring his protests, Minnie takes him in and hides him. "You are the first man I ever kissed," she says, "and I won't let you die." Rance comes back, looking for Ramerrez, and he is about to admit defeat when a drop of blood from the ceiling reveals Johnson's hiding place. Minnie offers to play poker with Rance. "If you win," she says, "I am yours; but if you lose, Johnson goes free." Minnie wins by cheating, but Rance keeps his word.

III. Nick and Rance are disgusted that Minnie loves Johnson. Ashby, hot on the trail of Johnson, catches him after an extended chase and delivers him up to the sheriff. Nick rushes off to get Minnie. The men call for Johnson's death, accusing him of robbery (which he admits) and murder (which he denies). Johnson accepts his sentence, but asks the men to let Minnie think he escaped. He is about to be hanged when she gallops in. Rance tries to proceed, but Minnie wins the miners over. They release Johnson and bid the pair a tearful farewell.

Faust

Composed by Charles François Gounod (June 17, 1818 – October 18, 1893). Libretto by Jules Barbier and Michel Carré. French. Based on the tragedy by Johann Wolfgang von Goethe. Premiered Paris, Théâtre Lyrique, March 19, 1859. Set in Germany in the 16th century. Lyric drama/Grand opera. Set numbers with recitative or dialogue. Introduction. Ballet. Revised by composer: dialogue replaced with recitative and ballet added.

Sets: 8. **Acts:** 5 acts, 8 scenes. **Length:** I: 25. II: 25. III: 50. IV: 25. V: 35. **Arias:** "Avant de quitter ces lieux" (Valentin), "Salut! demeure" (Faust), "Ah je ris"/Jewel Song (Marguerite), "Il ne revient pas"/Spinning Wheel Song (Marguerite), "Le veau d'or" (Méphistophélès). **Hazards:** I: Transformation of Faust into a young man. Visions of Marguerite. V: Apotheosis of Marguerite. **Scenes:** I. Faust's study. II. The Fair. III. Marguerite's garden. IVi. Marguerite's room. IVii. In church. IViii. Outside Marguerite's house. Vi. Walpurgis Night (Kingdom of Satan). Vii. Prison.

Major roles: Faust (tenor), Méphistophélès (bass or bass baritone), Marguerite (soprano), Valentin (baritone), Siebel (soprano or mezzo), Marthe Schwerlein (contralto or mezzo). **Minor role:** Wagner (baritone).

Chorus parts: SATTBB. **Chorus roles:** Soldiers, students, villagers, demons, priests, angels. **Dance/movement:** II: Waltz. IV: Walpurgis Night ballet (often omitted). **Orchestra:** 2 fl (picc), 2 ob (Eng hrn), 2 cl, 2 bsn, 4 hrn, 2 trp, 3 trb, tuba (in ballet), timp, perc, 4 harp, organ, strings. **Stageband:** IV: 2 cornets, 2 valve trp, 2 alto trb, ten trb, sop sax, bs sax, db bs sax. **Publisher:** Schirmer, Kalmus. **Rights:** Expired.

I. Contemplating suicide, Faust curses life and calls on Satan who—to his astonishment—appears. Faust longs for youth and love, which the devil promises to provide in return for his soul. After Faust signs the devil's contract, Méphistophélès transforms the poison Faust had been about to drink into an elixir of youth. Faust is transformed and the two go off in search of the young and beautiful Marguerite.

II. It is Sunday and the villagers are out drinking and flirting. In the presence of his friends Wagner and Siebel, Valentin commends the care of his sister to God while he is off to war. Méphistophélès appears and sings a drinking song. He foretells the deaths of both Valentin and Wagner, but when he insolently toasts Marguerite, Valentin challenges him. Before the youth can make good his threat, Méphistophélès magically breaks his sword, thus revealing his true identity. Faust appears looking for Marguerite. When she appears, Siebel (who also loves

Marguerite) tries to speak with her, but Méphistophélès prevents him.
Faust offers to escort her, but she declines. The village girls dance a
waltz.

III. First Siebel and then Faust sing of their love for Marguerite. Siebel
leaves a bouquet for his beloved; Faust leaves a casket of jewels. When
Marguerite appears, she sings a love ballad and wonders who that noble
gentleman was who approached her in the square. She discovers the two
presents. Marthe admires the jewels. Faust and Méphistophélès enter
and announce the death of Marthe's husband. This does not prevent her
from responding to Méphistophélès, while Faust and Marguerite slip off
for a walk in the garden and declare their love.

IVi. Faust has deserted Marguerite. Siebel swears his everlasting friendship and offers to seek revenge. IVii. Marguerite goes to church but her
prayers are stymied by Méphistophélès who tells her she is damned.
IViii. The soldiers return from battle victorious, among them Valentine,
who does not know what has happened to his sister. Siebel can't bring
himself to inform him. Faust returns and reluctantly agrees to fight
Valentine. Valentine is slain, cursing Marguerite as he dies.

Vi. Méphistophélès takes Faust into his kingdom for the feast of
Walpurgis Night. Faust demands to see Marguerite again. Vii.
Marguerite has gone mad and is in jail for killing her and Faust's child.
Faust tries to help her escape but Marguerite is too distracted to under-
stand. But she prays and her prayers are answered by a chorus of angels
who waft her soul to heaven.

La Favola d'Orfeo • The Fable of Orfeo

Composed by Claudio Monteverdi (May 15 [baptized], 1567 –
November 29, 1643). Libretto by Alessandro Striggio. Italian. Based on
the opera by Rinuccini and Peri. Premiered Mantua, Palazzo Ducale,
February 24, 1607. Set in Greece and the underworld in legendary times.
Musical fable. Set numbers with recitative. Prologue. Musical interlude
in II, III, IV, V. Entr'acte before II, III. Ballet. Composer published edi-
tions in 1609 and 1615. No significant differences. Realizations exist by
Respighi, Malipiero, Hindemith, Orff and Wenzinger.

Sets: 4. **Acts:** 5 acts, 5 scenes. **Length:** I: 25. II: 25. III: 25. IV: 15. V: 15.
Arias: "Tu sei morta" (Orfeo), "Qual onor di te sia degno" (Orfeo).
Hazards: V: Orfeo ascends to heaven with Apollo. **Scenes:** I – II. Banks
of the river Permessos. III. The gates of Hades. IV. Hades. V. The plains
of Thrace.

Major roles: Orfeo (tenor, soprano, baritone or mezzo), Euridice (soprano). **Minor roles:** Music (mezzo), Echo (soprano or mezzo), First shepherd/Apollo (tenor), Hope (mezzo), Caronte (bass), Proserpina (contralto), Plutone (bass). **Bit parts:** Second shepherd (soprano), Third shepherd (mezzo), Fourth shepherd (contralto), Messenger (mezzo), Four spirits (soprano, mezzo, tenor, bass).

Chorus parts: SSATTTBB. **Chorus roles:** Shepherds, nymphs, spirits. **Dance/movement:** I: Wedding ballet. **Orchestra:** 2 high recorders, 4 to 5 trb (modern instruments), 2 cornet, high trp (clarino), 3 trp, 2 harpsichord 1 or 2 harp, 2 or 3 large lute, 2 bs zither, 3 bs gamba, 2 organs with wood pipes, organ with reed pipes, 2 small vln, 10 viole da braccio (4 vln, 4 vla, 2 vlc), 2 cont bs viols. **Stageband:** None. **Publisher:** Amici della Musica, Editions Costallat. **Rights:** Expired.

Prologue. The spirit of music introduces the story.

I. Shepherds and nymphs celebrate the wedding of Orfeo and Euridice.

II. A messenger tells Orfeo that Euridice has died of a snake bite. Orfeo vows to use his gift of song to persuade Plutone, the king of the underworld, to return Euridice.

III. Hope accompanies Orfeo to the gates of Hades. The boatman, Caronte, tries to bar Orfeo's way, but Orfeo sings him to sleep.

IV. Proserpina pleads with Plutone to free Euridice. Plutone agrees on condition that Orfeo not look back while leading Euridice out of Hades. Orfeo is unable to resist temptation: He looks and Euridice again descends to Hades.

V. Orfeo mourns Euridice. Apollo brings him to heaven to dwell among the gods.

La Favorite • The Favorite

Composed by Gaetano Donizetti (November 29, 1797 – April 8, 1848). Libretto by Alphonse Royer and Gustave Vaëz. French (but often done in Italian translation). Based on "Le Comte de Comminges" by François-Thomas de Baculard d'Arnaud. Premiered Paris, Théâtre de l'Académie Royale de Musique, December 2, 1840. Set in the Kingdom of Castille in 1340. Drama. Set numbers with recitative. Overture. Entr'acte before each act. Ballet.

Sets: 5. **Acts:** 4 acts, 5 scenes. **Length:** I, II, III, IV: 170. **Arias:** "Léonor

viens" (Alphonse), "Ô mon Fernand" (Léonor), "Ange si pur" (Fernand).
Hazards: None. **Scenes:** Ii. One of the galleries surrounding the
monastery of St. James of Compostella. Iii. A beautiful view on the
shores of the island of St. Leon. II. An open gallery through which are
seen the gardens of the palace of Alcazar. III. A hall in the palace of
Alcazar. IV. The cloisters of the monastery of St. James.

Major roles: Fernand (tenor), Léonor/Leonora of Gusman (mezzo),
King Alphonse/Alfonso XI (baritone). **Minor roles:**
Balthazar/Baldassarre (bass), Inès (soprano), Don Gaspar (tenor). **Bit
part:** Lord (tenor).

Chorus parts: SATTB. **Chorus roles:** Courtiers, pages, guards, soldiers,
pilgrims, Spanish maidens, monks. **Dance/movement:** II: Ballet.
Orchestra: 2 fl (picc), 2 ob (Eng hrn), 2 cl, 2 bsn, 4 hrn, 2 trp, 4 trb (ophicléide), timp, perc, harp, strings. **Stageband:** II: perc. IV: organ.
Publisher: Ricordi, Garland Publishing. **Rights:** Expired.

Ii. Fernando has fallen in love and wants to leave his monastery.
Baldassare, the superior, is disappointed in him. Iii. A chorus of maidens
greets Fernando who questions them about their mistress, Leonora.
Leonora and Fernando meet and fall in love, but Leonora will not tell
him her name. She gives him a parchment and warns him to shun her.
When the king is announced, Leonora flees, so Fernando realizes she is
connected with the throne. He feels unworthy of her, but reading the
parchment, he sees Leonora has given him a commission that he may
prove his worth.

II. The king and his minister, Don Gaspare, wonder at the triumphs of
Fernando over the Moors. The king suspects his courtiers of trying to
frustrate his love for his mistress Leonora. She mourns her fate and
when Gaspare produces a love letter in her hand, she refuses to name
her beloved. Baldassare brings a Papal Bull that pronounces anathema
on the king unless Leonora is sent away immediately.

III. Ferrando returns triumphant and asks for Leonora's hand, which the
king feels pressured to grant. Skeptical of her good fortune, Leonora
sends a note to Ferrando, warning him of her past, but Gaspare arrests
Inez before she can deliver the message. The lovers are married and
Ferrando ennobled, Leonora believing that Ferrando knows—and forgives—her past. Realizing that the wedding is a ploy to fend off the
church, the courtiers spurn Ferrando. When Baldassare tells him the
truth, Ferrando renounces his titles, excoriates the king—and leaves.

IV. Ferrando has returned to the monastery while Baldassare is attending a young, heartbroken novice (Leonora in disguise). Praying to forget

his love, Ferrando is led to the altar to take his monastic vows, which Leonora witnesses. When she tells him she thought he knew the truth before they were married, he forgives her and suggests they run away. Leonora reminds him of his vows and sinks into death. The monks pray.

Fedora

Composed by Umberto Giordano (August 28, 1867 – November 12, 1948). Libretto by Arturo Colautti. Italian. Drama by Victorien Sardou. Premiered Milan, Teatro Lirico, November 17, 1898. Set in Russia, France and Switzerland in the late 19th century. Verismo tragedy. Through composed.

Sets: 3. **Acts:** 3 acts, 3 scenes. **Length:** I, II, III: 100. **Arias:** "Amor ti vieta" (Loris). **Hazards:** None. **Scenes:** I. The house of Count Vladimir Andreyevich in St. Petersburg. II. The house of Princess Fedora in Paris. III. The villa of Princess Fedora in Switzerland.

Major roles: Princess Fedora Romazov (soprano), De Siriex (baritone), Countess Olga Sukarev (light soprano), Count Loris Ipanov (tenor). **Minor roles:** Desiré (tenor), Dimitri (treble or contralto), Grech (bass), Lorek (baritone), Cirillo (baritone), Baron Rouvel (tenor), Dr. Borov (baritone). **Bit parts:** Nicola (bass or baritone), Sergio (tenor), Michele (tenor), Little savoyard (treble or mezzo). **Mute:** Boleslao Lazinski (pianist), Dr. Müller, Marka, Basilio, Ivan, Police agent.

Chorus parts: SATB. **Chorus roles:** Ladies, gentlemen, servants, Swiss mountain girls. **Dance/movement:** II: Ballroom dancing. **Orchestra:** picc, 2 fl, 2 ob, Eng hrn, 2 cl (bs cl), 2 bsn, 4 hrn, 3 trp, 3 trb, timp, perc, harp, strings. **Stageband:** I: electric bell. II: Boleslao Lazinski plays piano. III: fl (picc), hrn, accordion, perc. **Publisher:** Casa Musicale Sonzogno. **Rights:** Copyright 1898 by Casa Musicale Sonzogno.

I. Desiré, Nicola, Sergio and the other servants toast their master's upcoming marriage to the Princess Fedora—and hope that her dowry will ease the count's money troubles. Fedora arrives just before the wounded count, who is carried in by three policeman (Gretch, Ivan and another agent). The diplomat De Siriex, Lorek the surgeon and Doctor Müller also attend. Gretch questions the servants. Cirillo the coachman had discovered the count and flagged down De Siriex. Neither saw the assailant, but Desiré remembers a letter the count received from an old woman. Fedora swears to avenge her beloved. When they cannot find the letter, Dimitri remembers a mysterious visitor who left without giving his name. The concierge, Michele, knows the man's name: Loris

Ipanov. Gretch goes to apprehend Ipanov but he has fled. When Lorek announces the count's death, Fedora faints.

II. The Countess Olga Sukarev introduces Dr. Borov, Baron Rouvel and Boleslao Lazinski at a party. Fedora has made Ipanov fall in love with her. While she is not indifferent to him, she explains to De Siriex that she is only waiting for Ipanov to incriminate himself before taking her revenge. Borov counsels Ipanov to flee. Olga and De Siriex exchange barbed witticisms. While Ipanov tries to win Fedora's heart, Borov leaves for Russia. Fedora says she, too, will soon return. Ipanov is heart-broken. While Lazinski plays the piano, Ipanov confesses to Fedora that he cannot follow her because he murdered the count. He says it was punishment and promises to return with the proof. The party ends when news arrives of an attempt on the tsar's life. Fedora calls in Gretch and tells him to kidnap Ipanov and return him to Russia. Ipanov arrives and tells Fedora he killed the count because he was having an affair with Ipanov's late wife, Wanda. Fedora saves Ipanov from Gretch.

III. Ipanov and Fedora have fled to Fedora's villa in Switzerland. Olga is bored. She complains about Lazinski's desertion of her but agrees to go bicycling with De Siriex. While she is changing, De Siriex tells Fedora that Ipanov's brother and mother are both dead. The brother was killed by the count's father—who is chief of police—and Ipanov's mother died of grief. Fedora realizes that it is all her fault: It was she who told the chief of police about Ipanov's brother. Ipanov reads the letters he has received from Borov and learns of his own pardon, of his betrayal by a mysterious Russian woman living in Paris, and of the death of his broth-er and mother. Fedora begs Ipanov to forgive the mysterious lady, but Ipanov is relentless. When Ipanov guesses the truth, Fedora drinks poi-son. Borov, Olga and De Siriex return in time to see Fedora expire in the arms of the heartbroken Ipanov.

Die Feen • The Fairies

Composed by Richard Wagner (May 22, 1813 – February 13, 1883). Libretto by Richard Wagner. German. Based on "La Donna Serpente" by Carlo Gozzi. Premiered Munich, Königliches Hof- und Nationaltheater, June 29, 1888. Set in Tramond and the fairy kingdom at an unspecified time. Romantic opera. Set numbers with recitative. Overture. Ballet. Introduction before II, III.

Sets: 7. **Acts:** 3 acts, 8 scenes. **Length:** I: 65. II: 70. III: 30. **Arias:** "Wie muss ich doch beklagen" (Ada), "Wh' mir, so nah' die fürchterliche Stunde" (Ada), "Halloh!" (Arindal). **Hazards:** I: Gunther's and Morald's disguises are magically removed amid thunder and lightning. II: Ada makes a fiery abyss appear and hurls her two children into it. Ada sinks out of sight (she need not be turned into a stone onstage). III: Ada is transformed from a stone back into a fairy. **Scenes:** Ii. Fairy garden. Iii. Rocky wilderness. Iiii. The fairy garden. II. Entrance hall of the palace in the capital of Arindal's kingdom. IIIi. A decorated hall. IIIii. A fissure in a subterranean realm. IIIiii. A grotto. IIIiv. A magnificent fairy palace encircled by clouds.

Major roles: Gernot (bass), King Arindal of Tramond (tenor), Ada (soprano), Lora (soprano). **Minor roles:** Zemina or Jemina (soprano), Farzana (soprano), Morald (baritone), Günther (tenor), Drolla (soprano), Harald (bass), Offstage voice of the sorcerer Groma (bass), Fairy King (bass). **Bit parts:** Messenger (tenor). **Mute:** Ada and Arindal's two children.

Chorus parts: SSATTTTBBB (briefly AA). **Chorus roles:** Fairies, Morald's companions, warriors, people, earth sprites, bronze men, Groma's sprites (offstage), fairies, sprites. **Dance/movement:** I: Fairy ballet. **Orchestra:** picc, 2 fl, 2 ob, 2 cl, 2 bsn, 4 hrn, 2 trp, 3 trb, timp, perc, harp, strings. **Stageband:** II: 2 trp. III: 2 fl, 2 cl, 4 trb. **Publisher:** K. Ferd. Heckel. **Rights:** Expired.

Ii. The fairy Ada means to become mortal to be with her husband, King Arindal. (They were wed before the opera begins, but were separated when Arindal broke the fairy taboo and asked Ada's identity.) Ada's fairy friends band together to stop her from becoming mortal. Iii. Arindal's hunter, Gernot, is reunited with Morald and Gunther. He tells them how, eight years ago, Arindal met and married Ada. Arindal is desperate to find Ada. To persuade Arindal to abandon Ada, Gunther disguises himself as a holy man and Morald disguises himself as Arindal's father. Both disguises are magically revealed. Arindal agrees to return to his kingdom, but is charmed to sleep. Iiii. The fairies tell Ada that her mortal father has died, leaving her queen. She tells Arindal that they must again be separated and makes him swear not to curse her, no matter what happens.

II. Arindal's sister, Lora, defends his kingdom from attack. The king returns and Gernot is reunited with his sweetheart, Drolla. To become mortal, Ada must give Arindal reason to break his promise—but he must keep it. She throws their children into a fiery abyss and disperses the reinforcements brought by Arindal's general, Harald. Arindal curses Ada, thus dooming her to spend one hundred years transformed into a rock. Before her transfiguration, she returns their children and explains that Harald was conspiring against Arindal. Arindal's warriors are victorious.

IIIi. Arindal goes mad. The sorcerer Groma restores his senses and persuades him to try and save Ada. IIIii. With Groma's help, Arindal
defeats various evil spirits and locates Ada. IIIiii. Arindal dissolves the
spell that holds Ada by singing to her. IIIiv. The fairy king relents and
makes Arindal immortal.

Feuersnot • Beltane Fire

Composed by Richard Strauss (June 11, 1864 – September 8, 1949).
Libretto by Ernst von Wolzogen. German. Based on the Netherlandish
Sagas by J. W. Wolff. Premiered Dresden, Staatsoper, November 21,
1901. Set in Munich in the 12th century. Lyric poem. Through composed.
Introduction. Kunrad's monologues contain some not-so-subtle com-
ments on the public's original reception of Richard Wagner and Richard
Strauss.

Sets: 1. **Acts:** 1 act, 1 scene. **Length:** I: 90. **Hazards:** I: Conflagration seen
in distance. Kunrad hoisted partway up to Diemut's balcony in a basket.
Scenes: I. Sentlinger Street in Munich with the city gate in the background.

Major roles: Diemut (high soprano), Kunrad (high baritone). **Minor
roles:** Ortolf Sentlinger (low bass), Margret (high soprano), Elsbeth
(mezzo), Wigelis (low contralto), Jörg Pöschel (low bass), Kunz
Gilgenstock (bass), Hämerlein (baritone), Ortlieb Tulbeck (high tenor),
Ursula (contralto), Kofel (bass), Walpurg (high soprano), Ruger Asbeck
(tenor), Schweiker von Gundelfingen (low tenor). **Bit part:** Big girl
(soprano). **Mute:** policeman.

Chorus parts: SSAATTBB. **Chorus roles:** Citizens, women, retainers,
children (2 girl parts; 1 boy part, briefly 2). **Dance/movement:** None.
Orchestra: 3 fl (picc), 3 ob (Eng hrn), 3 cl (bs cl), 3 bsn (cont bsn), 4 hrn, 3
trp, 3 trb, tuba, timp, perc, glockenspiel, 2 harp, strings (12-12-8-8-6).
Stageband: I: 1 or 3 harp, harmonium, vln, vlc, 2 drums, glockenspiel,
perc. **Publisher:** Adolph Fürstner. **Rights:** Copyright 1901, 1910 by A.
Fürstner.

I. The children of Munich collect wood from the citizens to build a bon-
fire for midsummer's night. Kunrad surprises everyone by letting the
children pull down his house. He is the descendent of a pagan sorcerer
and has fallen in love with Diemut, the burgomaster's daughter. Kunrad
offends Diemut by kissing her in public and she decides to get even.
When he comes to her balcony at night, she agrees to draw him up in a
basket. But she only raises the basket halfway and suggests that he use
his magic to fly the rest of the way. The citizens laugh at Kunrad, who

casts a spell, quenching all the fires and lights in the town. After some heated exchanges, the people decide that Kunrad is not so bad. Diemut falls in love with him and when they kiss, all the lights are restored.

La Fiamma • The Flame

Composed by Ottorino Respighi (July 9, 1879 – April 18, 1936). Libretto by Claudio Guastalla. Italian. Based on "The Witch" by Hans Wiers Jenssen. Premiered Rome, Teatro Reale, January 23, 1934. Set in Ravenna at the end of the 7th century. Melodrama. Through composed. Entr'acte before III.

Sets: 5. **Acts:** 3 acts, 5 scenes. **Length:** I, II, III: 135. **Hazards:** None. **Scenes:** I. A spacious courtyard in the villa of the Exarch Basilio. II. A galley and room in the palace of Theodoric in Ravenna. IIIi. Donello's room in the palace. IIIii. Outside the basilica of San Vitale. IIIiii. Inside the basilica.

Major roles: Eudossia (mezzo), Silvana (soprano), Donello (tenor), Exarch Basilio (baritone). **Minor roles:** Monica (soprano), Sabina (mezzo), Agate (soprano), Lucilla (mezzo), Agnes (mezzo), Bishop (bass). **Bit parts:** Zoe (mezzo), Exorcist (bass), Mother Cesarios (soprano), Clergyman (tenor). **Bit parts:** Two pursuers (2 tenor).

Chorus parts: SSSAATTBB. **Chorus roles:** Women, people, clergy, councillors, servants, worshippers, prefects, henchmen, retainers, pursuers, children. **Dance/movement:** None. **Orchestra:** picc, 2 fl, 2 ob, Eng hrn, 2 cl, bs cl, 2 bsn, cont bsn, 4 hrn, 3 trp, 3 trb, tuba, timp, perc, harp, celeste, strings. **Stageband:** Eng hrn, 3 trp, 3 trb, bells. **Publisher:** G. Ricordi. **Rights:** Copyright 1935 by G. Ricordi.

I. Eudossia, the mother of Exarch Basilio of Ravenna, supervises the work of her handmaidens who chaff at her strictness. The crowd believes that Agnes is a witch and means to burn her. But Agnes appeals to Silvana, the exarch's wife, who hides her. Silvana greets her returned stepson, Donello. The mob captures Agnes who curses Eudossia.

II. Donello entertains the handmaidens with stories of his travels. Silvana has discovered her servant Monica's secret love and sends her to a convent. Basilio plans an expedition to subdue the pope's forces. Silvana asks about Agnes's trial. She realizes that Agnes was her mother. Basilio has known all along, but orders the truth suppressed because of his love for Silvana. Silvana realizes she has Agnes's magic powers—her flame—and uses them to call Donello to her.

IIIi. Donello and Silvana are having an affair. Eudossia suspects them and arranges for Donello to be summoned to Byzantium. Furious at losing Donello, Silvana tells Basilio about her infidelity and the shock kills him. IIIii. The crowd discusses the trial of Silvana. IIIiii. Silvana swears her innocence of the magic arts. Donello blames himself until Eudossia reveals Silvana's parentage—which she takes as proof of Silvana's guilt. The bishop and people—including Donello—anathematize Silvana.

Fidelio

Composed by Ludwig van Beethoven (December 15 or 16, 1770 – March 26, 1827). Libretto by Joseph Sonnleithner. German. Based on a libretto by Jean-Nicolas Bouilly. Premiered Vienna, Theater an der Wien, November 20, 1805. Set in Spain in the 18th century. Rescue opera. Set numbers with spoken dialogue and recitative. Overture. Introduction before II. Opus 72. Revised twice by composer with premieres on March 29, 1806 and May 23, 1814. Four versions of the overture. Libretto revised by Stefan von Breuning and Georg Friedrich Treitschke.

Sets: 4. **Acts:** 2 acts, 3 scenes (originally in 3 acts). **Length:** I: 68. II: 61. **Arias:** "O wär' ich schon mit dir vereint" (Marzelline), "Hat man nicht"/Gold aria (Rocco), "Ha! welch' ein Augenblick!" (Pizarro), "Abscheulicher!"/"Komm, Hoffnung" (Leonore), "In des Lebens Frühlingstagen" (Florestan). **Hazards:** None. **Scenes:** Ii. The jailer's quarters. Iii. The courtyard of a state prison. IIi. A dark, subterranean dungeon. IIii. A bastion before the castle.

Major roles: Leonore/Fidelio (soprano), Florestan (tenor), Pizarro (bass baritone), Rocco (bass). **Minor roles:** Marzelline (soprano), Jaquino (tenor), Fernando (bass). **Bit parts:** First prisoner (tenor), Second prisoner (bass).

Chorus parts: SATTBB. **Chorus roles:** Captains and officers, townspeople, guards, prisoners. **Dance/movement:** None. **Orchestra:** picc, 2 fl, 2 ob, 2 cl, 2 bsn, cont bsn, 4 hrn, 2 trp, 2 trb, timp, strings. **Stageband:** II: trp. **Publisher:** Schirmer, C. F. Peters. **Rights:** Expired.

Ii. Marcelline, the jailer's daughter, fends off the unwanted advances of the porter Jaquino. She loves Fidelio, the poor youth her father has taken in as an assistant. She does not suspect that Fidelio is really a woman (Leonora) in disguise. Fidelio/Leonora returns from the smith, where she has had prison chains repaired. The jailer, Rocco, is most impressed with Fidelio and plans to give "him" his daughter. Leonora complains about her bad luck while Rocco instructs the young couple on the value of money. She persuades Rocco to let her help him with his work in the prison. The jailer tells them about a mysterious political prisoner whom he has been starving on the orders of overseer Pizarro. Iii. Pizarro has wrongly imprisoned the man and is worried when he learns that the minister Fernando is arriving. When Rocco refuses to kill the prisoner, Pizarro decides to do it himself. Marcelline and Leonora persuade Rocco to let the prisoners out for a walk. Pizarro arrives, furious at Rocco's lenient treatment of the prisoners.

IIi. The mysterious prisoner is none other than Florestan, the husband whom Leonora has come to find. When Rocco and Leonora enter Florestan's cell and dig out an old well as a makeshift grave, Leonora recognizes him. She and Rocco give Florestan food and reveal that Pizarro is the overseer of the jail. It was for exposing Pizarro's crimes that Florestan landed in jail. When Pizarro tries to stab Florestan, Leonora reveals her true identity and draws a pistol. Trumpets announce the arrival of Fernando. Pizarro rushes out and husband and wife embrace. IIii. The prisoners and guards hail Fernando's arrival. The minister is surprised and pleased to learn that Florestan is still alive. Upon learning what has happened from Rocco, Fernando frees Florestan and has Pizarro arrested. All hail Leonora's courage and devotion.

Fierrabras

Composed by Franz Schubert (January 31, 1797 – November 19, 1828). Libretto by Josef Kupelwieser. German. Based on the play "La Puente de Mantible" by Calderón de la Barca, a story by Friedrich Heinrich Carl de la Motte Fouqué and a story by J. G. G. Büsching and F. H. von der Hagen. Premiered Karlsruhe, Hoftheater, February 9, 1897. Set in Southern France and Spain in the late 8th century. Heroic-romantic opera. Set numbers with recitative and spoken dialogue. Overture.

Sets: 8. **Acts:** 3 acts, 9 scenes. **Length:** I: 70. II: 45. III: 30. **Arias:** "Der Abend sinkt" (Eginhard), "In tiefbewegter Brust" (Fierrabras), "Die Brust, gebeugt von Sorgen" (Florinda). **Hazards:** None. **Scenes:** Ii. The women's quarters in the royal castle. Iii. Ceremonial room of state in the castle. Iiii. The garden outside in a brightly lit wing of the castle. IIi. An open region beyond the French frontier bounded by a height. IIii. An apartment in the palace of the Moorish prince, Boland of Agrimore. IIiii. A cell in a prison tower. IIIi. An apartment in the royal castle. IIIii. The tower. IIIiii. The square in front of the tower.

Major roles: Emma (soprano), Eginhard (tenor), King Karl (bass), Fierrabras (tenor), Roland (baritone), Florinda (soprano). **Minor roles:** Ogier (tenor), Gui von Burgund (tenor), Richard von der Normandie (bass), Gérard von Mondidier (bass), Brutamonte (bass), Maragond (mezzo), Prince Boland (bass), Olivier (tenor). **Speaking:** Moorish captain.

Chorus parts: SSAATTBB. **Chorus roles:** Frankish maidens, knights, ladies, pages, and vassals, Moorish prisoners, soldiers, people and priests. **Dance/movement:** None. **Orchestra:** picc, 2 fl, 2 ob, 2 cl, 2 bsn, 4 hrn, 2 trp, 3 trb, timp, strings. **Stageband:** I: 2 trp. II: 2 hrn, 2 trp, perc. III: 2 ob, 2 cl, 2 bsn, 2 hrn, 2 trp, 3 trb. **Publisher:** Dover Publications. **Rights:** Expired.

Ii. Emperor Charlemagne has defeated the Moors. Fearing the emperor's disapproval, his daughter, Emma, and the knight Eginhard keep their love secret. Iii. Charlemagne sends a group of knights—including Roland and Eginhard—as ambassadors to the Moorish camp. Roland had defeated and captured the Moorish prince's son, Fierrabras. They become friends and Roland secures his release. Fierrabras recognizes Emma as the woman he fell in love with in Italy years ago. He confesses to Roland and learns that his sister, Florinda, and Roland are in love. Iiii. Fierrabras discovers Eginhard and Emma eloping and agrees to help them. Charlemagne sees Fierrabras alone with Emma and orders his arrest.

IIi. Eginhard is overcome with guilt at his betrayal of Fierrabras. He is captured by a group of Moorish soldiers. IIii. Florinda pines for Roland. Eginhard confesses to Fierrabras's father, who treacherously imprisons all the ambassadors. IIiii. Florinda arms the knights. Eginhard escapes but Roland is recaptured.

IIIi. Charlemagne learns the truth and releases Fierrabras. Eginhard and Fierrabras go to rescue Roland. IIIii. Roland is lead to his execution. The imprisoned knights give up their defense of the tower to save him. IIIiii. They are captured. Florinda begs her father for mercy, but he refuses. The Franks defeat the Moors and release the knights. Charlemagne and the Moorish prince bless the marriages of Emma to Eginhard and Roland to Florinda.

Ognenny Angel • The Fiery Angel

Composed by Sergei Prokofiev (April 27, 1891 – March 5, 1953). Libretto by Sergei Prokofiev. Russian. After the novel by Valery Bryusov. Premiered Venice, Teatro la Fenice, September 14, 1955. Set in Germany in the 16th century. Tragedy. Through composed. Interludes before IIii and IIii. Op. 37. Fragments performed in Paris, June 14, 1928. Concert premiere in Paris, November 25, 1954.

Sets: 7. **Acts:** 5 acts, 7 scenes. **Length:** I: 30. II: 40. III: 10. IV: 15. V: 20 **Hazards:** III: Vision of Heinrich as fiery angel. IV: Mephistopheles swallows a serving boy. **Scenes:** I. The attic of an inn in Germany. IIi. A room in Köln. IIii. The library of Agrippa of Nettesheim. IIIi. A street in Köln. IIIii. A steep bank on the Rhine. IV. A quiet street in Köln. V. A convent.

Major roles: Ruprecht (baritone), Renata (dramatic soprano), Mephistopheles (tenor), Dr. Faustus (baritone). **Minor roles:** Hostess (mezzo), Laborer (baritone), Fortuneteller (mezzo), Jacob Glock (tenor), Agrippa of Nettesheim (tenor), Matthew (baritone), Abbess (mezzo), Inquisitor (bass),Two young nuns (2 soprano). **Bit parts:** Innkeeper (baritone), Three skeletons (soprano, 2 baritone), Physician (tenor), Three neighbors (3 bass). **Mute:** Count Heinrich, Boy.

Chorus parts: SSSAAATB (does not include small group of nuns). **Chorus roles:** Women (offstage), men of Köln, nuns (one small group of six and larger group). **Dance/movement:** V: Grotesque dance of possessed nuns. **Orchestra:** 3 fl (picc), 2 ob, Eng hrn, 2 cl, bs cl, 3 bsn (cont bsn), 4 hrn, 3 trp, 3 trb, tuba, 2 harp, timp, perc, strings. **Stageband:** V: bell, bs drum. **Publisher:** Boosey & Hawkes. **Rights:** Copyright 1957 by Boosey & Hawkes.

I. The knight Ruprecht lodges at an inn. Hearing screams next door, Ruprecht bursts in on Renata, who has had a vision. She explains that she was often visited by a fiery angel. Only when she fell in love with him did he abandon her. He came again to her in mortal form—as Count Heinrich—but Heinrich, too, has deserted her. The hostess is convinced Renata is a witch. Ruprecht tries to kiss Renata, but she rejects him. He repents and decides to help her get to Köln. Renata consults a fortuneteller, who sees blood.

IIi. Renata and Ruprecht have been in Köln a week without finding Heinrich. Renata dabbles in magic to no avail. Jacob Glock secures them an introduction to the great magician Agrippa. IIii. Agrippa is evasive in reply to Ruprecht's questions.

IIIi. Renata claims to have seen Heinrich, who again rejected her, and promises Ruprecht that she will be his if he murders Heinrich. When Ruprecht confronts Heinrich, Heinrich appears to Renata as a fiery angel. Ruprecht challenges Heinrich, but Renata has changed her mind. IIIii. Heinrich wounds Ruprecht. Renata tells Ruprecht she loves him.

IV. Renata is horrified by the sins she has committed with Ruprecht. Meaning to enter a convent, she stabs herself and runs away. Faust and Mephistopheles have dinner. They ask Ruprecht to show them around Köln.

V. The convent has been plagued with evil visitations since Renata's arrival. Warning Renata that the devil sometimes appears as a fiery angel, the inquisitor performs an exorcism. The other nuns become possessed and Renata accuses the inquisitor of being Beelzebub. He orders her to be burned.

Fiesta

Composed by Darius Milhaud (September 4, 1892 – June 22, 1974). Libretto by Boris Vian. French. Inspired by an actual event witnessed by the librettist. Premiered West Berlin, Städtische Opera, October 3, 1958. Set in Spain in the 20th century. Verismo opera. Through composed.

Sets: 1. **Acts:** 1 act, 1 scene. **Length:** I: 23. **Hazards:** I: A boat lands at the pier. **Scenes:** I. A pier of white stone.

Major roles: Mercedez (mezzo), Shipwreck survivor (baritone). **Minor roles:** Mario (tenor), Pedro (baritone), Esteban (bass), Julio (treble), Pia (soprano), Maria (mezzo), Concha (contralto), Nunez (bass). **Mute:** Fernan, Caracas, Alberto, Cortez, Raphael, Raquel.

Chorus parts: N/A. **Chorus roles:** None. **Dance/movement:** I: Mercedez dances for shipwreck survivor. **Orchestra:** fl (picc), ob, cl, bs cl, bsn, alto sax, trp, trb, perc, harp, 3 vln, 2 vlc, bs. **Stageband:** I: bell, guitar (played by Fernan). **Publisher:** Heugel & Co. **Rights:** Copyright 1958 by Heugel.

I. Esteban brings Mario and Pedro wine. Julio sees a boat with a castaway in it. The boat is brought in and the castaway fed. Nunez remembers when he was shipwrecked. Mercedez dances for the castaway. The castaway embraces her and the jealous Fernan kills him. Mario, Pedro and Esteban throw the corpse into the bay.

La Fille du Régiment • The Daughter of the Regiment

Composed by Gaetano Donizetti (November 29, 1797 – April 8, 1848). Libretto by Jean François Bayard and Jules-Henri Vernoy de Saint-Georges. French. Original work. Premiered Paris, Opéra Comique, February 11, 1840. Set in Swiss Tyrol in 1805. Comedy. Set numbers with recitative. Overture. Entr'acte before II. Recitatives sometimes replaced with spoken dialogue.

Sets: 2. **Acts:** 2 acts, 2 scenes. **Length:** I: 70. II: 40. **Arias:** "Ah! Chacun le sait chacun le dit" (Marie), "Ah mes amis" (Tonio), "Salut à la France"

(Marie). **Hazards:** None. **Scenes:** I. An army camp site in the Tyrol. II. A large drawing room in the Chateau Berkenfield.

Major roles: Marquise of Berkenfield (mezzo), Marie (soprano), Sulpice (bass), Tonio (tenor). **Minor roles:** Hortensius (bass), Corporal (baritone). **Bit part:** Peasant (tenor). **Speaking:** Duchess of Krackenthorp. **Mute:** Notary.

Chorus parts: SATTB. **Chorus roles:** French soldiers, Tyrolean peasants, ladies and gentlemen, servants of the Marquise. **Dance/movement:** None. **Orchestra:** 2 fl (picc), 2 ob (Eng hrn), 2 cl, 2 bsn, 4 hrn, 2 trp, 3 trb, timp, perc, strings. **Stageband:** I: drum. II: trps, hrns. **Publisher:** Schirmer, Schonenberger. **Rights:** Expired.

I. The Marquise and her steward, Hortensius, are surrounded by a battle on their way home. They meet up with a French regiment. Sergeant Sulpice expresses his pride in Marie, the spirited "daughter" of the regiment—a girl raised in camp by the soldiers. Still, he is concerned that she has been visiting a young Tyrolean peasant. This peasant, Tonio, is caught snooping about the camp and is brought in by the guards. The soldiers want to hang Tonio until they learn he once saved Marie's life by catching her fall. So they toast him and sing the regimental song until the drum is heard, calling the soldiers away. Marie remains behind and Tonio proposes to her. When the Marquise requests an escort to return home, Sulpice discovers that Marie is the Marquise's long-lost niece. Unaware of this, Tonio has enlisted. The regiment reluctantly gives its consent to the marriage of Tonio and Marie. Unfortunately, Marie's aunt objects and declares her intention to take Marie away. Marie bids the regiment—and Tonio—a tearful farewell.

II. The Marquise has arranged for Marie to marry the Duke of Krackenthorp. She calls in Sulpice to help her tame Marie so that she will make a good impression on the duchess (the duke's aunt). Marie practices the art song she has learned, but ends up singing the regimental song with Sulpice, shocking the Marquise. Marie is brooding on her happy past when her regiment appears with Tonio. Her love makes his case to the Marquise, but she is adamant. In private, the Marquise confesses to Sulpice that Marie must marry the duke because she is not the Marquise's niece, but her illegitimate daughter. Sulpice tells Marie. The party for the duchess is interrupted by the arrival of the regiment, who have come to rescue Marie. The duchess is scandalized but the Marquise is touched. She confesses to all that Marie is her daughter and promises to let her marry the man of her choice.

La Finta Giardiniera • The Pretend Gardener

Composed by Wolfgang Amadeus Mozart (January 27, 1756 – December 5, 1791). Libretto by Giuseppe Petrosellini and Marco Coltellini. Italian. Based on a libretto by Ranieri de Calzabigi. Premiered Munich, Salvatortheater, January 13, 1775. Set in the town of Lagonero in Italy in the mid-18th century. Dramma giocoso. Set numbers with recitative. Overture. Also exists in a singspiel version.

Sets: 7. **Acts:** 3 acts, 39 scenes. **Length:** I: 85. II: 80. III: 30. **Arias:** "Dento il mio petto" (Don Anchise), "Dolce d'amor compagna" (Ramiro), "Crudeli, oh Dio!" (Sandrina), "Va pure ad altri" (Ramiro). **Hazards:** None. **Scenes:** Ii – Iv. A charming garden with a wide staircase leading to the mayor's mansion. Ivi – Iix. A gallery. Ix – Ixv. A hanging garden. IIi – IIix. A hall in the mayor's residence. IIx – IIxiv. A room. IIxv – IIxvi. A deserted mountainous spot with ancient, partly ruined aqueducts. IIIi – IIIvi. A courtyard. IIIvii – IIIviii. The garden.

Major roles: Marchioness Violante Onesti / Sandrina (soprano), Ramiro (mezzo), Don Anchise (tenor or baritone), Roberto / Nardo (bass baritone), Serpetta (soprano), Arminda (soprano), Count Belfiore (tenor). **Speaking:** Doctor.

Chorus parts: N/A. **Chorus roles:** None. **Dance/movement:** None. **Orchestra:** 2 fl, 2 ob, 2 bsn, 4 hrn, 2 trp, timp, strings, continuo (harpsichord). **Stageband:** None. **Publisher:** Bärenreiter Kassel, Breitkopf & Härtel. **Rights:** Expired.

Ii. The mayor is waiting for his niece, Arminda, a noblewoman who is engaged to Count Belfiore. Cavalier Ramiro loves—and was jilted by—Arminda. Iii. The mayor proposes to his gardener, Sandrina. Iiii. Sandrina is really the Marchioness Violante Onesti who, with her servant Roberto, has disguised herself as a gardener. She was stabbed and deserted by Belfiore and has preferred to let everyone think she is dead. Iiv. The jilted lovers rail against the cruelty of fate. Iv. Roberto loves Serpetta, the mayor's maid. Ivi. Belfiore and Arminda arrive. Ivii. They are introduced. Iviii. Belfiore brags about his ancestors. Iix. Serpetta rejects Roberto. Ix. When Arminda tells Sandrina she is marrying Belfiore, Sandrina faints. Ixi. Belfiore recognizes Sandrina. Ixii. Ramiro confronts Arminda. Ixiii. The mayor is confused by all the commotion. Ixiv. He sees Sandrina with Belfiore. Ixv. Accusations fly.

IIi. Belfiore is upset. IIii. Arminda realizes he loves Sandrina. IIiii. She rebukes him for having deserted her. IIiv. Serpetta teases Roberto. IIv. Sandrina tells Belfiore she is not the marchioness: He killed the marchioness. IIvi. The mayor is offended by Sandrina's behavior. IIvii. After learning that Belfiore is wanted for murdering the marchioness, he breaks off Belfiore's engagement to his niece. IIviii. Arminda refuses to listen to Ramiro. IIix. He still loves her. IIx. The mayor confronts Belfiore, who lies unconvincingly. IIxi. Sandrina saves Belfiore by admitting she is the marchioness. But when Belfiore privately begs forgiveness, she tells him she only pretended to be the marchioness to help him. IIxii. The count is bewildered. IIxiii. Sandrina runs away. IIxiv. Serpetta privately muses that to succeed, one must be devious. IIxv. Sandrina loses her way. IIxvi. Everyone sets out after Sandrina. She and Belfiore go mad from the confusion.

IIIi. Everyone returns to town. IIIii. Roberto tries to reason with Sandrina and Belfiore. IIIiii. Arminda asks the mayor to marry her to Belfiore, while Ramiro demands Arminda marry him. IIIiv. The mayor wants to be left in peace. IIIv. Arminda tells Ramiro she hates him. IIIvi. Ramiro is unaware of his crime, but prefers death to life without Arminda. IIIvii. Sandrina and Belfiore recover their senses. They are reconciled and marry. IIIviii. Arminda admits it was she who made Belfiore so jealous he stabbed Sandrina. Sandrina forgives her. Arminda marries Ramiro and Roberto marries Serpetta.

La Finta Semplice • The Pretended Simpleton

Composed by Wolfgang Amadeus Mozart (January 27, 1756 – December 5, 1791). Libretto by Marco Coltellini. Italian. Based on a libretto by Carlo Goldoni. Premiered Salzburg, Palace of the Archbishop, May 1, 1769. Set in Cremona in the 18th century. Comic opera. Set numbers with recitative. Overture. KV 51/46a.

Sets: 5. **Acts:** 3 acts, 26 scenes. **Length:** I: 65. II: 50. III: 30. **Arias:** "Senti l'eco ove t'aggiri" (Rosina), "Amoretti, che ascosi qui siete" (Rosina). **Hazards:** None. **Scenes:** Ii – Iiii. A garden with an avenue of trees extending from an open space at the top of a hill to the facade of a small country mansion. Iiv – Iix. A room in Cassandro's house. IIi – IIiv. A balcony of Cassandro's house. IIv – IIxii. A room with chairs and lights. III. A country road.

Major roles: Giacinta (soprano), Captain Fracasso (tenor), Ninetta the chambermaid (soprano), Don Cassandro (bass), Rosina (soprano), Don Polidoro (tenor). **Minor role:** Simone (bass).

Chorus parts: N/A. **Chorus roles:** None. **Dance/movement:** None. **Orchestra:** 2 fl, 3 ob (2 Eng hrn), 2 bsn, 2 hrn, strings, continuo. **Stageband:** None. **Publisher:** Bärenreiter, Breitkopf & Härtel. **Rights:** Expired.

Iii. While quartered in the home of Don Cassandro, Captain Fracasso has fallen in love with Cassandro's sister, Giacinta. Fracasso and Giacinta want to marry—as do their servants Simone and Ninetta—but they know Cassandro will object. Iii. Ninetta devises a plan. Iiii. Cassandro admits he is a misanthrope. Iiv. Fracasso's sister, Rosina, agrees to follow Ninetta's plan to pose as a simpleton and make both Cassandro and

his foolish brother Polidoro fall in love with her. Polidoro proposes immediately. Iv. He tells Cassandro he is engaged to Rosina. Ivi. Cassandro is attracted to Rosina. Ivii. She reports her successes to Ninetta and Fracasso. Iviii. Ninetta helps Polidoro draft a love letter for Rosina. Iix. Fracasso intercepts the letter and pretends to be offended. Rosina swipes Cassandro's ring.

IIii. Ninetta is annoyed with Simone for being more interested in food than in her. IIii. Fracasso and Cassandro get drunk and exchange angry words. IIiii. Polidoro still believes Rosina plans to marry him. IIiv. Ninetta fetches Polidoro. IIv. Rosina coaches him for a confrontation with his brother. IIvi. Polidoro demands his half of the inheritance from Cassandro. IIvii. Rosina slips Cassandro's ring back on his finger while he is drunk. IIviii. Fracasso entraps Cassandro into saying that Rosina stole his ring—and then points out that Cassandro has the ring on his finger and challenges him for slandering his sister. IIix. Cassandro flees. IIx. Rosina and Fracasso congratulate each other. IIxi. They work out the rest of the plot. IIxii. Fracasso tells the brothers that Rosina and Ninetta have absconded with the family inheritance. The brothers promise to marry both girls to whoever can find them and bring them back and Fracasso and Simone volunteer.

IIIi. Simone catches up with Ninetta and they get married. IIIii. Giacinta is afraid her brother will not agree to her marrying Fracasso, but Fracasso assures her that Rosina has taken care of everything. IIIiii. Rosina tells Cassandro she wants to marry both him and Polidoro. IIIiv. Rosina teases Polidoro and rejects him. IIIv. Cassandro forgives Giacinta and marries Rosina.

Die Fledermaus • The Bat

Composed by Johann Strauss Jr. (October 25, 1825 – June 3, 1899). Libretto by Carl Haffner and Richard Genée. German. Based on "Le Réveillon" by Henri Meilhac and Ludovic Halévy. Premiered Vienna, Theater an der Wien, April 5, 1874. Set in Vienna in the 19th century. Operetta. Set numbers with spoken dialogue. Overture. Entr'acte before II and III. Ballet.

Sets: 3. **Acts:** 3 acts, 3 scenes. **Length:** I, II, III: 110. **Arias:** "Klänge der Heimat" (Rosalinda), "Mein Herr Marquis" / Laughing song (Adele), "Trinke, Liebchen" (Alfred), Orlofsky's aria (Orlofsky). **Hazards:** None. **Scenes:** I. Eisenstein's home. II. Prince Orlofsky's ball. III. In prison.

Major roles: Rosalinda (soprano), Gabriel Eisenstein (tenor), Adele (soprano), Alfred (tenor). **Minor roles:** Dr. Blind (tenor), Dr. Falke (baritone), Frank (baritone), Sally or Ida (soprano or speaking), Prince Orlofsky (mezzo). **Speaking:** Frosch.

Chorus parts: SSAATTB. **Chorus roles:** Guests at the party, four waiters, six soprano solo bits. **Dance/movement:** II: Ballet. Waltz. **Orchestra:** 2 fl (picc), 2 ob, 2 cl, 2 bsn, 4 hrn, 2 trp, 3 trb, timp, perc, chimes, harp, strings. **Stageband:** None. **Publisher:** Schirmer. **Rights:** Expired.

I. Alfred serenades Rosalinda while Rosalinda's chambermaid, Adele, wonders how she can go to Prince Orlofsky's ball. Adele asks for leave to see her poor sick aunt, but Rosalinda refuses. "Starting tonight, my husband, Eisenstein, must serve his five days in jail," Rosalinda reminds the maid. He hung a man's coat on the rack—with the man still in it. Eisenstein enters, furious with his lawyer Blind: after Blind's representations, the court extended the sentence from five days to eight. Dr. Falke persuades Eisenstein to go with him to Orlofsky's party instead of going to jail. Eisenstein reminds the doctor of the time he left him out in the park the night after a costume parade. The next morning, Falke was surrounded by all the Sunday promenaders and had to skulk home in his bat costume. The two men agree on a disguise for Eisenstein. Now that her husband is going to spend the night in jail, Rosalinda gives Adele the night off. Rosalinda's lover, Alfred, reappears. Falke leaves a note for Rosalinda telling her to come to Orlofsky's party disguised as a Hungarian countess. Frank, the prison warden, takes Alfred to jail, thinking he is Eisenstein.

II. Falke sets the stage for his practical joke: He introduces Eisenstein to the prince and gives out that Adele is an actress named Olga. The prince is bored. Eisenstein and Adele recognize each other. Falke and the guests laugh at Eisenstein for calling Adele a chambermaid. Rosalinda arrives wearing a mask. She is introduced as a Hungarian countess and immediately recognizes her husband and Adele. Eisenstein unknowingly woos his wife, with the aid of his charming watch. Rosalinda pockets the watch. The guests toast champagne and love. When the clock strikes six, Eisenstein hurries off to jail, arm in arm with Frank.

III. Frosch the jailer has been drinking. Frank staggers in, drunk, and falls asleep. Adele appears with her sister, Sally, hoping Frank will launch her on a stage career. Frank has the women locked up to get them out of the way. Eisenstein turns himself in, but Frank still believes that Alfred is Eisenstein. He tells the real Eisenstein how he found the prisoner (Alfred) kissing Rosalinda. Alfred demands a lawyer and Blind is sent for. Rosalinda comes to bail out Alfred. When Blind arrives, Eisenstein intercepts him and forces him to exchange clothes. Thus disguised, Eisenstein interrogates his wife and Alfred. Eisenstein removes his disguise and recriminations fly. Frank has Adele and Sally brought down to identify Eisenstein. Falke arrives with Orlofsky and his guests. "This was my revenge for your prank on me," Falke explains. Alfred claims that his visit to Rosalinda was part of the joke. The prince offers to sponsor Adele in the theater. All drink a toast to champagne.

Die Fliegende Holländer • The Flying Dutchman

Composed by Richard Wagner (May 22, 1813 – February 13, 1883). Libretto by Richard Wagner. German. Based on a story by Heinrich Heine. Premiered Dresden, Königliches Hoftheater, January 2, 1843. Set on the coast of Norway in the 18th century. Romantic opera. Through composed but with some set pieces. Overture. Entr'acte before II and III.

Sets: 3. **Acts:** 3 acts, 3 scenes. **Length:** I: 50. II: 55. III: 26. **Arias:** "Die frist ist um" (Dutchman), "Jo ho hoe"/Senta's ballad (Senta). **Hazards:** I: Appearance of the ghost ship. II: Storm around the ghost ship. Sinking of ship and image of Senta and dutchman in the sky. **Scenes:** I. Steep, rocky shore. II. Room in Daland's house. III. Bay with a rocky shore.

Major roles: Daland (bass), Dutchman (baritone), Senta (soprano), Erik (tenor). **Minor roles:** Steersman (tenor), Mary (mezzo).

Chorus parts: SSAATTTTBBBB. **Chorus roles:** Norwegian maidens, crew of Daland's vessel, crew of Dutchman's vessel. **Dance/movement:** III: sailor's dance. **Orchestra:** picc, 2 fl, 2 ob, Eng hrn, 2 cl, 2 bsn, 4 hrn, 2 trp, 3 trb, tuba, timp, harp, perc, strings. **Stageband:** I: 3 picc, perc, hrns. **Publisher:** Schirmer, Adolph Fürstner. **Rights:** Expired.

I. Daland's ship is thrown off course by a storm. The Dutchman's ghost ship appears. Seven years have passed and the Dutchman again goes ashore in search of true love: Only love will end the curse on him. The Dutchman offers Daland immense riches in return for a night's hospitality. He asks if Daland has a daughter—and asks for her hand. Daland agrees.

II. Mary and the women work at their spinning wheels. Senta is pensive; she has heard the ballad of the flying Dutchman and fallen in love with him. Erik begs Senta to marry him, having dreamt that the Dutchman came for Senta. Telling Senta his dream, Erik realizes she is in love. Daland brings the Dutchman home and leaves him alone with Senta. The two recognize in each other their true love.

III. The women prepare a feast for the sailors. They invite the Dutchman's crew, but are frightened away by the ghosts. Erik chides Senta for giving herself to the Dutchman so quickly. Overhearing their conversation, the Dutchman believes himself betrayed and sets sail. He promises that Senta will escape the damnation that is the normal fate of women who betray him. As proof of her faithfulness, Senta throws herself into the sea. The Dutchman's curse is lifted.

La Forza del Destino • The Force of Destiny

Composed by Giuseppe Verdi (October 9, 1813 – January 27, 1901). Libretto by Francesco Maria Piave. Italian. Based on the play "Don Alvaro" by Ángel Pérez de Saavedra. Premiered St. Petersburg, Imperial Theater, November 10, 1862. Set in Spain and Italy in the 18th century. Melodrama. Set numbers with recitative. Overture. Libretto later revised by Antonio Ghislanzoni.

Sets: 8. **Acts:** 4 acts, 8 scenes. **Length:** I: 30. II: 40. III: 45. IV: 35. **Arias:** "Madre, pietosa vergine" (Leonora), "O tu che in seno" (Don Alvaro), "Pace, pace" (Leonora), "Urna fatale" (Don Carlo). **Hazards:** None. **Scenes:** I. A large room hung with damask. IIi. The ground-floor kitchen of an inn in the village of Hornachuelos. IIii. A small mountain clearing before a church and monastery. IIIi. A wood in Italy near Velletri. IIIii. The quarters of a senior officer of the Spanish army. IIIiii. A military encampment near Velletri. IV. Interior of the monastery near Hornachuelos.

Major roles: Donna Leonora (dramatic soprano), Don Carlo of Vargas (baritone), Don Alvaro (tenor), Father superior (bass), Preziosilla (mezzo). **Minor roles:** Marquis of Calatrava (bass), Friar Melitone (baritone), Mayor (bass), Master Trabuco (tenor), Surgeon (baritone), Curra (mezzo). **Bit parts:** Woman (soprano, IVi), Three soldiers (tenor, baritone, bass).

Chorus parts: SSAATTTBBB. **Chorus roles:** Peasants, muleteers, pilgrims, Spanish and Italian soldiers, vivandières, conscripts, beggars, robbers, servants, orderlies, friars, country men and women. **Dance/movement:** II: Village girls and muleteers dance. III: Soldiers and vivandières dance. **Orchestra:** 2 fl (2 picc), 2 cl (bs cl), 2 ob, 2 bsn, 4 hrn, 2 trp, 3 trb, cimbasso, timp, perc, 2 harp, organ, strings. **Stageband:** III: 6 trp, 4 drums, onstage drums. **Publisher:** Dover. **Rights:** Expired.

I. The marquis kisses his daughter Leonora good night and retires. Leonora is wracked with guilt as she prepares to elope with Don Alvaro. She delays until the marquis, hearing them, rushes in. Alvaro drops his gun as a show of surrender, but it goes off, mortally wounding the marquis. Carlos leaves.

IIi. The village girls and muleteers dance and celebrate. Carlos, Leonora's brother, sits down to eat with them, disguised as a student. Leonora recognizes him and realizes he means to kill her. Preziosilla sings of war. Pilgrims are heard in the distance. Carlos questions the muleteer Trabuco about Leonora but learns nothing. Carlos tells Leonora's story, pretending, however, to be merely a friend of Leonora's brother. IIii. Leonora has been unaware that Alvaro is alive until she hears it in the inn. She seeks refuge in a monastery. Only the father superior knows who she is. He hides her in a cave.

IIIi. Alvaro, returned to the Spanish army, longs for death. He saves Carlos from robbers and the two men swear friendship—not knowing each other's true identity. IIIii. Alvaro is wounded in combat, but his army is victorious. Carlos is concerned for his friend until a chance remark awakens his suspicions. He goes through Alvaro's possessions and discovers the truth. He rejoices in Alvaro's recovery because it enables him to take his revenge. IIIiii. Ignoring Alvaro's assurance that he did not dishonor Leonora, Carlos challenges Alvaro. Alvaro is stunned to learn that Leonora is alive. The men fight but are separated by the guard. Preziosilla tells the soldiers' fortunes, while Trabuco sells them trinkets. The women and soldiers dance. Brother Melitone rails at them for indecency. When the soldiers try to beat him, Preziosilla distracts them with a song.

IVi. Five years have passed, and Brother Melitone reluctantly feeds a band of insolent beggars. Alvaro has joined the brotherhood, but Carlos discovers this and comes for him. Alvaro refuses to fight until Carlos slaps him. IVii. Leonora, longing for death, hears men approaching and retreats into her cave. It is Carlos and Alvaro. They fight and Carlos falls. Alvaro comes for a holy man to bless Carlos—and finds Leonora. Leonora goes to Carlos, but he stabs her. She blesses Alvaro and dies.

The Four Note Opera

Composed by Tom Johnson (b. November 18, 1939). Libretto by Tom Johnson. English. Original work. Premiered New York City, Cubiculo Theater, May 11, 1972. Set in an unspecified time and place. Absurdist comedy. Set numbers with recitative. Entire score built solely on the notes A, B, D and E.

Sets: 1. **Acts:** 1 act, 1 scene. **Length:** I: 60. **Hazards:** None. **Scenes:** I. Unspecified.

Major roles: Soprano, Contralto, Tenor, Baritone.

Chorus parts: N/A. **Chorus roles:** None. **Dance/movement:** None. **Orchestra:** Piano. **Stageband:** None. **Publisher:** Associated Music Publishers. **Rights:** Copyright 1973 by Associated Music Publishers Inc.

I. The four singers perform and explain each of the various opera forms: arias, trios, etc.

Four Saints in Three Acts

Composed by Virgil Thomson (November 25, 1896 – September 30, 1989). Libretto by Gertrude Stein. English. Original work based on a scenario by Maurice Grosser. Premiered Hartford, Connecticut, Hartford Atheneum, February 8, 1934. Set in Spain in the 16th century. Surrealist drama. Through composed with spoken lines. Prologue. Ballet. Intermezzo and prologue before IV. Libretto is non-linear and filled with word plays.

Sets: 5. **Acts:** 4 acts, 5 scenes. **Length:** Prologue: 11. I: 24. II: 21. III: 27. IV: 7. **Hazards:** None. **Scenes:** Prologue. Steps and portal of the cathedral, Avila. I. A garden at Avila in early spring. II. In the country out of doors. III. Monastery garden with low trees and a wall, behind the wall a bare Spanish horizon and an empty sky. IV. No scenery but the sky with tumultuous clouds and a sunburst.

Major roles: Compère (bass), Commère (mezo), St. Ignatius (baritone), St. Teresa I (soprano), St. Teresa II (mezzo), St. Chavez (tenor), St. Settlement (soprano). **Minor roles:** St. Plan (bass), St. Stephen (tenor), St. Cecilia (soprano), St. Sara (mezzo). **Bit parts:** St. Absalon (tenor), St. Eustace (baritone), St. Celestine (mezzo), St. Jean (baritone), St. Anne (soprano), St. Genevieve (soprano), St. Vincent (spoken), St. Placide (bass), St. Michael (baritone), St. Manuel (baritone), St. Sulpice (tenor), St. Hilyer (tenor), St. Andrew (tenor), St. Leonard (baritone), St. Arthur (tenor), St. Ferdinand (baritone), St. Sylvester (tenor), St. Henry (baritone), St. Philipp (baritone), St. Pelen (baritone), St. Gallo (baritone), St. Pilar (bass). (There are also unnamed solos for soprano, alto, tenor, baritone and bass. The bit parts come out of the chorus and many can be combined.)

Chorus parts: SSAATTBB. **Chorus roles:** Double chorus of saints. **Dance/movement:** III: Ballet of sailors and young girls. **Orchestra:** fl (picc), ob (Eng hrn), cl, bsn, 2 hrn, trp, trb, accordion, harmonium, 2 perc, strings. **Stageband:** None. **Publisher:** Schirmer. **Rights:** Copyright 1948 by Virgil Thomson.

I. In a series of tableaux, St. Teresa enacts scenes from her life.

II. The saints attend a garden party outside Barcelona. The Commère and Compère share a tender moment. The two St. Teresas have a vision.

III. In a monastery garden, the saints repair a fishing net and discuss the monastic life. St. Ignatius relates his vision of the holy ghost to a skeptical chorus. Sailors and young girls dance. St. Ignatius foretells the last judgment.

IV. Commère and Compère discuss whether there is to be a fourth act. The saints sing a hymn of communion.

Fra Diavolo • Brother Devil

Composed by Daniel François Esprit Auber (January 29, 1782 – May 12, 1871). Libretto by Eugène Scribe. French. Based on a historical character. Premiered Paris, Opéra Comique, January 28, 1830. Set in Italy in the late 18th century. Romantic opera. Set numbers with recitative. Overture. Entr'acte before III.

Sets: 3. **Acts:** 3 acts, 3 scenes. **Length:** I: 45. II: 35. III: 30. **Arias:** "Dès l'enfance les mêmes chaines" (Zerlina), "Je vois marcher sous ma bannière" (Fra Diavolo). **Hazards:** None. **Scenes:** I. Matteo's inn. II. Zerlina's bedroom. III. In the hills near Terracina.

Major roles: Lorenzo (tenor), Zerlina (soprano), Lord Cockburn (baritone), Lady Pamela (mezzo), Fra Diavolo/Marquis of San Marco (tenor). **Minor roles:** Matteo (bass), Beppo (tenor), Giacomo (bass). **Bit parts:** Farmer (tenor), Soldier (tenor), Miller (bass).

Chorus parts: SATTB. **Chorus roles:** People of Terracina, farmers, huntsmen, soldiers. **Dance/movement:** III: Optional ballet. **Orchestra:** 2 fl (2 picc), 2 ob, 2 cl, 2 bsn, 4 hrn, 2 trp, 3 trb, timp, perc, strings. **Stageband:** II: 4 hrn, 2 trp, 3 trb. III: perc. **Publisher:** Boosey & Co., Troupenas. **Rights:** Expired.

I. Matteo invites the soldiers to the wedding of his daughter Zerlina and a rich farmer's son. This upsets Lorenzo, the brigadier, who loves—and is loved by—Zerlina. Lord Cockburn and Lady Pamela have been robbed by Fra Diavolo and his brigand band and Lorenzo agrees to set out after them. Matteo explains that he will not let Zerlina marry Lorenzo because the brigadier is penniless. Cockburn offers a substantial reward for the recovery of his property. Cockburn objects to the marquis who has been hanging around, flirting with Lady Pamela. The marquis (who is actually Fra Diavolo) arrives and is regaled with stories of Fra Diavolo's fearsome deeds. In private, he confers with Beppo and Giacomo, two members of his gang who have come to Matteo's inn disguised as beggars. They report that the 500,000 francs supposedly in Cockburn's possession were not found when they robbed him. Diavolo woos Pamela. Cockburn and Pamela confess to him that they saved the 500,000 francs by sewing banknotes into their clothing. Lorenzo returns, having routed the bandits. He returns Pamela's jewel case to her and she rewards him handsomely.

II. Zerlina thinks of Lorenzo. Cockburn and Pamela go to bed. The marquis serenades Pamela. He and his men prepare to rob Cockburn, but wait until Zerlina leaves. Lorenzo arrives with his men, having found a farmer who can identify Diavolo. Diavolo's hiding place is discovered, but he explains that he was meeting Zerlina and Pamela. Lorenzo and Cockburn are furious and Lorenzo challenges him. The women are perplexed by their cold reception.

III. Diavolo rejoices in the life of a brigand. The village turns out to celebrate Easter morning. Beppo and Giacomo follow Diavolo's orders and watch for the bridal train. Lorenzo bids Zerlina farewell. She is surprised he suspects her fidelity. Beppo and Giacomo repeat the words they heard Zerlina speak to herself the night before. Lorenzo has them arrested and reads their instructions from Diavolo. He threatens the two bandits into helping him set a trap for Diavolo: they allow Diavolo to get Cockburn's money, and then catch him with it.

Francesca da Rimini • Francesca of Rimini

Composed by Sergei Rachmaninoff (April 1, 1873 – March 28, 1943). Libretto by Modest Tchaikovsky. Russian. Based on the fifth canto of Dante's epic poem "Inferno." Premiered Moscow, Bolshoi Theater, January 11 (24), 1906. Set in Hell and Rimini in the 13th century. Tragedy. Through composed. Prologue. Epilogue. Introduction before each scene. Opus 25.

Sets: 4. **Acts:** 2 acts, 5 scenes. **Length:** I, II: 65. **Hazards:** Prologue: Apparitions emerge from a hellish whirlwind. II: Clouds cover murder of Francesca and Paolo. **Scenes:** Prologue i. Cliffs in the first circle of hell. Prologue ii. A rocky, desert-like place with a distant horizon. I. Malatesta's palace in Rimini. II. A room in the palace. Epilogue. The rocky, desert-like place.

Major roles: Francesca (soprano), Paolo (tenor), Lanciotto Malatesta (baritone). **Minor roles:** Shade of Virgil (baritone), Dante (tenor). **Mute:** Cardinal.

Chorus parts: SSAATTB. **Chorus roles:** Specters of hell, retinue of Malatesta and the cardinal. **Dance/movement:** None. **Orchestra:** 3 fl (picc), 2 ob, Eng hrn, 2 cl, bs cl, 2 bsn, 4 hrn, 3 trp, 3 trb, tuba, timp, perc, harp, strings. **Stageband:** I: 2 hrn, 2 trp. **Publisher:** Boosey & Hawkes, State Music Publishers. **Rights:** Expired.

Prologue. The shade of Virgil leads Dante into hell. Dante asks the shades of Francesca and Paolo their story. Ii. At the Pope's command, Lanciotto Malatesta leads an army against the Ghibellines. Iii. Lanciotto laments that his wife Francesca loves his brother Paolo, not himself. Iiii. He asks for her love, but she says she cannot lie.

II. Paolo reads the story of Lancelot du Lac to Francesca and Francesca succumbs to Paolo's wooing. The lovers are surprised and murdered by Lanciotto. Epilogue. Francesca and Paolo are condemned to hell.

Francesca da Rimini • *Francesca of Rimini*

Composed by Riccardo Zandonai (May 30, 1883 – June 5, 1944). Libretto by Tito Ricordi. Italian. Based on the play by Gabriele d'Annunzio. Premiered Turin, Teatro Regio, February 19, 1914. Set in Ravenna and Rimini in the late 13th century. Lyric tragedy. Though composed. Entr'acte before III.

Sets: 4. **Acts:** 4 acts, 5 scenes. **Length:** I, II, III, IV: 125. **Arias:** "Chi ho veduto?" (Francesca), "Paolo, datemi pace!" (Francesca), "Inghirlandata di violette" (Paolo). **Hazards:** None. **Scenes:** I. A court in the house of the Polentani in Ravenna. II. Interior of a round tower in the house of the Malatesti in Rimini. III. A room painted in fresco in the house of the Malatesti. IVi. An octagonal hall in the house of the Malatesti. IVii. The room painted in fresco.

Major roles: Francesca (soprano), Giovanni or Gianciotto the lame (baritone), Paolo the handsome (tenor), Malatestino the one-eyed (tenor). **Minor roles:** Garsenda (soprano), Biancofiore (soprano or mezzo), Altichiara (mezzo), Jester (bass), Donella (soprano), Ostasio (baritone), Sir Toldo Berardengo (tenor), Samaritana (soprano), Tower guard (baritone), Slave Smaragdi (mezzo). **Bit part:** Archer (tenor).

Chorus parts: SSAATTBB (briefly SSSSAAA). **Chorus roles:** Women, archers, soldiers and musicians. **Dance/movement:** III: March calends celebration. **Orchestra:** picc, 2 fl, 2 ob, Eng hrn, 2 cl, bs cl, 2 bsn, cont bsn, 4 hrn, 3 trp, 3 trb, bs trb, harp, celeste, perc, timp, strings. **Stageband:** I: fl, fife, cl, vla pomposa, lute, vla (played by Giullare). II: trp, bugle, bells. III: fl, fife, ob, cl, lute. **Publisher:** G. Ricordi & Co. **Rights:** Copyright 1914, 1926 by G. Ricordi & Co.

I. A jester entertains Francesca's women servants. Francesca's brother, Ostasio, demands to know if the jester came with Paolo Malatesta, the brother of Francesca's fiancé, Giovanni. Ostasio and Sir Toldo fear that if Francesca meets her angry, crippled fiancé, she will call off the marriage. Francesca comforts her sister, Samaritana, who is upset because Francesca is leaving. Mistaking Paolo for her intended, Francesca falls in love and gives him a rose.

II. A tower guard and archer stand guard in Rimini, where the Guelf Malatesti battle the Ghibellines. Francesca—now married to Giovanni— encounters Paolo. She rebukes him for deceiving her but is interrupted by an attack. Undaunted, Francesca remains throughout the battle. Paolo is wounded, but the Guelfs are victorious. Giovanni praises his brother's fighting and receives a cup of wine from Francesca. Malatestino, the third brother, has been wounded in the eye.

III. Francesca reads aloud to her women. She confesses her fear of Malatestino to her slave. The women celebrate the calends of March. Paolo visits Francesca and she reads to him from "Lancelot." He kisses her.

IVi. Francesca is disturbed by a prisoner's screams so Malatestino kills him. The young man offers to help Francesca poison her husband. Francesca tells Giovanni that his youngest brother is cruel. Malatestino tells Giovanni that Francesca and Paolo are lovers. IVii. Francesca's women talk and watch Francesca sleep. She wakes from a nightmare and calls out for Paolo, who enters. The lovers are interrupted by Giovanni, who attacks Paolo. Francesca intercepts the mortal blow, but Giovanni now slays Paolo, too, and breaks his sword.

Lo Frate 'nnamorato • The Love Stricken Brother

Composed by Giovanni Battista Pergolesi (January 4, 1710 – March 16, 1736). Libretto by Gennarantonio Federico. Italian. Original work. Premiered Naples, Teatro dei Fiorentini, September 27, 1732. Set in Capodimonte in the 18th century. Comic opera. Set numbers with recitative. Overture.

Sets: 1. **Acts:** 3 acts, 3 scenes. **Length:** I: 75. II: 50. III: 35. **Arias:** "Chi disse c'a femmena" (Vannella). **Hazards:** None. **Scenes:** I – III. In front of Marcaniello and Carlo's houses.

Major roles: Vannella (soprano), Cardella (soprano), Don Pietro (bass baritone), Carlo (tenor), Nina (mezzo), Nena (soprano), Lugrezia (contralto), Marcaniello (comic bass), Ascanio (soprano).

Chorus parts: N/A. **Chorus roles:** None. **Dance/movement:** None. **Orchestra:** fl, strings, continuo. **Stageband:** None. **Rights:** Expired.

I. Two maids, Vannella and Cardella, gossip about their masters, Marcaniello and Carlo. Marcaniello and Carlo have arranged to join their families in a triple marriage: Marcaniello will marry Carlo's niece, Nina; Marcaniello's son, Don Pietro, will marry Carlo's other niece, Nena; and Carlo will marry Marcaniello's daughter, Lugrezia. None of the women is willing. All three love Ascanio, a young man brought up in Marcaniello's house; Ascanio loves both Nina and Nena. Pietro flirts with the maids. To cause trouble, Nena rebukes Pietro and Nina pretends to love him.

II. Nina pretends to think Marcaniello loves her maid. To prove her love for Ascanio, Nena scorns Pietro. Pietro worries that his disappointment is ruining his complexion, so Cardella helps him put on makeup. Nena and Nina confront Ascanio, but he cannot choose between them. Lugrezia overhears. Marcaniello blames his problems on his son, Pietro, and tries to hit him, but Pietro ducks and Marcaniello falls and has to be carried home.

III. Vannella and Cardella fight. To revenge himself on Nena, Pietro makes love to Vannella. Ascanio is wounded in a duel. While examining Ascanio's wound, Carlo finds a birthmark that proves that Ascanio is his long lost nephew. Ascanio marries Lugrezia and the other marriages are called off.

Die Frau Ohne Schatten • The Woman without a Shadow

Composed by Richard Strauss (June 11, 1864 – September 8, 1949). Libretto by Hugo von Hofmannsthal. German. Original work. Premiered Vienna, Volksoper, October 10, 1919. Set in the Empire of the Southeastern islands in legendary times. Fairy tale. Through composed. Orchestral interludes between scenes. Opus 65.

Sets: 8. **Acts:** 3 acts, 11 scenes. **Length:** I: 65. II: 65. III: 60. **Hazards:**

I: Magic cooking. Appearance out of thin air of nurse & empress, royal boudoir. II: Appearance of young man, cave, sword. Earth swallows Barak & wife and river floods house. III: Appearance of golden fountain. **Scenes:** Ii. A flat roof overlooking the imperial gardens. Iii – IIi. A bare room in the Barak's house. IIii. Outside the imperial falcon house in a lonely part of the woods. IIiii. Barak's house. IIiv. The empress's bedroom in the falcon house. IIv. Barak's house. IIIi. An underground vault. IIIii. A rocky terrace over a river. IIIiii. A temple-like hall. IIIiv. A beautiful landscape.

Major roles: Nurse (dramatic mezzo), Emperor (tenor), Empress (high dramatic soprano), Barak's wife (high dramatic soprano), Barak the dyer (bass baritone). **Minor roles:** Spirit messenger (high baritone), Voice of the falcon (soprano), Barak's one-eyed brother (high bass), Barak's one-armed brother (bass), Barak's hunchback brother (high tenor), Five servants (2 soprano, 3 mezzo), Child apparition (high tenor), Children's voices (3 soprano, 3 alto), Voices of the guards (3 high bass), Guard of the temple door (soprano or falsetto tenor). **Bit part:** Heavenly voice (contralto).

Chorus parts: SSAATTBB. **Chorus roles:** Slave girls, beggar children, watchmen, spirits, unearthly voices, unborn children. **Dance/movement:** None. **Orchestra:** 4 fl (2 picc), 3 ob (Eng hrn), 5 cl (basset hrn, bs cl), 4 bsn (cont bsn), 8 hrn (4 ten tuba), 4 trp, 4 trb, bs tuba, 2 celeste (glass harmonica), timp, perc, 2 harp, strings (16-16-6-6-6-6-8). **Stageband:** II: 6 trp, 6 trb, perc. III: 6 trp, 6 trb, perc, organ, 2 fl, ob, 2 cl, bsn, hrn. **Publisher:** Boosey & Hawkes. **Rights:** Copyright 1916, 1919 by Adolf Fürstner. Assigned 1943 to Boosey & Hawkes. Renewed 1946.

Ii. A spirit messenger from Keikobad tells the nurse that he will turn the emperor to stone in three days if the empress is still then without a shadow. The emperor goes hunting. When a falcon warns Keikobad's daughter (the empress) of her husband's danger, she asks the nurse how to get a shadow. The nurse explains that only a mortal woman has a shadow. (The shadow is an allegory for motherhood.) Iii. The wife of Barak the dyer wants to throw his three brothers out on the street. The dyer refuses and asks his wife when she will have children. The nurse and empress appear, offering to buy the wife's shadow in return for unbounded riches. Giving up her shadow means renouncing motherhood forever.

IIi. The nurse and empress pose as poor relations of the dyer's wife while she decides. The nurse produces a potential lover for the dyer's wife. They are interrupted by Barak, who returns laden with food. IIii. The falcon leads the emperor to a house in the woods. Seeing his wife, the emperor realizes she has been among mortals. Unwilling to kill her, he flees in despair. IIiii. The nurse drugs Barak and brings back the would-be lover. But the dyer's wife rejects him and wakes her husband. IIiv. The empress laments that she must sin against Barak or her husband. IIv. When Barak's wife says she has sold her shadow—even though the transaction is not really complete—Barak tries to kill her. The earth opens up, swallowing the pair.

IIIi. Underground, Barak and his wife repent. A staircase appears and they escape. IIIii. The empress hears Keikobad calling and rejects the nurse's advice to flee. The messenger sends the nurse away. IIIiii. The empress is offered the wife's shadow, but refuses. She tries to give her own life to save her husband's, thus proving that she has learned to be human: The emperor is released. IIIiv. Barak and his wife are reunited. A chorus of unborn children greet them.

Der Freischütz • The Free Shooter

Composed by Carl Maria von Weber (November 18, 1786 – June 5, 1826). Libretto by Friedrich Kind. German. Based on a folk tale in the "Gespentsterbuch" (book of ghosts) by Johann Apel and Friedrich Laun. Premiered Berlin, Schauspielhaus, June 18, 1821. Set in Bohemia in the 17th century. German romantic opera. Set numbers with spoken dialogue and some recitative. Overture. Entr'acte before III.

Sets: 5. **Acts:** 3 acts, 5 scenes. **Length:** I, II, III: 135. **Arias:** "Durch die Wälder" (Max), "Schweig! schweig!" (Caspar), "Leise, leise, fromme Weise" (Agathe). **Hazards:** II: Weird prodigies during the casting of the magic bullets. **Scenes:** I. An open space before an inn in the forest. IIi. A narrow antechamber in the forester's house. IIii. A weird, craggy glen. IIIi. Agnes's chamber. IIIii. A romantic landscape.

Major roles: Forester Max (tenor), Forester Caspar (bass), Agathe (soprano), Ännchen (soprano). **Minor roles:** Prince Ottokar (baritone), Heard ranger Cuno (bass), Hermit (bass), Kilian (bass), Bridesmaid (mezzo). **Speaking:** Zamiel.

Chorus parts: SATTTBB. **Chorus roles:** Huntsmen, villagers, bridesmaids, invisible spirits. **Dance/movement:** I: Bohemian waltz. **Orchestra:** 2 fl (picc), 2 ob, 2 cl, 2 bsn, 4 hrn, 2 trp, 2 trb, bs trb, timp, strings. **Stageband:** I: cl, 2 hrn, trp, 2 vln, vlc. **Publisher:** Kalmus, Dover, C. F. Peters. **Rights:** Expired.

I. Kilian has bested Max in a shooting contest and everyone congratulates him. Max is angered by Kilian's teasing until Cuno comes to his rescue. Caspar thinks Max has an evil spell on him, but Cuno dismisses this. He warns Max, however, that unless he can make the trial shot tomorrow, he cannot marry Cuno's daughter Agathe, nor become head ranger. The master shot, Cuno explains, is a test devised by the prince's great-grandfather, who gave the position of head ranger into Cuno's family in perpetuity. The test proves that the prospective forester is not under the devil's influence. Max loves Agathe and worries about the test. Caspar gives Max his own gun and instructs him to fire at a far away eagle. The eagle falls dead, demonstrating Caspar's magic bullets. Come to the Wolf's glen at midnight, he tells Max, and we will mold more charmed bullets. Caspar privately rejoices that he has ensnared Max, his rival for Agathe.

IIi. Agathe shares her worries with her cousin Ännchen, who is rehanging a picture of Cuno's great-grandfather that fell on Agathe. The hermit gave her some roses, Agathe relates, and warned her of a great danger. The women welcome Max home. He says he must go out again and is perturbed to realize that the picture fell on Agathe just at the time he shot the eagle. Agathe begs Max to be careful in the haunted Wolf's glen. IIii. Caspar has sold his soul to the devil Zamiel. He now purchases three more years of life by agreeing to entrap Max with more magic bullets. They agree to charm six bullets—the seventh will slay Agathe. Max arrives and Caspar and he cast the bullets.

IIIi. Agathe has dreamed she was a dove and Max shot her. Ännchen and the bridesmaids try to cheer up Agathe. The picture has fallen again and when Ännchen opens the box with the bridal wreath, she finds a funeral wreath. Agathe has the hermit's roses woven into a wreath instead. IIIii. The hunters rejoice in their manly lifestyle. Max is presented to the prince by Cuno. He takes his shot: Agathe and Caspar both fall. Agathe is unscathed, but Caspar has been hit. He dies, cursing heaven. The prince extorts a full confession from Max. He is horrified and banishes the young hunter until the hermit intervenes. He begs the prince to discontinue the trial of the free shot and to give Max one year to redeem himself. The prince agrees and all rejoice.

Friedenstag • Armistice Day

Composed by Richard Strauss (June 11, 1864 – September 8, 1949). Libretto by Josef Gregor. German. Based on "La Rendención de Breda" by Pedro Calderón de la Barca. Premiered Munich, Königliches Hof- und Nationaltheater, July 24, 1938. Set in Germany on October 24, 1648 (the last day of the thirty years' war). Historical drama. Through composed.

Sets: 1. **Acts:** 1 act, 1 scene. **Length:** I: 80. **Hazards:** I: Tower sinks into the earth to reveal sunlight and a surging sea of humanity. **Scenes:** I. A circular chamber in the citadel.

Major roles: Commandant of the besieged city (baritone), Maria (soprano). **Minor roles:** Sergeant of the guard (bass), Marksman (tenor), Youth from Piedmont (tenor), Munitions officer (baritone), Musketeer (bass), Officer (baritone), Mayor (tenor), Prelate (baritone), Commandant of the enemy army (bass). **Bit parts:** Bugler (bass), Front line officer (baritone), Woman from the village (soprano), Three deputies (1 tenor, 2 baritone).

Chorus parts: SSSSAAAATTTTBBBB. **Chorus roles:** Soldiers (TTBB), townspeople, deputies. **Dance/movement:** None. **Orchestra:** 3 fl (picc), 2 ob, Eng hrn, 3 cl, bs cl, 3 bsn, cont bsn, 6 hrn, 4 trp, 4 trb, tuba, timp, perc, strings (16-16-12-10-8). **Stageband:** I: organ, trp, bells. **Publisher:** Adolph Fürstner. **Rights:** Copyright 1938 by Richard Strauss. Renewed.

I. For thirty years, the city has been at war and now the civilians call on their commandant to surrender the city. He tells them to wait until noon. Determined not to surrender the city, the commandant prepares to blow it up. He begs his wife Maria to flee, but she refuses. Bells are heard announcing the end of the war. The city gates are thrown open. With Maria's help, the enemy commandant overcomes the commandant's anger and skepticism and the enemies embrace.

Z Mrtvého Domu • From the House of the Dead

Composed by Leoš Janáček (July 3, 1854 – August 12, 1928). Libretto by Leoš Janáček. Czech. Based on "Memoirs from the House of the Dead" by Fyodor Dostoevsky. Premiered Brno, National Theater, April 12, 1930. Set in Russia in the 19th century. Tragedy. Through composed. Overture. Entr'acte before II, III. Most of the dramatic action is in the form of stories told by individual prisoners.

Sets: 3. **Acts:** 3 acts, 4 scenes. **Length:** I: 30. II: 30. III: 30. **Arias:** Luka's story (Luka), Skuratov's story (Skuratov), Šapkin's story (Šapkin). **Hazards:** I: prisoners play with a pet eagle. **Scenes:** I. Prison courtyard in a Russian penal colony on the river Irtish. II. The bank of the Irtish river. IIIi. The prison hospital. IIIii. The prison courtyard.

Major roles: Filka Morozov/Luka Kuzmič (tenor), Alexandr Petrovič Gorjančikov (baritone), Skuratov (tenor), Šapkin (tenor), Siškov (baritone). **Minor roles:** Tall prisoner (tenor), Short prisoner (baritone), Commandant (bass), Aljeja (tenor), Old prisoner (tenor), Čekunov, (bass baritone), Prisoner/Don Juana (baritone), Kedril (tenor), Young prisoner (tenor), Prostitute (soprano), Čerevin (tenor). **Bit parts:** Guard (tenor),

Cook prisoner (baritone), Priest (baritone), Drunken prisoner (tenor), Blacksmith prisoner (bass). **Mute:** Elvira, Knight, Miller, Miller's Wife, Cobbler's wife, Priest's wife, Clerk, Devil.

Chorus parts: TTBB. **Chorus roles:** Prisoners and guards. **Dance/movement:** II: Don Juan, Kedril, Knight, Cobbler's wife and Priest's wife perform a pantomime and dance. III: Skuratov dances about in delirium. **Orchestra:** 4 fl (3 picc), 2 ob, Eng hrn, 3 cl (bs cl), 3 bsn (cont bsn), 4 hrn, 3 trp, bs trp (ten tuba), 3 trb, tuba, timp, perc, harp, celeste, strings. **Stageband:** None. **Publisher:** Universal Edition. **Rights:** Copyright 1930 by Universal Edition.

I. In a Russian penal colony, the prisoners are washing themselves and fighting. Gorjančikov, a political prisoner, is brought in and the commandant has him lashed for talking back. The prisoners mend boots, and Luka tells how he knifed the governor of Ukraine.

II. Gorjančikov promises to teach Aljea to read. Skuratov tells his story: He loved a German girl, Luisa, but her parents wanted her to marry a rich, old relation. Overcome with jealousy, Skuratov shot his rival. Some of the prisoners perform an opera (Don Juana) and a pantomime (The Fair Miller's Wife) for the other inmates. The prisoners abuse Gorjančikov and Aljea for having the money to buy tea.

IIIi. Many of the other prisoners are sick. Luka abuses Čekunov for serving Gorjančikov. Šapkin complains about having his ears pulled by the police and Skuratov admits he shot Luisa. Siškov tells his story: A certain Filka Morozov bragged about sleeping with Akulina, a rich merchant's daughter. But he refused to marry her and to erase the dishonor, Akulina's family married her to the drunken Siškov. On the wedding night, Siškov discovered that Akulina was still a virgin. He confronted Filka—who told Siškov he was too drunk to know whether she was or not. Infuriated by the situation, Siškov beat Akulina. Filka joined the army, but before leaving, he publicly admitted that Akulina was pure. Akulina bragged to Siškov that she loved Filka—so Siškov murdered her. When Siškov finishes his story, someone notices that one of the prisoners has died. Shishkov looks at the corpse and recognizes Filka. IIIii. Following orders, the commandant sets Gorjančikov free. Gorjančikov takes leave of Aljeja and the prisoners free their pet eagle.

The Gambler

Composed by Sergei Prokofiev (April 27, 1891 –
March 5, 1953). Libretto by Sergei Prokofiev.
Russian. Based on a story by Fyodor Dostoyevsky.
Premiered Brussels, Théâtre de la Monnaie, April 29,
1929. Set in the imaginary German spa town of Roulettenbourg in 1865.
Tragedy. Set numbers with recitative. Entr'actes before IVii and IViii.

Sets: 5. **Acts:** 4 acts, 6 scenes. **Length:** I, II, III, IV: 125. **Hazards:** None.
Scenes: I. The park of the Grand Hotel. II. The hall of the hotel. III. A
large room adjoining the casino. IVi. Alexei's hotel room. IVii. The casino. IViii. Alexei's hotel room.

Major roles: General (bass), Pauline (soprano), Alexei (tenor), Marquis
(tenor). **Minor roles:** Blanche (contralto), Grandmother/Babushka
(mezzo), Mr. Astley (baritone), Potapitch (baritone), First croupier
(tenor). **Bit parts:** Baron Würmerhelm (bass), Prince Nilsky (falsetto
tenor), Director (bass), Second croupier (tenor), Fat Englishman (bass),
Tall Englishman (bass), Gaudy lady (soprano), Pale lady (soprano), Lady
comme ci comme ça (mezzo), Venerable lady (mezzo), Rather dubious
old lady (contralto), Rash gambler (tenor), Hypochondriac gambler
(tenor), Hunchbacked gambler (tenor), Unlucky gambler (baritone),
Aged gambler (bass), Six gamblers (2 tenors, 2 baritones, 2 basses).
Mute: Baroness Würmerhelm, Head waiter, Bellboy, Two Feodors,
Martha.

Chorus parts: SATB. **Chorus roles:** Hotel guests, players, servants,
porters. **Dance/movement:** None. **Orchestra:** picc, 2 fl, 2 ob, Eng hrn, 2
cl, bs cl, 2 bsn, cont bsn, 4 hrn, 3 trp, 3 trb, tuba, timp, perc, 2 harp,
piano, strings. **Stageband:** IV: piano. **Publisher:** Boosey and Hawkes.
Rights: Copyright 1930 by Edition Russe de Musique. Assigned 1947 to
Boosey & Hawkes.

Ii. Pauline has had Alexei pawn her diamonds and gamble with the
money, but he lost everything. The general—who is Pauline's step-father
and Alexei's employer—receives a telegram that his mother (Babushka)
is at death's door. When quizzed about his losses by the general, Alexei
is insulting. Mr. Astley is impressed. Pauline admits to Alexei that she
needed the hoped-for winnings to pay a debt. Alexei guesses Pauline is
in debt to the marquis. Alexei pours out the passion—bordering on violence—he feels for Pauline. The marquis lends the general another 5,000
but makes him sign a note for 10,000. Pauline asks Alexei if he would
kill for her. She forces him to insult the old Baroness Würmerhelm.

II. The general is horrified by the insult to the baroness and dismisses Alexei. Mr. Astley explains the situation to Alexei: The general is engaged to Blanche, a disreputable woman who was once thrown out of the hotel by the baroness for flirting with her husband. The general has to prevent anyone from knowing about Blanche until his mother dies so that he can inherit her money, repay his debts to the marquis and marry Blanche. Astley thinks the marquis will marry Pauline to get her dowry. The marquis brings Alexei a letter from Pauline begging him not to make trouble. Alexei wonders about the marquis's power over Pauline but complies. Babushka astonishes everyone with her unannounced arrival. She is not fooled by their false good will and goes off to the casino to play.

III. Babushka has lost 30,000 and continues to gamble, rejecting the assistance of everyone except Alexei. The general is beside himself; Blanche is furious. Ask Alexei to help us, the marquis advises. While they try to persuade him, the losses mount. Alexei offers himself to Pauline one last time, but she is unmoved. Babushka has lost everything except her houses. She decides to return to Russia. The general is refused admittance to Babushka's room and Blanche has left him for Prince Nilsky.

IVi. Pauline shows Alexei the letter in which the marquis ends their affair and announces his intention to foreclose on the general's property. They have to raise 50,000 quickly if foreclosure is to be averted, but Pauline refuses to ask Babushka. Alexei asks her to wait for his return. IVii. He gambles and wins 90,000, breaking the bank. IViii. He tries to give 50,000 to Pauline but, disgusted with him and herself, she at first refuses. She swears she loves him, then takes the money and throws it in his face. He is too besotted with his winnings to care.

A Game of Chance

Composed by Seymour Barab (b. January 9, 1921). Libretto by Evelyn Manacher. English. Suggested by the play "All on a Summer's Day" by Florence Ryerson and Colin Clements. Premiered Rock Island, Illinois, Potter Hall, Augustana College, January 11, 1957. Set in a garden in the present. Comic opera. Set numbers with recitative. Some dialogue.

Sets: 1. **Acts:** 1 act, 1 scene. **Length:** I: 40. **Hazards:** None. **Scenes:** I. A garden with three chairs or a bench.

Major roles: First knitter (lyric soprano), Second knitter (soprano), Third knitter (mezzo), Representative (bass baritone).

Chorus parts: N/A. **Chorus roles:** None. **Dance/movement:** None.

Orchestra: fl, ob, cl, bsn, hrn, trp, trb, timp, perc, harps, strings.
Stageband: None. **Publisher:** Boosey & Hawkes. **Rights:** Copyright 1960
by Boosey & Hawkes, Inc.

I. Three women knit and talk about their dreams: One wants to be in
love, another to be famous, a third to be rich. The representative comes
to tell each in turn that she has her wish. Having gotten what they wanted, all three women realize that they should have asked for more.

La Gazza Ladra • The Thieving Magpie

Composed by Gioachino Rossini (February 29, 1792 – November 13,
1868). Libretto by Giovanni Gherardini. Italian. Based on a play by
Louis-Charles Caigniez and Jean-Marie-Théodore Baudouin d'Aubigny.
Premiered Milan, Teatro alla Scala, May 31, 1817. Set in Italy in the early
19th century. Melodrama. Set numbers with recitative. Overture.

Sets: 6. **Acts:** 2 acts, 34 scenes. **Length:** I: 105. II: 90. **Arias:** "Di piacer mi
balza il cor" (Ninetta), "A questo seno" (Lucia). **Hazards:** I: Magpie
talks. II: Magpie flies to bell tower. **Scenes:** Ii – Iix. The courtyard in
Fabrizio's house. Ix – Ixvi. A ground floor room in the house. IIi – IIvi.
The prison courtyard. IIvii – IIviii. A room in Fabrizio's house. IIix. The
village square. IIx – IIxii. The law court. IIxiii – IIxviii. The village
square.

Major roles: Ninetta Villabella (soprano), Giannetto Vingradito (tenor),
Mayor (bass). **Minor roles:** Pippo (tenor or mezzo), Lucia Vingradito
(mezzo), Fabrizio Vingradito (bass), Isacco (tenor), Fernando Villabella
(bass), Giorgio (bass), Antonio (tenor), Ernesto (bass). **Bit parts:** Judge
(bass). **Mute:** Clerk, Officer. **Speaking:** Magpie.

Chorus parts: SATTB. **Chorus roles:** Soldiers, peasants, servants, judges.
Dance/movement: I: country dances. **Orchestra:** 2 fl (picc), 2 ob, 2 cl, 2
bsn, 4 hrn, 2 trp, 3 trb, timp, perc, strings, continuo. **Stageband:** None.
Publisher: E. Girod. **Rights:** Expired.

Ii. Giannetto is expected home soon. His father Fabrizio knows he wants
to marry Ninetta, but Giannetto's mother, Lucia, distrusts the girl. Iii.
Fabrizio assures Ninetta of Giannetto's love. Iiii. Isacco sells his wares.
Iiv. The returning soldiers are sighted. Iv. Giannetto and Ninetta are
reunited. Ivi. Ninetta's father, Fernando, returns secretly: He has deserted after being condemned for fighting with a superior officer. Ivii. The
mayor woos Ninetta. Iviii. He receives a letter telling him of Fernando's
desertion. Iix. The mayor has Ninetta read him the letter, but she
changes the description to protect Fernando. Fernando gives Ninetta

some silverware to sell so he will have money for his escape. Fernando and Ninetta rebuke the mayor for making a pass at Ninetta. The mayor swears revenge. Ix. Ninetta sells her father's silverware to Isacco. Ixi. The servant Pippo witnesses the sale. Ixii. Ninetta intends to leave the money for her father. Ixiii. But Lucia counts her silverware and realizes a spoon is missing. She suspects Ninetta. Ixiv. The mayor sees an opportunity for revenge. He questions Ninetta and learns she got money from Isacco. Ixv. Isacco admits Ninetta sold him a spoon. Ixvi. The mayor orders Ninetta's arrest.

IIi. Antonio the jailer is kind to Ninetta. IIii. He lets Giannetto visit her. IIiii. Giannetto reminds Ninetta that the penalty for theft is death. He begs her to defend herself but she refuses. IIiv. Giannetto promises to do everything he can. IIv. The mayor offers to save Ninetta if she will be his, but she refuses. IIvi. Pippo promises Ninetta he will leave money for her father. IIvii. Lucia wonders if Ninetta is guilty. IIviii. Fernando learns of his daughter's predicament. IIix. Lucia prays for Ninetta's deliverance. IIx. Ninetta is found guilty. IIxi. Giannetto begs Ninetta to reveal her secret. IIxii. Fernando gives himself up, but is unable to save Ninetta. Ixiii. Ernesto arrives with a royal pardon for Fernando. Ixiv. Pippo's magpie steals a coin from him and flies to the bell tower. Ixv. Ninetta is lead off to execution. Ixvi. Pippo discovers the missing silverware in the bell tower: The magpie is the real thief. Ixvii. They save Ninetta. Ixviii. Everyone is reconciled.

The Ghosts of Versailles

Composed by John Corigliano (b. February 16, 1938). Libretto by William M. Hoffman. English. Suggested by "La Mère Coupable" by Pierre-Augustin Caron de Beaumarchais. Premiered New York City, Metropolitan Opera Association, December 19, 1991. Set in Marie Antoinette's theater in the Petit Trianon, Versailles in the present and the autumn of 1793. Grand opera buffa. Through composed. Opera within opera contains set numbers and recitative. Spoken lines. Opera alternates between the "ghost world" of the French court and Beaumarchais's opera, which the court is watching.

Sets: 13. Acts: 2 acts, 13 scenes. Length: I: 80. II: 70. Arias: "Long Live the Worm" (Bégearss), Samira's aria (Samira), Susanna's aria (Susanna). Hazards: I: The woman with hat descends to the stage in a fauteuil. Rosina's "clothes fly off," and she is transformed into herself twenty years ago. The ghosts fight and run each other through with swords. Pasha is portrayed by a large doll. Pasha doll's head explodes. II: A ghost audience member hovers overstage and descends into his seat. Beaumarchais takes Figaro into the ghost world; during the journey their images "disappear and distort, much like smoke." Quick set changes. Queen beheaded. **Scenes:** Prologue. Open stage with pieces of the private theater of Marie Antoinette at Versailles; within the private theater, the Almaviva mansion in Paris. Ii. The Almaviva mansion. Iii. The theater at Versailles. Iiii. Rosina's boudoir and a bower in the garden of the Almaviva family home in Spain. Iiv. Versailles. Iv. A gala reception in the embassy of the Sublime Porte. IIi. The theater at Versailles; Figaro and Rosina's bedroom. IIii. Figaro and Rosina's bedroom. IIiii. The temple of love at Versailles and the revolutionary tribunal in the palace of justice. IIiv. A Paris street. IIv. The ballroom in Almaviva's mansion. IIvi. The Gothic-vaulted interior of the Conciergerie prison. Finale. Place de la Révolution.

Major roles: Pierre-Augustin Caron de Beaumarchais (bass baritone), Marie Antoinette (soprano), Figaro (baritone), Susanna (mezzo), Count Almaviva (tenor), Patrick Honore Bégearss (tenor), Rosina (soprano). **Minor roles:** Woman with a hat/Duchess (mezzo), Louis XVI (bass), Marquis (tenor), Trio of gossips (2 sopranos, mezzo), Opera quartet (soprano, alto, tenor, bass), Léon (tenor), Florestine (coloratura soprano), Cherubino (mezzo), Suleyman Pasha (bass), British Ambassador (baritone), Samira (mezzo). **Bit parts:** Man in room (tenor), Man with lather (tenor), Woman holding infant (soprano), Three citizens (soprano, mezzo, tenor), Five witnesses (soprano, 2 altos, 2 tenors), Three jury members (3 baritones),Three Muscovite traders (3 baritones), Old man (tenor), Arab violist (plays viola; brief wailing bit). (All bit parts can be played by a twelve-person ensemble.) **Speaking:** Wilhelm, Page.

Chorus parts: SSAATTTBBB. **Chorus roles:** Figaro pursuers, Muscovite traders, revolutionary guards, Turkish duelists, dancing and harem girls, acrobats, revolutionary women, courtiers, dancers, prison guards, prisoners, soldiers, jury members, women with children, ball guests, witnesses, rhieta players, citizens. **Dance/movement:** I: Samira and harem girls belly dance. II: Almaviva's ball. **Orchestra:** 3 fl (2 picc), 3 ob (Eng hrn), 3 cl (bs cl), 3 bsn (cont bsn), 4 hrn, 4 trp, 3 trb, tuba, timp, 4 perc, synthesizer, harp, piano (celeste), strings. **Stageband:** I: small orchestra (guitars, vlcs, cbs, harp, mandolin), fl, ob, vla, 2 hrn, drums, 2 perc, "Rheita" (kazoo) players. II: Ballroom orchestra (fl, vln, vla, vlc), 2 hrn, 2 perc. **Publisher:** G. Schirmer. **Rights:** Copyright 1991 by G. Schirmer.

Prologue. The ghosts of Marie Antoinette and the French court amuse themselves. Beaumarchais loves Marie Antoinette and has written an opera for her. In the opera, Figaro is chased by his creditors, employers and old girlfriends. Beaumarchais borrows Marie Antoinette's necklace, promising to change history to eliminate the revolution—and the guillotine. Ii. He gives Count Almaviva (in the opera) the necklace so he can sell the jewels and help Marie Antoinette escape France. Beaumarchais introduces the other characters of the opera: the count's wife Rosina, his illegitimate daughter Florestine, and Rosina's illegitimate son Léon (by Cherubino). Florestine and Léon are in love, but Almaviva intends Florestine to marry Bégearss. The count fires Figaro for interfering. Bégearss sends his servant, Wilhelm, to spy on Almaviva since he means to betray him to the revolution. He styles himself a worm—and the king of the beasts. Iii. Marie Antoinette remembers how lonely she was when she first came to France. Beaumarchais comforts her—to the king's annoyance. Iiii. Rosina begs Almaviva to let Florestine marry Léon. She remembers her courtship with Cherubino twenty years before. Iiv. Louis is infuriated by his wife's increasing intimacy with Beaumarchais. He fights the poet, but since the ghosts are already dead, the sword thrusts have no effect. Iv. Almaviva meets the British Ambassador at the Turkish embassy. He tries to sell him the necklace, but is interrupted by Samira's performance. Disguised as a belly dancer, Figaro snatches the necklace and makes his escape.

Iii. Figaro refuses to return the necklace, intending to sell it to finance his own escape. Beaumarchais is furious that Figaro is not following his script and plunges into the opera to set things right. Iiii. Almaviva threatens to fire Susanna if she does not find Figaro and make him return the necklace. Susanna and Rosina commiserate about their husbands. Beaumarchais brings Figaro with him into the ghost world. Iiiii. Figaro is shown the trial of Marie Antoinette and is convinced of the queen's innocence. Iiiv. Bégearss stirs up a mob against Almaviva. IIv. Almaviva holds a ball. It is interrupted by Bégearss, who arrests the guests and extorts the necklace from Figaro. Beaumarchais is powerless to stop Bégearss, but he and Figaro escape. IIvi. In prison, Almaviva makes up with Léon. Marie Antoinette and the others pray. Figaro and Beaumarchais try to rescue them, but are surprised by Bégearss. Figaro denounces Bégearss and in the confusion, the players all escape. Beaumarchais goes to free Marie Antoinette, but she stops him, insisting that history play itself out. She tells Beaumarchais she loves him. Finale. The queen is beheaded.

Gianni Schicchi

Composed by Giacomo Puccini (December 22, 1858 – November 29, 1924). Libretto by Giovacchino Forzano. Italian. Based on a story in Dante's "Divina Commedia." Premiered New York City, Metropolitan Opera Association, December 14, 1918. Set in Florence in 1299. Opera buffa. Set numbers with accompanied recitative. Third opera in "Il Trittico."

Sets: 1. **Acts:** 1 act, 1 scene. **Length:** I: 50. **Arias:** "Firenze è come un albero fiorito" (Rinuccio), "O mio bambino caro" (Lauretta). **Hazards:** None. **Scenes:** I. The bedroom of Buoso Donati.

Major roles: Lauretta (soprano), Gianni Schicchi (baritone), Zita (mezzo), Rinuccio (tenor). **Minor roles:** Gherardo (tenor), Nella (soprano), Betto (baritone), Simone (bass), Marco (baritone), La Ciesca (soprano), Doctor Spinelloccio (bass), Amantio di Nicolao the notary (bass). **Bit parts:** Pinellino (bass), Guccio (bass), Gherardino (mezzo or treble).

Chorus parts: N/A. **Chorus roles:** None. **Dance/movement:** None. **Orchestra:** picc, 2 fl, 2 ob, Eng hrn, 2 cl, bs cl, 2 bsn, 4 hrn, 3 trp, 3 trb, bs trb, timp, perc, celeste, harp, strings. **Stageband:** I: low bell. **Publisher:** G. Ricordi. **Rights:** Expired.

I. Relatives of the deceased Buoso Donati kneel around his bedside, lamenting his passing—until they hear the rumor that Donati has left all his money to the monks. Simone realizes that their only hope is to find the will and a search is instituted. Rinuccio, who is in love with Gianni Schicchi's daughter, finds the will. If Donati has made me rich, will you let me marry Lauretta? Rinuccio asks his aunt Zita. To get the will, Zita agrees. The relatives are horrified to find that it is true that the money was left to the monks and they dismiss Rinuccio's assurances that Gianni Schicchi—whom Rinuccio has sent for—can help them. They forbid him to marry Lauretta. The relatives give Schicchi and Lauretta a cold reception, but the lovers convince Schicchi to help them. Schicchi sends his daughter out and reads the will. Hearing that nobody but the relatives know of Donati's death, Schicchi hides the body. When Doctor Spinelloccio calls, he is told that Donati is feeling better. Rinuccio goes to fetch the notary. They will dictate a new will, with Schicchi impersonating Donati. The relatives agree on the disposition of the lands, but fight over Donati's mule, saw mills and house. They leave the decision to Schicchi, but each individually tries to bribe him. Schicchi reminds everyone of the punishment for forgery if they are found out. The notary arrives, bringing Pinellino and Guccio as witnesses. Schicchi bestows the mule, the saw mills and house on himself. The relatives are furious, but when the lawyer leaves, Schicchi throws them out of the house. He asks the audience if he has done well.

La Gioconda • The Joyful Girl

Composed by Amilcare Ponchielli (August 31, 1834 – January 16, 1886). Libretto by Arrigo Boito under the pen name Tobia Gorrio. Italian. Based on "Angelo" by Victor Hugo. Premiered Milan, Teatro alla Scala,

April 8, 1876. Set in Venice in the 17th century. Lyric drama. Set numbers with recitative. Prelude. Ballet.

Sets: 5. **Acts:** 4 acts, 5 scenes. **Length:** I: 50. II: 35. III: 40. IV: 30. **Arias:** "Cielo e mar" (Enzo), "O monumento" (Barnaba), "Suicidio!" (Gioconda), "Voce di donna" (Cieca). **Hazards:** II: Enzo's ship burns and sinks. **Scenes:** I. The courtyard of the ducal palace. II. A ship in the lagoon. IIIi. A room in the Ca' d'Oro. IIIii. A sumptuous room. IV. The atrium of a palace on the Giudecca.

Major roles: Barnaba (baritone), Gioconda (dramatic soprano), Cieca (contralto), Enzo Grimaldo (dramatic tenor), Laura Adorno (mezzo), Alvise Badoero (bass). **Minor roles:** Zuàne (bass), Isèpo (tenor). **Bit parts:** Monk (baritone), Pilot (bass), Two street singers (2 baritones), Offstage singer (bass), Voice in the distance (tenor). **Mute:** Grand councillor, Councillor of the ten, Boatswain, Sail master, Moor, Doge.

Chorus parts: SSATTTBB. **Chorus roles:** Arsenal workers, senators, priests, nobles, masquers, people, sailors, monks, cavaliers, singers, children (in 2 parts). **Dance/movement:** I: Venetian masquers dance the furlana. III: ballet of the hours. **Orchestra:** picc, 2 fl, 2 ob (Eng hrn), 2 cl, 2 bsn, 4 hrn, 2 cornet, 2 trp, 4 trb, bombardone, timp, perc, organ, 2 harp, strings. **Stageband:** I: band. II: 2 cl, 3 trp, 2 trb, perc. III: 2 cl, 3 hrn, 2 bsn, harp, bells. **Publisher:** Ricordi, Broude Brothers. **Rights:** Expired.

I. The Venetians cheer the republic. Barnaba, an inquisition spy, loves the ballad singer Gioconda, but she scorns him. The Venetians hail the winner of the regatta. Barnaba tells Zuane—one of the losers—that his boat was bewitched by La Cieca, Gioconda's mother. He incites the crowd to burn La Cieca as a witch, but Enzo, whom Gioconda loves, State Inquisitioner Alvise, and Alvise's wife, Laura, intervene to save her. When Gioconda thanks Laura, Enzo realizes she is the woman he loved and lost. As Barnaba knows, Enzo was banished from Venice by Alvise and has risked his life by returning. The spy arranges for Enzo to meet Laura that night—and then anonymously warns Alvise. This way he can both demonstrate Enzo's faithlessness and get rid of him. Gioconda is heartbroken. The Venetians celebrate carnival.

II. Barnaba boards Enzo's ship. Laura joins Enzo and Gioconda curses her rival. Alvise is in pursuit of Laura, and when Gioconda realizes who Laura is, she helps her escape. Gioconda tells Enzo that Laura has deserted him. Disdaining to flee for his life, Enzo sets fire to his ship.

IIIi. Alvise gives Laura poison, insisting she kill herself before his guests have finished singing. Gioconda helps Laura substitute a sleeping potion for the poison. IIIii. Alvise entertains his guests, and Laura's death is announced. In despair, Enzo presents himself to Alvise, admitting his true identity. He is arrested. Gioconda offers to give herself to Barnaba if he saves Enzo. Alvise admits he killed Laura.

IV. Gioconda retrieves the sleeping Laura, but cannot find her mother. She considers killing either herself or Laura. Gioconda tries to goad Enzo into killing her, but Laura awakens. The lovers bless Gioconda who helps them escape. When Barnaba comes to claim his prize, Gioconda stabs herself. When the spy tries to tell her he killed her mother, he finds she is dead.

I Gioielli della Madonna • The Jewels of the Madonna

Composed by Ermanno Wolf-Ferrari (January 12, 1876 – January 21, 1948). Libretto by Carlo Zangarini and Enrico Golisciani. Italian (premiered in German). Inspired by the news account of a real event. Premiered Berlin, Kurfürstenoper, December 23, 1911. Set in Naples in the early 20th century. Verismo tragedy. Through composed. Intermezzo before II, III.

Sets: 3. **Acts:** 3 acts, 3 scenes. **Length:** I: 45. II: 45. III: 35. **Hazards:** None. **Scenes:** I. A small open square by the sea. II. The garden of Carmela's house. III. The haunts of the Camorra on the outskirts of Naples.

Major roles: Gennaro the blacksmith (tenor), Maliella (soprano), Carmela (mezzo), Rafaele (baritone). **Minor roles:** Two mora players (tenor, baritone), Totonno (tenor), Biaso the scribe (tenor), Ciccillo (comic tenor), Rocco (bass), Stella (soprano), Serena (contralto), Concetta (soprano). **Bit parts:** Flower girl (soprano), Water seller (soprano), Ice cream man (tenor), Macaroni seller (baritone), Blind man (bass), Three girls (2 soprano, 1 alto), Peasant girl (mezzo), Toy balloon man (tenor), Two young men (tenor, baritone), Father (bass), Nurse (contralto), Three women (2 soprano, 1 alto), Two distant voices (tenor, bass). **Speaking bit:** Fruit seller. **Dancer:** Grazia the "biondina."

Chorus parts: SSSAAATTTTTTBBB. **Chorus roles:** People, vendors, members of the Camorra, clergy, children, Neapolitan characters. **Dance/movement:** I: Maliella dances. III: Dance of Grazia and the Camorrists. **Orchestra:** 3 fl (picc), 2 ob, Eng hrn, 2 cl, bs cl, 2 bsn, cont bsn, 4 hrn, 3 trp, 3 trb, tuba, harp, piano, carillon, celeste, xylophone, min. 4 guitar, min. 6 mandolin, 3 timp, perc, strings. **Stageband:** I: picc, fl, cl, 2 hrn, cornet, 3 trp, 3 trb, tuba, bells, child's trps, perc, scietta rajasse, zerre-zerre, putipù, 6 mandolin, harmonica, glockenspiel. II: picc, fl, harmonium, piano, 6 mandolin, guitar, vla, vlc, bs, perc. III: trp, organ. **Publisher:** G. Schirmer, Josef Weinberger. **Rights:** Copyright 1911 by Josef Weinberger.

I. The Neapolitans celebrate the feast of the Madonna. Gennaro alone works, completing a candelabrum he has crafted as a present for the Madonna. Maliella objects to being kept cooped up in the house by Gennaro when everyone else is celebrating. She sings and dances, disappearing into the crowd. Her behavior is torture to Gennaro, who loves her. His mother, Carmela, explains how she took in Maliella as a little girl: she promised the Madonna to shelter an infant born of sin if Gennaro recovered from a childhood illness. Rafaele tries to kiss Maliella, but she defends herself with a hat pin. Even after she stabs him with the pin, he declares his love. The procession of the Madonna passes by and Rafaele offers to steal the jewels of the Madonna for Maliella. Gennaro warns Maliella against Rafaele, who is head of the outlaw Camorrists.

II. Maliella decides to leave rather than endure Gennaro's suffocating protectiveness. Gennaro prevents her—and pours out his love for her. She rejects him. Gennaro disappears and Rafaele persuades the besotted Maliella to go with him tomorrow. To prove his love, Gennaro has stolen the jewels of the Madonna, which he presents to Maliella. She can think only of Rafaele and swoons in Gennaro's arms.

III. The Camorrists enjoy their life of crime. They tease Rafaele about his new love. Maliella enters, pursued by Gennaro. She begs Rafaele to take revenge on Gennaro—who has taken advantage of her—but Rafaele spurns her. The Camorrists are horrified both that Gennaro stole the jewels of the Madonna and that Maliella is wearing them. Gennaro kills himself, believing that the Madonna has forgiven him.

Un Giorno di Regno • A One-Day Reign

Composed by Giuseppe Verdi (October 9, 1813 – January 27, 1901). Libretto by Felice Romani. Italian. Based on the play "Le faux Stanislas" by Alexandre Vincent Pineu-Duval. Premiered Milan, Teatro alla Scala, September 5, 1840. Set in Brest in August 1733. Comic opera. Set numbers with recitative. Overture.

Sets: 3. **Acts:** 2 acts, 5 scenes. **Length:** I, II: 120. **Arias:** "Pietoso al lungo pianto" (Edoardo). **Hazards:** None. **Scenes:** Ii. A large hall. Iii. A garden. Iiii – IIi. The hall. IIii. A glass-enclosed veranda overlooking the garden.

Major roles: Cavalier of Belfiore (baritone), Edoardo of Sanval (tenor), Giulietta of Kelbar (soprano), Marquise of Poggio (soprano). **Minor**

roles: Baron of Kelbar (bass baritone), La Rocca (comic bass). **Bit parts:** Delmonte (baritone), Servant (tenor), Count Ivrea (tenor).

Chorus parts: SSAATTBB. **Chorus roles:** Servants and retainers of the baron, peasants. **Dance/movement:** None. **Orchestra:** 2 fl, 2 ob, 2 cl, 2 bsn, 4 hrn, 2 trp, 3 trb, tuba, timp, perc, strings. **Stageband:** None. **Rights:** Expired.

Ii. The baron's daughter, Giulietta, is marrying La Rocca. The French king has sent the cavalier of Belfiore to attend, disguised as the deposed King Stanislas of Poland. This will distract Stanislas's enemies so he can slip back into Poland and gather his supporters. The cavalier fears he will be revealed by the marquise of Poggio, who is also getting married. La Rocca's nephew, Edoardo, loves Giulietta. Thwarted by his uncle, he offers his services to the cavalier. Iii. Giulietta returns Edoardo's love. The marquise promises to help the lovers. She recognizes the cavalier—whom she loves even though he left her. Iiii. The cavalier persuades La Rocca to call off his wedding to Giulietta by promising him a rich Polish princess. When La Rocca breaks the news to the baron, the baron demands revenge. They appeal to the cavalier.

IIi. The cavalier tells La Rocca to give his nephew Edoardo some of his money—which La Rocca does. The baron wants to fight La Rocca, but he agrees to forget it when La Rocca chooses a duel with explosives instead of swords. IIii. Pretending to believe that the chevalier is King Stanislas, the marquise tells him about her coming marriage to make him jealous. Edoardo tells Giulietta he must leave with the king. The cavalier learns that the real Stanislas is safely in Poland. He persuades the baron to let Edoardo marry Giulietta and then reveals his identity. The marquise marries the cavalier.

Giovanna d'Arco • Joan of Arc

Composed by Giuseppe Verdi (October 9, 1813 – January 27, 1901). Libretto by Temistocle Solera. Italian. Based on Friedrich von Schiller's "Die Jungfrau von Orleans." Premiered Milan, Teatro alla Scala, February 15, 1845. Set in France in the early 15th century. Lyric drama. Set numbers with recitative. Overture. Prologue.

Sets: 6. **Acts:** 3 acts, 6 scenes (prologue sometimes labelled I, in which case in 4 acts). **Length:** Prologue: 40. I: 30. II: 25. III: 25. **Arias:** "Sotto una quercia" (Carlo), "Sempre all'alba ed alla sera" (Giovanna), "So che per via di triboli" (Giacomo), "O fatidica foresta" (Giovanna), "T'arretri e palpiti!" (Giovanna), "Quale più fido amico" (Carlo). **Hazards:** None. **Scenes:** Prologue i. A great hall in Dom-rémy castle. Prologue ii. Dom-rémy forest. Ii. The encampment of the English near Rheims. Iii. A garden of the palace at Rheims. II. The main square of Rheims before the cathedral of St. Denis. III. A fortress in the camp of the English troops.

Major roles: King Carlo VII of France (tenor), Giacomo (baritone), Giovanna (soprano). **Minor roles:** Delil (tenor), Commander-in-chief of the English army Talbot (bass).

Chorus parts: SSAATTTTBBBB. **Chorus roles:** Officials of the king, nobles, people, French soldiers, English soldiers, demons, angels, heralds, pages, girls, deputies, knights, ladies, magistrates, guards. **Dance/movement:** None. **Orchestra:** picc, fl, 2 ob, 2 cl, 2 bsn, 4 hrn, 2 trp, 3 trb, cimbasso, timp, perc, harp, harmonium, accordion, strings. **Stageband:** II: band (trps). **Publisher:** Kalmus. **Rights:** Expired.

Prologue i. King Carlo decides to submit to the English invasion rather than allow more French blood to be shed. He takes an oath to visit the Virgin's shrine in the haunted forest. Prologue ii. Giacomo comes to the forest looking for his daughter, Giovanna. Angels grant Giovanna's wish that she be able to take up arms in defense of her country. Giacomo believes his daughter has made a pact with the devil.

Ii. Giovanna defeats the English. Giacomo promises to deliver Giovanna into their hands. Iiii. Carlo declares his love for Giovanna, who reluctantly admits she loves him too. She is tormented by visions of devils.

II. Giovanna crowns Carlo. Giacomo denounces her in public and her piety restrains her from defending herself.

III. Giacomo has turned Giovanna over to the English, but her purity touches him and he frees her. She saves Carlo's army from defeat, but is mortally wounded. Giovanna dies in Carlo's arms.

Giulio Cesare • Julius Caesar

Composed by George Frederic Handel (February 23, 1685 – April 14, 1759). Libretto by Nicola Francesco Haym. Italian. Based on a libretto by Giacomo Francesco Bussani. Premiered London, Opera Theater of the Royal Academy of Music, February 20, 1724. Set in Egypt in 48 BC. Opera seria. Set numbers with recitative. Overture.

Sets: 12. **Acts:** 3 acts, 31 scenes. **Length:** I: 45. II: 40. III: 35. **Arias:** "V'adoro pupille" (Cleopatra). **Hazards:** II: Cesare's vision of Virtue. Battle between Greeks and Egyptians. **Scenes:** Ii – Iiv. Egyptian countryside with a bridge over the Nile. Iv – Ivi. A room in Cleopatra's palace.

Ivii – Iviii. Quarters in Cesare's camp. Iix – Ixi. Vestibule in the palace of the Ptolemies. IIi – IIii. A grove of cedars before Mount Parnassus. IIiii – IIvi. The harem garden. IIvii – IIviii. The palace pleasure garden. IIix – IIxi. A room in the harem. IIIi – IIIv. A harbor near Alexandria. IIIvi. Cleopatra's apartments. IIIvii – IIIviii. A royal hall. IIIix. The harbor.

Major roles: Giulio Cesare (mezzo, contralto, countertenor or bass baritone), Cornelia (contralto), Sesto Pompeo (mezzo or tenor), Cleopatra (soprano). **Minor roles:** Curio (bass), Achilla (bass), Nireno (alto or bass), Tolomeo (alto, countertenor or bass).

Chorus parts: SATB. **Chorus roles:** Roman and Egyptian soldiers, Egyptians, suites of Cesare and Tolomeo, Cleopatra's attendants, Achilla's thugs. **Dance/movement:** II: spectacle of Mount Parnasso with Virtue enthroned among the muses. **Orchestra:** 2 fl, 2 ob, 2 bsn, 2 hrn, 2 trp (or 4 hrn, 0 trp), traversa, strings, continuo (cembalo). **Stageband:** II: ob, vla da gamba, theorbo, bsns, strings, 2 harp. **Publisher:** International, Gregg International Publishers. **Rights:** Expired.

Ii. Having defeated Pompeo's army at Pharsalia, Cesare chases Pompeo to Egypt. Iii. Pompeo's son, Sesto, and his wife, Cornelia, sue for peace, which Cesare grants. Iiii. Cesare is horrified when Achilla, commander of the Egyptian army, presents him Pompeo's severed head. Iiv. Curio prevents Cornelia from killing herself, admitting he loves her. Sesto swears revenge against the Egyptian King Tolomeo who betrayed his father. Iv. Cleopatra plans to rule in place of her brother Tolomeo. Ivi. Achilla agrees to arrange Cesare's death for Tolomeo in return for Cornelia's hand. Ivii. Cleopatra presents herself to Cesare under the name Lydia—and wins his heart. Iviii. She agrees to help Sesto assassinate Tolomeo. Iix. Cesare greets Tolomeo. Ix. Tolomeo has Sesto arrested and Cornelia put in the harem. Ixi. Cornelia takes a tearful farewell of her son.

IIi. Cleopatra tells Nireno to bring Cesare to her. IIii. Cesare has a vision of the goddess Virtue, but hurries off to Cleopatra. IIiii. Cornelia flees Achilla's proposals. IIiv. She also rejects Tolomeo. IIv. Nireno frees Sesto. IIvi. He leads him to the harem where Sesto can ambush Tolomeo. IIvii. Cesare sees Cleopatra sleeping. IIviii. Curio warns Cesare of the plot against his life. Cleopatra reveals her true identity. IIix. In the harem, Sesto attacks Tolomeo but is disarmed by Achilla. IIx. Achilla announces Cesare's death and Cleopatra's revolt. He demands Cornelia's hand but Tolomeo rebukes him. IIxi. Cornelia convinces Sesto to try again.

IIIi. Achilla deserts to Cleopatra's standard. IIIii. Tolomeo's army is victorious and Cleopatra is captured. IIIiii. Cleopatra laments. IIIiv. Cesare lives. Achilla, mortally wounded, gives him his seal to help him get into the palace to kill Tolomeo. Before dying, he confesses that the assassination of Pompeo was his idea. IIIv. Sesto feels victory is near. IIIvi. Cesare rescues Cleopatra. IIIvii. Cornelia draws a dagger on Tolomeo. IIIviii. Sesto, however, slays him first. IIIix. Sesto and Cornelia bow before Cesare. Cleopatra becomes queen. She and Cesare rejoice in their love.

Gloriana

Composed by Benjamin Britten (November 22, 1913 – December 4, 1976). Libretto by William Plomer. English. Original work based on historical incidents. Premiered London, Royal Opera House, Covent Garden, June 8, 1953. Set in England in the late 16th century. Historical drama. Set numbers with recitative. Prelude before each scene. Some spoken dialogue. Opus 53.

Sets: 8. **Acts:** 3 acts, 8 scenes. **Length:** I: 45. II: 50. III: 45. **Hazards:** III: Queen sees a vision of herself. **Scenes:** Ii. Outside a tilting ground. Iii. A private apartment at Nonesuch. IIi. The guild hall in Norwich. IIii. The garden of Essex House in the strand. IIiii. The great room in the palace of Whitehall. IIIi. The queen's ante-room in Nonesuch. IIIii. A street in the city of London. IIIiii. A room in the palace of Whitehall.

Major roles: Earl of Essex (tenor), Queen Elizabeth I (soprano). **Minor roles:** Henry Cuffe (baritone), Lord Mountjoy (baritone), Sir Walter Raleigh (bass), Sir Robert Cecil (baritone), Recorder of Norwich (bass), Spirit of the masque (tenor), Penelope Lady Rich (soprano), Frances Countess of Essex (mezzo), Lady in waiting (soprano), Master of ceremonies (tenor), Blind ballad singer (bass). **Bit parts:** Housewife (mezzo), City crier (baritone). **Speaking bits:** Mountjoy's page, Essex's page. **Dancers:** Concord, Time, Morris dancer.

Chorus parts: SSAATTBB. **Chorus roles:** Citizens, maids of honor, ladies and gentlemen of the household, courtiers, masquers, old men, men and boys (in three parts) of Essex's following, councillors. **Dance/movement:** II: Masque and country dances. III: Court galliard and lavolta. Morris dance. **Orchestra:** 3 fl (2 picc), 2 ob, Eng hrn, 2 cl, bs cl, 2 bsn, cont bsn, 4 hrn, 3 trp, 3 trb, tuba, timp, perc, harp, strings. **Stageband:** I: trps. II: 5 strings and/or woodwinds, pipe (fl), tabor. III: drums, cymbals, wind machine, harp. **Publisher:** Boosey & Hawkes. **Rights:** Copyright 1953 by Hawkes & Son Ltd.

Ii. Mountjoy wins a jousting tournament. Jealous, Essex challenges him to fight and is wounded. The queen rebukes the two men. Iii. Cecil warns the queen that Essex's sister Penelope and Mountjoy are having an affair. The Spanish king is preparing an armada to send against England. Essex plays the lute for the queen and manipulates her love to get permission to lead an army against Tyrone, the Irish rebel. The queen prays for strength.

IIi. A masque is given in the queen's honor. IIii. Mountjoy meets Penelope in the garden. Essex curses the queen and her advisors for holding him back. IIiii. The courtiers dance. The ladies retire to change. Lady Essex's dress is too splendid for her station and the queen wears it herself to chastise Lady Essex. Essex is appointed Lord Deputy of Ireland.

IIIi. Essex has made a truce with Tyrone. He bursts in on the queen while she is dressing, so anxious is he to explain his conduct. The angry queen orders his arrest. IIIii. Essex escapes and tries to raise an army against the queen. IIIiii. He is captured, tried and condemned, but Cecil fears the queen will pardon him. Penelope, Lady Essex and Mountjoy petition the queen on Essex's behalf, but they only succeed in persuading the queen to sign Essex's death warrant. The queen faces her own mortality and expresses her desire to rule well.

Die Glückliche Hand • The Lucky Hand

Composed by Arnold Schönberg (September 13, 1874 – July 13, 1951). Libretto by Arnold Schönberg. German. Original work. Premiered Vienna, Volksoper, October 14, 1924. Set in a wild landscape at an unspecified time. Music drama. Through composed. Opus 18.

Sets: 1. **Acts:** 1 act, 4 scenes. **Length:** I: 20. **Hazards:** I: A cat-like animal crouches on the man's back. Man climbs out of ravine with two dismembered Saracen's heads. Woman rolls a rock down on man. **Scenes:** Ii – Iii. Bare stage with various backdrops. Iiii. A wild, rocky landscape. Iiv. The bare stage.

Major role: Man (baritone or bass). **Minor roles:** Six women (3 soprano, 3 alto), Six men (3 tenor, 3 bass). **Mute:** Wife, Gentleman, Workers.

Chorus parts: N/A. **Chorus roles:** None. **Dance/movement:** None. **Orchestra:** picc, 3 fl (2 picc), 3 ob, Eng hrn, 4 cl, bs cl, 3 bsn, cont bsn, 4 hrn, 3 trp, 4 trb, tuba, harp, celeste, glockenspiel, xylophone, timp, perc, strings (16-14-10 to 12-10 to 12-8 to 10). **Stageband:** I: picc, cl, hrn, trp, 3 trb, perc. **Publisher:** Universal Edition. **Rights:** Copyright 1923 by Universal Edition. Renewed 1951 by Eduard Steuermann.

Ii. The chorus warns against longing for the unattainable. Iii. The man

admires a beautiful woman, but she prefers an elegant gentleman. Iiii.
The man emerges from a ravine with a bloody sword and two severed
heads. He forges a gold diadem and is almost overwhelmed by a storm.
He tries to reach the woman, but she rolls a rock down on him. Iiv. The
chorus pities the man.

Zolotoy Petuschok • The Golden Cockerel

Composed by Nicolai Rimsky-Korsakov (March 18, 1844 – June 21,
1908). Libretto by Vladimir Ivanovich Belsky. Russian (although usually
performed in French as "Le Coq d'Or"). Based on the poem by Pushkin.
Premiered Moscow, Solodovnikov Theater, October 7, 1909. Set in
Russia in legendary times. Fairy tale. Set numbers with accompanied
recitative. Overture.

Sets: 3. **Acts:** 3 acts, 3 scenes. **Length:** I: 40. II: 45. III: 40. **Arias:** Hymn to
the sun (Queen of Chémakhâ). **Hazards:** Golden cockerel flies. **Scenes:**
Prologue. Before the curtain. I. A vast hall in the palace of the King
Dodon. II. A narrow gorge covered with small bushes and hemmed in
by cliffs. III. Outside the royal palace. Epilogue. Before the curtain.

Major roles: Tsar Dodôn (bass), Queen of Chémakhâ (coloratura sopra-
no). **Minor roles:** Astrologer (tenor), Prince Gvidôn (tenor), General
Polkân (bass), Prince Aphrôn (baritone), Golden Cockerel (soprano),
Amelfa (contralto).

Chorus parts: SSAATTBB. **Chorus roles:** Subjects and servants of the
tsar, warriors. **Dance/movement:** II: The queen's slaves and the tsar
dance. **Orchestra:** 3 fl (2 picc), 2 ob, Eng hrn, 2 cl, bs cl, 2 bsn, cont bsn, 4
hrn, 3 trp, 3 trb, tuba, timp, 3 perc, xylophone, celeste, 2 harp, strings
(12-16; 10-14; 8-12; 6-10; 4-8). **Stageband:** None. **Publisher:** G. Schirmer.
Rights: Expired.

Prologue. The astrologer tells the audience that although his story is not
true, it will teach the audience something. I. Tsar Dodon calls his boyars
for advice on how to keep his foes quiet so that he can retire in peace.
Prince Gvidon suggests they provision the city and retire within the
walls. Prince Afron wants to disband the army until such time as they
know the enemy means to attack. The astrologer brings the tsar a golden
cockerel that will warn him of approaching danger. The astrologer asks
the tsar to put in writing his promise to reward him, but the tsar can
only think of the cockerel. Amelfa serves the tsar dinner. Everyone takes
a nap, but is awakened by the cockerel's warning crow. Gvidon and
Afron don't want to fight, but the tsar insists. When a second alarm is
given, the tsar himself leads the old men out to fight.

II. The tsar finds both of his sons slain. While searching for the enemy, he encounters the queen of Shamakhan. She says she means to capture his town, but since she has no soldiers, he thinks she is joking. The queen sings and the tsar is overcome by her beauty. The princes killed each other over her. At the queen's insistence, the tsar si gs and dances for her. He offers her his kingdom.

III. The tsar's subjects anxiously await his return. He comes back with his new queen in a splendid procession. As his reward, the astrologer demands the queen. The tsar refuses and strikes the astrologer with his scepter, killing him. The golden cockerel pecks the king, who dies; then the cockerel and the queen disappear.

Epilogue. The astrologer admits the tale is gory, but advises the audience not to worry.

The Good Soldier Schweik

Composed by Robert Kurka (December 22, 1921 – December 12, 1957). Libretto by Lewis Allan. English. Based on the unfinished novel by Jaroslav Hasek. Premiered New York City, New York City Center, April 23, 1958. Set in Bohemia in 1914. Satire. Through composed. Overture. Some spoken dialogue. Entr'acte before II. Prologue and epilogue. Orchestration completed by Hershey Kay after composer's death.

Sets: 17. **Acts:** 2 acts, 14 scenes. **Length:** I: 45. II: 60. **Hazards:** None. **Scenes:** Ii. Schweik's flat in Prague on the day of June 28, 1914. Iii. The Flagon tavern. Iiii. Police headquarters. Iiv. A prison cell. Iv. Another room in police headquarters. Ivi. The insane asylum. Ivii(a). Schweik's flat. Ivii(b). A busy street thronged with people. IIi. A hut used as an infirmary. IIii(a). In a guardhouse. IIii(b). A pulpit. IIiii. Lt. Lukash's flat. IIiv. The interior of the Prague-Budejovice Express, second class compartment. IIv. A private room in St. Stephen's Cross, a cafe in Budejovice. IIvi(a). Soprony street. IIvi(b). Interior of the Red Lamb tavern. IIvi(c). Soprony street. IIvii(a). A dugout at the front. IIvii(b). The front.

Major roles: Joseph Schweik (tenor), Army chaplain (tenor), Second psychiatrist/Second doctor/Army Doctor/Lt. Henry Lukash (baritone). **Minor roles:** Mrs. Müller/Katy Wendler/Madam Kakonyi (soprano), Palivec/General von Schwarzburg/Mr. Kakonyi (baritone), Bretschneider/First psychiatrist/First doctor (tenor), Police officer/Third psychiatrist/Colonel Kraus von Zillergut (bass), Three malingerers (tenor, baritone, bass), Baroness von Botzenheim (contralto), Mr. Wendler/Guard/Sergeant (tenor). **Bit parts:** Four prisoners (2 tenors, 2 basses), Consumptive (baritone). **Speaking:** Bohemian gentleman/Fox the dog/Voditchka/Sergeant Vanek, Newsboy, Several voices on train (IIiv: head guard, railway man, five people in the crowd).

Chorus parts: SATTBB. **Chorus roles:** Prisoners, mental patients, malingerers, wounded soldiers, baroness's retinue, tavern patrons. **Dance/movement:** I: Mental patients. II: Tavern patrons. **Orchestra:** picc, fl, ob, Eng hrn, cl, bs cl, bsn, cont bsn, 3 hrn, 2 trp, trb, timp, perc (no strings). **Stageband:** None. **Publisher:** Weintraub Music Co. **Rights:** Copyright 1962 by Lewis Allan and May Kurka.

Prologue. A Bohemian gentleman introduces the common, likable soldier Schweik. Ii. Mrs. Müller and Schweik discuss the assassination of Archduke Ferdinand. Iii. Bretschneider, the secret policeman, tries to entrap the customers in the inn. Palivec, the innkeeper, will not discuss the assassination, but Schweik freely spouts his theories. The secret policeman arrests both men. Iiii. Schweik confesses to the charges the police have trumped up against him. He was discharged from the army for being feeble-minded, he explains. Iiv. Schweik tries to cheer up his cell mates. Iv. He is examined by three psychiatrists who agree to send him to a mental institution. Ivi. Schweik is happy at the asylum. Ivii. Two doctors accuse Schweik of being a malingerer and evict him from the asylum. He is drafted and although his rheumatism confines him to a wheelchair, he enthusiastically goes to join his regiment.

IIi. A group of malingerers say that no matter what they do, the doctors pronounce them fit. The army doctor prescribes enemas. The baroness brings Schweik food and presents after having read about his going off to war in a wheelchair. The doctor is furious. IIii. He sees that all the malingerers are imprisoned. The chaplain abuses the men but is impressed by Schweik and hires him as his orderly. The chaplain gambles with Lt. Lukash, bets Schweik and loses. IIiii. Lukash returns to find that Schweik has: let his cat eat his canary; chased the cat away; acquired a dog; let in a girlfriend of Lukash's who is fleeing her husband; and called the husband. The lieutenant is furious. The dog turns out to belong to Lukash's superior, Colonel von Zillergut, who orders Lukash off to the front. IIiv. On the train, Schweik annoys a bald-headed man who turns out to be General von Schwarzburg. Lukash is again dressed down. Schweik pulls the train's emergency stop and is led off by the station master and a police sergeant. IIv. Lukash writes a love letter to a married woman. Surprised to see Schweik, who has found his way back to the regiment, he gives the letter to Schweik to deliver. IIvi. On his way to deliver the letter, Schweik runs into his old friend Voditchka and they have a drink. In delivering the letter, they alert Mr. Kakonyi. He and Schweik fight and a general riot ensues. Schweik swallows the letter. IIvii. Lukash, grateful that Schweik destroyed the letter, sends him and Sergeant Vanek off on patrol. They split up and Schweik disappears. Epilogue. The Bohemian gentleman wonders where Schweik went.

Götterdämmerung • The Twilight of the Gods

Composed by Richard Wagner (May 22, 1813 – February 13, 1883). Libretto by Richard Wagner. German. Original work based loosely on Norse mythology. Premiered Bayreuth, Festspielhaus, August 17, 1876. Set near the Rhine in legendary times. Epic music drama. Through composed with leitmotifs. Prelude before each act. Prologue. Musical interlude before I (Rhine journey) and in III (funeral march).

Sets: 4. **Acts:** 3 acts, 7 scenes. **Length:** Prologue: 30. I: 80. II: 60. III: 75. **Arias:** Immolation scene (Brünnhilde). **Hazards:** I: Siegfried arrives at Gunther's hall by boat. Siegfried uses the tarnhelm to disguise himself as Gunther. III: Siegfried finds Rheinmaidens swimming in the river. Brünnhilde rides her horse onto Siegfried's funeral pyre, setting fire to the world. **Scenes:** Prologue. Brünnhilde's rock. Ii. The Gibichung hall on the Rhine. Iii. Brünnhilde's rock. II. Banks of the Rhine before the Gibichung hall. IIIi – IIIii. A forest clearing in the Rhine valley. IIIii. The Gibichung hall.

Major roles: Brünnhilde (soprano), Siegfried (tenor), Gunther (bass or bass baritone), Hagen (bass). **Minor roles:** First norn (contralto), Second norn (mezzo), Third norn (soprano), Gutrune (soprano), Waltraute (mezzo), Alberich (bass), Woglinde (soprano), Wellgunde (mezzo), Flosshilde (contralto). **Bit parts:** Two vassals (tenor, bass). **Mute:** People (mute crowd of people often appears at end of opera).

Chorus parts: STTTBBBB (generally STTBB). **Chorus roles:** Gunther's vassals (several small groups), wedding guests. **Dance/movement:** None. **Orchestra:** picc, 3 fl (picc), 4 ob (Eng hrn), 3 cl, bs cl, 3 bsn (cont bsn), 8 hrn (2 ten tuba, 2 bs tuba), 3 trp, bs trp, 4 ten bs trb (cont bs trb), cont bs tuba, 2 timp, perc, 6 harps, strings (16-16-12-12-8). **Stageband:** Prologue: hrn. I: hrn, trp. II: 4 hrn, 2 trb, tuba. III: 4 hrn, 2 trp, tuba, 4 harps. **Publisher:** G. Schirmer Inc., B Schott's Söhne. **Rights:** Expired.

Prologue. The three Norns retell the story of the Ring thus far: how Wotan gave an eye for a drink from the spring that waters the world ash tree; how he killed the ash tree by breaking away a branch; and how he fashioned a spear from the branch on which are carved the treaties by which he rules the world. But a hero has broken the spear and Wotan now sits brooding in his castle. His heroes have piled the remains of the ash tree around the castle, preparing for the immolation of the world. As the day dawns, the cord of fate that the Norns have been spinning breaks. They disappear. Siegfried bids Brünnhilde a tearful farewell, leaving her the ring of the Nieblung.

Ii. Hagen suggests to the Gibichung king who is his half-brother, Gunther, that he marry Brünnhilde while his sister, Gutrune, marries Siegfried. Gunther thinks it is hardly possible—Brünnhilde is protected by a ring of fire that only Siegfried can penetrate. But Hagen reminds them of the love potion he has procured. Siegfried arrives and the plan is put into effect: Drugged by the potion, Siegfried agrees to disguise himself as Gunther (using the magic tarnhelm) to acquire Brünnhilde for Gunther. Gunther and Siegfried swear blood brotherhood and start off on their journey. Alone, Hagen longs for the ring—the ring that his father, Alberich, fashioned from the Rhine maidens' gold. Iii. Waltraute visits her sister Brünnhilde and begs her to return the ring to the Rhine maidens, thus ending Alberich's curse. Brünnhilde refuses to part with the ring since Siegfried gave it to her as a token of his love. Waltraute leaves. Siegfried returns, disguised as Gunther, and claims the mortified Brünnhilde as his bride. He takes the ring from her.

II. Alberich appears to Hagen during the night and makes him swear to get the ring. Siegfried speeds back to the Gibichung hall with news of his success. Hagen calls out the vassals to celebrate the double wedding. When Brünnhilde sees that Siegfried has forgotten her, she is overcome with bitterness. She asks how he got the ring, which Gunther—she believes—took from her. When she claims to be Siegfried's bride, Siegfried swears on Hagen's spear that she lies. He, Gutrune and the guests enter the hall. Hagen, Brünnhilde and Gunther remain behind to plot Siegfried's death. Brünnhilde's spells protect Siegfried—but she left his back unguarded since he would never retreat in battle.

IIIi. The men go hunting. Siegfried runs into the Rhine maidens who warn him he will die today unless he returns the ring to them. Siegfried refuses. IIIii. The rest of the hunters catch up and Siegfried tells them the story of his life. Hagen gives Siegfried a memory potion and Siegfried sings of his love for Brünnhilde—which Hagen uses as an excuse to slay him. IIIiii. The men return, bearing Siegfried's body. Gutrune is not deceived by their tales of a wild boar and Gunther admits that Hagen killed Siegfried. Hagen claims the ring. Gunther objects and is slain. When Hagen goes to recover the ring, Siegfried's arm rises. Brünnhilde demands a suitable funeral pyre for Siegfried. Promising to return the ring to the Rhine maidens, she rides into the flames on her horse, Grane. The Rhine overflows, extinguishing the fire. Hagen tries to grab the ring, but is drowned by the Rhine maidens who reclaim their prize. Walhalla and the gods burn up.

Goyescas

Composed by Enrique Granados (July 27, 1867 – March 24, 1916).
Libretto by Fernando Periquet y Zuaznabar. Spanish. Inspired by the
paintings of Goya. Premiered New York City, Metropolitan Opera
Association, January 28, 1916. Set in Spain about 1800. Tragedy. Set
numbers with recitative. Intermezzo before II and III. Inspired by Goya's
paintings.

Sets: 3. **Acts:** 3 acts, 3 scenes. **Length:** I, II, III: 65. **Arias:** "The Lover and
the Nightingale" (Rosario). **Hazards:** None. **Scenes:** I. A square in the
outskirts of Madrid. II. A large barn. III. Rosario's garden.

Major roles: Paquiro (baritone), Pépa (mezzo), Rosario (soprano),
Fernando (tenor). **Minor role:** Dancer (soprano or tenor).

Chorus parts: SSAATTBB. **Chorus roles:** Majas and Majos (flashy young
people from Madrid). **Dance/movement:** II: Peasant dances. **Orchestra:** 3
or 4 fl (picc), 2 or 3 ob (Eng hrn), 2 or 3 cl, 2 or 3 bsn, 4 hrn, trp (or 2 hrn,
3 trp), 3 or 4 trb, timp, perc, piano, 2 harp, guitar, strings. **Stageband:**
None. **Publisher:** G. Schirmer. **Rights:** Expired.

I. A group of Spaniards celebrates a holiday by tossing the "pelele." The
bullfighter Paquiro compliments the girls. Everyone welcomes Paquiro's
girlfriend, Pépa. Rosario, a highborn lady, comes looking for her lover,
Fernando. Paquiro reminds Rosario of the peasant ball she once attended and invites her to come again. Fernando is jealous of the bullfighter
and accepts for both of them.

II. Fernando refuses to be cowed by the threatening atmosphere at the
ball—or Rosario's embarrassment. His high-handed manner offends
everyone. Fernando goads Paquiro into a duel.

III. Rosario listens to the nightingale in her garden. She assures
Fernando that she loves only him, but Fernando ignores Rosario's pleas
not to fight Paquiro. Paquiro mortally wounds Ferrando, who dies in
Rosario's arms.

Gräfin Maritza • Countess Maritza

Composed by Emmerich Kálmán (October 24, 1882 – October 30, 1953).
Libretto by Julius Brammer and Alfred Grünwald. Original work.
Premiered Vienna, Theater an der Wien, February 28, 1924. Set in
Hungary in the early 20th century. Operetta. Set numbers with spoken
dialogue. Overture. Optional prologue. Ballet. Entr'acte before II, III.

Sets: 3 or 2 (without prologue). **Acts:** 3 acts, 4 or 3 (without prologue) scenes. **Length:** I, II, III: 110. **Arias:** "Höre ich Zigeunergeigen" (Maritza), "Grüss' mir mein Wien'" (Tassilo), "Komm Zigany!" (Tassilo). **Hazards:** None. **Scenes:** Prologue. A salon in château Enrody. I. The garden of Countess Maritza's country estate. II – III. Drawing room in the country estate.

Major roles: Count Tassilo/Bela Törek (tenor), Countess Maritza (soprano), Lisa (soprano). **Minor roles:** Manya (mezzo), Captain Karl Stefan (tenor), Baron Zsupán (tenor), Prince Populesco (tenor). **Speaking:** Zingo, Nepomuk, Lazlo, Tsheko, Freda, Princess Bozena, Auctioneer. (Nepomuk, Torek and Auctioneer only appear in prologue.)

Chorus parts: SSATTBB. **Chorus roles:** Village children (Juliska, Rosika, Etelka, Ilonka, Marischka, Miluschka, Rosemarie, Sari), farm hands, servants, gypsies, guests. **Dance/movement:** I: Farm hands and gypsies dance. Gypsy ballet. II: Cabaret dancing. III: Popolescu, Zsupan and Maritza dance. **Orchestra:** fl, 2 cl, ob (optional), bsn (optional), 2 hrn (optional), 2 trp, 1 or 2 trb, harp (optional), perc, strings. **Stageband:** I, II, III: gypsy violin or gypsy band. **Publisher:** Harms, Inc. **Rights:** Copyright 1924 by Octava Music Co. Copyright 1938 by B. Feldman.

I. Countess Maritza's country estate is managed by Tassilo—who is really Count Wittenburg in disguise. Tassilo is trying to earn money to pay off his father's debts and earn a dowry for his sister, Lisa. His friend Karl helps him sell his land. Maritza announces her engagement to Baron Zsupan. Lisa does not know that she and her brother are bankrupt. Tassilo is surprised to learn that Maritza has befriended Lisa—and brought her out to the country. Lisa recognizes Tassilo, but promises to keep his secret. Maritza confides to her friend Ilka that she has invented Baron Zsupán to scare away fortune-hunting suitors. She is surprised when a real Baron Zsupán appears and wants to get married. Maritza hears Tassilo singing, but when he refuses to sing for her, she fires him. A gypsy tells Maritza she will soon fall in love. Maritza forgives Tassilo.

II. Lisa falls in love with Zsupán. Maritza flirts with Tassilo. Prince Popolescu intercepts a letter Tassilo has sent to Karl. He shows it to Maritza and convinces her that Tassilo is trying to steal her fortune—and that he loves Lisa. Maritza publicly accuses Tassilo. He quits, but reveals that Lisa is his sister.

III. Tassilo asks Maritza for a reference, but they part on bad terms. Without Tassilo, Maritza is reduced to managing her own farm. Tassilo's rich aunt, the princess, learns about Tassilo's poverty. She buys back his property for him. Zsupán falls in love with Lisa and they become engaged. The princess arranges for Tassilo to marry Maritza.

Le Grand Macabre • The Grand Macabre

Composed by György Ligeti (b. May 28, 1923). Libretto by Michael Meschke and György Ligeti. German. Based on the play "La Balade du Grand Macabre" by Michel de Ghelderode. Premiered Stockholm, Royal Opera, April 12, 1978. Set in the imaginary principality of Breughelland in no particular century. Satire. Through composed. Spoken dialogue. Overture. Prelude before II. Intermezzi between scenes.

Sets: 3. **Acts:** 2 acts, 4 scenes. **Length:** I, II: 120. **Hazards:** I: Venus appears naked to Mescalina in a dream. II: The chief of police appears as a bird, spider and octopus; on roller skates and stilts. Ministers pelted with food from offstage. Explosion. Earthquakes. Heavy fog. Piet and Astradamors float away. Nekrotzar shrinks into a small ball and vanishes. **Scenes:** Ii. Countryside near a burial chamber. Iii. In the house of the court astronomer. IIi. The throne room of Prince Go-Go. IIii. The countryside near the burial chamber.

Major roles: Piet the Pot (high comic tenor), Nekrotzar (character baritone), Mescalina (dramatic mezzo), Astradamors (bass), Prince Go-Go (boy soprano or high countertenor). **Minor roles:** Clitoria (soprano), Spermando (mezzo), Venus/Chief of the secret police Gepopo (coloratura soprano). **Bit parts:** Ruffiack (baritone), Schobiack (baritone), Schabernack (baritone), Four people (2 soprano, 2 tenor). **Speaking:** White minister, Black minister. **Mute:** Detectives and executioners of the secret police, Henker of the secret police, dwarf master of ceremonies, pages, servants, Nekrotzar's infernal entourage. (Venus can be played by a naked striptease dancer with singer offstage.)

Chorus parts: SSSAAATTTBBB. **Chorus roles:** Children (offstage, 2 parts), people of Breughelland, spirits and echo of Venus (all offstage or in auditorium). **Dance/movement:** I: Mescalina and Astradamors dance. II: Astradamors dances with the prince to celebrate his wife's death. Final celebratory dance. **Orchestra:** 3 fl (2 picc), 3 ob (ob d'amore, Eng hrn), 3 cl (bs cl), 3 bsn (cont bsn), 4 hrn, 4 trp, bs trp, 3 trb (cont bs trb), tuba (cont bs tuba), perc, celeste (cembalo), flugel (electric piano), electric organ (regal), mandolin, harp, strings (3-0-2-6-4). **Stageband:** I: ob, Eng hrn, trp, bs trp. II: picc, cl, bsn, 2 trp, bs trp, 2 trb, perc, vln. **Publisher:** B. Schott's Söhne. **Rights:** Copyright 1978 by Schott's Söhne.

Ii. Two lovers (Amando and Amanda) hide in a tomb. Nekrotzar emerges, saying he is the Grand Macabre and will destroy Breughelland and its people at midnight. He employs the drunken Piet. Iii. Mescalina whips her husband, Astradamors, and then falls into a drunken sleep. She dreams of Venus and prays for a powerful man. Nekrotzar rapes and kills Mescalina. The light from a comet blinds everyone.

IIi. The ministers fight among themselves and abuse Prince Go-Go. The chief of police warns the prince about Nekrotzar. Astradamors and Piet get Nekrotzar drunk. As midnight approaches, there are earthquakes and explosions. IIii. Piet and Astradamors dream they are in heaven. Mescalina attacks Nekrotzar and the prince's ministers. A band of cutthroats kills Mescalina, the ministers and the prince. Prince Go-Go gets up and drinks with Astradamors and Piet. With the rising of the sun, Nekrotzar shrivels up and disappears. The lovers come out of the tomb disheveled. Everyone reflects that it is best to be merry, since no one knows when he will die.

La Grande Duchesse de Gérolstein • The Grand Duchess of Gérolstein

Composed by Jacques Offenbach (June 20, 1819 – October 5, 1880). Libretto by Henri Meilhac and Ludovic Halévy. French. Original work. Premiered Paris, Théâtre des Variétés, April 12, 1867. Set in the German duchy of Gerolstein in 1720. Operetta. Set numbers with spoken dialogue or recitative. Overture. Entr'acte before II, III.

Sets: 3. **Acts:** 3 acts, 4 scenes. **Length:** I, II, III: 115. **Arias:** "Ah que j'aime les militaires" (Grand Duchess). **Hazards:** None. **Scenes:** I. A soldiers' camp. II. A hall in the palace. IIIi. The red chamber. IIIii. The camp.

Major roles: Wanda (soprano), Fritz (tenor), General Boum (comic bass or baritone), Grand Duchess (mezzo). **Minor roles:** Aide-de-camp Nepomuc (tenor or baritone), Baron Puck (tenor or baritone), Iza (soprano), Prince Paul (tenor), Olga (soprano), Amelia (mezzo), Charlotte (mezzo), Baron Grog (baritone).

Chorus parts: SATTB. **Chorus roles:** Lords and ladies of the court, maids of honor, pages, ushers, soldiers, vivandières, country girls. **Dance/movement:** I: Soldiers and girls dance. **Orchestra:** 2 fl (picc), 2 ob, 2 cl, 2 bsn, 4 hrn, 2 trp, 3 trb, timp, perc, strings. **Stageband:** I: 3 trp, 3 trb, perc. **Publisher:** Bote & Bock. **Rights:** Expired.

I. The simple soldier Fritz and Wanda are in love, but General Boum is also attracted to Wanda. The general makes life difficult for Fritz. Boum's friend, Baron Puck, warns the general that they must start a war so as to maintain their hold on the twenty-year-old grand duchess. Puck's attempts to marry the grand duchess to Prince Paul have been unsuccessful. The grand duchess falls in love with Fritz and promotes him over General Boum. Boum, Puck and Paul plot revenge.

II. Fritz wins the war by first getting his enemies drunk. The grand duchess again puts off Baron Grog, the envoy of Prince Paul's father. Boum, Puck and Paul plan to murder Fritz. When Fritz asks permission to marry Wanda, the grand duchess decides to help the assassins.

IIIi. The grand duchess finally meets Grog—and falls in love with him. He persuades her to marry Paul and she calls off the assassination. Fritz and Wanda are married. IIIii. The grand duchess marries Paul. Fritz returns from a beating: Boum has sent him to his own mistress, knowing that the woman's husband was lying in wait to beat him. The grand duchess demotes Fritz. She plans to give his honors to Grog, until she learns Grog is married. Boum is again made general.

Řecké pašije • The Greek Passion

Composed by Bohuslav Martinů (December 8, 1890 – August 28, 1959). Libretto by Bohuslav Martinů. German, Czech or English. Based on the novel "Christ Recrucified" by Nikos Kazantzakis. Premiered Zürich, Städtisches Theater, June 9, 1961. Set in and around the village of Lykovrissi in the early 20th century. Tragedy. Through composed with spoken dialogue.

Sets: 7. **Acts:** 4 acts, 9 scenes. **Length:** I, II, III, IV: 115. **Hazards:** III: Manolios's dream. **Scenes:** I. The square in Lycovrissi, a village on the slopes of Mount Sarakina. IIi. Outside Jannakos's house. IIii. Outside the village at the spring of St. Basil. IIiii. A desolate spot on Mount Sarakina. IIIi. Manolios's hut on Mount Panagia. IIIii. A little room in Katerina's house. IIIiii. The road leading to Sarakina. IVi. The village square. IVii. On Mount Sarakina.

Major roles: Priest Grigoris (bass), Jannakos (tenor), Manolios (tenor), Widow Katerina (soprano). **Minor roles:** Kostandis (baritone), Panait (tenor), Michelis (tenor), Lenio (soprano), Priest Fotis (bass baritone), Old man (bass), Nikolios (soprano), Patriarcheas (bass), Andonis (tenor). **Bit parts:** Despinio (soprano), Old woman (contralto). **Speaking:** Ladas. **Speaking bit:** Man in crowd.

Chorus parts: SSSSAAAATTTTTTBBBBBB. **Chorus roles:** Villagers from Lycovrissi, refugees. **Dance/movement:** None. **Orchestra:** 3 fl (picc), 3 ob (Eng hrn), 3 cl, 3 bsn, 4 hrn, 3 trp, 3 trb, tuba, timp, perc, harp, piano, accordion, strings. **Stageband:** I: bells. III: Eng hrn, accordion. **Publisher:** Universal Edition. **Rights:** Copyright 1961 by Universal Edition.

I. The priest Grigoris assigns parts for a passion play the church plans to give. Lenio is engaged to Manolios. Greek refugees flood the village, led by the priest Fotis. Unwilling to help, Grigoris accuses them of bringing cholera into the village. Katerina, a fallen woman, gives them her shawl. Panait is furious but goes off with her. Manolios suggests the refugees settle on Mount Sarakina.

Ili. Katerina talks to Jannakos. Ladas persuades Jannakos to make money from the refugees by selling them food. Ilii. Katerina is tormented by dreams of Manolios. When she talks to him, he admits he has been thinking about her. She shrugs off his pity. Iliii. One of the Greeks, an old man, dies digging a foundation for their new village. Jannakos confesses his plan to Fotis and begs forgiveness.

IIIi. Manolios is tormented by the responsibility of playing Christ in the passion play. He dreams of Katerina. IIIii. Manolios begs Katerina to forget him. IIIiii. Jannakos finds Katerina taking food to the refugees. Because Manolios has taken to preaching that all men are brothers, Grigoris wants to drive him out of the village. Nikolios admits to Manolios that Lenio is going to marry him instead, and Manolios forgives him.

IVi. Nikolios weds Lenio. Manolios is excommunicated by Grigoris, but Jannakos, Michelis and Kostandis stand by him. Manolios admits his sinful fascination with Katerina and Panait—who was to play Judas— kills him. IVii. The starving refugees mourn for Manolios.

La Griselda • Griselda

Composed by Alessandro Scarlatti (May 2, 1660 – October 22, 1725). Libretto possibly by Francesco Maria Ruspoli. Italian. Based on libretto by Apostolo Zeno for Antonio Pollarolo. Premiered Rome, Teatro Capranica, January 1721. Set in Sicily at an unspecified time. Opera seria. Set numbers with recitative. Overture.

Sets: 10. **Acts:** 3 acts, 49 scenes. **Length:** I, II, III: 120. **Hazards:** None. **Scenes:** Ii – Iv. A room for receiving public audiences. Ivi – Ixi. A seaport with ships. Ixii – Ixv. An aristocratic antechamber. Ixvi – Ixviii. Royal quarters. IIi – IIv. Outside a rustic dwelling in the countryside. IIvi – IIix. A great gallery. IIx – IIxvii. A wood spot before Griselda's hut. IIIi – IIIvii. A royal apartment with a small throne. IIIviii – IIIxii. An avenue in the royal gardens. IIIxiii – IIIxiv. An amphitheater.

Major roles: Gualtiero (contralto or bass baritone), Griselda (soprano), Ottone (contralto or bass baritone), Constanza (soprano). **Minor roles:** Roberto (soprano or tenor), Corrado (tenor). **Mute:** Griselda's son Everardo, guards.

Chorus parts: STB. **Chorus roles:** Courtiers, people (chorus sings 4 measures in entire opera). **Dance/movement:** None. **Orchestra:** 2 fl, 2 ob, 2 hrn, 2 hunting horns, 2 trp, strings, continuo. **Stageband:** None. **Publisher:** Harvard University Press. **Rights:** Expired.

I. Gualtiero repudiates his wife, Griselda, on the grounds that a queen cannot be of humble birth. Ottone, who loves Griselda, decides to overthrow Gualtiero and abduct her. Griselda refuses to be a party to Ottone's plan. Gualtiero is engaged to Costanza—who loves Roberto.

II. Gualtiero orders his son by Griselda slain. Ottone tells Griselda he will save the boy in return for her love. Costanza befriends Griselda. Gualtiero forestalls Ottone's insurrection.

III. Roberto and Costanza are caught alone together. Gualtiero forgives Ottone and offers to help him win Griselda. Griselda refuses to marry Ottone and Gualtiero, realizing that virtue, not birth, make a queen, takes her back. Costanza turns out to be the long-lost daughter of Gualtiero and Griselda. Gualtiero sanctions her marriage to Roberto.

Grisélidis

Composed by Jules-Emile-Frédéric Massenet (May 12, 1842 – August 13, 1912). Libretto by Armande Silvestre and Eugène Morand. French. Based on story from Giovanni Boccaccio's "Decameron." Premiered Paris, Théâtre National de l'Opéra Comique, November 20, 1901. Set in Provence in the 14th century. Lyric tale. Set numbers with recitative. Some spoken lines. Prologue. Prelude before each act.

Sets: 3. **Acts:** 3 acts, 4 scenes. **Length:** Prologue, I, II, III: 120. **Hazards:** Marquis's sword disappears. Cross transformed into flaming sword. Loÿs returned by Saint Agnes. **Scenes:** Prologue. At the edge of a forest in Provence. I. The castle of the marquis. II. A terrace and garden before the castle. III. The castle.

Major roles: Alain (tenor), Marquis (baritone), Grisélidis (lyric soprano), Devil (baritone or bass). **Minor roles:** Gondebaut (baritone or bass), Prior (baritone), Bertrade (soprano), Fiamina (mezzo). **Speaking bit:** Loÿs (child).

Chorus parts: SSAATTBB. **Chorus roles:** Men at arms, spirits, voices of the night, servants, celestial voices. **Dance/movement:** IIv: Fiamina and devil dance for joy. **Orchestra:** 3 fl (picc), 2 ob, Eng hrn, 2 cl (bs cl), 2 bsn, 4 hrn, 2 trp, 3 trb, tuba, timp, perc, harps, strings.

Stageband: Prologue: bells. I: 4 trp. II: harp, celeste, bells, harmonium. **Publisher:** Heugel & Co. **Rights:** Expired.

Prologue. Alain loves Grisélidis. Gondebaut remarks that the marquis has yet to marry. Alain rashly praises Grisélidis's beauty. When the marquis sees her and proposes, she accepts. I. Bertrade sings while she works. The marquis leaves Grisélidis and their son, Loÿs, to fight the Saracens. The prior wants to keep a close watch on Grisélidis while the marquis is away, but the marquis insists she retain her freedom. He swears that she will be faithful, thus tempting the devil—who appears and bets that Grisélidis will forget her duty. The marquis reluctantly accepts and gives the devil his ring as a pledge. He is sorry to leave. Grisélidis bids him a tearful farewell.

II. The devil enjoys a few moments of peace away from his wife, Fiamina. She finds him. They fight and make up. Grisélidis longs for her husband. She is approached by the devil, who shows her the marquis's ring and commands her—in the marquis's name— to relinquish her position to Fiamina. Grisélidis obeys. The devil is vexed at Grisélidis's dutifulness and decides to tempt her with Alain's love. He calls spirits to his aid. Grisélidis listens to Alain's proposals, but the sight of her son recalls her to her duty. The devil abducts the child.

III. Grisélidis prays for her son's return, but the statue of Saint Agnes has disappeared. The devil tells Grisélidis that her son has been kidnapped by a pirate. In return for one kiss, the pirate will return the boy. Grisélidis agrees. Disguised as an old man, the devil tells the returned marquis that Grisélidis has been unfaithful. Seeing his ring on the devil's finger, the marquis realizes whom he is dealing with. He awaits his wife's return. Together, they unravel the devil's lies. The devil still has the child. The marquis reaches for his sword but it disappears. He prays and the cross on the altar is changed into a flaming sword. The statue of Saint Agnes reappears with Loÿs.

Guglielmo Ratcliff • William Ratcliff

Composed by Pietro Mascagni (December 7, 1863 – August 2, 1945). Libretto by Andrea Maffei. Italian. Based on the tragedy by Heinrich Heine. Premiered Milan, Teatro alla Scala, February 16, 1895. Set in Scotland around 1820. Tragedy. Set numbers with recitative. Overture. Intermezzo before IV.

Sets: 4. **Acts:** 4 acts, 4 scenes. **Length:** I: 35. II: 35. III: 20. IV: 30. **Hazards:** III: Ghosts of Maria's dead fiancés attack Ratcliff. IV: Ghostly figures haunt Ratcliff. Offstage gunshot. **Scenes:** I. A hall in MacGregor's castle.

II. A thieves' tavern. III. A savage spot near the black rock. IV. A room in the castle.

Major roles: MacGregor (bass), Count Douglas (baritone), Maria (soprano), Guglielmo Ratcliff (tenor). **Minor roles:** Margherita (mezzo), Tom (bass), Willie (mezzo), Lesley (tenor). **Bit parts:** Dick (tenor), Bell (baritone), Robin (bass), John (bass), Taddie (tenor), Servant (tenor).

Chorus parts: SATTTBaBaBBB. **Chorus roles:** Robbers, servants, wedding guests. **Dance/movement:** None. **Orchestra:** 2 fl, picc, 2 ob, Eng hrn, 4 cl, bs cl, 2 bsn, cont bsn, 4 hrn, 3 trp, 3 trb, tuba, timp, perc, 2 harp, strings. **Stageband:** II: ob, 2 bsn, hrn, bells. III: 5 trb. **Publisher:** Bote & Bock, Casa Musical Sonzogno. **Rights:** Expired.

I. MacGregor's daughter, Maria, marries Douglas. Douglas tells them how he was set upon by thieves in the forest, and only the intervention of a mysterious stranger saved him. MacGregor warns Douglas that William Ratcliff loves Maria and has killed two of her previous fiancés. Douglas receives an invitation from Ratcliff to meet him at the black rock and accepts.

II. In an inn frequented by thieves, Ratcliff tells his friend, Lesley, how Maria scorned his love. He has sworn to kill anyone who tries to marries her.

III. Ratcliff and Douglas fight. The ghosts of Maria's dead fiancés side with Douglas and he wins. Recognizing that Ratcliff was the man who saved him in the forest, Douglas spares his life.

IV. Maria's maid, Margherita, says that Maria's mother, Elisa, once loved Ratcliff's father, Edward. Elisa married MacGregor to spite Edward. When MacGregor found out, he killed Edward. Elisa died of terror and Margherita herself went mad. Ratcliff enters Maria's chamber and asks her to flee with him. She refuses, but kisses him. MacGregor finds them and attacks Ratcliff, but is slain. Ratcliff kills Maria and himself.

Guillaume Tell • William Tell

Composed by Gioachino Rossini (February 29, 1792 – November 13, 1868). Libretto by Victor Joseph Étienne de Jouy, Hippolyte Bis and Armand Marrast. Italian. Based on "Wilhelm Tell" by Friedrich von Schiller. Premiered Paris, Opéra, August 3, 1829. Set in Switzerland in the early 14th century. Grand opera. Set numbers with recitative. Overture. Ballet. Orchestral interlude in I.

Sets: 6. **Acts:** 4 acts, 6 scenes. **Length:** I, II, III, IV: 215. **Arias:** "Asile héréditaire" (Arnold), "Sois immobile" (Tell), "Sombre forêt" (Mathilde). **Hazards:** III: Tell shoots apple off Jemmy's head. **Scenes:** I. A landscape at Burglen, canton of Uri. II. The heights of Rütli above the Waldstetten lake. IIIi. Interior of a ruined chapel on the grounds of the governor's palace at Altdorf. IIIii. Open space in Altdorf decorated for a festival. IVi. Arnold's ancestral home. IVii. A rocky shore by the side of a lake.

Major roles: Guillaume Tell (baritone), Arnold (tenor), Mathilde (soprano). **Minor roles:** Ruodi (tenor), Hedwige (mezzo), Jemmy (soprano), Melcthal (bass), Leuthold (bass), Rudolph (tenor), Walter Fürst (bass), Gesler (bass). **Bit part:** Hunter (baritone).

Chorus parts: SSAATTTTTTBBBB. **Chorus roles:** Swiss peasants and shepherds, knights, pages, ladies, hunters, soldiers and guards of Gesler, three brides and their bridegrooms. **Dance/movement:** I: Wedding ballet. IIIii: Tyrolean dance. **Orchestra:** 2 fl (picc), 2 ob (Eng hrn), 2 cl, 2 bsn, 4 hrn, 2 or 4 trp, 3 trb, timp, perc, 1 or 2 harp, strings. **Stageband:** I: 4 hrn. II: perc, hrn. **Publisher:** Novello, Troupenas. **Rights:** Expired.

I. Tell is troubled by Austrian domination of his country. Following custom, three young couples are blessed by Melcthal, who wonders when his own son, Arnold, will marry. Arnold secretly loves Matilda, a Hapsburg princess. Tell approaches Arnold to plot a rebellion. While the wedding of the three couples is celebrated with singing and dancing, the shepherd Leuthold begs the assembled crowd to save him from Governor Gesler's vengeance. He has killed an Austrian guard who abducted his daughter. When Ruodi refuses to brave the tide to row Leuthold to shore, Tell does it. They narrowly escape Gesler's bodyguards, led by Rudolph. The peasants refuse to name Leuthold's accomplice, so Rudolph arrests Melcthal.

II. A group of hunters return from their sport. Matilda meets Arnold and they admit their love for each other, but when Tell and Walter approach, Matilda flees. The two men upbraid Arnold for forsaking his country. When they tell Arnold that his father (Melcthal) has been executed by the Austrians, the young man rejoins the patriot cause. Tell calls on all Swiss patriots to follow him.

IIIi. Arnold tells Matilda he must renounce her to pursue his vengeance against Gesler. IIIii. Gesler forces the Swiss to bow before a hat as token of their obedience to Austria. He orders a celebration in honor of the hundredth anniversary of the Austrian defeat of the Swiss. Refusing to bow, Tell is arrested. When Gesler orders Tell to shoot an apple off Tell's son Jemmy's head, Tell abases himself before the governor. His son's courage revives him, however, and he makes the shot successfully.

Gesler orders father and son imprisoned anyway, but Matilda intervenes and gets the boy released. The Swiss curse Gesler.

IVi. Arnold leads the patriots to free Tell. IVii. Matilda returns Jemmy to his mother, and Jemmy reports that Tell is being transferred to another prison by boat. Jemmy hastens to light the torches as a signal to begin the revolt. Tell escapes and kills Gesler with an arrow. The conspirators capture the Austrian fortress, freeing Switzerland.

Guntram

Composed by Richard Strauss (June 11, 1864 – September 8, 1949). Libretto by Richard Strauss. German. Based on historical incidents and an article in the Vienna Neue Freie Presse. Premiered Weimar, Hoftheater, May 10, 1894. Set in Germany in the 13th century. Drama. Through composed. Overture. Entr'acte before II, III. Revised in 1930s: orchestration lightened and half hour of music cut.

Sets: 3. **Acts:** 3 acts, 10 scenes. **Length:** I: 45. II: 35. III: 35. (shorter, revised version) **Hazards:** None. **Scenes:** I. A clearing in the woods. II. The festival banquet hall at the court of the old duke. III. The dungeon in the keep of the old duke's castle.

Major roles: Guntram (tenor), Freihild (soprano). **Minor roles:** Old man (tenor), First young man (bass), Old woman (contralto), Second young man (bass), Friedhold (bass), Old duke (bass), Duke Robert (baritone), Duke's jester (tenor), Messenger (baritone). **Bit parts:** Three vassals (3 bass), Jester (tenor), Four singers (2 tenor, 2 bass).

Chorus parts: TTBB. **Chorus roles:** Vassals of the duke, five monks, valets and soldiers. **Dance/movement:** None. **Orchestra:** 3 fl (picc), 3 ob (Eng hrn), 3 cl (bs cl), 3 bsn, cont bsn, 4 hrn, 3 trp, bs trp, 3 trb, tuba, 2 timp, 2 perc, lute, 2 harp, strings (16-16-12-19-8). **Stageband:** I: 4 hrn. II: 4 hrn, 4 trp, 3 bsn, 4 military drums. **Publisher:** Boosey & Hawkes, Josef Aibl. **Rights:** Copyright 1894 by Josef Aibl Verlag.

Ii. The people's rebellion against the oppressive Duke Robert fails and Robert takes bloody retribution. Guntram succors the survivors. Iii. Though disguised as a minstrel, Guntram is a knight of the secret order of "champions of love." He hopes to persuade Robert to rule more justly. Robert's wife, Freihild, cannot bear her husband's oppression of the poor. She tries to drown herself, but Guntram prevents her. Iiii. In gratitude for saving Freihild, the old duke (Freihild's father) promises to grant Guntram a request. Guntram uses it to free the poor people whom Robert has captured. The old duke invites Guntram to a feast.

IIi. Guntram sings at the feast. IIii. A messenger warns that the rebels have regrouped and are attacking the castle. Guntram blames the rebellion on Robert and when Robert attacks him, Guntram kills him. The old duke orders Guntram's arrest. IIiii. Freihild realizes she loves Guntram.

IIIi. In prison, Guntram insists he killed Robert in self defense—not because he loves Freihild. IIIii. Freihild sets Guntram free. IIIiii. Guntram's fellow knight, Friedhold, warns him that the brotherhood must punish him for the murder. Guntram answers that he must atone for his sins himself. IIIiv. He leaves Freihild to begin his penance.

Gwendoline

Composed by Emmanuel Chabrier (January 18, 1841 – September 13, 1894). Libretto by Catulle Mendès. French. Original work Premiered Brussels, Théâtre de la Monnaie, April 10, 1886. Set on the British coast in the 8th century. Tragedy. Set numbers with recitative. Overture. Prelude before II.

Sets: 3. **Acts:** 2 acts, 3 scenes. **Length:** I: 60. II: 40. **Hazards:** II: Danish ships are seen burning. **Scenes:** I. A valley not far from the sea. IIi. A nuptial chamber. IIii. A rocky ravine.

Major roles: Gwendoline (soprano), Harald (baritone). **Minor roles:** Armel (tenor), Aella (baritone), Erick (tenor). **Bit part:** Six girls (2 soprano, 2 mezzo, 2 contralto; only 1 from each part have solo lines: other 3 double), Five villagers (soprano, mezzo, tenor, baritone, bass).

Chorus parts: SSMMAATTTBaBBB. **Chorus roles:** Saxons, men, women, girls, Danes. **Dance/movement:** None. **Orchestra:** picc, 2 fl, 2 ob (Eng hrn), 2 cl, 4 bsn, 4 hrn, 4 trp, 3 trb, tuba, timp, perc, 2 harp, strings. **Stageband:** II: 2 picc, 3 trb, perc. **Publisher:** Enoch Frères et Costallat. **Rights:** Expired.

I. The Danes, led by Harald, invade Armel's kingdom. Harald and Armel's daughter Gwendoline fall in love. Armel agrees to let them marry, intending to ambush the Danes.

IIi. Armel gives Gwendoline a knife with which to kill Harald on their wedding night. Gwendoline warns Harald and gives him the knife. IIii. The Danes are massacred and Harald mortally wounded. Gwendoline stabs herself and dies with Harald.

Hamlet

Composed by Ambroise Thomas (August 5, 1811 – February 12, 1896). Libretto by Michel Carré and Jules Barbier. French. Based on the play by Shakespeare. Premiered Paris, Académie Impériale de Musique, March 9, 1868. Set in Denmark in the 14th century. Grand Opera. Set numbers with recitative. Musical interludes before Iii and IIii. Prelude before I. Entr'acte before II, III, IV. Ballet.

Sets: 7. **Acts:** 5 acts, 7 scenes. **Length:** I, II, III, IV, V: 175. **Arias:** "Partagez-vous mes fleurs" (Ophélie), "O vin, dissipe la tristesse" (Hamlet). **Hazards:** None. **Scenes:** Ii. The throne room in Elsinore castle. Iii. The castle ramparts. IIi. The palace gardens. IIii. A hall in the palace. III. A room in the palace. IV. A lake. V. A graveyard.

Major roles: King Claudius (bass), Queen Gertrude (mezzo), Ophélie (soprano), Hamlet (baritone). **Minor roles:** Laërte (tenor), Marcellus (tenor), Horatio (bass), Ghost of the king (bass), Polonius (bass), First grave digger (baritone). **Bit part:** Second grave digger (tenor). **Mute:** Player King, Player Queen, Player Villain.

Chorus parts: SATTBB. **Chorus roles:** Lords, ladies, soldiers, actors, servants, peasants, pages, officers. **Dance/movement:** IV: Ballet. **Orchestra:** 2 fl, 2 ob, 2 cl, bs cl, bar sax, 2 bsn, 4 hrn, 2 cornet, 2 trp, 3 trb, bs tuba, timp, perc, 2 harp, strings. **Stageband:** fl, cl, hrn, 3 trp, 4 trb, bs trb, 4 perc, 2 harp, cannon. **Publisher:** Heugel and Co. **Rights:** Expired.

Ii. Denmark celebrates the wedding of King Claudius to Gertrude, widow of the previous king (who was Claudius's brother and Hamlet's father). Hamlet assures Ophélie of his love. Ophélie's brother, Laërte, bound for Norway, entrusts Ophélie to Hamlet. Horatio and Marcellus have seen the ghost of Hamlet's father and come to the wedding feast looking for Hamlet. Iii. The ghost tells Hamlet to avenge his murder at the hands of Claudius.

IIi. Ophélie is convinced Hamlet no longer loves her. The queen believes otherwise and enlists Ophélie's aid in dispelling Hamlet's gloom. Hamlet appears to have lost his reason. In private, the king assures the queen that Hamlet knows nothing of the murder, but the queen is oppressed by fear. Hamlet invites the king to a play. To confirm Claudius's guilt, Hamlet arranges to have the players reenact the murder of his father. IIii. The king is horrified by the play. Hamlet's accusations are attributed to madness.

III. Hamlet struggles with his doubts. He finds the king praying and decides to delay his revenge for a less sacred moment. Polonius was an accomplice to the murder, Hamlet realizes. Hamlet rejects the queen's suggestion that he marry Ophélie. He abuses the queen for murdering her husband, but the ghost intercedes on her behalf.

IV. The villagers dance and celebrate the coming of spring. Ophélie, who has gone mad, drowns herself.

V. Laërte attacks Hamlet for causing the death of his sister, but the fight is interrupted by Ophélie's funeral procession. The ghost of Hamlet's father appears to the court. Hamlet kills Claudius and is hailed king in his place.

A Hand of Bridge

Composed by Samuel Barber (March 9, 1910 – January 23, 1981). Libretto by Gian Carlo Menotti. English. Original work. Premiered Spoleto, Italy, Festival of Two Worlds, June 17, 1959. Set in a room in the present. Comedy. Through composed.

Sets: 1. **Acts:** 1 act, 1 scene. **Length:** I: 9. **Hazards:** None. **Scenes:** I. A room.

Major roles: Sally (contralto), Bill (tenor), Geraldine (soprano), David (baritone).

Chorus parts: N/A. **Chorus roles:** None. **Dance/movement:** None. **Orchestra:** fl, ob, cl, bsn, trp, perc, string quintet. **Stageband:** None. **Publisher:** G. Schirmer. **Rights:** Copyright 1960 by G. Schirmer.

I. Two couples play bridge. While they play, Sally thinks about shopping; Bill about his mistress; Geraldine about her mother; and David about money.

Hänsel und Gretel • Hansel and Gretel

Composed by Engelbert Humperdinck (September 1, 1854 – September 27, 1921). Libretto by Adelheid Wette. German. Based on a story in Grimm's fairy tales. Premiered Weimar, Hoftheater, December 23, 1893. Set in a cottage in the Harz mountains at an unspecified time. Fairy opera. Set numbers with accompanied recitative. Overture. Entr'acte before II, III. After Wagner stylistically, although inspired by folk music.

Sets: 3. **Acts:** 3 acts, 10 scenes. **Length:** I: 35. II: 30. III: 45. **Arias:** "Der kleine Sandman bin ich" (Sandman). **Hazards:** II: Angels' descend. III: Witch rides her broom, oven explodes. **Scenes:** I. A small, meager room. II. A deep wood. III. A gingerbread house.

Major roles: Hänsel (mezzo), Gretel (soprano), Peter (baritone), Gertrude (mezzo), Witch (mezzo). **Minor roles:** Sandman (soprano), Dew fairy (soprano).

Chorus parts: SA (children). **Chorus roles:** Children. (Note that 8-measure offstage "echo" in II specifies 3 soprano, 2 alto.) **Dance/movement:** Various dances by principals and children's chorus. II: Ballet of the 14 angels over the sleeping children. **Orchestra:** picc, 2 fl, 2 ob (Eng hrn), 2 cl (bs cl), 2 bsn, 4 hrn, 2 trp, 3 trb, bs tuba, perc, timp, harp, strings. **Stageband:** II: Cuckoo. **Publisher:** Schirmer, B. Schott's Söhne. **Rights:** Expired.

Ii. Hänsel and Gretel are hungry and bored with their chores. Gretel teachers her brother to dance. Iii. Their mother catches them playing and in her fury, she spills the milk that was to be dinner. Thrusting a basket into Gretel's hands, the mother sends the children out to pick strawberries. She prays for relief. Iiii. Father returns with a basket piled high with food. "There was a great event in the town," he explains, "and the basket cost only half of what he earned." He asks where the children are and is upset when she tells him: "There is a witch in the woods who cooks children into gingerbread cookies." They rush out to rescue Hänsel and Gretel.

IIi. Hänsel has almost filled the basket with strawberries when he and Gretel begin to eat them. They empty the basket, but it is now too dark to pick more—and they are lost. IIii. The now-terrified children are pacified by the sand man who puts them to sleep with fairy sand. IIiii. Fourteen angels descend to watch over them.

IIIi. It is morning and the dew fairy wakes Hänsel and Gretel. Both children have dreamt of the angels who watched over them. IIIii. Hänsel and Gretel stare in wonder at the candy and gingerbread witch's house. Unable to control themselves, they begin to eat the house. IIIiii. The witch appears. Hänsel and Gretel try to escape but are caught in the witch's spell. With Hänsel locked in the stable and Gretel frozen in place, the witch fetches more food to fatten up Hänsel. Hänsel pretends to fall asleep and overhears the witch's plan to bake the children into gingerbread. The witch rides her broom around in anticipation of success. She tries to lure Gretel into the oven, but Gretel plays dumb so that the witch has to show her what to do. Once the witch is in front of the oven, Hänsel (who has escaped from the stable) and Gretel push the witch in. The children dance in pleasure while the witch burns. The oven collapses and Hänsel and Gretel are surrounded by all the children captured by the witch. IIIiv. Hänsel and Gretel set the children free. Mother and father arrive and father recounts the moral: God relieves those who suffer. Everyone dances.

Háry János

Composed by Zoltán Kodály (December 16, 1882 – March 6, 1967). Libretto by Béla Paulini and Zsolt Harsányi. Hungarian. Based on comic epic "The Veteran" by János Garay. Premiered Budapest, Royal Hungarian Opera House, October 16, 1926. Set in Hungary, Austria and Italy around 1810. Folk opera. Set numbers with spoken dialogue. Prologue. Epilogue. Overture after prologue. Intermezzo before II. Opus 15.

Sets: 5. **Acts:** 4 acts, 6 scenes. **Length:** Prologue, I, II, III, IV: 135. **Arias:** Marczi's song (Marczi), Chicken song (Örzse), Háry's song (Háry). **Hazards:** I: Háry moves the frontier building. II: Háry rides Lucifer (can be done offstage with chorus watching from onstage). Viennese musical clock. **Scenes:** Prologue. The inn in the village of Nagy Abony. I. The border post between Hungary and Russia. II. The palace garden in Vienna. III. A battlefield outside Milan. IV. The palace in Vienna. Epilogue. The inn.

Major roles: Háry János (baritone), Örzse (mezzo), Marczi (bass or baritone), Marie-Louise (contralto). **Minor role:** Empress of Austria (soprano). **Bit parts:** Three archdukes (2 sopranos, 1 alto). **Speaking:** Magistrate, Biro, Two peasants, Hary Janos as old man, Innkeeper, Hungarian sentry, Russian sentry, Bombazine, Two hussars, General Kaos, Emperor Napoleon, Emperor of Austria. **Mute:** Mayor, Old woman, Jewish family, Hussar sentry, Children in the Viennese musical clock.

Chorus parts: SSAAAATTBB. **Chorus roles:** People of Nagy Abony, peasant girls, attendants of Marie-Louise (one speaking line only), hussars, gypsies, courtiers, archdukes, archduchesses. **Dance/movement:** III: Country and Hussar dances. **Orchestra:** 3 fl (3 picc), 2 ob, 2 cl (alto sax), 2 bsn, 4 hrn, 3 trp, 3 cornets, 3 trb, tuba, timp, 4 perc, celeste, piano, cimbalon (can be played on harpsichord or second piano), strings. **Stageband:** I, II: fl, trps. III: trps, fiddlers. IV: gypsy fiddlers, brass band. **Publisher:** Universal Edition. **Rights:** Copyright 1929 by Universal

Edition. Assigned 1952 to Universal Edition (London). Renewed 1956 by Zoltán Kodály.

Prologue. Háry János tells stories to the people in the inn at Nagy Abony. I. On the Russo-Hungarian border, Háry's fiancée, Örzse, brings him freshly-roasted chicken. Napoleon's wife, Marie-Louise, and her entourage are stopped by the border sentry, but Háry moves the frontier building and gets them through. Háry, Örzse and the coachman Marczi reminisce. Marie-Louise promises to grant Háry three wishes. He asks for a double ration of oats for his horse, amnesty for Marczi's mustache (which he had been told to shave) and permission for Örzse to accompany them. They start for Vienna.

II. Marie-Louise looks out for Háry and Marczi at court, although her courtier, Bombazine, dislikes them. Bombazine challenges Háry to ride the unruly horse Lucifer, which Háry does. The empress is impressed and shows him her musical clock. Bombazine warns Örzse that Háry may soon forget her. He uses a declaration of war given him by Napoleon.

III. Háry singlehandedly defeats the French army. He captures Napoleon and forces him to pay war reparations. Marie-Louise promotes Háry to general. Örzse arrives to find the soldiers eating and dancing. She and Marie-Louise fight over Háry. Háry prevents Marie-Louise from jumping off the end of the world.

IV. Marie-Louise has divorced Napoleon and discusses with the empress whom she should marry now. She chooses Háry and the empress promises to talk to the pope about the problem of Háry being Protestant. The emperor feasts Háry and introduces him to the archdukes. Háry tells the emperor he cannot be the heir. Bombazine apologizes to Háry for his behavior. The emperor remits Háry's conscription time and Háry returns to Nagy Abony with Örzse. Epilogue. Háry concludes his story as the inn closes for the night.

Das Heimchen am Herd • The Cricket on the Hearth

Composed by Karl Goldmark (May 18, 1830 – January 2, 1915). Libretto by Alfred Maria Willner. German. Based on the novel by Charles Dickens. Premiered Vienna, Hofoperntheater, March 21, 1896. Set in England in the 19th century. Comedy. Set numbers with recitative. Overture. Prelude before III.

Sets: 2. Acts: 3 acts, 3 scenes. Length: I, II, III: 165. Hazards: I: Opera opens on a scene filled with clouds that part to reveal John's cottage. II: A woodland appears to John in his dream. **Scenes:** I. A large sitting room in John's cottage. II. The garden in front of John's cottage. III. The sitting room.

Major roles: Cricket (soprano), Dot (soprano), May (soprano), John (baritone), Edward (tenor), Tackleton (bass). **Bit parts:** Voice (baritone), Old Anne (soprano).

Chorus parts: SSAATTBB. **Chorus roles:** Elves (offstage), villagers, village lads, maidens. **Dance/movement:** II: Elven dance. III: Villagers dance around Tackleton, holding him captive. **Orchestra:** 3 fl (picc), 2 ob, Eng hrn, 2 cl, bs cl, 2 bsn, 4 hrn, 3 trp, 4 trb (tuba), timp, perc, harp, strings. **Stageband:** I: trp. **Publisher:** Emil Berté & Co. **Rights:** Expired.

I. The cricket on the hearth promises to complete the happiness of John the postman and Dot by bringing them a child. May confesses to Dot that she still loves Edward—who left her seven years ago—even though she will marry Tackleton tomorrow. John brings home an old sailor—who is actually Edward in disguise. John delivers letters to the assembled villagers.

II. Tackleton, Edward and May join John and Dot for dinner. May brushes off Tackleton's wooing. Questioned by Tackleton, Edward tells how he lost his parents and his one true love. He shows them a bag of jewels and whispers his identity to the surprised Dot. Tackleton tells John that Edward is a Lothario with designs on Dot. As proof, he has John spy on Edward while he is talking to Dot. The cricket brings John a dream of his future son.

III. Dot helps the sobbing bride to dress. When May decides to call off the marriage, Edward reveals himself. He invites the villagers to the wedding. The villagers hold off Tackleton while May and Edward make off in Tackleton's carriage. John and Dot fight until Dot reveals she is pregnant.

Heimkehr aus der Fremde • Return from Abroad

Composed by Felix Mendelssohn-Bartholdy (February 3, 1809 – November 4, 1847). Libretto by Karl Klingemann. German. Original work. Premiered Berlin, Mendelssohn home, December 26, 1829. Set in a village at an unspecified time. Operetta. Set numbers with recitative. Overture. Interlude. Published posthumously.

Sets: 1. **Acts:** 1 act, 1 scene. **Length:** I: 60. **Hazards:** None. **Scenes:** I. A village square.

Major roles: Ursula (mezzo), Lisbeth (soprano), Kauz the pedlar (baritone), Herrmann (tenor). **Minor roles:** Mayor (bass or baritone). **Minor roles:** Four people (soprano, alto, tenor, bass). **Mute:** Watchman Martin. **Chorus parts:** SATB. **Chorus roles:** Villagers. **Dance/movement:** None. **Orchestra:** 2 fl, 2 ob, 2 cl, 2 bsn, 2 hrn, 2 trp, strings. **Stageband:** None. **Publisher:** Novello. **Rights:** Expired.

I. The mayor's wife, Ursula, and his ward, Lisbeth, miss the mayor's son, Herrmann, who has gone away to seek his fortune. Herrmann returns. He loves Lisbeth. Jealous of the attention Lisbeth shows Herrmann, the pedlar, Kauz, first challenges Herrmann and then slanders him. Herrmann catches Kauz trying to rob the villagers, but the mayor releases Kauz. Hermann is welcomed home.

Die Heimsuchung • The Visitation

Composed by Gunther Schuller (b. November 22, 1925). Libretto by Gunther Schuller. German. Based on a story by Franz Kafka. Premiered Hamburg, Hamburgischen Staatsoper, October 11, 1966. Set in a city in the present. Tragedy. Through composed. Serial composition with jazz elements. Prologue. Epilogue. Recorded music used.

Sets: 10. **Acts:** 3 acts, 11 scenes. **Hazards:** Prologue: Carter sees a vision of the history of his race. **Scenes:** Prologue. A "colored" church of the 1880s and a slave auction. Ii. Carter's room and Miss Hampton's room next door. Iii. Miss Hampton and Carter's rooms seen from a different angle. Iiii. A drugstore. Iiv. A court or tribunal in a warehouse. IIi. One wing of the court house. IIii. A city square with a fountain. IIiii. Uncle Albert's home and lawyer Held's home. IIIi. A big, gaudy roadside nightclub. IIIii. Interior of a church. IIIiii. A deserted excavation pit in a desolate countryside.

Major roles: Carter Jones (baritone), Mrs. Claiborne (soprano), Teena (mezzo), Pulisi (tenor). **Minor roles:** Bill/First man (baritone), Frank/Second man (bass), Joe (tenor), Inspector (bass baritone), Landlady (mezzo), Miss Hampton (soprano), Mattie (tenor), Presiding officer (baritone), Chuck (tenor), Mr. Claiborne (tenor), Uncle Albert (bass), Held (baritone), Patterson (tenor), Deacon (bass). **Speaking:** Preacher. **Speaking bits:** Mill hand, Two men, Woman, Two companions of C. J., First policeman. **Mute:** Boy, Girl, Second policeman, Black preacher, Slave auctioneer, Two slave guards, Club stripper, Cleaning woman.

Chorus parts: STTBB. **Chorus roles:** People, members of the court.
Dance/movement: None. **Orchestra:** 3 fl (picc), 3 ob (Eng hrn), 3 cl (bs
cl), 3 bsn (cont bsn), 4 hrn, 3 trp, 3 trb, tuba, timp, perc, piano (harpsichord), celeste, harp, strings, jazz combo (cl, sax, trp, trb, perc, piano),
taped sound. **Stageband:** III: club band. **Publisher:** B. Schott's Söhne.
Rights: Copyright 1967 by Associated Music Publishers Inc.

Prologue. The black student Carter Jones has a vision of the history of
his race. Ii. Bill, Frank and Joe push their way into Carter's room and go
through his things. They bring him into the room of his neighbor, Miss
Hampton, where an inspector questions him. Iii. Carter apologizes to the
landlady and Miss Hampton for the men's visit. He kisses Miss
Hampton. Iiii. Two men visit Carter at work and tell him to meet them
by the steel mill warehouse tomorrow. Iiv. The mill houses a makeshift
court. The presiding officer makes racist remarks to Carter. Chuck, the
son of the mill owner, mauls Mrs. Claiborne.

IIi. Carter goes to the court house to find the lawyer Claiborne. He meets
Mrs. Claiborne, who promises to help him. She runs off with Chuck,
whom she claims to hate. Claiborne is angry about his wife's infidelities
but cannot do anything for fear of losing his job. IIii. Carter and his
friends are attacked by drunken punks. The police intercept the punks,
but let them go. IIiii. Carter visits his Uncle Albert, who recommends
him to the lawyer Held. They visit Held. Held is ill, but introduces them
to Patterson, the chief clerk of the court. Carter hears a crash and goes
into the next room to investigate. Patterson is insulted by Carter's sudden departure. Carter makes love to Held's nurse, Teena, while Held
and Albert discuss Carter's case.

IIIi. Carter is referred to Pulisi who promises to help him. Carter, now
accused of raping Mrs. Claiborne, has lost his job and apartment. IIIii.
Carter asks the deacon for help. The deacon hurries away to keep an
appointment with the sheriff. IIIiii. Chuck and his two companions brutally murder Carter.

Hérodiade

Composed by Jules-Emile-Frédéric Massenet (May 12, 1842 – August 13,
1912). Libretto by Paul Milliet and Henri Grémont (Georges) Hartmann.
French. Based on "Hérodias" by Gustave Flaubert. Premiered Brussels,
Théâtre de la Monnaie, December 19, 1881. Set in Jerusalem circa 30 AD.
Tragedy. Set numbers with recitative. Overture. Ballet. Prelude before
IV.

Sets: 7. **Acts:** 4 acts, 15 scenes. **Length:** I, II, III, IV: 155. **Arias:** "Vision

fugitive" (Hérode), "Il est doux, il est bon (Salomé). **Hazards:** None.
Scenes: I. A large court in Hérode's palace in Jerusalem. IIi – IIiii.
Hérode's chamber. IIiii. The palace. IIIi. Phanuel's home. IIIii – IIIv. The
temple. IVi. A subterranean vault. IVii – IViii. A great hall in the palace.

Major roles: Phanuel (bass), Salomé (soprano), Hérode (baritone),
Hérodiade (mezzo), Jean (tenor). **Minor roles:** Young Babylonian (soprano), Vitellius (baritone), Voice (tenor), High priest (baritone).

Chorus parts: SSATTTTBBBB (briefly TTTTTTBBBBBB). **Chorus roles:**
Slaves, merchants, chiefs, messengers, Pharisees, Sadducees, priests, soldiers, Canaanites, Hebrews, temple servants, Levites, children (1 part).
Dance/movement: I: Slave dance. II: Babylonian dance. III: Sacred
dance. IV: Ballet of the IV: Egyptians, Babylonians, Gauls and
Phoenicians. **Orchestra:** picc, 2 fl (picc), 2 ob, Eng hrn, 3 cl (bs cl), alto
sax, tenor sax, cont bs sax, 2 bsn, 4 hrn, 2 cornet, 2 trp, 4 trb, tuba, timp,
perc, piano, 2 harp, strings. **Stageband:** III: 2 picc, 2 fl, 2 cl, harmonica,
harp, piano, perc. **Publisher:** Heugel & Co. **Rights:** Expired.

Ii. Merchants and slaves bring their wares to Jerusalem. Phanuel loves
Salomé, who was sent away by her mother, Hérodiade, when she mar-
ried King Hérode. Salomé loves John the Baptist and has returned to
find him. Iii. Hérode loves Salomé. Iiii. The prophet has insulted
Hérodiade, who demands revenge. Hérode refuses, pointing out that
John has a large following. Iiv. Salomé admits her love to the prophet.
He gently reproves her.

IIi. Slaves dance for Hérode. A young Babylonian gives Hérode wine
that brings visions of his beloved. It also puts him to sleep. IIii. Hérode
asks Phanuel how he can rid himself of his obsession with Salomé, but
Phanuel is more concerned about the revolt brewing among Hérode's
subjects. IIiii. Hérode announces his intention to overthrow Jerusalem's
Roman masters. Vitellius, the Roman consul, arrives, squelching the
revolt. He agrees to let the Israelites reopen the temple.

IIIi. Phanuel wonders if John is mortal or divine. Hérodiade consults
Phanuel, who foretells blood and suffering to come. The queen does not
realize Salomé is her daughter. IIIii. Salomé calls on God to save John.
IIIiii. Now that Rome has taken control of the kingdom, Hérode intends
to free John. He declares his love to Salomé, but she scorns him. IIIiv.
The high priest presides over the sacred rites and dances. IIIv. The
priests demand that Vitellius condemn John, but he leaves them to judge
their own. Hérode is about to free John, when Salomé asks to die with
her beloved John. Furious, Hérode condemns them both.

IVi. John admits he loves Salomé. Salomé wishes to die with him, but

Hérode has ordered otherwise. IVii. In the palace, the Roman soldiers enjoy their victory. Slaves dance. IViii. Salomé begs Hérodiade for John's life. At last the queen recognizes her daughter, but too late to save John. Salomé kills herself.

L'Heure Espagnole • The Spanish Hour

Composed by Maurice Ravel (March 7, 1875 – December 28, 1937). Libretto by Franc Nohain. French. Based on comedy by Nohain. Premiered Paris, Opéra Comique, May 19, 1911. Set in Toledo in the 18th century. Musical comedy. Through composed. Orchestral introduction.

Sets: 1. **Acts:** 1 act, 21 scenes. **Length:** I: 50. **Hazards:** Moving around clocks with people inside. **Scenes:** I. Store of a Spanish watchmaker.

Major roles: Concepción (soprano), Gonzalve (tenor), Torquemada (tenor), Ramiro (baritone), Don Iñigo Gomez (comic bass).

Chorus parts: N/A. **Chorus roles:** None. **Dance/movement:** None. **Orchestra:** picc, 2 fl, 2 ob, Eng hrn, 2 cl, bs cl, 2 bsn, sarrusophone, 4 hrn, 2 trp, 3 trb, tuba, timp, perc, celeste, 2 harps, strings. **Stageband:** None. **Publisher:** Durand & Co. **Rights:** Expired.

Ii. Ramiro brings his watch to Torquemada the clockmaker to be repaired. He explains that as the government mule driver, he must always know the correct time. Iii. When Torquemada's wife, Concepción, reminds him that it is time to regulate the government clocks, he apologizes to Ramiro and asks him to await his return. Iiii. Concepción has been complaining that she has no clock in her bedroom so Ramiro carries one up for her. Iiv. Concepción's lover Gonzalve arrives. She tries to prod him into action, but he is caught up in his own poetic allusions. Iv. When Ramiro returns, Concepción persuades him to bring back the clock he just carried up—and then take up a different clock. Ivi. While Ramiro is fetching the first clock, Concepción hides Gonzalve in the second clock. Ivii. Inigo Gomez, an important—and heavy—official, arrives to court Concepción. It is he, he explains, who got her husband out of the house by appointing him to regulate the government clocks. She fends off his advances. Iviii. Concepción accompanies Ramiro upstairs with the second clock containing Gonzalve. Iix. Inigo decides to hide in another clock. Ix. Ramiro is pleased that Concepción has left him in charge of the shop. Ixi. Concepción complains that her clock does not keep time and begs Ramiro to carry it back down. Ixii. Inigo attracts Concepción's attention by imitating a cuckoo clock, a courtship technique that does not meet with success. Ixiii. Ramiro returns and offers to carry up the clock, which, he does not realize, contains Inigo. Concepción accepts. Ixiv. Disappointed by Gonzalve's dreamy silliness, Concepción tells him not to come back. Ixv. Gonzalve stays in the clock, composing poems. Ixvi. Ramiro is charmed that Concepción has found him something to do. He runs upstairs to fetch back the clock. Ixvii. "It is unfair to have two such foolish lovers," Concepción complains: "The entire afternoon has been wasted." Ixviii. Admiring Ramiro's biceps, she takes him back to her room—without any clocks. Ixix. Gonzalve tries to leave, but sees Torquemada returning. He opens a clock to hide, inadvertently exposing Inigo. Ixx. Torquemada sells a clock to each of the embarrassed men. Ixxi. Concepción's problem is solved when Torquemada asks Ramiro to tell her the time each morning on his daily rounds. All sing the moral: In love, the efficient lover succeeds and even the muleteer has his turn.

Histoire du Soldat • The Soldier's Tale

Composed by Igor Stravinsky (June 17, 1882 – April 6, 1971). Libretto by C. F. Ramuz. French. Original work. Premiered Lausanne, Municipal Theater, September 28, 1918. Set in two villages at an unspecified time. Morality play. Set numbers with spoken dialogue.

Sets: 5. **Acts:** 2 acts, 6 scenes. **Length:** I, II: 55. **Hazards:** None. **Scenes:** Ii. The banks of a stream. Iii. A village with the belfry visible in the distance. IIi. A village on the frontier and an inn. IIii. A room in the palace. IIiii. The princess's room. IIiv. The frontier.

Speaking: Narrator, Soldier, Devil. **Mute:** Princess (dancer).

Chorus parts: N/A. **Chorus roles:** None. **Dance/movement:** II: Princess dances tango, waltz and rag-time. Devil dances. **Orchestra:** cl, bsn, cornet, trb, timp, vln, db bs. **Stageband:** None. **Publisher:** Chester Music, Moscow State Music. **Rights:** Copyright 1924 by J. & W. Chester Ltd.

Ii. The devil persuades a soldier to trade his violin for a book that tells the future. The soldier goes home with the devil to learn how to use the book. Iii. When he returns to his village, the soldier finds that three years—not three days—have passed and his friends and relatives have forgotten him. He uses the book to become rich, but is still not happy. He tries to play his violin but cannot.

IIi. The soldier runs away. He hears that the princess is sick and will marry anyone who can cure her. IIii. The soldier realizes that his wealth gives the devil power over him. He gambles with the devil and loses everything. The devil grows weak and collapses. IIiii. The soldier plays his violin and cures the princess. The devil attacks, but the soldier defeats him. IIiv. As the devil has foreseen, the soldier tries to go home—and again falls into the devil's power.

Hugh the Drover

Composed by Ralph Vaughan Williams (October 12, 1872 – August 26, 1958). Libretto by Harold Child. English. Original work Premiered London, Royal College of Music, July 14, 1924. Set in the Cotswolds about 1812. Romantic ballad opera. Set numbers with recitative. Prelude. Optional extra scene in II.

Sets: 2. **Acts:** 2 acts, 2 scenes. **Length:** I: 55. II: 45. **Hazards:** I: Prize fight between Hugh and John. **Scenes:** I. A fair on the outskirts of town. II. The marketplace in the town.

Major roles: Mary (soprano), John the butcher (bass baritone), Hugh the drover (tenor). **Minor roles:** Cheap Jack (baritone), Shell fish seller (bass), Primrose seller (contralto), Showman (high baritone), Ballad seller (tenor), Aunt Jane (contralto), Turnkey (tenor), Constable (bass), Sergeant (high baritone). **Bit part:** Nancy (contralto), Robert (bass), Susan (soprano), William (tenor), Innkeeper (bass), Fool (baritone). **Mute:** Stall keepers, Showman's troupe, Morris men, Bugler, Drummer.

Chorus parts: SSSSAAAATTTTBBBB. **Chorus roles:** Townspeople, boys, soldiers, toy lamb sellers, primrose sellers. **Dance/movement:** None (Morris dancers do not dance). **Orchestra:** 2 fl (picc), 2 ob, 2 cl, 2 bsn, 4 hrn, 2 trp, 2 trb, bs trb, tuba, harp, timp, 2 perc, strings. **Stageband:** I: trp, drum, fife, pipe (tabor). II: hrns, bugle, drums. **Publisher:** Curwen Edition. **Rights:** Copyright 1924, 1951, 1978 J. Curwen and Sons Ltd.

I. The townsfolk attend a fair. The constable is annoyed that his daughter Mary objects to marrying John the butcher. Aunt Jane consoles Mary, but she and the constable are scandalized when Mary and Hugh the drover fall in love. Hugh agrees to a prize fight against John—with Mary as the prize. John cheats, but Hugh still wins. The constable and John accuse Hugh of being a French spy and have him arrested.

II. Hugh is in the town stocks awaiting execution. John beats him. Mary sets him free, but Hugh refuses to leave without her. She cannot run fast enough, so she tells Hugh to get back in the stocks—and locks herself up as well. The townspeople release Mary. The constable disowns Mary and John refuses to marry a pauper. The soldiers come for the spy, but are surprised to find it is their old friend Hugh. Annoyed at having to come all this way for nothing, they draft John. Mary leaves with Hugh.

Les Huguenots • The Huguenots

Composed by Giacomo Meyerbeer (September 5, 1791 – May 2, 1864). Libretto by Eugène Scribe and Émile Deschamps. French. Original work inspired by historical events. Premiered Paris, Opéra, February 29, 1836. Set in Touraine and Paris in August 1572. Grand opera. Set numbers with recitative. Overture. Entr'acte before each act. Ballet.

Sets: 6. **Acts:** 5 acts, 6 scenes. **Length:** I: 35. II: 35. III: 40. IV: 35. V: 15. **Arias:** "Nobles seigneurs" (Urbain), "Ô beau pays de la Touraine" (Marguerite), "Piff, paff" (Marcel). **Hazards:** III: Nevers and bridal suite arrive by boat. **Scenes:** I. A chamber in the castle of the count of Nevers. II. The castle and gardens of Chenonceaux. III. A meadow on the banks of the Seine. IV. A room in the castle of Nevers decorated with family portraits. Vi. A ballroom. Vii. A church cemetery.

Major roles: Count of Nevers (baritone), Raoul of Nangis (tenor), Queen Marguerite of Valois (soprano), Marcel (bass), Valentine (soprano). **Minor roles:** Count of Tavannes (tenor), Count of Cossé (tenor), Count of Méru (bass), Count of Retz (bass or baritone), Count of Thoré (bass), Urbain (mezzo or contralto), Two ladies in waiting (soprano, mezzo), Count of St. Bris (baritone or bass baritone), Bois-Rosé (tenor), Two gypsies (soprano, contralto), Maurevert (bass). **Bit parts:** Two young Catholics (soprano, alto), Archer (baritone), Page of Nevers (tenor), Three monks (2 tenor, bass).

Chorus parts: SSAATTTBBBB. **Chorus roles:** Soldiers, nobles, court ladies, village girls, Catholics, Huguenots, citizens, musicians, pages, knights, monks, assassins. **Dance/movement:** II: Ballet. III: Bohemian dance. V: ballet. **Orchestra:** picc, 2 fl, 2 ob (Eng hrn), 2 cl, 2 bsn, 4 hrn, 4 trp, 3 trb, ophicléide, timp, perc, harp, vla d'amore, strings. **Stageband:** III: bells, picc, 7 cl, 2 ob, 2 bsn, 2 hrn, 3 trp, 2 trb, ophicléide, timp, perc. IV: bells, 4 trp, cornet, 4 hrn, 2 trb. **Publisher:** Kalmus, Garland Publishing. **Rights:** Expired.

I. The Protestant Raoul meets his Catholic fellow officers. Nevers is soon to be married to Valentine, daughter of the Count of St. Bris. The men tell of their loves and Raoul recounts how he saved a mysterious lady (Valentine) from a group of rowdy students. His servant, Marcel, distrusts the Catholics. A lady arrives with a message inviting Raoul to court.

II. Valentine has persuaded Nevers to renounce his claim to her and the queen means to help her get her beloved Raoul. But Raoul, believing Valentine loves another, refuses her. The queen has to intervene to prevent St. Bris from fighting Raoul for this insult to his daughter.

III. Valentine is again engaged to Nevers. St. Bris challenges Raoul. Valentine overhears her father planning to ambush Raoul and warns Marcel. A general battle between Catholics and Huguenots is only prevented by the queen's arrival. Nevers claims his bride.

IV. Raoul comes to visit Valentine, but overhears St. Bris planning a massacre of the Huguenots. Troubled by the dishonorable nature of the plot, Nevers refuses to participate. St. Bris has him locked up. Valentine tells Raoul she loves him and begs him to stay with her. He is torn, but cannot betray his coreligionists.

V. The St. Bartholomew's day massacre is in progress. Nevers is killed defending Valentine. She converts and marries Raoul. They are killed by St. Bris and his soldiers.

The Ice Break

Composed by Michael Tippett (b. January 2, 1905). Libretto by Michael Tippett. English. Original work. Premiered London, Royal Opera House, Covent Garden, July 7, 1977. Set in a large, modern city in the present. Tragedy. Through composed. Interlude. Complex use of chorus. Electronic amplification of singers and instruments used.

Sets: 6. **Acts:** 3 acts, 29 scenes. **Length:** I, II, III: 75. **Hazards:** III: Psychedelic image of Astron. The paradise garden and chorus vanish as by explosion. **Scenes:** Ii – Ivii. An airport lounge. Iviii. Nadia's tiny apartment. Iix. The airport. Ix. Nadia's apartment. IIi – IIvi. The city at night. IIvii. Nadia's apartment. IIviii – IIx. The city at night. IIIi – IIIiv. Nadia's apartment. IIIv. The paradise garden. IIIvi. Luke's consulting room. IIIvii – IIIix. A hall within the hive of activity of a large hospital.

Major roles: Nadia (lyric soprano), Yuri (baritone), Lev (bass). **Minor roles:** Gayle (dramatic soprano), Hannah (mezzo), Olympion (tenor), Lieutenant (baritone), Luke (tenor), Astron (double voice: lyric mezzo and high tenor or countertenor).

Chorus parts: SSAAMMTTBaBaBB. **Chorus roles:** Double chorus: white and black. Fans, people, chorus of the paradise garden. **Dance/movement:** I: Olympion's fans dance at his return. II: mob tribal dances. III: Chorus from the paradise garden somersault and cartwheel down the hospital corridor. **Orchestra:** 2 fl, 3 ob, 3 cl, 3 bsn, 4 hrn, 2 trp, 3 trb, tuba, timp, 3 perc, xylophone, glockenspiel, jazz drum set, electric guitar, bs guitar, electric organ, harp, piano, celeste, strings. **Stageband:** None. **Publisher:** Schott & Co. **Rights:** Copyright 1977 Schott & Co. Ltd.

Ii. Nadia and her son Yuri await the arrival of her husband, Lev, who has spent twenty years in exile and prison. Iii. Yuri sees his girlfriend, Gayle, and her friend Hannah. Iiii. Hannah is meeting her boyfriend, the black champion Olympion. Fans mob him. Iiv. Yuri rebukes Hannah for spending time with blacks. Iv. Nadia wonders if the plane is late. Ivi. Olympion brags about his preeminence. Ivii. Lev returns. Iviii. Nadia listens to Lev's tale of imprisonment. Iix. Olympion makes racist remarks. Gayle tries to atone for injustice to blacks by kissing Olympion. Yuri attacks him, but Olympion hits Yuri first and kicks Gayle away. Ix. Lev asks Nadia about their son.

IIi. Yuri insists that violence rules and rebukes Lev for allowing himself to be beaten down. IIii. Whites band together in the Klan. IIiii. Olympion tells Hannah he must stand with his fellow blacks. IIiv. A black mob forms. IIv. Hannah is left alone. IIvi. White and black mobs perform a tribal dance. IIvii. Lev rushes out into the night. IIviii. The black mob kicks a white to death. The whites retaliate and shots ring out. IIix. Yuri is wounded, but Gayle and Olympion are dead. IIx. Lev and Hannah mourn.

IIIi. Lev reads to the dying Nadia. IIIii. Hannah and Luke (a medical intern) report that Yuri is going to live. IIIiii. Lev wonders why he came to this country—and if Yuri is not right about life being a constant fight. IIIiv. Nadia remembers scenes from her childhood and dies. IIIv. In the paradise garden, people smoke and have a psychedelic vision of Astron. IIIvi. Luke meditates on the death he confronts every day. IIIvii. Lev waits while Yuri undergoes an operation. IIIviii. The people from the paradise garden dance down the hospital corridor. IIIix. Having survived the operation, Yuri embraces his father.

Idomeneo

Composed by Wolfgang Amadeus Mozart (January 27, 1756 – December 5, 1791). Libretto by Giambattista Varesco. Italian. Based on libretto by Antoine Danchet. Premiered Munich, Cuvilliés Theater, January 29, 1781. Set in the port of Sidon on the island of Crete shortly after the Trojan war (12th century BC). Opera seria. Set numbers with recitative. Overture. Intermezzo in I. Ballet. K. 366. Revised version by Ermanno Wolf-Ferrari (premiered Munich, June 15, 1931).

Sets: 7. **Acts:** 3 acts, 28 scenes. **Length:** I: 60. II: 45. III: 65. **Arias:** "Fuor del mar" (Idomeneo), "Il padre adorato" (Idamante), "Torna la pace" (Idomeneo), "Zeffiretti lusinghieri" (Ilia), "Idol mio" (Elettra). **Hazards:** I, II: storm at sea. **Scenes:** Ii – Ivi. Apartments of Ilia in the royal palace. Ivii – Ixi. A beach. IIi – IIv. The royal apartments. IIvi – IIvii. The port of Sidon. IIIi – IIIv. The royal gardens. IIIvi. A square before the royal palace. IIIvii – IIIxi. Outside the temple of Nettuno.

Major roles: Ilia (soprano), Idamante (soprano or tenor), Elettra (soprano), Arbace (tenor or baritone), Idomeneo (tenor). **Minor roles:** High priest (tenor), Voice of Nettuno (bass). **Bit parts:** Two Trojans (tenor, bass), Two Cretan girls (soprano, alto).

Chorus parts: SATTTBBB. **Chorus roles:** Retinue of Idomeneo, retinue of Idamante, Trojan prisoners, people of Crete, sailors, warriors from Crete and Argos. **Dance/movement:** I: ballet of Cretan women. III: ballet. **Orchestra:** picc, 2 fl, 2 ob, 2 cl, 2 bsn, 4 hrn, 2 trp, 3 trb, timp, strings, continuo. (Trbs play only in III with Voice and can be stageband.) **Stageband:** None. **Publisher:** Bärenreiter, Breitkopf & Härtel. **Rights:** Expired.

Ii. The Trojan Ilia loves Idamante—Idomeneo's son and an enemy of Troy. She is afraid Idamante loves Elettra. Iii. But he loves her—and promises to mitigate the suffering of her countrymen. Iiii. Idamante consoles the Trojan prisoners. Iiv. Elettra rebukes him for this. Iv. Idomeneo is reported to have drowned returning from the war. Ivi. Elettra loves Idamante and plans revenge on Ilia. Ivii. The people are terrified by a storm at sea. Iviii. Idomeneo lands, having saved himself by promising Neptune to sacrifice the first mortal he meets. Iix. It is Idamante—though father and son do not at first recognize each other. Ix. Idomeneo flees. Ixi. The people honor Neptune.

IIi. Idomeneo explains his problem to Arbace. Arbace suggests they pack Idamante off to Argos while they find a way to placate Neptune. IIii. Idomeneo confirms Ilia's freedom and consoles her. IIiii. He guesses that she loves Idamante. IIiv. Elettra is grateful for Idomeneo's kindnesses. IIv. She is confident she can win Idamante's heart once she gets him away from Ilia. IIvi. Elettra prepares to leave. IIvii. Her departure is prevented by the rising up of the sea.

IIIi. Ilia adores Idamante. IIIii. She saves him from despair. IIIiii. The lovers are discovered by Idomeneo, who orders his son to depart. IIIiv. The priests of Neptune demand an explanation from Idomeneo. IIIv. Arbace offers himself as a sacrifice. IIIvi. Neptune has raised a sea monster that is causing death and destruction. IIIvii. Idomeneo publicly names Neptune's intended victim. IIIviii. Idamante slays the sea monster. IIIix. He persuades his father to sacrifice him. IIIx. Ilia asks to die in his place, but a heavenly voice intercedes: Idomeneo is forgiven but must abdicate in favor of his son.

L'Île de Tulipatan • The Island of Tulipatan

Composed by Jacques Offenbach (June 20, 1819 – October 5, 1880). Libretto by Henri Chivot and Alfred Duru. French. Original work. Premiered Paris, Théâtre des Bouffes Parisiens, September 30, 1868. Set on the island of Tulipatan 473 years before the invention of spittoons. Operetta. Set numbers with recitative or spoken dialogue. Overture.

Sets: 1. **Acts:** 1 act, 1 scene. **Length:** I: 55. **Hazards:** None. **Scenes:** I. The park of a stately mansion.

Major roles: Hermosa (tenor), Cacatois XXII (baritone), Alexis (soprano).

Minor roles: Théodorine (contralto), Romboïdal (tenor). **Mute:** Tetaclack.

Chorus parts: SATTB. **Chorus roles:** Officers, servants, people. **Dance/movement:** I: chorus dance during barcarole. **Orchestra:** 2 fl (picc), 2 ob, 2 cl, 2 bsn, 4 hrn, 2 trp, 3 trb, timp, perc, strings. **Stageband:** None. **Publisher:** Belwin Mills. **Rights:** Expired.

I. Grand Marshall Romboïdal complains to his wife, Théodorine, that their daughter, Hermosa, is a tomboy. Grand Duke Cacatois admits that his son, Alexis, is effeminate. Hermosa persuades Alexis to propose to her. Théodorine breaks the news to Hermosa that she is a man: she passed Hermosa off as a woman to protect him from fighting in Cacatois's wars. Romboïdal tells Hermosa that Alexis is really a woman: the grand duke kept starting wars every time he had a daughter, so the grand marshal told him Alexis was a boy. Cacatois tells Romboïdal that he means Alexis to marry Hermosa. Romboïdal and Théodorine admit the truth about Alexis and Hermosa. The lovers are united. Cacatois decides to remarry so he can have an heir.

Imeneo

Composed by George Frederic Handel (February 23, 1685 – April 14, 1759). Libretto by an anonymous author. Italian. Based on libretto by Silvio Stampiglia for Porpora. Premiered London, Theatre Royal, Lincoln's Inn Fields, November 22, 1740. Set in Greece in ancient times. Drama. Set numbers with recitative. Overture.

Sets: 1. **Acts:** 3 acts, 19 scenes. **Length:** I, II, III: 115. **Arias:** "Sorge nell'alma mia" (Tirinto), "Al voler di tua fortuna" (Rosmene), "Di cieca notte" (Argenio). **Hazards:** None. **Scenes:** I – III. A delightful glade.

Major roles: Tirinto (contralto), Imeneo (tenor or bass baritone), Clomiri (soprano), Rosmene (soprano). **Minor role:** Argenio (bass).

Chorus parts: SATB. **Chorus roles:** People. **Dance/movement:** None. **Orchestra:** 2 ob, strings, continuo. **Stageband:** None. **Publisher:** Oxford University Press, Gregg Press. **Rights:** Expired.

Ii. Tirinto loves Rosmene. Rosmene and Clomiri are kidnapped while sacrificing. Iii. They are rescued by Imeneo, who asks Rosmene's guardian, Argenio, for her hand. Clomiri loves Imeneo. Iiii. Rosmene gives Imeneo hope. Iiv. Tirinto is heartbroken at the thought of losing Rosmene. Iv. Clomiri tells Imeneo that a "friend" of hers loves him. Ivi. Rosmene assures Tirinto she will be his.

IIi. Imeneo asks Rosmene to marry him. IIii. She is torn between love and gratitude. IIiii. Tirinto is wracked with jealousy. IIiv. Clomiri decides to help Imeneo. IIv. Imeneo contemplates the pain of love. IIvi. Argenio tells Rosmene to choose between her suitors.

IIIi. Rosmene delays. IIIii. Both men threaten to kill themselves if she does not choose them. IIIiii. Clomiri asks Imeneo to take her friend if he cannot have Rosmene. IIIiv. Rosmene pretends she is insane. IIIv. Imeneo is surprised and concerned. IIIvi. So is Tirinto. IIIvii. Rosmene calls for divine inspiration and faints in Imeneo's arms. She chooses him.

The Impresario

See "Der Schauspieldirektor" entry.

In a Garden

Composed by Meyer Kupferman (b. July 3, 1926). Libretto by Gertrude Stein. English. Original work. Premiered New York City, After Dinner Opera Company, Finch Junior College, December 29, 1949. Set in a garden at an unspecified time. Fable. Through composed. Prelude.

Sets: 1. **Acts:** 1 act, 1 scene. **Length:** I: 20. **Hazards:** None. **Scenes:** I. A garden.

Major roles: Lucy Willow (soprano), Philip Hall (tenor), Kit Raccoon the first (baritone).

Chorus parts: N/A. **Chorus roles:** None. **Dance/movement:** None. **Orchestra:** fl, ob, cl, bsn, hrn, trp, trb, timp, perc, harp, strings. **Stageband:** None. **Publisher:** Mercury Music Corporation. **Rights:** Copyright 1951 by Mercury Music Corporation.

I. Lucy Willow insists she is a queen. Philip Hall and Kit Raccoon want her to be their queen, but she refuses. The two boys fight over her and kill each other.

L'Incoronazione di Poppea • The Coronation of Poppea

Composed by Claudio Monteverdi (May 15 (baptized), 1567 – November 29, 1643). Libretto by Giovan Francesco Busenello. Italian. Based on historical incidents in the Annals of Tacitus. Premiered Venice,

Teatro Santi Giovanni e Paolo, Autum 1642. Set in Rome in the mid-1st century. Historical drama. Set numbers with recitative. Overture. Prologue.

Sets: 7. **Acts:** 3 acts, 11 scenes. **Length:** Prologue, I, II, III: 210. **Arias:** "Solitudine amata" (Seneca), "Disprezzata regina" (Ottavia), "Oblivion soave" (Arnalta), "Felice cor mio" (Drusilla). **Hazards:** None. **Scenes:** Ii. Outside Poppea's house in Rome. Iii. Inside Poppea's house. Iiii. Ottavia's apartments in the palace. Iiv. Inside Poppea's house. Iv. Outside Poppea's house. Ivi. The palace garden. IIi. Seneca's garden. IIii. Nerone's apartments in the palace. IIiii. Ottavia's apartments. IIiv. Poppea's house. III. A street. (Arrangements with different numbers of scenes exist by Malipiero, Krenek, etc. Sometimes done in two acts. Raymond Leppard edition used most frequently.)

Major roles: Ottone (baritone), Poppea (mezzo), Nerone (tenor or mezzo), Arnalta (contralto or tenor), Ottavia (mezzo), Seneca (bass), Drusilla (soprano). **Minor roles:** Fortuna (mezzo), Virtù (mezzo), Amore (soprano), First soldier (tenor), Second soldier (tenor), Valetto (soprano), Nurse (contralto), Pallade (soprano), Damigella (soprano), Mercurio (tenor), Liberto (tenor), Lucano (tenor). **Bit part:** Lictor (bass).

Chorus parts: SATTB. **Chorus roles:** Friends of Seneca, consuls, tribunes, lictors, "loves" (not in Venetian version), virtues, servants, soldiers, senators. **Dance/movement:** None. **Orchestra:** Strings (vla da braccio, vla da gamba), 2 organs, chitarrone, harpsichord. (Benevenuti version: 3 fl, 2 ob, 2 cl, 2 bsn, 4 hrn, 2 trp, 3 trb, tuba, 2 harp, strings.) **Stageband:** III: 2 bands. **Publisher:** Universal Edition, Bocca Brothers. **Rights:** Expired.

Prologue. The goddesses of Virtue and Fortune argue their importance, but both acknowledge love's preeminence. Ii. Ottone still loves Poppea, although she has left him for Emperor Nerone. Nerone and Poppea take a tender farewell. Iii. Poppea's nurse, Arnalta, reminds her that she is playing a dangerous game: The empress Ottavia knows of Nerone's infidelity. Iiii. Ottavia resents her mistreatment. Seneca consoles her and tries to dissuade Nerone from putting her aside. Iiv. Nerone promises Poppea she will be empress. Her slanders convince Nerone to order Seneca's death. Iv. Realizing Poppea wants only power, Ottone transfers his affections to Drusilla. Ivi. Valetto woos Damigella.

IIi. Seneca follows Nerone's order and kills himself. IIii. Nerone revels in Seneca's death and Poppea's beauty. IIiii. Ottavia orders Ottone to kill Poppea. Ottone confides in Drusilla and borrows her cloak as a disguise. IIiv. The god of love prevents Ottone from murdering Poppea.

IIIi. Drusilla is arrested for the attempt, but Ottone confesses. Nerone banishes him and Ottavia. Ottavia bids Rome farewell. IIIii. Arnalta looks forward to the benefits of her mistress's advancement. Poppea is crowned Empress.

L'Infedeltà Delusa • Infidelity Deluded

Composed by Franz Joseph Haydn (March 31, 1732 – May 31, 1809). Libretto by Marco Coltellini. Italian. Original work. Premiered Esterháza, Court Theater, July 26, 1773. Set in Italy in the 18th century. Burletta per musica. Set numbers with recitative. Overture. Entr'acte before II.

Sets: 3. **Acts:** 2 acts, 15 scenes. **Length:** I: 65. II: 55. **Arias:** "Che imbroglio è questo" (Sandrina), "Ho un tumore" (Vespina), "Ho tesa la rete" (Vespina), "Trinche vaine allegramente" (Vespina), "È la pompa un grand' imbroglio" (Sandrina). **Hazards:** None. **Scenes:** Ii – Iiii. The countryside in front of Filippo's house. Iiv – Iv. The living room in Vespina's and Nanni's house. Ivi – IIvii. The countryside. IIviii – IIix. A room in Filippo's house.

Major roles: Filippo (tenor), Vespina (soprano), Nencio (tenor), Nanni (bass), Sandrina (soprano).

Chorus parts: N/A. **Chorus roles:** None. **Dance/movement:** None. **Orchestra:** 2 ob, 2 bsn, 2 hrn, 2 or 4 trp, timp, cembalo, strings. **Stageband:** None. **Publisher:** Haydn Mozart Press. **Rights:** Expired.

Ii. Filippo means his daughter, Sandrina, to marry Nencio. She and Nanni are in love, but Nanni is poor. Iii. Sandrina breaks the news to Nanni. Iiii. He refuses to submit to Filippo's decision. Iiv. Nanni's sister, Vespina, loves Nencio. Iv. Nanni tells her about Nencio's engagement to Sandrina. Ivi. Sandrina confesses to Nencio that she does not love him, but he wants to marry her anyway. Vespina and Nanni overhear and beat Nencio.

IIi. Vespina decides to prevent Nencio from marrying Sandrina. IIii. She dresses as a crone and pretends to have a daughter who married and was abandoned by Nencio. IIiii. Filippo is furious. IIiv. He slams the door in Nencio's face. IIv. Vespina next convinces Nencio that Filippo has found a rich marquis to marry Sandrina. IIvi. Masquerading as the marquis, Vespina convinces Nencio to help her trick Sandrina into marrying one of her "servants." IIvii. Vespina tells Nanni her plan. IIviii. Filippo agrees to marry Sandrina to the marquis. IIix. Vespina now draws up a contract marrying Sandrina to Nanni. Filippo is tricked into signing it with Nencio as a witness. The plot is revealed.

Intermezzo

Composed by Richard Strauss (June 11, 1864 – September 8, 1949). Libretto by Richard Strauss. German. Original work possibly based on the composer's own marriage. Premiered Dresden, Shauspielhaus of Staatsoper, November 4, 1924. Set in Grundlsee and Vienna in the 1920s. Bourgeois comedy. Through composed. Orchestral interludes between scenes. Opus 72.

Sets: 12. **Acts:** 2 acts, 13 scenes. **Length:** I: 65. II: 55. **Hazards:** None. **Scenes:** Ii. Robert's dressing room. Iii. On the tobaggan run. Iiii. Grundlsee inn. Iiv. A furnished room in the house of the notary. Iv. The sitting room in the Storch home. Ivi. The baron's room in the house of the notary. Ivii. The dining room at the Storch house. Iviii. The child's bedroom. IIi. A salon in the home of the merchant. IIii. The notary's office. IIiii. In the Prater. IIiv. Christine's dressing room. IIv. The festively decorated dining room.

Major roles: Christine Storch (soprano), Robert Storch (baritone), Baron Lummer (tenor). **Minor roles:** Anna the chambermaid (soprano), Notary (baritone), Merchant (baritone), Chamber singer (bass), Judge (baritone), Conductor Stroh (tenor). **Bit parts:** Notary's wife (soprano), Young maiden Resi (soprano). Speaking bits: Little Franzl, Therese. **Mute:** Chambermaids, house maids, cooks.

Chorus parts: N/A. **Chorus roles:** None. **Dance/movement:** None. **Orchestra:** 2 fl (picc), 2 ob (Eng hrn), 2 cl (bs cl), 2 bsn, 3 hrn, 2 trp, 2 trb, piano, harp, timp, perc, harmonium, strings (11-9-5-5-3). **Stageband:** None. **Publisher:** Adolph Fürstner. **Rights:** Copyright 1924 by Adolph Fürstner.

Ii. The composer and conductor Robert Storch packs for a trip to Vienna. His wife, Christine, is glad to get him out of the house: She dislikes the unusual hours associated with his job and complains that his work is nothing compared to her care for the household and their son. They argue. Iii. Christine goes tobagganing with a friend, where she meets Baron Lummer, the son of family friends. Iiii. She and Lummer attend a dance at the inn. Iiv. Having taken an interest in Lummer, Christine helps him find a room in the notary's house. Iv. But Lummer's visit to Christine's home is awkward. Lummer asks Christine to lend him money. Ivi. Alone, he admits his dislike for Christine. Still, he is afraid to see his girlfriend for fear that it will be reported back to Christine—and he will lose any chance of a loan. Ivii. Christine remembers her love for her husband—until she opens an incriminating letter to him from a young girl, Mieze Meier. Iviii. She decides to leave Robert.

IIi. Robert's friends wonder how he can put up with Christine. While they are playing cards with Robert, Robert receives Christine's farewell letter. Robert's friend Stroh is surprised that Robert knows Mieze Meier. IIii. Christine appeals to the notary to help her divorce Robert, but the notary is cautious and suspects Christine of an affair with Lummer. IIiii. Stroh and Robert realize that the Meier letter was a mistake: It was meant for Stroh not Robert (Storch). IIiv. Stroh goes to Robert's house to explain the letter to Christine. IIv. Robert returns and after further discussion, husband and wife are reconciled.

Introductions and Goodbyes

Composed by Lukas Foss (b. August 15, 1922). Libretto by Gian Carlo Menotti. English. Original work. Premiered Spoleto, Festival of Two Worlds, June 1960. Set in a room prepared for a cocktail party in the present. Comedy. Set numbers. Can be performed as a baritone solo with other parts omitted. Concert premiere in New York, New York Philharmonic, May 6, 1960.

Sets: 1. **Acts:** 1 act, 1 scene. **Length:** I: 9. **Hazards:** None. **Scenes:** I. A room prepared for a cocktail party.

Major role: Mr. McC (baritone). **Mute:** Nine guests (can be actors, dancers or life-sized marionettes).

Chorus parts: SATB. **Chorus roles:** Offstage guests (min. 4). **Dance/movement:** None. **Orchestra:** fl, cl, bsn, hrn, trp, xylophone (perc), harp, piano, strings. **Stageband:** None. **Publisher:** Carl Fischer. **Rights:** Copyright 1961 by Carl Fischer, Inc.

I. Mr. McC greets the guests at his cocktail party and introduces them to one another before he bids them goodbye.

Iolanta

Composed by Peter Ilyitch Tchaikovsky (May 7, 1840 – November 6, 1893). Libretto by Modest Tchaikovsky. Russian. Based on "Kong Renés Datter," a drama in verse by Henrik Hertz. Premiered St. Petersburg, Maryinsky Theater, December 18, 1892. Set in Provence in the 15th century. Lyric drama. Set numbers with recitative. Introduction.

Sets: 1. **Acts:** 1 act, 4 scenes. **Length:** I: 90. **Arias:** "Why did I not know this before?" (Iolanta). **Hazards:** None. **Scenes:** I. A beautiful garden on the estates of King René.

Major roles: Iolanta (soprano), King René (bass), Duke Robert (baritone), Gottfried Vaudémont (tenor). **Minor roles:** Marta (contralto), Brigitta (soprano), Laura (mezzo), Bertrand (bass), Almerik (tenor), Ibn-Hakia (baritone).

Chorus parts: SSAATTBB. **Chorus roles:** Servants, soldiers.
Dance/movement: None. **Orchestra:** 3 fl (picc), 2 ob, Eng hrn, 2 cl, 2 bsn, 4 hrn, 2 trp, 3 trb, tuba, 2 harp, timp, strings. **Stageband:** None.
Publisher: Kalmus, Moscow State Music. **Rights:** Expired.

Ii. King René's daughter, Iolanta, has been blind from birth, but the truth has been kept from her. Her friends bring her flowers and sing her to sleep. Iii. Almerik announces the king's arrival and Bertrand warns him not to speak of light in Iolanta's presence—or to tell her that her father is the king. Iolanta is betrothed to Robert, Duke of Burgundy, who does not know of her disability. The king brings a Moorish doctor, Ibn-Hakia, who insists that Iolanta must learn of her blindness—and wish to see—before he can treat her. The king refuses. Iiii. In fleeing his marriage, Robert has stumbled into Iolanta's garden with his friend Vaudemont. They ignore the signs telling them to go away. Vaudemont falls in love with Iolanta, but Robert fears she is a sorceress and goes off to gather his troop. Iolanta picks flowers for Vaudemont, but gives him white ones when he asks for red. He realizes she is blind and explains sight to her. Iiv. They are discovered. Vaudemont swears he loves Iolanta whether she is blind or not. Her desire to see is not strong enough, so the king threatens to execute Vaudemont if the treatment is unsuccessful. After the treatment has begun, the king releases Vaudemont. Robert arrives and admits he loves another. The king releases him from his promise and gives Iolanta to Vaudemont. The treatment is successful—Iolanta can see.

Iolanthe

Composed by Arthur Sullivan (May 13, 1842 – November 22, 1900). Libretto by W. S. Gilbert. English. Original work. Premiered London, Savoy Theater, November 25, 1882. Set in England in the 19th century. Operetta. Set numbers with recitative and spoken dialogue. Overture.

Sets: 2. **Acts:** 2 acts, 2 scenes. **Length:** I: 75. II: 45. **Arias:** "When I went to the bar as a very young man" (Lord Chancellor), "When you're lying awake with a dismal headache" (Lord Chancellor). **Hazards:** I: Iolanthe rises from the stream. II: Peers sprout wings. **Scenes:** I. An Arcadian landscape. II. The palace yard of Westminster.

Major roles: Lord Chancellor (baritone), Strephon (baritone), Queen of the Fairies (contralto), Iolanthe (mezzo), Phyllis (soprano). **Minor roles:** Lord Mountararat (baritone), Lord Tolloller (tenor), Private Willis (bass), Celia (soprano), Leila (soprano).

Chorus parts: SATTBB. **Chorus roles:** Fairies, peers. **Dance/movement:** I: Fairies dance. I, II: Finales and many numbers often done with simple choreography/dancing. **Orchestra:** 2 fl, ob, 2 cl, bsn, 2 hrn, 2 trp, trb, perc, strings. **Stageband:** None. **Publisher:** G. Schirmer. **Rights:** Expired.

I. Twenty-five years ago, Iolanthe was banished from fairy land for marrying a mortal. The queen of the fairies now yields to her subjects' pleas and ends Iolanthe's banishment. The fairies are astounded to learn that Iolanthe has a 24-year-old son (Strephon). He is a shepherd and loves Phyllis, a ward in chancery. Strephon is only a fairy down to the waist— below the waist he is mortal. He has not told Phyllis this and is determined to marry her today without the Lord Chancellor's permission. The whole House of Lords is in love with Phyllis and they meet to decide who should marry her. She means to marry Strephon without delay, but the Lord Chancellor has the lovers separated. Strephon is heartbroken and his mother promises to intervene. They are seen by the peers, who question Strephon's interest in an attractive 17-year-old (Iolanthe). Strephon explains that Iolanthe is his mother but is not believed and Phyllis, in despair, agrees to marry one of the peers—any one. The queen of the fairies forces the peers to accept Strephon into Parliament.

II. The peers are disgusted with Strephon's reforms and point out that during England's greatest triumphs the House of Lords made no pretense to intellectual eminence. The fairies are attracted to the peers, but their queen reminds them of the punishment for marrying a mortal. The choice of a husband for Phyllis has come down to two earls, but she does not care which. The men discuss it and decide to forget about Phyllis rather than imperil their friendship. Strephon finally confesses to Phyllis that he is half fairy. They forgive each other. The lovers beg Iolanthe to plead for them with the Lord Chancellor. She does so reluctantly—the chancellor is her husband and Strephon's father. Iolanthe's plea falls on deaf ears—the chancellor plans to marry Phyllis himself—until Iolanthe reveals her true identity. She had promised not to do this and the fairy queen threatens Iolanthe with death. When the other fairies reveal that they, too, have taken mortal husbands, their queen is stymied. The chancellor saves the situation by amending the statute to forbid a fairy not to marry a mortal. The peers marry the fairies and all is well.

Iphigénie en Aulide • Iphigénie in Aulide

Composed by Christoph Willibald Gluck (July 2, 1714 – November 15, 1787). Libretto by Marie François Louis Grand Bailli du Roullet. French. Based on the play by Jean Baptiste Racine. Premiered Paris, Académie Royale de Musique, April 19, 1774. Set in Greece at the time of the Trojan War. Melodrama. Set numbers with recitative. Overture. Ballet. Often performed in an edition prepared by Richard Wagner.

Sets: 2. **Acts:** 3 acts, 24 scenes. **Length:** I, II, III: 130. **Arias:** "Brillant auteur de la lumière" (Agamemnon), "Au faîte des grandeurs" (Calchas), "O toi, l'objet le plus aimable" (Agamemnon), "Par un père cruel" (Clytemnestre), "Jupiter, lance la foudre" (Clytemnestre). **Hazards:** III: Appearance of the goddess Diana. **Scenes:** I – IIIvi. The Greek camp and a wood. IIIvii – IIIix. A sea shore with an altar.

Major roles: Agamemnon (baritone), Clytemnestre (mezzo), Iphigénie (soprano), Achille (tenor). **Minor roles:** Calchas (bass or bass baritone), First Greek woman (soprano), Patrocle (bass), Arcas (bass), Diane (soprano). **Bit parts:** Second Greek woman (soprano), Third greek woman (mezzo), Two Greek generals (tenor, bass), Lesbian slave girl (soprano).

Chorus parts: SATTBB. **Chorus roles:** Greeks, guards, serving women, Thessalians, Lesbian slave women. **Dance/movement:** I: Greek dances accompany Iphigénie's entry into Aulide. II: Wedding dance and ballet. III: ballet. **Orchestra:** 2 fl, 2 ob, 2 cl, 2 or 3 bsn, 2 or 4 hrn, 2 or 3 trp, 3 trb, timp, strings. **Stageband:** None. **Publisher:** Bärenreiter, Marchand. **Rights:** Expired.

Ii. Agamemnon refuses to sacrifice his daughter, Iphigénie, to propitiate the goddess Diana. Since she is coming to Aulide to marry Achille, Agamemnon sends a note that Achille has broken faith. Iii. The Greeks demand that Calchas tell them whom Diana wants sacrificed. Iiii. Calchas tries to convince Agamemnon not to prevent the sacrifice. Iiv. Iphigénie and her mother, Clytemnestre, arrive, not having gotten Agamemnon's message. All admire Iphigénie's beauty. Iv. Iphigénie waits for Achille. Ivi. Clytemnestre breaks the news of Achille's betrayal to Iphigénie. Ivii. Iphigénie is heartbroken. Iviii. But Achille undeceives her and they are reconciled.

IIi. Iphigénie is concerned at the split between Achille and her father. IIii. Her marriage to Achille is to proceed. IIiii. The Greeks and Thessalians dance in celebration of the wedding. IIiv. Arcas reveals that Agamemnon means to sacrifice Iphigénie and Clytemnestre appeals to Achille to protect her. IIv. Achille sends Patrocle to assure Iphigénie that

he will protect her, but will not murder her father. IIvi. Achille and
Agamemnon exchange angry words. IIvii. Agamemnon is torn between
love and duty.

IIIi. The Greeks demand the sacrifice. IIIii. Iphigénie agrees to submit.
IIIiii. She refuses to flee with Achille. IIIiv. Achille is still determined to
save Iphigénie. IIIv. Iphigénie takes leave of her mother. IIIvi.
Clytemnestre curses her daughter's murderers. IIIvii. The Greeks pray to
the gods to favor their war against Troy. IIIviii. Achille comes to save
Iphigénie. IIIix. The goddess Diana descends and frees Iphigénie.

Iphigénie en Tauride • Iphigénie in Tauride

Composed by Christoph Willibald Gluck (July 2, 1714 – November 15,
1787). Libretto by Nicolas-François Guillard. French. Based on the play
by Euripides. Premiered Paris, Académie Royale de Musique, May 18,
1779. Set in Scythia after the Trojan War. Melodrama. Set numbers with
recitative. Overture. Ballet. Revised by composer in a German version
(includes lament; chorus at end of II replaced by funeral march).

Sets: 3. Acts: 4 acts, 4 scenes. Length: I, II, III, IV: 110. Arias: "O toi, qui
prolongeas mes jours" (Iphigénie), "De noirs pressentiments" (Thoas),
"O malheureuse Iphigénie" (Iphigénie), "Je t'implore et je tremble"
(Iphigénie). Hazards: None. Scenes: I. A temple and altar in the sacred
wood of Diana. II. The interior of the temple. III. Iphigénie's chamber.
IV. The temple and altar.

Major roles: Iphigénie (soprano), Thoas (bass or baritone), Pylade
(tenor), Oreste (baritone). Minor roles: First priestess (soprano),
Scythian (tenor or baritone), Greek woman (soprano), Diana (soprano).
Bit parts: Second priestess (soprano), Attendant (bass).

Chorus parts: SATTB. Chorus roles: Priestesses, Scythians, Furies,
Greeks, watchmen. Dance/movement: I: Scythian ballet. II: Optional ballet. Orchestra: 3 fl (picc), 2 ob, 2 cl, 2 bsn, 2 hrn, 2 trp, 3 trb, timp, perc,
strings. Stageband: None. Publisher: Bärenreiter Kassel, Bureau du
Journal de Musique. Rights: Expired.

I. Iphigénie, the high priestess of Diana in Tauride, dreams of her dead
father and her brother, Oreste, from whom she has been separated. King
Thoas announces the capture of some Greeks. He orders the priestesses
to sacrifice them to propitiate the gods. Iphigénie resists and prays for
death.

II. It is Oreste and his friend, Pylade, whom the Scythians have captured. Oreste welcomes death, but is sorry Pylade must die too. The furies torment Oreste for having murdered his mother, Clytemnestre. Oreste and Iphigénie do not recognize each other. Oreste relates how Clytemnestre murdered her husband, Agamemnon. He reports his own death to Iphigénie. She mourns her brother.

III. Iphigénie determines to save Oreste. She gives him a letter to deliver to their sister, Electre. Pylade is happy to die that Oreste may live, but Oreste begs Iphigénie to save Pylade instead. Pylade reluctantly agrees to deliver the letter in the hope that he can save Oreste.

IV. Iphigénie prays for release. She is about to sacrifice Oreste when he mentions Iphigénie's name. The brother and sister recognize each other. Thoas has learned of Pylade's escape and is determined to kill both Oreste and Iphigénie. He is prevented by Pylade who returns with a band of Greeks. The ensuing fight is interrupted by Diana, who forgives Oreste and returns him and his sister to Greece.

Iris

Composed by Pietro Mascagni (December 7, 1863 – August 2, 1945). Libretto by Luigi Illica. Italian. Original work. Premiered Rome, Teatro Costanzi, November 22, 1898. Set in Japan in legendary times. Verismo opera. Through composed. Overture. Entr'acte before III. Revised and repremiered at Teatro alla Scala, January 19, 1899.

Sets: 3. **Acts:** 3 acts, 3 scenes. **Length:** I, II, III: 125. **Hazards:** II: Iris throws herself off a precipice. III: Flowers grow around Iris's body and lift her up towards the sun. **Scenes:** I. In front of Iris's cottage. II. The house of Kyoto in Yoshiwara. III. A space outside the city.

Major roles: Blind man (bass), Osaka/Puppet Jor (tenor), Kyoto/Father puppet (baritone), Iris (soprano). **Minor roles:** Geisha/Puppet Dhia (soprano), First rag seller (tenor), Haberdasher (tenor). **Bit parts:** Three street vendors (2 tenor, 1 bass), Second rag seller (baritone). **Dancers:** Three geishas (beauty, death, vampire).

Chorus parts: SSAATTBB. **Chorus roles:** People, strolling players, samurai, geishas, street vendors, rag sellers. **Dance/movement:** I: Three geishas dance around Iris. **Orchestra:** picc, 2 fl, 2 ob, Eng hrn, 2 cl, bs cl, 2 bsn, cont bsn, 4 hrn, 3 trp, 3 trb, bs trb or tuba, timp, perc, Japanese sàmisen, 2 harp, strings. **Stageband:** I: 4 trp, 4 trb, ob, perc. II: fl, vla, vlc, bs, harp, 2 timp, 2 tam-tam. III: 4 trp, 4 trb. **Publisher:** G. Ricordi & Co. **Rights:** Expired.

I. Iris has dreamt that her doll was sick and was attacked by fantastic monsters. Osaka plots to abduct her. A group of working girls attend the puppet show being offered by Osaka and Kyoto. In the show Dhia, a young maiden, is treated cruelly by her father and her prayers for death are answered by Jor, the son of the sun. Three geishas dance to conclude the show. They surround Iris, hiding her from the rest of the crowd so that a group of samurai can abduct her. Iris's father is heartbroken at her disappearance. He finds money and a letter saying Iris left of her own accord. Cursing her, the old man follows her.

II. Kyoto wants to use Iris as a geisha, but Osaka wants her for himself. When Iris wakes in Kyoto's house, she believes herself dead and in paradise. She recognizes Osaka's voice from the puppet show as that of the god Jor. Osaka tries to bribe Iris with jewels and palaces, but she is homesick. The young man eventually loses interest and gives Iris up to Kyoto. Iris is dressed as a geisha and displayed to the public before Osaka repents and tries to buy her back. Iris's father throws mud at his disgraced daughter. She throws herself off a precipice.

III. A group of rag pickers discover Iris's broken body. She regains consciousness and hears the voices of her tormenters. Caressed by the rays of the rising sun, Iris dies while flowers wind themselves around her body.

Irmelin

Composed by Frederick Delius (January 29, 1862 – June 10, 1934). Libretto by Frederick Delius. Original work. Premiered Oxford, New Theatre, May 4, 1953. Set in a castle and its surroundings in mythical times. Comedy. Through composed. Prelude before I. Entr'acte before II, III.

Sets: 6. **Acts:** 3 acts, 6 scenes. **Length:** I, II, III: 135. **Hazards:** II: Nils tends a group of swine. **Scenes:** I. Irmelin's room in the royal castle. IIi. A swamp in the forest. IIii. A hall in Rolf's stronghold. IIiii. In the mountains. IIIi. A hall of the royal castle. IIIii. Outside the royal castle.

Major roles: Princess Irmelin (soprano), Prince Nils (tenor), Rolf the robber (bass baritone). **Minor roles:** Voice in the air (soprano), Maid (mezzo), King (bass), Third knight (bass), Woman (soprano). **Bit parts:** First knight (baritone), Second knight (tenor), Servant (baritone).

Chorus parts: SSAATTBB. **Chorus roles:** Young men and women (offstage), robbers, dancing girls, knights, wedding guests, wood nymphs, women. **Dance/movement:** II: Rolf's dancing women perform seductive dances for Nils. **Orchestra:** 3 fl, 2 ob, Eng hrn, 2 cl, bs cl, 3 bsn, 4 hrn, 3 trp, 3 trb, tuba, timp, harp, perc, strings. **Stageband:** I, III: hrns. **Publisher:** Hawkes & Son Ltd. **Rights:** Copyright 1953 by Hawkes & Son Ltd.

I. The king has decreed that Princess Irmelin must marry within six months. Irmelin, waiting for the man of her dreams, annoys her father by rejecting three knights who offer themselves as suitors.

IIi. Prince Nils loses his way while trying to follow a silver stream and is enslaved by the robber Rolf, who makes Nils tend his pigs. IIii. Rolf and his band celebrate. Nils leaves in spite of the efforts of Rolf's dancing women to make him stay. IIiii. Nils finds the silver stream and follows it.

IIIi. Nils arrives at the palace during the wedding feast for Irmelin and the warlike knight. He introduces himself as a swineherd and plays his pipe for the guests. When the guests leave, Irmelin speaks with Nils. They fall in love and agree to meet at midnight in the garden. IIIii. Irmelin and Nils run away into the forest.

Isabeau

Composed by Pietro Mascagni (December 7, 1863 – August 2, 1945). Libretto by Luigi Illica. Italian. Inspired by the legend of Lady Godiva. Premiered Buenos Aires, Teatro Cólon, June 2, 1911. Set in Italy in the Middle Ages. Lyric drama. Set numbers with recitative.

Sets: 3. **Acts:** 3 acts, 3 scenes. **Length:** I, II, III: 120. **Hazards:** I: A wild falcon lands on Folco's arm. II: Isabeau appears on horseback clad only in a white mantle. **Scenes:** I. The rotunda of the royal palace. II. The hanging gardens of the palace. III. The lower rooms in the palace containing the prison cells and opening on a small city square.

Major roles: Messer Cornelius (bass), King Raimondo (baritone), Isabeau (soprano), Giglietta/Giglieretta (mezzo), Folco (tenor). **Minor roles:** First herald (baritone), Outlaw knight (baritone), Ermyntrude (soprano), Ermyngarde (mezzo). **Bit parts:** Old man (baritone), Distant offstage voices (2 tenor, bass). **Mute:** Arundel of Westerne, Ethelberto of Argyle, Randolfo of Dublin, Ubaldo of Gascony.

Chorus parts: SSATTBB. **Chorus roles:** Dignitaries and counselors of the throne, pages, servants, young maidens, squires, heralds, equerries, people, vassals. **Dance/movement:** None. **Orchestra:** 3 fl (picc), 2 ob, Eng hrn, 2 cl, bs cl, 2 bsn, cont bsn, 4 hrn, 3 trp, 3 trb, tuba, timp, harp, celeste, perc, glockenspiel, xylophone, strings. **Stageband:** I: band (ob, 2 cl, hrn, 2 bsn, 2 vln, vla), 6 trp, timp. II: xylophone. III: 3 cl, clavichord (or harp). **Publisher:** Edoardo Sonzogno, G. Schirmer. **Rights:** Copyright 1910 by Edoardo Sonzogno. Copyright 1917 by G. Schirmer.

I. King Raimondo's adviser, Cornelius, persuades the king to hold a tournament with his daughter, Isabeau, as the prize. Raimondo breaks the news to his daughter, who agrees, stipulating only that she be allowed to wear her white mantle until she falls in love. The peasant Giglietta goes to the palace with her grandson, Folco, to get him a position. Folco presents two doves and a falcon to Isabeau and she agrees to make him her falconer. Isabeau rejects all of the entrants to the tournament, including an outlaw knight. The outlaw knight is the king's nephew, Ethelberto, who has disowned his father for contesting the succession. Cornelius incites the king against his people. When Isabeau intervenes, the king orders her to ride naked through the city streets.

II. The people petition the king to blind and kill anyone who sees Isabeau naked. Folco is imprisoned for witnessing Isabeau's ride. III. Isabeau promises Giglietta she will save Folco. The princess visits Folco in prison and is amazed to find him asleep. She tells him to flee, but he refuses until she admits she loves him. While Isabeau tells her father of her new-found love, Cornelius delivers Folco to the crowd. Isabeau returns to die with Folco.

Isis

Composed by Jean-Baptiste Lully (November 28, 1632 – March 22, 1687). Libretto by Philippe Quinault. French. Original work based loosely on Greek mythology. Premiered Saint Germain en Laye, Académie Royale de Musique, January 5, 1677. Set in Greece in legendary times. Lyric tragedy. Set numbers with recitative. Prologue. Overture. Entr'acte before II, IV, V.

Sets: 8. **Acts:** 5 acts, 9 scenes. **Hazards:** I: Jupiter descends from the heavens. III: Argus and Hiérax struck dead by Mercure's staff. V: Io tries to drown herself. Io transformed into a goddess. **Scenes:** Prologue. The palace of Renommée. I – Iii. Agreeable plains on the river Inachus. Iiii. The gardens of Hébé. III. A lake near a forest. IVi. Frozen lands of Scythia. IVii. The forges of Chalybes. IViii. Caves. V. The Nile delta.

Major roles: Renommée (soprano), Hiérax (bass), Io (soprano), Mercure (tenor), Jupiter (bass). **Minor roles:** Two Tritons (tenor), Neptune (bass), Callyope (mezzo), Thalie (mezzo), Apollon (tenor), Pirante (soprano), Micène (tenor), Isis (soprano), Junon (soprano), Hébé (soprano), Two nymphs (soprano, mezzo), Argus (baritone), Syrinx (mezzo), Two burgers (tenor, bass), Pan (bass), Fury (soprano). **Bit parts:** Melpomène (soprano), Hunger (soprano), War (bass), Flood (soprano), Fire (bass).

Chorus parts: SSSAATTB. **Chorus roles:** Sailors, nymphs, sylphs, satyrs, Renommée's suite, burgers, furies, spirits, people, celestial divinities, Egyptians, Scythians. **Dance/movement:** Dancing possible throughout. **Orchestra:** 3 fl (recorders), 2 ob, bsns, 5 trp, timp, strings, continuo. **Stageband:** None. **Publisher:** Théodore Michaelis, Ballard. **Rights:** Expired.

Prologue. The gods, along with the muses and the arts, sing the praises of the hero Louis XIV. I. Hiérax and the nymph, Io, are in love, but Hiérax is jealous of the attentions Jupiter pays to Io. Mercure tells Io that Jupiter wants to see her.

IIi. Jealous of Io, Jupiter's wife, Junon, sends Isis to locate Io. Jupiter hides himself and Io so that Isis cannot find them. IIii. When Jupiter suggests Junon add to her entourage, Junon spitefully names Io.

III. Junon has Argus guard Io, but Jupiter sends Mercure to tell Argus a story until he falls asleep. Hiérax wakes Argus, but Mercure kills them both. Argus is revived by Junon, who sends a Fury in pursuit of Io.

IVi. Pursued by the Fury, Io suffers from cold in Scythia. IVii. And from heat in the forges of Chalybes. IViii. She longs for death.

V. Io tries to drown herself, but the Fury pulls her out of the water. The dying Io begs for mercy, which Junon grants, elevating her into the pantheon as the goddess Isis.

L'Italiana in Algeri • The Italian Girl in Algiers

Composed by Gioachino Rossini (February 29, 1792 – November 13, 1868). Libretto by Angelo Anelli. Italian. Based on Anelli's libretto for Luigi Mosca. Premiered Venice, Teatro San Benedetto, May 22, 1813. Set in Algiers in the early 19th century. Comic opera. Set numbers with recitative. Overture.

Sets: 4. **Acts:** 2 acts, 8 scenes. **Length:** I, II: 135. **Arias:** "Languir per una bella" (Lindoro), "Già d'insolito ardore nel petto agitare" (Mustafà), "Per lui che adoro" (Isabella), "Le femmine d'Italia" (Ali), "Cruda sorte" (Isabella), "Pensa alla patria" (Isabella). **Hazards:** None. **Scenes:** Ii A small hall. Iii. A seashore. Iiii. The small hall. Iiv. A magnificent hall. IIi. The small hall. IIii. A magnificent apartment. IIiii. The small hall. IIiv. The magnificent hall.

Major roles: Mustafà (bass), Elvira (soprano), Lindoro (tenor), Isabella (contralto). **Minor roles:** Zulma (mezzo), Ali (bass), Taddeo (comic bass). **Mute:** Harem women.

Chorus parts: TTBB. **Chorus roles:** Eunuchs of the harem, Algerian pirates, Italian slaves, "pappatacci," sailors. **Dance/movement:** None. **Orchestra:** 2 fl, 2 ob, 2 cl, 2 bsn, 2 hrn, 2 trp, timp, perc, strings, harpsichord. **Stageband:** None. **Publisher:** Schirmer, V. Freddi. **Rights:** Expired.

Ii. Elvira knows that her husband, Mustafà, the bey of Algiers, does not love her. Ignoring the advice of Zulma, her personal slave, she confronts the bey who orders her out of his sight. He tells Ali he plans to get rid of her for good by marrying her to his Italian slave, Lindoro. "Get me an Italian woman," he orders Ali. Lindoro languishes for his love, Isabella, and Mustafà's proposition horrifies him. Iii. Ali and his pirates have captured Isabella, but she is confident she can outwit any man. Her companion, Taddeo, is captured with her. After a brief spat, they make up and agree to pose as uncle and niece. Iiii. Elvira and Lindoro do not want to be married. Mustafà sweetens the deal by freeing Lindoro. Zulma and Lindoro are astounded that Elvira still loves the bey. Iiv. Mustafà is impressed by Isabella's beauty but is confident that he will tame this woman as he has all the rest. Isabella wins him over just in time to save Taddeo from the block. Lindoro and Elvira say goodbye before leaving for Italy. Lindoro and Isabella recognize each other and Isabella insists that the party remain.

IIi. Mustafà's court is appalled at how completely he has capitulated to Isabella. Lindoro and Isabella plot their escape. Mustafà honors Taddeo in the hopes of insinuating himself with the niece. IIii. Isabella plans to teach Elvira how to control her husband. Taddeo has been told to leave Mustafà alone with Isabella when Mustafà sneezes, but Taddeo ignores this signal. Isabella invites Elvira in and insists the bey treat her well. Mustafà is furious. IIiii. Ali concludes that Italian women are superior. Taddeo confesses to Lindoro that Isabella loves him, but Lindoro is only amused. Taddeo tells Mustafà that Isabella plans to honor him with the title of Papadummy. "The duties of the position," Taddeo explains, "are to eat, drink and go to sleep." Mustafà is delighted. IIiv. Isabella assembles the Italian slaves and briefs them on her escape plan. She and the Papadummies welcome their initiate and make him swear not to leave his seat while he is eating. Isabella embarks the Italians on board ship. Taddeo now realizes he has been duped, but he is unable to rouse Mustafà from his dinner. Too late the bey realizes what has happened. Swearing he has learned his lesson, Mustafà returns to his loving wife.

Jakobín • The Jacobin

Composed by Antonín Dvořák (September 8, 1841 – May 1, 1904). Libretto by Marie Červinková-Riegrová. Czech. Original work. Premiered Prague, National Theater, February 12, 1889. Set in a Czech village in 1793. Folk opera. Set numbers with recitative. Introduction before I, II, III. Revised 1897.

Sets: 3. **Acts:** 3 acts, 3 scenes. **Length:** I, II, III: 140. **Arias:** The Mother's Song (Julie). **Hazards:** None. **Scenes:** I. The arcaded square of a small country town. II. A room in the schoolmaster's house. III. A hall in the chateau.

Major roles: Bohuš of Harasov (baritone), Julie (soprano), Jiří the gamekeeper (tenor), Benda the schoolmaster (tenor), Terinka (soprano). **Minor roles:** Filip the burgrave (bass), Adolf Harasov (baritone), Count Vilém (bass). **Bit part:** Lotinka the keeper of the keys (contralto).

Chorus parts: SSAATTBB. **Chorus roles:** Townspeople, youths, girls, children, servants, musketeers, country folk. **Dance/movement:** I: country dances. III: ballet, minuet and polka. **Orchestra:** picc, 2 fl (2 picc), 2 ob, Eng hrn, 2 cl, bs cl, 2 bsn, cont bsn, 4 hrn, 2 trp, 3 trb, tuba, harp, timp, perc, strings. **Stageband:** I: trp. **Publisher:** Národní Hudební Vydavatelství. **Rights:** Expired.

I. Bohuš married Julie against the wishes of his father, Count Vilém, and fled abroad. The couple return disguised as artists, hoping to make peace with the count. The young people of the town dance after church. Filip, the old burgrave, loves Benda's daughter, Terinka, but she loves Jiří, the gamekeeper. The village youths tease Jiří, who publicly ridicules the burgrave. Terinka chides Jiří for his behavior and the burgrave tells Jiří he will get even. Bohuš and Julie ask to see the count. Not recognizing them, the burgrave puts them off. He tells how the count's son ran off and became a Jacobin. The count arrives, still angry with his son and plans to make his nephew Adolf his heir.

II. Benda rehearses his choir to perform for the count. Terinka assures Jiří that she loves him, but begs him to be patient. They tell Benda they will ruin the performance if he insists on Terinka marrying the burgrave. The police search for a Jacobin couple who are reported to be plotting rebellion. Bohuš and Julie ask Benda to take them in, making him suspicious, but finally winning him over. The burgrave proposes to Terinka who puts him off. He is jealous of Jiří and threatens to have him drafted, but Benda needs Jiří for the performance. He asks the burgrave to relent. Adolf promises to promote the burgrave if he arrests the Jacobin couple. Bohuš intervenes to save Jiří from the burgrave. Adolf has Bohuš arrested.

III. Adolf prevents Jiří from telling the count his son has returned. Benda and Julie enter the chateau. Benda reminds the count of his son. Gathering her courage, Julie sings the song Bohuš used to sing as a little boy. The count is intrigued. Julie proves to the count that Bohuš is no Jacobin—and tells him that Adolf has had him imprisoned. At the performance, the count amnesties the prisoner. Father and son are reconciled.

Jeanne d'Arc au Bûcher • Joan of Arc at the Stake

Composed by Arthur Honegger (March 10, 1892 – November 27, 1955). Libretto by Paul Claudel. French. Based on historical characters. Premiered Zürich, Stadttheater, June 13, 1942. Set in France in the early 15th century. Dramatic oratorio. Through composed with spoken dialogue woven into the music. Prologue with chorus. Chorus onstage constantly. Concert premiere: May 12, 1938 in Basel.

Sets: 1. **Acts:** 1 act, 11 scenes. **Length:** Prologue, I: 90. **Hazards:** Dreamlike progression of events. **Scenes:** Ii. The voices from Heaven. Iii. The book. Iiii. The voices of the Earth. Iiv. Jeanne given up to the beasts. Iv. Jeanne at the stake. Ivi. The Kings or The invention of the game of cards. Ivii. Catherine and Marguerite. Iviii. The King sets out for Rheims. Iix. The sword of Joan. Ix. Trimazo. Ixi. The burning of Jeanne d'Arc.

Major speaking roles: Jeanne d'Arc, Brother Dominique. **Minor roles:** Porcus/Voice (tenor), First herald/Clerk (tenor), Second herald/Voice/ Second peasant (bass), Marguerite (soprano), Catherine (contralto), Virgin Mary (soprano), Child's voice/Voice (soprano). **Speaking:** Usher/Second reciter/Regnault de Chartres/Guillaume de Flavy/Perrot/Priest, Third herald/First reciter/Duke of Bedford/Jean de Luxembourg/Grinder Trusty/First peasant, Mother of Barrels. **Speaking bit:** Ass.

Chorus parts: SSAATTBB. **Chorus roles:** Narrators, assessors/sheep, people, children (in 3 parts). (Soprano solo in prologue. Spoken and hummed sections; sections in Latin.) **Dance/movement:** None. **Orchestra:** 2 fl (picc), 2 ob, 2 cl, bs cl, 3 sax, 3 bsn, cont bsn, 4 trp, 3 trb, bs trb (tuba), 2 pianos, timp, 2 perc, celeste, strings. **Stageband:** None. **Publisher:** Èditions Salabert. **Rights:** Copyright 1942 by Èditions Salabert.

Prologue. The chorus introduces Jeanne d'Arc. Ii. While the chorus hums, a dog is heard barking. Iii. Brother Dominique greets Jeanne and reads to her from the book he carries. Iiii. He and the chorus revile Jeanne as a heretic who should be burned. She wonders that she, who is so pious, stands condemned by the priests. "They were neither priests nor mortal men," Dominique answers: "They were beasts." Iiv. The usher and the third herald convene the court that is to judge Jeanne. The tiger, the fox and the serpent refuse to be her judges, but Porcus volunteers. The assessors are sheep and an ass is the recorder. The sheep laugh at the ass. Porcus pronounces sentence: Jeanne will be burned at the stake. He calls on Jeanne to confess that she did not overcome the English by her own strength, and she does. When he asked if it was the devil who helped her, Jeanne denies it, but the ass writes down that she agreed. Iv. Jeanne asks Dominique what dog is howling, but Dominique says it is Yblis howling alone in the depths of hell. "You were condemned by the card game of madmen," he says.

Ivi. The heralds introduce the kings of France and England and the Duke of Burgundy—three of the kings in the card game. The fourth is death. The queens are Stupidity, Bombast, Avarice and Lasciviousness; the knaves are the Duke of Bedford, Jean de Luxembourg, Regnault de Chartres and Guillaume de Flavy. They play cards three times and Guillaume de Flavy delivers Jeanne to Bedford and Regnault. Ivii. Jeanne hears Saints Catherine and Marguerite praying as they did long ago in Domremy when Jeanne was a little girl. Iviii. The chorus celebrates the reunion of Grinder Trusty and his wife, Mother of Barrels. The clerk chides them for drinking while the King goes to Rheims for his consecration. He leads them in a Latin hymn. Iix. Jeanne recalls that it was she who led the reluctant king to his consecration. Dominique asks Jeanne about her sword. Jeanne again hears the voices of Saints Catherine and Margaret calling her a daughter of God. She exults in her hope and faith. Ix. Jeanne asks for a little prayer. Ixi. A priest tries to make Jeanne confess, but she refuses. She glories in the love of God as she is burned at the stake.

Jenůfa

Composed by Leoš Janáček (July 3, 1854 – August 12, 1928). Libretto by Leoš Janáček. Czech. Based on the play "Její pastorkyňa" by Gabriela Preissová. Premiered Brno, Brno Theater, January 21, 1904. Set in Moravia in the 19th century. Tragedy. Through composed with integral recitative. Overture. Brief entr'actes. Revised version premiered in Prague, May 26, 1916.

Sets: 2. **Acts:** 3 acts, 3 scenes. **Length:** I: 40. II: 50. III: 30. **Arias:** "In a moment" (Kostelnička), Jenůfa's prayer (Jenůfa). **Hazards:** None.
Scenes: I. Grandmother Buryja's mill. II – III. Kostelnička's front room.

Major roles: Jenůfa (soprano), Laca Klemeň (tenor), Števa Buryja (tenor), Kostelnička Buryjovka (soprano). **Minor roles:** Grandmother Starenka Buryjovka (contralto), Mill foreman Stárek (baritone), Mayor (bass), Mayor's wife (mezzo), Karolka (mezzo). **Bit parts:** Jano (soprano), Barena (soprano), Maid (mezzo), Aunt (contralto).

Chorus parts: SATTTBBB. **Chorus roles:** Recruits, servants, girls, villagers, musicians. **Dance/movement:** I: Country dances. **Orchestra:** picc, 2 fl, 2 ob, Eng hrn, 2 cl, bs cl, 2 bsn, cont bsn, 4 hrn, 2 trp, 3 trb, tuba, timp, perc, harp, strings. **Stageband:** I: hrn, 2 vln I, vln II, vla, vlc, cont bs, bells, xylophone, trps (trps played by children). **Publisher:** Universal Edition. **Rights:** Copyright 1917 by Universal Edition.

I. Jenůfa prays that her sweetheart, Števa, will not be drafted. Starenka scolds her for falling behind at her work. Jenůfa has taught Jano how to read and Starenka thinks Jenůfa should have been a teacher. Stárek, Jenůfa's grandfather, sharpens Laca's knife for him. Laca is in love with Jenůfa and hopes to prevent her marriage to Števa, but the news comes that Števa was not drafted. Jenůfa does not want to join her mother, Kostelnička, inside. Števa arrives, drunk, with the rowdy new recruits and Jenůfa reproaches him for drinking. Kostelnička says she will not permit Števa to marry Jenůfa until he has gone one year without drinking. Jenůfa begs Števa not to provoke her mother. "It is bad enough having to conceal my guilt," she reminds him. She swears she would kill herself if Števa left her, but he assures her he never will. Laca tries to steal a kiss from Jenůfa, but, when she struggles, he accidentally slashes her cheek with his knife. Stárek accuses Laca of doing it on purpose.

II. The wound has left a scar on Jenůfa's face. Her mother was horrified to learn Jenůfa was pregnant. They pretended that Jenůfa was away during her confinement, but she has now given birth to a little boy. Kostelnička thinks it would be better if the baby died. Jenůfa goes to bed. Kostelnička laments that she has to marry Jenůfa to the worthless Števa. Števa did not once ask about Jenůfa during her confinement, but Kostelnička has called him to the house to settle things. Kostelnička begs Števa to marry Jenůfa, but he admits that with her beauty ruined, he no longer loves her. He offers to support the baby if the secret is kept, but he plans to marry Karolka. When Jenůfa cries out in her sleep, Števa runs away. Laca asks Kostelnička if he can marry Jenůfa. She tells him the whole story—but says that the baby died. Kostelnička resolves to kill the baby. Jenůfa wakes. When she cannot find her mother or her baby, she gets worried. Kostelnička returns and tells Jenůfa that the baby died while she lay in a fever. She recounts her interview with Števa. Jenůfa agrees to marry Laca.

III. Pastuchyňa wonders that Jenůfa is not nervous about her wedding. The mayor and his wife arrive. Kostelnička has gone into a decline. Jenůfa is grateful that Laca stood by her when Števa did not. Laca, still feeling guilty at having slashed her cheek, admits he only made peace with Števa because Jenůfa insisted. Števa and Karolka wish the bride and bridegroom well. Kostelnička cannot bear to see Števa again. Barena and the village girls bring flowers. The mayor blesses the couple. Jano announces that a baby has been found, frozen in the ice. Stárek comforts Kostelnička, who is agitated. Jenůfa recognizes the baby as her own. Hysterical, she ignores Laca's warning that people are listening. People accuse Jenůfa of murdering the baby, but Laca defends her. Kostelnička confesses she was the murderer. Karolka is horrified and breaks off her engagement to Števa. Jenůfa comforts her mother before she is led away. Jenůfa tries to send Laca away for his own sake, but he will not go. The lovers embrace.

Jessonda

Composed by Ludwig Spohr (April 5, 1784 – October 22, 1859). Libretto by Eduard Gehe. German. Based on "La Veuve de Malabar" by Antoine-Marin Lemièrre. Premiered Kassel, Hoftheater, July 28, 1823. Set in and about Groa on the coast of Malabar in the 16th century. Grand opera. Set numbers with recitative. Overture. Introduction before II, III.

Sets: 5. **Acts:** 3 acts, 25 scenes. **Length:** I, II, III: 130. **Arias:** "Als in mitternacht'ger Stunde" (Jessonda), "Der Kriegeslust ergeben" (Tristan), "Hohe Götter!" (Jessonda). **Hazards:** III: Altar struck by lightning. **Scenes:** Ii – Iiii. The interior of a pagoda. Iiv – Iv. Jessonda's apartment. II. An open country. IIIi – IIIiii. The interior of a tent. IIIiv – IIIx. The interior of a temple.

Major roles: Nadori (tenor), Jessonda (soprano), Amazili (soprano), Tristan d'Acunha (baritone). **Minor roles:** Two bayaderes (2 soprano), Dandau (bass), Pedro Lopes (tenor). **Bit part:** Indian officer (tenor).

Chorus parts: SATTTBBB. **Chorus roles:** Brahmins, bayaderes, Portuguese, Indian and Portuguese soldiers, Indian people, Jessonda's ladies in waiting, Portuguese people, Children. **Dance/movement:** I: Funeral dance. **Orchestra:** 2 fl (picc), 2 ob, 2 cl, 2 bsn, 4 hrn, 2 trp, 3 trb, timp, perc, strings. **Stageband:** III: 2 trp, 3 trb. **Publisher:** C. F. Peters. **Rights:** Expired.

Ii. The rajah is buried. Iii. By tradition, his wife, Jessonda, must throw herself onto the funeral pyre. The chief Brahmin, Dandau, sends Nadori to tell Jessonda. Iiii. The Portuguese besieging the city receive reinforcements led by Tristan d'Accunha. Iiv. Jessonda is resigned to death. She and her sister, Amazili, remember their childhood. Jessonda is faithful to the young soldier she loved as a girl: Her marriage to the rajah was never consummated. Iv. Nadori delivers his message, but falls in love with Amazili. Amazili asks Nadori to help Jessonda escape, but Jessonda refuses to be saved.

IIi. The Portuguese warriors prepare for battle. IIii. Tristan speaks to them. IIiii. Alone, Tristan remembers the woman he loves, but lost. IIiv. Jessonda says farewell to her sister. IIv. Nadori decides to save Jessonda. IIvi. He and Amazili agree to appeal to the Portuguese commander. IIvii. Jessonda prepares herself. IIviii. Tristan sees Jessonda and realizes she is the woman he loves. IIix. Jessonda and Tristan embrace, but the priests separate them. IIx. Tristan is about to forcibly free Jessonda when the chief Brahmin reminds Tristan that they swore a truce.

IIIi. Tristan's lieutenant worries about him. IIIii. Tristan is torn between love and honor. IIIiii. But the chief Brahmin himself has broken the truce by ordering a stealth attack on the Portuguese ships. Tristan prepares his defenses. IIIiv. The Brahmins pray. IIIv. Dandau hopes to destroy the Portuguese. During his prayers, lightning strikes and destroys the image of Brahma. IIIvi. Jessonda now wants to live. IIIvii. Amazili assures her rescue is on the way. The Portuguese attack the city. IIIviii. Dandau hastens the sacrificial rite. IIIix. But the Portuguese take the town. IIIx. Tristan saves Jessonda.

La Jolie Fille de Perth • The Pretty Maid of Perth

Composed by Georges Bizet (October 25, 1838 – June 3, 1875). Libretto by Jules-Henri Vernoy de Saint-Georges and Jules Adenis. French. Based on the novel by Sir Walter Scott. Premiered Paris, Théâtre Lyrique, December 26, 1867. Set in Perth in the 16th century. Comic opera. Set numbers with recitative. Prelude. Ballet. Entr'acte before III.

Sets: 4. **Acts:** 4 acts, 5 scenes. **Length:** I: 35. II: 35. III: 30. IV: 35. **Arias:** "Elle est là" (Henri Smith). **Hazards:** None. **Scenes:** I. The workshop of Henri Smith. II. The main square of Perth. III. An elegant boudoir in the palace of the Duke of Rothsay. IVi. A picturesque spot in the mountains. IVii. The main square of Perth.

Major roles: Henri Smith (tenor), Mab (soprano), Catherine Glover (soprano), Ralph (bass baritone), Duke of Rothsay (baritone or tenor).

Minor roles: Simon Glover (bass), Workman (bass), Major domo (bass), Nobleman (tenor). **Bit parts:** Gambler.

Chorus parts: SATTBB. **Chorus roles:** Blacksmiths, citizens' patrol, masqueraders, gypsy girls, gamblers, artisans, bachelors, young girls. **Dance/movement:** II: Gypsy ballet. **Orchestra:** 2 fl (picc), 2 ob, 2 cl, 2 bsn, 4 hrn, 2 trp, 3 trb, perc, timp, harp, strings. **Stageband:** I: anvil. II: chimes. III: fl, ob, 2 trp, 3 trb, harp, perc, 2 vln. **Publisher:** Kalmus, Choudens & Son. **Rights:** Expired.

I. It is carnival and the armorer, Henri Smith, sends his workers home early. He protects Mab, the gypsy queen, from an amorous nobleman. Mab predicts that Smith will win his beloved Catherine. She hears a knock at the door and hides. Catherine, her father, Simon Glover, and the apprentice, Ralph, pay a visit. Catherine agrees to marry Smith, making Ralph jealous. The Duke of Rothsay has been following Catherine and as an excuse to flirt with her, he brings a bent dagger to Smith for repair. The duke gives Catherine an enameled rose and invites her to his palace at midnight. Mab emerges from hiding to prevent Smith from attacking the duke. She takes the rose, which Catherine has thrown away. Catherine thinks Mab is Smith's lover.

II. Masqueraders and gypsies carouse in the square with the duke. The duke asks Mab to help him persuade Catherine to come to his palace. Smith watches Catherine's window until a workman persuades him to come into the inn for a drink. Ralph sees the duke's men leave with a lady they believe to be Catherine. He warns Smith, who sets off after her. After Smith is gone, Ralph hears Catherine singing at her window.

III. The duke gambles. Mab enters, disguised as Catherine. She escapes the duke's advances, but drops the enameled rose. Glover and Catherine come to ask the duke to assist at Catherine's wedding to Smith. While returning the duke's dagger, Smith denounces Catherine and shows her the enameled rose he has discovered in the palace.

IVi. Ralph and a group of artisans assure Smith that Catherine is innocent. Smith does not believe them and challenges Ralph to a duel. IVii. Mab tells Glover that the duke has prevented the duel. But Catherine believes Smith is dead and has lost her reason. To cure her, Mab dresses as Catherine and Smith woos her. The sight restores Catherine's sanity.

Le Jongleur de Notre Dame • The Juggler of Notre Dame

Composed by Jules-Emile-Frédéric Massenet (May 12, 1842 – August 13,

1912). Libretto by Maurice Léna. French. Based on a story by Anatole France in "L'Étui de Nacre" and a medieval miracle play. Premiered Monte Carlo, Théâtre de Monte Carlo, February 18, 1902. Set in Paris in the 14th century. Miracle opera. Set numbers with recitative. Introduction. Entr'acte before each act. Mystic pastoral before III.

Sets: 3. **Acts:** 3 acts, 3 scenes. **Length:** I, II, III: 120. **Arias:** "Liberté!" (Jean), "Chanson de guerre" (Jean), "Pastourelle de Robin et Marion" (Jean). **Hazards:** III: Painting of the Virgin comes to life. Assumption of the Virgin and Jean. **Scenes:** I. The square of Cluny. II. At the abbey. III. In the chapel of the abbey.

Major roles: Jean the juggler (tenor), Prior (bass), Boniface (baritone). **Minor roles:** Prankster (baritone), Musician monk (baritone), Sculptor monk (bass), Painter monk (baritone), Poet monk (tenor). **Bit parts:** Crier monk (baritone), Knight (tenor), Drunkard (bass), Voice (baritone), Two angels (soprano, mezzo).

Chorus parts: SSAATTBBB. **Chorus roles:** Citizens and their ladies, knights, clerks, peasants, populace, monks, voices of angels, merchants (3 soprano, 3 alto, 3 tenor, 3 baritone, 2 bass), beggars, children. **Dance/movement:** I: Peasant dances. III: juggler's dance. **Orchestra:** 3 fl (picc), 3 ob (Eng hrn), 3 cl (bs cl), 3 bsn, 4 hrn, 3 trp, 3 trb, tuba, timp, perc, harps, vla d'amore, strings. **Stageband:** II: harmonium. III: celeste, piano, organ. **Publisher:** Heugel & Co. **Rights:** Expired.

I. The people heckle Jean the juggler until he promises to sing a profane drinking song. The prior is scandalized and tells Jean he will only be forgiven if he becomes a monk. Though repentant, Jean does not want to give up his freedom—until he sees Brother Boniface bringing food for the monastery.

II. Jean is well fed in the monastery, but he cannot join in the singing as he does not know Latin. The monks offer to teach Jean their respective artistic skills—and argue over which art is the best. Boniface comforts Jean with the thought that the Virgin values even the humblest devotion.

III. In the dead of night, Jean sneaks into the chapel to juggle and sing for the Virgin. He is observed by the prior and the monks. All but Boniface are horrified at the sacrilege. As they are about to apprehend Jean, the painting of the Virgin smiles and the voices of angels are heard. The Virgin ascends to heaven with Jean.

Jonny Spielt Auf • Jonny Strikes Up

Composed by Ernst Křenek (b. August 23, 1900). Libretto by Ernst
Křenek. German. Original work. Premiered Leipzig, Opera House,
February 10, 1927. Set on and around a glacier in the Alps and in Paris in
the 1920s. Satiric jazz opera. Through composed. Musical interlude
before Iiii, IIiv, IIv, IIvi. Introduction.

Sets: 7. **Acts:** 2 acts, 11 scenes. **Length:** I: 55. II: 75. **Hazards:** II: Daniello
is hit by an oncoming train. Scene in a moving car. Jonny stands on the
north pole and plays his violin. **Scenes:** Ii. A narrow rock plateau above
a glacier in the Alps. Iii. Anita's hotel room near the Alps. Iiii – Iiv.
Longitudinal section of a hotel corridor in Paris. IIi – IIii. Anita's hotel
room near the Alps. IIiii. The rock plateau and the hotel front. IIiv. A
street. IIv. Platform of a railroad terminal. IIvi. Inside a moving car. IIvii.
The terminal and inside a train.

Major roles: Composer Max (tenor), Singer Anita (soprano),
Chambermaid Yvonne (soprano), Jazz band leader Jonny (baritone),
Violin virtuoso Daniello (baritone). **Minor roles:** Manager (comic bass),
Hotel director (tenor), First policeman (tenor), Second policeman (bari-
tone), Third policeman (bass). **Bit part:** Railway official (tenor). **Mute:**
Chambermaid, Bellboy, Hotel night watchman, Police official, Two
chauffeurs, Shop girl, Railroad porter.

Chorus parts: SATB. **Chorus roles:** Daniello's fans, hotel guests, rail passengers, public. **Dance/movement:** I: Pantomime of Yvonne and Jonny
breaking up. II: The public dances to Jonny's dance music. **Orchestra:** 2
fl (picc), 2 ob, 3 cl, 2 bsn, 2 hrn, 3 trb, 3 trb, tuba, timp, perc, xylophone,
piano, glockenspiel, flexatone, strings. **Stageband:** I: hotel jazz band (trp,
2 sax, bsn, piano, banjo, perc, vln, cont bs). II: harmonium, strings (solo
vln plus 5 string parts), flexatone, piano, electric bells, hotel jazz band
(recorded). **Publisher:** Universal Edition. **Rights:** Copyright 1927 by
Universal Edition.

Ii. The opera singer, Anita, loses her way in the Alps and meets the composer, Max. Iii. They become lovers, but Anita must leave to sing in one
of Max's operas being given in Paris. She promises Max she will return.
Iiii. Jonny, who plays jazz in a Paris hotel, is having an affair with
Yvonne, one of the chambermaids. Jonny starts to seduce Anita, but is
bought off by Daniello—who has designs on Anita himself. Yvonne and
Jonny break up. While Daniello seduces Anita, Jonny steals his violin
and hides it in Anita's baggage. Iiv. Anita leaves Daniello. He realizes
his violin is missing. The hotel manager suspects Yvonne and fires her,
but Anita takes her on. Hoping to make Max suspicious, Daniello gives
Anita's ring to Yvonne and tells her to give it to Max. Jonny quits.

IIi. Max impatiently expects Anita's return. IIii. When Yvonne gives Max Anita's ring, he despairs. Jonny follows them and recovers the violin. IIiii. Max tries to fling himself off the glacier, but the voice of the glacier orders him back. Daniello takes a vacation in the Alps and hears Jonny's new band on the radio. He recognizes his stolen violin. IIiv. Pursued by the police, Jonny decides to return to New York. IIv. Max comes to the train station to see Anita off, but Jonny hides the violin in his luggage and Max is arrested for the theft. Anita sends Yvonne to tell the police the truth. Daniello tries to prevent her, but falls in front of the oncoming train. IIvi. Yvonne asks Jonny to help Max. He disguises himself as a chauffeur, picks up Max and the policemen—and helps Max escape. IIvii. Jonny and Max hurry onto the train as it is about to depart. Jonny—the incarnation of jazz—is seen playing his violin atop the north pole.

Judith

Composed by Arthur Honegger (March 10, 1892 – November 27, 1955). Libretto by René Morax. French. Based on the Biblical story. Premiered Monte Carlo, Théâtre de Monte Carlo, February 13, 1926. Set in Bethulia and Holopherne's camp in Biblical times. Musical action. Through composed. Original, shorter work premiered Mézières, June 11, 1925.

Sets: 4. **Acts:** 3 acts, 5 scenes. **Length:** I, II, III: 105. **Hazards:** None. **Scenes:** I. The ramparts of Bethulia before the house of Judith. IIi. The base of a pair of towering crags. IIii. The tent of Holopherne. IIIi. The gates of the city. IIIii. The ramparts.

Major roles: Judith (mezzo), Holopherne (baritone). **Minor roles:** Ozias (bass), Servant (soprano). **Bit parts:** Two offstage voices (soprano, tenor), Bagoas (tenor), Offstage sentinel (tenor), Soldier (tenor), Wailer (soprano).

Chorus parts: SSAATTBB. **Chorus roles:** People of Bethulia, Hebrew and Assyrian warriors, Professional wailers, Assyrian slaves, Jewish virgins. **Dance/movement:** None. **Orchestra:** 2 fl (picc), 2 ob (Eng hrn), 2 cl (bs cl), 2 bsn, 4 hrn, 2 trp, 2 trb, harmonium, 2 piano, perc, timp, strings. **Stageband:** None. **Publisher:** Editions Maurice Senart. **Rights:** Copyright 1925 by Maurice Senart.

I. The Jews of Bethulia pray for deliverance from the Assyrian army. Ozias agrees to surrender the town if help does not come in five days. Disgusted by his defeatism, Judith prays for strength. She persuades the reluctant Ozias to let her go into the Assyrian camp.

IIi. Judith doubts her strength. IIii. The Assyrian army thirsts for the fall of Bethulia. Their general, Holopherne, is drunk and calls for Judith. He is attracted to her but refuses to have mercy on her people. When he falls asleep, Judith cuts off his head with his own sword and flees the camp.

IIIi. Judith brings the severed head back to the city and the Israelites attack and defeat the disoriented Assyrians. IIIii. The people hail Judith and their God.

La Juive • The Jewess

Composed by Jacques François Fromental Elie Halévy (May 27, 1799 – March 17, 1862). Libretto by Eugène Scribe. French. Original work. Premiered Paris, Opéra, February 23, 1835. Set in the city of Constance in 1414. Melodrama. Set numbers with recitative. Overture (two versions). Entr'acte before II. Ballet.

Sets: 5. **Acts:** 5 acts, 5 scenes. **Length:** I, II, III, IV, V: 180. **Arias:** "Rachel, quand du Seigneur" (Éléazar). **Hazards:** V: Rachel thrown into boiling oil. **Scenes:** I. A square in the city of Constance. II. The interior of Eleazor's house. III. The gardens of the imperial palace. IV. A Gothic ante chamber to the council room. V. The place of execution.

Major roles: Rachel (soprano), Éléazar (tenor), Prince Léopold (tenor), Eudoxie (soprano), Gian Francesco Cardinal of Brogni (bass). **Minor roles:** Ruggiero (baritone), Albert (bass). **Bit parts:** Herald (baritone), Two drinkers (bass, tenor), Major domo (baritone), Officer (tenor), Executioner (baritone). **Mute:** Emperor Sigismund.

Chorus parts: SATTBB. **Chorus roles:** Church choir, citizens of Constance, Jews and Jewesses, nobles, priests, soldiers, magistrates. **Dance/movement:** I: Waltz. III: pantomime ballet. V: funeral march. **Orchestra:** 2 fl (picc), 2 ob (2 Eng hrn), 2 cl, 2 bsn, 4 hrn, 4 trp, 3 trb, ophicléide or tuba, 3 perc, timp, harp, organ, 2 guitar, strings. **Stageband:** I: anvils, perc. **Publisher:** G. Ricordi, Lucie Ballard. **Rights:** Expired.

I. The people of Constance celebrate Prince Leopold's victory over the Hussites. Ruggiero condemns the Jew, Éléazar, and his daughter, Rachel, for working on a Christian holiday. They are brought before Cardinal Brogni, who once banished Éléazar from Rome. Brogni pardons Éléazar, but Éléazar's anger at Brogni continues unabated. Prince Leopold has been courting Rachel disguised as Samuel, a Jew. The soldiers return home. Seeing Éléazar and Rachel in the crowd, Ruggiero orders them arrested. The soldiers recognize Leopold with them and leave them alone.

II. Éléazar's Passover feast is interrupted by Eudossia, Leopold's wife, who buys a jewel from Éléazar. Leopold is wracked with guilt. When Rachel questions him about his odd behavior, he confesses to Rachel that he is Christian. Leopold asks her to run away with him, but Éléazar discovers them and Leopold flees.

III. A play is enacted for the emperor's amusement. Rachel and Éléazar deliver the jewel to Eudossia. Rachel recognizes Leopold and denounces him. The punishment for a Christian and Jew falling in love is death. Brogni anathematizes the lovers. Éléazar is condemned with them.

IV. Eudossia begs Rachel to save Leopold by perjuring herself. Rachel tells Brogni she has a confession that will save her lover. She offers no defense for herself. Brogni begs Éléazar to save himself by renouncing his faith. Éléazar refuses, telling Brogni that the daughter Brogni believes dead was saved by a Jew—whom he will not name. Éléazar realizes his secret will save Rachel's life, but cannot bring himself to divulge it.

V. Rachel's lie saves Leopold's life. Éléazar asks Rachel if she wishes to convert and live, but she refuses. After she has been thrown into the boiling oil, he tells Brogni that Rachel was his daughter. Éléazar goes to his death.

Julius Caesar

See "Giulio Cesare" entry.

The Jumping Frog of Calaveras County

Composed by Lukas Foss (b. August 15, 1922). Libretto by Jean Karsavina. English. Based on the short story by Mark Twain. Premiered Bloomington, Indiana, University of Indiana, May 18, 1950. Set in California during the gold rush. Comedy. Set numbers. Overture.

Sets: 2. **Acts:** 1 act, 2 scenes. **Length:** I: 45. **Arias:** "Each time I hit a town" (Stranger). **Hazards:** I: Not necessary to have a physical representation of the frog. **Scenes:** Ii. Uncle Henry's bar in Calaveras. Iii. The village square.

Major roles: Uncle Henry (baritone), Smiley (tenor), Lulu (mezzo), Stranger (bass). **Minor roles:** Guitar player (baritone), First crapshooter (tenor), Second crapshooter (bass).

Chorus parts: SATB. **Chorus roles:** Townspeople (chorus is optional). **Dance/movement:** None. **Orchestra:** fl, ob, 2 cl, bsn, hrn, 2 trp, trb, tuba, perc, piano, strings. **Stageband:** None. **Publisher:** Carl Fischer. **Rights:** Copyright 1951 by Carl Fischer Inc.

Ii. Smiley shows Uncle Henry and Lulu his champion frog, Daniel Webster, which can jump fourteen feet. A stranger makes fun of Daniel and Smiley bets him forty dollars that Daniel can out jump any frog the stranger can find. When everyone leaves, the stranger stuffs Daniel's mouth full of buckshot, explaining that as soon as he has fleeced people in a town, he moves on. Lulu makes the stranger dinner. Iii. The people of the town bet their money on Daniel. The stranger's frog wins, but Smiley discovers the buckshot and the people run the stranger out of town.

Der Junge Lord • The Young Milord

Composed by Hans Werner Henze (b. July 1, 1926). Libretto by Ingeborg Bachmann. German. Based on the story "The Sheik of Alexandria and His Slaves" by Wilhelm Hauff. Premiered Berlin, Deutsche Oper, April 7, 1965. Set in the little German town of Hülsdorf-Gotha in 1830. Comic opera. Through composed. Interludes between scenes.

Sets: 4. **Acts:** 2 acts, 6 scenes. **Length:** I: 60. II: 80. **Hazards:** II: Young lord revealed as a monkey. **Scenes:** Ii. The pretty little main square of Hülsdorf-Gotha. Iii. The Baroness von Greenweasel's salon. Iiii – IIi. The main square. IIii. Reception at Sir Edgar's house. IIiii. Grand ball at the town casino.

Major roles: Luise (soprano), Wilhelm (lyric tenor), Sir Edgar's secretary (baritone), Baroness von Greenweasel (mezzo). **Minor roles:** Chief Magistrate Harethrasher (baritone), Burgomaster (bass baritone), Professor von Mucker (comic tenor), Town Comptroller Sharp (baritone), Ida (light soprano), Frau von Hoofnail (mezzo), Frau Harethrasher (high soprano), Bègonia (mezzo), Amintore La Rocca (dramatic tenor), Lord Barrat (high tenor), Lamp lighter (baritone). **Bit parts:** Two girls (girl soprano), Boy (treble), Parlor maid (soprano), Three young men (3 tenor). **Mute:** Sir Edgar, Monsieur La Truiare, Meadows the butler, Jeremy the page, Schoolmaster, Street sweeper, Two men with brushes and paint. **Dancers:** Four circus performers (including monkey).

Chorus parts: SSAATTBB. **Chorus roles:** Ladies, gentlemen, young people of good society, common people, children (in two parts). **Dance/movement:** Iiii: Circus performance. IIiii: waltz. **Orchestra:** 2 fl (picc), 2 ob, 2 cl, 2 bsn, 4 hrn, 2 trp, 2 trb, tuba, timp, 6 perc, harp, celeste, piano, guitar, 2 mandolin, strings. **Stageband:** I: 2 picc, 2 ob, 2 cl, 2 trp, 2 trb, tuba, perc, piano. II: bells, picc, cl, trp, vln, vlc, db bs, perc. **Publisher:** B. Schott's Söhne. **Rights:** Copyright 1966 by B. Schott's Söhne.

Ii. The inhabitants of Hülsdorf-Gotha await the arrival of Sir Edgar, a rich British noble who has just bought an expensive house in town. Luise confesses to her friend Ida that she and Wilhelm are in love. She does not think her aunt, the baroness, approves. Three carriages arrive filled with animals, a Creole cook, a page, a butler, Sir Edgar's secretary—and Sir Edgar himself. The secretary politely rebuffs the mayor's invitations to Sir Edgar, offending the town officials. Iii. The baroness shows off Luise to her guests and wonders where they will find a suitor worthy of her. The ladies admire Sir Edgar's reserve until he sends word that he cannot come to tea. The baroness determines to revenge the insult. Iiii. The townspeople attend the circus, where Sir Edgar's kindnesses to the children are rebuffed by their parents. He refuses to speak to the town officials. Wilhelm persuades Luise to meet him behind Sir Edgar's house. The officials vent their frustration on the circus performers, but Sir Edgar invites the performers to dinner.

IIi. Jeremy is chased across the square by a group of children. Screams coming from Sir Edgar's house frighten the lamp lighter, who runs off as Wilhelm and Luise meet to exchange sweet nothings. The lamp lighter returns with the town fathers who demand an explanation from Sir Edgar. His secretary tells them that Sir Edgar is using beatings to teach his nephew, Lord Barrat, the local language and he promises to introduce them to the young lord in two weeks. Impressed, the officials apologize. IIii. At Sir Edgar's reception, Lord Barrat charms the ladies with his eccentric ways, but Wilhelm thinks him boorish. Sir Edgar tries to distract Wilhelm by showing him his scientific collection. Luise is taken with Barrat and when Wilhelm objects, she bursts into tears. IIiii. Lord Barrat flirts with Luise. All the young men copy Lord Barrat's uncouth manners. Lord Barrat's dancing gets more and more wild until he throws Luise against the wall. He is revealed to be Adam, the monkey from the circus. Luise begs Wilhelm's forgiveness.

Káťa Kabanová

Composed by Leoš Janáček (July 3, 1854 – August 12, 1928). Libretto by Vincenc Červinka. Czech. Based on the play "The Storm" by A. N. Ostrovsky. Premiered Brno, Brno Theater, November 23, 1921. Set in Russia in the 1860s. Tragedy. Through composed. Prelude. Intermezzo before Iii and IIii.

Sets: 5. **Acts:** 3 acts, 6 scenes. **Length:** Overture: 5. I: 30. II: 30. III: 30. **Arias:** "Early one morning" (Kudrjáš). **Hazards:** III: Káťa throws herself in the river. **Scenes:** Ii. Park on the banks of the Volga. Iii. A room in the Kabanová house. IIi. A cheerful workroom. IIii. The Kabanová garden. IIIi. In front of the arches and galleries of a decaying building. IIIii. A lonely bank of the Volga.

Major roles: Marfa Ignatěvna Kabanová (Kabanicha) (contralto), Boris Grigorjevič (tenor), Tichon Ivanyč Kabanov (tenor), Katěrina (Káťa) (soprano). **Minor roles:** Savěl Prokofjevič Dikoj (bass), Váňa Kudrjáš (tenor), Varvara (mezzo), Kullgin (baritone), Gláša Fekluša (mezzo). **Bit part:** Zena (contralto). **Mute:** Drunkard.

Chorus parts: SAATTB. **Chorus roles:** Bystanders (onstage very briefly). **Dance/movement:** None. **Orchestra:** 4 fl (2 picc), 3 ob (Eng hrn), 3 cl (bs cl), 3 bsn (cont bsn), 4 hrn, 3 trp, 3 trb (bs trb), tuba, timp, perc, harp, celeste, strings, vla d'amore (can do with 2 ob and 2 cl). **Stageband:** None. **Publisher:** Universal Edition. **Rights:** Copyright 1922 by Universal Edition.

Ii. Kudrjáš and Gláša see Dikoj bullying his nephew, Boris Grigorjevič. When Kudrjáš asks Boris why he puts up with Dikoj, Boris explains that his uncle controls his and his sister's inheritance. Boris is in love with Káťa, who is married to Tichon. Tichon's mother, Kabanicha, accuses him of loving his wife more than her. She thinks Káťa is having an affair. Iii. Káťa confesses to Varvara that she loves another man, insisting, however, that she will not see him. Káťa begs Tichon not to leave—or at least to take her with him. Kabanicha insists Tichon tell Káťa how to behave in his absence, which he does.

IIi. Varvara has duplicated the key to the garden, which Kabanicha locked, and gives it to Káťa. After struggling with herself, Káťa goes out to see Boris. Dikoj visits Kabanicha. IIii. Boris finds Kudrjáš in the Kabanov garden. He has come to meet Káťa, but Kudrjáš tries to convince him such an affair is dangerous. Varvara goes off with Kudrjáš. Káťa embraces Boris but is wracked with guilt.

IIIi. Kudrjáš takes shelter from the rain with his friend Kullgin. Dikoj and others join them. Varvara tells Boris that Káťa's husband has unexpectedly returned. Káťa confesses everything to Tichon and runs off into the storm. IIIii. Kudrjáš and Varvara run away. Tichon searches for Káťa, whom he still loves. She and Boris meet on the bank of the Volga. They part and Káťa throws herself in the river. Tichon recovers the body.

Khovanshchina • The Princes Khovansky

Composed by Modest Mussorgsky (March 21, 1839 – March 28, 1881). Libretto by Vladimir Stassov and Modest Mussorgsky. Russian. Based on a historical incident during the time of Peter the Great. Premiered St. Petersburg, Kononov Theater, February 21, 1886. Set in and around Moscow from 1682 to 1689. National music drama. Set numbers with accompanied recitative. Introduction. Ballet. Completed and orchestrated by N. Rimsky-Korsakov, premiered November 7, 1911. Version by Shostakovich premiered Leningrad, November 25, 1960.

Sets: 6. **Acts:** 5 acts, 6 scenes. **Length:** I, II, III, IV, V: 230. **Hazards:** V: Chorus jumps on funeral pyre in final scene. **Scenes:** I. Red Square, Moscow. II. The summer residence of Prince Galitsin. III. The guards quarters on the outskirts of Moscow. IVi. A richly furnished dining hall in Prince Ivan Khovansky's estate. IVii. The square in front of the Church of Vassily Blajeny, Moscow. V. A hermitage in the woods.

Major roles: Prince Ivan Khovansky (bass), Prince Andrei Khovansky (tenor), Prince Vassily Galitsin (tenor), Boyar Shaklovity (baritone), Dositheus (bass), Martha (mezzo). **Minor roles:** Scrivener (tenor), Emma (soprano), Varsonofiev (bass or baritone), Streshniev (tenor), Susanna (soprano). **Bit parts:** Kouzka (baritone or tenor), Three guards/streltsy (2 bass, tenor).

Chorus parts: SSAATTTBBB. **Chorus roles:** Guards (Streltsy) and their wives, old believers, chamber maids, troopers of Peter the Great (Poteshny), Moscow populace. **Dance/movement:** IV: Ballet of Persian slaves. **Orchestra:** Rimsky-Korsakov version: 3 fl (picc), 2 ob (Eng hrn), 2 cl, 2 bsn, 4 hrn, 2 trp, 3 trb, tuba, harp, piano, timp, perc, strings. Shostakovich version: picc, 2 fl, 2 ob, Eng hrn, 2 cl bs cl, 2 bsn, cont bsn, 4 hrn, 3 trp, 3 trb, tuba, timp, perc, 2 to 4 harp, piano, celeste, strings. **Stageband:** Shostakovich version: I & IV: trps, bell. V: trps. **Publisher:** W. Bessel & Co. **Rights:** Expired.

I. Two guardsmen brag and tease old Kouzka. Shaklovity, a spy for the czar, warns the government of a coup attempt by the Khovansky brothers, Ivan and his son Andrei. The guards welcome their leader, Prince Ivan. It is our duty, Ivan explains, to protect the czar. Prince Andrei loves a young German girl, Emma, whose family he has wronged, but she spurns him. Their interview is interrupted by Martha, an old believer, who reminds Andrei of his vows to her. Andrei draws his knife on her, but Martha parries with her own. Seeing Emma, Prince Ivan orders his men to bring her to him—over his son's protests. Emma is saved by the intervention of Dositheus, head of the old believers. Dositheus wonders if the old believers will prevail.

II. Prince Galitsin reads a letter from the princess regent. He realizes he must tread carefully to maintain control of the government. Martha is Galitsin's fortune teller. When she predicts only disgrace and exile, the prince orders her drowned. Ivan objects to Galitsin's tyrannical ways. Dositheus intervenes, berating Galitsin for ignoring the old customs. Martha returns after a narrow escape from Galitsin's assassin and begs for mercy. Shaklovity brings orders for the arrest of the Khovansky princes.

III. The old believers hope their faith will triumph. Martha sings of her betrayal. The old believer Susanna hears Martha's song and denounces her love as sinful. Martha confesses to Dositheus who consoles her. Shaklovity prays for a leader who can unite and protect Russia from her enemies. The guards awake after a late night of drinking and are berated by their wives. The scrivener breathlessly announces that the czar's troopers are pillaging the city. The guards beg Prince Ivan to lead them to (civil) war that they may protect their homes, but he refuses.

IVi. The chambermaids entertain Prince Ivan with a song. Varsonofiev brings a message from Galitsin to beware: Danger is near. Ivan is unconvinced. Ivan's Persian slaves dance for him. The prince is summoned by the regent, but is stabbed before he can go. IVii. A procession of troopers leads Prince Galitsin off to exile. Dositheus reflects that Prince Andrei, too, will likely to come to grief. He receives word from Martha that the council has decreed death to the old believers. When Martha tells Andrei of his father's murder, the young prince does not believe her. He asks where Emma has gone and threatens Martha. Seeing the guards being led out for execution for treason, Ivan begs Martha to save him. The guards are reprieved by order of the czar.

V. Dositheus prays. Hearing the approach of the troopers, the old believers prepare for death. Andrei begs Martha to help him escape, but they are surrounded. To the horror of the troopers, the old believers throw themselves onto a funeral pyre.

King Priam

Composed by Michael Tippett (b. January 2, 1905). Libretto by Michael Tippett. English. Based loosely on Homer's "Iliad" and Greek mythology. Premiered Coventry, Coventry Theater, May 29, 1962. Set in Troy and Sparta during the Trojan War. Tragedy. Through composed. Prelude. Sung interludes between scenes. Nurse, Old man, Serving woman and Young guard act as a Greek chorus during the interludes.

Sets: 7. **Acts:** 3 acts, 9 scenes. **Length:** I: 45. II: 25. III: 60. **Hazards:** I: Flashbacks and quick changes of scene. **Scenes:** Ii. The royal palace in Troy. Iii. The countryside around Troy. IIi. On the walls of Troy. IIii. Achilles' tent. IIiii. On the walls of Troy. IIIi. A room in the royal palace. IIIii. Priam's chamber in the palace. IIIiii. Achilles' tent. IIIiv. Before an altar.

Major roles: King Priam (bass baritone), Hector (baritone), Paris (tenor), Helen (mezzo), Achilles (heroic tenor), Andromache (lyric dramatic soprano). **Minor roles:** Hecuba (dramatic soprano), Nurse/Greek chorus (mezzo), Old man/Greek chorus (bass), Young guard/Greek chorus (lyric tenor), First huntsman (tenor), Second huntsman (tenor), Third huntsman (baritone), Young Paris (treble), Hermes (high light tenor), Athena (soprano), Hera (soprano), Patroclus (light baritone), Serving woman/Greek chorus (mezzo). **Bit part:** Aphrodite (mezzo). **Mute:** Neoptolemus.

Chorus parts: SSAATTB. **Chorus roles:** Hunters, wedding guests, serving women. **Dance/movement:** None. **Orchestra:** 2 fl (picc), ob, Eng hrn, 2 cl, bs cl, bsn, cont bsn, 4 hrn, 4 trp, 2 trb, tuba, timp, perc, guitar, piano (celeste), harp, strings. **Stageband:** None. **Publisher:** B. Schott's Söhne. **Rights:** Copyright 1962 by Schott & Co. Ltd.

Ii. Queen Hecuba dreams that her son, Paris, will someday cause the death of her husband, King Priam. She and the king decide to kill the baby. Unknown to them, the young guard entrusted with the baby gives him to a shepherd. Iii. Priam and his son, Hector, meet Paris while hunting. Hector befriends him and brings him back to the palace. Hector marries Andromache. Paris learns he is Priam's son. He visits Menelaus and Helen in Sparta and has an affair with Helen. Hermes gives Paris a golden apple and tells him to chose the most beautiful goddess: Athene, Hera or Aphrodite. Paris choses Aphrodite because she promises he can have Helen.

IIi. Paris's abduction of Helen has precipitated the Trojan War. Hector accuses Paris of cowardice. Achilles argues with Agamemnon and withdraws from combat. IIii. With Achilles' consent, Patroclus wears

Achilles' armor into battle to terrify the Trojans. IIiii. When Hector kills Patroclus, Achilles demands revenge.

IIIi. Andromache fears for Hector, but refuses to interfere in the war. She rebukes Helen for her adultery. Achilles kills Hector. IIIii. Paris breaks the news to Priam, who accuses Paris of cowardice. IIIiii. Priam begs Achilles for Hector's body, which Achilles gives him. IIIiv. Paris tells Priam he has killed Achilles. The city falls to the Greeks. Helen speaks kindly to Priam before he is killed by Achilles' son, Neoptolemus.

Die Kluge • The Wise Woman

Composed by Carl Orff (July 10, 1895 – March 29, 1982). Libretto by Carl Orff. German. Based on a fairy tale by the brothers Grimm. Premiered Frankfurt, Opernhaus, February 20, 1943. Set in an unspecified time and place. Allegorical opera. Set numbers with spoken dialogue. Sometimes performed with marionettes.

Sets: 1 (scenes are suggested with simple pieces on a bare stage). **Acts:** 1 act, 12 scenes. **Length:** I: 80. **Hazards:** None. **Scenes:** Ii. A jail cell. Iii. Bare stage. Iiii. The king's apartments. Iiv. Bare stage. Iv. Outside the palace. Ivi. Evening outdoors. Ivii – Iviii. The marketplace. Iix. The king's apartments. Ix – Ixi. Bare stage. Ixii. Before a blossoming tree.

Major roles: Peasant (bass), King (baritone), Peasant's daughter (soprano). **Minor roles:** Jailer (bass), First tramp (tenor), Second tramp (baritone), Third tramp (bass), Muleteer (baritone), Donkey man (tenor).

Chorus parts: N/A. **Chorus roles:** None. **Dance/movement:** I: The king performs a wild dance. **Orchestra:** 3 fl (3 picc), 3 ob (Eng hrn), 3 cl (bs cl), 2 bsn, cont bsn, 4 hrn, 3 trp, 3 trb, tuba, timp, harp, celeste, piano, 4 perc, strings. **Stageband:** I: drums, bells, 3 trp, organ. **Publisher:** B. Schott's Söhne. **Rights:** Copyright 1942 by B. Schott's Söhne.

Ii. The peasant laments that he did not take his daughter's advice and throw away the golden mortar he dug up. Instead, he took it to the greedy king, who demanded the pestle—and threw the peasant in jail when he could not produce it. Iii. Three tramps complain that times are bad. Iiii. The king summons the peasant's wise daughter and offers to free her if she can answer three riddles. When she answers correctly, he proposes to her and frees her father. Iiv. The tramps discuss the king's latest wife and the mule man tells them his plan. Iv. The mule man appeals to the king for judgment. He fraudulently claims the foal that the donkey man's donkey gave birth to while in the stable with his mule. The king gives the mule man the foal. Ivi. The wise woman comes

to the donkey man in disguise and promises to help him. Ivii. Bribing
the jailer to give them the king's wine, the tramps drink and carouse.
Iviii. The donkey man pretends to fish in the marketplace, and when the
king questions him, he replies that it is no more odd to fish on dry land
than it is to expect donkeys to give birth. The king realizes the wise
woman has put him up to this and orders him thrown in jail. Iix. He tells
his wife to pack a trunk with whatever she cannot live without and
leave. The wise woman drugs the king's wine so that he falls asleep. Ix.
The tramps watch the wise woman leave the palace with a large chest.
Ixi. On the king's orders, the jailer frees the donkey man and gives him
money. Ixii. The wise woman has brought the king home in the chest.
When he awakens, their love is rekindled.

The Knot Garden

Composed by Michael Tippett (b. January 2, 1905). Libretto by Michael
Tippett. English. Original work. Premiered London, Royal Opera House,
Covent Garden, December 2, 1970. Set in a shifting maze and rose garden in an industrial city in the present. Psychological drama. Through
composed.

Sets: 4. **Acts:** 3 acts, 32 scenes. **Length:** I: 30. II: 20. III: 30. **Arias:** "I want
no pity" (Denise). **Hazards:** Constant changing of maze and garden.
Scenes: Ii. A couch in a whirling storm. Iii – Ixiii. Entrance to the garden.
IIi – IIviii. The maze and rose garden. IIix – III. The rose garden.

Major roles: Faber (robust baritone), Thea (dramatic mezzo), Flora (light
high soprano), Denise (dramatic soprano), Mel (lyric bass baritone), Dov
(lyric tenor), Mangus (high tenor baritone).

Chorus parts: N/A. **Chorus roles:** None. **Dance/movement:** IIvi: Mel
and Dov do song and dance number. **Orchestra:** 2 fl (2 picc), ob, Eng
hrn, 3 cl (2 bs cl), bsn, cont bsn, 4 hrn, 4 trp, 2 trb, tuba, timp, perc, harp,
piano, celeste, electric guitar, electric harpsichord, strings. **Stageband:**
None. **Publisher:** Schott & Co. **Rights:** Copyright 1970 by Schott & Co.

Ii. Mangus presents himself to the audience as a new Prospero. Iii. Thea
refuses Mangus's offer to help her tend her garden. Iiii. Her husband,
Faber, arrives following their shrieking adolescent ward, Flora. Iiv. Thea
rebukes Faber for making advances to Flora. Iv. Faber is unhappy in his
marriage. Ivi. He defends himself to Mangus who notes the retreat of
husband and wife into their respective work. Ivii. Thea's sister, Denise,
is coming to visit, Flora tells her. Iviii. Flora hums to herself. Iix. Her
reveries are interrupted by Dov, a musician, and Mel, a writer, dressed
as Ariel and Caliban. Ix. Thea serves them drinks and takes Mel into the

garden. Mangus and Flora go off in search of more costumes with which to enact a play. Ixi. Faber returns home to find Dov whistling like a dog. Ixii. Dov introduces himself. Ixiii. Mangus brings costumes. Denise refuses pity for the torture that has twisted her body. She wonders how she can come home again. The characters release their emotions in a blues finale.

IIi. Denise and Thea wonder what they fear. IIii. Faber notices that Denise does not shun him the way Thea does. He approaches her but she is not interested. IIiii. Faber asks Flora what she is afraid of, but she is replaced by Thea. IIiv. She whips her husband. IIv. Dov sympathizes with Faber, having himself been mistreated by Mel. Faber and Dov start to kiss. IIvi. Mel and Dov have a lovers' quarrel. IIvii. Denise calls on Mel to fight for his fellow black man. IIviii. The characters confront each other. IIix. Dov comforts Flora and they sing. The garden appears around them. Mel appears and the garden fades.

IIIi. Mangus, Thea and Denise introduce the play. IIIii. Prospero (Mangus) tames Caliban (Mel) and frees Ariel (Dov). IIIiii. Denise revels in her clarity of purpose as a freedom fighter. Thea notes that love is not so clear. IIIiv. Caliban tries to tear off Miranda's (Flora's) clothes but is prevented by Denise. IIIv. She is attracted to Mel. Mangus and Thea watch Ferdinand (Faber) playing Chess with Miranda. IIIvi. Miranda knocks over the chess board and flees. IIIvii. Mangus, Thea and Faber reset the chess board. Thea finds her marriage has been repaired. IIIviii. Prospero frees Ariel but is reluctant to free Caliban. IIIix. Mangus notes that Prospero is a fake for trying to control Caliban, the personification of lust. The players examine what binds people together. Mel leaves with Denise; Flora and Dov leave alone. Mangus disappears. IIIx. Thea and Faber's desire transcends their hatred.

Die Königin von Saba • The Queen of Sheba

Composed by Karl Goldmark (May 18, 1830 – January 2, 1915). Libretto by Salomon Hermann von Mosenthal. German. Based on a Biblical story in the First Book of Kings. Premiered Vienna, Hofoperntheater, March 10, 1875. Set in Jerusalem and environs in Biblical times. Grand opera. Set numbers with recitative. Overture. Entr'acte before II. Ballet.

Sets: 5. Acts: 4 acts, 5 scenes. Length: I, II, III, IV: 195. Hazards: IV: Sandstorm. Scenes: I. A hall in the palace of King Solomon. IIi. A garden of cedars. IIii. A temple. III. A banquet hall. IV. In the desert.

Major roles: Assad (tenor), King Solomon (baritone), Queen of Saba (mezzo). Minor roles: Baal-Hanan (baritone), High priest (bass),

Sulamith (soprano), Astaroth (soprano). **Bit part:** Voice of the temple guard (bass).

Chorus parts: SSAAAATTTTBB. **Chorus roles:** Harem women, body guards, officers, slaves, suite of the queen, populace, priests, Levites, singers, harpists. **Dance/movement:** I: Processional entrance of the queen. III: bee ballet. **Orchestra:** 3 fl (picc), 2 ob, Eng hrn, 2 cl, bs cl, 2 bsn, 4 hrn, 3 trp, 3 trb, tuba, timp, perc, harp, strings. **Stageband:** I: perc (tambourines and triangles played by women onstage). III: 6 trb, tuba, perc. **Publisher:** Schirmer, Schweers & Haake. **Rights:** Expired.

I. King Solomon is acclaimed by his people. The high priest announces the return of Assad, who is betrothed to the high priest's daughter, Sulamith. He returns bringing the heathen Queen of Sheba. Assad tells Sulamith he can no longer marry her, but will not say why. The king, realizing that Assad has fallen in love with someone else, counsels the youth to forget this new infatuation and marry Sulamith. The Queen of Sheba is received by King Solomon. When she lifts her veil, Assad recognizes her as his mistress, but the queen pretends not to know him.

Iii. The queen admits to herself that she loves Assad and means to steal him from Sulamith. On the queen's orders, Astaroth lures Assad to her. The queen again seduces Assad. Baal-Hanan finds him the next morning and sends him home. Iiii. The high priest leads the people in prayers. Sulamith prepares for her wedding to Assad. The ceremony is interrupted when Assad sees the queen, who again publicly disowns him. Assad is driven into a fury and blasphemes—only to be condemned by the priests.

III. Entertainments are given in honor of the queen. She asks Solomon to spare Assad, and when he refuses, she threatens him. Privately, the king is determined to save Assad if he repents. Sulamith begs mercy for Assad, but says she means to devote her own life to God.

IV. Assad's sentence is commuted from death to banishment. The queen pleads with Assad to take her back, but he refuses. Assad prays for Sulamith and is overtaken by a sandstorm. Sulamith finds him in time for him to die in her arms.

Königskinder • The Royal Children

Composed by Engelbert Humperdinck (September 1, 1854 – September 27, 1921). Libretto by Ernst Rosmer. German. Based on an earlier melodrama. Premiered New York City, Metropolitan Opera Association, December 28, 1910. Set in Germany in legendary times. Fairy opera.

Through composed. Overture. Entr'acte before II, III. Opera grew out of incidental music Humperdinck wrote to Rosmer's play.

Sets: 2. **Acts:** 3 acts, 3 scenes. **Length:** I: 60. II: 40. III: 60. **Hazards:** I: A star falls from the sky onto a lily, which opens wide and glows, live geese. III: Dove leads the fiddler to the royal children. **Scenes:** I. A small sunlit glade before the witch's hut in the Hella woods. II. An open place in the town of Hellabrunn. III. The glade in the woods.

Major roles: Witch (contralto), Goose girl (soprano), King's son (tenor), Fiddler (baritone). **Minor roles:** Wood cutter (bass), Broom maker (tenor), Broom maker's daughter (treble), Stable maid (contralto), Innkeeper's daughter (mezzo), Innkeeper (bass), Senior councillor (baritone). **Bit parts:** Tailor (tenor), Two gatekeepers (baritones), Woman (mezzo).

Chorus parts: SSAATTTBBBB. **Chorus roles:** Citizens, peasants, maidens, councillors and their wives, burghers and their wives, artisans, musicians, children (in 3 parts). **Dance/movement:** II: Spring dance. **Orchestra:** picc, 2 fl, 2 ob, Eng hrn, 2 cl, bs cl, 2 bsn, cont bsn, 4 hrn, 3 trp, 3 trb, tuba, timp, perc, harp, xylophone, celeste, strings. **Stageband:** I: 2 vln, vla, vlc. II: perc, piano. III: vln, perc. **Publisher:** Max Brockhaus. **Rights:** Expired.

I. The witch berates the goose girl for not working hard enough. A king's son finds the goose girl alone and they fall in love. He offers her a crown, which she refuses. The goose girl tries to run away with the king's son, but the witch's magic prevents her from leaving the forest. Thinking she has scorned him, the king's son leaves. A fiddler, a wood cutter and a broom maker consult the witch on where their town can find a king to rule over it. The witch suggests they take the first person who enters the town gate at tomorrow's holiday feast. The fiddler thinks the goose girl should be queen and the witch admits the girl had royal parents. The goose girl is magically freed from the witch's control.

II. The innkeeper's daughter feeds and flatters the king's son, but he can only think of the goose girl. She leaves, insulted. Needing money, the king's son agrees to be a swineherd. He hears—and derides—the villagers' fantastic expectations of their hoped-for king so they beat him. The goose girl presents herself at the gate—fulfilling the witch's prophesy—but the villagers chase away her and the king's son. The fiddler is thrown in jail for taking their part.

III. The villagers have burnt the witch, but the village children long for the return of the royal couple. The wood cutter and broom maker find the fiddler in the woods and ask him to return home. They take over the witch's hut. When the king's son and the goose girl return, freezing and hungry, the wood cutter rudely turns them away. The king's son buys a scrap of bread from him with the pieces of his crown. Realizing what has happened, the fiddler searches for the royal children. He finds them—with the help of a dove—but it is too late: They have frozen to death in the snow. The fiddler and the children bear the bodies home.

Krapp ou La Dernière Bande • Krapp or The Last Tape

Composed by Marcel Mihalovici (October 22, 1898 – August 12, 1985). Libretto by Samuel Beckett. French. Original work. Premiered Bielefeld, Germany, Städtische Bühnen, February 25, 1961. Set in Europe some time ago. Monodrama. Through composed with spoken lines. Use of recorded singing. Opus 81.

Sets: 1. Acts: 1 act, 1 scene. Length: I: 60. Hazards: None. Scenes: I: Krapps' lodgings.

Major role: Krapp (baritone).

Chorus parts: N/A. Chorus roles: None. Dance/movement: None. Orchestra: fl (picc), ob, 2 cl, 2 bsn, 2 hrn, 2 trp, piano (celeste), 4 perc, strings. Stageband: None. Publisher: Heugel. Rights: Copyright 1961 by Heugel and Co.

I. Krapp dictates thoughts and memories into his tape recorder. He remembers old girlfriends and the death of his mother, then decides he does not want to relive the years of his youth.

Król Roger • King Roger

Composed by Karol Szymanowski (October 6, 1882 – March 29, 1937). Libretto by Jaroslaw Iwaszkiewicz. Polish. Original work inspired by historical personage and composer's novel. Premiered Warsaw, Teatr Wielki, June 19, 1926. Set in Sicily in the 12th century. Drama. Through composed. Entr'acte before II.

Sets: 3. Acts: 3 acts, 3 scenes. Length: I: 25. II: 35. III: 20. Arias: Roxane's aria (Roxane). Hazards: III: Roger and Roxane light a sacrificial fire. Scenes: I. The interior of a Byzantine church. II. The inner courtyard of Roger's palace. III. The ruins of an ancient theater.

Major roles: King Roger (baritone), Roxane (soprano), Shepherd (tenor).

Minor roles: Archbishop (bass), Deaconess (contralto), Edrisi (tenor). **Bit parts:** Woman (soprano), Man (tenor).

Chorus parts: SSAATTBB. **Chorus roles:** People, priests, ministers, monks, nuns, courtiers, eunuchs, shepherds, royal guards, followers of Dionysus, children (in 3 parts). **Dance/movement:** II: Hypnotic Dionysian dance. **Orchestra:** 3 fl (picc), 3 ob (Eng hrn), 3 cl, bs cl, 3 bsn (cont bsn), 4 hrn, 3 trp, 3 trb, tuba, timp, perc, celeste, 2 harp, piano, organ, strings. **Stageband:** II: Four musician companions of the shepherd (trps). **Publisher:** Universal Edition. **Rights:** Copyright 1925 by Universal Edition.

I. The archbishop calls on King Roger to punish a shepherd who claims to be the Savior. The shepherd wins over Queen Roxane. Roger tells him to appear at the palace for trial.

II. Roger confesses to his Arab advisor, Edrisi, that he fears the shepherd. The shepherd appears for trial and leads everyone in a hypnotic dance. Roger has the shepherd chained up, but the shepherd breaks the restraints. The shepherd leads Roxane and the people after him, with Roger following.

III. Roger finds Roxane and together they light a sacrificial fire. The shepherd appears as Dionysus. Roger sings a hymn to the rising sun.

Ledi Markbet Mtsenskovo Uyezda • Lady Macbeth of the Mtsensk District

Composed by Dmitri Shostakovich (September 25, 1906 – August 9, 1975). Libretto by Alexander Preis and Dmitri Shostakovich. Russian. Based on a short story by Nikolai Leskov. Premiered Leningrad, Maly Opera House, January 22, 1934. Set in Russia in 1865. Tragedy. Through composed. Interlude between scenes. Some spoken lines. Revised in 1935; then revised again as "Katerina Ismailova" and premiered Moscow, December 26, 1962.

Sets: 5. **Acts:** 4 acts, 9 scenes. **Length:** I: 50. II: 50. III: 25. IV: 30. **Hazards:** IV: Katerina jumps off a bridge into the river. **Scenes:** Ii. Katerina's bedroom. Iii. The courtyard of the Ismailov house. Iiii. Katerina's bedroom. IIi. The courtyard. IIii. Katerina's bedroom. IIIi. The courtyard. IIIii. At the police station. IIIiii. The garden of the Ismailov house. IV. On the way to Siberia.

Major roles: Boris Timofeyevich Ismailov (high bass), Zinovy Borisovich Ismailov (tenor), Katerina Lvovna Ismailova (soprano), Sergei (tenor). **Minor roles:** Aksinya (soprano), A drunkard (tenor), A priest (bass), Millhand/Police inspector (baritone or bass), Sonyetka (alto), An old convict (bass), Woman convict (soprano). **Bit parts:** Steward (bass), Porter (bass), Coachman/First foreman (tenor), Second foreman (tenor), Third foreman (tenor), Teacher (tenor), Drunken guest (tenor), Police officer (bass), Sentry (bass).

Chorus parts: SSAATTTBBBB. **Chorus roles:** Servants, laborers, policemen, wedding guests, convicts, guards. **Dance/movement:** None. **Orchestra:** picc, 2 fl, 2 ob, Eng hrn, 3 cl, bs cl, 2 bsn, cont bsn, 4 hrn, 3 trp, 3 trb, tuba, timp, 2 perc, 2 harp, celeste, organ (1935 version only), strings. **Stageband:** None (stageband of 5 cornets, 2 trp, 8 sax hrns in 1932 version only). **Publisher:** Musikverlag Hans Sikorski. **Rights:** Copyright 1979 by Musikverlag Hans Sikorski. Copyright 1963 by MCA Music.

Ii. Katerina Ismailova complains that she is bored as the wife of the merchant Zinovy. Her father-in-law, Boris, blames her for not giving Zinovy a son. "You are as cold as a fish," Boris says. He warns her not to have an affair since he is watching. A mill hand reports that the dam has burst. Zinovy introduces his new worker, Sergei, to his father—and makes Katerina swear to be faithful—before returning to the mill. Aksinya the cook notes that Sergei lost his last job for seducing the master's wife. Iii. Zinovy's servants have put Aksinya in a barrel and are pinching her. She is saved by Katerina, who berates the men. Sergei challenges Katerina to wrestle him, which they do. He throws Katerina, but when Boris enters, all pretend that Katerina tripped. Iiii. Katerina goes to bed alone, wondering if she will ever have a real lover. Sergei knocks on her door. She admits him and they become lovers.

IIi. Boris prowls the courtyard at night, looking for burglars. He remembers his own youthful philandering fondly, but when he observes Sergei leaving Katerina's bedroom he orders him flogged. Katerina tries to stop Boris, but she is locked in. She climbs out the window. Boris tires himself trying to make Sergei scream and orders him locked in the storeroom overnight. Boris calls for his favorite mushrooms, which Katerina laces with rat poison. He is found by the workers, who call a priest. Boris tries to explain he has been murdered, but dies first. Katerina and the others blame it on the mushrooms. IIii. Sergei says he longs to marry Katerina. She sees the ghost of Boris, who curses her. When Zinovy returns home and accuses Katerina of adultery, she and Sergei kill him and stuff the body in the cellar.

IIIi. Sergei and Katerina are to be married. The drunkard breaks into the cellar and discovers Zinovy's rotting corpse. IIIii. The police grouse that they are paid poorly and were not invited to the Ismailov wedding. A policeman locks up a teacher who he says is a nihilist. When the drunkard reports what he has found, the police eagerly head for the Ismailov house. IIIiii. The newlyweds and their guests are drunkenly celebrating the wedding when Katerina notices that the cellar door is open. They try to make a break for it, but are caught.

IV. Convicts are being led to Siberia. It is night and they sleep. Katerina bribes a guard so that she can sleep with Sergei, but he is angry and blames her for their capture. Sergei goes to Sonyetka and they both have a laugh at Katerina's expense. He tries to seduce her, but Sonyetka demands a pair of new stockings. Sergei procures them from Katerina by pretending to have a leg wound. Katerina realizes she has been duped, but the women convicts prevent her from following Sergei and Sonyetka. Sonyetka taunts Katerina who pushes her into the river and jumps in after her. Both drown and the convicts start on their way again.

Lakmé

Composed by Léo Delibes (February 21, 1836 – January 16, 1891). Libretto by Edmond Gondinet and Philippe Gille. French. Based on the play "Rarahu ou Le Mariage de Loti" by Gondinent. Premiered Paris, Opéra Comique, April 14, 1883. Set in India in the mid-19th century.

Tragedy. Set numbers with accompanied recitative and spoken dialogue. Overture. Entr'acte before II, III. Ballet.

Sets: 3. **Acts:** 3 acts, 3 scenes. **Length:** I: 50. II: 55. III: 30. **Arias:** "Où va la jeune Hindoue?"/Bell song (Lakmé). **Hazards:** None. **Scenes:** I. A heavily shaded garden. II. A public square in a Hindu city. III. A forest glade with a bamboo cabin.

Major roles: Gérald (tenor), Nilakantha (bass), Lakmé (soprano). **Minor roles:** Frédéric (baritone or bass), Mallika (mezzo), Hadji (tenor), Ellen (soprano), Rose (soprano), Mrs. Benson (mezzo). **Bit parts:** Fortune teller (tenor), Pick pocket (baritone), Chinese merchant (tenor), Six sailors (6 bass in unison).

Chorus parts: SATTBB (briefly SATTBBB). **Chorus roles:** English officers and ladies, Hindus, Brahmins, merchants, musicians, sailors, Chinese, dervishes, dancing girls. **Dance/movement:** II: Festival ballet. **Orchestra:** 2 fl (2 picc), 2 ob (Eng hrn), 2 cl, 2 bsn, 4 hrn, 2 trp, 3 trb, tuba, timp, perc, harp, strings. **Stageband:** I: harp. II: fifes, drums. III: picc, fl (picc), ob, cl, 2 hrn, perc, drum. **Publisher:** International. **Rights:** Expired.

I. Nilakantha (a Brahmin priest) and his daughter, Lakmé, lead the Hindus in prayer. Nilakantha leaves Lakmé in the care of two servants, Hadji and Mallika. A group of curious young British trespass on the temple grounds. They leave, except for Gérald, who stays behind to sketch the temple jewels. Lakmé warns him to leave before he is captured: Death is the penalty for trespassing. Gérald and Lakmé fall in love. Nilakantha discovers a breach in the gate and plots revenge for this sacrilege.

II. Miss Benson, the governess, is rescued from the crowd of Chinese and Hindu merchants by the young people. A festival in honor of the god Dourga is in progress and Nilakantha mingles with the crowd, disguised as a beggar. Only the trespasser's death will appease the god, Nilakantha declares. To discover Gérald's identity, Nilakantha has Lakmé sing the legend of the daughter of the Pariah. When Lakmé feels faint, Gérald catches her, thus giving himself away. Nilakantha instructs his co-conspirators to fall upon Gérald. Gérald meets Lakmé secretly and she tells him of a hidden bamboo hut. Gérald is struck down by the conspirators, but Hadji and Lakmé help him escape.

III. Lakmé has healed Gérald's wounds. Frederic discovers the lovers' hiding place and reminds Gérald that the British army is on the move. He convinces Gérald to desert Lakmé. Realizing what he intends, Lakmé bites a poisoned flower. The lovers vow eternal love and drink from the sacred well. They are discovered by Nilakantha. Lakmé dies.

Das Lange Weihnachtsmahl • The Long Christmas Dinner

Composed by Paul Hindemith (November 16, 1895 – December 28, 1963). Libretto by Thornton Wilder and Paul Hindemith. English (translated into German by composer). Based on Wilder's play. Premiered Mannheim, Nationaltheater, December 17, 1961. Set in the Bayard home over the course of a ninety-year period. Tragicomedy. Through composed. Orchestral introduction.

Sets: 1. **Acts:** 1 act, 1 scene. **Length:** I: 60. **Hazards:** I: Ninety years pass continuously during the course of the opera. **Scenes:** I. The dining room of the Bayard house.

Major roles: Lucia (soprano), Mother Bayard (contralto), Roderick (baritone), Cousin Brandon (bass), Charles (tenor), Genevieve (mezzo), Leonora (high soprano), Cousin Ermengarde (contralto), Sam (high baritone), Lucia II (soprano), Roderick II (tenor). **Mute:** Nursemaid. (Lucia can double Lucia II; Mother Bayard can double Ermengarde; Roderick can double Sam.)

Chorus parts: N/A. **Chorus roles:** None. **Dance/movement:** None. **Orchestra:** 2 fl (picc), ob, cl, bs cl, 2 bsn, cont bsn, hrn, 2 trp, 2 trb, tuba, harpsichord, perc, strings (6-0-4-4-3). **Stageband:** None. **Publisher:** B. Schott's Söhne. **Rights:** Copyright 1961 by B. Schott's Söhne.

I. Lucia, Roderick, Mother Bayard and Cousin Brandon celebrate Christmas dinner in their new house. Mother Bayard remembers how her family moved out west when the town was barely more than a single church. They toast Brandon and Bayard's business venture. Lucia fusses over her and Roderick's daughter, Genevieve. The years pass from one Christmas dinner to another. Mother Bayard has died. Genevieve and her brother, Charles, are grown. Roderick dies. Charles marries Leonora and they have a child, who dies young. Lucia dies and Leonora has three children: Sam, Lucia II and Roderick II. Cousin Ermengarde comes to live with them. Charles is furious with Roderick II for getting drunk at the ball. Roderick II refuses to join the firm of Bayard and Brandon. Leonora goes to live with her children, who are building a new house. Ermengarde is left alone in the house.

Lear

Composed by Aribert Reimann (b. March 4, 1936). Libretto by Claus H. Henneberg. German. Based on "King Lear" by Shakespeare. Premiered Munich, Königliches Hof- und Nationaltheater, July 9, 1978. Set in

England in legendary times. Tragedy. Through composed. Interludes between scenes. Extensive string division.

Sets: 11. **Acts:** 2 acts, 11 scenes. **Length:** I, II: 135. **Hazards:** II: Cornwall and Regan pluck out Gloucester's eyes. **Scenes:** Ii. The palace. Iii. The palace courtyard. Iiii. A heath. Iiv. A hovel. Ili. Gloucester's castle. Iliii. Albany's palace. Iliii. The French camp near Dover. IIiv. The country. IIv. The country on the coast. IIvi. In the French camp. IIvii. English camp near Dover.

Major roles: King Lear (baritone), Goneril (dramatic soprano), Cordelia (soprano), Regan (soprano), Edmund (tenor), Earl of Gloucester (bass baritone), Edgar (tenor and countertenor). **Minor roles:** Earl of Kent (tenor), King of France (bass baritone), Duke of Cornwall (tenor), Duke of Albany (baritone). **Bit parts:** Servant (tenor). **Speaking:** Fool, Knight. **Mute:** Guard, Two soldiers.

Chorus parts: TTBB. **Chorus roles:** Lear's followers, Gloucester's men. **Dance/movement:** None. **Orchestra:** alto fl, 3 fl (3 picc, bs fl), 2 ob, Eng hrn, 2 cl, bs cl, 2 bsn, cont bsn, 6 hrn, 4 trp, 3 trb, tuba, timp, perc, 2 harp, strings (24-10-8-6). **Stageband:** None. **Publisher:** B. Schott's Söhne. **Rights:** Copyright 1978 by B. Schott's Söhne.

Ii. King Lear decides to leave his kingdom to his daughters. When his daughter Cordelia refuses to flatter him, he disowns her and divides the kingdom between his daughters Goneril and Regan. Cordelia marries the King of France. The bastard Edmund tricks his father, Gloucester, into disowning Gloucester's legitimate son, Edgar. Iii. Goneril and Regan strip Lear of his followers. Iiii. Lear wanders out into a storm with only Kent and his jester. Iiv. They take shelter with Edgar, who has lost his wits. Gloucester rescues Lear.

Ili. Goneril and Regan accuse Gloucester of treason and blind him. Regan's husband, Cornwall, is killed by a servant who attempts to protect Gloucester. Ilii. Goneril promises to promote Edmund and plots with him to kill her own husband, Albany. Albany is horrified at the sisters' violence. Iliii. The French invade. IIiv. Gloucester searches for Lear. (Note: scenes Ilii, Iliii and IIiv occur simultaneously in different parts of the stage.) IIv. Gloucester tries to kill himself, but Edgar prevents him. IIvi. Cordelia tends Lear, who has gone mad. IIvii. Edmund's army defeats the French. He captures Cordelia and Lear and orders their immediate executions. Goneril and Regan fight. Regan dies, poisoned by Goneril. Edgar challenges, and mortally wounds, Edmund. Before he dies, Edmund reveals the plot against Albany and Goneril stabs herself. Cordelia is executed and Lear dies of grief.

Skazanie o nevidimom grade Kitezhe • The Legend of the Invisible City of Kitezh and the Maiden Fevronia

Composed by Nicolai Rimsky-Korsakov (March 18, 1844 – June 21, 1908). Libretto by Vladimir Ivanovich Belsky. Russian. Writings of the chronicler of Kitezh, oral traditions about the city of Kitezh and Fevronia of Murom. Premiered St. Petersburg, Maryinsky Theater, February 7 (February 20), 1907. Set in Russia in the year 6751 since the creation of the world. Romantic/fantasy opera. Set numbers with accompanied recitative. Introduction. Interlude to IIIii and IVii.

Sets: 5. **Acts:** 4 acts, 6 scenes. **Length:** I, II, III, IV: 195. **Arias:** "A dear forest deep" (Fevronia), "All the streams and swamps are overflowing" (Fevronia), "Day and night we praise" (Fevronia), "Dearest, without joy how can we live?" (Fevronia), "From deep Yara lake" (Dulcimer player). **Hazards:** Forest creatures including birds, elk and bear. Trained bear. Tartars arrive on horseback. Disappearance of the city of Kitezh. Reflection of the city visible in the lake. Flowers grow while Fevronia sleeps. Vision of Vsevolod's ghost. Birds of paradise. Lion and unicorn guarding Kitezh. **Scenes:** I. In the Kerzhenskii woods. II. In Little Kitezh on the Volga. IIIi. In Great Kitezh. IIIii. At the lake Svetlyi Iar. IVi. In the Kerzhenskii woods. IVii. In the invisible city.

Major roles: Fevronia (soprano), Prince Vsevolod Iurievich (tenor), Grishka Kuterma (tenor), Fedor Poiarok (baritone). **Minor roles:** Prince Iurii Vsevolodovich (bass), Dulcimer player (bass), Bear trainer (tenor), The Song Leader of the beggars (baritone), Tartar warrior Bediai (bass), Tartar warrior Burundai (bass), Child Otrok (mezzo), Bird of paradise Sirin (soprano), Bird of paradise Alkonost (contralto). **Bit parts:** Two of the "best people" (tenor, bass).

Chorus parts: SSSAAAAATTBBBB. **Chorus roles:** Prince's riflemen (8 basses), travelers, domra players, "best people" (i.e., nobles), beggars, people, Tartars. **Dance/movement:** II: Optional wedding dance. **Orchestra:** 3 fl (picc), alto fl, 2 ob, Eng hrn, 2 cl, bs cl, 2 bsn, cont bsn, 4 hrn, 3 trp, 3 trb, tuba, timp, perc, 2 harp, celeste, strings. **Stageband:** I: trp. II: ten tuba, bs tuba, bells, domras, balalaikas. III: bells. IV: ten tuba, bs tuba, bells. **Publisher:** Belwin Mills. **Rights:** Expired.

I. Fevronia sings to the forest in which she grew up. She feeds the animals of the forest until the appearance of Prince Vsevolod scares them off. Fevronia greets the prince and cures the wound he received killing a bear. She lives in the woods with her brother, she tells him. He wonders at her beauty and innocence and asks if she goes to church. The church is far away, Fevronia answers, and we are in the presence of God here. Vsevolod worries that the world is just a vale of tears but Fevronia sings of happiness and forgiveness. The prince, overcome, proposes to the maid and gives her a ring. He blows his horn to summon his riflemen, then takes his leave. In searching for the prince, Poiarok discovers Fevronia and tells her that Vsevolod is prince of Kitezh.

II. In little Kitezh, crowds assemble for the wedding. A bear trainer with his bear and a gusli (dulcimer) player entertain the crowd. The "best people" give money to Grishka Kuterma, a vagabond and drunkard, but sneer at the beggars. Kuterma praises alcohol and laughs at the bride's poor clothes. The wedding party arrives and showers the crowd with biscuits, ribbons and money. The crowd spurns Kuterma but Fevronia protects him. He warns her to fly before Grief sees her happiness and takes revenge. Poiarok tells Fevronia to ignore the beggar. Instead she exhorts Kuterma to pray, but he only mocks her. The procession is interrupted by the sound of horns. A frightened crowd rushes on: The enemy is burning the marketplace. The Tartars appear, killing everyone in their path. Bediai and Burundai kidnap Fevronia. They threaten Kuterma until he agrees to lead the Tartars to the great city of Kitezh. Fevronia prays to God to make the city disappear.

IIIi. Poiarok arrives in Kitezh having been blinded by the Tartars. He recounts the destruction of little Kitezh and the capture of Fevronia. The destruction is confirmed by a young boy whom Prince Iurii has made lookout. Iurii bids everyone pray to the Virgin Mother and prepare for a hopeless fight. Vsevolod leads the men forth to battle, while behind them the city is shrouded in a miraculous obscuring mist. IIIii. The Tartars arrive in front of Kitezh, having defeated Vsevolod's forces. Since they cannot see the city in the mist, they decide to make camp and wait until morning. The Tartars begin to divide the booty by lot but Bediai and Burundai quarrel over Fevronia and Burundai kills Bediai. The camp then retires to sleep while Fevronia sighs for her wounded lover. Kuterma begs her to release him. She points out that the Tartars would only punish her but Kuterma asks her what she has to live for. He admits that he has spread rumors that it is she, not he, who betrayed Kitezh. Pitying the drunkard, Fevronia releases him. Kuterma is overcome by the sound of bells from Kitezh but when he looks for the city, it is gone. Dawn has come and the soldiers awake. They see the reflection of the city in the lake, but the city itself is not there. They flee in holy terror.

IVi. Fevronia and Kuterma crawl through the forest. Kuterma mocks the princess but she reminds him of his own sins. Kuterma runs off into the forest raving. Fevronia sleeps and awakes to find herself surrounded by new-grown flowers. Alkonost, a bird of paradise, tells Fevronia that she will soon die. The ghost of Vsevolod appears and the lovers console each other. IVii. Sirin, the bird of joy and love, and Alkonost lead the lovers into Kitezh, which has been transformed into a living paradise. Fevronia grieves that Kuterma does not share her new-found happiness. She dictates a letter to him telling of the wondrous city of Kitezh. The lovers and assembled people of Kitezh enter the cathedral.

Let's Make an Opera

See "The Little Sweep" entry.

Die Liebe der Danae • The Love of Danae

Composed by Richard Strauss (June 11, 1864 – September 8, 1949). Libretto by Josef Gregor. German. Based on a scenario by Hugo von Hofmannsthal. Premiered Salzburg, Festspielhaus, August 14, 1952. Set on the island of Eos in ancient times. Mythological drama. Through composed. Prelude before II, III. Interludes between scenes.

Sets: 8. **Acts:** 3 acts, 8 scenes. **Length:** I: 45. II: 45. III: 70. **Hazards:** II: Danae turned into a statue. She and Midas disappear. **Scenes:** Ii. The throne room of King Pollux. Iii. Danae's bedroom. Iiii. Pillared hall in the palace. Iiv. The harbor. II. A room in the palace. IIIi. A country road in the Orient. IIIii. A mountain forest. IIIiii. Midas's hut.

Major roles: Pollux (tenor), Danae (soprano), Midas (tenor), Jupiter (baritone). **Minor roles:** Xanthe (soprano), Queen Semele (soprano), Queen Europa (soprano), Queen Alkmene (mezzo), Queen Leda (contralto), Four kings (2 tenor, 2 bass), Merkur (tenor). **Bit part:** Four guards (4 bass).

Chorus parts: SSAATTBB. **Chorus roles:** Retinue and servants of Pollux and Danae, people. **Dance/movement:** None. **Orchestra:** picc, 3 fl (2 picc), 2 ob, Eng hrn, 3 cl, basset hrn, bs cl, 3 bsn, cont bsn, 6 hrn, 4 trp, 4 trb, tuba, timp, perc, 2 harp, celeste, piano, glockenspiel, strings (16-16-12-10-8). **Stageband:** None. **Publisher:** J. Oertel, Boosey & Hawkes. **Rights:** Copyright 1944 by Richard Strauss.

Ii. King Pollux fends off his creditors with the hope that the king's daughter, Danae, will soon be married to the rich King Midas. Iii. Danae dreams of riches and vows not to have a poor husband. Iiii. Midas arrives disguised as his own servant. Iiv. Recognizing him from her dream, Danae believes Jupiter to be King Midas.

II. Jupiter warns Midas that he will make him poor if he attempts to woo Danae. When Midas confesses his true identity to Danae—and demonstrates his ability to turn objects into gold with his touch—Jupiter turns Danae into a statue. He makes her choose between himself and Midas, and when Danae chooses Midas, the god makes them both disappear.

IIIi. Stranded in the desert, Danae realizes that Midas has lost his golden touch. She is touched at what he has given up for her. IIIii. Merkur warns Jupiter that the gods are laughing at his rejection. IIIiii. Jupiter again tries to woo Danae, but she is steadfast in her love for Midas.

Das Liebesverbot • The Ban on Love

Composed by Richard Wagner (May 22, 1813 – February 13, 1883). Libretto by Richard Wagner. German. Play "Measure for Measure" by Shakespeare. Premiered Magdeburg, Stadttheater, March 29, 1836. Set in Palermo in the 16th century. Comic opera. Set numbers with recitative and spoken dialogue. Overture.

Sets: 6. **Acts:** 2 acts, 6 scenes. **Length:** I, II: 145. **Hazards:** None. **Scenes:** Ii. Outside Danieli's tavern in a suburb of Palermo. Iii. Cloister garden in the convent of St. Elizabeth. Iiii. A courtroom in Palermo. IIi. The prison garden. IIii. A room in Friedrich's palace. IIiii. A carnival at the end of the corso.

Major roles: Luzio (tenor), Isabella (soprano), Friedrich (bass). **Minor roles:** Antonio (tenor), Angelo (bass), Pontio Pilato (comic tenor), Danieli (bass), Dorella (soprano), Brighella (comic bass), Claudio (tenor), Mariana (soprano). **Bit part:** Young man. **Mute:** King and his entourage.

Chorus parts: SATTB (briefly SSAA). **Chorus roles:** Citizens of Palermo, policemen, judges, country people, revelers, musicians, nuns, guards. **Dance/movement:** II: Sicilian dance. **Orchestra:** picc, 2 fl, 2 ob, 2 cl, 2 bsn, 4 hrn, 4 trp, 3 trb, ophicléide, timp, perc, strings. **Stageband:** II: 2 picc, 5 cl, 4 bsn, 4 hrn, 6 trp, 3 trb, ophicléide, perc. **Publisher:** Breitkopf & Härtel. **Rights:** Expired.

Ii. The puritanical governor, Friedrich, outlaws carnival and arrests Claudio for flirting. Claudio sends for his sister, Isabella, to plead his case. Iii. Isabella has become a nun—as has Friedrich's wife, Mariana, whom he deserted after he rose to power. Claudio's messenger Luzio falls in love with Isabella. Iiii. Claudio is condemned, but Friedrich agrees to pardon him if Isabella will sleep with him. She is unable to expose him—his reputation for virtue is well known—so she agrees to cooperate.

IIi. Isabella is angry with Claudio for suggesting she should sleep with Friedrich to save him. She also suspects Luzio's fidelity. IIii. Isabella tells Friedrich to meet her at the carnival. IIiii. She sends Mariana in her place. Instead of freeing Claudio, Friedrich sends an order for his immediate execution. But Isabella intercepts the order and exposes Friedrich's hypocrisy. Claudio is pardoned and Isabella marries Luzio.

Zhizn' za Tsarya • A Life for the Tsar

Composed by Mikhail Ivanovich Glinka (June 1, 1804 – February 15, 1857). Libretto by Baron Gyorgy Rosen. Russian. Original work. Premiered St. Petersburg, Bolshoi Theater, December 9, 1836. Set in Russia from 1612 to 1613. Epic. Set numbers with recitative. Overture. Epilogue. Entr'acte before III, IV and epilogue.

Sets: 7. **Acts:** 4 acts, 7 scenes. **Length:** I: 50. II: 30. III: 65. IV: 70. **Hazards:** I: Sobinin's boat docks onstage. **Scenes:** I. A street in the village of Domnino with a river in the background. II. A magnificent ballroom. III. In Susanin's peasant hut. IVi. A dense forest. IVii. Part of a forest near the estate of a monastery. IViii. A different part of the forest. Epilogue. Red square in Moscow.

Major roles: Antonida (soprano), Ivan Susanin (bass), Bogdan Sobinin (tenor), Vanya (mezzo). **Minor roles:** Polish captain (bass), Messenger (tenor), Russian officer (bass). **Bit part:** Russian farmer (tenor).

Chorus parts: SSSSAAAATTTTBBBBB. **Chorus roles:** Russian peasants, oarsmen, Polish ball guests and knights, Russian maidens, Russian soldiers. **Dance/movement:** II: Polonaise, waltz, mazurka. **Orchestra:** 2 fl (picc), 2 ob (Eng hrn), 2 cl, 2 bsn, 4 hrn, 2 trp, 3 trb, ophicléide, timp, perc, harp, strings. **Stageband:** II: band. Epilogue: 2 bands, bells. **Publisher:** G. Ricordi, M. P. Belaïeff. **Rights:** Expired.

I. A group of Russian peasants rejoice that their boyar, young Romanov, has returned from captivity and swears to die for Russia. Antonida awaits the return of her beloved Sobinin from the wars. Her father, Susanin, fears that the Polish king will again subdue Russia, but Sobinin reports that the Russians have held Moscow. Susanin postpones the wedding until a new tsar is elected. "Romanov is rumored as the most likely candidate," Sobinin says.

II. The Poles anticipate the subjugation of Russia under a Polish tsar. A messenger arrives and announces the Muscovite victory and the election of Romanov as tsar. A group of knights leaves to help in the wars.

III. Susanin's young ward, Vanya, is eager to do his duty for the tsar. The preparations for Antonida's wedding are spoiled by the arrival of Polish knights seeking out the young tsar. Susanin agrees to help them, intending to lead them into a bog. He sends Vanya off to warn the tsar. Antonida has a premonition that her father will not return. Sobinin leads a rescue party.

IVi. Sobinin's band cannot find Susanin. IVii. Vanya warns the tsar and his soldiers arm for battle. IViii. Susanin knows he cannot fool the Poles much longer—and that they will kill him when they figure out the truth. Dawn breaks and Susanin, realizing that the tsar is now safe, confesses. The Poles kill him just before Sobinin's men arrive. Epilogue. At the tsar's victory parade, the warriors express their sympathy for Susanin's family. All hail the tsar.

The Lighthouse

Composed by Peter Maxwell Davies (b. September 8, 1934). Libretto by Peter Maxwell Davies. English. Based on a historical incident recorded by Craig Mair. Premiered Edinburgh, Edinburgh Festival, September 2, 1980. Set in Scotland in 1900. Chamber opera. Set numbers with recitative. Prologue.

Sets: 4. **Acts:** 1 act, 2 scenes. **Length:** I: 85. **Hazards:** Prologue: Lighthouse officers are caught in a storm at sea. I: Lighthouse keepers have a vision of lights, which they take to be the Antichrist. **Scenes:** Prologue. The Edinburgh courtroom, the lighthouse commissioner's ship and the steps leading to the lighthouse. I. Inside the lighthouse.

Major roles: First officer/Sandy (tenor), Second officer/Blazes (baritone), Third officer/Arthur/Voice of the cards (bass).

Chorus parts: N/A. **Chorus roles:** None. **Dance/movement:** None. **Orchestra:** fl (picc, alto fl), cl (bs cl), hrn, trp, trb, perc, piano (celeste, out-of-tune upright piano, flexatone, referee's whistle), guitar (banjo, bs drum), vln (tam tam), vla (2 flexatone), vlc, db bs. **Stageband:** I: hrn (optional; placed in audience if used). **Publisher:** Chester Music. **Rights:** Copyright 1982 by J & W Chester Edition.

Prologue. Three lighthouse keepers have disappeared without a trace from Flada Isle lighthouse. A court convenes and hears evidence from the officers who found the lighthouse abandoned. I. The lighthouse keepers are overdue to be relieved. The storm frightens them: Blazes thinks he sees an old woman he murdered; Arthur is sure the Antichrist is coming. In self-defense, the three officers kill the crazed lighthouse keepers. They agree among themselves not to tell anyone what happened.

Linda di Chamounix • Linda of Chamounix

Composed by Gaetano Donizetti (November 29, 1797 – April 8, 1848). Libretto by Gaetano Rossi. Italian. After "La Grâce de Dieu" by Adolphe Philippe d'Ennery and Gustave Lemoine. Premiered Vienna, Kärntnerthortheater, May 19, 1842. Set in the village of Chamounix and Paris circa 1760. Opera semi-seria. Set numbers with recitative. Overture.

Sets: 3. **Acts:** 3 acts, 3 scenes. **Length:** I, II, III: 155. **Arias:** "Ambo nati" (Antonio), "O luce di quest' anima" (Linda). **Hazards:** None. **Scenes:** I. Inside a farmhouse in the village of Chamounix. II. Apartment in a fine Parisian mansion. III. Square in the village of Chamounix.

Major roles: Marquis of Boisfleury (baritone), Linda (soprano), Pierotto (mezzo), Viscount Carlo (tenor). **Minor roles:** Maddalena (mezzo), Antonio (baritone), Intendent (tenor), Prefect (bass). **Bit parts:** Five villagers (soprano), Two fathers (tenor, baritone).

Chorus parts: SATTBB. **Chorus roles:** Villagers, savoyards, young people. **Dance/movement:** None. **Orchestra:** 2 fl (picc), 2 ob, 2 cl, 2 bsn, 4 hrn, 2 trp, 4 trb, ophicléide, timp, perc, strings. **Stageband:** None. **Publisher:** G. Ricordi. **Rights:** Expired.

I. The young people of Chamounix are leaving for Paris to earn money during the winter months. Linda's parents, Maddalena and Antonio, fear losing their farm and hope the marquis will extend the lease. The marquis agrees since he wants the beautiful Linda. Pierotto, an orphan savoyard, sings a farewell ballad for the villagers. Linda loves—and is loved by—Carlo, but at his insistence, they have kept their love secret. The prefect points out to Antonio that the marquis means to seduce Linda. Antonio, outraged, sends Linda away with the young people.

II. Linda is living in Paris as a lady—at Carlo's expense. The marquis offers her a palace, but she refuses. Unbeknownst to Linda, Carlo is really a viscount—and his mother is forcing him into a more appropriate marriage. Carlo tells Linda how much he loves her, but does not reveal his secret. Not recognizing his own daughter, Antonio begs Linda to intervene on his behalf with the viscount. He is horrified to realize that Linda is a kept woman. Pierotto brings the news of Viscount Carlo's marriage. Antonio curses Linda, who loses her sanity.

III. The young people of Chamounix return to the village. The viscount has convinced his mother to let him marry Linda, but learns from the prefect of Linda's madness. Pierotto brings Linda home. The marquis promises the villagers a magnificent wedding. In Carlo's arms, Linda regains her reason.

The Little Sweep

Composed by Benjamin Britten (November 22, 1913 – December 4, 1976). Libretto by Eric Crozier. English. Original work Premiered Aldeburgh, Jubilee Hall, Aldeburgh Festival, June 14, 1949. Set in Suffolk in 1810. Children's opera. Set numbers with spoken dialogue. Four songs sung by audience. In the three act version, "Let's Make an Opera," the children spend the first two acts preparing "The Little Sweep." Acts I and II are in play form.

Sets: 1. **Acts:** 1 act, 3 scenes. **Length:** I: 45. **Hazards:** None. **Scenes:** I. The children's nursery of Iken Hall, Suffolk.

Major roles: Sam (treble, age 8), Miss Baggott (contralto), Juliet Brook (soprano, age 14). **Minor roles:** Black Bob/Tom (bass), Clem/Alfred (tenor), Gay Brook (treble, age 13), Sophie Brook (soprano, age 10), Rowan (soprano), Jonny Crome (treble, age 15), Hughie Crome (treble, age 8), Tina Crome (soprano, age 8).

Chorus parts: N/A. **Chorus roles:** None. **Dance/movement:** None. **Orchestra:** string quartet, piano (four hands), percussion. **Stageband:** None. **Publisher:** Boosey & Hawkes. **Rights:** Copyright 1950 in USA by Hawkes & Son. Copyright 1967 for all countries.

Ii. Black Bob, the sweep master, and his son, Clem, are breaking in their new sweep boy, Sam. Miss Baggott, the housekeeper, insists the chimneys be swept but Rowan, nursery maid to the twins, feels sorry for the sweep boy. Sam pulls himself up the chimney but gets stuck. He calls for help and is pulled down by the children, who help him make black sooty footprints to the window, then hide him among their toys. Discovering the tracks, the adults are fooled and run off in search of the little sweep. The children share their secret with Rowan. Iii. Sam takes a bath. He explains that he was sold to the sweeps by his parents. Having come from the same area, Rowan knows his parents. The children beg Rowan to pack Sam in with her luggage and take him home. Miss Baggott returns in a foul mood and demands that everything be cleaned up. To prevent her discovering Sam's hiding place, Juliet pretends to faint. Iiii. The next morning, Juliet brings Sam breakfast and money. Sam climbs into the trunk for the journey home, but when Tom and Alfred come to take the trunk away, they cannot lift it. The men insist the trunk be unpacked until Rowan and the children volunteer to help lift it. With their assistance, the trunk is loaded onto the coach and Sam goes home.

Lizzie Borden

Composed by Jack Beeson (b. July 15, 1921). Libretto by Kenward Elmslie. English. Based on a scenario by Richard Plant and historical events. Premiered New York City, City Center of Music and Drama, March 25, 1965. Set in Fall River, Massachusetts in the 1880s. Lyric drama. Through composed. Prelude before I, II. Epilogue.

Sets: 2. **Acts:** 3 acts, 6 scenes. **Length:** I: 35. II: 40. III: 45. **Hazards:** III: Wedding dress Lizzie wears ripped. Lizzie smashes a mirror. Blood from double murder. **Scenes:** Ii. The living room of Andrew Borden's house. Iii. Lizzie and Margret's room and garden. II. The living room. IIIi. Lizzie and Margret's room and garden. IIIii. The living room. Epilogue. The living room.

Major roles: Elizabeth Andrew Borden (mezzo), Andrew Borden (bass baritone), Abigail Borden (spinto soprano with coloratura). **Minor roles:** The Reverend Harrington (tenor), Margret Borden (lyric soprano), Captain Jason MacFarlane (lyric baritone). **Bit parts:** Two children (2 treble).

Chorus parts: Trebles or SA. **Chorus roles:** Children and young people. **Dance/movement:** None. **Orchestra:** 2 fl (picc), 2 ob, (Eng hrn), 2 cl (bs cl), 2 bsn, 2 hrn, 2 trp, 2 trb, 2 tuba (tenor, bs), timp, 2 perc, harp, harmonium, strings. **Stageband:** I: reed organ (played by Lizzie & child), fog horns. II: harmonium (played by Abbie), door bell, fog horns. III: door bell. **Rights:** Copyright 1966 by Boosey & Hawkes.

Ii. Lizzie and her sister, Margret, are treated harshly by their father, Andrew, and his new wife, Abigail. Andrew refuses to help the Reverend Harrington's church or to give Lizzie money for a new dress. Iii. Lizzie warns Margret she will lose her beau, Jason, if she keeps putting him off out of fear of her father.

II. Abigail persuades Andrew to buy her a new piano. Abigail and Lizzie argue; Andrew makes Lizzie apologize to her step-mother. Jason and the Reverend Harrington pay a call at the Borden house. Andrew thinks Jason is after his money and suggests he marry Lizzie instead of Margret.

IIIi. Andrew makes Margret promise not to see Jason. Abigail and Andrew go out to celebrate their anniversary and Jason and Margret elope. Lizzie fantasizes about marrying Jason, putting on her mother's wedding dress. Abigail and she argue. IIIii. Jason takes Margret's things. Lizzie kills Abigail and her father. Epilogue. Lizzie has been acquitted in the murders, but the townspeople shun her. She lives alone, managing her father's fortune. Harrington pays her a visit but cannot accept her donation for the church.

Lodoletta

Composed by Pietro Mascagni (December 7, 1863 – August 2, 1945). Libretto by Giovacchino Forzano. Italian. Based on a novel by Ouida. Premiered Rome, Teatro Costanzi, April 30, 1917. Set in Holland and Paris in 1853. Lyric drama. Set numbers with recitative.

Sets: 2. **Acts:** 3 acts, 3 scenes. **Length:** I, II, III: 100. **Arias:** "Flammen, perdonami" (Lodoletta), "Ah, ritrovarla" (Flammen). **Hazards:** I: Flammen arrives in a carriage. **Scenes:** I – II. In front of Lodoletta's cottage. III. A garden and boulevard outside Flammen's villa in Paris.

Major roles: Lodoletta (soprano), Flammen (tenor). **Minor roles:** Antonio (bass), Giannotto (baritone), Franz (baritone), Crazy woman (contralto), Vanard (soprano), Voice (tenor). **Bit parts:** Mailman (tenor), Child (treble), Maud (soprano).

Chorus parts: SSSAAATTTBBB. **Chorus roles:** Dutch women, villagers, neighbors, children (2 parts), Parisian friends, crowd on the boulevard, fugitives. **Dance/movement:** III: Shadows of couples dancing seen through the window. **Orchestra:** 3 fl (picc), 2 ob, Eng hrn, 3 cl, bs cl, 2 bsn, 4 hrn, 3 trp, 3 trb, tuba, timp, perc, harp, celeste, carillon, xylophone, strings. **Stageband:** I: old fiddler. **Publisher:** Casa Musicale Sonzogno. **Rights:** Expired.

I. The villagers give Lodoletta gifts on her birthday. The painter Flammen arrives. Seeing a portrait of the Madonna, Flammen persuades Lodoletta's guardian, Antonio, to rent him the painting to copy. With the money from Flammen, Antonio buys Lodoletta a pair of red shoes. Antonio falls from a peach tree and dies. Flammen meets Lodoletta and consoles her.

II. Lodoletta has been ostracized for befriending Flammen. Giannotto proposes to her—and suggests that Flammen will eventually desert her. Lodoletta sends Flammen away.

III. Flammen finds that life in Paris no longer has any attractions. He misses Lodoletta, who has disappeared from her village. Lodoletta arrives, starving and exhausted. Seeing a party in Flammen's house, she quietly dies in the garden. Flammen finds Lodoletta's body.

Lohengrin

Composed by Richard Wagner (May 22, 1813 – February 13, 1883). Libretto by Richard Wagner. German. Based on medieval legends. Premiered Weimar, Hoftheater, August 28, 1850. Set in Antwerp in the early 10th century. Romantic opera. Through composed. Overture. Introduction before III.

Sets: 3. **Acts:** 3 acts, 11 scenes. **Length:** I: 60. II: 75. III: 55. **Arias:** "Einsam in trüben Tagen"/Elsa's dream (Elsa), "In fernam Land" (Lohengrin). **Hazards:** I, III: Swan boat appears. III: Swan transformed into Gottfried. **Scenes:** I. A plain on the banks of the Scheldt. II. The citadel of Antwerp. IIIi – IIIii. The bridal chamber. IIIiii. The plain on the Scheldt.

Major roles: Lohengrin (tenor), Frederick Count Telramund (baritone), Elsa of Brabant (soprano), Heinrich I (bass), Ortrud (mezzo). **Minor roles:** Royal herald (bass or baritone). **Bit parts:** Four nobles of Brabant (2 tenors, 2 basses), Four pages (2 sopranos, 2 altos), Eight ladies (4 sopranos, 4 altos). **Mute:** Gottfried.

Chorus parts: SSAATTTTTTBBBBBB. **Chorus roles:** Saxon, Brabantian and Thuringian nobles, ladies, pages, people. **Dance/movement:** None. **Orchestra:** 3 fl (picc), 3 ob (Eng hrn), 3 cl (bs cl), 3 bsn, 4 hrn, 3 trp, 3 trb, tuba, perc, timp, harp, organ, strings. **Stageband:** I: 4 trp. II: picc, 2 fl, 3 ob, 3 cl, 2 bsn, 3 hrn, 12 trp, 3 trb, timp, perc. III: 3 fl, 2 ob, 2 cl, 2 bsn, 4 hrn, 12 trp, perc, harp. **Publisher:** Schirmer, Breitkopf & Härtel. **Rights:** Expired.

Ii. King Henry comes to Brabant to raise an army against the Hungarians. He finds the land leaderless, the heir, Gottfried, having mysteriously disappeared. Frederick accuses Gottfried's sister, Elsa, of having killed him. He has renounced Elsa and married Ortrud instead, and he now claims the duchy in his own right. Iii. The king sends for Elsa and questions her, but she is engrossed by a vision of her knight in shining armor. The question of Elsa's guilt is submitted to mortal combat. When the herald announces the challenge, Lohengrin appears in a swan boat. Iiii. Lohengrin proposes to marry Elsa if he is victorious, making her swear she will never ask his name. Lohengrin fights and defeats Frederick.

IIi. Frederick blames Ortrud for his disgrace, but she says that Lohengrin's power will end when his name is revealed. "We must therefore convince Elsa to ask him," she concludes. IIii. Ortrud begs Elsa's pardon and is forgiven. She plants doubts in Elsa's mind about Lohengrin. IIiii. The king exiles Frederick and declares Lohengrin guardian of Brabant. After his wedding, Lohengrin will lead his new subjects against the Hungarians. Frederick confesses his plans to four nobles who conceal him from the crowd. IIiv. Ortrud declares publicly that Lohengrin's strength lies in magic and demands to know his heritage. IIv. Frederick repeats the charge before the king, but Lohengrin says he answers to no one but Elsa. Frederick tells Elsa he can rob Lohengrin of his magic powers by cutting off a tiny piece of flesh. The bridal pair is led to the altar.

IIIi. The nobles escort Elsa and Lohengrin to the bridal chamber. IIIii. Elsa asks Lohengrin his name. Frederick and the four nobles burst in, but Lohengrin slays Frederick and orders the body brought before the king. IIIiii. King Henry's army gathers. Lohengrin explains how Frederick attacked him and complains that Elsa has been duped into betraying him. He reveals his name and says he is the son of Parsifal and a knight of the holy grail. This breaks the spell, Lohengrin announces, so he must now leave. The magic swan appears and is revealed to be the missing Gottfried. The young prince is turned back into himself. Lohengrin departs and Elsa falls to the ground.

I Lombardi alla Prima Crociata • The Lombards at the First Crusade

Composed by Giuseppe Verdi (October 9, 1813 – January 27, 1901). Libretto by Temistocle Solera. Italian. Based on the epic poem by Tommaso Grossi. Premiered Milan, Teatro alla Scala, February 11, 1843. Set in Milan, Antioch and Jerusalem in the late 11th century. Lyric drama. Set numbers with recitative. Prelude. Later revised and presented under the title "Jérusalem" at the Paris Opéra, November 26, 1847.

Sets: 9. **Acts:** 4 acts, 11 scenes. **Length:** I: 40. II: 35. III: 35. IV: 25. **Arias:** "Sciagurata! Hai tu creduto" (Pagano), "Salve Maria" (Giselda), "La mia letizia" (Oronte). **Hazards:** IV: large battle scenes. **Scenes:** Ii. The square of S. Ambrogio in Milan. Iii. A gallery in the Folco palace. IIi. A room in the Acciano palace in Antioch. IIii. A prominence of a hill before a cave. IIiii. The enclosure of the harem. IIIi. The valley of Josaphat. IIIii. Arvino's tent. IIIiii. The mouth of the cave. IVi. A cavern near Jerusalem. IVii. The Lombard tents near the sepulcher of Rachele. IViii. Arvino's tent.

Major roles: Pagano/Hermit (bass), Arvino (tenor), Giselda (soprano),

Oronte (tenor). **Minor roles:** Pirro (bass), Viclinda (soprano), Acciano (bass), Sofia (soprano). **Bit parts:** Prior of Milan (tenor).

Chorus parts: SSATTBB. **Chorus roles:** Citizens of Milan, monks, priors, nuns, retainers, soldiers, senators, servants, Persians, Medians, Damascan and Chaldean ambassadors, crusaders, pilgrims, Lombard ladies, harem girls, celestial virgins, people. **Dance/movement:** None. **Orchestra:** picc, fl, 2 ob, 2 cl, 2 bsn, 4 hrn, 2 trp, 3 trb, cimbasso (serpent), timp, 3 perc, 2 harp, organ, strings. **Stageband:** I, II, IV: band. **Publisher:** Kalmus. **Rights:** Expired.

Ii. Years ago, Pagano attacked his brother, Arvino, for marrying Viclinda and was exiled from Milan. Pagano has now returned, supposedly repentant, but actually looking for revenge. Arvino is made leader of the crusaders. Pagano confers with Pirro and his henchmen. Iii. They attack Arvino's household. Viclinda and her daughter, Giselda, promise to make a pilgrimage to the holy land if they survive. Pagano realizes he has killed his father, not Arvino. He is exiled again.

IIi. Acciano, the tyrant of Antioch, prays for deliverance from the crusaders. His son, Oronte, loves Giselda—who has been captured by the Moslems. IIii. Pirro seeks out a hermit to ask atonement for his part in the patricide. He is now general of Antioch and the hermit tells him to betray the city to the crusaders, promising him victory. IIiii. Giselda returns Oronte's love. To her horror, her father and the crusaders sack Antioch.

IIIi. A group of pilgrims comes to Jerusalem. Oronte returns for Giselda and they flee together. IIIii. Learning that Pagano is in the camp, Arvino decides to punish him. IIIiii. Oronte is mortally wounded. He and Giselda make their way to the hermit's cave, where the hermit baptizes Oronte before he dies.

IVi. Giselda has a vision of Oronte among the angels. He brings hope for the crusaders. IVii. Fired by Giselda's vision, the crusaders attack. IViii. The crusaders are victorious but the hermit is mortally wounded. He reveals that he is actually Pagano and dies with Arvino and Giselda's forgiveness.

Lord Byron

Composed by Virgil Thomson (November 25, 1896 – September 30, 1989). Libretto by Jack Larson. English. Original work inspired by historical character. Premiered New York City, Juilliard Theater, Lincoln

Center, April 20, 1972. Set in London from 1812 to 1824. Historical drama. Through composed. Ballet.

Sets: 5. **Acts:** 3 acts, 7 scenes. **Length:** I, II, III: 120. **Hazards:** None. **Scenes:** I – Ili. Inside Westminster Abbey, 1824. Ilii. Morning party at Lady Melbourne's, March 1812. Iliii. Victory ball at Burlington House, July 1814. Iliv. Lady Melbourne's house and Byron's club, New Year's Eve 1814. IIli. Mrs. Leigh's country house, August 1815. IIlii. The Abbey.

Major roles: John Hobhouse (bass baritone), Augusta Leigh (soprano), Lady Byron (mezzo), Lord Byron (tenor). **Minor roles:** John Murray (tenor), Thomas Moore (baritone), Gray (tenor), Thomson (tenor), Spenser (baritone), Dryden (baritone), Milton (bass), Johnson (bass), Countess Guiccioli (soprano), Count Gamba (baritone), Lady Charlotte (soprano), Lady Jane (mezzo), Lady Melbourne (soprano), John Ireland (bass), Shelley (baritone). **Bit parts:** Two English noblemen (baritones), Young lady (contralto).

Chorus parts: SSAATTBB. **Chorus roles:** People of London, Abbey choir, women. **Dance/movement:** II: Victory ball. **Orchestra:** 2 fl (picc), 2 ob (Eng hrn), 2 cl (bs cl), 2 bsn, 4 hrn, 2 trp, 3 trb, bs tuba, timp, perc, harp, organ, strings. **Stageband:** None. **Publisher:** Southern Music Publishing Co. **Rights:** Copyright 1971, 1975 by Virgil Thomson.

I. The people of London—seconded by the poets Gray, Thomson, Spenser, Dryden, Milton and Johnson—mourn the death of Lord Byron. Byron's friends Hobhouse and Moore, his publisher, Murray, his sister, Augusta Leigh, and Lady Byron agree to look out for the poet's posthumous fame. Byron's last mistress, the Countess Guiccioli, has brought a statue of Byron. Hobhouse plans to give it to John Ireland, the dean of Westminster Abbey, in the hope it will help get Byron buried in the poet's corner of the abbey. Byron's friends recall the last verses he sent each of them. Moore tells everyone that Byron left a memoir. He gave the rights to Moore—who received an advance on it from Murray. Murray tells them the memoir would damn Byron's name forever. Sailors set up the statue. Lord Byron himself appears, praising the abbey's beauty.

Ili. Moore insists they read the memoir, which he proceeds to do. Ilii. Byron attends a morning party and entertains the ladies. He is introduced to the defiant Miss Milbank (the future Lady Byron). They talk and Miss Milbank tries to rouse the poet from his bitterness. Iliii. Byron attends a ball celebrating the English victory over Napoleon, but is derisive. He flirts with his sister, Augusta. Lady Melbourne advises him to avert a scandal by getting married. Miss Milbank tries to console him. Iliv. Byron and Miss Milbank are to be married tomorrow on New

Year's Day. Miss Milbank is set on reforming the poet. Byron goes out drinking with his friends.

IIIi. Lady Byron catches Byron embracing his sister, Augusta, but still hopes to reform him. The poet calls his wife a fool but Augusta sides with her. He is bitter about his lame foot. At Lady Byron's prodding, Augusta vows never to see Byron again. IIIii. Moore has finished reading the memoir. He vows to buy back the manuscript and give it to Augusta. Hobhouse lends Moore the money. Over the countess's objections, they burn the memoir. Dean Ireland refuses Byron burial in the abbey. The poets point out that Byron's genius and fame live on.

Lord Byron's Love Letter

Composed by Raffaello De Banfield (b. June 2, 1922). Libretto by Tennessee Williams. English. Original work inspired by real occurrence. Premiered New Orleans, Dixon Hall, Tulane University, January 17, 1955. Set in New Orleans in the late 19th century. Lyric drama. Through composed. Overture.

Sets: 1. **Acts:** 1 act, 6 scenes. **Length:** I: 60. **Hazards:** None. **Scenes:** I. Parlor of a faded house in the French quarter of New Orleans.

Major roles: Old woman (dramatic soprano or mezzo), Spinster (soprano), Matron (contralto). **Minor roles:** Husband (tenor). **Bit parts:** Middle-aged woman (contralto), Young girl (soprano). **Mute:** Handsome young man (Lord Byron).

Chorus parts: N/A. **Chorus roles:** None. **Dance/movement:** None. **Orchestra:** 3 fl, 3 ob, 2 cl, 2 bsn, 4 hrn, 3 trp, 3 trb, tuba, timp, perc, celeste, harp, strings (reduced orchestration: 2 fl, ob, 2 cl, bsn, 2 hrn, 2 trp, trb, timp, perc, celeste, strings). **Stageband:** I: piano, band. **Publisher:** G. Ricordi. **Rights:** Copyright 1955 by G. Ricordi and Company.

Ii. The old woman is furious at the spinster's inept piano playing. Iii. A matron has come to see the old woman's love letter from Lord Byron, which she displays in a case in the parlor. (Byron wrote it to her grandmother.) The matron is in town with her husband for Mardi Gras. The women tell their guest about the deaths of Byron and Shelley. Iiii. The matron fetches her husband who shows little interest in a reading from the grandmother's journal. Iiv. The spinster reads the grandmother's account of meeting Byron on the Acropolis. Iv. The reading stops and the spinster displays the letter—at a safe distance. While the old woman is reciting her grandmother's sonnet to Byron, the Mardi Gras parade passes by. The husband rushes off, ignoring the old women's plea for a small donation. Ivi. The ladies put the letter away.

Loreley

Composed by Alfredo Catalani (June 19, 1854 – August 7, 1893). Libretto by Carlo d'Ormeville and Angelo Zanardini. Italian. Based on legends. Premiered Turin, Teatro Regio, January 31, 1880. Set on the banks of the Rhine circa 1300. Romantic opera. Set numbers with recitative. Prelude before I, II. Ballet. Revised version premiered Turin, February 16, 1890.

Sets: 4. **Acts:** 3 acts, 4 scenes. **Length:** I, II, III: 135. **Arias:** "Amor, celeste ebbrezza" (Anna). **Hazards:** I: Nymphs seen swimming in the Rhine. Loreley flings herself into the river and reappears transformed. II: Image of Loreley disrupts the wedding procession. III: Walter flings himself into the river. **Scenes:** Ii. A rocky landscape on the banks of the Rhine. Iii. An Alpine landscape with deep black caverns. II. A bank of the Rhine before the margrave's castle and a church. III. The beach at Oberwesel.

Major roles: Baron Hermann (baritone), Lord Walter (tenor), Loreley (dramatic soprano). **Minor roles:** Anna of Rehberg (soprano), Margrave Rudolfo (bass).

Chorus parts: SSAATTBBB. **Chorus roles:** Fishermen, foresters, archers, vassals, old women, nymphs of the Rhine, spirits of the air, children, peasants, priests, acolytes. **Dance/movement:** II: Waltz of the flowers (peasant wedding dance). III: Water nymph dance. **Orchestra:** picc, 2 fl, 2 ob, Eng hrn, 2 cl, bs cl, 2 bsn, 4 hrn, 3 trp, 3 trb, cimbasso, perc, harp, strings. **Stageband:** I: trps. II: organ, trps (trps can be 2 trp, 3 trb, 2 cornet). **Publisher:** G. Ricordi and Co. **Rights:** Expired.

Ii. Walter is engaged to Anna of Rehberg. He admits to his friend Herrmann that he loves Loreley—a maid he met on the riverbank—not Anna. Herrmann loves Anna, but counsels Walter to forget Loreley and marry Anna. Walter breaks the news to Loreley, who swoons. Herrmann decides to avenge Anna. Iii. Loreley agrees to be the Rhine king's consort if he will help her captivate Walter. The Rhine nymphs make Loreley irresistibly beautiful.

II. Anna prepares for her wedding. Herrmann warns her that Walter does not love her, but she does not believe him. Loreley interrupts the wedding. Seeing her, Walter rejects Anna.

III. Anna dies of grief. Loreley appears to Walter and forgives him, but she is married to the Rhine king. Walter drowns himself.

Louise

Composed by Gustave Charpentier (June 25, 1860 – February 18, 1956). Libretto by Gustave Charpentier. French. Original work. Premiered Paris, Opéra Comique, February 2, 1900. Set in Paris and Montmartre in 1900. Romantic opera. Set numbers with accompanied recitative. Ballet. Prelude before each act. Interlude before IIii.

Sets: 4. **Acts:** 4 acts, 23 scenes. **Length:** I: 35. II: 45. III: 35. IV: 25. **Arias:** "Depuis le jour" (Louise). **Hazards:** None. **Scenes:** I. A room in the mansard of a working man's tenement. IIi – IIviii. An open thoroughfare at the foot of the hill of Montmartre. IIix – IIxi. A dressmaker's working room. III. A little garden on the side of Montmartre. IV. The tenement room.

Major roles: Julien (tenor), Louise (soprano), Mother (mezzo), Father (baritone). **Minor roles:** Young rag picker (mezzo), Noctambulist / King of the Fools (tenor), Junk man (bass), Newspaper girl (soprano), Milk woman (soprano), Ragman (bass), Street sweeper (mezzo), Street Arab (soprano), Painter (bass), Sculptor (baritone), Song writer (baritone), Student (tenor), Young poet (baritone), First philosopher (tenor), Second philosopher (bass), Old Bohemian (baritone), Blanche (soprano), Marguerite (soprano), Suzanne (mezzo), Gertrude (mezzo), Irma (soprano), Camille (soprano), Errand girl (soprano), Madeleine (mezzo), Élise (soprano). **Bit parts:** Coal gatherer (mezzo), Two policemen (2 baritone), Apprentice (baritone), Old clothes vendor (tenor), Forewoman (mezzo). **Mute:** Dancer.

Chorus parts: SSATTBB. **Chorus roles:** Street vendors, working girls, the voice of Paris, Bohemians, children, prowlers, beggars, people of Montmartre. (Many bit parts for vendors. Also, the minor characters are used as ensemble / choral groups.) **Dance/movement:** III: Bohemians crown Louise. **Orchestra:** 3 fl (picc), 2 ob (Eng hrn), 3 cl (bs cl), 2 bsn, 4 hrn, 3 trp, 3 trb, tuba, 2 harp, perc, timp, celeste, strings. **Stageband:** II: guitar, picc, cl, 3 trp, 2 trb, tuba, perc. III: fl, 4 trp, trb, tuba, perc. IV: 2 trp. **Publisher:** Heugel & Co. **Rights:** Copyright by Heugel 1900. Renewed 1927.

Ii. Julien asks Louise to run away with him, but she refuses. He remembers how he first saw her, walking home one night. Iii. Louise's mother throws Julien out. Iiii. She considers him to be a vagabond and a drunk. Iiv. When Louise defends him, her mother threatens to tell Father everything. Iv. Louise's father returns from work in a philosophical mood. Julien has sent another letter asking for Louise's hand. Father explains to Louise that he is only trying to use his greater experience of life to save her pain.

IIi. A group of Parisians admits they cannot protect their daughters from the city's temptations. IIii. A street sweeper reminisces. IIiii. Julien waits for Louise. His bohemian friends laugh at Louise's family's middle class pretensions. IIiv. Julien wonders how he will persuade Louise to elope with him. IIv. The girls arrive at the dressmaker's workroom. IIvi. Louise is brought by her mother. IIvii. Julien begs her to run away with him but she refuses. IIviii. The vendors go about their business. IIix. The working girls tease Louise about being in love. IIx. Julien serenades Louise in the work house. IIxi. She runs away with him.

IIIi. Louise is happy with Julien. The lovers laugh at Louise's overprotective parents. IIIii. Bohemians gather beneath Julien's window. IIIiii. They crown Louise their queen. Louise's mother interrupts. IIIiv. Father is ill. She begs Louise to come home and promises to let Louise return to Julien.

IVi. Louise's father is bitter that his daughter is no longer content to be a child. IVii. He refuses to let her return to Julien, but Louise goes anyway. IViii. Father despairs.

Lyubov k Tryom Apelsinam • The Love for Three Oranges

Composed by Sergei Prokofiev (April 27, 1891 – March 5, 1953). Libretto by Sergei Prokofiev. Russian. Based on "L'Amore delle Tre Melarance" by Carlo Gozzi. Premiered Chicago, Chicago Opera Company, December 30, 1921. Set in a theater and a mythical kingdom at an unspecified time. Satire. Through composed. Prologue.

Sets: 7. **Acts:** 4 acts, 11 scenes. **Length:** Prologue, I: 30. II: 25. III, IV: 50. **Hazards:** Transformation of oranges into young women. Giant cook and kitchen. **Scenes:** Prologue. In front of a cabalistic curtain. Ii. The palace of the king. Iii. In front of a cabalistic curtain. Iiii. The palace. IIi. The prince's room. IIii. The grand court of the palace. IIIi. The desert. IIIii. The courtyard in Creonte's castle. IIIiii. The desert. IVi. In front of a cabalistic curtain. IVii. The throne room of the palace.

Major roles: King of clubs (bass), Prince (tenor), Léandre (baritone), Trouffaldino (tenor), Fata Morgana (soprano). **Minor roles:** Princess Clarice (contralto), Pantalon (baritone), Magician Tchélio (bass), Ninette (soprano), Cook Cleonte (bass), Sméraldine (mezzo). **Bit parts:** Linette (contralto), Nicolette (mezzo), Farfarello (bass), Master of ceremonies (tenor), Herald (bass). **Instrumentalist:** Trompette. **Mute:** monsters, drunkards, gluttons, guards, servants, soldiers.

Chorus parts: SAATTTTBBBB. **Chorus roles:** Ten spectators (5 tenor, 5 bass), tragedians, comedians, empty heads, little devils, doctors, courtiers, "lyriques." **Dance/movement:** I: Little devils dance. **Orchestra:** 3 fl (picc), 3 ob, 3 cl (bs cl), 3 bsn (cont bsn), 6 hrn, 3 trp, 3 trb, tuba, timp, 3 perc, 2 harp, xylophone, strings. **Stageband:** I: bs trb (played by character Trompette). II, III, IV: 3 trp, 2 trb, harp, perc. **Publisher:** Boosey & Hawkes. **Rights:** Copyright 1922 Breitkopf and Härtel. Assigned 1947 to Boosey & Hawkes.

Prologue. A group of spectators argues over what kind of show to see. The herald announces that the king of clubs is desperate because his son is an incurable hypochondriac. Ii. Doctors tell the king that unless the prince laughs and has fun, he will not survive the day. Pantalon suggests that Trouffaldino might be able to make the prince laugh. The king orders festivities and dancing, but Léandre, the prime minister, does not believe this will help. Iii. Fata Morgana beats the magician Tchélio at cards. It is she who prevents the prince from laughing. Iiii. If the prince dies, Clarice will inherit the throne. She is in league with Léandre but criticizes his methods. Léandre kills the prince with melancholy plays and poetry, but Clarice thinks it would be more direct to poison or shoot him. Sméraldine has been listening. He warns the conspirators that Tchélio is aiding Trouffaldino. Fata Morgana will help you, he assures them.

Ili. Trouffaldino is unable to make the prince laugh. The prince does not want to attend the entertainments prepared for him. He pops his pills. Iliii. The entertainments proceed, but the prince only wants to go back to bed. Trouffaldino throws Fata Morgana out. She falls—and the prince laughs. Her plans thwarted, Fata Morgana casts a spell on the prince: he must seek out and fall in love with three oranges. Taking Trouffaldino with him, the prince sets out to rescue the oranges from the giantess, Creonte.

IIIi. Tchélio invokes the devil Farfarello and orders him to return the oranges from Creonte's kitchen. Farfarello refuses, explaining that Fata Morgana's magic has won the day. Trouffaldino tries to tell the prince how dangerous Creonte's giant cook is, but the prince will not listen. Tchélio gives them a magic ribbon. If you get the oranges, he warns them, cut them open near water. IIIii. The prince and Trouffaldino arrive in Creonte's kitchen. The cook catches Trouffaldino but is fascinated by the magic ribbon and lets him go. The men escape with the oranges. IIIiii. They recross the desert, but the oranges weigh them down and they are overcome with thirst. While the prince sleeps, Trouffaldino opens two oranges—which turn into the princesses Linette and Nicolette. When Trouffaldino cannot give the princesses water, they die of thirst. He runs away. The prince opens the third orange, which becomes the Princess Ninetta. The prince finds her water and they pledge their love. Come back with me, the prince urges, but the princess insists he fetch proper clothing for her. While the prince is gone, Ninetta is transformed into a rat by Fata Morgana. The witch leaves Sméraldine behind to impersonate the princess. The court comes for Ninetta. The prince recognizes the substitution and is horrified, but the king insists the prince keep his word and marry Sméraldine.

IVi. Fata Morgana and Tchélio fight and Tchélio is victorious. IVii. The master of ceremonies uncovers the throne and discovers a rat. It is Ninetta, whom Tchélio transforms back into herself. Sméraldine is revealed as an accomplice of Léandre and Clarice. The king orders all three to be hanged, but Fata Morgana saves them. The prince and princess are married.

The Lowland Sea

Composed by Alec Wilder (February 16, 1907 – December 24, 1980). Libretto by Arnold Sundgaard. English. Based on various pictures and memories of the librettist. Premiered Montclair, New Jersey, Hillside Junior High School Auditorium, Montclair State Teachers College Players, May 8, 1952. Set in a port town, at sea and in Singapore around 1845. Folk drama. Through composed with dialogue spoken over music.

Sets: 5. **Acts:** 1 act, 7 scenes. **Length:** I: 55. **Hazards:** None. **Scenes:** Ii. A dock. Iii. A ship. Iiii. Dorie's house. Iiv. A dock in Singapore. Iv. A hill. Ivi. The dock in Singapore. Ivii. Dorie's house. (Score indicates that scenery can be extremely minimal, suggested only by chairs, a table, a bench, etc.)

Major roles: Dorie Davis (soprano or mezzo), Johnny Dee (baritone). **Minor roles:** Captain Jesse (bass baritone), Nathaniel Hazard (tenor), Three children (treble) [One girl, two boys preferred: Abraham, Isaac and Delight; three boys—Abraham, Isaac and Mordecai—or three girls—Delight, Patience and Submit—acceptable], Four sailors (2 tenor, 2 bass). **Bit parts:** Hannah (mezzo or soprano), Belinda (soprano). **Speaking:** Amos, Ship's doctor.

Chorus parts: SSATTBB. **Chorus roles:** Sailors and their wives and girl-friends. **Dance/movement:** I: Nathaniel dances for joy while proposing to Dorie. Sailors dance. **Orchestra:** fl, ob, 2 cl, bsn, 2 hrn, 2 trp, 2 trb, timp, perc, piano (and/or harp), strings. **Stageband:** None. **Publisher:** G. Schirmer Inc. **Rights:** Copyright 1952 by G. Schirmer Inc.

Ii. Johnny Dee says goodbye to his fiancée, Dorie, before sailing away.

They promise to wait for each other. Iii. Aboard ship, Johnny wonders if Dorie will be true. Iiii. Nathaniel proposes to Dorie, but she refuses. Iiv. Johnny gets malaria in Singapore and the ship has to sail without him. The captain promises him to take a message to Dorie. Iv. Dorie learns that Johnny's ship sank and mistakenly believes Johnny dead. Ivi. Eventually, Johnny finds a ship that will take him home. Ivii. Dorie has married Nathaniel. She stays home while Nathaniel and the children go to church. Johnny returns and talks with Dorie. He learns the truth and leaves before Nathaniel or the children see him.

Lucia di Lammermoor • Lucia of Lammermoor

Composed by Gaetano Donizetti (November 29, 1797 – April 8, 1848). Libretto by Salvatore Cammarano. Italian. Based on the novel "The Bride of Lammermoor" by Walter Scott. Premiered Naples, Teatro San Carlo, September 26, 1835. Set in Scotland in the late 17th century. Tragedy. Set numbers with recitative.

Sets: 6. **Acts:** 3 acts, 7 scenes. **Length:** Prelude: 5. I: 35. II: 43. III: 56. **Arias:** "Ardon gl'incensi"/Mad scene (Lucia), "Cruda funesta" (Enrico), "Fra poco a me" (Edgardo), "Regnava nel silenzio" (Lucia). **Hazards:** None. **Scenes:** Ii. The grounds of Ravenswood castle. Iii. Entrance to a park with a fountain in the foreground. IIi. Lord Ashton's chamber. IIii. A hall prepared for Arturo's reception. IIIi. A ground floor chamber in the tower of Wolf's Crag. IIIii. The hall prepared for Arturo's reception. IIIiii. The tombs of the Ravenswoods.

Major roles: Enrico Ashton (baritone), Lucia (soprano), Edgardo of Ravenswood (lyric tenor). **Minor roles:** Arturo Bucklaw (tenor), Raimondo Bidebent (bass), Alisa (mezzo), Normanno (tenor).

Chorus parts: SATTBB. **Chorus roles:** Edgardo's retainers, knights and ladies, relatives and friends of Ashton, people of Lammermoor, pages, servants, guards. **Dance/movement:** III: Optional ballet, often omitted. **Orchestra:** picc, 2 fl, 2 ob, 2 cl, 2 bsn, 4 hrn, 2 trp, 3 trb (tuba part exists doubling 3rd trb but not in score), timp perc, harp, strings. **Stageband:** II: band. **Publisher:** Ricordi. **Rights:** Expired.

Ii. Enrico complains to Raimondo that the family name can only be saved if his sister Lucia makes an advantageous marriage. Enrico fumes when Raimondo reminds him that she is still in mourning for her mother, and Normanno reveals that Lucia loves her brother's mortal enemy, Edgardo. Iii. Lucia leads Alisa to a fountain in the park where she meets Edgardo. Alisa worries that no good will come of this. Edgardo must go to France, but before he goes, he plans to ask Enrico to end the feud and give him Lucia's hand. Lucia dissuades him from further enraging her brother and they exchange vows.

IIi. Enrico has found Lucia a noble suitor—Arturo—who will wed her that very day. To make her forget Edgardo, Enrico gives Lucia a forged letter stating that Edgardo has fallen in love with another. Lucia is overwhelmed. Mary has replaced William on the throne of Scotland, Enrico tells her: "If we do not ally ourselves with Arturo, I am dead." Raimondo (who had been helping Lucia get letters to Edgardo) also advises Lucia to submit. IIii. Arturo and Lucia sign the marriage contract. Edgardo bursts in, but Raimondo prevents a fight. Edgardo is shown the signed wedding contract and he leaves, cursing Lucia.

IIIi. Enrico visits Edgardo and challenges him to a duel at dawn. IIIii. Raimondo interrupts the wedding festivities with the news that Lucia has gone mad and murdered her husband. Lucia appears, thinking she is talking to Edgardo. Her relatives are overcome with remorse. IIIiii. Edgardo longs for death. Seeing Lucia's funeral procession, he stabs himself.

Lucio Silla

Composed by Wolfgang Amadeus Mozart (January 27, 1756 – December 5, 1791). Libretto by Pietro Metastasio and Giovanni di Gamerra. Italian. Inspired by historical events. Premiered Milan, Teatro Regio Ducal, December 26, 1772. Set in Rome and environs in the 1st century BC. Opera seria. Set numbers with recitative. Overture.

Sets: 5. Acts: 3 acts, 7 scenes. Length: I, II, III: 210. Arias: "Ah se il crudel periglio" (Giunia), "Parto, m'affretto" (Giunia), "Pupille amate" (Aufidio), "Frà i pensier più funesti" (Giunia). Hazards: None. Scenes: Ii. In exile. Iii. Silla's dwelling. Iiii. The hall of heroes. IIi. Silla's dwelling. IIii. The Capitol. IIIi. A prison. IIIii. The Capitol.

Major roles: Lucio Silla (tenor), Giunia (soprano), Cecilio (soprano), Cinna (soprano), Celia (soprano). Minor role: Aufidio (tenor).

Chorus parts: SATB. Chorus roles: Guards, senators, patricians, soldiers, people. Dance/movement: None. Orchestra: 2 fl, 2 ob, 2 bsn, 2 hrn, 2 trp, timp, strings, continuo. Stageband: None. Publisher: Bärenreiter Kassel. Rights: Expired.

Ii. Rome is ruled by the dictator Silla. Cecilio, banished for plotting against Silla, learns from his friend Cinna that Silla is chasing Cecilio's fiancée, Giunia. He decides to return to Rome. Iii. Silla woos Giunia without success. Iiii. Cecilio meets Giunia in secret and they renew their vows of love.

IIi. Cinna tells Giunia to marry Silla and then murder him, but she refuses. IIii. Silla's public proposal to Giunia is interrupted by Cecilio, who appears, armed, in the Capitol. He is arrested.

IIIi. Cinna visits Cecilio in prison and works for his release. IIIii. Silla has a change of heart. He rescinds his condemnation of Cecilio and abdicates as dictator. The lovers are reunited.

Lucrezia Borgia

Composed by Gaetano Donizetti (November 29, 1797 – April 8, 1848). Libretto by Felice Romani. Italian. Based on "Lucrèce Borgia" by Victor Hugo. Premiered Milan, Teatro alla Scala, December 26, 1833. Set in Venice and Ferrara in the early 16th century. Melodrama. Set numbers with recitative. Prologue. Introduction.

Sets: 5. **Acts:** 2 acts, 5 scenes. **Length:** I, II: 135. **Arias:** "Com'è bello" (Lucrezia Borgia), "Il segreto per esser felice" (Orsini), "Vieni, la mia vendetta" (Don Alfonso). **Hazards:** I: Lucrezia arrives in a gondola. **Scenes:** Prologue. Terrace in the Grimani palace in Venice. Ii. Square in Ferrara. Iii. Room in the ducal palace. IIi. Small courtyard of Gennaro's house. IIii. Room in the Negroni palace.

Major roles: Maffio Orsini (contralto), Gennaro (tenor), Lucrezia Borgia (soprano), Don Alfonso (bass). **Minor roles:** Don Apostolo Gazella (bass), Ascanio Petrucci (bass), Giuseppe Liverotti (tenor), Oloferno Vitellozzo (tenor), Gubetta (bass), Rustighello (tenor), Astolfo (bass). **Bit part:** Usher (tenor). **Mute:** Princess Negroni.

Chorus parts: SATTBB. **Chorus roles:** Lords and ladies, pages, retainers, guards, masquers, soldiers, ushers, halberd bearers, cup bearers, gondoliers. **Dance/movement:** None. **Orchestra:** 2 fl (picc), 2 ob, 2 cl, 2 bsn, 4 hrn, 2 trp, 3 trb, timp, perc, harp, strings. **Stageband:** I, II, III: military band. **Publisher:** G. Ricordi. **Rights:** Expired.

Prologue. A masked party is in progress at the Barbarigo palace. Orsini tells how Gennaro saved his life after a fight and how together the two men fled into the woods, where a specter warned Orsini that Lucrezia Borgia threatens his life. Lucrezia loves Gennaro, but she is so universally hated that she can only travel in disguise. She kisses the sleeping Gennaro. Lucrezia's husband, Duke Alfonso of Ferrara, has followed her to Venice with his henchman, Rustighello. Gennaro returns Lucrezia's love and tells how his mother sent him away to protect him from her enemies. The guests return and reveal Lucrezia's identity to Gennaro. All anathematize her.

Iii. The duke swears to kill Gennaro because Lucrezia loves him. To prove he has forgotten Lucrezia, Gennaro incautiously knocks the "b" off the Borgia family arms. Astolfo has been sent by Lucrezia to fetch Gennaro, but Rustighello's henchmen scare him away. Iii. Lucrezia appeals to the duke for revenge against the man who defaced her palace. Horrified when she learns that Gennaro was the culprit, she then begs the duke for mercy. He pretends to relent, but gives Gennaro poisoned wine. Convincing Gennaro to drink the antidote by invoking the name of his mother, Lucrezia warns him to flee Ferrara.

IIi. Gennaro feels a foreboding. Rustighello's men stake out Gennaro's house. When Orsini convinces Gennaro that Lucrezia set him up to win his trust and they leave for a party at the Negroni palace, Rustighello's men retire. IIii. At the party, Orsini takes offense at Gubetta's supercilious manner. They return to their drinking, but the lamps are extinguished. Lucrezia has poisoned the guests—including Gennaro. When Orsini threatens to kill her, she reveals that she is his mother. Rather than take the antidote, he dies.

Luisa Miller

Composed by Giuseppe Verdi (October 9, 1813 – January 27, 1901). Libretto by Salvatore Cammarano. Italian. Based on Friedrich von Schiller's play "Kabale und Liebe." Premiered Naples, Teatro San Carlo, December 8, 1849. Set in a village in the Tyrol in the early 17th century. Tragic melodrama. Set numbers with recitative. Overture.

Sets: 5. **Acts:** 3 acts, 7 scenes. **Length:** I: 55. II: 40. III: 40. **Arias:** "Tu puniscimi, O signore" (Luisa), "Quando le sere al placido" (Rodolfo), "Sacra la scelta" (Miller). **Hazards:** None. **Scenes:** Ii. Before Miller's house in the village. Iii. A room in Walter's castle. Iiii – IIi. Inside Miller's house. IIii. Walter's apartments in the castle. IIiii. The castle garden. III. Miller's house.

Major roles: Miller (baritone), Luisa (soprano), Rodolfo (tenor), Wurm (bass), Count Walter (bass). **Minor roles:** Laura (mezzo), Federica (contralto). **Bit part:** Peasant (tenor).

Chorus parts: SSAATTTTBB. **Chorus roles:** Ladies in waiting to Federica, pages, servants, archers, villagers. **Dance/movement:** None. **Orchestra:** picc, 2 fl, 2 ob, 2 cl, 2 bsn, 4 hrn, 2 trp, 3 trb, cimbasso (serpent, ophicléide), timp, perc, harp, strings. **Stageband:** I: church bell, 2 hrn. III: organ. **Publisher:** G. Ricordi. **Rights:** Expired.

Ii. The village celebrates Luisa Miller's birthday. She has fallen in love with Carlo, a young hunter, who is actually Rodolfo, son of Count Walter, in disguise. Luisa's father fears for his daughter. He promised her to Wurm—if Luisa consents. Wurm reveals Rodolfo's identity, confirming in Miller's mind his fear that Carlo means to seduce Luisa. Iii. Walter learns of Rodolfo's adventure from Wurm and is upset by this threat to his plans. He tells Rodolfo that he means him to marry the well-connected Federica. Left alone with Federica, Rodolfo begs her to understand. She is unconvinced. Iiii. Miller tells Luisa she has been betrayed, but Rodolfo swears he loves only Luisa. Walter orders Luisa and her father arrested. He rescinds the order when Rodolfo threatens to reveal how Walter became a count.

IIi. The villagers tell Luisa that her father has been taken away by the count's soldiers. Wurm persuades her to save her father by writing a letter renouncing Rodolfo. She must say she loves Wurm and come to the castle to "prove" it. IIii. Wurm reports to Walter that the plan is working. They recall how they slew the previous count—and gave out that he had been killed by bandits. Only Rodolfo knows the truth. Luisa convinces Federica she loves Wurm. IIiii. A peasant gives Rodolfo a love letter addressed from Luisa to Wurm. Rodolfo challenges Wurm, but Wurm escapes. Betrayed, as he thinks, by Luisa, Rodolfo agrees to marry Federica.

III. The villagers try to comfort Luisa. Miller returns home, freed by Luisa. She gives him a letter for Rodolfo telling all—and asking him to join her in suicide. Miller persuades Luisa to tear up the letter. Rodolfo drinks poison with the unsuspecting Luisa. She reveals the truth. Rodolfo slays Wurm before he and Luisa expire.

Lulu

Composed by Alban Berg (February 9, 1885 – December 24, 1935). Libretto by Alban Berg. German. Based on the plays "Erdgeist" and "Die Büchse der Pandora" by Frank Wedekind. Premiered Paris, Opéra, February 24, 1979. Set in Germany, France and England in the late 19th or early 20th century. Tragedy. Through composed. Spoken dialogue. Highly symmetric forms. Twelve-tone serialism. Use of musical form to reflect dramatic content. Musical interludes between scenes. Prologue. Third act left unfinished. A performance of the first two acts only was given in Zürich on June 2, 1937.

Sets: 6. Acts: 3 acts, 7 scenes. Length: I: 62. II: 54. III: 56. Arias: "Pussi" (Lulu), "Wach auf!" (Painter), Lulu's lied (Lulu), Alwa's hymn/"Kuss! Einen Kuss!" (Alwa). Hazards: None. Scenes: Ii. A shabbily equipped studio. Iii. An elegant drawing room. Iiii. A dressing room in the theater. IIi. A magnificent room in German Renaissance style. IIIi. A spacious drawing room in Paris. IIIii. An attic in a London slum.

Major roles: Alwa (heldentenor), Dr. Schön/Jack the Ripper (helden baritone), Lulu (high soprano), Countess Geschwitz (dramatic mezzo), Schigolch (high character bass). Minor roles: Animal trainer/Rodrigo (helden bass), Painter/Negro (lyric tenor), Prince/Manservant/Marquis (comic tenor), Theater dresser/Gymnast/Groom (contralto), Theater director (comic bass), Professor of Medicine/Banker (bass). Mute: Clown, Stagehand. Bit parts: Fifteen-year-old girl (soprano), Girl's mother (contralto), Lady artist (mezzo), Journalist (baritone), Servant (baritone). Speaking: Police officer.

Chorus parts: N/A. Chorus roles: None. Dance/movement: None. Orchestra: 3 fl (2 picc), 3 ob (Eng hrn), alto sax, 3 cl, bs cl, 3 bsn (cont bsn), 4 hrn, 3 trp, 3 trb, tuba, 4 timp, perc, vibraphone, harp, piano, strings. Stageband: I: 3 cl (ten sax), alto sax, 2 jazz trp, sousaphone, jazz band, banjo, piano, 3 vln, bs. Publisher: Universal Edition. Rights: Copyright 1936 by Universal Edition.

Prologue. The animal trainer invites the audience to see his human "zoo." Ii. The composer Alwa picks up his father, Dr. Schön, from the studio where the painter is painting Lulu, a dancer. When the amorous painter is chasing Lulu around the room, Lulu's husband, a professor of medicine, breaks into the studio only to drop dead of a stroke. Lulu realizes she is now rich. Iii. The painter, now married to Lulu, has become successful. Lulu receives a notice of Dr. Schön's engagement. Schigolch, an old man, comes to beg money, which Lulu gives him. He leaves as Dr. Schön arrives. The doctor is surprised that the painter allows Schigolch—Lulu's father—into the house. He has come to break off his affair with Lulu. She is reluctant, but Dr. Schön tells the painter everything and advises him to watch her closely. The painter locks himself in his room and a cry is heard from within. Alwa arrives and helps Dr. Schön break down the door: The painter has cut his own throat. Dr. Schön fears the scandal will endanger his engagement; Lulu announces that Dr. Schön will eventually marry her. Iiii. Alwa drinks champagne with Lulu in her dressing room before a performance. During Lulu's performance, the prince enters and admits he wants to marry Lulu. Lulu rushes in, followed by the dresser, the theater manager and Dr. Schön: she has fainted upon seeing Dr. Schön and his fiancée in the audience. Lulu and Dr. Schön quarrel. Lulu dictates a letter from the doctor—unbeknownst to him—breaking off his engagement.

IIi. Lulu and Dr. Schön are now married. The countess Geschwitz visits them and invites Lulu to a ball for lady artists. When Dr. Schön and Lulu leave the room, the countess hears people coming and hides. She overhears Schigolch, the athlete Rodrigo, and the schoolboy all admit they are in love with Lulu. (Schigolch is not, he explains, Lulu's father.) When Dr. Schön returns, the men hide. While Alwa talks to Lulu, Dr. Schön, too, conceals himself to eavesdrop on them. Alwa tries to control himself but at last concedes his passion for Lulu. Dr. Schön pulls out a gun, meaning to revenge himself, but cannot shoot, and in despair gives the gun to Lulu. The countess and schoolboy are discovered; Rodrigo runs off. Lulu shoots and kills Dr. Schön. With his dying breath, Dr. Schön warns Alwa not to fall victim to Lulu. Lulu begs Alwa not to hand her over to the police. During a musical interlude, a silent film is played that shows: Lulu arrested, tried and condemned; Lulu in prison; Lulu ill. IIiii. Rodrigo, the countess and Schigolch plan to spring Lulu from jail. Schigolch enters with passports for himself and Lulu and Schigolch and the countess go to free Lulu. The schoolboy has his own plot to free Lulu but is told she is dead. Lulu returns, playing her part of invalid to the hilt. Rodrigo storms out, disgusted. Lulu explains how she was freed: She and the countess intentionally contracted cholera and were admitted to the same hospital. When the countess was discharged, she returned, swapped clothes with Lulu—and selflessly remained behind in Lulu's place. Lulu seduces Alwa and they run off to Paris together.

IIIi. Lulu and Alwa are throwing a party, at which guests admire the 15-year-old girl. Various people try to buy Jungfrau shares from the banker. The Marquis proposes to sell Lulu to an Egyptian and threatens to expose her as Dr. Schön's murderer if she protests. Rodrigo is also trying to blackmail Lulu. The countess reminds Lulu of the love vows she made to her in the hospital. Lulu persuades Schigolch to murder Rodrigo. She tells Rodrigo to get money from the countess by sleeping with her, then persuades the countess to lead Rodrigo into Schigolch's trap. A messenger arrives with news of the crash of Jungfrau's stock, and Alwa and the guests realize they are bankrupt. Lulu switches clothes with a groom and she and Alwa escape before the police arrive. IIIii. Lulu has taken to prostitution. When she returns to her attic with a customer (a professor), Alwa and Schigolch hide. The now-impoverished countess arrives with the painter's portrait of Lulu. Alwa objects to Lulu's new business but is himself too sick to work, having contracted a social disease from Lulu. Lulu returns with a Negro—who gets into a fight with Alwa and kills him—and then with Jack the Ripper. Jack kills Lulu and the countess.

Die Lustige Witwe • The Merry Widow

Composed by Franz Lehár (April 30, 1870 – October 24, 1948). Libretto by Viktor Léon and Leo Stein. German. Based on "L'Attaché de l'Ambassade" by Henri Meilhac. Premiered Vienna, Theater an der Wien, December 30, 1905. Set in Paris in the early 20th century. Operetta. Set numbers with spoken dialogue. Overture (added for London premiere).

Sets: 3. **Acts:** 3 acts, 3 scenes. **Length:** I, II, III: 150. **Arias:** Vilja-Lied (Hanna), "O Vaterland" (Danilo). **Hazards:** None. **Scenes:** I. The Pontevedrian embassy in Paris. II. Hanna's house. III. Maxim's.

Major roles: Hanna Glawari (soprano), Baron Zeta (tenor), Prince Danilo (tenor). **Minor roles:** Cascada (tenor), Olga (mezzo), St. Brioche (tenor), Kromow (tenor), Count Camille de Rosillon (tenor), Valencienne (soprano), Sylviane (soprano), Prascowia (mezzo), Bogdanowitsch (baritone), Pritschitsch (baritone), Njegus (baritone), Zo Zo (mezzo). **Bit parts:** Lady (mezzo), Lolo (mezzo), Dodo (mezzo), Jou Jou (mezzo), Frou Frou (mezzo), Clo Clo (mezzo). **Speaking:** Maitre d'hôtel at Maxim's.

Chorus parts: SATTBB. **Chorus roles:** Pontevedrians, Parisians, grisettes. **Dance/movement:** II: Ballroom dancing. Danilo and Anna dance the Kolo. III. Ballet at Maxim's. **Orchestra:** 3 fl (picc), 3 ob (Eng hrn), 3 cl (bs cl), 3 bsn (cont bsn), 4 hrn, 2 trp, 3 trb, tuba, timp, perc, harp, celeste, strings. (Reduced version with double winds.) **Stageband:** I: strings, perc. II: perc. III: perc, guitar, strings. **Publisher:** Glocken Verlag, Ltd. **Rights:** Copyright 1905 by Glocken Verlag Ltd.

I. Baron Zeta, the Pontevedrian ambassador in Paris, gives a party. Camille declares his passion for Valencienne, but she reminds him she is Zeta's devoted wife. Everyone awaits the rich widow, Hanna Glawari. Since her money represents the entire capital of the National Bank of Pontevedro, there is concern that her marrying a foreigner would bankrupt the country. Hanna is unimpressed by the men's compliments, suspecting everyone is after her money. Hanna invites everyone to a party. Valencienne wants Hanna to marry Camille. Prince Danilo arrives. Hanna upbraids him for deserting her when she was poor. Danilo says he had no choice—and points out she quickly married a rich banker. Valencienne sends Camille in search of her fan—on which he had written "I love you." Kromow finds the fan and thinks his wife Olga is having an affair. To pacify Kromow, Zeta claims the fan belongs to his wife. Zeta tells Danilo he must marry Hanna to keep her money in Pontevedro. Danilo refuses, but agrees to keep all eligible foreigners away from Hanna. All the men beg for a dance with the widow. Hanna chooses Danilo, who scares the other men off by offering to sell the dance for ten thousand francs.

II. Hanna entertains her guests. Dinner is served. Zeta is furious to hear that Danilo does not plan to attend. However, Danilo does come. They worry that Camille is after Hanna and determine to learn the identity of Camille's mistress. Danilo flirts with Hanna. He inadvertently gets Olga to confess to an affair with St. Brioche, and Sylviane confesses to a fling with Cascada. Prascowia thinks Danilo is in love with her. Danilo blackmails Cascada and St. Brioche into leaving. Hanna asks Danilo whom she should marry, but he pretends not to care. When Danilo drops the fan, Hanna picks it up and thinks the words of love are meant for her. The two dance the Kolo and reminisce. The Pontevedrian government presses Zeta to end the crisis. Valencienne recovers her fan. When she bids Camille farewell, Zeta sees Camille in the pavilion with his wife. Hanna takes Valencienne's place and convinces Zeta he was mistaken. Hanna announces her engagement to Camille. Danilo storms off to Maxim's.

III. Valencienne, Sylviane and Olga go to Maxim's to persuade Danilo to marry Hanna. The grisettes dance and sing. Cascada and St. Brioche fight over a grisette. Zeta tells Danilo that Hanna loves him. Danilo and Hanna bribe the maitre d'hôtel to clear out the restaurant. Hanna admits she has no intention of marrying Camille. She says that by her husband's will she would lose her money if she married again. Danilo is overjoyed and confesses he loves her. She explains that she would lose her money because it would go to her new husband. All drink a toast to love.

Die Lustigen Weiber von Windsor • The Merry Wives of Windsor

Composed by Otto Nicolai (June 9, 1810 – May 11, 1849). Libretto by Salomon Hermann von Mosenthal. German. Based on the play by Shakespeare. Premiered Berlin, Royal Opera House, March 9, 1849. Set in the town of Windsor in the 15th century. Singspiel. Set numbers with recitative and spoken dialogue. Overture. Ballet.

Sets: 7. **Acts:** 3 acts, 7 scenes. **Length:** I: 50. II: 55. III: 40. **Arias:** "Horche, die Lerche singt" (Fenton), Drinking song (Falstaff). **Hazards:** None. **Scenes:** Ii. A court. Iii. A room in Ford's house. IIi. A room in the Garter Inn. IIii. The garden of Page's house. IIiii. Mrs. Ford's room. IIIi. A room in Page's house. IIIii. Windsor forest.

Major roles: Alice Ford or Mrs. Fluth (soprano), Meg Page or Mrs. Reich (mezzo), Fenton (tenor), Sir John Falstaff (bass), Mr. Ford or Fluth (baritone), Anne Page (soprano). **Minor roles:** Mr. Page or Reich (bass), Slender (tenor), Dr. Cajus (bass). **Bit parts:** First neighbor (tenor).

Speaking bits: Second neighbor, Third neighbor, Fourth neighbor, Landlord, Waiter. **Mute:** John, Robert.

Chorus parts: SSAATTBB. **Chorus roles:** Neighbors, elves, spooks, insects. **Dance/movement:** III: Elf and insect ballet. **Orchestra:** 2 fl, 2 ob, 2 cl, 2 bsn, 4 hrn, 2 trp, 3 trb, timp, perc, harp, strings. **Stageband:** III: bells. **Publisher:** G. Schirmer, Inc., Bote & Bock. **Rights:** Expired.

Ii. Alice Ford and Meg Page both receive love letters from Sir John Falstaff. The two women agree to revenge themselves on Falstaff for his presumption. Meg's husband, Mr. Page, promises his daughter, Anne, to Slender; Meg hopes Anne will marry Cajus, but Anne loves Fenton. Page rejects Fenton because he is poor. Iii. Alice invites Falstaff over and has her husband warned anonymously. By prearrangement, Meg interrupts them to say that Ford is on his way to catch them. The two women stuff Falstaff into a laundry basket and order the servants to dump the basket in the pond. Ford searches the house, but does not find Falstaff. He apologizes to Alice for his unfounded jealousy.

IIi. Disguised as Mr. Brook, Ford pays Falstaff to seduce Alice. Falstaff reveals that he has an assignation with Alice that very day. IIii. Cajus and Slender overhear Fenton and Anne declaring their love. IIiii. Meg again interrupts Falstaff and Alice to warn them that Ford is coming. The women dress Falstaff as an old woman whom Ford hates. Ford beats the old woman and throws her out. He then searches the house, but finds nothing.

IIIi. Alice and Meg tell their husbands the whole story. Together, they plan to lure Falstaff into the forest and scare him. Privately, Page and his wife each arrange for Anne to sneak off—he with Cajus and she with Slender. Anne has her own plans. IIIii. Alice and Meg both flirt with Falstaff, then slip away. The neighbors, disguised as elves and spirits, torment Falstaff. Fenton and Anne get married. The joke is revealed to Falstaff.

Macbeth

Composed by Ernest Bloch (July 24, 1880 – July 15, 1959). Libretto by Edmond Fleg. English. Based on the play by Shakespeare. Premiered Paris, Opéra Comique, November 30, 1910. Set in Scotland in an unspecified time. Lyric drama. Through composed. Prologue. Entr'acte before II, III. Intermezzo before Iii, IIii, IIIii.

Sets: 7. **Acts:** 3 acts, 7 scenes. **Hazards:** II: Macbeth's vision of Banquo's ghost. III: Apparitions raised by witches for Macbeth. **Scenes:** Prologue. A wind-swept hearth. Ii. A room in Macbeth's castle. Iii. The inner courtyard of Macbeth's castle. IIi. A room of state in Macbeth's castle. IIii. A garden in Macduff's castle. IIIi. A dark cave. IIIii. A room in Macbeth's castle with a balcony opening onto Birnam wood.

Major roles: Macbeth (baritone), Lady Macbeth (soprano). **Minor roles:** First witch (soprano), Second witch (mezzo), Third witch (contralto), Banquo (low tenor), Macduff (lyric bass), Servant (tenor), Duncan (tenor), Porter (baritone), Lennox (low tenor), Malcolm (tenor), Old man (bass), Murderer (bass), Lady Macduff (soprano), Son of Macduff (mezzo), Third apparition (contralto). **Bit part:** First apparition (bass). **Mute:** Fleance, Second murderer, Attendant, Eight kings in Macbeth's vision.

Chorus parts: SSSAAAATTTTBBBB. **Chorus roles:** Lords, ladies (several solo ejaculations), soldiers, peasants, ghosts. **Dance/movement:** Prologue: witches' dance. **Orchestra:** 3 fl, 3 ob, 4 cl, 4 bsn, 4 hrn, 3 trp, 3 trb, tuba, timp, celeste, harp, perc, strings. **Stageband:** I: 3 trp, 2 hrn, 3 fl, piano, harp, drums, bells, tam tam. **Publisher:** Suvini Zerboni. **Rights:** Copyright 1951 by Suvini Zerboni.

Prologue. Macbeth and Banquo meet three witches who tell them Macbeth will be king, as will Banquo's sons. One of the witches' prophesies is confirmed when Macbeth is named Thane of Cawdor. Ii. King Duncan spends the evening in Macbeth's castle. Lady Macbeth persuades her husband to murder him. Iii. The deed is done and Macduff discovers the bodies. Malcolm flees the country.

IIi. Macbeth is king. Rather than let Fleance succeed him, Macbeth pays assassins to kill him and his father, but Fleance escapes. Macbeth is frightened by a vision of Banquo's ghost. IIii. Macbeth's men murder Lady Macduff and her children. Malcolm and Macduff return with their army and swear revenge.

IIIi. Macbeth consults the witches who tell him he is safe until Birnam Wood comes to his castle. IIIii. Wracked by guilt, Lady Macbeth kills herself. Malcolm's army attacks Macbeth's castle using the trees of Birnam wood for camouflage. Macduff kills Macbeth and Malcolm's army is victorious.

Macbeth

Composed by Giuseppe Verdi (October 9, 1813 – January 27, 1901). Libretto by Francesco Maria Piave and Andrea Maffei. Italian. Based on the play by Shakespeare. Premiered Florence, Teatro della Pergola, March 14, 1847. Set in Scotland in the mid-11th century. Melodrama. Set numbers with recitative. Prelude. Ballet. Later revised with a French translation, premiered at Théâtre-Lyrique, Paris, April 21, 1865.

Sets: 9. **Acts:** 4 acts, 9 scenes. **Length:** I: 50. II: 30. III: 20. IV: 40. **Arias:** "Ah, la paterna mano" (Macduff), "Come dal ciel precipita" (Banquo), "La luce langue" (Lady Macbeth), "Una macchia" (Lady Macbeth), "Mal per me" (Macbeth), "Pietà, rispetto, amore" (Macbeth), "Vieni, t'affretta" (Lady Macbeth). **Hazards:** None. **Scenes:** Ii. A deserted spot. Iii. The atrium of Macbeth's castle. IIi. A room in the castle. IIii. A park far from the castle. IIiii. A magnificent banquet room in the castle. III. An obscure cavern. IVi. A deserted spot on the English border. IVii. The room in the castle. IViii. A battlefield.

Major roles: Macbeth (baritone), Lady Macbeth (soprano). **Minor roles:** Banquo (bass), Macduff (tenor), Lady-in-waiting (mezzo), Malcolm (tenor), Doctor (bass). **Bit parts:** Servant to Macbeth (bass), Herald (bass), Assassin (bass), Three apparitions (bass, 2 soprano). **Mute:** King Duncano, Fleanzio. **Dancer:** Ecate.

Chorus parts: SSATTTBB. **Chorus roles:** Witches, king's messengers, Scottish nobles, English soldiers, attendants, Scottish refugees, spirits of the air, apparitions, assassins. **Dance/movement:** III: Spirits and apparitions ballet. **Orchestra:** 2 fl, 2 ob (Eng hrn), 2 cl (bs cl), 2 bsn, 4 hrn, 2 trp, 3 trb, tuba, timp, perc, harp, strings. **Stageband:** I: military band. III: wind ensemble. IV: trps. **Publisher:** G. Ricordi. **Rights:** Expired.

Ii. Banquo and Macbeth discover three covens of witches who predict that Macbeth will be king of Scotland—as will Banquo's children. Iii. Lady Macbeth inflames her husband's ambition. Macbeth murders King Duncan (who is his guest), but leaves Lady Macbeth to disguise the evidence. Macduff and Banquo discover the murder.

IIi. Macbeth and Lady Macbeth agree that Banquo must die. IIii.

Macbeth's assassins kill Banquo but Banquo's son, Fleance, escapes. IIiii.
A banquet is given for Macbeth and Lady Macbeth. Macbeth cringes in
terror at the sight of Banquo's ghost. Macduff flies the country.

III. Macbeth calls on the witches to predict his future. The witches call
forth three apparitions, which tell Macbeth: to fear Macduff; that no man
of woman born can harm him; and that he shall be king until Birnam
wood uproots itself. Macbeth asks about Banquo's descendants and is
shown a line of eight kings. The witches disappear and Macbeth vows to
kill Fleance and Macduff.

IVi. Macbeth has killed Macduff's wife and children. Macduff and
Malcolm lead an English army against Macbeth. Let every man take a
branch from Birnam wood to use as cover, Malcolm orders. IVii. Lady
Macbeth's maid and physician watch the queen sleepwalk through the
palace, reliving her husband's murders. IViii. Macbeth is told the queen
is dead. He observes Birnam forest moving against him. Macduff
explains he is not born of woman: he was torn from his mother's womb.
He fights and kills Macbeth. Malcolm is hailed King of Scotland.

Madama Butterfly • Madam Butterfly

Composed by Giacomo Puccini (December 22, 1858 – November 29,
1924). Libretto by Luigi Illica and Giuseppe Giacosa. Italian. Based on
play by David Belasco (itself based on story by John Luther Long).
Premiered Milan, Teatro alla Scala, February 17, 1904. Set in Nagasaki in
the present. Japanese tragedy. Through composed. Entr'acte before III.
In original, 2-act version, acts II and III were IIi and IIii. Revised version
premiered in Brescia, May 28, 1904. Third revision premiered in London,
July 10, 1905.

Sets: 1. **Acts:** 3 acts, 3 scenes. **Length:** I: 50. II: 50. III: 35. **Arias:** "Addio
fiorito asil" (Pinkerton), "Un bel dì" (Butterfly). **Hazards:** None. **Scenes:**
I-III. A Japanese house, terrace and garden.

Major roles: Madame Butterfly/Cio-Cio-San (soprano), Lieutenant B. F.
Pinkerton (tenor), Sharpless (baritone). **Minor roles:** Suzuki (mezzo),
Kate Pinkerton (mezzo), Goro (tenor), Prince Yamadori (tenor), The
Bonze (bass), Imperial commissioner (bass). **Bit parts:** Official registrar
(baritone), Butterfly's mother (mezzo), Butterfly's aunt (mezzo),
Butterfly's cousin (soprano), Butterfly's uncle Yakusidé (bass). **Mute:**
Butterfly's child Sorrow.

Chorus parts: SSAATT. **Chorus roles:** Cio-cio-san's relations and
friends, sailors. **Dance/movement:** None. **Orchestra:** 3 fl (picc), 2 ob, Eng

hrn, 2 cl, bs cl, 2 bsn, 4 hrn, 3 trp, 3 trb, tuba, timp, perc, harp, strings. **Stageband:** I: tam tam. II: bells, viola d'amore. **Publisher:** G. Ricordi. **Rights:** Expired.

I. Goro the marriage broker shows Lieutenant Pinkerton the house Pinkerton has bought for himself and his Japanese bride-to-be, Madam Butterfly. Goro introduces Suzuki, Butterfly's maid. Pinkerton receives Sharpless, the American consul. The lieutenant hints that he considers this imminent marriage temporary, which worries the consul. Butterfly is escorted by her female friends. She answers the American men's questions about her family, which, she says, was once rich and important. Butterfly is 15 years old. The relations are divided about Pinkerton's worth. In private, Butterfly shows Pinkerton her keepsakes, including the knife with which her father committed suicide. She has converted to Christianity, she confides. The imperial commissioner marries Butterfly and Pinkerton. The toasts afterwards are interrupted by Butterfly's uncle, the Bonze, who is furious. He has discovered Butterfly's conversion and he and the relatives all renounce her. Pinkerton consoles his new wife and they watch the sun set.

II. Pinkerton is long gone from their home, but Butterfly is convinced her husband will return to her. Sharpless has a letter from Pinkerton, but Butterfly's solicitousness prevents him from speaking. Goro presents Prince Yamadori, who wishes to wed Butterfly. They argue that Pinkerton's abandonment is equivalent to divorce in Japan. Butterfly disagrees and rejects the prince. When she goes to help Suzuki with the tea, Sharpless confesses to Goro and Yamadori that Pinkerton does not want to see Butterfly when he returns. Sharpless tries to read her Pinkerton's letter, but her hopeful misinterpretations break his heart. He begs her to marry Yamadori. In tears, Butterfly shows Sharpless her three-year-old son by Pinkerton. She declares her intention to die rather than return to being a geisha. "The child's name is Sorrow," she explains. Promising to inform Pinkerton about his son, Sharpless leaves. Suzuki and Butterfly attack Goro for spreading rumors. They sight Pinkerton's ship in the harbor. Butterfly is overjoyed and has Suzuki fill the house with flowers. She dresses up for her husband's return.

III. Dawn breaks but Pinkerton has not arrived. Butterfly and Sorrow go to bed. Sharpless arrives with Pinkerton—and Pinkerton's new American wife, Kate. They have come for the child and ask Suzuki to help them. Pinkerton, overcome with guilt, leaves. Butterfly realizes what has happened. She agrees to hand over the child if Pinkerton will come for him in half an hour. Pinkerton returns to find that Butterfly has killed herself with her father's knife.

Madame Chrysanthème • Madame Chrysanthemum

Composed by André Charles Prosper Messager (December 30, 1853 – February 24, 1929). Libretto by Henri Grémont (Georges) Hartmann and André Messager. French. After Pierre Loti. Premiered Paris, Théâtre Lyrique Renaissance, January 26, 1893. Set in Japan in the 19th century. Lyric comedy. Set numbers with recitative and spoken dialogue. Prologue. Epilogue. Entr'acte before II, III, IV. Ballet.

Sets: 5. **Acts:** 4 acts, 6 scenes. **Hazards:** Prologue and Epilogue set on a ship at sea. **Scenes:** Prologue. The bridge of a man-of-war at sea. I. The port of Nagasaki with pagodas and houses in the background. II. A vestibule in Chrysanthème's home. III. A public square near the temple of Osueva. IV. The garden of Chrysanthème's house. Epilogue. The man-of-war.

Major roles: Pierre (tenor), Yves (bass), Madame Chrysanthème (soprano), Kangourou (tenor). **Minor roles:** Voice of a sailor (tenor), Mr. Sugar (tenor), Madam Prune (mezzo), Oyouki (soprano). **Bit parts:** Charles (tenor), Raoul (tenor), René (bass), Mrs. Campanule (soprano), Madam Jonquille (mezzo), Madam Strawberry (mezzo).

Chorus parts: SSAATTTTBBBB. **Chorus roles:** Merchants, French officers and sailors, geishas, priests, bonzes, temple attendants, jugglers, Japanese people. **Dance/movement:** I: Geishas dance to Chrysanthème's song. III: Ballet of the holiday dancers. **Orchestra:** 2 fl (picc), 2 ob (Eng hrn), 2 cl, 2 bsn, 4 hrn, 2 trp, 3 trb, sarrusophone (or cont bsn), timp, perc, harp, strings. **Stageband:** I: trps, drums. III: temple bell. IV: harp, celeste, perc. **Publisher:** Choudens Fils. **Rights:** Expired.

Prologue. Two French naval officers, Pierre and Yves, fantasize about the brides they will find in Japan. Ii. The French sailors are accosted by merchants and geishas in the port of Nagasaki. Iii. Pierre is attracted to one of the geishas, Madame Chrysanthème. Iiii. They talk and Chrysanthème leaves. Iiv. A Japanese merchant, Kangourou, offers his services in finding a bride. Iv. He brings back Madame Chrysanthème with her parents, Mr. Sugar and Mrs. Prune.

IIi. Mrs. Prune says her prayers. IIii. Kangourou brings a marriage contract for Pierre and Chrysanthème. IIiii. Yves admires Mr. Sugar's paintings of storks. IIiv. Pierre praises the beauty of Japan. IIv. Pierre tells Chrysanthème how much he loves her. IIvi. The newlyweds' friends serenade them.

IIIi. The Japanese celebrate a holiday. IIIii. Pierre and his friends attend. IIIiii. Chrysanthème confesses to Yves that she misses her days as a street singer. IIIiv. Pierre is jealous of Yves. IIIv. One of Kangourou's singers runs away. IIIvi. Pierre goes off with his friends. IIIvii. Chrysanthème agrees to take the missing singer's place. IIIviii. Dancers entertain the crowd. IIIix. Chrysanthème sings. IIIx. Pierre recognizes her and is furious. IIIxi. Kangourou offers to find Pierre a new Japanese bride. IIIxii. The priests parade through the temple square.

IVi. Chrysanthème and Oyouki sing for themselves. IVii. Pierre overhears and is touched. IViii. He makes up with Chrysanthème. IViv. She knows that Pierre will eventually have to leave her and is not surprised when Yves arrives for Pierre. IVv. The ship is leaving that very night. IVvi. Pierre makes his farewells. IVvii. Chrysanthème asks Pierre to visit her one last time before he leaves. IVviii. Pierre prepares to depart. IVix. Seeing Yves and Chrysanthème together reawakens Pierre's jealousy and he stalks off in disgust. Epilogue. On the ship home, Pierre asks Yves about Chrysanthème. Yves produces a letter from her to Pierre telling him she truly did love him.

Madame Sans-Gêne • Madam Free-and-Easy

Composed by Umberto Giordano (August 28, 1867 – November 12, 1948). Libretto by Renato Simoni. Italian. Based on the comedy by Victorien Sardou and E. Moreau. Premiered New York City, Metropolitan Opera Association, January 25, 1915. Set in France in 1792 and 1811. Comedy. Through composed.

Sets: 3. **Acts:** 4 acts, 4 scenes. **Length:** I, II, III, IV: 115. **Arias:** "Alle giubbe scarlatte diam la caccia" (Lefebvre), "Questa tua bocca" (Lefebvre), "Ah non guardarmi" (Lefebvre). **Hazards:** None. **Scenes:** I. Madame Sans-Gêne's laundry in Ste. Anne street. II. A large drawing room in the château of Compiègne. III – IV. The cabinet of the emperor.

Major roles: Caterina Hubscher/Madame Sans-Gêne (soprano), Fouché (baritone), Lefebvre (tenor). **Minor roles:** Toniotta the washer woman (soprano), Giulia the washer woman (soprano), La Rossa the washer woman (soprano), Vinaigre a drummer (tenor), Count of Neipperg (tenor), Despréaux a ballet master (tenor), Gelsomino a valet (baritone), Leroy a tailor (baritone), Queen Carolina (soprano), Emperor Napoleon (baritone). **Bit parts:** Princess Elisa (soprano), Chamberlain de Brigode (baritone), Roustan (baritone), Madame de Boulow (soprano), Offstage voice of the empress (soprano or mezzo). **Mute:** Maturino, Caterina's maid, Napoleon's servant Constant.

Chorus parts: SSAATTTBB. **Chorus roles:** People, vendors, nobles, national guardsmen, archers, court ladies, officials, diplomats, academics, valets, hunters. **Dance/movement:** None. **Orchestra:** picc, 2 fl, 2 ob, 2 cl, 2 bsn, 4 hrn, 3 trp, 3 trb, tuba, timp, perc, harp, celeste, strings. **Stageband:** I: drums, bells, perc. IV: 2 hrn, 2 trp, 2 trb. **Publisher:** Casa Musicale Sonzogno. **Rights:** Copyright 1914 by Edoardo Sonzogno.

I. The laundress Caterina recounts her adventures in the revolution-torn streets of Paris. Fouché asks about her fiancé, Sergeant Lefebvre, while his fellow revolutionaries capture the palace. The wounded Count of Neipperg appeals to Caterina, who agrees to hide him. When Lefebvre visits, the locked bedroom door arouses his suspicion and he wrests the key from Caterina. He finds the count and agrees to help save him.

II. The servants marvel that Napoleon has made Caterina and Lefebvre Duke and Duchess of Danzig. The emperor is scandalized by Caterina's behavior and tells Lefebvre to divorce her, but he refuses. The count of Neipperg is banished because of rumors that he loves the empress. Caterina embarrasses herself before Queen Carolina and Princess Elisa and insults them.

III. Napoleon summons Caterina. She wins him over by recalling to him the days when she used to do his laundry. Napoleon catches the count of Neipperg on his way to a secret meeting with the empress and arrests him.

IV. Napoleon persuades Caterina to knock on the empress's door and announce the count. When she does so, the empress gives her a letter. It is addressed to the Austrian king and merely asks him to entertain the count in exile. The empress is exonerated and Napoleon tells Lefebvre not to divorce Caterina.

The Magic Flute

See "Die Zauberflöte" entry.

The Magic Fountain

Composed by Frederick Delius (January 29, 1862 – June 10, 1934). Libretto by Frederick Delius. English. Original work. Premiered London, BBC Radio Broadcast, November 20, 1977. Set in Florida in the 16th century. Lyric drama. Through composed. Prelude. Musical interlude before Iii and IIiii. Entr'acte before II and III.

Sets: 5. **Acts:** 3 acts, 5 scenes. **Length:** I: 30. II: 35. III: 30. **Hazards:** I: Storm at sea. III: Magic fountain appears out of the mist. **Scenes:** Ii. On board ship. Iii. On the coast of Florida. IIi. Indian village in the forest. IIii. Talum Hadjo's abode in the Everglades. III. The Everglades.

Major roles: Solano (tenor), Watawa (soprano), Wapanacki (bass or baritone). **Minor roles:** Talum Hadjo (bass). **Bit parts:** Spanish sailor (bass). **Mute:** Unktahí.

Chorus parts: SSATTBB. **Chorus roles:** Sailors, Indian warriors and women, night mists and invisible spirits of the fountain. **Dance/movement:** II: A wild, Indian war dance. III: Ballet of the night mists. **Orchestra:** picc, 3 fl, 3 ob, Eng hrn, 3 cl, bs cl, 3 bsn, sarrusophone, 4 hrn, 3 trp, 3 trb, bs tuba, timp, perc, glockenspiel, 2 harps, strings. **Stageband:** None. **Publisher:** Delius Trust. **Rights:** Copyright 1979 by Delius Trust.

Ii. The Spaniard Solano has sailed in search of the fountain of eternal youth. His ship is becalmed and the crew discouraged, but Solano promises them gold. A storm wrecks the ship off the coast of Florida. Iii. Solano is discovered on the beach by a young Indian girl, Watawa.

IIi. Wapanacki, the Indian chief, tells Solano that only the seer Talum Hadjo knows how to find the magic fountain. Angry over the death of her father at the hands of the white man, Watawa seeks to revenge herself on Solano. Wapanacki prefers to be friendly, as Solano is unarmed— and has gold. The Indians perform a war dance. IIii. Watawa guides Solano through the Everglades to Talum Hadjo's hut. Going ahead, Watawa reveals her murderous plans to Hadjo and asks his advice. Hadjo tells Watawa that the waters of the magic fountain will kill Solano, unprepared as he is for its magic.

III. Watawa leads Solano to the fountain. She has fallen in love with him, but still means to have her revenge. Solano declares his love for Watawa and she confesses. The lovers fall asleep in each other's arms. They are awakened by invisible spirits who reveal to them the god Unktahí and the magic fountain. Watawa tells Solano that the magic water will kill him, but he does not believe her. She drinks the water herself and falls dead. Realizing he has killed his love, Solano also drinks of the fountain and dies.

Mahagonny

See "Aufstieg und Fall der Stadt Mahagonny" entry.

Orleanskaya Deva • The Maid of Orleans

Composed by Peter Ilyitch Tchaikovsky (May 7, 1840 – November 6, 1893). Libretto by Peter Ilyitch Tchaikovsky. Russian. Based on "Die Jungfrau von Orleans" by Friedrich von Schiller. Premiered St. Petersburg, Maryinsky Theater, February 13 (25), 1881. Set in France in the early 15th century. Tragedy. Set numbers with accompanied recitative. Ballet.

Sets: 6. **Acts:** 4 acts, 6 scenes. **Length:** I: 45. II: 60. III: 50. IV: 25. **Arias:** "Farewell, O native hills and fields" (Joan), "Holy father, they call me Joan" (Joan). **Hazards:** IV: Joan is burned at the stake. **Scenes:** I. By a stream and chapel. II. A hall in the Chinon palace. IIIi. A location near the battlefield. IIIii. A square before the cathedral of Reims. IVi. A forest glade. IVii. A square in Rouen.

Major roles: Thibault (bass), Joan (soprano or mezzo), King Charles VII (tenor), Lionel (baritone). **Minor roles:** Raimond (tenor), Bertran (bass), Voice of an angel (soprano), Dunois (baritone), Agnès (soprano), Cardinal or archbishop (bass). **Bit parts:** Soldier (bass), Lore (bass). **Mute:** Executioner, Priest.

Chorus parts: SSAATTBB. **Chorus roles:** Maidens, offstage angels, people, cavaliers and court ladies, French and English soldiers, knights, monks, pages, minstrels, people. **Dance/movement:** II: Gypsies, dwarfs and buffoons dance for the king. **Orchestra:** picc, 2 fl, 2 ob, Eng hrn, 2 cl, 2 bsn, 4 hrn, 2 cornet, 2 trp, 3 trb, tuba, timp, perc, harp, organ, strings. **Stageband:** II: trps, band. **Rights:** Expired.

I. Joan's father, Thibault, wants her to marry Raimond, but she refuses. Refugees flee the conquering British army. Joan prophesies the death of the British general. The voice of an angel tells her she must lead France against her enemies.

II. The French king is about to flee for his life when word arrives that Joan has led the army to victory. The court is deeply impressed by her divine inspiration and she is named commander of the army.

IIIi. Joan defeats Lionel in combat, but falls in love with him. He agrees to fight for France. IIIii. Thibault publicly accuses his daughter of being in league with the devil. Guilty over her love for Lionel, Joan refuses to defend herself.

IVi. Joan and Lionel declare their love. An angel warns Joan that she will be punished for succumbing to earthly love. British soldiers kill Lionel and capture her. IVii. Joan is burned at the stake.

Le Maître de Chapelle • The Music Master

Composed by Ferdinando Paër (June 1, 1771 – May 3, 1839). Libretto by Sofie Gay. French. Based on "Le Souper Imprévu" by Alexandre Duval. Premiered Paris, Théâtre Feydeau, March 29, 1821. Set near Milan in the late 18th century. Comic opera. Set numbers with recitative and spoken dialogue in II. Overture. Entr'acte before II. A one-act version exists, which is essentially just the first act.

Sets: 1. **Acts:** 2 acts, 2 scenes. **Length:** I, II: 90. **Arias:** "Ah! quel bonheur de pressentir sa gloire" (Barnabé). **Hazards:** None. **Scenes:** I – II. A modestly furnished apartment.

Major roles: Gertrude (soprano), Barnabé (baritone), Benetto (tenor). **Minor roles** (not in 1-act version): Sans-Quartier (bass), Captain Firmin (tenor), Coélénie (soprano).

Chorus parts: SSATTB (only in 2-act version). **Chorus roles:** Villagers and soldiers. **Dance/movement:** I: Barnabé imitates the dance in his new opera. **Orchestra:** 2 fl (picc), 2 ob, 2 cl, 2 bsn, 2 hrn, timp, perc, strings. **Stageband:** None. **Publisher:** Colombier. **Rights:** Expired.

I. Gertrude, cook to the music master Barnabé, complains about her master and his nephew Benetto. She frightens the two men by telling them the French are attacking. Barnabé sends Benetto out for wine. Barnabé imagines the premiere of his opera "Cleopatra."

II. Barnabé rehearses his student, Coélénie. The soldier Sans Quartier returns for his love, Gertrude, and Benetto and Coélénie declare their love.

Věc Makropulos • The Makropulos Affair

Composed by Leoš Janáček (July 3, 1854 – August 12, 1928). Libretto by Leoš Janáček. Czech. Based on the play by Karel Capek. Premiered Brno, Brno Theater, December 18, 1926. Set in Prague in 1920s. Tragedy. Through composed. Prelude.

Sets: 3. **Acts:** 3 acts, 3 scenes. **Length:** I: 35. II: 30. III: 30. **Hazards:** None. **Scenes:** I. The clerk's room in Dr. Kolenaty's office. II. The stage of a large theater. III. A hotel room.

Major roles: Albert Gregor (tenor), Emilia Marty (dramatic soprano), Kolenatý (bass baritone), Jaroslav Prus (baritone). **Minor roles:** Vítek (tenor), Kristina/Krista (mezzo), Cleaning woman (contralto),

Stagehand (bass), Janek (tenor), Hauk-Šendorf (tenor), Chambermaid (contralto).

Chorus parts: TTBB. **Chorus roles:** Offstage at end of opera. **Dance/movement:** None. **Orchestra:** 4 fl (2 picc), 2 ob, Eng hrn, 3 cl (bs cl), 2 bsn, cont bsn, 4 hrn, 3 trp, 3 trb, tuba, timp, perc, harp, celeste, strings. **Stageband:** I, III: 2 hrn, 2 trp, timp. **Publisher:** Universal Edition. **Rights:** Copyright 1926, 1970 by Universal Edition.

I. Kolenatý's law clerk, Vítek, digs out the file on Gregor v. Prus, a case that has been in the courts for almost one hundred years. Vítek's daughter, Krista, impressed by the diva Emilia Marty, wants to be an opera singer. Marty asks Kolenatý about the Gregor case. The lawyer explains that when Baron Prus died a century ago, he left conflicting instructions: His heir was either Ferdinand Gregor or Mac Gregor. Marty points out that "Mac Gregor" was Ferdinand's nickname, his mother being the Scottish opera singer Ellian MacGregor. Marty claims that among Baron Prus's papers is a written will. Although Kolenatý thinks Marty is lying, he agrees to try. Gregor tells Marty he is so in debt that if he loses his case, he will have to kill himself. Marty's beauty captivates him and he offers her anything she wants. She asks for the Greek documents willed to him, but he does not know what she is talking about. Kolenatý returns with the will. Prus asks for proof that Ferdinand was Baron Prus's son, which Marty provides.

II. Marty's admirers visit her after her performance. Krista breaks up with Prus's son Janek. Marty is rude to everyone except Hauk-Šendorf, a crazy old man who thinks Marty is a gypsy girl he loved fifty years ago. Along with the will, Prus found an envelope addressed to Elina Makropulos—the mother listed on the birth certificate of the illegitimate Ferdinand Makropulos. Marty tries unsuccessfully to buy the envelope from Prus. Gregor tells her he loves her. She convinces Janek to steal the envelope for her, but Prus overhears.

III. After sleeping with Marty, Prus gives her the letter himself. They learn that Janek has killed himself for love of Marty. Deciding to run away with Hauk-Šendorf, Marty is stopped by Kolenatý, Prus and Gregor: They have discovered that the note from Ellian MacGregor proving Ferdinand's parentage was written in modern ink. Marty admits she was Ellian—and Elina—and many other women. She is 337 years old, her father having given her a potion that kept her young. The youth formula is in the envelope, but Marty has lost interest in living. "Being mortal is the only thing that gives life meaning," she explains. Marty gives the Makropulos formula to Krista who burns it.

Malady of Love

Composed by Lehman Engel (September 14, 1910 – August 29, 1982). Libretto by Lewis Allan. English. Original work. Premiered New York City, May 27, 1954. Set in An office in the present. "Sham" opera. Set numbers with recitative.

Sets: 1. **Acts:** 1 act, 1 scene. **Length:** I: 25. **Hazards:** None. **Scenes:** I. A psychoanalyst's office.

Major roles: Dr. Stanley Barlow (baritone), Emily Brown (soprano). (Score suggests using doubles to act out dream sequences.)

Chorus parts: N/A. **Chorus roles:** None. **Dance/movement:** I: Doctor and Emily waltz. **Orchestra:** fl, cl, hrn, trp, trb, drums, piano, strings. **Stageband:** None. **Publisher:** Harold Flammer, Inc. **Rights:** Copyright 1954 by Harold Flammer, Inc.

I. Emily Brown consults a psychiatrist she met at a cocktail party about a dream she has been having. Doctor and patient fall in love.

Les Malheurs d'Orphée • The Misfortunes of Orphée

Composed by Darius Milhaud (September 4, 1892 – June 22, 1974). Libretto by Armand Lunel. French. Inspired by Greek mythology. Premiered Brussels, Théâtre de la Monnaie, May 7, 1926. Set in France at an unspecified time. Tragedy. Set numbers with recitative.

Sets: 3. **Acts:** 3 acts, 3 scenes. **Length:** I, II, III: 40. **Hazards:** None. **Scenes:** I. The last houses of a village on the edge of the open country. II. A natural clearing formed by steep walls at the back of the landscape. III. The interior of Orphée's house.

Major roles: Orphée (baritone), Eurydice (soprano). **Minor roles:** Blacksmith (tenor), Cartwright (baritone), Basket maker (bass), Fox (soprano), Boar (tenor), Bear (bass), Wolf (contralto), Younger gypsy sister (mezzo), Elder gypsy sister (contralto), Twin gypsy sister (soprano).

Chorus parts: N/A. **Chorus roles:** None. **Dance/movement:** None. **Orchestra:** fl, ob (Eng hrn), cl, bs cl, bsn, trp, timp, perc, harp, solo strings. **Stageband:** None. **Publisher:** Heugel & Co. **Rights:** Copyright 1926 by Heugel.

I. The village tradesmen warn their healer, Orphée, to spend his time among people, not animals. Orphée promises to do so, having fallen in love with the gypsy girl Eurydice. She leaves her family to be with Orphée, but the gypsies pursue her, and Orphée and Eurydice flee into the mountains.

II. Eurydice, dying, makes their animal protectors promise to watch over Orphée. III. Heartbroken, Orphée has returned to the village where Eurydice's sisters blame him for her death and beat him to death.

Les Mamelles de Tirésias • The Breasts of Tirésias

Composed by Francis Poulenc (January 7, 1899 – January 30, 1963). Libretto by Guillaume Apollinaire. French. Based on Apollinaire's play. Premiered Paris, Opéra Comique, June 3, 1947. Set in Zanzibar in 1910. Comic opera. Through composed. Prologue. Entr'acte with singing and dancing before II. Revised January 1963.

Sets: 1. **Acts:** 2 acts, 17 scenes. **Length:** I, II: 55. **Hazards:** I: Thérèse's breasts turn into balloons and blow up. **Scenes:** Prologue. Before the curtain. I – II. The main square of Zanzibar.

Major roles: Thérèse/Tirésias/Fortune teller (soprano), Husband (baritone), Gendarme (baritone). **Minor roles:** Manager (baritone), Presto (baritone), Lacouf (tenor), Newspaper seller (mezzo), Journalist (tenor), Son (baritone). **Bit parts:** Newborn (tenor), Elegant lady (mezzo), Heavy woman (mezzo), Bearded gentleman (bass).

Chorus parts: SSAATTBB. **Chorus roles:** Offstage (4 tenor, 4 baritone), people of Zanzibar, infants. **Dance/movement:** I: Presto and Lacouf dance a polka. Husband and gendarme dance. II: Singing and dancing during the entr'acte. Thérèse and her husband dance seductively. **Orchestra:** 2 fl (picc), 2 ob (Eng hrn), 2 cl, bs cl, 2 bsn, 2 hrn, 2 trp, trb, tuba, timp, perc, celeste, xylophone, glockenspiel, harp, piano, strings (10-8-6-4-3). **Stageband:** None. **Publisher:** Heugel & Co. **Rights:** Copyright 1947, 1963 by Heugel & Co.

Prologue. The theater manager introduces the opera. Ii. Thérèse tells her husband that she wants to be a soldier, not a mother. Her breasts turn into balloons—which she blows up—and she grows a beard. Iii. Thérèse's husband no longer recognizes her. She changes her name to Tirésias. Iiii. Thérèse moves out of their house. Iiv. Presto and Lacouf are drunk and have been gambling. The two old friends goodnaturedly decide to fight a duel. Iv. They shoot and kill each other. Ivi. The gendarme investigates. He is attracted to the husband, who is dressed as a woman. Ivii. Since women want equality—and refuse to have children—

the husband decides to have the children. Iviii. He promises to show the gendarme how.

IIi. The husband nurses his infants. IIii. A journalist interviews him about his children. The husband shows him the novel one of the infants has written—and then throws the journalist out. IIiii. The husband explains that having children makes him richer. IIiv. His son blackmails him. IIv. He considers disowning the son. IIvi. The gendarme tells the husband that the people of Zanzibar are starving because he has had so many thousands of children. The husband recommends they talk to the clairvoyant, who has food cards. IIvii. She tells the husband that only the fecund will be rich—and reveals that she is really his wife Thérèse. The husband is overcome with love for her. IIviii. The people of Zanzibar tell the audience to go have children.

Manon

Composed by Jules-Emile-Frédéric Massenet (May 12, 1842 – August 13, 1912). Libretto by Henri Meilhac and Philippe Gille. French. Based on the novel by the Abbé Antoine-François Prévost. Premiered Paris, Opéra Comique, January 19, 1884. Set in Paris and Amiens in the early 18th century. Tragic romance. Set numbers with accompanied recitative and spoken dialogue. Prelude. Entr'acte to III. Ballet.

Sets: 6. **Acts:** 5 acts, 6 scenes. **Length:** I: 35. II: 25. III: 50 IV: 20. V: 15. **Arias:** "Adieu, notre petite table" (Manon), "Ah, fuyez douce image" (Des Grieux), "En fermant les yeux" (Des Grieux). **Hazards:** None. **Scenes:** I. The courtyard of an inn at Amiens. II. Apartment of Des Grieux and Manon in the Rue Vivienne, Paris. IIIi. Cours la Reine, Paris. IIIii. Reception room of the seminary of St. Sulpice. IV. The Hotel Transylvanie, Paris. V. On the road to Le Havre.

Major roles: Chevalier des Grieux (tenor), Lescaut (baritone), Guillot de Morfontaine (tenor), De Brétigny (baritone), Manon Lescaut (soprano). **Minor roles:** Count des Grieux (bass), Innkeeper (baritone), Poussette (soprano), Javotte (mezzo), Rosette (mezzo). **Bit parts:** Two guards (tenor, bass), Sergeant (tenor), Maid (mezzo). **Speaking:** Porter of the seminary, gambler.

Chorus parts: SSAATTTTTTBB. **Chorus roles:** People of Amiens and Paris, travelers, post boys and porters (many solo lines in I), vendors and dressmakers (many solo lines in III), devoted women, lords and ladies, card sharks, gamblers, guards. **Dance/movement:** III: Ballet. **Orchestra:** 2 fl (picc), 2 ob (Eng hrn), 2 cl, 2 bsn, 4 hrn, 2 trp, 3 trb, timp, perc, harp, strings. **Stageband:** III: 2 vln, cl, bsn, vlc, bs, organ. **Publisher:** Schirmer, Musicus. **Rights:** Expired.

I. Guillot and Brétigny and a trio of actresses loudly demand dinner from the innkeeper. The innkeeper remembers that he promised to reserve a seat on the first coach for the Chevalier des Grieux. People gather to see who will arrive on the coach. Lescaut leaves his companions at the inn while he awaits his cousin, Manon, who is on her way to a convent. When the coach arrives, all the passengers try to get their luggage at once. Lescaut is charmed by Manon's beauty and innocence. Guillot makes a pass at her, but she only laughs. Lescaut leaves Manon in the courtyard while he goes off to gamble, abjuring her not to do anything that might stain the family name. Seeing Manon, Des Grieux decides not to leave Amiens. He introduces himself and the pair fall in love. Des Grieux invites her to come with him to Paris and Manon hits on the idea of stealing Guillot's carriage. Lescaut returns and accuses the carriage-less Guillot of abducting Manon, but Guillot sets him straight.

II. Manon is living with Des Grieux in Paris. He wants to marry her and writes to his father for permission. Lescaut, who has caught up with them, is abrasive, but he only wants to know that Des Grieux will marry Manon. Brétigny, one of Manon's would-be lovers, has come along to warn her that Des Grieux's father will abduct Des Grieux that night. He promises to make her life easy if she leaves Des Grieux. Manon struggles with herself, but, feeling herself unworthy of him, does not warn Des Grieux and he is abducted.

IIIi. On the Cours la Reine, Parisians shop and toast the king. Brétigny and Guillot discuss women's fickleness. Manon, now living with Brétigny, is the toast of the town and Guillot plots to steal her. Brétigny and Manon meet Des Grieux's father, the count, who tells them his son has taken holy orders. Guillot hires the opera ballet to entertain Manon, but she flees to St. Sulpice and Des Grieux. IIIii. Des Grieux has impressed the women of the congregation with his religious discourse. He is furious with Manon for her betrayal, but he succumbs to her pleading to return.

IV. Lescaut gambles in the hotel Transylvania, and Manon badgers Des Grieux into playing to replenish their depleted fortunes. When he wins, Guillot accuses him of cheating. Des Grieux's father brings the police, who lock up Des Grieux and Manon.

V. Des Grieux's father gets him out of jail, but Manon is to be deported. Des Grieux and Lescaut bribe a sergeant to speak with Manon who feels guilty about how she treated Des Grieux. Her strength exhausted by prison life, Manon dies in Des Grieux's arms.

Manon Lescaut

Composed by Giacomo Puccini (December 22, 1858 – November 29, 1924). Libretto by Marco Praga, Giuseppe Giacosa, Domenico Oliva, Giulio Ricordi and Luigi Illica. Italian. Based on the novel by the Abbé Antoine-François Prévost. Premiered Turin, Teatro Regio, February 1, 1893. Set in France and America in the second half of the 18th century. Lyric drama. Through composed. Intermezzo before III.

Sets: 4. **Acts:** 4 acts, 4 scenes. **Length:** I: 35. II: 40. III: 20. IV: 20. **Arias:** "Donna non vidi mai" (Des Grieux), "In quelle trine morbide" (Manon), "No! pazzo son!" (Des Grieux), "Sola, perduta, abbandonata" (Manon). **Hazards:** None. **Scenes:** I. Spacious square near the Paris gate at Amiens. II. Elegant room in Geronte's house in Paris. III. Square near the harbor in Le Havre. IV. Vast plain on the borders of New Orleans.

Major roles: Manon Lescaut (soprano), Lescaut (baritone), Cavalier Renato des Grieux (tenor). **Minor roles:** Geronte di Ravoir (bass), Edmondo (tenor), Innkeeper (bass), Singer (mezzo), Dancing master (tenor), Sergeant of the royal archers (bass), Lamp lighter (tenor), Naval captain (bass). **Mute:** Hair dresser.

Chorus parts: SSSAATTTB. **Chorus roles:** Old men, abbés, girls, villagers, nobles, citizens, students, people, courtesans, archers, sailors, soldiers, prisoners. **Dance/movement:** II: Manon's dance lesson. **Orchestra:** 3 fl (picc), 2 ob, Eng hrn, 2 cl, bs cl, 2 bsn, 4 hrn, 3 trp, 3 trb, tuba, timp, perc, harp, bells, celesta, strings. **Stageband:** I: drum, trp. II: string quartet. **Publisher:** Schirmer, Ricordi. **Rights:** Expired.

I. Edmondo and the other students, who are wooing the girls, wonder if Des Grieux is in love. The coach from Arras arrives carrying Lescaut, his sister Manon and Geronte. While Lescaut makes arrangements with the innkeeper, Manon is approached by Des Grieux. She is being sent to a convent by her father and is easily persuaded to meet Des Grieux later. The students laugh at Des Grieux's new adventure. Lescaut, confiding in Geronte that he disagrees with the decision to make Manon a nun, sits down to wine and cards with the students. Geronte, meanwhile, arranges for a carriage. He is overhead by Edmondo, who warns Des Grieux that the old man means to abduct Manon for himself. Des Grieux quickly persuades Manon to fly with him instead—in Geronte's carriage. Geronte is frantic when he discovers what has happened, but Lescaut is philosophical. "We will go to Paris tomorrow," Lescaut assures Geronte. "Manon is used to comfort," he explains, "and she will be only to grateful to have you when the purse of her young student is exhausted."

II. Manon has moved into Geronte's Paris home, where she is having her hair done. Lescaut compliments her on her desertion of the penniless Des Grieux, but Manon misses him. "As his good friend," Lescaut says, "I have taught him how to cheat at cards so he may win a fortune for you." A group of singers bore the siblings with Geronte's latest composition while the dancing master gives Manon a lesson. Geronte's friends pay court to her. When they leave, Des Grieux appears, disgusted with Manon. She wins him over, but their professions of love are interrupted by Geronte who reproaches Manon for her ingratitude and storms out. While the lovers are laying their plans, Lescaut warns them that Geronte has denounced them. Manon's attempt to take her jewels with her slows them down and she is arrested.

Intermezzo. Unable to secure Manon's release, Des Grieux decides to follow her into exile. III. At the port of Le Havre, Lescaut and Des Grieux bribe a guard to release Manon, but the attempted jail break fails. The women are put on the ship for America. Des Grieux begs the captain to take him along and the captain agrees. IV. Manon and Des Grieux are alone in the desert. Manon dies.

Maria Golovin

Composed by Gian Carlo Menotti (b. July 7, 1911). Libretto by Gian Carlo Menotti. English. Original work Premiered Brussels, International Exposition Pavilion Theater, August 20, 1958. Set in Donato's villa near a frontier in a European country a few years after a recent war. Tragedy. Through composed. Prelude before I, III. Interludes between scenes. Revised version premiered Washington, D.C., January 22, 1965.

Sets: 2. **Acts:** 3 acts, 7 scenes. **Length:** I: 40. II: 35. III: 35. **Hazards:** None. **Scenes:** I. The living room of Donato's villa. II. A terrace in front of the house. III. The living room.

Major roles: Agata (mezzo), Donato (bass baritone), Donato's mother (contralto), Maria Golovin (soprano). **Minor roles:** Dr. Zuckertanz (tenor), Prisoner (baritone). **Bit part:** Another prisoner (tenor). Speaking bit: Trottolò (8 years old). **Mute:** Manservant.

Chorus parts: TTBB. **Chorus roles:** Male prisoners (offstage). **Dance/movement:** None. **Orchestra:** 2 fl (picc), 2 ob (Eng hrn), 2 cl (bs cl), 2 bsn, 4 hrn, 3 trp, 3 trb, tuba, timp, 2 perc, harp, xylophone, strings. **Stageband:** III: jazz band (piano, cl, vln, vlc). **Publisher:** Belwin-Mills. **Rights:** Copyright 1958, 1959, 1978 by Belwin-Mills Publishing Corp.

Ii. Agata is derisive of Donato's mother's obsequiousness before Maria

Golovin, her new tenant. Maria and her son, Trottolò, are introduced to
Donato and the tutor, Dr. Zuckertanz. Donato—who was blinded in the
war—asks Agata if Maria is beautiful. The sounds from the camp for
prisoners of war remind Maria that her own husband has not returned.
Donato confesses his loneliness. They discuss their hobbies: Maria
paints, Donato makes bird cages. Maria allows Donato to touch her face.
When Maria tells Trottolò that Donato made the cage for him, Donato is
infuriated and throws his chair across the room. Iii. Agata tells Donato
that everyone knows about his affair with Maria and warns him not to
trust Maria. While teaching Maria Braille, Donato asks about her past
affairs. She hides when Trottolò appears.

IIi. Agata tells Donato about a letter addressed to Maria from one of her
former lovers. She offers to spy for him. An escaped prisoner
demands—at gunpoint—that they hide him. When he promises to leave
after dark, Donato agrees. Mother complains that Maria spoils Trottolò.
Donato tells his mother that while he loves Maria, he knows she lies to
him. In private, he asks Maria why she did not come last night. She
answers that Trottolò has been spying on her. Donato entraps Maria into
lying about the letter. The three women reminisce. IIii. Mother and the
tutor take Trottolò off to a neighbor's party. When Donato accuses Maria
of lying she calls Agata to read the—innocent—letter. Donato begs forgiveness but Maria runs off. The prisoner—who has lost everything—
finds Donato's problems trivial. He leaves Donato his gun.

IIIi. Dr. Zuckertanz and Maria sing duets. A telegram arrives announcing the release of Maria's husband. IIIii. Mother orders Maria out of the
house, but is chastened by Maria's suffering. She notes that Donato's
love has become obsessive. Donato objects to the party Maria is throwing for her husband's return. She agrees to visit him at midnight—her
birthday. Donato begs Maria never to leave him. IIIiii. It is two o'clock
when Maria finally comes. She tells Donato she must leave him. He pulls
his gun to shoot her but cannot find her. Mother returns and directs his
shot into empty space. Letting him think he has killed Maria, Mother
plans their escape across the border.

Maria Stuarda

Composed by Gaetano Donizetti (November 29, 1797 – April 8, 1848).
Libretto by Giuseppe Bardari. Italian. Based on the play by Johann
Friedrich von Schiller. Premiered Milan, Teatro alla Scala, December 30,
1835. Set in England in the late 16th century. Lyric tragedy. Set numbers
with recitative. Prelude. Later reset in the 12th century in an attempt to
allay concerns of the censor. Premiered as "Buondelmonte" in Naples,
Teatro San Carlo, October 18, 1834. Can also be done in two acts.

Sets: 4. **Acts:** 3 acts, 5 scenes. **Length:** I: 35. II: 35. III: 75. **Arias:** "Deh! tu di una umile preghiera" (Maria). **Hazards:** None. **Scenes:** I. A gallery in the palace of Westminster. II. The park at Fotheringhay. IIIi. The gallery. IIIii. Maria Stuarda's private chamber in the castle of Fotheringhay. IIIiii. The hall next to the place of execution.

Major roles: Queen Elisabetta (soprano or mezzo), Leicester (tenor), Maria Stuarda (soprano). **Minor roles:** Talbot (bass), Cecil (baritone), Anna (contralto). **Bit part:** Offstage voice (tenor).

Chorus parts: SATTB. **Chorus roles:** Lords, ladies and attendants of Queen Elisabetta's court, courtiers, guards, hunters, servants of Maria Stuarda, sheriff and his officers. **Dance/movement:** None. **Orchestra:** picc, 2 fl, 2 ob, 2 cl, 2 bsn, 4 hrn, 2 trp, 3 trb, timp, perc, harp, strings. **Stageband:** II: 2 trp. **Publisher:** F. Gerard, G. Ricordi. **Rights:** Expired.

I. Queen Elisabetta's courtiers anticipate her marriage to the King of France. Talbot asks the queen to pardon Maria Stuarda, but Cecil councils death: Alive, Maria is a threat to the throne. It vexes the queen that Leicester loves Maria, not her. Through Talbot, Leicester receives a letter from Maria and determines to save her. The queen interrogates Leicester. She reads Maria's letter and is moved. Leicester asks the queen to visit Maria.

II. Maria wishes she were free. But the sound of the royal hunt—and the possibility of a meeting with the queen—unnerves her. Leicester assures Maria the queen will forgive her. He brings Elisabetta. But the queen insults Maria, who answers in kind. The queen orders Maria's execution.

IIIi. Cecil extinguishes the queen's remaining doubts about the execution and Leicester is unable to change her mind. IIIii. Maria worries that association with her will hurt Leicester. Cecil brings Maria the signed death warrant. Talbot visits Maria in the vestments of a Catholic priest. He hears her confession and absolves her sins. IIIiii. Maria's servants are horrified by the preparations for the execution. They fall silent in their mistress's presence. Maria takes her leave of them. Leicester is overcome with grief, but Maria goes to her death with forgiveness on her lips.

Mârouf

Composed by Henri Rabaud (November 10, 1873 – September 11, 1949). Libretto by Lucien Népoty. French. Based on the "Thousand and One Nights." Premiered Paris, Opéra Comique, May 15, 1914. Set in Cairo and Khaïtân at an unspecified time. Comic opera. Through composed. Introduction. Entr'acte before II, IV. Ballet.

Sets: 5. **Acts:** 5 acts, 5 scenes. **Length:** I, II, III, IV, V: 140. **Hazards:** V: Fellah turns into a genie. Dwarves appear out of the ground bearing riches for Mârouf. **Scenes:** I. A poor cobbler's booth off an alley of the market in Cairo. II. The marketplace of Khaïtân. III. An inner court in the sultan's palace. IV. The Harem at Khaïtân. V. A plain in the environs of Khaïtân.

Major roles: Mârouf (tenor), Sultan of Khaïtân (bass), Princess Saamcheddine (soprano). **Minor roles:** Fattoumah (soprano), Pastry cook Ahmad (bass), Two policemen (tenor, bass), Ali (baritone), First merchant (tenor), Second merchant (bass), Beggar (tenor), Vizier (bass), Fellah/Genie (tenor). **Bit parts:** Kâdi (bass), Sea captain (tenor), First off-stage muezzin (tenor), Second offstage muezzin (tenor), First slave (bass), Second slave (bass). **Speaking:** Sheik al Islam (reads in an under-tone but words are not meant to be heard).

Chorus parts: SSAATTBB. **Chorus roles:** Neighbors, sailors, mamelukes, caravaneers, slaves, ladies of the harem, populace. **Dance/movement:** III: Ballet of the sultan's slaves. **Orchestra:** 3 fl (picc), 3 ob (Eng hrn), 3 cl, 2 bsn, 4 hrn, 3 trp, 3 trb, tuba, timp, perc, xylophone, celeste, harp, strings. **Stageband:** II: tambourine, drum. III: fl (picc), perc, harp. **Publisher:** Choudens. **Rights:** Copyright 1914 by Choudens.

I. Mârouf envies men who have young, beautiful wives. His wife, Fattoumah, demands he bring her a sweet cake. Mârouf does not have the money to buy cake, but his friend Ahmad the pastry cook gives him one free. The cake is made with honey from sugar cane, but Fattoumah insists on bee honey. Mârouf eats the cake himself. Fattoumah is infuri-ated and runs off. She returns with the Kâdi, who has Mârouf beaten for supposedly beating his wife. Mârouf takes ship to leave his wife.

II. Mârouf has been shipwrecked. He is saved by Ali—Ahmad the pastry cook's son and the richest merchant in Khaïtân. He dresses Mârouf in his best clothes and tells everyone that Mârouf is the richest merchant in the world. They are impressed. The sultan and his vizier enter the mar-ketplace disguised as merchants. Mârouf lies and says he is expecting a rich caravan. The sultan invites him to dinner.

III. The sultan decides to wed Mârouf to his daughter. He promises to bear the wedding costs himself since Mârouf's caravan has not arrived. Mârouf distributes the sultan's money liberally. He is reluctant to take a second wife, but the princess's beauty so overcomes him that he blurts out his real identity and faints.

IV. The sultan listens to his vizier's doubts about Mârouf. His son-in-law's expenses have emptied the treasury. The vizier questions the princess, who defends her husband vigorously. Nevertheless, she promises her father she will find out when the caravan is due to arrive. Mârouf tells the princess the truth (which she already knew). She swears she loves him anyway and the lovers flee the palace.

V. A fellah sings to his donkey. He takes in Mârouf and the princess. While working the fellah's fields, Mârouf discovers a buried staircase and cavern. It is guarded by the fellah—who is really a genie. The genie promises to grant Mârouf his rich caravan. The vizier discovers them and arrests Mârouf. Mârouf and Ali are about to be beheaded by order of the sultan when Mârouf's caravan appears.

The Marriage of Figaro

See "Le Nozze di Figaro" entry.

Martha

Composed by Friedrich von Flotow (April 27, 1812 – January 24, 1883). Libretto by Friedrich Wilhelm Riese. German. Based on the ballet "Lady Henriette" by Jules-Henri Vernoy de Saint-Georges which was itself based on the vaudeville "La Comtesse d'Egmont." Premiered Vienna, Kärntnerthortheater, November 25, 1847. Set near Richmond circa 1710. Romantic comedy. Set number with recitative. Overture. Ballet.

Sets: 5. **Acts:** 4 acts, 5 scenes. **Length:** I: 45. II: 25. III: 20. IV: 25. **Arias:** "Ach so fromm" (Lionel), Porterlied/Drinking song (Plunkett). **Hazards:** None. **Scenes:** Ii. Boudoir of Lady Harriet. Iii. Fairground at Richmond. II. A room in Plunkett's farmhouse. III. Forest near Richmond. IVi. The farmhouse. IVii. Lady Harriet's park.

Major roles: Lady Harriet Durham/Martha (soprano), Nancy/Julia (mezzo), Plunkett (bass baritone), Lionel (tenor). **Minor roles:** Lord Tristan of Mickleford (bass), Sheriff (bass). **Bit parts:** Three servants (tenor, 2 bass), Three servant maids (soprano or mezzo). **Mute:** Queen Anne.

Chorus parts: SSSSAATTBB. **Chorus roles:** Courtiers, ladies, maids, servants, vendors, farmers and their wives, country girls, hunters, huntresses, people of Richmond. **Dance/movement:** I: Fairground ballet. **Orchestra:** 2 fl (picc), 2 ob, 2 cl, 2 bsn, 4 hrn, 2 trp, 3 trb, ophicléide, timp, perc, harp, strings. **Stageband:** I: perc. **Publisher:** Schirmer, Kalmus. **Rights:** Expired.

Ii. Lady Harriet Durham is bored by wealth and pomp and even more bored by her would-be suitor Sir Tristram. Seeing a group of country girls on their way to the fair, Lady Harriet and her maid Nancy decide to join them in disguise. They take Sir Tristram along, disguised as Farmer Bob. Iii. The tradition at the fair is for farmers to "bid" to hire the fairest girls for the coming year. Farmer Plunkett and his foster brother, Lionel, have come to the fair to find a farm girl to help with the work now that their mother is dead. They recount how Lionel's father came to the Plunkett farm; he died leaving Lionel only a ring. The sheriff oversees the auction to insure the bidding is fair. Overcoming their shyness, Lionel and Plunkett hire Lady Harriet and Nancy while Sir Tristram makes a futile attempt to buy the ladies back.

II. The women have adopted false names. Martha (Lady Harriet) and Julia (Nancy) refuse to hang up the men's coats and have to be taught how to spin. Lionel proposes to Martha, who rejects him. When night falls, the girls are relieved to be rescued by Tristram.

III. Plunkett and a group of huntsmen accompany the queen on the hunt. Lady Harriet misses Lionel, but she pretends not to know him when she meets him. When he asserts his contract with her, Tristram has him arrested. Lionel realizes what has happened and tries to tell his story to the courtiers. He gives his ring to the queen, who rides off.

IV. Lionel is furious with Lady Harriet even though she has repented. She brings a message from the queen: Lionel is to be restored to the fortunes of his father, the Earl of Derby. Nancy and Plunkett tease each other, but agree to be married. The court dresses up as peasants to reenact the Richmond fair. Seeing his own Martha, Lionel relents.

Mary, Queen of Scots

Composed by Thea Musgrave (b. May 27, 1928). Libretto by Thea Musgrave. English. Based on the play "Moray" by Amalia Elguera. Premiered Edinburgh, Scottish Opera, Edinburgh International Festival, September 6, 1977. Set in Edinburgh in the 1560s. Tragedy. Set numbers with recitative. Orchestral prelude before III. Interlude in III.

Sets: 8. **Acts:** 3 acts, 9 scenes. **Length:** I: 55. II: 45. III: 30. **Hazards:** None. **Scenes:** Ii. Cardinal Beaton's house in Edinburgh. Iii. The quay at Leith. Iiii. Outdoors. Iiv. A ballroom. IIi. An antechamber. IIii. Mary's supper room. IIiii. The council chamber. IIIi. Mary's supper room. IIIii. The palace courtyard.

Major roles: James Stuart Earl of Moray (baritone), Mary Queen of Scots (soprano), James Hepburn Earl of Bothwell (tenor), Henry Stuart Lord Darnley (tenor). **Minor roles:** Cardinal Beaton/David Riccio (bass baritone), Earl of Morton (baritone), Earl of Ruthven (tenor), Lord Gordon (bass), Mary Seton (soprano). **Bit parts:** Mary Beaton (soprano), Mary Livingstone (mezzo), Mary Fleming (mezzo), First lord (tenor), Second lord (baritone).

Chorus parts: SSAATTTTBBBB. **Chorus roles:** Monks, soldiers, courtiers, lords of the congregation and people of Edinburgh (minimum total 32). **Dance/movement:** I: Courtly dances (pavane, saltarello, reel). **Orchestra:** 2 fl (picc), 3 ob (2 Eng hrn), 2 cl (bs cl), 2 bsn (cont bsn), 3 hrn, 2 trp, trb, timp, perc, chamber organ, harp, strings (8-6-5-4-2). **Stageband:** I: fl (picc), ob, Eng hrn, bsn, trp, perc (whole group can be drawn from pit). **Publisher:** Novello. **Rights:** Copyright 1976, 1978 Novello & Co., Ltd.

Ii. James Stewart, the bastard son of King James V —and brother of Mary, Queen of Scots—returns to the home of his foster father, Cardinal Beaton. Beaton has been advising Mary to trust the Earl of Bothwell, because he suspects James wants to be king. James has the cardinal arrested. Iii. Mary returns to Scotland, ignoring Bothwell's warnings about James. Iiii. Beaton dies in prison. Lord Gordon fails to raise a rebellion against James. Iiv. Mary is attracted to Darnley and ignores James and Bothwell's warnings about him. Bothwell and Darnley argue and Mary orders Bothwell to leave to guard the frontier.

IIi. Mary and Darnley are married, but the Scottish lords refuse to make Darnley king. James's henchmen, Ruthven and Morton, convince Darnley that Mary is having an affair with her secretary, Riccio. James refuses to support Mary unless she abdicates in his favor. She refuses. IIii. Riccio consoles Mary. In a drunken fit, Darnley kills Riccio. IIiii. Some of the lords ask James to become regent. James tells the people that Mary has fled, but Mary appears and banishes James.

IIIi. Mary recalls Bothwell to protect her against James's army. Gordon warns Mary that the people hate and fear Bothwell. Bothwell murders Darnley and seduces Mary. James and his men defeat Bothwell. The crowd calls for Mary's death. Gordon tells her to flee to England, which she reluctantly does. IIIii. Gordon kills James. Morton holds up Mary's infant son and heir.

Masaniello

Composed by Daniel François Esprit Auber (January 29, 1782 – May 12, 1871). Libretto by Eugène Scribe and Germain Delavigne. French. Based on historical events. Premiered Paris, Opéra, February 29, 1828. Set in Italy in 1647. Grand opera. Set numbers with recitative. Overture. Introduction before II. Ballet. Also known as "La Muette de Portici."

Sets: 5. **Acts:** 5 acts, 5 scenes. **Length:** I: 30. II: 25. III: 15. IV: 30. V: 15. **Hazards:** V: Fenella throws herself into a volcano. **Scenes:** I. Before a church. II. On the coast. III. The market square. IV. Masaniello's cottage. V. Before the castle.

Major roles: Alfonso (tenor), Elvira (soprano), Masaniello (tenor). **Minor roles:** Lorenzo (tenor), Selva (bass), Borella (bass), Pietro (baritone). **Bit parts:** Emma (soprano or mezzo), Moreno (bass). **Mute dancer:** Fenella.

Chorus parts: SSAATTTTBB. **Chorus roles:** Courtiers, nobles, ladies, soldiers, fishermen, bridesmaids, rebels, people. **Dance/movement:** I: Spanish dances. III: ballet. **Orchestra:** picc, 2 fl, 2 ob, 2 cl, 2 bsn, 4 hrn, 2 trp, 3 trb, ophicléide, timp, perc, organ, strings. **Stageband:** III: church bells. **Publisher:** Boosey & Co., Troupenas. **Rights:** Expired.

I. Alfonso, son of the Neapolitan viceroy, is guilt stricken over his betrayal of Fenella to marry his new love, Elvira. His friend Lorenzo can learn nothing of Fenella's fate. Elvira, a Spanish princess, prepares for her wedding. Her countrywomen dance. Fenella, pursued by soldiers, throws herself at Elvira's feet. She has escaped from prison, where she was confined for her affair with Alfonso. Since Fenella cannot speak, she is unable to name her seducer. The wedding takes place. Elvira returns to help Fenella and learns that Alfonso is the guilty one.

II. Masaniello's fellow fishermen call on him to cheer them with a song. Pietro has failed to locate Masaniello's sister (Fenella). He and Masaniello swear vengeance on her abductor. Fenella considers taking her own life, but returns, instead, to her brother. At his urging she reveals her lover's identity. Masaniello rouses the fishermen to rebellion.

III. Alfonso begs Elvira to forgive him, which she eventually does. The village market is in full swing. Selva sees Fenella and tries to recapture her, but Masaniello and the fishermen come to her rescue and subdue Selva's soldiers.

IV. Masaniello is horrified by the bloodshed he has caused but calls on God to harden him to complete his task. The rebels lay siege to the castle. Fenella is distraught but her brother comforts her. Pietro reminds Masaniello of their agreement to murder the tyrant and his son. Alfonso and Elvira beg Fenella's mercy. Not recognizing Alfonso, Masaniello takes him in. When Alfonso is identified, Masaniello refuses to break his word: he orders his enemy returned to the castle unharmed.

V. The viceroy's soldiers are turning the tide and Masaniello has gone mad. Masaniello recovers enough to lead the rebels into battle but is slain by his own men for protecting Elvira. Alfonso's men triumph. Fenella throws herself into the erupting Vesuvius.

Maskarade • Masquerade

Composed by Carl Nielsen (June 9, 1865 – October 3, 1931). Libretto by Wilhelm Andersen. Danish. Comedy by Ludvig Holberg. Premiered Copenhagen, Royal Theater, November 11, 1906. Set in Copenhagen in 1723. Comic opera. Set numbers with recitative. Overture. Entr'acte before II. Ballet.

Sets: 3. **Acts:** 3 acts, 3 scenes. **Length:** I: 45. II: 40. III: 55. **Hazards:** None. **Scenes:** I. A room in Jeronimus's house. II. The street in front of Jeronimus's house. III. The main hall of the Grønnegade playhouse.

Major roles: Leander (tenor), Henrik (bass baritone), Jeronimus (bass). **Minor roles:** Magdelone (mezzo), Leonard (tenor or baritone), Arv (tenor), Night watchman (bass), First student (tenor), Officer (baritone), Pernille (soprano), Leonora (soprano), Mask vendor (baritone), Tutor (baritone), Master of the masquerade/Corporal Mars (bass baritone). **Bit parts:** Doorman at the playhouse (baritone), First maiden (soprano), Second student (tenor), Third Student (tenor), Flower vendor (soprano), Second maiden (soprano), Third maiden (alto), Fourth student (tenor), Fifth student (tenor). **Dancers:** Mars (speaking bit), Venus (speaking bit), Vulcan (mute). **Mute:** Dancing master.

Chorus parts: SSATTBB. **Chorus roles:** Students, officers, girls, maskers. **Dance/movement:** I: Magdelone dances for her son. II: Girls dance on the way to the masquerade. III: Cotillion. Dance of the Cockerels. Pantomime and ballet. **Orchestra:** 3 fl (picc), 2 ob, Eng hrn, 2 cl, 2 bsn, 4 hrn, 3 trp, 3 trb, tuba, timp, perc, harp, strings. **Stageband:** None. **Publisher:** Wilhelm Hansen. **Rights:** Expired.

I. Leander and his servant, Henrik, sleep off a long night of dancing and drinking at the masquerade. Leander has fallen in love with a girl he met there, but his father, Jeronimus, insists he marry Leonard's daughter, Leonora. Leander's mother, Magdelone, wants to go to the dance. Jeronimus is angry that Leander will not marry Leonora, but learns from Leonard that Leonora is equally reluctant to marry Leander. Jeronimus forbids his family to attend the masquerade.

II. Jeronimus posts his servant, Arv, at the gate to prevent anyone from leaving the house. Henrik disguises himself as a ghost and frightens Arv into confessing he slept with the kitchen maid. He then blackmails Arv into letting him and Leander go to the masquerade. Leander finds his love. It is Leonora, who he does not realize is Leonard's daughter. Jeronimus realizes his son has escaped and follows him. While Jeronimus is buying a mask, Magdelone sneaks out of the house.

III. Inside the playhouse, the maskers dance. Leander woos Leonora and Henrik woos Pernille. Leonard and Magdelone flirt. Henrik enlists a tutor's aide who gets Jeronimus drunk during the pantomime and ballet. Everyone unmasks and Jeronimus discovers that Leander and Leonora are in love.

I Masnadieri • The Bandits

Composed by Giuseppe Verdi (October 9, 1813 – January 27, 1901). Libretto by Andrea Maffei. Italian. Based on "Die Räuber" by Friedrich von Schiller. Premiered London, Her Majesty's Theatre, July 22, 1847. Set in Germany in the 18th century. Tragedy. Set numbers with recitative. Prelude.

Sets: 8. **Acts:** 4 acts, 9 scenes. **Length:** I, II, III, IV: 130. **Arias:** "Lo sguardo avea degli angeli" (Amalia), "Un ignoto, tre lune or saranno" (Massimiliano). **Hazards:** II: Prague is seen burning in the distance. **Scenes:** Ii. A tavern on the border with Saxony. Iii. A room in Moor castle in Franconia. Iiii. A bedroom in the castle. IIi. An enclosure adjoining the church chapel. IIii. The Bohemian forest. IIIi. A lonely place giving onto the forest near the castle. IIIii. The ruins of an ancient keep within the forest. IVi. A series of rooms. IVii. The ruins.

Major roles: Carlo (tenor), Francesco (baritone), Amalia (soprano), Massimiliano Count of Moor (bass). **Minor roles:** Rolla (tenor), Arminio (tenor), Moser (bass).

Chorus parts: SSATTBB. **Chorus roles:** Fallen women, bandits, ladies, girls, servants. **Dance/movement:** None. **Orchestra:** picc, fl, 2 ob, 2 cl, 2 bsn, 4 hrn, 2 trp, 3 trb, cimbasso, timp, perc, strings. **Stageband:** None. **Publisher:** Kalmus. **Rights:** Expired.

Ii. Carlo repents his dissipated life and hopes to return home to his father, Count Massimiliano, and his sweetheart, Amalia. He receives a letter from the count who has disowned him. Infuriated, Carlo forms his companions into a band of brigands. Iii. The letter was forged by Carlo's jealous younger brother, Francesco, who plans to do away with the count. Iiii. Francesco's servant, Arminio, arrives in disguise and reports that Carlo died fighting at the battle of Prague. He reads a letter from

Carlo telling Amalia to marry Francesco. The count faints and is believed dead.

IIi. Amalia visits the count's tomb, but her contemplation is interrupted by the sounds of Francesco's rejoicing. Arminio tells Amalia that he lied about Carlo's death. Francesco woos Amalia, but she rejects him. He threatens her and she defends herself with a dagger. IIii. Carlo frees one of his brigands from prison by setting fire to Prague. The brigands are surrounded by soldiers, but fight their way out.

IIIi. Amalia flees the castle and meets Carlo. IIIii. He leaves her rather than reveal the truth. Carlo finds his father the count imprisoned in the forest by Francesco and swears to revenge him.

IVi. Francesco wakes from a nightmare and calls for the priest, Moser. He asks what crimes most offend God. "Fratricide and patricide," Moser responds. Arminio reports that the brigands are attacking the castle. Francesco cannot bring himself to pray. IVii. Carlo admits his guilt to Amalia and the count. Amalia forgives him, but the brigands remind him of his oath. Carlo kills Amalia and goes voluntarily to the gallows.

Mathis der Maler • Mathis the Painter

Composed by Paul Hindemith (November 16, 1895 – December 28, 1963). Libretto by Paul Hindemith. German. Based on the life of the 16th century painter Mathias Grünewald. Premiered Zürich, Stadttheater, May 28, 1938. Set in Mainz in 1524. Tragedy. Through composed. Overture.

Sets: 8. **Acts:** 1 act, 8 scenes. **Length:** I: 190. **Hazards:** VI: Visions of St. Anthony/Mathis. **Scenes:** I. The yard of a cloister of the order of St. Anthony on the Main river. II. A hall in the cardinal's residence in Mainz. III. The interior of Riedinger's house on the town square of Mainz; the square visible in the background. IV. A small square surrounded by war-damaged houses in the village of Koenigshofen. V. The cardinal's study in Mainz. VIi. A forest. VIii. Hermitage of St. Paul. VII. Mathis's study in Mainz. (Seven "tableau" or scenes; no act divisions given.)

Major roles: Albrecht Cardinal of Brandenburg (tenor), Mathis (baritone), Riedinger (bass), Ursula (soprano), Regina (soprano). **Minor roles:** Lorenz of Pommersfelden (bass), Wolfgang Capito (tenor), Hans Schwalb (tenor), Prefect of Waldburg (bass), Sylvester of Schaumberg (tenor), Countess of Helfenstein (contralto). **Bit parts:** Count's piper (tenor), Four peasants (2 tenors, 2 basses). **Mute:** Count of Helfenstein.

Chorus parts: SSSAATTTTTBB. **Chorus roles:** Monks, Papist and Lutheran burghers (TTTTBB), humanist students (SAT), women (SSA), mercenaries of the chapter, peasants, soldiers. **Dance/movement:** None. **Orchestra:** 2 fl (picc), 2 ob, 2 cl, 2 bsn, 4 hrn, 2 trp, 3 trb, tuba, timp, 2 perc, strings. **Stageband:** IV: 3 trp. **Publisher:** B. Schott's Söhne. **Rights:** Copyright 1935 by B. Schott's Söhne.

I. Mathis, painter to the cardinal, wonders if a life of art is enough. In escaping their pursuers, the wounded Schwalb and his daughter, Regina, enter the cloister. Regina washes herself in the fountain and sings. Schwalb berates Mathis for painting while the world is immersed in war. Schwalb's pursuers discover him and Mathis hurries him and Regina away. Sylvester demands Schwalb and Mathis admits he helped him escape. He submits himself to the judgement of the cardinal.

II. A group of students and burghers fight in the cardinal's waiting room. Cardinal Albrecht thanks everyone for coming and announces he has retrieved the body of Saint Martin. The cardinal greets Ursula and Mathis. Ursula's father, Riedinger, warns the cardinal that people are angry over the book burning ordered by the Pope. The cardinal wants to rescind the order, but Pommersfelden persuades him not to. The cardinal is short of money. Sylvester brings a message from the prefect of Waldburg, asking the cardinal for reinforcements with which to fight the peasants. Sylvester accuses Mathis of helping the enemy. Mathis renounces painting and makes an impassioned plea for the peasantry. The cardinal's advisers want Mathis hanged, but the cardinal protects him.

III. Riedinger helps his fellow Lutherans hide their books, but the mercenaries find them. Capito produces a letter from Luther to the cardinal bidding him set an example for all Germany by taking a wife. The Lutherans decide to use the cardinal's money problems to their advantage by finding him a wealthy bride. Reidinger approaches his daughter, Ursula, about marrying the cardinal. Ursula does not want to marry the cardinal. She begs Mathis to take her with him, but he refuses: The painter intends to go to war. The book burning begins. Ursula agrees to marry the cardinal.

IV. A group of peasants executes the Count of Helfenstein, ignoring his wife's pleas for mercy. Mathis scolds the peasants for their cruelty and protects the countess. Schwalb leads the peasants into battle. He is slain, his army defeated. The victorious army enters the town. The countess intercedes with the prefect on Mathis's behalf. Mathis, feeling he has failed, flees with Regina.

V. The cardinal is furious with Capito for using his poverty to blackmail him into marriage. He chides Ursula for her cold-hearted zeal, but she makes a passionate plea for her faith. Deeply moved, the cardinal decides to retire to the life of a hermit.

VIi. Mathis and Regina rest. Mathis appears as St. Anthony. He is tempted by visions and tormented by demons. VIii. St. Paul (the cardinal) tells Mathis not to waste his God-given gifts.

VII. Mathis has returned to Mainz and his painting. His work has been prolific, but has broken him. He and Ursula comfort Regina, who dies. Mathis takes leave of his friend, the cardinal. Mathis packs his things and anticipates death.

Il Matrimonio Segreto • The Secret Marriage

Composed by Domenico Cimarosa (December 17, 1749 – January 11, 1801). Libretto by Giovanni Bertati. Italian. After "A Clandestine Marriage" by George Colman and David Garrick. Premiered Vienna, Burgtheater, February 7, 1792. Set in Bologna in the 18th century. Comic opera. Set numbers with accompanied recitative. Overture.

Sets: 2. **Acts:** 2 acts, 35 scenes. **Length:** I, II: 180. **Arias:** "Udite, tutti udite" (Geronimo), "Pria che spunti in ciel l'aurora" (Paolino). **Hazards:** None. **Scenes:** Ii – Iviii. A room in Geronimo's house. Iix – II. Geronimo's study.

Major roles: Paolino (tenor), Carolina (soprano), Geronimo (comic bass), Elisetta (high mezzo or soprano), Fidalma (contralto), Count Robinson (bass or baritone).

Chorus parts: N/A. **Chorus roles:** None. **Dance/movement:** None. **Orchestra:** 2 fl, 2 cl, 2 ob, 2 bsn, 2 hrn, 2 trp, timp, perc, strings. **Stageband:** None. **Publisher:** Ricordi, Imbault. **Rights:** Expired.

Ii. Carolina and Paolino plan to marry secretly. Paolino thinks it will be easier to break the news to Carolina's father, Geronimo, if he can arrange a marriage between Carolina's older sister, Elisetta, and his former employer, Count Robinson. Elisetta's dowry will be a powerful incentive for the count, Paolino knows. Iii. Geronimo receives a letter from the count announcing his intentions. Iiii. He announces the marriage to the family. Carolina is sad, which her father and sister mistake for envy. Iiv. The sisters fight. Geronimo's sister, Fidalma, begs them to behave. Iv. Fidalma confesses to Elisetta that she is in love—with Paolino. Ivi. Geronimo tries unsuccessfully to cheer up Carolina. Ivii.

The count is complimentary but nervous. Iviii. He mistakes both Carolina and Fidalma for his bride-to-be. The thought of marrying the ugly Elisetta horrifies him. Iix. Paolino decides to enlist the count's help. Ix. The count, however, asks his help in persuading Geronimo to let him marry Carolina instead of Elisetta. Ixi. Carolina rebuffs the count's advances. Ixii. The count guesses Carolina has a lover. Ixiii. Elisetta is upset by her fiancé's rudeness. Ixiv. The count continues to importune Carolina. Ixv. Elisetta catches them. Ixvi. The ensuing fight arouses Geronimo.

IIi. When the count agrees to take only a portion of the dowry if he can wed Carolina, Geronimo is convinced. He stipulates that Elisetta must agree. IIii. The count informs Paolino. IIiii. Paolino tries to confide in Fidalma, but she thinks he is trying to propose. He faints. IIiv. Carolina thinks Paolino has betrayed her. IIv. Paolino suggests they get married as planned. IIvi. Carolina refuses. IIvii. The count tries to persuade Elisetta to refuse him. IIviii. Fidalma and Elisetta decide to get their rival, Carolina, put in a convent. IIix. They try to convince Geronimo. IIx. He agrees. IIxi. And breaks the news to Carolina. IIxii. Carolina is heartbroken. IIxiii. Seeing her sad, the count swears to help her. IIxiv. Carolina begs her father for a reprieve. IIxv. Elisetta forgives the count. IIxvi. Geronimo entrusts Paolino with his letter to the convent. IIxvii. Paolino goes to Carolina. IIxviii. The count wants to help Carolina, but Elisetta will not let him out of her sight. IIxix. Paolino and Carolina get married. Elisetta catches them before they can flee and they plead for understanding. Geronimo disowns them. Only when the count agrees to marry Elisetta does Geronimo relent.

Mavra

Composed by Igor Stravinsky (June 17, 1882 – April 6, 1971). Libretto by Boris Kochno. Russian. Based on "The Little House at Kolomna" by Alexander Pushkin. Premiered Paris, Théâtre National de l'Opéra, June 3, 1922. Set in Russia in the 17th century. Comic opera. Set numbers. Overture.

Sets: 1. **Acts:** 1 act, 1 scene. **Length:** I: 25. **Hazards:** None. **Scenes:** I. A room in Parasha's home.

Major roles: Parasha (soprano), Hussar (tenor), Mother (contralto). **Minor role:** Neighbor (mezzo).

Chorus parts: N/A. **Chorus roles:** None. **Dance/movement:** None. **Orchestra:** picc, 2 fl, 2 ob, Eng hrn, 3 cl, 2 bsn, 4 hrn, 4 trp, 3 trb, tuba, timp, strings. **Stageband:** None. **Publisher:** Boosey & Hawkes, Russian

Music Edition. **Rights:** Copyright 1925 by Edition Russe de Musique. Assigned 1947 to Boosey & Hawkes.

I. Parasha loves a hussar. She questions his comings and goings, but agrees to see him again. Parasha's mother sends her next door to inquire about a new cook and she returns with the hussar, whom she introduces as Mavra, a young girl looking for employment. Left alone, the hussar removes his disguise to shave, which makes the mother mistake him for a robber. The hussar escapes through the window and the mother faints.

Maiskaya Noch • May Night

Composed by Nicolai Rimsky-Korsakov (March 18, 1844 – June 21, 1908). Libretto by Nicolai Rimsky-Korsakov. Russian. Based on a story by Nicolai Gogol. Premiered St. Petersburg, Maryinsky Theater, January 9 (January 21), 1880. Set in the Ukraine in legendary times. Fairy tale opera. Set numbers with accompanied recitative. Overture. Entr'acte before III.

Sets: 4. **Acts:** 3 acts, 4 scenes. **Length:** I: 55. II: 25. III: 50. **Arias:** "It happened long ago" (Levko), "Sleep, my beauty" (Levko). **Hazards:** Rusalki (water sprites) appear out of the lake. **Scenes:** I. A village street with Hanna's cottage front. IIi. The interior of the mayor's cottage. IIii. A street in the village near the clerk's hut. III. On the banks of the lake in front of the old squire's house.

Major roles: Levko (tenor), Hanna (mezzo), Mayor (bass). **Minor roles:** Kalenik (baritone or bass), Sister-in-law (contralto), Distiller (tenor), Clerk (bass), First nymph (mezzo), Nymph queen (soprano), Second nymph (mezzo). **Bit part:** Third nymph (mezzo).

Chorus parts: SSAATTBB. **Chorus roles:** Village boys and girls, bailiffs, Rusalki. **Dance/movement:** I: Charcoal burner drunkenly dances the "hopak." III: Dance of the Rusalki. **Orchestra:** picc, 2 fl, 2 ob (Eng hrn), 2 cl, 2 bsn, 4 hrn, 2 trp, 3 trb, timp, perc, 2 harp, piano, strings. **Stageband:** II: 2 picc, 2 cl, 2 hrn, trb, perc, string quintet. **Publisher:** Verlag Musik. **Rights:** Expired.

I. Levko and Hanna are in love, but Levko's father (the mayor) refuses his permission to let them marry. Hanna persuades Levko to tell her the story of the squire's house: a beautiful lieutenant's daughter was persecuted by her witch stepmother and eventually drowned herself. The daughter became a water sprite (Rusalka) and she and her fellow Rusalki drowned the stepmother. The daughter wants to complete her revenge, but she does not recognize which water sprite is the stepmother. Kalenik the charcoal burner comes home drunk. The mayor proposes to Hanna, who rejects him. Levko wants revenge.

Iii. Kalenik mistakenly enters the mayor's house to sleep off his drinking. Levko and the village boys throw a rock through the mayor's window and sing taunting songs. The mayor tries to capture Levko, but in the dark he grabs his sister-in-law instead. Iiii. The clerk thinks he has imprisoned Levko in his cottage, but the boys have substituted the sister-in-law. The mayor orders the boys arrested.

III. Levko sits by the lake at night, thinking of Hanna. A chorus of water sprites appear, including the beautiful daughter—who is still looking for her stepmother. Levko recognizes the stepmother and the water sprites drag her into the lake. Out of gratitude, the daughter gives Levko a letter to give to his father. The mayor orders Levko's arrest—until he sees the letter. It is from the commissar ordering the mayor to allow Hanna and Levko to marry.

Mazeppa

Composed by Peter Ilyitch Tchaikovsky (May 7, 1840 – November 6, 1893). Libretto by Peter Ilyitch Tchaikovsky and Viktor Burenin. Russian. Based on the epic poem "Poltava" by Alexander Pushkin. Premiered Moscow, Bolshoi Theater, February 15, 1884. Set in the Ukraine in the 18th century. Tragedy. Set numbers with recitative. Overture. Battle of Poltava enacted (without words) in Act III. Entr'acte before II, III. Interlude between IIi and IIii.

Sets: 6. **Acts:** 3 acts, 6 scenes. **Length:** I: 65. II: 65. III: 40. **Hazards:** I: Girls sail down the river. **Scenes:** Ii. Kotschubei's garden overlooking the river Dnieper. Iii. A room in Kotschubei's house. IIi. A dank dungeon in the palace at Whitechurch (Belaya Tserkov). IIii. A room with terrace in Mazeppa's palace. IIiii. A field with a scaffold. III. Battle of Poltava and Kotschubei's garden.

Major roles: Maria (soprano), Andrei (tenor), Mazeppa (baritone), Kotschubei (bass). **Minor roles:** Lyubov (mezzo), Iskra (tenor), Orlik (bass), Drunken cossak (tenor).

Chorus parts: SSAATTBB. **Chorus roles:** Cossacks, women, Kotschubei's servants, guests, musicians, servants, dancers, Mazeppa's bodyguards, monks, executioners. **Dance/movement:** I: People dance the "hopak." **Orchestra:** 3 fl (picc), 2 ob, Eng hrn, 2 cl, 2 bsn, 4 hrn, 4 trp, 3 trb, tuba, timp, perc, harp, strings. **Stageband:** II, III: Band. **Publisher:** State Music Publishers. **Rights:** Expired.

Ii. Maria stays behind while the other girls sail down the river. She loves the hetman (chieftan) Mazeppa. The cossak Andrei loves her. The people dance a hopak to honor Mazeppa. Mazeppa asks Maria's father, Kotschubei, for her hand, but Kotschubei says Mazeppa is too old for her and refuses his consent. Maria admits she loves Mazeppa and leaves with him. Iii. Kotschubei sends Andrei to Moscow to denounce Mazeppa to the tsar for conspiring with the Swedes.

IIi. The tsar does not believe Kotschubei's accusations and condemns him. Orlik tortures Kotschubei, but is unable to learn where his money is hidden. IIii. Mazeppa regrets Kotschubei's condemnation. He and Maria reaffirm their love. Maria's mother, Lyubov, tells her that Kotschubei is to be executed. IIiii. But Maria is too late to save her father.

III. Mazeppa's forces are defeated in the battle of Poltava. Andrei attacks Mazeppa and is wounded. Mazeppa finds Maria wandering about in a daze, but is forced to flee without her. Andrei dies in Maria's arms.

McTeague

Composed by William Bolcom (b. May 26, 1938). Libretto by Robert Altman and Arnold Weinstein. English. Based on the novel by Frank Norris. Premiered Chicago, Lyric Opera of Chicago, October 31, 1992. Set in San Francisco and Death Valley in the late 19th or early 20th century. Tragedy. Through composed. Prelude before II. Many flashbacks.

Sets: 6. **Acts:** 2 acts, 12 scenes. **Length:** I: 55. II: 70. **Arias:** Gold aria (Trina). **Hazards:** None. **Scenes:** Ii. A desert bathed in blinding sun. Iii. Polk Street in San Francisco and McTeague's dental office, 1900. Iiii. The desert. Iiv. The fairgrounds. Iv. The dental parlor/living room of the McTeagues. IIi. The desert. IIii. Polk Street. IIiii. McTeague's office/apartment. IIiv. Polk street. IIv. The desert. IIvi. The new dentist's office and Trina's small room. IIvii. The desert.

Major roles: McTeague (tenor), Maria Miranda Macapa (mezzo), Marcus Schouler (baritone), Trina (soprano). **Minor roles:** Sheriff (tenor), Papa Sieppe (bass baritone), Mama Sieppe (mezzo), Owgooste (treble), Lottery agent/Health inspector (bass), New dentist (bass). **Bit parts:** Posse solos (2 tenor, baritone, bass).

Chorus parts: SSAATTTBBB. **Chorus roles:** Men, waiters, wedding guests, neighbors, posse, clients. (Can be done with a small ensemble rather than a full chorus: 12 guests/neighbors who double as 4 waiters and 8 posse.) **Dance/movement:** None. **Orchestra:** 3 fl (picc, alto fl), 3 ob (Eng hrn), 3 cl (bs cl), 3 bsn (cont bsn), 4 hrn, 3 trp (flügelhrn), 2 trb, bs trb, tuba, 3 perc, 2 timp, harp, Kurzweil piano sampler (composer specifies synthesizer not acceptable), strings. **Stageband:** None. **Rights:** Copyright 1992 by William Bolcom and Arnold Weinstein.

Ii. McTeague wanders through the desert. Iii. We flash back to San Francisco where McTeague is opening a dental practice. His friend Schouler asks him to fix his girlfriend Trina's broken tooth. Maria the cleaning lady soliloquizes about the gold she once had. McTeague worked in the gold mines and hated it. Maria sells Trina a lottery ticket. McTeague gives Trina ether and, overcome by her beauty, kisses her. Iiii. In the present, the sheriff is after McTeague for murder. Although McTeague is loaded with gold, no one wants to follow him into Death Valley. Iiv. Schouler realizes McTeague is in love with Trina and gives her up. McTeague meets Trina's parents. Clumsily, he proposes to her and is accepted. Iv. The McTeagues finish their wedding feast. A lottery agent tells Trina she has won five thousand dollars in gold. Schouler thinks the money should have been his and demands half of it. McTeague points out it is not his to give. Trina's parents leave for Los Angeles to become artichoke farmers. Schouler leaves in a huff, having mortally offended McTeague.

IIi. The posse sights McTeague and tries to dissuade him from going into Death Valley. IIii. Schouler pumps Maria for information about the gold she had in Nevada. IIiii. Trina insists that the lottery money not be used—even as a loan to her parents. Schouler brings the health inspector to McTeague's office. When McTeague admits he has no diploma, the health inspector shuts him down. IIiv. McTeague comes home having failed to find work. Trina has sold everything to the new dentist. She refuses to dip into the lottery money and lies about what she got for the dental equipment. Furious, McTeague takes her purse. IIv. In Nevada, Schouler discovers that Maria imagined all that gold. He runs into the posse and learns that McTeague is a wanted man. Schouler volunteers to go after him. IIvi. Trina caresses her gold. She refuses to let McTeague in or give him money so he breaks in and strangles her. IIvii. Back in the desert, McTeague has run out of water. Schouler tries to arrest him. During the struggle, the gun goes off piercing Schouler's canteen—their last water. Schouler handcuffs himself to McTeague before McTeague kills him.

Médée

Composed by Luigi Cherubini (September 14, 1760 – March 15, 1842). Libretto by François Benoît Hoffman. French. Based on Thomas Corneille's libretto for Charpentier. Premiered Paris, Theatre Feydeau, March 13, 1797. Set in Corinth in legendary times. Tragedy. Set numbers

with spoken dialogue. Recitatives composed later by Franz Lachner.
Overture. Introduction to II, III. Often performed in Italian translation.

Sets: 3. **Acts:** 3 acts, 3 scenes. **Length:** I, II, III: 140. **Arias:** "Hymen, viens
dissiper une vaine frayeur" (Glauce), "Ah! du moins accordez un azile"
(Médée), "Chers enfants" (Médée), "Eh quoi, je suis Médée" (Médée).
Hazards: III: Médée burns to death in the temple. **Scenes:** I. Atrium of
the royal palace of Creonte in Corinth. II. A wing of the palace. III. A
temple in a mountainous place covered with heavily-leafed trees.

Major roles: King Créon of Corinth (bass), Jason (tenor), Médée (dramatic soprano). **Minor roles:** First handmaid (soprano), Second handmaid (soprano or mezzo), Glauce (lyric soprano), Néris (mezzo). **Bit
part:** Captain of the guards (baritone or bass). **Mute:** Jason's two sons.

Chorus parts: SATTB. **Chorus roles:** Handmaidens of Glauce,
Argonauts, people of Corinth, warriors, priests. **Dance/movement:**
None. **Orchestra:** 2 fl (picc), 2 ob, 2 cl, 2 bsn, 4 hrn, timp, perc, strings.
Stageband: II: band (2 fl, 2 ob, 2 cl, 2 bsn, 2 hrn, trb). **Publisher:** Ricordi,
Gregg International Publisher. **Rights:** Expired.

I. Glauce, daughter of king Créon, hopes that Médée has lost her power
over Glauce's fiancé, Jason. She and her father agree to save Jason's two
sons by Médée from public wrath. Jason assures Glauce that he loves
only her. Médée arrives in disguise and threatens Jason . Créon orders
her out of his kingdom. Médée promises revenge.

II. Créon remains deaf to Médée's pleas for asylum to be with her sons.
He agrees to grant her one day before she must go into exile. Jason
agrees to let Médée spend the day with their children. Médée sends a
magic diadem and mantle to her rival. While the others pray, Médée
plots.

III. Glauce is killed by the magic in Médée's diadem. Jason comes for
their sons to find Médée has murdered them. Médée curses Jason and
sets fire to the temple, burning herself to death.

Médée

Composed by Darius Milhaud (September 4, 1892 – June 22, 1974).
Libretto by Madeleine Milhaud. French. Based on the play by Euripides.
Premiered Antwerp, Opéra Royal Flamand d'Anvers, October 7, 1939.
Set in Corinth in ancient times. Tragedy. Through composed. Prelude.

Sets: 2. **Acts:** 3 acts, 9 scenes. **Length:** I, II, III: 70. **Arias:** Invocation à

Hécate (Médée). **Hazards:** II: Magic incantation. III: Robe burns Créuse and Créon to death. Bodies of Médée's dead children revealed. **Scenes:** I. A square in Corinth before Créon's palace and Médée's house. II. A cavern. III. The square.

Major roles: Créuse (soprano), Médée (soprano), Créon (baritone). **Minor roles:** Nurse (contralto), Jason (tenor).

Chorus parts: SSAATTBB. **Chorus roles:** People of Corinth. **Dance/movement:** None. **Orchestra:** 3 fl (picc), 2 ob, Eng hrn, 2 cl, bs cl, alto sax, 2 bsn, cont bsn, 2 hrn, 3 trp, 3 trb, tuba, timp, perc, celeste, harp, strings. **Stageband:** None. **Publisher:** Heugel & Co. **Rights:** Copyright 1939 by Heugel.

I. King Créon's daughter, Créuse, is to marry Jason, the hero who recovered the Golden Fleece. Créon banishes Médée, fearing that she, who helped Jason get the fleece, will take revenge on him for jilting her. Médée begs to be allowed one last day with her and Jason's children and Créon relents.

II. Using her magic powers, Médée makes a poisoned robe, which she sends to Créuse as a wedding present.

III. The robe burns Créuse to death, also killing Créon when he attempts to rescue her. Médée kills her children and shows the bodies to Jason.

The Medium

Composed by Peter Maxwell Davies (b. September 8, 1934). Libretto by Peter Maxwell Davies. English. Original work. Premiered Stromness, Orkney, Academy Hall, June 21, 1981. Set in an unspecified time and place. Monodrama. Through composed.

Sets: 1. **Acts:** 1 act, 1 scene. **Length:** I: 60. **Hazards:** None. **Scenes:** I. A bare stage with a single chair. (Composer recommends a small audience and claustrophobic space.)

Major role: Medium (mezzo).

Chorus parts: N/A. **Chorus roles:** None. **Dance/movement:** None. **Orchestra:** None. **Stageband:** None. **Publisher:** Boosey & Hawkes. **Rights:** Copyright 1981 by Boosey and Hawkes.

I. The medium tells her clients' fortunes. She is possessed by spirits, including that of her dead daughter, a dog and a crab.

The Medium

Composed by Gian Carlo Menotti (b. July 7, 1911). Libretto by Gian Carlo Menotti. English. Original work. Premiered New York City, Brander Matthews Hall, Columbia University, May 8, 1946. Set in a squalid room in a flat on the outskirts of a great city in the 1940s. Tragedy. Through composed.

Sets: 1. **Acts:** 2 acts, 2 scenes. **Length:** I:25. II: 30. **Hazards:** Optional apparitions during seance. **Scenes:** I – II. Madame Flora's parlor.

Major roles: Monica (soprano), Madame Flora/Baba (contralto). **Minor roles:** Mrs. Gobineau (soprano), Mr. Gobineau (baritone), Mrs. Nolan (mezzo). **Mute:** Toby.

Chorus parts: N/A. **Chorus roles:** None. **Dance/movement:** None. **Orchestra:** fl, ob, cl, bsn, hrn, trp, 2 piano, perc, strings. **Stageband:** None. **Publisher:** G. Schirmer. **Rights:** Copyright 1947, 1967 by G. Schirmer, Inc.

I. Madame Flora (Baba) catches her daughter, Monica, and Toby, a mute gypsy, playing with her silks. They prepare for the evening's seance. Mrs. Nolan is visiting Baba for the first time, in hope of communicating with her dead daughter. Mr. and Mrs. Gobineau are longstanding customers who have come to hear their dead two-year-old. The seance begins: Mrs. Nolan's daughter (Monica in disguise) appears to console her mother. The laughter of the Gobineaus' son is heard. In the dark, something touches Baba, terrifying her. She throws the customers out and accuses Toby of trying to frighten her. Monica suspects she has been drinking again and comforts her. The sound of a child's laugh is heard.

II. Toby and Monica play at being lovers. Desperate to know what really happened at the seance, Baba cajoles, bribes and finally beats Toby— who admits nothing. The Gobineaus and Mrs. Nolan return for another session, but Madame Flora confesses she cheated them. Persisting in believing that the visions were real, they refuse to take back their money. Baba throws them—and Toby—out on the street. She hears voices and starts to drink. Toby returns and hides behind a curtain. Seeing movement, Baba fires a gun into the curtain, killing Toby. She wonders if the voices and touches were Toby's doing.

Mefistofele

Composed by Arrigo Boito (February 24, 1842 – June 10, 1918). Libretto by Arrigo Boito. Italian. Based on "Faust" by Johann von Goethe.

Premiered Milan, Teatro alla Scala, March 5, 1868. Set in Germany and Greece in the 16th century. Tragedy. Set numbers with recitative. Ballet. Prologue with instrumental scherzo. Epilogue. Revised by composer and repremiered October 4, 1875.

Sets: 7. **Acts:** 4 acts, 8 scenes. **Length:** Prologue: 25. I: 25. II: 30. III: 20. IV: 20. Epilogue: 15. **Arias:** "Son lo spirito che nega" (Mefistofele), "Ecco il mondo" (Mefistofele), "L'altra notte" (Margherita), "Dai campi" (Faust). **Hazards:** None. **Scenes:** Prologue. In the heavens. Ii. Frankfurt-am-Main, Easter Sunday. Iii. Faust's laboratory. IIi. A rustic garden. IIii. A wild spot in Schirk Valley, the night of the Sabbath. III. A prison. IV. The shore of Peneus near a Doric temple. Epilogue. Faust's laboratory.

Major roles: Mefistofele (bass), Faust (tenor), Margherita (soprano). **Minor roles:** Marta (mezzo or contralto), Wagner (tenor), Elena (soprano), Pantalis (mezzo or contralto), Nereò (tenor).

Chorus parts: SSAATTTTBBBB. **Chorus roles:** Mystic chorus, cherubs, penitents, promenaders, students, villagers, people, nobles, witches, Greek chorus, sirens, dryads, fauns, soldiers, children (in 2 parts). **Dance/movement:** I: Peasant ballet. II: Witches' round. IV: Greek dances. **Orchestra:** 3 fl (picc), 2 ob, Eng hrn, 2 cl, bs cl, 2 bsn, 4 hrn, 2 trp, 3 trb, ophicleide, cimbasso, 3 timp, perc, 2 harps, strings. **Stageband:** Prologue: 2 hrn, 2 trp, 3 trb, harmonium, accordion, perc, organ. I: 2 trp, 3 trb, bells, perc. II: hrns (infernal fanfare), perc. Epilogue: 2 hrn, 2 trp, 3 trb, accordion, perc. **Publisher:** Ricordi. **Rights:** Expired.

Prologue. The angels rejoice in heaven. Mefistofele mocks Man's pitiful state and wagers the mystic choir that he can tempt Faust. A group of penitents prays for forgiveness. Ii. Back on earth, the people watch the prince's cavalcade pass by and a group of peasants dance. While going for a walk, Faust and Wagner observe a suspicious gray friar who follows them out. Iii. Faust returns to his study to contemplate but is interrupted by the scream of the gray friar. The friar reveals himself as the spirit of chaos and death. He offers to serve Faust in this world if Faust will serve him in the next. Faust agrees.

IIi. Faust walks in the garden with Margherita, speaking of love, while Mefistofele does the same with Marta. Faust has given out his name as Enrico. He gives Margherita a supposedly-harmless sleep potion and persuades her to use it on her mother so that they may spend the night together. IIii. Mefistofele takes Faust to the witches' Sabbath where the witches bow down to their master. They offer Mefistofele a glass globe in representation of the world and he sings of the world he would enslave. He smashes the globe. Faust sees Margherita in fetters and is overcome with sadness.

III. Margherita is in prison for having killed her mother and drowned her child. Faust tries to help her escape, but she is raving. In spite of her love for Faust, she realizes who Mefistofele is and renounces them both. A heavenly chorus announces Margherita's salvation.

IV. Mefistofele has transported Faust to Greece in the time of Helen. A chorus of choretids dances and sings and Helen remembers the destruction of Ilium. She is approached by Faust and they sing of their love. Epilogue. Faust is dying and Mefistofele grants him one last wish: that he may see the angels in heaven. Clutching a holy book, Faust expires, having at last found what he was seeking. The angels forgive Faust.

Die Meistersinger von Nürnberg • The Master Singers of Nürnberg

Composed by Richard Wagner (May 22, 1813 – February 13, 1883). Libretto by Richard Wagner. German. Original work with historical personages. Premiered Munich, Königliches Hof- und Nationaltheater, June 21, 1868. Set in Nürnberg in the 16th century. Comic opera. Through composed. Overture. Prelude before III.

Sets: 4. **Acts:** 3 acts, 11 scenes. **Length:** I: 80. II: 65. III: 110. **Arias:** "Am stillen Herd" (Walter), "Fanget an!" (Walter), "Jerum! Jerum!" (Hans Sachs), "Morgenlich leuchtend'"/Prize song (Walter), "Wahn! Wahn!" (Hans Sachs). **Hazards:** Enormous cast. **Scenes:** I. Inside Saint Catherine's church. II. A street in Nuremberg. IIIi. Sachs's workshop. IIIii. A meadow outside Nuremberg.

Major roles: Walter von Stolzing (tenor), Eva (soprano), Hans Sachs (bass or bass baritone). **Minor roles:** Magdelena (mezzo or soprano), David (tenor), Veit Pogner (bass), Sixtus Beckmesser (bass or bass baritone), Kunz Vogelgesang (tenor), Konrad Nachtigall (bass), Fritz Kothner (bass or bass baritone), Balthasar Zorn (tenor), Augustin Moser (tenor), Ulrich Eisslinger (tenor), Hans Foltz (bass), Hans Schwarz (bass), Hermann Ortel (bass), Night watchman (bass or bass baritone). **Bit parts:** First apprentice (tenor), Second apprentice (tenor), First neighbor (bass), Second neighbor (bass).

Chorus parts: SSSSAAATTTTTTBBBB. **Chorus roles:** Citizens of all guilds and their wives, ladies, maidens, master singers, neighbors, journeymen, apprentices, young women, people. **Dance/movement:** III: Ballet. **Orchestra:** picc, 2 fl, 2 ob, 2 cl, 2 bsn, 4 hrn, 3 trp, 3 trb, tuba, timp, perc, glockenspiel, harp, lute, strings. **Stageband:** I: organ. II: hrn. III: trps, drums. **Publisher:** C. F. Peters, B. Schott's Söhne. **Rights:** Expired.

Ii. Walter, a young knight, sees Eva in church and learns she is to marry the winner of the master singing competition. He decides to compete and Eva and her nurse, Magdalena, turn him over to David, apprentice to the cobbler, and song master Hans Sachs. Iii. David tells Walter what one must learn to become a master singer. Iiii. Beckmesser asks Pogner to intercede on his behalf with Eva (Pogner's daughter). Pogner says that although Eva may refuse the winner of the singing competition, she must wed a master singer. Hans Sachs's suggestion that the people—not the master singers—judge the competition is rejected. Pogner proposes Walter for the master singers' guild and Walter performs a trial song while Beckmesser chalks up the compositional mistakes. Walter's violations of the guild rules disqualify him, but Sachs insists they hear Walter's song to the end.

IIi. Magdalena learns of Walter's defeat from David. IIii. Eva is distraught. IIiii. Sachs remembers Walter's song with pleasure. IIiv. He is approached by Eva, who hopes Sachs will save her from Beckmesser. Her questions about Walter reveal her love to Sachs. Beckmesser sends a message to Eva that he means to serenade her, and Eva decides to send Magdalena in her place. IIv. Walter asks Eva to elope with him, but Sachs moves his work into the street where he can keep an eye on the lovers. IIvi. He sings to annoy Beckmesser—who is trying to serenade Eva—and to prevent the lovers' escape. To quiet Sachs, Beckmesser agrees to let him use his hammer to mark mistakes in Beckmesser's song. David recognizes his beloved Magdalena at the window and attacks Beckmesser. A riot ensues.

IIIi. David brings sausage and cake for Hans Sachs on his name day. Sachs contemplates the riot of the night before. When Walter recounts a dream he had, Sachs helps him shape the dream into a prize song. But after the two men retire to dress for the festivities, Beckmesser discovers Walter's poem and pockets it, thinking Sachs wrote it. Discovering the theft, Sachs makes Beckmesser a present of the song, assuring him that he himself will not sing it. Eva comes in, complaining that her shoes pinch. Although Sachs knows better, he pretends to fix them and takes the opportunity to tell Eva he will not compete for her hand. Sachs christens Walter's song in the traditional way. IIIii. Each guild praises its own craft. The master singers arrive and Sachs sings for the crowd. When Beckmesser's prize song is a failure, he blames Walter's poem. Sachs defends the poem and presents a witness to back him up: Walter—who sings the song to general acclaim. Walter wins Eva and Sachs reminds the people to honor the German masters.

The Merry Widow

See "Die Lustige Witwe" entry.

The Midsummer Marriage

Composed by Michael Tippett (b. January 2, 1905). Libretto by Michael
Tippett. English. Original work. Premiered London, Royal Opera House,
Covent Garden, January 27, 1955. Set in a woods in the present.
Psychological fantasy. Set numbers with recitative. Introduction before
each act.

Sets: 2. **Acts:** 3 acts, 3 scenes. **Length:** I: 60. II: 35. III: 60. **Arias:** Sosostris's
aria (Sosostris), Cosmetics aria (Bella), "How can I such lovely visions of
the mind deny?" (Jenifer), "Where stallions stamp" (Mark). **Hazards:** I:
Transformation of Mark into Dionysus and Jenifer into Athena. III:
Sosostris disrobed to reveal an enormous bud containing Mark and
Jenifer. Ritual dance of fire uses burning sticks. Temple wrapped in mist,
but reduced to ruins. **Scenes:** I. A clearing in the woods before a temple.
II. The clearing from a different angle. III. The clearing at the original
angle.

Major roles: Mark (tenor), Jenifer (soprano), King Fisher (baritone), Bella
(soprano), Jack (tenor). **Minor roles:** Priest/He Ancient (bass),
Priestess/She Ancient (mezzo), Sosostris the clairvoyant (contralto). **Bit
parts:** Half tipsy man (baritone), Dancing man (tenor), Man (tenor), Girl
(soprano). **Dancers:** Strephon, temple dancers.

Chorus parts: SSAATTBB. **Chorus roles:** Mark's and Jenifer's friends.
Dance/movement: I: Temple dancers perform a ritual dance. II: Solo
dance by Strephon. Ritual dances of "The Earth in Autumn," "The
Waters in Winter" and "The Air in Spring." III: Mark and Jenifer's
friends dance to a fiddle. Ritual dance "Fire in Summer." **Orchestra:** 2 fl
(picc), 2 ob, 2 cl, 2 bsn, 4 hrn, 2 trp, 3 trb, timp, perc, celeste, harp,
strings. **Stageband:** I: trps. **Publisher:** Schott & Co. **Rights:** Copyright
1954 by Schott & Co.

I. Mark and Jenifer, who are to be married, rendezvous with their
friends before a temple in the woods. The temple dancers perform a ritual dance, but Mark wants something stranger. To make the point that
not all change is good, the priest trips one of the dancers. Mark loves
Jenifer, but she calls off the wedding, saying that she seeks truth. She
enters the temple and Mark goes into a cave. Jenifer's father, King
Fisher, arrives looking for his daughter and tries to follow Mark into the
cave, but cannot open the gates. Fisher bribes Mark's friends to help him

and Bella's boyfriend, Jack, tries to force the gates. Jenifer and Mark reappear, transfigured into the gods Athena and Dionysus, respectively. Mark enters the temple, while Jenifer descends into the cave.

II. Bella decides to marry Jack. The temple priests perform three ritual dances that frighten Bella, so Jack reassures her.

III. Mark and Jenifer's friends eat, drink and dance. King Fisher summons his personal clairvoyant, Madame Sosostris, and challenges the temple priests, whom he believes to have kidnapped his daughter. Sosostris arrives and King Fisher asks her to locate Jenifer, but is angry when she reports a vision of Jenifer and Mark together in a field. Jack refuses King Fisher's order to unveil Sosostris, so King Fisher does it himself only to find an enormous bud containing Mark and Jenifer. King Fisher draws a pistol on Mark, but dies of a heart attack. The temple dancers perform a ritual dance of fire and Mark and Jenifer marry.

A Midsummer Night's Dream

Composed by Benjamin Britten (November 22, 1913 – December 4, 1976). Libretto by Benjamin Britten and Peter Pears. English. Based on the play by Shakespeare. Premiered Aldeburgh, Jubilee Hall, Aldeburgh Festival, June 11, 1960. Set in Athens and environs in the age of Theseus. Fairy opera. Through composed.

Sets: 2. **Acts:** 3 acts, 4 scenes. **Length:** I: 50. II: 50. III: 50. **Arias:** "I know a bank where the wild thyme blows" (Oberon). **Hazards:** II: Bottom's head is turned into that of an ass. **Scenes:** I – IIIi. The woods. IIIii. Theseus's palace.

Major roles: Oberon (counter tenor or contralto), Tytania (coloratura soprano), Lysander (tenor), Demetrius (baritone), Hermia (mezzo), Helena (soprano), Bottom (bass-baritone). **Minor roles:** Theseus (bass), Hippolyta (contralto), Quince (bass), Flute (tenor), Snug (bass), Snout (tenor), Starveling (baritone), Cobweb (treble), Peaseblossom (treble), Mustardseed (treble), Moth (treble). **Mute:** Puck.

Chorus parts: SS (or trebles). **Chorus roles:** Fairies. **Dance/movement:** II: Tytania and Oberon dance. III: Bergomask dance by the rustics. **Orchestra:** 2 fl (2 picc), ob (Eng hrn), 2 cl, bsn, 2 hrn, trp, trb, 2 perc, 2 harp, harpsichord, celeste, strings (min. 4-2-2-2-2). **Stageband:** II: soprano recorders, perc. III: 2 hrn. **Publisher:** Boosey & Hawkes. **Rights:** Copyright 1960 by Hawkes & Son.

I. Oberon, king of the fairies, is furious with his wife Tytania because she will not give him her changeling servant. Lysander asks Hermia to flee Athens and wed him instead of Demetrius. They are pursued by Demetrius (who loves Hermia) and Helena (who loves Demetrius). Having sent Puck to fetch a love-inducing flower, Oberon orders him to use it on Tytania—to make a fool of her. To help Helena, he also orders Puck to bewitch Demetrius. A group of rustics plan their play for the duke's wedding. Puck lays his spell on the sleeping Lysander—instead of Demetrius, and when Lysander awakes, he falls in love with Helena. Oberon lays the spell on Tytania.

II. While the rustics rehearse, Puck affixes an ass's head on Bottom. Bottom's friends run away, but Tytania awakes only to fall in love with him. Oberon discovers Puck's mistake and attempts to fix it. The result is that now both men love Helena—who thinks they are playing a joke on her. Demetrius and Lysander are about to fight when Puck intervenes and sets everything right.

IIIi. Having abducted the changeling, Oberon undoes the spell on Tytania. Bottom is restored to normal and the mortals return to Athens. IIIii. The lovers tell Theseus their story and watch the rustics perform "Pyramus and Thisbe." The fairies bid the audience farewell.

The Mighty Casey

Composed by William Howard Schuman (b. August 4, 1910). Libretto by Jeremy Gury. English. Based on the poem "Casey at Bat" by Ernest L. Thayer. Premiered Hartford, Connecticut, Moss Music Group, May 4, 1953. Set in Mudville, U.S.A. not long ago. Baseball opera. Set numbers with spoken dialogue. Overture. Extensive pantomime during overture.

Sets: 3. **Acts:** 1 act, 3 scenes. **Length:** I: 80. **Hazards:** I: Baseballs pitched and hit. **Scenes:** Ii. Main street and exterior of Mudville stadium. Iii. Outside the stadium. Iiii. Inside the stadium.

Minor roles: Watchman (baritone), Merry (mezzo or soprano), Thatcher (baritone), Fireball Snedeker (baritone), Concessionaire (bass or baritone), Charlie (treble), Male fan (tenor), Female fan (soprano), Manager (bass), Umpire Buttenheiser (bass or baritone). **Mute:** The Mighty Casey. **Bit parts:** Mudville team (Jones, O'Toole, Burrows, Perrone, Blake, Cooney, Flynn, Rabensky; tenors).

Chorus parts: SATBaB. **Chorus roles:** Hawkers, fans. **Dance/movement:** I: Dance of the hawkers. "Rhubarb" dance of angry fans gesticulating at the umpire. **Orchestra:** fl (picc), ob, 2 cl, bsn, 2 trp, 3 trb, perc, piano, xylophone, glockenspiel, strings. **Stageband:** None. **Publisher:** Schirmer. **Rights:** Copyright 1954 by G. Schirmer Inc.

Ii. The citizens of Mudville prepare for the state baseball championship. The watchman and Casey's girlfriend, Merry, are excited. Thatcher and Snedeker realize they can defeat Casey with the proper strategy. The concessionaire trains his hawkers and the team is introduced. Charlie wants Casey's autograph. The watchman admits that everyone knows what happened to Casey—but we can hope. Iii. Mudville is behind four to two in the bottom of the ninth inning with two outs. Merry prays. Casey has two strikes. The fans scream at the umpire. Casey strikes out. Iiii. Charlie gets Casey's autograph and Casey leaves with Merry.

Mignon

Composed by Ambroise Thomas (August 5, 1811 – February 12, 1896). Libretto by Michel Carré and Jules Barbier. French. Based on the novel "Wilhelm Meister's Lehrjahre" by Goethe. Premiered Paris, Opéra Comique, November 17, 1866. Set in Germany and Italy at the end of the 18th century. Romance. Set numbers with recitative (original version with dialogue). Overture. Entr'acte before II. Revised version premiered London, July 5, 1870.

Sets: 4. **Acts:** 3 acts, 4 scenes. **Length:** I: 55. II: 50. III: 30. **Arias:** "Oui, je veux par le monde" (Wilhelm), "Connaistu le pays" (Mignon), "Adieu, Mignon!" (Wilhelm). **Hazards:** None. **Scenes:** I. The courtyard of a German inn. Iii. An elegant dressing room. IIii. In the park adjoining the baron's castle. III. A gallery adorned with statues in an Italian villa.

Major roles: Mignon (mezzo or soprano), Filina (soprano), Wilhelm Meister (tenor). **Minor roles:** Frederick (contralto or tenor), Laertes (tenor), Lothario (bass), Giarno (bass), Antonio (bass or speaking). **Chorus parts:** SSAATTTBBB. **Chorus roles:** Townspeople, peasants, actors and actresses, gypsies, guests of the baron. **Dance/movement:** I: Gypsy dance. **Orchestra:** 2 fl (picc), 2 ob, 2 cl, 2 bsn, 4 hrn, 2 trp, 3 trb, timp, perc, harp, strings. **Stageband:** III: harp. **Publisher:** Schirmer. **Rights:** Expired.

I. The townspeople drink in the inn and are entertained by gypsy dancers. An old nobleman, Lothario, rants about his lost Speranta. The gypsy Giarno introduces Mignon, but she refuses to dance and he threatens her with a stick. A student (Wilhelm) intervenes. Mignon is grateful. After the villagers have gone home, the actor Laertes has a drink with Wilhelm. Filina (an actress and old companion of Laertes's) flirts with Wilhelm. Mignon tells Wilhelm how she was kidnapped by gypsies as a child. Wilhelm buys Mignon's freedom from Giarno. Frederick has come to visit Filina, who receives a note from Frederick's uncle, the Baron von Rosenberg, inviting her and the whole troupe to his castle. Filina invites Wilhelm along. To show her gratitude, Mignon offers to accompany Wilhelm, disguised as his man-servant. He accepts her proposal only after she threatens to go off with the old Lothario. Wilhelm is enchanted with Filina. The comedians and actors accompany Filina to the baron's castle.

IIi. Laertes is impressed at the ease with which Filina has enchanted the baron and taken over his household. Filina laughs at Mignon's naive loyalty to Wilhelm. Alone, Mignon borrows Filina's clothes and makeup to spruce herself up. Frederick and Wilhelm both come looking for Filina. They end up fighting, but are interrupted by Mignon. Wilhelm again thinks it would be best to send Mignon off to some of his friends. Mignon decides to go back to the gypsy life. Filina bears Wilhelm away in triumph. IIii. Mignon considers drowning herself, but encounters Lothario and pours out her troubles to him. She wishes the palace were struck by lighting. The performance of "Midsummer Night's Dream" ends and the actors and guests flood into the garden praising Filina. To Mignon's dismay, Lothario confesses he set the theater on fire for her sake. Not realizing this, Filina asks Mignon to fetch for her a bouquet left in the theater. Mignon goes. Laertes alerts everyone to the fire and Wilhelm rushes back and saves Mignon.

III. Wilhelm is considering purchasing a mansion in the Italian country-side. A servant tells him how the former owner went mad with despair when his daughter and wife drowned in the lake. Lothario reports that Mignon's fever has abated. It has finally dawned on Wilhelm that Mignon loves him. He avows his own love for her and ignores Filina's attempts to get him back. Lothario reveals that this is his house. He shows them the scarf he has kept that belonged to his lost daughter Speranta. Mignon realizes she is Speranta and Father and daughter embrace.

The Mikado

Composed by Arthur Sullivan (May 13, 1842 – November 22, 1900). Libretto by W. S. Gilbert. English. Original work. Premiered London, Savoy Theater, March 14, 1885. Set in Japan at an unspecified time. Operetta. Set numbers with recitative and spoken dialogue. Overture.

Sets: 2. **Acts:** 2 acts, 2 scenes. **Length:** I: 55. II: 35. **Arias:** "A wandering minstrel I" (Nanki-Poo), "The sun, whose rays are all ablaze" (Yum-Yum), "A more humane Mikado" (Mikado), "Tit Willow" (Ko-Ko).

Hazards: None. **Scenes:** I. Courtyard of Ko-Ko's official residence. II. Ko-Ko's garden.

Major roles: Nanki-Poo (tenor), Ko-Ko (baritone), Yum-Yum (soprano), Katisha (mezzo). **Minor roles:** Pish-Tush (tenor or baritone), Pooh-Bah (bass baritone), Pitti-Sing (mezzo), Peep-Bo (soprano), Mikado (bass). **Speaking bit:** Japanese nobleman.

Chorus parts: SATTBB. **Chorus roles:** Japanese nobles, people, school girls, the troops and suite of the Mikado. **Dance/movement:** I, II: Finales and many numbers often done with simple choreography/dancing. **Orchestra:** 2 fl, ob, 2 cl, bsn, 2 hrn, 2 trp, trb, perc, timp, strings. **Stageband:** None. **Publisher:** G. Schirmer Inc. **Rights:** Expired.

I. Nanki-Poo, the son of the Mikado, has disguised himself as a wandering minstrel and fallen in love with Yum-Yum. But Yum-Yum is betrothed to her guardian, Ko-Ko. Hearing that Ko-Ko is condemned to death for flirting, Nanki-Poo returns for Yum-Yum. Pish-Tush tells him that Ko-Ko was reprieved at the last minute and raised to the rank of lord high executioner. This shrewd move has delayed the enforcement of the flirting law since Ko-Ko is both executioner and condemned. Ko-Ko's wedding to Yum-Yum is back on. Nanki-Poo pleads with Yum-Yum to refuse Ko-Ko, but she points out that as her guardian, Ko-Ko, would refuse to let her marry Nanki-Poo. Nanki-Poo reveals his true identity and how he fled the court to avoid marrying the elderly Katisha. A letter from the Mikado says that unless an execution takes place forthwith, Ko-Ko's job will be abolished and the town reduced to the rank of a village. Ko-Ko is frantic. He persuades Nanki-Poo to let himself be executed, provided he is first allowed to marry Yum-Yum. Katisha appears and claims Nanki-Poo, but her attempts to reveal Nanki-Poo's identity are drowned out by the crowd.

II. Yum-Yum prepares for her wedding, although she is upset that Nanki-Poo is to be beheaded in a month. Yum-Yum calls off the wedding when Ko-Ko reveals that when a man is beheaded the law demands his wife be buried alive. Nanki-Poo reneges on his bargain with Ko-Ko just as the Mikado arrives. Nanki-Poo changes his mind and agrees to die, but Ko-Ko cannot bring himself to behead anyone. He tells Nanki-Poo to marry Yum-Yum while he gives a false death warrant to the Mikado. Katisha and the Mikado are shocked to learn that Ko-Ko has beheaded the heir apparent. Ko-Ko, Pooh-Bah and Pitti-Sing are sentenced to be boiled in oil. The condemned try to persuade Nanki-Poo to show himself, but he refuses. Now that he is married, he points out, Katisha will insist he be executed for breaking his pledge to her. Desperate, Ko-Ko marries Katisha. Katisha pleads for the release of her husband and Nanki-Poo reappears. The Mikado grants his pardon.

Mireille

Composed by Charles François Gounod (June 17, 1818 – October 18, 1893). Libretto by Michel Carré. French. Based on the poem "Mirèio" by Frédéric Mistral. Premiered Paris, Théâtre Lyrique, March 19, 1864. Set in Arles in the 19th century. Grand opera. Set numbers with recitative. Overture. Prelude before III. Ballet. Three-act version premiered December 15, 1864 in Paris.

Sets: 4. **Acts:** 3 acts, 17 scenes (originally in 5 acts). **Length:** I, II, III: 150. **Arias:** "Anges du Paradis" (Vincent). **Hazards:** None. **Scenes:** I. A mulberry plantation. II. The arena of Arles. IIIi. Exterior of Raimondo's farm house with distant view of the town of Arles. IIIii – IIIiii. A valley with distant country in background.

Major roles: Mireille (soprano), Vincent (tenor), Taven (mezzo), Ourrias (baritone), Ramon (bass). **Minor roles:** Clémence (soprano), Vincenette (soprano), Ambroise (bass), Young shepherd Andreloun (mezzo). **Bit parts:** Boatman (baritone or bass), Arlesien (baritone), Celestial voice (soprano).

Chorus parts: SSATTBB. **Chorus roles:** Villagers, citizens, peasants, spirits. **Dance/movement:** II: Country dance (farandola). III: Ballet of the spirits. **Orchestra:** 2 fl (picc), 2 ob (Eng hrn), 2 cl, 2 bsn, 4 hrn, 2 trp, 3 trb, tuba, timp, perc, harp, strings. **Stageband:** IV: organ, cornet. **Publisher:** Choudens. **Rights:** Expired.

Ii. The Arlesian girls collect mulberry leaves and dance. Iii. The girls tease Mireille about her interest in Vincent. Iiii. The fortune teller, Taven, worries about Mireille and her lover and offers her help. Iiv. Vincent tells Mireille about his sister, Vincenette. He and Mireille declare their love.

IIi. Villagers dance the farandola. IIii. The lovers are again teased by the crowd. IIiii. The villagers persuade the lovers to sing them a song. IIiv. Taven warns Mireille that she has other suitors than Vincent—ones her father may consider more worthy. IIv. Mireille loves only Vincent. IIvi. Ourrias proposes to Mireille, but she refuses. IIvii. He tells her father, Ramon. IIviii. Vincent's father, Ambroise, approaches Ramon, but is rebuffed. IIix. Mireille begs her father to relent, but the old man is furious. IIx. He sends Ambroise and Vincent away.

IIIi. Andreloun the shepherd tends his flocks. Vincenette tells Mireille that Vincent has been attacked by Ourrias, but will recover. IIIii. Mireille is overcome by the strength of the sun while crossing the desert. IIIiii. Being reunited with Vincent restores Mireille and her father relents.

Skupoy Ritsar • The Miserly Knight

Composed by Sergei Rachmaninoff (April 1, 1873 – March 28, 1943). Libretto by Alexander Pushkin. Russian. Based on a blank verse drama by Pushkin. Premiered Moscow, Bolshoi Theater, January 11 (24), 1906. Set in Russia at an unspecified time. Tragedy. Through composed. Introductions before each scene.

Sets: 3. **Acts:** 1 act, 3 scenes. **Length:** I: 60. **Hazards:** None. **Scenes:** Ii. A tower. Iii. A cellar. Iiii. A palace.

Major roles: Albert (tenor), Baron (baritone). **Minor roles:** Servant (bass), Jewish moneylender (tenor), Duke (baritone).

Chorus parts: N/A. **Chorus roles:** None. **Dance/movement:** None. **Orchestra:** 3 fl (picc), 2 ob, Eng hrn, 2 cl, bs cl, 2 bsn, 4 hrn, 3 trp, 3 trb, tuba, timp, perc, harp, strings. **Stageband:** None. **Publisher:** Boosey & Hawkes. **Rights:** Expired.

Ii. Albert complains bitterly about his poverty. His father, the baron, refuses to give him an allowance and the money lender will not extend his credit. When the money lender suggests Albert poison his father, Albert angrily sends him away. Albert decides to apply to the duke. Iii. The baron revels in his golden treasure and fears that his son will squander his inheritance. Iiii. Promising to help Albert, the duke summons the baron, who tells him that Albert has been plotting to kill him. Albert calls him a liar. The baron challenges his son to a fight, which Albert accepts. The baron is overcome and dies.

Miss Havisham's Wedding Night

Composed by Dominick Argento (b. October 27, 1927). Libretto by John Olon-Scrymgeour. English. Based on character from novel "Great Expectations" by Charles Dickens. Premiered Minneapolis, Tyrone Guthrie Theater, The Minnesota Opera, May 1, 1981. Set in Satis House, Essex, England circa 1850. Monodrama. Through composed. Meant to be performed with Argento's other monodrama, "A Water Bird Talk."

Sets: 1. **Acts:** 1 act, 1 scene. **Length:** I: 30. **Hazards:** None. **Scenes:** I. Miss Havisham's dressing room.

Major role: Miss Havisham (soprano). **Mute:** Estella, Chambermaid.

Chorus parts: N/A. **Chorus roles:** None. **Dance/movement:** None. **Orchestra:** fl, ob, cl, bsn, hrn, trp, tuba, perc, harp, piano (celeste), organ (harmonium), string quintet. **Stageband:** None. **Publisher:** Boosey & Hawkes. **Rights:** Copyright 1979, 1987 by Boosey & Hawkes.

I. Having been deserted by her fiancé years ago, Miss Havisham sits alone in her dressing room at night drinking. In her imagination, she relives the morning of her wedding and talks with her fiancé. The night over, Estella comes to visit Miss Havisham.

Miss Julie

Composed by Ned Rorem (b. October 23, 1923). Libretto by Kenward Elmslie. English. Based on the play by August Strindberg. Premiered New York City, New York City Opera, November 4, 1965. Set on a country estate in Sweden in the 1880s. Tragedy. Through composed with some recitative.

Sets: 1. **Acts:** 2 acts, 2 scenes. **Length:** I: 60. II: 55. **Hazards:** None. **Scenes:** I – II. Servants' quarters of a country estate in Sweden.

Major roles: Christine (mezzo), Miss Julie (soprano), John (bass baritone). **Minor roles:** Niels (tenor), Wildcat boy (soprano or boy soprano), Young boy (tenor), Young girl (soprano). **Bit parts:** Three girls (soprano, 2 altos), Stable boy (bass).

Chorus parts: SATB. **Chorus roles:** Servants, farm hands, revelers disguised as birds and beasts. **Dance/movement:** I: Julie and revelers dance. **Orchestra:** 2 fl (picc), 2 ob (Eng hrn), 2 cl (alto sax), 2 bsn, 3 hrn, 2 trp, 2 trb, timp, perc, harp, strings. **Stageband:** None. **Publisher:** Boosey and Hawkes. **Rights:** Copyright 1965 by Boosey and Hawkes.

I. Christine the cook is engaged to John the valet. She is annoyed by the noisy Midsummer Eve revelers. Miss Julie joins the revelers with her fiancé, Niels. He is put out that Julie, the daughter of a count, mingles so easily with the servants. Disgusted with her cruel games, Niels stalks off. Christine makes John dinner and they discuss Julie's wild ways. Julie makes John get dressed up and dance with her. He kisses her boot. After Christine falls asleep, Julie and John discuss their dreams. John tells Julie about growing up poor and how he pined for the count's daughter. Julie wants to go boating, but John is afraid they will be seen. To escape the revelers, they hide in John's room.

II. John is convinced the other servants know that Julie spent the night with him. He decides to flee to Lake Como with her and start an exclusive hotel—with the count's money. John admits he was surprised Julie was a virgin. They fight and drink. Julie tells how her mother slept around and her father tried to kill himself. Julie suggests they get married but John is cold. He tells her to get money for the trip. When Christine learns what happened, she is shocked and decides to quit. Julie returns with money stolen from the count's desk. She wants to bring her bird along, but John refuses and kills it. The count's carriage is heard. Julie asks John what to do and he hands her his razor. She slits her wrists.

Mitridate

Composed by Wolfgang Amadeus Mozart (January 27, 1756 – December 5, 1791). Libretto by Vittorio Amadeo Cigna-Santi. Italian. Based on the tragedy by Jean Baptiste Racine. Premiered Milan, Teatro Regio Ducal, December 26, 1770. Set in Ninfea in the 2nd century BC. Opera seria. Set numbers with recitative. Overture. KV 87. Large number of soldier supers.

Sets: 8. **Acts:** 3 acts, 8 scenes. **Length:** I, II, III: 195. **Hazards:** None. **Scenes:** Ii. A square in Ninfea with a view into the distance from the city gate. Iii. The temple of Venus. Iiii. A sea port with two fleets anchored on opposite sides of the harbor. IIi. The royal apartments. IIii. Mitridate's camp. IIIi. Hanging gardens. IIIii. The interior of a tower adjoining the walls of Ninfea. IIIiii. A ground floor hall adjoining a great courtyard in the palace of Ninfea.

Major roles: Sifare (soprano), Aspasia (soprano), Farnace (alto), King Mitridate (tenor). **Minor roles:** Arbate (soprano), Marzio (tenor), Ismene (soprano).

Chorus parts: N/A. **Chorus roles:** None. **Dance/movement:** None. **Orchestra:** 2 fl, 2 ob, 2 bsn, 4 hrn, 2 trp, strings, continuo. **Stageband:** None. **Publisher:** Breitkopf & Härtel. **Rights:** Expired.

Ii. Arbate, the governor of Ninfea, welcomes Mitridate's younger son, Sifare. Mitridate is believed dead. Sifare is contending against his elder brother, Farnace—and the Romans—and Arbate promises to back Sifare. Mitridate's betrothed, Aspasia, is loved by both of Mitridate's sons. Sifare promises to defend Aspasia against Farnace's advances. Aspasia's words raise Sifare's hopes. Iii. Farnace accosts Aspasia, who rebukes him. But Sifare intervenes. Arbate announces Mitridate's return. Aspasia is distraught. Farnace considers opposing Mitridate's return, but Sifare refuses to help him. The Roman tribune Marzio agrees to back Farnace. Iiii. Mitridate has been defeated—but not killed—in battle by Pompey. He urges Farnace to wed Ismene, daughter of the Parthian king, to strengthen the kingdom. Mitridate intentionally told Arbate to spread word of his death to test his sons. Mitridate swears revenge against Farnace.

IIi. Ismene berates Farnace for his infidelity, but he remains indifferent. Mitridate promises to avenge Ismene. Aspasia's reluctance to marry Mitridate infuriates him. He mistakenly believes that Aspasia loves Farnace. In private, Aspasia admits to Sifare that she loves him. Mitridate calls everyone to the camp. At Aspasia's urging, Sifare agrees to leave. Aspasia is torn between love and duty. IIii. Mitridate confides in Ismene his fears that Farnace intends to betray him to the Romans. He tells his sons that he means to attack Rome. Farnace discourages him, while Sifare offers to lead the army. Marzio's appearance determines Mitridate and he has Farnace arrested. Ismene takes Farnace's disgrace stoically. Farnace incriminates Sifare. Mitridate tricks Aspasia into admitting her love for Sifare. Sifare and Aspasia decide to die together.

IIIi. Ismene intervenes with Mitridate on Aspasia's behalf. Mitridate offers to forgive Aspasia if she will marry him, but she refuses—and asks that he spare Sifare. The Romans attack. Aspasia decides to take poison. Sifare stops her and goes to help his father. Sifare prays for an honorable death. IIIii. The Romans release Farnace from prison. Marzio promises to make Farnace king. Overcome with remorse, Farnace decides to back his father. IIIiii. Mitridate has given himself a mortal wound, rather than be captured by the Romans. He forgives Sifare and gives him Aspasia. Ismene shows Mitridate the destruction Farnace has wrought on the Roman army. Mitridate forgives Farnace and dies happy.

Der Mond • The Moon

Composed by Carl Orff (July 10, 1895 – March 29, 1982). Libretto by Carl Orff. German. Based on "Children's and Household Tales" by the brothers Grimm. Premiered Munich, Königliches Hof- und Nationaltheater, February 5, 1939. Set in a village and a crypt in legendary times. Comedy. Set numbers with spoken dialogue. Musical interludes when moon is stolen and to mark passage of time. Revised version premiered in Munich, November 26, 1950.

Sets: 3. Acts: 1 act, 4 scenes. Length: I: 75. Hazards: I: Earthquakes, storms and lightning when the dead fight. Peter is of enormous size. He looks down through the clouds at the dead and hurtles a comet at them, causing an explosion. A magic aura emanates from Peter while he is drinking with the dead. Scenes: Ii. In front of a tavern, to the left an oak tree. Iii – Iiii. In front of a tavern, to the right an oak tree. Iiv. The vaults of the dead.

Major roles: Narrator (high tenor), Four fellows who steal the moon
(tenor, 2 baritone, bass), Old man named St. Peter (bass). **Minor role:**
Old peasant (baritone). **Bit parts:** Eight dead people (2 alto, 2 soprano, 2
tenor, 2 bass; includes three carpenters, four drinkers and one girl),
Three dead dice players (bass). **Speaking:** Village mayor, Innkeeper,
Small child who discovers the moon in the sky. **Speaking bit:** Three card
players, Two dead brawlers. **Mute:** Another village mayor.

Chorus parts: SSSAATTTBB. **Chorus roles:** Farmers drinking at the inn
who have the moon stolen from them, people who enjoy having the
stolen moon and who bury the dead, people long dead and wakened by
the moon, children, prerecorded offstage chorus (TTTBBB).
Dance/movement: I: Farmers dance around their new moon. Dance of
the dead. **Orchestra:** 3 fl (3 picc), 3 ob (Eng hrn), 3 cl (bs cl), 2 bsn (cont
bsn), 4 hrn, 3 trp, 3 trb, tuba, 5 perc, timp, harmonium, accordian,
celeste, piano, harp, zither, strings. **Stageband:** I: tape recording, organ,
perc. **Publisher:** B. Schott's Söhne. **Rights:** Copyright 1939, 1973 by B.
Schott's Söhne.

Ii. Four fellows arrive from a land without a moon. Seeing a moon for
the first time, they decide they want one, so they steal it. The people discover their moon is missing and demand the mayor buy them a new
one. Iii. The fellows bring the moon home and explain its usefulness to
the people. Iiii. Time passes. Each of the four owners of the moon dies in
turn and is buried with his quarter of the moon. Iiv. The dead arise and
reassemble the moon. They drink and play cards and dice. One of the
dead cheats and a fight ensues. Peter, the guardian of heaven, hears the
noise and hurls a comet at the dead to silence them. Impressed by their
moon, Peter joins the party of the dead. They all drink until the dead get
sleepy. Peter tells them to return to their coffins. He takes the moon and
hangs it in the sky.

Il Mondo della Luna • The World on the Moon

Composed by Franz Joseph Haydn (March 31, 1732 – May 31, 1809).
Libretto by Carlo Goldoni. Italian. Based on the drama by Carlo
Goldoni. Premiered Esterháza, Court Theater, August 3, 1777. Set in
Venice in the 18th century. Comic opera. Set numbers with recitative.
Overture. Ballet. Intermezzi in I and before III.

Sets: 4. **Acts:** 3 acts, 4 scenes. **Length:** I, II, III: 165. **Arias:** "Che mondo
amabile" (Bonafede). **Hazards:** II: Garden redressed to look like moon.
Women arrive on moon in a machine. **Scenes:** Ii. A terrace above
Ecclitico's house. Iii. A room in Buonafede's house. II. The garden of

Ecclitico's house made up to look like the moon. III. A room in Ecclitico's house.

Major roles: Ecclitico (tenor), Buonafede (bass), Ernesto (contralto), Cecco (tenor), Clarice (soprano), Flaminia (soprano), Lisetta (mezzo). **Bit part:** Echo (baritone). **Mute:** Pages, Soldiers of the moon.

Chorus parts: TTBB. **Chorus roles:** Students, lunar knights, pages and footmen (can be four choristers throughout). **Dance/movement:** II: Lunar ballet. **Orchestra:** 2 fl, 2 cl, 2 ob, 2 bsn, 2 hrn, 2 trp, timp, strings, continuo (cembalo). **Stageband:** II: 2 hrn, 2 bsn. **Publisher:** Bärenreiter. **Rights:** Expired.

Ii. Ecclitico poses as an astrologer to dupe others. He tells Buonafede, his latest victim, that he has built a telescope so strong that he can see people on the moon. When Buonafede looks into the telescope, Ecclitico puts a mechanical box at the other end to convince him. Buonafede is delighted by the moon people's strange behavior. Ecclitico is after Buonafede's beautiful daughter, Clarice. His friend Ernesto loves (and is loved by) Buonafede's other daughter, Flaminia, while Ernesto's servant Cecco loves the maid, Lisetta. Buonafede has turned down all three matches. Iii. Clarice and Flaminia chafe under their father's strictness. They prefer marriage since a husband is easier to rule than a father. Buonafede fights with Clarice. He tells Lisetta—who pretends to love him—about Ecclitico's telescope. Ecclitico announces his intention of visiting the moon. Buonafede wants to go, too. He drinks an elixir Ecclitico gives him and falls asleep. The daughters think Buonafede has died, but Ecclitico enlightens them.

II. Buonafede wakes up in Ecclitico's garden, which the astrologer has made look like the moon. He gives Buonafede lunar clothing and takes him to meet the emperor of the moon (Cecco). The emperor agrees to bring Buonafede's daughters and Lisetta to the moon. Ernesto, disguised as a star, tells Buonafede that on the moon, men are not subservient to their women. Lisetta and Buonafede are drugged and brought to the garden, where Lisetta agrees to wed the emperor. Buonafede gives up the key to his money box and Clarice and Flaminia marry their lunar beaux. The sham is revealed. Buonafede is furious.

III. The men plead with Buonafede to forgive them. He relents when they return the key to his money box. Both daughters and Lisetta are granted generous dowries.

Monsieur Choufleuri • Mister Choufleuri

Composed by M. de St. Rémy and Jacques Offenbach (June 20, 1819 – October 5, 1880). Libretto possibly by Ernest Lépine, Ludovic Halévy and Hector-Jonathan Crémieux. French. Original work. Premiered Paris, Palais Bourbon, May 31, 1861. Set in Paris on January 24, 1833. Operetta. Set numbers with spoken dialogue and recitative. Overture. First public performance given at the Théâtre des Bouffes Parisiens, Paris, September 14, 1861.

Sets: 1. **Acts:** 1 act, 1 scene. **Length:** I: 60. **Hazards:** None. **Scenes:** I. Choufleuri's living room in the Marais section of Paris.

Major roles: Ernestine (soprano), Chrysodule Babylas (tenor), Mr. Choufleuri (baritone). **Minor roles:** Petermann (tenor), Balandard (tenor), Madame Balandard (soprano).

Chorus parts: SATTB. **Chorus roles:** Guests. **Dance/movement:** None. **Orchestra:** 2 fl (picc), ob, 2 cl, bsn, 2 hrn, 2 trp, trb, timp, perc, strings. **Stageband:** I: bsn, piano, bell. **Publisher:** Belwin Mills. **Rights:** Expired.

I. Ernestine loves the young composer Babylas, but her father, Choufleuri, refuses to invite him to his musical evening because he is not well known. When the famous Italian singers whom Choufleuri has engaged for the musical evening cancel, Ernestine suggests that she, Babylas and Choufleuri impersonate them. Choufleuri agrees and the evening is a tremendous success. Babylas threatens to expose the scam if Choufleuri does not agree to let him marry Ernestine. Choufleuri reluctantly gives his consent.

Montezuma

Composed by Roger Sessions (December 28, 1896 – March 16, 1985). Libretto by Giuseppe Antonio Borgese. English. Based on the memoirs of Bernal Díaz del Castillo. Premiered Berlin, Deutsche Oper, April 19, 1964. Set in Mexico from March 1519 to June 1520. Historical drama. Through composed. Pantomimed scenes to musical accompaniment in IIi. Interludes.

Sets: 11. **Acts:** 3 acts, 11 scenes. **Length:** I, II, III: 150. **Hazards:** III: Natives fire arrows, stones and darts at Montezuma. **Scenes:** Ii. An open space on the Mexican coast. Iii – Iiv. The main center of Villa Rica on the Mexican gulf coast. Iv. The marketplace of Tlaxcala. IIi. The causeway across Lake Texcoco to the city of Tenochtitlan and the great plaza of the city. IIii. The gardens, palace and royal gallery of Montezuma. IIIi. The

palace of Axayaca. IIIii. A retired quarter of Tenochtitlan between
palaces and gardens. IIIiii. The great hall of the fortress. IIIiv. The floor
of the palace with the roof visible.

Major roles: Old Bernal Díaz del Castillo/Narrator (bass), Hernán
Córtez (baritone), Pedro de Alvarado (tenor), Malinche (soprano),
Emperor Montezuma (tenor). **Minor roles:** Fray Olmedo de la Merced
(bass), Young Bernal Díaz del Castillo (tenor), Jeronimo Aguilar (tenor
or baritone), First conquistador/Deacon (tenor), Second
conquistador/Veteran (baritone), Teuhtililli (tenor), Cuanuhtemoc (baritone), Netzahualcoyotl (bass), Indian princess Itlamal (soprano), Indian
princess Cuaximatl (mezzo), Cacamatzin (tenor). **Bit parts:** Third conquistador (bass), Seven Indian girls (7 soprano), Cacique of Cempoalla
(tenor), Offstage voice of a soldier of Cortez's army (tenor), Lord of
Tacuba (tenor), Two passers-by (2 baritone), Three crowd members (3
tenor), Offstage voice of the negro Guidela (high baritone). **Mute:**
Cuitalpitoc, Spanish conquistadors and soldiers, Aztec nobles, warriors,
priests, slaves, citizens, Indian sacrificial victims, Tlaxcalan warriors.

Chorus parts: SSSSAAAATTTTBBB. **Chorus roles:** Spanish soldiers,
men of Narvaez, Aztecs, offstage Nephelai (clouds). **Dance/movement:**
I: Alvarado and sailors dance around the cross. II: Indian dance representing the female dieties and celebration of the corn harvest. **Orchestra:**
picc, 2 fl (picc), 2 ob, Eng hrn, 3 cl, bs cl, 2 bsn, cont bsn, 4 hrn, 4 trp, 3
trb, tuba, timp, piano, celeste, perc, 6 harp, 2 xylophones, marimba,
vibraphone, strings. **Stageband:** I: Mexican drums, 3 trp. II: Spanish
drum, trp. III: piccs, fls, cl, 2 sax, 2 hrn, drums, perc, timp, Four drummers of Narvaez's army. **Publisher:** Marks Music Corporation. **Rights:**
Copyright 1965 by B. Marks Music Corporation.

Ii. Cortez and his conquistadors land in Mexico. Iii. They are searching
for gold, but the natives claim to have none. Iiii. Ambassadors arrive
from Emperor Montezuma bearing gifts. Cortez wants to meet
Montezuma and the slave girl Malinche promises to show him the way.
The ambassadors are awed by the Spaniards' horses. Iiv. The Spaniards
baptize the Indians. They attack and take Tlaxcala. Iv. Malinche asks
Cortez questions about Christianity and wonders if he is a god or a
demon.

IIi. The Spaniards enter the capital city of Tenochtitlan where
Montezuma gives Cortez a warm welcome. IIii. Cortez imprisons
Montezuma.

IIIi. The Spaniards use Montezuma as a figurehead to execute the
natives who oppose them. Hearing that another conquistador has landed in Mexico, Cortez rushes to challenge him. IIIii. Cuanuhtemoc and

Cacamatzin conspire against the Spaniards. IIIiii. Cortez is angry with
Alvarado for his cruelty, but the rival conquistador is killed and his
army subdued. IIIiv. The natives storm the palace. Cortez sends
Montezuma onto the roof to address them and make peace. The crowd
showers Montezuma with darts and stones, killing him. They attack the
palace, massacring the Spaniards.

Mosè in Egitto • Moses in Egypt

Composed by Gioachino Rossini (February 29, 1792 – November 13,
1868). Libretto by Andrea Leone Tottola. Italian or French. Based on
"L'Osiride" by Francesco Ringhieri. Premiered Naples, Teatro San Carlo,
March 5, 1818. Set in Egypt in Biblical times. Tragedy. Set numbers with
recitative. Introduction before I, II. Ballet. Revised in 1819: Amaltea's
second act aria omitted and third act rewritten. More extensively revised
and premiered in Paris as "Moïse" on March 26, 1827.

Sets: 3 (5 in revised version). **Acts:** 3 acts, 5 scenes (4 acts, 16 scenes in
revised French version). **Length:** I, II, III: 145. **Arias:** "Eterno! immenso!
incomprensibil Dio!" (Mosè). **Hazards:** I: Mosè brings down hail and
fire. II: Osiride is struck dead by lightning. III: Mosè parts the Red Sea.
The Israelites cross safely, but the Egyptian army drowns. **Scenes:** I – IIi.
A courtyard in the Pharaoh's palace. IIii. A cave. IIiii. The courtyard. III.
The shores of the Red Sea. (Four act version: I. The camp of the
Midanites. II. A gallery inside the pharaoh's palace. III. The portico of
the temple of Iside. IVi -IVii. The desert. IViii. On the bank of the Red
Sea.)

Major roles: Osiride (tenor/bass), Mosè/Moïse (bass), Elcia/Anaíde
(soprano), Aménosi/Aménofis (mezzo/tenor). **Minor roles:** Marie
(mezzo), Aronne/Éliéser (tenor), Amaltea/Sinaïde (mezzo), Aufide
(tenor), Pharaoh (bass). **Bit part:** Mysterious voice (bass).

Chorus parts: SSAATTBB. **Chorus roles:** Jews, Midanites, Egyptians,
priests, guards, soldiers, dancers. **Dance/movement:** III: Ballet.
Orchestra: 2 fl (picc), 2 ob, 2 cl, 2 bsn, 4 hrn, 2 trp, 3 trb, ophicléide, timp,
perc, harp, strings. **Stageband:** None. **Publisher:** Kalmus, Brandus.
Rights: Expired.

I. God has brought plagues on Egypt, because the Pharaoh refuses to
release the Israelites. The Pharaoh relents and tells Mosè and Aronne
their people are free to go. The Pharaoh's son, Osiride, objects because
he is in love with the Israelite maiden Elcia. He appeals to the Egyptian
priest Mambre for help. Elcia takes a tearful farewell of Osiride. Mambre
and Osiride persuade the king to revoke his decree over the objections of

the Pharaoh's wife, Amaltea. Osiride breaks the news to Mosè, who brings down a storm of hailstones and fire.

IIi. The Pharaoh again orders the Israelites to depart. He arranges a marriage between Osiride and a foreign princess. The Pharaoh sees Osiride's unhappiness, but cannot learn the cause. Aronne and Mosè learn that Osiride has abducted Elcia. IIii. The lovers have hidden in a cave where Osiride explains that he wishes to live out his life as a shepherd with Elcia. They are surprised by Aronne and Amaltea who take Elcia away. IIiii. Pharaoh once again forbids the Israelites from leaving on the pretext that the neighboring kingdoms would object. Mosè warns him that God will smite Egypt's first born children—including Osiride. The Pharaoh raises Osiride to rule with him. Elcia appeals to Osiride to free the Israelites. Osiride is struck dead by lightning.

III. The Israelites flee Egypt, pursued by Pharaoh's army. Mosè parts the waters of the Red Sea and the Israelites pass through. When Pharaoh's soldiers attempt to follow, the waters close over them.

Moses und Aron • Moses and Aron

Composed by Arnold Schönberg (September 13, 1874 – July 13, 1951). Libretto by Arnold Schönberg. German. Original work based on Biblical story. Premiered Zürich, International Society for Contemporary Music, June 6, 1957. Set in Egypt and Judaea in Biblical times. Oratorio. Through composed. Twelve-tonal composition. Interlude between I and II. Music never completed for third act. Concert premiere of acts I and II on July 2, 1951.

Sets: 2. **Acts:** 3 acts, 10 scenes. **Length:** I: 50. II: 55. III: 5. **Hazards:** I: Burning bush. **Scenes:** I. Egypt. II – III. The mountains of Judaea.

Major roles: Aron (tenor), Moses (speaking or bass baritone). **Minor roles:** Young girl (soprano), Young man (tenor), Another man (baritone), Priest (bass), Ephraimite (baritone). **Bit parts:** Invalid woman (contralto), Naked youth (tenor), Four naked virgins (2 soprano, 2 alto).

Chorus parts: SMATBaB (exclusive of small groups noted below). **Chorus roles:** Voice from the burning bush (soprano, boys, alto, tenor, baritone, bass), beggars (6-8 altos, 6-8 basses), several elderly persons (tenors), seventy elders (25 basses, the rest supernumeraries), twelve tribal leaders (6 tenors, 6 basses), six solo voices (in the orchestra; soprano, mezzo, alto, tenor, baritone, bass). **Dance/movement:** II: Dance of the butchers and bacchanalia. **Orchestra:** 3 fl (3 picc), 3 ob (Eng hrn), 3 cl, bs cl, 2 bsn, cont bsn, 4 hrn, 3 trp, 3 trb, tuba, timp, perc, harp, piano, celeste, 2 mandolins, strings. **Stageband:** II: picc, fl, Eng hrn, cl, hrn, 2 trp, 2 trb, 2 mandolins, 2 guitars, timp, perc, piano. **Publisher:** B. Schott's Söhne. **Rights:** Copyright 1958 by Gertrud Schönberg.

Ii. God appears in a burning bush and calls on Moses to lead his people out of Egypt. Moses begs to be released, doubting that people would follow him. "Aron will be your voice," God replies. Iii. Moses meets Aron in the desert and tells him of his visitation. They discuss God's almighty but unseen presence. Iiii. The people, skeptical of the new God, nevertheless agree to worship him if he frees them from the Pharaoh's might. They watch Moses and Aron approach. Iiv. Moses and Aron tell the people not to make offerings to their new God or graven images of Him. The Israelites reject this God until Aron convinces them of His power by changing Moses's rod into a serpent. Moses's hand becomes leprous—a symbol of the weakened spirit of the Israelites—and is cured. Aron, who proposes to lead them through the desert to a land of milk and honey, turns Nile water to blood, symbolizing the toil of the Israelites on behalf of their Egyptian masters. Interlude. The Israelites fear they have been abandoned by their leader.

IIi. The seventy elders, who have waited for Moses before the mountain of revelation for forty days, complain that life in Judaea is harder than it was in Egypt: Might rules. IIii. An angry crowd demands the restoration of order and the old gods. Aron tells them to gather their gold and he will fashion an image of their God. IIiii. The Israelites sacrifice to a golden calf and dance, and when an invalid woman is cured, the beggars and old men give the calf their last scraps of food; Ephraimite and the tribal leaders abase themselves before the altar. A youth who conjures the people to destroy the false idol is slain by the tribal leaders. A bacchanalia and fight ensues, and four virgins are sacrificed to the calf. IIiv. The crowd flees before Moses who destroys the golden calf. IIv. Moses rebukes Aron and gives him the commandments. Aron explains that he loves the people and they need an Image to sustain the Idea that Moses loves. In despair, Moses breaks the tablets of the commandments. A pillar and cloud of fire are seen. Moses fears that in expressing the Idea, he, too, is teaching but a false image.

III. Soldiers detain Aron. Moses tries to explain to him that Image is not enough: He must follow the word and the Idea. Aron is freed, but drops dead. (Opera left incomplete.)

The Mother of Us All

Composed by Virgil Thomson (November 25, 1896 – September 30, 1989). Libretto by Gertrude Stein. English. Scenario by Maurice Grosser based loosely on historical events. Premiered New York City, Brander Matthews Hall, Columbia University, May 7, 1947. Set in America in the 19th century. Historical drama. Through composed. Prelude before Iiv and Iv.

Sets: 5. **Acts:** 2 acts, 8 scenes. **Length:** I: 65. II: 40. **Hazards:** None.
Scenes: Ii. A room in the house of Susan B. Anthony. Iii. A political rally. Iiii – Iv. A village green adjoining the house of Susan B. Anthony. IIi – IIii. The drawing room of Susan B. Anthony. IIiii. The congressional hall.

Major roles: Susan B. Anthony (dramatic soprano), Anne (contralto), Daniel Webster (bass), John Adams (romantic tenor), Jo the loiterer (tenor). **Minor roles:** Gertrude S. (soprano), Virgil T. (baritone), Chris the citizen (baritone), Indiana Elliot (contralto), Angel More (light lyric soprano), Anthony Comstock (bass), Thaddeus Stevens (tenor), Constance Fletcher (high mezzo), Isabel Wentworth (mezzo), Anna Hope (contralto), Lillian Russell (lyric soprano), Jenny Reefer (mezzo). **Bit parts:** Henrietta M. (soprano), Gloster Heming (baritone), Ulysses S. Grant (bass baritone), Herman Atlan (high baritone), Donald Gallup (baritone), Andrew Johnson (tenor), Indian Elliot's brother (bass baritone), Henry B. (bass baritone). **Speaking bits:** Somebody else, Negro man, Negro woman.

Chorus parts: SATB (briefly SSAATTB). **Chorus roles:** Spectators, page boys or postilions, citizens. **Dance/movement:** I: Waltz. **Orchestra:** fl (picc), ob (Eng hrn), 2 cl (bs cl), bsn, 2 hrn, 2 trp, trb, harp, celeste, xylophone, bells, 2 perc, piano, strings. **Stageband:** None. **Publisher:** G. Schirmer. **Rights:** Copyright 1947 by Virgil Thomson.

Ii. Susan B. Anthony and her companion, Anne, discuss how gullible men are. Iii. Susan debates Daniel Webster on the issue of political rights for women. Iiii. Andrew Johnson and Thaddeus Stevens argue. Constance Fletcher is wooed by John Adams. Everyone waltzes. Iiv. In a dream, Susan wonders if her support of suffrage for black men will win them to the cause of women's suffrage. Jo asks Susan about the nature of poverty. Iv. Susan tells her fellow suffragettes that there is nothing wrong with marriage. Indiana Elliot's brother objects to her marrying Jo the loiterer. Indiana renounces his brother.

IIi. Anne and Jenny Reefer tell Susan that she has been asked to speak at a political meeting. Susan is bitter that suffrage laws are not being passed. IIii. Fear of the suffragette movement has caused the male politicians to insert the word "male" in a constitutional amendment. Lillian Russell becomes a suffragette. Indiana decides to change her last name now that she is married. IIiii. Women win the right to vote.

Mourning Becomes Electra

Composed by Marvin David Levy (b. August 2, 1932). Libretto by Henry Butler. English. Based on the play by Eugene O'Neill. Premiered New York City, Metropolitan Opera Association, March 17, 1967. Set on the outskirts of a small New England seaport town from 1865 to 1866. Lyric tragedy. Through composed. Orchestral interlude before Iliii, IIIii. Revised after premiere: Interludes expanded and chorus eliminated.

Sets: 4. **Acts:** 3 acts, 7 scenes. **Length:** I: 50. II: 60. III: 45. **Arias:** "Too weak to kill the man I hate" (Adam). **Hazards:** None. **Scenes:** Ii. Exterior of the Mannon house. Iii. The master bedroom. IIi. Downstairs in the house. IIii. Aboard Brant's clipper ship in Boston harbor. IIiii. Exterior of the house. IIIi. Downstairs in the house. IIIii. Exterior of the house.

Major roles: Christine Mannon (dramatic soprano), Lavinia Mannon (spinto or dramatic soprano), Adam Brant (dramatic baritone), Orin Mannon (high baritone or tenor). **Minor roles:** Jed (bass), Peter Niles (lyric baritone), Helen Niles (lyric soprano), General Ezra Mannon (bass baritone). **Mute:** Servants, townspeople, field workers.

Chorus parts: N/A. **Chorus roles:** None. **Dance/movement:** II: Helen and Orin waltz. **Orchestra:** 3 fl (picc), 3 ob (Eng hrn), 3 cl (bs cl, sax), 3 bsn (cont bsn), 4 hrn, 3 trp, 3 trb, tuba, timp, 1 or 2 harp, organ, piano, celeste, electric guitar, 2 perc, strings. **Stageband:** I: Military band. **Publisher:** Boosey & Hawkes. **Rights:** Copyright 1967 by Boosey & Hawkes.

Ii. General Ezra Mannon is coming home from the Civil War to his wife, Christine, and daughter, Lavinia. His son, Orin, has been wounded, but is also returning. When Christine tells Lavinia she invited Captain Adam Brant to visit, Lavinia quizzes the old servant Jed about him. "He is the bastard son of your uncle," Jed says. Brant reminds Lavinia of their affair, but she knows Brant is having an affair with her mother. When Lavinia confronts the lovers with her knowledge, they agree not to see each other again. In private, Christine tells Brant she means to kill her husband. Lavinia's boyfriend, Peter Niles, brings by his sister Helen. Iii. General Mannon begs his wife not to leave him—while also accusing her of wishing his death. Christine confesses her affair with Brant. When Mannon has a seizure, Christine gives him poison instead of medicine. The general accuses Christine and dies.

IIi. As Helen and Peter welcome Orin home, Lavinia and Christine try to make Orin believe their version of the general's death. Orin threatens to kill Brant if he sets foot in the house again. Lavinia confronts Christine with the poison and Christine begs for Brant's life. IIii. Christine meets

Brant on his boat. Lavinia and Orin have followed her and after Christine leaves, Orin kills Brant. They try to make it look like the work of thieves. IIiii. Orin tells his mother what he did. Christine has a vision of Brant. She goes into the house and shoots herself. Lavinia sends Jed to fetch the doctor—and to tell him that Christine killed herself in a fit of grief over the general's death.

IIIi. Orin and Lavinia return to the house after a year away. Orin is wracked with guilt, but Lavinia comforts him. Peter and Lavinia are engaged. Orin repulses Helen. He tries to give her a written confession of his and Lavinia's crimes, but Lavinia prevents him. Orin realizes he and Lavinia are reenacting their parents' conflict. He tries to kiss his sister and then shoots himself. IIIii. Lavinia still loves Brant. She sends Peter away and shuts herself up in the house.

Mozart i Salieri • Mozart and Salieri

Composed by Nicolai Rimsky-Korsakov (March 18, 1844 – June 21, 1908). Libretto by Nicolai Rimsky-Korsakov. Russian. Based on a verse drama by Aleksandr Pushkin. Premiered Moscow, Solodovnikov Theater, December 7, 1898. Set in Vienna in the 18th century. Tragedy. Set numbers with accompanied recitative. Intermezzi between scenes. Opus 48.

Sets: 2. **Acts:** 2 acts, 2 scenes. **Length:** I, II: 80. **Hazards:** None. **Scenes:** I. A room. II. A private room in a tavern.

Major roles: Salieri (bass), Mozart (tenor). **Mute:** Blind violinist.

Chorus parts: SATB. **Chorus roles:** Requiem chorus offstage. **Dance/movement:** None. **Orchestra:** fl, ob (Eng hrn), cl, bsn, 2 hrn, 3 trb, timp, piano, strings. **Stageband:** None. **Rights:** Expired.

Ii. Salieri realizes that in spite of his enormous influence at court and his consummate skill, his music is uninspired. He berates God for giving such gifts to a silly boy like Mozart. Mozart brings in a blind violinist who plays an abominable version of "Voi che sapete." Salieri is not amused. He is overwhelmed by Mozart's latest musical sketches and invites him to dinner. Salieri decides to poison his competitor. Iii. Over dinner, Mozart tells Salieri how a mysterious man in black came to his house to commission a requiem. Salieri poisons Mozart, who plays a portion of the requiem and then goes home sick.

La Muette de Portici

See "Masaniello" entry.

Nabucco

Composed by Giuseppe Verdi (October 9, 1813 – January 27, 1901). Libretto by Temistocle Solera. Italian. Based on biblical story and play by Anicet-Bourgeois and Francis Cornu. Premiered Milan, Teatro alla Scala, March 9, 1842. Set in Jerusalem and Babylon in Biblical times. Lyric drama. Set numbers with recitative. Overture.

Sets: 5. **Acts:** 4 acts, 24 scenes. **Length:** Overture: 7. I: 35. II: 30. III: 25. IV: 25. **Arias:** "Anch'io dischiuso" (Abigaille), "Dio di Giuda" (Nabucco), "Tu sul labbro" (Zaccaria). **Hazards:** II: Nabucco hit by lightning. IV: Destruction of statue of Baal. **Scenes:** I. Interior of the temple of Solomon at Jerusalem. IIi – IIii. Royal apartment in Nabucco's palace in Babylon. IIiii – IIviii. Hall in the palace. IIIi – IIIii. Banks of the Euphrates. IIIiii – IIIv. Hanging gardens. IVi – IVii. Royal apartment. IViii – IViv. Hanging gardens.

Major roles: Nabucodonosor/Nabucco (baritone), Ismaele (tenor), Zaccaria (bass), Fenena (mezzo), Abigaille (soprano). **Minor roles:** Anna (soprano), High Priest of Baal (bass), Abdallo (tenor).

Chorus parts: SSATTBB. **Chorus roles:** Babylonian and Hebrew soldiers, Levites, Hebrew virgins, Babylonian women, Magi, Babylonian courtiers, people. **Dance/movement:** None. **Orchestra:** 2 fl (picc), 2 ob, 2 cl, 2 bsn, 4 hrn, 2 trp, 3 trb, cimbasso, 2 harp, timp, perc, strings. **Stageband:** I, IV: band. **Publisher:** Ricordi, University of Chicago Press. **Rights:** Expired.

Ii. The Hebrews bemoan their defeat by the King of the Assyrians. Iii. But Zaccaria, the chief priest, has a hostage: Nabucco's daughter, Fenena. Iiii. He turns her over to Ismaele. Iiv. Fenena once freed Ismaele from prison and he resolves to return the favor. Iv. They are captured by Nabucco's other daughter, Abigaille, who loves Ismaele. Ivi. Nabucco himself approaches the temple on horseback. Ivii. Zaccaria forces Nabucco to dismount by holding a knife to Fenena's throat. Abigaille hopes Zaccaria will kill her sister and thus dispose of a rival. Ismaele saves Fenena, but Nabucco orders the destruction of the temple. The Hebrews curse Ismaele.

IIi. Abigaille discovers she is not Nabucco's daughter, but the child of a slave. She vows to overthrow Fenena, who rules in Nabucco's absence. IIii. Horrified that Fenena has freed the Hebrews, the high priest of Baal

offers to back Abigaille in a bid for the throne. IIiii. Zaccaria visits
Fenena to instruct her in the Hebrew religion. IIiv. Zaccaria has called
the Levites to the palace. Seeing Ismaele, they curse him. IIv. He is saved
by the intervention of Anna, Zaccaria's sister. IIvi. Abdallo falsely
announces the death of Nabucco and the ascension of Abigaille. IIvii.
Abigaille demands Fenena's scepter, but she refuses. IIviii. Nabucco
declares himself God. Fenena says she worships only the God of Israel.
The king is struck by lightning and Abigaille assumes the throne.

IIIi. The Israelites again suffer under the Babylonian yoke. IIIii. Zaccaria
foresees a brighter day. IIIiii. The high priest asks Abigail to destroy the
Hebrews. IIIiv. Reduced to madness, Nabucco seeks to remount his
throne. IIIv. Abigaille tricks him into signing the warrant for the destruction of Israel. He is horrified at the thought of Fenena's death, but is
powerless to prevent it. Abigaille destroys the document proving she is
a slave and ignores Nabucco's pleas to spare his real daughter.

IVi. Nabucco prays to the God of Israel and his reason is restored. IVii.
He marshals his soldiers about him. IViii. Fenena prepares for death.
IViv. Nabucco halts the execution. The statue of Baal falls to pieces and
Abigaille drops dead. All bow to Jehovah.

La Navarraise • The Girl from Navarre

Composed by Jules-Emile-Frédéric Massenet (May 12, 1842 – August 13,
1912). Libretto by Jules Clarétie and Henri Cain. French. After "La
Cigarette" by Henri Cain. Premiered London, Royal Opera House,
Covent Garden, June 20, 1894. Set in the Basque provinces of Spain in
1874. Lyric verismo episode. Set numbers with recitative. Overture.
Nocturne before II.

Sets: 1. Acts: 2 acts, 2 scenes. Length: I, II: 50. Arias: "O bien-aimée"
(Araquil). Hazards: None. Scenes: I – II. A small, picturesque square
with houses in a village near Bilbao in the Basque provinces.

Major roles: Garrido (baritone), Anita (soprano), Araquil (tenor). Minor
roles: Ramon (tenor), Remigio (bass), Sergeant Bustamente (baritone).
Bit part: Soldier (tenor).

Chorus parts: TB. Chorus roles: Officers, soldiers, villagers, peasants.
Dance/movement: None. Orchestra: picc, 2 fl, 2 ob, Eng hrn, 2 cl, bs cl, 2
bsn, cont bsn, 4 hrn, 3 trp, 3 trb, tuba, timp, 3 perc, 2 harp, strings.
Stageband: I: 6 trp, timp. II: bells. Publisher: Heugel & Co. Rights:
Expired.

I. General Garrido hopes to recapture Bilbao from the Carlists. Anita warmly welcomes her beloved Araquil home from battle. But Araquil's father, Remigo, refuses to sanction their marriage unless Anita can produce a handsome dowry. For his bravery in combat, Araquil is made lieutenant. Anita hears Garrido venting his hatred of the rebel Zuccaraga who has killed so many of his soldiers. She promises to kill the rebel for a dowry. The general asks her name. Lt. Ramon warns Araquil that Anita has been seen sneaking into the rebel camp. The soldiers carouse.

II. Shots are heard in the camp and Anita returns, disheveled. Garrido pays Anita and promises to keep her secret. Araquil is mortally wounded trying to retrieve Anita from the rebel camp. He accuses Anita of selling herself to Zuccaraga to get the money. Hearing of Zuccaraga's death, Araquil realizes the truth before he dies. Anita goes mad.

Nerone

Composed by Arrigo Boito (February 24, 1842 – June 10, 1918). Libretto by Arrigo Boito. Italian. Based on historical incidents and a play by Pietro Cossa. Premiered Milan, Teatro alla Scala, May 1, 1924. Set in Rome and environs in the 1st century AD. Tragedy. Through composed. Orchestral introduction before IV. Fifth act never completed. First four acts edited by Arturo Toscanini after the composer's death.

Sets: 5. **Acts:** 4 acts, 5 scenes. **Length:** I: 45. II: 30. III: 30. IV: 40. **Arias:** "Queste ad un lido fatal" (Nerone). **Hazards:** I: Asteria appears on Agrippina's grave with snakes around her neck. II: Asteria appears to Nerone. Nerone destroys part of the temple. Dositeo's beard and clothes catch fire. IV: Oppidum burns down. A section of the spoliary collapses. Simon thrown from roof. Christians killed in arena. **Scenes:** I. A grassy field situated along the right side of the Appian way. II. A large, underground temple. III. An orchard outside Rome where Christians meet. IVi. The interior of the Oppidum leading to the arena and the forum. IVii. A subterranean chamber of the circus where the dead and dying are thrown.

Major roles: Simon Mago (baritone), Nerone (tenor), Asteria (soprano), Rubria (mezzo), Fanuèl (baritone). **Minor roles:** Tigellino (bass), First traveler (tenor), Dositèo/Voice of the oracle (baritone), Gobrias (tenor), Cerinto (contralto), Pèrside (soprano). **Bit parts:** Offstage voices (2 soprano, 1 alto, 1 tenor, 1 bass), Second traveler (baritone), Slave advisor (baritone), Temple attendant (tenor). **Mute:** Terpnos.

Chorus parts: SSSAATTBaBaBBB. **Chorus roles:** Distant voices, Roman people, Praetorians, Augustinian cavalry, legionnaires, Dionysiacs, worshipers, priests, Christians, partisans of the green and blue factions, actors, freemen, champions, slaves, plebes, senators, matrons. **Dance/movement:** None. **Orchestra:** 3 fl (2 picc), 3 ob (2 Eng hrn), 4 cl (bs cl), 4 bsn (sarrusophone), 5 hrn, 3 trp, 3 trb, tuba, timp, perc, organ, piano, carillon, celeste, 2 harp, strings. **Stageband:** I: ob, guitar, 8 trp, 3 bugle, perc. II: ob. IV: 2 ob, hrn, timp, 8 trp, 3 bugle, perc, crotali. **Publisher:** G. Ricordi & Co. **Rights:** Copyright 1924 by G. Ricordi & Co.

I. Emperor Nerone has murdered his mother, Agrippina. With the help of the guard, Tigellino, and the pagan priest Simon Mago, Nerone quietly buries her. The ceremony is interrupted by the appearance of Asteria, a young girl in love with Nerone. Simon realizes that he can use Asteria to gain power over the superstitious emperor. He meets the Christian prophet Fanuel and offers him money for his help in ruling the empire, but Fanuel curses him. Tigellino assures Nerone that the Senate believes Agrippina was caught plotting against Nerone and took her own life. The people of Rome come out to welcome Nerone home.

II. Simon performs a religious service. He helps Asteria masquerade as a goddess to enslave Nerone, but Nerone discovers the deception and smashes the altar and temple statues. He orders Simon and Asteria arrested.

III. Fanuel preaches to his flock. Asteria has escaped from the snake pit and comes to warn the Christians that Simon is out for blood. Fanuel calls a Christian woman, Rubria, to confess her sins. Simon gets into the Christian camp disguised as a beggar, where he has Fanuel arrested.

IVi. A plot is underway to free Simon by setting fire to Rome. Tigellino warns Nerone, but Nerone likes the idea of rebuilding the city after a fire. The Christians are sent into the arena. A vestal virgin who begs mercy for them is revealed to be Rubria. She joins the Christians. Simon is thrown to his death from the roof of the arena. Flames break out in the circus. IVii. Rubria confesses her sin to Fanuel and dies of the wounds received in the arena. Asteria and Fanuel escape.

Neues vom Tage • News of the Day

Composed by Paul Hindemith (November 16, 1895 – December 28, 1963). Libretto by Marcellus Schiffer. German. Original work. Premiered Berlin, Kroll Opera, June 8, 1929. Set in Germany in the late 1920s. Satire. Set numbers with some recitative. Overture. Orchestral introduction before II. Ballet. Revised 1953 and reduced to two acts with significant change in the ending. Repremiered in Naples, April 7, 1954.

Sets: 9. **Acts:** 2 acts, 10 scenes (3 acts, 11 scenes in original version). **Length:** I: 40. II: 30. III: 25. (original version) **Arias:** "Wie lange ist's her" (Laura). **Hazards:** I: Laura takes a bath onstage. **Scenes:** Ii. The living room of Eduard and Laura. Iii. A room. Iiii. An office. Iiv. A museum. Iv. Bathroom in a "Universum" hotel. IIi. A "Universum" hotel room. IIii. The office. IIiii. Laura and Eduard's dressing room in the theater. IIiv. Theater auditorium. IIv. Onstage.

Major roles: Laura (soprano), Eduard (baritone), Mrs. Pick (mezzo), Mr. Hermann (tenor). **Minor roles:** Elli (soprano), Olli (contralto), Ali (tenor), Uli (bass), Registrar (bass), Baron d'Houdoux (bass), Tour guide (bass), Six managers (2 tenor, 2 baritone, 2 bass). **Bit parts:** Hotel manager (bass), Head waiter (baritone), Chambermaid (soprano). (First manager can double head waiter; Fourth manager can double tour guide.)

Chorus parts: SSAATTTTBBBB. **Chorus roles:** People. **Dance/movement:** II: Optional ballet. **Orchestra:** 2 fl (picc), ob, Eng hrn, 2 cl, bs cl, alto sax, 2 bsn, cont bsn, hrn, 2 trp, 2 trb, tuba, 2 perc, 2 pianos (1 two-hands, 1 four-hands), harp, mandolin, banjo, timp, xylophone, glockenspiel, 3 electric bells, strings (6-0-4-4-4). **Stageband:** None. **Publisher:** B. Schott's Söhne. **Rights:** Copyright 1929 by B. Schott's Söhne. Copyright 1954 by Schott & Co. Ltd.

Ii. A newlywed couple, Eduard and Laura, argue and throw things at each other. Iii. They decide to get a divorce. Iiii. They engage Mr. Hermann to handle things. Hermann typically falls in love with his female clients and Laura is no exception: he arranges an assignation at a museum. Iiv. Eduard catches them at the museum and smashes an expensive vase over Herrman's head, thereby getting himself arrested. Iv. Laura lounges in the bath in the hotel room Herrman has found for her, praising the joys of modern plumbing.

IIi. Laura is seen in the hotel room with Herrman by the staff and their affair quickly becomes a scandal in the local press. IIii. Laura and Eduard become celebrities. IIiii. A theater engages them to enact their domestic squabbles. IIiv. Tired of their new-found fame, Laura and Eduard are reconciled. IIv. They leave the stage and return to private life. (In the original version, their public does not allow them to resign.)

The New Moon

Composed by Sigmund Romberg (July 29, 1887 – November 9, 1951). Libretto by Frank Mandel, Lawrence Schwab and Oscar Hammerstein II. English. Original work Premiered New York City, Imperial Theater, September 19, 1928. Set in New Orleans, at sea and on the Isle of Pines in

1788. Musical romance. Set numbers with spoken dialogue. Overture. Intermezzo before II.

Sets: 7. **Acts:** 2 acts, 11 scenes. **Length:** I: 90. II: 80. **Arias:** "Marianne" (Robert), "Lover, come back to me" (Marianne). **Hazards:** II: Naval battle between "The New Moon" and a pirate ship. **Scenes:** Ii. Grand salon of M. Beaunoir's mansion near New Orleans. Iii. Entrance to Chez Creole. Iiii. Interior of Chez Creole. Iiv. Entrance to Chez Creole. Iv. Grand salon of M. Beaunoir's mansion. IIi. The deck of "The New Moon." IIii. The road from the beach on the isle of Pines. IIiii. The stockade. IIiv. The road from the beach. IIv. Marianne's cabin. IIvi. The stockade.

Major roles: Robert (tenor), Alexander (tenor), Marianne (soprano), Julie (soprano). **Minor roles:** Besace (bass), Captain Georges Duval (tenor), Philippe (tenor), Clotilde (mezzo). **Bit parts:** First girl (soprano), Captain Dejean (bass). **Speaking:** Mr. Beaunoir, Viscount Ribaud, Jacques, Doorman of the tavern, Flower girl, Dancer, Fouchette. **Speaking bits:** Seamstress, Second girl, Beaunoir's butler, Emile, Brunet, Sailor, Girl at Chez Creole, Woman at Chez Creole, Proprietor of Chez Creole, Spaniard, Man at the cotillion, Woman at the cotillion, Sailor, Crying baby, Two French sailors. **Mute:** Waiter, Dancer.

Chorus parts: SATTBB. **Chorus roles:** Courtiers, ladies, servants, sailors, pirates. **Dance/movement:** I: Julie dances for Alexander. Tango. Cotillion. II: Sailors' dance. **Orchestra:** 2 fl (picc), ob, Eng hrn, 2 cl (alto sax), 2 hrn, 2 trp, trb (optional euphonium), timp, perc, harp, piano, strings. **Stageband:** None. **Publisher:** Harms, Tams Witmark. **Rights:** Copyright 1928 by Harms Inc.

Ii. Beaunoir receives the great detective Vicomte Ribaud who has come to America to search for the revolutionary nobleman Robert Misson. To escape France, Misson sold himself and his servant Alexander as bond-servants to Beaunoir. Robert loves Beaunoir's daughter Marianne. Beaunoir wants his sailors to deliver a cargo of brides to Martinique, but the men want land and pay. Marianne uses the sailors love for her to convince them to obey. Julie loves Alexander, but discovers he is already married to Clotilde—whose name is tattooed on his chest. Captain Duval serenades Marianne, but Robert continually interrupts. Marianne overhears Robert admit he loves her and they fight. Her complaints to Ribaud convince him Robert is his man. Ribaud tries to shoot Robert, but a mysterious stranger shoots the gun out of Ribaud's hand. Iii. Robert's friend Philippe goes to Chez Creole to meet him. Iiii. In the tavern, Ribaud hears the revolutionary sentiments of the sailors. Robert has Ribaud tied up. Robert and Philippe plan to found a free country on the Isle of Pines. Iiv. While Philippe goes to gather men, Robert disguises himself in Ribaud's clothes and returns to the Beaunoir mansion. Iv.

Marianne is throwing a cotillion. Clotilde and the brides arrive and she and Julie fight over Alexander. The sailor Besac is also married to Clotilde. Ribaud returns in disguise, having escaped from the tavern. Robert kisses Marianne and tells her he loves her. Ribaud captures and unmasks Robert. When Beaunoir orders Duval to sail Robert back to France for trial, Marianne decides to go too.

IIi. On board "The New Moon," Duval questions Robert about an uprising in New Orleans the night of Robert's arrest. Robert is defiant. Besac and Alexander fight over which of them will satisfy Clotilde. Julie and Clotilde fight over Alexander. The ship is attacked by pirates. When Duval decides to surrender, Robert takes over the ship. But the pirates are led by his friend Philippe and they agree to sail to the Isle of Pines. Marianne thinks their ideals are a delusion. IIii. Alexander infuriates Marianne by telling her that Robert means to "remake" her. The men have passed a law that all women on the island must marry. Alexander wants to marry Julie, but first has to convince Clotilde to stay with Besac. IIiii. A year has passed. Robert has married Marianne in accordance with the law, but is no closer to winning her heart. Ribaud tells the men that the French warships in the harbor have only come to get Marianne. Robert agrees to let Marianne go. IIiv. Alexander tries to quiet his baby. As Ribaud knows, the French have not come for Marianne at all: but Ribaud wants them to storm the colony. IIv. He sends Robert a message telling him to come to Marianne's cabin. Once there, he tells the lovers about their sacrifices for each other, thus reconciling them. As Ribaud intended, Robert is then distracted when the French attack. IIvi. The French arrive. But the French captain explains that the French have executed their king. He arrests Ribaud.

Solovey • The Nightingale

Composed by Igor Stravinsky (June 17, 1882 – April 6, 1971). Libretto by Stepan Nikolayevich Mitusov. Russian. Based on a fairy tale by Hans Christian Andersen. Premiered Paris, Opéra, May 26, 1914. Set in China in legendary times. Lyric tale. Through composed with introduction. Entr'acte with chorus ("breezes") before II. Entr'acte before III.

Sets: 3. **Acts:** 3 acts, 3 scenes. **Length:** I, II, III: 45. **Arias:** Nightingale's song (Nightingale). **Hazards:** None. **Scenes:** I. The edge of a forest by the sea. II. The porcelain palace of the emperor. III. A room in the palace.

Major roles: Fisherman (tenor), Voice of the nightingale (soprano), Cook (soprano), Emperor of China (baritone), Chamberlain (bass). **Minor roles:** Bonze (bass), Death (contralto). **Bit parts:** Three courtiers in entr'acte (tenor, alto, soprano), Three Japanese envoys (2 tenor, 1 bass).

Chorus parts: SSAATTBB. **Chorus roles:** Courtiers, specters. **Dance/ movement:** None. **Orchestra:** picc, 2 fl, 2 ob, Eng hrn, 3 cl (bs cl), 3 bsn (cont bsn), 4 hrn, 4 trp, 3 trb, tuba, timp, perc, piano, celeste, 2 harp, guitar, mandolin, strings. **Stageband:** None. **Publisher:** Boosey & Hawkes. **Rights:** Copyright 1923 by Édition Russe de Musique. Assigned 1947 to Boosey & Hawkes.

I. The fisherman is enchanted by the song of the nightingale. Guided by the Cook, the Bonze, the chamberlain and a group of courtiers have come to invite the nightingale to court to sing for the emperor. The nightingale accepts.

II. The courtiers ask the cook about the nightingale. The Emperor of China arrives in a solemn procession and at his command, the nightingale sings. The Japanese envoys present the emperor with a mechanical nightingale, but he interrupts its performance wanting to hear the real nightingale again. Upon discovering that the nightingale has fled, the emperor pronounces its banishment and proclaims the mechanical bird first singer of the court.

III. The ghosts of the emperor's past deeds have come to haunt him, but are silenced by the nightingale's song. Death has usurped the crown and scepter. When the nightingale falls silent, Death agrees to relinquish the crown and scepter if the nightingale will resume its song. It does. The emperor tries to appoint the nightingale first singer, but the nightingale feels sufficiently rewarded that the emperor has shed tears at his song and he promises to come every night and sing. The courtiers are surprised to find their emperor alive. The voice of the fisherman is heard, praising the birds' songs.

Nina

Composed by Giovanni Paisiello (May 9, 1740 – June 5, 1816). Libretto by Giovanni Battista Lorenzi and Giuseppe Carpani. Italian. Based on a libretto by Benoît-Joseph Marsollier. Premiered Caserta, San Leucio, June 25, 1789. Set in Italy in the 18th century. Opera semi-seria. Set numbers with recitative and spoken dialogue. Overture.

Sets: 1. **Acts:** 2 acts, 2 scenes. **Length:** I: 75. II: 55. **Arias:** "Il mio ben quando verrà" (Nina), "Lontano da te, Lindoro" (Nina), "Già il sol si cela dietro la montagna" (Shepherd). **Hazards:** None. **Scenes:** I – II. A garden between a road and a park.

Major roles: Elisa (soprano), Count (bass), Nina (soprano), Lindoro (tenor). **Minor roles:** Giorgio (baritone), Shepherd (tenor). **Bit parts:** Six country girls. **Mute:** Servants of the count.

Chorus parts: SATB. **Chorus roles:** Country people. **Dance/movement:** None. **Orchestra:** 2 fl, 2 ob, 2 cl, 2 bsn, 2 hrn, 2 trp, strings, continuo. **Stageband:** I: bagpipe (accompanies shepherd's aria). **Publisher:** Carisch S.A. **Rights:** Expired.

I. Nina loved her fiancée Lindoro, but at the last minute Nina's father, the count, decided on a wealthier suitor. Lindoro fought the suitor and was mortally wounded and Nina went mad with grief. The count asks after his daughter and repents his actions. The servant, Giorgio, comforts him. Nina wakes, but the count cannot face her. She waits for Lindoro as some country girls sing with her. Nina speaks kindly to the count, but does not recognize him.

II. Nina's nurse, Elisa, refuses to take money for looking after her. The count's servants crowd around a young man. It is Lindoro, who was wounded, but not fatally. To Lindoro's surprise, the count welcomes him as his son. He tells Lindoro about Nina's madness. Lindoro prays that Nina will recover. She recognizes Lindoro and her reason returns. The count blesses the couple.

Nixon in China

Composed by John Adams (b. February 15, 1947). Libretto by Alice Goodman. English. Based on historical events and persons. Premiered Houston, Brown Theater, Wortham Center, October 22, 1987. Set in China in 1972. Historic drama. Through composed. Ballet. Minimalist.

Sets: 6. **Acts:** 3 acts, 6 scenes. **Length:** I, II, III: 145. **Arias:** "News has a kind of mystery" (Nixon), "This is prophetic" (Pat), "I am the wife of Mao Tse-tung" (Chiang Ch'ing). **Hazards:** I: Airplane onstage. **Scenes:** Ii. The tarmac at Beijing airport. Iii. Chairman Mao's study. Iiii. The great hall of the people. IIi. Chinese factory, school, and park. IIii. A theater. III. Unspecified.

Major roles: Chou En-lai (bass), Richard Nixon (bass), Henry Kissinger (bass), Mao Tse-tung (tenor). **Minor roles:** Nancy T'ang/First secretary (mezzo), Second secretary (mezzo), Third secretary (mezzo), Pat Nixon (soprano), Chiang Ch'ing/Madame Mao Tse-tung (soprano). **Dancer:** Wu Ching-hua.

Chorus parts: SSSAAATTBB. **Chorus roles:** Chinese people, guests at

state dinner, workers. **Dance/movement:** II: Communist ballet.
Orchestra: 2 fl (picc), 2 ob (Eng hrn), 3 cl (2 bs cl), 4 sax, 3 trp, 3 trb, perc,
synthesizer, 2 piano, strings. **Stageband:** None. **Publisher:** Boosey &
Hawkes. **Rights:** Copyright 1987 by Red Dawn Music BMI.

Ii. President Nixon's plane lands in China where he is greeted by
Chinese reciting Communist slogans. He chats with Prime Minister
Chou and contemplates his place in history. Iii. Mao welcomes Nixon
and Kissinger but refers them to Chou for the political negotiations.
They discuss the confusion of the political extremes of right and left and
Mao's caution about China's entry into world markets. Nixon and Mao
agree they are both pragmatists first and ideologues second. Iiii. Chou
and Nixon give speeches and toasts at a state dinner in Nixon's honor.

IIi. Mrs. Nixon is taken on a tour of Chinese factories, schools and parks.
IIii. The Nixons attend a ballet dramatizing the Communist revolution.
Mrs. Nixon is upset by the violence. Chiang Ch'ing, Mao's wife, lectures
from Mao's little red book.

IIIi. Nixon reminisces about his war experiences with Pat while Mao,
Chou and Chiang Ch'ing remember the revolution.

Norma

Composed by Vincenzo Bellini (November 3, 1801 – September 23,
1835). Libretto by Felice Romani. Italian. Based on the tragedy by Louis
Alexandre Soumet. Premiered Milan, Teatro alla Scala, December 26,
1831. Set in Gaul in about 50 BC. Opera seria. Set numbers with recitative. Overture. Introduction before II.

Sets: 5. **Acts:** 4 acts, 5 scenes. **Length:** Overture: 6. I: 57. II: 27. III: 23. IV:
43. **Arias:** "Casta diva" (Norma), "Ite sul colle" (Oroveso), "Meco
all'altar di Venere" (Pollione). **Hazards:** II: Norma ascends funeral pyre.
Scenes: I. Sacred forest of the druids. II. Norma's dwelling. III. Interior
of Norma's dwelling. IVi. A solitary spot near the druids' wood surrounded by rocky caverns. IVii. The temple of Irminsul.

Major roles: Oroveso (bass), Pollione (tenor), Norma (soprano),
Adalgisa (soprano). **Minor roles:** Flavio (tenor), Clotilde (mezzo). **Mute:**
Two children of Norma.

Chorus parts: SATTBB. **Chorus roles:** Gallic soldiers, druids, priestesses,
priests, Gauls. **Dance/movement:** None. **Orchestra:** 2 fl (picc), 2 ob, 2 cl,
2 bsn, 4 hrn, 2 trp, 3 trb, cimbasso, timp, perc, harp, strings. **Stageband:**
I: brass band. **Publisher:** G. Schirmer, Dover. **Rights:** Expired.

I. Oroveso promises his fellow Druids that Norma, his daughter, will cut the sacred mistletoe. The Roman proconsul Pollione and his friend Flavio seek out Norma. She is the mother of Pollione's children, but he now loves Adalgisa, a young priestess. Norma counsels the Druids against armed revolt against Rome, knowing that the empire's end is not yet come. She presides over the sacred rites and wonders how to shield Pollione from her countrymen's wrath. Adalgisa is torn between love of Pollione and her sacred vows, but Pollione persuades her to accompany him to Rome.

II. Norma fears that Pollione means to leave without her. Adalgisa confides in Norma, who is sympathetic—until she realizes that Adalgisa loves Pollione. Norma curses Pollione.

III. Norma cannot bring herself to kill her own children. Instead, she decides to kill herself and asks Adalgisa to take the children to Pollione whom Adalgisa insists she no longer loves.

IVi. Oroveso reports that the Roman military presence is being augmented and reluctantly agrees that the time is not right for a revolt. IVii. Norma summons the Druids and orders them to attack the legions. Pollione is dragged in by soldiers, having profaned the holy precincts in his search for Adalgisa. Norma offers to free Pollione if he forswears Adalgisa, but he refuses. She threatens their children, Adalgisa, and the Roman soldiers. Norma admits her adultery to all and begs her father to take care of her children. She is led to the pyre, where Pollione—his love for her reawakened—joins her.

Nos • The Nose

Composed by Dmitri Shostakovich (September 25, 1906 – August 9, 1975). Libretto by Alexander Preis, Yevgeny Zamyatin, Georgy Yonin and Dmitri Shostakovich. Russian. Based on the story by Gogol. Premiered Leningrad, Maliy Theater, January 18, 1930. Set in St. Petersburg in the 19th century. Comic opera. Through composed. Some spoken lines. Overture. Epilogue. Intermezzo before epilogue. Interlude before Iiii and Ivi. Entr'acte before II.

Sets: 11. **Acts:** 3 acts, 12 scenes. **Length:** I, II, III: 105. **Hazards:** I: Kovalioff loses his nose; the nose appears as a life-size character. II: coach driven onstage. III: Nose transformed back to actual size during a scuffle. **Scenes:** Ii. The barber's house. Iii. A quay. Iiii. Kovalioff's bedroom. Iiv. A cathedral. IIi. Outside the police chief's house. IIii. A newspaper office. IIiii. An anteroom. IIIi. A railway station. IIIii. Kovalioff's

living room and Podtotchina's living room. IIIiii. A street. IIIiv.
Kovalioff's bedroom. IIIv. The street.

Major roles: Platon Kusmitsch Kovalioff (baritone), Ivan Iakovlevitsch
(bass baritone), Police inspector (tenor), Ivan (tenor), Nose (tenor).
Minor roles: Alexandra Grigorievna Podtotschina (mezzo), Alexandra's
daughter (soprano), Distinguised matron (alto), Praskovia Ossipovna
(soprano), Pretzel vendor (soprano), Editor (bass baritone), Doctor (bass
baritone), Yarizhkin (tenor). **Bit parts:** Mother/Traveling Mother (soprano), Porter/Second policeman/First man/First student (tenor), Fifth
policeman/Second man/First Dandy/Acquaintance of Kovalioff (tenor),
Seventh policeman/Third man/Second student (tenor), Eighth police-
man/Seventh man/Fifth student (tenor), Ninth policeman/Another
man/Sixth student (tenor), First son/Iarischkin a friend of Kovalioff/
Eighth man (tenor), Piotr Fiodorovitsch/Seventh student (tenor),
Lackey/Coachman/First servant/First policeman/Fourth man/
Acquaintance of Kovalioff (bass), Second servant /Third policeman/
Fifth man/Major (bass), Third servant/Fourth policeman/Speculator
(bass), Fourth servant/Sixth policeman/Fourth student (bass), Fifth ser-
vant/Tenth policeman/Ninth man (bass), Sixth servant/Father/Second
Dandy (bass), Seventh servant/Kutscher/Sixth man (bass), Eighth ser-
vant/Second son/Third student (bass), Salesman/Ivan Ivanovitsch/
Eighth student (bass), Two wives' voices (2 sopranos), Two children of
the traveling mother (1 bass, 1 mute). **Speaking:** Friends of Ivan
Iakovlevitsch, Tourist, Accompanying man, Accompanying woman,
Male voice, Khan Chosrow Mirsa. **Mute:** Countess, Salesgirl.

Chorus parts: SSAATTTBB. **Chorus roles:** Police, vendors, pedestrians,
beggars, travelers, servants, eunuchs, people. **Dance/movement:** None.
Orchestra: 2 fl (picc), 2 ob (Eng hrn), 2 cl (bs cl), 2 bsn (cont bsn), hrn,
trp, trb, 2 harp, piano, 3 perc, strings. **Stageband:** I: balalaikas.
Publisher: Universal Edition. **Rights:** Copyright 1962 by Universal
Edition.

Ii. The barber Yakovlevich cuts off Kovalioff's nose. Iii. Yakovlevich is
horrified and gets rid of the evidence by throwing the nose in the river.
Iiii. Kovalioff realizes he has lost his nose. Iiv. He sees it in church, but
the nose denies belonging to him.

IIi. Kovalioff goes to the police. IIii. He tries to advertise in the paper for
his nose, but the newspapermen laugh at him. IIiii. Kovalioff fears his
career is ruined.

IIIi. The nose is caught at the train station stealing a handkerchief. IIIii.
The police chief returns the nose to Kovalioff but neither Kovalioff nor
his doctor can get it to stay on his face. Kovalioff decides his fiancée's

mother has cursed him and writes her a letter breaking the engagement. Her response convinces him she is innocent. IIIiii. A mob forms to watch the nose promenade. IIIiv. Kovalioff wakes up and finds his nose is back on his face. IIIv. He goes for a walk and decides to delay his marriage.

Noye's Fludde

Composed by Benjamin Britten (November 22, 1913 – December 4, 1976). Libretto by an anonymous author. English. Based on the Biblical story. Premiered Aldeburgh, Orford Church, June 18, 1958. Set aboard Noye's ark in Biblical times. Miracle play. Through composed with spoken lines. Text written in the late 16th century for the Chester miracle play.

Sets: 1. **Acts:** 1 act, 1 scene. **Length:** I: 50. **Hazards:** I: The flood. A rainbow appears after the flood. **Scenes:** I. Before and onboard the Noye's ark.

Major role: Noye (bass baritone). **Minor roles:** Mrs. Noye (contralto), Sem (boy treble), Ham (boy treble), Jaffett (boy treble), Mrs. Sem (girl soprano), Mrs. Ham (girl soprano), Mrs. Jaffett (girl soprano), Two gossips (girl sopranos). **Speaking:** The voice of God.

Chorus parts: SATB. **Chorus roles:** Mrs. Noye's gossips (girl sopranos), Noye's children, animals and birds (seven "well balanced" groups of children), congregation. **Dance/movement:** None. **Orchestra:** Professionals: 2 vln, vla, vlc, db bs, treble recorder, piano (four hands), organ, timp. Children or amateurs: 3 recorders, 4 bugles, hand bells, strings, perc. **Stageband:** None. **Publisher:** Hawkes & Sons. **Rights:** Copyright 1958 Hawkes & Son (London) Ltd.

I. God is angered by mankind's evil ways and determines to wipe out everyone except Noye and his family. Noye and the children set to build the ark, mocked by Mrs. Noye and her gossips. The animals board the ark. Mrs. Noye does not want to join them, but her children carry her on board. For forty days, the earth is flooded. At last, Noye sends out a raven, which does not return. But a dove returns with an olive branch in its mouth. God shows Noye a rainbow in token that he will never again flood the earth.

Le Nozze di Figaro • The Marriage of Figaro

Composed by Wolfgang Amadeus Mozart (January 27, 1756 – December 5, 1791). Libretto by Lorenzo Da Ponte. Italian. Play by Pierre-Augustin

Caron de Beaumarchais. Premiered Vienna, Imperial Court Theater, May 1, 1786. Set in the castle of Count Almaviva, three leagues from Seville, in the 18th century. Comedy. Set numbers with recitative. Overture.

Sets: 5. **Acts:** 4 acts, 5 scenes. **Length:** I: 40. II: 45. III: 40. IV: 40. **Arias:** "Se vuol ballare" (Figaro), "La vendetta" (Bartolo), "Non so più cosa son, cosa faccio" (Cherubino), "Non più andrai" (Figaro), "Porgi, amor" (Countess), "Voi, che sapete" (Cherubino), "Vedrò mentr'io sospiro" (Count), "Dove sono?" (Countess), "Il capro e la capretta" (Marcellina), "In quegli anni" (Basilio), "Aprite un po'" (Figaro), "Deh vieni non tardar" (Susanna), "Venite inginocchiatevi" (Susanna). **Hazards:** None. **Scenes:** I. An incompletely furnished room in the castle of Count Almaviva. II. A luxurious room. III. A richly decorated hall prepared for a wedding. IVi. A small room. IVii. A thickly grown garden.

Major roles: Figaro (bass baritone), Susanna (soprano), Count Almaviva (baritone), Countess Almaviva (soprano). **Minor roles:** Bartolo (bass), Marcellina (mezzo), Cherubino (soprano or mezzo), Basilio (tenor), Antonio (bass), Don Curzio (tenor), Barbarina (soprano). **Bit parts:** Two girls.

Chorus parts: SATB. **Chorus roles:** Country men and women, hunters, servants. **Dance/movement:** III: Wedding dance. **Orchestra:** 2 fl, 2 ob, 2 cl, 2 bsn, 2 hrn, 2 trp, timp, strings. **Stageband:** None. **Publisher:** Schirmer, Breitkopf and Härtel. **Rights:** Expired.

I. Figaro measures the bedroom that Count Almaviva has given him and his bride-to-be, Susanna. Susanna objects to being so close to the count, who has been importuning her, and Figaro decides to turn the tables. Marcellina hopes to force Figaro into marrying her since he cannot repay the money he owes her. She and Susanna cut each other dead. Cherubino confesses to Susanna that the count caught him visiting Barbarina and fired him. He is also in love with the countess and has written her a love song. As the count approaches, Cherubino hides behind a chair. The count tries to seduce Susanna but is interrupted by Basilio and hides behind the chair while Cherubino jumps into it. Susanna covers Cherubino with a dressing gown. Basilio gossips about Cherubino's love for the countess. The count jumps up, intending to punish Cherubino—until he realizes the page has overheard everything. Figaro arrives with a group of villagers. They praise the count for giving up his *droit de signor*. The count forgives Cherubino, but makes him captain of his regiment—and orders him to leave town immediately.

II. Susanna tells the countess about the count's attentions. Figaro decides to distract the count by telling him the countess has a lover. Meanwhile,

Susanna will agree to meet him in the garden, but send Cherubino instead. Cherubino sings his love song and they dress him as a woman for his rendezvous. Cherubino's commission was never sealed, the countess notes. The count returns and Cherubino hides in the next room. The noise he makes alerts the count, but the countess refuses to unlock the door. The count goes off to fetch tools. While he is gone, Cherubino jumps out the window and Susanna takes his place. The countess admits Figaro's warning to the count was a setup and the count begs forgiveness. Antonio the gardener complains that a man jumped out of the window onto his flowers. The count is again suspicious, but Figaro claims he jumped upon hearing the count's angry voice. Antonio gives Cherubino's commission to the count and the count quizzes Figaro about it. With much coaching from the women, Figaro explains he brought the commission back to be sealed. Marcellina pleads her case.

III. Basilio goes to Seville to check that Cherubino arrived. Susanna promises to meet the count in the garden. Don Curzio, the judge, declares that Figaro must pay Marcellina or marry her. In desperation, Figaro reveals he was a noble foundling and from his birthmark Marcellina recognizes him as her long lost son. Bartolo is his father, and Bartolo and Marcellina decide to marry. Barbarina steals away with Cherubino. The countess mourns the loss of her husband's love. Cherubino is still in the castle, Antonio tells the count. Susanna writes a letter to the count and closes it with a pin. Country women—including Barbarina and Cherubino dressed as a girl—present flowers to the countess. Antonio reveals Cherubino's disguise, but Barbarina blackmails the count with their past liaison and claims Cherubino as her own. Susanna slips her note to the count. He invites everyone to a celebration in honor of the pending marriages.

IVi. Barbarina has lost the pin she was supposed to return to Susanna. From her, Figaro learns of Susanna's interview with the count. Marcellina urges caution and Barbarina wonders why men are so unfaithful. IVii. Figaro has brought Basilio and Bartolo to witness Susanna's assignation. Basilio notes that a little humility goes a long way. Figaro rails against woman's fickleness. Susanna and the countess exchange clothes. Cherubino addresses the countess but is scared away by the count. The count gives the countess (who is disguised as Susanna) a diamond and invites her into the pavilion. Figaro takes revenge by making love to Susanna (disguised as the countess). She is furious and boxes his ears. The count sees them and calls for help, thinking his wife has betrayed him. Susanna begs forgiveness but the count is adamant. He discovers his mistake when the countess emerges from the pavilion. The count begs forgiveness and all rejoice.

Oberon

Composed by Carl Maria von Weber (November 18, 1786 – June 5, 1826). Libretto by James Robinson Planché. English. Based on a poem by Christoph Martin Wiel and "Huon de Bourdeaux" from the collection of French romances entitled "La Bibliothèque Bleue." Premiered London, Royal Opera House, Covent Garden, April 12, 1826. Set in the fairy kingdom, Bagdad, Tunis and France in the early 9th century. Romantic fairy opera. Set numbers with recitative and spoken dialogue. Overture. Ballet. Many revised versions, including one by Gustav Mahler.

Sets: 8. **Acts:** 3 acts, 9 scenes. **Length:** I: 45. II: 40. III: 35. **Arias:** "Ocean, thou mighty monster" (Reiza), "From boyhood trained" (Sir Huon). **Hazards:** I: Huon has a vision of Reiza. Droll vanishes. II: Droll transports Huon to Tunis in a chariot of blossoms. **Scenes:** Ii. A garden in Oberon's fairy kingdom. Iii. A road from Oberon's magic wood to Baghdad. Iiii – IIi. A splendid hall in the palace of Harun al Raschid in Baghdad. IIiii. A rock strewn landscape. IIIi. The palace garden of Emir Almansor in Tunis. IIIii. A colonnade in the Emir's palace. IIIiii. The market place of Tunis. IIIiv. The throne room of the Emperor Charlemagne.

Major roles: Oberon (tenor), Sir Huon of Bordeaux (tenor), Sherasmin (baritone), Reiza (soprano), Fatima (mezzo). **Minor roles:** Puck (contralto), Droll (contralto), First mermaid (soprano), Second mermaid (soprano). **Mute:** Titania, Charlemagne. **Speaking:** Harun al Rashchid (Caliph of Bagdad), Babekan, Almansor, Roshana, Nadina, Abdallah, Chief of Harun's palace guard.

Chorus parts: SSAATTBB. **Chorus roles:** Elves, fairies, harem guards, nymphs, followers of Charlemagne, followers of the caliph, slaves, guard, eunuchs, pirates, lords of the realm, spirits of earth, air, water and fire, courtiers. **Dance/movement:** II: Slave ballet. Dance of the spirits. Mermaid dance. III: Slave dance. **Orchestra:** 2 fl, 2 picc, 2 ob, 2 cl, 2 bsn, 4 hrn, 2 trp, 3 trb, timp, perc, strings. **Stageband:** I: 2 ob, 2 cl, 2 bsn, perc. **Publisher:** Universal Edition, Schlesinger. **Rights:** Expired.

Ii. Oberon, the fairy king, fights with his wife, Titania, over who is less faithful: men or women. Oberon decides to find a pair of faithful lovers and test them. He settles on Huon of Bordeaux, a knight exiled from Charlemagne's court until he should travel to Baghdad, kill the man on the caliph's left and marry the caliph's daughter, Reiza. Oberon sends

Huon a vision of Reiza and gives him a magic horn to help him find her. Huon's servant, Sherasmin, is given a magic goblet. Oberon transports Huon to Baghdad. Iii. Hüon decides he could not live without honor. Iiii. Reiza and her serving lady, Fatima, wait for Huon to rescue them from the caliph.

IIi. The caliph plans for Reiza to marry Prince Babekan, but Huon kills Babekan, abducts Reiza—and puts the caliph and his men to sleep with his magic horn. Fatima flees with Sherasmin. IIii. The lovers set sail for France, but Puck raises a storm and shipwrecks them. They lose the magic horn and goblet. Reiza is captured by pirates. The elves and mermaids dance.

IIIi. Reiza , Fatima and Sherasmin are sold as slaves to Almansor, the Emir of Tunis. Huon follows them and is reunited with Fatima and Sherasmin. He is hired as a gardener in the emir's gardens. IIIii. Reiza rejects the emir's advances. His wife, Roshana, tries to seduce Huon, but fails. The emir sees them together and condemns Huon to death. IIIiii. Neither the emir nor his servant Abdallah realize the value of the magic horn that they have recovered from the sea. Abdallah gives it to Sherasmin. The emir is infuriated by Reiza's pleas for Huon and condemns her with him, but Sherasmin uses the magic horn to save them. IIIiv. Oberon transports the lovers to France where they are welcomed into Charlemagne's court.

Oberto

Composed by Giuseppe Verdi (October 9, 1813 – January 27, 1901). Libretto by Temistocle Solera. Italian. Based on a libretto by Antonio Piazza. Premiered Milan, Teatro alla Scala, November 17, 1839. Set in Bassano and environs in 1228. Drama. Set numbers with recitative. Overture.

Sets: 4. **Acts:** 2 acts, 4 scenes. **Length:** I: 70. II: 50. **Arias:** "Oh chi torna l'ardente pensiero" (Cuniza), "L'orror del tradimento" (Oberto), "Sotto il paterno tetto" (Leonora). **Hazards:** None. **Scenes:** Ii. The countryside around Bassano. Iii. A magnificent room in the castle of Ezzelino. IIi. The princess's room. IIii. A remote site near the castle gardens.

Major roles: Riccardo (tenor), Leonora (soprano), Oberto (bass), Cuniza (mezzo). **Minor role:** Imelda (mezzo).

Chorus parts: SATTB. **Chorus roles:** Knights, ladies, vassals. **Dance/ movement:** None. **Orchestra:** 2 fl, 2 ob, 2 cl, 2 bsn, 4 hrn, 2 trp, 3 trb, tuba, timp, perc, harp, strings. **Stageband:** None. **Publisher:** G. Ricordi & Co. **Rights:** Expired.

Ii. Oberto has been defeated in battle by the Ghibelline despot Ezzelino and Count Riccardo has deserted Oberto's daughter, Leonora, to marry Ezzelino's sister, Cuniza. Leonora resolves to attend the wedding and Oberto comes looking for her. He rebukes her for dishonoring him and encourages her to exact revenge. Iii. The wedding guests assemble. Cuniza has evil forebodings. Leonora goes to the palace. She and Oberto confront Cuniza. They reveal Riccardo's betrayal and Cuniza agrees to help them. Leonora publicly accuses Riccardo.

IIi. Cuniza is determined that Riccardo shall marry Leonora. IIii. A group of knights ponders the situation. Oberto awaits Riccardo—whom he has challenged to a duel. Riccardo is reluctant to fight a man so much older than himself, but Oberto's insults infuriate him. Cuniza intervenes and Oberto and Riccardo pretend to make peace. The knights hear the sounds of a fight. Riccardo kills Oberto. Cuniza and Leonora learn what has happened and Leonora blames herself. Riccardo leaves a letter asking Leonora's forgiveness and pledging her his faith and property. She decides to enter a convent.

Oedipus Rex

Composed by Igor Stravinsky (June 17, 1882 – April 6, 1971). Libretto by Jean Cocteau. Latin. Based on the play by Sophocles. Premiered Vienna, Staatsoper, February 23, 1928. Set in Thebes in legendary times. Opera oratorio. Through composed. Spoken prologue. Concert premiere Théâtre Sarah Bernhardt, Paris, May 30, 1927. Revised 1948.

Sets: 1. **Acts:** 2 acts, 2 scenes. **Length:** I: 24. II: 28. **Arias:** "Liberi vos liberabo" (Oedipus), "Nonne erubeskite, reges clamáre" (Jocasta). **Hazards:** None. **Scenes:** I – II. Before the Acropolis.

Major roles: Oedipus (tenor), Créon/Messenger (bass baritone), Tirésias (bass), Jocasta (mezzo). **Minor roles:** Shepherd (tenor). **Speaking:** Speaker.

Chorus parts: TTBB. **Chorus roles:** People of Thebes. **Dance/movement:** None. **Orchestra:** 3 fl (picc), 2 ob, Eng hrn, 3 cl, 2 bsn, cont bsn, 4 hrn, 4 trp, 3 trb, tuba, timp, perc, harp, piano, strings. **Stageband:** None. **Publisher:** Boosey & Hawkes. **Rights:** Copyright 1927 by Édition Russe de Musique. New version copyright 1949 by Boosey & Hawkes.

Prologue. The narrator sets the scene in Thebes where Oedipus has

saved Thebes from the Sphinx by answering its riddle. I. Oedipus tells
the Thebans that Créon, the queen's brother, has gone to consult the oracle. Créon reports that the gods demand that King Laius's murderer be
punished. Oedipus learns from Tirésias that the murderer is himself a
king. He accuses Tirésias of plotting against him with Créon.

II. When Queen Jocasta describes Laius's death, Oedipus realizes he may
be the murderer. A messenger reports the death of King Polybus of
Corinth and says that Polybus was not Oedipus's father. Jocasta realizes
that she is Oedipus's mother and that Oedipus killed his own father. A
shepherd tells how Oedipus was discovered on a mountain as a baby
and reveals that Laius and Jocasta were Oedipus's true parents. The people mourn Jocasta, who has hanged herself. Oedipus puts out his eyes
with a pin. The Thebans bid their king farewell.

Of Mice and Men

Composed by Carlisle Floyd (b. June 11, 1926). Libretto by Carlisle
Floyd. English. Based on the novel and play by John Steinbeck.
Premiered Seattle, Seattle Opera Association, January 22, 1970. Set in an
agricultural valley in northern California in the 1930s or 1940s. Music
drama. Through composed. Musical interludes before Iii and IIIii. Some
spoken lines.

Sets: 3. **Acts:** 3 acts, 5 scenes. **Length:** I: 50. II: 25. III: 40. **Hazards:** I, II:
George has pet dogs. II: George shoots Lennie in the head. **Scenes:** Ii. A
clearing in the woods. Iii – II. The bunkhouse. IIIi. The barn. IIIii. A
clearing in the woods.

Major roles: Lennie Small (tenor), George Milton (bass baritone), Curley
(tenor), Candy (bass), Curley's wife (soprano). **Minor roles:** Carlson
(tenor), Slim (baritone), Ballad singer (tenor). **Bit parts:** Haygood (tenor),
Luke (bass), Pete (tenor), Johnson (baritone). **Speaking bits:** Three men.

Chorus parts: TB. **Chorus roles:** Ranch hands (minimum 8; Luke,
Haygood, Pete and Johnson are ranchhands, but each has one solo line).
Dance/movement: None. **Orchestra:** 2 fl (picc), 2 ob (Eng hrn), 2 cl (bs
cl), 2 bsn, 4 hrn, 2 trp, 2 trb, tuba, timp, 2 or 3 perc, harp, celeste, strings.
Stageband: None. **Publisher:** Belwin Mills. **Rights:** Copyright 1971 by
Belwin Mills Publishing Corporation.

Ii. Lennie and George escape from the police after Lennie frightened a
woman by stroking her dress. George is convinced his life would be easier without Lennie, but he promised Lennie's aunt he would look after
him. George takes away the mouse Lennie accidentally killed while pet-

ting it and promises to get Lennie a pet—when they have the house and farm they both dream about. Iii. Curley impatiently awaits Lennie and George, his new farm hands. Curley's wife is bored and wants to have a night on the town, but her husband refuses. Lennie and George meet the other farm hands. Curley's wife is attracted to Slim—and Lennie. Slim convinces Candy that his dog is so old and smelly it has to be put out of its misery. Lennie begs George to let him accept one of the puppies that Slim is giving away.

II. The ranch hands pitch horseshoes. Slim observes that all ranch hands dream of owning their own farms—but few succeed. George reads the advertisements and finds a small farm house for sale. He and Lennie agree to purchase it with Candy. Curley's wife visits the men. Knowing her presence could cost them their jobs, the men try to make her leave, but Curley discovers them. Words are exchanged. Curley picks a fight with Lennie and Lennie thrashes him. The men promise not to tell how Curley got hurt so long as he does not fire Lennie or George. George warns Lennie they cannot afford to get in trouble.

IIIi. Curley's wife finds Lennie in the barn, mourning his puppy. She tells him her plan to run away to Hollywood. When she lets him stroke her hair, he won't let go. Frightened, Curley's wife struggles and Lennie—trying to keep her quiet—accidentally breaks her neck. George and Candy discover the body and decide they have to kill Lennie. Candy realizes they will never get their farm. IIIii. Curley and the farm hands search for Lennie. George finds him first. He tells Lennie about their dream farm and, when Lennie is not looking, shoots him.

The Old Maid and the Thief

Composed by Gian Carlo Menotti (b. July 7, 1911). Libretto by Gian Carlo Menotti. English. Original work. Premiered Philadelphia, Philadelphia Opera Company, February 11, 1941. Set in a small town in the United States in the present. Grotesque opera. Through composed with overture. Radio premiere by NBC, April 22, 1939.

Sets: 1. **Acts:** 1 act, 14 scenes. **Length:** I: 60. **Arias:** "When the air sings of summer (Bob), "Steal me, sweet thief" (Laetitia). **Hazards:** None. **Scenes:** I. Various rooms in Miss Todd's house. (One set.)

Major roles: Miss Todd (contralto), Laetitia (soprano), Miss Pinkerton (soprano), Bob (baritone). **Speaking bit:** Store keeper. **Mute:** Policeman.

Chorus parts: N/A. **Chorus roles:** None. **Dance/movement:** None. **Orchestra:** picc, fl, ob, cl, bsn, 2 hrn, 2 trp, trb, perc, piano, strings.

Stageband: None. **Publisher:** Ricordi. **Rights:** Copyright 1943 by
G. Ricordi & Co.

Ii. Miss Pinkerton and Miss Todd gossip about former boyfriends. A
beggar (Bob) appears at the door and is taken in by Miss Todd. Iii. Miss
Todd and her maid, Laetitia, agree that Bob is clever and charming.
They want him to stay. Iiii. Laetitia asks Bob to stay and he agrees. To
avoid gossip, he pretends to be Cousin Steve. Iiv. Miss Pinkerton warns
Miss Todd that a thief has escaped from jail. From the description, Miss
Todd realizes the thief is Bob. Iv. Miss Todd tells Laetitia, but the maid
thinks Bob should stay. "If we steal money for him he will stay," Laetitia
suggests. Ivi. Laetitia and Miss Todd are both attracted to Bob, but he
makes no advances. Ivii. Miss Pinkerton reports robberies all over town.
Iviii. Bob is bored and threatens to leave unless they buy him liquor. Iix.
Miss Todd fears that buying liquor will ruin her reputation. Ix. Instead,
she and Laetitia rob the liquor store. Ixi. Miss Pinkerton tells Miss Todd
that a famous detective has been hired to catch the thief. Ixii. Laetitia
and Miss Todd warn Bob to flee but he says he is not the escaped thief.
When he tells Miss Todd he does not love her, she decides to accuse him
of her own crimes. Ixiii. Seeing no alternative, Bob and Laetitia steal
Miss Todd's valuables and escape in her car. Ixiv. Miss Todd returns to
an empty house.

Olympie

Composed by Gaspare Luigi Pacifico Spontini (November 14, 1774 –
January 24, 1851). Libretto by Michel Dieulafoy and Charles Brifaut.
French. Based on the tragedy by Voltaire. Premiered Paris, Opéra,
December 22, 1819. Set in Ephesus in 332 BC. Lyric tragedy. Set numbers
with recitative. Overture. Ballet. Heavily revised by composer with new
German libretto by E. T. A. Hoffmann, later translated back into French.
(Entry follows Hoffmann version.)

Sets: 2. **Acts:** 3 acts, 3 scenes. **Length:** I: 45. II: 40. III: 40. **Hazards:** III:
Lightning strikes the altar steps. **Scenes:** I. Outside the temple of Diana.
II – III. Inside the temple.

Major roles: Cassandre (tenor), Antigone (bass baritone), Olympie
(soprano), Statira (mezzo). **Minor roles:** High Priest (bass). **Bit parts:**
Hermas (bass), Three priestesses (1 soprano, 2 mezzo).

Chorus parts: SSATTTTBBB. **Chorus roles:** Priests, priestesses, soldiers,
people. **Dance/movement:** I: Ballet, bacchanal. III: triumphal march, ballet. **Orchestra:** picc, 2 fl, 2 ob, Eng hrn, 2 cl, 3 bsn, 4 hrn, 2 trp, 2 trb, bs

trb, timp, perc, harp, strings. **Stageband:** III: 2 hrn, 4 trp, bs trb, ophicléide, perc. **Publisher:** G. Brandus. **Rights:** Expired.

I. Alexandre the Great is murdered, leaving behind a widow, Statira,
and a daughter, Olympie. Several claimants to his throne appear, including his general, Antigone, and Cassandre, the son of King Antipâtre of
Macedonia. Cassandre and Antigone form an alliance. It is generally
believed that Alexandre was murdered by Antipâtre, but the real murderer was Antigone. Cassandre is engaged to one of his slaves, who
Antigone shrewdly realizes is Olympie in disguise. The priestess of
Diana is called to bless Cassandre's marriage. It is Statira (Alexandre's
widow) and she publicly accuses Cassandre of murdering her husband.

II. The high priest learns Statira's true identity and Statira recognizes her
daughter, Olympie. Cassandre is unable to convince Statira of his innocence. Antigone takes Statira's side.

III. Statira wants Olympie to marry Antigone, but Olympie remains
faithful to Cassandre. The soldiers of Cassandre and Antigone fight in
the temple and Antigone is mortally wounded. Before he dies, Antigone
confesses he murdered Alexandre. Statira is reconciled to Cassandre and
blesses his marriage to Olympie.

L'Oracolo • The Oracle

Composed by Franco Leoni (October 24, 1864 – February 8, 1949).
Libretto by Camillo Zanoni. Italian. Based on Chester Bailey Fernald's
"The Cat and the Cherub." Premiered London, Royal Opera House,
Covent Garden, June 28, 1905. Set in Chinatown in San Francisco in the
19th century. Tragedy. Through composed.

Sets: 1. **Acts:** 1 act, 1 scene. **Length:** I: 65. **Hazards:** None. **Scenes:** I. A
street in Chinatown.

Major roles: Chim-Fen (baritone), San-Lui (tenor), Uin-Scî (baritone),
Ah-Yoe (soprano). **Minor roles:** Hua-Quî (contralto), Hu-Tsin (bass),
Fortuneteller (mezzo). **Bit parts:** Two voices from afar (2 baritone), Four
vendors (soprano, alto, tenor, baritone). **Mute:** Hu-Cî (child), Policeman,
Opium addict.

Chorus parts: SSATTBB. **Chorus roles:** Gamblers, vendors, children,
Chinese citizens. **Dance/movement:** None. **Orchestra:** 2 fl (picc), 2 ob, 2
cl, 2 bsn, 4 hrn, 3 trp, 4 trb, timp, perc, lyre, harp, strings. **Stageband:**
None. **Publisher:** Chappell & Co. **Rights:** Copyright 1905, 1919 by
Chappell & Co., Ltd. Copyright renewed.

I. Chim-Fen expels an opium addict from his den. Hua-Quî complains that Hu-Tsin never lets her leave the house. She promised Chim-Fen she would steal the fan on which San-Lui composed a love letter to Hu-Tsin's daughter, Ah-Yoe. Chim-Fen threatens to dump her if she does not steal the fan and asks Uin-Scî for advice. San-Lui and Ah-Yoe are in love. The people celebrate Chinese New Year. Chim-Fen asks Hu-Tsin for Ah-Yoe's hand in marriage—what he really wants is her dowry—but Hu-Tsin rejects him. Chim-Fen consults a fortune teller, who tells him he has a dirty past and a damned future. Uin-Scî makes a gloomy but obscure prediction about Hu-Tsin and his son, Hu-Cî. Chim-Fen kidnaps Hu-Cî while Hua-Quî is not looking. Hu-Tsin agrees that Ah-Yoe will marry whoever can recover Hu-Cî. When Chim-Fen is cold to Hua-Quî, she complains to San-Lui. Realizing that Chim-Fen is the kidnapper, San-Lui retrieves the child from the opium den—only to be brutally murdered by Chim-Fen. Chim-Fen hides Hu-Cî in a sewer. Ah-Yoe has gone mad with grief. Uin-Scî divines the boy's whereabouts and returns him to Hu-Tsin. He then tells Chim-Fen how he discovered the murderer. Before Chim-Fen can stab him, Uin-Scî strangles Chim-Fen with his own ponytail. He props up the body and repeats his advice of yesterday until the policeman passes by.

Orfeo ed Euridice • Orfeo and Euridice

Composed by Christoph Willibald Gluck (July 2, 1714 – November 15, 1787). Libretto by Ranieri di Calzabigi. Italian and French (2 versions). Based on Greek mythology. Premiered Vienna, Burgtheater, October 5, 1762. Set in Greece in legendary times. Lyric tragedy. Set numbers with recitative. Overture. Ballet. Revised in a French version by composer and Pierre-Louis Moline premiered in Paris August 2, 1774.

Sets: 5. Acts: 3 acts, 5 scenes. Length: I: 45. II: 25. III: 40. Arias: "Che farò senza Euridice?" (Orfeo), "Che puro ciel" (Orfeo), "Che fieso momento" (Euridice). Hazards: None. Scenes: I. A beautiful but solitary grove around Euridice's tomb. Iii. The gates of Erebus. II. Elysium. IIIi. An obscure cavern, which through winding paths leads out of the infernal regions. IIIii. A magnificent temple dedicated to Amore.

Major roles: Orfeo (male contralto; tenor in French version), Love (soprano), Euridice (soprano). Minor role: Happy spirit (soprano).

Chorus parts: SATB. Chorus roles: Shepherds and shepherdesses, nymphs, demons, furies, specters, heroes. Dance/movement: II: Ballet of the furies and spirits. III: Ballet of the heroes. Orchestra: 2 fl, 2 ob, 2 cl, 2 bsn, 2 hrn, 2 trp, 3 trb, harp, timp, strings. Stageband: II: harp, strings. Publisher: G. Ricordi, Des Lauriers. Rights: Expired.

Ii. Orfeo mourns Euridice and determines to win her back from the gods of the underworld. Love tells Orfeo that he will get Euridice back so long as he does not look at her while in the underworld. Orfeo is frightened of the task before him, but elated by the promise of success. Iii. He charms the demons of hell with his lyre.

II. A happy shade delights in the peacefulness of Elysium. Orfeo is charmed, but he has not forgotten his purpose. He is reunited with Euridice.

IIIi. She is upset that Orfeo will not look at her. But when Orfeo does look, Euridice is drawn back into the abyss. IIIii. Orfeo tries to kill himself, but Love intervenes and saves Euridice. Reunited, Orfeo and Euridice praise love.

Orlando

Composed by George Frederic Handel (February 23, 1685 – April 14, 1759). Libretto by Dr. Braccioli. Italian. Based on Carlo Sigismondo Capeci libretto, itself based on Lodovico Ariosto's "Orlando Furioso." Premiered London, King's Theater, Haymarket, January 27, 1733. Set in the countryside at an unspecified time. Pastoral. Set numbers with recitative. Overture. Prelude before III.

Sets: 4. **Acts:** 3 acts, 5 scenes. **Length:** I, II, III: 165. **Arias:** "Fammi combattere" (Orlando), "Verdi allori" (Medoro), "Cielo! se tu il consenti" (Orlando), "Amor è qual vento" (Dorinda), "Sorge infausta una procella" (Zoroastro). **Hazards:** I: Zoroastro makes mountain disappear and fountain appear. II: Cloud bears Angelica away into the air.
III: Zoroastro makes a cave appear, which later turns into a temple of Mars. Genii and an eagle descend. Statue of Mars appears. **Scenes:**
Ii. Countryside with a mountain in view. Iii. A woods with shepherds' huts. IIi. The woods. IIii. A garden with a view of the sea in the distance. III. A grove of palm trees.

Major roles: Zoroastro (bass), Orlando (contralto or countertenor), Dorinda (soprano), Angelica (soprano), Medoro (alto or tenor). **Mute:** people.

Chorus parts: N/A. **Chorus roles:** None. **Dance/movement:** None. **Orchestra:** 2 recorder, 2 ob, 2 bsn, 2 hrn, strings, continuo. **Stageband:** None. **Publisher:** Gregg Press. **Rights:** Expired.

Ii. The magician Zoroastro contemplates the motion of the stars. He counsels Orlando to shake off love's lethargy and pursue deeds of valor.

Orlando loves Angelica, queen of Cathay. He points out that even the ancient heroes loved. Iii. The shepherdess Dorinda is in love with the African prince Medoro. Angelica no longer loves Orlando: She now dotes on Medoro. Medoro assures Dorinda that he has not forgotten her, although he owes his life and love to Angelica. Dorinda is confused. Angelica conceals her betrayal of Orlando by accusing him of infidelity. Zoroastro uses his magic to conceal Medoro. Orlando promises to prove his love. Angelica and Medoro plan their departure. Dorinda confronts them and Angelica gives her a jewel.

Iii. Dorinda is sad. She shows Angelica's jewel to Orlando, who realizes he has been betrayed. Orlando contemplates revenge and suicide. Iiii. Zoroastro helps the lovers escape. Medoro carves his and Angelica's initials into a tree. Angelica philosophizes that lovers are ungrateful. Orlando sees the initials carved into the tree. He chases Angelica. Medoro follows. Angelica is rescued by a cloud that bears her away. Orlando is furious. He discovers Zoroastro in the grotto.

III. Having been separated from Angelica, Medoro takes refuge in Dorinda's cottage. Dorinda still loves him. Orlando, who has gone mad, woos Dorinda. Angelica learns about Orlando's condition from Dorinda. Dorinda wonders about love's power. Zoroastro makes a cave appear. Angelica reports to Dorinda that Orlando has destroyed her cottage and killed Medoro. Angelica gives herself up to Orlando's fury. The hero falls asleep. Zoroastro restores Orlando to his senses with a magic liquor. Overcome with grief at the murders he has committed, Orlando tries to throw himself off a precipice. Angelica stops Orlando and Zoroastro reveals that he saved both Medoro and Angelica. Orlando blesses Angelica and Medoro.

Orlando Furioso

Composed by Antonio Vivaldi (March 4, 1678 – July 28 (buried), 1741). Libretto by Grazio Braccioli. Italian. Based on the poem by Ariosto. Premiered Venice, Teatro Sant' Angelo, Autumn 1727. Set on Alcina's island at an unspecified time. Drama. Set numbers with recitative.

Sets: 8. **Acts:** 3 acts, 25 scenes. **Length:** I: 55. II: 60. III: 50. **Arias:** "Nel profondo cieco mondo" (Orlando), "Sol da te, mio dolce amore" (Ruggiero). **Hazards:** III: Destruction of the temple of Hecate. **Scenes:** I. A delightful garden in which two springs are seen. Iii – Iiii. A grove with green secluded spots. Iiiii – Iiiv. A mountainous alpine region with a high, precipitous cliff. IIv. A cavern. IIvi – IIviii. A countryside at the foot of a hill. IIIi – IIIii. Entrance hall before the temple of Hecate. IIIiii – IIIvi. Inside the temple of Hecate. IIIvii – IIIix. A deserted island.

Major roles: Orlando (mezzo), Angelica (soprano), Medoro (tenor), Alcina (mezzo), Ruggiero (baritone or contralto), Bradamante (contralto). **Minor role:** Astolfo (bass). **Bit part:** Voice in the cavern (bass).

Chorus parts: SATB. **Chorus roles:** Wedding guests, soldiers. **Dance/movement:** III: Orlando dances in his madness. **Orchestra:** fl, 2 hrn, 2 trb, strings, continuo. **Stageband:** None. **Rights:** Expired.

Ii. Orlando notes that love will conquer with the help of valor. Iii. Medoro escapes from a shipwreck into the arms of his beloved Angelica. Iiii. Alcina magically heals Medoro and he recounts how he was first captured, then shipwrecked. Iiv. Orlando is jealous of Medoro, but Angelica lies and says Medoro is her brother. Iv. Alcina is attracted to the knight Ruggiero. She uses her magic to make him forget Bradamante and love her instead. Ivi. Bradamante discovers Ruggiero's betrayal. Ivii. She shows him the ring he gave her, thus breaking Alcina's spell. Iviii. Ruggiero is wracked with guilt by his actions, but Orlando consoles him.

IIi. Astolfo loves Alcina, but is tormented by her unfaithfulness. IIii. Bradamante makes Ruggiero look at Alcina that she may be convinced of his change of heart. IIiii. Angelica and Medoro swear their love and part. IIiv. To rid herself of Orlando, Angelica sends him to fight a monster who guards an elixir of youth. IIv. Orlando enters a cavern and is trapped. Realizing Angelica's faithlessness, he digs his way out. IIvi. Angelica and Medoro are married. IIvii. They carve their vows on a nearby tree. IIviii. Orlando reads the inscription and goes mad. He destroys the trees.

IIIi. Astolfo believes Orlando dead. With Ruggiero and Bradamante, he plots revenge against Alcina. IIIii. The secret of Alcina's power lies in an urn, which is locked in the temple of Hecate. The conspirators await Alcina's return. IIIiii. Bradamante disguises herself as a man with a vendetta against Ruggiero. Alcina falls in love with her. IIIiv. Orlando raves. IIIv. He reproaches Angelica. IIIvi. In his madness, Orlando fights with the temple statues, inadvertently destroying Alcina's power. IIIvii. Alcina tries to attack the sleeping Orlando, but is prevented by Ruggiero and Bradamante. IIIviii. Medoro begs Angelica to flee. IIIix. Astolfo returns to arrest Alcina. Orlando regains his reason and forgives Angelica and Medoro.

L'Ormindo • Ormindo

Composed by Pier Francesco Cavalli (February 14, 1602 – January 14, 1676). Libretto by Giovanni Faustini. Italian. Original work. Premiered Venice, Teatro San Cassiano, Spring 1644. Set in the city of Fez in North

Africa at an unspecified time. Comedy. Set numbers with recitative. Overture. Realized by Raymond Leppard.

Sets: 7. **Acts:** 2 acts, 9 scenes. **Length:** I, II: 135. **Arias:** "Chi mi toglie al dìe" (Sicle), "Mai volsi ch'il mio core" (Erice), "Che città!" (Nerillo). **Hazards:** II: Erice's magic incantation. **Scenes:** Ii. Fez in North Africa. Iii. The royal garden. Iiii. The palace. Iiv – IIi. The harbor. IIii. A cave outside the city walls. IIiii. The harbor. IIiv. On the way to prison. IIv. The prison.

Major roles: Prince Ormindo (tenor), Prince Amida (baritone), Princess Sicle (mezzo), Queen Erisbe (soprano). **Minor roles:** Nerillo (mezzo), Melide (mezzo), Erice the nurse (tenor), Mirinda (mezzo), King Ariadeno (bass), Captain Osmano (baritone).

Chorus parts: N/A. **Chorus roles:** None. **Dance/movement:** None. **Orchestra:** 2 harpsichords, harp, 2 lutes, theorbo, guitar, flue organ, 3 vlc, 2 db bs, strings. **Stageband:** None. **Publisher:** Faber Music. **Rights:** Expired.

Ii. Ormindo and Amida are friends—until they discover they both love Queen Erisbe. Sicle comes looking for Amida, who abandoned her. Pretending to be an Egyptian fortuneteller, she learns of Amida's new attachment. Sicle's nurse, Erice, reflects that it is better not to get too attached to one's lovers. Iii. Erisbe fumes against her frigid old husband, but is comforted by the thought of her two lovers. Confronted by the two men, Erisbe tells them both to hope. The king asks Erisbe to befriend his allies, Ormindo and Amida. Erisbe's waiting woman, Mirinda, warns old men not to believe they are loved by young wives. Iiii. Erisbe is interested in Sicle's fortunetelling. Sicle exposes Amida's faithlessness and tells the queen to favor Ormindo. Meaning to mislead Amida, Erice agrees to help him win the queen. Sicle's waiting woman, Melide, swears she will never fall in love. Iiv. Ormindo must lead his troops out of the city and Erisbe decides to go with him.

IIi. The servant Nerillo is scandalized by the people of Fez. IIii. Erice disguises herself as a sorceress and leads Amida to a cavern. There she tells Amida that Sicle is dead and conjures up Sicle's ghost. Amida falls in love with Sicle again and Sicle reveals she is not dead. Mirinda applauds Erisbe for leaving her husband. IIiii. Osmano reports to the king that Erisbe and Ormindo have been captured. The king orders them poisoned. IIiv. Osmano tells Mirinda that he means to save Ormindo and Mirinda agrees to be Osmano's. IIv. Ormindo and Erisbe drink the potion given them by Osmano—and fall asleep. Seeing their unconscious forms, the king repents. Osmano admits it was only a sleeping potion. The king gives his throne and wife to Ormindo.

L'Orontea • Orontea

Composed by Antonio Cesti (August 5, 1623 – October 14, 1669).
Libretto by Giovanni Filippo Apolloni and Giacinto Andrea Cicognini.
Italian. Original work. Premiered Innsbruck, Teatro Sala, February 19,
1656. Set in Egypt in ancient times. Comedy. Set numbers with recitative. Overture. Prologue. Cesti may have first set the opera in 1649
(revising it in 1656), but if he did, the manuscript is lost.

Sets: N/A. **Acts:** 3 acts, 52 scenes (including prologue). **Length:** I: 65. II:
55. III: 65. **Arias:** "Intorno all'idol mio" (Orontea). **Hazards:** None.
Scenes: Score does not specify locations.

Major roles: Queen Orontea of Egypt (soprano), Alidoro/Floridano
(tenor), Silandra (soprano). **Minor roles:** Philosophy (soprano), Love
(soprano), Creonte (baritone), Tibrino (soprano), Aristea (contralto),
Gelone (bass), Corindo (countertenor), Giacinta/Ismero (soprano).

Chorus parts: N/A. **Chorus roles:** None. **Dance/movement:** None.
Orchestra: Strings, continuo (harpsichord with lute, harp or organ).
Stageband: None. **Publisher:** Wellesley. **Rights:** Expired.

Prologue. Love and Philosophy argue. Ii. Queen Orontea refuses to take
a husband. Iii. Her advisor, Creonte, tells her she must marry for the
good of Egypt. Iiii. The page Tibrino rescues Alidoro from a mysterious
assailant. Iiv. Alidoro is accompanied by his mother, Aristea. Iv. Orontea
falls in love with Alidoro. Ivi. The servant Gelone likes his wine. Ivii.
Corindo prefers love. Iviii. And his love for Silandra is reciprocated. Iix.
Alidoro admits to Orontea that he is fleeing the love of the Phoenician
princess Arnea. Ix. He asks fate to be kind. Ixi. Silandra falls in love with
Alidoro. Ixii. Gelone drinks heavily. Ixiii. The queen summons him, but
Tibrino finds him dead drunk.

IIii. Orontea wants to marry Alidoro. IIiii. Giacinta begs an audience with
the queen. IIiii. She is disguised as a boy, having been sent by Princess
Arnea to kill Alidoro. IIiv. Creonte protects Giacinta from the queen's
anger. IIv. He learns that Orontea loves Alidoro. IIvi. Aristea falls in love
with Giacinta (who she thinks is a boy). IIvii. She chases her. IIviii.
Silandra waits for Alidoro. IIix. She breaks off with her old love,
Corindo. IIx. Corindo wonders at woman's faithlessness. IIxi. Alidoro
decides to paint Silandra. IIxii. He has fallen in love with her. IIxiii.
Orontea warns them to avoid each other. IIxiv. Alidoro is overcome by
the queen's words and faints. IIxv. Gelone awakes and finds Alidoro.
IIxvi. The queen rebukes Gelone for ignoring her summons. IIxvii.
Orontea leaves a love letter for Alidoro. IIxviii. Alidoro awakes, reads
Orontea's letter-and realizes he returns her affection.

IIIi. Silandra pines for Alidoro. IIIii. But Alidoro wants to be king. IIIiii. Tibrino and Gelone wonder at the queen's love-struck behavior. IIIiv. Creonte warns Orontea that Alidoro is beneath her. IIIv. The queen agrees and rejects Alidoro. IIIvi. Alidoro tries unsuccessfully to patch things up with Silandra. IIIvii. Silandra decides she still loves Corindo. IIIviii. Corindo agrees to take her back after he kills Alidoro. IIIix. Tibrino overhears. IIIx. Giacinta falls in love with Alidoro. Aristea gives Giacinta a royal medallion as a love token. IIIxi. Alidoro anticipates Corindo by challenging him. IIIxii. Giacinta tells Alidoro she is really a woman. She gives him Aristea's medallion. IIIxiii. Gelone believes Alidoro has stolen the medallion. IIIxiv. Corindo complains that Alidoro, being a commoner, has no right to challenge him. Orontea offers to ennoble Alidoro. IIIxv. Creonte objects. IIIxvi. Alidoro is accused of theft. IIIxvii. The queen decides to examine the facts. IIIxviii. Alidoro says he got the medallion from Giacinta. IIIxix. But she points out that it came originally from Aristea. IIIxx. Aristea explains that the medallion was stolen by her pirate husband-along with the baby Alidoro. Creonte realizes Alidoro must be the rightful king of Phoenicia. Alidoro marries Orontea and Silandra marries Corindo.

Orphée aux Enfers • Orpheus in the Underworld

Composed by Jacques Offenbach (June 20, 1819 – October 5, 1880). Libretto by Hector Crémieux and Ludovic Halévy. French. Parody of Greek mythology and French society. Premiered Paris, Théâtre des Bouffes Parisiens, October 21, 1858. Set in Thebes, Mount Olympus and Hell in legendary times. Operetta. Set numbers with recitative and spoken dialogue. Overture. Entr'acte before II, III, IV. Ballet. Revised version premiered in Paris, February 7, 1874.

Sets: 4. **Acts:** 4 acts, 4 scenes (originally in 2 acts). **Length:** I, II, III, IV: 165 (revised version) **Arias:** "Quand j'étais roi de Béotie" (John Styx), "Moi, je suis Aristée" (Aristée), "La mort m'apparaît souriante" (Eurydice). **Hazards:** I: Aristée is transformed into Pluton. Pluton writes in flame on the door of Orphée's cottage. III: Jupiter and and Styx fight over Jupiter's thunder. Jupiter is transformed into a fly. A crowd of John Styxes appear. Cupidon transforms Pluton's boudoir into a hothouse. IV: Orphée navigates the river Styx in a boat. Jupiter creates a noisy, electric spark. **Scenes:** I. Countryside in the neighborhood of Thebes. II. Mount Olympus. III. Pluton's boudoir and a hothouse. IV. The bank of the river Styx.

Major roles: Eurydice (soprano), Orphée (tenor), Aristée/Pluton (tenor), Jupiter (tenor). **Minor roles:** Public opinion (soprano or mezzo), Vénus (soprano or mezzo), Cupidon (soprano or mezzo), Diane (soprano),

Mercure (tenor), Junon (mezzo), John Styx (tenor). **Bit parts:** Lictor (tenor), Counselor (bass), Mars (baritone), Morphée (tenor), Minerve (soprano), Cybèle (soprano), Pomone (soprano), Flore (soprano), Cérès (soprano), Minos (tenor), Eaque (tenor), Rhadamante (bass), Four policemen (4 tenor). **Speaking:** Neptune, Plutus, Saturne, Vulcain, Pan, Hercule, Apollon, Bacchus, Éole, Hébé, Thalie, Vesta, Polynnie, Iris, Euterpe, Clio, Fortune, Pandore, Éhato. **Barking:** Cerbère.

Chorus parts: SATTBB. **Chorus roles:** Shepherds, shepherdesses, Thebes city council members, children, gods, policemen, nymphs. **Dance/movement:** I: Pastoral ballet. II: Ballet of the nights and hours. III: ballet of the flies. IV: Jupiter, Pluton and two bacchanites dance a minuet. Gods dance the infernal gallop. **Orchestra:** 2 fl (picc), ob, 2 cl, bsn, 2 hrn, 2 trp, trb, timp, perc, strings. **Stageband:** None. **Publisher:** Heugel & Co. **Rights:** Expired.

I. Eurydice leaves flowers for her beloved shepherd, Aristée, while her husband, Orphée, serenades a nymph. Husband and wife scold each other and Orphée warns Eurydice that he means to kill her lovers. He has laid poisonous snakes for Aristée, but they bite Eurydice. Aristée reveals that he is really Pluton, god of the underworld. Orphée is thrilled to learn of his wife's death, but Public Opinion harries him into going to her rescue.

II. The goddess Diane is upset that Jupiter has turned her mortal lover into a deer. The gods learn of Eurydice's abduction, Mercure reporting that it was Pluton's doing. Jupiter scolds Pluton, but the other gods rebel against Jupiter's authority and remind him of his own peccadilloes. Egged on by Public Opinion, Orphée demands the return of his wife and Jupiter agrees.

III. Eurydice is bored in hell. John Styx, Pluton's servant, has fallen in love with her. Jupiter convenes a court to determine if Pluton really abducted Eurydice. The court gets nowhere, but Cupidon calls his police, who locate Eurydice. Cupidon transforms Jupiter into a fly so he can get into Eurydice's boudoir. Jupiter disguises Eurydice and leaves with her. A horde of John Styxes appear. Cupidon transforms the boudoir into a hothouse. Pluton is furious.

IV. The gods attend a banquet by the river Styx. Pluton recognizes Eurydice in spite of her disguise and confronts Jupiter, forcing him to turn Eurydice back over to Orphée. Jupiter tells Orphée he can only have Eurydice if he does not look back while leading her out of hell. Jupiter then gets Orphée to turn around by making a loud noise. Rather than keep Eurydice for himself, Jupiter turns her into a bacchante.

Otello

Composed by Gioachino Rossini (February 29, 1792 – November 13, 1868). Libretto by Francesco Maria Berio di Salsa. Italian. Based on the play by Shakespeare. Premiered Naples, Teatro del Fondo, December 4, 1816. Set in Venice in the late 15th century. Opera seria. Set numbers with recitative. Overture. In the 1823 revision, Desdemona survives.

Sets: 6. **Acts:** 3 acts, 6 scenes. **Length:** I: 35. II: 35. III, IV: 70. **Arias:** "Assisa a piè d'un salice" / Willow song (Desdemona). **Hazards:** None. **Scenes:** Ii. The Doge's palace. Iii. A room in Elmiro's house. Iiii. A magnificent hall. IIi. A garden. IIii. Otello's house. III. Desdemona's bedroom.

Major roles: Otello (tenor), Iago (tenor), Rodrigo (tenor), Desdemona (soprano). **Minor roles:** Doge of Venice (tenor), Elmiro Barberigo (bass), Emilia (mezzo), Lucio (tenor). **Bit part:** Gondolier (tenor).

Chorus parts: SATTBB. **Chorus roles:** Populace, senators, maids of honor, maidens, confidants, friends of Otello. **Dance/movement:** None. **Orchestra:** 2 fl (2 picc), 2 ob, 2 cl, 2 bsn, 4 hrn, 2 trp, 3 trb, timp, perc, strings. **Stageband:** I, II: 2 trp, 3 trb. **Publisher:** G. Ricordi. **Rights:** Expired.

Ii. The Moor Otello returns to a Venice grateful for his military victories over its enemies. He hopes to marry Desdemona, daughter of Elmiro. Rodrigo (who loves Desdemona) and Iago (who hates Otello) plot against him. Iii. Desdemona is happy at Otello's return, but realizes his fame only increases her father's hatred for him. Elmiro tells Iago to arrange the wedding of his daughter to Rodrigo. Iiii. Desdemona is brought to the altar with Rodrigo, where she is rescued by Otello. Elmiro and Rodrigo curse Desdemona.

IIi. Desdemona admits to Rodrigo that she is already married to Otello. Realizing Rodrigo means Otello harm, she asks advice of her confidant Emilia. IIii. Iago convinces Otello that Desdemona is unfaithful by showing him one of her love letters—a letter that was really meant for Otello himself, but which Elmiro intercepted. Desdemona is unable to prevent Rodrigo and Otello from fighting, and Elmiro is furious.

III. Desdemona has abandoned hope. Otello comes to kill her. He tells her that Iago has slain Rodrigo, and then kills her. Lucio reports that it was actually Rodrigo who slew Iago—and that Iago's plots have been revealed. All welcome Otello and bid him marry Desdemona. He kills himself.

Otello

Composed by Giuseppe Verdi (October 9, 1813 – January 27, 1901).
Libretto by Arrigo Boito. Italian. Tragedy by Shakespeare. Premiered
Milan, Teatro alla Scala, February 5, 1887. Set in a seaport on the island
of Cyprus at the end of the 15th century. Lyric drama. Through composed with some recitative.

Sets: 4. **Acts:** 4 acts, 21 scenes. **Length:** I: 33. II: 36. III: 37. IV: 30. **Arias:**
"Piangea cantando"/Willow song (Desdemona), "Ave Maria"
(Desdemona), "Niun mi tema" (Otello), "Credo in un dio crudel" (Iago),
"Dio, mi potevi" (Otello), "Era la notte" (Iago), "Inaffia
l'ugola"/Drinking song (Iago), "Ora è per sempre addio" (Otello).
Hazards: I: Otello's ship tossed by storms (generally offstage). **Scenes:** I.
Exterior of Otello's castle. II. Courtyard of Otello's castle. III. Great hall
of the castle. IV. Desdemona's bed chamber.

Major roles: Otello (dramatic tenor), Iago (baritone), Desdemona (sopra-
no). **Minor roles:** Cassio (tenor), Roderigo (tenor), Lodovico (bass),
Montàno (bass), Emilia (mezzo). **Bit parts:** Herald (bass). **Mute:**
Innkeeper.

Chorus parts: SSATTTBB. **Chorus roles:** Soldiers and sailors of the
Venetian republic, Venetian ladies and gentlemen, Cypriot men, women
and children, Cypriots, Greek, Dalmatian and Albanian soldiers, townspeople, people, children. (Many small groups.) **Dance/movement:** None.
Orchestra: 3 fl (picc), 2 ob (Eng hrn), 2 cl, bs cl, 4 bsn, 4 hrn, 4 trp, 4 trb
(bs trb), timp, perc, harp, strings. **Stageband:** I: perc, organ. II: bag pipe
(or cornemuse or Eng hrn or 2 ob), mandolin (or 2 harp), guitar (or 2
harp). III: 6 trp, 4 trb. **Publisher:** Schirmer, Kalmus. **Rights:** Expired.

Ii. The Cypriots watch Otello's ship being tossed about in the storm, but
Otello lands safely and announces the defeat of the Moslems. Roderigo
pines for the love of Otello's bride—Desdemona—and Iago promises to
help him. Iago confesses he hates Otello for promoting Cassio over himself. He and Roderigo get Cassio drunk and provoke him into a fight.
Iago has Roderigo wake up the neighborhood. Iii. Otello demotes Cassio
for brawling. Iiii. Desdemona keeps Otello company outdoors while he
waits for the town to settle down.

IIi. Iago persuades Cassio to ask Desdemona to intervene with Otello on
his behalf. IIii. Iago declares his evil intentions. IIiii. Otello sees Cassio
talking to Desdemona and Iago fuels his natural jealousy. Women, children and sailors shower Desdemona with flowers. IIiv. When
Desdemona pleads Cassio's cause, Otello turns a deaf ear. He throws
Desdemona's proffered handkerchief to the ground. Emilia picks it up,

but Iago takes it from her. IIv. Suspicion has ruined his life, Otello complains. He demands proof, which Iago provides. I overheard him speaking of Desdemona in his sleep, Iago claims. And Desdemona made him a present of her handkerchief, he adds. The moor swears vengeance.

IIIi. Otello lays a trap for Desdemona and Cassio. IIIii. He demands Desdemona present the handkerchief he gave her, telling her that there is a curse on anyone who loses it. When she cannot, he openly accuses her of infidelity, which Desdemona denies. IIIiii. Otello asks God why He has taken Desdemona's faithfulness from him. IIIiv. He swears to kill his wife once Cassio has confessed. IIIv. Otello hides on the terrace while the unsuspecting Cassio is lead on by Iago. When Cassio produces the handkerchief—which Iago planted on him—Otello has his proof. Trumpets announce the arrival of the Venetian delegates. IIIvi. Otello promotes Iago to captain and the two men plot Cassio and Desdemona's deaths. IIIvii. The Venetian ambassador, Lodovico, arrives and is welcomed by Otello. When Desdemona again pleads for Cassio, Otello has to be restrained from striking her. He calls for Cassio. Lodovico is amazed at Otello's behavior. IIIviii. I am returning to Venice, Otello announces. He appoints Cassio governor in his absence. Iago is furious and sets Roderigo to attack Cassio. IIIix. Otello faints away with grief in front of Iago.

IVi. Desdemona, having a premonition of her own death, sings the "Willow Song" her mother sang to her when she was a child. IVii. Desdemona says her prayers. IViii. When Otello accuses her of infidelity, she denies it. He strangles her. Emilia announces that Cassio has killed Roderigo. IViv. The others arrive and Iago's scheming is revealed. He runs out. Otello sends his attendants after Iago and then stabs himself. He kisses Desdemona's lifeless form and dies.

Owen Wingrave

Composed by Benjamin Britten (November 22, 1913 – December 4, 1976). Libretto by Myfanwy Piper. English. Based on the short story by Henry James. Premiered London, Royal Opera House, Covent Garden, May 10, 1973. Set in London and the Wingrave family seat in the country in the late 19th century. Tragedy. Through composed. Prelude before I, II. Interlude between scenes set in different locations. Opus 85. Television premiere by the BBC TV, May 24, 1971.

Sets: 7. **Acts:** 2 acts, 9 scenes. **Length:** I: 64. II: 42. **Arias:** Peace aria (Owen). **Hazards:** II: Owen's vision of the father and son of the Wingrave legend. **Scenes:** Ii. The study of Coyle's military cramming establishment. Iii. Miss Wingrave's lodgings in Hyde Park and in

London. Iiii. A room in Coyle's establishment. Iiv. The hall of Paramore, the Wingrave family seat. Iv. An abstract scene. Ivi. The hall of Paramore. Ivii. The dining room at Paramore. Prologue to II. Unspecified. IIi. The gallery at Paramore. IIii. The Coyles' bedroom and the gallery.

Major roles: Coyle (bass baritone), Lechmere (tenor), Owen Wingrave (baritone), Miss Wingrave (dramatic soprano), Mrs. Coyle (soprano), Mrs. Julian (soprano), Kate Julian (mezzo), General Sir Philip Wingrave (tenor). **Minor role:** Narrator/Ballad singer (tenor). **Mute:** Young Wingrave, Friend, Old General.

Chorus parts: Trebles (2 parts). **Chorus roles:** Offstage. **Dance/movement:** None. **Orchestra:** 2 fl (2 picc), 2 ob, 2 cl (bs cl), 2 bsn (cont bsn), 2 hrn, 2 trp, 2 trb, tuba, harp, piano, timp, 4 perc, strings. **Stageband:** II: trp, hrn, perc. **Publisher:** Faber Music Ltd. **Rights:** Copyright 1970, 1973 by Faber Music Ltd.

Ii. Lechmere and Owen Wingrave are studying to become soldiers but Owen is disgusted by war and tells his teacher, Coyle, that he means to withdraw. Horrified, Coyle wonders how Owen's family—with its long history of military service—will take the news. Iii. Coyle tells Miss Wingrave. Iiii. Mrs. Coyle and Lechmere are unable to make Owen change his mind. Iiv. Owen receives a frosty reception at home. Iv. Owen's aunt, grandfather, Mrs. Julian and her daughter, Kate, all revile Owen. Ivi. Coyle, his wife, and Lechmere come to visit Owen. They are more sympathetic than his family. Ivii. The family and guests sit down to an acrimonious dinner.

Prologue to II. A ballad singer and chorus sing of how a Wingrave once killed his son for being a coward. The room where it happened is haunted. IIi. Sir Philip disinherits Owen. Kate flirts with Lechmere. Owen has a vision of the father and son of the ballad. He approaches Kate, but she calls him a coward and challenges him to sleep in the haunted room. He agrees. IIii. Lechmere tells the Coyles about Kate's challenge. They hear Kate screaming and run downstairs to find Owen dead.

Paganini

PComposed by Franz Lehár (April 30, 1870 – October 24, 1948). Libretto by Paul Knepler and Béla Jenbach. German. Based loosely on historical events. Premiered Vienna, Johann Strauss Theater, October 30, 1925. Set in Lucca and environs in 1809. Operetta. Set numbers with spoken dialogue.

Sets: 3. **Acts:** 3 acts, 3 scenes. **Length:** I, II, III: 145. **Arias:** "Gern hab' ich die Frau'n geküsst" (Paganini). **Hazards:** None. **Scenes:** I. An idyllic landscape in the neighborhood of the village of Capannari near Lucca. II. The great hall in the prince's palace in Lucca. III. "The Rusty Horseshoe," a disreputable smugglers' inn on the frontier of the principality of Lucca.

Major roles: Marquis Giacomo Pimpinelli (tenor), Princess Maria Anna Elisa (soprano), Niccolo Paganini (tenor), Marquess Bella Giretti (soprano). **Minor roles:** Prince Felice Bacchiocchi (tenor), Beppo the hunchback (baritone). **Bit parts:** Countess De Laplace (contralto), Foletto (tenor). **Speaking:** Bartucci, Count Hédouville, Tofolo the smuggler. **Speaking bits** (can sing with chorus): Landlord, Anitta, Marco, Philippo, Emanuele, Julia, Corallina. **Instrumental:** Two violin soloists (one onstage, one in pit).

Chorus parts: SATTBB. **Chorus roles:** Villagers, gentlemen, courtiers, girls, smugglers. **Dance/movement:** I: Bella and Pimpinelli dance. II: witches and bacchanites dance during Paganini's performance. III: Neapolitan dance. **Orchestra:** 2 fl (picc), 2 ob, 2 cl, 2 bsn, 4 hrn, 2 trp, 3 trb, tuba, timp, perc, 2 mandolin, celeste, harp, strings. **Stageband:** I, II: vln. **Publisher:** Glocken-Verlag. **Rights:** Copyright 1925, 1936 by Glocken-Verlag.

I. Paganini plays for the people of Capannari. He is heard by the Princess Anna Elisa, Napoleon's sister, who has stopped at the village inn. Without knowing who she is, Paganini invites her to his concert. She accepts, but Paganini's impresario, Bartucci, tells Paganini that his performance has been banned. Paganini angrily insults the town and its princess. Instead of being offended, the princess falls in love with Paganini. The princess's chamberlain, Pimpinelli, tries unsuccessfully to win the love of Bella Giretti, the leading lady of the Lucca opera—and the mistress of the princess's husband, Prince Felice. After Paganini apologizes to the princess and admits he loves her, he learns who she is. The princess persuades her husband to let Paganini's concert happen.

II. Playing cards with Pimpinelli, Paganini loses his money and violin. Pimpinelli returns the violin but asks Paganini about his success with women. Paganini sings the princess a song he has composed for her. Bartucci warns Paganini that he is courting trouble by making love to both the prince's wife and his mistress. Paganini assures the princess that he loves only her. Count Hédouville arrives with orders from Napoleon to put an end to Paganini's affair with the princess. Bella persuades Paganini to dedicate his song to her. She uses the song—and the gossip about the princess and Paganini—to thwart the princess's attempt to send her away. The princess tells the count to arrest Paganini during his performance, but is so moved by Paganini's performance she changes her mind.

III. Paganini flees Lucca, but Pimpinelli helps Bella track Paganini to an inn on the border. Bella begs Paganini to take her with him, but when he refuses, she agrees to marry Pimpinelli. The princess arrives disguised as a street singer. Paganini recognizes her. She realizes that art is Paganini's only true mistress and lets him go.

Pagliacci • The Clowns

Composed by Ruggero Leoncavallo (April 23, 1857 – August 9, 1919). Libretto by Ruggero Leoncavallo. Italian. Original work. Premiered Milan, Teatro dal Verme, May 21, 1892. Set in Calabria near Montalto in the late 1860s. Verismo drama. Through composed. Prologue. Orchestral intermezzo.

Sets: 1. Acts: 2 acts, 5 scenes. Length: I: 45. II: 25. Arias: "Stridono lassù" (Nedda), "Vesti la giubba" (Canio), "Si può?" (Tonio). Hazards: None. Scenes: I. Crossroads in front of a village where a traveling theater has been set up.

Major roles: Canio/Pagliaccio (tenor), Nedda/Colombina (soprano), Tonio/Taddeo (baritone). Minor roles: Silvio (baritone), Beppe/Arlecchino (tenor). Bit parts: Two villagers (tenor, bass).

Chorus parts: SATTBB. Chorus roles: Peasants, villagers, boys. Dance/movement: None. Orchestra: picc, 2 fl, 2 ob (Eng hrn), 2 cl, bs cl, 3 bsn, 4 hrn, 3 trp, 3 trb, bs tuba, 3 timp, perc, 2 harp, strings. Stageband: I: ob, trp, bs drum, bells. II: trp, bs drum. Publisher: Schirmer, Broude Brothers. Rights: Expired.

Prologue. Tonio asks the audience to understand that the opera, though drama, portrays the hard truths of love. Ii. The boys and villagers noisily welcome the troupe of clowns. The show begins at eleven, Canio tells them. The villagers invite Canio out for a drink. When Tonio tries to help Nedda down from the cart, Canio amuses the villagers by shooing him off. Tonio is furious. The villagers joke about the incident, but Canio points out that betrayal would not be funny in real life. The villagers go off to church. Iii. Nedda wonders if Canio knows of her infidelities. She sings until she realizes Tonio has been listening. He tries to kiss her but she hits him in the face with her whip and Tonio swears revenge. Iiii. Silvio appears and asks Nedda to run away with him. She loves him, but is unsure. The lovers are overheard by Tonio. He fetches Canio, who arrives in time to hear Nedda agree to run off with Silvio at midnight. Canio chases Silvio but the villager escapes. At knife point, Canio tries to force a confession from Nedda. She refuses to name her lover and is only saved by the intervention of Beppe. People are arriving for the play and Canio forces himself to prepare for the performance.

IIi. Silvio approaches Nedda while she is collecting money from the audience. She tells Silvio that Canio did not see him and Silvio confirms their midnight rendezvous. IIii. The play begins. It is the story of the opera itself: Colombina (Nedda) is loved by Taddeo (Tonio) but scorns him. She betrays her husband Pagliaccio (Canio) with Harlequin (Beppe). Pagliaccio confronts Colombina with her infidelity, but Canio cannot help interjecting his own unhappiness into the scene. He accuses Nedda of ingratitude and tries to force from her the name of her lover. She refuses to reveal it and Canio stabs her. As she dies, Nedda calls out to Silvio. The villager tries to come to her aid, but Canio strikes him down. The horrified audience calls for Canio's arrest.

Palestrina

Composed by Hans Pfitzner (May 5, 1869 – May 22, 1949). Libretto by Hans Pfitzner. German. Original work. based on historical events. Premiered Munich, Königliches Hof- und Nationaltheater, June 12, 1917. Set in Italy and Germany in 1563. Musical legend. Through composed. Overture. Prelude before II, III.

Sets: 2. **Acts:** 3 acts, 3 scenes. **Length:** I: 105. II: 70. III: 35. **Arias:** Palestrina's prayer (Palestrina). **Hazards:** I: Spirits of dead composers and angels appear to Palestrina. II: Soldiers fire on the council delegates. **Scenes:** I. A room in Palestrina's house. II. A great hall in the palace of Madruscht in Trent. III. Palestrina's house.

Major roles: Carlo Cardinal Borromeo (baritone), Giovanni Pierluigi Palestrina (tenor), Bernardo Cardinal Novagerio (tenor), Giovanni Cardinal Morone (baritone). **Minor roles:** Silla (mezzo), Ighino (soprano), Voice of the first angel (soprano), Offstage voice of Lukrezia (alto),

Bishop Ercole Severolus Master of Ceremonies (bass baritone), Christoph Cardinal Madruscht (bass), Cardinal of Lorraine (bass), Count Luna (baritone), Bishop of Budoja (tenor), Theophilus Bishop of Imola (tenor), Dandini of Grosseto (tenor), Abdisu Patriarch of Assyria (tenor), Anton Brus of Müglitz Archbishop of Prague (bass), Five choir singers of Santa Maria Maggiore (3 bass, 2 tenor), Pope Pius IV (bass), Avosmediano Bishop of Cadiz (bass baritone). **Bit parts:** Voice of the second angel (soprano), Voice of the third angel (soprano), Bishop of Feltre (bass), Young doctor of theology (alto), Bishop of Fiesole (tenor). **Mute:** Two papal nuncios, Láinez, Salmeron, Jesuit general, Massarelli, Council secretary, Giuseppe.

Chorus parts: SSAATTTTTBBBB. **Chorus roles:** Angels, servants, Spanish, French and Italian ecclesiastics, soldiers, papal singers, nine masters from the past (TTTBaBaBaBBB). **Dance/movement:** None. **Orchestra:** 4 fl (3 picc), alto fl, 3 ob (Eng hrn), 3 cl, bs cl, 3 bsn, cont bsn, 6 hrn, 4 trp, 4 trb, tuba, 2 harp, celeste, 2 mandolin, organ, timp, 3 perc, strings (vla d'amore). **Stageband:** III: church bells. **Publisher:** Adolph Fürstner. **Rights:** Copyright 1917 by Adolph Fürstner.

I. Silla is unhappy with the traditional approach of his composition master, Palestrina, and plans to leave him. Palestrina's son, Ighino, fears his father is unhappy. Cardinal Borromeo warns Palestrina that the council of Trent nearly outlawed polyphony in church services until Emperor Ferdinand interceded; the Pope has agreed to listen to a new mass if one can be found. Borromeo asks Palestrina to write this mass, but Palestrina refuses—he is old and tired of life. The ghosts of past composers appear to Palestrina and persuade him to write the mass, which he does with the inspiration of angels. Silla and Ighino collect Palestrina's manuscript pages.

II. Preparations are made for the conclusion of the council of Trent. Borromeo arrives and he and Cardinal Novagerio discuss the political situation. Not realizing Palestrina's mass is complete, Borromeo has the composer thrown in prison. The national delegations arrive. Cardinal Morone asks the delegates to agree, but the meeting breaks up in mutual recrimination. The delegates confer privately. Fighting breaks out. Cardinal Madruscht brings in soldiers who fire on the delegates.

III. Ighino gives up Palestrina's mass to save him from prison. Pope Pius is so impressed by Palestrina's mass he comes in person to ask him to lead the Sistine choir. Borromeo is overcome with regret for what he did, but Palestrina forgives him. Ighino tells Palestrina that Silla has gone to Florence. He rejoices at his father's good fortune.

Paradise Lost

Composed by Krzysztof Penderecki (b. November 23, 1933). Libretto by Christopher Fry. English. Based on the poem by John Milton. Premiered Chicago, Lyric Opera of Chicago, November 29, 1978. Set in Heaven, Hell and on the Earth shortly after the Creation. Allegorical drama. Through composed.

Sets: 12. **Acts:** 2 acts, 19 scenes. **Length:** I: 95. II: 85. **Hazards:** I: God creates the garden of Eden and animals from the void. Ithuriel touches Satan with his spear changing him from a toad-like figure into a blazing fiend. Constellation of the scales shines brightly in the sky and the balance tips. Glittering figure of the serpent rises up in the garden. II: Satan takes the form of a serpent. The garden fades after Adam and Eve taste the fruit. The bridge over chaos (a raging sea and high winds). Messias materializes in the tree. Animals dance. Projected images from the beginning of time to the present showing disease, war and natural disasters. Flaming swords of of the archangel. **Scenes:** Ii. Dark stage. Iii. The garden of Eden after the fall. Iiii. Hell. Iiv. In the presence of God. Iv. Hell. Ivi. A void and the garden of Eden. Ivii. The gates of hell. Iviii. Chaos and confusion. Iix. The garden of Eden. Ix. A mountain top. Ixi. Another part of Eden. IIi. Dark stage. IIii. Near the tree of knowledge. IIiii. The bridge over chaos. IIiv. The garden of Eden. IIv. Heaven. IIvi. Hell. IIvii. Eden. IIviii. Atop the highest mountain.

Major roles: Adam (lyric baritone), Eve (lyric soprano), Satan (dramatic baritone). **Minor roles:** Beelzebub (tenor), Moloch (low bass), Belial (tenor), Mammon (baritone), Death (countertenor), Sin (mezzo), Ithuriel/Raphael (countertenor), Zephon (coloratura soprano), Gabriel (tenor), Messias (baritone), Archangel Michael (tenor). **Speaking:** Milton, God's voice.

Chorus parts: SSSSAAAATTTTBBBB. **Chorus roles:** Angels, fallen angels, animals in the garden of Eden, children. **Dance/movement:** I: The creation of Adam. The creation of Eve. Courtship and marriage of Adam and Eve. II: Animals in the garden dance with Eve. Adam and Eve dance drunkenly after tasting the fruit. Birds, a panther, hart and hind dance. Dance enactment of Cain killing Abel. **Orchestra:** 4 okarinen, picc, 2 fl (picc), 3 ob (Eng hrn), 3 cl (bs cl), soprano sax, 3 bsn (cont bsn), 5 hrn, 3 trp, 2 Wagner tuba, 6 trb, tuba, timp, perc, harp, celeste, organ, strings. **Stageband:** None. **Publisher:** European American Music. **Rights:** Copyright 1978 by European American Music.

Ii. Milton introduces his story. Iii. After the fall, Adam rails against God and Eve. Iiii. Satan rallies the fallen angels and persuades them to attempt the conquest of mankind. Iiv. God creates man in his image. Iv.

Satan makes his way up from hell. Ivi. From the void, God creates the garden of Eden, which he gives to Adam, commanding him not to eat the fruit of the tree of knowledge. Ivii. Sin and Death oppose Satan's exit from hell, but he wins them over. Iviii. Satan passes through chaos to the garden of Eden. Iix. Adam names all the animals. He is lonely, so God creates Eve. Ix. Satan embraces evil. Ixi. Adam and Eve fall in love. Jealous, Satan decides to tempt them with the forbidden fruit. The angels protect the sleeping Adam and Eve from Satan. But Eve has dreamed of the forbidden fruit, so God sends Raphael to warn Adam of the danger. The figure of the serpent is seen.

IIi. Milton recounts how Satan got into the garden disguised as a serpent. IIii. Satan tells Eve he has eaten the forbidden fruit and grown wise. Eve tastes the fruit. Adam is aghast, but he, too, tries the fruit. IIiii. Sin and Death rejoice that Satan has freed them from hell. IIiv. Embarrassed at their nakedness, Adam and Eve clothe themselves in fig leaves. Messias pleads with God to mitigate his punishment of mankind. Eve is sentenced to the pain of childbirth; Adam, to sweat and toil. They pray. IIv. God agrees to let Adam and Eve live for a time. IIvi. Satan returns to hell to lead forth his troops, but they all fall to the ground, writhing like snakes. IIvii. The angel Michael visits Adam and Eve. IIviii. He shows Adam and Eve their son Cain killing his brother Abel—and disease, war and natural disasters. Adam cries, but is encouraged by God's goodness. He and Eve go forth into the world.

Parisina d'Este • Parisina of Este

Composed by Gaetano Donizetti (November 29, 1797 – April 8, 1848). Libretto by Felice Romani. Italian. Based on the poem by Lord Byron. Premiered Florence, Teatro della Pergola, March 17, 1833. Set in Belvedere and Ferrara in the early 15th century. Melodrama. Set numbers with recitative. Overture.

Sets: 5. **Acts:** 3 acts, 5 scenes. **Length:** I, II, III: 135. **Hazards:** None. **Scenes:** Ii. Apartment in the ducal palace. Iii. Palace gardens. IIi. Parisina's apartments. IIii. Gallery of the palace. III. Chapel.

Major roles: Ernesto (bass), Azzo (baritone), Ugo (tenor), Parisina (soprano). **Minor roles:** Imelda (soprano).

Chorus parts: SATTTTBB. **Chorus roles:** Cavaliers, ladies, gondoliers, soldiers. **Dance/movement:** None. **Orchestra:** 2 fl (picc), 2 ob, 2 cl, 2 bsn, 4 hrn, 2 trp, 3 trb, cimbasso, timp, perc, harp, strings. **Stageband:** I: trp, 2 hrn, 2 bsn, 2 trb. III: hrn, 2 trp, 2 bsn, 2 trb, drum. **Publisher:** Belwin Mills, Garland Publishing. **Rights:** Expired.

Ii. The jealous Azzo, Duke of Ferrara, has banished young Ugo, fearing that he and Azzo's wife, Parisina, are in love. Ernesto, one of Azzo's courtiers, who has raised Ugo as his own son, points out that the duke's unbounded jealousy led to the death of his first wife. Ernesto's news that the wars are going well does nothing to cheer up Azzo. When Azzo leaves to prepare a tournament to celebrate the victory, Ugo returns. Ernesto begs Ugo not to be caught breaking his banishment and Ugo agrees to leave—after he has seen Parisina. Iii. Ugo meets Parisina in the garden and although she begs him to leave, he realizes she returns his love. Azzo catches them together, but Parisina protects Ugo. Azzo invites Ugo to the tournament.

IIi. Ugo has won the tournament and been crowned by Parisina. Back in her apartments, Parisina worries that her love for Ugo is too obvious. She sleeps. Azzo, watching her sleep, convinces himself of her innocence, until he hears her whisper Ugo's name in her sleep. Waking Parisina, Azzo threatens to kill Ugo. IIii. Azzo's soldiers arrest Ugo at a party. To protect Ugo, Ernesto reveals the truth: that Ugo is Azzo's own son by his first marriage. Rather than condemn his own son, Azzo again banishes him.

III. While praying, Parisina receives a message from Ugo demanding that she flee with him. But Azzo has already heard about the plot. He confronts Parisina and shows her the body of Ugo, whom he has slain.

Parsifal

Composed by Richard Wagner (May 22, 1813 – February 13, 1883). Libretto by Richard Wagner. German. Epic medieval poem by Wolfram von Eschenbach. Premiered Bayreuth, Festspielhaus, July 26, 1882. Set in Montsalvat in the Spanish Pyrenees in the Middle Ages. Stage-consecrational-festival-play (Bühnenweihfestspiel). Through composed with leitmotifs. Preludes before each act.

Sets: 5. **Acts:** 3 acts, 6 scenes. **Length:** I: 110. II: 60. III: 75. **Arias:** Herzeleide (Kundry). **Hazards:** I: Dying swan flies onstage. Presentation of the grail to the brotherhood. I, III: continuous scene change from forest to castle. II: Appearance of Klingsor's magic garden. Throwing and catching of holy spear. Destruction of Klingsor's castle and garden. **Scenes:** Ii. Forest near a lake. Iii. Temple of the grail. IIi. Klingsor's enchanted castle. IIii. Klingsor's gardens. IIIi. Landscape near the temple of the grail. IIIii. Temple of the grail.

Major roles: Gurnemanz (bass), Kundry (dramatic soprano), Amfortas (baritone), Parsifal (dramatic tenor), Klingsor (bass). **Minor roles:** Titurel (bass), First knight (tenor), Second knight (baritone), First squire (soprano), Second squire (mezzo), Third squire (tenor), Fourth squire (tenor), Six flower maidens (soprano), Voice (mezzo).

Chorus parts: SSSAAATTTTBBBB. **Chorus roles:** Flower maidens, brotherhood of the knights, esquires and boys. Small solo groups among flower maidens and knights. **Dance/movement:** None. **Orchestra:** 3 fl, 3 ob, Eng hrn, 3 cl, bs cl, 3 bsn, cont bsn, 4 hrn, 3 trp, 2 ten trb, bs trb, bs tuba, timp, bells 2 harps, strings. **Stageband:** I: 6 trp, 6 trb, drums, bells. **Publisher:** Schirmer, Dover, C. F. Peters, Leipzig. **Rights:** Expired.

Ii. Gurnemanz awakes. The balm brought by Gawain for King Amfortas has not eased the King's wound, and the wild Kundry returns with an Arabian balsam for the King. The Knights wonder if Kundry might not be trying to poison the King, but Gurnemanz points out that Kundry has always been helpful. Gurnemanz remembers the reign of Titurel, the King who founded the holy brotherhood. To support Titurel in his fight against the heathens, Gurnemanz explains, angels brought him the holy grail and the holy spear. Klingsor disfigured himself in the hope that it would win him the grail, but was scorned by Titurel. Klingsor then turned to magic, building a pleasure garden with which to lure knights away from the brotherhood. Titurel's son, Amfortas, tried to defeat Klingsor, but was distracted by one of the sorcerer's women and wounded with the holy spear. Klingsor took the spear, and when Amfortas prayed to get it back, a holy voice spoke to him, telling him to wait for the "holy fool." Gurnemanz is interrupted by shouts from offstage. A swan flies onstage and dies, shot by Parsifal. The knights demand that Parsifal be punished for murdering an animal within the sacred forest. Parsifal expresses his remorse, but is unable to remember where he is from, who his father is, who sent him or what his name is. He tells Gurnemanz that he lived with his mother and fashioned his own sword. His father is Gamuret, Kundry explains, who died in battle. To protect Parsifal from a similar fate, his mother raised him ignorant of all weapons. Then, one day, Parsifal saw some knights and chased after them, leaving behind his mother who, Kundry tells us, is now dead. Gurnemanz takes Parsifal to the hall of the grail castle. Iii. The knights enter the hall. Titurel's voice is heard, telling Amfortas to present the grail that it may again feed the assembled knights. Weary of the pain that presenting the grail causes, Amfortas begs Titurel to do it, but the old king is too enfeebled. Only the grail keeps Titurel alive. Amfortas presents the grail, the knights are fed and they depart. Parsifal has been watching, but he is mute in response to Gurnemanz's questions. Disgusted with the boy's simplicity, Gurnemanz sends him away.

IIi. Klingsor uses his magic to command Kundry to seduce Parsifal, reminding her that it was she who seduced Amfortas. They watch from the ramparts as Parsifal fights his way into the castle. The tower sinks into the ground and is replaced by the magic garden. IIii. The flower maidens first weep over Parsifal's defeat of their lovers, then fight over the youth until he shoos them away. Kundry appears and explains that Parsifal's name comes from "fal-par-si," meaning "foolish pure one." She tells Parsifal that his mother died of a broken heart when he deserted her. Parsifal is overcome by remorse, but when Kundry kisses him he remembers Amfortas's wound and pushes her away. Impressed by the boy's purity, Kundry reveals that her sin was to mock the Redeemer. She now seeks forgiveness, but when it is offered her, she only repeats her sin. Klingsor attacks Parsifal with the holy spear, but the spear will not harm him. Kundry curses Parsifal to wander. Parsifal takes the spear and makes the sign of the cross. The castle falls and the garden withers.

IIIi. Gurnemanz, now grown old, discovers Kundry, asleep among the bushes and wakes her. Parsifal appears in black armor. Gurnemanz chides him for wearing weapons in the holy forest on Good Friday and when Parsifal removes his armor, he and Gurnemanz recognize each other. In his attempt to return the spear, Parsifal has been continually led astray by Kundry's curse. Meanwhile, the brotherhood has withered away since Amfortas refuses to present the grail. Titurel is dead, Gurnemanz says. Kundry washes Parsifal's feet and dries them with her hair. Parsifal baptizes Kundry and forgives her. Gurnemanz leads Parsifal to the hall of the grail. IIIii. Titurel's funeral is in progress. Amfortas has agreed to present the grail one last time. He prays for death. Parsifal appears and cures Amfortas with a touch of the holy spear. Parsifal, the new guardian of the grail, presents it. Kundry sinks to the ground, lifeless.

Il Pastor Fido • The Faithful Shepherd

Composed by George Frederic Handel (February 23, 1685 – April 14, 1759). Libretto by Giacomo Rossi. Italian. Based on play by Giovanni Battista Guarini. Premiered London, Haymarket Theater, November 22, 1712. Set in Arcadia in legendary times. Pastoral. Set numbers with recitative. Overture. Extensively rewritten by the composer for revival of May 18, 1734.

Sets: 4. **Acts:** 3 acts, 4 scenes. **Length:** I, II, III: 150. **Arias:** "Mi lasci, mi fuggi" (Dorinda). **Hazards:** None. **Scenes:** I. Shepherds' cottages in a grove. II. Before Ericina's cave. IIIi. A wood. IIIii. Before the temple of Diana.

Major roles: Mirtillo (soprano), Amarilli (soprano), Eurilla (soprano), Silvio (mezzo), Dorinda (soprano). **Minor role:** High priest Tirenio (bass). **Mute:** huntsmen, priests. Apollo, Erato and Terpsichore added in 2nd version.

Chorus parts: SATB. **Chorus roles:** People. **Dance/movement:** I, II, III: Ballet (2nd version only). **Orchestra:** 2 fl, 2 ob, 2 bsn, strings, continuo (theorbo, organ 2 hrn added in 2nd version). **Stageband:** None. **Publisher:** Gregg Press Ltd. **Rights:** Expired.

I. Mirtillo pines for his lovely Amarilli. But she is betrothed to Silvio to fulfill a command of the goddess Diana: Two descendants of the gods must marry so that "the love of a shepherd can cancel the ancient crime of a perfidious maid." Amarilli returns Mirtillo's love. She sends him away. Mirtillo decides to kill himself. Amarilli's confidante, Eurilla, stops Mirtillo by promising that Amarilli will not always be so cold. Privately, Eurilla wonders how she will turn Mirtillo's affections towards herself. Silvio rejects Dorinda's declarations of love. He prefers hunting.

II. Mirtillo falls asleep waiting for Eurilla. Eurilla leaves him a forged love letter. Mirtillo wakes and is overjoyed. His reaction is noted by Amarilli—who believes he has found someone else. Eurilla pretends to confirm Mirtillo's betrayal, but Amarilli says she will remain faithful to him. Silvio again rejects Dorinda's advances. Dorinda continues to hope. Eurilla tells Mirtillo that Amarilli will meet him in the cave. She then offers to prove to Amarilli that Mirtillo loves another. On Eurilla's instructions, Amarilli hides in the cave. Eurilla arranges for the two to be discovered together, knowing that Amarilli will then be executed for adultery.

IIIi. Dorinda hides to watch Silvio. Seeing something move, Silvio throws his dart—and wounds Dorinda. He is overcome by love for Dorinda. Silvio reproaches himself for his past behavior and prays for Dorinda's recovery. Eurilla thinks her plan has succeeded. Dorinda recovers and marries Silvio. Eurilla is horrified to learn that Mirtillo has been condemned to death with Amarilli. IIIii. Amarilli prepares for her execution. She tells Mirtillo she always loved him. He asks to be allowed to die in her stead. The high priest of Diana discovers that Mirtillo is also descended from the gods. In the goddess's name he forgives the transgressors.

Paul Bunyan

Composed by Benjamin Britten (November 22, 1913 – December 4, 1976). Libretto by W. H. Auden. English. Based on American folklore. Premiered New York City, Brander Matthews Hall, Columbia

University, May 5, 1941. Set on the American frontier in the 19th century. Operetta. Set numbers with spoken dialogue. Ballad interludes. Opus 17. Revised in 1974.

Sets: 2. **Acts:** 2 acts, 5 scenes. **Length:** Prologue, I: 65. II: 50. **Arias:** Slim's song (Slim). **Hazards:** None. **Scenes:** Prologue – Ii. A clearing in the forest. Iii. The camp. IIi. The clearing in the forest. IIii. The camp.

Major roles: Narrator (baritone or tenor), Johnny Inkslinger (tenor), Hot Biscuit Slim (tenor), Tiny (soprano). **Minor roles:** Four young trees (2 sopranos, 2 tenors), Wild Geese (2 mezzos, 1 soprano), Andy Anderson (tenor), Pete Peterson (tenor), Jen Jenson (bass), Cross Corsshaulson (bass), Western Union boy (tenor), Hel Helson (baritone), Sam Sharkey (tenor), Ben Benny (bass), Moppet the cat (mezzo), Poppet the cat (mezzo), Fido the dog (high soprano), John Shears (baritone), Four cronies of Helson (4 baritones). **Bit parts:** Quartet of the defeated (contralto, tenor, baritone, bass), Two farmers (tenor, bass). **Speaking:** Paul Bunyan (offstage throughout). **Speaking bits:** Heron, Moon, Wind, Beetle, Squirrel. (Moppet, Poppet and Fido can double as wild geese.)

Chorus parts: SATTBB. **Chorus roles:** Old trees, lumberjacks, farmers, frontier women. **Dance/movement:** None. **Orchestra:** 2 fl (picc), ob, 2 cl (alto sax), bs cl, bsn, 2 hrn, 2 trp, 2 trb, tuba, timp, perc, harp, piano (celeste), strings. **Stageband:** I: trp, perc. Interludes: guitar (or banjo), vln, db bs. **Publisher:** Faber Music Ltd. **Rights:** Copyright 1941 by Hawkes & Son. Renewed 1968.

Prologue. The old trees in the forest are content to watch time pass, but the young trees hanker for more. A trio of wild geese tell the trees that Paul Bunyan is coming to give them a new life as homes, ships and furniture. The narrator tells how Paul was born and grew to be as tall as the Empire State Building. His dream was to fell trees and he set out west with his enormous cow, Babe. Ii. Paul assembles his lumberjacks and names Hel Helson foreman. Sam Sharkey and Ben Benny are appointed cooks, while Johnny Inkslinger reluctantly becomes the bookkeeper. The narrator recounts Paul's unsuccessful marriage to Carrie. Carrie died, leaving their daughter, Tiny, in Paul's care. Iii. While Paul is away at the funeral, the men grumble about the food. Johnny represents the complaints to Sam and Ben, who quit. Slim takes their place. The lumberjacks are smitten with Tiny and crowd around her.

IIi. Paul asks his lumberjacks which of them want to settle down and become farmers. While Paul is leading the farmers to their land, four lumberjacks suggest to Helson that he take over the operation. Helson follows their advice and is bested in a fight with Paul. Tiny and Slim fall in love, and Paul and Helson make up. IIii. As the frontier is pushed

back, Paul's operation dwindles. The lumberjacks throw a farewell
Christmas party. Slim is taking charge of a Manhattan hotel and is
engaged to Tiny; Helson is going to administer public works in
Washington; and Inkslinger gets a job as a Hollywood scriptwriter. Paul
wishes them all well.

Le Pauvre Matelot • The Poor Sailor

Composed by Darius Milhaud (September 4, 1892 – June 22, 1974).
Libretto by Jean Cocteau. French. Original work. Premiered Paris,
Théâtre National de l'Opéra Comique, December 16, 1927. Set in France
in the early 20th century. Lament. Through composed. Entr'acte before
III.

Sets: 1. **Acts:** 3 acts, 3 scenes. **Length:** I, II, III: 45. **Hazards:** None.
Scenes: I – III. A seaport with the wife's bar (left), friend's wine shop
(right) and street.

Major roles: Wife (soprano), Friend (baritone), Father-in-law (bass),
Sailor (tenor).

Chorus parts: N/A. **Chorus roles:** None. **Dance/movement:** None.
Orchestra: fl, ob, cl, bsn, hrn, trp, trb, timp, perc, 2 vln, vla, vlc, cb.
Stageband: None. **Publisher:** Heugel. **Rights:** Copyright 1927, 1930 by
Heugel.

I. A sailor has been gone for 15 years, but his wife waits for him.
Although she is poor, she rejects her father's suggestion that she remarry. The sailor returns and stays with an old friend.

II. The wife does not recognize her husband. He says he has seen her
husband, who is deeply in debt. He shows her an expensive necklace
and asks her if she will rent him a room.

III. While the sailor is sleeping, the wife kills him and steals the necklace.
She means to use it to save her husband. The wife and her father dispose
of the body.

Les Pêcheurs de Perles • The Pearl Fishers

Composed by Georges Bizet (October 25, 1838 – June 3, 1875). Libretto
by Michel Carré and Eugène Cormon. French. Original work. Premiered
Paris, Théâtre Lyrique, September 30, 1863. Set in Ceylon in ancient
times. Grand opera. Set numbers with recitative. Prelude. Entr'acte

before III. Ballet. Several revisions of the opera were done after Bizet's death by his editors. These included changes to IIIi and a new trio in III. Originally set in Mexico, but moved to Ceylon for political reasons.

Sets: 4. **Acts:** 3 acts, 4 scenes. **Length:** I, II, III: 105. **Arias:** "Je crois entendre encore" (Nadir), "O Nadir, tendre ami" (Zurga), "Comme autrefois" (Léïla). **Hazards:** None. **Scenes:** I. A beach on the island of Ceylon. II. The ruins of an Indian temple. IIIi. An Indian hut. IIIii. The forest.

Major roles: Léïla (soprano), Nadir (tenor), Zurga (baritone). **Minor role:** Nourabad (bass).

Chorus parts: SATTBB. **Chorus roles:** Pearl fishers. **Dance/movement:** I: Dance of pearl fishers. III: Ballet of the divers before executing Nadir. **Orchestra:** 2 fl, 2 ob (Eng hrn), 2 cl, 2 bsn, 4 hrn, 2 trp, 3 trb, timp, perc, harp, strings. **Stageband:** II: 2 picc, perc, harp. **Publisher:** Choudens, Kalmus. **Rights:** Expired.

I. The pearl fishers dance and sing about the danger of their work. They elect Zurga as their leader. All are delighted when their friend Nadir—a former pearl fisher—returns to their band after 12 months as a hunter. Zurga and Nadir remember when, years ago, they saw the lovely priestess of the Candi temple. Both loved her and their jealousy turned friendship to hatred. They had sworn never to see her again. Friends again, the two men greet the veiled, virgin priestess of Brahma who has come to pray for the divers and protect them from evil. Zurga swears the priestess to chastity and anonymity—she can never reveal her face to the divers. He promises her the rarest pearl they can find. "But if you break your vow," he warns, "the punishment is a watery death." Léïla swears the oath, but trembles when she recognizes Nadir. The high priest, Nourabad, and the temple guards lead Léïla up to the temple. Nadir has also recognized in the priestess his love—whom he sought out in violation of his oath to Zurga. From a high rock, Léïla sings to keep away the demons. Nadir tells Léïla not to be afraid: He is here.

II. Léïla tells Nourabad how she once saved a man's life by hiding him from brigands who threatened to kill him. The man gave her a chain in thanks. The high priest leaves Léïla to sleep in the temple, protected by the guards. When Nadir enters, Léïla tries to send him away. Nadir laments that Léïla never loved him—even years ago when he used to wait in the garden, listening to her singing. He learns otherwise. They separate but the guards have heard Nadir and give chase. A powerful storm blows over the waters. Nadir is caught. The fishers demand his and Léïla's deaths but Nadir holds them off until Zurga intervenes. When Nourabad tears off Léïla's veil, Zurga recognizes Léïla as the priestess he and Nadir both loved. In a fury, he condemns the lovers.

IIIi. Zurga is racked with guilt that he must condemn his friend until Léïla begs him to spare Nadir's life. This proof of her love for Nadir hardens Zurga's resolve to execute them both. Léïla curses Zurga. On her way to her execution, she gives her chain to a young diver. Zurga recognizes the chain. IIIii. The drunken divers dance around the stake on which the lovers will burn at break of day. Zurga runs in with news that the camp is burning and the divers rush off to save their children. "I started the fire myself," Zurga explains as he cuts Nadir and Léïla free: "I was the man whose life you saved and who gave you the chain." The lovers escape.

Pelléas et Mélisande • Pelléas and Mélisande

Composed by Claude Debussy (August 22, 1862 – March 25, 1918). Libretto by Maurice Maeterlinck. French. Almost exact setting of the play by Maeterlinck. Premiered Paris, Opéra Comique, April 30, 1902. Set in the Kingdom of Allemande during the Middle Ages. Lyric drama. Through composed with scenes separated by brief musical interludes.

Sets: 9. **Acts:** 5 acts, 15 scenes. **Length:** I: 30. II: 30. III: 34. IV: 40. V: 27. **Hazards:** III: Mélisande's hair must reach from the tower to the ground. **Scenes:** Ii. A forest. Iii. A room in the castle. Iiii. Before the castle. IIi. A well in the park. IIii. A room in the castle. IIiii. Outside a grotto. IIIi. One of the towers of the castle. IIIii. The vaults of the castle. IIIiii. A terrace at the entrance of the vaults. IIIiv. Before the castle. IVi – IVii. A room in the castle. IViii – IViv. A well in the park. V. A bed chamber in the castle.

Major roles: Golaud (baritone), Mélisande (soprano), Pelléas (tenor or baritone). **Minor roles:** Geneviève (mezzo), Arkël (bass), Yniold (mezzo or soprano), Doctor (bass). **Bit part:** Shepherd (baritone or bass). **Mute:** Serving women, Three paupers.

Chorus parts: AATBB. **Chorus roles:** Offstage sailors. **Dance/movement:** None. **Orchestra:** 3 fl, 2 ob, Eng hrn, 2 cl, 3 bsn, 4 hrn, 3 trp, 3 trb, tuba, timp, perc, 2 harps, strings. **Stageband:** I, IV: bells. **Publisher:** Belwin Mills Publishing Corp., Kalmus, Dover, E. Fromont, Paris. **Rights:** Expired.

Ii. While hunting in the forest, Prince Golaud discovers the frightened, weeping Mélisande, sitting by a shallow pond in which a crown is visible. It is Mélisande's crown, but she refuses to let Golaud retrieve it. In answer to his questions, Mélisande confesses only her name. He persuades her to come back with him as it will soon be dark. Iii. Six months have passed and Geneviève reads to the nearly blind King Arkel a letter from his grandson, Golaud. Golaud wishes to marry Mélisande, but fears his grandfather's displeasure. He asks Pelléas to light a lamp in one of the towers of the castle if the King consents to the marriage: If no lamp is lit, Golaud will not return. Arkel expresses his concern over Golaud's loneliness since the death of his first wife. Although the King had arranged a marriage with Princess Ursula, he consents to his grandson's change of plans. Pelléas enters. His friend Marcellus is dying and begs Pelléas to come to him. Arkel thinks Pelléas should wait for the return of Golaud and reminds Pelléas of his own father, lying sick in bed in the castle. Iiii. Geneviève and Mélisande encounter Pelléas in the garden as they watch Golaud's ship returning. Pelléas and Mélisande go in and Pelléas, taking Mélisande's hand, says that he may have to go away the next day.

IIi. Pelléas shows Mélisande the well in the park. While they talk, Mélisande toys with the ring Golaud gave her and accidentally drops it into the well. "What should I say if Golaud asks about it?" Mélisande asks. "Tell him the truth," Pelléas answers. IIii. Golaud is in bed, having fallen from his horse while hunting. Mélisande begs him to take her away from the castle. Golaud takes her hand and asks about the missing ring. "It must have fallen off," Mélisande says, mentioning a cave by the sea. Even though it is dark, Golaud insists she go and recover the ring before high tide. "Take Pelléas along to help you," he suggests. IIiii. Pelléas and Mélisande approach the grotto where they discover three white-haired paupers. They return to the castle without the ring.

IIIi. Pelléas sees Mélisande in one of the tower windows, singing and arranging her hair. He asks to touch her hand but cannot reach it and must content himself with caressing her hair. Golaud discovers them but dismisses the scene as childish playing. IIIii. Golaud shows Pelléas the castle vaults. IIIiii. Golaud tells Pelléas that Mélisande is pregnant and warns his brother not to repeat the scene by the tower. IIIiv. Golaud goes out with his son (by his first marriage) Yniold. The boy admits that he once saw Pelléas and Mélisande kiss. Golaud lifts the boy on his shoulders to spy on Pelléas and Mélisande but discovers nothing.

IVi. Pelléas's father is getting better and has decided to send Pelléas away. Pelléas arranges a last meeting with Mélisande. IVii. Arkel sympathizes with Mélisande, living always in the shadow of age and death. Golaud appears looking for his sword. He is furious with Mélisande and disparages her innocent air. Grabbing her by the hair, he drags her around before relapsing into a morose acceptance of fate. IViii. Yniold is unable to recover his golden ball which has become trapped behind a rock. He watches a flock of sheep being led away from the stables and wonders where they will sleep with night coming on. IViv. Pelléas and Mélisande meet by the well in the park and confess their love. Golaud has been watching them. When they embrace passionately, Golaud emerges from hiding and kills Pelléas. He chases Mélisande through the woods.

V. The wounded Mélisande sleeps while the physician assures Golaud that the wound he gave her is minor. Overcome with guilt, Golaud asks the physician and Arkel to leave the room so he can speak with Mélisande alone. He blames himself for everything and begs Mélisande's forgiveness, saying that he will soon die. He presses Mélisande to confess her own guilt, but she maintains her innocence. Arkel and the doctor return, bringing Mélisande's infant daughter. Mélisande quietly dies.

Pénélope

Composed by Gabriel-Urbain Fauré (May 12, 1845 – November 4, 1924). Libretto by René Fauchois. French. Based on the "Odyssey" by Homer. Premiered Monte Carlo, Théâtre de Monte Carlo, March 4, 1913. Set in Greece after the Trojan War. Lyric poem. Set numbers with accompanied recitative. Prelude. Introduction before II, III.

Sets: 3. **Acts:** 3 acts, 3 scenes. **Length:** Prelude: 7. I: 55. II: 29. III: 34. **Arias:** "Ulysse! fier époux!" (Pénélope), "O mon hôte, à présent" (Ulysse). **Hazards:** III: Ulysse fires one arrow offstage and with another kills Eurymaque. **Scenes:** I. A vestibule outside Pénélope's bedroom. II. The top of a hill overlooking the sea. III. The great hall of Ulysse's palace.

Major roles: Euryclée (mezzo), Pénélope (soprano), Ulysse (tenor). **Minor roles:** Cléone (mezzo), Mélantho (soprano), Alkandre (mezzo), Eurymaque (baritone), Antinoüs (tenor), Léodès (tenor), Ctésippe (baritone), Eumée (baritone), Pisandre (baritone). **Bit parts:** Phylo (soprano), Lydie (soprano), Eurynome (soprano or mezzo), Shepherd (tenor).

Chorus parts: SSAATTBB. **Chorus roles:** Serving maids, shepherds, people. **Dance/movement:** I, III: Girl flautists play and dance. **Orchestra:** 2 fl, picc, 2 ob, Eng hrn, 2 cl, bs cl, 2 bsn, cont bsn, 4 hrn, 2 trp, 3 trb, tuba, timp, perc, harp, strings. **Stageband:** None. **Publisher:** Heugel & Co. **Rights:** Expired.

I. Pénélope's maids are surprised that after ten years their mistress continues to expect the return of her husband, Ulysse. Pénélope's suitors demand to see her. But she has asked not to be disturbed. Pénélope rebukes the suitors. They remind her that she promised to marry one of them as soon as she finished making the shroud for Ulysse's father. Ulysse returns disguised as a beggar and Pénélope takes him in.

Ulysse's old nurse, Euryclée, recognizes Ulysse, but promises not to reveal his secret. The suitors catch Pénélope undoing her work on the shroud and insist she choose one of them. Euryclée and Ulysse encourage Pénélope to hope. Ulysse is pleased by his wife's fidelity. The three go to watch for Ulysse's ship.

II. Eumée tends his sheep. Ulysse assures Pénélope that her husband loves her and will return. To put off her suitors, he suggests Pénélope agree to marry the man who can bend Ulysse's bow. Ulysse reveals his identity to his shepherds and calls on them to help him revenge himself on the suitors.

III. Ulysse arms himself. He tells Euryclée to make sure Pénélope asks the suitors to bend the bow. Eumée reports that the shepherds are ready. The suitors anticipate their victory. No one can bend Ulysse's bow except Ulysse himself. He and the shepherds kill the suitors. Ulysse and Pénélope are reunited. The people of Ithaca welcome Ulysse back.

La Périchole • Périchole

Composed by Jacques Offenbach (June 20, 1819 – October 5, 1880). Libretto by Henri Meilhac and Ludovic Halévy. French. Based on "La Carrosse du Saint Sacrement" by Prosper Mérimée. Premiered Paris, Théâtre des Variétés, October 6, 1868. Set in Peru in the mid-19th century. Operetta. Set numbers with recitative and spoken dialogue. Overture. Entr'acte before II and III. Revised version premiered in Paris, April 25, 1874.

Sets: 3. Acts: 3 acts, 4 scenes (originally in 2 acts). Length: I: 50. II: 40. III: 40. Arias: "O mon cher amant" (Périchole), "Tu n'es pas beau" (Périchole). Hazards: None. Scenes: I. A square in Lima. II. Throne room in the viceroy's palace. IIIi. The cell for recalcitrant husbands in Lima jail. IIIii. A square in Lima.

Major roles: Piquillo (tenor or high baritone), Viceroy Don Andrès de Ribiera (baritone), La Périchole (soprano or mezzo). Minor roles: Don Pedro (tenor or baritone), Count of Panatellas (tenor or baritone), Pablo the notary (tenor), Carlos the notary (tenor), Guadelena (soprano), Estrella (soprano), Virginella (mezzo), Frasquinella (soprano), Violetta (soprano), Bambilla (mezzo), Ninetta (mezzo). Speaking: The Marquis de Santarem.

Chorus parts: SATTB. Chorus roles: Ladies and gentlemen of the court, citizens, pages, guards. Dance/movement: I, II: Ballet. Orchestra: 2 fl (picc), 1 or 2 ob, 2 cl, 1 or 2 bsn, 2 or 4 hrn, 2 trp, 1 or 3 trb, timp, perc, strings (smaller numbers are from original version). **Stageband:** None. **Publisher:** Kalmus. **Rights:** Expired.

I. The patrons of the Three Cousins' Inn drink to the viceroy on his birthday—and at his expense. The viceroy arrives incognito—though, in fact, everyone knows it is him. He flirts with Anita and the customers dance. Two street singers—La Périchole and Piquillo—perform in hopes of earning the price of the wedding fee so they can marry. Piquillo goes off to try his hand elsewhere. While he is gone, the viceroy offers Périchole a position at court, which she reluctantly accepts. She writes Piquillo a farewell letter. Since unwed women cannot reside in the palace, the viceroy tells his first lord, Gomez, to get La Périchole married. Gomez unwittingly chooses Piquillo for La Périchole's husband. The lovers do not know they are to marry each other and are reluctant. The viceroy and his cronies get them drunk and perform the service. The lovers are separated and led off to the palace.

II. The ladies of the court wake Piquillo and inform him that he has been made Count of Trocadero. He is to present his unknown wife at court. The courtiers are full of malicious gossip about the new count and countess. Piquillo discovers he is married to La Périchole, but he is jealous of the viceroy and denounces his wife before the full court. The viceroy orders Piquillo arrested and thrown in the dungeon. IIIi. La Périchole visits Piquillo in jail and the lovers are reconciled. They attempt to bribe the jailer, but it is the viceroy in disguise. He locks La Périchole up with her husband. An old prisoner, the Marquis de Santarem, manages to unchain the pair. Together they seize the viceroy, bind him—and escape. IIIii. Pedro and Gomez are unable to discover the fugitives, who have hidden in the Three Cousins' Inn. The three cousins are astounded that the lovers have abandoned wealth so easily. La Périchole and Piquillo reveal themselves and beg the viceroy for mercy. He forgives them.

Peter Grimes

Composed by Benjamin Britten (November 22, 1913 – December 4, 1976). Libretto by Benjamin Britten and Montagu Slater. English. Based on the poem "The Borough" by George Crabbe. Premiered London, Sadler's Wells Theatre, June 7, 1945. Set in The Borough, a small fishing town on the East Coast of England around 1830. Tragedy. Through composed. Prologue. Orchestral "sea" interludes between scenes.

Sets: 4. **Acts:** 3 acts, 7 scenes. **Length:** I: 55. II: 50. III: 40. **Arias:** "Now the Great Bear" (Grimes), "Embroidery" (Ellen). **Hazards:** II: John falls off a cliff. III: Grimes sails his boat out and sinks it. **Scenes:** Prologue. Interior of the Moot hall arranged for a coroner's inquest. Ii. Street by the sea before Moot hall and The Boar. Iii. Interior of the Boar. IIi. The street. IIii. Grimes's hut. IIIi – IIIii. The street.

Major roles: Peter Grimes (tenor), Ellen Orford (soprano), Captain Balstrode (baritone). **Minor roles:** Hobson the carrier (bass), Swallow the lawyer (bass), Bob Boles (tenor), The Reverend Horace Adams (tenor), Two nieces (sopranos), Mrs. Sedley (mezzo), Ned Keene (baritone), Auntie (contralto). **Bit parts:** Fisherman (bass), Lawyer (tenor), Fisher woman (mezzo), Six burgesses (2 bass, 2 baritone, 2 tenor), Village woman (soprano). **Speaking bit:** Grimes' boy John (scream from off-stage when he falls). **Mute:** Dr. Crabbe or Dr. Thorp.

Chorus parts: SSAATTBB. **Chorus roles:** Townspeople and fisherfolk. **Dance/movement:** None. **Orchestra:** 2 fl (2 picc), 2 ob (Eng hrn), 2 cl, 2 bsn, cont bsn, 4 hrn, 3 trp, 3 trb, tuba, timp, 2 perc, celeste, harp, strings. **Stageband:** II: organ, bells, drums. III: 2 cl, vln, db bs, perc, tuba (can be same as pit tuba; meant to sound like a fog horn). **Publisher:** Boosey & Hawkes. **Rights:** Copyright 1945, 1963 by Boosey & Hawkes.

Prelude. Peter Grimes gives evidence in court about the death at sea of his apprentice, William Spode. "The wind turned against us," Grimes explains, "and we ran out of drinking water." The crowd is biased against Grimes and Judge Swallow recounts the scene in the village square when Grimes came ashore. Noting that Grimes saved Spode from drowning in the March storms, he rules the apprentice's death an accident. The judge suggests Grimes hire a fisherman instead of an apprentice to help him, but Grimes points out that he needs an apprentice just like every other fisherman. He objects that people will still accuse him even though the court has acquitted him. Ellen Orford, the school teacher, tries to comfort Grimes.

Ii. The fishermen haul in their boats and head for a drink in the Boar. When Grimes comes ashore, only Balstrode and Keene will help him land the boat. Keene has found him a new apprentice, but Hobson refuses to bring the boy in his cart and he only relents when Ellen insists. Mrs. Sedley asks after her laudanum and Keene tells her to meet him in the pub. A storm approaches and Balstrode asks Grimes why he does not ship out. Grimes insists the village is his home and he plans to win people over with money when he makes his fortune. Then he can marry Ellen. Balstrode points out that Ellen would have him now, but Grimes disdains her pity. Balstrode fears more tragedy is in store. Iii. Balstrode is surprised to find Mrs. Sedley in the Boar. Auntie (the publican) objects to his screaming. Her "nieces" are hysterical. Boles, the methodist preacher, is drunk and paws the nieces until Balstrode puts him in his seat. Keene arrives with the news that the road is flooded. Grimes's appearance almost starts a riot, but Keene begins a song. Hobson, Ellen and Grimes's new apprentice, John, arrive, chilled to the bone, but Peter insists that the boy go with him.

IIi. On Sunday when Ellen takes John out, she discovers a bruise on his neck. Grimes intends to fish again, but Ellen pleads for a day of rest for the boy. Money cannot buy respect, she notes. Grimes hits her and takes the boy. Church services having ended, the villagers gossip about Grimes. They ask Ellen what happened and the men go to Grimes's hut. IIii. In his haste to get to sea, Grimes manhandles his apprentice and the boy falls over the cliff. The villagers find a neat and empty hut.

IIIi. There is a dance in the Moot hall and Swallow chases Auntie's nieces. Mrs. Sedley takes Keene aside and insists John has been murdered, neither he nor Grimes having been seen for days. Keene ignores her. The dance breaks up. Mrs. Sedley eavesdrops while Ellen and Balstrode discuss Grimes's arrival. His boat has been in for an hour, but they cannot find him or the boy. Mrs. Sedley rouses Swallow and Hobson who go looking for Grimes. IIIii. Balstrode finds Peter and tells him to sail his boat out and sink it. He does.

Phaëton

Composed by Jean-Baptiste Lully (November 28, 1632 – March 22, 1687). Libretto by Philippe Quinault. French. Based on the "Metamorphoses" by Ovid. Premiered Versailles Palace, January 6, 1683. Set in Egypt and the abodes of the gods in legendary times. Lyric tragedy. Set numbers with recitative. Overture. Prologue. Ballet.

Sets: 5. **Acts:** 5 act, 30 scenes. **Length:** Prologue, I: 55. II: 25. III: 25. IV: 20. V: 15. **Arias:** "Il me fuit, l'inconstant!" (Théone), "Je plains ses malheurs" (Phaëton), "Vous êtes sons fils, je le jure" (Clymène). **Hazards:** I: Protée, Triton and Neptune's flocks emerge from the sea. Protée transforms into a lion, a tree, a sea monster, a fountain and a flame. III: Temple doors swing closed. Flames and furies pour out of the temple. Winds bear Phaëton to the Sun palace. V: Phaëton rides the chariot of the Sun across the sky. Jupiter strikes him with a thunderbolt and he falls from the sky. **Scenes:** Prologue. The gardens of Astrée's palace. I. A garden in the foreground, a grotto in the middle and the sea in the distance. II. Inside the palace of the king of Egypt. III. The temple of Isis. IV. The palace of the Sun. V. A pleasant countryside.

Major roles: Princess Libye (soprano), Théone (soprano), Phaëton (tenor), Queen Clymène (soprano), Epaphus (bass). **Minor roles:** Astrée (soprano), Saturne (baritone), Protée (bass), Triton (tenor), Mérops (baritone), Autumn (tenor), Sun god (tenor), Egyptian shepherdess (soprano), God of the earth (tenor). **Bit parts:** First tributary king (bass), Hour of the day (soprano), Jupiter (bass). **Mute:** Furies, Ghosts, Second tributary king.

Chorus parts: SSAATTB. **Chorus roles:** Followers of Astrée, Saturne, Phaëton and Protée, sea gods, Indians, Ethiopians, Egyptians, priestesses of Isis, hours, seasons, shepherds, shepherdesses, furies, phantoms. **Dance/movement:** Prologue: Followers of Astrée and Saturne dance. I: Sea gods dance. II: Egyptian ballet. III: Priestesses dance. IV: Seasons dance. V: Shepherds dance. **Orchestra:** 3 fl, recorder, 4 ob, 2 bsn, perc, strings, continuo (2 harpsichord, 3 theorbo, guitar, 2 vla di gamba, 5 basses de vln). **Stageband:** None. **Publisher:** Théodore Michaelis, Académie Royale de la Musique. **Rights:** Expired.

Prologue. Astrée and Saturne introduce the hero, Phaëton. Ii. Princess Libye is upset. Iii. She tells Théone she fears her father will not let her marry her beloved Epaphus. Iiii. Théone worries that Phaëton no longer loves her. Iiv. But Phaëton is more interested in being king. He appeals to his mother, Queen Clymène. She says he will have to marry Libye if he wants to be the heir, since his father was the sun god, not the king. Phaëton agrees. Iv. The god Protée and his followers tend Neptune's fish. Ivi. Clymène calls on Triton to help her learn the future from Protée. Ivii. Protée is reluctant to tell the future. Iviii. He warns that Phaëton's ambition will be fatal.

IIi. Phaëton brushes aside Clymène's fears for his life. IIii. Theone pines for Phaëton. IIiii. She and Libye console each other. IIiv. Epaphus tells Libye that the king means to marry her to Phaëton. IIv. The king announces the marriage.

IIIi. Théone curses Phaëton. IIIii. Phaëton pities her, but is more interested in power. IIIiii. Epaphus suggests that the sun god is not really Phaëton's father. IIIiv. Phaëton makes offerings to Isis, but the gates of the temple swing closed. IIIv. Phaëton forces the gates, but flames and furies pour out. IIIvi. At Phaëton's urging, Clymène swears that the sun god is Phaëton's father. Winds bear Phaëton away.

IVi. In the sun palace, the hours and seasons revere the sun god. IVii. The god promises to silence Phaëton's detractors. Phaëton asks to drive the sun chariot across the sky. The sun god tries to dissuade Phaëton since the task will kill him.

Vi. The people of Egypt watch Phaëton guiding the sun chariot across the sky. Vii. Epaphus calls on Jupiter to punish Phaëton's hubris. Viii. He hopes he may yet win Libye. Viv. The Egyptians celebrate the new day. Vv. Phaëton loses control of the sun chariot and singes the earth. Vvi. The goddess of the earth calls on Jupiter to protect her. Vvii. The people do likewise. Vviii. Jupiter strikes down Phaëton with a thunderbolt.

Il Piccolo Marat • Little Marat

Composed by Pietro Mascagni (December 7, 1863 – August 2, 1945). Libretto by Giovanni Targioni-Tozzetti and Giovacchino Forzano. Italian. Based on Victor Martin's novel "Sous la Terreur." Premiered Rome, Teatro Costanzi, May 2, 1921. Set in Nantes in 1793. Lyric drama. Through composed.

Sets: 3. **Acts:** 3 acts, 3 scenes. **Length:** I: 45. II: 50. III: 25. **Hazards:** III: Ogre fires a pistol at Little Marat. **Scenes:** I. A square. II. A gloomy room in the ogre's house. III. The ogre's bedroom.

Major roles: Carpenter (baritone), Mariella (soprano), President of the board/Ogre (bass), Prince of Fleury/Little Marat (tenor). **Minor roles:** Captain of the Marats (baritone), Spy (baritone), Tiger (bass), Thief (bass), Soldier (baritone), Courier (baritone). **Bit parts:** Voice (tenor), Princess (mezzo), Voice (baritone), Bishop (baritone).

Chorus parts: SSSSAATTTTTTBBBBBB. **Chorus roles:** Prisoners, hungry crowd, Marats, American cavalry. **Dance/movement:** None. **Orchestra:** 3 fl (picc), 2 ob, Eng hrn, 2 bsn, 3 cl, clarone, cont clarone, 4 hrn, 3 trp, 3 trb, tuba, timp, perc, 2 harp, celeste, carillon, xylophone, strings. **Stageband:** None. **Publisher:** Casa Musicale Sonzogno. **Rights:** Copyright 1921 by Casa Musicale Sonzogno.

I. A hungry crowd, seeing Mariella with a basket of food, gives chase. She is saved by a young man, Little Marat, who pledges loyalty to her uncle, the president of the revolutionary committee, known as "the ogre" for his terrible cruelty. The ogre has commissioned a carpenter to build a boat that can be exploded to kill those inside. When the carpenter expresses horror at what he has created, the ogre condemns him to witness all public executions. A soldier criticizes the ogre for his treatment of his prisoners. Little Marat is really the prince of Fleury in disguise and he has joined the ogre's committee to get close to his mother, the princess, who is in prison. To Little Marat's horror, the ogre sends a batch of prisoners off to their deaths in the carpenter's boat.

II. Little Marat has become the ogre's right hand man, and when the carpenter appeals to Mariella to get him excused from attending further executions, she goes to Little Marat, who agrees to help. The ogre interrogates his prisoners and has the soldier arrested for criticizing his methods. Won over by Little Marat's confession that he has only wormed his way into the ogre's confidence to save his mother, Mariella admits her love for Little Marat and together they plan their escape.

III. Catching the ogre while he is asleep, Little Marat binds him and threatens to kill him if he does not sign a safe conduct for Little Marat, his mother, Mariella and the carpenter. When a crowd announces the revolutionary committee's latest military victory, the ogre frees one of his hands and shoots Little Marat. The wounded Little Marat convinces Mariella to leave him and save his mother. While she is gone, the ogre frees himself, but before he can finish off Little Marat, the carpenter appears and strikes the ogre dead. The carpenter and Little Marat escape with Mariella and Little Marat's mother.

La Pietra del Paragone • The Touchstone

Composed by Gioachino Rossini (Feburary 29, 1792 – November 13, 1868). Libretto by Luigi Romanelli. Italian. Original work. Premiered Milan, Teatro alla Scala, September 26, 1812. Set in Tuscany in the 19th century. Comic opera. Set numbers with recitative. Overture. Storm interlude in II.

Sets: 3. **Acts:** 2 acts, 8 scenes. **Length:** I: 70. II: 50. **Hazards:** None. **Scenes:** Ii. A hall in the count's castle. Iii. The castle garden. Iiii. Before the curtain. Iiv – IIi. The hall. IIii. A gazebo in the park. IIiii. Before the curtain. IIiv. The hall.

Major roles: Count Asdrubal (bass or bass baritone), Baroness Clarice (contralto), Pacuvio (baritone or bass baritone), Macrobio (bass or bass baritone). **Minor roles:** Fabrizio (bass), Donna Fulvia (soprano), Marquise Ortensia (soprano or mezzo), Giocondo (tenor).

Chorus parts: TTB. **Chorus roles:** Friends and guests of the count, hunters, servants, soldiers. **Dance/movement:** None. **Orchestra:** 2 fl (2 picc), 2 ob, 2 cl, 2 bsn, 2 hrn, 2 trp, timp, perc, strings. **Stageband:** II: Turkish band. **Publisher:** Bärenreiter Kassel. **Rights:** Expired.

Ii. The count wants to marry, but is not sure whom. He is surrounded by flatterers and adventurers. The Marquise Ortensia hopes to snag the count, as do Baroness Clarice and Fulvia. Fulvia and the painter Pacuvio promise to work together. The count has decided to test the women before making his choice. The poet Giocondo takes Clarice's part. Iii. Clarice loves the count and he is attracted to her, but refuses to commit himself. As part of his test, the count sends himself a (fake) letter saying he is bankrupt. Pacuvio paints Fulvia and wonders at women's ways. The count accepts Pacuvio's painting without comment. The corrupt journalist and critic Macrobio arrives. Giocondo is indignant that Macrobio expects to be bribed in return for favorable reviews. Macrobio's attempts at blackmail come to nothing when Giocondo threatens him. The count receives his own letter. Iiii. Word spreads that the count is bankrupt. Iiv. The count's creditor (who is really the count in disguise) takes charge of the house. The count's guests fawn over the creditor, ignoring the count's appeals for help—except Clarice who determines to save him.

IIi. The guests wonder how to get the most out of the situation. The creditor employs each of them, except Clarice who defies him. Giocondo loves Clarice, but realizes he cannot have her. IIii. Pacuvio paints the creditor and his hunters. They are caught in a downpour and the count angrily destroys Pacuvio's painting. The other guests discover Pacuvio's misfortune. Macrobio has written an article exposing the count's misfortunes—and vilifying Clarice for her sudden, mysterious departure. Both Giocondo and the count challenge Macrobio. IIiii. Rather than fight, Macrobio agrees to write a letter admitting his own cowardice and villainy. IIiv. Macrobio lies to the other guests about what happened. Clarice's brother, Lucindo, is announced. It is Clarice, disguised and in command of a regiment of soldiers. Ortensia and Fulvia fall in love with Lucindo. The count wonders about Clarice. Hearing of Lucindo's arrival, he fears his test has driven Clarice away. Lucindo tells the creditor he will pay the count's debts. The count now reveals his true identity—and Clarice reveals hers. The lovers are reunited.

Pimpinone

Composed by Georg Philipp Telemann (March 14, 1681 – June 25, 1767). Libretto by Johann Peter Praetorius. German. Based on an Italian libretto by Pietro Pariati for Albinoni. Premiered Hamburg, Theater am Gänsemarkt, September 27, 1725. Set in Pimpinone's house in the 18th century. Intermezzo. Set numbers with recitative.

Sets: 2. **Acts:** 3 acts, 3 scenes. **Length:** I, II, III: 40. **Hazards:** None. **Scenes:** I. A street. II – III. Pimpinone's house.

Major roles: Vespetta (soprano), Pimpinone (baritone).

Chorus parts: N/A. **Chorus roles:** None. **Dance/movement:** None. **Orchestra:** Strings, continuo (harpsichord). **Stageband:** None. **Publisher:** B. Schott's Söhne. **Rights:** Expired.

I. The serving girl Vespetta persuades the rich Pimpinone to hire her. II. By pretending to be modest and retiring, Vespetta persuades Pimpinone to propose to her. III. Once they are married, Vespetta threatens and torments Pimpinone until she gets her way.

Pique Dame

See "The Queen of Spades" entry.

Il Pirata • The Pirate

Composed by Vincenzo Bellini (November 3, 1801 – September 23, 1835). Libretto by Felice Romani. Italian. Based on "Bertram, or the Castle of St. Aldobrand" by Charles Maturin. Premiered Milan, Teatro alla Scala, October 27, 1827. Set in Sicily in the mid-13th century. Opera seria. Set numbers with recitative. Overture.

Sets: 5. **Acts:** 2 acts, 6 scenes. **Length:** I: 75. II: 70. **Arias:** "Sì, vincemmo" (Ernesto), "Tu vedrai" (Gualtiero), "Col sorriso d'innocenza" (Imogene). **Hazards:** I: Ship battered by a storm seen out to sea. **Scenes:** Ii. The seashore near Caldora. Iii. The terrace of the castle of Caldora overlooking the gardens. Iiii. Outside the palace. IIi. An antechamber in Imogene's apartments. IIii. The terrace. IIiii. The castle entrance hall.

Major roles: Gualtiero (tenor), Imogene (soprano), Ernesto (baritone). **Minor roles:** Goffredo (bass), Itulbo (tenor), Adele (soprano). **Mute:** Imogene's son, Messenger.

Chorus parts: SSATTB. **Chorus roles:** Fishermen and their wives, pirates, knights, ladies in waiting. **Dance/movement:** None. **Orchestra:** 2 fl (picc), 2 ob, 2 cl, 2 bsn, 4 hrn, 2 trp, 3 trb, serpent, harp, timp, perc, strings. **Stageband:** II: band. **Publisher:** Kalmus, Garland Publishing. **Rights:** Expired.

Ii. Gualtiero is driven into exile by his rival, Ernesto, and turns to piracy. After being defeated by Ernesto in a sea battle, Gualtiero and his men run aground in their native Sicily. Gualtiero meets his beloved Imogene. Iii. Imogene has been forced to marry Ernesto to save her father, but she still loves Gualtiero. Ernesto and Imogene have a son. Iiii. Gualtiero and his men are presented to Ernesto disguised. Ernesto is suspicious, but Imogene protects them.

IIi. Ernesto badgers Imogene into admitting her love for Gualtiero. He learns from a messenger that Gualtiero is in Sicily. IIii. Imogene tells

Gualtiero she cannot leave with him. Ernesto overhears them and challenges Gualtiero. IIiii. Gualtiero slays Ernesto and gives himself up to the authorities. Imogene goes mad. Gualtiero is condemned and led off to execution.

The Pirates of Penzance

Composed by Arthur Sullivan (May 13, 1842 – November 22, 1900). Libretto by W. S. Gilbert. English. Original work. Premiered New York City, New Fifth Avenue Theater, December 31, 1879. Set in Cornwall in the 19th century. Operetta. Set numbers with recitative and dialogue. Overture. Near-simultaneous premieres in New York and London.

Sets: 2. **Acts:** 2 acts, 2 scenes. **Length:** I: 60. II: 45. **Arias:** "Oh, better far to live and die" (Pirate King), "When Frederic was a little lad" (Ruth), "I am the very model of a modern major general" (Major General Stanley). **Hazards:** None. **Scenes:** I. A rocky seashore on the coast of Cornwall. II. A ruined chapel by moonlight.

Major roles: Frederic (tenor), Mabel (soprano), Pirate King (bass baritone), Major General Stanley (baritone), Ruth (mezzo). **Minor roles:** Samuel (baritone), Sergeant of police (bass), Edith (mezzo), Kate (soprano), Isabel (soprano).

Chorus parts: SATTBB. **Chorus roles:** Pirates, police, wards of General Stanley. **Dance/movement:** None. **Orchestra:** 2 fl, ob, 2 cl, bsn, 2 hrn, 2 trp, trb, timp, perc, strings. **Stageband:** None. **Publisher:** Kalmus, G. Schirmer Inc. **Rights:** Expired.

I. The pirates toast Frederic's coming of age. They expect him to become a full-fledged member of the band, but Frederic admits he abhors piracy and served his apprenticeship only out of a sense of duty. He was supposed to be apprenticed to a pilot and only came here because Ruth, his nursemaid, was hard of hearing. Frederic explains that he feels bound to destroy the pirates. Since his indentures last until noon, however, he is still loyal and suggests that the pirates are too tender-hearted. Being orphans themselves, they let other orphans go and consequently everyone they meet claims to be an orphan. The pirates encourage Frederic to take the middle-aged Ruth with him. He is reluctant to marry her, having never met another woman with whom to compare her. Ruth's assurances that she is a "fine woman" make Frederic's indignation great when he beholds a bevy of beautiful, young maidens. These are the daughters of Major General Stanley who are unswayed by Frederic's appeal for companionship—all except Mabel, who gets to know her new beau while her sisters discreetly discuss the weather. Frederic suddenly remembers the proximity of the pirates, but his warning is too late. The pirates swoop down and claim the sisters as their brides. Only Stanley's assurance that he, too, is an orphan saves his daughters.

II. Stanley's conscience bothers him for the lie he told the pirates. Frederic intends to lead a police force against the pirates. No sooner has he obtained the general's blessing than he is accosted by Ruth and the Pirate King. They have discovered that since Frederic was born in leap year, he is not yet out of his indentures—being only a boy of five and a quarter. Reluctantly, Frederic reveals the general's lie and all three plot revenge. Mabel's pleas prove unavailing against Frederic's sense of duty but they promise to wait for each other. The police hide and await the arrival of the pirates. A struggle ensues in which the police are soundly defeated. Realizing that the pirates are loyal Englishmen, the sergeant of police charges them to yield in the Queen's name—which they do. Ruth now reveals that the pirates are actually noblemen gone wrong. Impressed, Stanley invites them to wed his daughters.

The Poisoned Kiss

Composed by Ralph Vaughan Williams (October 12, 1872 – August 26, 1958). Libretto by Evelyn Sharp. English. Based on "The Poisoned Maid" by Richard Garnett and "Rapaccini's Daughter" by Nathaniel Hawthorne. Premiered Cambridge, Arts Theatre, May 12, 1936. Set in Golden Town and environs in legendary times. Romantic extravaganza. Set numbers with spoken dialogue. Introduction before II, III. Overture.

Sets: 3. **Acts:** 3 acts, 3 scenes. **Length:** I, II, III: 120. **Arias:** "Day is dawning" (Angelica), "There was a time" (Tormentilla), "I thought I loved Maria" (Amaryllus). **Hazards:** I: Noise from offstage of owls, bats, cats, larks, cuckoos, crowing cocks, etc. Tormentilla cuddles her pet snake. Dipsacus raises a hurricane. Shower of golden rain when Angelica rubs the philosopher's stone. II: The Empress's mediums float. III: Huge image of Dipsacus appears. Angelica comes through the floor, summoned by the empress's magic. **Scenes:** I. The magician's haunt in the forest. II. Tormentilla's apartment in Golden Town. III. Boudoir of the Empress Persicaria in her palace at Golden Town.

Major roles: Gallanthus (baritone), Angelica (soprano), Prince Amaryllus (tenor), Tormentilla (soprano). **Minor roles:** Dipsacus (bass), Hob (tenor), Gob (baritone), Lob (bass), First medium (soprano), Second medium (mezzo), Third medium (contralto), Empress Persicaria (contralto). **Speaking:** Physician.

Chorus parts: SSATTBB. **Chorus roles:** Day and night voices, hobgoblins, witches, forest, creatures, messengers, milliners, flower girls, off-stage lovers, courtiers, guards, attendants. **Dance/movement:** I: Hobgoblins dance, Angelica and Dipsacus dance, chorus dance. II: flower girls dance. III: Gallanthus and Angelica dance. **Orchestra:** 2 fl (picc), ob (Eng hrn), 2 cl, bsn, 2 hrn, 2 trp, trb, timp, 2 perc, harp (can substitute piano for harp), strings. **Stageband:** I: gong, bells. II: bells. III: trps, drums. **Publisher:** Oxford University Press. **Rights:** Copyright 1936 by Oxford University Press.

I. Disguised as a humble shepherd, Prince Amaryllus meets the magician's daughter Tormentilla in the woods and falls in love. The prince's attendant, Gallanthus, loves Tormentilla's maid, Angelica. Tormentilla's father, Dipsacus, is furious and uses his magic to get rid of the men. He explains to Tormentilla that he has raised her on poisons so that her first kiss will be fatal. He means her to kiss the prince, whose mother (the empress) jilted him twenty years ago. When Tormentilla refuses, Dipsacus disowns her.

II. Jealous of Tormentilla's reputed beauty, the empress sends her poisoned candies—which have no effect. Dipsacus's hobgoblins bring Amaryllus to Tormentilla and they kiss. Tormentilla learns for the first time that Amaryllus is the prince. He falls unconscious.

III. The court physicians fear the prince will die if he is not reunited with his beloved Tormentilla. The empress remembers Dipsacus, whom she loved but whom her parents forced her to renounce. Tormentilla convinces the empress that the best revenge on Dipsacus would be to let Tormentilla marry the prince. The empress admits she knew Dipsacus's plan all along and raised her son on antidotes so the poison would have no affect. She and Dipsacus are reconciled and decide to marry. Tormentilla marries the prince, Angelica marries Gallanthus and Dipsacus's hobgoblins marry the empress's mediums.

Les Pont des Soupirs • The Bridge of Sighs

Composed by Jacques Offenbach (June 20, 1819 – October 5, 1880). Libretto by Hector Crémieux and Ludovic Halévy. French. Original work. Premiered Paris, Théâtre des Bouffes Parisiens, March 23, 1861. Set in Venice in 1321. Operetta. Set numbers with recitative and spoken dialogue. Introduction. Entr'acte before III, IV. Ballet.

Sets: 4. **Acts:** 4 acts, 4 scenes. **Length:** I, II, III, IV: 100. **Arias:** "Catarina, je chante" (Amoroso), "Les affaires sont les affaires" (Malatromba). **Hazards:** II: Baptiste and Cornarino stuff Malatromba's spies into the clock and barometer; then hide there themselves. IV: Malatromba and

Cornarino joust from boats on the Orfano canal. **Scenes:** I. A square in front of the Cornarini palace. II. A hall in the Cornarini palace. III. The hall of the Council of Ten. IV. The Lido.

Major roles: Baptiste (comic tenor), Doge Cornarino Cornarini (tenor), Amoroso (mezzo), Catarina Cornarino (soprano), Fabiano Fabiani Malatromba (tenor). **Minor roles:** Cascadetto (tenor), Astolfo (bass), Franrusto (bass), Fiammetta (soprano), Chief of the Council of Ten (tenor). **Bit parts:** Three women (2 soprano, 1 alto), Colombine (soprano), Pierrot (soprano), Léandre (soprano), Isabelle (soprano), Arlequin (soprano). **Speaking:** Laodice. **Speaking bits:** Rigolo, Paillumido, Fiorella, Ninetta, Marietta, Zerlina, Usher, Cassandre, Officer.

Chorus parts: SSATTBB. **Chorus roles:** Members of the Council of Ten, Venetians, guards, bravi, maskers, lady gondoliers, ladies in waiting, servants. **Dance/movement:** II: Astolfo, Franrusto, Cornarino and Baptiste dance the bolero. IV: Carnival dances. **Orchestra:** 2 fl (picc), ob, 2 cl, bsn, 2 hrn, 2 cornet, trb, timp, perc, strings. **Stageband:** None. **Publisher:** E. Gérard & Co. **Rights:** Expired.

I. Doge Cornarino flees his first battle and returns to Venice in disguise with his servant, Baptiste. He finds the page Amoroso wooing Cornarino's wife, Caterina. Malatromba also loves Caterina—and he has Amoroso arrested. Cascadetto announces the destruction of the fleet and the reward offered by the Council of Ten for Cornarino's capture.

II. While Malatromba tries to woo Caterina, Cornarino and Baptiste knock out Malatromba's two bodyguards and take their places. Malatromba threatens to harm Amoroso. Caterina goes mad. Amoroso escapes from prison and challenges Malatromba. Malatromba calls his spies and has everyone arrested. Cornarino is discovered, still disguised. To save himself, he claims to have proof that the doge is dead. Malatromba bribes the populace to elect him doge.

III. Malatromba finds the Council of Ten flirting with a group of young maidens. He presents Cornarino, but Cornarino's testimony is contradicted by Amoroso and Caterina. Cornarino's true identity is discovered and he is condemned to death. Malatromba is elected doge. Before Cornarino can be hanged, news arrives that his flight was a ruse and the fleet is victorious.

IV. Since Venice now has two doges, the council decrees that Malatromba and Cornarino must fight for the dogeship. Malatromba is victorious. He banishes Cornarino, Caterina and Amoroso to Spain.

Porgy and Bess

Composed by George Gershwin (September 26, 1898 – July 11, 1937).
Libretto by Du Bose Heyward and Ira Gershwin. English. Based on the
play "Porgy" by Du Bose and Dorothy Heyward. Premiered Boston,
Alvin Theatre, September 30, 1935. Set in Charleston, South Carolina in
the recent past. Music drama. Set numbers with recitative and some spoken lines. Orchestral introduction. Boston premiere was a Broadway try-
out. Moved to New York City and opened on October 10, 1935.

Sets: 3. **Acts:** 3 acts, 9 scenes. **Length:** I: 60. II: 85. III: 40. **Arias:** "I got
plenty o' nuttin'" (Porgy), "It ain't necessarily so" (Sporting Life),
"Summertime" (Clara). **Hazards:** II: Porgy leaves for New York in a goat
cart. **Scenes:** Ii. Catfish row. Iii. Serena's room. IIi. Catfish row. IIii.
Kittiwah island. IIiii. Catfish row. IIiv. Serena's room. III. Catfish row.

Major roles: Sporting Life (tenor), Porgy (bass baritone), Crown (baritone), Bess (soprano). **Minor roles:** Clara (soprano), Jake (baritone),
Mingo (tenor), Serena (soprano), Robbins (tenor), Jim (baritone), Peter
(tenor), Lily (mezzo), Maria (contralto), Undertaker (baritone), Annie
(mezzo), Frazier (baritone), Crab man (tenor). **Bit parts:** Four crap shoot-
ers (2 baritones, 2 basses), Two mourners (soprano and baritone), Scipio
(treble), Nelson (tenor), Strawberry woman (mezzo), Praying people (2
sopranos, alto, tenor, 2 basses), Nursing woman (alto). **Speaking:**
Detective, Policeman, Mr. Archdale, Coroner. **Speaking bits:** Resident,
Woman.

Chorus parts: SSAATTBB. **Chorus roles:** Residents of Catfish row, fish-
ermen, children, stevedores, children (one part). **Dance/movement:** I:
Residents dance to blues piano. II: Residents dance at picnic. **Orchestra:**
2 fl (picc), 2 ob (Eng hrn), 3 cl (2 alto sax), bs cl (tenor sax), bsn, 3 hrn, 3
trp, 2 trb, tuba, timp, 2 perc, piano, banjo, strings. **Stageband:** I, II: piano.
II: mouth organs, comb, bones played by choristers, hurricane bell.
Publisher: Chappell Music Co. **Rights:** Copyright 1935 by Gershwin
Publishing Corp. Renewed and assigned to Chappell & Co. Inc.

Ii. Residents of Catfish Row dance and play at dice. The cripple Porgy
loves Crown's girl, Bess. Crown gets drunk and loses at dice. He kills
Robbins, but takes off before the police arrive. Porgy is the only person
willing to take in Bess. Iii. Porgy and Bess pay a call on Robbins's widow
and contribute money to pay for the burial. A detective drags Peter off
to be a witness in the murder investigation. The undertaker agrees to
bury Robbins.

IIi. Porgy is happy living with Bess. The lawyer Frazier swindles him
into paying for a fake divorce for Bess and Crown. Mr. Archdale puts up

Peter's bond. Bess does not want to go to the picnic since Porgy is not going, but Porgy insists. IIii. Bess meets Crown at the picnic and agrees to leave with him. IIiii. Bess returns to Porgy delirious. She recovers and tells Porgy she does not want to go away with Crown. He promises to protect her. IIiv. The residents of the row take refuge from a hurricane. Crown comes for Bess. Jake's boat overturns. Clara rushes out into the hurricane and Crown goes after her.

IIIi. Sporting Life knows that Crown is not—as people believe—dead. Crown returns and Porgy kills him. IIIii. The detective investigates Crown's death, but learns nothing. He takes Porgy away to view Crown's body. Sporting Life convinces Bess that Porgy will never return. He gives her dope and she leaves with him. IIIiii. Porgy returns after a week in jail for contempt of court. He brings presents that he bought with money he won gambling. Realizing that Bess has left for New York, Porgy sets out after her in his goat cart.

Postcard from Morocco

Composed by Dominick Argento (b. October 27, 1927). Libretto by John Donahue. English. Original work. Premiered Minneapolis, Minnesota Opera, Cedar Village Theater, October 14, 1971. Set in the Shamula railway station in Morocco in 1914. Psychological drama. Through composed. Orchestral interlude before Iii.

Sets: 1. **Acts:** 1 act, 2 scenes. **Length:** I: 95. **Arias:** "When I was a young man" (Mr. Owen). **Hazards:** None. **Scenes:** I. A railway station in Morocco.

Major roles: Lady with a hand mirror/Operetta singer (coloratura soprano), Lady with a cake box (soprano), Lady with a hat box/Foreign singer (mezzo), Man with old luggage/First puppet/Operetta singer (lyric tenor), Man with a paint box/Mr. Owen (tenor), Man with a shoe sample kit/Second puppet (baritone), Man with a cornet case/Puppet maker (bass).

Chorus parts: N/A. **Chorus roles:** None. **Dance/movement:** None (train station entertainers may dance). **Orchestra:** cl (alto sax, bs cl), trb (bs trb), classical guitar, piano (celeste), vln, vla, db bs (string parts may be doubled), perc. **Stageband:** None. **Publisher:** Boosey & Hawkes. **Rights:** Copyright 1972 by Boosey & Hawkes.

Ii. A group of travelers chats while waiting for the train. The coloratura soprano explains the many uses of a hand mirror. Leaping forward in time, we see everyone watching the puppet show. The two puppets discuss the ship they will build. A foreign singer performs. The bass asks Mr. Owen about his suitcase. "It is old," Owen says, explaining that he does not travel with anything valuable that might be stolen. The bass displays his cornet case but refuses to unlock it and the baritone grabs the case and parades around before giving it back. The women coo over the mezzo's hat box. I make hats for movies, the mezzo explains. The women ask the name of her business. The travelers are entertained with a musical interlude. Iii. The baritone—a shoe salesman—talks about his wares. Having learned that Owen is a painter, the travelers pester him with questions. They next turn on the soprano, who is carrying a box. "I keep my lover in this box," she explains. Owen thinks he saw her and her lover near a church once. He kisses her. "When I was a young man," Owen recalls, "I imagined a magical sailing vessel." The bass tells the mezzo about the puppets he makes. The travelers quiz Mr. Owen about his paint kit and try to get him to paint a group portrait. He defends himself by asking about their luggage and occupations. When Owen does open his paint box, it is empty. The puppet show is now given. The train arrives, and everyone but Owen leaves. Getting up on the stage, Owen acts out his boat dream with one of the puppets and sails off into the distance.

Le Postillon de Lonjumeau • The Postilion of Lonjumeau

Composed by Adolphe Adam (July 24, 1803 – May 3, 1856). Libretto by Adolphe de Leuven and Léon Lévy Brunswick. French. Original work. Premiered Paris, Opéra Comique, October 13, 1836. Set in France in the 1770s. Comic opera. Set numbers with recitative. Overture. Entr'acte before II, III.

Sets: 3. **Acts:** 3 acts, 3 scenes. **Length:** I: 50. II: 50. III: 20. **Arias:** "Mes amis, écoutez l'histoire" (Chapelou), "Oh qu'il était beau" (Chapelou). **Hazards:** III: Madelaine must convince St. Phar that both of her characters (Madelaine and Madame de Latour) are onstage together. **Scenes:** I. The yard of a village inn in Lonjumeau. II. A handsome salon in the chateau of Madam de Latour in Fontainebleau opening onto a garden. III. Madam de Latour's country house.

Major roles: Chapelou the postilion/St. Phar (tenor), Madeleine/ Madam de Latour (soprano). **Minor roles:** Marquis of Corcy (tenor), Bijou the wheelwright/Alcindor (bass), Bourdon (bass), Rose (soprano).

Chorus parts: SATTB. **Chorus roles:** Peasants, singers and coryphées at the opera, neighbors and friends of Madame de Latour, soldiers, domestics. **Dance/movement:** None. **Orchestra:** 2 fl (2 picc), 2 ob, 2 cl, 2 bsn, 4 hrn, 2 trp, 3 trb, timp, perc, strings. **Stageband:** None. **Publisher:** Schott & Co., Schlesinger. **Rights:** Expired.

I. Chapelou and Madeleine are married. Chapelou asks his friend Bijou to take his duties as postilion on the wedding night, but Bijou refuses. The marquis is in search of replacement opera singers for the king's theater. He hears Chapelou sing for the villagers and persuades him to leave Madeleine and become an opera singer.

II. Ten years have passed and Chapelou is a famous opera singer under the name of St. Phar. He ignores Madeleine's letters, not realizing that her rich aunt has died and she has taken the name Madame de Latour. The marquis (who loves Madeleine) introduces her to St. Phar. Denying that he is already married, St. Phar proposes to Madame de Latour. He instructs Bijou (who has also joined the opera) to fetch a fake priest, but Madeleine substitutes a real one.

III. St. Phar believes he has unwittingly committed bigamy. By moving between hiding places, Madeleine has both Madeleine and Madam de Latour confront St. Phar. The marquis fetches soldiers to arrest St. Phar, but Madeleine reveals the truth and St. Phar swears his fidelity.

The Postman Always Rings Twice

Composed by Stephen Paulus (b. August 24, 1949). Libretto by Colin Graham. English. Based on the novel by James M. Cain. Premiered St. Louis, Opera Theatre of St. Louis, June 17, 1982. Set in the United States in 1934. Tragedy. Through composed. Prelude. Interludes between scenes. Scenery other than Twin Oaks can be minimal and requires quick changes.

Sets: 5. **Acts:** 2 acts, 20 scenes. **Length:** I, II: 120. **Arias:** "There was a boat drifting out at sea" (Nick), Katz's aria (Katz), Frank's dreams (Frank). **Hazards:** I: Scene in a moving car. Frank and Cora push Nick's car off the road with him in it. **Scenes:** Ii. A darkened stage. Iii – Ivii. Interior and exterior of the Twin Oaks tavern, a roadside sandwich joint. Iviii. A road and Twin Oaks. Iix. Twin Oaks. Ix. Inside Nick's car. IIi. A hospital bed, a corridor, a courtroom. IIii – IIiii. A room. IIiv – IIix. Twin Oaks. IIx. Death row.

Major roles: Frank Chambers (baritone), District Attorney Sackett (bass), Nick Papadakis (tenor), Cora (soprano). **Minor roles:** Second cop (baritone), Katz (tenor). **Mute:** First cop. **Speaking:** Kennedy. (The role of the motorcycle cop was removed after the premiere.)

Chorus parts: N/A. **Chorus roles:** None. **Dance/movement:** None.
Orchestra: 2 fl (picc), ob, cl, alto sax, bsn, hrn, 2 trp, 2 trb (bs trb), timp, 2
perc, guitar, harp, piano, strings (8-6-4-4-2). **Stageband:** I: Nick mimes
guitar, which is played in pit. **Publisher:** European American Music
Corporation. **Rights:** Copyright 1982 European American Music
Corporation.

Ii. Frank wakes from a nightmare in which he is being electrocuted. Iii.
District attorney Sackett asks him about his arrival at the Twin Oaks tavern, a roadside joint run by Nick Papadakis. Frank agrees to work for
Nick and meets Nick's sultry wife, Cora. Iiii. Nick sings and plays the
guitar. Frank and Cora persuade him to go into town to buy a new neon
sign for the tavern. Iiv. Frank kisses Cora. She tells him how Nick saved
her from the hash house. Frank asks her to run away with him and live
on the road. She refuses and suggests they kill Nick. Iv. They make love.
Ivi. Cora tries to kill Nick in the bath while Frank puts up the new sign.
The sign blows a fuse and Nick comes around, thinking he hit his head.
Ivii. Frank leaves without Cora. Iviii. He travels and gambles, finally
returning to the Twin Oaks. Iix. Cora wants Frank to leave. She tells him
Nick wants a baby. Ix. Nick, Cora and Frank are driving home from
Santa Barbara when Cora stops the car. They get out to see what's
wrong and Frank hits Nick with a wrench. He and Cora make love on
the car trunk, then push Nick and the car into a ravine.

IIi. Sackett interviews Frank, who insists he was driving the car—
although he was found in the backseat of the wreckage. Sackett surprises Frank by telling him that Nick had a $10,000 life insurance policy. He
persuades him to sign a complaint against Cora. A cop recommends the
lawyer Katz to Frank. Sackett charges Cora with murder and assault.
Katz—who is also representing Cora—pleads her guilty. IIii. Cora gives
a complete deposition to Kennedy rather than bear the blame alone.
Katz and Sackett bet on the outcome of the trial. IIiii. Katz silences
Kennedy. Cora gets off because the insurance company realizes that if
Cora did murder Nick and assault Frank, then they are liable for Frank's
injuries. IIiv. Frank and Cora return to Twin Oaks. IIv. They find it difficult to trust each other. Frank wants to go, but Cora insists they stay.
IIvi. They make love. IIvii. Frank is wracked by guilt. IIviii. Kennedy
threatens to blackmail Frank, but he and Cora overpower Kennedy and
destroy the incriminating deposition. IIix. Frank catches Cora trying to
run away. They admit to trying to kill each other and Cora says she is
pregnant. Cora goes into labor. IIx. Cora is killed in an auto accident on
the way to the hospital. Frank is convicted of murder. As he awaits execution, he thinks of his love for Cora.

Il Prigioniero • The Prisoner

Composed by Luigi Dallapiccola (February 3, 1904 – February 19, 1975). Libretto by Luigi Dallapiccola. Italian. Based on "La torture par l'espérance" by Count Villiers de l'Isle-Adam and "La légende d'Ulenspiegel et de Lamme Goedzak" by Charles de Coster. Premiered Florence, Teatro Comunale, May 20, 1950. Set in Saragossa in the late 16th century. Tragedy. Through composed. Prologue. Choral intermezzo before Ii, Iiv. Radio premiere on Radio Turin, December 1, 1949.

Sets: 3. **Acts:** 1 act, 5 scenes. **Length:** I: 55. **Hazards:** None. **Scenes:** Prologue. Before the curtain. Ii – Iii. A prison cell in a dungeon in Saragossa. Iiii. An underground passage in the dungeon. Iiv. A vast garden.

Major roles: Mother (dramatic soprano), Prisoner (baritone), Jailer/Grand Inquisitor (tenor). **Minor roles:** Two priests (tenor, baritone). **Mute:** Fra Redemptor.

Chorus parts: SSAATTBB. **Chorus roles:** Offstage. **Dance/movement:** None. **Orchestra:** 3 fl (picc), 2 ob, Eng hrn, 3 cl, bs cl, 2 sax, 2 bsn, cont bsn, 4 hrn, 3 trp, 3 trb, tuba, timp, perc, vibraphone, xylophone, celeste, glockenspiel, 2 harp, piano, strings. Reduced orchestration by composer exists. **Stageband:** Prologue, I: organ, 2 trp, trb. **Publisher:** Suvini Zerboni. **Rights:** Copyright 1947 by S. A. Edition Suvini Zerboni.

Prologue. The prisoner's mother fears that this visit to her son will be the last. She has a vision of the evil King Philip. Ii. The prisoner tells his mother how a few kind words from his jailer reawakened his desire to live. Iii. Flanders is in revolt and the jailer tells his prisoner that the king will be defeated. The jailer goes away, leaving the cell door unlocked. Iiii. The prisoner makes his way up out of the dungeon. Iiv. But he is recaptured by the jailer—who is actually the grand inquisitor. Hope, the prisoner realizes, is the ultimate torture.

Knyaz' Igor' • Prince Igor

Composed by Alexander Borodin (November 12, 1833 – February 27, 1887). Libretto by Alexander Borodin. Russian. Based on the medieval epic "The Tale of Igor's Campaign." Premiered St. Petersburg, Maryinsky Theater, November 4, 1890. Set in Russia in 1185. Epic drama. Set numbers with recitative. Overture. Prologue. Ballet. Completed after the composer's death and orchestrated by A. Glazounov and N. A. Rimsky-Korsakov.

Sets: 5. **Acts:** 4 acts, 6 scenes. **Length:** Prologue: 20. I: 35. II: 35. III: 25. IV: 25. **Arias:** "I hate a dreary life" (Galitsky), "No little time has passed" (Jaroslavna), "Unhappy, prince?" (Kontchak), Jaroslavna's lament (Jaroslavna). **Hazards:** None. **Scenes:** Prologue. A square in Poutivle. Ii. The courtyard of Prince Galitsky's house. Iii. A room in the Terem. II – III. In the camp of the Polovtsi. IV. The city walls and public square in Poutivle.

Major roles: Prince Igor Svïatoslavitch (baritone), Prince Vladimir Galitsky (bass), Vladimir Igorevitch (tenor), Jaroslavna (soprano), Kontchakovna (contralto), Khan Kontchak (bass). **Minor roles:** Skoula (bass), Eroshka (tenor), Young Polovtsi girl (soprano), Ovlour (tenor). **Bit part:** Nurse (soprano). **Mute:** Gzak.

Chorus parts: SSAATTTTBBBB. **Chorus roles:** Russian princes and princesses, boyars and their wives, villagers, soldiers, youths, people, khans, prisoners of war, slaves, sentinels. **Dance/movement:** II: Dance of the Polovtsi maidens and the slaves. III: Polovtsi march. Dance of the drunken guards. **Orchestra:** picc, 2 fl (picc), 2 ob (Eng hrn), 2 cl (bs cl), 2 bsn, 4 hrn, 2 trp, 3 trb, tuba, timp, perc, harp, piano, strings. **Stageband:** III: 2 alto hrn, 2 tenor hrn, 2 bs hrn, 2 trp, tuba, perc. **Publisher:** M. P. Belaïeff, Edition Musicus. **Rights:** Expired.

Prologue. Prince Igor leads his army against the khans who have enslaved Russia. A solar eclipse frightens the people, but Igor presses on. He leaves his wife, Yaroslavna, in the care of her brother, Prince Galitsky. Ii. Galitsky is living it up in the prince's absence. Having bribed the populace with wine and song, he persuades them to depose Igor and elect him. Iii. No news has come of the prince and Yaroslavna misses him. She receives a delegation of maidens who complain that Galitsky has carried off one of their number against her will. When Yaroslavna demands her release, Galitsky complies. He reminds her that he is ruler now. The boyards bring news that the khan's army is at the gate. Igor has been taken captive.

II. Prince Igor's son, Vladimir Igorievich, has fallen in love with the khan's daughter, Konchakovna. Alone, Igor prays for freedom. He nevertheless refuses his captor Ovlour's help in a dishonorable escape. Kahn Konchak admits his admiration for Igor and tries to cheer him up with dances.

III. Konchak welcomes the return of Khan Gzak and his army. When Ovlour proposes to take advantage of the guards' drunkenness to escape, Igor agrees. Vladimir is torn between duty and love. While he hesitates, Konchakovna sounds the alarm. Igor escapes.

IV. Igor returns home to a loving wife—and a countryside devastated by Khan Gzak. He vows to raise a new army and defeat the khans. The people welcome Igor home.

Die Prinzessin auf der Erbse • The Princess and the Pea

Composed by Ernst Toch (December 7, 1887 – October 1, 1964). Libretto by Benno Elkan. German. Based on the fairy tale by Andersen. Premiered Baden Baden, Chamber Music Festival, July 17, 1927. Set in a royal castle at an unspecified time. Fairy tale. Set numbers with recitative and some dialogue. Prelude.

Sets: 2. **Acts:** 1 act, 11 scenes. **Length:** I: 55. **Hazards:** None. **Scenes:** Ii – Ivi. A throne room. Ivii – Ixi. A bedroom.

Major roles: King (bass), Queen (soprano), Foreign princess (soprano), Nurse (mezzo). **Minor roles:** Chancellor (baritone), Minister (tenor), Prince (tenor).

Chorus parts: SATB. **Chorus roles:** Ladies of the court, maids, servants, pages. **Dance/movement:** None. **Orchestra:** 2 fl (picc), ob, cl, bsn (cont bsn), hrn, trp, tuba, timp, perc, strings. **Stageband:** None. **Publisher:** B. Schott's Söhne. **Rights:** Copyright 1927 by B. Schott's Söhne.

Ii. The king is worried about the succession because his son will not marry. Iii. The queen insists that any prospective daughter-in-law be of the most royal blood. Iiii. A foreign princess arrives at court fleeing her stepmother. Iiv. The prince falls in love with her. Iv. The queen decides to test the princess. Ivi. The nurse suggests putting a pea in the princess's bed: Only a true princess would have the delicacy to feel it. Ivii. A bed is prepared. Iviii. The nurse puts a pea under the mattress. Iix. The princess prepares for bed. Ix. But she cannot sleep. Ixi. She wakes the household, complaining bitterly about the bed. The queen begs the princess's forgiveness and welcomes her as a daughter-in-law.

The Prodigal Son

Composed by Benjamin Britten (November 22, 1913 – December 4, 1976). Libretto by William Plomer. English. Based on the gospel of St. Luke. Premiered Suffolk, English Opera Group, Orford Church, June 10, 1968. Set in a farm and city in Biblical times. Parable for church performance. Through composed. Opus 81.

Sets: 2. **Acts:** 1 act, 3 scenes. **Length:** I: 70. **Hazards:** None. **Scenes:** Ii. The father's farm. Iii. The city. Iiii. The father's farm.

Major roles: Tempter/Abbot (tenor), Father (bass or baritone), Elder son (baritone), Younger son (tenor). (Roles and orchestra are drawn from a group of 1 abbot, 11 monks, 5 acolytes and 8 lay brothers.)

Chorus parts: 3 tenors, 3 baritones, 2 basses, 5 trebles. **Chorus roles:** Monks, acolytes and lay brothers play all roles, soloist and chorus. Servants, parasites, beggars, young servants (trebles), offstage voices (trebles). **Dance/movement:** None. **Orchestra:** fl (picc), trp, hrn, vla, bs, harp, perc, chamber organ (instruments played by lay brothers). **Stageband:** None. **Publisher:** Faber Music Ltd. **Rights:** Copyright 1968 by Faber Music Limited.

Ii. The father sends his two sons out to the fields to supervise the tilling. The tempter convinces the younger son to explore the world. The father agrees to let his young son go and gives him his portion. Iii. In the city, the younger son loses all his money on wine, women and gambling and is reduced to begging. Iiii. The younger son returns home, repentant, and is received joyfully by his father. The elder son objects to this special treatment. The abbot explains that there is more rejoicing in heaven for one sinner who is saved than for ninety-nine who have nothing to repent.

Prometheus

Composed by Carl Orff (July 10, 1895 – March 29, 1982). Libretto by Aeschylus. Greek. Setting of the play by Aeschylus. Premiered Stuttgart, Staatstheater, March 24, 1968. Set on an ocean coast in legendary times. Tragedy. Through composed with extensive rhythmic speaking.

Sets: 1. **Acts:** 1 act, 1 scene. **Length:** I: 130. **Hazards:** I: Prometheus chained to a rock. Daughters of Okeanos arrive in a winged car. Okeanos arrives on a winged horse. **Scenes:** I. A plateau overhanging a cliff near the ocean.

Major roles: Prometheus (baritone), Io (soprano). **Speaking:** Power, Hephaistos, Okeanos, Hermes. **Mute:** Force.

Chorus parts: SSAA. **Chorus roles:** Daughters of Okeanos. **Dance/movement:** None. **Orchestra:** 4 piano (8 performers), 6 fl (6 picc), 6 ob (2 Eng hrn), 6 trp, 6 trb, 4 ten banjo, 4 harp, electric organ, 9 bs, 15 to 18 perc, timp. **Stageband:** I: organ, perc, 3 piano. **Publisher:** B. Schott's Söhne. **Rights:** Copyright 1967 by B. Schott's Söhne.

I. Hephaistos and the gods of Power and Force chain Prometheus to a rock in punishment for giving fire to mankind. Prometheus complains of the injustice of the new king of the gods, Zeus. He tells the daughters of Okeanos how he protected mankind from Zeus. Okeanos offers to speak to Zeus on Prometheus's behalf, but Prometheus tells him not to make Zeus angry. Prometheus lists the boons he granted mankind. Because Zeus loves Io, Io is hounded around the world by Zeus's jealous wife, Hera. Prometheus tells Io's future. He reveals that Zeus's downfall is preordained. Prometheus refuses to tell Hermes who will overthrow Zeus. Zeus adds torture to Prometheus's punishment.

Le Prophète • The Prophet

Composed by Giacomo Meyerbeer (September 5, 1791 – May 2, 1864). Libretto by Eugène Scribe. French. Based on a historical incident. Premiered Paris, Opéra, April 16, 1849. Set in Holland and Germany in the early 16th century. Grand opera. Set numbers with recitative. Prelude. Ballet. Entr'acte before III, IV, V.

Sets: 8. **Acts:** 5 acts, 9 scenes. **Length:** I: 35. II: 35. III: 55. IV: 50. V: 40. **Arias:** "Ô Prêtres de Baal" (Fidès). **Hazards:** II: Girls ice skate. V: Palace explodes and burns. **Scenes:** I. Outside Count Oberthal's castle in Dordrecht. II. Jean's inn in Leyden. IIIi. The Anabaptists' camp near Münster. IIIii. Inside Zacharie's tent in the camp. IIIiii. The Anabaptists' camp. IVi. The city hall square in Münster. IVii. Interior of Münster cathedral. Vi. Dungeon in the palace of Münster. Vii. Banqueting hall of the palace.

Major roles: Berthe (soprano), Fidès (mezzo), Jonas (tenor), Mathisen (bass or baritone), Zacharie (bass), Count of Oberthal (bass or bass baritone), Jean of Leyde (tenor). **Bit parts:** Two children (soprano, mezzo), Two peasants (tenor, bass), Soldier (tenor), Two bourgeois men (2 tenor), Two officers (tenor, bass), Elector of Westphalia (bass), Laborer (tenor).

Chorus parts: SSAATTTTBBB. **Chorus roles:** Shepherds, peasants, soldiers, Anabaptists, noble prisoners, citizens of Münster, children (in 2 parts). **Dance/movement:** II: Waltzing. III: skating ballet. V: girls dance at the prophet's coronation. **Orchestra:** picc, 2 fl, 2 ob, Eng hrn, 2 cl, bs cl, 4 bsn, 4 hrn, 2 cornet, 2 trp, 3 trb, ophicléide, 4 timp, perc, 2 harp, strings. **Stageband:** I: 2 cl or 2 reed pipes. III: 4 trp, military drums. IV: 2 small sax, 4 sop sax, 4 alto sax, 2 ten sax, 4 bs sax, 2 cont bs sax, military drums, 2 cornet, 2 trp, organ (4 hands). **Publisher:** G. Ricordi & Co., Garland Publishing, Breitkopf & Härtel. **Rights:** Expired.

I. Jean has sent his mother, Fidès, to fetch Berthe, his fiancée. Three anabaptist preachers—Jonas, Zacharie and Mathisen—preach revolt to the peasants and are arrested by the Count of Oberthal. He refuses permission for Berthe to marry Jean.

II. A crowd gathers in Jean's inn. The anabaptist preachers are surprised by Jean's resemblance to a painting of King David. Jean tells them of his dreams, which they interpret to mean he will be a king. They beg him to go with them, but Jean refuses. Berthe arrives, pursued by Oberthal. When Oberthal threatens to kill Fidès, Jean reluctantly turns over Berthe. Jean leaves his mother to become the preachers' prophet.

IIIi. The anabaptists celebrate their victories and ransom their noble captives. IIIii. The preachers plan to besiege Münster and kill Oberthal and his father, the governor. Oberthal has gotten lost in the dark. Discovered by the anabaptists, he claims to be a follower. He and Jonas recognize each other. The preachers order Oberthal's instant execution, but Jean intervenes. He learns that Berthe escaped Oberthal by jumping from the castle wall. Oberthal was following her to Münster to beg forgiveness. IIIiii. On the preachers' orders, Jean's soldiers attack Münster —and are defeated. Jean regroups and leads them to victory.

IVi. Fidès believes the prophet has killed Jean. She is reduced to begging when she is reunited with Berthe. Berthe decides to murder the prophet. IVii. Jean has been crowned king. He and his mother recognize each other. Warned by Mathisen that a reunion with Fidès will mean her death, Jean pretends not to know her. He asks the anabaptists to kill him if she is really his mother. Faced with this choice, Fidès says she was mistaken.

Vi. The three preachers agree to betray Jean to the emperor to save themselves. Jean visits his mother in jail. She calls him a tyrant and demands he relinquish his crown. Berthe has stockpiled gunpowder under the palace. Realizing Jean is the prophet, she curses him and stabs herself. IVii. Forewarned of the preachers' betrayal—and knowing about the gunpowder—Jean returns to the coronation celebration. Oberthal and his soldiers break in. An explosion rocks the palace and it is engulfed in flame.

Der Protagonist • The Protagonist

Composed by Kurt Weill (March 2, 1900 – April 3, 1950). Libretto by Georg Kaiser. German. Based on Kaiser's play. Premiered Dresden, Dresden State Opera, March 27, 1926. Set in England in the late 16th or early 17th century. Tragedy. Through composed. Some spoken dialogue.

Sets: 1. **Acts:** 1 act, 1 scene. **Length:** I: 75. **Hazards:** None. **Scenes:** I. A dilapidated bar hall in a country inn.

Major roles: Protagonist (tenor), Catherine (soprano). **Minor roles:** Innkeeper (bass), First player Jonathan (bass), Second player Richard (baritone), Third player Henry (mezzo or contralto), Duke's major domo (tenor), Young man (baritone).

Chorus parts: N/A. **Chorus roles:** None. **Dance/movement:** I: Two pantomimes, dance-like movement in the first pantomime. **Orchestra:** 2 ob, 2 bs cl, 3 hrn, 3 bsn, perc, strings. **Stageband:** I: 2 fl, 2 cl, 2 trp, 2 bsn (the 8 musicians of the duke). **Publisher:** Universal Edition. **Rights:** Copyright 1926 by Universal Edition.

I. The protagonist rents a room from the innkeeper in which to rehearse his troupe. He apologizes to his sister, Catherine, for bringing her along on his tours, but her presence anchors his sanity. The protagonist sends a note to the duke announcing his arrival. Catherine and a young man are in love, but Catherine worries how to break the news to her brother. She knows the fact that she initially lied about the affair will wound him deeply. The duke sends his major domo to ask for a light pantomime. The players rehearse. In the pantomime, a husband has an affair with a girl while his wife does likewise with a priest. The wife begs the husband to come home and lets him bring the girl with him. The sister tells the protagonist about her love. The major domo returns to say the duke now wants a serious ending. The protagonist portrays jealousy and is swept away by the part. When his sister returns with the young man, the protagonist stabs her in a jealous fury. The protagonist runs off to perform.

Purgatory

Composed by Hugo Weisgall (October 13, 1912 – March 11, 1997). Libretto by William Butler Yeats. English. A literal setting of the play by Yeats. Premiered Washington, D.C., Library of Congress, February 17, 1961. Set in a ruined house in the present. Tragedy. Through composed.

Sets: 1. **Acts:** 1 act, 1 scene. **Length:** I: 35. **Hazards:** None. **Scenes:** I. A ruined house and a bare tree in the background.

Major roles: Old man (bass), Young boy (high tenor or baritone with high and strong falsetto). **Mute:** Vision of old man's father.

Chorus parts: N/A. **Chorus roles:** None. **Dance/movement:** None. **Orchestra:** fl (picc), 2 cl (bs cl), bsn, hrn, trp, perc, timp, piano, strings.

Stageband: None. **Publisher:** Merion Music. **Rights:** Copyright 1959 by Merion Music.

I. An old man revisits the ruins of the house in which he grew up. He tells his son how his own mother married the stable boy and died in child birth. The uneducated stable boy refused to educate his son (the old man) and burned down the house in a drunken fury. While the house burned, the old man stabbed and killed his father. The old man imagines the night of his own conception, and he and his son fight over a bag of money. The old man sees an image of his father in the window. He kills his son rather than allow his polluted line to continue.

I Puritani • The Puritans

Composed by Vincenzo Bellini (November 3, 1801 – September 23, 1835). Libretto by Carlo Pepoli. Italian. Based on "Têtes Rondes et Cavaliers" by Jacques-Arsène Ancelot and Joseph-Xavier Boniface Saintine (based in turn on "Old Morality" by Sir Walter Scott). Premiered Paris, Théâtre Italien, January 25, 1835. Set in a Puritan fortress in the south of England near Plymouth in the mid-17th century during the Civil War soon after Charles I's execution. Melodramma serio. Set numbers with recitative. Introduction.

Sets: 5. **Acts:** 3 acts, 5 scenes. **Length:** Introduction: 5. I: 65. II: 40. III: 30. **Arias:** "A te, o cara" (Arturo), "Cinta di fiori" (Giorgio), "Qui la voce" (Elvira). **Hazards:** None. **Scenes:** Ii. Spacious terrace in the fortress. Iii. Elvira's apartments. Iiii. Armory. II. Room in the fortress. III. Arbor in a wooded garden near Elvira's house.

Major roles: Elvira (soprano), Arturo Talbo (tenor), Riccardo Forth (baritone), Sir Giorgio (bass). **Minor roles:** Sir Bruno Roberton (tenor), Lord Gualtiero Valton (bass), Enrichetta of France (mezzo).

Chorus parts: SATTBB. **Chorus roles:** Cromwell's soldiers, guards, armorers, heralds, pages, men and women of the castle, ladies, puritans, bridesmaids. **Dance/movement:** None. **Orchestra:** 2 fl (picc), 2 ob, 2 cl, 2 bsn, 4 hrn, 2 trp, 3 trb, timp, perc, harp, strings. **Stageband:** I: organ (or 2 cl, 2 bsn, 2 hrn), 4 hrn. II: harp, perc. III: 4 hrn. **Publisher:** Ricordi, Kalmus. **Rights:** Expired.

Ii. Bruno and the soldiers hear the morning hymn. Riccardo confides to Bruno that, although Elvira's hand was promised him by her father, Elvira loves Arturo Talbot, the cavalier. Bruno suggests he seeks solace in religion and duty. Iii. Giorgio comes to tell Elvira she is to be married. She refuses until her uncle Giorgio reveals that he persuaded her father to let her marry her beloved Arturo. They hear the horns that signal Arturo's arrival. Iiii. The inhabitants of the castle greet Arturo. Valton says he cannot attend the wedding as he must escort the prisoner, Enrichetta, before Parliament. He gives Arturo a safe conduct to the church. Giorgio points out that Enrichetta is widely believed to be a spy for the Stuarts. This seals her fate, Arturo realizes with pity. When she reveals to him (in private) that she is the queen of the murdered King Charles, he promises to save her. Elvira has Enrichetta try on her wedding veil, giving Arturo an idea: He will smuggle Enrichetta out of the fortress disguised as Elvira. As they are leaving, Riccardo challenges him to a duel. They fight, but Enrichetta intervenes and her veil slips to reveal her face. Riccardo allows the pair to leave the castle. Just as they clear the gates, Riccardo and Valton sound the alarm. Elvira goes mad at Arturo's betrayal. All curse Arturo and Enrichetta.

II. Giorgio describes Elvira's madness to the inhabitants of the castle. Riccardo enters with Parliament's judgments: Arturo is condemned; Valton, honored. Elvira enters, plainly mad. Giorgio takes Riccardo aside and insists that he save Arturo's life. The two men swear themselves to liberty and victory.

III. Arturo has secretly returned. He explains his past actions to Elvira and swears his undying love. Riccardo and the Puritans swarm in to arrest Arturo, but he is oblivious, having finally recognized Elvira's madness. She is restored to sanity by the shock of hearing Arturo's death sentence. Elvira demands to die by his side, but a message arrives announcing the defeat of the Stuarts and the pardon of Arturo.

I Quattro Rusteghi • The Four Rustics

Composed by Ermanno Wolf-Ferrari (January 12, 1876 – January 21, 1948). Libretto by Giuseppe Pizzolato. Venetian dialect (premiered in German). Based on the play by Carlo Goldoni. Premiered Munich, Königliches Hof- und Nationaltheater, March 19, 1906. Set in Venice in the late 18th century. Lyric comedy. Set numbers with recitative. Prelude. Intermezzo before II. Interlude before Iv.

Sets: 3. **Acts:** 3 acts, 4 scenes. **Length:** I: 55. II: 40. III: 25. **Hazards:** None. **Scenes:** Ii. A room in Lunardo's house. Iii. The roof terrace of Marina's house. II. A large room in Lunardo's house. III. The room in Lunardo's house.

Major roles: Lucieta (lyric soprano), Margarita (mezzo), Lunardo (bass), Marina (soprano), Filipeto (tenor). **Minor roles:** Maurizio (bass), Simon (bass), Cancian (bass), Count Riccardo (tenor), Felice (soprano). **Bit part:** Marina's maid (mezzo).

Chorus parts: N/A. **Chorus roles:** None. **Dance/movement:** None. **Orchestra:** 2 fl (picc), 2 ob (Eng hrn), 2 cl, 2 bsn, 4 hrn, 3 trp, 3 trb, tuba, 3 perc, timp, harp, strings. **Stageband:** None. **Publisher:** Josef Weinberger. **Rights:** Copyright 1934 by Josef Weinberger.

Ii. Lunardo tyrannizes over his second wife, Margarita, and his daughter, Lucieta. He has invited three fellow merchants to dinner: Maurizio, Simon and Cancian. Lunardo wants Lucieta to marry Maurizio's son, Filipeto, but he thinks it improper for the couple to meet before the wedding. Iii. Marina promises to help Filipeto see his fiancée.

II. Lucieta makes do with Margarita's cast off clothes and jewelry. Filipeto comes to the dinner disguised as a girl and meets Lucieta. The two fall in love. Filipeto hides when Lunardo returns but is quickly discovered. Lunardo and Maurizio are furious.

III. The men agree that the wedding must be called off and their wives disciplined. Cancian's wife, Felice, tells them they are being foolish. She engineers a general reconciliation and Lucieta weds Filipeto.

Pikovaya Dama • The Queen of Spades

Composed by Peter Ilyitch Tchaikovsky (May 7, 1840 – November 6, 1893). Libretto by Modest Tchaikovsky. Russian. Based on a story by Pushkin. Premiered St. Petersburg, Maryinsky Theater, December 19, 1890. Set in St. Petersburg in the late 18th century. Tragedy. Set numbers with recitative. Introduction and entr'actes. Orchestral interludes. Opus 68.

Sets: 7. **Acts:** 3 acts, 7 scenes. **Length:** I, II, III: 165. **Arias:** "I don't even know her name" (Herman), "But why these tears" (Lisa), "Forgive me, adorable creature" (Herman), "I love you beyond measure" (Yeletsky), "Ah, I am worn out by grief" (Lisa), "If pretty girls could fly like birds" (Tomsky). **Hazards:** None. **Scenes:** Ii. An open space in the summer garden, St. Petersburg. Iii. Lisa's room. IIi. A large reception room in the house of a rich dignitary. IIii. The countess's bedroom. IIIi. Herman's quarters in the barracks. IIIii. The canal opposite the winter palace. IIIiii. The gambling house.

Major roles: Herman (tenor), Countess (mezzo), Lisa (soprano). **Minor roles:** Count Tomsky/Plutus (baritone), Prince Yeletsky (baritone), Tchekalinsky (tenor), Sourin (bass), Tchaplitsky (tenor), Master of ceremonies (tenor), Pauline/Daphnis (contralto), Governess (mezzo), Chloë (soprano). **Bit parts:** Naroumov (bass), Mary (soprano). **Mute:** Child, Amor, Hymen.

Chorus parts: SSSAATTBB. **Chorus roles:** Children (boys and girls), nurses, maids, governesses, promenaders, Lisa and Pauline's girlfriends, singers, shepherds and shepherdesses, guests, gamblers. **Dance/movement:** II: Pauline and girlfriends dance, quadrille, shepherds and shepherdesses. **Orchestra:** 3 fl (picc), 2 ob (Eng hrn), 2 cl, bs cl, 2 bsn, 4 hrn, 2 trp, 3 trb, tuba, timp, perc, harp, strings. **Stageband:** III: drum, trp. **Publisher:** Schirmer, Moscow State Music Publisher. **Rights:** Expired.

Ii. The children play. Tchekalinsky asks Sourin about his card playing. "Herman was there," Sourin says, "but he just drank and watched—as usual." Tchekalinsky taxes Herman with his moroseness and Herman admits he is in love and paralyzed by fear of failure. A group of promenaders enjoys the spring weather. Tchekalinsky and Sourin congratulate the prince on his engagement—to Lisa, Herman's beloved. The countess asks Tomsky about Herman. The withered countess was once a great card player and beauty, Tomsky tells his friends, and her nickname was the queen of spades. The Count Saint-German, Tomsky continues, tempted her into a dalliance by telling her three secret cards. With them, she won back all the money she had lost. The countess revealed the three cards to her husband and a young gallant, but a ghost told her she would die if she told anyone else. A storm disperses the promenaders. Herman swears not to give up Lisa. Iii. Lisa, Pauline and their girlfriends sing and dance. Pauline asks Lisa why she is so glum, but Lisa only begs her not to tell the prince. The governess chides the girls for making noise and sends them home. Herman appears on Lisa's balcony threatening to kill himself for love of her. Lisa returns his love.

IIi. A dance and party are in progress. The prince asks Lisa to confide in him. Herman has a letter from Lisa asking him to wait for her after the performance. For fun, Sourin, Tchekalinsky and Tomsky hide near Herman and whisper about the three cards, making Herman think he is hearing a ghost. A pastoral, "The Faithful Shepherdess" is now performed: Daphnis, a poor shepherd, wins the hand of Chloë, beating out his rich rival, Plutus. Lisa gives Herman a key that will get him into her room via her grandmother's. The empress arrives. IIii. Herman enters the countess's chamber and hides. The ladies retire to bed. Herman begs the countess to tell him her secret, but when he threatens her with a gun, the shock kills her. Blaming Herman for the countess's death, Lisa sends him away.

IIIi. Herman reads a letter from Lisa, forgiving him and begging him to meet her near the Winter Palace. The ghost of the countess appears and tells Herman the three cards: seven, ace and three. IIIii. Lisa's doubts are dispelled by Herman's arrival—until he reveals his intention to use the secret cards. When he pushes Lisa away, she throws herself into the river. IIIiii. Tomsky, Tchekalinsky and Sourin are all at the gambling house when the prince arrives, intent on revenge. Tomsky sings. Herman enters, looking pale. He bets on the three and the seven, winning both times. When he tries to double again, only the count will bet against him. Instead of an ace, Herman draws the queen of spades. The ghost of the countess appears and Herman stabs himself. Dying, Herman asks Lisa and the count to forgive him.

A Quiet Place

Composed by Leonard Bernstein (August 25, 1918 – October 14, 1990). Libretto by Stephen Wadsworth. English. Original work. Premiered Houston, Houston Grand Opera, Jones Hall, June 17, 1983. Set in Suburban America in the early 1980s and 1950s. Psychological drama. Set numbers with recitative and spoken dialogue. Prologue. Postlude after I. Prelude before III. Quiet Place is a sequel to the one-act opera Trouble in Tahiti (premiered June 12, 1952). The revised Quiet Place includes Tahiti in its second act (IIii & IIiv).

Sets: 6. **Acts:** 3 acts, 6 scenes. **Length:** I: 40. II: 65. III: 35. **Hazards:** None.

Scenes: I. A room in a well-appointed funeral parlor. IIi. The master bedroom in Sam's house. IIii. Sam and Dinah's house, young Sam's office, office of Dinah's psychiatrist, a street. IIiii. Two bedrooms in Sam's house. IIiv. A gym, a movie theater, a hat shop, a bus stop, the house. III. Dinah's garden behind the house.

Major roles: Old Sam (bass), Dede (soprano), François (tenor), Junior (baritone), Young Sam (bass baritone), Dinah (mezzo). **Minor roles:** Bill (baritone), Susie (mezzo), Mrs. Doc (mezzo), Doc (bass), Analyst (tenor), Funeral director (tenor), Jazz trio (soprano, tenor, baritone).

Chorus parts: SSAATTBB. **Chorus roles:** Offstage (onstage for funeral scene at premiere, but completely offstage in subsequent productions). **Dance/movement:** None. **Orchestra:** 3 fl (alto fl, picc), 2 ob, Eng hrn, 3 cl, bs cl, 2 bsn, cont bsn, 4 hrn, 3 trp, 2 trb, bs trb, tuba, timp, 3 or 4 perc, electric bs, piano (electronic keyboard), harp, strings (12, 8, 6, 6, 6). **Stageband:** None. **Publisher:** Boosey and Hawkes. **Rights:** Copyright 1983, 1988 by L. Bernstein and S. Wadsworth.

Prologue. A ghostly chorus witnesses Dinah's death in a car accident. I. The funeral director asks Dinah's friends to describe her two children, Dede and Junior. Sam, the widower, has never met Dede's husband, François. The mourners chat awkwardly. Junior arrives late, interrupting the readings. Sam is furious. After a brief flashback of the children growing up, Junior curses his father and begins to undress. A scuffle ensues and someone knocks the coffin.

IIi. Sam reads Dinah's diary and learns that she was sick of her marriage. Although he is angry, he misses her. IIii. In a flashback, Sam and Dinah fight. Dinah reminds Sam that today is the day of Junior's play, but Sam has an appointment at the gym. Dinah asks for money to pay her analyst. Sam goes to his office, where his day's encounters convince him of his own shrewdness and generosity. Dinah tells her analyst about a dream in which she is trapped in a garden. Sam and Dinah see each other on the street. To avoid having lunch together, both lie and say they have appointments. IIiii. Back in the present, Sam and Dede go through Dinah's things. Next door, François chides Junior for his behavior at the funeral parlor. Junior caresses François, but François says that their days as lovers are over. Junior torments François by telling him he had sex with Dede. Dede changes into one of her mother's dresses. Junior slips into the nonsense syllables and rhyming that characterize his bouts of mental illness. François puts him to bed and goes to Dede. Sam looks in on his sleeping son. IIiv. The young Sam revels in his victory in the handball match. Dinah is first skeptical of, then carried away by, the south-sea fantasy movie "Trouble in Tahiti." Later that evening, Sam wants to have an intimate conversation with her but cannot. Instead he takes her to "Trouble in Tahiti."

III. Junior and Dede have breakfast in their mother's garden. They play games from their childhood and kiss. In a flashback, Junior introduces his boyfriend, François, to Dede. The old Sam and François join Junior and Dede's game of tag. Sam welcomes François to the family and reads them portions of Dinah's diary in which she says how much she loves her family. To Sam's delight, the children decide to stay on with him for another week. They discuss all the wonderful things they mean to do but end up fighting over the sleeping arrangements. Peace again descends when Junior tosses the pages of Dinah's diary into the air. Junior and Sam, Dede and François are reconciled.

Radamisto

Composed by George Frederic Handel (February 23, 1685 – April 14, 1759). Libretto by Nicola Francesco Haym. Italian. Based on "L'Amor Tirranico" by Domenico Lalli and "Zenobia" by Matteo Noris. Premiered London, King's Theater, Royal Academy of Music, April 17, 1720. Set in Armenia in 53 AD. Historical drama. Set numbers with recitative. Overture. Two revisions by composer, the first done months after the premiere to accommodate changes in available singers and including extensive rewrites and new material.

Sets: 7. Acts: 3 acts, 7 scenes. Length: I, II, III: 190. Arias: "Ombra cara" (Radamisto). Hazards: II: Zenobia throws herself into the river. Scenes: Ii. A camp with tents and a view of the city. Iii. A square before Radamisto's palace. IIi. A plain through which runs the river Arasse. IIii. Part of the garden with a view of the royal palace. IIIi. A courtyard of the royal palace. IIIii. A royal chamber. IIIiii. A temple.

Major roles: Polissena (soprano), Tigrane (soprano), Tiridate (tenor; bass in 2nd version), Radamisto (countertenor or soprano; contralto in 2nd version), Zenobia (contralto; soprano in 2nd version). Minor roles: Farasmane (bass), Fraarte (soprano; eliminated in 2nd version).

Chorus parts: SATB. Chorus roles: Guards, soldiers, people. Dance/movement: None. Orchestra: traversa, 2 ob, bsns, 2 hrn, 2 trp, strings, continuo (cembalo). Stageband: None. Publisher: Gregg Press Ltd. Rights: Expired.

Ii. King Tiridate has attacked the kingdom of his father-in-law, Farasmane. Tiridate is in love with Farasmane's daughter-in-law, Zenobia, who is married to Radamisto. Prince Tigrane loves Tiridate's wife, Polissena, but she loves her husband. Farasmane's army is defeated. He is captured. Zenobia affirms her undying loyalty to her husband (Radamisto). Radamisto is still in command of the town, but Tiridate threatens to kill Farasmane if he does not capitulate. Farasmane tells his son he is ready to die. Tigrane intervenes to save Farasmane. Tiridate leads his troops against the city. Polissena hopes to be able to save her brother (Radamisto). Iii. Tiridate's soldiers take the town but cannot find Radamisto or Zenobia. Polissena pleads her case with Tiridate. She thanks Tigrane for saving her father.

IIi. Zenobia throws herself in the river to avoid capture. Tigrane captures Radamisto and offers to disguise him and convey him to Polissena.

Tiridate's soldiers fish Zenobia out of the river. Iiii. Tigrane reports to Tiridate. Tiridate offers Zenobia his kingdom. Tigrane reunites Radamisto with his sister, Polissena. Polissena refuses to help her brother kill her husband. Torn between conflicting duties, Polissena decides to save Tiridate from Radamisto. Tigrane falsely reports Radamisto's death. He introduces the disguised Radamisto to Tiridate. Tiridate promises to reward Radamisto if he can persuade Zenobia to marry him (Tiridate). In private, Radamisto and Zenobia rejoice at their reunion.

IIIi. Tiridate divorces and banishes Polissena. Tigrane decides to stop Tiridate. IIIii. Radamisto hides in Zenobia's room. Tiridate presses his attentions on Zenobia, who rejects him. Radamisto emerges from hiding, but Polissena prevents him from killing Tiridate. Tiridate again gains the upper hand. He repeats his offer to marry Zenobia. Zenobia refuses. IIIiii. Tiridate nevertheless prepares for the wedding. Zenobia again refuses to cooperate. Tigrane raises the army against Tiridate. Radamisto is restored to his throne and forgives Tiridate. Tiridate and Polissena are reconciled.

The Rake's Progress

Composed by Igor Stravinsky (June 17, 1882 – April 6, 1971). Libretto by W. H. Auden and Chester Kallman. English. Inspired by a series of eight paintings by Hogarth. Premiered Venice, Teatro la Fenice, September 11, 1951. Set in England in the 18th century. Morality play. Set numbers with recitative. Based on 18th century forms. Prelude. Epilogue.

Sets: 6. **Acts:** 3 acts, 10 scenes. **Length:** I: 40. II: 40. III, Epilogue: 55. **Arias:** "Here I stand" (Tom), "Quietly night" (Anne), "In youth the panting slave" (Nick). **Hazards:** I: Clock runs backwards. II: Baba breaks dishes. III: Nick sinks into the earth. **Scenes:** Ii. The garden of Trulove's house in the country. Iii. Mother Goose's brothel in London. Iiii. The garden. IIi. The morning room of Tom's house in London. IIii. A street in front of Tom's house. IIiii – IIIi. The morning room. IIIii. A churchyard. IIIiii. Bedlam. Epilogue. Bare stage.

Major roles: Anne Trulove (soprano), Tom Rakewell (tenor), Nick Shadow (baritone). **Minor roles:** Father Trulove (bass), Mother Goose (mezzo), Baba the Turk (mezzo), Sellem (tenor). **Bit parts:** Keeper of the Madhouse (bass).

Chorus parts: SAATTB (generally SATB). **Chorus roles:** Roaring boys, whores, townspeople, respectable citizens, servants, madmen. (Many solo bids in IIIi.) **Dance/movement:** None. **Orchestra:** 2 fl (picc), 2 ob (Eng hrn), 2 cl, 2 bsn, 2 hrn, 2 trp, timp, cembalo (piano), strings.

Stageband: III: bell. **Publisher:** Boosey & Hawkes. **Rights:** Copyright 1951 by Boosey & Hawkes.

Ii. Father Trulove does not approve of Tom Rakewell as a suitor for his daughter, Anne. Sure of his own prospects, Tom brushes off Trulove's offer of a job. Nick Shadow arrives with the news that Tom is a rich man, a wealthy but forgotten uncle having died. Shadow proposes to work for Tom for a year and a day, after which Tom will pay Shadow whatever both agree is fair. He hurries Tom off to London to settle accounts. Iii. Shadow has brought Tom to Mother Goose's, a London brothel. There roaring boys and whores brag of their triumphs. Mother Goose and Shadow quiz Tom on the cynical epigrams they have taught him. When they ask him about love, Tom remembers Anne. He resolves to go "before it is too late," but Shadow persuades him to stay by turning back time. Tom sings a song about love. All present are moved, but Mother Goose claims him for her own. Iiii. Knowing Tom's weak character, Anne decides to go to London to find him.

IIi. Tom is disgusted with the hypocrisy of London and wishes he were happy. Shadow convinces him to wed Baba the Turk, the bearded lady of the circus. Tom can only be happy if he is not governed by his conscience or his appetites, Shadow reasons. And marrying Baba will prove his freedom. IIii. Anne arrives to discover Tom returning home with his new bride, Baba. IIiii. Baba talks incessantly over breakfast. Tom's coldness infuriates her and she throws a tantrum. She freezes when Tom places a wig over her head. Tom sleeps and dreams of a machine that turns stones into bread. He awakes to find Shadow holding the machine. Tom is ecstatic at the thought of doing a good deed by which he will deserve Anne; Shadow is amused that his master has fallen for such an obvious fraud.

IIIi. Tom's business venture has ruined him and his property is being auctioned off. Anne is looking for him. When Sellem, the auctioneer, tries to auction off Baba, she comes back to life. "Tom still loves you," she tells Anne before returning to the circus. IIIii. Shadow brings Tom to a graveyard to get his "wages." He offers Tom a choice of deaths, but— to make things more interesting—suggests they play a game. If Tom can correctly guess three cards that Shadow will pull out of the deck, he is free. If not, his soul is forfeit. Through luck and a hint from Shadow, Tom guesses the first two cards: the queen of hearts and the two of spades. Anne's voice gives Tom the last clue: he correctly guesses that Shadow has again picked the queen of hearts. Mortified, Shadow makes Tom insane before sinking into hell. IIIiii. Tom is in bedlam where he raves that he is Adonis. When Anne visits him, Tom acclaims her as his Venus. She forgives him. Epilogue. Baba, Tom, Shadow, Anne and

Trulove draw the moral: "for idle hands and hearts and minds the devil finds a work to do."

The Rape of Lucretia

Composed by Benjamin Britten (November 22, 1913 – December 4, 1976). Libretto by Ronald Duncan. English. Based on the play "Le Viol de Lucrèce" by André Obey. Premiered Glyndebourne, Mr. and Mrs. John Christie's Opera House, July 12, 1946. Set in Rome in 500 BC. Tragedy. Set numbers with recitative. Interludes with male and female chorus between scenes. Epilogue.

Sets: 3. **Acts:** 2 acts, 4 scenes. **Length:** I: 49. II: 60. **Arias:** "Flowers alone are chaste" (Lucretia). **Hazards:** None. **Scenes:** Ii. In front of curtain and outside a Roman camp. Iii. The hall of Lucretia's home. IIi. Lucretia's bedroom. IIii. Hall of Lucretia's home.

Major roles: Collatinus (bass), Prince Tarquinius (baritone), Lucretia (contralto), Male chorus (tenor), Female chorus (soprano). **Minor roles:** Junius (baritone), Bianca (mezzo), Lucia (soprano).

Chorus parts: N/A. **Chorus roles:** None. **Dance/movement:** None. **Orchestra:** fl (picc), ob (Eng hrn), cl (bs cl), bsn, hrn, perc, harp, strings (1-1-1-1-1), piano (for recitatives; can be played by conductor). **Stageband:** None. **Publisher:** Boosey & Hawkes. **Rights:** Copyright 1946 by Boosey & Hawkes Ltd.

Ii. The male and female chorus explain how the evil Tarquinius bribed, flattered and murdered his way onto the throne: Rome is now ruled by a degenerate Etruscan. In camp, Prince Tarquinius and two of his generals, Junius and Collatinus, drink and discuss the infidelity of Roman wives. The generals went home last night to check on their wives—only to discover their infidelities. The only chaste one was Collatinus's wife Lucretia. Tarquinius calls Junius a cuckold and Junius attacks the prince's licentiousness and his foreign birth. Junius is furious that his wife's philandering elevates Lucretia—and hence Collatinus. Collatinus retires to bed while the other men reflect bitterly on Lucretia's chastity. Tarquinius expresses interest in his general's wife and leaves for Rome. Iii. Lucretia and her maids, Bianca and Lucia, are at home, spinning and sewing. Lucretia misses her husband. As the women are preparing for bed, Tarquinius arrives. Hospitality demands that Lucretia put the prince up for the night, even though his palace is only across town. Tarquinius and the women bid each other good night.

IIi. The Romans express their hatred of Etruscan rule. Tarquinius sneaks into Lucretia's bedroom. When she rejects his advances, Tarquinius rapes her at sword point. Iiii. Lucia and Bianca arrange flowers and coo over the beautiful spring morning. Lucretia sends an orchid to Collatinus telling him to hurry home. "Say it comes from a Roman harlot," she says. Realizing something of what has happened, Bianca tries to prevent the messenger from going, but is too late. Junius and Collatinus appear. The heartbroken Lucretia tells her husband what happened. Collatinus points out that the shame is on Tarquinius, not her, but Lucretia kills herself. While Collatinus mourns, Junius uses the incident to incite the crowd against Tarquinius, hoping to rule instead of the Etruscans. The participants wonder if sin and grief is all there is. "No, for Christ died that we might live," the chorus sings.

Un Re in Ascolto • A King Listens

Composed by Luciano Berio (b. October 24, 1925). Libretto by Italo Calvino. Italian. Inspired by an article about listening. Premiered Salzburg, Kleines Festspielhaus, August 7, 1984. Set in a theater in the present. Musical action. Through composed.

Sets: 2. **Acts:** 2 acts, 2 scenes. **Length:** I: 50. II: 40. **Arias:** Aria I, II, III, IV, VI (Prospero), Aria V (Protagonist). **Hazards:** Extensive spectacle of the play being produced. **Scenes:** I – II. A theater set of an island.

Major roles: Prospero (baritone), Director (tenor), Protagonist (soprano), Venerdi (actor). **Minor roles:** Three singers (tenor, baritone, bass), First soprano (soprano), Pianist (tenor), Mezzo (mezzo), Wife (mezzo), Doctor (tenor), Nurse (soprano), Lawyer (bass), Second soprano (soprano). **Mute:** Mime, Messenger, Theatrical designer and his assistants, Acrobats, Woman who is sawed in two, Clown, Three ballerinas.

Chorus parts: SSAATTBB. **Chorus roles:** Players, chorus. **Dance/movement:** I, II: Ballet corps performs during larger scenes. Ballroom couple. **Orchestra:** 3 fl (picc), 2 ob, Eng hrn, 3 cl, bs cl, tenor sax, 2 bsn, cont bsn, 3 hrn, 3 trp, 3 trb, tuba, celeste/electric organ, perc, strings. **Stageband:** I: wind machine, chorus plays percussive instruments. I, II: 2 piano (pianist who sings, tenor; and "her pianist"), accordion player. **Publisher:** Universal Edition. **Rights:** Copyright 1983 by Universal Edition.

I. The members of Prospero's theater company rehearse a musical version of "The Tempest." The director auditions several singers and discusses the play with Prospero.

II. The doctor tends the dying Prospero. The protagonist of Prospero's play appears to rebuke the impresario. The company members leave Prospero and he dies.

Il Re Pastore • The Shepherd King

Composed by Wolfgang Amadeus Mozart (January 27, 1756 – December 5, 1791). Libretto by Pietro Metastasio. Italian. Original work. Premiered Salzburg, Palace of the Archbishop, April 23, 1775. Set in Sidon in the 4th century BC. Drama. Set numbers with recitative. Overture. KV 208.

Sets: 2. **Acts:** 2 acts, 2 scenes. **Length:** I: 55. II: 52. **Arias:** "L'amerò sarò costante" (Aminta), "Voi che fausti" (Alessandro). **Hazards:** None. **Scenes:** I. The bank of a stream. II. A tent in the Greek camp.

Major roles: Aminta (soprano), Elisa (soprano), Agenore (tenor), King Alessandro of Macedonia (tenor), Tamiri (soprano).

Chorus parts: N/A. **Chorus roles:** None. **Dance/movement:** None. **Orchestra:** 2 fl, 2 ob (2 Eng hrn), 2 bsn, 4 hrn, 2 trp, strings, continuo. **Stageband:** None. **Publisher:** Breitkopf & Härtel. **Rights:** Expired.

I. Elisa assures her beloved Aminta that the war between King Alessandro and Strato, the tyrant of Sidon, will not affect them. Having defeated Strato, Alessandro searches for the rightful heir to Sidon. Alessandro comes to Aminta in disguise, suspecting he is the heir. He offers to take him to Alessandro, but Aminta wants to remain a shepherd. Alessandro is now convinced Aminta is the heir. Agenore encounters his beloved Tamiri, the daughter of the tyrant Strato, and tries to convince her that Alessandro will be her friend. Tamiri is comforted to learn that Agenore still loves her. Elisa obtains permission from her father to marry Aminta. Agenore tells Aminta that he is the rightful king—his father was driven out by Strato when he was a baby. Aminta promises to return to Elisa after claiming his throne.

II. Agenore prevents Elisa from seeing Aminta. He discourages Aminta from pursuing Elisa. Alessandro tells Aminta to dress like a king so he can be presented to his subjects. He decides to show his clemency by marrying Tamiri to Aminta. Aminta is unhappy. Agenore misunderstands Aminta to say that he will marry Tamiri. Agenore is upset. He breaks the news to Elisa. Tamiri does not want to marry Aminta. Agenore, too, is tormented by the planned marriage. Tamiri tells Alessandro that she and Agenore are in love. Elisa begs Alessandro to give her back Aminta. Aminta refuses to be king. Alessandro tells Tamiri to marry Agenore and Aminta to marry Elisa. Aminta is crowned king of Sidon.

Punainen Viiva • The Red Line

Composed by Aulis Sallinen (b. April 9, 1935). Libretto by Aulis
Sallinen. Finnish. Based on the novel by Ilmari Kianto. Premiered
Helsinki, Finnish National Opera, November 30, 1978. Set in Finland in
1907. Music drama. Through composed. Some spoken lines. Epilogue.

Sets: 4. **Acts:** 2 acts, 8 scenes. **Length:** I: 70. II, Epilogue: 40. **Hazards:** I:
Topi dreams he is in the vicarage. **Scenes:** Ii. Topi's house. Iii. Topi's
house and the vicarage. Iiii. Topi's house. Iiv. An election rally. IIi.
Topi's house. IIii. A polling station. IIiii – Epilogue. Topi's house.

Major roles: Topi the crofter (baritone), Riika (soprano), Puntarpää the
agitator (tenor). **Minor roles:** Rector (tenor), Simana Arhippaini the ped-
lar (bass), Boy (treble), Girl (girl soprano), Young priest (bass baritone),
Jussi (bass), Epra (tenor), Kaisa (contralto). **Bit parts:** Tiina (soprano),
Policeman Pirhonen (bass). **Speaking:** Raappana the cobbler, Kunilla.
Speaking bit: Two peasants. **Mute:** Third child.

Chorus parts: SSAATTBB. **Chorus roles:** Poor villagers. **Dance/move-
ment:** None. **Orchestra:** 3 fl (picc), 2 ob, 3 cl (bs cl), 2 bsn (cont bsn), 4
hrn, 3 trp, 3 trb, tuba, timp, 4 perc, harp, celeste, strings. **Stageband:** I:
brass band. **Publisher:** Novello. **Rights:** Copyright 1982 Novello & Co.

Ii. Topi tells his wife, Riika, he will kill the bear that has been stealing
their sheep. She reproaches him with their poverty. Iii. Topi dreams the
children have died and the vicar is rebuking him for not going to
church. Iiii. The pedlar Simana visits Riika. Topi is invited to a political
meeting about the coming elections. Iiv. The agitator Puntarpää rouses
the crowd.

IIi. Topi and his neighbors talk about the election and the red line they
will draw on the ballot. IIii. Topi and Riika go to vote. IIiii. The children
die. Kaisa tells Riika voting was a sin. Epilogue. The reform party in
Helsinki is victorious. Topi is killed by the bear.

El Retablo de Maese Pedro • Master Pedro's Puppet Show

Composed by Manuel de Falla (November 23, 1876 – November 14,
1946). Libretto by Manuel de Falla. Spanish. An episode from "Don
Quixote" by Miguel de Cervantes. Premiered Paris, Salon of the Princess
de Polignac., June 25, 1923. Set in Aragon in the late 16th or early 17th
century. Marionette opera. Set numbers with recitative. Overture.
Prologue. Epilogue. Concert premiere March 23, 1923 in Spain.

Sets: 1. **Acts:** 1 act, 8 scenes (prologue, epilogue and 6 scenes of the puppet show). **Length:** Prologue, I, Epilogue: 30. **Hazards:** I: All onstage characters (including those in the inn) are played by puppets. Inn puppets should be larger than puppets in the show. **Scenes:** I. The stable of an inn in La Mancha. (The six scenes of the puppet show are set as follows: Ii. Hall in Charlemagne's palace. Iii. Tower of the Alcázar at Saragossa. Iiii. A public square in Saragossa. Iiv. A winding path through the Pyrenees. Iv. A road. Ivi. The square.)

Major roles: Boy (treble or soprano), Master Pedro (tenor), Don Quijote (bass or baritone). **Mute:** Sancho Panza, Innkeeper, Scholar, Page, Man with lances and halberds. **Puppets in the show:** Charlemagne, Don Gayferos, Don Roldán, Melisendra, King Marsilio, Enamored moor. **Other puppets in the show:** heralds, knights, men-at-arms, soldiers of King Marsilio, criers, executioners, moors.

Chorus parts: N/A. **Chorus roles:** None. **Dance/movement:** None. **Orchestra:** fl (picc), 2 ob, Eng hrn, cl, bsn, 2 hrn, trp, timp, cembalo, lute, perc, xylophone, harp, strings. **Stageband:** None. **Publisher:** J & W Chester Ltd. **Rights:** Copyright 1924 by J & W Chester Ltd.

Prologue. Master Pedro introduces his puppet show about Don Gayferos, whose wife, Melisendra, has been imprisoned by moors. Ii. Pedro's boy narrates the story: Melisendra's father, Charlemagne, rebukes Gayferos for not rescuing his daughter. Gayferos sets out after her. Iii. A Moor forces a kiss from Melisendra. The spectator Don Quijote rebukes Pedro's boy for embellishing the story. Iiii. In the show, the Moorish king, Marsilio, has the man publicly whipped. Iiv. Gayferos searches for Melisendra. Iv. He finds her, but she does not immediately recognize him. They flee together. Ivi. King Marsilio and his men give chase and recapture them. Epilogue. Quijote draws his sword and attacks the puppet show to free Gayferos and Melisendra. He salutes his beloved Dulcinea and praises knighthood.

Das Rheingold • The Rhinegold

Composed by Richard Wagner (May 22, 1813 – February 13, 1883). Libretto by Richard Wagner. German. Original work based on German and Icelandic legend, particularly the Niebelungenlied and Volsunga Saga. Premiered Munich, Königliches Hof- und Nationaltheater, September 22, 1869. Set near the Rhine in mythological times. Epic music-drama. Through composed with leitmotifs and overture. Musical interludes between scenes.

Sets: 3. **Acts:** 1 act, 4 scenes. **Length:** I: 147. **Hazards:** I: Opening scene

underwater. Tarnhelm makes Alberich disappear and transforms him
into a dragon and a toad. Quick changes of scene. Mysterious appearance of Erda. Rainbow bridge to Valhalla. **Scenes:** Ii. At the bottom of
the Rhine. Iii. Open space on a mountain height near the Rhine. Iiii.
Subterranean caves of Nibelheim. Iiv. Open space on mountain heights.

Major roles: Wotan (bass-baritone), Loge (tenor), Alberich (baritone),
Fricka (mezzo). **Minor roles:** Donner (baritone), Froh (tenor), Mime
(tenor), Fasolt (baritone), Fafner (bass), Freia (soprano), Erda (mezzo),
Woglinde (soprano), Wellgunde (soprano), Flosshilde (mezzo). **Mute:**
Nieblungs (or speaking bit if they scream).

Chorus parts: None. **Chorus roles:** N/A. **Dance/movement:** None.
Orchestra: picc, 3 fl (picc), 4 ob (Eng hrn), 3 cl, bs cl, 3 bsn (cont bsn), 8
hrn (2 ten tuba, 2 bs tuba), cont bs tuba, 3 trp, bs trp, 4 ten bs trb (cont bs
trb), 2 timp, perc, 6 harps, strings (16-16-12-12-8). **Stageband:** I: 18 anvils,
6 harps. **Publisher:** Schirmer, B. Schott's Söhne. **Rights:** Expired.

Ii. Underwater, the three Rhinemaidens play, when they should be
guarding the Rheingold, and taunt the dwarf Alberich for being in love
with them. The glistening of the Rheingold catches Alberich's eye and
they tell him that whoever renounces love and fashions a ring out of the
gold will have measureless power and wealth. Alberich steals the gold
and curses love. Iii. Fricka awakens Wotan and they look at the newly-
completed castle of the gods. Fricka is distraught that her husband has
promised her sister Freia in payment to the giants who built the castle.
"You begged for a home," Wotan answers, but Fricka explains that her
real desire was to keep Wotan home—and faithful. Wotan reminds
Fricka that he gave his eye to win her. "Besides," he says, "I never
intended to hand over Freia." Fasolt and Fafner claim their payment.
Wotan is counting on Loge, the tricky god of fire, to get him out of his
predicament, but Loge is nowhere to be found. When Wotan tries to
renege, Fasolt reminds him that his power is bound up in the treaties he
has made. Only Freia knows how to tend the golden apples that keep
the gods forever young, Fafner notes. Loge finally arrives, pointing out
that he only promised to try to find a way out. "There is nothing more
precious than love," he says, "unless it is Alberich's ring." All present
discover a motive for having the ring. Loge proposes that Wotan steal it.
The giants agree to accept the Nieblung gold instead of Freia, but take
her away as a hostage. Without Freia's apples, the gods grow weak.
Wotan decides to steal the gold. Iiii. Alberich has had his brother Mime
forge a magic tarnhelm, which allows the owner to change shape or disappear at will. Alberich tests it by becoming invisible and beating his
brother. Mime confesses to Wotan and Loge what has happened: "The
ring allows Alberich to find gold deposits," he says, "which he forces the
Nieblung to mine." Alberich appears, driving the enslaved Nieblung

before him, and confronts Wotan and Loge, who alternately abuse and flatter the dwarf. Falling into their trap, Alberich explains that he will enslave the world by means of its own greed. The tarnhelm will protect him from thieves. To demonstrate its power, Alberich transforms himself first into a dragon and then—at Loge's suggestion—into a toad. Wotan and Loge bind the toad and drag him away. Iiv. Wotan and Loge extort from Alberich the Nieblung gold, the tarnhelm and the ring, but the dwarf curses the ring so it will bring death to its owner. Returning for the gold, Fasolt and Fafner demand that the gold be piled up until it completely hides Freia. Wotan throws in the tarnhelm and ring only after Erda appears and warns him he must. When Fasolt claims his fare share of the ransom, Fafner kills him. Donner calls forth a storm and a rainbow bridge appears, stretching to Valhalla. Loge foretells the end of the gods and the Rhinemaidens are heard crying for their lost gold.

Riders to the Sea

Composed by Ralph Vaughan Williams (October 12, 1872 – August 26, 1958). Libretto by John Millington Synge. English. Based on Synge's play. Premiered London, Royal College of Music, November 30, 1937. Set on an island off the west coast of Ireland in the present. Tragedy. Through composed.

Sets: 1. **Acts:** 1 act, 1 scene. **Length:** I: 30. **Hazards:** None. **Scenes:** I. A cottage kitchen on an island off the west coast of Ireland.

Major roles: Nora (soprano), Cathleen (soprano), Maurya (contralto). **Minor role:** Bartley (baritone). **Bit parts:** Woman (mezzo).

Chorus parts: SSAA. **Chorus roles:** Old women. **Dance/movement:** None. **Orchestra:** 2 fl, ob, Eng hrn, bs cl, bsn (use 2nd bsn if bs cl not available), 2 hrn, trp, timp, perc, strings (not more than 6-6-4-4-2). **Stageband:** None. **Publisher:** Oxford University Press. **Rights:** Copyright 1936 by Oxford University Press, London.

I. Maurya's son, Michael, has been missing and presumed drowned for nine days. Michael's clothing is recovered, but his sisters, Nora and Cathleen, hide it from their mother. Maurya hopes her other son, Bartley, will not take the horses to the Galway fair, but he goes without her blessing. Maurya is convinced that Bartley will drowned like her five other sons. Her daughters show her Michael's clothes and a woman reports that Bartley has drowned. Maurya mourns her sons.

Rienzi

Composed by Richard Wagner (May 22, 1813 – February 13, 1883). Libretto by Richard Wagner. German. Based on play by Mary Russell Mitford and novel by Edward Bulwer Lytton. Premiered Dresden, Königliches Hoftheater, October 20, 1842. Set in Rome in the mid-14th century. Grand tragic opera. Set numbers with recitative. Ballet. Overture. Entr'acte before each act.

Sets: 6. **Acts:** 5 acts, 6 scenes. **Length:** I: 45. II: 40. III: 30. IV: 16. V: 20. **Arias:** "Allmächt'ger Vater" (Rienzi), "Gerechter Gott" (Adriano). **Hazards:** V: The Roman capitol is razed. **Scenes:** I. A street showing in the background the church of the Lateran and the home of Rienzi. II. A large room in the capitol. III. A large public place in Rome. IV. A wide street in front of the church of the Lateran. Vi. A hall in the capitol. Vii. A street before the capitol.

Major roles: Irene (soprano), Adriano (mezzo), Cola Rienzi (tenor). **Minor roles:** Paolo Orsini (baritone or bass), Steffano Colonna (bass), Raimondo (bass), Baroncelli (tenor), Cecco del Vecchio (bass), Messenger of Peace (soprano). **Bit part:** Herald (tenor).

Chorus parts: SSSAATTTTTTTTBBBB. **Chorus roles:** Roman nobles, people, Colonna's attendants, priests and monks, messengers of peace, Roman senators and subjects, ambassadors from the Italian cities, Roman soldiers, conspirators. **Dance/movement:** II: Ballet of Roman warriors and maidens. **Orchestra:** picc, 2 fl, 2 ob, 3 cl, 3 bsn (serpent), 4 hrn, 4 trp, 3 trb, ophicléide, timp, perc, harp, strings. **Stageband:** I: 4 trp. III: 12 trp, 6 trb, 4 ophicléide, 8 drums, bells, tam tam. IV: organ. **Publisher:** Adolph Fürstner. **Rights:** Expired.

I. Orsini and a group of nobles abduct Rienzi's sister, Irene. Colonna and his men attack, intending to steal her. Colonna's son, Adriano, tries to save Irene, as does Raimondo, the Papal ablegate. But only Rienzi's appearance quiets the combatants. Rienzi berates the nobles for the dishonor their banditry has brought on Rome. He wins Adriano to his side. When Colonna and Orsini leave the city to fight a duel, Rienzi calls on the people to shut the gates against the nobles.

II. Rienzi has forced the nobles to swear to obey the laws. He has leveled the nobles' castles and brought peace to Rome and her colonies. Orsini and Colonna plot to murder Rienzi, but Adriano overhears them. While Rienzi is receiving ambassadors from the Italian cities, Adriano warns him to be on his guard. Colonna's men attack, but the plebeian guards overpower them. The nobles are condemned to death. Only Adriano's pleas—supported by Rienzi—save the nobles.

III. The nobles have taken up arms against Rienzi and the plebeians. Adriano fails to persuade Rienzi to let him go to the nobles as an emissary of peace.

IV. The emperor of Germany and the Pope have joined the number of Rienzi's enemies. Thinking that Rienzi has betrayed their cause, the plebeians turn against him. With Colonna dead, Adriano, too, wants revenge. The conspirators fear Rienzi, but Raimondo closes the church doors against him. Irene chooses her brother over Adriano.

Vi. Rienzi prays and tells Irene to save herself. Irene rejects Adriano.
Vii. The people burn down the capitol with Rienzi and Irene in it.

Rigoletto

Composed by Giuseppe Verdi (October 9, 1813 – January 27, 1901). Libretto by Francesco Maria Piave. Italian. Based on play "Le roi s'amuse" by Victor Hugo. Premiered Venice, Teatro la Fenice, March 11, 1851. Set in Mantova and environs in the 16th century. Melodrama. Set numbers with recitative. Prelude.

Sets: 4. **Acts:** 4 acts, 4 scenes (originally 3 acts). **Length:** I: 15. II: 40. III: 30. IV: 30. **Arias:** "La donna è mobile" (Duke), "Caro nome" (Gilda), "Cortigiani" (Rigoletto), "Parmi veder le lagrime" (Duke), "Questa o quella" (Duke), "È il sol dell'anima" (Duke). **Hazards:** None. **Scenes:** I. A magnificent hall in the ducal palace. II. Rigoletto's house and courtyard. III. A room in the ducal palace. IV. A lonely spot before Sparafucile's inn.

Major roles: Duke of Mantova (tenor), Gilda (soprano), Rigoletto (baritone). **Minor roles:** Borsa (tenor), Countess Ceprano (mezzo), Count Ceprano (bass), Marullo (baritone), Count Monterone (baritone), Sparafucile (bass), Giovanna (mezzo), Maddalena (contralto). **Bit parts:** Duchess's page (mezzo), Court usher (baritone or tenor). **Mute:** Ladies.

Chorus parts: TTBB. **Chorus roles:** Cavaliers, pages, soldiers. **Dance/movement:** I: Short dance. **Orchestra:** 2 fl (picc), 2 ob (Eng hrn), 2 cl, 2 bsn, 4 hrn, 2 trp, 3 trb, cimbasso (bombardone), timp, perc, strings. **Stageband:** I: band, 2 vln, 2 vla, cont bs. III: timp, perc. **Publisher:** Schirmer, Ricordi. **Rights:** Expired.

I. The duke discusses his latest romantic adventure with Borsa, one of his courtiers. To the courtiers' amusement, the duke flirts with the Countess of Ceprano in front of her husband. Marullo, another courtier, tells everyone that the hunchback jester, Rigoletto, has a mistress. The

Count of Ceprano is furious when he overhears Rigoletto advising the duke to banish or behead Ceprano so he can bed the countess. He swears revenge. Monterone, too, wants revenge: The duke has dishonored his daughter. His accusations serve only as material for Rigoletto's barbs and the nobleman is led off to prison, cursing the duke and his jester.

II. Sparafucile offers his services as assassin to Rigoletto. "If I am a monster," Rigoletto says, "it is the world that has made me so." He hates being a jester and worries about Monterone's curse. Rigoletto's daughter, Gilda, comforts him. They discuss Gilda's dead mother. Rigoletto takes his leave, reminding Gilda and her nurse, Giovanna, not to go out. The duke, meanwhile, has sneaked into the courtyard where he bribes Giovanna and declares his love to Gilda. Gilda—who has seen the duke in church, though she does not know his name—admits she loves him. Voices are heard and the duke hurries away. It is the courtiers. Rigoletto returns and Marullo persuades him to help abduct Ceprone's wife. When Rigoletto agrees, Marullo blindfolds him and has him hold the ladder while they abduct not the countess, but Gilda. Rigoletto discovers the truth too late.

III. The duke is livid that Gilda has been abducted, until the courtiers hand her over. Realizing Gilda is in the duke's bedroom, Rigoletto begs the courtiers to restore his daughter to him. They bar his way. Gilda is at last released. Rigoletto comforts her and swears revenge—ignoring Gilda's pleas of forgiveness for the duke. Monterone is led off to execution.

IV. Hoping to convince Gilda of the duke's faithlessness, Rigoletto brings her to Sparafucile's inn. They spy on the duke as he woos Maddalena, Sparafucile's sister. Gilda is convinced and Rigoletto sends her off to Verona, disguised as a man. After paying Sparafucile to murder the duke, Rigoletto leaves. Gilda returns. The duke retires to rest. Maddalena begs her brother not to kill the handsome stranger. If someone else comes to the inn before midnight, I will kill that person instead, Sparafucile agrees. Having overheard their agreement, Gilda enters, intending to give her life for the duke's. Sparafucile kills her and hands the body—wrapped in a sack—to Rigoletto. Rigoletto is overjoyed until he hears the voice of the duke and cuts open the sack. He is horrified. With her dying breath, Gilda explains what she has done.

Rinaldo

Composed by George Frederic Handel (February 23, 1685 – April 14, 1759). Libretto by Aaron Hill and Giacomo Rossi. Italian. After episodes in Torquato Tasso's epic poem "Gerusalemme liberata." Premiered London, Queen's Theatre in the Haymarket, February 24, 1711. Set in Palestine in 1099 (during the first crusade). Medieval drama. Set numbers with recitative. Overture. Prelude before III. Sinfonia in I, III. Large numbers of super spirits, demons, etc. Extensively revised by composer for February 10, 1731 revival.

Sets: 6. **Acts:** 3 acts, 8. **Length:** I: 60. II: 40. III: 30. **Arias:** "Lascia ch'io pianga" (Almirena). **Hazards:** II: The mermaid's boat sinks. Armida transforms herself into Almirena. III: Magician enters riding a fire-breathing dragon. Rinaldo magically turns Armida's garden into a desert. Goffredo and Argante's armies do battle. **Scenes:** Ii. A Christian encampment outside the gates of Jerusalem. Iii. A desolate rock with Armida's castle in the background. Iiii. Almirena's garden. IIi. A boat at anchor on a great and tranquil sea. IIii. Armida's enchanted palace. IIIi. An awesome mountain with Armida's palace on its summit and a grotto at its foot. IIIii. Armida's enchanted palace. IIIiii. The gates of Jerusalem.

Major roles: Goffredo (contralto; tenor in 2nd version), Rinaldo (countertenor or soprano; contralto in 2nd version), Almirena (soprano), Argante (bass; contralto in 2nd version), Armida (soprano; contralto in 2nd version), Eustazio (contralto; deleted in 2nd version). **Minor roles:** Herald (tenor), Mermaid (soprano), Magician (contralto; bass in 2nd version). **Mute:** Spirits, Demons.

Chorus parts: N/A. **Chorus roles:** None. **Dance/movement:** None. **Orchestra:** flageolet, 2 recorders, 2 ob, 2 bsn, 4 trp, timp, strings, continuo (cembalo) (2 hrn added and 2 trp removed in 2nd version). **Stageband:** None. **Publisher:** Gregg Press Ltd. **Rights:** Expired.

Ii. The hero Rinaldo and his general, Goffredo, anticipate their success over the heathen rulers of Jerusalem. Rinaldo is betrothed to Goffredo's daughter, Almirena. Argante, the king of Jerusalem, visits Goffredo's camp to ask for a three-day truce. He loves Armida, an enchantress and the queen of Damascus. Iii. Armida tells Argante that he can win if Rinaldo withdraws from the fight. She promises to accomplish this herself. Iiii. Armida and her evil minions overpower Rinaldo and steal Almirena from him.

IIi. Goffredo and Rinaldo search out a Christian magician who can help them defeat Armida. A mermaid tempts Rinaldo into a magic boat, which puts out to sea and sinks. IIii. Argante falls in love with Almirena.

He attempts to free her, but Armida subdues him. Armida loves Rinaldo, who scorns her. She confuses him by assuming Almirena's form.

IIIi. The Christian magician arms Rinaldo with a magic wand and he uses the wand to ward off Armida's evil spirits. IIIii. Armida and Argante make up. Rinaldo uses the wand to turn Armida's enchanted garden into a desert. Rinaldo and Goffredo are reunited with Almirena. IIIiii. A battle takes place before the gates of Jerusalem. Rinaldo is victorious. Armida breaks her magic wand.

Der Ring des Nibelungen

See entries for "Das Rheingold," "Die Walküre," "Siegfried," and "Götterdämmerung."

The Rise and Fall of the City of Mahagonny

See "Aufstieg und Fall der Stadt Mahagonny" entry.

Il Ritorno d'Ulisse in Patria • The Return of Ulisse to his Country

Composed by Claudio Monteverdi (May 15 [baptized], 1567 – November 29, 1643). Libretto by Giacomo Badoaro. Italian. Based on the "Odyssey" by Homer. Premiered Venice, Teatro San Cassiano, February 1640. Set in Greece shortly after the Trojan war. Drama. Set numbers with recitative. Prologue. Ballet. Composer's manuscript not extant. Contemporary copies lack orchestration. Numerous problems associated with period practice and ornamentation. Version edited by Luigi Dallapiccola.

Sets: 5. **Acts:** 3 acts, 13 scenes. **Length:** I: 75. II: 70 III: 45. **Arias:** "O gran figlio d'Ulisse" (Eumete), "Godo anc'io" (Ulisse), "Illustratevi o cieli" (Penelope). **Hazards:** I: Nettuno turns the Feaci and their ship into stone. Ulisse transformed into an old man. II: A scene on a moving chariot. A ray of fire comes down from the sky, the earth opens and Ulisse disappears into the rift. An eagle flies over the heads of Penelope's suitors. **Scenes:** Prologue. Unspecified. Ii. The royal palace. Iii. At sea. Iiii. A seashore. Iiv. The palace. Iv. A forest. IIi. On a chariot. IIii. The seashore. IIiii. The palace. IIiv. In the forest. IIv. The palace. IIIi. The palace. IIIii. The sea. IIIiii. The palace.

Major roles: Penelope (soprano), Melanto (soprano), Ulisse (tenor), Telemaco (tenor). **Minor roles:** Human frailty (soprano), Time (bass), Fortune (soprano), Cupid (soprano), Giunone (soprano), Eurimaco (tenor), Nettuno (bass), Giove (tenor), Phaeacian (tenor), Minerva (soprano), Eumete (tenor), Iro (tenor), Antinoo (bass), Pisandro (tenor), Anfinomo (countertenor or contralto). **Bit part:** Ericlea (mezzo).

Chorus parts: SSATTB. **Chorus roles:** Sailors, heavenly spirits. **Dance/movement:** II: Ballet of the Moors for Penelope. **Orchestra:** Strings, continuo (theorbo, cembalo, harp, etc.). **Stageband:** None. **Publisher:** Zerboni. **Rights:** Expired.

Prologue. The gods confess they will make Ulisse miserable. Ii. Penelope prays for the return of her husband, Ulisse. Her maid, Melanto, agrees to help Penelope's suitors. Iii. Giove allows Nettuno to punish the Feaci. Nettuno turns the Feaci and their ship into stone. Iiii. Ulisse wakes on an abandoned seashore, abandoned—he believes—by the Feaci. Minerva disguises Ulisse as an old beggar to demonstrate Penelope's faithfulness. Minerva goes to fetch Ulisse's son, Telemaco. Iiv. Melanto tries to persuade Penelope to take a lover. Iv. The shepherd Eumete ponders the unhappiness of kings. He chases away Penelope's gluttonous suitor, Iro. He does not recognize Ulisse, but takes him in.

IIi. Minerva brings Telemaco home. IIii. Still disguised, Ulisse assures Telemaco that Ulisse is returning. He is swallowed by the earth and reappears in his natural form for Telemaco. IIiii. Melanto cannot convince Penelope. Antinoo, Pisandro and Anfinomo woo Penelope. They entertain her with a dance. Eumete tells Penelope of Ulisse's return. The suitors wonder how to defend themselves when Ulisse returns. IIiv. Minerva instructs Ulisse that she will have Penelope propose an archery contest. Eumete reports back to Ulisse. IIv. Telemaco tells his mother of Helen's beauty. Ulisse returns, again disguised as an old beggar. He beats Iro in a fight and is welcomed by Penelope. She proposes to give herself to anyone who can bend Ulisse's bow. The suitors try and fail. Ulisse succeeds and kills all the suitors but Iro.

IIIi. Iro is frightened and (as usual) hungry. Penelope is distraught. Eumete explains that the old man is Ulisse, but Penelope does not believe him. Telemaco tries to convince her. IIIii. Minerva persuades Giunone to intercede with Giove on Ulisse's behalf. Giove and Nettuno both agree to let Ulisse return home. IIIiii. Ericlea wonders if she should reveal her secret. Telemaco has not yet convinced Penelope. Even Ulisse's appearance in his own form does not convince her until Ericlea confirms his identity—and Ulisse describes Penelope's bed. Penelope welcomes Ulisse home.

Robert le Diable • Robert the Devil

Composed by Giacomo Meyerbeer (September 5, 1791 – May 2, 1864).
Libretto by Eugène Scribe. French. Based on a sketch by Germain
Delavigne. Premiered Paris, Opéra, November 21, 1831. Set in Sicily in
the 13th century. Grand opera. Set numbers with recitative. Overture.
Entr'acte before each act. Ballet.

Sets: 6. **Acts:** 5 acts, 6 scenes. **Length:** I, II, III, IV, V: 165. **Arias:** "En vain
j'espère un sort prospère" (Isabelle), "Je t'ai trompé je fus coupable"
(Bertram). **Hazards:** III: Flames issue from the cave. Stone figures
become animated. V: Bertram sinks into the earth. **Scenes:** I. The Lido
with a view of the port of Palermo. II. The ruins of an ancient temple on
the mountainous rocks of St. Irene. IIIi. The mysterious vaults. IIIii. An
apartment in the palace of the King of Sicily. IV. Isabelle's private apartments. V. A cloister.

Major roles: Robert (tenor), Bertram (bass), Alice (soprano), Isabelle
(soprano). **Minor roles:** Alberti (bass or baritone), Raimbaut (tenor),
Maid of honor (soprano or mezzo). **Bit parts:** First knight (tenor), Second
knight (tenor), Third knight (bass or baritone), Gambler (baritone),
Herald (tenor), Master of ceremonies (tenor), Fourth knight (bass), Priest
(baritone or bass). **Mute:** Helen the abbess, King of Sicily, Prince of
Grenada.

Chorus parts: SSAATTBB. **Chorus roles:** Knights, courtiers, heralds,
pages, pilgrims, peasants, chaplains, priests, servants, ladies, nuns, gamblers. **Dance/movement:** II: Dance. III: Nun ballet. **Orchestra:** picc, 2 fl, 2
ob (Eng hrn), 2 cl, 2 bsn, 4 hrn, 2 trp, 3 trb, ophicléide, timp, perc, 2 harp,
strings. **Stageband:** II: 2 hrn, 4 trp, trb, drum. IV: picc, 4 trp, 4 hrn, 3 trb,
ophicléide, perc. V: organ. **Publisher:** Bergère, Garland Publishing.
Rights: Expired.

I. Robert comes to Sicily, having been banished from his native
Normandy. He is infuriated by his countryman Raimbaut, who spreads
the story that Robert's father was a devil. Raimbaut is engaged to
Robert's foster sister, Alice, who tells him his mother has died and gives
him her will. Robert does not feel up to reading the will, but he tells
Alice of his hopeless love for the Princess Isabelle. Alice suspects
Robert's friend Bertram of evil. Bertram convinces Robert to gamble and
Robert loses everything.

II. Bertram seduces Raimbaut with gold. Alice sees Bertram conversing
with fiends in a cavern, but he threatens her into silence. Bertram only
has until midnight to win Robert's soul, so he persuades him to try to
win a magic vault out of the mystic vaults.

IIIi. Bertram calls forth dead nuns to seduce Robert, but Robert wrests the mystic branch from them. IIIii. Isabelle rebukes Robert for deserting her until Alice delivers a letter from him.

IV. Bertram entrances Robert so that he misses the tournament at which Isabelle is the prize. Robert uses the magic branch to put the court to sleep so he can abduct Isabelle. He is only prevented by Isabelle herself, who appeals to his better nature.

V. Robert realizes that Bertram is his father—and the devil. Alice tells him he has not lost Isabella: she still waits for him. She reads him his mother's will, which warns him against Bertram. Midnight strikes and Bertram sinks into the earth, having failed to win Robert's soul.

Roberto Devereux

Composed by Gaetano Donizetti (November 29, 1797 – April 8, 1848). Libretto by Salvatore Cammarano. Italian. Based on "Élisabeth d'Angleterre" by François Ancelot. Premiered Naples, Teatro San Carlo, October 29, 1837. Set in London in the late 16th century. Lyric tragedy. Set numbers with recitative. Prelude.

Sets: 5. **Acts:** 3 acts, 7 scenes. **Length:** I: 65. II: 25. III: 45. **Arias:** "A te dirò" (Roberto), "Vivi, ingrato" (Elisabetta). **Hazards:** None. **Scenes:** I. Hall in Westminster Palace. IIi. Magnificent state apartment. IIii. Apartments of the duchess in Nottingham Palace. IIiii. The hall in Westminster Palace. IIIi. Apartments of the duchess. IIIii. Prison in the tower of London. IIIiii. Royal apartments.

Major roles: Duchess Sara (mezzo), Queen Elisabetta (soprano), Count Roberto Devereux (tenor), Lord Nottingham (baritone). **Minor roles:** Lord Cecil (tenor), Sir Gualtiero Raleigh (bass). **Bit parts:** Page (bass), Friend of Nottingham (bass). **Mute:** Messenger.

Chorus parts: SATTB. **Chorus roles:** Lords, ladies, knights, soldiers, pages, guards, retainers. **Dance/movement:** None. **Orchestra:** picc, 2 fl, 2 ob (Eng hrn), 2 cl, 2 bsn, 4 hrn, 2 trp, 3 trb, timp, perc, strings. **Stageband:** None. **Publisher:** G. Ricordi, Garland publishing. **Rights:** Expired.

I. Sara, Duchess of Nottingham, is oppressed by a secret grief. She and Queen Elisabetta await the return of the banished Earl of Essex, Roberto Devereux. The queen loves Roberto, but he stands accused of treason. Roberto denies the charges, but the queen realizes he loves another. Roberto refuses to name his love and the queen meditates revenge.

IIi. Roberto confides his problem to his friend the Duke of Nottingham. Parliament convenes to try Roberto. IIii. Sara loves Roberto. Roberto accuses Sara of betraying him, but she explains the queen forced her to marry Nottingham. Sara begs Roberto to flee. IIiii. The trial occurs. Roberto is condemned. Gualtiero gives the queen a scarf knitted by Sara, but found on Roberto. Nottingham begs the queen to pardon Roberto. She refuses. The queen confronts Roberto with the scarf. Nottingham recognizes it. The queen offers to spare Roberto's life if he names Sara. He refuses and the queen signs his death warrant.

IIIi. Sara awaits news of the trial. She remembers the ring Roberto gave her: he received it from the queen, who said that if he ever presented it back to her, she would ensure his safety. Nottingham prevents Sara from taking the ring to the queen. IIIii. Roberto hopes for a pardon. He is horrified to realize there will be no pardon and blames Sara. IIIiii. The queen's anger has subsided and she hopes Roberto will present the ring in time to save himself. Sara is announced. She brings the ring and admits she is the queen's rival. Elisabetta orders the execution halted, but it is too late. Crushed, Elisabetta decides to abdicate.

Le Roi d'Ys • The King of Ys

Composed by Édouard Lalo (January 27, 1823 – April 22, 1892). Libretto by Édouard Blau. French. Based on a Breton legend. Premiered Paris, Opéra Comique, May 7, 1888. Set in the Kingdom of Ys in legendary times. Tragedy. Through composed. Overture.

Sets: 5. **Acts:** 3 acts, 5 scenes. **Length:** I, II, III: 110. **Arias:** "Vainement ma bien-aimée" (Mylio). **Hazards:** II: Statue of Saint Corentin comes to life. III: Ys floods. Margared throws herself into the sea. Vision of Saint Corentin over the waters. **Scenes:** I. A terrace in the palace of the Kings of Ys. IIi. A great hall in the palace of Ys. IIii. An immense plain before Ys. IIIi. A gallery in the palace of Ys. IIIii. A flat hill top.

Major roles: Rozenn (soprano), Margared (mezzo), King (bass). **Minor roles:** Jahel (baritone), Karnac (baritone), Mylio (tenor), Saint Corentin (bass or baritone).

Chorus parts: SSSAAATTTBBB. **Chorus roles:** People of Ys, maids of honor, Karnac's warriors, soldiers of Ys, young lords, companions of Mylio, young girls, attendants and friends of Rozenn. **Dance/movement:** None. **Orchestra:** 2 fl, 2 cl, 2 ob, 2 bsn, 4 hrn, 4 trp, 3 trb, tuba, timp, 2 perc, organ, strings. **Stageband:** I, II: 4 trp. **Publisher:** Heugel & Co. **Rights:** Expired.

I. The citizens of Ys rejoice that the Princess Margared's marriage to Prince Karnac will end the war. Princess Rozenn senses her sister's unhappiness. Margared secretly loves Mylio—who is believed dead— but is determined to do her duty. Mylio is not dead and he returns to Rozenn—whom he loves and who loves him. The king welcomes Karnac. Hearing that Mylio lives, Margared calls off her wedding. Karnac swears to revenge himself on Ys, but Mylio defies him.

IIi. Margared is furious that Mylio loves Rozenn. Mylio prepares for battle. The king promises Mylio Rozenn's hand if he is victorious. Margared curses her sister and hopes Mylio dies in battle. IIiii. Mylio's army is victorious, but Margared flees Ys and tells Karnac how to flood the city by raising the sluice gates. Saint Corentin appears and warns the pair to repent.

IIIi. Mylio comes to wed Rozenn. The thought of the happy couple persuades Margared to help Karnac in spite of the saint's warning. She overhears Rozenn and the king hoping for her own return. Overcome with remorse, she warns them of the impending flood. Mylio kills Karnac. IIIii. The survivors of the flooded city have fled to a hill top, but the waters continue to rise. Margared realizes she must sacrifice herself to save the others. Over Rozenn and the king's objections, she throws herself into the sea. Saint Corentin appears and the waters recede.

Le Roi Malgré Lui • The King in Spite of Himself

Composed by Emmanuel Chabrier (January 18, 1841 – September 13, 1894). Libretto by Émile de Najac and Paul Burani. French. Based on the play by Jacques-Arsène Ancelot. Premiered Paris, Opéra Comique, May 18, 1887. Set in Cracow, Poland in 1574. Comic opera. Set numbers with recitative. Prelude. Introduction before II. Entr'acte before III. Revised by Albert Carré in 1929.

Sets: 3. **Acts:** 3 acts, 3 scenes. **Length:** I, II, III: 130. **Arias:** "L'amour ce divin maître" (Minka). **Hazards:** None. **Scenes:** I. A winter garden of a palace. II. A banquet room at the estate of the grand palatine, Laski. III. A room in a tavern.

Major roles: Count of Nangis (tenor), Duke of Fritelli (comic baritone), Minka (soprano), King Henri of Valois (baritone), Alexina (soprano). **Minor roles:** Caylus (baritone), Liancourt (tenor), Maugiron (baritone), Villequier (bass), D'Elbeuf (tenor), Laski (bass), Basile (tenor). **Bit parts:** Soldier (bass), Six servants (3 soprano, 3 alto).

Chorus parts: SSAATTTTBBBB. **Chorus roles:** Pages, French gentlemen gamblers, Polish ladies and gentlemen, soldiers, people. **Dance/movement:** II: Ballroom dancing at Laski's estate. **Orchestra:** 2 fl (picc), 2 ob, 2 cl, 2 bsn, 4 hrn, 3 trp, 3 trb, timp, perc, 2 harp, strings. **Stageband:** None. **Publisher:** Enoch & Co. **Rights:** Expired.

I. Henri of Valois is poised to become king of Poland. Minka falls in love with the Count of Nangis, who has rescued her from a soldier's advances. Alexina is ambitious for her husband, Fritelli. Not realizing who Henri is, Minka warns him of a plot against the throne. The king's play acting deceives Alexina—who concludes that Nangis is the king—while the king himself misunderstands and arrests the loyal Nangis. Disguised as a commoner, Henri encounters Alexina with whom he had an affair in Venice years ago. Her husband, Fritelli, knows the king's true identity. Alexina incites Henri against the king. Nangis escapes from prison.

II. Laski and his fellow Polish aristocrats conspire against Henri. Alexina introduces Henri to Laski as a fellow plotter. Fritelli is loath to participate in their plans, but Henri eggs on the conspirators. The conspirators mistake Nangis for the king and Henri orders him to play along. When Henri realizes that the conspirators mean to kill Nangis, he reveals himself, but no one believes him. Henri is chosen to kill the king. Minka frees Nangis. Henri promises to find and kill the king.

III. Minka is overjoyed to find that Nangis has escaped. Henri and Nangis reveal their true identities. The king pardons Nangis and promotes Fritelli.

Roméo et Juliette • Romeo and Juliet

Composed by Charles François Gounod (June 17, 1818 – October 18, 1893). Libretto by Jules Barbier and Michel Carré. French. Based on the play by Shakespeare. Premiered Paris, Théâtre Lyrique, April 27, 1867. Set in Verona in the 14th century. Romantic tragedy. Set numbers with recitative. Overture-prologue with chorus. Ballet. Entr'actes before II, III and V.

Sets: 6. **Acts:** 5 acts, 6 scenes. **Length:** I, II, III, IV, V: 220. **Arias:** "Mab, la reine des mensonges"/Ballad of Queen Mab (Mercutio), "Je veux vivre" (Juliette), "L'amour, oui, son ardeur a troublé" (Roméo), "Que fais-tu blanche tourterelle" (Stéphano), "Amour ranime mon courage" (Juliette). **Hazards:** None. **Scenes:** I. Capulet's Palace. II. The garden of Juliet. IIIi. The cell of Friar Laurence. IIIii. A public square before Capulet's palace. IV. Juliet's chamber. V. Tomb of the Capulets.

Major roles: Juliette (soprano), Roméo (tenor), Mercutio (baritone), Capulet (bass). **Minor roles:** Gertrude (mezzo), Tybalt (tenor), Stéphano (soprano or mezzo), Friar Laurent (bass), Duke (bass), Grégorio (baritone), Pâris (baritone), Benvolio (tenor). **Bit parts:** Manuela (soprano), Pepita (mezzo), Angelo (tenor) (All three of these parts occur only in the act IV finale, which is usually omitted.)

Chorus parts: SATTBB. **Chorus roles:** Guests of Capulet, friends of Roméo (6 tenors, 6 basses), relatives and retainers of the Capulets and Montagues. **Dance/movement:** I: Capulet's ball. IV: Wedding procession ballet. **Orchestra:** 2 fl (picc), 2 ob (Eng hrn), 2 cl, 2 bsn, 4 hrn, 2 trp (2 cornet), 3 trb, tuba, timp, perc, 2 harp, strings. **Stageband:** I: 2 harps (can be in pit). IV: organ. **Publisher:** Schirmer, Kalmus. **Rights:** Expired.

Prologue. The chorus recounts the feud between two powerful families, which nothing but the deaths of Roméo and Juliette could overcome. I. Capulet's guests dance at the ball. Tybalt points out Juliette to Paris. It is Juliette's birthday and she is overcome by the splendor of the party. Capulet invites everyone to dance. Roméo, Mercutio and their friends retire to a corner of the palace where Mercutio sings the ballad of Queen Mab. Roméo has a premonition of trouble to come; he sees Juliette and is overcome with love. Mercutio is amused at how quickly Roméo has forgotten his love for Rosaline. Juliette's nurse, Gertrude, draws her attention to Paris, but Juliette says she is not yet ready to give up the daydreams of youth. Gertrude is called off to supper, leaving Roméo alone with his love. Roméo woos Juliette but is interrupted by Tybalt. Only now does Roméo realize that Juliette is the daughter of his family's sworn enemy. Juliette is brought to the same realization when Tybalt identifies Roméo in spite of his disguise. Tybalt swears to kill Roméo but Capulet forbids him to ruin the party.

II. Roméo slips into Juliette's garden. He overhears Juliette confess her love and presents himself at her balcony. They hear the approach of Gregorio and company who are angrily searching for Roméo. Gregorio explains to Gertrude what has happened. Juliette promises Roméo to arrange a meeting place where they may be married. They say their farewells.

IIIi. Roméo, Juliette and Gertrude meet in Friar Laurence's cell. The friar consents to marry the lovers in hopes of ending the feud. IIIii. Roméo's page, Stephano, cannot find his master. He provokes the Capulets by singing to them to guard their "dainty darling." Gregorio and Stephano fight followed by Tybalt and Mercutio. Roméo appears but ignores Tybalt's insults. Infuriated by Roméo's apparent cowardice, Mercutio fights Tybalt and is slain. In revenge, Roméo kills Tybalt. The Prince banishes Roméo.

IV. Roméo visits Juliette in her room. She forgives him for Tybalt's death and they bid a fond farewell. Capulet says it was Tybalt's dying wish that Juliette marry Paris. All is prepared, and Capulet leaves the friar with Juliette while he goes to greet the wedding guests. Friar Laurence gives Juliette a potion that simulates death. Once everyone has given her up for dead, Roméo will spirit her away, he says. Juliette has misgivings but takes the potion. A ballet of the wedding procession. Juliette falls, apparently dead, at Capulet's feet.

V. Friar Laurence tries, unsuccessfully, to deliver a letter to Roméo outlining his plans. Roméo enters Juliette's tomb, thinking she is dead. He poisons himself. Juliette awakes in time to see Roméo die. She stabs herself.

La Rondine • The Swallow

Composed by Giacomo Puccini (December 22, 1858 – November 29, 1924). Libretto by Giuseppe Adami. Italian. Based on libretto by Dr. Alfred Maria Willner and Heinz Reichert. Premiered Monte Carlo, Théâtre de Monte Carlo, March 27, 1917. Set in Paris in the mid-19th century. Lyric comedy. Set numbers with accompanied recitative. Prelude.

Sets: 3. **Acts:** 3 acts, 3 scenes. **Length:** I: 40. II: 30. III: 35. **Arias:** "Che il bel sogno" (Magda). **Hazards:** None. **Scenes:** I. An elegant salon in Magda's house in Paris. II. At Bullier's. III. A small summer house on a hill.

Major roles: Magda (soprano), Lisette (soprano), Rambaldo (baritone), Ruggero (tenor), Prunier (tenor). **Minor roles:** Périchaud (bass baritone), Gobin (tenor), Crébillon (bass baritone), Yvette (soprano), Bianca (soprano), Suzy (mezzo), Rabonniero (bass). **Bit parts:** Major Domo (bass), Georgette (soprano), Gabriella (soprano), Lolette (soprano), Adolfo (tenor), Two women (2 soprano), Three men (3 tenor), Youth (tenor), Two students (2 tenor), Three girls (3 soprano).

Chorus parts: SATTBB. **Chorus roles:** Students, artists, men about town, grisettes, demimondaines, dancers, waiters, four flower girls. There are many small groups and solo bits in II; groups involving fewer than 4 on a part are shown in role classifications above. **Dance/movement:** II: Customers and grisettes as Bullier's. **Orchestra:** picc, 2 fl, 2 ob, Eng hrn, 2 cl, bs cl, 2 bsn, 4 hrn, 3 trp, 3 trb, tuba, harp, glockenspiel, celeste, timp, perc, strings. **Stageband:** None. **Publisher:** Universal/Casa Sonzogno. **Rights:** Expired.

Ii. In Magda's Paris home, Prunier tells the women that love and passion are all the fashion in Paris. He sings his latest composition. Magda is intrigued, but she is a kept woman, supported by Rambaldo. She accepts Rambaldo's presents, but admits she does not love him. Magda remembers the night she escaped her ever-watchful aunt and went dancing. She fell in love with a young student, but they parted. Prunier predicts each woman's future. Ruggero enters with a letter of introduction to Rambaldo. Rambaldo asks Prunier how his guest should spend his first night in Paris. Prunier scoffs but everyone gathers around, offering sight-seeing suggestions. Magda's guests take their leave. Prunier meets Lisette in secret. He is fascinated by the maid, he admits. On a sudden inspiration, Magda disguises herself as a grisette and leaves for the cabaret.

II. The customers at Bullier sing, dance and drink. Magda is accosted by several students. She dances with Ruggero and they fall in love. Prunier scolds Lisette. The maid recognizes Magda, but Prunier convinces her it is a different person. They introduce themselves and Lisette confesses to Magda that she borrowed her mistress's clothes without permission. The crowd showers the four lovers with flowers. Rambaldo appears. At Magda's insistence, Prunier hurries Ruggero away. Rambaldo recognizes Magda and demands an explanation. She says she loves Ruggero and means to stay with him. Magda and Ruggero vow their eternal love.

III. Ruggero and Magda have escaped to a cottage on the Riviera. He wonders how they will pay their bills and confesses that he has asked his parents for permission to marry her. She is overcome and realizes she must tell him the truth. Lisette and Prunier come looking for Magda. They fight over Lisette's disastrous and brief stage career and Prunier's constant criticism. Lisette begs Magda for her old job back, and Magda agrees. Prunier points out to Magda that she cannot live this way forever and transmits a message from "one who would help her." Ruggero returns with a letter from his parents: They have agreed to the marriage. Magda confesses her past. Fulfilling Prunier's prediction, she bids her griefstricken lover farewell—and flies back to her former life.

Der Rosenkavalier • The Cavalier of the Rose

Composed by Richard Strauss (June 11, 1864 – September 8, 1949). Libretto by Hugo von Hofmannsthal. German. Original work. Premiered Dresden, Hofoper, January 26, 1911. Set in Vienna in the 1740s (early years of the reign of Maria Theresia). Music comedy. Through composed. Introduction before I & III. Pantomime before III. Opus 59.

Sets: 3. **Acts:** 3 acts, 3 scenes. **Length:** I: 65. II: 55. III: 60. **Arias:** "Di rigori

armato il seno" (Italian tenor), "Die Zeit" (Marschallin). **Hazards:** None.
Scenes: I. The bedroom of the princess. II. Room in Herr von Faninal's
house. III. A private room in an inn.

Major roles: Princess von Werdenberg the Marschallin (soprano),
Octavian (mezzo), Baron Ochs of Lerchenau (bass), Sophie (high soprano). **Minor roles:** Herr von Faninal (high baritone), Major domo of the
Princess (tenor), Four footmen of the princess (2 tenor, 2 bass), Italian
Singer (high tenor), Princess's attorney (bass), Valzacchi (tenor), Annina
(contralto), Mistress Marianne Leitmetzer (high soprano), Major domo
of Faninal (tenor), Innkeeper (tenor), Four waiters (1 tenor, 3 bass),
Commissary of police (bass). **Bit parts:** Three noble orphans (soprano,
mezzo, alto), Milliner (soprano), Animal vendor (tenor). **Mute:** Scholar,
Flute player, Hairdresser, Hairdresser's assistant, Widow of noble family, Indian servant boy.

Chorus parts: SAATTBBBB. **Chorus roles:** Footmen, couriers, heyducks,
cook boys, guests, musicians, two watchmen, four little children, various
personages of suspicious appearance. **Dance/movement:** None.
Orchestra: 3 fl (picc), 3 ob (Eng hrn), 3 cl, bs cl (basset hrn), 3 bsn (cont
bsn), 4 hrn, 3 trp, 3 trb, tuba, timp, 3 perc, celeste, 2 harp, strings (16-16-
12-10-8). **Stageband:** III: 2 fl, ob, 3 cl, 2 bsn, 2 hrn, trp, perc, harmonium,
piano, string quintet (2 vln, vla, vlc, cont bs). **Publisher:** Boosey &
Hawkes. **Rights:** Copyright 1910 by Adolph Fürstner. Renewed 1938.
Assigned 1943 to Boosey & Hawkes.

I. The princess and Octavian exchange vows of love. The princess
dreamed that her husband came home. They hear a noise and Octavian
hides in the curtains. It is the oafish Baron Ochs. Octavian tries to leave,
disguised as a maid, but the baron is attracted to "her." The baron
announces his intention to marry the 15-year-old Sophia, daughter of the
merchant, Faninal. He asks the princess who he should have convey a
silver rose to Sophia and brags about his love affairs. The princess proposes he send Octavian—who is the twin of the maid, she claims. A
group of petitioners pesters the princess. The baron insists the princess's
lawyer find a way of requiring his bride-to-be to pay him a dowry.
When Valzacchi and Annina offer to spy for the baron, he sets them to
find out about the princess's maid. Once everyone has gone, the princess
remembers her own marriage at a young age and contemplates her mortality. She greets Octavian's renewed vows of love with a worldly skepticism, telling him that he will leave her some day. Octavian denies it.
She sends him away and sends the rose after him.

II. Herr von Faninal and Sophia receive Octavian. The two young people
fall in love. The baron enters and behaves like a boor, although his title
dazzles all but Sophia. When the baron retires to talk with his lawyer,

Octavian promises to help Sophia escape the baron's clutches. Valzacchi and Annina catch the pair, but the baron is only amused. The baron tries to drag Sophia into the next room, but Octavian challenges him to fight. Octavian wounds the baron, but is grabbed by the servants. Faninal insists Sophia will marry the baron. The baron meanwhile has recovered and still means to marry Sophia. He receives a letter supposedly from the princess's maid who wants to see him.

III. Octavian bribes Valzacchi and Annina to help him. They lay a trap for the baron and Octavian again disguises himself as the maid. The baron tries to seduce the maid, but finds her resemblance to Octavian unnerving. He catches glimpses of Octavian's men who are concealed in the room. Annina interrupts, claiming to be the baron's wife. A scene ensues and the police are called. To escape the charge of leading a young girl astray, the baron claims Octavian is Sophia. He is surprised when Faninal arrives thinking that the baron has sent for him. Faninal is furious at being drawn into a scandal. The princess arrives and introductions are made. Sophia tells the baron to stay away from her. The joke is explained to him and the princess orders him out. He is chased out by the servants who demand payment. Painfully, the princess resigns Octavian to Sophia.

Le Rossignol

See "The Nightingale" entry.

The Ruby

Composed by Norman Dello Joio (b. January 24, 1913). Libretto by William Mass. English. Based on the play "A Night at an Inn" by Lord Dunsany. Premiered Bloomington, Indiana, University of Indiana, Mary 13, 1955. Set in England in the late 19th/early 20th century. Lyric drama. Set numbers with recitative. Prelude.

Sets: 1. **Acts:** 1 act, 1 scene. **Length:** I: 55. **Hazards:** I: Ruby gives off a fiery glow. Scott's men stab the three priests to death. The stone idol returns, covered in blood, and puts the ruby back in its eye socket. **Scenes:** I. The main room of a lonely house on the moors.

Major roles: Scott (baritone), Laura (soprano). **Minor roles:** Sniggers (tenor), Bull (bass), Albert (tenor). **Mute:** Three Indian priests, Stone idol.

Chorus parts: N/A. **Chorus roles:** None. **Dance/movement:** None.
Orchestra: picc, 2 fl, 2 ob, Eng hrn, 2 cl, bs cl, 2 bsn, 4 hrn, 3 trp, 2 trb, bs

trb, tuba, timp, celeste, harp, perc, strings. **Stageband:** None. **Publisher:** G. Ricordi & Co. **Rights:** Copyright 1955 by G. Ricordi & Co.

I. Sniggers, Bull, Albert and Scott have stolen the ruby out of a stone idol and are being tracked by three Indian priests. Albert sees the priests in town and wants to flee, but Scott insists they stay. Scott persuades his wife, Laura, to come back to him. The priests arrive, but Scott's men kill them. Laura is horrified. The stone idol kills Scott's men and summons Scott to follow.

Rusalka

Composed by Antonín Dvořák (September 8, 1841 – May 1, 1904). Libretto by Jaroslav Kvapil. Czech. Based on "Ondine" by Friedrich de la Motte Fouqué, "The Little Mermaid" by Hans Christian Andersen and "Die Versunkene Glocke" by Gerhard Hauptmann. Premiered Prague, Nationaltheater, March 31, 1901. Set near a lake and castle in legendary times. Lyric fairy tale. Set numbers with accompanied recitative. Overture. Ballet. Entr'actes before II and III. Opus 114.

Sets: 2. **Acts:** 3 acts, 3 scenes. **Length:** I: 55. II: 45. III: 50. **Arias:** "O silver moon" (Rusalka). **Hazards:** I, III: Water gnome and Rusalka enter from, and remain in, the lake. **Scenes:** I. A meadow on the edge of a lake. II. The grounds of the prince's castle. III. The meadow.

Major roles: Water gnome (bass), Rusalka (soprano), Witch (mezzo), Prince (tenor). **Minor roles:** Three wood sprites (2 sopranos, alto), Gamekeeper (tenor), Turnspit (soprano), Foreign princess (soprano). **Bit parts:** Hunter (baritone).

Chorus parts: SSSAATTBB. **Chorus roles:** Wood sprites, hunters, guests at the castle. **Dance/movement:** I, III: Wood sprites dance. II: Ballet of the wedding guests. **Orchestra:** picc, 2 fl, 2 ob, Eng hrn, 2 cl, bs cl, 2 bsn, 4 hrn, 3 trp, 3 trb, tuba, timp, 2 perc, harp, strings. **Stageband:** I: hunting horns. III: accordian. **Publisher:** Supraphon. **Rights:** Expired.

I. The water gnome tries to catch one of the water sprites but they run away. The gnome is Rusalka's father and Rusalka begs him to let her become human. He rightly guesses that she loves a mortal and is heartbroken. Rusalka wonders where her love is. She asks the witch to help her become mortal. The witch agrees on condition that Rusalka be mute forevermore. If she loses her love, Rusalka must forever return to the waters—and her lover will be damned. The witch makes Rusalka mortal. Rusalka's prince, exhausted from hunting, finds Rusalka and falls in love.

II. A turnspit and his uncle, a gamekeeper, wonder at the bustle in the castle. They fear Rusalka is an evil spirit and hope the prince will forget her. A foreign princess wants the prince for herself and chides him for being an inattentive host. She tries to get Rusalka to speak. The water gnome comforts Rusalka, who fears the prince has forgotten her. Father and daughter overhear the prince declare his love for the foreign princess. The water gnome reclaims Rusalka and the prince falls unconscious.

III. Rusalka, abandoned by her love and shunned by the other water nymphs, wishes for death. She appeals to the witch, who tells her she can go back to her old life if she kills the prince. Rusalka refuses. The gamekeeper and his nephew come to ask the witch's help. The prince is sick, cursed—they believe—by Rusalka. The water gnome drives them away. The water sprites play. The prince comes in search of Rusalka. She warns him away, but he is determined to join her. They kiss and he dies in her arms.

Russlan and Ludmilla

Composed by Mikhail Ivanovich Glinka (June 1, 1804 – February 15, 1857). Libretto by Valerian Fyodorovich Shirkov, Nestor Vasileyvich Kukolnik, K. A. Bakturin, Mikhail Alexandrovich Gedeonov, Nikolai Andreyevich Markevich and Mikhail Glinka. Russian. Based on the poem by Pushkin. Premiered St. Petersburg, Bolshoi Theater, November 27 (December 9), 1842. Set in the Ukraine in the 10th century. Romantic opera. Set numbers with recitative. Overture. Entr'acte before each act. Ballet.

Sets: 7. **Acts:** 5 acts, 8 scenes. **Length:** I, II, III, IV, V: 190. **Arias:** "Oh field, who has bestrewn thee with dead bones?" (Russlan), "Sultry heat has supplanted shade of night" (Ratmir), "Far from my beloved and constrained" (Chernomor). **Hazards:** II: Severed head of Chernomor's brother (voice sung by the chorus). III: Naina's castle transformed into a forest. Table with food rises out of the ground. Magic battle between Russlan and Chernomor. **Scenes:** I. Svetozar's palace in Kiev. IIi. Finn's cell. IIii. On the road. IIiii. A desert. III. Naina's magic castle. IV. Chernomor's magic gardens. Vi. A wide field before a warrior's camp. Vii. Svetozar's palace in Kiev.

Major roles: Ratmir (contralto), Farlaf (bass), Russlan (baritone), Ludmilla (soprano), Finn (tenor), Naina (mezzo). **Minor roles:** Grand Duke Svetozar (bass), Gorislava (soprano), Minstrel (tenor). **Mute:** Dwarf Chernomor.

Chorus parts: SATTBB. **Chorus roles:** Wedding guests, Naina's servants, subjects and slaves, fairies, Chernomor's slaves. **Dance/movement:** III: Ballet of Naina's girls dancing to bewitch Ratmir. IV: Ballet of the ondines and fairies. Oriental dances. **Orchestra:** picc, 2 fl, 2 ob (Eng hrn), 2 cl, 2 bsn, cont bsn, 4 hrn, 2 trp, 3 trb, timp, perc, piano, strings. **Stageband:** I: 6 hrn, 3 cornet, 2 tuba. IV: picc, 2 fl, 2 ob, 2 bsn, cont bsn, 6 cl, 4 hrn, 2 cornet, 4 trp, 3 trb, basset hrn, tuba, perc. V: picc, 2 fl, 2 ob, 2 bsn, cont bsn, 6 cl, 2 cornet, 4 hrn, 2 alto hrn, 2 tenor hrn, bs hrn, 4 trp, 3 trb, 2 tuba, perc. **Publisher:** Suvini Zerboni. **Rights:** Expired.

I. Bayan the minstrel entertains the guests at the wedding feast of Russlan, a Russian knight, and Ludmilla, daughter of Grand Duke Svetozar. Ratmir and Farlaf are present, although they both love Ludmilla. The thought of living abroad worries Ludmilla. Farlaf considers kidnaping her. The sky darkens and two weird creatures carry Ludmilla off. Svetozar promises half his kingdom—and Ludmilla—to the man who rescues her. All three suitors set off in pursuit.

IIi. Russlan consults the magician Finn who says Ludmilla is being held captive by the sorcerer Chernomor. IIii. Farlaf encounters the sorceress Naina who promises to help him. IIiii. Russlan wins a sword from the giant severed head that guards it. The head belongs to the brother of Chernomor.

III. Out of love, Gorislava has followed Ratmir. Naina and her dancing girls seduce Ratmir and Russlan. The men are rescued by Finn, who destroys Naina's castle.

IV. Chernomor's servants try to console Ludmilla. Chernomor puts her into a magic sleep before he is defeated in battle by Russlan. Russlan takes the unconscious Ludmilla home.

Vi. Ratmir renounces his harem for Gorislava. Ludmilla is kidnapped by Naina. Finn gives Ratmir a magic ring to give to Russlan. Vii. With Naina's help, Farlaf returns Ludmilla—still unconscious—to her father. Russlan uses the magic ring to revive her. The lovers are reunited.

Sadko

Composed by Nicolai Rimsky-Korsakov (March 18, 1844 – June 21, 1908). Libretto by Nicolai Rimsky-Korsakov and Vladimir Ivanovich Belsky. Russian. Based on the 11th century Novgorod Cycle.

Premiered Moscow, Solodovnikov Theater, January 7, 1898. Set in Novgorod in legendary times. Lyric legend. Set numbers with accompanied recitative. Introduction. Orchestral interludes before IIIii, IIIiii. Can also be done in 5 acts (2 scenes in II and IV; 1 in I, III, V).

Sets: 8. **Acts:** 3 acts, 7 scenes. **Length:** I: 55. II: 55. III: 60. **Arias:** Song of the Varangian merchant (Varangian merchant), Song of the Indian trader (Hindu merchant). **Hazards:** I: Swans transformed into young girls and back into swans. II: Sadko recovers golden fish from the lake. III: Scene set onboard a ship becalmed at sea. Sadko floats away on a plank. He descends to the sea king's underwater palace in a conch drawn by sea-gulls. Wedding procession of the marvels of the sea (scaled fish, whale, etc.). Dancing causes a hurricane. Sadko and princess sail to Novgorod on a conch. Volkhova turns into a river. Sadko's ships sail into the lake and anchor. **Scenes:** Ii. The vast halls of the sumptuous palace of the merchant's guild of Novgorod. Iii. On the banks of Lake Ilmen. IIi. A room in Sadko's house. IIii. The port of Novgorod. IIIi. The open sea. IIIii. The sea king's palace. IIIiii. At sea in a conch and a green meadow on Lake Ilmen.

Major roles: Sadko (tenor), Princess Volkhova (soprano), Sea King (bass), Lioubava Bousslaevna (mezzo). **Minor roles:** Sheriff Foma Nazaritch (tenor), Sheriff Luka Zinovitch (bass), Douda the jester (bass), Sopiel the jester (tenor), Niejata the singer (contralto), Varangian merchant (bass), Hindu merchant (tenor), Venetian merchant (baritone), Apparition (baritone). **Bit parts:** Two commediennes (2 tenor), Two spirits (2 tenor). **Mute:** Sea Queen.

Chorus parts: SSAATTBB. **Chorus roles:** Merchants, clowns, jester, young sea princesses, people, sailors, pilgrims, soothsayers, Sadko's companions, citizens of the undersea kingdom. **Dance/movement:** I: Clowns and jesters dance for the merchants. Sea princesses dance to Sadko's song. III: Dance of the inhabitants of the undersea kingdom; dance of the little fish with gold and silver scales. **Orchestra:** 3 fl (picc), 2 ob, Eng hrn, 3 cl (bs cl), 2 bsn, cont bsn, 4 hrn, 3 trp, 3 trb, tuba, timp, perc, 2 harp, piano, strings. **Stageband:** I: tambourines. II: bells, organ, harp. III: 3 trp. **Rights:** Expired.

Ii. The merchants of Novgorod, who are celebrating, invite Sadko to entertain them with a song. Instead he tells them he would not spend his time feasting if he had their money. They throw him out. Iii. By Lake Ilmen, Sadko sees swans transformed into the daughters of the sea king. He and the sea princess, Volkhova, fall in love. The daughters again become swans.

IIi. Sadko's wife, Lioubava, welcomes him home, but he rebuffs her. IIii. Sadko wagers his head that there are fish with golden scales in the lake. With Volkhova's help, he is proved correct. Sadko collects a group of followers and buys ships with which to explore and trade. After talking to three foreign merchants, Sadko sets sail for Venice.

IIIi. For twelve years Sadko has plied the sea without paying homage to the sea king. The king now takes revenge by becalming Sadko's ships. Sadko appeases the king by setting himself adrift on a plank. IIIii. He descends to the sea king's underwater palace. Impressed by Sadko's singing, the king lets him marry Volkhova. The dancing after the wedding is so frenzied it causes a hurricane. An apparition appears to put a stop to the destruction and admonishes Sadko for wasting his time. IIIiii. Volkhova and Sadko return to Novgorod. When Volkhova is turned into a river, Sadko goes back to his wife, Lioubava. The people of Novgorod praise Volkhova for giving them direct access to the sea.

Saffo

Composed by Giovanni Pacini (February 17, 1796 – December 6, 1867). Libretto by Salvatore Cammarano. Italian. Based on the play by Pietro Beltrame. Premiered Naples, Teatro San Carlo, November 29, 1840. Set in Greece at the time of the forty-second Olympiad. Lyric tragedy. Set numbers with recitative. Overture. Entr'acte before II.

Sets: 5. **Acts:** 3 acts, 5 scenes. **Length:** I, II, III: 130. **Hazards:** III: Saffo casts herself into the sea. **Scenes:** I. Exterior of the circus. IIi. Alcandro's apartments off of the temple of Apollo. IIii. Interior of the great temple. IIIi. A remote place. IIIii. The promontory of Leucadia overlooking the sea.

Major roles: High priest Alcandro (baritone), Faone (tenor), Saffo (soprano), Climene (mezzo). **Minor roles:** Ippio (tenor), Lisimaco (bass), Dirce (mezzo).

Chorus parts: SATTB. **Chorus roles:** Auspices, Climene's attendants, Greek citizens, people of Leucade, guards, guitar players, dancers. **Dance/movement:** None. **Orchestra:** 2 fl (picc), 2 ob, 2 cl, 2 bsn, 4 hrn, 2 trp, 3 trb, cimbasso, timp, perc, harp, strings. **Stageband:** I, II, III: band (trps, hrns, trbs, bsns, cimbasso). **Publisher:** Garland Publishing Inc. **Rights:** Expired.

I. Saffo publicly denounces the rites of Apollo, humiliating Apollo's high priest, Alcandro, who swears revenge. Alcandro tells Saffo's lover, Faone, that she is unfaithful to him. Faone believes him and rejects Saffo, ignoring her protestations of love.

IIi. Faone is engaged to Climene, Alcandro's daughter. Saffo begs Apollo's forgiveness and is received kindly by Climene. IIii. She recognizes Faone too late to stop the wedding. Infuriated, Saffo tears down the altar and is driven from the temple.

IIIi. Saffo again repents and begs to be allowed to perform the rite she denounced: the Leucadian leap, in which a penitent jumps—to his death—into the Aegean. The gods agree to allow the jump. Lisimaco reveals how he found the child Saffo on the beach and Alcandro realizes Saffo is his long-lost daughter. He asks the gods to release Saffo from the jump, but they refuse. IIIii. Saffo goes to cast herself into the sea.

Saint François d'Assise • Saint Francis of Assisi

Composed by Olivier Messiaen (December 10, 1908 – April 28, 1992). Libretto by Olivier Messiaen. French. Based on the 14th century religious texts "Fioretti" and "Considérations Sur les Stigmates." Premiered Paris, Palais Garnier, Opéra, November 28, 1983. Set in Italy in the 13th century. Religious drama. Through composed. Two orchestral episodes.

Sets: 6. **Acts:** 3 acts, 8 scenes. **Length:** I: 70. II: 105. III: 60. **Hazards:** II: Birds listen to St. François's preaching and then fly off. **Scenes:** Ii. A road. Iii. Interior of a little, cloistered church. Iiii. A room in the leper hospital, the Hospice of Saint Savior by the Walls. IIi – IIii. A monastery room and road on the mountain of La Verna. IIiii. Before the hermitage of the Carceri. IIIi. The mountain of La Verna. IIIii. Interior of the church of the Porziuncola at Saint Mary of the Angels.

Major roles: St. François (baritone). **Minor roles:** Brother Léon (baritone), Brother Sylvestre (bass), Brother Rufin (bass), Brother Bernard (bass), Leper (tenor), Angel (soprano), Brother Massée (tenor), Brother Élie (tenor).

Chorus parts: SSMAATTBaBB. **Chorus roles:** Offstage and visible upstage as indistinct black shapes (150 choristers total). **Dance/movement:** None. **Orchestra:** 3 picc, alto fl, 3 fl, 3 ob, Eng hrn, 5 cl, bs cl, cont bs cl, 3 bsn, cont bsn, 6 hrn, 4 trp, 3 trb, 2 tuba, bs tuba, perc, xylophone, xylorimba, marimba, glockenspiel, vibraphone, timp, strings (16-16-14-12-10). **Stageband:** None. **Rights:** Copyright 1983 by Olivier Messiaen.

Ii. St. François explains to Brother Léon that perfect happiness consists of willingly bearing injury and discomfort. Iii. He prays for strength to face and love his greatest fear: lepers. Iiii. St. François comforts a leper. An angel heals the leper.

IIi. An angel visits the monastery and asks the brothers about predestination. IIii. St. François has a vision of an angel who speaks to him about music. IIiii. St. François preaches to the birds.

IIIi. St. François receives the stigmata. IIIii. He dies, surrounded by his fellow monks.

The Saint of Bleecker Street

Composed by Gian Carlo Menotti (b. July 7, 1911). Libretto by Gian Carlo Menotti. English. Original work. Premiered New York City, Broadway Theatre, December 27, 1954. Set in New York City in the present. Music drama. Through composed with several musical interludes.

Sets: 5. **Acts:** 3 acts, 5 scenes. **Length:** I: 50. II: 30. III: 40. **Arias:** "Oh sweet Jesus, spare me this agony" (Annina), "I know that you all hate me" (Michele). **Hazards:** None. **Scenes:** Ii. A cold-water flat in the tenements of Bleecker Street. Iii. An empty lot on Mulberry Street. II. An Italian restaurant in the basement of a house on Bleecker Street. IIIi. A deserted passageway in a subway station. IIIii. Annina's room.

Major roles: Carmela (soprano), Don Marco (bass), Annina (soprano), Michele (tenor), Desideria (mezzo). **Minor roles:** Assunta (mezzo), Maria Corona (soprano), Young man (tenor), Young woman (soprano). **Bit parts:** Old man (bass) (can be done as soprano line by an old woman), Bartender (bass), First guest (tenor), Second guest (baritone), Salvatore (baritone), Women (soprano), Man's voice (tenor). **Speaking bits:** Maria's son (1 word), Screaming children (1 boy and 1 girl with spoken lines), Concettina (5-year-old girl). **Mute:** Nun, Young priest.

Chorus parts: SSAATTBB. **Chorus roles:** Neighbors, relatives and guests at Carmela's wedding. **Dance/movement:** II: Wedding guests dance. **Orchestra:** 3 fl, 2 ob (Eng hrn), 2 cl (bs cl), 2 bsn (cont bsn), 4 hrn, 3 trp, 3 trb, tuba, timp, perc, harp, piano, strings. **Stageband:** I: picc, 3 trp, trb, tuba, 2 perc. **Publisher:** G. Schirmer. **Rights:** Copyright 1953, 1954 by G. Schirmer Inc.

Ii. Assunta and the neighbors pray. They are waiting for Annina to heal and bless them. Maria Corona doubts Annina's powers, but Carmela and Assunta enumerate Annina's miracles and visions. The priest Don Marco brings in Annina, who has a vision of the Crucifixion and receives a stigmata. When everyone crowds in to touch her wounds, Annina's brother, Michele, throws them out. He is furious with Don Marco for exploiting his sister's pain and the neighbors' credulity. Iii. Carmela and Annina are dressing up Concettina as an angel for the parade. Michele has forbidden Annina to participate. When Carmela admits to Annina that she plans to marry rather than enter a convent with Annina, Annina is happy for her. The two women discuss heaven with Assunta. Maria Corona warns Annina that the Sons of San Gennaro insist that she participate in the procession. They are threatening to harm Michele. Maria Corona—a believer since Annina's touch cured her mute son—promises to protect Annina. Michele tells Annina that her visions are a product of illness, but her faith is unshakable. The procession appears. Some of the boys beat Michele and tie him up. In triumph, they lead off the frightened Annina. Desideria unties Michele and kisses him.

II. The guests dance at Carmela's and Salvatore's wedding and toasts are offered. Desideria arrives, uninvited, in search of her lover—Michele. She is bitter that sleeping with Michele has made her an outcast. As a proof of his love, Desideria asks Michele to take her into the banquet with him. He refuses, then relents, but Don Marco blocks his way. Do not make everyone hate you even more, he begs Michele. The guests rush in and Salvatore is angry with Michele for spoiling the wedding. "At least I am proud of my Italian heritage," Michele says: "I do not accept defeat as easily as you." The guests disperse. Desideria accuses Michele of being in love with his sister. When she refuses to take back the accusation, Michele stabs her. He flees as Desideria dies in Annina's arms.

IIIi. Annina and Maria Corona meet Michele in a subway station. A fugitive from the police, he says he lives only for Annina. She tells him she will die soon. When Annina announces her intention to take the veil, they argue and Michele curses his sister. IIIii. Carmela and Annina await the church's permission for Annina to take the veil. When Annina realizes she has no white dress for the ceremony, Carmela donates her wedding dress. The permission arrives. Don Marco tells Salvatore to guard the door in case Michele tries to interfere. Michele bursts in, but is too late. Don Marco completes the ceremony and Annina dies.

Salome

Composed by Richard Strauss (June 11, 1864 – September 8, 1949). Libretto by Richard Strauss. German. Based on the play by Oscar Wilde. Premiered Dresden, Staatsoper, December 9, 1905. Set in the Palace of Herod in Judaea in the 1st century AD. Music drama. Through composed with orchestral interludes (longest before Iiv). Opus 54.

Sets: 1. **Acts:** 1 act, 5 scenes. **Length:** I: 105. **Hazards:** I: Severed head of Jokanaan. **Scenes:** I. A great terrace in the Palace of Herod.

Major roles: Herod Antipas (tenor), Herodias (mezzo), Princess Salome (dramatic soprano), Prophet Jokanaan (baritone). **Minor roles:** Narraboth (tenor), Page of Herodias (contralto), Five Jews (4 tenors, 1 bass), Two Nazarenes (tenor, bass), Two soldiers (bass). **Bit parts:** Cappadocian (bass), Slave (mezzo).

Chorus parts: N/A. **Chorus roles:** None. **Dance/movement:** Iv: Salome's dance of the seven veils. **Orchestra:** picc, 3 fl, 2 ob, Eng hrn, heckelphone, 5 cl, bs cl, 3 bsn, cont bsn, 6 hrn, 4 trp, 4 trb, bs tuba, 2 timp, 6 or 7 perc, 2 harp, celeste, strings (16-16-10 or 12-10-8). **Stageband:** I: harmonium, organ. **Publisher:** Belwin Mills, Kalmus, Dover, Adolph Fürstner. **Rights:** Copyright 1905 by Richard Strauss.

Ii. To the page's dismay, Narraboth will not stop talking about Princess Salome's beauty. Two soldiers complain about the commotion in the palace. From a cistern below, the imprisoned prophet, Jokanaan, is heard prophesying about the Messiah. Iii. Salome escapes from the dinner table and Tetrarch Herod's lecherous looks. The tetrarch sends a slave to fetch her, but she will not go. Instead, she listens to the prophet, who has said terrible things about her mother. When she asks the soldiers to bring the prophet to her, they refuse: even the high priest is forbidden to see Jokanaan. But Salome persuades Narraboth to grant her wish. Iiii. Released, the prophet calls on Herodias to repent her incestuous marriage to Herod. The princess lusts for the prophet, but her praise of his features only earns repeated rebukes. Narraboth kills himself rather than listen to Salome begging Jokanaan for a kiss. The prophet advises the princess to seek out the Son of Man and beg forgiveness for her sins. Declaring Salome accursed, Jokanaan returns to his cistern. Iiv. Herod and Herodias enter. The tetrarch slips in Narraboth's blood; he hears the beating of wings. Herodias asks Herod not to look at Salome but he instead tries to tempt the princess with wine, fruit—and an offer of her mother's place on the throne. Salome refuses. When Jokanaan is again heard, Herodias asks why the prophet is allowed to live. She accuses Herod of being afraid. The Jews bicker about the prophet Elias. Two Nazarenes say that Jokanaan is right: The Messiah has come and is performing miracles, raising people from the dead. Over the objections of Herodias, Herod persuades Salome to dance for him—by promising her anything she desires. The tetrarch again hears the beating of wings. Iv. Salome dances the dance of the seven veils. As her reward, she claims the head of Jokanaan—on a silver shield. Herod offers her wealth and power instead, but she is adamant and he acquiesces. The prophet submits to his death in silence. The executioner returns with the severed head, which Salome kisses. She laments that her passion for the prophet will never be satisfied. Horrified, Herod has the soldiers crush Salome to death.

Samson et Dalila • Samson and Dalila

Composed by Camille Saint-Saëns (October 9, 1835 – December 16, 1921). Libretto by Ferdinand Lemaire. French (premiered in German). Based on the Biblical story in the Book of Judges. Premiered Weimar, Grand Ducal Theater, December 2, 1877. Set in Palestine in 1150 BC. Drama. Set numbers with recitative. Prelude before II. Musical interlude before IIIii. Ballet.

Sets: 4. **Acts:** 3 acts, 12 scenes. **Length:** I: 45. II: 40. III: 30. **Arias:** "Amour, viens aider ma faiblesse" (Dalila), "Mon coeur s'ouvre à ta voix" (Dalila). **Hazards:** III: Destruction of the temple of Dagon. **Scenes:** I. A public square in the city of Gaza in Palestine. II. The valley of Soreck before Dalila's house. IIIi. A prison in Gaza. IIIii – IIIiii. Interior of the Temple of Dagon.

Major roles: Dalila (mezzo or contralto), Samson (dramatic tenor), High priest of Dagon (baritone). **Minor roles:** Abimélech (bass), Old Hebrew (bass). **Bit parts:** Philistine Messenger (tenor), First Philistine (tenor), Second Philistine (bass).

Chorus parts: SSAATTBB. **Chorus roles:** Hebrews and Philistine soldiers, priests and women. **Dance/movement:** I: Dance of the Philistine priestesses. III: Ballet in the temple of Dagon. **Orchestra:** 3 fl (picc), 2 ob, Eng hrn, 2 cl, bs cl, 2 bsn, cont bsn, 4 hrn, 2 trp, 2 cornet, 3 trb, tuba, 2 ophicléide, 2 harps, timp, 4 to 5 perc, strings. **Stageband:** None. **Publisher:** Schirmer, Durand and Son. **Rights:** Expired.

Ii. The Hebrews pray for deliverance from their enemies, the Philistines. Samson bolsters their morale. Iii. Abimelech, the Philistine satrap of Gaza, belittles the god of the Hebrews. He attacks Samson, but Samson grabs his sword from him and runs him through. Iiii. The Philistine high priest calls for vengeance for the satrap's death, but his warriors are weak and afraid. Iiv. A Philistine messenger announces the success of

Samson's rebellion. The high priest flees, cursing Samson and his race. Iv. The Israelites praise God. Ivi. The maidens of the temple of Dagon dance for the Hebrew soldiers. In spite of the warnings of an old Hebrew, Samson is drawn to Dalila, a priestess of Dagon.

IIi. Dalila plots to bring Samson down. IIii. She confers with the high priest, but scorns his offers of gold. "I hate Samson," she says, "and need no reward." IIiii. Though he knows he should stay away, Samson succumbs to Dalila's charms. As a token of trust, she demands to know the secret of his strength. Giving in, Samson follows her inside where he is betrayed into the hands of the Philistine soldiers.

IIIi. Samson, his hair shorn, grinds at a mill in prison. He prays that God's wrath be visited on himself and not on his countrymen. IIIii. In the temple of Dagon, the Philistines pray and dance. IIIiii. Dalila and her countrymen delight in their victory over Samson. They torment the blinded Samson and insult his God. Samson is led to the altar to bow before Dagon, but he tells the boy to position him between the temple columns. Praying for one last burst of strength, Samson breaks the columns, bringing the temple down on the screaming Philistines.

Sapho

Composed by Charles François Gounod (June 17, 1818 – October 18, 1893). Libretto by Émile Augier. French. Loosely based on the historical figure. Premiered Paris, Opéra, April 16, 1851. Set in Greece in the 6th century BC. Grand opera. Set numbers with recitative. Introduction. Entr'acte before III.

Sets: 3. **Acts:** 3 acts, 3 scenes. **Length:** I: 50. II: 45. III: 35. **Arias:** "Ô ma lyre immortelle" (Sapho). **Hazards:** III: Sapho throws herself into the sea. **Scenes:** I. A square before the temple of Jupiter at Olympia. II. In Phaon's house on Lesbos. III. A rocky cliff dominating the seashore.

Major roles: Pythéas (bass), Phaon (tenor), Sapho (mezzo), Glycère (soprano). **Minor roles:** Two men (tenor, bass), Alcée (baritone), Cratès (tenor), High Priest Cygénire (bass), Shepherd (tenor). **Bit parts:** Woman (soprano), Two heralds (tenor, bass). **Mute:** Phèdre.

Chorus parts: SATTTTBBBB. **Chorus roles:** Procession, athletes, escort, people, priests, conspirators, travelers, maidens, young men. **Dance/movement:** None. **Orchestra:** picc, 2 fl, 2 ob (Eng hrn), 2 cl, 3 bsn, 4 hrn, 2 cornet, 2 trp, 2 trb, tuba, timp, perc, harp, strings. **Stageband:** None. **Publisher:** Choudens Pére & Fils. **Rights:** Expired.

I. Phaon is torn between his love for Glycère and for Sapho. Alcée calls on his fellow Greeks to overthrow the tyrant who oppresses them. His words are received enthusiastically. Sapho's song wins the Olympic competition and Phaon leaves Glycère for her.

II. The conspirators draw lots to see who will assassinate the tyrant and Phaon is chosen. The conspirator Pythéas reveals the plot to Glycère, who uses her knowledge to blackmail Sapho. Reluctantly, Sapho agrees to send Phaon away. Thinking Sapho does not love him, Phaon leaves with Glycère.

III. Sapho throws herself off a cliff rather than live without Phaon.

Sapho

Composed by Jules-Emile-Frédéric Massenet (May 12, 1842 – August 13, 1912). Libretto by Henri Cain and Arthur Bernède. French. Based on the novel of Alphonse Daudet. Premiered Paris, Opéra Comique, November 27, 1897. Set in France in the 19th century. Musical play. Set numbers with recitative. Prelude before I, IV. Revised in 1909 with expansion of III.

Sets: 5. **Acts:** 5 acts, 5 scenes. **Hazards:** None. **Scenes:** I. A large drawing room behind which is the studio of Caoudal. II. The lodgings of Jean Gaussin on the rue d'Amsterdam in Paris. III. In the garden of a restaurant at Ville d'Avray. IV. The homestead of the Gaussin's. V. The dismantled room of the little house at Ville d'Avray.

Major roles: Jean Gaussin (tenor), Fanny Legrand/Sapho (soprano). **Minor roles:** Caoudal (baritone), Borderie (tenor), Césaire (bass), Divonne (soprano), Irène (soprano), Restaurant keeper (bass).

Chorus parts: SSAATTB. **Chorus roles:** Guests at a masked ball, youths, people, friends. **Dance/movement:** I: Ballroom dancing (masked ball). **Orchestra:** 3 fl, 3 ob, 2 cl, 2 bsn, 4 hrn, 2 trp, 3 trb, tuba, timp, perc, celeste, harp, strings. **Stageband:** 2 vln, vlc, bs, fl, harmonium, piano, tuba, cornet. **Publisher:** Heugel & Co. **Rights:** Expired.

I. The sculptor Caoudal gives a masked ball. He and his friend, La Borderie, greet Jean. Jean is embarrassed by his provincial manners and dreams of Provence. Fanny (known to her friends as Sapho) has been singing to the assembled artists. All the men, including Jean, are in love with her. Fanny takes Jean into dinner with her.

II. Jean entertains his father, Césaire, in his lodgings in Paris. Jean's mother, Divonne, arrives with Irene, a niece who is going to live with Jean's parents. Jean and Irene grew up together and they reminisce about the games they used to play. Jean's parents catch their son kissing Irene. They take their leave. Now that Jean's parents and Irene are gone, Fanny returns. She admires Jean's lodgings, including a statue of her done by Caoudal. They pledge their love.

III. A year has passed and Jean and Fanny are living in the country. Caoudal, La Borderie and their friends dine nearby. They greet Jean and ask if he is still living with Sapho. He denies it. They tell Jean about all the other men Fanny has loved and left—and about her child. Jean confronts Fanny, who dismisses him haughtily. But her love for Jean is real and she berates the artists for ruining her happiness.

IV. Jean returns home to his parents, who comfort him. Irene asks about Jean's sad looks. Césaire sends Irene away. He warns Jean that Fanny has come looking for him. Fanny still loves Jean passionately and she pleads with him to come back to her. Jean's resolve weakens, but his mother intervenes and sends Fanny away.

V. Fanny tearfully leaves the house she shared with Jean. Jean has abandoned his family to return to Fanny, but she knows he is making a mistake. When Jean goes to sleep, Fanny leaves him.

Šárka

Composed by Leoš Janáček (July 3, 1854 – August 12, 1928). Libretto by Julius Zeyer. Czech. Based on Bohemian legends. Premiered Brno, Brno Theater, November 11, 1925. Set in Bohemia in pagan times. Heroic opera. Through composed. Overture. Revised in 1888, 1918/1919 and 1924/1925. Orchestration of the third act and final revision of acts one and two done by Janáček's student, Oswald Chlubna.

Sets: 3. **Acts:** 3 acts, 3 scenes. **Length:** I, II, III: 80. **Hazards:** III: Šárka throws herself on Ctirad's funeral pyre. **Scenes:** I. The castle of Libice. II. A wild empty valley in the moonlight. III. A courtyard with lime trees.

Major roles: Šárka (soprano), Chieftan Ctirad (tenor), Lumír (tenor). Minor role: Duke Přemysl (bass).

Chorus parts: SATB. **Chorus roles:** Women and men warriors, headmen, people, youths. **Dance/movement:** None. **Orchestra:** 2 fl, 2 ob, Eng hrn, 2 cl, bs cl, 2 bsn, cont bsn, 4 hrn, 2 trp, 3 trb, tuba, timp, perc, harp, strings. **Stageband:** None. **Publisher:** Universal Edition. **Rights:** Copyright 1925 by Universal Edition.

I. Libuše, the ruler of Bohemia, has died leaving her consort, Přemysl, in control of the country. Infuriated over the loss of their special privileges under Libuše's rule, the women of Bohemia revolt, led by Vlasta and her captain, Šárka. Šárka's troops are routed by the forces of the young hero, Ctirad. The women swear revenge.

II. In an attempt to ambush Ctirad, Šárka has herself tied to a tree while her warriors hide nearby. When Ctirad finds her, she claims to have been ostracized by Vlasta. Ctirad and Šárka fall in love. Nevertheless, Šárka gives the signal and her warriors kill Ctirad.

III. Heartbroken, Šárka throws herself onto Ctirad's funeral pyre.

Satyagraha

Composed by Philip Glass (b. January 31, 1937). Libretto by Constance De Jong. Hindu. Adapted from the Bhagavad-Gita and historical incidents. Premiered Rotterdam, Nederlandse Operastichting, September 5, 1980. Set in South Africa, Russia and India in the late 19th and early 20th century. Historical drama. Set numbers with spoken monologues. Musical interludes between scenes. Minimalist.

Sets: 6. **Acts:** 3 acts, 7 scenes. **Length:** I, II, III: 120. **Hazards:** None. **Scenes:** Ii. The Kuru field of justice. Iii. The Tolstoy farm. Iiii. An empty field in South Africa. IIi. A European settlement in South Africa. IIii. Part of the communal residence housing the publication "Indian Opinion." IIiii. The empty field. III. The mythical battlefield and a plain in South Africa.

Major roles: M. K. Gandhi (tenor), Miss Schlesen (soprano), Mrs. Naidoo (soprano), Kasturbai (mezzo), Mr. Kallenbach (baritone), Parsi Rustomji (bass). **Minor roles:** Prince Arjuna (tenor or baritone), Krishna (bass), Mrs. Alexander (alto). **Speaking:** Count Leo Tolstoy, Rabindranath Tagore, Martin Luther King Jr.

Chorus parts: SSSAATTTBB. **Chorus roles:** Soldiers of the Kuruva and Pandava families, European men in South Africa, farm and commune residents, satyagrahi (minimum 40 singers total). **Dance/movement:** None. **Orchestra:** 3 fl, 3 ob, 3 cl, bs cl, 2 bsn, electric organ, strings. **Stageband:** None. **Rights:** Copyright 1980 by G. Schirmer.

Ii. The Kuruva and Pandava families face each other in battle. Gandhi narrates how Prince Arjuna sought Lord Krishna's advice. Iii. Gandhi and his satyagrahi start Tolstoy Farm where they can come together in "self-purification and self-reliance." Iiii. Parsi Rustomji addresses a public protest against the British proposal to register and fingerprint all Indians in South Africa.

IIi. Gandhi is greeted on his return to South Africa by a crowd of angry European men. He is protected by Mrs. Alexander, the wife of the superintendent of police. IIii. Gandhi's followers publish "Indian Opinion," a weekly publication devoted to satyagraha principles. IIiii. The satyagrahi defy the government by publicly burning their registration cards.

III. A group of miners joins Gandhi in a march to the Transvaal border. They are protesting the government's breech of promises.

La Scala di Seta • The Silken Ladder

Composed by Gioachino Rossini (February 29, 1792 – November 13, 1868). Libretto by Giuseppe Foppa. Italian. Based on a libretto by François-Antoine-Eugène de Planard for Gaveaux. Premiered Venice, Teatro San Moisè, May 9, 1812. Set in France in the 18th century. Farce. Set numbers with recitative. Overture.

Sets: 1. **Acts:** 1 act, 1 scene. **Length:** I: 85. **Hazards:** None. **Scenes:** I. Apartment of Giulia in the house of her guardian Dormont.

Major roles: Giulia (soprano), Germano (comic bass), Dorvil (tenor), Blansac (baritone). **Minor roles:** Lucilla (mezzo), Dormont (tenor). **Bit part:** Servant (comic bass).

Chorus parts: N/A. **Chorus roles:** None. **Dance/movement:** None. **Orchestra:** 2 fl (2 picc), 2 ob, 2 cl, bsn, 2 hrn, strings, continuo. **Stageband:** None. **Publisher:** Edizioni Musicale Otos. **Rights:** Expired.

I. Giulia chases away her talkative servant, Germano, and her cousin, Lucilla. She has secretly married her lover, Dorvil, and he is hiding in the closet until she can let him out by a silken ladder. Her guardian, Dormont, wants her to marry Blansac, but Giulia plans to marry him to Lucilla instead. Meanwhile, Dorvil uses his friendship with Blansac to try and talk him out of the marriage. Giulia accuses Blansac of being fickle, but he swears he will be faithful. Dorvil and Germano spy on this conversation, which makes Dorvil jealous. Blansac flirts with Lucilla. Germano overhears Giulia's plans for a midnight rendezvous and— thinking she is meeting Blansac—reveals the details to him and Lucilla. Lucilla and Germano both hide as Giulia receives Dorvil. She tries to sooth his jealousy, but hides him when she hears Blansac coming. Giulia rebukes Blansac for his presumption and the noise brings Dormont.

Everyone is discovered. Dorvil admits that he and Giulia are already married and Blansac marries Lucilla.

Scaramouche

Composed by Jean Sibelius (December 8, 1865 – September 20, 1957). Libretto by Poul Knudsen. Based on a play by Poul Knudsen and M. Bloch. Premiered Copenhagen, Copenhagen Theater, May 12, 1922. Set in Lelion's country estate at an unspecified time. Tragic pantomime. Through composed. All spoken dialogue over music. Introduction before II.

Sets: 1. **Acts:** 2 acts, 21 scenes. **Length:** I, II: 65. **Hazards:** II: Scaramouche's bloody corpse revealed. **Scenes:** I – II. A room in Lelion's house.

Major speaking roles: Lelion, Blondelaine (significant dancing required). **Minor speaking roles:** Gigolo, Mezzetin, Second dandy, First dandy. **Bit speaking part:** Old servant. **Musicians:** Scaramouche (a few spoken lines), Boy (a few spoken lines). **Mute:** Woman, violinist, horn player, guests.

Chorus parts: N/A. **Chorus roles:** None. **Dance/movement:** I: Ballroom dancers seen in distance. Blondelaine dances a bolero for her guests. II: Blondelaine dances wildly for Scaramouche. **Orchestra:** 2 fl (picc), 2 ob, 2 cl, 2 bsn, 4 hrn, timp, perc, piano, strings (minimum 6-4-3-3-2). **Stageband:** I: 2 cl, 2 ob, vla, vlc, perc, piano (note that act I band can be drawn from pit players). II: cornet. **Publisher:** Wilhelm Hansen. **Rights:** Copyright 1918, 1919 by Wilhelm Hansen.

Ii. Lelion watches the dancers. Iii. He has the candles lit. Iiii. Gigolo takes his leave and the two men talk about loneliness and love. The dancers urge Lelion to dance with his young wife, Blondelaine. Iiv. At Lelion's suggestion, Blondelaine dances for the guests. They hear the music of a wandering troupe and invite them in. Iv. Scaramouche and his troupe play for Blondelaine. She dances wildly, as if enchanted. Worried, Lelion dismisses the musicians. Ivi. Mezzetin tells Blondelaine he loves her, but she is not interested. Ivii. Everyone goes in to dinner except Blondelaine. Iviii. She hears Scaramouche playing and runs into the garden. Iix. Lelion realizes Blondelaine has left. Ix. The guests find him sobbing.

IIi. Lelion broods. IIii. Gigolo sits with him. IIiii. Gigolo asks Lelion to come away with him. IIiv. The servant brings wine. IIv. Gigolo tells Lelion that the same thing happened to him—and that Blondelaine is not coming back. IIvi. Lelion contemplates his wife's picture. IIvii.

Blondelaine returns and tells Lelion how much she loves him. He threatens her with his dagger, but eventually they are reconciled. IIviii. Lelion goes to fetch more wine. IIix. Scaramouche returns and threatens to tell Lelion about their tryst if Blondelaine does not leave with him. She kills him with Lelion's dagger and hides the body. IIx. Blondelaine dances for Lelion, but she is haunted by the murder. She reveals Scaramouche's body and dances for the corpse until she, too, drops dead. Lelion is horrified. IIxi. The woman and boy from Scaramouche's troupe come looking for him and discover the body.

The Scarf

Composed by Lee Hoiby (b. February 17, 1926). Libretto by Harry Duncan. English. Based on a story by Chekhov. Premiered Spoleto, Festival of Two Worlds, June 20, 1958. Set in an isolated farmhouse in the present. Tragedy. Through composed. Orchestral introduction. Opus 12.

Sets: 1. **Acts:** 1 act, 1 scene. **Length:** I: 45. **Hazards:** None. **Scenes:** I. The kitchen-bedroom of an isolated farmhouse.

Major roles: Miriam (soprano) Reuel (tenor), Postman (baritone).

Chorus parts: N/A. **Chorus roles:** None. **Dance/movement:** None. **Orchestra:** ob, cl, bsn, 2 hrn, trp, trb, timp, perc, piano, celeste, strings. **Stageband:** None. **Publisher:** G. Schirmer. **Rights:** Copyright 1959 by G. Schirmer Inc.

I. Reuel accuses his wife, Miriam, of being a witch. He believes that she raises snowstorms with her spells and lures young men to the farmhouse. The postman gets lost and takes shelter with Miriam and Reuel. Miriam kisses the postman while Reuel is not looking and gives him a scarf. Reuel hurries the postman out of the house, but Miriam, left alone, casts a spell to bring the postman back. Reuel returns instead, wearing the scarf. Miriam strangles him with it and calls out into the night for the postman.

Der Schauspieldirektor • The Impresario

Composed by Wolfgang Amadeus Mozart (January 27, 1756 – December 5, 1791). Libretto by Gottlieb Stephanie. German. Original work. Premiered Suburb of Vienna, Schönbrunn Palace, February 7, 1786. Set in Salzburg or Vienna in the late 18th century. Comedy/singspiel. Set numbers with recitative or spoken dialogue. Overture. K. 486. Various versions extant with or without Frank and additional auditionees; numbers changed. Scenery and script often adapted for local conditions.

Sets: 1. **Acts:** 1 act, 1 scene. **Length:** I: 55. **Arias:** "Da schlägt die Abschiedsstunde" (Herz), "Bester Jüngling" (Silverklang). **Hazards:** None. **Scenes:** I. The impressario's office.

Major roles: Mr. Buff (bass), Mr. Vogelgesang (tenor), Madam Silverklang (soprano), Miss Herz (soprano). **Speaking:** Frank.

Chorus parts: N/A. **Chorus roles:** None. **Dance/movement:** None. **Orchestra:** 2 fl, 2 ob, 2 cl, 2 bsn, 2 hrn, 2 trp, timp, strings. **Stageband:** None. **Publisher:** G. Schirmer, Breitkopf & Härtel. **Rights:** Expired.

I. Frank is ambivalent about his appointment as general manager of the court theater—especially when his assistant, Mr. Buff, informs him that the court has decreed that the season must be exclusively opera. Buff—who wants to be a singer himself—tells Frank how he can produce opera at a profit if he puts aside his artistic scruples. Vogelgesang, the rich, star-struck banker, offers to support the company if they will make use of his aging diva mistress, Madame Silverklang. As soon as Frank has reluctantly accepted Madame Silverklang, Vogelgesang makes another donation—and pushes another soprano on him, his younger mistress, Miss Herz. Frank makes her an offer, which she haughtily refuses. Silverklang returns and wonders why Vogelgesang has offered to pay Herz's fee. A fight ensues. Frank announces his retirement and Vogelgesang ends up as the new impresario. His money ensures better discipline from the singers.

School for Wives

Composed by Rolf Liebermann (b. September 14, 1910). Libretto by Heinrich Strobel. English. Based on the comedy by Molière. Premiered Louisville, Kentucky, Louisville Orchestra Society, December 3, 1955. Set in France in the 18th century. Comedy. Through composed. Overture. Revised 3-act version premiered as "Die Schule der Frauen" in Salzburg, 1957.

Sets: 1. **Acts:** 1 act, 1 scene. **Length:** I: 72. (Three-act version: 90.) **Hazards:** None. **Scenes:** I. Before two houses with a common entrance.

Major roles: Molière/Poquelin/Alain/Old woman/Henry (baritone), Arnolphe (baritone), Horace (lyric tenor), Agnes (lyric soprano). **Minor roles:** Georgette (contralto), Oronte (bass).

Chorus parts: N/A. **Chorus roles:** None. **Dance/movement:** None.
Orchestra: fl (picc), ob, cl, bsn (cont bsn), 2 hrn, trp, trb, timp, perc, cembalo, strings. **Stageband:** I: 2 cl, bsn, 2 hrn, trp, trb, tuba, timp.
Publisher: Universal Edition. **Rights:** Copyright 1955 by Universal.

Ii. Arnolphe has had Agnes brought up in a convent to be the perfect
bride for him. Horace—the son of Arnolphe's best friend, Oronte—
comes to visit Arnolphe. Not realizing that Arnolphe means to marry
Agnes, Horace confesses that he and Agnes have fallen in love and
Arnolphe promises to help. When Horace leaves, he instructs (and
bribes) his servants not to let Horace in. Horace gets back in anyway and
hides while Arnolphe berates Agnes for her behavior. Horace and Agnes
agree to elope. Iii. Later that night, Horace comes for Agnes, but is beaten
by Arnolphe's servants. Horace tells Agnes to stay with a friend of
his—and turns her over to Arnolphe. He now discovers (too late)
Arnolphe's real plans. Horace's father, Oronte, and Agnes's father,
Henry, arrive and tell Horace to marry Agnes. Arnolphe makes his
peace with the young lovers.

Schwanda the Bagpiper

See "Švanda Dudák" entry.

Die Schweigsame Frau • The Silent Woman

Composed by Richard Strauss (June 11, 1864 – September 8, 1949).
Libretto by Stefan Zweig. German. Based on "Epicoene" by Ben Jonson.
Premiered Dresden, Staatsoper, June 24, 1935. Set in London in the late
18th century. Comic opera. Set numbers with recitative and spoken dialogue. Overture. Entr'acte before III.

Sets: 1. **Acts:** 3 acts, 3 scenes. **Length:** I: 60. II: 70. III: 45. **Hazards:** None.
Scenes: I – III. Morosus's living room.

Major roles: Barber Pankrazius Schneidebart (high baritone), Sir
Morosus (comic bass), Henry Morosus (high tenor), Aminta (coloratura
soprano). **Minor roles:** Housekeeper (contralto), Vanuzzi (bass), Morbio
(baritone), Isotta (coloratura soprano), Carlotta (mezzo), Farfallo (bass).
Speaking bit: Parrot.

Chorus parts: SATTTBB. **Chorus roles:** Comediennes and neighbors.
Dance/movement: III: Jurists' dance. **Orchestra:** 3 fl (picc), 2 ob, Eng hrn,
3 cl, bs cl, 3 bsn (cont bsn), 4 hrn, 3 trp, 3 trb, tuba, 2 timp, perc, xylophone, glockenspiel, celeste, harp, strings (14-12-8-8-5 or 6). **Stageband:**

III: organ, cembalo, trps, bagpipes, drums. **Publisher:** Adolph Fürstner. **Rights:** Copyright 1935 by Richard Strauss.

I. Morosus's housekeeper loves her master, but fails to persuade the barber to hint that Morosus should marry her. Morosus cannot stand noise. The barber suggests he marry a young, silent woman—whom the barber undertakes to find. Morosus's favorite nephew, Henry, arrives with his new wife—the opera singer Aminta—and her opera troupe. Morosus disowns Henry for taking up singing and agrees to let the barber find him a wife. The barber conspires with the opera singers to fool Morosus into a mock marriage with one of them. The girl can then annoy Morosus until he demands a divorce and reinstates Henry as his heir.

II. The barber presents the lady opera singers, and Morosus choses Aminta. The impressario, Vanuzzi, performs a fake marriage. The rest of the troupe pretend to be old sea comrades of Morosus's and make a great deal of noise. Aminta pities Morosus, but plays her part as a shrew. Henry sends her to her room and promises to help Morosus get a divorce.

III. Aminta has the house redone and practices her singing. Members of the opera troupe arrive disguised as distinguished jurists to hear the divorce. They drive Morosus to distraction before Henry reveals the plot. Morosus is so amused that he forgives everyone and becomes an opera lover.

The Second Hurricane

Composed by Aaron Copland (November 14, 1900 – December 2, 1990). Libretto by Edwin Denby. English. Original work. Premiered New York City, Grand Street Playhouse, April 21, 1937. Set in Midwest America in the 1930s. Play opera. Set numbers with spoken dialogue. Overture. Meant for high school performance.

Sets: 3. **Acts:** 2 acts, 4 scenes. **Length:** I, II: 50. **Hazards:** I: Hurricane. **Scenes:** Ii. A high school. Iii. A radio station. Iiii – II. A rise of ground in a waste country near a great river.

Major roles: Gwen (contralto), Butch (tenor), Lowrie (tenor), Gyp (baritone), Fat (bass), Queenie (soprano), Jeff (soprano). **Speaking:** Principal Lester, Mr. MacLenahan, Radio operator. **Speaking bits:** Fresh boy, Three parents, Two children.

Chorus parts: SSAATTBB. **Chorus roles:** Adult chorus (SATB) and student chorus (SATB). **Dance/movement:** None. **Orchestra:** fl, picc, ob, 2

cl, sax, bsn, 2 trp, trb, timp, perc, piano, glockenspiel, xylophone, strings.
Stageband: I, II: sound effects (airplanes, thunder, roaring water).
Publisher: Boosey & Hawkes, C. C. Birchard & Co. **Rights:** Copyright
1938, 1939 by C. C. Birchard and Co. Assigned to Boosey & Hawkes Inc.,
1957.

Ii. The aviator MacLenahan is trying to rescue people from a hurricane
and flood. Principal Lester lets MacLenahan take six student volunteers:
Gwen, Butch, Lowrie, Fat, Gyp and Queenie. Iii. The radio operator
reports a second hurricane approaching. He loses contact with
MacLenahan's plane. Iiii. MacLenahan puts the children down and continues alone. The children fight among themselves. They feed Jeff, a
young abandoned farm boy, and then help themselves to the emergency
rations. The parents are disappointed by the children's behavior.
MacLenahan's plane crashes. The children strike off in different directions. The hurricane strikes.

II. The children regroup and help one another, but the water is rising.
All the supplies have been washed away except a rubber boat the children cannot inflate and a flashlight. They sing until a plane finds and
rescues them.

Il Segreto di Susanna • Susanna's Secret

Composed by Ermanno Wolf-Ferrari (January 12, 1876 – January 21,
1948). Libretto by Enrico Golisciani. Italian (premiered in German).
Based on the 18th century intermezo form. Premiered Munich,
Königliches Hof- und Nationaltheater, December 4, 1909. Set in
Piedmont in 1910. Interlude. Through composed. Overture.

Sets: 1. **Acts:** 1 act, 1 scene. **Length:** I: 45. **Hazards:** None. **Scenes:** I. A
handsome apartment in the count's palace.

Major roles: Count Gil (baritone), Countess Susanna (soprano). **Mute:**
Sante.

Chorus parts: N/A. **Chorus roles:** None. **Dance/movement:** None.
Orchestra: 3 fl (picc), 2 ob, 2 cl, 2 bsn, 4 hrn, 2 trp, 3 trb, timp, harp,
strings. **Stageband:** None. **Publisher:** Schirmer. **Rights:** Copyright 1911
by Josef Weinberger.

I. Count Gil smells tobacco. Since neither he nor his wife, Susanna,
smokes, Gil worries that she may have a lover. Ashamed of his own suspicions, the count embraces Susanna—and smells tobacco. Susanna begs
her husband to overlook her failing (she smokes). Gil thinks she is

telling him to ignore a love affair and they fight. Susanna promises to reform. When Gil leaves for his club, she starts smoking again. Gil tries to catch Susanna, but cannot find the imagined lover. The second time he returns, he catches Susanna smoking. Relieved that his suspicions were groundless, the count decides to take up smoking himself.

Semirama

Composed by Ottorino Respighi (July 9, 1879 – April 18, 1936). Libretto by Alessandro Cerè. Italian. Loosely based on historical events. Premiered Bologna, Teatro Comunale, November 20, 1910. Set in Babylon in legendary times. Lyric tragedy. Through composed. Introduction before I, III.

Sets: 2. **Acts:** 3 acts, 3 scenes. **Length:** I: 45. II: 50. III: 55. **Hazards:** None. **Scenes:** I. The hanging gardens of the royal palace in Babylon. II. The temple of Baal. III. The hanging gardens.

Major roles: Queen Semirama (soprano), Princess Susiana (soprano), General Merodach (tenor). **Minor roles:** High Priest Ormus (bass), Tetrarch Falasar (baritone). **Bit parts:** Two serving maids (2 sopranos), Prophet Satibara (bass). **Mute:** Farno, Two executioners.

Chorus parts: SSAATTBB. **Chorus roles:** People, guests, revelers. **Dance/movement:** II: Ritual dance in honor of Baal. **Orchestra:** 3 fl, 3 ob, 4 cl, 3 bsn, 6 hrn, 3 trp, 3 trb, tuba, timp, perc, celeste, xylophone, harp, organ, strings. **Stageband:** fl, 2 ob, harmonium, harp, perc. **Publisher:** G. Ricordi & Co. **Rights:** Expired.

I. Susiana confesses to Queen Semirama that she and General Merodach are in love. When the general returns from the wars, his prisoners beg for mercy, but Semirama is ruthless. She orders King Farno's execution, but Merodach prevents it. Susiana suspects Semirama's intentions and tells Merodach that Semirama means to steal him away from her.

II. Ormus tries to learn the future. He prays. Semirama's former lover Falasar still hopes to marry the queen, but the omens are bad. Ormus and Falasar warn Semirama to appease the gods for the murder of her husband, King Nino. She belittles their fear and says she will marry Merodach. Falasar threatens to involve Semirama's son—whom the queen banished when Falasar murdered Nino. Semirama warns him she will drown Babylon in a river of blood.

III. Merodach and Semirama celebrate their upcoming wedding. Ormus warns Semirama that such a wedding would be shameful. Falasar tells

Susiana that Merodach is Semirama's banished son. Meanwhile, Semirama herself has had a frightening vision of the dead King Nino. Merodach comforts her. Susiana reveals that Semirama is Merodach's mother. She also tells Merodach it was Falasar who killed his father. Swearing to kill Falasar, Merodach chases him into the tomb, but in the darkness he accidentally stabs Semirama. The queen dies and Merodach goes mad.

Semiramide

Composed by Gioachino Rossini (February 29, 1792 – November 13, 1868). Libretto by Gaetano Rossi. Italian. Based on "Sémiramis" by Voltaire. Premiered Venice, Teatro la Fenice, February 3, 1823. Set in Babylon in the 8th century BC. Opera seria or tragic melodrama. Set numbers with recitative. Overture.

Sets: 8. **Acts:** 2 acts, 8 scenes. **Length:** I: 95. II: 75. **Arias:** "Bel raggio lusinghier" (Semiramide). **Hazards:** None. **Scenes:** Ii. A magnificent temple erected to the glory of Baal. Iii. The hanging gardens. Iiii. A magnificent throne room in the palace. IIi. A hall in the palace. IIii. The interior of the sanctuary. IIiii. Semiramide's apartments. IIiv. A remote corner of the palace adjacent to Ninus's tomb. IIv. The interior of Ninus's monument.

Major roles: Semiramide (soprano), Arsace (contralto), Assur (bass or baritone). **Minor roles:** High priest Oroe (bass), Idreno (tenor), Mitrane (tenor), Nino's ghost (bass), Azema (soprano).

Chorus parts: SSAATTBB. **Chorus roles:** Satraps, Magi, Babylonians, princesses, cithara players, foreign women, royal guards, temple priests, Indians, Scythians, Egyptians, slaves, Queen's attendants. **Dance/movement:** None. **Orchestra:** 2 fl (2 picc), 2 ob, 2 cl, 2 bsn, 4 hrn, 2 trp, 3 trb, timp, perc, strings. **Stageband:** I: ob, 2 bsn, 3 trb, timp. II: 2 trp, 2 bsn. (Band only partially specified by Rossini.) **Publisher:** Kalmus, Garland Publishing. **Rights:** Expired.

Ii. Oroe declares the day sacred to Baal and calls upon Queen Semiramide to chose her successor to the throne of Assyria. Prince Assur hopes to be chosen. As Semiramide calls upon Ninus, her dead husband, there is a clap of lightning and the sacred fire on the altar goes out. Arsace, commander of the army, returns at the command of Semiramide. He eagerly anticipates his reunion with his beloved Princess Azema. Before his death, Arsace's father told his son to give certain possessions to the high priest. This Arsace does. The high priest tells Arsace that his father was murdered—and implicates Prince Assur. The prince is furious that Arsace has returned to the capital. Assur tells Arsace that he intends to marry Azema. Iii. Semiramide herself loves

Arsace. She is comforted by an oracle that predicts her sufferings will end when Arsace marries. Iiii. Semiramide names Arsace as her king— and husband. Assur protests. The queen gives Azema to Idreno. An earthquake indicates the wrath of the gods. Ninus returns from the grave and commands Arsace to avenge his father.

IIi. Assur reminds Semiramide that she mixed the poison that he administered to Ninus. "You convinced me that I was about to be banished," the queen responds. She places her hopes in Arsace. Assur swears revenge. IIii. Oroe reveals to Arsace that he is Ninias, son of Ninus— Semiramide is his mother. IIiii. Arsace tells Semiramide the truth. She begs him to kill her, but he forgives her. Idreno longs for Azema's love. IIiv. The satraps loyal to Assur warn him that he has been exposed by Oroe. The prince decides to catch Arsace and kill him when he enters Ninus's tomb. An invisible hand grabs Assur and thrusts him to the ground, but the prince recovers and ignores the warning. IIv. Oroe, Arsace, Semiramide and Assur all descend into Ninus's tomb. Arsace kills Assur and is hailed by the people.

Serse • Xerxes

Composed by George Frederic Handel (February 23, 1685 – April 14, 1759). Libretto by Niccolò Minato. Italian. Based on libretto by Nicolò Minato for Cavalli. Premiered London, Haymarket Theater, April 15, 1738. Set in Persia in the 5th century BC. Opera seria. Set numbers with recitative. Overture. Symphony before III.

Sets: 8. Acts: 3 acts, 8 scenes. Length: I, II, III: 180. Arias: "Ombra mai fù" (Serse). Hazards: II: Bridge of boats destroyed by thunderstorm. Scenes: I. A pavilion giving onto a beautiful garden. Iii. A public place. IIi. A piazza in the city with an arcade. IIii. A bridge of boats across the sea joining Asia and Europe and Serse's camp. IIiii. A retreat near the city. IIIi. A gallery. IIIii. A wood. IIIiii. A brightly lit room with an altar.

Major roles: King Serse of Persia (soprano, mezzo or countertenor), Arsamene (soprano, mezzo or countertenor), Amastre (mezzo), Romilda (soprano), Elviro (bass or baritone). Minor roles: Ariodate (bass), Atalanta (soprano).

Chorus parts: SATB. Chorus roles: Soldiers, sailors and ministers. Dance/movement: None. Orchestra: 2 recorders or 2 fl, 2 ob, 2 hrn, trp, strings, continuo (harpsichord, cello, db bs, bsn). Stageband: None. Publisher: Chester Music, Deutschen Händelgesellschraft, Leipzig. Rights: Expired.

Ii. Serse contemplates the shade of his garden. His brother, Arsamene, arrives accompanied by the servant, Elviro, for an assignation with Romilda. They encounter Serse, who admits his own love for Romilda. Arsamene tries, unsuccessfully, to talk the king out of marrying Romilda and refuses to propose to her on the king's behalf. Arsamene tells Romilda, but she swears she loves only him. Romilda's sister, Atalanta, is not pleased, since she, too, loves Arsamene. At the approach of the king, Arsamene and Elviro hide. The king proposes to Romilda, but she says she is unworthy; he blames his brother for having defamed him. When Arsamene steps out of hiding to defend himself, Serse banishes him from court. Serse asks Romilda why she does not love him. Alone at last, Romilda promises to be faithful to Arsamene. Iii. Amastre, dressed as a man, admits that no disguise can conceal the fury of love. Ariodate and his troops return, victorious. The general hears with pleasure Serse's intention to give his daughter, Romilda, a royal husband. Serse muses that society must approve whatever the king does. "Liar!" Amastre responds. Serse does not recognize his consort in disguise. She claims her outcry was against her companion for predicting the failure of the bridge Serse is building between Europe and Asia. Arsamene sends Elviro off with a letter to Romilda. Amastre swears revenge on Serse for jilting her. Atalanta tries to convince Romilda that Arsamene has forsaken her. When she says she plans to have Arsamene herself, Romilda insists that Arsamene will always love her. Atalanta outlines how she will win Arsamene and says women cannot be blamed for their deceits.

IIi. Elviro is in disguise selling flowers in the city square. In venting his thoughts about the king's love for Romilda, he attracts the attention of Amastre—who is also in disguise. She guesses that the letter that Elviro carries is from Arsamene and bemoans the king's faithlessness. Elviro approaches Atalanta and gives her the letter, upon which Atalanta tells him that Romilda has forgotten Arsamene and loves Serse. Atalanta now gives Arsamene's love letter to the king, saying that it was addressed to her—rather than Romilda. "Arsamene only pretends to love Romilda," she explains, "but he really loves me." The king gives Atalanta his blessing. Hoping to change Romilda's mind, the king gives her Arsamene's letter. Romilda believes that Arsamene has betrayed her but swears that she will still be true to him. Alone, Romilda gives voice to her grief at betrayal. Amastre contemplates suicide. The deception comes full circle as Elviro tells Arsamene that Romilda has betrayed him. IIii. The king, Ariodate and the king's sailors rejoice in the bridge of boats they have built to Europe. Arsamene's hopes are accidentally raised by the king, who promises to marry him to the recipient of Arsamene's letter. When he realizes that the recipient was Atalanta, not Romilda, Arsamene curses his brother. The king now realizes his mistake and counsels Atalanta to forget her love for his brother. The two agree that life would be easier if it were possible to fall in and out of love voluntarily. Elviro is caught in a thunderstorm that destroys the bridge of boats. IIiii. Serse mistakes Amastre for one of his own soldiers. When Serse again proposes to Romilda, Amastre calls him a traitor. The king orders Amastre's arrest, but Romilda intervenes.

IIIi. Arsamene, Romilda and Atalanta meet. Atalanta claims that what she did was done to protect her sister. The lovers renew their vows of love. When the king arrives, Romilda puts him off by saying he must ask her father's consent. She will abide by his decision, she says. Serse goes off in search of Ariodate, sure of success. Romilda sends Arsamene away. IIIii. Having gained Ariodate's approval, Serse tells him to wait for the arrival of the royal bridegroom. The king's vague wording leads Ariodate to think that Arsamene will be Romilda's husband. He applauds the choice. Romilda has determined to refuse the king. In a desperate attempt to fend him off, Romilda says Arsamene once kissed her. The king orders Arsamene's execution. Romilda sends Amastre off to warn Arsamene. Arsamene returns and accuses Romilda of fabricating tales of danger to get rid of him. IIIiii. The lovers' quarrel is ended when Ariodate follows the king's command and has them wed. The king is furious when he finds out. A page delivers a letter from Amastre accusing the king of infidelity and swearing vengeance. The king demands vengeance on those who have betrayed him. All claim that they were only following the king's orders. Amastre reveals her true identity and points out that the king has betrayed her. He admits it but she forgives him.

La Serva Padrona • The Maid as Mistress

Composed by Giovanni Battista Pergolesi (January 4, 1710 – March 16, 1736). Libretto by Gennarantonio Federico. Italian. Based on the play by Jacopo Angello Nelli. Premiered Naples, Teatro San Bartolomeo, August 28, 1733. Set in Italy in the 18th century. Comic intermezzo. Set numbers with recitative and spoken dialogue.

Sets: 1. Acts: 1 act, 1 scene (originally done in 2 parts between acts of an opera seria). Length: I: 50. Arias: "Sempre in contrasti" (Uberto), "Stizzoso, mio stizzoso" (Serpina), "A Serpina penserete" (Serpina), "Son imbogliato io già" (Uberto). Hazards: None. Scenes: I. The apartment of Uberto.

Major roles: Uberto (bass), Serpina (soprano). Mute: Vespone.

Chorus parts: N/A. Chorus roles: None. Dance/movement: None. Orchestra: Strings, continuo. Stageband: None. Publisher: Kalmus. Rights: Expired.

I. Uberto complains that the interest he has shown in his serving maid, Serpina, has spoiled her. She bosses Uberto around. To free himself from Serpina's tyranny, Uberto decides to marry. Serpina insists he can marry only her. Dressing Vespone up as a soldier, she presents him as her intended to make Uberto jealous. She says Vespone demands a dowry from Uberto. Without the dowry he will not marry Serpina—but insists that Uberto do so. Uberto marries Serpina. Vespone reveals his true identity and the newlyweds declare their love.

The Shepherds of the Delectable Mountains

Composed by Ralph Vaughan Williams (October 12, 1872 – August 26, 1958). Libretto by Ralph Vaughan Williams. English. Based on Bunyan's "Pilgrim's Progress." Premiered London, Parry Opera Theatre, Royal College of Music, June 11, 1922. Set in a mountain pass at an unspecified time. Pastoral episode. Through composed. Later incorporated into Vaughan Williams's opera "The Pilgrim's Progress."

Sets: 1. Acts: 1 act, 1 scene. Length: I: 25. Hazards: None. Scenes: I. A mountain pass.

Major roles: First shepherd (baritone), Pilgrim (baritone), Second shepherd (tenor), Third shepherd (bass). Minor roles: Offstage voice of a bird (soprano), Celestial messenger (tenor).

Chorus parts: SSAAAA. Chorus roles: Offstage voices from the celestial city. Dance/movement: None. Orchestra: 2 fl, ob, Eng hrn, strings (min. 2-2-2-2-1, max. 6-6-4-4-2). Stageband: I: 2 trp, harp, bells. Publisher: Oxford University Press. Rights: Copyright 1925, 1926 by Oxford University Press.

I. A pilgrim meets three shepherds while seeking out the celestial city of God. He is tested, but eventually enters the city.

Le Siège de Corinthe • The Siege of Corinth

Composed by Gioachino Rossini (February 29, 1792 – November 13, 1868). Libretto by Luigi Balocchi and Alexandre Soumet. French. Based on Cesare della Valle's libretto for "Maometto II." Premiered Paris, Opéra, October 9, 1826. Set in Corinth in 1459. Lyric tragedy or grand opera. Set numbers with recitative. Overture. "Siège" is a revised but significantly different version of "Maometto Secondo." Several versions of both operas exist, including 1969 version by Randolph Mickelson.

Sets: 4. **Acts:** 3 acts, 4 scenes. **Length:** I, II, III: 155. **Hazards:** III: Catacombs collapse revealing Corinth in flames. **Scenes:** Ii. The vestibule of the Senate. Iii. The square of Corinth. II. Maometto's tent or flagship. III. The catacombs of Corinth.

Major roles: Néoclès (tenor or contralto), Pamira (soprano), Emperor Maometto II (bass). **Minor roles:** Governor Cléomène (tenor), Iero (bass), Omar (bass), Ismene (mezzo). **Bit part:** Adrasto (tenor).

Chorus parts: SSAATTTTBBBB. **Chorus roles:** Greek citizens, warriors and women, Turkish warriors and women, Imams. **Dance/movement:** None. **Orchestra:** 2 fl (picc), 2 ob, 2 cl, 2 bsn, 4 hrn, 2 trp, 3 trb, ophicléide, timp, perc, 2 harp, strings. **Stageband:** None. **Publisher:** G. Ricordi. **Rights:** Expired.

Ii. Governor Cléomène calls on the citizens of Corinth to decide whether to surrender to the Moslem emperor, Maometto II. Néoclès and Iero persuade the citizens to fight on. The governor has promised his daughter Pamira to Néoclès, but Pamira loves the Athenian Almanzor. Iii. Maometto conquers the city, but not the fortress. He tells his friend Omar about the girl he fell in love with while traveling under the name of Almanzor. Cléomène and Pamira are taken prisoner. Maometto and Pamira recognize each other and he asks her to marry him, but her father curses her.

II. Maometto tries to console Pamira. Néoclès has been captured attempting to fight his way to freedom. To save Néoclès, Pamira says he is her brother. The Greeks rise in revolt and Pamira decides to die with them rather than marry Maometto.

III. Néoclès and Pamira join the Greek resistance in the catacombs beneath the city. Maometto comes alone to plead for Pamira's hand. He learns that Néoclès is her intended. Pamira makes peace with her father. Admitting that the fight is hopeless, Iero leads the Greeks out to battle. The defeated Greeks set fire to the city rather than leave it to the Turks.

Siegfried

Composed by Richard Wagner (May 22, 1813 – February 13, 1883). Libretto by Richard Wagner. German. Original work based loosely on Norse mythology. Premiered Bayreuth, Festspielhaus, August 16, 1876. Set in a woods and mountain in mythical times. Epic music drama. Through composed with leitmotifs. Prelude before each act.

Sets: 4. **Acts:** 3 acts, 9 scenes. **Length:** I: 80. II: 70. III: 80. **Arias:**

"Nothung! Nothung!" (Siegfried). **Hazards:** I: Siegfried brings home a bear and reforges his father's sword. Anvil splits. II: Siegfried fights and slays the dragon Fafner. Siegfried talks to a bird. III: Siegfried shatters Wotan's spear. Brünnhilde's rock is surrounded by fire. **Scenes:** I. A cave in the forest. II. The depths of the forest. IIIi – IIIii. A wild region at the foot of a rocky mountain. IIIiii. Summit of Brünnhilde's rock.

Major roles: Mime (tenor), Siegfried (heldentenor), Wanderer/Wotan (bass or bass baritone), Brünnnhilde (dramatic soprano). **Minor roles:** Alberich (bass), Fafner (bass), Voice of the Forest Bird (soprano), Erda (contralto).

Chorus parts: None. **Chorus roles:** N/A. **Dance/movement:** None. **Orchestra:** picc, 3 fl (picc), 4 ob (Eng hrn), 3 cl, bs cl, 3 bsn (cont bsn), 8 hrn (2 ten tuba, 2 bs tuba), 3 trp, bs trp, 4 ten bs trb (cont bs trb), cont bs tuba, 2 timp, perc, 6 harps, strings (16-16-12-12-8). **Stageband:** II: hrn, Eng hrn. **Publisher:** G. Schirmer Inc., B. Schott's Söhne. **Rights:** Expired.

Ii. Alberich's brother, Mime, rears Siegfried after his mother Sieglinde's death. Mime wants the ring and the gold, which are being guarded by Fafner who is disguised as a dragon. Unfortunately, Mime cannot reforge the shattered sword of Siegfried's father, Siegmund. Iii. The wanderer (Wotan) visits Mime and agrees to answers his questions. Iiii. Siegfried returns and reforges the sword himself.

IIi. Wotan, finding Alberich keeping vigil by Fafner's cave, tells the dwarf that Siegfried is coming to slay Fafner. IIii. Mime has brought Siegfried to the lair to learn fear, but Siegfried is unmoved and kills Fafner. IIiii. The dragon's blood gives Siegfried the power to hear people's thoughts and he soon realizes that Mime means to kill him. Siegfried kills Mime first and follows a wood bird to the rock where Brünnhilde lies, surrounded by a ring of fire.

IIIi. Wotan consults Erda. IIIii. He encounters Siegfried and is upset by Siegfried's arrogance. The young hero breaks Wotan's spear to get to Brünnhilde. IIIiii. Siegfried makes his way through the ring of fire, awakens Brünnhilde—and falls in love with her.

Il Signor Bruschino • Mister Bruschino

Composed by Gioachino Rossini (February 29, 1792 – November 13, 1868). Libretto by Giuseppe Foppa. Italian. Based on "Le Fils par Hazard" by Alisan de Chazet and E.-T. Maurice Ourry. Premiered Venice, Teatro San Moisè, January 27, 1813. Set in Italy in the 18th century. Farce. Set numbers with recitative. Overture.

Sets: 1. **Acts:** 1 act, 15 scenes. **Length:** I: 85. **Arias:** "Ah! donate il caro sposo" (Sofia). **Hazards:** None. **Scenes:** I. A ground floor room in Gaudenzio's house exiting onto the garden.

Major roles: Florville (tenor), Sofia (soprano), Gaudenzio (comic bass or baritone), Bruschino the father (bass baritone). **Minor roles:** Marianna (mezzo), Filiberto (baritone or bass), Police commissioner (bass). **Bit part:** Bruschino the son (tenor). **Mute:** servants.

Chorus parts: N/A. **Chorus roles:** None. **Dance/movement:** None. **Orchestra:** 2 fl, 2 ob (Eng hrn), 2 cl, 2 bsn, 2 hrn, strings. **Stageband:** None. **Publisher:** G. Ricordi. **Rights:** Expired.

Ii. Florville and Sofia are in love, but Sofia's father, Gaudenzio, has promised her to Bruschino's son. Iii. Bruschino, junior, has run up an enormous bill at the inn and been imprisoned by the innkeeper for non-payment. He writes a repentant letter to his father. Introducing himself as a relative of Bruschino's, Florville pays Filiberto, the innkeeper, part of the money, takes the letter and tells Filiberto to keep Bruschino, junior, locked up. Iiii. Florville decides to take Bruschino junior's place. Iiv. He forges a letter from Bruschino, senior, to Gaudenzio, enclosing his own likeness. Iv. Florville then tells Gaudenzio how sorry he is to have been such a rake. Ivi. Gaudenzio pleads Florville's case with Bruschino, senior. But Bruschino, senior, insists he does not know Florville. Ivii. Gaudenzio takes this to mean he is disowning his son. Iviii. He asks Sofia to talk to Bruschino, senior. Iix. She does, but without success. Ix. The commissioner of police gets Bruschino, senior, to say that the letter from Bruschino, junior, is in fact in his son's handwriting. Ixi. Since Florville brought the letter, the commissioner concludes that Florville is Bruschino, junior. The innkeeper further confuses matters by addressing Florville as Bruschino. Ixii. Bruschino, senior, at last learns the truth from Filiberto. Ixiii. Gaudenzio sounds his daughter out about the proposed marriage and finds she is agreeable. Ixiv. Bruschino, senior, learns that Florville is the son of Gaudenzio's old enemy. Since he feels that Gaudenzio has treated him poorly, Bruschino, senior, decides to help Florville. The marriage is celebrated. Ixv. Bruschino, senior, pays off Filiberto and Bruschino, junior, is released. Gaudenzio learns the truth, but eventually forgives Florville.

Simon Boccanegra

Composed by Giuseppe Verdi (October 9, 1813 – January 27, 1901). Libretto by Francesco Maria Piave. Italian. Based on a play by Antonio García Gutiérrez. Premiered Venice, Teatro la Fenice, March 12, 1857. Set in Genoa and environs in the mid-14th century. Melodrama. Set num-

bers with recitative. Prologue. Revised version premiered Teatro alla
Scala, March 24, 1881. Libretto revised by Arrigo Boito.

Sets: 5. **Acts:** 3 acts, 5 scenes (including prologue). **Length:** Prologue: 25.
I: 55. II: 55. **Arias:** "Come in quest'ora bruna" (Amelia), "Il lacerato spiri-
to" (Fiesco), "Plebe! Patrizi!" (Boccanegra). **Hazards:** None. **Scenes:**
Prologue. A square in Genoa. Ii. Garden of the Grimaldi palace outside
Genoa. Iii. Council chamber in the Abati palace. II. Doge's room in the
ducal palace. III. Inside the ducal palace.

Major roles: Simon Boccanegra (baritone), Jacopo Fiesco (bass), Amelia
Grimaldi/Maria Boccanegra (soprano), Gabriele Adorno (tenor). **Minor
roles:** Paolo Albiani (bass), Pietro (baritone), Captain of archers (tenor).
Bit part: Amelia's maid (mezzo).

Chorus parts: SSATTTTTTBBB. **Chorus roles:** Sailors, people, Fiesco's
servants, soldiers, senators, members of the Doge's court. **Dance/move-
ment:** None. **Orchestra:** 2 fl (picc), 2 ob, 2 cl, bs cl, 2 bsn, 4 hrn, 2 trp, 3
trb, tuba, timp, perc, harp, strings. **Stageband:** Prologue: drums. I: 4 trp,
harp. II: 4 trp, 4 trb, 2 drums. III: trp, chime. **Publisher:** Kalmus. **Rights:**
Expired.

Prologue. Paolo arranges with Pietro to support Boccanegra for doge of
Genoa. In the hope of getting back his beloved Maria from her father,
Fiesco, Boccanegra agrees to accept the post—and to share his power
with Paolo. Maria dies. Boccanegra begs Fiesco's forgiveness, but Fiesco
demands Maria's daughter by Boccanegra. Boccanegra does not have
her. He enters Fiesco's palace and discovers Maria's casket. Emerging
into the square, he is hailed as doge.

Ii. Twenty five years later, Amelia Grimaldi fears for her beloved
Gabriele Adorno under Boccanegra's rule. Fiesco, under the assumed
name of Andrea, has adopted Amelia. He admits to Gabriele that she is
not really a Grimaldi, but a penniless foundling. Gabriele does not care
and Fiesco blesses their marriage. Boccanegra forgives the Grimaldis
and discovers that Amelia is really his daughter, Maria. Paolo wishes to
marry Amelia but when the doge refuses, he decides to abduct her. Iii.
The ducal council is interrupted by a mob demanding Boccanegra's
head. Boccanegra causes the palace doors to be thrown open. Gabriele
explains he killed Lorenzino for abducting Amelia. He accuses
Boccanegra of masterminding the abduction. Boccanegra has Gabriele
arrested but Amelia pleads for him. Boccanegra makes Paolo lay a curse
upon the real kidnapper.

II. Paolo and Pietro plan to poison the doge and ask both Fiesco and
Gabriele to do the deed. Gabriele is convinced that Amelia is

Boccanegra's mistress, but Amelia assures him she loves him. He hides behind the curtain when Boccanegra arrives. Amelia tells the doge she loves Gabriele. Boccanegra drinks the poisoned wine and falls asleep. Gabriele tries to kill Boccanegra but is stopped by Amelia and begs forgiveness. A crowd has again gathered to fight the doge. Gabriele promises to fight on Boccanegra's side.

III. Fiesco and Paolo's forces have been defeated and are condemned. Paolo tells Fiesco that Boccanegra is dying from the poisoned wine. Fiesco learns Amelia's true identity from Boccanegra. All forgive one another. Boccanegra asks that Gabriele be made doge after him. He dies and Fiesco proclaims Gabriele doge.

Sir John in Love

Composed by Ralph Vaughan Williams (October 12, 1872 – August 26, 1958). Libretto by Ralph Vaughan Williams. English. Based on Shakespeare's play "The Merry Wives of Windsor." Premiered London, Royal College of Music, March 21, 1929. Set in Windsor in the 15th century. Comedy. Through composed. Entr'acte before each act. Interludes between scenes. Ballet.

Sets: 6. Acts: 4 acts, 7 scenes. Length: I: 35. II: 30. III: 30. IV: 35. Arias: "O that joy so soon should waste" (Falstaff). Hazards: None. Scenes: I. A street in Windsor. IIi. A room in Page's house. IIii. The parlor of the Garter Inn. IIIi. A field near Windsor. IIIii. A room in Ford's house. IVi. A room in Ford's house. IVii. Windsor forest.

Major roles: Page (baritone), Sir John Falstaff (baritone), Anne Page (soprano), Fenton (tenor), Mrs. Quickly (mezzo or contralto), Ford (bass), Mrs. Ford (mezzo), Mrs. Page (soprano). Minor roles: Shallow (tenor or baritone), Sir Hugh Evans (high baritone), Slender (tenor), Bardolph (tenor), Pistol (bass), Nym (baritone), Dr. Caius (high baritone), Rugby (bass), Peter Simple (tenor or baritone), Host of the Garter Inn (baritone). Bit parts: John (baritone), Robert (baritone). Speaking: Robin (boy), William (boy), Alice Shortcake, Jenny Pluckpears.

Chorus parts: SATB. Chorus roles: Young men and women, neighbors, servants, fairies. Dance/movement: II: Country dance. IV: fairy ballet and wedding dance. Orchestra: 2 fl, 2 ob (Eng hrn), 2 cl, 2 bsn, 2 hrn, 2 trp, trb, timp, perc, harp, strings. Stageband: III: perc. IV: perc, fl. Publisher: Oxford University Press. Rights: Copyright 1930 by Oxford University Press.

I. Shallow, Slender and Evans complain that they have been mistreated by Falstaff and his men. Falstaff's men deny the charges. Page intends to marry his daughter, Anne, to Slender, but Mrs. Page wants Anne to marry Dr. Caius. Anne herself loves Fenton. Falstaff decides to repair his dwindling fortunes by making love to both Mrs. Page and Mrs. Ford. Falstaff insults his men, who take revenge by telling Ford Falstaff's plans.

IIi. Mrs. Page and Mrs. Ford receive identical love letters from Falstaff. They agree to take revenge jointly and enlist Mrs. Quickly in their scheme. IIii. Mrs. Quickly arranges a rendezvous between Mrs. Ford and Falstaff. Ford introduces himself to Falstaff as Master Brook, a rich man in love with Mrs. Ford. He pays Falstaff to seduce Mrs. Ford on the theory that once she has fallen once, a second suitor will have an easier time. Caius challenges his rival, Evans, to a duel.

IIIi. Anne and a party of young people go out for a picnic. Fenton joins them and woos Anne. The host and Shallow break up the duel between Evans and Caius. IIIii. Falstaff tries to woo Mrs. Ford, but is interrupted by Ford's return. While Ford searches the house, the women smuggle Falstaff out in a laundry basket.

IVi. Mrs. Page and Mrs. Ford show their husbands Falstaff's letters. Together, they plan revenge. Mrs. Page arranges for Caius to secretly marry Anne; Page arranges for Slender to marry her. IVii. Falstaff meets Mrs. Ford in the forest, but runs away. The town people enter, dressed as fairies and pinch Falstaff. They reveal the plot and have a laugh at Falstaff's expense. Caius and Slender's plans have gone awry: Anne and Fenton snuck away and were married. Page forgives them.

Six Characters in Search of an Author

Composed by Hugo Weisgall (October 13, 1912 – March 11, 1997). Libretto by Denis Johnston. English. Based on the play by Luigi Pirandello. Premiered New York City, New York City Opera, April 26, 1959. Set in a provincial opera house in the present. Drama. Set numbers with recitative.

Sets: 1. **Acts:** 3 acts, 3 scenes. **Length:** I: 48. II: 47. III: 41. **Hazards:** None. **Scenes:** I. A stage set for a rehearsal. II. The stage and a set of Madame Pace's shop. III. The stage and a set of the father's garden.

Major roles: Director Burt Betts (tenor), Father (dramatic baritone), Stepdaughter (dramatic soprano). **Minor roles:** Accompanist Sam Stein (baritone), Stage Manager Mike Pampanickli (comic bass), Mezzo Gwen Thomas (mezzo), Tenore Buffo Terence O'Flaherty (tenor), Prompter

Gertrude Glubb (soprano), Basso Cantante Pasquale Subito (bass), Wardrobe Mistress Mrs. Harbinger (contralto), Coloratura Lili Klein (soprano), Son (high lyric baritone), Mother (mezzo), Madame Pace (contralto). **Mute:** Boy, Child.

Chorus parts: SSAATTBB. **Chorus roles:** Seven deadly sins (Pride, soprano; Envy, soprano; Sloth, alto; Lust, alto; Anger, tenor; Avarice, baritone; Gluttony, bass; Unheardof sin, tenor), actors, carpenters, electricians, ushers, front-office, men, actresses, cleaning women, seamstresses, secretaries. (Eight choristers total to be bolstered by the performers in ensemble sections.) **Dance/movement:** None. **Orchestra:** 2 fl (alto fl, picc), 2 ob (Eng hrn), 2 cl (bs cl), 2 bsn (cont bsn), 2 hrn, 2 trp, 2 trb, tuba, timp, perc, celeste, strings (min. 6-5-4-4-2). **Stageband:** I, II, III: piano. **Publisher:** Merion Music. **Rights:** Copyright 1957, 1960 by Merion Music Inc.

I. The mezzo works on her aria with the accompanist while the other members of the troupe arrive for rehearsal. The soprano is late and the wardrobe mistress is concerned about getting the costumes done. The chorus is to represent the seven deadly sins. They are rehearsing the "Temptation of St. Anthony" by Weisgall when six characters appear, searching for an author. The stepdaughter tells how *her* father was her mother's lover. The mother claims she was sent away by the father (her husband), but he says he did not want to stand between the mother and her lover. The father turned to Madame Pace, a dressmaker, who fixed him up with his own stepdaughter. The director agrees to be the characters' author.

II. The characters reluctantly acquiesce in the director's rewrites, which include setting the scene in Madame Pace's shop. The father suggests the characters play themselves, but the professional players are outraged and the director points out he cannot use non-union people. Madame Pace arrives. She is unhappy with the stepdaughter's work and threatens to send her back home if she does not perform in other ways. The outraged mother interrupts the rehearsal and has to be dragged off. The father and stepdaughter reenact their meeting, after which the professionals do the scene. The director critiques them and the characters laugh at the performers. The stepdaughter insists that in real life she took her dress off, but the director will not have it. They are interrupted by the mother, who recognizes the father and screams.

III. The characters and performers argue over which scenes to perform and whose reality is more real. All agree to set the next scene in the garden of the father's house. The boy and child play. The son refuses to play out the scene with his mother and they fight. The child is found dead in the fountain, drowned by her brother. The boy has stolen the son's gun and in a blackout, the gun goes off. When the lights come up, the characters have disappeared. The players disperse.

Snegurochka • Snow Maiden

Composed by Nicolai Rimsky-Korsakov (March 18, 1844 – June 21, 1908). Libretto by Nicolai Rimsky-Korsakov. Russian. Based on the play by Alexander Nikolayevich Ostrovsky. Premiered St. Petersburg, Maryinsky Theater, February 10, 1882. Set in Russia in legendary times. Fairy tale opera. Set numbers with accompanied recitative. Dramatic prologue. Orchestral interludes before I, III, IV.

Sets: 5. **Acts:** 4 acts, 5 scenes. **Length:** Prologue, I, II, III, IV: 190. **Arias:** Lell's songs (Lell). **Hazards:** III: Miskir chases illusions of the snow maiden that become trees. IV: The spirit of spring rises from the lake. **Scenes:** Prologue. Red mountain near the Tsar's capital. I. The village of Berendey. II. Inside the Tsar's palace. III. In the sacred forest. IV. In the valley of Yarilo.

Major roles: Snegourouchka/Snow Maiden (soprano), Shepherd Lell (contralto), Coupava (soprano), Miskir (baritone). **Minor roles:** Fairy Spring (mezzo), The spirit of the woods (tenor), Tsar Berendey (tenor), King Frost (bass), Bobil (tenor), Bermata (bass), King of the carnival (bass), First herald (tenor), Second herald (bass). **Bit parts:** Bobilicka (mezzo), Page (mezzo). **Mute:** Echo.

Chorus parts: SSSSAAAATTTTBBBB. **Chorus roles:** The Tsar's retinue, boyards and their wives, blind singers, tumblers, shepherds, people, birds, youths, pages, flowers. **Dance/movement:** I: Birds dance. III: Young people, tumblers' ballet. **Orchestra:** 3 fl (2 picc), 2 ob (Eng hrn), 2 or 3 cl (bs cl), 2 bsn, 4 hrn, 2 trp, 3 trb, tuba, timp, perc, harp, celeste, strings. **Stageband:** None. **Publisher:** W. Bessel & Co. **Rights:** Expired.

Prologue. Fairy Spring tells the birds it is her fault the spring is so cold: She allowed herself to be ruled by the Frost King, who will not release their daughter, Snegourouchka, the snow maiden. The parents argue over their daughter's freedom and safety. The snow maiden wishes to sing with her mortal friends, including the shepherd Lell. Fairy Spring tells her daughter to come to her in the vale of Yarilo if she ever needs help. The Frost King instructs the spirit of the woods to guard the snow maiden from all intruders. The people welcome the spring. Snegourochka appears to them and is adopted by Bobil and Bobilicka.

I. Lell sings to Snegourochka, but quickly tires of her. Coupava announces her wedding to the merchant Miskir. Coupava's friends are reluctant to part with her, but Miskir wins them over with gold, spices and cakes. Before the wedding can be celebrated, Miskir falls in love with Snegourochka. When Miskir accuses Coupava of having previous lovers, she calls for revenge. The villagers are appalled at Miskir's behavior and advise Coupava to appeal to the tsar.

II. A chorus of blind singers praises the tsar. Bermata tells the tsar all is well, but the tsar knows that the weather is too cold to give good harvests. He proposes a celebration in honor of the god Yarilo. Coupava pleads her case. Moved, the tsar orders Miskir's arrest. A court is convened and the tsar banishes Miskir. Snegourochka is presented. When she declares she has no lover, the tsar promises rich gifts to him who can awaken love within her heart. He consults the boyards' wives on a suitable husband for Snegourochka and they name Lell. Miskir wishes to try for the snow maiden's hand as well.

III. The people dance and celebrate in a sacred grove and the tsar rewards Lell's singing with a kiss from the maiden of his choice. To Snegourochka's dismay, Lell chooses Coupava. Miskir woos Snegourochka unsuccessfully. When his advances become more forceful, the spirit of the woods rears up and seizes him. The spirit leads Miskir astray with a vision of the snow maiden. Snegourochka interrupts Lell and Coupava exchanging vows of love.

IV. Snegourochka goes to the valley of Yarilo to enlist her mother's aid. "I do not know how to love," the snow maiden laments. Fairy Spring calls on the flowers to fill her daughter's heart with love. Snegourochka falls in love with Miskir, but her mother warns her she will die if Yarilo, the god of summer, beholds her. Miskir insists he must present her before the tsar to prove he has won her love. A chorus of brides and bridegrooms are blessed by the tsar. Miskir presents Snegourochka, but she melts in the hot summer sun. Miskir drowns himself in the lake. The tsar reveals that these misfortunes are blessings in disguise: The snow maiden's presence angered the god Yarilo. Now that she is gone, summer will come in its proper time.

Il Sogno di Scipione • The Dream of Scipio

Composed by Wolfgang Amadeus Mozart (January 27, 1756 – December 5, 1791). Libretto by Pietro Metastasio. Italian. Based on "Somnium Scipionis" by Cicero. Premiered Salzburg, Palace of the Archbishop, April or May, 1772. Set in North Africa circa 200 BC. Azione teatrale. Set numbers with recitative. Overture.

Sets: 1. **Acts:** 1 act, 1 scene. **Length:** I: 110. **Arias:** "Quercia annosa"

(Scipione). **Hazards:** None. **Scenes:** I. Massinissa's palace in Africa and the temple of heaven.

Major roles: Fortuna (soprano), Costanza (soprano), Scipione (tenor). **Minor roles:** Publio (tenor), Emilio (tenor), Licenza (soprano).

Chorus parts: SATB. **Chorus roles:** Heroes. **Dance/movement:** None. **Orchestra:** 2 fl, 2 ob, 2 hrn, 2 trp, timp, strings, continuo. **Stageband:** None. **Publisher:** Breitkopf & Härtel. **Rights:** Expired.

I. Scipione's sleep is disturbed by the goddesses of constancy and fortune who demand he choose between them. He questions them about the temple of heaven and its inhabitants. Scipione's father and adopted grandfather appear before him. Scipione chooses the goddess of constancy. Licenza praises the archbishop Colloredo for whom the piece was composed.

Die Soldaten • The Soldiers

Composed by Bernd Alois Zimmermann (March 20, 1918 – August 10, 1970). Libretto by Bernd Alois Zimmermann. German. Based on the play by Jakob Michael Reinhold Lenz. Premiered Cologne, Opernhaus, February 15, 1965. Set in Armentières and Lille in Flanders in the 18th century. Tragedy. Through composed. Twelve tone style with jazz, Bach chorales. Spoken dialogue. Prelude before I, III, IV. Intermezzo before IIiii.

Sets: 10. **Acts:** 4 acts, 15 scenes. **Length:** I: 35. II: 25. III: 30. IV: 15. **Hazards:** III: Film presentations over stage action. **Scenes:** Ii. In Wesener's house. Iii. Stolzius's house. Iiii. Wesener's house. Iiv. The city moat of Armentières. Iv. Marie's room in Wesener's house. IIi. A coffee house in Armentières. IIii. Wesener's house and Stolzius's house. IIIi. The filled-in city moat. IIIii. Mary's quarters in Lille. IIIiii. Wesener's house. IIIiv. The house of the Countess de la Roche. IIIv. Wesener's house. IVi. Dream sequence set in the coffee house, a ballroom in the house of Madame Bischof, and a tribunal. IVii. Mary's quarters in Armentières. IViii. On the shores of the Lys.

Major roles: Charlotte (mezzo), Marie (dramatic coloratura soprano), Stolzius the draper (high baritone), Baron Desportes (high tenor), Wesener (bass), Pirzel (high tenor), Eisenhardt the army chaplain (helden baritone), Lieutenant Mary (baritone). **Minor roles:** Stolzius's mother (high dramatic contralto), Major Haudy (helden baritone), Three young officers (3 high tenor), Young Count de la Roche (high lyric tenor), Obrist Count of Spannheim (bass), Wesener's old mother (low contralto), Countess de la Roche (mezzo). **Speaking:** Madam Roux (or mute), Young Hunter, Young ensign, Drunken officer, Three Captains, Countess de la Roche's servant. **Dancers:** Three ensigns, Andalusian waitress.

Chorus parts: N/A. **Chorus roles:** Officers and ensigns (rhythmic speech, not sung). **Dance/movement:** II: Three young ensigns dance a glorification of army life. Andalusian waitress dances. III: Twist and waltzing in film clips. Drunken soldiers dance. **Orchestra:** 4 fl (picc, alto fl), 3 ob (Eng hrn, ob d'amore), 4 cl (bs cl), alto sax, 3 bsn (cont bsn), 5 hrn (5 tenor tuba, bs tuba), 4 trp, bs trp, 4 trb (bs trb), tuba, timp, 8 or 9 perc, 2 harp, cembalo, piano (celeste), 1 or 2 organ, guitar, strings (14-12-10-10-8). **Stageband:** I, II, III, IV: 3 perc. II, IV: jazz combo (cl, trp, guitar, cont bs). **Publisher:** B. Schott's Söhne. **Rights:** Copyright 1966 by B. Schott's Söhne.

Ii. Charlotte teases her sister, Marie, about her love for Stolzius the draper. Iii. Stolzius receives a letter from Marie and begs his mother to let him reply. Iiii. Baron Desportes woos Marie. He asks Wesener to be allowed to take her to the theater. Fearing for Marie's reputation, Wesener refuses. Iiv. A group of soldiers returns from the theater arguing philosophy. Iv. Although Marie loves Stolzius, she prefers to be a baroness.

IIi. Soldiers carousing at the inn anger Stolzius by dropping hints about Marie and Desportes. IIii. Marie gets a proposal via letter from Stolzius. Desportes tells her to refuse and they end up roughhousing. Stolzius's mother complains about Marie's faithlessness.

IIIi. Eisenhardt and Pirzel philosophize. IIIii. Stolzius joins the army and is assigned as Field Officer Mary's servant. IIIiii. Charlotte chides Marie for being so attentive to Mary. IIIiv. The countess has words with her son, the young count, over the time he spends with Marie. She is concerned because of Marie's bad reputation, but promises to help her. IIIv. The young count takes up with another woman. The countess takes in Marie.

IVi. Marie runs away to join Desportes—who leaves her to be raped by his gamekeeper. IVii. Desportes defends his actions to Mary, but Stolzius poisons Desportes. IViii. Marie's family sets out to find her. Wesener finds her begging on the street and gives her money—without recognizing her.

La Sonnambula • The Sleepwalker

Composed by Vincenzo Bellini (November 3, 1801 – September 23, 1835). Libretto by Felice Romani. Italian. Based on a vaudville by Eugène Scribe J. P. Aumer. Premiered Milan, Teatro Carcano, March 6, 1831. Set in a Swiss village in the early 19th century. Melodrama. Set numbers with recitative. Brief prelude.

Sets: 4. **Acts:** 2 acts, 4 scenes. **Length:** I, II: 120. **Arias:** "Ah! non credea mirarti" (Amina), "Come per me sereno" (Amina), "Vi ravviso" (Rodolfo), "Ah! non giunge!" (Amina), "Prendi, l'anel ti dono" (Elvino). **Hazards:** Amina walking on the mill roof. **Scenes:** Ii. Outskirts of a Swiss village. Iii. A room in Lisa's inn. IIi. A shady vale between the village and the castle. IIii. The village.

Major roles: Count Rodolfo (bass), Amina (soprano), Elvino (tenor), Lisa (soprano). **Minor roles:** Teresa (mezzo), Alessio (bass). **Bit part:** Notary (tenor).

Chorus parts: SSATTBB. **Chorus roles:** Villagers. **Dance/movement:** None. **Orchestra:** 2 fl (picc), 2 ob, 2 cl, 2 bsn, 4 hrn, 2 trp, 3 trb, timp, perc, strings. **Stageband:** I: hrns, military band. **Publisher:** Schirmer, G. Ricordi. **Rights:** Expired.

Ii. The villagers have assembled to celebrate the wedding of Amina while Lisa privately laments her lost love for the bridegroom, Elvino. She spurns Alexis's advances. Amina thanks the villagers and her mother, Teresa, for their devotion. She prods Alexis about his attachment to Lisa who is cold to him. Elvino and Amina sign the marriage contract. Count Rodolfo arrives after a hard journey, making everyone wonder about the stranger who appears so oppressed by grief. Amina apparently reminds Rodolfo—who is the son of the late lord of the castle—of someone in his past. It grows dark and the villagers disperse, hoping to avoid the ghostly woman who roams at night. The count retires to Lisa's inn. Elvino is jealous of Rodolfo. Iii. Rodolfo is flattering Lisa when they are interrupted by Amina, who enters through the window—sleepwalking. She is dreaming aloud of her coming marriage. Rodolfo flees and Lisa slips away, dropping her veil. The villagers come to pay their respects to Rodolfo—and discover Amina instead. She awakes and Elvino accuses her of faithlessness. None believe Amina's protestations of innocence.

IIi. A delegation of villagers goes to the castle to beg Rodolfo to clear Amina's name. On their way home, Amina and her mother pass Elvino's house and see him grieving. But he still spurns Amina, even though Rodolfo has declared her innocent. IIii. Lisa again rejects Alexis and is wooed by Elvino. They are heading off to church to be married when Rodolfo catches up with them and explains that Amina is a sleepwalker—and innocent. But still no one believes him. When Lisa brags that she was not found in Rodolfo's chamber, Theresa refutes her by producing Lisa's veil, which confounds Elvino. He is only convinced of Amina's innocence when she appears on the mill roof, fast asleep. She successfully avoids the wheel mill and approaches Elvino who awakens her, whereupon they renew their pledges of love.

The Spanish Lady

Composed by Edward Elgar (June 2, 1857 – February 23, 1934). Libretto by Edward Elgar. English. Based on "The Devil is an Ass" by Ben Jonson. Premiered London, BBC Radio Broadcast, December 4, 1969. Set in London and Hell in 1616. Comedy. Set numbers with spoken dialogue. Prologue. Introduction before II. Unfinished at the composer's death. Fifteen excerpts orchestrated by Percy M. Young. Stage premiere London, St. John's, Smith Square, May 15, 1986.

Sets: 3. **Acts:** 2 acts, 6 scenes (including prologue). **Length:** I, II: 80. **Hazards:** Prologue: Satan conjures up an image of Fitzdottrel. **Scenes:** Prologue. In hell. Ii. A street outside an inn. Iii. Lady Tailbush's drawing room. Iiii. The street. IIi. The drawing room. IIii. The street.

Major roles: Fitzdottrel (bass), Meercraft (baritone), Lady Tailbush (mezzo), Wittipol (tenor), Frances (soprano). **Minor roles:** Ananias (bass), Everill (baritone), Manly (tenor), Citizen (tenor), Lady Eitherside (coloratura soprano). **Speaking:** Satan, Pug, Engine the clothes man, Parson Palate. **Speaking bits:** Tobie, Washerwoman, Captain, Crowd member, Adventurer.

Chorus parts: SATB. **Chorus roles:** Citizens. **Dance/movement:** I: Teenagers dance in the street. II: Gigue, country dance and gavotte at Lady Tailbush's reception. **Orchestra:** 2 fl (picc), ob, 2 cl, bsn, 2 hrn, trp, harp, perc, strings. **Stageband:** None. **Publisher:** Novello. **Rights:** Copyright 1990 by Novello & Company (Young arrangement).

Prologue. Satan agrees to send Pug on a mission to London. He disguises him as a cut purse who is servant to the squire Fitzdottrel. Ii. In London, Meercraft sells his various get-rich-quick schemes to the crowd. A group of adventurers sings the praises of the New World. Iii. Meercraft hawks cosmetics to Lady Tailbush, who is in love with Frank Manly. Iiii. Meercraft sells Fitzdottrel on a scheme to reclaim lands that are underwater. Wittipol woos Fitzdottrel's ward, Frances, but is chased

away by Fitzdottrel. Meercraft tells Fitzdottrel about a Spanish lady who
he should meet.

IIi. Fitzdottrel and Frances attend a reception at Lady Tailbush's where
they meet the Spanish lady (really Wittipol in disguise). Wittipol has a
tête-à-tête with Frances. IIii. Frances and Wittipol are secretly married.
Fitzdottrel discovers the lovers, but forgives them. Pug returns to hell,
defeated.

Lo Speziale • The Apothecary

Composed by Franz Joseph Haydn (March 31, 1732 – May 31, 1809).
Libretto by Carlo Goldoni. Italian. Original work. Premiered Esterháza,
Court Theater, Autumn 1768. Set in an apothecary's shop in the 18th
century. Dramma giocoso. Set numbers with recitative. Overture.

Sets: 3. **Acts:** 3 acts, 6 scenes. **Length:** I: 40. II: 20. III: 5. **Arias:** "Questa e
un'altro novità" (Sempronio), "Per quel che ha mal di stomaco"
(Mengone), Grilletta mocking aria (Grilletta). **Hazards:** None. **Scenes:** Ii.
The apothecary's dispensary. Iii – IIi. The inner chamber of the dispen-
sary. IIii. The dispensary. IIIi. The garden of the apothecary's house. IIIii.
The dispensary.

Major roles: Mengone (tenor), Sempronio (tenor), Volpino (soprano),
Grilletta (soprano).

Chorus parts: N/A. **Chorus roles:** None. **Dance/movement:** None.
Orchestra: fl, 2 ob, bsn, 2 hrn, cembalo, strings. **Stageband:** None.
Publisher: Haydn Mozart Press. **Rights:** Expired.

Ii. Mengone fills prescriptions while his employer, the apothecary,
Sempronio, reads the newspaper. Sempronio plans to marry his ward,
Grilletta. Volpino brings a fake prescription to Mengone. He loves
Grilletta and while Mengone is trying to read the prescription, he talks
to Grilletta. Volpino hopes Grilletta will marry him, but she is more
interested in Mengone. Volpino decides to fight Mengone to win
Grilletta. Iii. Grilletta confesses her feelings to Mengone. Sempronio sees
them holding hands and is furious.

IIi. Volpino asks Sempronio for Grilletta's hand, but the apothecary
refuses. Sempronio accuses all women of infidelity. Mengone and
Grilletta fight and Grilletta storms out. Mengone repents his words.
IIii. In a rage, Grilletta agrees to marry Sempronio. Sempronio summons
a notary to draw up the marriage contract. Volpino comes disguised as
the notary. Mengone also disguises himself as a notary. To quiet the two

men, Sempronio agrees to pay for two copies of the marriage contract. Sempronio discovers the fraud when each notary writes in his own name as the bridegroom.

IIIi. Volpino tells Sempronio that a rich Turk wants to hire him. Volpino disguises himself as a Turk. IIIii. Mengone and Grilletta make up. Sempronio accepts the Turk's terms and agrees to let him marry Grilletta. Mengone disguises himself as a Turk. Mengone and Grilletta are married. Volpino and Sempronio discover the deception too late.

Die Spieler • The Gamblers

Composed by Dmitri Shostakovich (September 25, 1906 – August 9, 1975) and Krzysztof Meyer (b. August 11, 1943). Libretto by Krzysztof Meyer. German. Based on the play by Nikolay Gogol. Premiered Wuppertal, Opernhaus, June 12, 1983. Set in a provincial inn at an unspecified time. Drama. Through composed. Preludes before I and III. Composed largely by Meyer from some music left by Shostakovich.

Sets: 1. **Acts:** 3 acts, 3 scenes. **Length:** I: 60. II: 40. III: 35. **Hazards:** None. **Scenes:** I – III. A room in a provincial inn.

Major roles: Ikharyov (tenor), Shvokhnyev (bass), Uteshityelny (baritone). **Minor roles:** Alexey (bass), Gavryushka (bass), Krugel (tenor), Mikhayl Glov (bass), Alexander Glov (baritone), Zamukhrishkin (tenor).

Chorus parts: N/A. **Chorus roles:** None. **Dance/movement:** None. **Orchestra:** 3 fl (alto fl, picc), 2 ob, Eng hrn, 3 cl, bs cl, 3 bsn (cont bsn), 4 hrn, 3 trp, 3 trb, tuba, timp, perc, xylophone, balalaika, 2 harp, piano, strings. **Stageband:** None. **Publisher:** Moscow Soviet Composers. **Rights:** Copyright 1983 by Moscow Soviet Composers.

I. Alexey shows the card shark Ikharyov and his servants to their rooms in the inn. Krugel and Shvokhnyev are suspicious, but they and Uteshityelny agree to gamble with Ikharyov. Paying Alexey to substitute a marked deck, Ikharyov wins handsomely. His opponents—themselves card sharks—propose an alliance. Ikharyov accepts and they discuss methods, deciding to fleece the landowner Mikhayl Glov.

II. Glov is in town to mortgage his estate to pay his daughter's dowry. Since he is leaving town, he asks Uteshityelny to look out for his son, Alexander. As soon as Glov leaves, the gamblers win all the mortgage money from Alexander and persuade him to go straight to his Hussar regiment.

III. The gamblers try to hurry up the bank's payment of the mortgage money. When they can't, Uteshityelny and his friends—claiming urgent business elsewhere—persuade Ikharyov to advance them half the sum and take the bank note. They fly town, leaving Alexander to explain to Ikharyov that he's been swindled: The whole thing was a fraud.

Stiffelio

Composed by Giuseppe Verdi (October 9, 1813 – January 27, 1901). Libretto by Francesco Maria Piave. Italian. Play "Le Pasteur" by Émile Souvestre and Eugène Bourgeois. Premiered Trieste, Teatro Grande, November 16, 1850. Set in Austria in and around Stankar's castle by the river Salzbach in the early 19th century. Lyric drama. Set numbers with recitative. Overture. "Stiffelio" later used by Verdi as the basis for his opera "Aroldo."

Sets: 5. Acts: 3 acts, 5 scenes. Length: I, II, III: 110. Arias: "Vidi dovunque gemere" (Stiffelio), "Ah, dagli scanni eterei" (Lina). Hazards: None. Scenes: Ii. A hall on the ground floor of Stankar's castle. Iii. A reception hall in the castle. II. An old cemetery near a church. IIIi. An anteroom in Stankar's castle. IIIii. The interior of a Gothic church.

Major roles: Stiffelio/Rudolfo Müller (tenor), Count Stankar (baritone), Lina (soprano), Raffaele (tenor). Minor roles: Jorg (bass), Dorotea (mezzo). Bit parts: Federico di Frengel (tenor). Mute: Fritz.

Chorus parts: SSATTBB. Chorus roles: Count's friends, Stiffelio's disciples, members of the Assasverian congregation. Dance/movement: None. Orchestra: 2 fl (picc), 3 ob (Eng hrn), 2 cl, 2 bsn, 4 hrn, 2 trp, 3 trb, cimbasso, timp, perc, celeste, organ, strings. Stageband: None. Rights: Expired.

Ii. The Protestant minister Rodolfo Müller (known as Stiffelio) returns to the castle of his father-in-law, Count Stankar. Stiffelio hears that a man was seen escaping from a woman's chamber eight days ago. He does not realize it was Raffaele, who is having an affair with Stiffelio's wife, Lina. Stiffelio burns the papers the man dropped rather than discover a guilty secret. He notices that Lina does not have her wedding ring and warns her he will not forgive infidelity. Realizing the truth, Stankar insists that Lina hide the past. Raffaele leaves a letter for Lina, but is overseen by Jorg. Iii. Stiffelio's followers welcome him home. Jorg mistakenly tells Stiffelio that a letter was left for Lina by her cousin Federico. Stiffelio retrieves the letter, but Stankar tears it up before Stiffelio can read it. Stankar challenges Raffaele to a duel.

II. Raffaele meets Lina in the cemetery. She asks him to return her ring and leave, but he refuses. Stankar reveals that Raffaele is not a noble, but a foundling. They fight until Stiffelio interrupts them. Stiffelio tries to make peace, but when Stankar inadvertently reveals Raffaele's crime, Stiffelio wants to continue the duel himself. The voices of the congregation recall Stiffelio to his priestly duties and he collapses.

IIIi. Stankar considers suicide. Stiffelio asks Raffaele what he would do if Lina were free. He hides Raffaele in the room while he offers Lina a divorce. With some reluctance, Lina agrees. She reaffirms her love for Stiffelio and begs forgiveness. Raffaele seduced her, she says. Stankar emerges from Raffaele's hiding place, having killed Raffaele. IIIii. Lina comes to hear Stiffelio preach. While delivering his sermon, Stiffelio pardons Lina.

Kamennyi Gost • The Stone Guest

Composed by Alexander Dargomyzhsky (February 14, 1813 – January 17, 1869). Libretto by Alexander Dargomyzhsky. Russian. Based on the dramatic poem by Pushkin. Premiered St. Petersburg, Maryinsky Theater, February 28, 1872. Set in Spain in the 17th century. Tragedy. Set numbers with accompanied recitative. Prelude. Completed after composer's death by Cui and Rimsky-Korsakov.

Sets: 4. **Acts:** 3 acts, 4 scenes. **Length:** I: 40. II: 20. III: 15. **Hazards:** II: Statue of the commander moves. III: Commander and Don Juan sink into the earth. **Scenes:** Ii. In the precincts of a monastery. Iii. A chamber in Laura's house. II. The mausoleum of the commander. III. A room in Doña Anna's house.

Major roles: Don Juan (tenor), Leporello (bass), Doña Anna (soprano), Laura (mezzo). **Minor roles:** Monk (bass), First guest (tenor), Second guest (bass), Don Carlos (baritone). **Bit parts:** Third guest (tenor), Fourth guest (bass), Commander (bass).

Chorus parts: TTBB. **Chorus roles:** Laura's guests. **Dance/movement:** None. **Orchestra:** 2 fl (picc), 2 ob, 2 cl, 2 bsn, 4 hrn, 2 trp, 3 trb, timp, harp, perc, strings. **Stageband:** None. **Publisher:** Leningrad Music, W. Bessel & Co. **Rights:** Expired.

Ii. Don Juan returns to Madrid in spite of having been banished for killing the commander. He is intrigued by rumors that the commander's widow, Doña Anna, is beautiful. Iii. Don Juan's mistress, Laura, sings for her guests. She is attracted to Don Carlos and when Don Juan returns, Laura admits she loves him. Don Carlos challenges Don Juan and is killed.

II. Disguised as a monk, Don Juan awaits Doña Anna in the mausoleum of her husband. He tells her he is really Don Diego and she invites him to her house. As a joke, Don Juan invites the statue of the dead commander to accompany him. The statue accepts.

III. Anna is attracted to Don Juan. He confesses he killed her husband, but says he has never loved anyone but her. The statue of the commander arrives and drags Don Juan down to hell.

La Straniera • The Foreign Woman

Composed by Vincenzo Bellini (November 3, 1801 – September 23, 1835). Libretto by Felice Romani. Italian. After "L'Étrangère" by Victor-Prévôt and Vicomte d'Arlincourt. Premiered Milan, Teatro alla Scala, February 14, 1829. Set in Brittany in the 14th century. Opera seria. Set numbers with recitative. Introduction.

Sets: 6. **Acts:** 2 acts, 7 scenes. **Length:** I, II: 140. **Arias:** "Sì li sciogliete" (Valdeburgo), "Ah! se non'mami più" (Isoletta). **Hazards:** I: Wedding celebrations on boats on the lake. Valdeburgo falls into the lake. Arturo jumps in after him. **Scenes:** Ii. Vestibule in the castle of Montolino. Iii. Interior of a cottage. Iiii. A forest. Iiv. A remote spot. IIi. A grand hall. IIii. The forest. IIiii. The vestibule of the chapel of the knights of Malta.

Major roles: Baron of Valdeburgo (baritone), Arturo (tenor), Alaide (soprano). **Minor roles:** Isoletta (mezzo), Montolino (bass), Osburgo (tenor), Prior of the knights of Malta (bass). **Bit parts:** Four distant voices.

Chorus parts: SATTB. **Chorus roles:** Ladies in waiting, knights, gondoliers, fishermen, huntsmen, guards, vassals. **Dance/movement:** None. **Orchestra:** 2 fl (picc), 2 ob, 2 cl, 2 bsn, 4 hrn, 2 trp, 3 trb, serpent, cimbasso, timp, perc, strings. **Stageband:** I: 2 hrn, bsn. II: 4 hrn, 2 bsn, serpent, 2 cl, harp. **Publisher:** Schlesinger, Garland Publishing. **Rights:** Expired.

Ii. Arturo is engaged to Isoletta, but Arturo's friend Valdeburgo suspects that Arturo does not love his fiancée. His fears are confirmed by Isoletta, who knows that Arturo loves the outcast stranger, Alaide. Osburgo promises Isoletta's father that Arturo will marry Isoletta. Iii. Arturo visits Alaide. They love each other, but Alaide does not want Arturo to share her misfortunes. Iiii. Osburgo spies on Alaide. Valdeburgo and Alaide recognize each other, making Arturo jealous. Valdeburgo begs

Arturo to leave. Iiv. Osburgo tells Arturo that Valdeburgo and Alaide are lovers. This appears to be confirmed when Arturo overhears Alaide and Valdeburgo planning to run away. Arturo challenges Valdeburgo and they fight, whereupon Valdeburgo is wounded and falls into the lake. Alaide explains that Valdeburgo is her brother. Arturo plunges into the lake to save Valdeburgo. Osburgo's men find Alaide with Arturo's bloody sword and arrest her.

IIi. Osburgo accuses Alaide of Valdeburgo's murder. At the trial, Alaide swears her innocence, but refuses to give evidence or reveal her identity. Arturo tries to save Alaide by confessing, but the court condemns them both. Valdeburgo returns alive. Without a crime, the court is forced to release Alaide, but they demand to know her identity. She reveals her face only to the judge. IIii. Valdeburgo persuades Arturo that he must forget Alaide and marry Isoletta. IIiii. The nuptials begin. Isoletta realizes Arturo does not love her and stops the wedding. But Alaide appears and persuades them to go through with it. Alaide's identity is at last revealed: she is the exiled queen. Arturo kills himself and Alaide faints.

Street Scene

Composed by Kurt Weill (March 2, 1900 – April 3, 1950). Libretto by Langston Hughes. English. Based on the play by Elmer Rice. Premiered New York City, Adelphi Theater, January 9, 1947. Set on a sidewalk in New York City in the present. American opera. Set numbers with spoken dialogue. Interlude before IIii.

Sets: 1. **Acts:** 2 acts, 3 scenes. **Length:** I, II: 150. **Arias:** "I got a marble and a star" (Henry Davis), "Somehow I never could believe" (Anna), "Lonely house" (Sam), "Wouldn't you like to be on Broadway?" (Harry Easter), "What use would the moon be?" (Rose). **Hazards:** None. **Scenes:** I – II. A sidewalk in New York City.

Major roles: Sam Kaplan (tenor), Anna Maurrant (dramatic soprano), Frank Maurrant (bass baritone), Rose Maurrant (lyric soprano). **Minor roles:** Greta Fiorentino (high soprano), Emma Jones (mezzo), Olga Olsen (contralto), Abraham Kaplan (tenor), Henry Davis (high baritone), Willie Maurrant (treble), Daniel Buchanan (comic tenor), George Jones (baritone), Lippo Fiorentino (tenor), Jennie Hildebrand (mezzo), Charlie Hildebrand (child), Mary Hildebrand (child), Grace Davis (child), Harry Easter (light baritone), Mae Jones (singer/dancer, mezzo), Dick McGann (singer/dancer, tenor), Joan (child), Myrtle (child), Joe (child). **Bit parts:** Negro woman (soprano), Two Salvation Army girls (soprano, mezzo), Carl Olsen (bass), Mrs. Hildebrand (mezzo), First graduate (soprano), Second graduate (mezzo), First nursemaid (soprano), Second nursemaid (mezzo). **Speaking:** Shirley Kaplan, Steve Sankey, Vincent Jones, City Marshall James Henry, Fred Cullen, Officer Murphy. **Speaking bits:** Dr. Wilson, Policeman, Milkman, Workman, Old clothes man, Man, Another man, Grocery boy, Ambulance driver, Girl violin student, Medical intern, Married couple.

Chorus parts: SSAATTBB. **Chorus roles:** Passersby, neighbors, children (2 parts). **Dance/movement:** I: Mrs. Maurrant and Lippo Fiorentino dance. I: Mae and Dick dance. **Orchestra:** fl, ob 2 cl, bs cl, bsn, 2 hrn, 2 trp, 2 trb, harp, piano, perc, strings. **Stageband:** II: siren. **Publisher:** Chappell Music Company. **Rights:** Copyright 1948 by Kurt Weill, Elmer Rice and Langston Hughes. Copyright renewed.

I. The neighborhood women complain about the heat and discuss Anna Maurrant's affair with Steve Sankey. Sam Kaplan calls on Rose Maurrant, but she is not yet home. Mrs. Buchanan is pregnant and her husband is a nervous wreck. Frank Maurrant is upset that his daughter (Rose) is out so late. His wife, Anna, continues to believe in a dream of love—in spite of a disappointing marriage and her growing distance from her two children. Sankey and Anna Maurrant sneak off together. Lippo Fiorentino adores ice cream. When Frank Maurrant threatens to discipline his son, Kaplan lectures him on the immorality of capitalism. Maurrant insists he means to bring up his children in the old ways. The neighbors congratulate Jennie Hildebrand on her art scholarship. Mrs. Hildebrand is proud of Jennie but cannot forget that they are to be evicted tomorrow. Lippo and Mrs. Maurrant dance, but are interrupted by Sankey's arrival. Frank Maurrant asks about Sankey and learns that his son, Willie, has been in a fight. Sam is angry with the women for gossiping about Mrs. Maurrant. Harry Easter brings Rose home from a date. He tells her he loves her and tries to persuade her to go on the stage. Rose is not interested in Easter (who is married) or Broadway. Buchanan asks Rose to call the doctor for his wife. Mae and Dick have been out drinking. They dance. Vincent Jones manhandles Rose. When Sam comes to her rescue, Vincent punches him. Rose talks over her mother's infidelities with Sam. They kiss.

IIi. Mrs. Buchanan has given birth. The children play but end up fighting. Rose asks her father to be more tender with Anna. Frank and Anna fight. Frank has started drinking. Rose hints to her mother that Sankey should not show himself so often in the neighborhood. Anna fusses over her son, Willie. Shirley Kaplan hopes that Rose will not distract Sam from his studies. Desperate, Rose considers Easter's offer of a stage career. Sam suggests they run away, but Rose says she has to think about it. Easter invites Rose out, but she declines. With Frank supposedly off to New Haven, Anna invites Sankey into the apartment. A city marshal comes to evict the Hildebrands. Frank returns drunk. When

Sam blocks his path, Frank pushes him out of the way. Frank shoots his wife and Sankey and makes his escape. Anna is taken to the hospital. IIii. Two nursemaids gawk at the crime scene. Anna dies. Sam and Shirley comfort Rose. After a brief gun battle, Frank is taken into custody. He tells Rose he loved Anna and is sorry. He expects a death sentence. Rose tells Sam she must go away by herself. "Perhaps some day we can be together," she says. She leaves. The women gossip.

The Student Prince

Composed by Sigmund Romberg (July 29, 1887 – November 9, 1951). Libretto by Dorothy Donnelly. English. Based on "Old Heidelberg" by Rudolf Bleichmann, itself based on the novella "Alt Heidelberg" by Wilhelm Meyer-Forster. Premiered New York City, Jolson Theater, December 2, 1924. Set in Karlsburg and Heidelberg in 1860. Light opera. Set numbers with spoken dialogue. Introduction before II. Opening and ballet before III. Prologue. Serenade intermezzo before IV.

Sets: 4. **Acts:** 4 acts, 5 scenes (including prologue). **Length:** I, II, III, IV: 100. **Hazards:** None. **Scenes:** Prologue. Antechamber in the palace at Karlsberg. I. Garden of the inn of the "Three Golden Apples" at the university of Heidelberg. II. Sitting room of Prince Karl at the inn. III. A room of state in the royal palace of Karlsberg. IV. The garden of the inn.

Major roles: Prince Karl Franz (tenor), Kathie (soprano). **Minor roles:** First lackey (tenor), Second lackey (tenor), Third lackey (tenor), Fourth lackey (tenor), Dr. Engel (baritone), Gretchen (soprano), Ruder (baritone), Von Asterberg (tenor), Lucas (bass), Count Hugo Detlef (tenor), Captain Tarnitz (tenor), Princess Margaret (soprano). **Speaking:** Prime Minister Von Mark, Toni the waiter, Nicolas, Lutz the valet, Hubert the footman, Grand Duchess Anastasia, Countess Leydon, Baron Arnheim, Rudolph Winter. **Speaking bits:** Freshman, Captain of the guard, Second guard. **Bit parts:** Waiter, Big student.

Chorus parts: SATTBB. **Chorus roles:** Girls, students, courtiers, officers. **Dance/movement:** I: Girls' dance. II: can can. III: waltz, gavotte. **Orchestra:** 2 fl (picc), ob, 2 cl, bsn, 2 hrn, 2 trp, 2 trb, harp, piano, timp, perc, strings. **Stageband:** I: Nicolas plays pipe. II: bell. **Publisher:** Chappell & Co., Tams Witmark. **Rights:** Copyright 1932 by Harms, Inc. Copyright renewed.

Prologue. Prince Karl Franz is sent off to attend university at Heidelberg. I. The prince's valet Lutz inspects the inn where the prince is to live. He is horrified by the rowdy students, but the prince decides to remain. He meets Kathie, the niece of the proprietor and makes friends with his fellow students.

II. Lutz hates student life. The prince and his friends return after a night of drinking and carousing. His fiancée, Prince Margaret, calls unexpectedly with her mother. The prince and Kathie have fallen in love. Word comes that the king is dying and the prince reluctantly says goodbye to Kathie.

III. Two years have passed since the king's death and still the new king puts off his marriage to the princess. A waiter from Heidelberg tells the king how things have changed at his old inn and the king decides to return for Kathie.

IV. The princess convinces Kathie to give up the prince. When the prince returns, Kathie tells him she is engaged to her cousin.

Summer and Smoke

Composed by Lee Hoiby (b. February 17, 1926). Libretto by Lanford Wilson. English. Based on the play by Tennessee Williams. Premiered St. Paul, Minnesota, St. Paul Opera Association, June 19, 1971. Set in Glorious Hill, Mississippi in the late 19th, early 20th century. Psychological drama. Through composed. Some spoken lines. Prologue. Epilogue. Interludes between scenes. Prelude before II.

Sets: 5. **Acts:** 2 acts, 14 scenes. **Hazards:** None. **Scenes:** Prologue – Ii. A small park. Iii – Iiii. The rectory. Iiv. Dr. Buchanan's office. Iv. The Moon Lake Casino. Ivi. The rectory and the Moon Lake Casino. IIi. The rectory and Dr. Buchanan's office. IIii. The doctor's office and house. IIiii. The rectory. IIiv. The doctor's office. IIv. The park. IIvi. The doctor's office. Epilogue. The park.

Major roles: Alma Winemiller (soprano), John Buchanan Jr. (baritone). **Minor roles:** The Reverend Winemiller (bass baritone), Nellie Ewell (lyric soprano), Vernon (baritone), Mrs. Bassett (mezzo), Roger Doremus (tenor), Rosemary (soprano), Rosa Gonzales (mezzo, dancer), Archie Kramer (baritone). **Bit part:** Dr. Buchanan (bass baritone). **Speaking:** Young Alma, Young John, Mrs. Winemiller, Papa Gonzales. **Mute:** Townspeople.

Chorus parts: N/A. **Chorus roles:** None. **Dance/movement:** II: Rosa dances for John. **Orchestra:** 2 fl (picc), 2 ob (Eng hrn), 2 cl (bs cl), 2 bsn, 4 hrn, 2 trp, 2 trb, timp, perc, glockenspiel, xylophone, harp, celeste, strings. **Stageband:** I: piano, guitar. II: 2 vln, 2 trp, cont bs, taped marching band. **Publisher:** Belwin Mills. **Rights:** Copyright 1976 by Belwin Mills Publishing Corp.

Prologue. Two young children, Alma and Johnny, examine a statue of an angel in the park. They kiss. Johnny yanks the ribbon from Alma's hair and runs away. Ii. The adult Alma attends a fourth of July celebration with her parents, the Reverend and Mrs. Winemiller. Alma stays behind to wait for Roger. John, who is now a doctor and has returned home for the summer, approaches her and they talk. He asks her out. Iii. Alma gives Nellie her singing lesson, but Mrs. Winemiller keeps interrupting. (Mrs. Winemiller has severe psychological problems.) Alma learns that her mother has stolen a hat from Mr. Gilliam's store. Nellie tells Alma she saw John out with Rosa Gonzales from the Moon Lake Casino. Mrs. Winemiller says Alma is in love with John. Alma sends Nellie away and berates her mother for always acting like a child. She tries to retrieve the stolen hat from her mother. Iiii. Alma hosts her literary group and John attends. The guests vote to postpone the reading of Vernon's play in favor of Rosemary's paper on William Blake. Mrs. Bassett heckles the reading and the guests squabble. John leaves and Mrs. Winemiller's hallucinations scare the others away. Iiv. John gets home at two in the morning with Rosa. He has a knife wound in his arm. Alma demands to see Dr. Buchanan, John's father, but John calms her down. While Rosa waits outside, John examines Alma. Dr. Buchanan comes down in time to see John go out with Rosa. Iv. John takes Alma to the Moon Lake Casino. He is only interested in self-gratification and has decided to give up medicine. John's presumptuousness offends the ladylike Alma. Ivi. Separately, Alma and John wonder about the coming fall.

IIi. Roger shows Alma photographs. They hear the sounds of a party next door at the Buchanan house. Roger tells Alma that John and Rosa have taken out a marriage license. Alma calls Dr. Buchanan at work and tells him to come home. John goes to the rectory to see Alma. Dr. Buchanan returns home and orders Rosa and her father out of the house, but Papa Gonzalez shoots him. IIii. Outside Dr. Buchanan's sick room, Alma confronts John with his weakness. He tries to reduce all human yearnings to biological necessity. Dr. Buchanan dies. IIiii. The Reverend Winemiller returns home, disgusted at his wife's behavior. Alma has lost the will to live, but John has completed his father's work and is being honored with a parade. IIiv. Back from school, Nellie flirts with John. IIv. Alma's literary group has disintegrated. Nellie tells Alma that John considers her to have been an inspiration to him. IIvi. Alma congratulates John on his achievements. She tells him she has always loved him. They are interrupted by Nellie—who is engaged to John. Epilogue. Alma goes off to the Moon Lake Casino with a young traveling salesman she has just met.

Sunday Excursion

Composed by Alec Wilder (February 16, 1907 – December 24, 1980). Libretto by Arnold Sundgaard. English. Original work Premiered New York City, National Federation of Music Clubs Convention, Grassroots Opera Company, April 17, 1953. Set on a railway coach on the New York, New Haven and Hartford Railroad around 1910. Curtain raiser. Set numbers. Overture.

Sets: 1. **Acts:** 1 act, 1 scene. **Length:** I: 25. **Hazards:** I: Motion of the train starting and stopping. **Scenes:** I. A section of a Sunday excursion coach on the New York, New Haven and Hartford Railroad.

Major roles: Alice (soprano), Veronica (contralto), Marvin (baritone), Hillary (tenor), Tim the candy butcher (bass baritone).

Chorus parts: N/A. **Chorus roles:** None. **Dance/movement:** None. **Orchestra:** fl, ob, 2 cl, bsn, trp, hrn, perc, piano, strings. **Stageband:** None. **Publisher:** G. Schirmer, Inc. **Rights:** Copyright 1953 by G. Schirmer, Inc.

I. Alice and Veronica return home from a disappointing excursion to the city. They eye Marvin and Hillary, who also had a disappointing trip. Marvin and Alice have botany class together. Veronica and Hillary want to meet, so they nudge their companions to make an introduction. Marvin and Alice talk, but forget to introduce their friends. Veronica and Hillary introduce themselves. All four talk about what a wonderful trip they had.

Suor Angelica • Sister Angelica

Composed by Giacomo Puccini (December 22, 1858 – November 29, 1924). Libretto by Giovacchino Forzano. Italian. Original work. Premiered New York City, Metropolitan Opera Association, December 14, 1918. Set in a convent near Siena in the latter part of the 17th century. Verismo opera. Set numbers with accompanied recitative. Second opera of "Il Trittico."

Sets: 1. **Acts:** 1 act, 1 scene. **Length:** I: 53 **Arias:** "Senza mamma" (Angelica). **Hazards:** None. **Scenes:** I: Interior of a convent.

Major roles: Sister Angelica (soprano), Princess (contralto). **Minor roles:** Abbess (mezzo), Monitor (mezzo), Mistress of the novices (contralto), Sister Genevieve (soprano), Nursing sister (mezzo), First attending nun (mezzo). **Bit parts:** Two lay sisters (soprano and mezzo), Sister Osmina (mezzo), Sister Dolcina (mezzo), Two novices (mezzo), Second attending nun (mezzo).

Chorus parts: SSATB. **Chorus roles:** Nuns, offstage angels, offstage children, offstage men. **Dance/movement:** None. **Orchestra:** picc, 2 fl, 2 ob, Eng hrn, 2 cl, bs cl, 2 bsn, 4 hrn, 3 trp, 3 trb, bs trb, timp, perc, celeste, harp, strings. **Stageband:** I: picc, 3 trp, piano, organ, bells. **Publisher:** Ricordi. **Rights:** Expired.

I. The monitor rebukes two lay sisters who were late for worship. They belong to a convent where three nights a year the fountain is turned golden by the sunset. The sisters talk and Genevieve confesses she misses the lambs she used to tend. Sister Angelica claims not to have any desires, but the sisters all know that she longs for news of her noble relations. It has been seven years since she has heard anything. Since she is good with herbs and medicines, Angelica helps the infirmary nurse. The tourières bring food and report that they have seen a grand coach approaching the convent. The abbess announces Angelica's aunt, the princess, who explains that Angelica's sister, Anna Viola, is to be married and Angelica must sign a parchment renouncing all claims to her inheritance. The princess is unmoved when Angelica says she has repented her past indiscretion. "Your child died two years ago," the princess tells Angelica. Overcome with grief, Angelica signs the renunciation and when the princess departs, Angelica poisons herself. She begs forgiveness and sees a vision of the Madonna and child.

Susannah

Composed by Carlisle Floyd (b. June 11, 1926). Libretto by Carlisle Floyd. English. Based on a story in the Apocrypha. Premiered Tallahassee, Florida, Florida State University, February 24, 1955. Set in New Hope Valley, Tennessee in the 1950s. Music drama. Through composed with some set numbers and spoken lines.

Sets: 4. **Acts:** 2 acts, 10 scenes. **Length:** I: 41. II: 53. **Arias:** "Ain't it a pretty night" (Susannah), "The trees on the mountains" (Susannah), "Hear me, O Lord" (Blitch). **Hazards:** None. **Scenes:** Ii. Outside New Hope Church. Iii. The porch of the Polk farmhouse. Iiii. A woods close to the Polk place. Iiv. Outside the church. Iv – IIi. The porch of the Polk farmhouse. IIii. Interior of the New Hope church. IIiii. The porch of the Polk farmhouse. IIiv. Interior of the New Hope church. IIv. The porch of the Polk farmhouse.

Major roles: Olin Blitch (bass baritone), Susannah Polk (soprano), Little Bat McLean (tenor), Sam Polk (tenor). **Minor roles:** Mrs. Gleaton (soprano), Mrs. Hayes (soprano), Mrs. McLean (mezzo), Mrs. Ott (contralto), Elder McLean (bass), Elder Hayes (tenor), Elder Ott (bass), Elder Gleaton (tenor). **Bit parts:** First man (bass), Second man (bass).

Chorus parts: SATB. **Chorus roles:** People of New Hope Valley. **Dance/movement:** I: Square dancing. **Orchestra:** 2 fl (picc), 2 ob (Eng hrn), 2 cl (bs cl), 2 bsn (cont bsn), 4 hrn, 2 trp, 3 trb, tuba, timp, perc, celeste, harp, xylophone, strings. **Stageband:** None. **Publisher:** Boosey & Hawkes. **Rights:** Copyright 1956, 1957 by Boosey & Hawkes. Copyright renewed.

Ii. While the young people square dance, Mrs. McLean, Gleaton, Hayes and Ott discuss the arrival of the Reverend Olin Blitch. They agree that pretty, young Susannah is a shameless flirt. Blitch notices Susannah and the women tell him she was brought up by her drunken brother, Sam. The preacher joins her in the square dance. Iii. Little Bat, though not very bright, is in love with Susannah. He walks her home from the dance in spite of his fear of Sam. Susannah wonders what it would be like to live in the valley. Little Bat makes a hasty exit when Sam returns. Brother and sister talk and sing. Iiii. The elders search for a creek that Blitch can use for baptisms. They encounter Susannah, bathing nude, and convert their feelings of lust to righteous indignation. This girl is of the devil, they agree. Iiv. The elders have spread their story throughout the valley and when Susannah shows up for the communal picnic she is ostracized. Iv. Little Bat tells Susannah what people are saying. When he admits that they cowed him into swearing that Susannah seduced him, she tells him never to come back. Sam wonders at how hard-hearted people are.

IIi. Susannah asks why God is punishing her when she didn't do anything wrong. Sam, who has to go away for the evening, persuades Susannah to go to the preacher's meeting where, he hopes, she will be safe. IIii. In church, Blitch collects the offering and gives an impassioned sermon calling on sinners to repent. He tries to force Susannah to come forward and make public confession, but she will not. IIiii. Blitch visits Susannah at home. He first tries to make her repent and then seduces her. IIiv. Horrified at what he has done, the preacher prays for himself and Susannah. His attempts to convince the elders that they have sinned against Susannah meet with haughty disbelief. Susannah ignores his own pleas for forgiveness. IIv. Sam returns drunk and when Susannah tells him what has happened, he grabs a shotgun and runs off. A shotgun blast is heard and Susannah falls on her knees to pray. Little Bat runs in with the news that Sam has killed the preacher. When the men come for Susannah, she laughs and chases them away with Sam's gun. Little Bat again approaches and Susannah slaps him.

Švanda Dudák • Švanda the Bagpiper

Composed by Jaromír Weinberger (January 8, 1896 – August 8, 1967). Libretto by Miloš Kareš. Czech. Based on a story by J. K. Tyl. Premiered Prague, Czech National Opera, April 27, 1927. Set in Bohemia and hell in legendary times. Folk opera. Through composed. Overture. Intermezzo before Iii. Some spoken dialogue. Ballet. Often known by the German spelling, "Schwanda."

Sets: 4. **Acts:** 2 acts, 5 scenes. **Length:** I: 85. II: 45. **Hazards:** I: Flames blaze from the ground and the earth swallows Švanda. II: Devil conjures up a vision of Dorotka. Devils prepare a flaming kettle for Švanda. Hell sinks out of sight. **Scenes:** Ii. Švanda's farmyard. Iii. The Queen's apartments. Iiii. An open place outside the town. IIi. Hell. IIii. Švanda's farmyard.

Major roles: Dorotka (soprano), Babinský (tenor), Švanda (baritone). **Minor roles:** Queen (mezzo), Magician (bass), Judge (tenor), Devil (bass), Devil's familiar (tenor). **Bit parts:** First forester (tenor), Second forester (bass), Captain of Hell (tenor), Executioner (tenor). **Mute:** Twelve headsmen, Warder.

Chorus parts: SSAATTBB. **Chorus roles:** Stewards, courtiers, attendants of the queen, soldiers, guards, people, devils, villagers. **Dance/movement:** I: The queen's attendants dance a polka to amuse her. Executioners and soldiers dance to Švanda's bagpiping. II: Ghosts and witches appear and dance a polka while the devil plays Švanda's bagpipes. Hell ballet. **Orchestra:** 3 fl (picc), 2 ob (Eng hrn), 2 cl (bs cl), 2 bsn (cont bsn), 4 hrn, 3 trp, 3 trb, tuba, 1 or 2 harps, celeste, organ, timp, perc, strings. **Stageband:** II: 4 trp. **Publisher:** Universal Edition. **Rights:** Copyright 1928, 1929 by Universal Edition.

Ii. The robber Babinský hides on Švanda's farm and is invited to dinner by Švanda and his wife, Dorotka. Over dinner, Babinský persuades Švanda to leave Dorotka and go to court, where the queen has promised to marry anyone who can restore her good humor. Iii. A magician holds queen and court captive until Švanda's bagpipe playing frees them. Dorotka interrupts preparations for the queen to marry Švanda. Furious, the queen has both Dorotka and Švanda imprisoned. Iiii. Švanda is narrowly saved from execution by Babinský. Švanda is reunited with Dorotka, but when he swears he did not kiss the queen, the earth opens and swallows him. Babinský loves Dorotka, but promises to save Švanda.

IIi. Švanda refuses to play his bagpipes for the devil, but the devil tricks him into signing away his soul. Babinský appears and out-cheats the devil at cards. He wins half of the devil's kingdom, but agrees not to claim his prize if Švanda is allowed to go free. Before leaving, Švanda plays for the devil. IIii. Babinský tries to scare Švanda away from Dorotka by saying (incorrectly) that twenty years have passed on earth while they were in hell. Švanda does not care and is reunited with Dorotka.

Il Tabarro • The Cloak

Composed by Giacomo Puccini (December 22, 1858 – November 29, 1924). Libretto by Giuseppe Adami. Italian. Based on the play "La Houppelande" by Didier Gold. Premiered New York City, Metropolitan Opera Association, December 14, 1918. Set in a boat on the Seine in 1910. Verismo opera. Set numbers with accompanied recitative. First opera in "Il Trittico."

Sets: 1. **Acts:** 1 act, 1 scene. **Length:** I: 50. **Arias:** "Nulla, silenzio" (Michele). **Hazards:** I: Michele hides Louis's dead body under his cloak. **Scenes:** I. Michele's barge, anchored in the Seine.

Major roles: Michele (baritone), Luigi (tenor), Giorgetta (soprano), Frugola (mezzo). **Minor roles:** Tinca (tenor), Talpa (bass), Song vendor (tenor). **Bit parts:** Two lovers (soprano, tenor). **Mute:** Organ grinder, Harpist.

Chorus parts: SATBB. **Chorus roles:** Midinettes, stevedores (or sung off-stage and stevedores mute). **Dance/movement:** I: Georgette dances with stevedores. **Orchestra:** picc, 2 fl, 2 ob, Eng hrn, 2 cl, bs cl, 2 bsn, 4 hrn, 3 trp, 3 trb, bs trb, timp, perc, celeste, hand organ, bells, harp, strings. **Stageband:** I: harp, bugle or cornet. **Publisher:** Ricordi. **Rights:** Expired.

I. While the stevedores empty the cargo from Michele's boat, Michele wonders if his wife Giorgetta still loves him. She serves wine to the stevedores, Luigi, Tinca, and Talpa, and dances with Tinca to the music of an organ grinder. Talpa's wife, Frugola, comes looking for him, displaying the odds and ends she has collected on the streets of Paris and talking about her cat. Frugola scolds the men about their drinking and Luigi contemplates the bleakness of life. He and Giorgetta reminisce about the neighborhood in which they both grew up. Luigi asks Michele to take him along to Rouen, but Michele refuses. Luigi and Giorgetta, who are lovers, arrange a night rendezvous. Michele reminds Giorgetta of life before their baby died, when he used to hold them both within his cloak. He knows she has a lover but is trying to win her back. Luigi returns, having mistaken Michele's lit pipe for Georgette's signal. Michele forces Luigi to confess, then kills him and hides the body in his cloak, which he opens to show Giorgetta her lover's corpse.

Skazka o Tsarie Saltanie • The Tale of Tsar Saltan

Composed by Nicolai Rimsky-Korsakov (March 18, 1844 – June 21,

1908). Libretto by Vladimir Ivanovich Belsky. Russian. Based on the poem by Alexander Pushkin. Premiered Moscow, Solodovnikov Theater, November 3, 1900. Set in Russia in legendary times. Fantasy opera. Set numbers with accompanied recitative. Prologue. Preludes before each act and scene. Includes the interlude "The Flight of the Bumble Bee."

Sets: 7. **Acts:** 4 acts, 8 scenes (including prologue). **Length:** I, II, III, IV: 165. **Hazards:** II: Millitrisa and Gvidon washed ashore in a barrel. Swan chased by a kite. Kite shot and killed by Gvidon. Magical city appears. III: Gvidon turns into a bee. IV: Swan transformed into a princess. Tsar shown the wonders of the city (a magic squirrel and 33 magic heroes who emerge from the waves). **Scenes:** Prologue. A rural winter evening. I. A room in the royal palace. II. An island shore. IIIi. A forest. IIIii. A hall in the palace. IVi. The shore. IVii. Inside the citadel of Dedenets. IViii. The entrance to the palace.

Major roles: Tsar Saltan (bass), Tsaritsa Millitrisa (soprano), Povarika (soprano), Tkachika (mezzo), Baba Babarika (contralto), Prince Gvidon (tenor), Swan Princess (soprano), Old grandfather (tenor), Shomorch (bass). **Minor roles:** Courier (baritone), Three Shipmasters (tenor, baritone, bass).

Chorus parts: SSAATTBB. **Chorus roles:** Enchanters, spirits, nurses, guards, boyars, people. **Dance/movement:** None. **Orchestra:** picc, 2 fl, 2 ob, Eng hrn, 3 cl (bs cl), 2 bsn, cont bsn, 4 hrn, 3 trp, 3 trb, tuba, timp, perc, xylophone, celeste, 1 or 2 harps, strings. **Stageband:** II: trp, bells, bs drum. **Rights:** Expired.

Prologue. Watched by the witch Barbarika, three sisters—Povarika, Tkachika and Millitrisa—discuss what they would do if they became Tsaritsa. Povarika says she would cook an enormous feast, while Tkachika decides she would weave cloth for everyone. When Millitrisa says she would bear the tsar a hero for a son, the tsar, who has been listening, bursts into the room and claims Millitrisa as his bride. He appoints the elder sisters as his cook and weaver. Angry and jealous, the two elder sisters plot revenge.

I. Millitrisa has borne the tsar a son, Prince Gvidon, and she anxiously awaits her husband's return from the war. But Millitrisa's elder sisters and Barbarika intercept the letter and replace it with a fake, telling the tsar that Millitrisa has given birth to a monster. Orders arrive from the tsar that Millitrisa and the baby be put to sea in a barrel. The saddened populace complies.

II. Millitrisa and Gvidon wash ashore on a desert island. The now-fully-grown Gvidon saves a swan, which turns out to have magical powers. An enchanted city appears and the populace hails Gvidon as their ruler.

IIIi. The swan shows the homesick Gvidon how to turn himself into a bumble bee so that he can fly home. IIIii. Travellers tell the tsar about Gvidon's wondrous kingdom and the tsar decides to visit it. Gvidon, who has been watching, disguised as a bee, stings Millitrisa's elder sisters when they try to dissuade the tsar from the voyage by telling him about a beautiful princess.

IVi. Gvidon pines for the beautiful princess. It is the swan, he discovers, who transforms herself back into a woman and they declare their love for each other. IVii. The tsar arrives on the island and is shown the wonders of the city. IViii. He is astonished to find his wife and son. They are reconciled and Millitrisa's elder sisters flee in disgrace.

A Tale of Two Cities

Composed by Arthur Benjamin (September 18, 1893 – April 10, 1960). Libretto by Cedric Cliffe. English. Based on the novel by Charles Dickens. Premiered London, Sadler's Wells Theatre, July 23, 1957. Set in Paris and London from 1783 to 1790. Romantic melodrama. Through composed. Radio premiere by the BBC, April 17, 1953.

Sets: 5. **Acts:** 1 act, 6 scenes. **Length:** I: 135. **Hazards:** I: Jacques bring in 2 severed heads on spikes. Beheadings in the final scene are seen as shadows projected on a screen. **Scenes:** Ii. A Parisian wine shop. Iii. Dr. Manette's garden in Soho. Iiii. The wine shop. Iiv. The great hall of the revolutionary tribunal. Iv. A prison cell in Paris. Ivi. The Place de la République. (Composer recommends intermissions after Ii, Iiii. Also optional intermission after Iiv.)

Major roles: Madame Defarge (dramatic soprano), Lucie Manette (lyric soprano), Doctor Manette (tenor), Sydney Carton (baritone), Charles Darnay (tenor). **Minor roles:** Jacques I (baritone), Defarge (bass), Jacques II the cripple (bass), Jacques III (baritone), Jacques IV (tenor), First woman (soprano), Second woman (mezzo), Third woman (contralto), Marquis of Saint Evremonde (baritone), Gabelle (bass), Spy (tenor), Lorry (baritone), Miss Pross (contralto), Old marquis (bass), Young countess (lyric soprano). **Bit parts:** Hurdy-gurdy man (baritone), Four members of the revolutionary tribunal (soprano, contralto, tenor, bass), Apple seller (contralto), Two men in the crowd (tenor, bass), Woman in the crowd (alto). **Speaking:** Corporal. **Speaking bits:** Crowd member, Old count, Old marquise, First prison guard. **Mute:** Son of Jacques IV, Second prison guard.

Chorus parts: SSAATTBaBaBB. **Chorus roles:** Revolutionaries and people of Paris. **Dance/movement:** I: Revolutionaries celebrate the fall of the Bastille. Aristocrats dance in prison. **Orchestra:** picc, 2 fl, 2 ob (Eng hrn), 2 cl (bs cl), 2 bsn, 4 hrn, 3 trp, 2 trb, bs trb, tuba, timp, perc, harp, piano (celeste), strings. **Stageband:** I: fl, guitar, fiddler. **Publisher:** Hawkes & Son Ltd. **Rights:** Copyright 1954 by Hawkes & Son Ltd.

Ii. Madame Defarge assures the Paris revolutionaries that their time will come. The son of Jacques IV is killed by the carriage of the marquis of Saint Evremonde and the marquis gives Jacques IV money. A spy sounds Madame Defarge out, but she tells him nothing. Lorry and Lucie come to retrieve Lucie's father, Doctor Manette, who has been cared for by the Defarges since his release from the Bastille. Manette has forgotten his name and his daughter, but Lucie takes him home.

Iii. Six years have passed. Dr. Manette has recovered and is living with his daughter in London. Lucie is engaged to Charles Darnay, the son of the marquis who has left France in disgust over his father's cruelty. Sydney Carton also loves Lucie—and he looks just like Charles. Iiii. The Paris revolutionaries celebrate the taking of the Bastille. They capture the marquis's servant, Gabelle, and threaten to kill him unless he writes to Charles, asking him to come to France.

Iiv. Charles and Lucie are married. Charles returns to France to save Gabelle. He is followed by Lucie, Dr. Manette—and Sydney Carton. The revolutionaries arrest Charles and try him. When Madame Defarge produces evidence that Dr. Manette was imprisoned by Charles's father, the court condemns Charles. Iv. Sydney switches places with Charles in prison. Ivi. Sydney dies at the guillotine. Madame Defarge realizes that all of her enemies have escaped.

The Tales of Hoffmann

See "Le Contes d'Hoffmann" entry.

Tamerlano

Composed by George Frederic Handel (February 23, 1685 – April 14, 1759). Libretto by Nicola Francesco Haym. Italian. Based on libretto by Agostino Piovene. Premiered London, King's Theatre, Haymarket, Royal Academy of Music, October 31, 1724. Set in the capital of Bythnia in the early 15th century. Medieval drama. Set numbers with recitative. Overture.

Sets: 6. **Acts:** 3 acts, 6 scenes. **Length:** I: 75. II: 35. III: 65. **Arias:** "Forte e lieto" (Andronico), "Benchè mi sprezzi" (Andronico), "Bella Asteria" (Andronico), "Se non mi vuol amar" (Asteria), "Par che mi nasca" (Irene), "A suoi piedi" (Bajazet), "Cor di padre" (Asteria). **Hazards:** None. **Scenes:** Ii. The courtyard of Tamerlano's palace. Iii. Bajazet's rooms in the palace. Iiii. Atrium of the palace. II. An anteroom leading to Tamerlano's study. IIIi. Courtyard of the harem. IIIii. The throne room.

Major roles: Andronico (countertenor or contralto), Bajazet (tenor), Tamerlano (countertenor, contralto or bass baritone), Asteria (soprano). **Minor roles:** Leone (bass), Irene (mezzo). **Mute:** Zaida, guard, courtiers.

Chorus parts: N/A. **Chorus roles:** None. **Dance/movement:** None. **Orchestra:** 2 fl, 2 recorders, 2 ob, 2 bsn, 2 trp or 2 hrn, strings, continuo (harpsichord). **Stageband:** None. **Publisher:** Gregg Press Ltd. **Rights:** Expired.

Ii. Bajazet, who is Tamerlano's prisoner, longs for death. Tamerlano loves Bajazet's daughter, Asteria. He decides to get his fiancée, Irene, out of the way by marrying her to the Greek Prince Andronico. Tamerlano does not realize that Asteria and Andronico are in love. Iii. He proposes to Asteria. Asteria fears that Andronico no longer loves her. Bajazet refuses to let Tamerlano marry Asteria. Irene and her escort, Leone, hope to change Tamerlano's mind. Iiii. Irene loves Tamerlano. Andronico complains that everyone is mad at him.

II. Tamerlano is confident of success. Suspecting Asteria's fidelity, Andronico decides to take his case to Bajazet. Irene argues with Tamerlano but cannot persuade him to forget Asteria. Asteria assures Irene she will not marry Tamerlano and Irene's hopes revive. Bajazet agrees to help Andronico. Tamerlano threatens Bajazet and Asteria.

IIIi. As a last resort, Bajazet provides Asteria with a vial of poison. Tamerlano asks Andronico to argue his case with Asteria, but Andronico publicly declares his own love for Asteria. Tamerlano summons all three for judgment. Bajazet rebukes Asteria and Andronico for not showing more spirit. Asteria and Andronico swear their love. IIIii. Irene admits she can only love Tamerlano if he returns her love. Leone hopes Irene will succeed. Bajazet wants to kill himself. Tamerlano decides to marry Irene. Bajazet poisons himself and dies, cursing Tamerlano. Tamerlano repents and lets Asteria marry Andronico. He begs Irene's forgiveness.

The Taming of the Shrew

Composed by Vittorio Giannini (October 19, 1903 – November 28, 1966).
Libretto by Vittorio Giannini and Dorothy Fee. English. Based on the
play by Shakespeare. Premiered Cincinnati, Cincinnati Symphony,
January 31, 1953 (concert premiere). Set in Padua in the 16th century.
Comic opera. Through composed. Overture. Entr'acte before III.
Sets: 3. **Acts:** 3 acts, 4 scenes. **Length:** I: 35. II: 40. III: 35. **Hazards:** None.
Scenes: I. A street in Padua showing a small square with houses facing
it. II. The garden of Baptista's house. III. A room in Petruchio's house.

Major roles: Lucentio/Cambio (tenor), Baptista (bass), Katharina (dramatic soprano), Hortensio/Licio (baritone), Bianca (lyric soprano),
Petruchio (baritone). **Minor roles:** Gremio (tenor), Tranio (baritone),
Biondello (bass), Grumio (tenor), Curtis (bass), Vincentio (bass), Pedant
(tenor). **Bit part:** Tailor (tenor). **Mute:** Servants, maids.

Chorus parts: N/A. **Chorus roles:** None. **Dance/movement:** None.
Orchestra: 4 fl (picc), 4 ob (Eng hrn), 4 cl, 3 cl, 3 bsn, 4 hrn, 3 trp, 3 trb, 2
tuba, perc, timp, harp, celeste, xylophone, strings. Reduced version: 3 fl
(picc), 2 ob (Eng hrn), 2 cl, 2 bsn, 4 hrn, 3 trp, 2 trb, bs trb, tuba, timp,
perc, harp, piano, strings. **Stageband:** None. **Publisher:** G. Ricordi.
Rights: Copyright 1953, 1954 by G. Ricordi & Co.

I. Hortensio and Gremio are in love with Bianca, but her father, Baptista,
will not allow her to marry until a husband is found for her older sister,
the shrewish Katharina. Lucentio, too, falls in love with Bianca. To woo
her, he swaps identities with his servant, Tranio. Hearing of Katharina's
large dowry, Hortensio's friend Petruchio agrees to marry her. He presents himself while Hortensio tries to see Bianca by posing as a music
teacher. Tranio woos Bianca in Lucentio's name, while Lucentio himself
poses as a Latin teacher. Hortensio tries to give Katharina a music lesson, but she thrashes him. Petruchio faces her down, insisting he means
to marry her on Sunday.

IIi. Hortensio and Lucentio both try to give Bianca her lesson, but Bianca
favors Lucentio. Petruchio threatens to get married in tattered old clothing. Katharina fights with Bianca. Baptista is furious and insists that
Katharina marry Petruchio. Lucentio reveals his true identity to Bianca
and they agree to elope. IIiii. Katharina is frantic on her wedding day.
Hortensio decides to help Lucentio win Bianca. Petruchio does not show
up for the wedding ceremony, but sends a letter promising to be at the
church exactly at noon. Baptista is furious at Petruchio's insolence, but
the others persuade him to let the marriage proceed.

III. Petruchio tames Katharina by being more unpleasant and demanding than she. Lucentio and Bianca have been married secretly. They flee to Katharina who hides them. Lucentio's father, Vincentio, arrives, followed by Baptista, Tranio (still disguised as Lucentio)—and a pedant impersonating Vincentio. The real Vincentio fears Tranio has murdered Lucentio. Everyone's true identities are revealed and Baptista forgives his daughter and Lucentio. Alone, Petruchio tells Katharina he loves her, now that he has tamed her shrewish ways.

Tancredi

Composed by Gioachino Rossini (February 29, 1792 – November 13, 1868). Libretto by Gaetano Rossi. Italian. Based on "Tancrède" by Voltaire and "Gerusalemme Liberata" by Torquato Tasso. Premiered Venice, Teatro la Fenice, February 6, 1813. Set in Syracuse in the 11th century. Opera seria or heroic melodrama. Set numbers with recitative. Overture. An alternate, happy ending exists.

Sets: 6. **Acts:** 2 acts, 7 scenes. **Length:** I, II: 165. **Arias:** "Di tanti palpiti" (Tancredi). **Hazards:** None. **Scenes:** Ii. A gallery in the palace of Argirio. Iii. A park near the palace with a view of the sea. Iiii. A public place near a Gothic temple. IIi. The gallery. IIii. A prison. IIiii. The great square in Syracuse. IIiv. A mountain scene with a waterfall.

Major roles: Argirio (tenor), Amenaide (soprano), Tancredi (contralto). **Minor roles:** Isaura (mezzo), Orbazzano (bass), Roggerio (contralto or tenor).

Chorus parts: TTB. **Chorus roles:** Knights, noblemen, maidens, squires, soldiers, people. **Dance/movement:** None. **Orchestra:** 2 fl (picc), 2 ob, 2 cl, 2 bsn, 2 hrn, 2 trp, timp, strings, Turkish band, continuo. **Stageband:** None. **Publisher:** G. Ricordi. **Rights:** Expired.

Ii. Argirio, his daughter Amenaide, and other Syracusans celebrate the end of the civil war. Iii. Ignoring a sentence of death, Tancredi returns to Syracuse to see his beloved Amenaide. Argirio intends Amenaide for Orbazzano. Amenaide warns Tancredi to flee. Iiii. At the altar, Amenaide refuses to wed Orbazzano. He threatens to kill her, but is prevented by Tancredi. Orbazzano now reveals a letter Amenaide has sent to Solamir, enemy of Syracuse, bidding him take her and the kingdom. Amenaide protests her innocence but everyone curses her.

IIi. Argirio reluctantly signs his daughter's death warrant. IIii. Amenaide languishes in prison. Although he believes her guilty, Tancredi comes in disguise to fight for her. He defeats Orbazzano. IIiii. Amenaide tries to convince Tancredi of her continued faithfulness. IIiv.

Tancredi defends Syracuse from Solamir's forces, but is mortally wounded. Before Tancredi dies, Argirio reveals that Amenaide's letter was written to Tancredi, not Solamir. Tancredi renews his vows of love to Amenaide and dies.

Tannhäuser

Composed by Richard Wagner (May 22, 1813 – February 13, 1883). Libretto by Richard Wagner. German. Based on a medieval legend. Premiered Dresden, Königliches Hoftheater, October 19, 1845. Set in the Wartburg in the early 13th century. Romantic opera. Through composed with leitmotifs. Overture. Introduction before second and third acts. Ballet.

Sets: 3. **Acts:** 3 acts, 11 scenes. **Length:** I: 65. II: 60. III: 60. **Arias:** "Dich, teure Halle" (Elisabeth), "O du, mein holder Abendstern" (Wolfram), Tannhäuser's hymn to Venus (Tannhäuser), "Inbrunst im Herzen" (Tannhäuser). **Hazards:** III: Pope's staff sprouts leaves. **Scenes:** Ii – Iiii. Hill of Venus. Iiii – Iiv. Valley before the Wartburg. II. Hall of the minstrels in the Wartburg. III. Valley before the Wartburg.

Major roles: Hermann, Landgrave of Thuringia (bass), Tannhäuser (tenor), Minstrel Wolfram von Eschenbach (baritone), Elisabeth (soprano), Venus (soprano). **Minor roles:** Minstrel Walther von der Vogelweide (tenor), Minstrel Biterolf (bass), Minstrel Heinrich der Schreiber (tenor), Minstrel Reinmar von Zweter (bass), Young shepherd (soprano). **Bit parts:** Four noble pages (soprano and alto).

Chorus parts: SSAATTBB. **Chorus roles:** Thuringian nobles and knights, ladies, pages, pilgrims, fauns, nymphs and bacchantes. **Dance/movement:** I: Bacchanale ballet. **Orchestra:** 3 fl (picc), 2 ob, 2 cl, 2 bsn, 4 hrn, 3 trp, 2 ten trb, bs trb, bs tuba, perc, timp, harp, strings. **Stageband:** I: 2 fl, 2 ob, 2 cl, 2 bsn, 12 hrn, harp, Eng hrn. II: 12 trp. III: 2 picc, 4 fl, 4 ob, 6 cl, 4 bsn, 4 hrn, perc. **Publisher:** Schirmer, Ernst Eulenburg, Leipzig. **Rights:** Expired.

Ii. Nymphs dance around the hill of Venus. Iii. The minstrel Tannhäuser is tired of the pleasures of Venus's domain and longs to return to earth. Venus releases him but warns that earth will not receive him kindly. Iiii. Tannhäuser is returned to his home, where he hears a shepherd singing and encounters a group of pilgrims bound for Rome. Iiv. The Landgrave Hermann and the minstrels discover the return of their friend. They beg him to stay, but their efforts are unsuccessful until they recount Elisabeth's sorrow at Tannhäuser's absence.

IIi. Elisabeth returns to the hall of the minstrels, where Tannhäuser's song first won her heart. IIii. She is reunited with Tannhäuser. Wolfram laments that now Elisabeth will never love him. IIIiii. The Landgrave is pleased to see his niece Elisabeth once again in the hall of minstrels. He calls together the tournament of song. IIIiv. The Landgrave welcomes his guests and announces the theme for the minstrels' songs: "What is love; by what signs shall we know it?" Wolfram sings first. The opening of his song is praised by the spectators, but Tannhäuser interrupts, objecting to Wolfram's idealized love and pointing out that the fulfill-ment of love is pleasure. The spectators are outraged and Biterolf chal-lenges Tannhäuser to fight. The Landgrave steps in to restore peace and Wolfram resumes his song. Again, Tannhäuser interrupts to praise Venus. Everyone now realizes the sinful company Tannhäuser has kept. The minstrels denounce Tannhäuser and close in on him. He is protect-ed by Elisabeth who reminds them all that it is for God, not them, to judge Tannhäuser. It is our duty to save him from damnation, she insists. The Landgrave disowns and banishes Tannhäuser. He advises the bard to accompany the band of pilgrims to Rome, which Tannhäuser does.

IIIi. Elisabeth prays for the forgiveness and return of Tannhäuser and Wolfram hopes that her prayers will be answered. The pilgrims return without Tannhäuser. Elisabeth longs for death. IIIii. Wolfram sings of Elisabeth's suffering. IIIiii. Tannhäuser appears and tells Wolfram about his pilgrimage. Instead of granting Tannhäuser forgiveness, the Pope told him that he would never be forgiven—until the pontiff's staff sprouts leaves. In bitter despair, Tannhäuser calls on Venus. She appears, but Wolfram restrains him. When Elisabeth's funeral train appears, Tannhäuser forgets all thought of Venus. He begs Elisabeth's soul to pray for him and falls dead. The pilgrims return, marveling at a sign from heaven: the Pope's staff has sprouted leaves.

Tartuffe

Composed by Kirke Mechem (b. August 16, 1925). Libretto by Kirke Mechem. English. Based on the play by Molière. Premiered San Francisco, San Francisco Opera, Herbst Theater, May 27, 1980. Set in Paris in the 17th century. Comic opera. Through composed. Opus 47.

Sets: 1. Acts: 3 acts, 4 scenes. Length: I, II, III: 110. Hazards: None. Scenes: I – III. The salon of Orgon's house.

Major roles: Elmire (mezzo), Dorine (soprano), Mariane (soprano), Orgon (bass), Valère (tenor), Tartuffe (baritone). Minor roles: Mme. Pernelle (mezzo), Damis (high baritone). Mute: Flipote.

Chorus parts: N/A. **Chorus roles:** None. **Dance/movement:** None.
Orchestra: Full: 2 fl (picc), 2 ob, 2 cl (bs cl), 2 bsn (cont bsn), 2 hrn, trp,
trb, 2 perc, timp, harp, strings (min. 6-5-4-4-2). Reduced: fl (picc), ob, cl,
bsn, hrn, trp, trb, perc, harp, strings. **Stageband:** None. **Publisher:** G.
Schirmer. **Rights:** Copyright 1980 by G. Schirmer Inc.

I. Orgon's mother, Mme. Pernelle, is convinced that the holy man
Tartuffe is saving her son from moral ruin. But Orgon's second wife,
Elmire, is surprised that her husband has been taken in by Tartuffe's
sham piety. She asks him about his promise to his daughter Mariane
that she could marry Valère. Orgon is evasive. Orgon tells Mariane he
wants her to marry Tartuffe. Mariane is horrified, but cannot bring herself to contradict her father. Valère and Mariane argue but make up.

II. Elmire allows Tartuffe to make a pass at her. She then threatens to tell
her husband if he does not relinquish all claim to Mariane. Orgon's son,
Damis, overhears. He insists on more direct action: he tells Orgon—who
does not believe him. Orgon disowns Damis and makes Tartuffe his
heir.

IIIi. Elmire has Orgon hide under a table while she meets with Tartuffe.
Tartuffe makes a pass at Elmire, but Orgon does not intervene until
Tartuffe says Orgon is a fool. When Orgon confronts Tartuffe, Tartuffe
points out he has the deed to the house. IIIii. Damis returns disguised as
a bailiff to help Tartuffe evict Orgon. While Tartuffe fetches a police officer, Damis explains his plan: The officer whom Tartuffe finds is Valère
in disguise. Mariane presents herself as an envoy from the king and gets
Tartuffe to give her the deed. Mariane reads a list of Tartuffe's crimes
and encourages him to flee—which he does. Orgon apologizes to his
family. Preparations begin for Valère's and Mariane's wedding.

The Telephone

Composed by Gian Carlo Menotti (b. July 7, 1911). Libretto by Gian
Carlo Menotti. English. Original work. Premiered New York City,
Heckscher Theater, February 18, 1947. Set in Lucy's apartment in the
mid-20th century. Comic opera. Through composed. Prelude.

Sets: 1. **Acts:** 1 act, 1 scene. **Length:** I: 25. **Hazards:** None. **Scenes:** I.
Lucy's apartment.

Major roles: Lucy (soprano), Ben (baritone).

Chorus parts: N/A. **Chorus roles:** None. **Dance/movement:** None.
Orchestra: fl, ob, cl, bsn, hrn, trp, perc, piano, strings. **Stageband:**

None. **Publisher:** G. Schirmer, Inc. **Rights:** Copyright 1947 by G. Schirmer, Inc.

I. Ben comes to propose to Lucy, but cannot find the words. He gives her a present and tells her his train leaves in an hour. The telephone rings. It is Margaret and she and Lucy gossip. Just as Lucy hangs up, a wrong number calls. Next, George calls, furious at Lucy over something he has heard. Lucy goes to dry her eyes but returns in time to prevent Ben from cutting the telephone cord. She insists on calling Pamela to discuss her fight with George. While Lucy relates the fight to Pamela, Ben slinks out. He proposes to Lucy over the telephone and she accepts. Remember to call me every day you are away, Lucy says.

The Tempest

Composed by Lee Hoiby (b. February 17, 1926). Libretto by Mark Shulgasser. English. Based on the play by William Shakespeare. Premiered Des Moines, Iowa, Des Moines Metro Opera, June 21, 1986. Set on an uninhabited island at an unspecified time. Comedy. Through composed. Prelude before I, II. Interlude in II. Masque in III.

Sets: 4. **Acts:** 3 acts, 10 scenes. **Length:** I, II, III: 150. **Hazards:** III: Juno descends in the masque. **Scenes:** I. Before Prospero's cell. IIi. Another part of the island. IIii – IIiiii. Another part of the island. III. Another part of the island.

Major roles: Miranda (soprano), Prospero (bass baritone), Ariel (coloratura soprano), Ferdinand (lyric baritone), Caliban (dramatic tenor). **Minor roles:** Trinculo (baritone), Stephano (bass), Gonzalo (tenor), Alonso (bass), Antonio (baritone), Sebastian (baritone), Goddess Iris (lyric soprano), Goddess Ceres (mezzo), Goddess Juno (contralto).

Chorus parts: SSAATTBB. **Chorus roles:** Spirits (offstage), courtiers. **Dance/movement:** III: Masque. **Orchestra:** 2 fl, 2 ob, 2 cl, 2 bsn, 4 hrn, 2 trp, 2 trb, tuba, timp, 3 perc, harp, piano, strings. **Stageband:** None. **Publisher:** G. Schirmer. **Rights:** Copyright 1986 by G. Schirmer, Inc.

Ii. Twelve years ago, Antonio had deposed his brother, Prospero, from the dukedom of Milan and set Prospero and his daughter, Miranda, adrift at sea. But Prospero and Miranda made it to an island where Prospero used his magic to help an island spirit, Ariel. At Prospero's command, Ariel shipwrecks Antonio, Antonio's ally King Alonso of Naples and Alonso's court on the island. Prospero is severe with Alonso's son, Ferdinand, knowing his injustice will make Miranda sympathetic to the young man. Iii. The savage Caliban objects that Prospero has enslaved him, but Prospero answers that he treated him with every kindness until Caliban tried to violate Miranda. Iiii. Caliban falls in with two drunken members of Alonso's court, Stephano and Trinculo.

IIi. Alonso believes his son drowned. Antonio suggests to Alonso's brother, Sebastian, that they kill Alonso in his sleep. But Ariel wakes the king up before the murder can be accomplished. IIii. Caliban persuades Stephano to kill Prospero, but Ariel overhears. IIiii. Ariel torments Alonso and Antonio and drives them mad.

IIIi. Ferdinand and Miranda declare their love for each other. Prospero shows the lovers a masque and blesses their union. IIIii. Prospero decides to renounce his magic once his plan is complete. IIIiii. He restores Alonso and the courtiers to their right minds. IIIiv. Caliban realizes he was a fool to follow Stephano and Trinculo. Alonso begs Prospero's forgiveness. Prospero shows them Ferdinand and Miranda. Prospero releases Ariel from his service.

The Tender Land

Composed by Aaron Copland (November 14, 1900 – December 2, 1990). Libretto by Horace Everett. English. Based on "Let Us Now Praise Famous Men" by James Agee. Premiered New York City, New York City Opera, April 1, 1954. Set in Midwest America in the early 1930s. Folk drama. Set numbers with recitative and dialogue. Revised version premiered Berkshire, August 2, 1954 (expanded to three acts from two).

Sets: 1. **Acts:** 3 acts, 3 scenes. **Length:** I, II, III: 100. **Arias:** Laurie's song (Laurie). **Hazards:** None. **Scenes:** I – III. A lower-middle-class farm in the midwest.

Major roles: Ma Moss (contralto), Laurie Moss (soprano), Top (baritone), Martin (tenor), Grandpa Moss (bass). **Minor roles:** Mr. Splinters (tenor), Mrs. Splinters (mezzo). **Bit parts:** Mrs. Jenks (soprano), Mr. Jenks (baritone), First man (tenor), Second man (baritone). **Speaking:** Beth Moss (child).

Chorus parts: SATB (briefly SSATTB). **Chorus roles:** Party guests (four or more couples). **Dance/movement:** II: Country dancing and waltz. **Orchestra:** 2 fl (picc), ob, Eng hrn, 2 cl (bs cl), 2 bsn, 2 hrn, 2 trp, 2 trb, 2 perc, harp, piano, strings. **Stageband:** None. **Publisher:** Boosey & Hawkes. **Rights:** Copyright 1956 by Boosey & Hawkes.

I. Beth daydreams about living in a big house while her mother, Ma Moss, does chores. Mr. Splinters, the postman, brings Laurie Moss's mail-order dress. Ma Moss invites Splinters and his wife to Laurie's graduation party. He tells her how the Gray girl was surprised by two men out in the fields. Iii. Beth runs off to invite the Jenkses to the party. Ma Moss tells Laurie not to upset her grandfather by dawdling and Laurie confesses her anger at Grandpa Moss for sending away her boyfriend. Ma Moss promises to help Laurie have her own life, but Laurie doubts her ability to convince Grandpa. Two drifters, Martin and Top, approach Laurie. They convince Grandpa to hire them to help with the harvest. Top tells Martin to keep Grandpa busy at the party so he can talk to Laurie.

II. The guests at Laurie's graduation party drink and dance. Ma Moss suspects Top and Martin and asks Mr. Splinters to fetch the sheriff. Top distracts Grandpa with his stories while Martin kisses Laurie. The young people exchange vows of love. They are interrupted by Grandpa, who is furious. Mr. Splinters returns with the report that the men who bothered the Gray girl were apprehended. Ignoring Laurie's protests, Grandpa sends Martin and Top away.

III. Laurie makes plans to run away with Martin at dawn. Top convinces Martin that Laurie would hate life on the road. Reluctantly, Martin flees before daybreak. Laurie is distraught, but decides to leave home anyway.

Die Teufel von Loudun • The Devils of Loudun

Composed by Krzysztof Penderecki (b. November 23, 1933). Libretto by Krzysztof Penderecki. German. Based on John Whiting's dramatization of Aldous Huxley's "The Devils of Loudun." Premiered Hamburg, Hamburgischen Staatsoper, June 20, 1969. Set in Loudun in the 1630s. Tragedy. Set numbers with declamatory recitative and spoken dialogue.

Sets: 14. **Acts:** 3 acts, 30 scenes. **Length:** I, II, III: 150. **Hazards:** I: Jeanne has visions of Grandier, Ninon, soldiers. II: Barré performs an enema. III: Grandier tortured and burned alive. **Scenes:** Ii. Jeanne's cell in the convent of St. Ursula. Iii. A street in Loudun. Iiii. Ninon's bathtub. Iiv. The street. Iv – Ivi. In the church of St. Peter. Ivii. The street. Iviii. A confessional. Iix. On the town wall. Ix. The street. Ixi. A cloister. Ixii. A pharmacy. Ixiii. Jeanne's cell. IIi – IIii. In the church. IIiii – IIiv. A cell. IIv. In the church. IIvi. The pharmacy. IIvii. The convent garden. IIviii. On the town wall. IIix – IIx. In the church. IIIi – IIIii. A prison. IIIiii – IIIiv. A public place. IIIv. The upper room of the prison. IIIvi. The street. IIIvii. Before the church and convent.

Major roles: Jeanne the prioress (dramatic soprano or high mezzo), Urbain Grandier the parish priest of St. Peter's (baritone), Father Barré (bass). **Minor roles:** Sister Claire of St. John (mezzo), Mannoury the surgeon (baritone), Adam the pharmacist (tenor), Philippe Trincant (high soprano), Baron of Laubardemont (tenor), Father Mignon (tenor), Voice of the devil Asmodeus (deep bass), Father Rangier (deep bass), Sister Louise of Jesus (contralto), Sister Gabrielle of the Incarnation (soprano), Prince Henri of Condé (baritone), Bontemps the goaler (bass baritone), Father Ambrose (bass). **Bit parts:** Ninon (contralto), Voice of the devil Isacaaron (bass), Voice of the devil Beherit (bass), Two nuns (basses). **Speaking:** Jean d'Armagnac Mayor of Loudun, Judge Guilleaume de Cerisay, Clerk of the court. **Mute:** Captain of the guard.

Chorus parts: SSSSSSAAAAAATTTTBBBB. **Chorus roles:** Ursuline sisters, Carmelite sisters, people, children, guards, soldiers. **Dance/movement:** None. **Orchestra:** 4 fl (picc, alto fl), 2 Eng hrn, cl, cont bs cl, 2 alto sax, 2 baritone sax, 3 bsn, cont bsn, 6 hrn, 4 trp, 4 trb, 2 tuba, perc, bs electric guitar, harp, piano, harmonium, organ, strings (20-0-8-8-6), tape recording. **Stageband:** None. **Publisher:** B. Schott's Söhne. **Rights:** Copyright 1969 by B. Schott's Söhne.

Ii. Jeanne, the humpback prioress of the convent of St. Ursula, has a vision of Father Grandier. Iii. Adam the pharmacist and Mannoury the surgeon repeat the rumors that the widow Ninon and Grandier are having an affair. Iiii. Grandier and Ninon take a bath together. Iiv. Grandier passes Adam and Mannoury in the street. Iv. Grandier prays. Ivi. Upon seeing Grandier at church, Jeanne screams and flees. Ivii. Adam and Mannoury agree to denounce Grandier. Iviii. Philippe confesses to Grandier her love for him. Iix. The baron of Laubardemont delivers Cardinal Richelieu's order to Governor d'Armagnac to demolish the city walls. (The cardinal wants to forestall protestant resistance.) Ix. Adam and Mannoury collect evidence against Grandier. Ixi. Jeanne tells Father Mignon her visions. Ixii. Laubardemont asks about Grandier. Ixiii. Father Barré discovers that Jeanne has been possessed by the devil. She blames Grandier.

IIi. When a normal exorcism fails, Barré gives Jeanne an enema. IIii. D'Armagnac and Cerisay, the town judge, ask Grandier about Jeanne's accusations, but he denies them. IIiii. Jeanne tells how she and other sisters were debauched by Grandier. IIiv. Grandier supports D'Armagnac's decision not to pull down the walls. IIv. Philippe tells Grandier she is pregnant and he abandons her. IIvi. The archbishop prevents Barré from entering the convent or performing exorcisms. IIvii. The people shun the convent. IIviii. The king orders the walls demolished. IIix. Jeanne and the sisters assure Mignon that they truly are possessed—not playing parts as people suspect. IIx. Barré performs a public exorcism of the nuns. The nuns congratulate themselves on their new-found fame. Laubardemont arrests Grandier for sorcery.

IIIi. Grandier prays and confesses his sins to Father Ambrose. IIIii. He is shaved. IIIiii. The court condemns him. Laubardemont asks Grandier to sign a confession of sorcery, but Grandier refuses. IIIiv. Jeanne tries to hang herself, but is prevented by the nuns. IIIv. Barré tortures Grandier, but he will not make false confession. IIIvi. Soldiers take Grandier to the execution place. IIIvii. They instruct him to beg forgiveness of the nuns. Grandier is burned at the stake while praying for forgiveness for his enemies.

Thaïs

Composed by Jules-Emile-Frédéric Massenet (May 12, 1842 – August 13, 1912). Libretto by Louis Gallet. French. Based on the novel by Anatole France. Premiered Paris, Opéra, March 16, 1894. Set in Egypt, near Thebes and Alexandria in the late 4th century. Lyric drama. Set numbers with recitative. Ballet. Musical interlude before Iiii. Prelude before III.

Sets: 6. Acts: 3 acts, 7 scenes. Length: I, II, III: 140. Arias: "Voilà donc la terrible cité" (Athanael), "Ô mon miroir fidèle" (Thaïs), "O messager de Dieu" (Thaïs). Hazards: I, III: Athanael's visions of Thaïs. Scenes: Ii. Huts of the Cenobites on the bank of the Nile. Iii. The terrace of the house of Nicias at Alexandria. IIi. At the house of Thaïs. IIii. Square facing the house of Thaïs. IIIi. Oasis in the desert. IIIii. Huts of the cenobites on the Nile. IIIiii. The garden of the convent.

Major roles: Athanael (baritone), Nicias (tenor), Thaïs (soprano). Minor roles: Palémon (bass), Crobyle (soprano), Myrtale (mezzo), Enchantress dancer (soprano). Bit parts: Five Cenobites (3 tenor, 2 bass), Servant (baritone), Albine (mezzo).

Chorus parts: SSAATTTTBB (briefly SSSAAA). Chorus roles: Cenobite monks, historians, comediennes, philosophers, friends of Nicias, people of Alexandria, crazy women, nuns. Dance/movement: II: Slave ballet. Orchestra: picc, 2 fl, 2 ob, Eng hrn, 2 cl, bs cl, 2 bsn, cont bsn (or sarrusophone), 4 hrn, 2 trp, 3 trb, tuba, timp, perc, 1 to 4 harps, strings. Stageband: I: fl, Eng hrn, cl, 1 or 2 harp, harmonium. II: ob, Eng hrn, clavier de timbres, piano, Arab drum, perc. III: organ, perc. Publisher: Heugel & Co. Rights: Expired.

Ii. Athanael returns to his fellow cenobite monks and reports on the sinfulness of the city. The monks sleep, but Athanael is wakened by a vision of the Venus-worshiping courtesan Thaïs. Ignoring Palemon's advice, Athanael returns to Alexandria to save Thaïs's soul. Iii. Athanael goes to his former friend Nicias. Thaïs has been carrying on an affair with Nicias for the past week. She is dining with Nicias that evening and Athanael allows Nicias's beautiful slaves to dress him. Thaïs warns Nicias that she means to leave him. She is intrigued by Athanael.

IIi. Thaïs is bored with life and fearful of growing old. Athanael's divine vision touches her. IIii. She agrees to destroy all her possessions and accompany Athanael to a convent. Nicias's slaves dance for his amusement. When Athanael tries to take Thaïs away, an angry mob gathers. Only Nicias's gold prevents them from stoning the holy man.

IIIi. Athanael conveys Thaïs through the desert to the convent of Albine. He is thunderstruck when he realizes he will never again see Thaïs. IIIii. For some time, Athanael has lived among the monks trying to forget Thaïs. He has a vision of her on her deathbed. IIIiii. Athanael confesses his love to the dying Thaïs, but she has eyes only for heaven.

The Three Penny Opera

See "Die Dreigroschenoper" entry.

Tiefland • The Lowland

Composed by Eugène d' Albert (April 10, 1864 – March 3, 1932). Libretto by Rudolph Lothar. German. Based on a story by Angel Guimerà. Premiered Prague, German Opera House, November 15, 1903. Set in the Pyrenees and Catalonia in the early 20th century. Music drama. Through composed. Prologue. Prelude. Revised, two-act version premiered Magdeburg, January 16, 1905.

Sets: 2. **Acts:** 2 acts, 3 scenes (including prologue; originally in 3 acts). **Length:** Prologue: 25. I: 60. II: 45. **Hazards:** None. **Scenes:** Prologue. A rocky slope high up in the Pyrenees. I – II. The interior of the mill.

Major roles: Pedro (tenor), Marta (mezzo), Sebastiano (baritone). **Minor roles:** Nando (tenor), Tommaso (bass), Moruccio (baritone), Pepa (soprano), Antonia (soprano), Rosalia (contralto), Nuri (soprano). **Bit part:** Voice (baritone). **Mute:** Priest.

Chorus parts: SATB. **Chorus roles:** Peasants. **Dance/movement:** IIvii: Marta dances for Sebastiano. **Orchestra:** 3 fl (3 picc), 2 ob, Eng hrn, 2 cl, bs cl, 2 bsn, cont bsn, 4 hrn, 3 trp, 3 trb, tuba, timp, perc, harp, strings.

Stageband: Prologue: cl. I: bells. **Publisher:** Bote and G. Bock. **Rights:** Expired.

Prologue. Two shepherds, Nando and Pedro, lead out their flocks. Although Pedro glories in his lonely life, he wishes for a wife. He has dreamed that the Virgin Mary promised him a bride. To determine the direction from which his bride will come, Pedro throws a rock—and hits the wealthy landlord Sebastiano. Sebastiano intends that his servant Marta marry Pedro, but she refuses. Nevertheless, he offers Pedro Marta's hand and the job of miller—and Pedro accepts both. Tommaso, the village elder, says it was he who recommended Pedro for promotion. Pedro bids Nando farewell and descends to his new life in the lowlands.

I. Pepa, Antonia, and Rosalia pester Moruccio for news of Marta's engagement. Moruccio is sulking because he wants to marry Marta himself. Nuri tells the women about Pedro—and the conversation she once overheard in which Sebastiano told Marta she would always be his and he, hers. The women laugh at Pedro's naivete. Marta throws them out of the mill. She is sorry she did not have the strength to drown herself. Moruccio tells the real story to a disbelieving Tommaso: Sebastiano is throwing over Marta so he will be free to find himself a rich wife who can pay off his debts. The villagers turn out to welcome Pedro, but they laugh at him and Pedro gets angry. Tommaso insists on speaking to Sebastiano before the ceremony. When Marta begs Sebastiano not to make her marry Pedro, Sebastiano insists. Marta agrees, but refuses to continue being Sebastiano's lover. The peasants start for the chapel. Moruccio refuses to go, so Sebastiano fires him. Tommaso asks about the rumors and Sebastiano denies them. He is not convinced, but it is too late. Pedro finds his new bride extremely cold. To impress her, he tells her how he killed a wolf. A light appears in Marta's room: Sebastiano is waiting for her as usual. The newlyweds do not go to their bedrooms.

II. Pedro wants revenge. Seeing Pedro with Nuri, Marta turns her out of the house, but Pedro leaves with her. Marta is upset and tells Tommaso how Sebastiano rescued her from penury after her mother died. Now she has fallen in love with Pedro. Tommaso counsels her to tell Pedro the truth. Nuri refuses to satisfy the curiosity of the gossips, who laugh at Pedro. Marta begs Pedro not leave her, but to kill her. When she taunts him, he stabs her in the arm, but admits that he still loves her. They decide to flee. Sebastiano arrives and forces Marta to dance for him. He has Pedro thrown out when he tries to take Marta away. Tommaso ruins Sebastiano's planned marriage by telling his father-in-law-to-be the truth. Pedro fights and kills Sebastiano, and then Pedro carries his bride up to the mountains.

Tom Jones

Composed by François André Philidor (September 7, 1726 – August 31, 1795). Libretto by Antoine Alexandre Henri Poinsinet. French. Based on the novel by Henry Fielding. Premiered Paris, Comédie Italienne, February 27, 1765. Set in England in the 18th century. Lyric comedy. Set numbers with recitative and spoken dialogue. Overture. Prelude before II, III. Revised and repremiered January 30, 1766.

Sets: 3. **Acts:** 3 acts, 3 scenes. **Length:** I, II, III: 125. **Arias:** "Respirons un moment" (Sophia). **Hazards:** None. **Scenes:** I. Salon in Mr. Western's country house. II. Garden of Mr. Western's house. III. The Upton Inn.

Major roles: Sophia (soprano), Mr. Western (bass baritone), Tom Jones (tenor). **Minor roles:** Mrs. Western (mezzo), Mrs. Honour (soprano), Blifil (tenor), Allworthy (baritone), Four drunks (2 tenor, 2 bass).
Speaking: Dowling. **Speaking bit:** Landlord's daughter.
Chorus parts: TB. **Chorus roles:** Huntsman. **Dance/movement:** None.
Orchestra: 2 ob, bsn, 2 hrn, strings, continuo. **Stageband:** None.
Publisher: Boosey & Hawkes, Monthulay. **Rights:** Expired.

I. Sophia is encouraged in her love for the bastard Tom Jones by her companion, Mrs. Honour. Sophia's aunt, Mrs. Western, thinks Sophia loves Squire Allworthy's heir, Blifil. She approves and gets her brother, Mr. Western, to arrange a marriage. When she learns that Sophia loves Tom, Mrs. Western is furious and threatens to ruin Tom.

II. Blifil persuades Dowling to wait before revealing that Tom is, in fact, Blifil's legitimate—and elder—brother. Sophia begs her uncle to postpone the marriage, admitting she hates Blifil. But Western insists she marry Blifil. Western and Allworthy catch Tom confessing his love to Sophia. Allworthy disowns and banishes Tom.

III. Dowling meets Tom at an inn and promises to help him. Sophia runs away from home. She and Mrs. Honour are pestered by the drunks in the inn until Tom rescues them. Dowling tells Western and Allworthy the truth. They are horrified at Blifil's perfidy and agree that Tom should marry Sophia—and inherit Allworthy's fortune.

Tosca

Composed by Giacomo Puccini (December 22, 1858 – November 29, 1924). Libretto by Giuseppe Giacosa and Luigi Illica. Italian. Based on the play by Victorien Sardou. Premiered Rome, Teatro Costanzi, January 14, 1900. Set in Rome in June 1800. Verismo opera. Through composed.

Sets: 3. **Acts:** 3 acts, 3 scenes. **Length:** I: 45. II: 40. III: 30. **Arias:** "Vissi d'arte" (Tosca), "E lucevan le stelle" (Cavaradossi), "Recondita armonia" (Cavaradossi). **Hazards:** III: Cavaradossi is executed by firing squad. Tosca throws herself from the parapet of the Castel San Angelo. **Scenes:** I. Inside the church of Sant'Andrea della Valle. II. Scarpia's apartment in the Farnese palace. III. The parapet of Castel Sant'Angelo.

Major roles: Mario Cavaradossi (tenor), Floria Tosca (soprano), Baron Scarpia (baritone). **Minor roles:** Cesare Angelotti (bass), Sacristan (baritone or bass), Spoletta (tenor), Sciarrone (bass), Offstage shepherd (treble). **Bit part:** Jailer (bass). **Mute:** Roberti the executioner, cardinal, judge, clerk, officers, sergeant.

Chorus parts: SSATTBB. **Chorus roles:** Soldiers, police agents, ladies, nobles, citizens, priests, acolytes, choir boys, Swiss guardsmen. **Dance/movement:** None. **Orchestra:** 3 fl (picc), 2 ob, Eng hrn, 2 cl, bs cl, 2 bsn, cont bsn, 4 hrn, 3 trp, 3 trb, tuba, timp, perc, bells, celeste, harp, strings. **Stageband:** I: 4 hrn, 3 trb, bells, organ, cannon. II: fl, vla, drums, harp. III: bells. **Publisher:** Ricordi. **Rights:** Expired.

I. Angelotti hides in the chapel of the church of St. Andrea. The sacristan complains about having to clean up after Cavaradossi the painter. He is scandalized that Cavaradossi has painted the Marchesa Attavanti as his Madonna. Cavaradossi contrasts her beauty with that of his opera singer love, Tosca. He is astonished at the appearance of his friend Angelotti— consul of the outlawed Roman Republic—who has escaped from jail. Hearing Tosca's voice, Cavaradossi hurries Angelotti back into hiding. Tosca's suspicions are aroused by the locked door and Cavaradossi's distracted air. She recognizes the woman in Cavaradossi's painting, but succumbs to his professions of love. Reluctantly, she goes. Angelotti emerges and explains his plan: he means to stay in hiding for a week, then cross the border in women's clothing. His sister—who is helping him escape—is the very woman Cavaradossi has painted. Cavaradossi sends Angelotti to his villa and tells him about a secret hiding place beneath the garden well. The sacristan tells the choir that Napoleon was defeated. The choir's celebration is cut short by Scarpia and his police agents looking for Angelotti. In the chapel, Scarpia discovers a fan with the crest of Angelotti's sister, the Marchesa Attavanti. Scarpia suspects Cavaradossi. He uses the fan to inflame Tosca's jealousy—and, he hopes, forward his own cause. When Tosca runs out, Scarpia has her followed.

II. Scarpia anticipates a violent victory over Cavaradossi and Tosca. He sends Sciarrone with a note for Tosca and questions his spy, Spoletta. "We ransacked Cavaradossi's villa," Spoletta reports, "but were unable to find Angelotti." Scarpia is partially mollified by the news of

Cavaradossi's arrest. Under interrogation, the painter insists he does not know Angelotti's whereabouts. While he is tortured, Scarpia works on Tosca. Hearing Cavaradossi's screams, she reveals Angelotti's hiding place. Cavaradossi is furious with her but Scarpia's triumph is interrupted by Sciarrone, who announces a victory for Napoleon. Cavaradossi triumphantly declares for Napoleon and is dragged off to prison. Scarpia will free Cavaradossi only if Tosca sleeps with him. Spoletta reports that Angelotti has killed himself rather than be captured. Scarpia orders the body hanged anyway. Tosca accepts Scarpia's terms. As evidence that he will keep his part of the bargain, Scarpia orders Spoletta to give Cavaradossi a mock execution—"like Count Palmieri," he adds. Tosca demands free passage out of Rome. When Scarpia finishes writing the order, he turns to claim his prize—and is stabbed to death by Tosca. After retrieving the safe conduct and placing candles around the corpse, Tosca flees.

III. A shepherd can be heard singing in the distance. In prison, Cavaradossi bribes the jailer to allow him to write a farewell letter. Tosca arrives and tells Cavaradossi of Scarpia's death and the mock execution. She coaches him on how to fake death. After the execution, Tosca goes to wake Cavaradossi—and discovers the execution was real. The soldiers have located Scarpia's body. They rush Tosca, but she flings herself over the parapet, cursing Scarpia.

Die Tote Stadt • The Dead City

Composed by Erich Wolfgang Korngold (May 29, 1897 – November 29, 1957). Libretto by the composer and his father, Julius Korngold, under the pen name Paul Schott. German. Based on the novel "Bruges la Morte" by Georges Rodenbach. Premiered Hamburg and Cologne simultaneously, Stadttheater (Hamburg) and Opernhaus (Cologne), December 4, 1920. Set in Bruges in the late 19th century. Tragedy. Through composed. Entr'acte before II, III. Opus 12.

Sets: 2. Acts: 3 acts, 3 scenes. Length: I: 50. II: 55. III: 40. Arias: "Glück, das mir verblieb" (Marietta). Hazards: I: Visions of Marie and Marietta. II: Dancers arrive by boat. Scenes: I. A room in Paul's house. II. A deserted quay in Bruges. III. The room in Paul's house.

Major roles: Frank (baritone), Paul (tenor), Marietta/Apparition of Marie (soprano). Minor roles: Brigitta (contralto), Offstage voice of Gaston/Victorin (tenor); Juliette (soprano), Lucienne (mezzo), Count Albert (tenor), Fritz (baritone). Mute: Gaston. (Marietta, Juliette, Lucienne and Gaston should be dancers.)

Chorus parts: SSAATTB. **Chorus roles:** Dancers, monks, nuns, offstage children (1 part) and other participants in the procession. **Dance/movement:** I: Marietta dances for Paul. II: Marietta's ballet. III: Marietta dances holding Marie's braid. **Orchestra:** 3 fl (2 picc), 2 ob, Eng hrn, 2 cl, bs cl, 2 bsn, cont bsn, 4 hrn, 3 trp, bs trp, 3 trb, tuba, mandolin, 2 harp, celeste, piano, harmonium, timp, 3 or 4 perc, glockenspiel, xylophone, strings. **Stageband:** I: perc. II: organ, perc. III: 2 cl, 2 trp, 2 trb. **Publisher:** B. Schott's Söhne. **Rights:** Copyright 1920 by Schott. Renewed 1948.

I. Brigitta, Paul's housekeeper, tells Frank how Paul suddenly came out of his lethargy after his wife's death. Paul has met a woman who he is convinced is his dead Marie returning to him. Frank counsels him to leave the dead in peace. At Paul's invitation, the dancer Marietta pays him a visit. She dances and sees the portrait of Marie before leaving for rehearsal. Paul converses with the dead Marie and assures her he is faithful. She shows him a vision of Marietta.

II. Paul has a vision in which Brigitta has left his service because of his sinful infatuation with Marietta. Frank is also having an affair with Marietta and he and Paul have a falling out. Marietta's friends and fellow dancers visit. They introduce Count Albert who is paying for their supper. Paul finds Marietta dancing in the street and is horrified. He curses her and tells her he never cared for her—only for Marie. Marietta seduces Paul and makes him take back his words.

III. Still in the vision, Marietta taunts the portrait of Marie. Paul is angry with her for entering Marie's room. Together they watch a religious procession pass by. Marietta taunts Paul about Marie and he strangles her with the braid of Marie's hair that Marietta has stolen. Paul's vision ends and he realizes he cannot allow his mourning to consume his life.

Transformations

Composed by Conrad Susa (b. April 26, 1935). Libretto by Conrad Susa. English. Based on the book of poems by Anne Sexton. Premiered Minneapolis, Minnesota Opera, Cedar Village Theater, May 5, 1973. Set in a ward in a hospital or institution in the present and mythological time. An entertainment. Set numbers with recitative. Prologue. The fairy tales have extensive and explicit sexual overtones dealing with issues such as child abuse and homosexuality.

Sets: 1. **Acts:** 2 acts, 10 scenes. **Length:** I, II: 120. **Hazards:** None. **Scenes:** I. A ward in a hospital or institution.

Major roles: Witch/Anne Sexton (soprano), Princess (soprano), Good fairy (mezzo), Wizard (tenor), Magic object (tenor), Prince (tenor), King (high baritone), Neighboring King (bass baritone).

Chorus parts: N/A. **Chorus roles:** None. **Dance/movement:** None. **Orchestra:** cl (sax), trp, trb, db bs, piano (electric harpsichord, electric piano, electric celeste), electric organ, perc (N.B., score calls for full orchestra to be in view of audience). **Stageband:** None. **Publisher:** G. Schirmer Inc. **Rights:** Copyright 1973, 1976 by E. C. Schirmer Music Company.

Ii. The witch talks about a sixteen-year-old boy who has found a key and who wants some answers. Iii. The inmates of an asylum act out fairy tales. They narrate how Snow White's stepmother ordered a hunter to kill Snow White. She escaped and was taken in by seven dwarves. The queen tried to kill Snow White, but she was rescued by a prince. Iiii. In the second fable, a servant ate the white snake that made the king wise. He did favors for the animals, who, in turn, helped him win a princess. Iiv. A king discovered a wild man (Iron Hans) while hunting and locked him up in an iron cage. The wild man convinced the king's son to free him, and the two went back to the woods. The wild man helped the son to win a princess—which freed him from the spell he was under. Iv. A king locked a young girl in a room and threatened to kill her if she did not spin straw into gold. A dwarf appeared and spun the gold for her— on condition that she give him her first born. The king married the girl and they had a child. But when the dwarf claimed the child, the mother resisted. The dwarf agreed to forgo his reward if she could guess his name—Rumplestiltskin—which she did.

Iii. Two women love each other. A pregnant woman persuaded her husband to steal a magic root from a witch's garden, but the witch caught the husband and demanded the child as ransom. The witch named the child Rapunzel and locked her in a tower, but a prince stole her away. Iiii. Godfather death struggled to claim a king's child. Iiiii. A musician trapped a wolf, a fox and a hare with his music. When they came after him for revenge, the musician was saved by a wood cutter. Iiiv. Hansel and Gretel's parents turned them out into the wood, where they were captured by a witch. The witch intended to cook and eat the children, but Gretel trapped the witch in the oven. The children returned home. Iiv. A king invited twelve fairies to the christening of his daughter, Briar Rose. The thirteenth fairy took revenge by prophesying that Briar Rose would prick her finger and die on her fifteenth birthday. Another fairy commuted this doom into a hundred-year sleep. The time came and Briar Rose fell asleep. One hundred years later, she was rescued by a prince. But the prince was her father, circling over her bed.

La Traviata • The Fallen Woman

Composed by Giuseppe Verdi (October 9, 1813 – January 27, 1901).
Libretto by Francesco Maria Piave. Italian. Based on the novel and play
"La Dame aux Camélias" by Alexandre Dumas. Premiered Venice,
Teatro la Fenice, March 6, 1853. Set in Paris and environs about 1850.
Tragedy. Set numbers with recitative. Prelude.

Sets: 4. **Acts:** 3 acts, 4 scenes. **Length:** I: 30. II: 65. III: 55. **Arias:** "Sempre
libera" / "Ah! fors'è lui" (Violetta), "De'miei bollenti spiriti" (Alfredo),
"Di provenza il mar" (Germont), "Addio del passato" (Violetta).
Hazards: None. **Scenes:** I. A salon in Violetta's house. IIi. A country
house near Paris. IIii. A richly furnished and illuminated room in Flora's
house. III. The bedroom of Violetta.

Major roles: Violetta Valery (soprano), Alfredo Germont (tenor),
Giorgio Germont (baritone). **Minor roles:** Flora Bervoix (mezzo), Annina
(soprano), Gastone (tenor), Baron Douphol (baritone), Marquis
d'Obigny (bass), Doctor Grenvil (bass). **Bit parts:** Giuseppe (tenor),
Servant to Flora (bass), Messenger (bass).

Chorus parts: SSATTBB. **Chorus roles:** Friends of Violetta and Flora,
matadors, picadors, gypsies, servants. **Dance/movement:** II: Ballet of
gypsies and matadors. **Orchestra:** 2 fl (picc), 2 ob, 2 cl, 2 bsn, 4 hrn, 2 trp,
3 trb, cimbasso, timp, perc, strings. **Stageband:** I: band, harp. III: 2 picc, 4
cl, 2 hrn, 2 trb, perc. **Publisher:** Schirmer, Ricordi. **Rights:** Expired.

I. Violetta greets her guests, including Gastone who has brought Alfredo
Germont, one of her admirers. "Alfredo asked about you every day of
your illness," Gastone tells Violetta. The young swain obliges his hostess
by singing a drinking song. When the guests go to the ballroom,
Violetta, overcome by a spell of weakness, remains behind. Alfredo
seizes the moment to declare his love to Violetta. She promises to allow
him to return the next day. After the guests have taken their leave,
Violetta is torn between love for Alfredo and for her life of freedom.

IIi. Violetta has abandoned Paris and is living in the country with
Alfredo. To pay for it all, she has been selling off her possessions.
Alfredo learns this from Violetta's servant Annina and rushes off to
Paris to get money. An invitation to a ball in Paris arrives from Flora.
Germont, Alfredo's father, is announced. He pleads with Violetta to
leave Alfredo, as her reputation is ruining Alfredo and his sister.
Reluctantly, she agrees, asking only that when she is dead Germont tell
Alfredo of her sacrifice. Violetta takes a tearful farewell of Alfredo and
leaves for Paris. He is only aware that she has left for good when a mes-
senger delivers a letter from her. Alfredo thinks she has gone back to a

previous lover, the baron. Ignoring his father's pleas, he swears revenge. IIii. Flora tells her guests about Alfredo and Violetta's split. Gypsies and dancers provide entertainment. Alfredo beats the baron at cards, and Violetta begs him to leave before there is trouble. When this has no effect, Violetta says she loves the baron. Infuriated, Alfredo throws his winnings at Violetta in front of all the guests. This turns everyone— including Germont—against Alfredo and the baron challenges him.

III. Violetta is now confined to bed because of her consumption. Germont has written to her to say that Alfredo has learned of her sacrifice and is returning. He will be too late, Violetta laments. Carnival revelers can be heard outside. Alfredo returns and the lovers sing of happier times to come. Violetta wants to go to church, but does not have the strength to get dressed. After a brief moment of elation, she falls dead.

Treemonisha

Composed by Scott Joplin (November 24, 1868 – April 1, 1917). Libretto by Scott Joplin. English. Original work Premiered Atlanta, Morehouse College, January 28, 1972. Set in Arkansas in 1884. Folk opera. Set numbers with recitative or spoken dialogue. Overture. Prelude before III. No orchestration by composer. Later orchestrated separately by Gunther Schuller and T. J. Anderson. Produced in concert form in 1915.

Sets: 4. **Acts:** 3 acts, 4 scenes. **Length:** I: 40. II: 15. III: 35. **Arias:** "The sacred tree" (Monisha). **Hazards:** II: Eight bears frolic and search for food. **Scenes:** I. On the plantation. IIi. In the woods at a conjurors' meeting. IIii. A cotton field. III. Interior of Ned and Monisha's cabin.

Major roles: Monisha (soprano), Ned (bass), Treemonisha (soprano), Remus (tenor). **Minor roles:** Zodzetrick (high baritone or tenor), Lucy (soprano), Parson Alltalk (bass), Simon (bass), Luddud (bass or baritone), Male quartet (2 tenor, 2 bass). **Bit parts:** Andy (tenor), Cephus (tenor).

Chorus parts: SSAATTBB. **Chorus roles:** Corn huskers, conjurors, cotton pickers, people. **Dance/movement:** I: Corn huskers perform ring dance. III: Everyone does the "slow drag." **Orchestra:** fl (picc), ob, 2 cl, bsn, 2 hrn, 2 trp, trb, tuba, piano, timp, perc, harp, banjo, strings. **Stageband:** None. **Publisher:** Scott Joplin, Dramatic Publishing Co. **Rights:** Copyright 1911 by Scott Joplin.

I. The conjuror Zodzetrick tries to sell Monisha a good luck bag, but her husband, Ned, is suspicious. Treemonisha and Remus rebuke Zodzetrick for fostering superstition. Zodzetrick threatens to bring them bad luck. The corn huskers dance. Treemonisha decides to make herself a wreath of leaves. To please Monisha, she avoids one particular tree—the one under which, Monisha admits, she found the baby Treemonisha. Everyone is surprised to learn that Monisha is not Treemonisha's mother. While Parson Alltalk lectures his parishioners, Zodzetrick and Luddud kidnap Treemonisha.

IIi. The conjurors determine to push Treemonisha into a wasps' nest as punishment for spoiling their livelihood. Remus, disguised as a scarecrow, scares the conjurors away and frees Treemonisha. IIii. The young pair encounters cotton pickers on their way home.

III. Treemonisha returns to her parents. Andy and the corn huskers have captured the conjurors. At Treemonisha's insistence, the conjurors are not beaten but set free. The people proclaim Treemonisha their leader to protect them from ignorance and superstition. Everyone dances.

Tristan und Isolde • Tristan and Isolde

Composed by Richard Wagner (May 22, 1813 – February 13, 1883). Libretto by Richard Wagner. German. Based on a medieval legend. Premiered Munich, Königliches Hof- und Nationaltheater, June 10, 1865. Set at sea, in Cornwall and in Brittany in the Middle Ages. Romantic tragedy. Through composed. Prelude before each act.

Sets: 3. **Acts:** 3 acts, 11 scenes. **Length:** I: 80. II: 75. III: 75. **Arias:** "Mild und leise"/Liebestod (Isolde). **Hazards:** I: Set aboard ship. **Scenes:** I. At sea on the deck of Tristan's ship on the voyage from Ireland to Cornwall. II. King Marke's castle in Cornwall. III. Tristan's castle in Brittany.

Major roles: Isolde (dramatic soprano), Brangäne (mezzo or soprano), Tristan (tenor), King Marke (bass). **Minor roles:** Sailor (tenor), Kurwenal (baritone), Melot (tenor), Shepherd (tenor).

Chorus parts: TTBB. **Chorus roles:** Sailors, knights, attendants. **Dance/movement:** None. **Orchestra:** 3 fl (picc), 2 ob, Eng hrn, 2 cl, bs cl, 3 bsn, 4 hrn, 3 trp, 3 trb, bs tuba, timp, perc, harp, strings. **Stageband:** II: 3 trp, 3 trb, 6 hrn. III: Eng hrn. **Publisher:** G. Schirmer, Könemann Music Budapest. **Rights:** Expired.

I. Tristan is returning to Cornwall with Isolde, the intended of King Marke. Isolde is angry with Tristan for killing her previous fiancé and then tricking her into nursing Tristan through his own convalescence. She taunts Tristan and plans to poison him, but Isolde's maid, Brangäne, replaces the poison with a love potion and Tristan and Isolde fall in love.

II. In Cornwall, Tristan and Isolde attempt to meet in secret, but the King bursts in on them: Tristan's friend Melot has betrayed them to the King. Tristan and Melot fight and Tristan falls, mortally wounded.

III. Tristan has returned to his country estate to await Isolde—and death. He dies in her arms. Melot, the king and Brangäne now arrive, intending to forgive and forget. Tristan's friend Kurwenal, not realizing their intentions, resists their advance and is killed. Isolde dies of love.

Il Trittico

See entries for "Il Tabarro," "Suor Angelica" and "Gianni Schicchi."

Troilus and Cressida

Composed by William Walton (March 29, 1902 – March 8, 1983). Libretto by Christopher Hassall. English. Based on stories by Chaucer and Boccaccio. Premiered London, Royal Opera House, Covent Garden, December 3, 1954. Set in Troy in the 12th century BC. Tragedy. Set numbers with accompanied recitative. Interlude before IIii. Revised version premiered London, November 12, 1976.

Sets: 3. **Acts:** 3 acts, 4 scenes. **Length:** I: 40. II: 45. III: 45. **Arias:** "If one last doubt, one lurking fear remain" (Troilus), "You gods, you deathless gods" (Cressida). **Hazards:** None. **Scenes:** I. The citadel of Troy before the temple of Pallas. II. An upper room in the house of Pandarus. III. The Greek camp.

Major roles: Calkas (bass), Prince Troilus (tenor), Cressida (soprano; mezzo in revised version), Pandarus (tenor). **Minor roles:** Captain Antenor (baritone), Evadne (mezzo), Horaste (baritone), Four ladies in attendance on Cressida (2 soprano, 2 contralto), Prince Diomede (baritone). **Bit parts:** First priest (tenor), First soldier (tenor), Second soldier (bass), Priest (bass). **Speaking bit:** woman.

Chorus parts: SSSSSAAAAATTTTBBBB. **Chorus roles:** Priests and priestesses of Pallas, Trojan soldiers, worshipers and people, Greek soldiers and women of the camp. **Dance/movement:** None. **Orchestra:** 3 fl, 3 ob (Eng hrn), 3 cl (bs cl), 2 bsn, cont bsn, 4 hrn, 3 trp, 3 trb, tuba, timp, 4 or 5 perc, 2 harp, celeste, strings. **Stageband:** II: drums. III: hrn, 4 trp. **Publisher:** Oxford University Press. **Rights:** Copyright 1954 by Oxford University Press.

I. After ten years of war, the Trojans' faith in their gods is slipping. Their priest, Calkas, angers his countrymen by arguing for negotiations with the Greeks. Only Prince Troilus's arrival saves Calkas from the mob. Troilus loves Cressida, Calkas's daughter and a temple novice. But Cressida prefers the peace of religious service. Her uncle, Pandarus, offers himself to Troilus as a go-between. While Pandarus is making Troilus's case with Cressida, news arrives that Calkas has fled to the Greeks and Antenor has been captured. Pandarus gives Troilus Cressida's scarf.

IIi. Pandarus gives a dinner party and persuades his guests—including Cressida—to stay the night. He manufactures a misunderstanding between Troilus and Cressida, then introduces Troilus into Cressida's bedroom so they can make up. IIii. The next morning, a contingent of Greek soldiers visits Pandarus. Their captain, Diomede, announces that both sides have agreed to exchange Antenor for Cressida. Troilus returns Cressida's scarf and promises to visit her secretly in the Greek camp.

III. Cressida has been ten weeks in the Greek camp without a word from Troilus. Both Calkas and Cressida's maid, Evadne, beg Cressida to forget Troilus and look more favorably on the handsome Diomede. Worn down with waiting, Cressida agrees and gives Diomede her scarf. Troilus and Pandarus visit the Greek camp under flag of truce, not realizing that Evadne has destroyed all of Troilus's messages. Troilus has negotiated Cressida's release, but the wedding procession is already gathering. Troilus sees Diomede with Cressida's scarf, and challenges him. They fight, but Calkas stabs Troilus in the back, killing him. Diomede banishes Calkas and curses Cressida. She stabs herself with Troilus's sword.

Trouble in Tahiti

See "A Quiet Place" entry.

Il Trovatore • The Troubadour

Composed by Giuseppe Verdi (October 9, 1813 – January 27, 1901). Libretto by Leone Emanuele Bardare and Salvatore Cammarano. Italian. Play by Antonio García Gutiérrez. Premiered Rome, Teatro Apollo, January 19, 1853. Set in Spain in the 15th century. Tragedy. Set numbers with accompanied recitative.

Sets: 8. **Acts:** 4 acts, 8 scenes. **Length:** I: 30. II: 40. III: 20. IV: 40. **Arias:** "Ah sì, ben mio" (Manrico), "Il Balen" (Count di Luna), "Di quella pira"

(Manrico), "Miserere" / "D'amor sull' ali rosee" (Leonora), "Stride la vampa" (Azucena), "Tacea la notte" / "Di tale amor" (Leonora). **Hazards:** None. **Scenes:** Ii. Hall in the Aliaferia palace. Iii. Palace garden. IIi. Gypsy camp in the mountains of Biscaglia. IIii. Cloister of a convent in the neighborhood of Castellor. IIIi. Military camp. IIIii. Hall at Castellor. IVi. Wing of the Aliaferia palace. IVii. Horrible dungeon.

Major roles: Leonora (soprano), Count di Luna (baritone), Manrico (tenor), Azucena (mezzo). **Minor roles:** Ferrando (bass), Inez (mezzo), Ruiz (tenor). **Bit parts:** Gypsy (bass), Messenger (tenor).

Chorus parts: SSAATTTTBBBB. **Chorus roles:** Retainers of the count, nuns, monks, Manrico's men, gypsies, soldiers. **Dance/movement:** None. **Orchestra:** 2 fl (picc), 2 ob, 2 cl, 2 bsn, 4 hrn, 2 trp, 3 trb, cimbasso, timp, perc, harp, organ, bells, strings. **Stageband:** I: drum, anvils, harp. II: hrn. **Publisher:** Ricordi. **Rights:** Expired.

Ii. To pass the time on guard duty, Ferrando tells his men about the count's brother, Garcia. When Garcia was a baby, a gypsy crept into his bedroom and cast a spell on him. As punishment, the gypsy was burned alive. The gypsy's daughter then kidnapped Garcia and burned him alive. The men are frightened by stories that the dead gypsy's spirit has been seen. Iii. Leonora confides to Inez that she loves the troubadour Manrico who has been serenading her. The count, too, loves Leonora and in the dark she mistakes him for Manrico. The mistake is rectified, but the count challenges Manrico.

IIi. A band of gypsies sings while working. Manrico, who spared the count, but barely escaped from the count's men, asks his mother, the gypsy Azucena, about her past. She recounts how her mother was burned by the count's men. "In revenge, I stole the count's son," Azucena says, "but when I went to throw him in the fire, I found I had killed my own son instead." Manrico is surprised at this revelation, but Azucena assures Manrico he is her son. A messenger brings word that Leonora is going to take the veil. Manrico hurries off to stop her, ignoring his mother's warning that his wounds have not yet healed. IIii. The count and his men hide outside Leonora's convent, meaning to seize her. The count surprises the nuns but is himself surprised by Manrico and his men. Leonora leaves with Manrico.

IIIi. The count's army besieges Manrico's castle of Castellor. Azucena is captured spying and brought before the count, who realizes it was she who killed Garcia. Her admission that Manrico is her son fuels his hatred. IIIii. Manrico assures Leonora he will defeat the count. When he sees the pyre lit for Azucena, he orders his men to arms.

IVi. Manrico's men have been defeated. Leonora and Ruiz sneak into the palace where Manrico is imprisoned. Leonora offers herself to the count in exchange for Manrico and the count accepts. She drinks poison. IVii. In prison, Manrico comforts Azucena. Leonora enters and bids Manrico flee. He guesses the price she has paid for his freedom and curses her. He repents, however, when Leonora is overcome by the effects of the poison. The count enters the cell. Leonora dies and the count has Manrico executed. Azucena reveals to the count that Manrico was his brother—the gypsy has avenged her mother.

Les Troyens • The Trojans

Composed by Hector Berlioz (December 11, 1803 – March 8, 1869). Libretto by Hector Berlioz. French. Based on the "Aeneid" of Virgil. Premiered Paris, Théâtre Lyrique, November 4, 1863. Set in Troy and Carthage towards the end of the Trojan War. Grand opera. Set numbers with recitative. Prelude. Entr'acte before II. Ballet. Orchestral interludes. Original 5-act version split into two operas: "La Prise de Troie" and "Les Troyens à Carthage," the former not premiered until December 6, 1890. Small parts can be double cast.

Sets: 8. **Acts:** 5 acts, 9 scenes. **Length:** I, II, III, IV, V: 240. **Arias:** "Je vais mourir" (Dido), "Vallon sonore" (Hylas). **Hazards:** V: Vision of Rome's legions. **Scenes:** I. The abandoned Greek camp on the plains of Troy. IIi. A room in Énée's palace. IIii. A room in Priam's palace. III. A vast hall of greenery in Didon's palace at Carthage. IVi. An African forest. IVii. Gardens of Didon by the sea. Vi. The sea shore covered with Roman tents. Vii. A room in Didon's palace. Viii. Didon's gardens. (When split, part I comprises acts I and II; part II comprises acts III, IV and V.)

Major roles (part I): Cassandre (soprano), Chorèbe (baritone), Énée (tenor). **Major roles (part II):** Didon (mezzo or soprano), Anna (contralto), Énée (tenor), Narbal (baritone or bass). **Minor roles (part I):** Hélénus (tenor), Panthée (bass), Ascagne (soprano), Ghost of Héctor (bass), Hécube (mezzo), Priam (bass), Polyxena (soprano). **Mute (part I):** Andromaque, Astyanax. **Minor roles (part II):** Ascagne (soprano), Panthée (bass), Iopas (tenor), Hylas (tenor), Mercure (baritone), Two soldiers (baritone, bass), Ghost of Cassandre (soprano), Ghost of Chorèbe (baritone), Ghost of Héctor (baritone), Ghost of Priam (bass).

Chorus parts: SSATTBB. **Chorus roles:** People of Troy and Carthage, Trojan and Greek soldiers, ghosts, priests of Pluto, children, courtiers, Nubian slaves, Tyrians, laborers, sailors, workers, invisible spirits, naiads, fawns, saytrs. **Dance/movement:** I: Trojans celebrate the Greeks' retreat; wrestlers' dance. IV: royal hunt (pantomime), ballet of Egyptian dancing girls and Nubian slaves. **Orchestra:** picc, 2 fl (picc), 2 ob (Eng hrn), 2 cl (bs cl), 4 bsn, 4 hrn, 2 trp, 2 cornet, 3 trb, tuba (ophicléide), timp, perc, 3 harp, strings. **Stageband:** I: high saxhorn, 2 sop saxhrn, 2 tenor saxhrn, 3 trb, bs saxhrn. II: 2 sop saxhrn, 2 alto saxhrn, 2 ten saxhrn, 2 bs saxhrn, perc. III: 3 ob, harp (trps and tubas can be substituted for saxhrns). **Publisher:** Kalmus, Choudens & Co. **Rights:** Expired.

I. After ten years of war, the Trojans celebrate the retreat of the Greeks from their shores. They prepare to bring the wooden horse left behind by the Greeks within the city walls. Cassandre realizes that Troy will fall. She begs her beloved Chorèbe to flee, but he refuses. Andromaque and her son, Astyanax, mourn for Hector. Énée tells how Laocoon was devoured by serpents for suspecting the wooden horse. Cassandre is unable to prevent the horse's entrance into the city.

IIi. The shade of Hector tells Énée to escape to Italy. He leads the Trojans in a last defense of the city. IIii. Before the altar of Vesta, Cassandre tells how Énée saved the citadel. Cassandre and the other women kill themselves rather than be enslaved. Énée escapes with the city's treasures. III. Didon rewards her adoring subjects and calls on them to defeat Numidian advances. Her sister Anna assures Didon that some day Didon will again take a husband. The Trojans ask for a few days of shelter, which Didon grants. Narbal brings news of an imminent Numidian attack. Énée offers to fight for the besieged Didon.

IVi. Énée joins the royal hunt. IVii. The Numidians have been defeated, but Narbal worries that Didon does not pay attention to matters of state as she once did. Anna points out that she is in love with Énée. Slaves dance for the queen and Iopas recites. Énée relates how Andromaque married Pyrrhus, her father's murderer. Alone, Didon and Énée enjoy the night. Mercure orders Énée on to Italy.

Vi. Hylas, a young sailor, sings of his homeland. The Trojans prepare to leave Carthage—to the consternation of two sentries. Énée is heartbroken, but a visitation of ghosts strengthens his resolve. Didon curses the faithless Énée. Vii. Caught between love and hate, Didon decides to kill herself. Viii. Didon looks forward to the day that Hannibal will avenge Carthage. She stabs herself. A vision appears of Rome's legions.

Tsarskaya Neviesta • The Tsar's Bride

Composed by Nicolai Rimsky-Korsakov (March 18, 1844 – June 21, 1908). Libretto by Nicolai Rimsky-Korsakov and Ilya Fyodorovich Tuymenev. Russian. Based on a play by Lev Alexandrovich Mey. Premiered Moscow, Private Russian Opera, November 3, 1889. Set in

Russia in 1572. Tragedy. Set numbers with accompanied recitative.
Overture. Entr'acte before II, III, IV. Intermezzo before IIiv. Ballet.

Sets: 4. **Acts:** 4 acts, 20 scenes. **Length:** Overture: 7. I: 45. II: 40. III: 25. IV:
25. **Hazards:** None. **Scenes:** I. A large sitting room in Gryaznoy's home.
II. A street in the Alexandrovsky suburb before Sobakin's and
Bomelius's houses. III. A sitting room in Sobakin's house. IV. A hall in
the tsar's palace.

Major roles: Vassily Stepanovich Sobakin (bass), Grigory Grigoryevich
Gryaznoy (baritone), Boyar Ivan Sergeyevich Lyikov (tenor), Lyubasha
(mezzo), Martha (soprano). **Minor roles:** Grigory Lukianovich Maliuta
Skuratov (bass), Elisey Bomelius (tenor), Dunyasha (contralto), Domna
Ivanovna Saburova (soprano). **Bit parts:** Young man (tenor), Petrovna
(mezzo), Chambermaid (mezzo), Tsar's valet (bass). **Mute:** Tsar Ivan the
Terrible.

Chorus parts: SSAATTBB. **Chorus roles:** Oprichniks, people.
Dance/movement: I: Guest ballet. **Orchestra:** 3 fl (picc), 3 ob (Eng hrn), 3
cl, 2 bsn, 4 hrn, 3 trp, 3 trb, tuba, timp, perc, harp, piano, strings.
Stageband: None. **Rights:** Expired.

Ii. Gryaznoy loves Marfa, but she is already engaged. Iii. He throws a
party. Iiii. The guests praise the new tsar and dance. Iiv. Gryaznoy's
mistress, Lyubasha, sings for them. Iv. Gryaznoy pays Bomelius to make
him a love potion. Ivi. Lyubasha realizes she has lost Gryaznoy's love.

IIi. The tsar has summoned his female subjects so he can chose a bride.
IIii. Marfa tells her friend Dunyasha about her fiancé, Lyikov. IIiii. The
girls are observed by the tsar. IIiv. Lyubasha persuades Bomelius to
make a potion that will destroy Marfa's beauty. IIv. She agrees to come
be Bomelius's mistress. IIvi. The dreaded Oprichniks murder the tsar's
enemies.

IIIi. Marfa and Dunyasha are summoned to appear before the tsar. IIIii.
Gryaznoy prepares the love potion. IIIiii. The tsar speaks to Dunyasha.
IIIiv. Gryaznoy puts the potion in Marfa's wine, not realizing that
Lyubasha has switched it for the poison. IIIv. A message from the tsar
announces his intention to marry Marfa.

IVi. Marfa is mortally ill. IVii. Gryaznoy accuses Lyikov of sorcery and
has him executed. He fears the potion has made Marfa ill and confesses.
IViii. Lyubasha explains she switched the potions. Gryaznoy kills her
and is arrested.

Turandot

Composed by Ferruccio Busoni (April 1, 1866 – July 27, 1924). Libretto by Ferruccio Busoni. German. Based on the play by Carlo Gozzi. Premiered Zurich, Stadttheater, May 11, 1917. Set in Peking in ancient times. Chinese fable. Set numbers with recitative. Some spoken dialogue. Introduction before Ii and Iii. Ballet. Intermezzo before IIii.

Sets: 4. **Acts:** 2 acts, 4 scenes. **Length:** I: 45. II: 30. **Arias:** "Konfutse, dir hab' ich geschworen" (Altoum), "Es pocht mein Herz" (Turandot).
Hazards: I: Executioner impales a freshly severed head on a pike.
Scenes: Ii. One of the vast city gates of Peking. Iii. The throne room of the emperor's palace. IIi. Turandot's apartments. IIii. The throne room.

Major roles: Prince Kalaf (tenor), Turandot (dramatic soprano). **Minor roles:** Barak (baritone), Mother of the prince of Samarkand (mezzo), Truffaldino (tenor), Emperor Altoum (bass), Pantalone (baritone), Tartaglia (baritone), Adelma (mezzo), Singer (soprano). **Mute:** Executioner.

Chorus parts: SSATTBB. **Chorus roles:** Mourners, slaves, doctors of law (4 tenor, 4 bass), guards, heralds, attendants of the emperor, attendants of Turandot. **Dance/movement:** II: ballet of Turandot's slaves.
Orchestra: 2 fl (picc), 2 ob (Eng hrn), 2 cl (bs cl), 2 bsn (cont bsn), 4 hrn, 3 trp, 3 trb, timp, perc, harp, celeste, strings. **Stageband:** I: 6 trp, 3 trb, bs trb, 2 sax. II: 6 trp, 3 trb, bs trb, drum, 2 sax. III: I, III: 6 trp, 3 trb, bs trb, 2 sax, gong. **Publisher:** Breitkopf and Härtel. **Rights:** Copyright 1926, 1955 by G. Ricordi.

Ii. After being defeated in battle by his enemies, Prince Kalaf flees to Peking where he meets his old servant Barak. Barak warns Kalaf of the beautiful Princess Turandot who beheads suitors who cannot answer her three riddles. A Moorish prince is now paying the price of courting the princess and his mother mourns him. Kalaf sees the princess's picture and falls in love. Iii. Truffaldino, the chief eunuch, gloats over the executions. The emperor dislikes the executions and tries to dissuade Kalaf from taking the challenge. Turandot is moved by Kalaf's appearance, while her confidante, Adelma, recognizes him as her childhood love. When Kalaf answers all three riddles correctly, Turandot tries to kill herself. Kalaf agrees to leave if Turandot can guess his name.

IIi. Truffaldino has failed to discover Kalaf's name. The emperor has lost patience with Turandot and looks forward to her embarrassment. Adelma tells Turandot Kalaf's name. IIii. Turandot correctly names Kalaf, but she loves him and they marry.

Turandot

Composed by Giacomo Puccini (December 22, 1858 – November 29, 1924). Libretto by Giuseppe Adami and Renato Simoni. Italian. Based on play by Carlo Gozzi. Premiered Milan, Teatro alla Scala, April 25, 1926. Set in Peking in the time of fables. Lyric drama. Through composed. Last duet and finale composed by Franco Alfano after Puccini's death.

Sets: 4 or 5. **Acts:** 3 acts, 5 scenes. **Length:** I: 30. II: 40. III: 35. **Arias:** "In questa reggia" (Turandot), "Del primo pianto" (Turandot), "Nessun dorma" (Calaf), "Signor, ascolta" (Liù). **Hazards:** I: Severed head of the Prince of Persia appears. **Scenes:** I. In front of the walls of the imperial city. IIi. A large tent. IIii. Courtyard of the imperial palace. IIIi. Garden of the imperial palace. IIIii. Outside the imperial palace.

Major roles: Princess Turandot (soprano), Prince Calaf (tenor), Liù (soprano). **Minor roles:** Timur (bass), Mandarin (baritone), Emperor Altoum (tenor), Ping (baritone), Pang (tenor), Pong (tenor). **Bit parts:** Prince of Persia (one line, delivered offstage). **Mute:** Executioner.

Chorus parts: SSATTBBB. **Chorus roles:** Imperial guards, children, heralds, priests, mandarins, officials, eight wise men (bass), Turandot's ladies-in-waiting, soldiers, musicians, servants, 12 assistants of the executioner (bass), nine girls (soprano), eight ghosts of Turandot's suitors, people. Solo lines and small groups. **Dance/movement:** None.
Orchestra: 3 fl (picc), 2 ob, Eng hrn, 2 cl, bs cl, 2 bsn, cont bsn, 4 hrn, 3 trp, 3 trb, tuba, timp, perc, bells, celeste, 2 xylophone, 2 harps, organ, strings. **Stageband:** I: 2 sax, 6 trp, 3 trb, bs trb. II: 2 sax, 6 trp, 3 trb, bs trb, drum. III: 2 sax, 6 trp, 3 trb, bs trb, Chinese gong (can be in pit).
Publisher: Ricordi. **Rights:** Copyright 1926 by G. Ricordi and Co.

I. A mandarin reads the royal decree stating that the Princess Turandot will marry any royal suitor who answers her three riddles. To take the test and fail means death. The Prince of Persia has already forfeited his life. In the pushing of the crowd, Timur is knocked to the ground. He is found by his long lost son, Calaf, who warns him that the usurper of Timur's throne still pursues them. When asked, Liù explains that although she is a slave, she has helped the deposed Timur because Calaf once smiled at her. The executioner's men hone his sword. At the appearance of the Prince of Persia, the crowd—which has been screaming for the Prince's blood—begs pity for him. Calaf is overcome by Turandot's beauty when she appears to condemn the Prince. He goes to sound the gong, indicating his acceptance of the challenge, just as the last cry of the Prince of Persia is heard from offstage. Ping, Pang and Pong (the chancellor, marshal and chief cook respectively) try to dissuade Calaf. The ghosts of Turandot's dead suitors appear and egg Calaf on. Timur and Liù make one final, unsuccessful attempt to restrain him. Calaf sounds the gong three times.

IIi. Ping, Pang and Pong lament that because of Turandot they have become ministers of the executioner. They long for their country homes. IIii. The Emperor Altoum tries to talk Calaf out of the ordeal, but Calaf insists. Turandot explains that the ordeal of the riddles is her revenge on the man who, centuries ago, killed Turandot's ancestor, the Princess Lou-Ling. The test begins. "What phantom is it that everyone calls to that dies every morning and is reborn every night?" Turandot asks. "Hope," Calaf answers correctly. "What burns like a flame, but is not a flame?" she asks; it grows cold if you die, but flares up at dreams of conquests. "Blood," Calaf says. "What is lily white and dark?" Turandot asks. "What makes you a King if it accepts you as a slave?" "Turandot," Calaf responds. The Emperor pronounces Calaf the victor in spite of Turandot, who begs her father not to give her to any man. She asks Calaf if he would take a bride by force. "No," Calaf answers. He offers her a challenge of his own: "If you can discover my name by dawn," he says, "my life is forfeit to you."

IIIi. Heralds proclaim Turandot's order that no one is to sleep all night. Anyone who does not discover Calaf's name risks execution. Ping, Pang and Pong try to bribe Calaf with women, riches and promises of escape from Turandot's wrath; the crowd threatens him. Liù and Timur are discovered and arrested but Liù offers herself up to torture to save Timur. Love gives her strength to resist and she stabs herself without having revealed Calaf's name. Before dying, she predicts that Turandot will love Calaf by morning. All mourn Liù's untimely death. Calaf forcibly kisses Turandot who is transformed and admits her love for (and fear of) Calaf. The prince confesses his name, putting his fate in Turandot's hands. IIIii. Turandot announces the stranger's name to the crowd. "His name," she says, "is love."

Il Turco in Italia • The Turk in Italy

Composed by Gioachino Rossini (February 29, 1792 – November 13, 1868). Libretto by Felice Romani. Italian. Based on a libretto by Caterino Mazzolà for Franz Seydelmann. Premiered Milan, Teatro alla Scala, August 14, 1814. Set in Naples in the 18th century. Comic opera. Set numbers with recitative. Overture.

Sets: 4. **Acts:** 2 acts, 6 scenes. **Length:** I, II: 150. **Arias:** "Perchè mai se son tradito" (Narciso). **Hazards:** None. **Scenes:** Ii. The seashore near Geronio's house outside Naples. Iii. Elegantly furnished apartment in the house of Geronio. Iiii. The seashore. IIi. A room in an inn. IIii. A hall brilliantly lighted for a ball. IIiii. The seashore.

Major roles: Don Geronio (bass), Fiorilla (soprano), Selim (bass), Narciso (tenor), Zaida (mezzo or soprano), Poet (bass baritone). **Bit parts:** Albazar (tenor).

Chorus parts: SATTB. **Chorus roles:** Gypsies, Turks, people. **Dance/movement:** None. **Orchestra:** 2 fl, 2 ob, 2 cl, 2 bsn, 2 hrn, 2 trp, trb, timp, perc, strings, continuo. **Stageband:** None. **Publisher:** Kalmus. **Rights:** Expired.

Ii. The poet encounters a group of gypsies and decides they would make a perfect opening for his drama. He directs them towards old Geronio who always wants to have his fortune told. Geronio is plagued by his young wife, Fiorilla. Selim the Turk disembarks, where he meets—and flirts with—Fiorilla. The poet is overjoyed at this spicy material for his play but Geronio and his friend Narciso are indignant. Iii. Geronio interrupts his wife serving the Turk coffee. When Fiorilla explains Geronio is her husband, Selim draws his knife. The cowardly Geronio has to kiss Selim's coat to smooth things over. Narciso—who also loves Fiorilla—is indignant. Geronio pours out his troubles to the poet, but his attempt to discipline Fiorilla fails. Iiii. The gypsy Zaida offers to tell Selim's fortune. The two are long lost lovers; they are reunited. Fiorilla and Zaida fight over Selim.

IIi. Selim tries to persuade Geronio to sell Fiorilla, but Geronio refuses. The men threaten each other. Fiorilla is determined to defeat Zaida even though she does not want Selim. The two women confront Selim—who ends up with Fiorilla. The poet warns Geronio that Selim means to run off with Fiorilla. "She is going to a party in disguise where she will meet him," he explains. Geronio disguises himself as a Turk and Zaida as an Italian. IIii. Narciso also disguises himself as a Turk and finds Fiorilla first. Selim pairs off with Zaida. Geronio is presented with two Fiorillas and two Selims. He tries, unsuccessfully, to prevent both couples from leaving. IIiii. Fiorilla repents and is reunited with her husband. Zaida and Selim take their farewell.

The Turn of the Screw

Composed by Benjamin Britten (November 22, 1913 – December 4, 1976). Libretto by Myfanwy Piper. English. Based on the novel by Henry James. Premiered Venice, Teatro la Fenice, September 14, 1954. Set in Bly, a country-house in the East of England in the mid-19th century.

Psychological/supernatural tragedy. Through composed with prologue. Each scene based on a variation of the same theme.

Sets: 11. **Acts:** 2 acts, 16 scenes. **Length:** I: 53. II: 52. **Hazards:** None.
Scenes: Ii. Interior of a coach. Iii. The porch of Bly. Iiii. Side of the house. Iiv. Outside the house with the tower visible. Iv. Interior of the hall at Bly. Ivi. The schoolroom. Ivii. The lake in the park. Iviii. Garden in front of the house, night. IIi. Nowhere. IIii. Churchyard. IIiii. Schoolroom. IIiv – IIv. Miles's bedroom. IIvi. The music room. IIvii. The lake. IIviii. The house and grounds.

Major roles: Governess (soprano), Miles (boy treble), Flora (girl soprano), Mrs. Grose (soprano), Quint (tenor). **Minor roles:** Prologue (tenor), Miss Jessel (soprano). (Peter Quint often plays Prologue.)

Chorus parts: N/A. **Chorus roles:** None. **Dance/movement:** None. **Orchestra:** fl (picc, bs fl), ob (Eng hrn), cl (bs cl), bsn, hrn, harp, perc, piano (celeste), strings (1-1-1-1-1). **Stageband:** None. **Publisher:** Boosey & Hawkes. **Rights:** Copyright 1955 by Boosey & Hawkes.

Prologue. A young governess is given charge of two children, Miles and Flora. "Handle everything," their guardian tells her, "and never disturb me." Ii. In the train, the governess wrestles with her insecurities. Iii. She arrives at Bly, where she is greeted warmly by Mrs. Grose, the housekeeper, and charmed by the children. Iiii. Miles is expelled from school for being "an injury to his friends." The governess and Mrs. Grose dismiss the charges as preposterous. Iiv. The governess catches a glimpse of Peter Quint in the tower and wonders who he is. Iv. The children are playing. When the governess sends them off, she sees Quint at the window. Mrs. Grose recognizes Quint from the governess's description: he was the master's valet. Left in charge in the master's absence, Quint "made free" with Miles and the former governess, Miss Jessel. But Quint and Jessel are both dead. The governess determines to protect Miles from Quint. Ivi. The children have their lesson. Miles sings an old song he "found." Ivii. The governess takes the children out to the lake but hurries inside when Miss Jessel appears to her. Iviii. Quint and Miss Jessel visit the children.

IIi. Miss Jessel offers to be the friend that Quint seeks, but he rejects her. The governess feels overwhelmed by the evil around her. IIii. It is Sunday. When the governess hears the children blaspheming, she fears she has lost them. Miles challenges the governess to act by asking her about "the others." IIiii. When the governess finds Miss Jessel in the schoolroom, she breaks down and writes to the children's guardian. IIiv. The governess tells Miles about the letter and asks him to confide in her but he hears Quint and refuses. IIv. At Quint's urging, Miles steals the letter. IIvi. Miles distracts the governess by playing the piano while Flora slips off to meet Miss Jessel. IIvii. The governess and Mrs. Grose catch up with Flora by the lake. Miss Jessel is there, but only the governess can see her. Flora bursts into tears when the governess tries to force her to admit she can see Miss Jessel. IIviii. Mrs. Grose takes Flora away to London. The governess's letter was never sent and Mrs. Grose and the governess realize that Miles stole it. When the governess again tries to draw Miles out, Quint appears and they struggle for the boy's soul. Miles curses Quint and falls dead.

Ulisse

Composed by Luigi Dallapiccola (February 3, 1904 – February 19, 1975). Libretto by Luigi Dallapiccola. Italian. Based on the "Odyssey" by Homer. Premiered Berlin, Deutsche Oper, September 29, 1968. Set in the Mediterranean islands and Greece shortly after the Trojan War. Opera. Through composed. Prologue with symphonic intermezzo. Epilogue. Musical interlude before IIii and IIiv. Score calls for amplified sound.

Sets: 10. **Acts:** 2 acts, 11 scenes. **Length:** Prologue, I, II: 135. **Hazards:** I: Ulisse's boat lands on the beach. Shade of Ulisse's mother disappears. II: Ulisse shoots the suitors with his bow. Final scene set on a boat at sea. **Scenes:** Prologue i. A beach on the island of Ogygia. (Prologue ii is a symphonic intermezzo.) Prologue iii. A beach on the island of the Phaeacians. Ii. A great hall in Alcinoo's palace. Iii. A beach. Iiii. Luxuriant countryside on the island of Aeaea. Iiv. The kingdom of the Cimmerians. Iv. The hall in Alcinoo's palace. IIi. An open space in Ithaca surrounded by hills. IIii. A courtyard before the palace. IIiii. The interior of the palace. IIiv. A small boat on the open sea.

Major role: Ulisse (baritone). **Minor roles:** Calypso/Penelope (soprano), First handmaid (contralto), Nausicaa (light soprano), King Alcinoo (bass baritone), Demodoco/Tiresia (tenor), Circe/Melanto (mezzo or contralto), Ulisse's mother Anticlea (dramatic soprano), Antinoo (baritone), Pisandro (baritone), Eurimaco (tenor), Eumeo (tenor), Telemaco (countertenor). **Bit parts:** Second handmaid (soprano), Lotus eater (soprano). **Dancers:** Six ballerinas.

Chorus parts: SSAATTBaBB (Second parts are spoken, not sung). **Chorus roles:** Maidservants (6 soprano, 6 contralto), subjects of Alcinoo, sailors, lotus eaters, shades, shepherds, peasants, suitors, women,. **Dance/movement:** I: Handmaidens dance on the beach (score specifies 6 ballerinas). II: Melanto's lascivious dance for the suitors. **Orchestra:** picc, 3 fl (picc), 2 ob, Eng hrn, 3 cl, bs cl, contralto sax, tenor sax, 2 bsn, cont bsn, 4 hrn, 3 trp, bs trp, 3 trb, tuba, 2 harps, celeste, glockenspiel, piano, vibraphone, xylomarimba, xylophone, organ, timp, perc, strings. **Stageband:** None. **Publisher:** Suvini Zerboni. **Rights:** Copyright 1970 by Suvini Zerboni.

Prologue i. Calypso marvels that Ulisse refused her offer of immortality. [Prologue ii is symphonic intermezzo.] Prologue iii. Princess Nausicaa tells her handmaidens of a dream in which she marries a stranger from the sea. Ulisse—the man from her dreams—appears on the beach. Ii. Demodoco tells Nausicaa's father, King Alcinoo, the fate of the Greek leaders after the Trojan War. The king welcomes Ulisse and asks about his travels. Iii. In a flashback, Ulisse's sailors complain that they want to go home. They land on the island of the lotus eaters, where some of the sailors join the lotus eaters. Iiii. Ulisse takes his leave of Circe. Iiv. In the world of shades, Ulisse finds his mother. Tiresia promises Ulisse he will see his home again, but warns of much bloodshed. Iv. Back in King Alcinoo's palace, Ulisse tells how his shipmates died. The king promises to take Ulisse home.

IIi. Many men hope to marry Ulisse's wife, Penelope. One of them, Antinoo, lays an ambush for Ulisse's son, Telemaco. Ulisse returns disguised as a beggar and is taken in by the herdsman, Eurimaco. Telemaco avoids the ambush and lands safely. IIii. Ulisse returns home. No one recognizes him except Melanto. IIiii. The suitors hold a drunken banquet. Melanto dances for them with Ulisse's bow. Telemaco and Ulisse interrupt. Ulisse strings his old bow and kills the suitors one by one. Penelope welcomes Ulisse home. IIiv. Now an old man, Ulisse has once again set to sea in search of truth.

Der Vampyr • The Vampire

Composed by Heinrich Marschner (August 16, 1795 – December 14, 1861). Libretto by Wilhelm August Wohlbrück. German. Based on "The Vampyre" by John Polidori. Premiered Leipzig, Sächsisches Hoftheater, March 29, 1828. Set in Scotland in the 18th century. Romantic opera. Set numbers with recitative and spoken dialogue. Overture. Introduction before II. Revised by Hans Pfitzner.

Sets: 3. **Acts:** 2 acts, 4 scenes. **Length:** I: 70. II: 75. **Arias:** "Ha, noch einen ganzen Tag" (Ruthven), "Dort am jenen Felsenhang" (Emmy), "Ha, wie das grauenvolle Bild" (Aubry). **Hazards:** II: Ruthven killed by a bolt of lightning. **Scenes:** Ii. A deserted spot. Iii. A hall in Lord Davenaut's castle. II. In front of the castle. IIii. The hall.

Major roles: Lord Ruthven (baritone), Edgar Aubry (tenor), Malwina (soprano), Emmy (soprano). **Minor roles:** Sir Humphrey (bass), Janthe (soprano), Sir Berkley (bass), Davenaut (bass), Georg Diddin (tenor), James Gadshill (tenor), Richard Scrop (tenor), Robert Green (bass), Toms Blunt (bass), Suse (mezzo). **Bit parts:** Four dancers (1 soprano, 1 alto, 1 tenor, 1 bass). **Speaking:** Vampire Master, John Perth.

Chorus parts: SATTBB. **Chorus roles:** Witches, ghosts, youths, peasants. **Dance/movement:** II: Wedding dance. **Orchestra:** 2 fl (picc), 2 ob, 2 cl, 2 bsn, cont bsn, 4 hrn, 2 trp, 3 trb, timp, perc, strings. **Stageband:** I: 2 hrn, 2 trp. **Publisher:** Peters Edition. **Rights:** Expired.

Ii. Ruthven has become a vampire, but the witches promise him another year of life if he kills three young girls within twenty-four hours. His first victim is Janthe, who has run away from home to be with Ruthven. Her father, Berkley, finds her body drained of blood and severely wounds Ruthven. Aubry saves Ruthven, who swears him to silence on pain of becoming a vampire. Iii. Malwina welcomes her beloved Aubry home. Her father, Davenaut, is determined to marry her to Ruthven. Aubry recognizes Ruthven, but his oath prevents him from exposing the vampire.

IIi. Ruthven seduces and kills Georg's girlfriend, Emmy. Aubry decides to expose Ruthven, but Ruthven threatens him with damnation. IIii. The wedding feast begins. Aubry tells the truth, but no one believes him. A bolt of lightning kills Ruthven. Aubry marries Malwina.

Vanessa

Composed by Samuel Barber (March 9, 1910 – January 23, 1981). Libretto by Gian Carlo Menotti. English. Based on a story in "Seven Gothic Tales" by Isak Dinesen (Karen Blixen). Premiered New York City, Metropolitan Opera Association, January 15, 1958. Set at Vanessa's country house in a northern country about 1905. Tragedy. Set numbers with accompanied recitative. Orchestral interludes before acts. Intermezzo before IIIii. Revised 1964.

Sets: 4. **Acts:** 4 acts, 5 scenes. **Length:** I: 25. II: 30. III: 21. IV: 40. **Hazards:** None. **Scenes:** I. Vanessa's drawing room. II. The winter garden. III. Entrance hall with the ballroom beyond. IVi. Erika's bedroom. IVii. The drawing room.

Major roles: Vanessa (soprano), Erika (mezzo), Anatol (tenor), Old doctor (baritone or bass baritone). **Minor roles:** Nicholas the major domo (bass), Old Baroness (contralto). **Bit part:** Footman (bass). **Mute:** Young pastor.

Chorus parts: SATB. **Chorus roles:** Servants, guests, peasants, their children, musicians. **Dance/movement:** II: Doctor, Vanessa and Anatol waltz. III: Guests ballroom dance. **Orchestra:** picc, 2 fl, 2 ob, Eng hrn, 2 cl, bs cl, 2 bsn, 4 hrn, 3 trp, 3 trb, tuba, timp, perc, celeste, harp, strings. **Stageband:** I: bells. II: organ. III: dance orchestra: fl, ob, 2 cl, 2 bsn, 2 hrn, 1 or 2 trp, drum, accordion, strings. IV: hrn. **Publisher:** Schirmer. **Rights:** Copyright 1957, 1958, 1964 by G. Schirmer.

Ii. Vanessa, her niece Erika, and her mother, the baroness, await Anatol's arrival. Twenty years have passed since Vanessa and Anatol have met and Vanessa refuses to reveal her face until Anatol says he still loves her. He does, but when Vanessa turns around she does not recognize him. It is Anatol's father who loved Vanessa—but he is dead. Anatol and Erika dine at the table set for Vanessa and his father.

II. The baroness rebukes Erika for letting Anatol seduce her. Erika loves Anatol; he is willing to marry her—but she hesitates, not believing he truly loves her. The doctor is pleased to see the house alive again. Vanessa confesses to Erika that she loves Anatol; she ignores Erika's warning that this is not the same man. The baroness counsels Erika to fight for Anatol. "He will do what is easiest for him," she says. "Then he is not worth fighting for," Erika concludes. Anatol again proposes, but Erika refuses him.

III. A New Year's Eve ball is in progress and the doctor is tipsy. He is to announce Vanessa's and Anatol's engagement, but the baroness and

Erika refuse to come downstairs. The doctor goes after them and Vanessa confesses her fears to Anatol. While the doctor is making the announcement, Erika faints on the steps, clutching her stomach. Recovered, she rushes off towards the lake. The baroness cries out and Anatol chases after Erika.

IVi. The search for Erika continues. Vanessa is elated when Erika is returned alive. She questions Anatol about Erika's behavior, but Anatol swears Erika does not love him. Vanessa begs him to take her away. Alone, Erika confesses to the baroness that she was pregnant—though no longer. IVii. Vanessa and Anatol prepare to leave. Vanessa presses Erika to confess why she ran from the party that night, but Erika says it was only a fond foolishness. After the newlyweds depart, Erika has the house shut up and the mirrors covered like Vanessa before her.

I Vespri Siciliani • The Sicilian Vespers

Composed by Giuseppe Verdi (October 9, 1813 – January 27, 1901). Libretto by Charles Duveyrier and Eugène Scribe. French or Italian. Based on a historical event. Premiered Paris, Opéra, June 13, 1855. Set in Palermo and environs in 1282. Drama. Set numbers with recitative. Overture. Ballet. "Les Vêpres Siciliennes" in the original French.

Sets: 6. **Acts:** 5 acts, 6 scenes. **Length:** I: 25. II: 25. III: 30. IV: 30. V: 15. **Arias:** "O tu Palermo" (Procida), "In braccio alle dovizie" (Monforte), "Giorno di pianto" (Arrigo), "Mercé, dilette amiche" (Elena). **Hazards:** None. **Scenes:** I. The great square in Palermo. II. A valley outside Palermo. IIIi. A room in the Monforte palace. IIIii. A magnificent room prepared for a ball. IV. The courtyard of a fortress. V. The gardens of the Monforte palace.

Major roles: Guido di Monforte (baritone), Giovanni da Procida (bass), Duchess Elena (soprano), Arrigo (tenor). **Minor roles:** Sire di Bethune (bass), Count Vaudemont (bass), Ninetta (contralto), Danieli (tenor), Tebaldo (tenor), Roberto (bass), Manfredo (tenor). **Mute:** Executioner.

Chorus parts: SSAATTTTBB. **Chorus roles:** Sicilians, French soldiers, pages, nobles, officers, monks. **Dance/movement:** II: Tarantella nuptial dances. III: Ballet of the four seasons. **Orchestra:** 2 fl (picc), 2 ob, 2 cl, 2 bsn, 4 hrn, 4 trp, 3 trb, tuba, timp, perc, harp, strings. **Stageband:** None. **Publisher:** Kalmus. **Rights:** Expired.

I. Tebaldo, Roberto and the other French soldiers carouse. The Sicilians plot revenge against their French oppressors. Bethune and Vaudemont, two French officers, admire the beauty of the Duchess Elena, sister of the beheaded Duke Federigo. Roberto bids Elena sing, which she does, calling on the Sicilians to be brave. They draw their daggers, but Monforte, the French governor appears, and frightens the Sicilians off with his presence alone. Arrigo, a young Sicilian, is welcomed home, having been acquitted by a French court. He confronts Monforte and praises the dead Federigo. The governor is impressed by his daring and forgives the youth. He warns Arrigo to shun Elena's house as love will be his undoing. Ignoring Monforte's warning, Arrigo enters the house.

II. The patriot Procida returns from exile with his followers. He is greeted by Arrigo and Elena. Together they plot an uprising at the upcoming nuptials of twelve Sicilian couples. Arrigo and Elena fall in love. Bethune brings Arrigo an invitation to the ball. When Arrigo refuses, Bethune's soldiers disarm him and lead him away. The nuptial festivities are interrupted by the French soldiers who steal the brides. Elena and Procida dress down the Sicilian men for their cowardice. Procida plans to fall on the French tyrant at the upcoming ball.

IIIi. Monforte receives word from his dying wife that Arrigo is none other than Monforte's son. He tells Arrigo the truth, hoping to win his love. Arrigo flies from Monforte, blaming him for his mother's death. IIIii. Procida, Arrigo and Elena all attend the ball in disguise wearing silk ribbons. Arrigo warns Monforte that he will be assassinated, but the governor refuses to leave. Arrigo protects him and Monforte has the conspirators arrested. The conspirators curse Arrigo for his betrayal.

IV. Arrigo visits Elena in prison and tells her Monforte is his father. Elena forgives him. Monforte orders the prisoners executed. He agrees to forgive them if Arrigo calls him "father." At the last moment, Arrigo does so. Monforte forgives the prisoners and blesses Arrigo's union with Elena. V. Elena and Arrigo prepare for their wedding. Procida tells Elena that the exchange of vows is the signal for a general uprising in Palermo. Unable to reconcile her conflicting loyalties, Elena tries to call off the marriage. The wedding bells sound and the Sicilians murder the French.

La Vestale • The Vestal

Composed by Gaspare Luigi Pacifico Spontini (November 14, 1774 – January 24, 1851). Libretto by Victor Joseph Étienne de Jouy. Italian. Based partly on "Monumenti Antichi Inediti" by Johann Joachim Winckelmann. Premiered Paris, Opéra, December 16, 1807. Set in Rome in the Roman year 269. Lyric tragedy. Set numbers with recitative. Overture. Ballet.

Sets: 4. **Acts:** 3 acts, 4 scenes. **Length:** I: 50. II: 45. III: 45. **Arias:** "Dans le sein d'un ami fidèle" (Cinna), "Licinius, je vais donc te revoir" (Julia), "Toi que j'implore" / "Impitoyables dieux" (Julia), "Non, non je vis encore" (Licinius), "Toi que je laisse sur la terre mortel" (Julia). **Hazards:** I: Grand triumphal procession. III: Volcano erupts in flames, which engulf priestess and relight Vestal flame. **Scenes:** I. The Roman forum. II. The interior of the temple of Vesta. IIIi. The field of the accursed. IIIii. The circus of Flore and the temple of Venus.

Major roles: Licinius (tenor), Julia (soprano). **Minor roles:** Cinna (tenor or baritone), Grand vestal (mezzo), High priest (bass). **Bit parts:** Consul (bass), Auspice (bass).

Chorus parts: SSSAATTBB. **Chorus roles:** Vestals, Romans, warriors, people, priests, priestesses of Venus. **Dance/movement:** I: Triumphal dances and games. III: dances peculiar to the cult of the Erycine Venus. **Orchestra:** picc, 2 fl, 2 ob, 2 cl, 2 bsn, 4 hrn, 2 trp, 3 trb, timp, perc, 2 harp, strings. **Stageband:** I: 2 fl, 2 ob, 2 cl, 2 bsn, 2 hrn, 2 trp, perc. **Publisher:** C. F. Peters, Erard. **Rights:** Expired.

I. Before the latest war, Licinius had fallen in love with Julia and asked to marry her. But since Licinius had not yet made a name for himself, Julia's father refused. Licinius has now returned as a victorious general, but the father is dead and Julia has become a Vestal virgin. At his triumphal procession, Licinius tells Julia he will meet her in the temple of Vesta after dark.

II. Licinius meets Julia in the temple, where she has been left to guard the sacred flame. While they talk, the flame goes out. Alerted about the rendezvous, a crowd gathers. Licinius asks Julia to flee with him, but she refuses. She is arrested and condemned by the priests for violating her oath.

IIIi. Licinius's friend Cinna promises to stand by him. Licinius appeals to the pontifex to spare Julia, but the pontifex refuses. The general gathers his soldiers. A fight is about to break out when a nearby volcano erupts. The flames relight the vestal flame. Taking it as a sign, the pontifex frees Julia. IIIii. Licinius and Julia are married.

Il Viaggio a Reims • The Voyage to Reims

Composed by Gioachino Rossini (February 29, 1792 – November 13, 1868). Libretto by Luigi Balocchi. Italian. Partly based on "Corinne ou l'Italie" by Anne-Louise de Staël. Premiered Paris, Théâtre Italien, June 19, 1825. Set in the Spa hotel in Plombières in May 1825. Comic opera.

Set numbers with recitative. Composed for the coronation of King Charles X of France.

Sets: 2. **Acts:** 1 act, 2 scenes. **Length:** I: 135. **Arias:** "Invan strappar dal core" (Sidney), "Medaglie incomparabili" (Profondo). **Hazards:** None. **Scenes:** Ii. A hall in a spa hotel giving onto rooms. Iii. The garden.

Major roles: Madame Cortèse (soprano), Countess of Folleville (soprano), Baron Trombonok (bass), Don Profondo (bass), Marquise Melibea (mezzo), Count Libenskof (tenor), Corinna (soprano), Lord Sidney (bass), Cavalier Belfiore (tenor). **Minor roles:** Maddalena (soprano), Don Prudenzio (bass), Antonio (bass), Modestina (mezzo), Don Luigino (tenor), Don Alvaro (baritone), Zefirino (tenor), Gelsomino (tenor). **Bit part:** Delia (mezzo).

Chorus parts: SSAATTB. **Chorus roles:** Strolling players, countrymen and women, gardeners, hotel staff dancers, servants of the hotel guests. **Dance/movement:** I: Dance troupe entertains the hotel guests. **Orchestra:** picc, 2 fl, 2 ob, 2 cl, 2 bsn, 4 hrn, 2 trp, 3 trb, harp, timp, perc, strings. **Stageband:** None. **Publisher:** G. Ricordi & Co. **Rights:** Expired.

Ii. A group of nobles from all over Europe has stopped in a French spa on their way to the coronation of Charles X. The hotel housekeeper, Maddalena, berates the staff. The staff doctor, Don Prudenzio, checks the food. Madame Cortèse, the spa owner, reminds the staff to leave the guests with a good impression of the hotel. The countess and her chambermaid, Modestina, have words. The countess's clothes are lost in a stagecoach accident. She faints but is revived by the doctor. Modestina recovers the countess's bonnet from the wreckage. Baron Trombonok makes arrangements for the guests' departure. Don Alvaro introduces Don Profondo to the Marquise Melibea. He and Count Libenskof both love Melibea. Libenskof and Alvaro argue. Lord Sidney loves the poetess Corinna. Profondo annoys Lord Sidney by asking for mythical objects. He assures Corinna that everything will soon be ready for their departure. The cavalier Belfiore courts Corinna, but she spurns him. Profondo checks the baggage and tells the Countess of Folleville that he saw Cavalier Belfiore with Corinna. Everyone is ready to go, but Baron Trombonok has bad news. Zefirino explains that there are no horses to be found. Madame Cortèse consoles everyone by inviting them to her house in Paris. In the meantime, the guests arrange a feast at the hotel to celebrate the coronation. The baron tells Count Libenskof that Melibea loves him. Libenskof begs Melibea to forgive him for his jealousy, which she does. Iii. A traveling company arrives and agrees to entertain at the banquet. Each of the guests performs a song from his native country. Corinna improvises a poem about the coronation of Charles X. The entertainment concludes with a dance and tribute to the new king.

La Vida Breve • A Brief Life

Composed by Manuel de Falla (November 23, 1876 – November 14, 1946). Libretto by Carlos Fernández-Shaw. Spanish (premiered in French). Original work. Premiered Nice, Casino Municipal, April 1, 1913. Set in Grenada about 1900. Lyric drama. Through composed. Interlude before IIii.

Sets: 4. **Acts:** 2 acts, 4 scenes. **Length:** I: 35. II: 30. **Hazards:** None. **Scenes:** Ii. The inner court of a gypsy house in the Albaicin quarter. Iii. A panoramic view of Grenada. IIi. A small street in Grenada. IIii. The patio of Carmela's home.

Major roles: Grandmother (mezzo or contralto), Salud (soprano), Paco (tenor), Uncle Sarvaor (bass or baritone). **Minor roles:** Voice from the forge (tenor), Singer (baritone), Carmela (mezzo), Manuel (baritone). **Bit parts:** Voice from a distance (tenor), Voice of a vendor (tenor), Four vendors (3 soprano, 1 mezzo).

Chorus parts: SSAATTBB. **Chorus roles:** Street vendors and forge workers, wedding guests. **Dance/movement:** II: Wedding dance. **Orchestra:** 3 fl, 3 ob, 3 cl, 3 bsn, 4 hrn, 2 trp, 3 trb, tuba, timp, perc, 2 harp, celeste, strings. **Stageband:** II: guitar, bells. **Publisher:** B. Schott's Söhne. **Rights:** Copyright 1913 by Max Eschig.

Ii. Salud's grandmother attends her birds. She comforts Salud, who is distraught that Paco is late. Salud meditates on the bleak life of the poor. Iii. Paco arrives. The two swear their love. But Salud's uncle has learned that the rich Paco means to marry a girl of his own class. The lovers part.

IIi. Paco celebrates his wedding to Carmela. Salud discovers the truth and is comforted by her grandmother and uncle. IIii. She confronts Paco, who pretends not to know her. Salud swoons and dies.

La Vie Parisienne • Parisian Life

Composed by Jacques Offenbach (June 20, 1819 – October 5, 1880). Libretto by Henri Meilhac and Ludovic Halévy. French. Original work. Premiered Paris, Palais-Royal, October 31, 1866. Set in Paris in the 19th century. Operetta. Set numbers with recitative. Spoken dialogue. Overture. Entr'acte before II, III, IV.

Sets: 4. **Acts:** 4 acts, 4 scenes. **Length:** I, II, III, IV: 100. **Arias:** "Je suis Brésilien" (Brazilian). **Hazards:** III: Quick costume changes as Bobinet's servants double as distinguished guests. **Scenes:** I. The outside of a railway station in Paris. II. Gardefeu's apartments. III. The Quimper-Karadec townhouse. IV. A private room in a restaurant.

Major roles: Bobinet (baritone), Raoul of Gardefeu (tenor), Métella (soprano), Baron of Gondremarck (baritone), Frick the boot maker (baritone), Gabrielle the glover (soprano). **Minor roles:** Baroness of Gondremarck (mezzo), Brazilian (tenor), Pauline the chambermaid (soprano), Prosper the servant (baritone), Léonie the concierge's niece (mezzo), Urbain the servant (baritone), Alfred the major domo (baritone). **Bit parts:** Gontran (tenor), Clara the concierge's niece (soprano), Louise the concierge's niece (mezzo), Madame Folle Verdure, Madame Quimper Karadec. **Speaking:** Joseph, Alphonse. **Speaking bit:** Railway clerk.

Chorus parts: SSAATTBB. **Chorus roles:** Railway workers, train travelers, tourists, friends of Gabrielle and Frick, servants, waiters. **Dance/movement:** IV: ball. **Orchestra:** 2 fl (picc), 2 ob, 2 cl, 2 bsn, 4 hrn, 2 trp, 3 trb, timp, perc, strings. **Stageband:** I, II, IV: 2 trp, 3 trb, timp. III: 3 trb, timp. **Publisher:** Editions Salabert, Bote & Bock. **Rights:** Expired.

I. Bobinet and Raoul de Gardefeu are not on speaking terms because Gardefeu stole Bobinet's last mistress. Both have come to the train station to meet Bobinet's current mistress, Métella. But Métella gets off the train arm in arm with another man. The jilted suitors decide to find more fashionable mistresses. Gardefeu bribes a guide to turn over his charges—a Swedish baron and baroness—to him. A rich Brazilian comes to Paris to squander his fortune.

II. Gardefeu brings home the baron and his wife and tells them they are in the grand hotel. Gardefeu promises to deliver a letter of introduction the baron has to Métella. The baron wants to sit at the hotel common table, so Gardefeu has Bobinet, Frick the boot maker, Gabrielle the glover and their friends impersonate hotel guests. Métella returns to make explanations to Gardefeu, but finds him with the baroness.

III. Bobinet borrows his aunt's townhouse to entertain the baron so Gardefeu can spend time alone with the baroness. Bobinet's servants impersonate distinguished guests and get the baron drunk.

IV. The Brazilian is in love with Gabrielle and he hires a restaurant to throw a masked ball. Métella rejects the baron, but fixes him up with a masked lady (the baroness). Having figured out Gardefeu's scheme, the baron challenges him to fight. The baroness intervenes. Métella and Gardefeu admit they still love each other.

A Village Romeo and Juliet

Composed by Frederick Delius (January 29, 1862 – June 10, 1934). Libretto by Frederick Delius. German and English. Based on a story by Gottfried Keller. Premiered Berlin, Komische Oper, February 21, 1907. Set in Seldwyla, Switzerland in the mid-19th century. Music drama. Through composed. Introduction. Musical interludes between scenes.

Sets: 5. **Acts:** 1 act, 6 scenes. **Length:** I: 110. **Hazards:** Iiv: Sali and Vreli's dream. **Scenes:** Ii. A piece of land luxuriously overgrown on a hill. Iii. Outside Marti's house. Iiii. The piece of land overgrown with red poppies in full bloom. Iiv. Interior of Marti's house and the old church of Seldwyla. Iv. A square before an inn and a circus. Ivi. The paradise garden.

Major roles: Manz (baritone), Marti (baritone), Sali (tenor), Vrenchen (soprano), Dark fiddler (baritone). **Minor roles:** Gingerbread woman (soprano), Wheel-of-fortune woman (soprano), Cheap jewelry woman (contralto), Showman (tenor), Merry-go-round man (baritone), Shooting-gallery man (bass), Slim girl (soprano), Wild girl (contralto), Poor horn player (tenor), Hunchbacked bass fiddler (bass), First barge man (baritone). **Bit parts:** First peasant (baritone), Second peasant (baritone), First woman (soprano), Second woman (soprano), Third woman (alto), Second barge man (baritone), Third barge man (tenor).

Chorus parts: SATBB. **Chorus roles:** Church congregation, vagabonds, peasants and barge men. **Dance/movement:** Iv: Circus dancers. **Orchestra:** 3 fl (picc), 3 ob, Eng hrn, 3 cl, bs cl, 3 bsn, cont bsn, 6 hrn, 3 trp, 3 trb, tuba, xylophone, 2 timp, perc, 2 harp, strings. **Stageband:** I: vln, 6 hrn, 2 cornet, 2 alto trb, perc, organ (hrns and vln can be played in pit). **Publisher:** Boosey & Hawkes, Harmonie. **Rights:** Expired.

Ii. Two rich farmers, Manz and Marti, work while their children, Sali and Vrenchen, play together. The dark fiddler appears. Although his father owned the land between Manz and Marti's farms, the dark fiddler is a bastard and has no rights. Manz and Marti both mean to buy the land. When each realizes the other has surreptitiously been annexing portions of this land, they argue and drag the two children apart. Iii. Six years later, Sali comes back for Vrenchen. Their fathers' feud—and the ensuing lawsuits—have bankrupted everyone. Vrenchen fears her father will discover Sali but promises to meet him later in the fields. Iiii. Sali and Vrenchen are visited by the dark fiddler. The lovers kiss. Marti tries to separate them, and Sali hits him. Iiv. Marti's mind is gone and Vrenchen has taken him to Seldwyla and sold the farm. The lovers sleep and dream of getting married. Iv. They attend a fair, but people recognize them and stare. Ivi. The dark fiddler tells his fellow vagabonds

Vrenchen's and Sali's story. He toasts the couple and invites them to join his gang in the mountains. They demure. Seeing a boat, the lovers ecstatically cast off and sink the boat that they may be united in death.

Le Villi • The Fairies

Composed by Giacomo Puccini (December 22, 1858 – November 29, 1924). Libretto by Ferdinando Fontana. Italian. Based on "Les Willis" by Alphonse Karr. Premiered Milan, Teatro dal Verme, May 31, 1884. Set in the black forest in the Middle Ages. Opera ballet. Set numbers with recitative. Prelude before I, II. Ballet. Intermezzo divides acts. Revised version (1 act expanded to 2) premiered Turin, December 26, 1884.

Sets: 1. **Acts:** 2 acts, 2 scenes. **Length:** I: 25. II: 40. **Arias:** "Se come voi" (Anna), "No! possibile non è" (Guglielmo), "Dio, che orrenda notte!" (Roberto). **Hazards:** None. **Scenes:** I – II. A clearing in the forest before Guglielmo's house.

Major roles: Guglielmo Wolf (baritone), Anna (soprano), Roberto (tenor). **Speaking:** Narrator (generally omitted).

Chorus parts: SATTBB. **Chorus roles:** Mountaineers, spirits. **Dance/movement:** I: Mountaineers' dance. II: ballet of the spirits. **Orchestra:** picc, 2 fl, 2 ob, Eng hrn, 2 cl, 2 bsn, cont bsn, 4 hrn, 5 trp, 3 trb, cimbasso, timp, perc, harp, strings. **Stageband:** None. **Publisher:** G. Ricordi. **Rights:** Expired.

I. Celebrations are in progress for Roberto's coming wedding to Anna. The wedding guests dance. Roberto has to go away before the wedding and Anna fears she will never see him again. He reassures her. Intermezzo. Roberto is bewitched by a siren. He forgets his love, who dies in his absence. The narrator explains the legend of the Villis: When a maiden dies of love, they wait for her betrayer and force him to dance until he dies. II. Guglielmo is angry with Roberto for causing the death of his daughter. Roberto is lured into the forest by an image of Anna. She and the Villis pull him into their dance. He dies, exhausted, at Anna's feet.

Violanta

Composed by Erich Wolfgang Korngold (May 29, 1897 – November 29, 1957). Libretto by Hans Müller. German. Original work. Premiered Munich, Hoftheater, March 28, 1916. Set in Venice in the 15th century. Tragedy. Through composed. Overture.

Sets: 1. **Acts:** 1 act, 1 scene. **Length:** I: 75. **Hazards:** None. **Scenes:** I. The house of Captain Simone Trovai on the Giudecca canal.

Major roles: Simone Trovai (bass baritone), Violanta (soprano), Alfonso (tenor). **Minor roles:** Second soldier (baritone), Matteo (tenor), Bice (soprano), Barbara (contralto), Giovanni Bracca (tenor). **Bit parts:** Second woman (mezzo), First woman (soprano), First soldier (tenor).

Chorus parts: SSSAAATTTBBB. **Chorus roles:** Boatmen, soldiers, maids, maskers. **Dance/movement:** None. **Orchestra:** 4 fl (picc), 2 ob, Eng hrn, 3 cl, bs cl, 2 bsn, cont bsn, 4 hrn, 3 trp, 3 trb, tuba, perc, timp, glockenspiel, xylophone, mandolin, piano, celeste, 2 harp, strings. **Stageband:** I: 2 trp, 2 trb, perc. **Publisher:** B. Schott's Söhne. **Rights:** Copyright 1916, 1927 by B. Schott's Söhne.

I. Violanta mourns her sister, who committed suicide after being seduced by Alfonso, the illegitimate son of the King of Naples. Violanta's husband, Simone, learns that Alfonso is in Venice for the Festival of the Redentore. Violanta has arranged an assignation with Alfonso—who does not know who she is—so Simone can kill him. But when Alfonso comes, Violanta realizes she loves him. She tells her husband, who attacks Alfonso. Violanta intervenes and receives a mortal wound. She dies pure.

The Visitation

See "Die Heimsuchung" entry.

Viva la Mamma • Long Live Mother

Composed by Gaetano Donizetti (November 29, 1797 – April 8, 1848). Libretto by Gaetano Donizetti. Italian. Based on a comedy by Antonio Sografi. Premiered Naples, Teatro Nuovo, November 21, 1827. Set in the Rimini Opera House during rehearsals for the opera "Romulus and Ersilia" in 1840. Comedy. Set numbers with recitative. Overture. Some spoken dialogue. Ballet. Revised and expanded to two acts, premiered April 20, 1831 in Milan. Title role played by a man.

Sets: 1. **Acts:** 2 acts, 2 scenes. **Length:** I, II: 100 (60 for 1-act version). **Arias:** Audition song (Mamma Agatha). **Hazards:** None. **Scenes:** I – II. A stage set for the opera "Romulus and Ersilia."

Major roles: Composer Vincenzo Biscroma (bass), Prima Donna Corilla Sartinecchi (soprano), Guglielmo Antolstoinolonoff (tenor), Stefano (baritone), Impresario (bass), Mamma Agatha (bass). **Minor roles:** Luigia Boschi (soprano), Dorotea Caccini (mezzo), Librettist Orazio Prospero (tenor), Procolo (bass). **Mute:** Stage doorman, Messenger.

Chorus parts: SATTB. **Chorus roles:** Rimini opera chorus dressed as Roman patricians. **Dance/movement:** II: Rehearsal of the ballet from "Romulus and Ersilia." **Orchestra:** 2 fl (picc), 2 ob, 2 cl, 2 bsn, 4 hrn, 2 trp, 3 trb, timp, perc, strings. **Stageband:** None. **Publisher:** Universal. **Rights:** Expired.

I. Biscroma, an opera composer, rehearses the singers for his opera, "Romulus and Ersilia." The tenor is foreign and does not speak Italian well. When Corilla, the soprano, demands that the tenor be in chains during her big scene, the librettist tries to point out that Romulus has returned victorious. The posters arrive. Agatha, the mother of Luigia, the second soprano, insists that her daughter sing the rondo. Corilla's husband, Stefano, demands that his wife be listed first on the poster. They argue over the order of the bows and Stefano brags about his wife's career. Agatha and Corilla fight. When Dorotea, the mezzo, walks out both Stefano and Agatha offer to take the role. Agatha gets the part but then the tenor (Guglielmo) walks out and is replaced by Stefano. When word comes that the council may be cutting the theater's funding, all the singers demand advances. They claim illness and the impresario threatens to sue them.

II. Agatha importunes the impresario for money, but he threatens to fire her. She begs and agrees to sell her jewels to help finance the opera. Corilla sings her aria. The ballet, Roman triumphal march and funeral procession rehearse. Corilla asks Biscroma to expand her husband's scene. The council cuts the opera house's funding because of doubts about the artistic quality. The opera is saved by Agatha's donation. The participants anticipate a great success.

La Voix Humaine • The Human Voice

Composed by Francis Poulenc (January 7, 1899 – January 30, 1963). Libretto by Jean Cocteau. French. Original work. Premiered Paris, Opéra Comique, February 6, 1959. Set in a woman's bedroom in the present. Monodrama. Through composed.

Sets: 1. **Acts:** 1 act, 1 scene. **Length:** I: 45. **Hazards:** None. **Scenes:** I. A woman's bedroom.

Major role: Woman (soprano).

Chorus parts: N/A. **Chorus roles:** None. **Dance/movement:** None. **Orchestra:** 2 fl (picc), ob, Eng hrn, 2 cl, bs cl, 2 bsn, 2 hrn, 2 trp, trb, tuba, timp, perc, xylophone, harp, strings. **Stageband:** None. **Publisher:** G. Ricordi. **Rights:** Copyright 1959 by G. Ricordi.

I. The woman is on the telephone with her former lover, recounting her day and arranging for him to pick up his things. She is determined to be brave. They are disconnected but he calls back. The woman admits she did not go out to dinner—as she had said—but spent the whole evening waiting for him to call. Last night, she despaired and took 12 sleeping pills. At the last moment, she repented and called her friend Martha who brought a doctor. Living without him is painful. "The dog, too, misses you," she tells him. She assures him she will not attempt suicide again, but she winds the telephone cord around her neck. Swearing her love for him, she lets the receiver fall.

Volo di Notte • Night Flight

Composed by Luigi Dallapiccola (February 3, 1904 – February 19, 1975). Libretto by Luigi Dallapiccola. Italian. Based on "Vol de nuit" by Antoine de Saint-Exupéry. Premiered Florence, Teatro della Pergola, May 18, 1940. Set in Buenos Aires in the early 1930s. Poetic drama. Through composed. Prelude.

Sets: 1. **Acts:** 1 act, 6 scenes. **Length:** I: 60. **Hazards:** None. **Scenes:** I. Rivière's apartment and an office.

Major roles: Mr. Rivière (bass baritone), Inspector Robineau (bass), Mrs. Fabien (soprano). **Minor roles:** Third employee (tenor), Old squadron leader Leroux (bass), Offstage voice (soprano), Pilot Pellerin (tenor), Second employee (baritone), First employee (tenor), Fourth employee (bass), Radio operator (tenor).

Chorus parts: SSSAATTTBB. **Chorus roles:** Airport workers, people. **Dance/movement:** None. **Orchestra:** picc, 3 fl (picc), 2 ob, Eng hrn, 3 cl, 2 sax, 2 bsn, cont bsn, 4 hrn, 4 trp, 3 trb, tuba, timp, perc, xylophone, celeste, piano, 2 harp, strings. **Stageband:** I: 2 cl, 3 sax, 2 trp, trb, xylophone, vibraphone, piano, 2 perc, 3 vln, 2 bs. **Publisher:** Universal Edition, G. Ricordi & Co. **Rights:** Copyright 1940 by Universal-Edition. Copyright 1940 by G. Ricordi & Co.

I. The director of air services, Mr. Rivière, believes that night flying is practical. With the aid of the radio telegrapher, he guides various planes along their routes. One plane avoids a patch of foul weather, but a second plunges right into it. Rivière and the pilot try to save the plane, but all attempts are futile: a last ditch effort to crash land comes to nothing when the pilot realizes the storm has blown him out to sea. The plane is lost. Rivière prepares to guide out the next night flight.

Von Heute auf Morgen • From Evening to Morning

Composed by Arnold Schönberg (September 13, 1874 – July 13, 1951). Libretto by Gertrud Kolisch Schönberg under the pen name Max Blonda. German. Original work. Premiered Frankfurt, Opernhaus, Feburary 1, 1930. Set in an apartment in the present. Comic opera. Through composed. Twelve tone harmony.

Sets: 1. **Acts:** 1 act, 1 scene. **Length:** I: 50. **Hazards:** None. **Scenes:** I. A modern bed/sitting room with built-in cupboards and beds.

Major roles: Husband (baritone), Wife (soprano). **Minor roles:** Singer (tenor), Friend (soprano). **Speaking:** Child.

Chorus parts: N/A. **Chorus roles:** None. **Dance/movement:** None. **Orchestra:** 2 fl (2 picc), 2 ob (Eng hrn), 3 cl, bs cl, 2 sax, 2 bsn (cont bsn), 2 hrn, 2 trp, 3 trb, tuba, timp, flexatone, xylophone, glockenspiel, perc, harp, piano (celeste), mandolin, guitar (banjo), strings (8-10; 8-10; 6-8; 6-8; 6-8). **Stageband:** None. **Publisher:** B. Schott's Söhne. **Rights:** Copyright 1930, 1961 by Arnold Schönberg.

I. A husband and wife entertain an opera tenor and a friend of the wife's, to whom the husband is attracted. To regain her husband's love, the wife dresses up fashionably and pretends to be in love with the tenor. Becoming jealous, the husband realizes he loves only his wife and persuades her to put off her act. The friend and tenor try to woo the husband and wife, but get nowhere and eventually give up.

The Voyage of Edgar Allan Poe

Composed by Dominick Argento (b. October 27, 1927). Libretto by Charles Nolte. English. Based on the life of Edgar Allan Poe. Premiered Minneapolis/St. Paul, O'Shaughnessy Auditorium, College of St. Catherine, April 24, 1976. Set on a dock at Richmond and aboard a vessel sailing from there in the 19th century. Tragedy. Through composed with some recitative. Prologue. Epilogue.

Sets: 5. **Acts:** 2 acts, 12 scenes. **Length:** I: 65. II: 60. **Hazards:** I: Virginia switched with rag doll. Scene set on a drifting boat. II: Women throw parts of their bodies (arms, wigs, torsos) at Poe. I, II: Dream-like scene changes. **Scenes:** Prologue. A pool of light. Ii. The dock. Iii. A ship's passenger lounge with a small stage. Iiii. Two drifting boats. Iiv – Iv. The lounge. IIi. The lounge and a courtroom. IIii. Poe's cottage at Fordham. IIiii. The stage with a mirror frame. IIiv. Virginia Poe's bedroom. IIv. The courtroom. Epilogue. The dock.

Major roles: Edgar Allan Poe (tenor), Griswold/Captain/Mr. Allan (baritone), Virginia Poe (lyric soprano). **Minor roles:** Doctor/Wedding Guest/Passenger (tenor), Mrs. Poe/Ballad Singer/Rosy (soprano), Mrs. Clemm/Aunt Nancy (mezzo), Mrs. Allan/Granny Poe (alto), Theater Director/M. Dupin (bass). **Bit parts:** Willie (baritone). **Mute:** Young Virginia.

Chorus parts: SSAATTBB. **Chorus roles:** Passengers (minimum 24), jurors, wedding guests. **Dance/movement:** II: Women dance wildly around Poe during the auction. **Orchestra:** 2 fl (picc), 2 ob (Eng hrn), 2 cl (bs cl), 2 bsn, 3 hrn, 2 trp, 2 trb, tuba, timp, perc, harp, piano (celeste), strings (min. 6-5-5-4-3). **Stageband:** None. **Publisher:** Boosey & Hawkes. **Rights:** Copyright 1976 by Boosey & Hawkes Inc.

Prologue. Edgar Allan Poe's doctor recalls his last visit before Poe's death. The author speaks of a cruise he plans to take to Baltimore that has been arranged by his literary executor, Griswold. The doctor advises Poe not to drink—and not to trust Griswold. Ii. At the dock, Poe boards a ghost ship. Iii. On board, he finds a troupe of actors reenacting the death of his mother. Poe's stepfather appears and they fight. Iiii. Poe goes boating with his wife, Virginia. Iiv. Back on the boat, Poe walks into a reenactment of his wedding. Everyone is scandalized at Virginia's age (she's 12) and Poe's stepfather disinherits him. Poe promises to stop drinking and earn some money. Iv. He gives unsuccessful speeches on "the poetic principle." The death of Virginia is reenacted.

IIi. The second act centers around the "trial" of Poe, directed by the detective Dupin. The court wishes to determine if Poe is mad and accuses Poe of wanting Virginia's death because it provided him with artistic inspiration. IIii. Attempting to vindicate Poe, Dupin invites the court to look into the past where they see Virginia's death. The scene then changes to an auction where women are offered as Poe's next muse. IIiii. As a final test, Virginia is brought back to life on condition that Poe not ask her about the afterworld. Unable to resist, Poe asks and thus kills Virginia. He begs the court for mercy. IIiv. Griswold—who has been Poe's stepfather, judge and literary agent, in turn—admits to being Poe's own soul. Poe stabs Griswold and the ghost ship dissolves back to the empty dock. Epilogue. Poe collapses; his body is discovered by the doctor.

Der Wald • The Forest

Composed by Ethel Smyth (April 22, 1858 – May 9, 1944). Libretto by Ethel Smyth. German. Original work. Premiered Berlin, Opera, April 9, 1902. Set in a virgin forest in the latter half of the Middle Ages. Music drama. Set numbers with recitative. Epilogue. Prologue.

Sets: 1. **Acts:** 1 act, 11 scenes. **Length:** Prologue, I, Epilogue: 65. **Hazards:** I: Pedlar leads a live bear. Jolanthe appears on horseback. **Scenes:** I. Before a cottage in a forest.

Major roles: Röschen (soprano), Heinrich (tenor), Jolanthe (soprano or mezzo). **Minor roles:** Pedlar (baritone), Peter (bass), Landgrave Rudolf (baritone), First huntsman (bass). **Bit part:** Youth (tenor).

Chorus parts: SSAATTBB. **Chorus roles:** Peasants, huntsmen, spirits of the woods. **Dance/movement:** I: "Rough and rustic" dance. **Orchestra:** picc, 2 fl, 2 ob, Eng hrn, 2 cl, bs cl, 2 bsn, 4 hrn, 3 trp, 3 trb, tuba, timp, perc, harp, strings. **Stageband:** I: hrn. **Publisher:** B. Schott's Söhne. **Rights:** Expired.

Prologue. The spirits of the woods avoid mankind. Ii. The peasants congratulate Röschen on her engagement to Heinrich. Iii. They celebrate. Iiii. The sound of Jolanthe's hunting horn scares the villagers and they return home. Iiv. Heinrich hides a deer he has poached. Iv. Jolanthe tries to seduce Heinrich, but he loves Röschen. Ivi. Landgrave Rudolf loves Jolanthe, but she spurns him. Ivii. The deer is discovered and, to save himself, a peddler admits he saw Heinrich hide it. Iviii. Rudolf tells Jolanthe that Heinrich will die for his crime. Iix. Jolanthe offers to save Heinrich if he will come with her, but he refuses. On Jolanthe's order, the huntsmen stab Heinrich to death. Epilogue. The wood spirits comment on the transitory nature of human happiness.

Die Walküre • The Valkyrie

Composed by Richard Wagner (May 22, 1813 – February 13, 1883). Libretto by Richard Wagner. German. Original work based loosely on Norse mythology. Premiered Munich, Königliches Hof- und Nationaltheater, June 26, 1870. Set in a hut and on a mountain in mythical times. Epic music drama. Through composed. Prelude before I, II.

Sets: 3. **Acts:** 3 acts, 11 scenes. **Length:** I: 65. II: 95. III: 70. **Arias:** Todesverkündigung (Brünnhilde), "Winterstürme" (Siegmund).

Hazards: II: Wotan breaks Siegmund's sword in battle. III: Valkyries appear on horseback bearing the corpses of dead heroes. Wotan surrounds Brünnhilde with a ring of fire. **Scenes:** I. Inside Hunding's dwelling. II. Wild, rocky height. III. On top of a rocky mountain.

Major roles: Siegmund (dramatic tenor), Sieglinde (dramatic soprano), Wotan (baritone or bass baritone), Brünnhilde (dramatic soprano), Fricka (mezzo or soprano). **Minor roles:** Hunding (bass), Gerhilde (soprano), Helmwige (soprano), Waltraute (mezzo), Schwertleite (mezzo), Ortlinde (soprano), Siegrune (mezzo), Grimgerde (mezzo), Rossweisse (mezzo).

Chorus parts: N/A. **Chorus roles:** None. **Dance/movement:** None. **Orchestra:** picc, 3 fl (picc), 4 ob (Eng hrn), 3 cl, bs cl, 3 bsn (cont bsn), 8 hrn (2 ten tuba, 2 bs tuba), 3 trp, bs trp, 4 ten bs trb (cont bs trb), cont bs tuba, 2 timp, perc, 6 harps, strings (16-16-12-12-8). **Stageband:** II: stierhorn. III: perc. **Publisher:** G. Schirmer, B Schott's Söhne. **Rights:** Expired.

I. Siegmund seeks refuge from a storm in Hunding's house. He is tended by Hunding's wife, Sieglinde (who he does not realize is his long lost sister). In defending a young woman who was being married against her will, Siegmund has become Hunding's mortal enemy. Nevertheless, Hunding refuses to break the sacred duties of hospitality. He promises Siegmund safety for the night, but swears to fight him in the morning. Sieglinde gives Hunding a sleeping potion and shows Siegmund the sword stuck into a tree by Wotan on Sieglinde's wedding day. Siegmund draws the sword out of the tree. He and Sieglinde fall in love. They discover they are brother and sister and flee the house together.

IIi. Wotan tells his warrior daughter, Brünnhilde, to help his son Siegmund defeat Hunding. Wotan's wife, Fricka—the patroness of marriage—demands vengeance on Siegmund. Wotan explains that only a hero independent of the gods can free the gods from the ring's curse, but Fricka wins her point. Wotan orders Brünnhilde not to help Siegmund. IIii. Brünnhilde appears to Siegmund to tell him that he is about to die, but his passion persuades Brünnhilde to disobey Wotan and protect him. During the fight, Wotan breaks Siegmund's sword. Hunding kills Siegmund and Wotan, in disgust, kills Hunding.

III. Brünnhilde flees with Sieglinde to her Valkyrie sisters, but they are horrified that Brünnhilde has disobeyed Wotan. Sieglinde herself prefers death—until Brünnhilde tells her that she is pregnant with Siegmund's child. Brünnhilde helps Sieglinde make her escape and then waits for Wotan. The king of the gods is furious and condemns Brünnhilde to finish out her life as a mortal, the property of the first man who finds her.

She persuades him to surround her with a ring of fire so that only the bravest mortal may claim her.

La Wally

Composed by Alfredo Catalani (June 19, 1854 – August 7, 1893). Libretto by Luigi Illica. Italian. Novel "Die Geyer-Walley" by Wilhelmine von Hillern. Premiered Milan, Teatro alla Scala, January 20, 1892. Set in the Swiss Tyrol circa 1800. Tragedy. Set numbers with accompanied recitative. Prelude before I, III, IV.

Sets: 4. **Acts:** 4 acts, 4 scenes. **Length:** I: 35. II: 30. III: 25. IV: 30. **Arias:** "Nè mai dunque" (Wally). **Hazards:** III: Gellner pushes Hagenbach off the bridge into the ravine. Wally retrieves him from the ravine. IV: Avalanche kills Hagenbach and Wally throws herself off a precipice. **Scenes:** I. A large square in the village of Hochstoff before Stromminger's house. In the background, a bridge over a ravine and mountains are visible. II. The square at Sölden before a church and the Eagle Inn. III. Stromminger and Wally's house and a street in Hochstoff leading across the bridge spanning the ravine. IV. Wally's hut on the Murzoll.

Major roles: Vincenzo Gellner (baritone), Walter (soprano), Giuseppe Hagenbach (tenor), Wally (soprano). **Minor roles:** Stromminger (bass), Old soldier (bass), Afra (mezzo).

Chorus parts: SSATTTTBBBB. **Chorus roles:** Inhabitants of the Alps, shepherds, citizens, old women, farmers, peasants huntsmen, children (2 parts). **Dance/movement:** II: Villagers dance a ländler. **Orchestra:** picc, 2 fl, 2 ob, Eng hrn, 2 cl, bs cl, 2 bsn, 4 hrn, 3 trp, 3 trb, bs trb or tuba, timp, perc, harp, organ, strings. **Stageband:** I: 6 hrn, 2 trp, bells. II: Tyrolean band. IV: perc. **Publisher:** Belwin Mills, G. Ricordi & Co. **Rights:** Expired.

I. The wealthy landowner Stromminger celebrates his seventieth birthday. He toasts Gellner's shooting. Walter asks after Stromminger's daughter, Wally, and sings a song written by her. When Hagenbach arrives with his fellow huntsmen from Sölden bragging about killing a bear, Stromminger belittles his achievement but Wally's arrival prevents a fight. Gellner—himself a former suitor of Wally's—points out to Stromminger that Wally loves Hagenbach. Furious, Stromminger insists that Wally marry Gellner, whom she does not love. She appeals to Gellner's better nature not to insist, but Gellner loves her. Wally appeals to her father, who is adamant. Wally decides to run off with Walter.

II. One year later, the villagers of Sölden celebrate a holiday. An old soldier teases Walter about his friendship with Wally. Wally, who has declared that she will kiss no one, teases Gellner, who still loves her. Surprised at her brazenness in attending public fairs and adorning herself with pearls, he tells her that Hagenbach is engaged to Afra. Furious, Wally throws money at Afra's feet. Hagenbach determines to avenge her. He bets he can extort a kiss from Wally and the villagers start the kissing dance. Wally pours out her love to Hagenbach, who is genuinely touched. They kiss and the crowd—who know about Hagenbach's wager—laugh. Wally tells Gellner to kill Hagenbach.

III. Gellner tries to comfort Wally. He learns from the old soldier that Hagenbach is on his way over to Hochstoff. Wally repents of her anger at Hagenbach and goes to bed. Gellner intercepts Hagenbach on the bridge and pushes him into the ravine. Wally, horrified, rouses the villagers and retrieves Hagenbach, who has survived. Wally gives everything she has to Afra.

IV. Walter has followed Wally into the mountains, but urges her to return to escape the avalanches. She persuades Walter to return alone. Hagenbach finds her and confesses his love. An avalanche kills Hagenbach and Wally throws herself over a precipice.

The Wandering Scholar

Composed by Gustav Holst (September 21, 1874 – May 25, 1934). Libretto by Clifford Bax. English. From "The Wandering Scholars" by Helen Waddell. Premiered Liverpool, David Lewis Theater, January 31, 1934. Set in France in the 13th century. Chamber opera. Set numbers with recitative.

Sets: 1. Acts: 1 act, 1 scene. Length: I: 30. Hazards: None. Scenes: I. The kitchen of a farmhouse.

Major roles: Louis (baritone), Alison (soprano), Father Philippe (bass), Pierre (tenor).

Chorus parts: N/A. Chorus roles: None. Dance/movement: None. Orchestra: picc, fl, ob, Eng hrn, 2 cl, 2 bsn, 2 hrn, strings. Stageband: None. Publisher: G. Schirmer. Rights: Copyright 1971 by Faber Music.

I. Alison receives Father Philippe after the departure of her husband, Louis. Their dalliance is interrupted by Pierre, a wandering scholar who begs for some food. Philippe throws him out, but Louis comes home with Pierre. Philippe hides, but Pierre gives him away.

Voyna i Mir • War and Peace

Composed by Sergei Prokofiev (April 27, 1891 – March 5, 1953). Libretto by Sergei Prokofiev and Mira Mendelssohn-Prokofieva. Russian. Based on the novel by Leo Tolstoy. Premiered Leningrad, Maly Theater, June 12, 1946. Set in Russia in the early 19th century. Epic drama. Through composed. Overture. Extensive revisions made at various points.

Sets: 13. **Acts:** 1 act, 13 scenes (originally 2 acts/evenings). **Length:** I: 240. **Hazards:** I: A cannonball lands onstage near Napoleon. Moscow burns. Staggeringly large cast. **Scenes:** Ii. The garden and house of the Rostovs' estate. Iii. A ball at an old nobleman's house. Iiii. A small reception room in Prince Bolkonski's mansion at Vozdvijhenka. Iiv. A small drawing room in Pierre Bezukhov's house. Iv. Dolokhov's study. Ivi. A reception room in Marya Dmitrievna Akhrosimova's mansion in Staraya Koniushennaya Street. Ivii. Pierre Bezukhov's study. Iviii. Before the battle of Borodino. Iix. The redoubt of Shevardino during the battle of Borodino. Ix. A cottage at Fili. Ixi. A Moscow street under French occupation. Ixii. A dark cottage. Ixiii. The Smolensk road.

Major roles: Prince Andrei Bolkonski (baritone), Natasha Rostova (soprano), Pierre Bezukhov (tenor), Marshal Kutuzov (bass). **Minor roles:** Sonya (mezzo), Master of ceremonies (tenor), Count Rostov (bass baritone), Marya Dmitrievna Akhrosimova (mezzo), Madame Peronskaya (soprano), Helene Bezukhova (mezzo), Anatol Kuragin (tenor), Dolokhov (bass baritone), Princess Marya Bolkonskaya Akhrosimova (mezzo), Old prince Nicolai Bolkonski (bass), Coachman Balaga (bass), Dunyasha the Rostov chamber maid (soprano), Denisov (bass baritone), Fyodor (tenor), Tikhon Shcherbaty (bass), Matveyev (baritone), Vasilisa (mezzo), Kutuzov's aide-de-camp (tenor), Napoleon (baritone), General Compans's aide-de-camp (tenor), Murat's aide-de-camp (contralto or treble), Marshal Berthier (bass baritone), Monsieur de Beausset (tenor), General Benigsen (bass), General Barclay du Tolly (tenor), General Rayevski (baritone), Soldier (baritone), Ramballe (bass), Lt. Bonnet (tenor), Captain Jacquot (bass), Gerard (tenor), Young workman (tenor), Woman shopkeeper (soprano), Rostov's maid Mavra Kuzminishna (contralto), French officer (bass baritone), Platon Karatayev (tenor), Marshall Davout (bass). **Bit parts:** Footman (tenor), Bolkonskis' old footman (bass), Bolkonskis' chamber maid (contralto), Bolkonski's valet (baritone), Gypsy girl Matryosha (contralto), Akhrosimova's footman Gavrila (bass baritone), French doctor Metivier (bass baritone), French abbe (tenor), Trishka (contralto), Prince Andrei Bolkonski's orderly (tenor), Two staff officers (tenor, bass baritone), General Belliard (bass baritone), Voice offstage (tenor), Napoleon's aide-de-camp (bass), Prince Yevgeni's aide-de-camp (tenor), General Yermolov (bass), General Konovnitsin (tenor), Ivanov (tenor), Three madmen (tenor, bass baritone), Two French actresses (soprano, mezzo), Voice backstage (bass). **Speaking:** Two German generals. **Mute:** Tsar Alexander, Maria Antonovna, Josef, Marquis de Caulaincourt, French Ambassador to Russia, Peasant's daughter.

Chorus parts: SSAATTBB. **Chorus roles:** Ball guests, home guards, Smolensk peasants, Russian soldiers, grenadiers, chasseurs, Izmailov life guards, Cossacks, French soldiers, Muscovites, liberated prisoners. **Dance/movement:** Iii: Polonaise and waltz. Iiv: ballroom dancing. **Orchestra:** picc, 2 fl, 2 ob, Eng hrn, 2 cl, bs cl, 2 bsn, cont bsn, 4 hrn, 3 trp, 3 trb, tuba, timp, perc, harp, strings. **Stageband:** I: dance band and military band. **Publisher:** State Music Publishers. **Rights:** Copyright 1946 by State Music Publishers.

Ii. Prince Andrei falls in love with Natasha Rostov while visiting her family. Iii. He dances with her at a ball and proposes. Iiii. Andrei's father disapproves and refuses to see Natasha and her father, Count Rostov, but Andrei's sister receives them. Iiv. At a dance thrown by Pierre and Helene Bezukhov, Anatol asks Natasha to elope with him. She is attracted to him, but Sonya is determined not to let her disgrace herself. Iv. Dolokhov helps Anatol plan his seduction of Natasha. Ivi. Natasha's godmother, Marya Dmitrievna Akhrosimova, thwarts the elopement and berates Natasha. Pierre Bezukhov tells Natasha that Anatol is already married and promises to bear her apologies to Andrei. Ivii. Pierre forces Anatol to go abroad. He wishes he could escape his own unhappy marriage. The French declare war on Russia. Iviii. The contending armies meet before Borodino. The French have captured Smolensk but the peasants burn their goods rather than let them fall into enemy hands. Pierre has freed his serfs to provide soldiers. Kutuzov fires the troops' enthusiasm and the battle begins. Iix. Napoleon directs his army through hard fighting. Ix. Kutuzov decides on a strategic retreat from Moscow. Ixi. The French occupy and loot Moscow. Disguised as a coachman, Pierre plans to assassinate Napoleon. He hears how Natasha helped a group of wounded soldiers—including Prince Andrei—to escape the city. The peasants set fire to the city. Pierre is captured, but is pardoned before his execution can take place. Two madmen are carted off. Ixii. Andrei forgives Natasha and dies in her arms. Ixiii. Pierre is rescued from the retreating French army. The Russians celebrate their victory.

A Water Bird Talk

Composed by Dominick Argento (b. October 27, 1927). Libretto by Dominick Argento. English. Freely adapted from "On the Harmfulness of Tobacco" by Anton Chekhov and "The Birds of America" by J. J.

Audubon. Premiered Brooklyn, Brooklyn Academy of Music, May 19, 1977. Set in Maryland or Virginia in the second half of the 19th century. Monodrama. Set numbers with recitative. Work is a single theme with six variations and a coda.

Sets: 1. **Acts:** 1 act, 1 scene. **Length:** I: 45. **Hazards:** I: Sound of birds offstage, lecture accompanied by slides, slide projector explodes pouring out smoke. **Scenes:** I. The rostrum of a provincial club.

Major role: Lecturer (baritone or low tenor). **Speaking bit:** Offstage woman coughs.

Chorus parts: N/A. **Chorus roles:** None. **Dance/movement:** None. **Orchestra:** fl, ob, cl, hrn, harp, piano (celeste), perc, string quintet. **Stageband:** I: piano (played by lecturer). **Publisher:** Boosey & Hawkes. **Rights:** Copyright 1980 by Boosey & Hawkes, Inc.

I. Egged on by his wife, a middle-aged man gives a lecture on water birds. When she leaves the room, the lecturer interrupts himself to talk about his wife's music school, his own feelings of failure and what an ogre his wife is.

Werther

Composed by Jules-Emile-Frédéric Massenet (May 12, 1842 – August 13, 1912). Libretto by Édouard Blau, Paul Milliet and Henri Grémont (Georges) Hartmann. French. Based on novel by Johann von Goethe. Premiered Vienna, Opéra Impérial de Vienne, February 16, 1892. Set in Wetzlar near Frankfurt circa 1780. Lyric drama. Set numbers with accompanied recitative. Preludes before each act.

Sets: 4. **Acts:** 4 acts, 5 scenes. **Length:** I: 40. II: 30. III: 35. IV: 20. **Arias:** "Ô Nature" (Werther), "Va, laisse couleur" (Charlotte), "Pourquoi me réveiller?" (Werther). **Hazards:** None. **Scenes:** I. Garden of the bailiff's house. II. Village square in Wetzlar. III. Albert's house. IV. Werther's apartment, Christmas Eve.

Major roles: Werther (tenor), Charlotte (mezzo), Albert (baritone), Sophie (15 years old, soprano). **Minor roles:** Bailiff (bass or baritone), Schmidt (tenor), Johann (bass or baritone). **Bit parts:** Bruhlmann (sings 2 notes), Katchen (sings 4 notes). **Mute:** Peasant, Servant.

Chorus parts: SSA. **Chorus roles:** Townsfolk, six children (Fritz, Max, Hans, Karl, Gretel, Clara; children, sing in 3 parts). (Women sing with children in final scene.) **Dance/movement:** None. **Orchestra:** 2 fl (picc), ob, Eng hrn, 2 cl, alto sax, 2 bsn, 4 hrn, 2 trp, 3 trb, tuba, harp, timp, perc, strings. **Stageband:** None. **Publisher:** Heugel. **Rights:** Expired.

I. The bailiff rehearses Christmas carols with his children, which surprises Johann and Schmidt, since it is July. Sophie tells the men that the bailiff's daughter, Charlotte, is dressing for the ball at Wetzlar. They discuss Werther's gloomy manner and the return of Albert, Charlotte's intended. Werther approaches the house, overcome with the splendor of Nature, and is welcomed by the bailiff. Charlotte apologizes for keeping him waiting, explaining that she must take care of the children now that their mother is dead. She and Werther leave for the ball. Sophie persuades the bailiff to join Johann and Schmidt at the inn. Albert, returning after six months away to find only Sophie, promises to come back later. Werther and Charlotte return, he professing his love for her, she thinking of her mother's death. The bailiff announces Albert's arrival and Charlotte remembers she promised her mother she would marry Albert.

II. It is Sunday in the village square and Johann and Schmidt, who have been drinking, toast Albert and Charlotte's marriage. Werther is tormented by his loss. Johann and Schmidt assure Bruhlmann that his Katchen will come back to him and they go into church. Suspecting Werther's feelings, Albert tells him he is grateful for his continued loyalty and friendship. Sophie tries to cheer up the two men. Werther is torn: He hates to lie and tell everyone that he has gotten over Charlotte; but he cannot bear the thought of leaving her. When Werther speaks to Charlotte of his love, she sends him away. "You may return on Christmas day," she says. Sophie bursts into tears when Werther takes his leave.

III. In love with Werther, Charlotte is terrified at the insinuation in his letters that he may not be able to return at Christmas. Everyone is sad at home since Werther left, Sophie laments. Charlotte agrees to come home for a visit, since Albert is away. She prays for guidance and Werther appears. He realizes Charlotte loves him, but she flies from his embraces. Resolving to kill himself, Werther leaves Albert a letter asking to borrow his pistols. Albert returns and has Charlotte send them. Too late, she realizes the reason for the request.

IVi. [Musical interlude.] IVii. Charlotte finds Werther in his apartment, dying. He begs her to forgive him. They kiss and Werther dies. In the background, the children can be heard singing Christmas carols.

Čím člověk žije • What Men Live By

Composed by Bohuslav Martinů (December 8, 1890 – August 28, 1959). Libretto by Bohuslav Martinů. Czech. Based on a story by Leo Tolstoy. Premiered New York, May 20, 1953. Set in a small village at an unspecified time. Miracle opera. Through composed with spoken lines.

Sets: 1. **Acts:** 1 act, 5 scenes. **Length:** I: 40. **Hazards:** I: Martin sees a vision of the people he has helped. **Scenes:** I. A street in a small town. A basement with a window looking onto the street at foot-level.

Major roles: Speaker (tenor), Martin Avdeitch (baritone). **Minor roles:** Old soldier Stepanitch (bass), Woman with child/Second Voice (soprano), Old woman/First Voice (contralto). **Bit part:** Old peasant pilgrim (bass). **Speaking:** Boy.

Chorus parts: SSATB. **Chorus roles:** Offstage. **Dance/movement:** None. **Orchestra:** picc, fl, 2 ob, 2 cl, 2 bsn, 2 hrn, trp, trb, timp, perc, piano, strings (6-6-4-3-2). **Stageband:** None. **Publisher:** Boosey & Hawkes. **Rights:** Copyright 1953 by Boosey & Hawkes.

Ii. The speaker introduces Martin Avdeitch, a cobbler living in a basement. Iii. Having lost his wife and child, Martin wishes to die. But an old pilgrim reminds Martin of his faith. Martin reads the Bible and hears voices saying that he will be visited. Iiii. He invites Stepanitch for tea. Iiv. Martin feeds a woman and her child and reads the story of how a Pharisee invited Jesus into his home. He continues to wait for his visitor. Iv. A boy steals an apple from an old woman, but gets caught. The woman wants to call the police, but Martin pays for the apple and makes the boy apologize. The boy helps the woman carry her things home. Martin sees a vision of the people he has helped and realizes that they were his visitation.

Where the Wild Things Are

Composed by Oliver Knussen (b. June 12, 1952). Libretto by Maurice Sendak. English. Based on the children's book by Sendak. Premiered Brussels, Théâtre de la Monnaie, November 28, 1980. Set in Max's room and on an island in the present. Fantasy opera. Through composed. Overture. Revised version premiered January 9, 1984 by Glyndebourne Opera at the National Theater, London.

Sets: 5. **Acts:** 1 act, 9 scenes. **Length:** I: 40. **Hazards:** Magical changes of scene. **Scenes:** Ii – Iii. The hallway outside Max's room. Iiii. Max's room and a forest. Iiv. A boat at sea and an island. Iv – Ivii. The island. Iviii. At sea and in the forest. Iix. Max's room.

Major roles: Max (soprano). **Minor roles:** Mama (mezzo), Tzippy (mezzo), Wild thing with beard/Goat wild thing (tenor), Wild thing with horns (baritone), Rooster wild thing (bass baritone), Bull wild thing (bass).

Chorus parts: N/A. **Chorus roles:** None. **Dance/movement:** Ivi: The wild rumpus. **Orchestra:** 3 fl (picc), ob, Eng hrn, 3 cl, bsn, cont bsn, 4 hrn, 3 trb, 4 perc, piano 4-hands, harp, strings. **Stageband:** None. **Publisher:** G. Schirmer. **Rights:** Copyright 1980 by G. Schirmer Inc.

Ii. Max plays at being a wolf. Iii. His antics upset his mother who sends him to bed without supper. Iiii. Max continues to jump about as his room is transformed into a forest. A boat appears. He sails to an island, warding off a sea monster on the way. Iiv. The wild things jabber at Max but he silences them. Iv. They crown him king. Ivi. Max and the wild things dance about in a wild rumpus. Ivii. Max is hungry and decides to go home. Iviii. The wild things are angry with Max for leaving. Iix. Max tastes the soup his mother has cooked.

Wiener Blut • Viennese Blood

Composed by Johann Strauss Jr. (October 25, 1825 – June 3, 1899). Libretto by Viktor Léon and Leo Stein. German. Original work. Premiered Vienna, Wiener Carltheater, October 25, 1899. Set in Vienna and environs in 1815. Operetta. Set numbers with spoken dialogue. Overture. Musical interlude in II. Entr'acte before III. The opera was created from existing Strauss music by Adolf Müller Jr.

Sets: 3. **Acts:** 3 acts, 3 scenes. **Length:** I, II, III: 100. **Hazards:** None. **Scenes:** I. Cagliari's home in Döbling. II. The palace of Countess Bitowsky. III. The casino in Hietzing.

Major roles: Josef the valet (tenor), Franzi Cagliari (soprano), Count Zedlau (tenor), Pepi Pleininger (soprano), Prince Ypsheim-Gindelbach Prime Minister of Reuss-Greiz-Schleiz (baritone), Countess Gabriele Zedlau (soprano), Kagler (tenor). **Bit parts:** Lisi or Sali the laundry maid (soprano or mezzo), Lori or Mali the laundry maid (soprano or mezzo). **Speaking bits:** English ambassador, Dutch envoy, Count Bitowski, Waiter.

Chorus parts: SATTBB. **Chorus roles:** Ball guests, nobles. **Dance/movement:** II: Polonaise. Dance of the countesses. **Orchestra:** 2 fl (picc), 2 ob, 2 cl, 2 bsn, 4 hrn, 2 trp, 3 trb, timp, perc, strings. **Stageband:** None. **Publisher:** Belwin Mills. **Rights:** Expired.

I. Josef the valet looks for his master, Count Zedlau, at the count's mistress's house. But the mistress—the ballerina Franzi—has not seen the count either and worries he has a new girlfriend. The count arrives and assures Franzi that he has only been with his wife. In fact, the count is chasing a young dress fitter named Pepi—not realizing that Pepi is Josef's girlfriend. Pepi brings Franzi her dress for the ball, but it does not fit, so Franzi tells Pepi to go in her place. The prime minister pays his respects to Franzi—he thinks she is the countess—and her father Kagler. The countess now arrives, hoping to discover her husband's secret. The prime minister believes the countess is the count's mistress. The count confuses everyone by persuading the prime minister to present the countess as his own wife.

II. At the ball, the countess decides that the problem with her marriage is her husband's lack of Viennese blood. The count asks Pepi to meet him at the fair. She agrees only after having a lover's quarrel with Josef. The count refuses the countess's and Franzi's request to accompany them to the fair. The minister misintroduces the women, giving the countess and Franzi a clue to what is going on.

III. The minister, the countess, Franzi and Josef all come to the fair to catch the count. The count tells Josef to distract Pepi while he sees Franzi. But the countess and Franzi have joined forces. They conclude that the only way to keep a man's interest is not to give in too easily. Josef is angry with Pepi, but the count swears nothing happened between them. Josef reveals that he and Pepi are married. Everyone makes up and toasts Viennese blood.

The Wife of Martin Guerre

Composed by William Laurence Bergsma (b. April 1, 1921). Libretto by Janet Lewis. English. Based on historical events. Premiered New York City, Juilliard Opera Theatre, February 15, 1956. Set in France in the mid-16th century. Tragedy. Set numbers with accompanied recitative.

Sets: 5. **Acts:** 3 acts, 9 scenes. **Length:** I, II, III: 110. **Hazards:** Real and false Martin must look alike. **Scenes:** I – II. A farm kitchen and courtyard. IIIi. A curtained alcove. IIIii. A court room. IIIiii. A street in Toulouse. IIIiv. A second courtroom.

Major roles: Bertrande (soprano), Catherine (contralto), Pierre Guerre (bass), Martin Guerre (baritone). **Minor roles:** First worker (baritone or bass), Annette (mezzo), Diane (soprano), Second worker (baritone or tenor), Third worker (baritone), Fourth worker (baritone), Steward/ Second judge, in red (tenor), Old Guerre/Third soldier/Real Martin Guerre (bass baritone), First soldier/First court crier (tenor), Father Antoine (tenor), Sanxi (treble), Second soldier, from Rochefort/First judge, in black (bass), Espagnol (tenor), Carter/Second court crier (bass), Jean du Tilh (baritone). **Bit parts:** Man-at-arms (bass or tenor), Man (baritone), Woman (mezzo), Bagpiper (tenor), Shepherd (tenor), Musician (bass).

Chorus parts: SATB. **Chorus roles:** Workers, servants, witnesses, spectators. **Dance/movement:** I, II: Workers perform a country dance.
Orchestra: 2 fl (picc), ob, cl (bs cl), bsn, trp, hrn, harp, perc, strings (written for 2 vln, vla, 2 vlc, bs, but in big hall should be 6-4-4-4-2).
Stageband: None. **Rights:** Copyright 1956 by William Laurence Bergsma.

I. The Guerre household sits down to dinner and Old Guerre questions his steward about some missing grain seed. Martin Guerre has had it planted, but ran away for fear of his father's anger. Martin's wife, Bertrande, and her servant, Catherine, wonder at Martin's continued absence. A young soldier pretends to have news about Martin, knowing that Bertrande will feed him. Old Guerre dies in a fall from his horse and Bertrande asks the soldier to tell Martin that he may return home now that Old Guerre is dead.

IIi. After eight years, Martin returns. IIii. Bertrande wonders if Martin is really the harsh, disciplined man she married. IIiii. She gives birth to a daughter. Bertrande is more convinced than ever that Martin is an impostor who has tricked her into adultery. He cautions her against such mad ideas. IIiv. A soldier from Rochefort claims the real Martin lost a leg in battle.

IIIi. Bertrande has Martin arrested. IIIii. Witnesses at Martin's trial suggest that his relatives are doing this to steal his farm. Only Pierre believes Bertrande. Espagnol testifies that Martin is really Arnaud du Tilh and that Martin sold him the right to impersonate him. The court declares Martin an impostor and orders his execution. IIIiii. He appeals. Annette, Father Antoine and Catherine beg Bertrande to withdraw her charge. IIIiv. At the new trial, Arnaud du Tilh's brother, Jean, refuses to testify. The real Martin returns and treats Bertrande harshly. The false Martin realizes that part of his punishment is that Bertrande will be left with the real Martin after he is executed.

Der Wildschütz • The Poacher

Composed by Gustav Albert Lortzing (October 23, 1801 – January 21, 1851). Libretto by Gustav Albert Lortzing. German. Based on a comedy by August von Kotzebue. Premiered Leipzig, Altes Theater, December 31, 1842. Set in Germany in the early 19th century. Comedy. Set numbers with recitative. Spoken dialogue. Overture.

Sets: 3. **Acts:** 3 acts, 3 scenes. **Length:** I: 60. II: 55. III: 30. **Arias:** "Fünf Tausend Thaler" (Baculus). **Hazards:** None. **Scenes:** I. A country scene in front of the schoolmaster's house. II. An elegant salon in Eberbach castle. III. The park of the count's castle with a pavilion and arbor in the foreground.

Major roles: Gretchen (soprano), Baculus (bass), Baroness Freimann (soprano), Baron Kronthal (tenor), Count of Eberbach (baritone), Countess of Eberbach (mezzo). **Minor roles:** Nanette (mezzo), Pancratius (bass). **Bit parts:** Women (soprano, alto).

Chorus parts: SSAATTBB. **Chorus roles:** Peasants, hunters, villagers, servants, cooks, girls (2 parts). **Dance/movement:** I: country folk dance a quadrille. III: Count waltzes with village girls. **Orchestra:** 2 fl (picc), 2 ob, 2 cl, 2 bsn, 4 hrn, 2 trp, 3 trb, perc, timp, strings. **Stageband:** None. **Publisher:** C. F. Peters. **Rights:** Expired.

I. Gretchen and Baculus the schoolmaster are engaged. Baculus receives a note from the count dismissing him for poaching on the count's land to get venison for his wedding feast. The count's sister, Baroness Freimann, returns, disguised as a man because she wants to have a secret look at Baron Kronthal, the man her brother wants her to marry. Hearing Baculus's problem, the baroness proposes to disguise herself as a girl and plead with the count on Baculus's behalf. Her maid, Nanette— who is disguised as a man—woos Gretchen. Baculus insists Gretchen remain home. The baron resists the idea of marrying the count's sister. The countess does not realize that the baron is her long-lost brother. The count and baron wander into Baculus's wedding celebration. Both men are impressed by Gretchen's beauty, but the baron falls in love with the baroness. The count invites everyone to his birthday celebration.

II. The countess reads Greek dramas to her servants. The steward Pancratius tells Baculus to learn Sophocles to impress the countess. The baron flirts with the countess (his sister), making the countess think he loves her. Baculus approaches the countess and together they plan to stage a Greek drama. The count interrupts and orders Baculus out of his sight. The baron works up his courage to approach the baroness. The baroness tells the count she is Baculus's fiancée, but the count refuses to pardon Baculus. Baculus and the baroness argue, but Baculus gladly leaves his "fiancée" with the baron. The baron proposes to the baroness, who plays hard to get. The countess convinces the count to reconsider Baculus's case. Since it is raining, Baculus and the baroness stay the night. The baron tries to get the count out of the room so he can seduce the baroness. Their noise awakens the countess, who takes the baroness into her own room. The baron bribes Baculus to renounce his fiancée. Baculus agrees.

III. The count celebrates his birthday. The baron waits for the baroness. The count dances with the village girls and the baron joins in the dancing, but the countess interrupts. Baculus is jealous of Nanette—who is still disguised as a boy and whom he found talking with Gretchen. He tells Gretchen that the baron wants to marry her. The baron confirms this bargain and pays the money, but is surprised to discover that Gretchen is not the baroness. Baculus tells him that the baroness is a man, but the baroness tells the baron the truth. The baroness wonders about the relationship between the countess and the baron. Meanwhile, the countess sees the count embracing the baroness. She is angry—until the baron reveals that the baroness is the count's sister. The baron admits he is the countess's brother. Having learned that Baculus shot his own donkey—not one of the count's deer—the count forgives him.

Willie Stark

Composed by Carlisle Floyd (b. June 11, 1926). Libretto by Carlisle Floyd. English. Based on the novel "All the King's Men" by Robert Penn Warren. Premiered Houston, Houston Grand Opera, April 24, 1981. Set in a state capital in the deep south in 1935. Music drama. Set numbers with spoken dialogue. Radio announcer (prerecorded) details Stark's life and career in interludes scattered throughout the opera. Prerecorded chorus (SSAATTBB).

Sets: 8. **Acts:** 3 acts, 9 scenes. **Length:** I, II, III: 210. **Hazards:** III: Assassination of Willie Stark. **Scenes:** Ii. A city street adjacent to the state capitol grounds and the governor's offices in the capitol building. Iii. The living room and library of Judge Burden's home. Iiii. The courthouse steps in Willie's home town. IIi. The governor's office. IIii. The Stark home. IIiii. The library of the governor's mansion and the street outside. IIIi. The living room and library of Judge Burden's home. IIIii. Sadie's office and the reception room of the governor's offices. IIIiii. The state capitol and grounds.

Major roles: Willie Stark (baritone), Jack Burden (tenor), Sadie Burke (mezzo), Anne Stanton (soprano). **Minor roles:** Senator Jeff (tenor),

Lieutenant-Governor "Tiny" Duffy (tenor), Judge Courtney Burden (bass baritone), Sugar Boy (tenor), Mrs. Stark (soprano), Lucy (soprano), Two women (soprano, alto). **Bit parts:** Senator Hugh (baritone or speaking), Four men (2 tenor, 2 bass). **Speaking:** Radio announcer, Reporter (prerecorded), Jarvis, Mayor. **Speaking bit:** George William.

Chorus parts: SSAATTBB. **Chorus roles:** Football players, people, banjo and harmonica players, reporters and news photographers, mounted police, medical aides, stretcher bearers. **Dance/movement:** None. **Orchestra:** fl (picc), ob (Eng hrn), cl (bs cl), bsn (cont bsn), 2 hrn, 2 trp, trb, tuba, timp, perc, harp, strings. **Stageband:** None. **Publisher:** Belwin Mills. **Rights:** Copyright 1981 by Belwin Mills Publishing Corp.

Ii. A group of poor farmers protests the legislature's attempt to impeach Governor Stark. Stark is assembling a petition of support. He is blackmailing Senator Jeff for his vote using information about the senator's father's illegal business dealings. Stark's aide, Jack Burton, is appalled but he believes in Stark's advocacy of the poor. Senator Hugh changes his vote too, but warns Stark that Judge Burden—Jack's father—means publicly to support impeachment. Sadie tells Jack and Duffy that she taught Stark everything he knows. She secretly loves Stark and is annoyed to hear he has a new girlfriend. Iii. Jack tries to persuade his father to meet Stark, but the judge refuses. Jack is reproached by his fiancée, Anne, for not spending time with her. The judge refuses to see Stark when he calls, but Stark forces his way in. He is seeing Anne and arranges an assignation. Unable to change the judge's mind, Stark decides to search for blackmail material. Anne goes to meet Stark. Iiii. Stark holds a political rally in Mason City, his home town.

IIi. Stark dreams about being elected president. Duffy receives information that Judge Burden accepted a bribe from a power company. Jack is disgusted by Stark's tactics. IIii. Anne visits Stark at the home of his mother and daughter, Lucy, and Stark proposes to Anne. Duffy gets confirmation that the judge accepted a bribe and Stark agrees to let Jack take the news to his father. Stark's conscience bothers him. Anne decides to marry Stark even if it means being disowned by her friends and family. IIiii. Stark watches an old newsreel of himself. Anne agrees to marry him. Sadie interrupts them and insists she will not give Stark up.

IIIi. Jack confronts his father and is horrified to learn that he did accept a bribe. Left alone, the judge shoots himself. IIIii. Sadie inadvertently tells Jack about Anne and Stark. IIIiii. A crowd gathers before the capitol to support Stark, who wins the impeachment vote. Jack assassinates Stark and is himself shot to death by Stark's bodyguard. Stark's followers and friends mourn him.

The Wings of the Dove

Composed by Douglas Moore (August 10, 1893 – July 25, 1969). Libretto
by Ethan Ayer. English. Based on the novel by Henry James. Premiered
New York City, New York City Opera, October 12, 1961. Set in London
and Venice in 1900. Drama. Through composed. Ballet.

Sets: 4. **Acts:** 1 act, 6 scenes. **Length:** I: 115. **Hazards:** None. **Scenes:** Ii –
Iii. The parlor of Mrs. Lowder at Lancaster Gate. Iiii. A room in the
National Gallery. Iiv. A courtyard and balcony of the Palazzo Leporelli
in Venice. Iv. Milly's apartment in the Palazzo Leporelli. Ivi. Mrs.
Lowder's parlor.

Major roles: Kate Croy (mezzo), Miles Dunster (baritone), Aunt Maud
Lowder (contralto), Milly Theale (soprano). **Minor roles:** Steffens (baritone), Homer Croy (baritone), Lord Mark (tenor), Susan Stringham
(soprano), Lecturer at the National Gallery (tenor), Major domo Guiliano
(baritone). **Mute:** Museum guard, Janus, Minstrel, Maiden in masque,
Sister of Mercy.

Chorus parts: S. **Chorus roles:** Party guests (one line of spoken ejaculations), Madrigal chorus (6 minimum; sing minstrel part while he mimes
it). **Dance/movement:** I: Polka and waltz at Aunt Maud's party.
Venetian ballet "The Masque of Janus" (minimum 12 dancers).
Orchestra: 2 fl (picc), 2 ob (Eng hrn), 2 cl (bs cl), 2 bsn, 3 hrn, 2 trp, 2 trb,
timp, perc, strings. **Stageband:** I: chamber orchestra. **Publisher:** G.
Schirmer. **Rights:** Copyright 1961, 1963 by G. Schirmer Inc.

Ii. Homer Croy visits his daughter, Kate, who is living with her aunt,
Maud Lowder. He has gambled away the money Kate gave him and
wants more, but she refuses. Kate and a young journalist, Miles Dunster,
are in love, but Kate insists Miles win over her rich aunt so that they will
not be poor. Aunt Maud is too shrewd to banish Miles, preferring to
appeal to his better nature. Kate admits she has rejected Lord Mark's
proposal. Iii. Aunt Maud throws a party for the rich young American
Milly Theale. Everyone is impressed by Milly's resemblance to a portrait
of Constanza Leporelli, the daughter of a Venetian doge, who died
young. Lord Mark courts her. Kate realizes Milly loves Miles. Iiii. Milly
runs into Kate in the National Gallery and thanks her for her solicitude
while she was ill. She invites Kate and Miles to come to Venice with her.
Believing that Milly will die within the year, Kate wants Miles to marry
Milly. Iiv. Kate leaves Miles in Venice with Milly. They watch a masque.
Lord Mark tells Milly that Kate and Miles are lovers. Iv. Maud apologizes to Miles for coming between him and Kate. He is distraught. Ivi.
Back in London, Kate learns of Milly's death. Milly has left half her for-
tune to Miles. Miles returns with the money, which he gives to Kate.

Kate goads him into admitting he no longer loves her. She tears up the money.

Wozzeck

Composed by Alban Berg (February 9, 1885 – December 24, 1935). Libretto by Alban Berg and Georg Büchner. German. Based on the play by Georg Büchner. Premiered Berlin, Berlin Staatsoper, December 14, 1925. Set in Germany in the early 19th century. Sprechstimme music drama. Through composed with extensive use of established musical forms (symphony, pasacaglia, etc.) in complex tonalities. Orchestra interludes between scenes. Opus 7.

Sets: 10. **Acts:** 3 acts, 15 scenes. **Length:** I: 34. II: 33. III: 22. **Hazards:** III: Wozzeck wades into lake and drowns. **Scenes:** Ii. Captain's room. Iii. Open field outside the town. Iiii. Marie's room. Iiv. Doctor's study. Iv. Street before Marie's door. IIi. Marie's room. IIii. Street in town. IIiii. Street before Marie's door. IIiv. Tavern garden. IIv. Guardroom in the barracks. IIIi. Marie's room. IIIii. Forest path by a pool. IIIiii. A low tavern. IIIiv. Forest path by a pool. IIIv. Street before Marie's door.

Major roles: Captain (comic tenor), Wozzeck (baritone), Doctor (comic bass), Drum major (helden tenor), Marie (soprano). **Minor roles:** Andres (lyric tenor), Margret (contralto), First apprentice (bass), Second apprentice (baritone). **Bit parts:** Soldier (tenor), Fool (tenor), Marie's child (treble).

Chorus parts: SATTBBBB. **Chorus roles:** Soldiers, men, women, children (2 parts, 3 solo spoken lines). **Dance/movement:** II: Artisans, soldiers and girls dance in inn. III: Artisans, soldiers and girls dance in tavern. **Orchestra:** 4 fl (picc), 4 ob (Eng hrn), 4 cl, bs cl, 3 bsn, cont bsn, 4 hrn, 4 trp, 4 trb, tuba, 2 timp, perc, celeste, harp, strings. **Stageband:** I: drum, military band (picc, 2 fl, 2 ob, 2 cl, 2 bsn, 2 hrn, 2 trp, 3 trb, tuba, perc). II: 2 vln, cl, accordian, guitar, bombardon or bs tuba. III: piano. **Publisher:** Universal Edition. **Rights:** Copyright 1926 by Universal Edition.

Ii. While Wozzeck shaves him, the captain chides Wozzeck for having a child out of wedlock. "It is hard for the poor to be virtuous," Wozzeck replies. Iii. Andres and Wozzeck gather sticks in a field. Iiii. A military band passes Marie's window and she and the drum major wave to each other. When Margret calls Marie a slut, Marie slams the door in her face. Marie sings to her child, whose father, Wozzeck, visits but is too absorbed by his ideas to pay attention to his son. Marie rails bitterly against poverty. Iiv. The company doctor pays Wozzeck to participate in bizarre medical experiments. He needs the extra money to give to Marie,

Wozzeck explains. Iv. When the drum major embraces Marie, she first resists, but soon gives in and disappears with him into her room.

IIi. Marie is playing with her new earrings and trying to get the child to go to sleep when Wozzeck surprises her. He sees the earrings but gives her money and when he leaves, Marie feels remorse. IIii. The captain stops the doctor on the street but is horrified by the doctor's morbid (and unasked for) diagnoses. Seeing Wozzeck, the two men drop innuendoes about Marie's infidelity. IIiii. Wozzeck confronts Marie with her faithlessness. "Better to stab me than touch me," she tells him coldly. IIiv. Wozzeck sees Marie dancing with the drum major in the inn. He is approached by the idiot, who smells blood. IIv. The drum major returns to barracks bragging about his fling with Marie. He beats Wozzeck.

IIIi. Marie reads the Bible and prays for mercy. IIIii. Wozzeck takes Marie into the woods where he kisses her and then kills her with his knife. IIIiii. He gets drunk in the tavern and flirts with Margret, who sees the blood on his hand. IIIiv. Wozzeck returns to the murder scene to collect the knife and throw it in the lake. Afraid he has not hidden it well enough, Wozzeck wades into the lake and drowns. Hearing him drowning, the doctor and captain hurry away. IIIv. A group of children go off to see Marie's corpse. Her son, who has been riding his hobby horse, rides off after them.

The Wreckers

Composed by Ethel Smyth (April 22, 1858 – May 9, 1944). Libretto by Henry Brewster. French (translated into English & German). Based on Brewster's own play, itself inspired by historical existence of "wreckers" in Cornwall. Premiered Leipzig, Neues Theater, November 11, 1906. Set in a Cornish village on the sea in the late 18th century. Lyric drama. Set numbers with recitative. Overture. Prelude before II. Originally written in French. Premiered in German.

Sets: 3. Acts: 3 acts, 17 scenes. Length: I: 60. II: 40. III: 30. Hazards: III: Mark and Thirza drown in rising tide. Scenes: I. A Cornish village on a cliff above the sea. II. A desolate part of the seashore. III. The interior of a huge cave.

Major roles: Pascoe (bass baritone), Avis (soprano), Thirza (mezzo), Mark (tenor). Minor roles: Tallan (tenor), Harvey (bass), Lawrence (baritone), Jack (mezzo). Bit parts: Man (bass).

Chorus parts: SSAATTBB. Chorus roles: Villagers, congregation. Dance/movement: I: Wild wreckers dance. Orchestra: 2 fl (picc), 2 ob

(Eng hrn), 2 cl (bs cl), 2 bsn (cont bsn), 4 hrn, 2 trp, 3 trb, tuba, timp, perc, harp, strings. **Stageband:** I: organ, perc, hrn, canon. II: hrn. III: perc. **Publisher:** Forsyth Brothers. **Rights:** Expired.

Ii. The villagers intentionally lure ships onto the rocks and plunder them, believing it is God's way of providing for them. Iii. The preacher Pascoe rebukes the villagers for drinking on Sunday. Iiii. Avis tells the villagers that someone has been lighting a beacon to warn ships off. Iiv. Pascoe's wife, Thirza, shuns the villagers. Iv. Avis confronts Mark, who admits he no longer loves her. Ivi. Avis is heartbroken. Ivii. Thirza and Mark have been having an affair. Iviii. Pascoe demands Avis give up her necklace to feed the poor. She hints at Thirza's infidelity. Iix. Thirza tells Pascoe she hates him and the villagers for wrecking passing ships. Ix. Pascoe has a vision of a pillar of fire. Ixi. Avis suspects Pascoe is lighting the beacon. The villagers agree to lie in wait for the traitor.

IIi. Avis eggs on the villagers, including the young Jack. IIii. Mark waits for Thirza. IIiii. She warns him not to light the beacon tonight and promises to run away with him. They light the beacon one last time. Pascoe sees them embracing and faints. IIiv. He is discovered next to the beacon.

IIIi. Pascoe refuses to defend himself before a court of the villagers. Avis accuses Thirza of being a witch. IIIii. Mark and Thirza admit their guilt and are condemned. The villagers lock them in a cavern to be drowned by the rising tide.

Wuthering Heights

Composed by Carlisle Floyd (b. June 11, 1926). Libretto by Carlisle Floyd. English. Novel by Emily Brontë. Premiered Santa Fe, Santa Fe Opera, July 16, 1958. Set in Northern England in 1835 and from 1817 to 1821. Music drama. Through composed. Prologue. Prelude. Interlude before IIii.

Sets: 3. **Acts:** 3 acts, 8 scenes. **Length:** Prologue, I: 40. II: 40. III: 50. **Arias:** "I've dreamt in my life" (Catherine), "Oh Nelly, I've fallen in love with him" (Isabella). **Hazards:** None. **Scenes:** Prologue – Ii. The living room and kitchen of a craggy, weather-hewn house (Wuthering Heights) with the exterior also visible. Iii. Wuthering Heights and exterior of Thrushcross Grange. II. Wuthering Heights. III. The living room and drawing room of Thrushcross Grange.

Major roles: Isabella Linton (soprano), Heathcliff (baritone), Catherine Earnshaw (soprano), Nelly (mezzo), Hindley Earnshaw (tenor), Edgar

Linton (tenor). **Minor roles:** Lockwood (tenor), Joseph (tenor), Mr. Earnshaw (bass). **Mute:** Servants, Mr. Linton, Mrs. Linton.

Chorus parts: SATB. **Chorus roles:** Party guests. **Dance/movement:** III: party guests dance a minuet and waltz. **Orchestra:** 2 fl (picc), 2 ob (Eng hrn), 2 cl (bs cl), 2 bsn, 2 hrn, 2 trp, 2 trb, timp, perc, harp, strings. **Stageband:** None. **Publisher:** Boosey & Hawkes. **Rights:** Copyright 1961 by Boosey & Hawkes.

Prologue. Heathcliff's tenant, Lockwood, gets lost on the moors and finds himself at Heathcliff's house, Wuthering Heights. Heathcliff reluctantly agrees to let Lockwood stay the night. Lockwood goes to sleep reading the diaries of Catherine Linton—and is awakened by a vision of her ghost. Heathcliff runs out onto the moor after the ghost.

Ii. The young Heathcliff has been shirking his chores, but Cathy's father, Mr. Earnshaw, protects him from the wrath of Cathy's brother, Hindley. Hindley is furious that Earnshaw cares more for the foundling Heathcliff than for him. He challenges his father, who has a heart attack and dies. Cathy and Heathcliff swear to love each other always. Iii. They rebel against the sermons of the old servant Joseph and against Hindley's tyranny. The two run across the moors to the Lintons' home, Thrushcross Grange. Cathy twists her ankle and is taken in by the Lintons.

IIi. Four weeks later, Cathy returns to Wuthering Heights filled with ideas of being a lady. Heathcliff feels humiliated in front of her new friends, Edgar and Isabella Linton. Hindley beats Heathcliff for his boorishness, but Catherine nurses him. IIii. Heathcliff is jealous of Edgar. Edgar visits Cathy, but Cathy throws a tantrum when Nelly refuses to leave the room. Cathy cries and Edgar proposes to her. She accepts, knowing that she really loves Heathcliff. Heathcliff runs away.

IIIi. Three years later, Heathcliff returns, a gentleman. Cathy is now married to Edgar, but Heathcliff asks her to run away with him. He wins Wuthering Heights from Hindley in a card game. Edgar forbids Cathy to see Heathcliff and Nelly begs her not to. IIIii. To revenge himself on Cathy, Heathcliff proposes to Isabella. Edgar disowns Isabella and Cathy vents her fury on both Heathcliff and her husband. IIIiii. Hearing that Cathy is sick, Heathcliff forces his way into her bedroom. They reaffirm their love and Cathy dies in his arms.

Wuthering Heights

Composed by Bernard Herrmann (June 29, 1911 – December 24, 1975).

Libretto by Lucille Fletcher. English. Based on the novel and poems by Emily Brontë. Premiered Portland, Oregon, Portland Opera, November 6, 1982. Set in Northern England in 1840. Lyric drama. Through composed. Spoken dialogue. Prologue. Orchestral interlude before Iii and during IV. Offstage voice should match that of Catherine Earnshaw, but Catherine's corpse remains onstage while voice is heard.

Sets: 3. **Acts:** 4 acts, 6 scenes. **Length:** Prologue, I, II, III, IV: 195.
Hazards: None. **Scenes:** Prologue. A small upper bedroom at Wuthering Heights. I – II. The main hall at Wuthering Heights twenty years earlier. III. The drawing room at Thrushcross Grange three years later. IV. The main hall at Wuthering Heights the following March.

Major roles: Nelly Dean (mezzo or contralto), Heathcliff (baritone), Catherine Earnshaw (soprano), Hindley Earnshaw (baritone), Edgar Linton (tenor), Isabella Linton (mezzo). **Minor roles:** Mr. Lockwood (baritone), Joseph (bass), Offstage voice (soprano). **Speaking bit:** Hareton Earnshaw (child).

Chorus parts: SATB. **Chorus roles:** Offstage carolers (SATB: 3-2-2-2).
Dance/movement: None. **Orchestra:** 3 fl (picc), 2 ob, Eng hrn, 2 cl, bs cl, 2 bsn, cont bsn, 4 hrn, 3 trp, 3 trb, tuba, timp, perc, 2 harp, strings (min. 12-12-10-8-5). **Stageband:** III: chime, piano (played by Isabella if possible). IV: harmonium or electronic organ. **Publisher:** Broude Brothers.
Rights: Copyright 1957 by Novello & Co.

Prologue. Heathcliff's tenant, Mr. Lockwood, has been stranded at Wuthering Heights by a snowstorm. The maid, Nelly Dean, puts him in a guest room where he has a nightmare about Catherine Earnshaw. Heathcliff bursts in and, hearing Lockwood's dream, runs out into the snow in search of Cathy. Ii. Twenty years earlier, Cathy and Heathcliff delight in the freedom of the moors. Heathcliff was taken in as a child by Cathy's father, but Cathy's brother, Hindley, is now master—and he hates Heathcliff. Hindley has Joseph read a prayer, but Joseph falls asleep and Cathy and Heathcliff slip out onto the moor. Iii. Cathy has spent five weeks at Thrushcross Grange with the Lintons and Nelly tries to persuade Heathcliff to clean himself up for her return. Heathcliff is contemptuous of the Lintons' son, Edgar. Heathcliff's rough look and manner prompt Edgar to tease him and Hindley to beat him.

II. Heathcliff objects to the time Cathy spends with Edgar. When Edgar comes, Cathy has a tantrum, pinches Nelly and slaps Edgar. Edgar starts to leave, but he and Cathy make up. Hindley attacks Nelly and his son, Hareton, in a drunken stupor. Cathy admits to Nelly that she has agreed to marry Edgar, although she really loves Heathcliff. Heathcliff overhears and runs away.

III. Three years later, Heathcliff pays a call on Cathy—and her husband Edgar. To punish Cathy, Heathcliff allows Edgar's sister, Isabella, to love him. Cathy fights with everyone and is taken ill.

IV. Isabella is married to Heathcliff, but he has made her life at Wuthering Heights a hell. Hindley is in debt to Heathcliff and decides to kill him, but fails. Cathy dies in Heathcliff's arms. Hearing Cathy's voice, Heathcliff rushes out onto the moors.

Yeomen of the Guard

Composed by Arthur Sullivan (May 13, 1842 – November 22, 1900). Libretto by W. S. Gilbert. English. Original work. Premiered London, Savoy Theater, October 3, 1888. Set in the Tower Green, London in the 16th century. Operetta. Set numbers with spoken dialogue. Overture.

Sets: 1. **Acts:** 2 acts, 2 scenes. **Length:** I: 55. II: 40. **Arias:** "When maiden loves" (Phoebe), "When our gallant Norman foes" (Carruthers), "Were I thy bride" (Phoebe). **Hazards:** None. **Scenes:** I – II. Tower Green, a grass-covered yard overlooking the river.

Major roles: Phoebe Meryll (mezzo), Dame Carruthers (mezzo), Sergeant Meryll (bass), Colonel Fairfax (tenor), Elsie Maynard (soprano), Jack Point (baritone). **Minor roles:** Wilfred Shadbolt (baritone), Second Yeoman (baritone), Leonard Meryll (tenor), Sir Richard Cholmondely (baritone), First Yeoman (tenor), Kate (soprano). **Speaking bits:** Two citizens.

Chorus parts: SSAATTTBBB. **Chorus roles:** Yeomen of the guard, citizens. **Dance/movement:** None. **Orchestra:** fl, cl, ob, 2 hrn (or trp and trb), trp, trb, timp, perc, strings. **Stageband:** None. **Publisher:** G. Schirmer, Inc. **Rights:** Expired.

I. Sergeant Meryll's daughter, Phoebe, has fallen in love with Colonel Fairfax, who is to be beheaded for alchemy. Wilfred, the assistant jailer, loves Phoebe. Meryll welcomes home his son Leonard, who has been made a yeoman of the guard. Fairfax twice saved Meryll's life, so Meryll sends Leonard away so that Fairfax can impersonate him. Fairfax has been condemned because of the machinations of his heir and arranges to thwart his heir by marrying. Two strolling performers, Jack Point and Elsie Maynard, entertain the crowd. Elsie agrees to marry Fairfax even though she and Jack are engaged. Phoebe gets the keys to Fairfax's cell from Wilfred and she and her father present Fairfax as Leonard. Fairfax's escape is discovered.

II. Wilfred wants to become a jester. Jack agrees to train him if Wilfred will claim he shot Fairfax escaping—thereby leaving Elsie a widow. Fairfax woos Elsie. She returns his love, but admits she is already married. Jack and Wilfred describe Fairfax's death. Jealous of Fairfax's interest in Elsie, Phoebe inadvertently reveals his identity to Wilfred. She buys Wilfred's silence by agreeing to marry him. Leonard returns with a pardon for Fairfax. Dame Carruthers, too, learns Fairfax's secret. Sergeant Meryll agrees to marry her. Fairfax reveals his identity. Jack is heartbroken.

Yerma

Composed by Heitor Villa-Lobos (March 5, 1887 – November 17, 1959). Libretto by Heitor Villa-Lobos. Spanish. Based on the play by Federico García Lorca. Premiered Santa Fe, Santa Fe Opera, August 12, 1971 (posthumous). Set in Spain in the 20th century. Tragedy. Through composed. Prelude. Interlude before Iii.

Sets: 5. **Acts:** 3 acts, 6 scenes. **Length:** I: 45. II: 25. III: 25. **Hazards:** None. **Scenes:** Ii. Yerma's house. Iii. A field. IIi. The bank of a river. IIii. Yerma's house. IIIi. Dolores's house. IIIii. Hermitage in a mountain.

Major roles: Yerma (dramatic soprano), Juan (tenor). **Minor roles:** Maria (mezzo), Victor (baritone), Old woman (mezzo), First laundress (soprano), Second laundress (soprano), Dolores (mezzo), Masked man (tenor), Masked woman (soprano). **Bit parts:** Third laundress (soprano), Fourth laundress (mezzo), Fifth laundress (mezzo), Sixth laundress (mezzo).

Chorus parts: SSAATTBBB. **Chorus roles:** Offstage voices, workers, children (3 parts) (several bit chorus parts). **Dance/movement:** III: Ritual ballet (optional). **Orchestra:** picc, fl, ob, Eng hrn, 2 cl (2 sax, bs cl), bsn, cont bsn, sax, 2 hrn, 2 trp, 3 trb, tuba, timp, 2 perc, glockenspiel, harp, piano, celeste, strings. **Stageband:** None. **Publisher:** Max Eschig. **Rights:** Copyright 1971 by Max Eschig.

Ii. Yerma desparately wants a child, but her husband Juan is indifferent. Iii. Her friend Maria is pregnant.

IIi. The village women gossip about Yerma while doing their washing. IIii. Yerma's family confines her to the house for her own good.

IIIi. Yerma escapes. She considers, but rejects, the advances of her childhood sweetheart. IIIii. She goes to a shrine to pray, but to no avail. When Juan finds her and upbraids her for being out on her own, Yerma, in a fit of anger, strangles him. Yerma realizes that her last chance of having a child died with Juan.

Der Zar Lässt sich Photographieren • The Tsar Has His Photograph Taken

Composed by Kurt Weill (March 2, 1900 – April 3, 1950). Libretto by Georg Kaiser. German. Original work. Premiered Leipzig, Leipzig Opera, February 18, 1928. Set in Paris in the late 19th or early 20th century. Comedy. Set numbers with recitative and spoken dialogue.

Sets: 1. **Acts:** 1 act, 1 scene. **Length:** I: 45. **Hazards:** None. **Scenes:** I. A fashionable photographer's studio.

Major roles: False Angèle (soprano), Tsar (baritone). **Minor roles:** Angèle (soprano), Boy (mezzo), Assistant (tenor), Leader (tenor), False boy (mezzo), False assistant (tenor), Tsar's equerry (bass). **Speaking bits:** Two detectives.

Chorus parts: TTTBBB. **Chorus roles:** Conspirators, police. **Dance/movement:** None. **Orchestra:** 2 fl, 2 ob, 2 cl, 2 bsn, 3 hrn, 2 trp, 2 trb, timp, perc, piano, strings. **Stageband:** None. **Publisher:** Universal. **Rights:** Copyright 1927, 1978 by Universal Edition.

I. The Tsar calls the studio of Madame Angèle to arrange for his photograph to be taken. Before he arrives, a group of conspirators take over the studio and impersonate the owners, planning to assassinate the tsar with a gun hidden in the camera. The tsar asks the false Angèle about the photographs on the walls and he insists on taking a photo of Angèle before she photographs him. She is terrified and the tsar tries to kiss her. They are interrupted by the tsar's equerry, who explains that the chief of police has uncovered an assassination plot and is on his way to the studio. The conspirators are surrounded, but they cover the tsar in pillows and make their escape. The real Angèle takes the photograph of the tsar—who is none the wiser about what almost happened.

Zar und Zimmermann • Tsar and Carpenter

Composed by Gustav Albert Lortzing (October 23, 1801 – January 21, 1851). Libretto by Gustav Albert Lortzing. German. Based on "Der Burgermeister von Saardam" by Georg Christian Römer itself based on "Le Bourgmestre de Sardam" by Anne-Honoré Joseph de Mélesville, Jean Toussaint Merle and Eugène Centiran de Boirie. Premiered Leipzig,

Stadttheater, December 22, 1837. Set in Saardam in Holland in 1698. Comic opera. Set numbers with recitative and spoken dialogue. Overture. Introduction before II, III. Ballet.

Sets: 3. **Acts:** 3 acts, 3 scenes. **Length:** I: 65. II: 40. III: 40. **Arias:** "O sancta justitia" (Van Bett). **Hazards:** None. **Scenes:** I. Inside the shipyards at Saardam. II. Interior of a spacious tavern. III. Great chamber in Saardam's city hall.

Major roles: Peter Michaelov/Tsar of Russia (baritone), Peter Ivanov (tenor), Marie (soprano), Burgomaster Van Bett of Saardom (comic bass). **Minor roles:** Admiral Lefort (bass), Widow Browe (contralto), Marquis of Chateauneuf (tenor), Lord Syndham (bass). **Speaking bits:** Officer, Council servant.

Chorus parts: SATTBB. **Chorus roles:** Servants, Dutch officers, magistrates, sailors, inhabitants of Saardam, soldiers, waiters, carpenters, shipbuilders, women, wedding guests. **Dance/movement:** II: Wedding guests dance. III: national ballet. **Orchestra:** 2 fl (picc), 2 ob, 2 cl, 2 bsn, 4 hrn, 2 trp, 3 trb, timp, perc, strings. **Stageband:** I: picc, cl, 2 bsn, 2 hrn. **Publisher:** Universal Edition, C. F. Peters. **Rights:** Expired.

I. The tsar has spent a year working in the shipyards of Amsterdam disguised as the carpenter Peter Michaelov. Peter Ivanov confesses to the tsar that he deserted from the Russian army. His sweetheart, Marie, fears that her uncle, Burgomaster van Bett, will not allow them to marry. Admiral Lefort warns the tsar of rebellion at home. Two envoys, the French Marquis de Chateauneuf and the English Lord Syndham, are looking for the tsar. The marquis recognizes Michaelov and arranges an interview. Syndham bribes Van Bett to help him.

II. At a wedding celebration, Van Bett leads Syndham to Ivanov while the marquis works out a treaty with the tsar. Syndham is convinced Ivanov is the tsar. The inn is surrounded by Dutch soldiers who order the arrest of any foreigner who cannot properly identify himself. A scuffle ensues.

III. Van Bett still believes Ivanov is the tsar. The real tsar tries to return to Russia, but the harbor is blockaded. Syndham gives Ivanov a ship and men, which Ivanov gives to the tsar. Van Bett entertains Ivanov while the tsar escapes. Van Bett discovers his mistake and Ivanov shows him a letter giving the tsar's consent to the marriage of Ivanov and Marie.

Die Zauberflöte • The Magic Flute

Composed by Wolfgang Amadeus Mozart (January 27, 1756 – December 5, 1791). Libretto by Emanuel Schikaneder. German. Original work based on popular fairy tales, Masonic practices and "Sethos" by Jean Terrasson. Premiered Vienna, Theater an der Wien, September 30, 1791. Set in Sarastro's kingdom at an unspecified time. Singspiel. Set numbers with recitative and spoken dialogue. Overture. K. 620.

Sets: 12. **Acts:** 2 acts, 14 scenes. **Length:** I: 70. II: 80. **Arias:** "Der Vogelfänger bin ich ja" (Papageno), "Dies Bildnis" (Tamino), "Der Hölle Rache" (Queen of the night), "In diesen heilgen Hallen" (Sarastro), "Ach, ich fühl's" (Pamina), "Ein Mädchen oder Weibchen" (Papageno), "O Isis und Osiris" (Sarastro), "O zitt're nicht" (Queen). **Hazards:** I: Papagena transformed from an old woman into herself. II: Rapid scene changes, trials by fire and water. **Scenes:** Ii. A rough, rocky landscape. Iii. An elaborate Egyptian room. Iiii. A grove in the middle of which stand three temples. IIi. A forest of palm trees. IIii. Court of the temple at night. IIiii. A garden. IIiv. A short hallway. IIv. Interior of a pyramid. IIvi. A palm garden. IIvii. Rocky caves. IIviii. The temple. IIix. Garden. IIx. Rocky landscape. IIxi. Temple of the Sun.

Major roles: Tamino (tenor), Papageno (baritone), Queen of the night (coloratura soprano), Pamina (soprano), Sarastro (bass). **Minor roles:** First lady (soprano), Second lady (soprano or mezzo), Third lady (mezzo), Monostatos (tenor), Three genii (treble), Speaker of the temple (bass), Two priests (tenor, bass), Papagena (soprano), Two armored men (tenor, bass). **Speaking:** Three slaves. **Speaking bits:** Three priests.

Chorus parts: SATTBB. **Chorus roles:** Priests, slaves, people. **Dance/movement:** I: Magic bells set Monostatos and slaves dancing. **Orchestra:** 2 fl (picc), 2 ob, 2 cl (basset hrn), 2 bsn, 2 hrn, 2 trp, 3 trb, timp, glockenspiel, celeste, strings. **Stageband:** I, II: bs drum, perc. **Publisher:** Schirmer, Breitkopf and Härtel. **Rights:** Expired.

Ii. Prince Tamino is saved from a giant serpent by three ladies, who fight over who will tell the queen of the night. They go together. Recovering, the prince is convinced that Papageno, the bird catcher, is his savior. As punishment for this lie, Papageno has his mouth padlocked by the three ladies. They give Tamino a picture of Pamina, the queen's daughter. She is yours, the queen promises him—if you get her back from Sarastro, her father. Tamino is given a magic flute and Papageno a set of magic bells. Three young spirits guide them to Sarastro's castle. Iii. Monastatos's slaves are distraught that Monastatos has foiled Pamina's attempted escape. Papageno and Monostatos terrify each other. Pamina and Papageno escape. Iiii. The prince himself has been led to Sarastro's temple. He is met by a priest, who dismisses the queen's complaints as lies. A chorus of voices assures him that Pamina lives. Monastatos tries to recapture Papageno and Pamina but is foiled by the magic bells. Sarastro appears with his suite and says that he cannot let Pamina go as she must be guided by a man's hand. He punishes Monastatos. Tamino and Papageno are taken off for initiation into the brotherhood.

IIi. The priests concur in Sarastro's decision to test Tamino and Papageno. IIii. Two priests abjure Tamino and Papageno to silence and warn them against the wiles of women. The three ladies appear, but cannot get Tamino or Papageno to talk. IIiii. Seeing Pamina asleep in the garden, Monastatos is moved to kiss her. He is prevented by the arrival of the queen of the night, who gives Pamina a dagger and orders her to kill Sarastro. Monastatos has overheard everything and tries to use the information to blackmail Pamina. When she does not submit, he attacks her, but is stopped by Sarastro. Monastatos decides to throw in his lot with the queen of the night. IIiv. Papageno talks to an old woman. By order of Sarastro, the three spirits return Tamino's flute and Papageno's bells. When Pamina tries to speak with Tamino, he silently rebuffs her and she is griefstricken. IIv. Tamino is led off to the final trials. The gods forgive Papageno's weakness, the speaker tells him, but he cannot be admitted to the brotherhood. He again meets the old woman. She reveals herself as the young and pretty Papagena, but the speaker whisks her away. IIvi. Pamina contemplates suicide, but the spirits assure her that Tamino loves her. IIvii. Pamina is allowed to accompany Tamino through the trials of fire and water. The flute protects them. IIviii. The lovers are welcomed into the temple. IIix. Despairing of Papagena, Papageno tries to hang himself. He is prevented by the three spirits who tell him to summon Papagena with his magic bells. It works. IIx. The queen of the night, her ladies and Monastatos attack the temple and are defeated. IIxi. Sarastro, Tamino, Pamina and the brotherhood celebrate the triumph of good.

Zazà

Composed by Ruggero Leoncavallo (April 23, 1857 – August 9, 1919). Libretto by Ruggero Leoncavallo. Italian. After the play by Pierre Berton and Charles Simon. Premiered Milan, Teatro Lirico, November 10, 1900. Set in France in the 1890s. Lyric comedy. Through composed.

Sets: 3. **Acts:** 4 acts, 4 scenes. **Length:** I, II, III, IV: 120. **Arias:** "Zazà, piccola zingara" (Cascart), "Mamma usciva da casa" (Zazà). **Hazards:** None. **Scenes:** I. Backstage at the "Alcazar" in St. Étienne with Zazà's dressing room visible. II. The living room of Zazà's apartment. III. Drawing room in Dufresne's home in Paris. IV. Zazà's living room.

Major roles: Zazà (soprano), Milio Dufresne (tenor), Cascart (baritone).
Minor roles: Impressario Courtois (baritone), Floriana (soprano),
Journalist Bussy (baritone), Anaide (mezzo), Waiter Augusto (tenor),
Natalia (soprano), Mrs. Dufresne (soprano). **Bit part:** Marco (tenor),
Antonietta "Totò" Dufresne (treble). **Mute:** Theatrical performers
(includes Four Spanish dancers, Two singers in costume, Two gardero-
bières, Fireman, Two clowns, Gentleman, Singer in a soldier's uniform,
Two machinists, Scene shifter), Michelin the journalist, Duclou the stage
manager, Malardot, Lartigon, Claretta, Simona.

Chorus parts: N/A. **Chorus roles:** None. **Dance/movement:** None.
Orchestra: 2 fl (picc), 2 ob (Eng hrn), 2 cl, 2 bsn, 4 hrn, 3 trp, 3 trb, tuba,
timp, perc, 2 harp, strings. **Stageband:** III: Totò plays piano. **Publisher:**
Casa Musicale Sonzogno. **Rights:** Expired.

I. Zazà is a successful singer, having been rescued from poverty by her
lover and singing partner, Cascart. Her mother, Anaide, is an alcoholic.
Zazà seduces Dufresne.

II. Zazà and Dufresne are lovers. She convinces him not to make a four-
month trip to the United States. After Dufresne leaves for Paris, Cascart
tells Zazà that Dufresne has another love. Zazà follows Dufresne to
Paris.

III. Dufresne means to go to America—with his wife and daughter. Zazà
visits his house. He is out, but she meets his daughter, Totò. The thought
of her own impoverished and fatherless upbringing makes Zazà cry and
she leaves without telling Mrs. Dufresne the truth.

IV. Zazà returns to the theater. Dufresne visits her. She tells him she told
his wife everything. His fury—and his evident love for his wife—convinces Zazà that she must give him up. Heartbroken, she sends him
away.

Die Zigeunerbaron • The Gypsy Baron

Composed by Johann Strauss Jr. (October 25, 1825 – June 3, 1899).
Libretto by Ignatz Schnitzer. German. Based on "Saffi" by Maurus Jókai.
Premiered Vienna, Theater an der Wien, October 24, 1885. Set in
Hungary and Vienna in the mid-18th century. Operetta. Set numbers
with recitative and spoken dialogue. Overture. Entr'acte before II, III.

Sets: 3. **Acts:** 3 acts, 3 scenes. **Length:** I, II, III: 120. **Arias:** "So elend und
so treu" (Sáffi). **Hazards:** None. **Scenes:** I. Barinkay's ancestral lands in
Hungary. II. The ruins of an old castle in a gorge on the property. III.
The gates of Vienna, the "Kätnertor."

Major roles: Ottokar (tenor), Czipra (mezzo), Carnero (tenor, baritone or bass), Gypsy Baron Sandor Barinkay (tenor), Sáffi (soprano), Kalman Zsupán (comic baritone), Arsena (soprano). **Minor roles:** Mirabella (mezzo), Count Peter Homonay (tenor or baritone). **Bit parts:** Two girls (soprano, alto), Pali (soprano). **Speaking bit:** Boatman, servant, Laczi, Joszi, Ferko, gypsy, herald, Viennese man, chimney sweep, boy.

Chorus parts: SSAATTBB. **Chorus roles:** Boatmen, peasants, gypsies, soldiers, citizens of Vienna. **Dance/movement:** II: Dance of the Czardas. III: Optional ballet. **Orchestra:** 2 fl (picc), 2 ob, 2 cl, 2 bsn, 4 hrn, 2 trp, 3 trb, timp, perc, harp, glockenspiel, strings. **Stageband:** None. **Publisher:** Boosey & Hawkes. **Rights:** Expired.

I. Ottokar searches for the treasure purportedly buried by the owner of the estate before he died. Czipra, an old gypsy woman, laughs at his hopeless search and teases him about his love for Arsena. The estate now belongs to Barinky, who has come home to claim it. Barinky and Carnero (the Austrian commissioner of public morals) persuade Czipra and a rich pig farmer, Zsupan, to witness the document reinstating Barinkay as owner of the estate. Barinkay proposes to Zsupan's daughter, Arsena, who refuses to marry anyone less noble than a baron. Arsena's governess, Mirabella, recognizes Carnero as her long lost husband—and the father of Ottokar. Arsena loves Ottokar but her meeting with him is overheard by Barinkay. Ottokar gives Arsena a locket with his picture in it. The gypsies pledge alliegance to Barinkay. Barinkay uses this to claim he is noble—a gypsy baron. But he now wants to marry the gypsy Sáffi, not Arsena. Arsena, Zsupan and their friends are stung.

II. Guided by a dream of Sáffi, Barinkay locates the treasure. The gypsies work at their forges. Zsupan's wagon gets stuck in the mud. He sends a message to Barinkay, but while he is waiting the gypsies steal all his posessions. Careno objects that Barinkay's marriage to Sáffi is not legal. When Carnero realizes that Barinkay has found the hidden treasure, he demands it on behalf of the government. Barinkay refuses. Barinkay's friend Count Homonay comes to recruit for the army. Ottokar volunteers, and Zsupan is tricked into joining. Barinkay donates his money to Homonay's cause. Czirpa reveals that Sáffi is not really a gypsy: She is a princess and daughter of the last Pasha of Hungary. Barinkay despairs because Sáffi is now too high above him and he joins the hussars.

III. After two years, the Hungarian army returns victorious. Zsupan has managed to avoid battle. Barinkay is made a baron as reward for his bravery and his father's treasure is returned to him. Barinkay asks for Arsena's hand—for Ottokar. Carnero retires as commissioner of public morals. Barinkay is reunited with Sáffi.

INDICES

LIBRETTIST INDEX

SOPRANO ARIAS

"A dear forest deep" (Fevronia in "Skazanie o nevidimom grade Kitezhe")
"A Serpina penserete" (Serpina in "La Serva Padrona")
"Abscheulicher!"/"Komm, Hoffnung" (Leonore in "Fidelio")
"Ach ich liebte" (Konstanze in "Die Entführung aus dem Serail")
"Ach, ich fühl's" (Pamina in "Die Zauberflöte")
"Addio del passato" (Violetta in "La Traviata")
"Adieu, notre petite table" (Manon in "Manon")
"Ah fuggi il traditor!" (Elvira in "Don Giovanni")
"Ah je ris"/Jewel Song (Marguerite in "Faust")
"Ah se il crudel periglio" (Giunia in "Lucio Silla")
"Ah! Chacun le sait chacun le dit" (Marie in "La Fille du Régiment")
"Ah! donate il caro sposo" (Sofia in "Il Signor Bruschino")
"Ah! du moins accordez un azile" (Médée in "Médée")
"Ah! non credea mirarti" (Amina in "La Sonnambula")
"Ah! non giunge!" (Amina in "La Sonnambula")
"Ah, dagli scanni eterei" (Lina in "Stiffelio")
"Ah, I am worn out by grief" (Lisa in "Pikovaya Dama")
"Ah, love's sweet dream" (Mařenka in "Prodaná Nevěsta")
"Ain't it a pretty night" (Susannah in "Susannah")
"Al dolce guidami" (Anna in "Anna Bolena")
"Al voler di tua fortuna" (Rosmene in "Imeneo")
"All the streams and swamps are overflowing" (Fevronia in "Skazanie o nevidi-
    mom grade Kitezhe")
"Als in mitternacht'ger Stunde" (Jessonda in "Jessonda")
Alzira's cavatina (Alzira in "Alzira")
"Amor è qual vento" (Dorinda in "Orlando")
"Amor, celeste ebbrezza" (Anna in "Loreley")
"Amoretti, che ascosi qui siete" (Rosina in "La Finta Semplice")
"Amour ranime mon courage" (Juliette in "Roméo et Juliette")
"Amours divins" (Hélène in "La Belle Hélène")
"Anch'io dischiuso" (Abigaille in "Nabucco")
"Après avoir pris à droite" (Fiorella in "Les Brigands")
"Ardon gl'incensi"/Mad scene (Lucia in "Lucia di Lammermoor")
Aria V (Protagonist in "Un Re in Ascolto")
"As when the dove laments" (Galatea in "Acis and Galatea")
"Assisa a piè d'un salice"/Willow song (Desdemona in "Otello")
"Ave Maria" (Desdemona in "Otello")
"Batti, batti, o bel Masetto" (Zerlina in "Don Giovanni")
"Bel raggio lusinghier" (Semiramide in "Semiramide")
"Bester Jüngling" (Silverklang in "Der Schauspieldirektor")
"But why these tears" (Lisa in "Pikovaya Dama")
"C'est ici" (Béatrice in "Béatrice")
"Care selve" (Meleagro in "Atalanta")
"Caro nome" (Gilda in "Rigoletto")

"Casta diva" (Norma in "Norma")
"Che fieso momento" (Euridice in "Orfeo ed Euridice")
"Che il bel sogno" (Magda in "La Rondine")
"Che imbroglio è questo" (Sandrina in "L'Infedeltà Delusa")
"Chers enfants" (Médée in "Médée")
"Chi disse c'a femmena" (Vannella in "Lo Frate 'nnamorato")
"Chi ho veduto?" (Francesca in "Francesca da Rimini")
"Col sorriso d'innocenza" (Imogene in "Il Pirata")
"Com'è bello" (Lucrezia Bórgia in "Lucrezia Borgia")
"Come in quest'ora bruna" (Amelia in "Simon Boccanegra")
"Come per me sereno" (Amina in "La Sonnambula")
"Come scoglio" (Fiordiligi in "Così fan tutte")
"Comme autrefois" (Léïla in "Les Pêcheurs de Perles")
Composer's aria (Composer in "Ariadne auf Naxos")
"Connaistu le pays" (Mignon in "Mignon")
"Cor di padre" (Asteria in "Tamerlano")
Cosmetics aria (Bella in "The Midsummer Marriage")
Countess's final scene (Countess in "Capriccio")
"Crudeli, oh Dio!" (Sandrina in "La Finta Giardiniera")
"Da schlägt die Abschiedsstunde" (Herz in "Der Schauspieldirektor")
"Das war sehr gut" (Arabella in "Arabella")
"Day and night we praise" (Fevronia in "Skazanie o nevidimom grade Kitezhe")
"Day is dawning" (Angelica in "The Poisoned Kiss")
"Dearest, without joy how can we live?" (Fevronia in "Skazanie o nevidimom grade Kitezhe")
"Deh vieni non tardar" (Susanna in "Le Nozze di Figaro")
"Deh! tu di una umile preghiera" (Maria in "Maria Stuarda")
"Del primo pianto" (Turandot in "Turandot")
"Depuis le jour" (Louise in "Louise")
"Der Hölle Rache" (Queen of the night in "Die Zauberflöte")
"Der kleine Sandman bin ich" (Sandman in "Hänsel und Gretel")
"Dès l'enfance les mêmes chaines" (Zerlina in "Fra Diavolo")
"Di piacer mi balza il cor" (Ninetta in "La Gazza Ladra")
"Dich, teure Halle" (Elisabeth in "Tannhäuser")
"Die Brust, gebeugt von Sorgen" (Florinda in "Fierrabras")
"Die Zeit" (Marschallin in "Der Rosenkavalier")
"Divinités du Styx" (Alceste in "Alceste")
"Dort am jenen Felsenhang" (Emmy in "Der Vampyr")
"Dove sono?" (Countess in "Le Nozze di Figaro")
"È la pompa un grand' imbroglio" (Sandrina in "L'Infedeltà Delusa")
"Ecco l'orrido campo" (Amelia in "Un Ballo in Maschera")
"Eh quoi, je suis Médée" (Médée in "Médée")
"Einsam in trüben Tagen" / Elsa's dream (Elsa in "Lohengrin")
"Elle a fui" (Antonia in "Le Contes d'Hoffmann")
"Embroidery" (Ellen in "Peter Grimes")
"En proie à la tristesse" (Countess in "Le Comte Ory")
"En vain j'espère un sort prospère" (Isabelle in "Robert le Diable")

"Er ist der Richtige nicht für mich!" (Arabella in "Arabella")
"Er mein-ich sein" (Arabella in "Arabella")
"Ernani involami" (Elvira in "Ernani")
"Es pocht mein Herz" (Turandot in "Turandot")
"Espoir si cher et si doux" (Cybèle in "Atys")
"Falsacappa voici ma prise" (Fragoletto in "Les Brigands")
"Farewell, O native hills and fields" (Joan in "Orleanskaya Deva")
"Felice cor mio" (Drusilla in "L'Incoronazione di Poppea")
"Flammen, perdonami" (Lodoletta in "Lodoletta")
"Frà i pensier più funesti" (Giunia in "Lucio Silla")
"Già riede primavera" (Rosina in "Il Barbiere di Siviglia")
"Glitter and be Gay" (Cunegonde in "Candide")
"Glöcklein im Thale" (Euryanthe in "Euryanthe")
"Glück, das mir verblieb" (Marietta in "Die Tote Stadt")
Gold aria (Trina in "McTeague")
Grilletta mocking aria (Grilletta in "Lo Speziale")
"Grossmächtige Prinzessin" (Zerbinetta in "Ariadne auf Naxos")
Herzeleide (Kundry in "Parsifal")
"Ho tesa la rete" (Vespina in "L'Infedeltà Delusa")
"Ho un tumore" (Vespina in "L'Infedeltà Delusa")
"Hohe Götter!" (Jessonda in "Jessonda")
"Holy father, they call me Joan" (Joan in "Orleanskaya Deva")
"Höre ich Zigeunergeigen" (Maritza in "Gräfin Maritza")
"How can I such lovely visions of the mind deny?" (Jenifer in "The Midsummer
     Marriage")
"How sad it is in the castle" (Princess in "Čert a Káča")
"Hymen, viens dissiper une vaine frayeur" (Glauce in "Médée")
Hymn to the sun (Queen of Chémakhâ in "Zolotoy Petuschok")
"I am the wife of Mao Tse-tung" (Chiang Ch'ing in "Nixon in China")
"I dreamt that I dwelt in marble halls" (Arline in "The Bohemian Girl")
"I want no pity" (Denise in "The Knot Garden")
"I've dreamt in my life" (Catherine in "Wuthering Heights")
"Idol mio" (Elettra in "Idomeneo")
"Il est doux, il est bon (Salomé in "Hérodiade")
"Il me fuit, l'inconstant!" (Théone in "Phaëton")
"Il mio ben quando verrà" (Nina in "Nina")
"Il ne revient pas" / Spinning Wheel Song (Marguerite in "Faust")
"Il padre adorato" (Idamante in "Idomeneo")
"Il vecchioto cerca moglie" (Berta in "Il Barbiere di Siviglia")
"Illustratevi o cieli" (Penelope in "Il Ritorno d'Ulisse in Patria")
Immolation scene (Brünnhilde in "Götterdämmerung")
"In a moment" (Kostelnička in "Jenůfa")
"In quelle trine morbide" (Manon in "Manon Lescaut")
"In questa reggia" (Turandot in "Turandot")
"In uomini" (Despina in "Così fan tutte")
"Intorno all'idol mio" (Orontea in "L'Orontea")
Invocation à Hécate (Médée in "Médée")

"Io son l'umile ancella" (Adriana in "Adriana Lecouvreur")
"It was a beautiful dream" (Ludiše in "Braniboři v Čechách")
Jaroslavna's lament (Jaroslavna in "Knyaz' Igor'")
"Je dis que rien" (Micaëla in "Carmen")
"Je t'implore et je tremble" (Iphigénie in "Iphigénie en Tauride")
"Je vais le voir" (Héro in "Béatrice et Bénédict")
"Je vais mourir" (Dido in "Les Troyens")
"Je veux vivre" (Juliette in "Roméo et Juliette")
Jenůfa's prayer (Jenůfa in "Jenůfa")
"Jo ho hoe" / Senta's ballad (Senta in "Die Fliegende Holländer")
Joy aria (Milada in "Dalibor")
"Klänge der Heimat" (Rosalinda in "Die Fledermaus")
"L'altra notte" (Margherita in "Mefistofele")
"L'amerò sarò costante" (Aminta in "Il Re Pastore")
"L'amour ce divin maître" (Minka in "Le Roi Malgré Lui")
"L'année en vain" (Lia in "L'Enfant Prodigue")
"La luce langue" (Lady Macbeth in "Macbeth")
"La mamma morta" (Maddalena in "Andrea Chénier")
"La mort m'apparaît souriante" (Eurydice in "Orphée aux Enfers")
"Lascia ch'io pianga" (Almirena in "Rinaldo")
Laurie's song (Laurie in "The Tender Land")
"Leise, leise, fromme Weise" (Agathe in "Der Freischütz")
"Les oiseaux dans la charmille" (Olympia in "Le Contes d'Hoffmann")
Letter aria (Baby Doe in "The Ballad of Baby Doe")
Letter aria (Tatyana in "Yevgeny Onyegin")
"Licinius, je vais donc te revoir" (Julia in "La Vestale")
"Lo sguardo avea degli angeli" (Amalia in "I Masnadieri")
"Lontano da te, Lindoro" (Nina in "Nina")
"Love sounds th'alarm" (Acis in "Acis and Galatea")
"Lover, come back to me" (Marianne in "The New Moon")
Lulu's lied (Lulu in "Lulu")
"Madre, pietosa vergine" (Leonora in "La Forza del Destino")
"Mamma usciva da casa" (Zazà in "Zazà")
"Martern aller Arten" (Konstanze in "Die Entführung aus dem Serail")
"Mein Herr Marquis" / Laughing song (Adele in "Die Fledermaus")
"Mercé, dilette amiche" (Elena in "I Vespri Siciliani")
"Mi chiamano Mimì" (Mimì in "La Bohème")
"Mi lasci, mi fuggi" (Dorinda in "Il Pastor Fido")
"Mi tradì quell'alma ingrata" (Elvira in "Don Giovanni")
"Mild und leise" / Liebestod (Isolde in "Tristan und Isolde")
"Miserere" / "D'amor sull' ali rosee" (Leonora in "Il Trovatore")
"Morrò, ma prima in grazia" (Amelia in "Un Ballo in Maschera")
Musetta's aria (Musetta in "La Bohème")
"Musette svaria sulla bocca viva" (Mimì in "La Bohème")
"Nè mai dunque" (Wally in "La Wally")
"Nel villaggio d'Edgar" (Fidelia in "Edgar")
Nightingale's song (Nightingale in "Solovey")

"No little time has passed" (Jaroslavna in "Knyaz' Igor'")
"Non mi dir" (Anna in "Don Giovanni")
"Non pianger, mia compagna" (Elisabetta in "Don Carlo")
"Non più di fiori" (Vitellia in "La Clemenza di Tito")
"Non so più cosa son, cosa faccio" (Cherubino in "Le Nozze di Figaro")
"Now I flee" (Etherea in "Výlet pana Broučka do XV století/Výlet pana Broučka
    do Měsíce")
"O Bastien" (Bastienne in "Bastien und Bastienne")
"Ô beau pays de la Touraine" (Marguerite in "Les Huguenots")
"O cieli azzurri"/"O patria mia"/Nile aria (Aïda in "Aïda")
"O fatidica foresta" (Giovanna in "Giovanna d'Arco")
"O luce di quest' anima" (Linda in "Linda di Chamounix")
"O malheureuse Iphigénie" (Iphigénie in "Iphigénie en Tauride")
"O messager de Dieu" (Thaïs in "Thaïs")
"O mio bambino caro" (Lauretta in "Gianni Schicchi")
"O mon cher amant" (Périchole in "La Périchole")
"Ô mon miroir fidèle" (Thaïs in "Thaïs")
"O quante volte" (Giulietta in "I Capuleti e i Montecchi")
"O silver moon" (Rusalka in "Rusalka")
"O toi, qui prolongeas mes jours" (Iphigénie in "Iphigénie en Tauride")
"O wär' ich schon mit dir vereint" (Marzelline in "Fidelio")
"O zitt're nicht" (Queen in "Die Zauberflöte")
"Ocean, thou mighty monster" (Reiza in "Oberon")
"Oh Nelly, I've fallen in love with him" (Isabella in "Wuthering Heights")
"Oh sweet Jesus, spare me this agony" (Annina in "The Saint of Bleecker Street")
"Ombra cara" (Radamisto in "Radamisto")
"Ombra mai fù" (Serse in "Serse")
"Or sai, chi l'onore" (Anna in "Don Giovanni")
"Où va la jeune Hindoue?"/Bell song (Lakmé in "Lakmé")
"Pace, pace" (Leonora in "La Forza del Destino")
"Paolo, datemi pace!" (Francesca in "Francesca da Rimini")
"Partagez-vous mes fleurs" (Ophélie in "Hamlet")
"Parto, m'affretto" (Giunia in "Lucio Silla")
"Per pietà" (Fiordiligi in "Così fan tutte")
"Piangea cantando"/Willow song (Desdemona in "Otello")
"Più non vive!" (Lucrezia in "I Due Foscari")
"Pleurez mes yeux" (Chimène in "Le Cid")
"Porgi, amor" (Countess in "Le Nozze di Figaro")
"Poveri fiori" (Adriana in "Adriana Lecouvreur")
"Pussi" (Lulu in "Lulu")
"Qual onor di te sia degno" (Orfeo in "La Favola d'Orfeo")
"Que fais-tu blanche tourterelle" (Stéphano in "Roméo et Juliette")
"Qui la voce" (Elvira in "I Puritani")
"Quietly night" (Anne in "The Rake's Progress")
"Regnava nel silenzio" (Lucia in "Lucia di Lammermoor")
"Respirons un moment" (Sophia in "Tom Jones")
"Ritorna vincitor!" (Aïda in "Aïda")

Roxane's aria (Roxane in "Król Roger")
Sabre song (Margot in "The Desert Song")
"Salut à la France" (Marie in "La Fille du Régiment")
"Salve Maria" (Giselda in "I Lombardi alla Prima Crociata")
"Se come voi" (Anna in "Le Villi")
"Se non mi vuol amar" (Asteria in "Tamerlano")
"Sempre all'alba ed alla sera" (Giovanna in "Giovanna d'Arco")
"Sempre così sul margine del sogno" (Ginevra in "La Cena delle Beffe")
"Sempre libera"/"Ah! fors'è lui" (Violetta in "La Traviata")
"Senti l'eco ove t'aggiri" (Rosina in "La Finta Semplice")
"Senza mamma" (Angelica in "Suor Angelica")
"Sì, ma d'un altro Amore" (Silvia in "Ascanio in Alba")
"Signor, ascolta" (Liù in "Turandot")
Silver aria (Baby Doe in "The Ballad of Baby Doe")
"So anch'io la virtù magica" (Norina in "Don Pasquale")
"So elend und so treu" (Sáffi in "Die Zigeunerbaron")
"Sola, perduta, abbandonata" (Manon in "Manon Lescaut")
"Sombre forêt" (Mathilde in "Guillaume Tell")
"Somehow I never could believe" (Anna in "Street Scene")
"Sotto il paterno tetto" (Leonora in "Oberto")
"Steal me, sweet thief" (Laetitia in "The Old Maid and the Thief")
"Stizzoso, mio stizzoso" (Serpina in "La Serva Padrona")
"Stridono lassù" (Nedda in "Pagliacci")
"Suicidio!" (Gioconda in "La Gioconda")
"Sul fil d'un soffio" (Nannetta in "Falstaff")
"Summertime" (Clara in "Porgy and Bess")
"T'arretri e palpiti!" (Giovanna in "Giovanna d'Arco")
"Tacea la notte"/"Di tale amor" (Leonora in "Il Trovatore")
"The Lover and the Nightingale" (Rosario in "Goyescas")
The Mother's Song (Julie in "Jakobín")
The Plaint (Juno in "The Fairy Queen")
"The sacred tree" (Monisha in "Treemonisha")
"The sun, whose rays are all ablaze" (Yum-Yum in "The Mikado")
"The trees on the mountains" (Susannah in "Susannah")
"The world is wide" (Minette in "Die Englische Katze")
"There was a time" (Tormentilla in "The Poisoned Kiss")
"This is prophetic" (Pat in "Nixon in China")
"Thrice happy lovers" (Juno in "The Fairy Queen")
"To this we've come" (Magda in "The Consul")
Todesverkündigung (Brünnhilde in "Die Walküre")
"Toi que j'implore"/"Impitoyables dieux" (Julia in "La Vestale")
"Toi que je laisse sur la terre mortel" (Julia in "La Vestale")
"Traurigkeit" (Konstanze in "Die Entführung aus dem Serail")
"Trinche vaine allegramente" (Vespina in "L'Infedeltà Delusa")
"Tristes apprêts" (Télaïre in "Castor et Pollux")
"Tu che la vanità conoscesti del mondo" (Elisabetta in "Don Carlo")
"Tu n'es pas beau" (Périchole in "La Périchole")

"Tu puniscimi, O signore" (Luisa in "Luisa Miller")
"Tu sei morta" (Orfeo in "La Favola d'Orfeo")
"Ulysse! fier époux!" (Pénélope in "Pénélope")
"Un bel dì" (Butterfly in "Madama Butterfly")
"Una donna di quindici anni" (Despina in "Così fan tutte")
"Una macchia" (Lady Macbeth in "Macbeth")
"Una voce poco fa" (Rosina in "Il Barbiere di Siviglia")
"V'adoro pupille" (Cleopatra in "Giulio Cesare")
"Vedrai, carino" (Zerlina in "Don Giovanni")
"Venite inginocchiatevi" (Susanna in "Le Nozze di Figaro")
"Verdi prati" (Ruggiero in "Alcina")
"Vieni, t'affretta" (Lady Macbeth in "Macbeth")
Vilja-Lied (Hanna in "Die Lustige Witwe")
"Vissi d'arte" (Tosca in "Tosca")
"Vivi, ingrato" (Elisabetta in "Roberto Devereux")
"Voi lo sapete o mamma" (Santuzza in "Cavalleria Rusticana")
"Voi, che sapete" (Cherubino in "Le Nozze di Figaro")
"Volta la terrea" (Oscar in "Un Ballo in Maschera")
"Vorrei spiegarvi il giubilo" (Fanny in "La Cambiale di Matrimonio")
"Vous êtes sons fils, je le jure" (Clymène in "Phaëton")
"Welche Wonne, welche Lust" (Blöndchen in "Die Entführung aus dem Serail")
"Were I ever to learn that you had ceased to care" (Mařenka in "Prodaná
     Nevĕsta")
"Wh' mir, so nah' die fürchterliche Stunde" (Ada in "Die Feen")
"What shall I do to show how much I love?" (Polly in "The Beggar's Opera")
"What use would the moon be?" (Rose in "Street Scene")
"When I am laid in earth" (Dido in "Dido and Æneas")
"Why did I not know this before?" (Iolanta in "Iolanta")
"Wie lange ist's her" (Laura in "Neues vom Tage")
"Wie muss ich doch beklagen" (Ada in "Die Feen")
Willow song (Baby Doe in "The Ballad of Baby Doe")
"Wird Philomele trauern" (Fatime in "Abu Hassan")
"You gods, you deathless gods" (Cressida in "Troilus and Cressida")
"Zeffiretti lusinghieri" (Ilia in "Idomeneo")
"Zu ihm! zu ihm!" (Euryanthe in "Euryanthe")

MEZZO ARIAS

"A questo seno" (Lucia in "La Gazza Ladra")
"Ah que j'aime les militaires" (Grand Duchess in "La Grande Duchesse de
     Gérolstein")
"Ah! se non'mami più" (Isoletta in "La Straniera")
"Amour, viens aider ma faiblesse" (Dalila in "Samson et Dalila")
"Ardo, sospiro e piango" (Diana in "La Calisto")
Augusta's lament (Augusta in "The Ballad of Baby Doe")
"Bethörte!" (Eglantine in "Euryanthe")

"Catarina, je chante" (Amoroso in "Les Pont des Soupirs")

"Che città!" (Nerillo in "L'Ormindo")

"Chi mi toglie al dìe" (Sicle in "L'Ormindo")

Chicken song (Örzse in "Háry János")

"Cieca notte" (Ariodante in "Ariodante")

"Con l'ali di costanza" (Ariodante in "Ariodante")

"Connaistu le pays" (Mignon in "Mignon")

"Da quel suon soavemente" (Musette in "La Bohème")

"Dieu! que viens-je d'entendre" / "Il m'en souvient" (Béatrice in "Béatrice et Bénédict")

"Disprezzata regina" (Ottavia in "L'Incoronazione di Poppea")

"Dolce d'amor compagna" (Ramiro in "La Finta Giardiniera")

"Dopo notte" (Ariodante in "Ariodante")

"Farewell, O native hills and fields" (Joan in "Orleanskaya Deva")

"Gerechter Gott" (Adriano in "Rienzi")

"Holy father, they call me Joan" (Joan in "Orleanskaya Deva")

"Il capro e la capretta" (Marcellina in "Le Nozze di Figaro")

"Il vecchioto cerca moglie" (Berta in "Il Barbiere di Siviglia")

"Je vais mourir" (Dido in "Les Troyens")

"Jupiter, lance la foudre" (Clytemnestre in "Iphigénie en Aulide")

"L'amour est un oiseau rebelle" (Carmen in "Carmen")

"Les tringles des sistres tintaient" (Carmen in "Carmen")

"Mon coeur s'ouvre à ta voix" (Dalila in "Samson et Dalila")

"Nel giardin del bello" / Veil song (Eboli in "Don Carlo")

"Nel profondo cieco mondo" (Orlando in "Orlando Furioso")

"Nobles seigneurs" (Urbain in "Les Huguenots")

"Non so più cosa son, cosa faccio" (Cherubino in "Le Nozze di Figaro")

"Nonne erubeskite, reges clamáre" (Jocasta in "Oedipus Rex")

"O don fatale" (Eboli in "Don Carlo")

"Ô ma lyre immortelle" (Sapho in "Sapho")

"O mein Leid" (Eglantine in "Euryanthe")

"O mon cher amant" (Périchole in "La Périchole")

"Ô mon Fernand" (Léonor in "La Favorite")

"Ô Prêtres de Baal" (Fidès in "Le Prophète")

"Oh chi torna l'ardente pensiero" (Cuniza in "Oberto")

"Oh London is a fine town" (Mrs in "The Beggar's Opera")

"Ombra mai fù" (Serse in "Serse")

Orlofsky's aria (Orlofsky in "Die Fledermaus")

"Par che mi nasca" (Irene in "Tamerlano")

"Par un père cruel" (Clytemnestre in "Iphigénie en Aulide")

"Parto, parto" (Sesto in "La Clemenza di Tito")

"Près des remparts de Séville" / Seguidilla (Carmen in "Carmen")

"Qual onor di te sia degno" (Orfeo in "La Favola d'Orfeo")

"Quand la femme a vingt ans" (Dulcinée in "Don Quichotte")

"Que fais-tu blanche tourterelle" (Stéphano in "Roméo et Juliette")

Samira's aria (Samira in "The Ghosts of Versailles")

"Scherza infida" (Ariodante in "Ariodante")

"Stride la vampa" (Azucena in "Il Trovatore")
Susanna's aria (Susanna in "The Ghosts of Versailles")
"Toi, le coeur de la rose" (Child in "L'Enfant et les Sortilèges")
"Tu il cuor mi strazi" (Tigrana in "Edgar")
"Tu n'es pas beau" (Périchole in "La Périchole")
"Tu sei morta" (Orfeo in "La Favola d'Orfeo")
"Una voce poco fa" (Rosina in "Il Barbiere di Siviglia")
"Va pure ad altri" (Ramiro in "La Finta Giardiniera")
"Va, laisse couleur" (Charlotte in "Werther")
"Verdi prati" (Ruggiero in "Alcina")
"Vivere in fretta" (Bersi in "Andrea Chénier")
"Voi, che sapete" (Cherubino in "Le Nozze di Figaro")
"Were I thy bride" (Phoebe in "Yeomen of the Guard")
"When Frederic was a little lad" (Ruth in "The Pirates of Penzance")
"When maiden loves" (Phoebe in "Yeomen of the Guard")
"When our gallant Norman foes" (Carruthers in "Yeomen of the Guard")
"You gods, you deathless gods" (Cressida in "Troilus and Cressida")

CONTRALTO ARIAS

"Ah si pera" (Malcolm in "La Donna del Lago")
"Ah, sì, morrò" (Admeto in "Admeto")
"Ah, Tanya, Tanya" (Olga in "Yevgeny Onyegin")
"Amour, viens aider ma faiblesse" (Dalila in "Samson et Dalila")
"Bella Asteria" (Andronico in "Tamerlano")
"Benchè mi sprezzi" (Andronico in "Tamerlano")
"Cieca notte" (Ariodante in "Ariodante")
"Cielo! se tu il consenti" (Orlando in "Orlando")
"Con l'ali di costanza" (Ariodante in "Ariodante")
"Cruda sorte" (Isabella in "L'Italiana in Algeri")
"Di tanti palpiti" (Tancredi in "Tancredi")
"Dopo notte" (Ariodante in "Ariodante")
"Fammi combattere" (Orlando in "Orlando")
"Flowers alone are chaste" (Lucretia in "The Rape of Lucretia")
"Forte e lieto" (Andronico in "Tamerlano")
"I know a bank where the wild thyme blows" (Oberon in "A Midsummer
    Night's Dream")
"Il segreto per esser felice" (Orsini in "Lucrezia Borgia")
Lell's songs (Lell in "Snegurochka")
"Mon coeur s'ouvre à ta voix" (Dalila in "Samson et Dalila")
"Nobles seigneurs" (Urbain in "Les Huguenots")
"Oblivion soave" (Arnalta in "L'Incoronazione di Poppea")
"Ombra cara" (Radamisto in "Radamisto")
"One charming night" (Secrecy in "The Fairy Queen")
"Pensa alla patria" (Isabella in "L'Italiana in Algeri")
"Per lui che adoro" (Isabella in "L'Italiana in Algeri")

"Rè dell'abisso" (Ulrica in "Un Ballo in Maschera")
"Scherza infida" (Ariodante in "Ariodante")
"Sol da te, mio dolce amore" (Ruggiero in "Orlando Furioso")
"Sorge nell'alma mia" (Tirinto in "Imeneo")
Sosostris's aria (Sosostris in "The Midsummer Marriage")
"Sultry heat has supplanted shade of night" (Ratmir in "Russlan and Ludmilla")
"Una volta c'era un re" (Angelina in "La Cenerentola")
"Unhappy, prince?" (Kontchak in "Knyaz' Igor'")
"Verdi allori" (Medoro in "Orlando")
"Voce di donna" (Cieca in "La Gioconda")

COUNTERTENOR ARIAS

"Ah, sì, morrò" (Admeto in "Admeto")
"Bella Asteria" (Andronico in "Tamerlano")
"Benchè mi sprezzi" (Andronico in "Tamerlano")
"Care selve" (Meleagro in "Atalanta")
"Cielo! se tu il consenti" (Orlando in "Orlando")
"Fammi combattere" (Orlando in "Orlando")
"Forte e lieto" (Andronico in "Tamerlano")
"I know a bank where the wild thyme blows" (Oberon in "A Midsummer
      Night's Dream")
"Lucidissima face" (Endimione in "La Calisto")
"Ombra cara" (Radamisto in "Radamisto")
"Ombra mai fù" (Serse in "Serse")
"One charming night" (Secrecy in "The Fairy Queen")
"Thus the gloomy world" (Chinese man in "The Fairy Queen")
"Verdi prati" (Ruggiero in "Alcina")

TENOR ARIAS

"A suoi piedi" (Bajazet in "Tamerlano")
"A te dirò" (Roberto in "Roberto Devereux")
"A te, o cara" (Arturo in "I Puritani")
"A wandering minstrel I" (Nanki-Poo in "The Mikado")
"Ach so fromm" (Lionel in "Martha")
"Addio fiorito asil" (Pinkerton in "Madama Butterfly")
"Adieu, Mignon!" (Wilhelm in "Mignon")
"Ah mes amis" (Tonio in "La Fille du Régiment")
"Ah non guardarmi" (Lefebvre in "Madame Sans-Gêne")
"Ah sì, ben mio" (Manrico in "Il Trovatore")
"Ah, fuyez douce image" (des Grieux in "Manon")
"Ah, la paterna mano" (Macduff in "Macbeth")
"Ah, ritrovarla" (Flammen in "Lodoletta")
"Al infelice veglio conforta" (Jacopo in "I Due Foscari")
"Alle giubbe scarlatte diam la caccia" (Lefebvre in "Madame Sans-Gêne")

"Allmächt'ger Vater" (Rienzi in "Rienzi")
"Alwa's hymn/"Kuss! Einen Kuss!" (Alwa in "Lulu")
"Am stillen Herd" (Walter in "Die Meistersinger von Nürnberg")
"Amor ti vieta" (Loris in "Fedora")
"Ange si pur" (Fernand in "La Favorite")
"Anges du Paradis" (Vincent in "Mireille")
"Antri ch'a miei lamenti" (Orfeo in "Euridice")
"Asile héréditaire" (Arnold in "Guillaume Tell")
"Celeste Aïda" (Radamès in "Aïda")
"Cercherò lontana terra" (Ernesto in "Don Pasquale")
"Ces airs joyeux" (Azaël in "L'Enfant Prodigue")
"Cessa di più resistere" (Almaviva in "Il Barbiere di Siviglia")
"Ch'ella mi creda" (Dick Johnson in "La Fanciulla del West")
"Chanson de guerre" (Jean in "Le Jongleur de Notre Dame")
"Che farò senza Euridice?" (Orfeo in "Orfeo ed Euridice")
"Che gelida manina" (Rodolfo in "La Bohème")
"Ciel! Quelle vapeur m'environne" (Atys in "Atys")
"Cielo e mar" (Enzo in "La Gioconda")
"Com'è gentil" (Ernesto in "Don Pasquale")
"Come un bel dì di Maggio" (Chénier in "Andrea Chénier")
"Dai campi" (Faust in "Mefistofele")
"Dal labbro" (Fenton in "Falstaff")
"Dalla sua pace" (Ottavio in "Don Giovanni")
"Dans le sein d'un ami fidèle" (Cinna in "La Vestale")
"De'miei bollenti spiriti" (Alfredo in "La Traviata")
"Dento il mio petto" (Don Anchise in "La Finta Giardiniera")
"Der Abend sinkt" (Eginhard in "Fierrabras")
"Di provenza il mar" (Germont in "La Traviata")
"Di quella pira" (Manrico in "Il Trovatore")
"Di rigori armato il seno" (Italian tenor in "Der Rosenkavalier")
"Dies Bildnis" (Tamino in "Die Zauberflöte")
"Dio, che orrenda notte!" (Roberto in "Le Villi")
"Dio, mi potevi" (Otello in "Otello")
"Donna non vidi mai" (des Grieux in "Manon Lescaut")
"Durch die Wälder" (Max in "Der Freischütz")
"È il sol dell'anima" (Duke in "Rigoletto")
"E lucevan le stelle" (Cavaradossi in "Tosca")
"Early one morning" (Kudrjáš in "Káťa Kabanová")
"Ecco ridente" (Almaviva in "Il Barbiere di Siviglia")
"Elle est là" (Henri Smith in "La Jolie Fille de Perth")
"En fermant les yeux" (des Grieux in "Manon")
"Fanget an!" (Walter in "Die Meistersinger von Nürnberg")
"Firenze è come un albero fiorito" (Rinuccio in "Gianni Schicchi")
"Forgive me, adorable creature" (Herman in "Pikovaya Dama")
"Fra poco a me" (Edgardo in "Lucia di Lammermoor")
"From a clear sky" (Žvný in "Osud")
"From boyhood trained" (Sir Huon in "Oberon")

"Funeste piagge, ombrosi orridi campi" (Orfeo in "Euridice")
"Fuor del mar" (Idomeneo in "Idomeneo")
"Gern hab' ich die Frau'n geküsst" (Paganini in "Paganini")
"Già il sol si cela dietro la montagna" (Shepherd in "Nina")
"Gioite al canto mio" (Orfeo in "Euridice")
"Giorno di pianto" (Arrigo in "I Vespri Siciliani")
"Godo anc'io" (Ulisse in "Il Ritorno d'Ulisse in Patria")
"Grüss' mir mein Wien'" (Tassilo in "Gräfin Maritza")
"Ha, wie das grauenvolle Bild" (Aubry in "Der Vampyr")
"Halloh!" (Arindal in "Die Feen")
"Here I stand" (Tom in "The Rake's Progress")
"Herz, verzage nicht geschwind" (Zuniga in "Der Corregidor")
"Horche, die Lerche singt" (Fenton in "Die Lustigen Weiber von Windsor")
"I accept their verdict" (Vere in "Billy Budd")
"I don't even know her name" (Herman in "Pikovaya Dama")
"I know that you all hate me" (Michele in "The Saint of Bleecker Street")
"I know you all" (Hal in "At the Boar's Head")
"I thought I loved Maria" (Amaryllus in "The Poisoned Kiss")
"I, an unhappy shepherd" (Jirka in "Čert a Káča")
"Ich baue ganz" (Belmonte in "Die Entführung aus dem Serail")
"Ich hab' kein Geld" (Symon in "Der Bettelstudent")
"Ich sehe einen jungen Mann dort stehn" (Boccaccio in "Boccaccio")
"If one last doubt, one lurking fear remain" (Troilus in "Troilus and Cressida")
"Il était une fois à la cour d'Eisenbach" / La légende de Kleinzach (Hoffmann in
     "Le Contes d'Hoffmann")
"Il mio tesoro intanto" (Ottavio in "Don Giovanni")
"Il padre adorato" (Idamante in "Idomeneo")
"In des Lebens Frühlingstagen" (Florestan in "Fidelio")
"In fernam Land" (Lohengrin in "Lohengrin")
"In quegli anni" (Basilio in "Le Nozze di Figaro")
"In tiefbewegter Brust" (Fierrabras in "Fierrabras")
"Inbrunst im Herzen" (Tannhäuser in "Tannhäuser")
"Inghirlandata di violette" (Paolo in "Francesca da Rimini")
"Io la vidi" (Carlo in "Don Carlo")
"Io trar non voglio" (Gerardo in "Caterina Cornaro")
"It ain't necessarily so" (Sporting Life in "Porgy and Bess")
"It happened long ago" (Levko in "Maiskaya Noch")
"Je crois entendre encore" (Nadir in "Les Pêcheurs de Perles")
"Je plains ses malheurs" (Phaëton in "Phaëton")
"Je suis Brésilien" (Brazilian in "La Vie Parisienne")
"Je vois marcher sous ma bannière" (Fra Diavolo in "Fra Diavolo")
"Jour et nuit" (Franz in "Le Contes d'Hoffmann")
Katz's aria (Katz in "The Postman Always Rings Twice")
"Komm Zigany!" (Tassilo in "Gräfin Maritza")
"L'amour, oui, son ardeur a troublé" (Roméo in "Roméo et Juliette")
"La donna è mobile" (Duke in "Rigoletto")
"La fleur que tu m'avais jetée" / Flower song (José in "Carmen")

"La mia letizia" (Oronte in "I Lombardi alla Prima Crociata")
"Là rivedrà nell'estasi" (Riccardo in "Un Ballo in Maschera")
"Languir per una bella" (Lindoro in "L'Italiana in Algeri")
Lenski's aria (Lenski in "Yevgeny Onyegin")
"Les affaires sont les affaires" (Malatromba in "Les Pont des Soupirs")
"Liberi vos liberabo" (Oedipus in "Oedipus Rex")
"Liberté!" (Jean in "Le Jongleur de Notre Dame")
"Lonely house" (Sam in "Street Scene")
"Long Live the Worm" (Bégearss in "The Ghosts of Versailles")
"Love sounds th'alarm" (Acis in "Acis and Galatea")
Luka's story (Luka in "Z Mrtvého Domu")
"Ma se m'è forza perderti" (Riccardo in "Un Ballo in Maschera")
"Ma-ma-ma-ma, so dear" (Vašek in "Prodaná Nevěsta")
"Mac the Knife" (Macheath in "Die Dreigroschenoper")
"Mai volsi ch'il mio core" (Erice in "L'Ormindo")
"Marianne" (Robert in "The New Moon")
"Meco all'altar di Venere" (Pollione in "Norma")
"Merci doux crépuscule" (Faust in "La Damnation de Faust")
"Mes amis, écoutez l'histoire" (Chapelou in "Le Postillon de Lonjumeau")
"Moi, je suis Aristée" (Aristée in "Orphée aux Enfers")
"Morgenlich leuchtend'"/Prize song (Walter in "Die Meistersinger von
    Nürnberg")
"Nel pur ardor" (Tirsi in "Euridice")
"Nessun dorma" (Calaf in "Turandot")
"Niun mi tema" (Otello in "Otello")
"No! pazzo son!" (des Grieux in "Manon Lescaut")
"Non maledirmi" (Jacopo in "I Due Foscari")
"Non piango e non sospiro" (Orfeo in "Euridice")
"Non, non je vis encore" (Licinius in "La Vestale")
"Nothung! Nothung!" (Siegfried in "Siegfried")
"Now the Great Bear" (Grimes in "Peter Grimes")
"O bien-aimée" (Araquil in "La Navarraise")
"O gran figlio d'Ulisse" (Eumete in "Il Ritorno d'Ulisse in Patria")
"O mon hôte, à présent" (Ulysse in "Pénélope")
"Ô Nature" (Werther in "Werther")
"Ô Paradis" (Vasco di Gama in "L'Africaine")
"O soave vision" (Edgar in "Edgar")
"Ô souverain" (Rodrigue in "Le Cid")
"O tu che in seno" (Don Alvaro in "La Forza del Destino")
"O Vaterland" (Danilo in "Die Lustige Witwe")
"Oblivion soave" (Arnalta in "L'Incoronazione di Poppea")
"Oh fiamma soave" (Uberto in "La Donna del Lago")
"Oh qu'il était beau" (Chapelou in "Le Postillon de Lonjumeau")
"Ora è per sempre addio" (Otello in "Otello")
"Oui, je veux par le monde" (Wilhelm in "Mignon")
Palestrina's prayer (Palestrina in "Palestrina")
"Parmi veder le lagrime" (Duke in "Rigoletto")

"Pastourelle de Robin et Marion" (Jean in "Le Jongleur de Notre Dame")
"Per quel che ha mal di stomaco" (Mengone in "Lo Speziale")
"Perchè mai se son tradito" (Narciso in "Il Turco in Italia")
"Pietoso al lungo pianto" (Edoardo in "Un Giorno di Regno")
"Plus j'observe ces lieux" (Renaud in "Armide")
"Pourquoi me réveiller?" (Werther in "Werther")
"Prendi, l'anel ti dono" (Elvino in "La Sonnambula")
"Pria che spunti in ciel l'aurora" (Paolino in "Il Matrimonio Segreto")
"Pupille amate" (Aufidio in "Lucio Silla")
"Qual onor di te sia degno" (Orfeo in "La Favola d'Orfeo")
"Quale più fido amico" (Carlo in "Giovanna d'Arco")
"Quand j'étais roi de Béotie" (John Styx in "Orphée aux Enfers")
"Quand l'atteindrai je donc" (Lorenzo in "Béatrice")
"Quando le sere al placido" (Rodolfo in "Luisa Miller")
"Quanto è bella" (Nemorino in "L'Elisir d'Amore")
"Quercia annosa" (Scipione in "Il Sogno di Scipione")
"Questa e un'altro novità" (Sempronio in "Lo Speziale")
"Questa o quella" (Duke in "Rigoletto")
"Questa tua bocca" (Lefebvre in "Madame Sans-Gêne")
"Queste ad un lido fatal" (Nerone in "Nerone")
"Qui sosteniamo"/"Che intesi" (Norfolk in "Elisabetta")
"Rachel, quand du Seigneur" (Éléazar in "La Juive")
"Recondita armonia" (Cavaradossi in "Tosca")
"Salut! demeure" (Faust in "Faust")
"Séjour de l'éternelle paix" (Castor in "Castor et Pollux")
"Seul pour lutter" (Cellini in "Benvenuto Cellini")
"Seul sur la terre" (Sébastien in "Dom Sébastien")
Skuratov's story (Skuratov in "Z Mrtvého Domu")
"Sleep, my beauty" (Levko in "Maiskaya Noch")
Slim's song (Slim in "Paul Bunyan")
Song of the Indian trader (Hindu merchant in "Sadko")
"Sotto una quercia" (Carlo in "Giovanna d'Arco")
Šapkin's story (Šapkin in "Z Mrtvého Domu")
Tannhäuser's hymn to Venus (Tannhäuser in "Tannhäuser")
The peasant lad's Dumka (Gritzko in "Sorochinskaya Yarmarka")
"There was a boat drifting out at sea" (Nick in "The Postman Always Rings
      Twice")
"Torna la pace" (Idomeneo in "Idomeneo")
"Tradito schernito" (Ferrando in "Così fan tutte")
"Trinke, Liebchen" (Alfred in "Die Fledermaus")
"Tu sei morta" (Orfeo in "La Favola d'Orfeo")
"Tu vedrai" (Gualtiero in "Il Pirata")
"Un dì all'azzurro spazio" (Chénier in "Andrea Chénier")
"Un'aura amorosa" (Ferrando in "Così fan tutte")
"Una furtiva lagrima" (Nemorino in "L'Elisir d'Amore")
"Vainement ma bien-aimée" (Mylio in "Le Roi d'Ys")
"Vallon sonore" (Hylas in "Les Troyens")

"Verdi allori" (Medoro in "Orlando")
"Vesti la giubba" (Canio in "Pagliacci")
"Vidi dovunque gemere" (Stiffelio in "Stiffelio")
"Viva il vino"/Drinking song (Turiddù in "Cavalleria Rusticana")
"Vivi tu" (Riccardo Percy in "Anna Bolena")
"Voi che fausti" (Alessandro in "Il Re Pastore")
"Wach auf!" (Painter in "Lulu")
"Was nun zu machen" (Abu Hassan in "Abu Hassan")
"Wehen mir Lüfte Ruh!" (Adolar in "Euryanthe")
"What magic is this?" (Dalibor in "Dalibor")
"When I was a young man" (Mr in "Postcard from Morocco")
"Where stallions stamp" (Mark in "The Midsummer Marriage")
"Winterstürme" (Siegmund in "Die Walküre")

BARITONE ARIAS

"Adamastor" (Nélusko in "L'Africaine")
"Ah! m'abbraccia d'esultanza" (Rolando in "La Battaglia di Legnano")
"Ah! quel bonheur de pressentir sa gloire" (Barnabé in "Le Maître de Chapelle")
"Ah! qui pourrait me résister" (Fieramosca in "Benvenuto Cellini")
"Ambo nati" (Antonio in "Linda di Chamounix")
"Aria I, II, III, IV, VI (Prospero in "Un Re in Ascolto")
"Avant de quitter ces lieux" (Valentin in "Faust")
"Bella siccome un angelo" (Malatesta in "Don Pasquale")
"Billy Budd, king of the birds!" (Budd in "Billy Budd")
"Brillant auteur de la lumière" (Agamemnon in "Iphigénie en Aulide")
"Come paride" (Belcore in "L'Elisir d'Amore")
"Cortigiani" (Rigoletto in "Rigoletto")
"Credo in un dio crudel" (Iago in "Otello")
"Cruda funesta" (Enrico in "Lucia di Lammermoor")
"Dagl' immortali vertici" (Ezio in "Attila")
"Dans le sein d'un ami fidèle" (Cinna in "La Vestale")
"De noirs pressentiments" (Thoas in "Iphigénie en Tauride")
"Dento il mio petto" (Don Anchise in "La Finta Giardiniera")
"Der Kriegeslust ergeben" (Tristan in "Jessonda")
"Der Vogelfänger bin ich ja" (Papageno in "Die Zauberflöte")
"Die frist ist um" (Dutchman in "Die Fliegende Holländer")
"Dio di Giuda" (Nabucco in "Nabucco")
"È sogno?" (Ford in "Falstaff")
"Ein Mädchen oder Weibchen" (Papageno in "Die Zauberflöte")
"Era la notte" (Iago in "Otello")
"Eri tu" (Renato in "Un Ballo in Maschera")
Frank's dreams (Frank in "The Postman Always Rings Twice")
"Ha, noch einen ganzen Tag" (Ruthven in "Der Vampyr")
Háry's song (Háry in "Háry János")

"I am the very model of a modern major general" (Major General Stanley in
    "The Pirates of Penzance")
"I got a marble and a star" (Henry Davis in "Street Scene")
"I love you beyond measure" (Yeletsky in "Pikovaya Dama")
"I'm sleepy" (Budd in "Billy Budd")
"Ich möchte" (Philippides in "Des Esels Schatten")
"Ich sehe einen jungen Mann dort stehn" (Boccaccio in "Boccaccio")
"If pretty girls could fly like birds" (Tomsky in "Pikovaya Dama")
"Il Balen" (Count di Luna in "Il Trovatore")
"In braccio alle dovizie" (Monforte in "I Vespri Siciliani")
"In youth the panting slave" (Nick in "The Rake's Progress")
"Inaffia l'ugola" / Drinking song (Iago in "Otello")
"Io morrò" (Rodrigo in "Don Carlo")
"L'onore! Ladri!" / Honor monologue (Falstaff in "Falstaff")
"La calunnia, mio signor" (Basilio in "Il Barbiere di Siviglia")
"Largo al factotum" (Figaro in "Il Barbiere di Siviglia")
"Léonor viens" (Alphonse in "La Favorite")
"Mab, la reine des mensonges" / Ballad of Queen Mab (Mercutio in "Roméo et
    Juliette")
"Mal per me" (Macbeth in "Macbeth")
"Man makes his world" (Tom in "Die Englische Katze")
Marczi's song (Marczi in "Háry János")
"Mon fils est revenu" (Siméon in "L'Enfant Prodigue")
"Mondo ladro" (Falstaff in "Falstaff")
"Nemico della patria" (Gérard in "Andrea Chénier")
"No! possibile non è" (Guglielmo in "Le Villi")
"Nulla, silenzio" (Michele in "Il Tabarro")
"O du, mein holder Abendstern" (Wolfram in "Tannhäuser")
"O Lisbonne" (Camoëns in "Dom Sébastien")
"O monumento" (Barnaba in "La Gioconda")
"O Nadir, tendre ami" (Zurga in "Les Pêcheurs de Perles")
"O that joy so soon should waste" (Falstaff in "Sir John in Love")
"O toi, l'objet le plus aimable" (Agamemnon in "Iphigénie en Aulide")
"O vecchio cor, che batti" (Doge in "I Due Foscari")
"O vin, dissipe la tristesse" (Hamlet in "Hamlet")
"Oh field, who has bestrewn thee with dead bones?" (Russlan in "Russlan and
    Ludmilla")
Peace aria (Owen in "Owen Wingrave")
"Pietà, rispetto, amore" (Macbeth in "Macbeth")
"Plebe! Patrizi!" (Boccanegra in "Simon Boccanegra")
"Qual onor di te sia degno" (Orfeo in "La Favola d'Orfeo")
"Questo amor" (Frank in "Edgar")
"Rimorso in lei?" (Filippo in "Beatrice di Tenda")
"Sacra la scelta" (Miller in "Luisa Miller")
"Scorsi già molti paesi" (Figaro in "Il Barbiere di Siviglia")
"Se al nuovo dì pugnando" (Rolando in "La Battaglia di Legnano")
"Sì li sciogliete" (Valdeburgo in "La Straniera")

"Si può?" (Tonio in "Pagliacci")
"Sì, vincemmo" (Ernesto in "Il Pirata")
"So che per via di triboli" (Giacomo in "Giovanna d'Arco")
"Sois immobile" (Tell in "Guillaume Tell")
"Sol da te, mio dolce amore" (Ruggiero in "Orlando Furioso")
"Tit Willow" (Ko-Ko in "The Mikado")
"Too weak to kill the man I hate" (Adam in "Mourning Becomes Electra")
"Traum der Jugend" (Faust in "Doktor Faust")
"Tu sei morta" (Orfeo in "La Favola d'Orfeo")
"Urna fatale" (Don Carlo in "La Forza del Destino")
"Vedrò mentr'io sospiro" (Count in "Le Nozze di Figaro")
"Vision fugitive" (Hérode in "Hérodiade")
"Voilà donc la terrible cité" (Athanael in "Thaïs")
"Votre toast"/Toreador's song (Escamillo in "Carmen")
"Were I a man whom fate intended" (Onegin in "Yevgeny Onyegin")
"When I went to the bar as a very young man" (Lord Chancellor in "Iolanthe")
"When the air sings of summer (Bob in "The Old Maid and the Thief")
"When you're lying awake with a dismal headache" (Lord Chancellor in
    "Iolanthe")
"Wo berg' ich mich?" (Lysiart in "Euryanthe")
"Wouldn't you like to be on Broadway?" (Harry Easter in "Street Scene")
"Your picture" (Tausendmark in "Braniboři v Cechách")
"Zazà, piccola zingara" (Cascart in "Zazà")

BASS BARITONE ARIAS

"A un dottor" (Bartolo in "Il Barbiere di Siviglia")
"Aprite un po'" (Figaro in "Le Nozze di Figaro")
"Au faîte des grandeurs" (Calchas in "Iphigénie en Aulide")
Chanson de la Puce (Méphistophélès in "La Damnation de Faust")
"Deh vieni alla finestra" (Giovanni in "Don Giovanni")
"Finch' han dal vino"/Champagne aria (Giovanni in "Don Giovanni")
"Ha! welch' ein Augenblick!" (Pizarro in "Fidelio")
"Hear me, O Lord" (Blitch in "Susannah")
"I got plenty o' nuttin'" (Porgy in "Porgy and Bess")
"I have attained the highest power" (Boris in "Boris Godunov")
"Jerum! Jerum!" (Hans Sachs in "Die Meistersinger von Nürnberg")
"Le veau d'or" (Méphistophélès in "Faust")
"Non più andrai" (Figaro in "Le Nozze di Figaro")
"Oh, better far to live and die" (Pirate King in "The Pirates of Penzance")
Porterlied/Drinking song (Plunkett in "Martha")
"Scintille diamant"/Diamond aria (Dappertutto in "Le Contes d'Hoffmann")
"Se vuol ballare" (Figaro in "Le Nozze di Figaro")
"Wahn! Wahn!" (Hans Sachs in "Die Meistersinger von Nürnberg")
"Warm as the autumn night" (Horace Tabor in "The Ballad of Baby Doe")

BASS ARIAS

"A more humane Mikado" (Mikado in "The Mikado")
"Au faîte des grandeurs" (Calchas in "Iphigénie en Aulide")
Audition song (Mamma Agatha in "Viva la Mamma")
"Bella cosa" (Annibale in "Il Campanello")
"Bin Akademiker" (Abul in "Der Barbier von Bagdad")
"C'est vers ton amour" (Quichotte in "Don Quichotte")
"Che mondo amabile" (Buonafede in "Il Mondo della Luna")
"Cinta di fiori" (Giorgio in "I Puritani")
"Come dal ciel precipita" (Banquo in "Macbeth")
"Da bilden sich die guten Leute" (Kenteterion in "Des Esels Schatten")
"De noirs pressentiments" (Thoas in "Iphigénie en Tauride")
"Di cieca notte" (Argenio in "Imeneo")
Drinking song (Falstaff in "Die Lustigen Weiber von Windsor")
"Each time I hit a town" (Stranger in "The Jumping Frog of Calaveras County")
"Ecco il mondo" (Mefistofele in "Mefistofele")
"Ella giammai m'amò" (Filippo in "Don Carlo")
"Eterno! immenso! incomprensibil Dio!" (Mosè in "Mosè in Egitto")
"From deep Yara lake" (Dulcimer player in "Skazanie o nevidimom grade
        Kitezhe")
"Fünf Tausend Thaler" (Baculus in "Der Wildschütz")
"Già d'insolito ardore nel petto agitare" (Mustafà in "L'Italiana in Algeri")
Goaler aria (Beneš in "Dalibor")
"Grazie, grazie" (Slook in "La Cambiale di Matrimonio")
"Ha wie will ich triumphieren" (Osmin in "Die Entführung aus dem Serail")
"Hat man nicht" / Gold aria (Rocco in "Fidelio")
"I hate a dreary life" (Galitsky in "Knyaz' Igor'")
"Il lacerato spirito" (Fiesco in "Simon Boccanegra")
"In diesen heilgen Hallen" (Sarastro in "Die Zauberflöte")
"Infelice, e tu credevi" (Silva in "Ernani")
"Invan strappar dal core" (Sidney in "Il Viaggio a Reims")
"It is a little far" (Marbuel in "Čert a Káča")
"Ite sul colle" (Oroveso in "Norma")
"Je t'ai trompé je fus coupable" (Bertram in "Robert le Diable")
"Jerum! Jerum!" (Hans Sachs in "Die Meistersinger von Nürnberg")
"Konfutse, dir hab' ich geschworen" (Altoum in "Turandot")
"L'orror del tradimento" (Oberto in "Oberto")
"La calunnia" (Basilio in "Il Barbiere di Siviglia")
La Roche's aria (La Roche in "Capriccio")
"La vendetta" (Bartolo in "Le Nozze di Figaro")
"Le femmine d'Italia" (Ali in "L'Italiana in Algeri")
"Le veau d'or" (Méphistophélès in "Faust")
"Madamina! Il catalogo è questo" / Catalog aria (Leporello in "Don Giovanni")
Marczi's song (Marczi in "Háry János")
"Medaglie incomparabili" (Profondo in "Il Viaggio a Reims")

"Miei rampolli femminili" (Magnifico in "La Cenerentola")
"News has a kind of mystery" (Nixon in "Nixon in China")
"O Isis und Osiris" (Sarastro in "Die Zauberflöte")
"O sancta justitia" (Van Bett in "Zar und Zimmermann")
"O tu Palermo" (Procida in "I·Vespri Siciliani")
"Piff, paff" (Marcel in "Les Huguenots")
"Schweig! schweig!" (Caspar in "Der Freischütz")
"Sciagurata! Hai tu creduto" (Pagano in "I Lombardi alla Prima Crociata")
"Sempre in contrasti" (Uberto in "La Serva Padrona")
"Solitudine amata" (Seneca in "L'Incoronazione di Poppea")
"Son imbogliato io già" (Uberto in "La Serva Padrona")
"Son lo spirito che nega" (Mefistofele in "Mefistofele")
Song of the Varangian merchant (Varangian merchant in "Sadko")
"Sorge infausta una procella" (Zoroastro in "Orlando")
"Taci, lo voglio e basti" (Douglas in "La Donna del Lago")
"Tu sul labbro" (Zaccaria in "Nabucco")
"Udite, tutti udite" (Geronimo in "Il Matrimonio Segreto")
"Udite, udite o rustici" (Dulcamara in "L'Elisir d'Amore")
"Un ignoto, tre lune or saranno" (Massimiliano in "I Masnadieri")
"Vecchia zimarra" / Coat song (Colline in "La Bohème")
"Veiller sans cess" (Tutor in "Le Comte Ory")
"Veramente ha torto" (Bartolo in "Il Barbiere di Siviglia")
"Vi ravviso" (Rodolfo in "La Sonnambula")
"Vieni, la mia vendetta" (Don Alfonso in "Lucrezia Borgia")
"Wahn! Wahn!" (Hans Sachs in "Die Meistersinger von Nürnberg")

ONE-ACT OPERA INDEX

Other titles of interest

ALL AMERICAN MUSIC
Composition in the Late
Twentieth Century
John Rockwell
New preface by the author
294 pp.
80750-5 $14.95

THE ART OF ACCOMPANYING
AND COACHING
Kurt Adler
260 pp., 21 illus.
80027-6 $15.95

ARTURO TOSCANINI
Contemporary Recollections
of the Maestro
B. H. Haggin
Edited by Thomas Hathaway
544 pp., 8 photos
80356-9 $13.95

BRAHMS
His Life and Work
Karl Geiringer
416 pp.
80223-6 $13.95

CHARLES IVES REMEMBERED
An Oral History
Vivian Perlis
256 pp., 80 illus.
80576-6 $13.95

THE COMPANION TO
20th-CENTURY MUSIC
Norman Lebrecht
440 pp., 151 illus.
80734-3 $16.95

THE COMPLETE OPERAS
OF MOZART
Charles Osborne
349 pp., 23 photos
80190-6 $14.95

THE COMPLETE OPERAS
OF PUCCINI
Charles Osborne
282 pp., 16 photos
80200-7 $14.95

THE COMPLETE OPERAS OF
RICHARD STRAUSS
Charles Osborne
248 pp., 19 illus.
80459-X $13.95

THE COMPLETE OPERAS
OF RICHARD WAGNER
Charles Osborne
304 pp., 25 illus.
80522-7 $13.95

THE COMPLETE OPERAS
OF VERDI
Charles Osborne
458 pp.
80072-1 $14.95

THE DA CAPO CATALOG OF
CLASSICAL MUSIC
COMPOSITIONS
Jerzy Chwialkowski
1,412 pp.
80701-7   paperback $29.50
79666-X   hardcover $85.00

AN ENCYCLOPEDIA OF
QUOTATIONS ABOUT MUSIC
Compiled by Nat Shapiro
418 pp., 14 photos
80138-8 $14.95

AN ENCYCLOPEDIA
OF THE VIOLIN
Alberto Bachmann
470 pp., 78 illus.
80004-7 $16.95

GENESIS OF A MUSIC
Harry Partch
517 pp., 40 photos, 28 diagrams
80106-X $17.95

GREATNESS IN MUSIC
Alfred Einstein
298 pp.
80046-2 $9.95